The Concise Oxford Dictionary of
Archaeology

204 THAN THAT

Timothy Darvill is Professor of Archaeology at
Bournemouth University, and is a Fellow of
the Society of Antiquaries. He graduated from
Southampton University and has worked for
the Western Archaeological Trust and the
Council for British Archaeology. He has directed a number of excavations, was Secretary
of the Committee for Archaeology in Gloucestershire, and Secretary of CBA Group 13. He has
also served on the Council of the National
Trust and was Chairman of the Institute of
Field Archaeologists. He is currently chairman
of the board of directors of the Cotswold
Archaeological Trust Ltd. His previous publications include numerous reports and papers in
academic and popular journals, and he has
written several books including: *The Archaeology
of the Uplands* (1986), *Prehistoric Britain* (1987), and
Prehistoric Britain from the Air (1996).

Oxford
Paperback
Reference

The most authoritative and up-to-date reference
books for both students and the general reader.

ABC of Music
Accounting
Allusions
Archaeology
Architecture
Art and Artists
Art Terms
Astronomy
Better Wordpower
Bible
Biology
British History
British Place-Names
Buddhism
Business
Card Games
Catchphrases
Celtic Mythology
Chemistry
Christian Art
Christian Church
Classical Literature
Computing
Contemporary World History
Dance
Dates
Dynasties of the World
Earth Sciences
Ecology
Economics
Engineering*
English Etymology
English Folklore
English Grammar
English Language
English Literature
Euphemisms
Everyday Grammar
Finance and Banking
First Names
Food and Drink
Food and Nutrition
Foreign Words and Phrases
Geography
Handbook of the World
Humorous Quotations
Idioms
Internet
Irish Literature
Jewish Religion
Kings and Queens of Britain
Language Toolkit
Law
Linguistics

Literary Quotations
Literary Terms
Local and Family History
London Place-Names
Mathematics
Medical
Medicinal Drugs
Modern Design*
Modern Slang
Music
Musical Terms*
Musical Works*
Nursing
Ologies and Isms
Philosophy
Phrase and Fable
Physics
Plant Sciences
Pocket Fowler's Modern
  English Usage
Political Quotations
Politics
Popes
Proverbs
Psychology
Quotations
Quotations by Subject
Reverse Dictionary
Rhyming Slang
Sailing Terms
Saints
Science
Scientists
Shakespeare
Ships and the Sea
Slang
Sociology
Spelling
Statistics
Synonyms and Antonyms
Twentieth-Century Art
Weather
Weights, Measures, and Units
Who's Who in the Classical
  World
Who's Who in the Twentieth
  Century
World History
World Mythology
World Religions
Writers' Dictionary
Zoology

*forthcoming

The Concise Oxford Dictionary of

Archaeology

TIMOTHY DARVILL

OXFORD
UNIVERSITY PRESS

OXFORD

UNIVERSITY PRESS

Great Clarendon Street, Oxford OX2 6DP

Oxford University Press is a department of the University of Oxford.
It furthers the University's objective of excellence in research, scholarship,
and education by publishing worldwide in

Oxford New York

Auckland Bangkok Buenos Aires Cape Town Chennai
Dar es Salaam Delhi Hong Kong Istanbul Karachi Kolkata
Kuala Lumpur Madrid Melbourne Mexico City Mumbai Nairobi
São Paulo Shanghai Singapore Taipei Tokyo Toronto

Oxford is a registered trade mark of Oxford University Press
in the UK and certain other countries

Published in the United States
by Oxford University Press Inc., New York

First published 2002
First published as an Oxford University Press paperback, 2003

British Library Cataloguing in Publication Data
Data available

Library of Congress Cataloging in Publication Data
Data available

ISBN 0–19–280005–1

10 9 8 7 6 5 4 3 2 1

Typeset by SNP Best-set Typesetter Ltd., Hong Kong

Printed in Great Britain by Clays Ltd
Bungay, Suffolk

Contents

Preface

Over the last few decades archaeology has come to be practised in most countries of the world, adopting, adapting, and extending traditions of investigation and interpretation that had their roots in Europe in the 18th century. The modern discipline of archaeology would probably be unrecognizable to the early practitioners, now drawing as it does on a wide range of scientifically based techniques and methods, and cast within an intellectual and theoretical framework that is increasingly heterogeneous.

As a result of these changes there have developed an extensive vocabulary and a wide range of technical terms. Some are peculiar to archaeology while others are borrowed from a range of disciplines either directly or with modification to their traditionally accepted meanings and applications. This dictionary of terms is intended as a guide to words likely to be commonly encountered in the archaeological literature or in the presentation of archaeological material through lectures, television, or video films. It is thus primarily intended for those who are essentially unfamiliar with the vocabulary and technical terms used by archaeologists, for example students starting out on a career in archaeology or seeking to expand their areas of special interest, journalists popularizing the scholarly outpourings of archaeologists, and other professionals who have cause to dip into the archaeological literature.

Selecting the words and terms included in this dictionary has not been easy, but has been informed by a number of general criteria. Temporally, the words and terms selected mainly relate to the period from about 3 million years ago down to about AD 1700. Some terms relevant to still later periods have been included, although it is recognized that the overlap between the vocabulary of archaeologists and historians becomes considerable when dealing with recent centuries.

Geographically, the range of words and terms included here focuses on Europe, the Mediterranean, and English-speaking countries in which archaeology has become an established academic and vocational subject. The selection of sites included was probably the most difficult choice, as there are so many important and interesting places. One of the criteria applied here was the inclusion of sites that illustrate some of the main kinds of monuments described. There are, however, many regional guides to the archaeology of particular places and countries, amongst them volumes in the *Ancient People and Places* series published by Thames and Hudson and the *Oxford Archaeological Guides* published by OUP.

Within these parameters, emphasis has been given to what may be termed 'mainstream' archaeology. A few words and terms derived from highly specialist branches of archaeology, such as industrial archaeology, classical archaeology, or maritime archaeology, have been included where they may be encountered in general works. For more technical terms a specialist dictionary should be consulted, for example:

T. Barfield, 1997, *The dictionary of anthropology*. Oxford: Blackwell.

L. Flanagan, 1992, *A dictionary of Irish archaeology*. Dublin: Gill and Macmillan.

W. Jones, 1998, *Dictionary of industrial archaeology*. Stroud: Alan Sutton.

G. Leick, 1999, *Who's who in the ancient Near East*. London: Routledge.

M. Symes, 1993, *A glossary of garden history*. Princes Risborough: Shire.

Atlases are also extremely useful in exploring some of the words listed in this dictionary, and special mention may be made of the following:

J. Haywood, 2000, *The Cassell atlas of world history: the ancient and classical worlds*. London: Cassell.

A. Mackay with D. Ditchburn (eds.), 1996, *Atlas of medieval Europe*. London: Routledge.

C. Scarre (ed.), 1993, *Past worlds. The Times atlas of archaeology*. London: Times Books.

R. J. A. Talbert (ed.), 2000, *Barrington atlas of the Greek and Roman worlds*. London: Barrington.

This dictionary is not intended to be a comprehensive encyclopedia of archaeology; a number of these are available and provide short essays on a wide range of topics, some of which will be found briefly described herein. The following are particularly useful:

G. Barker (ed.), 1999, *Companion encyclopedia of archaeology*. London: Routledge.

B. Fagan (ed.), 1996, *The Oxford companion to archaeology*. Oxford: OUP.

P. N. Peregrine and M. Ember (eds.), 2001, *Encyclopedia of prehistory*. Higham MA: Kluwer and Plenum.

A. Sherratt (ed.), 1980, *The Cambridge encyclopedia of archaeology*. Cambridge: CUP.

Where words and terms included in this dictionary are usually spelt in the Latin alphabet this has been followed, but words and terms in other alphabets have been anglicized for ease of listing and access. Cross-referencing terms into other languages is always fraught with difficulties and is not attempted here. The following concordance provides a useful guide for those wishing to move between English, German, Russian, and Latvian, and has illustrations of commonly found objects to help:

J. Graudonis, 1994, *Arheoloģijas terminu vārdnīca*. Riga: Zinātne.

In order to assist with the usage of the entries in this dictionary, all the terms have been classified into a series of main groupings. These are indicated by abbreviations in square brackets set immediately after the word or term and before the definition. The following categories have been used:

[Ab]   Abbreviation
[Ar]   Artefact
[Bi]   Biographical entry
[Co]   Component or feature of a recognized class of monument
[CP]   Cultural phase, period, tradition, or defined grouping
[De]   Descriptive term
[Di]   Deity
[Do]   Document (usually a historical text relevant to archaeological enquiry)
[Eq]   Equipment used in archaeological work

[Ge]   General term
[Le]   Legal term
[Ma]   Material
[MC]   Monument class or category
[Na]   Name of historical or mythical person
[Or]   Organization, association, society, institution, or company
[Sp]   Plant or animal species/genus
[Si]   Site, monument, or area of archaeological importance
[Sl]   Slang
[Te]   Technique commonly used in archaeological work
[Th]   Theoretical perspective, model, or set of principles underpinning archae-
       ological work

In the case of biographical entries, references to published biographies, auto-biographies, notes, or obituaries have been included where known. For the sites listed, a reference to a general summary or excavation report is given; most of these have further references for those wishing to find out more. Legal terms are restricted to those which apply in the United Kingdom and North America and take account of legislation enacted up until July 2000. Where appropriate, reference is made to the relevant Acts.

Some entries simply refer to another entry, indicating that they are synonyms or that they are conveniently explained, together with any other related terms, in another entry. Major terms cross-referenced in this way are indicated in SMALL CAPITALS.

Dating is one of the topics covered by entries in the dictionary, but by way of introduction it is important to note that throughout the dictionary dates are expressed in calendar years BC or AD on the Gregorian chronology used widely in Europe and America. Where radiocarbon dates have been used as the basis for local or regional chronologies they have been calibrated using available curves. Other chronological systems are defined in the text.

Archaeological interpretations are constantly changing in the light of new evidence and ongoing research; in some spheres of interest such change can be quite rapid. Accordingly, the entries included here are point-in-time statements reflecting available knowledge and accepted understandings of what are undoubtedly complicated phenomena.

Finding out how words and terms have been used has been an interesting experience, and I would like to thank all those individuals whom I have talked to about the current use of the archaeological language, and also all the writers whose work I have consulted on the library shelves to gain an understanding of words and terms, insights into the way they are used, and an appreciation of the nature and extent of modern treatment. Dictionaries can only reflect usage and commonly understood meanings; accordingly, any authors who find definitions herein which resemble their own usage will, I hope, feel flattered.

In preparing the text of this dictionary a number of friends and colleagues have helped immensely and deserve special thanks for their efforts: Gennadii Afanas'ev, Kevin Andrews, Bettina Arnold, Fiona Ashmore, Mark Brisbane, Steve Burrow, Anne Chojnacki, Vanessa Constant, Penny Dale, Margarita Díaz-Andreu, Roger Doonan, Lindsay Drew, Bruce Eagles, Thomas Emersen, Andy Fulton,

Christopher Gerrard, David Gilbertson, Norman Hammond, Nicola King, Mark Maltby, Liz McCrimmon, Louise Pearson, Włodzimierz Rączkowski, Bronwen Russell, Miles Russell, Alan Saville, Liz Slater, Alexander Smirnov, Helen Smith, Alexei Sorokin, Paul Stamper, Gareth Talbot, Deborah Wildgust, and Eileen Wilkes. At Oxford University Press Angus Phillips, Vicki Rodger, and Ruth Langley have been a constant source of advice and encouragement, and models of patience in waiting for the final text to arrive.

Timothy Darvill
Bournemouth
December 2000

Abbreviations

Abio.	Autobiography
AD	*anno Domini*
BC	Before Christ (expressed in conventional calendar/solar years)
Bio.	Biography
c.	*circa*
CoE	Council of Europe
CUP	Cambridge University Press
d.	died
EC	European Commission
EU	European Union
HMSO	Her Majesty's Stationery Office
Not.	Biographical note/review
Obit.	Obituary
OUP	Oxford University Press
pl.	plural
RAF	Royal Air Force
RCHME	Royal Commission on the Historical Monuments of England
Rep.	Report on a major excavation or survey of the site/region
Rev.	Review
Sum.	Summary overview or synthesis of excavation and survey work
TV	Television
UK	United Kingdom
USA	United States of America
WW1	World War 1
WW2	World War 2

AAS [Ab]. *See* ATOMIC ABSORPTION SPECTROMETRY.

abacus [Ar]. The uppermost member of a capital, set atop a pillar, and, on classical buildings, in contact with the bottom of the ENTABLATURE. The abacus resembles in form the flat slab on which it was modelled.

Abbasids [CP]. An Arab dynasty descended from Abbas, uncle of Muhammad, who supplanted the Umayyads in AD 750.

Abbeville, France [Si]. A gravel pit in the 45 m gravel terrace of the Somme Valley, France, from which numerous handaxes were obtained by Boucher de Perthes and others from AD 1836 onwards and which in 1939 gave its name to the ABBEVILLIAN.

[Sum.: F. Bordes, 1956, Some observations on the Pleistocene succession in the Somme Valley. *Proceedings of the Prehistoric Society*, 22, 1–5]

Abbevillian [CP]. Now obsolete, this term was originally proposed by Abbé Breuil in AD 1939 to describe the pre-ACHEULIAN flint industries of western Europe on the basis of material from ABBEVILLE in France. Also known as the Chellean.

abbey [De]. A community of monks or nuns ruled by an abbot or abbess.

abbey [MC]. A general term used to describe the buildings inhabited by a community of monks or nuns. *See* MONASTERY.

ABC Model [De]. A scheme for the cultural history of the British Iron Age first proposed Christopher HAWKES in 1931, but expanded and elaborated in the late 1950s as the opening paper at a conference on the Southern British Iron Age organized by the CBA and held in London in December 1958, subsequently published in *Antiquity* (1959, 170–82). The ABC refers to cultures, each of which appears in each of three periods that are designated 1, 2, and 3. Period 1 broadly equates to the late Hallstatt on the continent, period 2 to La Tène I, and period 3 to La Tène II and III. Hawkes's scheme is often recalled but rarely used.

Abejas Phase [CP]. Fourth main phase of activity in the Tehuacán Valley of Mexico, dating to the period 4300–3000 BC, marked archaeologically by the appearance of semi-permanent villages of pit houses, new species of plant food, long obsidian blades, and possibly the cultivation of cotton. Agriculture supplies up to 25 per cent of food requirements during this phase.

Abercromby, Lord John (1841–1924) [Bi]. Scottish antiquary who specialized in the prehistory of northwest Europe. Born the 5th Baron of Aboukir and Tullibody, he served in the army from 1858 to 1870 before devoting himself to scholarship and especially philology, archaeology, and folklore. He travelled widely and mastered several European languages, including Finnish. In 1904 he introduced the term 'BEAKER' into the literature to refer to the late Neolithic decorated drinking vessels often associated with burials of the period. The term has remained in use ever since, although Abercromby's original subdivision into three types—A, B, and C—has since been modified. In 1912 he published in two volumes *A study of Bronze Age pottery in Great Britain and Ireland* (Oxford: Clarendon Press). Throughout his later life he supported the work of the Society of Antiquaries of Scotland and was their President from 1913 to 1918. In his will he founded and endowed the Abercromby Chair of Archaeology in the University of Edinburgh, the first two incumbents being Gordon Childe and Stuart Piggott respectively.

[Obit: *Proceedings of the Society of Antiquaries of Scotland*, 59, 4–6]

Åberg, Nils (1888–1957) [Bi]. Swedish archaeologist and scholar with wide interests in European prehistory. A pupil of Oscar Montelius and Professor of Archaeology at Stockholm University, his typological studies of Bronze Age, Iron Age, and migration period metalwork are fundamental to modern interpretation of European chronology and cultural groupings. The results were published in his five-volume work *Bronzezeitliche u. früheisenzeitliche Chronologie* (1930–5, Stockholm: Kungl Vitterhets och Antikvitets Akademien).

[Obit: *Kuml*, 1957, 192–5]

Abingdon ware [Ar]. A type of middle Neolithic round-bottomed decorated pottery found in the upper Thames valley and central parts of England, one of the regional variations of the so-called Southern Decorated series. Dates mainly to the 4th millennium BC.

aborigines [Ge]. Derived from the Latin word 'aborigine' extended to mean the original inhabitants of a country. When used as a proper noun the term usually refers to the indigenous peoples of Australia.

absolute dating [De]. General term applied to a range of techniques that provide estimates of the age of objects, materials, or sites in real calendar years either directly or through a process of calibration with material of known age. Such techniques rely on principles that lie outside the influence of the makers and users of the material being dated, for example RADIOCARBON DATING. Various calendars are used to express absolute dates. Some sciences preferring BP as 'before present', the scientific present being conventionally taken as AD 1950. In archaeology the use of BC and AD based on the Gregorian Calendar is commonly used in Europe and America, although other calendars apply to specific cultures in other regions and these are used too where appropriate. *Compare* RELATIVE DATING.

Abu Simbel, Egypt [Si]. A pair of rock-cut temples in Lower Nubia, now overlooking the artificially created Lake Nasser 230 km up-river from Aswan. Both temples were built by Ramesses II in the 13th century BC. The Great Temple is dedicated to him and has as its facade two pairs of colossal seated figures of him (each about 22 m tall). The main part of the temple is cut into solid rock, 55 m deep, and the main walls are decorated with reliefs showing the king's military campaigns in Syria and Nubia. The Small Temple is more modest and is dedicated to his principal queen, Neferirkare. Both temples were sawn into blocks, dismantled, moved upslope, and re-erected in their present positions in 1968 as part of the Nubian Rescue Campaign to save important archaeological sites from the rising waters of Lake Nasser.

[Rep.: T. Säve-Söderbergh (ed.), 1987, *Temples and tombs of ancient Nubia: the international rescue campaign at Abu Simbel, Philae, and other sites*. London: Thames & Hudson and UNESCO]

abutment [Co]. Masonry platform or earth embankment supporting the central structure of a bridge.

accelerator mass spectrometry (AMS) [Te]. A method for detecting atoms of specific elements according to their atomic weights. There are a number of archaeological applications, the most common being in radiocarbon dating. Here, the addition of a series of magnetic lenses and a high-voltage 'accelerator' to a mass spectrometer allows ^{14}C atoms to be detected in an ancient sample and the amount present determined in a matter of minutes. The technique provides an alternative to the conventional approach which relies on measuring the decay of ^{14}C in a sample over a defined period (usually weeks or months). In addition to being relatively quick, AMS determinations can be made on far smaller samples of carbon (1 mg), allowing, for example, the dating of individual cereal grains. AMS is also used for determining ^{18}O/^{16}O ratios (*see* OXYGEN ISOTOPE ANALYSIS).

acculturation [Th]. Transference of ideas, beliefs, traditions and sometimes artefacts by long-term, personal contact and interaction between communities or societies. Adoption through assimilation by prolonged contact. *Compare* DIFFUSION.

accuracy [De]. The closeness of an estimate to the true value. *Compare* PRECISION.

aceramic [De]. A term applied to a culture, region, or period in which pottery was not made, used, or traded on a regular basis. Instead, containers may have been made from leather, basketry, bark, gourds or other pliable materials. The **aceramic Neolithic** is taken to be the period when plant and animal domestication was already underway but ceramics were not used.

Achaeans [CP]. Name used by Homer to refer to the Greeks at TROY and other places. Perhaps applicable to Bronze Age communities in the region that are known archaeologically as the MYCENAEANS.

Achaemenids [Na]. A group of Persian communities that moved into western Iran during the early 1st millennium BC. The founding father of the ruling house was Achaemenes who lived in the 7th century BC, his descendants expanding the area of influence to create an empire that extended from central Asia and northern India to France and Egypt in the 6th century BC. Notable later rulers of the Achaemenids include Cyrus II (559–530 BC), Darius (522–486 BC), and Xerxes I (485–465 BC). The Achaemenid period was an important one for Iranian civilization and was one of the richest in terms of contacts between the classical world and the Near East. It saw the appearance and spread of Zoroastrianism, and some spectacular architecture at, for example, Darius' capital at Persepolis. However, tensions between the Achaemenids and the Greeks were always in the background, and erupted into several key battles: Darius was defeated by the Greeks at Marathon in 490 BC and the same fate befell Xerxes ten years later. In 330 BC Alexander the Great conquered and destroyed the Achaemenid empire.

Acheulian [CP]. Lower Palaeolithic toolmaking tradition, found throughout Europe, western Asia, and Africa, which is closely associated with *Homo erectus*. The tradition was initially named, after the type-site assemblage from ST ACHEUL, Amiens, France, as the Epoque de St Acheul by de Mortillet in 1872, and after 1925 as the Acheulian. The most distinctive stone tools were ovate and pear-shaped handaxes, but assemblages also include flake tools and waste flakes which show considerable regional variation. In Europe the Acheulian Tradition spans the period from about 1 million years ago down

to about 100 000 years ago. In Africa the Acheulian follows the OLDOWAN and spans the period 1.5 million years ago down to 150 000 years ago.

achira [Sp]. Tropical plant with bright flowers (*Canna edulis*), native to the Caribbean and lower eastern slopes of the Andes. Domesticated from *c*.3000 BC and used as a food source.

ACRA [Ab]. *See* AMERICAN CULTURAL RESOURCES ASSOCIATION.

acropolis (akropolis) [MC]. Hill-top enclosure found in classical Greek cities to give protection to the temple of the patron deity and, in early times, to the king's palace. The acropolis was the nucleus of a community living outside its walls, although it might provide refuge in times of danger. The most famous acropolis is the one in Athens, which was of ancient foundation as a fortified site. Through the influence of Pericles in the 5th century BC it was adorned with a number of exceptional buildings including the Erechtheum and the PARTHENON.

acroterion [Co]. The sculptured figure, tripod, disc or urn, of bronze, marble, or terracotta, placed on the apex of the pediment of a Greek temple or other substantial building; sometimes also above the outer angles of the pediment triangle.

activity area [De]. A patterning of artefacts in a site, indicating that a specific set of tasks or operations took place there, for example flint-knapping.

activity set [De]. A set of artefacts that reveals the activities of an individual.

Acton Park Tradition [CP]. Industrial stage of the British early Bronze Age named after a hoard of bronze tools and weapons found at Acton Park, Clwyd in *c*.1875 AD. Dating to the period around 1500 BC, the traditions of this stage fit within Colin Burgess's BEDD BRANWEN PERIOD. The metalwork includes palstaves, half-flanged axes, socket-looped spearheads, dirks, rapiers, and daggers. In Scotland the Caverton Phase and the Auchterhouse Phase are concurrent with the Acton Park Tradition.

ad/AD [Ab]. Anno Domini. The Christian era in the Gregorian calendar, starting from the year AD 1 as the calculated and back-projected year in which Christ was believed to have been born. Widely used in western societies. The use of lower-case initials is often taken to indicate that the date has been calculated from a radiocarbon determination by subtracting 1950 from the radiocarbon age. The use of upper-case letters denotes a historical date or a calibrated radiocarbon age in calendar years.

adaptation [Ge]. The ability of a biological organism to survive within a given environment by changing its behaviour or physical attributes. Extended to include human adaptation to the environment in which communities find themselves and therefore a major explanatory tool in developing archaeological understandings of periods of change.

Adena Complex [CP]. A group of related native American cultures of the early Woodland period centred on the Ohio area of the USA and dating to the period 1000 BC to 100 BC. Named after the type-site of Adena, these communities lived in small villages, perhaps seasonally, supported by an essentially hunter-gatherer economy with limited small-scale horticultural use of sunflowers, marsh elder, squashes, and gourds. Distinctive material culture includes cord-decorated pottery, engraved stone tablets ('birdstones' and 'boatstones'), and ornamented smoking tubes. Copper bracelets, beads, crescents, axes and other items were imported from areas around Lake Superior. Drawing on earlier prototypes, the most impressive and distinctive Adena constructions after about 500 BC were the burial mounds, of which several types have been found. Important individuals were typically interred in log-lined tombs which were burnt and then covered by a conical earth mound up to 20 m high. In other cases corpses were cremated in a clay oven and the remains then buried under a mound. Elaborate grave goods were often placed with the dead. Adena earthworks also included large geometrically shaped ceremonial constructions and circles. One of the best known is the Great Serpent Mound, Ohio. Adena Complex groups were locally ancestral to the HOPEWELLIAN CULTURE.

Adena Mound, Ross County, Ohio, USA [Si]. Burial mound beside the Scioto River which gives its name to the Adena Complex of early Woodland cultures. Excavated by William C. Mills in the early 20th century.

[Rep.: W. C. Mills, 1902, Excavations of the Adena Mound. *Ohio Archaeological and Historical Publications*, 10, 452–79]

adit [MC]. An early style of mining in which a tunnel is driven into a hillside in order to follow or intercept seams of useful stone or veins of ore. Generally, adits are dug at a slight angle so that water naturally drains out of the tunnel.

adobe [Ar]. American term for sun-dried, unfired, clay bricks used as a building material.

adze [Ar]. A woodworking tool which has its working edge perpendicular to the long axis of the haft. It therefore contrasts with an axe, the working edge of which is parallel with the plane of the haft. Adzes are generally used for trimming and shaping timbers, and for hollowing out large cavities such as in making a dug-out canoe.

aedes [Co]. Latin term for the shrine in a Roman military headquarters, centrally situated, usually at the rear of the *principia*, to house the standards and an image of the emperor.

aeolian deposits (eolian deposits) [De]. Wind-blown sediments characteristic of relatively dry periods, e.g. interpluvials or glacials with low precipitation. Aeolian deposits can easily bury sites and create well-preserved archaeological deposits, like many sand-dune-covered sites.

aerial photography (AP) [Me]. A form of remote sensing that involves the detection and photographic recording of sites from satellites, aircraft, or balloons. Amongst other things such studies can help to understand the shape of large sites which are not clear at ground level. VERTICAL AERIAL PHOTOGRAPHS, taken from greater heights, are useful for surveys of large areas especially for crop marks and similar phenomena. OBLIQUE AERIAL PHOTOGRAPHS, from lower altitudes, and normally of specific areas, detect shadows created by slight 'earthworks' and permit more detailed interpretations of known sites.

aerobic [De]. A term to describe environments in which oxygen is present and in which microbial decay of organic materials takes place. *Compare* ANAEROBIC.

aestiva [MC]. Latin term for the summer quarters of a military force on manoeuvres in the field.

Aethelberht [Na]. Anglo-Saxon king of Kent from *c*.AD 560. Defeated by Ceawlin of Wessex in 568. Married to Bertha, daughter of Charibert, king of Paris, as a result of which he accepted the Catholic faith from St Augustine *c*.AD 597; the first of the Anglo-Saxon kings to be baptized a Christian. A code of laws based on Roman law is attributed to him.

Aethelred II [Na]. King of England from AD 978 to 1016. Nicknamed 'Unready' because of his vacillating policy towards the Danish Vikings. Married Emma, daughter of Richard, duke of Normandy, to whom he fled during the invasion of King Svein of Denmark. After Svein's death (AD 1014) he returned to his throne until his own death in AD 1016.

Aethelweard [Na]. Chronicler, who called himself an EALDORMAN, and may have been the ealdorman who arranged a treaty for Aethelred II in 994. His chronicle (from the Creation to AD 973) contains some otherwise unknown material in 10th-century history. Died *c*.AD 998.

Aetius, Flavius [Na]. Roman general who was effective ruler of the west from about AD 430 until his assassination in AD 454. His 'realm' lay in Gaul, whose boundaries he maintained with the aid of Hunnic and other barbarian mercenaries, and in alliance with the Visigoths he defeated Attila's invasion of Gaul in AD 451.

Afanasievo Culture [CP]. Late Neolithic communities in southern Siberia living around the headwaters of the Ob and Yenisei rivers during the early 3rd millennium BC. Reliant on breeding cattle, sheep, and horses, these communities also engaged in hunting; they do not appear to have used agriculture. The culture is best known through its burials which typically comprise groups of round barrows (kurgans), each up to 12 m in diameter with a stone kerb and covering a central pit grave containing multiple inhumations. Pottery suggests contacts with the slightly earlier KELTAMINAR CULTURE of the Aral and Caspian Sea area. The Afanbasievo Culture was succeeded by the ANDRONOVO CULTURE in the mid 2nd millennium BC.

Afontova Culture [CP]. Upper Palaeolithic communities in south-central Siberia in the period 20 000 to 10 000 years ago. Distinguished on the basis of their worked stone industries which includes wedge-shaped microcores, microblades, and scrapers. The culture was defined by F. A. Abramova in 1979, drawing on material recovered in the early 20th century from a series of sites at Afontova Gora on the Yenisei River.

African Replacement Model [Th]. *See* HOMO *SAPIENS*.

agency [Th]. The proposition that human beings think about the intentional actions they perform and the resources they need to achieve their ends. Trying to apply such thinking to archaeology has led John Barrett to suggest that archaeologists should seek to understand how people may once have lived out their lives rather than restricting their enquiries to simply interpreting the archaeological record.

agger [Co]. **1.** Latin name for a cambered, artificially raised causeway or ridge of consolidated earth or stone carrying a Roman road. **2.** The rampart of a Roman camp.

aggregate [Ge]. A collection of people present in a public setting, all going their separate ways rather than composing a homogeneous group.

Agilulf [Na]. King of the Lombards, a nobleman selected by Queen Theudelinda as her second husband in AD 590. After threatening the Byzantine states he agreed to a truce, and after 605 was at peace with his neighbours in Italy. During his reign Catholics in northern Italy were re-established. Died *c*.AD 615.

agora [MC]. The market-place or centre of a Greek town with shopping and commercial facilities, the main public buildings, and open space where the citizens would gather for markets and sporting events. Many agoras were delimited by boundary stones. *See also* FORUM.

agrarian societies [Ge]. Societies whose means of subsistence is based on agricultural production, crop-growing and the husbandry of animals.

Agricola [Na]. Gnaeus Julius Agricola was governor of Britain between AD 78 and AD 84. Thanks to the biography by his son-in-law TACITUS, we know a good deal about his life. He was born in the *colonia* of Forum Iulii, now Fréjus, in France and served in Britain on two occasions before succeeding Frontinus as governor. During his period of office he campaigned extensively in north Wales, northern England, and Scotland where he inflicted a crushing defeat on the Caledonian tribes at Mons Graupius, probably near Aberdeen. Plans for the total conquest of Scotland were unfulfilled.

Aguada Culture [CP]. A South American culture found around the Valliserrana region of northwest Argentina of the period AD 700–1000, characterized by finely made ceramics and ceremonial objects of bronze and copper, some perhaps made under the influence of craftsmen working at Tiahuanco, Bolivia. Incised and polychrome decoration is common on pottery vessels, as too are feline and dragon motifs, depictions of warriors and weaponry, and images of trophy heads. Warfare was endemic, and many burials contain the remains of decapitated individuals. The disappearance of the Aguada Culture, apparently rather sudden, may have been the result of an invasion from the east.

AH [Ab]. Anno Hegirae. Years according to the Islamic calendar starting in 1 AH when Mohammad was banished from Mecca. Year 1 AH is equivalent to AD 622 in the Christian calendar.

AHM [Ab]. Archaeological heritage management. *See* ARCHAEOLOGICAL RESOURCE MANAGEMENT.

Ahmose (Ahmosis) [Na]. Prince of Thebes and first Pharaoh of the 18th Dynasty and the New Kingdom who reigned in the period *c.*1550–1525 BC. During this time the HYKSOS were expelled from Egypt and territorial gains made in Nubia and Palestine.

Ahrensburgian [CP]. An early post-glacial culture of north Germany and the Low Countries dating to the period around 8500 BC. The stone-tool industries include scrapers, burins,

and tanged points probably used as arrow tips. More than 50 wooden arrow shafts of this culture were found at the type-site of Ahrensburg near Hamburg in Schleswig-Holstein, together with clubs that were possibly used in hunting reindeer.

ahu [MC]. A kind of ceremonial platform constructed on Easter Island and the Society Islands in the period *c.*AD 600 through to AD 1500. Rectangular in plan, the platforms were built of stone slabs covering a rubble core. Stone statues (MOAI) were sometimes set on the ahu. Ahu are probably related to the MARAE found in ceremonial contexts in Polynesia.

AIA [Ab]. *See* ARCHAEOLOGICAL INSTITUTE OF AMERICA.

aisle [Co]. The part of a church on either side of the nave or chancel.

aisled hall [MC]. A timber structure in which the weight of the roof is borne on rows of internal posts which divide the interior into a 'nave' and flanking 'aisles'. The regular plan for north German and Scandinavian houses in the migration period, the type has an ancestry which runs back to the 4th or 5th millennium BC.

aisled house (aisled building, aisled villa) [MC]. A class of Roman villa in which a simple rectangular building was divided into a nave and two flanking aisles by lines of timber roof supports. Sometimes divided by internal partitions, these houses seem to have belonged to the poorer families. Some aisled houses had specific agricultural or industrial functions rather than a domestic use.

Ajalpan Phase [CP]. Sixth main phase of settlement recognized in the Tehuacán Valley of Mexico, broadly dating to the period 1500–830 BC. Agriculture is believed to have provided about 40 per cent of the food consumed, the remainder being derived in roughly equal parts from hunting and gathering. Settlements took the form of hamlets and were occupied all the year round, although by this time the Tehuacán Valley was already becoming marginal to the more complex societies developing in other parts of Mexico.

Ajanta, India [Si]. A Buddhist shrine in central India where a series of 28 rock-cut temples were constructed along the northern shore of the Waghora River between the 1st century BC and the 5th century AD. On the walls are scenes from the Jatakas, stories about the lives of the Buddha in earlier incarnations. At its height, Ajanta was home to more than 200 monks.

[Sum.: R. Gupte and B. D. Mahajan, 1962, *Ajanta, Ellora and Aurangabad caves*. Bombay: Taraporevala]

Ajuereado Phase [CP]. Earliest main phase of settlement in the Tehuacán Valley of Mexico, dating to 9500–7000 BC. This phase was characterized by Palaeo-Indian communities using spears with leaf-shaped points to hunt horse, antelope, and deer. The tool kit is dominated by butchering and hide-working equipment. In the early part of the phase there is little evidence for the use of plant resources; the exploitation of the valley seems to have involved small mobile hunting groups. About 8000 BC, horse, antelope, and several other animal species became extinct, perhaps because of over-hunting, forcing the population to greater reliance on plant food.

Akhenaten (Ikhnaton, Amenophis IV) [Na]. Pharaoh of Egypt in the period *c*.1349–1333 BC, towards the end of the 18th Dynasty of the New Kingdom. Together with his queen Nefertiti, he rejected the traditional pantheon of Egyptian gods, preferring instead the monotheistic worship of ATEN as the state religion. During his reign he moved the capital of Egypt from THEBES to El-Amarna. On Akhenaten's death there was a rapid return to the worship of AMUN in Thebes.

Akerman, John Yonge (1806–73) [Bi]. English antiquary, who worked as secretary to William Cobbett. Akerman had a life-long interest in the study of coins and helped found the Numismatic Society of London in 1836. Soon afterwards he began editing the *Numismatic Journal*. He was influential as the secretary of the Society of Antiquaries of London (1848–60), and in 1855 published *Remains of Pagon Saxondum*, a synthesis of recent discoveries.

[Bio.: *Dictionary of National Biography*, I, 211]

Akkadian [CP]. A cultural grouping named after an archaeologically unlocated site in the northern part of SUMER (possibly BABYLON) that became the capital city of the Akkadian state founded by Sargon in *c*.2370 BC. Under Sargon and his grandson Naram-Sin the dynasty extended the city-state into a larger empire covering northern and southern Mesopotamia as well as the neighbouring area of Elam. The Semitic language that was associated with the Akkadian empire is also called Akkadian and replaced Sumerian as the official language of the region. It was also written in CUNEIFORM script which had originally been devised to record the unrelated and quite different Sumerian language. Through the later 3rd millennium BC the Akkadian language became extensively used throughout the Near East and into Anatolia and Egypt, in the 2nd and 1st millennia BC becoming Assyrian and Babylonian.

ala (pl. *alae*) [De]. Latin term for an auxiliary cavalry unit of either 500 or, more rarely, 1000 men.

alabaster [Ma]. *See* GYPSUM.

Alaca Hüyük, Turkey [Si]. Multi-period settlement site covering more than 7 ha near Alaca to the east of Ankara on the Anatolian Plateau. Extensive excavations by Hamit Kosay during the period 1935–49 established the long and complicated history of the site spanning the Chalcolithic through to the late Roman period. Related to the early Bronze Age II Phase (early 3rd millennium BC) of the settlement is a group of 13 'royal graves' situated just outside the town. These tombs comprise rectangular stone or timber-lined pits containing single or double inhumations accompanied by extremely rich grave goods. These include royal standards in the form of animal figures plated in precious metals, and a range of weapons, jewellery, and vessels in precious metal. Notable is the very early occurrence of two daggers made of iron with gold-plated handles. As a final act animal skins had been spread over the top of the grave pits, the skulls and hooves being found upon excavation.

From the 2nd millennium BC is an extensive Hittite occupation consisting of a walled town containing several temples, residential areas, and a monumental gateway known as the Sphinx Gate. There was an iron foundry within the town, the whole complex perhaps being identified with the Old Hittite period cult centre known as Arinna.

[Rep.: H. Z. Kosay, 1973, *Alaca Hoyuk Kazisi: 1963–1967 calismalari ve kesiflere ait ilk rapor*. Ankara: Turk Tarih Kuruma yayinlarindan]

Alamanni [CP]. A confederation of several Germanic tribes who amalgamated in the 3rd century AD. In c.AD 260 they conquered the Roman frontier lands between the Rhine and the Danube, and remained there, despite their defeat by the Romans in AD 357, until the Frankish expansions of the 6th century AD incorporated their territory into Francia.

Alans [CP]. Nomadic people of southeastern Russia, who migrated eastwards as their lands were taken over by the Goths during the 3rd century AD. The advance of the HUNS caused a movement westwards. Some Alans joined the Huns in the 370s AD. A tribe of Alans crossed into Spain in AD 409, where they joined forces with the VANDALS.

Alaric [Na]. Visigoth leader who in AD 395 led a migration of his people into Greece and devastated the Balkans. The eastern government encouraged him to turn his attention westwards and he invaded Italy in 401. In an attempt to find lands for his people he marched south but failed to cross to Sicily, and died in southern Italy c.AD 410.

Alaric II [Na]. King of the Visigoths, who succeeded his father Euric in AD 484 and ruled the Catholics with toleration. In 506 he issued a code of laws abstracted from Roman practice for the use of his Roman subjects. He was defeated and killed by Clovis in AD 507 at Vuillé.

Albany [CP]. A late Stone Age industry of southern and eastern Cape Province, South Africa, dating to the period 10 000 to 6000 BC. Also known as the Oakhurst, this industry has few distinctive tool types except large scrapers more than 20 mm long. The Albany industries directly precede the appearance of WILTON industries.

albarello [Ar]. A type of late medieval drug-jar, made in Spain, with a particularly fine thin tin glaze over blue designs that draw heavily on contemporary forms of Arabic script. Albarello ware were traded and have been found in the Netherlands and Britain.

Albion [Na]. *See* AVIENUS.

Alboin [Na]. King of the Lombards, succeeding his father c.AD 565. With Avar assistance he destroyed the Gepids and withdrew into Italy with his people, where he overthrew the new Byzantine state. He was murdered in AD 572.

Alcuin [Na]. Theologian born at York in c.AD 735 and educated in the cathedral school. In AD 778, when master of the school, he was chosen by Charlemagne to found the Palace School at Aachen. He settled in Francia and from AD 796 to his death he was abbot of Tours. He wrote theological and philosophical works and his influence was widespread in court circles. He died c.AD 804.

Aldbourne cup [Ar]. Type of miniature cup or accessory vessel found in early Bronze Age (WESSEX II) graves in southern England. Generally less than 15 cm across, Aldbourne cups are characterized by a wide mouth and straight-sided body decorated with geometric incised and *pointillé* decoration.

Aldbourne–Edmonsham group [CP]. Term for the burials of the second phase of the Wessex Culture (WESSEX II) in southern Britain, named after two typical examples: Aldbourne, Wiltshire, and Edmonsham, Dorset. Burials of this tradition are mainly cremations. Both males and females are represented and grave goods typically include Camerton–Snowshill daggers, bone tweezers, ALDBOURNE CUPS, bronze or bone pins, and shaft-hole battle-axes. The few dates available cluster in the 15th century BC.

alembic [Ar]. The upper part of a two-piece round container used in distillation. A downward-sloping spout allows a condensed distillate to run into another vessel.

Aleutian Tradition [CP]. Hunter-gatherer tradition found in western Alaska and the Aleutian Islands from about 3000 BC down to AD 1800. Characterized by a distinctive core and flake stone industry and an elaborate bone-working tradition. Most distinctive are the bifacially trimmed projectile points, tanged and untanged knives, and adzes. Among the bone artefacts special note may be made of the finely worked harpoon heads and figurines. The subsistence base was marine mammals and sea fish such as cod and halibut. Houses were elliptical or rectangular in plan, dug about 0.5 m into the ground, roofed with driftwood and sod, and probably entered through an opening in the roof.

Alexander I (The Fierce) [Na]. King of Scotland. Born *c*.1077, fifth son of Malcolm III and Margaret. Married Sybilla, illegitimate daughter of Henry I of England. Died in AD 1124 aged 47, having reigned seventeen years.

Alexander II [Na]. King of Scotland. Born 1198, son of William I. Married: (1) Joan, daughter of John, king of England; (2) Marie, daughter of Ingelram de Coucy. Died in 1249 aged 50, having reigned 34 years.

Alexander III [Na]. King of Scotland. Born 1241, son of Alexander II and Marie. Married: (1) Margaret, daughter of Henry III of England; (2) Yoland, daughter of the count of Dreux. Killed accidentally in AD 1285 aged 44, having reigned 36 years.

Alexander the Great [Na]. Leader of the Macedonians. Born in 356 BC, Alexander was tutored in his early years by Aristotle before succeeding his father Philip as king of Macedonia and the mainland of Greece in 336 BC. Early in his reign he set about releasing the Greeks from Persian domination, but continued his campaigns into a programme of imperialist aggrandizement that eventually created a massive, albeit short-lived, empire from India to Egypt. After his death from fever in 323 BC his hastily constructed dominion fell apart, the most lasting tribute to his achievement being the town of Alexandria, which he founded in Egypt in 331 BC.

Alexandria, Egypt [Si]. Coastal city and Hellenistic capital in the northwestern area of the Nile Delta, established by Alexander the Great in 331 BC. It soon replaced Memphis as the capital of Egypt, establishing itself as a hub of eastern Mediterranean trade with its famous double harbour and favourable position at the natural intersection of shipping routes. Important buildings within this trading port included the tomb of Alexander, the temple of Serapis, the great library, and the Pharos which rates as one of the SEVEN WONDERS OF THE ANCIENT WORLD. Built of white limestone, the Pharos had three tiers and is estimated to have been 110 m high. It was destroyed by an earthquake in the 14th century AD.

[Sum.: G. L. Sheen (ed.), 1993, *Alexandria: the site and its history*. New York: New York University Press]

Alfred the Great [Na]. King of Wessex whose exploits are known from the *ANGLO-SAXON CHRONICLE* and the biography written by his friend Asser. Born in Wantage, Oxfordshire, in AD 849, he succeeded to the throne of Wessex in AD 871. After numerous encounters with Viking raiders and a period in hiding in the remote area of Athelney, Somerset, he drove the invaders out of Wessex and forced the DANELAW upon then. In consolidating his victory he established stronger links with the Carolingian empire, created an English fleet, and developed a series of fortified towns, known as *Burhs*, across central southern England. He died in AD 899.

Alice Holt ware [Ar]. Major Romano-British pottery industry based around Farnham in Surrey, England, producing a wide range of wares between the mid 1st century AD and the 4th century AD. Grey and cream-coloured fabrics predominate.

alidade [Eq]. At its most simple, a flat wooden or metal strip with a scaled straight edge on one side and sighting mounts at each end so that it can be aligned on specific target points when used in conjunction with a plane table. More sophisticated alidades are equipped with telescopic sights and a series of levels and scales to measure vertical angles. *See* PLANE TABLE.

alien [De]. An ecclesiastical establishment which was directly dependent on a foreign monastery. *See* MONASTERY.

alienation [Th]. The sense that our own abilities, as human beings, are taken over by other entities. The term was originally used by Karl Marx to refer to the projection of human powers on to gods. Subsequently he employed the term to refer to the loss of control on the part of workers over the nature of the labour task, and over the products of their labour. Archaeologically it provides a useful set of concepts for dealing with the development of state-based societies and early industrialization.

alignment [De]. A straight line formed by connecting three or more significant or related points. *Compare* ORIENTATION.

Ali Kosh, Iraq [Si]. Early Neolithic TELL on the Deh Luran plain in lowland Khuzistan, western Iran. Excavated by Frank Hole and Kent Flannery in the 1960s, the work was innovative in successfully using a flotation unit to sample deposits for carbonized plant remains. The cultural sequence begins at about 8000 BC and runs through for about two millennia, spanning the period when farming developed in the region. In the earliest, Bus Mordeh, phase (c.8000–7000 BC) the settlement comprised simple rectangular houses built of mud brick. The occupants lived through a combination of simple farming, hunting, and gathering. Domesticates included herded sheep and goats together with hulled barley, and emmer and einkorn wheat. The inhabitants collected a wide range of plants and also fished. In the succeeding Ali Kosh Phase (c.7000–6200 BC) the same range of domesticates were found and some hunting and fishing still occurred, but the contribution made by wild plants decreased dramatically as the use of cultivated plants increased. The settlement was larger, with more substantial buildings. In the third, Muhammad Jaffar, phase (c.6200–5800 BC) there were further innovations, including the introduction of pottery, and farming had become firmly established. The site appears to have been abandoned in the mid 6th millennium BC.

[Rep.: F. Hole, K. V. Flannery and J. A. Neely, 1969, *Prehistory and human ecology of the Deh Luran Plain*. Ann Arbor: University of Michigan Press]

All Hallows (All Saints) [Ge]. Autumn/winter festival traditionally celebrated in northwest Europe on 1 November in the Gregorian calendar. This was the time when stock were excluded from fields in tillage and when the sowing of winter corn was expected to be completed. The night before, All Hallows Eve, was regarded as a time when the spirits of the dead were at large amongst the living.

Allectus [Na]. Roman finance minister to the usurper Carausius and his murderer in AD 293. Allectus was defeated and deposed by Constantius Chlorus, in AD 296.

allée couverte [MC]. Class of Neolithic chambered tomb found in central and northern France. It comprises long rectangular chambers with little or no evidence of differentiation within them, although some have antechambers at the entrance and a small inaccessible cell beyond the back wall of the main chamber. This end-cell sometimes has

pairs of raised lumps carved on to the faces of the wall stones that are interpreted as female breasts. Low stone and earth mounds cover the chambers, and in some cases there are kerbs around the outer edge of the mound. They date to the 3rd millennium BC and are especially common in Brittany and the Paris basin (SEINE-OISE-MARNE CULTURE). Where excavated, the chambers are found to contain the remains of several hundred individuals.

Allen, Derek Fortrose (1910–75) [Bi]. British numismatist and archaeologist well known for his work on early coinage in Britain and Gaul. From 1935 until 1939 he was Assistant Keeper in the Department of Coins and Medals at the British Museum. Subsequently he worked in the Ministries of Shipping and Transport, rising to become Under-Secretary in the Ministry of Aviation. Celtic coins remained his great love and he maintained his interest in them, finding time to publish numerous papers and reports throughout the 1950s and 1960s. On his retirement from the civil service he was appointed Secretary of the British Academy, successor to Sir Mortimer Wheeler, a post he held until 1973. He was elected a Fellow of the Society of Antiquaries in 1947 and a Fellow of the British Academy in 1963.

[Obit.: *The Times*, 16 June 1975]

Allen, Major George W. G. (1891–1940) [Bi]. A mechanical engineer who pioneered the use of aerial photography for archaeological research. Born in Oxford, he was educated at Boxgrove School, Guildford, and Clifton College, before attending the Royal Military Academy in Woolwich. He resigned his commission, however, to become an engineer, working for some years on the east coast of Africa. During WW1 he served in the Royal Tank Corps, after the war joining his family business and finding time to become an enthusiastic airman. Piloting his own aircraft, the first privately owned aircraft in Oxford, and using a hand-made camera, he became well known for his pictures of archaeological sites in the Oxford area, which were mostly taken between 1933 and 1938. In 1936 he was elected a Fellow of the Society of Antiquaries. He was killed in a motor-cycle accident in November 1940.

[Bio.: D. N. Riley, 1984, Introduction. *Aerial Archaeology*, 10, 1–16]

Allerød Interstadial [CP]. A warm phase during the Devensian glaciation of the Pleistocene Ice Age in Europe, dated to approximately 9850–8850 BC. Equivalent to the Two Creeks Interval in the North American sequence.

allotment [MC]. Land allocated in parcels or blocks to the different proprietors in a parish under the Enclosure Acts of the 18th and 19th centuries AD in lieu of former scattered open-field arable, meadow, and rights of pasture.

all-over-corded beakers (AOC) [Ar]. *See* BEAKERS.

all-over-ornamented beakers (AOO) [Ar]. *See* BEAKERS.

alloy [Ma]. Any deliberate mixture of two or more metals to enhance the properties of one or other in some way. Alloys involving just two main metals are known as binary alloys. The earliest alloy in most parts of the world was bronze, essentially a combination of copper and tin although lead and arsenic were later added.

alluvium [Ge]. A general term for sediment deposited by rivers, including that on the river bed, along its margins, across its floodplain, and in an estuary, if it has one. Alluvium tends to be rich in organic matter and may contain archaeological material. The onset of periods of rapid alluviation may also have the effect of sealing old land surfaces under the alluvium.

Almerian Culture [CP]. A Neolithic culture dating to the 5th and 4th millennia BC in southeastern Spain, and particularly associated with the settlement at El Garcel. Many of the settlements were built on hilltops with circular houses built from wattle and daub. Inside were hearths and storage pits. The tombs are also round, built of dry-stone walling and used for single or multiple inhumation. Almerian pottery was plain with rounded or pointed bases. Some copper objects are found in late Almerian contexts.

alpaca [Sp]. Camelid mammal (*Lama pacos*) with long shaggy hair, native to the high Andean grasslands of Peru and Ecuador, related to the llama. Domesticated by *c*.5000 BC and widely used as a source of food and raw material for the manufacture of textiles.

alphabet [Ge]. *See* WRITING.

Altamira, Spain [Si]. An extensive cave system in the Cantabrian Mountains near Santander in northern Spain. Between 1875 and 1879 Don Marcelino de Sautuola explored the 280 m deep caves and discovered paintings on the walls. He believed them to be Palaeolithic in date because of their style and the flintwork and faunal remains found in the entrance to the caves. It took a while for this to be accepted, but the works are now recognized as being late SOLUTREAN and early MAGDALENIAN in date, broadly 13 000 to 11 500 BC. The motifs and figures represented include polychrome images of bison, masks, and quadrilateral signs of unknown meaning. Some of the figured animals are large, up to 2 m across, the most spectacular group being on the ceiling of a low hall near the entrance which depicts bison, deer, and horses.

[Rep.: H. Breuil and H. Obermaier, 1935, *The cave of Altamira at Santilana der Mar, Spain*. Madrid: El Viso]

altar-pace [Co]. The steps or platform on which an altar stands in a church.

Altithermal [Ge]. Holocene climatic optimum centred on *c*.5500–3500 BC recognized in the western part of North America and broadly equivalent to the Atlantic Phase in Europe.

AMAAA [Ab]. *See* ANCIENT MONUMENT.

AMAC [Ab]. *See* ANCIENT MONUMENTS ADVISORY COMMITTEE.

amaranth [Sp]. Flowering herb (*Amaranthus hypochondriacus*) with the flowers bunched together in long conspicuous racemes, native to Mexico and central America. Domesticated from *c*.4500 BC in Mexico, but rather later elsewhere in South America.

amber [Ma]. Fossilized pine resin, relatively soft and easily carved, extensively used in prehistoric and later times for the manufacture of ornaments and jewellery. There are few sources of the material, but items were traded widely. It is mostly derived from the Baltic coastlands but sources around the North Sea are also known. Amber also occurs in the Mediterranean but can be chemically distinguished from north European sources.

ambo [Co]. The raised pulpit in a Byzantine or Orthodox Christian church.

ambulatory [Co]. Covered portico surrounding the inner shrine of a temple.

Amen (Amon, Amun) [Di]. God of Thebes in Upper Egypt who came to prominence during the rise of the Theban dynasties in the Middle and New Kingdoms. Though represented in human form, he is associated with the ram, and later came to be assimilated with the sun god RA and as Amen-Ra was patron god of the Egyptian empire.

Amenemhet (Amenemmes) [Na]. Four pharaohs took this name during the 12th Dynasty when the Middle Kingdom of Egypt reached the peak of its development c.2100–1785 BC.

Amenhoptep (Amunhotep, Amenophis) [Na]. Alternative names for four pharaohs of the 18th Dynasty between c.1525 and 1333 BC.

American Cultural Resources Association (ACRA) [Or]. A trade association established in March 1995 to serve the needs of the cultural resources industry in the USA. Covering the fields of historic preservation, history, archaeology, architectural history, historical architecture, and landscape architecture, the aim is to promote professional, ethical, and business practices for the benefit of the resources, the public, and the members of the association.

American Indian (Amerindian) [Ge]. A general term applied rather indiscriminately to the members of any of the various first nation aboriginal peoples of North America south of the Arctic, or of South America, or the West Indies. Sometimes regarded as synonymous with 'Native American', but this latter term is generally regarded as being more all-embracing by including, among others, Hawaiians and Aleuts.

amino-acid racemization [Te]. A biological dating method used on human and animal bone and carbonate shells. Within living organisms amino acids are molecularly structured in what is known as the L-isomer configuration, but at death they restructure to what is known as the D-isomer configuration through a process known as racemiza- tion. This restructuring takes place relatively slowly, so that from a zero point at the time of death the D/L ratio gradually increases so that equilibrium is reached after anything from 150 000 years to more than 2 million years. The main problem with the technique is that the rate of racemization varies according to temperature and groundwater conditions so that regional differences according to latitude can be seen as well as, over long periods, uneven rates of change through time. This means that turning the D/L ratios into absolute ages is difficult, although as data about a particular area is built up fairly reasonable sequences can be developed.

Ammianus Marcellinus [Na]. One of the last great Roman historians. Originally from Antioch, born c.AD 330, he served in the army and settled in Rome c.AD 378. His *History*, written in Latin for a Roman audience, spanned the years AD 96 to 378. Only the section from AD 353 survives, providing an account of events and of society in the years before the barbarian incursions into the empire. Died c.AD 395.

Amon [Di]. Egyptian god. *See* AMEN.

Amorites [CP]. Nomadic people of western Mesopotamia, instrumental in the collapse of the UR III kingdom around 2000 BC, who then settled amongst the Babylonians and integrated with them. The first eminent Amorite king was Gungunum, part of the Larsa Dynasty. In the early 2nd millennium BC an Amorite Dynasty emerged at Babylon under Sumuabum, initiating the Old Babylonian period from soon after 2000 BC down to 1600 BC. The later Amorite capital was Mari on the middle Euphrates. The Amorites eventually amalgamated with the Canaanites, and in later times can be identified with a small kingdom and associated language group in northern Syria.

amphictiony [De]. An association of neighbouring city-states for joint supervision of religious institutions, such as control of the Delphic oracle in Greece in the 1st millennium BC.

amphitheatre [MC]. A Roman building of elliptical form, open to the elements, with an arena surrounded by tiers of seats. Public spectacles were held in the arena.

amphora [Ar]. A large two-handled ceramic jar with narrow neck and pointed or rounded base. Used for the storage and transportation of liquid commodities such as wine, olive oil, and fish sauce around the ancient world. One of the most abundant forms of finds in Roman and later sites. The earliest amphorae, known as Canaanite jars, originated on the Lebanese–Syrian coast in the 15th century BC. The latest amphorae date to the 7th century AD, by which time wooden and skin containers seem to have taken over the traditional roles. The study of amphorae is facilitated by the distinctive typological form of vessels from different areas and of different dates. Petrological work also helps with the definition of sources for vessels found at the end of their journey as containers. Stamps and painted inscriptions (*tituli picti*) assist in the recognition of the original contents.

Several classificatory schemes have been proposed for amphorae, most notably by Dressel in 1899 who illustrated 45 main forms (D1–D45). Pélichet (1946) and Almagro (1955) added further forms to the list, while Schumacher (1936), Callender (1965), and Lamboglia (1955) have attempted to group the basic types into broad groups. Most recently, David Peacock and David Williams have provided a new classification based on form and origin (based on petrological work) with 66 classes. The more common classes can be summarized as follows (with Dressel numbers in brackets): 1. brindisc amphorae from Apani, Italy—olive oil; 2. Greco-Italic amphorae from a range of sources in Sicily, Corsica, Spain, and the Aegean—probably wine; 3. (D1A) from Campania, Latium, and Etruria in Italy—wine and occasionally shells, resin, and hazel nuts; 5. (D1C) from Campania and Etruria—wines and olives; 6. (D1) from Catalan coast of Spain and ?Aspiran, France—wine; 7. (D21–22) possibly from Campania and Lazio, Italy—fruit; 8. (D6) from Apulia and Istrian peninsula of Yugoslavia—mainly olive oil; 9. Rhodian amphorae from Rhodes—wine and sometimes figs; 10. Greco-Roman amphorae (D2–4) from a range of sources in Campania, Latium, and Etruria, Italy, Catalonia and Baetica in Spain, southern and central France, and perhaps Brockley Hill in England—mainly wine, sometimes figs and fish sauce; 14. (D12) southern Spain and used for fish-based products; 16. (D7–11) from southern Spain—fish sauce; 24. (D25) southern Spain, possibly olive oil; 25. (D20) globular amphorae, Baetica,

southern Spain—olive oil; 26. (D23) southern Spain—olive-oil-based products; 26. (D23) southern Spain—olive-based products. 32. Neo-Punic amphorae, Morocco and Tunisia—?olive oil; 43. (British Bi) Aegean or Black Sea region, content unknown, possibly resin; 44. (British Bii) Northern Syria or Cyprus—?oil; 45. (British Biv) eastern Mediterranean—content not known; 49. (Almagro 54), Gaza, Palestine—?wine.

Amratian [CP]. Egyptian predynastic culture named after the site of El Amrah and dating to the period *c*.3250 to 2850 BC, emerging out of the earlier BADARIAN Culture. Few settlements are known, but large cemeteries such as the one at Nagada provide much information about the culture which displays a high level of skill in stoneworking and in the production of painted pottery. Copper also began to be worked in this period. The dead were buried in a couched position with rich grave goods including pottery, personal ornaments, ivory combs, and figurines, all probably intended for use in the afterlife.

AMS [Ab]. *See* ACCELERATOR MASS SPECTROMETRY.

Amudian [CP]. Name given to a distinctive middle Palaeolithic lithic industry comprising blades and burins found at sites close to the Mediterranean coast in the Near East and dating to the last interglacial, between *c*.50 000 and 40 000 years ago. At Amud, Israel, excavations by M. Suzuki have yielded the remains of five Neanderthal people associated with Amudian material culture.

amulet [Ar]. An object which is believed by its owner to have the power to ward off evil. Sometimes bears a magical inscription to ensure efficacy.

Amun [Di]. *See* AMEN.

anaerobic [De]. Term describing preservational environments in which oxygen is lacking and in which microbial decay is halted or greatly slowed. Such environments are typically waterlogged or deeply buried under very fine grained sediments and lead to the preservation of organic materials such as animal and plant remains.

analogy [Th]. A process of reasoning whereby two entities or processes that share some similarities are assumed to share many others. Alison Wylie has usefully defined two kinds of analogy in archaeological reasoning: **formal analogy** is based on a straightforward comparison of some aspect of form, or observable characteristics, which can be transferred from one case to another; **relational analogy** is based on understanding the causal relationships between the variables that can be observed.

analytical type [Ge]. Arbitrary grouping that an archaeologist defines for classifying human-manufactured artefacts. Analytical types consist of groups of attributes that define convenient types of artefacts for comparing sites in space and time. They do not necessarily coincide with actual tool types used by prehistoric people.

Ananatuba Complex [CP]. South American cultural grouping, defined almost entirely by ceramic styles, from Marajo Island, Amazonia, and tentatively dated to *c*.1400 BC. The ceramic assemblages belong to the Zone Hachure Horizon defined in the Amazon Basin. Typical vessel forms include rounded bowls and jars. Some are decorated with fine parallel or cross-hatched lines with zones defined by deeply incised outlines. There is no evidence for agriculture associated with groups using this pottery. Settlements were small, perhaps multi-family communal residences.

Anangula Island, Alaska, USA [Si]. Cliff-top coastal settlement site of Palaeo-Arctic communities on an islet off the coast of Umnak Island in the eastern Aleutians. The site was occupied from before 7000 BC down to *c*.5000 BC. There were traces of elliptical houses partially dug into the ground. The economy probably relied on sea mammals and fish, although little of the tool assemblage recovered appears to have been designed for such use.

[Rep.: J. Aigner, 1970, The unifacial, core and blade sites on Anangula Island, Aleutians. *Arctic Anthropology*, 7, 59–88]

Anasazi [CP]. A regional cultural grouping of peoples living along the Arizona–Utah borderlands of the USA, emerging within the Basketmaker Phase defined in the prehistory of the southwestern part of North America. Dating to *c*.AD 400–1300, the Anasazi tradi-

tion is the largest cultural grouping of the period and covers the northwestern quarter of New Mexico, much of southwestern and western Colorado, the northern half of Arizona, and most of Utah: an area known as the 'Four Corners'. Much of this area has inadequate rainfall for the size of populations involved and some basic irrigation measures were used, although not extensively. Alongside agriculture, hunting and the collecting of wild foodstuffs was also practised. Ceremonial centres near the settlements remained important. Exchange links with Mississippian Cultures are evident from, among other things, similarities in the form of some ceramic containers. The distinctive characteristics of the Anasazi tradition developed during the Basketmaker III Phase (AD 450–750). Beans were added to the diet and communities became more committed to agriculture. Domesticated turkeys were introduced to supplement deer and rabbit meat obtained through hunting and trapping. A sophisticated ceramic technology developed with the resultant bowls and jars often internally decorated with black painted geometric patterns. There was also a transition from scattered village life to nucleated settlements. At first these comprised pit-houses with domed roofs and a central hearth.

After AD 750, in the Pueblo I and II Phases, the size of the settlements increased considerably. These large settlements or 'pueblos' comprised multi-storey and multi-roomed houses, some with over 100 rooms and constructed from masonry. By about AD 1300 many of the classic sites of this culture had been abandoned, perhaps because of climatic factors, erosion, intergroup conflicts, or demographic changes. One theory holds that Anasazi communities migrated away from their former homeland.

Anastasius [Na]. Emperor of the eastern Roman empire who succeeded Zeno in AD 491. Born *c*.AD 430 he was a careful and prudent administrator who reformed the currency, and spent much time in attempts to reconcile the irreconcilable viewpoints of theologians in the empire. Died *c*.AD 518.

Anat [Di]. Syrian war goddess worshipped in Egypt.

anchor [Ar]. A heavy weight or hook-shaped attachment carried on a boat or ship for use in mooring the vessel in shallow water. Early anchors are large perforated stones, but from classical times onwards specially designed anchors occur, usually with a weighted stock at the end of which is one or more hooks. Different types of anchor are needed for different types of sea-bed.

anchorite [De]. A hermit.

anchor ornament [Ar]. An anchor-shaped ceramic object with a perforation through the shank. Widespread in the early Bronze Age of Greece and slightly later in Sicily and Malta.

ancient cottage [Ge]. A cottage having long-established rights of common. After the 17th century, newly established cottages had fewer or no rights.

Ancient Monument [Le]. Although generally referring to recognized archaeological sites and ancient structures, this term also has a specific legal meaning set out in Section 61(12) of the *Ancient Monuments and Archaeological Areas Act 1979* (AMAAA) for England, Wales, and Scotland. Here 'Ancient Monuments' are either SCHEDULED Monuments or 'any other MONUMENT which in the opinion of the Secretary of State is of public interest by reason of the historic, architectural, traditional, artistic, or archaeological interest attaching to it'. Section 33(8) of the *National Heritage Act 1983* also defines the term Ancient Monument with reference to the work of English Heritage as: 'any structure, work, site, garden or area which in the Commission's opinion is of historic, architectural, traditional, artistic or archaeological interest'.

Ancient Monuments Advisory Committee (AMAC) [Or]. A small committee of archaeologists established by the Commissioners of English Heritage to provide counsel on matters relating to archaeology and the work of the Commission.

Andernach Grit [De]. *See* NIEDERMENDIG LAVA.

Andersson, John Gunnar (1874–1960) [Bi]. A Swedish geologist who in 1921, while working in China, demonstrated for the first time the presence of prehistoric settlement in the country. He is credited with the discovery of *Homo erectus* remains at Zhoukoudian during his excavation there between 1921 and 1926,

and also the identification of the Neolithic painted pottery sites.

[Not.: G. Daniel, 1950, *One hundred years of Archaeology*. London: Duckworth 267–8]

Andjety [Di]. Egyptian god Busiris whose symbols, the crook and the flail, were incorporated into the iconography of Osiris.

Andrai, Walter (1875–1956) [Bi]. German archaeologist and prehistorian who undertook large-scale excavations at the city of Assur, Iraq, between 1903 and 1914.

[Not.: G. Daniel, 1950, *One hundred years of Archaeology*. London, Duckworth, 199–200]

Andronovo Culture [CP]. Bronze Age communities living in western Siberia, Russia, and adjacent parts of Kazakhstan in the period 1500–800 BC, which were closely involved with the exploitation of copper ores in the Altai Mountains. Named after the settlement site of Andronovo in Siberia, typical villages of the culture consist of up to ten large semi-subterranean houses of log-cabin-type construction, each anything up to 30 m by 60 m in extent. Burials were made either in stone cists or stone enclosures with underground timber chambers. The Andronovo Culture was succeeded by the KARASUK CULTURE.

Angles [CP]. A Germanic people who originated on the Baltic coastlands of Jutland.

Anglian Stage [CP]. A group of deposits representing a geostratigraphic stage within the PLEISTOCENE series of the British QUATERNARY system, mainly found in East Anglia and dating to between 450 000 and 300 000 years ago. The Anglian Stage is generally seen as a full glacial phase, the deposits stratigraphically overlying CROMERIAN INTERGLACIAL material and below HOXNIAN interglacial deposits. Formerly known as the Lowestoft glaciation. The Alpine equivalent is the MINDEL, the North American equivalent the Kansas. The Anglian is perhaps equated to the Elster glacial maximum in Europe.

Anglo-Norman [CP]. **1.** General term used to refer to cultural traditions, especially architectural styles, current in England in the period after the Norman conquest, broadly AD 1066 to 1200. During this time Norman and Romanesque designs were being applied by English buildings in the construction of churches, palaces, and castles. **2.** In Ireland the Anglo-Normans were the invaders who arrived in Ireland in AD 1176 at the instigation of Dermot Mac Murrough.

Anglo-Saxon Chronicle [Ar]. A principal source for Anglo-Saxon history, compiled from a series of annals between *c*.AD 871 and AD 890 during the reign of Alfred the Great. Some manuscripts were augmented by further annals which give variant and near-contemporary accounts of 10th- to 12th-century history. The annals were probably composed in major monasteries including Abingdon, Canterbury, Peterborough, Winchester, and Worcester.

Anglo-Saxon palace [MC]. A high-status occupation site used by a king or bishop, comprising one or more large structures assumed to be halls, together with associated buildings and sometimes enclosed by a bank and ditch. They date to the period from the 5th century AD through to the 11th century AD. Excavated examples include those at Cheddar, Somerset, and Yeavering, Northumberland.

Anglo-Saxons [CP]. **1.** A compound name used to describe amalgamated groups of Angles, Saxons, and others who from the 5th century AD were living away from their homelands, and to distinguish them from their kindred still on the continent. **2.** The period in early English history between the collapse of British power *c*.AD 550 and the Norman conquest of AD 1066 when the eastern part of the country was dominated by migrant Angles and Saxons. The period is generally divided into three chronological subdivisions: the early Saxon period up to about AD 650, the middle Saxon period from about AD 650 to AD 850, and the late Saxon period from AD 850 down to AD 1066. The first of these broadly equates with what is also sometimes referred to as the PAGAN SAXON period. The Anglo-Saxon period saw the emergence of a series of seven kingdoms in England (the Heptarchy), the most important of which were MERCIA, NORTHUMBRIA, and WESSEX. The Anglo-Saxons were also responsible for the establishment of the English language and a pattern of settlement that became characteristic of the medieval period and in part still survives today.

animal pound [MC]. *See* POUND.

animism [Ge]. A belief that events in the world are mobilized by the activities of spirits.

ankh [Ge]. The Egyptian hieroglyph for 'life', consisting of T surmounted by a loop. Representations of this symbol carried by the gods and pharaohs are often seen on wall paintings.

Annales School [Th]. A French school of historical thought, established by Marc Bloch and Lucien Febvre in the late 1920s and developed by Fernand Braudel in the 1950s and 1960s, which focuses on the idea of the history of ideologies, worldviews, and mental structures: the historical context. Key to this is the matter of time and the interrelationships between different timescales in the way that human beings perceive and operate within the world. History becomes a dialogue between the past and the present, the task of the investigator being to explore simultaneously both the interests and ideas of the society to which the investigator belongs and those things which are specific to the culture of the people being studied.

Anne [Na]. Queen of the United Kingdom from the House of Stuart. Born 1665, younger daughter of James II and Anne Hyde. Married Prince George of Denmark, son of Frederick III of Denmark. Died in 1714 aged 49, having reigned twelve years.

annealing [Ge]. A metallurgical process involving the heating and then slow cooling of metal during the course of working it in order to increase its ductility and reduce any brittleness caused by hammering and bending. Annealing is especially important when working gold, silver, copper, and bronze.

Ansur [Di]. *See* OSIRIS.

anta [Co]. The end of a wall of a building if it projects and is architecturally treated.

antefix [Ar]. A Latin word for a terracotta plaque covering the end of an *IMBREX* at eaves level, and usually decorated with an APOTROPAIC subject.

anthracology [De]. Studies of wood charcoal from archaeological sites in order to develop an understanding of the ways communities used the plants and trees around them.

anthropogenic [De]. Referring to things, events, or actions whose origins can be traced to the activities of individual people or human groups.

anthropology [De]. The study or science of man, which began to develop as a separate discipline in the 19th century. In its widest sense anthropology embraces human physiology and psychology as well as the study of human societies and all other aspects of human culture past and present.

In North America anthropology is traditionally divided into four main fields: cultural anthropology, which deals with the description and analysis of the forms and styles of social life past and present; archaeology, which looks at sequences of social and cultural evolution under diverse natural and cultural conditions; anthropological linguistics, which focuses on the formation and relationships between human languages and the relationships between language and culture; and physical anthropology, which concentrates on the animal origins of humans, the development of human anatomy, and the distribution of hereditary variations amongst contemporary populations.

In Britain archaeology is seen as a separate but related discipline, while the non-physical side of anthropology is traditionally divided into social anthropology and cultural anthropology. Cultural anthropology covers the whole range of human activities which are learned and transmitted. Social anthropology is more concerned with social institutions, social values, social organization, and social structure.

anthropomorphic [De]. Referring to objects or structures that resemble or have human form, attributes, or personality. Usually applied to figurines or the representation of gods or animals.

antiquarianism [Th]. An intellectual tradition of enquiry that developed in Europe in the 16th and early 17th centuries AD as a result of new interests in nature, antiquity, the Renaissance of learning, and the addition of time-depth to people's view of the world. It was in some senses a substitute for the study of classical antiquities, and a reflection of emergent national pride. It may also have been prompted by a reaction to the Reformation, when the monasteries were destroyed and great libraries disposed of. In the 18th century it was invigorated by the rediscovery of ancient Greece and the classical world, the Romantic movement, and the rapid development of natural history.

antiquary/antiquarian [De]. A person whose interest in the past is based upon the traditions of antiquarianism.

antiquity [Le]. In the context of the *American Antiquities Act* this term is used to refer to historic or prehistoric monuments and ruins, or objects of great age, or objects used in conjunction with ancient rituals or American Indian religious practices.

Antiquity [Ge]. The principal independent international academic journal devoted to the field of archaeology. Established in 1927 by O. G. S. CRAWFORD, the quarterly journal is published by the Antiquity Trust and includes papers, reports, reviews, news, and editorial comment relating to archaeology of all periods in all countries.

antler [Ma]. Bone-like structures found on the heads of male red deer, fallow deer, roe deer, and elk (moose), and on both male and female reindeer (caribou). Antlers are grown in the spring and shed annually in the winter, except in reindeer which shed their antlers in the spring. Antler was a valuable material for making tools and equipment of various kinds throughout northern Europe, northern Asia, and North America from Palaeolithic times through into the medieval period and beyond.

antler comb [Ar]. A type of tool found in the Neolithic in southern Britain, and occasionally elsewhere, comprising a section of red-deer antler cut across and with the cut end grooved into a ring of teeth which are carefully pointed and in most specimens show a high degree of polish from wear. On the basis of ethnographic analogy these tools are believed to have been used for removing hair and dressing animal hides.

antler pick [Ar]. A type of tool found widely amongst the sites of Neolithic communities in northwestern Europe. They are formed from a red-deer antler from which all but the brow tine has been removed; the beam forms the handle and the brow tine the 'pick'. They were used for excavating soil and quarrying out stone and bedrock. The marks left by their use have been detected on the sides of ditches, pits, and shafts. Experiments suggest that they were used rather more like levers than the kind of pickaxe that is swung from over the shoulder.

antler sleeve [Ar]. A piece of deer antler which fits over a stone axe to form a sleeve between the axehead and the wooden haft into which the combined axe and sleeve is fitted. Being more resilient to shock than wood, the antler sleeve lessens the risk of splitting the wooden haft while the axe is in use.

Antonine Wall, UK [Si]. Roman frontier work in northern Britain extending across Scotland across the Forth–Clyde isthmus for a distance of 60 km between Carriden in the east to Old Kilpatrick in the west. There were also flanking forts along the coast on either side. Built in stages in the early 140s AD after a series of successful military campaigns in Scotland led by Antoninus Pius. The main frontier comprises a stone foundation about 4.3 m wide on which stood a turf bank up to 3 m high, fronted by a berm and a ditch normally about 12 m wide and 3 m deep. The boundary was built by troops from all three legions in Britannia at the time: the II Augusta, the VI Vitrix, and the XX Valeria Vitrix. Forts were constructed at intervals of about 3 km, nineteen of them in all, attached to the back of the wall, many with annexes to the south for storage. A road, the Military Way, linked the forts. Signal stations were also built between some forts. The Antonine Wall succeeded Hadrian's Wall as the northern frontier of Britannia in AD 143, but was abandoned in AD 158 following a retreat southwards to Hadrian's Wall. After some limited re-use the Antonine Wall was finally abandoned by AD 214.

[Sum.: J. F. Keppe and J. F. Lawrence (eds.), 1990, *The Antonine Wall: a handbook to the surviving remains by Robertson*. Glasgow: Glasgow Archaeological Society]

Antonitus [Na]. Roman emperor AD 138–161.

Anu [Di]. The Sumerian sky god and chief divinity whose seat was at URUK.

Anubis [Di]. Jackal-headed god of ancient Egypt mainly responsible for guarding tombs and the underworld and closely associated with embalming. Local god of the 16th and 17th nomes of Upper Egypt. Shown as a man with a jackal's head or as a black jackal seated on a hill, a chest, or a pylon.

Anuket [Di] Egyptian goddess, associated with Khnum at the First Cataract and in Nubia. Shown as a woman with a crown of feathers, grasping a papyrus staff. Chief centre is the island of Seheil where she has a temple. Equivalent to the Greek Anukis.

Anuradhapura, Sri Lanka [Si]. Ancient capital city from the introduction of Buddhism to the island in the 3rd century BC through to the 8th century AD when it was abandoned because of Tamil incursions from southern India. The site covers more than 100 ha and amongst the numerous and important buildings in the city are palaces, monasteries, and STUPAS.

[Rep.: R. A. E. Coningham and F. R. Allchin, 1995, The rise of the cities in Sri Lanka. In F. R. Allchin (ed.), *The archaeology of early Historic South Asia: the emergence of cities and states*. Cambridge: CUP]

anvil technique [De]. A method of removing flakes by swinging the core against an anvil. Produces large thick flakes. Used extensively in the CLACTONIAN toolmaking industries. Also called the block-on-block technique.

Anyang, China [Si]. An early city of the late SHANG period near modern-day Anyang City in Henan Province, northern China. Excavations between 1928 and 1937 by Li Chi and more recent work by the Academia Sinica show that occupation starts in the 13th century BC. The town consists of an oval area about 3.75 km by 9.75 km, mainly unenclosed, but incorporating a temple complex, residential buildings, clusters of aristocratic houses, and workshops. The distinctive Anyang style of bronze working with prominent TA'O T'IEH designs suggests a strong interest in death and ancestor worship. Its ORACLE BONES provide important information on early social organization. Perhaps the most important finds from the city relate to the cemeteries, which included over a dozen royal tombs. Each consists of a large square pit 14 m across and 4 m deep entered by either two or four ramps. At the centre an inner pit contained the body of the king set in a large wooden coffin. A small pit below the coffin held the bones of a dog. Around the central burial pit and on the ramps there were placed many grave goods and the bodies of the king's retinue (men and horses). Around the tomb, excavations have revealed numerous smaller pit graves and these seem to represent the accumulation of burials over a long period after the central prestige grave had been completed.

[Rep.: Li Chi, 1977, *Anyang: a chronicle of the discovery, excavation, and reconstruction of the ancient capital of the Chang Dynasty*. Folkstone: Daveson]

AOC [Ab]. *See* AREA OF COMPETENCE.

AOC beaker [Ab]. All-over-corded beaker. *See* BEAKER.

aonach [De]. A fair or assembly place in the early medieval period in Ireland. The word occurs fairly frequently in PLACE-NAMES. By the 11th century AD the aonach had become more or less synonymous with a market.

AOO beaker [Ab]. All-over-ornamented beaker. *See* BEAKER.

AP [Ab]. Aerial photograph. *See* AERIAL PHOTOGRAPHY.

apadana [Co]. The principal audience hall of a Persian palace.

Apennine Culture [CP]. A middle and late Bronze Age culture which developed about 1600 BC in peninsular Italy with some influence from the Balkans. Characterized by the variety of its pottery types, which included bowls with elaborate, upstanding handles, and vessels decorated with curvilinear and zig-zag geometric designs. Many of the sites lie high in the mountains and may have been occupied by transhumant pastoralists. Inhumation cemeteries are known.

Apet (Opet, Epet) [Di]. Egyptian goddess, sometimes claimed as mother of Osiris. Shrine at Karnak.

Aphrodite [Di]. Greek goddess, probably derived from a Phoenician fertility goddess whose domain embraced all nature: vegetable, animal, and human. Later she became the goddess of love in its noblest as well as in its most degraded form. She also became a marine deity. Homer describes her as the daughter of Zeus and Dione, but a more compelling story has her rising from the sea on Cyprus. Equated with the Roman Venus.

Apis [Di]. Egyptian god, the sacred bull of Memphis, a form of Ptah-Osiris. Recognized by a blaze on the forehead, marks on the tongue and certain hairs on the back. Buried in Serapeum at Sakkara which was the main sanctuary. Many representations of him with sun disc on his head between horns.

AP : NAP ratio [Ge]. In looking at the results of POLLEN ANALYSIS, the proportion of tree pollen (arboreal pollen) can be compared with the amount of pollen from other plants (non-arboreal pollen) to provide a general impression of whether the landscape was wooded or not. This is known as the AP : NAP ratio.

apodyterium [Co]. Latin name for the changing room in a Roman bath building. Some examples are equipped with wall niches for storing clothes and belongings.

Apollo [Di]. Greek and Roman god of uncertain derivation: possibly in origin a Hittite god or a Hellenic double of the Arab god Hobal. He was the god of light, a sun god (but not the sun itself, which was Helios), who delighted in high places. He made the fruits of the earth to ripen and in some areas the first fruits were dedicated to him. He was also the god of divination and prophecy. Traditions record that Apollo was the son of Leto, first wife of Zeus. His retinue includes the Muses and his chosen land was Delphi. Apollo is often depicted carrying a bow and arrows which he uses in hunting.

apotropaic [De]. Referring to an image or device which is designed to ward off unwanted influences.

appliqué [Ge]. A decorative figure or motif made separately, usually in a mould, and applied or fixed to the surface of a pot before slip-coating and fitting.

apse [Co]. The semi-circular recess usually in the short end wall of the long basilica or Roman law court in which was the dais for the tribunal. When early Christians built churches on the basilica plan, the seats of the Elders were ranged around the apse to the east of the altar, as in the early Christian church at Delos.

apsidal [De]. In architecture, having one end of a building rounded in plan.

apsidiole [Co]. A small subsidiary apse.

aquatic civilizations [De]. A general term applied to those early civilizations whose subsistence base depended on water management for the cultivation of crops and the maintenance of the land: for example, Egypt, Mesopotamia, and the Indus Valley.

aqueduct [MC]. An artificial conduit used to supply water to a city from a source some distance away.

Aramaens [CP]. A group of SEMITIC peoples who moved out of the Syrian desert to conquer the Canaanites of Syria and set up their own city-states in the 12th and 13th centuries BC.

Arawak [CP]. Linguistically associated peoples who inhabited parts of the Caribbean and the adjacent mainland of northeastern South America at the time of Columbus in the 16th century AD. All were pottery-using agricultural societies.

Arbogastes [Na]. Barbarian general, probably Frankish, served under Theodosius the Great and sent by him to assist Valentinian II. At Valentinian's death in AD 392, Arbogastes proclaimed Eugenius emperor, the first of the barbarian generals to take this step, but he and his protégé were defeated in AD 394 and he committed suicide.

Arcadius [Na]. Roman emperor, the eldest son of Theodosius the Great, and successor in AD 395 to the eastern half of the empire. His influence on events can scarcely be traced, and his government is assumed to have been controlled by his ministers. Died c.AD 408.

archaeo-astronomy [Ge]. The study of ancient astronomy through archaeological remains. Sometimes known as astro-archaeology.

archaeobotany [Ge]. *See* PALAEOBOTANY.

archaeological assessment [Ge]. *See* ASSESSMENT.

archaeological context [Ge]. *See* CONTEXT.

archaeological culture [Th]. *See* CULTURE.

Archaeological Institute of America (AIA) [Ge]. Founded in 1879, the AIA is dedicated to the greater understanding of archaeology, the protection and preservation of the world's archaeological resources and the information they contain, and the encouragement and support of archaeological research and publication.

A non-profit-making cultural and educational organization, it is chartered by the US Congress and is the oldest and largest archaeological organization in North America. In 1995, its membership was approximately 11 000.

The AIA has its headquarters in Boston University, Boston, Massachusetts. It publishes the magazine *Archaeology* and the *American Journal of Archaeology*, as well and an annual bulletin of archaeological opportunities around the world, a newsletter, and monographs. There is an annual meeting at which professionals present the latest results of archaeological fieldwork and research, mainly in the classical domain.

archaeological interest [Le]. In the administration of legislation and related guidance a site or object is said to have archaeological interest if is capable of contributing to the scientific or humanistic understanding of past human behaviour, cultural adaptation, or related topics through the application of scientifically based or scholarly techniques such as structured observation, contextual measurement, controlled collection, analysis, interpretation, and explanation.

archaeological region [Ge]. In North American archaeology this term refers to areas which exhibit a degree of cultural homogeneity in a particular period. Often defined by appropriate topographical features such as drainage systems, coastlines, or upland plateaux.

archaeological resource [Ge]. Any material remains of the past which offer potential for archaeological investigation and analysis as a means of contributing to the understanding of past human communities.

archaeological resource management (ARM) [Ge]. A branch of archaeology that is concerned with the identification, mapping, recording, assessment, evaluation, and documentation of archaeological sites and objects at all scales in order to assist in their conservation, protection, preservation, presentation, and exploitation through effective mitigation strategies, excavation, and non-destructive study. Major aspects of this work involve: the administration of legislation that bears on archaeological remains; informing the decision-making process as it applies to the potential impacts of development on archaeological remains; issuing permits and licences; monitoring and managing contract archaeology; the definition and application of research policies; and the development of public education programmes. In the USA and Australia this branch of archaeology is often referred to as **cultural resource management (CRM)** where it also covers the management of the contemporary material culture of the indigenous populations. The term **archaeological heritage management (AHM)** is also used in the international context.

Archaeological Resources Protection Act 1979 [Le]. Principal piece of legislation in the USA for the protection of archaeological resources: that is, the material remains of past human existence, of archaeological interest, which are more than 100 years old. The legislation also includes procedures for the issuing of permits to lawfully excavate archaeological sites.

archaeological survey [Ge]. A systematic attempt to locate, identify, and record the distribution, structure, and form of archaeological sites on the ground and in relation to their natural geographic and environmental setting.

archaeological theory [Ge]. A body of philosophical and theoretical concepts providing both a framework and a means for archaeologists to look beyond the facts and material objects for explanations of events that took place in prehistory.

archaeological unit [Ge]. **1.** Arbitrary unit of classification set up by archaeologists to separate conveniently one grouping of artefacts in time and space from another. **2.** In Britain, a general term for any organization established for the purpose of carrying out archaeological surveys and investigations. An archaeological contractor.

archaeologist [De]. Someone who studies the past using archaeological methods and in the context of established archaeological theory, with the motive of recording, interpreting, and understanding ancient cultures and what they did.

archaeology (archeology) [De]. Literally, 'the study of ancient things'; the term archaeology has developed and grown to embrace a much wider set of meanings through common usage as the discipline itself has expanded and matured. Walter Taylor writing in 1948 was confidently able to assert that: 'Archaeology is neither history nor anthropology. As an autonomous discipline, it consists of a method and a set of specialized techniques for the gathering or "production" of cultural information.'

Operationally, archaeology has come to mean the study of past human societies and their environments through the systematic recovery and analysis of material culture or physical remains. The primary aims of the discipline are thus: to recover, record, analyse, and classify archaeological material; to describe and interpret the patterns of human behaviours that led to its creation; and to explain or develop an understanding of the reasons for this behaviour. In Europe and the Old World archaeology has tended to focus on the material remains themselves (sites and monuments), the techniques of recovering material, and theoretical and philosophical underpinnings inherent to achieving its goals. In the New World attention is directed more towards the subject matter and past human societies, and as such is considered one of the four fields of ANTHROPOLOGY. In both traditions, the attainment of a broadly based archaeology involves multidisciplinary and interdisciplinary endeavour, and it can fairly be said that the discipline of archaeology is a broad church embracing an increasingly large number of different subdiscipline areas or branches.

Originally, archaeology was a descriptive science, documenting, defining, and classifying everything it came across and mainly concerned with the material itself. This developed into an explanatory discipline where interest focused on understanding the causes behind the patterns and the reasons for what could be observed with a consequent obsession with the processes and the methodology whether at the practical level or the theoretical level. Increasingly, attention is being directed to what archaeologists actually produce, the end result of their labours, with an inevitable swing towards concerns over the nature of discourse and the production of knowledge.

archaeomagnetic dating [Ge]. A method of determining absolute dates for certain kinds of archaeological materials, particularly in-situ hearths, kilns, and furnaces. The method works because the materials used to construct these facilities contain fine particles of iron-rich elements such as haematite. When these materials are heated above about 650 °C (the Curie point) all previous alignments in the magnetic particles are destroyed, and as the material cools the particles realign themselves on the Earth's natural magnetic field. Since the prevailing magnetic field moves over the course of time, local and regional sequences in the pattern of magnetic declination, dip, and intensity can be established and in-situ remains related to it to show when the last major episode of heating took place. The technique is very sensitive and can sometimes be used to show the time lapse between the inner and outer walls of a long-lived kiln or furnace. *Compare* PALEOMAGNETIC DATING.

archaeometry [De]. The application of techniques and procedures from the hard sciences (physics, chemistry, biology, etc.) and engineering to archaeological questions and problems.

archaeozoology [De]. A branch of archaeology focused around the recovery and analysis of animal remains in order to examine their physiology and ecology in relation to cultural activities and contribute to an understanding of animals in society. Major themes of investigation include animal domestication, exploitation and use patterns, butchery practices, and dietary contributions.

archaic [Ge]. **1.** In America, this term refers in a generic sense to a simple hunter-gatherer lifestyle involving small bands of people pursuing a pattern of seasonal movements linked to the migrations and periodic abundance of animal and plant foods. **2.** Of ancient or early form. The term 'archaic period' is often used

to describe the early phases in the development of a civilization.

Archaic [CP]. The second of five general cultural stages proposed by G. Willey and P. Phillips in 1958 as a framework for the study of ancient communities in the Americas. The Archaic Stage (which in the original scheme succeeded the LITHIC) embraced all the post-Pleistocene hunter-gatherer communities from the period after about 8000 BC. The Archaic Stage ends when sedentary agriculture becomes the main means of subsistence; its duration is therefore subject to considerable local variation.

The Archaic Stage is characterized by subsistence economies based on sedentary resources such as nuts, seeds, and shellfish, and a closer adjustment to the forest or desert environment. As a general term still in regular use, the Archaic Stage covers a series of local and regional traditions and the cultures they embrace.

On the west coast of North America the early, middle, and late phases within the Archaic are defined, each with numerous local variations, but extending down to modern times. In the Great Basin and western interior, the Archaic is usually divided into the early Desert Archaic, middle Archaic, and late Archaic, again extending in a continuous series down to modern times. In the southwest, a single Southwestern Archaic is recognized spanning the period *c.*6000–100 BC, followed by a series of FORMATIVE STAGE traditions (e.g., ANASAZI, MOGOLLON, HOHOKAM). In the eastern woodlands an early, middle, and late Archaic is recognized, followed by the Woodland Stage after about 1000 BC.

Archaic period [CP]. In the Old World from 700 BC to the end of the Persian Wars in the early 5th century BC.

archaistic [Ge]. Referring to a style or tradition which imitates an earlier form.

archer's wrist guard [Ar]. *See* BRACER.

architrave [Co]. The horizontal member above two columns spanning the interval between them.

archon [De]. Strictly 'one who rules', but in classical Greek times the term was applied to one of the chief magistrates of Athens, and of certain other city-states.

arc style [De]. An early style of Celtic art, an eastern subgroup in Bavaria, Bohemia, and Austria in which compass-drawn geometric motifs predominate.

Arctic Small Tool Tradition [CP]. Small-scale hunter-gatherer communities settled around the Alaskan Peninsula and the eastern shores of the Baring Strait from about 2000 BC. They may have originated among the Bel'kachinsk farmers of the Aldan River in Siberia. At about the same time, Arctic Small Tool Tradition communities also appear among the islands of northern Canada and in western Greenland.

Arctic Small Tool Tradition groups, also known in Alaska as the Denbigh Flint Complex, shared the widespread use of a microlithic stone industry. Stone tools include delicately made blades, microburins, burins, scrapers, and adzes. The most important innovation they brought to North America was the bow and arrow. Bifacially worked projectile points were made to tip the wooden arrowshafts. The main quarry was caribou and waterfowl.

Settlements were often small, represented archaeologically by stone scatters and traces of a tented encampment. More permanent structures in the form of square semi-subterranean houses are known where settlements take advantage of especially abundant food resources. By c.800 BC, the Arctic Small Tool Tradition had given way to a series of localized distinctive traditions, for example the Pre-Dorset Tradition and the Norton Tradition.

ard [Ar]. A simple form of plough in which the share (point) is dragged through the soil, parting it rather than turning it over. The earliest examples from the Near East date to the 4th millennium BC. *See also* PLOUGH.

area excavation [De]. *See* OPEN AREA EXCAVATION.

area of competence (AOC) [Ge]. Specialist areas of archaeological endeavour identified and defined by the INSTITUTE OF FIELD ARCHAEOLOGISTS and used by them in assessing the capabilities of applicants for full membership of the Institute (MIFA). Validated areas of competence are subsequently listed in the directory of members. The following AOCs have been defined: archaeological field practice; archaeological resource management; finds and environmental study, collections research and conservation; archaeological research and development; and recording and analysis of buildings.

Arenal Complex [CP]. Hunter-gatherer communities living on the Peruvian coast c.6000–5000 BC. Small temporary campsites are known and the relative abundance of debris from marine as against terrestrial food sources suggests that fishing was more important than hunting. A few grinding stones suggest that seeds from wild plants made a small contribution to diet.

Argar Culture [CP]. An early Bronze Age culture of southeastern Spain, named for the type-site in Almeria. Settlements are generally fortified with rectilinear layout of houses and streets, as at El Oficio, and include extensive burials within the settlement area. Burials are individual or paired, rather than communal, in cists in the early phase of the culture and subsequently in jars. Characteristic artefacts including triangular bronze daggers and halberds and silver ornaments, the principal pottery forms being plain, carinated bowls and tall, pedestaled 'fruit stands'. The culture spans the first half of the second millennium BC.

Argonne ware [Ar]. Pottery type of the 4th century AD, usually with a red colour-coat. Vessels are decorated with horizontal bands of impressed geometric patterns, executed with a roller stamp. The ware was made in the Argonne in northeast Gaul. Its distribution in Britain is mainly confined to the south and southeast band. Also known as Marne ware.

Arikara [CP]. *See* MIDDLE MISSOURI TRADITION.

Ariuşd, Romania (Erosal) [Si]. One of a small number of tell mounds in Transylvania situated in the upper Olt Valley, the site gives its name to a regional variant of the CUCENTENI CULTURE. Excavations by F. László between 1907 and 1913 revealed seven main occupation levels. Levels I–VI contained Ariuşd-style painted wares together with a range of gold jewellery and copper ornaments, weapons, and tools. Abundant evidence for craft activities was recovered, including a workshop in which pottery was made. The final phase, Level VII, belongs to the late Copper Age of the region.

[Sum: A. Laszlo, 1993, Asezari intarite ale culturii Ariusd-Cucureni in sud-estul Transilvaniei. Fortificarea asezarii Malnas-Bai. *Arheologia Moldovei*, 16, 33–48]

ARM [Ab]. *See* ARCHAEOLOGICAL RESOURCE MANAGEMENT.

Armorican axe [Ar]. Rather plain and shoddily made type of socketed bronze axe produced in the period 600–650 BC at the very end of the Bronze Age of northern France (Hallstatt II). Mostly found in large hoards, in which few examples appear to have been finished or used. This has led to the suggestion that they were somehow connected with emergency trade in metal rather than finished products.

Armorican coins [Ar]. Collective name for coinage issued by a range of tribes living in Brittany during the early 1st century BC, including the Coriosolites, Baiocasses, Redones, Unelli, and Osismii.

Armorico-British dagger [Ar]. Type of bronze dagger found in the WESSEX I Phase of the early Bronze Age (*c*.1700–1500 BC) in southern Britain which has similarities with examples from Brittany. It has a flat triangular blade, lateral grooves, and six rivets for attaching the blade to the hilt. Sometimes a small tang or languette is present to assist securing the blade to the hilt. Traces of wooden and leather sheaths have been found with some blades; the hilts were probably of wood and in the case of an example found in the Bush Barrow, Wiltshire, were inlaid with gold tacks.

ARPA [Ab]. *See* ARCHAEOLOGICAL RESOURCES PROTECTION ACT.

Arras Culture [CP]. Middle and later Iron Age culture in eastern Yorkshire, distinguished by its use of square-ditched as well as circular-ditched barrows, and among richer graves the practice of burying a two-wheeled cart with the dead, reminiscent of the funerary practices of earlier La Tène groups in Champagne. While it is generally agreed that the culture reflects an intrusive movement from across the Channel, the chronology and exact region of its origins are debatable. The later Iron Age tribe in the region was known to the Romans as the PARISI.

Arretine ware [Ar]. Red-coloured pottery with a glossy surface produced between the 1st century BC and the mid 1st century AD at Arretium (modern Arezzo) in Tuscany, Italy. The forms of the vessels are copies of metal prototypes; some are highly decorated. This ware was traded throughout the Roman empire of the time, and sometimes beyond.

Arreton Down Tradition [CP]. Early industrial stage of the British early Bronze Age spanning the 16th and 15th centuries BC and part of Burgess's BEDD BRANWEN PERIOD. Named after a small hoard of weapons found at Arreton Down on the Isle of Wight in December 1735, the industry is characterized by the production of flat axes, tanged spearheads, end-looped spearheads, tanged and collared spearheads, chisels and tracers.

arris [De]. The sharp edge formed, for instance, at the meeting point of two flutes in the Doric column, a vulnerable feature of the order, rectified in the Ionic by the substitution of a flat narrow fillet between the flutes.

arrowhead [Ar]. Stone or metal tip for mounting at the business end of a wooden arrow shaft to increase the penetrating power or modify the impact of the arrow when it strikes its target. The earliest arrowheads are of upper Palaeolithic date; in Britain Neolithic arrowheads are typically of leaf-shaped form, while Bronze Age examples are triangular in outline, with a tang for hafting and barbs for increasing attachment to the target.

arrow straighteners [Ar]. A single block of stone, or more unusually a pair of stones, with a straight groove on one face which was rubbed up and down the shaft of an arrow to straighten and smooth it.

arroyo [De]. The dry bed of a seasonal stream.

arsenic [Ma]. A steel-grey semi-metallic element (As) that is highly toxic but which occurs naturally in many copper deposits and which was later sought after and added to bronze by early European metalworkers in order to improve the casting properties of their metal.

arsenical bronze [Ma]. Bronze that contains a high proportion (up to 30 per cent) of arsenic.

artefact (artifact) [Ge]. Any object which has been modified, fashioned, or manufactured according to a set of humanly imposed attributes, including tools, weapons, ornaments, utensils, houses, buildings, etc. Artefacts are the basic components of MATERIAL CULTURE.

artefact attribute [De]. A logically irreducible characteristic or independent variable within a specific artefact.

Arthur [Na]. Legendary king and champion of the British against the Anglo-Saxon invaders, immortalized in the 15th century AD by Malory's chivalric tales about the Knights of the Round Table and the search for the Holy Grail. Most of the stories about Arthur belong to the 12th century and later, and even his existence is disputed.

artillery castle [MC]. A powerful defensive structure built specifically to house heavy guns in multiple tiers. The castle walls were built of stone, sometimes with earthen outworks. They were usually constructed to protect a harbour entrance or anchorage from attack by sea. Accommodation inside the castle was usually limited to that needed for the garrison and to store munitions. One of the earliest examples is Dartmouth Castle, Devon, built in AD 1481; the majority were constructed in the 16th century AD.

Aruã Complex [CP]. South American farming cultures found in the Marajo area of Amazonia and tentatively dated to c.AD 1300–1500, characterized by their ceramic assemblages which belong to the Incised and Punctuate Horizon defined in the Amazon Basin. The Aruã Complex was a successor to, and apparently simpler than, the Marajoara Culture that spread widely in Amazonia in the early 1st millennium AD.

Aryans [CP]. Groups of people who called themselves Arya, and who spoke the Indo-European SANSKRIT language, are known from the *Rigveda* and other early Indian historical sources. They probably invaded India from the northwest during the 2nd millennium BC, spreading east and south over the succeeding centuries. By about 500 BC the Aryan language was probably common over most of the Indian subcontinent, the

area in which Indo-Aryan is now spoken. Archaeologically, Aryan peoples are more or less invisible, despite much searching. Some authorities link them to cultures using PAINTED GREY WARES, and as such the spread of the Aryans may have contributed to the downfall of the HARAPPAN civilization.

aryballus [Ar]. A kind of jar with a conical base, tall narrow neck, and flaring rim. Used to carry liquids. Found in INCA assemblages of Peru.

as [Ar]. Roman brass or copper coin worth one sixteenth of a DENARIUS.

ascencus [Co]. Latin term for the sloping ramp giving access to the walkway along the top of a rampart.

ashlar [De]. Masonry comprising square-finished or square-hewn stone laid in regular courses with fine joints, and an even face.

Ashmole, Elias (1617–92) [Bi]. Antiquarian, solicitor, alchemist, and creator of the first public museum in Britain. Born in Lichfield he became a solicitor in 1638 before embracing the Royalist cause in the Civil War. In 1644 he was appointed by the king as commissioner of excise in Lichfield, which led to him to Oxford where the Royalist parliament sat. He entered Brasenose College to study physics and mathematics, but further changes of employment took him to Worcester and London. Following the Restoration he was appointed Windsor herald and from that time he developed his antiquarian interests alongside increasing influence at court. In a life full of twists and turns he inherited from John Tradescant (Keeper of the Botanic Garden at Chelsea) a collection of antiquities and in 1677 he determined to give the collection, plus his own additions, to the University of Oxford on condition that they find a suitable building for it. This was agreed and the building opened in 1682, Dr Plot being appointed its curator. At least twelve wagon-loads of material were taken to the museum. In 1690 the university conferred on Ashmole the degree of MD and in turn he bequeathed his library to them. The Ashmolean Museum, though really formed by Tradescant, has secured its donor a celebrity that remains today.

[Bio.: *Dictionary of British biography: earliest times to 1900*, 644–6]

Ashunasirpal II [Na]. King of Assyria from 883 to 859 BC.

Ashurbanipal [Na]. King of Assyria from 668 to 627 BC.

askos [Ar]. Asymmetrical pottery vessel, often duck-shaped, with one handle and its mouth off-centre. The form was common in the Aegean Bronze Age from early Helladic times and through into the classical period.

Aspero, Peru [Si]. A Preceramic Stage ceremonial centre on the coastal plain near the mouth of the Rio Supe, dating to c.2800 BC. The complex comprises perhaps as many as seventeen platform mounds. Each mound was built in stages, having two or three steps or tiers rising to about 10 m above the surrounding ground surface. On the summit was a masonry structure comprising a series of rooms or cells of different sizes, each elaborated with niches and adobe friezes. Dedicatory caches are found within the structures, including feathers, cotton, string and cane objects, clay figurines, wooden bowls, and carved wooden items.

One mound, Huaca de los Idolos, measures 30 m by 50 m in plan and 10 m high. A large settled population must have lived in the Supe Valley round about.

[Sum.: R. A. Feldman, 1987, Architectural evidence for the development of non-egalitarian social systems in coastal Peru. In J. Hass, S. Pozorski, and T. Pozorski (eds.), *The origins and development of the Andean state*. Cambridge: CUP, 9–14]

assart [MC]. In medieval times an assart was an area of land taken from the waste or forest and cultivated or used to build a smallholding or farm. The process of 'assarting' was particularly common in the later 11th and early 12th centuries.

assemblage [De]. **1.** An associated set of contemporary artefacts that can be considered as a single unit for record and analysis. **2.** All of the artefacts found at a site, including the sum of all sub-assemblages at the site.

assessment [Ge]. A review of the known archaeology in a known area based on searches and checks through available records and documentation such as those in the relevant sites and monuments record, national monuments record, local record offices, museum archives, and other sources such as historic maps and aerial photographs. An assessment may also, however, involve some non-destructive methods of site reconnaissance such as earthwork surveys and geophysical surveys. In Britain, assessments are regarded as an essential preliminary stage in identifying whether there is an archaeological dimension to a development proposal. They are also used in preparing research designs. Also known as archaeological assessments and desk-top assessments.

assimilation [Ge]. The absorption of a minority group into a majority population, during which the group takes on the values and norms of the dominant culture.

association [Th]. The relationship between an artefact and other archaeological finds and a site level, or other artefact, structure, or feature in the site. *See* CLOSED ASSOCIATION, SPATIAL ASSOCIATION, STRATIGRAPHIC ASSOCIATION.

Assur (Ashur) [Di]. Solar deity, chief god of the city of Assur and Assyria.

Assyrian civilization [CP]. A city-state in the northern part of Mesopotamia with its capital at ASSUR. From about 1300 BC the Assyrian kings, all great warriors, developed an empire that, at its maximum, included Egypt, much of the area west of Mesopotamia as far as the Mediterranean, Elam to the east and parts of Anatolia to the north. Assurnasirpal II transferred the centre of government to Calah (NIMRUD) where he rebuilt the city; NINEVEH and for a while Khorsabad were co-capitals. He was also the first king to create pictorial reliefs to supplement CUNEIFORM inscriptions. The fortunes of the empire were fairly turbulent between the 9th and 7th centuries BC and in 614 BC the empire collapsed when the Medes invaded Assyria capturing Calah and destroying Assur.

Asterte (Asherah) [Di]. Goddess of love and war, the mythical mother and fertility goddess of the PHOENICIANS and Canaanites, variously equated with the Egyptian Isis, Babylonian ISHTAR, Carthaginian TANIT, and Greek APHRODITE.

Aten [Di]. Egyptian god of the sun, shown as a gold disc with rays ending in hands.

Worshipped by AKHENATEN as a great creator god, the sole god of his monotheistic state religion.

Aterian [CP]. Name given to an evolved middle Palaeolithic stoneworking tradition in the Atlas Mountains of North Africa. Among the distinctive tools are tanged points and basically worked leaf-shaped points.

Athaulf [Na]. Leader of the Visigoths, successor of Alaric, who led the Visigoths out of Italy into southern Gaul in AD 412. In AD 414 he married Placidia, sister of Honorius, who had been captured in AD 410 at the sack of Rome. Athaulf is said to have intended to create a Gothic empire, but changed his mind because of his people's savagery. Died c.AD 415.

Athenaeus [Na]. Provincial Greek writer of the period around 200 AD whose sole surviving work is cast in the genre of symposium literature, in which learned guests at a banquet debate philosophical, literary, and allied topics. Its archaeological relevance derives from brief descriptions of Celtic feasting customs which are borrowed virtually verbatim from POSIDONIUS.

Athens, Greece [Si]. The modern capital of Greece, situated at the upper corner of a small coastal plain on the western side of the peninsula of Attica. The site has an exceptionally long, more or less continuous, history extending back into prehistoric times. Numerous excavations and surveys have been carried out in the city, the biggest programme of work in the late 20th century being that connected with the construction of a metro.

Traces of occupation in late Neolithic and Mycenaean times have been found, but it is from the 7th century BC onwards that the town develops into a major city-state and enters a period of alternating phases of success and failure that lasts down to Roman times. Amongst the first buildings to be set out in the new Hellenistic city were the agora and the monumental temples on the ACROPOLIS. At the same time Athenian black-figure ware of high artistic quality was developed and came to be widely traded in the Mediterranean world. Red-figure ware succeeded it from about 500 BC. The sack of Athens by the Persians in 480 BC provided a major setback with most of the major buildings and structures flattened. Outstanding

buildings constructed in the 5th-century rebirth of Athens include the PARTHENON and Erechtheum on the acropolis. After the defeat of Athens by Sparta in the Peloponnesian Wars (432–404 BC) building nearly ceased again, but from the early 4th century new private finances were found and the city again entered a period of prosperity. This tradition continued down the centuries: the east side of the agora was filled with a stoa financed by Attalos, king of Pergamum, in the 2nd century, while, for example, Ptolemy VI, the Roman emperor Hadrian, and others built libraries.

[Sum.: J. M. Hurwit, 1999, *The Athenian Acropolis: history, mythology and archaeology from the Neolithic era to the present*. Cambridge: CUP]

Atkinson, Kathleen Mary Tyrer (d. 1979) [Bi]. British archaeologist and classical scholar. Born Kathleen Chrimes, she married Donald Atkinson, and became Professor of Ancient History in Queen's University, Belfast. In addition to excavating at Caistor-by-Norwich with her husband, she worked at Psart and Kouklia in Cyprus. Her published works include *Ancient Sparta* (1949, Manchester: Manchester University Press).

[Obit.: *Antiquaries Journal*, 60 (1980), 463]

Atkinson, Richard John Copland (1920–94) [Bi]. British archaeologist and academic, well known for his excavations in Neolithic and Bronze Age sites. Born in Dorset and educated at Sherborne School and Magdalen College, Oxford, where he read PPE. As a Quaker he was a non-combatant during WW2, employed instead on ditch-digging and hospital duties. In 1944 he returned to Oxford as Assistant Keeper of Archaeology in the Ashmolean Museum. Almost immediately he began excavating at Dorchester-on-Thames, later with help from Stuart Piggott. In 1949 he was appointed to a lectureship in archaeology at Edinburgh University, and in 1958 became the first Professor of Archaeology at Cardiff where he remained until his retirement in 1983. Throughout these years he was active in the field, excavating at Stonehenge in 1953–6, the West Kennet long barrow with Piggott in 1955–6, and at Wayland's Smithy in 1962–3. In 1968–9 he undertook an examination of Silbury Hill under the watchful eye of the BBC television cameras. University administration was a call on his time later in life: between 1966 and 1970 he was Dean of Arts at Cardiff and between 1970 and 1974 he was Vice-Principal of the University. This stood him in good stead for being a member of the University Grants Committee between 1973 and 1982. He was elected a Fellow of the Society of Antiquaries in 1946 and appointed a CBE in 1979. At the time of his death many of his excavations remained unpublished, but this has since been rectified through the diligent work of his successors at Cardiff.

[Obit.: *British Archaeological News*, NS 18 (November 1994), 11]

Atlantic Phase [CP]. A biostratigraphic subdivision of the FLANDRIAN in which conditions were warmer and damper than today, the climatic optimum of the Flandrian. Godwin's POLLEN ZONE VII (*c*.5500–3000 BC) characterized by the development of mixed forest of oak, elm, alder, and lime in southern Britain. Some woodland clearance by late Mesolithic groups during this period has been found, but the Atlantic traditionally ends with the ELM DECLINE.

Atlantis [Ge]. An earthly paradise described by Plato in his *Timaeus*, that has tantalized and exasperated explorers and romantics ever since. Perhaps drawing on earlier sources, but probably based largely on folk myth, Plato describes Atlantis as an island in the Atlantic west of Gibraltar that was destroyed because of the wickedness of its inhabitants. Many guesses have been made as to its location, and numerous attempts have been made to find traces of its existence.

atlatl [Ar]. American term used for a spear-thrower. An atlatl provided a means of increasing the thrust exerted on a spear or other projectile by artificially extending the length of the thrower's arm and thus the leverage available.

atom bomb effect [Ge]. Increase in the atmospheric concentration of radiocarbon caused by the nuclear explosions of the mid 20th century AD and after.

atomic absorption spectrometry (AAS) [Te]. A technique used in archaeology to determine the chemical composition of metals, pottery, minerals, and rocks of various kinds. A powdered sample of the material to be examined (typically 10–100 mg) is dissolved in an aqueous liquid which is then atomized in a flame.

A beam of light of controlled wavelength is shone through the flame to a detector on the other side. The wavelength is selected so that atoms of the element under study will absorb some of the light and so will not reach the detector. The amount of energy absorbed is directly proportional to the concentration of the element in the sample.

Atrebates [CP]. The pre-Roman Iron Age tribe living in central southern England between the BELGAE to the south and the CATUVELLAUNI to the north. Their capital appears to have been at SILCHESTER, a site which later became the *civitas capital* after the Roman conquest. The Atrebates minted coins from about 75 BC onwards and from these it is possible to know the names of some of their leaders including Commius, Tincommius, and Verica. By the early 1st century AD it is likely that the Atrebatic territory had been subdivided into at least six socio-economic zones, in three of which there were substantial, semi-urbanized settlements or *OPPIDA*.

atrium [Co]. Literally, the 'place made black by the smoke', but more generally used to refer to a small court or hall, open to the sky, sometimes colonnaded with four or more columns supporting the roof, and rooms opening on to the colonnade. In some Roman examples there is a central pond or basin to collect rainwater.

Attic black-figure ware [Ar]. Type of pottery manufactured in the Attica region of southern Greece from about 720 BC. Vase-painters in Athens and Corinth developed a characteristic style of decoration in which one or more friezes of human and animal figures are presented in silhouette in black against a red ground. The delineation of the figures is sometimes heightened by the use of incised lines and the addition of white or purple colouring agents. Around 530 BC the style was replaced by its inverse: RED-FIGURE WARE.

Attila [Na]. King of the Huns from AD 445 who, for a short period, united his people against the Roman Empire and invaded Gaul and Italy. He was defeated in battle by Aetius in AD 452, and died in AD 453 while preparing to resume the attack. His death destroyed the Hunnic 'empire' and the nomads were crushed by revolts of their German subjects.

attribute [Ge]. A minimal characteristic of an artefact such that it cannot be further subdivided; attributes commonly studied include aspects of form, style, decoration, colour, and raw material.

attritional age profile [De]. The distribution of ages in an animal population that results from selective hunting or predation.

Atum [Di]. Egyptian god, one of the great creator gods of Egypt. Main cult centre Heliopolis, but worshipped all over Egypt. Always represented in human form as man leaning on a stick. An ancient god who become identified with RA.

Atwater, Caleb (1778–1867) [Bi]. American antiquarian whose pioneering work included surveys of the burial mounds and earthworks around Cleveland, Ohio, which were disappearing during the early 19th century. Atwater was the postmaster at Circleville, Ohio, and devoted much of his spare time to studying earthworks in the neighbourhood. His careful descriptions and plans earned him great respect among his peers and later generations, although some of his speculative interpretations involving migrations of Hindus from India are clearly incorrect.

[Bio.: *American National Biography*, I, 728–30]

Aubrey, John (1626–97) [Bi]. Best known of the British 17th-century antiquaries, a pioneer of field archaeology, who was also a scientist, biographer, and writer. Born in Kingston St Michael in north Wiltshire, Aubrey went to school in Blandford, Dorset, before going up to Oxford in 1642. His studies were interrupted by the Civil War so that throughout the 1650s and 1660s he lived as a country gentleman in Wiltshire. Lawsuits and a disastrous courtship reduced him to poverty, however, and in the early 1670s his life changed and he devoted himself to scholarship. His researches were centred mainly on Wiltshire, in particular on the sites of Stonehenge and Avebury, and were written up in his unpublished *Monumenta Britannica*. While at Stonehenge he recognized the presence of shallow pits just inside the inner lip of the bank; these are now known to be postholes but have been named the 'Aubrey Holes'. He was one of the first Fellows of the Royal Society in 1663.

[Bio.: M. Hunter, 1975, *John Aubrey and the realm of learning*. London: Duckworth]

auger [Eq]. A boring tool for removing samples of sediment or rock from the ground. A number of different kinds are widely used in archaeology. The **screw auger** comprises a screw thread attached to a bar and surmounted by a cross-handle. The thread is twisted into the ground, thus drilling a hole (typically 2–4 cm in diameter) while trapping the deposit being drilled through in the thread. By repeatedly drilling in and pulling out the auger a sample of deposit can be examined. For shallow holes a **posthole auger**, either hand-powered or attached to the power takeoff on a Land Rover or similar vehicle, provides a good and quick glimpse of what is below the ground. A **gouge auger** is similar, but instead of a screw thread there is a sharp-ended tube with a slot cut in the side. This can be pushed into the ground, twisted, and then carefully extracted with a thin sample of the material through which the auger has passed trapped in the tube. For deep deposits of soft material where samples are needed, a **Hiller auger** can be used. This has a chamber at the end of the main shaft, and usually extension bars can be added to achieve depths of up to 20 m.

Augustine, St [Na]. Church Father, born *c*.AD 354, who, after a varied life as a teacher and philosopher, was ordained bishop of Hippo, Africa, in AD 395. His letters, polemics, and theological and philosophical works transformed the Christianity of the west, and his autobiographical *Confessions* (*c*.AD 400) inspired generations of writers. He died *c*.AD 430 in the early stages of the Vandal conquest of Africa.

Augustine Pattern [CP]. Name given to successor communities of the BERKELEY PATTERN living on the Pacific shore of the central west coast of North America in the period *c*.AD 300 to recent times. Essentially hunter-gatherer fishing populations, widespread and scattered, these groups are characterized by technical innovations such as the use of bows and arrows, harpoons, tubular tobacco pipes, and the custom of burning artefacts in a grave before the body was interred. These developments are associated with the movement of Utian-speaking Wintun people of the Sacramento Valley. After AD 1400 population numbers and density rose steeply. Inter-community exchange assumed great importance and clam shell 'money' came into circulation.

Augustinian [Ge]. A monastic order of ordained canons; most Augustinian houses were founded in the mid to late 12th century.

Augustus [Na]. First Roman emperor. Born c.63 BC, great-nephew and heir of Julius Caesar, after whose murder he rose to power. In 30 BC he made himself supreme ruler of the Roman world, his long reign being the turning point from the republic to the empire. He developed a new constitutional arrangement whose details owe much to his personal viewpoint. Died AD 14.

Aulnat, France [Si]. An extensive Iron Age settlement near Clermont Ferrand, Auvergne, southern France. Extensive excavations began under the leadership of M. Robert Périchon in 1966, joined by John Collis and a British team from 1973. This work has established that occupation began in the 3rd century BC. As well as the remains of an extensive agricultural settlement there is abundant evidence for industrial activity at the site, including gold-working, silversmithing, and the use of coral, glass, bone, and textiles. Gold and silver coins were amongst the products. Imported luxury items from the Mediterranean show that it was heavily involved in long-distance trade. The site was abandoned between 40 BC and 20 BC, soon after the Roman conquest of the area, when the *oppidum* of Gergovie was founded.

[Sum.: J. R. Collis, 1980, Aulnat and urbanisation in France: second interim report. *Archaeological Journal*, 137, 40–9]

Aulus Plautius [Na]. The Roman general who led the invasion of Britain in AD 43. He then became Britain's first governor. On returning to Rome in AD 47 he became the last man to receive an *ovatio*—a form of triumphal celebration.

aumbry [Co]. A small cupboard or closed recess in a wall.

Aunjetitz [CP]. German and Czech variation of UNETICE Culture.

Aurelius [Na]. Roman emperor, AD 270–5.

aureus [Ar]. A high-value Roman gold coin.

Aurignacian [CP]. Refers to an upper Palaeolithic toolmaking industry named after the Aurignac rock-shelter in the French Pyrenees. The tradition appears to have begun in the Near East around 40 000 years ago and from there spread westwards. It was present in France by about 32 000 years ago where it post-dates the CHÂTELPERRONIAN and precedes the SOLUTREAN, GRAVETTIAN, and MAGDALENIAN. Aurignacian assemblages are characterized by a high proportion of burins, but they also contain long blades, steeply retouched scrapers, and split-based bone points.

aurochs [Sp]. The wild ancestor of domestic cattle (*Bos primigenius*), found widely throughout Europe and Asia in early post-glacial times. It generally inhabited open woodland, and with its dark coat and great bulk (up to 1.8 m high at the shoulder and weighing up to 1 tonne) it was an impressive beast. Aurochs became extinct during the late medieval period in Europe as a result of hunting and interbreeding.

Australian Small Tool Tradition [CP]. Stone tool assemblages characteristic of hunter-gatherer communities across Australia, but not Tasmania, during the period 3000 BC through to European contact. The tool types represented include hafted implements, such as Bondi points, a range of bifacial and unifacial points and projectile tips, microliths in geometric forms, and a variety of blade-based items. There is considerable spatial variation in the composition of the Australian Small Tool Tradition, and its unity and integrity has been called into question. The introduction of the dingo into Australia has sometimes been linked with the adoption and spread of the Australian Small Tool Tradition.

Australopithecus [Sp]. Early hominid reconstructed as being bipedal but small-brained. The earliest specimens, classified as *Australopithecus afarensis* come from East Africa and date to about 3.75 million years ago, although claims of still greater age have been made on fragments of fossil bone from Lothagam in Kenya which date to about 5 million years ago. *Australopithecus africanus* has been recognized at about 2–3 million years ago in southern Africa. Both *A. afarensis* and *A. africanus* have a relatively light build and are considered 'gracile' australopithecines. Many regard them as direct human ancestors. A more robust australopithecine (*A. robustus/ paranthropus*) is known from a number of sites in Kenya at about 2 million years ago when it seems to have been contemporary with *Homo habilis* and *Homo erectus*.

autocratic military rule [Ge]. Rule by a specific military leader, who concentrates power in his own hands.

autonomous invention [Th]. The development of a new technology, artefact, or style which is similar to one that already exists in another time or place but which has come about completely independently. Many important discoveries and inventions have been made several times over, for example: the domestication of plants and animals; metalworking; and writing.

auxilia [Ge]. Latin name for the units comprising auxiliaries or non-citizens in the Roman army, usually 500 or 100 strong.

Avebury, Lord (1834–1913) [Bi]. *See* LUBBOCK.

Avebury, Wiltshire, UK [Si]. The largest and finest henge monument in Britain set on the rolling chalk downlands of southern England near the headwaters of the River Kennet. The great ditch encloses an area of 11.5 ha and has a diameter of 350 m. On the inner edge of the ditch stood a ring of 98 stones. Near the centre of the henge were two smaller stone circles with internal settings. Limited excavation within the interior of the site revealed very little, as is the case at most henge monuments. It is, however, known that prior to its construction in about 2100 BC some or all of the area was under cultivation.

Two avenues of upright stones led away from Avebury, connecting it to the wider landscape. The Beckhampton Avenue to the southwest has largely disappeared, but the West Kennet Avenue to the southeast remains, in part reconstructed.

At the southeastern end of the West Kennet Avenue is the Sanctuary, a complicated and long-lived monument that started its life as a series of timber circles. Two rings of stone slabs were later added and it is the outer of these that connects to the Avenue and thence to Avebury.

[Sum.: A. Burl, 1979, *Prehistoric Avebury*. London and New Haven: Yale University Press]

avenue [MC]. A more or less parallel-sided strip of ground whose sides are defined or marked by lines of upright stones or timber posts and/or low earthworks. Such features are found widely in different cultures at different times, often connected with the formal approaches to ceremonial monuments or buildings. In the later Neolithic of the British Isles a number are associated with approaches to STONE CIRCLES, as at AVEBURY and STONEHENGE.

Avienus, Rufus Festus [Na]. Roman writer of fables in elegiac verse of the late 4th century AD. His poem, *Ora Maritima*, contains borrowings from the *Massiliote Periplus* an account of a sea voyage from Massilia (Marseilles) along the western Mediterranean, thought to date back to the 6th century BC at the latest. It includes reference to the islands of Ierne and Albion, Ireland and Britain, whose inhabitants reputedly traded with the Oestrymnides of Brittany.

avocado [Sp]. A pear-shaped fruit with soft oily edible flesh (*Persea americana*). Native to Mexico. Domesticated from about 1800 BC.

awl [Ar]. A hand-held bone, flint, or metal piercing tool with a strong sharp point used for making holes in such materials as leather, wood, or cloth.

axe [Ar]. Stone or metal cutting tool mounted on a wooden or bone haft with the cutting edge parallel to the haft.

axe factory [MC]. A place where stone axeheads were manufactured from fine-grained rock during the Neolithic period in Europe. Axe factories include quarry sites where ADITS and pits follow bands of the desired rock into the ground, but in other cases exploited surface outcrops or detached boulders of suitable rock. Primary working involving the production of ROUGH-OUTS is usual, only a few sites having evidence for polishing and finishing. Very extensive axe factories are known at Great Langdale, England, Graig Llwyd, Wales, Tievebulliagh, Ireland, and Plussulien, Brittany.

axe-hammer [Ar]. A large and usually heavy kind of perforated stone axe with a broad flat butt at one end, a tapered blade at the other, and a shaft-hole towards the butt end. The stone examples found in Neolithic and early Bronze Age contexts in northwestern Europe are probably copies of copper and bronze examples current at the time in central Europe. Their purpose is unknown. *See also* BATTLE-AXE.

Ayampitín points [Ar]. Bifacially worked stone missile tips of willow-leaf outline found among archaic hunter-gatherer communities of the Peruvian highlands and coasts in 9000–7000 BC. Typical examples are 60–70 mm long.

Aylesford–Swarling Culture [CP]. Late La Tène regional culture in southeastern England, named after two cemeteries in Kent, and conventionally associated with immigrants of the 1st century BC from Belgic Gaul. Innovations of the period include the introduction of coinage and of wheel-thrown pottery, including characteristic jars with pedestal bases and cordon ornament, platters, cups, and beakers. There were imports of Italic-type bronzes as well as wine amphorae from continental Europe, and this continued after the Roman conquest of Gaul with the import of Gaulish and Arretine wares.

Azilian [CP]. A late upper Palaeolithic industry of northern Spain and southwest France dating to the period 9000 to 8000 BC named after the site of Le Mas D'Azil near Toulouse on the French side of the Pyrenees. The industry is characterized by microlithic tools, notably the so-called Azilian point, which is a kind of double-pointed backed blade. Flat perforated and barbed harpoons of red-deer antler are also known. Azilian communities also had small schist pebbles covered in red dots or stripes. Of unknown purpose, such objects are also found amongst the material culture of communities further east in Italy and Switzerland.

azimuth [Ge]. A compass bearing taken from true north. An azimuth of 90 degrees is due east, 180 degrees due south, etc.

Aztec [CP]. The dominant polity of the late Post-Classic period in the densely populated Basin of Mexico, which came to control large areas of Mesoamerica north of the Gulf of Tehuantepec.

The origins of the Aztecs are bound up in the population movements of Toltec refugees and Chichimec immigrants settling in the Basin of Mexico around 1000 AD, each establishing itself as a tiny state whose ruling dynasties claimed descent from the Toltecs and adopted Toltec ideologies and divinely authorized kingship.

The Aztecs, also known as the Tenochca or Mexica, were the last Chichimec tribe to arrive, possibly forced to leave their home at Aztlan by drought or over-population. There was little available land for occupation and the Aztecs lived a peripatetic existence, periodically being moved on by one state after another appalled by their savage ways and liking for human sacrifice. Eventually, they settled on some uninhabited swampy islands near the western shore of Lake Texcoco where, according to legend, they saw a sign previously prophesied as indicating the site for their capital: an eagle with a snake in its beak sitting on a cactus. The twin Aztec towns of Tenochtitlán and Tlatelolco were founded in AD 1325 or AD 1345.

In AD 1367 the Aztecs started serving as mercenaries for the ruler of the Tepanec city-state of Azcapotzalco, then in competition with the rulers of Texcoco for recognition as paramount lords of new Chichimec states. Through a series of alliances and rebellions the Aztec cities grew larger and more wealthy, with the Aztecs themselves gradually accruing more and more power. In 1434 the rulers of the Aztec city of Tenochtitlán formed the so-called Triple Alliance with the rulers of Texcoco and Tlacopan. All the other small states in the Basin became tribute-paying vassals of the Alliance. By 1500 the Triple Alliance controlled an area of 200 000 square kilometres and a population of perhaps 10 million. Aztec domination of the Alliance came in 1502.

The Aztecs invested much time and effort into the construction of their cities and the agricultural systems round about. The centre of Tenochtitlán was a sacred precinct dominated by a 60 m high pyramid on which stood the temples of Tlaloc the rain god and Huitzilopochtli the war god. The precinct also included the priest's residence, a large ball court, and a *tzompantli* on which the skulls of many thousands of sacrificed victims were displayed. Surrounding the precinct were the palaces of Tenochtitlán's rulers, two major market-places, and, beyond these, the houses of the town's inhabitants.

Agriculture was intensive and heavily dependent on water control systems established in the Basin of Mexico by the Teotihuacan state. These water control systems were crucial both for irrigation and the draining of lakes. The Aztecs also made use of floating gardens by dredging lakes and piling the silt up to form raised surfaces.

Aztec society was stratified into three main classes: nobles (*pilli*), who were relatives of the king; commoners (*macehuales*), who belonged by birth to one of twenty clans; and displaced and conquered people (*mayeques*), who worked as tenants. Craftsmanship was important and Aztec artists excelled in stone sculpture. Other nations, particularly the Mixtec of Oaxaca were engaged to make featherwork, polychrome ceramics, superb gold jewellery, and intricate mosaics.

The Aztec state was a militaristic regime, constantly at war in order to conquer other states and force them to pay tribute, and as a way of obtaining captives to sacrifice.

The Aztecs inherited from the Toltec and the Maya the practice of human sacrifice. It was believed that the main Aztec deities, Huitzilopochtli and Tezcatlipoca, needed regular nourishment from the blood and heart of sacrificed victims in order to perpetuate the continued existence of the universe. Up to 15 000 people a year were sacrificed, mainly by ripping out the beating heart of the victim who was stretched out on a stone in front of the temple of the god. High-status warriors, nobles, and priests ate the flesh of those sacrificed.

The Aztec empire came to an abrupt end on 13 August 1521 when Hernan Cortés and his Spanish *conquistadors* took the Aztec capital and its emperor Montechzuma (Montezuma) II.

Baal [Di]. Principal god of the CANAANITES, usually depicted as a young warrior, armed, and with bull's horns springing from his helmet. Identified by the Hyksos with the Egyptian deity SETH. The PHOENICIANS carried the worship of Baal westwards into the Mediterranean region in the 1st millennium BC.

Babylon, Iraq [Si]. One of the largest and most ancient cities in Mesopotamia, 80 km south of modern Baghdad on the River Euphrates. Excavations by the German archaeologist Robert Koldewey between 1899 and 1917, together with more recent work, provide the plan of the ancient city and allow some understanding of its main elements.

In the early 2nd millennium BC it was the centre of a city-state, the so-called old Babylonian, reaching prominence in 1792 BC under the 6th ruler of the 1st Dynasty, Hammurabi. It was destroyed by the HITTITES in c.1595 BC and then ruled by the KASSITES until c.1157 BC. Thereafter followed a period of further decline under short-lived dynasties and with frequent wars with ELAM and ASSYRIA.

In the 7th century BC the city-state rose again under the rulers of the 11th Dynasty, destroying Assyria and, under Nebuchadnezzar, conquering an empire from the Persian Gulf through to the Mediterranean, the so-called neo-Babylonian. The city itself covered some 850 ha and is estimated to have had a population in excess of 100 000 souls. Within it were many famous monuments including the Ishtar Gate, the ziggurat long identified with the biblical Tower of Babel, and the palace of Nebuchadnezzar which contained a structure that Koldeway identified as the famous Hanging Gardens (*see* SEVEN WONDERS OF THE WORLD).

In 539 BC Babylon was overthrown by the PERSIANS under Cyrus, after which it continued to exist only as a regional capital for successive occupants of the area. Alexander the Great died in the town in 323 BC. The site was abandoned after the Muslim conquest of the area in AD 641.

[Rep.: J. Oates, 1986, *Babylon*. London: Thames & Hudson]

Babylonia [CP]. A region taking in the whole of the southern alluvial plain of Mesopotamia, which although traditionally linked with the city of Babylon was not always connected to it or ruled from it.

Bacaudae [Ge]. Celtic name of obscure meaning applied to the peasant rebels of northern Spain and Gaul from the 3rd to the 5th century AD. After c.AD 400 massive outbreaks of revolt in Armorica contributed to the breakdown of Roman power in the northern provinces.

bacini [Ar]. Ceramic vessels placed for decorative reasons high in the walls of Christian churches in southern Europe between the 11th and 15th centuries AD.

backed blade [Ar]. Blade tool blunted on one side by the removal of small steep flakes, the other side being left sharp. Some small examples may have been used as projectile tips, larger examples were probably knives with the blunted edge providing a finger-rest or to ease hafting.

backside [Co]. Yard behind a house or cottage.

Badarian [CP]. A predynastic agrarian culture of the Period 4500–3250 BC in Egypt, named after the site of El Badari in Middle Egypt. Its most distinctive material culture is its fine pottery, thin-walled and ripple-burnished, with a black band around the top of brown or red walls. Long-distance trade was carried out by Badarian communities who also developed the use of native copper for making beads. Barley and wheat were grown and cattle and sheep herded. Flax was grown and made into linen.

Baden Culture (Baden–Pécel Culture) [CP]. Final Copper Age communities living in central Europe, especially Poland, the Czech Republic, Austria, Hungary, and parts of Germany in the early and mid 3rd millennium BC. The early phase of the Baden Culture (*c*.2750–2450 BC) equates with the Bolzeráz Culture of the Hungarian Plain, while in the middle and later phases (*c*.2600–2200 BC) there is greater similarity of material culture over a wider area. The settlements are generally dispersed with thin occupation layers. Metal tool types include axe-hammers and TORCS of twisted copper wire. The pottery is usually plain and dark in colour, sometimes with channelled decoration and moulded handles. Domestic horses are represented, and carts running on four solid disc wheels were introduced. The presence of ceramic vessels tentatively identified with milk processing, draft animals, and evidence for spinning suggests that the economy of these communities include strong elements of the SECONDARY PRODUCTS REVOLUTION.

Badorf ware [Ar]. A type of pottery made in the Vorgebirge Hills west of Cologne in the 8th and 9th centuries AD with a cream-coloured fabric. Globular pitchers are the best-known forms and appear to have been traded widely. In the 9th century red paint was also used for decoration.

baffle [Co]. An obstacle, such as a low wall, bollard, or screen, usually positioned in the stokehole or flue of a kiln to prevent a rapid rush of cold air directly into the kiln chamber.

Bahía [CP]. A regional tradition occupying the central coast of Ecuador in the period *c*.500 BC to AD 500. Characterized by large stone-lined terraced platform mounds at ceremonial centres. At Manta (Ecuador), one such mound is said to have been 175 m by 50 m. Pottery styles include everted rim wares, perforated rim wares, and polypod vessels. Elaborate anthropomorphic figurines are known, some stylized and grotesque, others naturalistic. Ceramic models of houses are also found.

bailey [Co]. Fortified enclosed courtyard or ward within a medieval castle. *See* MOTTE AND BAILEY CASTLE.

bailiwick [De]. Area under the jurisdiction of a bailiff in medieval times.

Bajada Phase [CP]. A subdivision of the Archaic of southwestern parts of North America dating to *c*.4800–3200 BC and characterized by increasing numbers of flake scrapers and choppers in lithic assemblages. This hints at greater reliance on plant food in the diet of Bajada communities. Bajada succeeds the Jay Phase and precedes the Cochise Phase.

balk [De]. *See* BAULK.

ball court [Co]. An open court, usually in the shape of an elongated H, originating in Mesoamerica in the later 1st millennium BC, and used for a game known by the Nahuatl word for it: *tlatchli*. This game, which was both recreational and of ritual significance, involved two opposing teams or individuals attempting to keep a large and heavy rubber ball in motion without the use of their hands or feet. Rules and arrangements changed over time and between regions, but some Post-Classic examples had stone rings set high on the walls of the court. When a team managed to get the ball through such a ring they automatically won the game. The loss of a game could sometimes result in the sacrifice of the losing team.

Ballintober swords [Ar]. Type of late Bronze Age sword found in the British Isles, named after finds from Ballintober in Ireland. Produced during the Penard Phase (*c*.1200–1000 BC). Distinctive in having a leaf-shaped bronze blade with an lozenge cross-section and swept-back ricasso. The hilt is secured in place by being riveted to a rectangular tang.

ballista [Ar]. A large military catapult which fired projectiles of iron or stone. Roman examples were made up of a framework in which twisted tendons, rope or leather thongs provided elasticity and force. When the twist was suddenly released, a stone of up to 45 kg in weight could be thrown a considerable distance to batter a wall. The most famous ballista bolt in Britain is that piercing the spine of a man buried at Maiden Castle.

Ballistaria or ballista platforms can still be detected in some forts. In the later Roman period ballistae were mounted on bastions projecting from fort walls.

Ballyalton bowl [Ar]. A type of well-made decorated Neolithic pottery found in Ireland and dating to the late 4th and early 3rd millennia BC. The forms are round-based and shouldered, with a blunted section at the top of the blade and with the diameter of the rim less than that of the shoulder, sometimes markedly so. Decoration includes vertical linear grooved and whipped cord impressions arranged in lines or arcs. Relief ornament is sometimes present. A revised scheme for Irish Neolithic pottery put forward by Alison Sheridan places these vessels within a longer-lived tradition of fineware bipartite bowls spanning the early and middle Neolithic.

baluster jug [Ar]. General term for a style of tall medieval jug used in Europe whose height is about three times its diameter.

balustrade [Co]. A row of ornamented supports to a railing or low colonnade.

BANANA [Ab]. The abbreviated form of the principle 'Build Absolutely Nothing Anywhere Near Anything' used as a slogan by radical environmentalists, and some archaeologists, attempting to curb property development.

Banas Culture [CP]. The name given to a series of early Bronze Age agricultural communities living along the Banas River in Rajasthan, India, in the early 2nd millennium BC. Their material culture is characterized by black-on-red pottery which sometimes has white painted decoration, red-ware pottery, and copper and bronze tools and ornaments made from local ore sources. Their houses are made in stone and mud brick.

band [Ge]. A simple, small, autonomous family-based group, the definition of which may be no more than the fact that its members feel closely enough related not to intermarry. There are no specialized or formalized institutions or groups which can be recognized as economic, political, or religious, for the band itself is the organization that undertakes all roles. Leadership and the division of labour is usually by age or sex differentia-

tions. This simple form of human social organization flourished for most of prehistory. Bands consist of a family or a series of families, usually ranging from 20 to 50 people.

Bandkeramik Culture [CP]. *See* LINEARBANK-CERAMIC.

banjo enclosure [MC]. A class of middle Iron Age settlement site found widely across southern Britain. It comprises a small round enclosure, usually less than 6 ha in extent, bounded by a bank and outer ditch. The enclosure has a single main entrance that is approached by a long narrow trackway defined on either side by a low bank and ditch. The outer ends of earthworks defining the approach track are sometimes turned outwards to create a funnel entrance, the ground plan as a whole having the appearance of a banjo. Mainly constructed between 400 BC and 100 BC, banjo enclosures are essentially farmsteads or small hamlets with pretentious driveways, in some cases occupied by important and influential people to judge by the quality of the material culture represented.

bank barrow [MC]. A distinctive class of Neolithic ceremonial monument found in parts of the British Isles, especially England and southern Scotland. Generally over 150 m long, bank barrows comprise narrow parallel-sided mounds of earth and stone with a length/breadth ratio in excess of 6:1. Flanking ditches were used as quarries to obtain the material to make the mound. Few have been extensively excavated, but from surface surveys and limited investigations it seems that some were built by extending earlier LONG BARROWS while others developed as the episodic enlargement of a simple mound. They date mainly to the early 3rd millennium BC, in some cases post-dating the abandonment of causewayed enclosures. Some are closely associated with CURSUS monuments. Also known as long mounds.

Ban Na Di, Thailand [Si]. A small prehistoric settlement occupied from about 1500 BC through to about AD 300 south of Ban Chiang in Khorat. After about 500 BC the site was important for metalworking and as the centre of a local tin–bronze industry that specialized in jewellery, axes, and projectile heads. From about 100 BC onwards, iron was also worked at the site, smelted and forged to produce hoes, knives, spearheads, and ornaments. Lead–bronze was also being cast to make, amongst other thing, bells and bowls.

[Rep.: C. Higham, 1984, *Prehistoric investigations in northeast Thailand*. Oxford: British Archaeological Reports International Series 231]

Bann Culture [CP]. A general term for the late Mesolithic flint industries of Northern Ireland and the Isle of Man characterized by the use of heavy blades and distinguished most especially by the presence of basally retouched flakes (BANN FLAKES) and tanged points, and the use of the LARNIAN flint-working technique. Peter Woodman has shown that the Bann Culture industries are part of more widely distributed late Mesolithic cultures in Ireland, dating to between 5500 BC and about 3800 BC.

banner stone [Ar]. A ground and polished flattish stone object with a single longitudinal perforation commonly found in the American midwest and east. Possibly an ATLATL weight or a ceremonial artefact.

Bann flake (Bann point) [Ar]. A term variously used by different authorities, but at its minimum it is simply a kind of leaf-shaped flake found widely amongst the later Mesolithic assemblages of Northern Ireland and the Isle of Man, one component of the BANN CULTURE. More strictly, Peter Woodman defines them as large flakes having no significant tang, with light retouch, either as elongated or laminar forms less than 3.2 cm across, or as leaf-shaped forms which are broader and have only very peripheral retouch at the butt.

Banpo, China [Si]. Site of an early Yangshao village, now preserved in a museum at Xi'an, Shaanxi Province, dating to the 5th millennium BC. The residential area was enclosed by a ditch, outside of which were cemeteries and an industrial area that included pottery kilns. Dogs and pigs were domesticated while millet was the staple crop. Coarse pottery was cord-marked or stamped, but the finewares were painted in black and red with geometric designs or drawings of animals.

[Rep.: S. Lin, 1981, *Banpo yi zhi zong shu*. Xianggang: Zhong wen da xue chu ban she]

baptistery [Co]. The place, usually a separate room entered from one of the aisles, of an early Christian church in which a pool of water provided with steps down into it was used for the baptism of adult converts by immersion, e.g., in the Twin Churches of St Mary at Ephesus, or at Philerimos in Rhodes.

barbarous radiate [Ar]. Late and inferior copies of RADIATE coins that circulated in the Roman empire. Most were made in regional mints scattered throughout the provinces.

barbed and tanged arrowhead [Ar]. Triangular-shaped flint arrowheads of the later Neolithic and early Bronze Age in Europe. Distinctive in having a short rectangular tang on the base opposite the point, symmetrically set either side of which is a barb. The tang was used to secure the arrow tip to its shaft and usually projects slightly below the ends of the barbs.

barbican [Co]. A tower or advance work defending the entrance to a castle.

barbotine decoration [De]. A method of relief decoration executed by trailing semi-liquid clay through the end of an implement on to a finished pottery vessel before firing, a process identical to icing a cake.

Bare Creek Phase [CP]. Hunter-gatherer communities occupying parts of the northwest corner of the Great Basin in California 2500–100 BC. Successors to the Menlo Phase, Bare Creek communities lived in small domed brush wickiups each of which probably held a nuclear family. They hunted bison, deer, and sheep, but relied for food on the meat of rabbits and waterfowl. Artefacts include the bifurcate chipped stone Pinto points.

Bargrennon group [CP]. Regional style of middle Neolithic SIMPLE PASSAGE GRAVES found in southwestern Scotland. Only about twelve sites are known, but all have round mounds covering one or more small single-celled chambers with a passage giving access to them.

Barker, Philip Arthur (1920–2001) [Bi]. British archaeologist well known for his work developing excavation methodology and recording systems. Born in Wembley, London, he left school with no significant qualifications. During WW2 he served in the RAF and subsequently trained as a schoolmaster. His first post was teaching art at the Priory Boys' School in Shrewsbury, Shropshire. It was here that he became interested in archaeology, quickly developing practical work in excavation and especially the application of his training as an artist. He was appointed first to a lectureship and later a readership in the Department of Extramural Studies in the University of Birmingham, a post he retained until retirement in 1987. He was a driving force in the establishment of RESCUE in the 1970s and the Institute of Field Archaeologists in the 1980s. For many years he was the archaeologist at Worcester Cathedral, but he is remembered most for his work at Wroxeter in Shropshire and Hen Domen in Montgomeryshire. His much translated book *Techniques of archaeological excavation* was first published in 1977 (London: Batsford) and has since gone through several editions.

[Obit.: *The Times*, 30 March 2001]

barley [Sp]. Staple cereal of the Old World of the genus *Hordeum*. Two main groups are recognized. Two-row barley (*Hordeum distichum*) derives from the wild form *Hordeum spontameum* that was distributed from the Aegean through to the Hindu Kush, and is recorded as early as 7000 BC at JARMO. Six-row barley (*Hordeum hexastichum*) derives from the wild *Hordeum distichum* whose distribution extended from China westwards to Egypt. Modern barley (*Hordeum tetrastichum*) is a development of the original domesticated six-row types. Wild barley is of hulled form with the seed firmly held in the glume with a fragile stalk attached to the ear. Domesticated barley has a stronger spike which does not break during harvesting and includes hulled forms as well as the rather easier to thresh, so-called free threshing, naked forms.

Barley, Maurice Willmore (1910–91) [Bi]. British archaeologist specializing in medieval settlement and historic buildings, with a lifelong commitment to socialism, working-class origins, and the study of traditional buildings and folklore. Born in Lincoln, he studied history at Reading University before becoming involved in teaching adults in the Extramural Department of Nottingham University. In 1962 he transferred to a newly created post in archaeology in the Classics Department where he stayed until retirement in 1974. From 1951 he was actively involved in the development of the Council for British

Archaeology, first as a member of the Executive Committee and later as its Secretary (1954–64) and President (1964–7). Between 1957 and 1963 he was President of the Vernacular Architecture Group and between 1972 and 1990 Chairman of the York Archaeological Trust. Medieval buildings and towns were his speciality and his publications include *The English farmhouse and cottage* (1961, London: Routledge and Kegan Paul) and *Guide to British topographical collections* (1974, London: CBA).

[Obit.: *British Archaeological News*, 6.5 (1991), 60–1]

barmkin [Co]. A defensive farmyard enclosure, usually attached to a towerhouse or SHIEDING, in which animals are sheltered and crops stored. In Ireland it is know as a **bawn**, an anglicized version of the Irish word *badhun* or *bo-dhaingan* meaning a cattle fortress.

barn [MC]. Any timber or stone agricultural structure built expressly for the storage and primary processing of field crops, hay, or straw.

Barnenez, France [Si]. One of the earliest Neolithic chambered tombs in western France, set on a hilltop in Finistère, discovered during quarrying operations in 1953–4. Excavation of the site by P. R. Giot between 1955 and 1957 showed that there were two main phases to its construction. The first monument, dating to about 4000 BC, was a rectangular stone cairn 30 m by 20 m and perhaps 4 m high, with stepped sides. Five chambers lay inside the cairn, each approached by a separate passage opening into the south side of the cairn. One of the chambers has a number of carvings on the orthostats, including three axes. The monument was extended to the southwest around 3700 BC, with the cairn being more than doubled in length and a further six chambers added.

[Rep.: P. R. Giot, 1970, *Barnenez*. Rennes: University of Rennes]

Barrancoid [CP]. Refers to a ceramic sequence developed by Irving Rouse and José Cruxent to facilitate interregional comparisons. The sequence spans the period 1000 BC to AD 1000 and is based on material from the site of Barrancas on the Belize River. The most distinctive features of the pottery include curvilinear incised decoration, and applied, modelled animal and human faces called *adornos*. Griddles imply the cultivation of bitter manioc by Barrancoid pottery-using communities.

In the Orinoco Delta area the Barrancoid sequence succeeds the Saladoid series, although elsewhere Barrancoid ware is contemporary with the later phases of Saladoid.

barrel urn [Ar]. Type of large middle Bronze Age pot found within the overall repertoire of the DEVEREL–RIMBURY ceramic tradition of southern Britain in the period 1500 BC through to 1200 BC. Usually over 60 cm high, barrel urns have a distinctive profile, wider in the middle than at the base or the rim, often with applied cordons that are decorated with finger-tip impressions. Found on domestic sites where they were presumably used as storage vessels and as containers for cremations often found as SECONDARY BURIALS in earlier ROUND BARROWS.

barrel vault [De]. An arrangement for constructing a stone roof over an open space which took a semi-circular form rather like an elongated arch. Such vaults can only be used to span narrow spaces and rely for their strength on the tight packing of the stones. Barrel vaults are the earliest kind of vaulting used. Also known as a tunnel vault.

barrow [MC]. General term used to describe a mound of earth and stone heaped up to cover one or more burials. Burial beneath a barrow is one of the most enduring traditions of burial practice in Europe, and is also found in many other parts of the world. Many different kinds of barrow can be recognized on the basis of shape, construction detail, date, position, and relationships to other things. Round, long, oval, and square forms are the most common styles found. Round barrows in England are often called tumuli; those made almost entirely of stone in upland regions are termed CAIRNS. *See also* KURGAN, SQUARE BARROW, LONG BARROW, BANK BARROW, OVAL BARROW, ROUND BARROW, FANCY BARROW, POND BARROW.

barrow cemetery (barrow field) [MC]. A general term for a group of barrows, typically anything between 5 and 300, clustered together and representing the gradual build-up of burials and their associated monuments and structures over a period of time. Anglo-Saxon cemeteries that comprise numerous small barrows are generally referred to as barrow fields. *See also* ROUND BARROW CEMETERIES.

bar-shaped ingot [Ar]. Term applied to flat rectangular ingots of silver of Roman date.

Barton–Bendish Tradition [CP]. *See* TAUNTON PHASE.

Barumini, Sardinia [Si]. A NURAGHE site towards the southern end of the island, well inland, which was excavated by Giovanni Lilliu in the 1940s. It began as a single fortified tower, 17 m high and with three corbelled chambers one above the other, in the early 2nd millennium BC. Four round towers around the base of the central tower, and a perimeter wall with smaller towers enclosing a village were built in the 8th century BC. In the 6th century BC the site was sacked by the CARTHAGINIANS.

[Rep.: L. Giovanni, 1988, *Su nuraxi ali Barumini*. Sassari: C. Delfino]

basal-looped spearhead [Ar]. Type of leaf-shaped socketed spearhead of the European middle Bronze Age which has two small holes or loops at the base of the blade, one either side of the socket. It is assumed that these were to assist in securing the metal spearhead to the wooden shaft, but they might also have been used to tie streamers of some kind to the top of the spear.

basilica [MC]. A Roman public hall providing the administrative and commercial centre of a Roman town. Usually situated along one side of the FORUM and containing one or more tribunals for magistrates, the standard form of the basilica was a long rectangular building with two rows of pillars dividing it into a central nave and two outer aisles. Behind the basilica there was usually a range of rooms containing the CURIA, a shrine for the TUTELA, and offices. The aisled-hall plan characteristic of most basilicas was adopted for use by numerous religious cults, including Christianity, that needed space for communal worship.

basilican church [MC]. A church modelled on the form of a Roman BASILICA which would typically have a broad nave and aisles.

Basketmaker Tradition [CP]. Late Archaic and Post-Archaic sedentary communities living in southwestern parts of North America between *c*.1000 BC and AD 750. Identified in the late 19th century and codified into three main phases by Alfred Kidder in 1927, it is now recognized that much of what was formerly classified as Basketmaker Tradition is more comfortably seen as belonging to more clearly identified traditions and cultures. Basketmaker Phase I, dated to *c*.1000–1 BC, is essentially the same as the Archaic; Phase II, *c*.AD 1–450 is the same as the Desert Archaic and represents the beginning a long-lived cultural tradition on the Colorado Plateau which is referred to as the ANASAZI from the Navajo word for 'ancient alien ones'. Basketmaker Phase III, *c*.AD 450–750, equates to a developed phase of Anasazi, when beans were added to the diet and there was a greater commitment to agriculture.

bas-relief [De]. A technique of sculpture in which subjects are defined by being slightly raised from a flat background. Also known as low-relief.

bastion [Co]. An outward projection from a defensive wall.

Bastis (Bast, Bastet) [Di]. The cat goddess of Lower Egypt. Her main cult centre was at Bubastis in the Nile Delta.

bastle (bastle house) [MC]. A type of defended farmhouse dating to the 16th and 17th centuries found in northern England and southern Scotland. Bastles are generally two-storeyed buildings, roughly constructed, with the main living area on the first floor and storerooms and animal shelters below. The thick walls, small doorways, and narrow slit-windows provided a measure of defence in time of trouble along the English/Scottish borders. Also known as peel houses.

Bat Cave, New Mexico, USA [Si]. A series of rock-shelters containing stratified occupation over a long period. The earlier evidence of settlement takes the form of intermittent usage by hunter-gatherer groups over the period 8000–800 BC.

Between 800 BC and 250 BC more regular usage occurred, and the occupants constructed large pits and hearths. The pits contained maize and squash and thus represent some of the earliest evidence for the cultivation of these crops in North America.

[Rep.: H. W. Dick, 1952, Evidence of early man in Bat cave and on the Plains of San Augustin, New Mexico. In S. Tax (ed.), 1952, *Indian tribes of aboriginal America*. Chicago: Chicago University Press, 158–63]

Bateman, Thomas (1821–61) [Bi]. British antiquarian well known for his exploits in excavating barrows in the Peak District of central England. Born in Rowsley, Derbyshire, Bateman began his antiquarian work at the age of three when he accompanied his father, William Bateman (1787–1835), on the excavation of a barrow. Both Thomas's parents died when he was young and he was brought up by his stern but wealthy grandfather. He began excavating barrows on his own account in 1843, working assiduously over a period of about a decade. It seems that Bateman was a colourful character and throughout his early life carried on an affair with a young married woman, Mary Mason, setting up house with her in 1844. Things came to a head with the death of his grandfather in 1847 and the prospect of being disinherited. Thomas saved himself by marrying his housekeeper, Sarah Parker, after which he reverted to a life of unblemished respectability. In 1848 he published the results of his excavations as *Vestiges of the antiquities of Derbyshire* (London: J. R. Smith). At this time he employed various excavators to work for him in order to speed the flow of antiquities to his blossoming museum. Two weeks before his death at the young age of 39 he published *Ten years' diggings* (1861, London: J. R. Smith). He was buried at Middleton-by-Youlgrave in an impressive tomb, still visible today, with a stone replica of a Bronze Age urn on top.

[Bio.: B. M. Marsden, 1984, *Pioneers of prehistory*. Ormskirk: Hesketh, 53–6]

bath-house [Co]. A feature of all Roman towns and cities as well as private houses throughout the empire. From the 1st century BC onwards, the tradition of bathing became a major social institution. *See* THERMAE.

bâton de commandement [Ar]. An implement made from antler with a cylindrical hole at one end. Often decorated, and dating from the AURIGNACIAN through to the Upper MAGDALENIAN. Interpretations vary from the symbolic to it being a spear-thrower or arrow-straightener. Also referred to as a *bâton percé*.

batter [De]. The slope back from vertical given to a ditch side or trench face in order to increase its stability. The most effective batter would be the natural angle of rest of the material through which the cutting was made.

battle-axe [Ar]. **1.** Type of perforated stone implement dating to the later Neolithic and early Bronze Age in southern, eastern, and northern Europe with a solid body, centrally placed shaft-hole, slightly concave outline when viewed in profile, and expanded blades and butts. Some have a blade at both ends. There is great variety in form: Fiona Roe recognized nine main types in Britain alone, and taking Europe as a whole they were made and used over a very long period from the mid 3rd millennium through to the mid 2nd millennium BC. The name was rather fancifully applied to these implements by 19th-century antiquaries; there is no evidence that they were ever used in war. *See also* AXE-HAMMER. **2.** Type of copper, bronze, or gold implement with a centrally placed shaft-hole, believed to be of ceremonial function and probably derived from the earlier stone versions. **3.** Iron weapon used by VIKING warriors in the later 1st millennium AD and remaining a popular weapon through into the Middle Ages in Europe.

Battle-axe Culture [MC]. *See* CORDED WARE CULTURE.

battlement [Co]. A crenellated parapet along the top of a wall constructed to aid defence with merlons (the solid portion) alternating with embrasures (the gaps).

battleship curve [De]. Shape on a seriation graph formed by plotted points representing, for instance, the rise in popularity of an artefact, its period of maximum popularity, and its eventual decline.

baulk (balk) [De]. An artificial wall of unexcavated archaeological deposits left standing between the trenches of an excavation in order to provide access to the working areas and preserve until the last possible moment a sample of the stratigraphy for study and recording.

bawn [Co]. *See* BARMKIN.

bay [Ge]. Structural division in the length of a building or roof. The unit within a building between a pair of piers or buttresses; the division of a roof marked by its main trusses.

BB1/BB2 [Ab]. *See* BLACK-BURNISHED WARE.

bc/BC/BCE [Ab]. Before Christ, meaning the pre-Christian era in the Gregorian calendar, running backwards from the year 1 BC as the year before the calculated, and back-projected, year in which Christ was believed to have been born. The term is widely used in western societies in modern times, but when applied to prehistory it is simply the back-projection of a relatively recent chronological system which cannot have had any meaning to ancient people. The use of lower-case initials is often taken to indicate that the date has been calculated from a radiocarbon determination by subtracting 1950 from the radiocarbon age (sometimes expressed as RCYBC—Radiocarbon Years Before Christ). Although common in literature of the 1960s through to the 1980s, such a date is fundamentally wrong because radiocarbon years are not the same as calendar years and thus such calculations have been made without subtracting like from like. The use of upper-case letters conventionally denotes a CALIBRATED RADIOCARBON AGE in calendar years or, exceptionally, a historically determined age in calendar years. The alternative term BCE, meaning Before the Christian Era, is increasingly popular.

Beacharra ware [Ar]. Style of decorated middle Neolithic pottery found in western parts of Scotland and classified by Stuart Piggott into three groups: unornamented bag-shaped bowls (A); decorated carinated bowls with a rim diameter less than the diameter at the carination and incised or channelled ornament (B); and small bowls with panel ornament in fine whipped cord (C).

beacon [MC]. General term for the place where a fire was deliberately lit to give some kind of warning or predetermined message to others, usually by smoke during the day and flames by night. Beacons are generally situated in prominent positions and are usually part of a group, chain, or line that allows the essential message to be spread over a wide area relatively quickly. Most were used to warn of the approach of hostile forces, and during periods of general unrest and the threat of war some beacons became well-established structures with temporary accommodation for those tending them. Roman, medieval, and post-medieval examples are known in northern Europe. *See also* SIGNAL STATION.

bead rim [De]. A rim in the form of a small, rounded moulding, in section at least two-thirds of a circle. It was often used on bowls, dishes, and jars.

beaker [Ar]. **1.** Generally, a ceramic or metal drinking vessel of suitable size and shape to hold in the hands. The precise type is normally specified by reference to form or fabric, thus BUTT BEAKER, ROUGH-CAST BEAKER, etc. **2.** Specifically, a kind of late Neolithic and early Bronze Age ceramic vessel characteristic of the BEAKER CULTURE. First defined by Lord ABERCROMBY in the early 20th century AD, beaker pottery, also known as drinking cups by earlier scholars, is distinctive in its range of shapes and style of decoration. Three main forms are recognized—the bell beaker, the short-necked beaker, and the long-necked beaker—each with numerous variations.

Bell beakers are often decorated with twisted cord impressions across the whole outer surface and these are known as all-over-corded beakers (AOC beakers). Where the outer surface of a beaker is covered in decoration, whether corded or using comb-impressed motifs, they are referred to as all-over-ornamented (AOO) beakers. Some beakers have a single looped handle making a mug. In some cases the impressed decoration was inlaid with a white paste which, against the traditional red fabric of beaker ware, makes the decoration look all the more impressive. Beaker pottery is found from northern Scotland to North Africa and from western Spain across to western Russia. It is particularly common in the Low Countries and northern France, and a good case has been made for its development out of local protruding foot beaker wares in the lower Rhine valley during the later 3rd millennium BC.

There has been much debate about the topological development of beaker styles and the role of regional traditions in the evolution of the forms. In general, bell beakers appear to be the earliest and the most widely distributed common form, especially AOC types. They are sometimes known as maritime beakers, reflecting something of the distribution itself and the means of transportation by which the ideas behind their manufacture spread. In the traditional chrono-topological sequence, short-necked forms follow the bell beakers, with the long-necked forms following still later. However, through studies of the British material, Humphrey Case suggested in 1993 that these rather crude stereotypes masked a series of three rather more broadly definable 'styles' which were in fact used contemporaneously in different regions. In this model each area has its own trajectory of topological development but within the overall limits of its chosen style.

Beaker Culture (Beaker Folk) [CP]. A general term for widely scattered groups of late Neolithic and early Bronze Age communities of the late 3rd and early 2nd millennia BC, whose material culture includes substantial amounts of BEAKER pottery. The distribution of these communities is wide: from the North African coast in the south to Scotland in the north; and from Spain and Portugal in the west to the Dnieper in the Ukraine in the east. The greatest concentrations of beaker-using communities is in fertile agricultural regions, especially in the lower Rhine Valley and around the North Sea coastlands where they seem to have developed from the local protruding foot beaker corded ware ceramics.

Because of the ubiquity of beaker ceramics, their distinctive forms and fabrics, and the fact that in most parts of Europe they appear to contrast markedly with existing later Neolithic styles, diffusionist explanations seemed highly appropriate. During early decades of the 20th century this expanded to embrace not only the pottery, but also the spread of metalworking in northern Europe, links to preferred burial rites (well-furnished crouched single inhumations), the extensive use of round barrows over their burial places, and biometrical data suggestive of intrusive racial groups in some areas. Together these were seen as the Beaker Folk, described in 1940 by Gordon Childe as 'warlike invaders imbued with domineering habits and an appreciation of metal weapons and ornaments which inspired them to impose sufficient political unity on their new domain for some economic unification to follow'.

Most of these connections can now be seen as erroneous, with beaker ceramics and certain aspects of the early metalworking traditions being added to rather than replacing local late Neolithic traditions. Following suggestions made in 1976 by Colin Burgess and Steven Shennan, what was once seen as a

Beaker Culture is increasingly viewed as a 'package' in which exotic elements such as pottery (and maybe whatever was drunk from it) and new styles of metalwork were acquired and adapted by indigenous communities.

bean [Ge]. The general term 'bean' relates to two genera of plants: *Phaseolus* which comprises a number of species and varieties including the haricot bean, french bean, runner bean and butter bean, all of which originate in Mexico and South America; and *Vicia* which comprises only one cultivated species, the horsebean (also known as the field bean or broad bean), which originated in the Near East before being spread all over Europe by the later first millennium BC.

Beazley, Sir John Davidson (1885–1970) [Bi]. British scholar and art historian who identified the various potters responsible for making Attic black-figure ware and red-figure ware. Educated at Balliol College, Oxford, where he read classics, he was appointed a tutor at Christchurch College in 1908. In 1925 he was made Professor of Classical Archaeology in the University of Oxford. In addition to recognizing the various forms and styles of decoration characteristic of the potters whose names appear on the vessels themselves, he identified a series of anonymous potters whom he named either by the museum in which some of their best work is represented, a former owner of an exemplar of the style, or a mannerism of the style itself. He was elected a Fellow of the British Academy in 1927, and held many offices and appointments in professional and academic bodies. He was knighted in 1949 and became a Companion of Honour in 1959.

[Bio.: *Dictionary of National Biography*, 1960–70, 84–6]

bed [De]. In geology, this term refers to the smallest formally recognized division in a sediment or rock formation within a defined stratigraphic series. In much Palaeolithic archaeology, these geological units form the contextual units for assemblages of stone tools, faunal remains, and fossil hominid remains.

Bedd Branwen Period [CP]. A phase of the British early Bronze Age spanning the period 1650–1400 BC which was defined by Colin Burgess in the late 1970s. Coming immediately after the BEAKER Tradition and the rich early WESSEX CULTURE graves of the preceding OVERTON PERIOD, Bedd Branwen times saw the almost universal adoption of cremation as the main mode of burial, the tendency to use existing round barrows as the focus for flat cremation cemeteries (although some barrows continued to be built), the emergence of DEVEREL–RIMBURY ceramics alongside existing collared urns, and the development of metallurgy through the ARRETON DOWN and ACTON PARK industrial phases.

bedding trench [Co]. A straight slot dug in the ground into which a large timber is laid so that wall posts can be recessed into it and thus held securely in place.

Bede, The Venerable [Na]. English monk and historian born c.AD 673, who spent most of his life in the monastery at Jarrow, Northumbria, teaching Latin, Greek, and Hebrew. Most of his works were biblical, but his principal composition, *The ecclesiastical history of the English*, completed in 731, is the most valuable source for the study of the 7th century, and is arguably the greatest historical writing of the early Middle Ages in Europe. Died c.AD 735.

bedrock [Ge]. Undisturbed natural substrate below any archaeological deposits, accumulative overburden such as alluvium or colluvium, or established soil profile. The bedrock is not necessarily solid rock: gravels, sands, glacial tills, and many other kinds of relatively soft materials are, in archaeological terms, bedrock.

beehive quern [Ar]. Type of ROTARY QUERN common in Roman times which had an extremely thick dome-shaped upper stone with a slightly flared base; some authorities believe such querns have a phallic symbolism.

beehive tomb [MC]. *See* THOLOS.

behavioural archaeology [Th]. An approach to the study of archaeological materials formulated by Michael Schiffer in the mid 1970s that privileged the analysis of human behaviour and individual actions, especially in terms of the making, using, and disposal of material culture. In particular this focused on observing and understanding what people actually did, while refraining from considering people's thoughts and intentions in explaining that behaviour. *See also* FORMATION PROCESSES.

Belev Culture [CP]. Early Neolithic communities forming part of the Volga-Oka Culture group in the forest zone of western Russia in the later 4th millennium BC. The Belev Culture occupied a territory to the south of the LIALOVO CULTURE around the upper Oka. It is named after the site of Belev beside the Oka, north of Orel. Characteristic of the Belev Culture are elongated ceramic vessels, similar in form to those of the Lialovo Culture, but decorated with rhomboid-shaped impressed pits. Flint implements typical of the culture include large chopping tools and massive knives. By the middle of the 3rd millennium BC the Belev Culture had spread southwards into the middle Donetz River system.

belfry [MC]. A tower or wooden structure, sometimes simply a frame, in which bells are hung so that when rung the sound can escape. Often associated with churches and religious sites, early examples are often free-standing structures away from the church building itself. In Ireland the tall round towers associated with monastic sites were probably used as belfries as well as refuges. The tradition of incorporating the bell-tower into the main church structure dates to the period after the 11th century AD.

Belgae [CP]. The name given by Caesar and other Roman authors to communities living in northern Gaul during the 2nd and 1st centuries BC. They were divided into at least 27 different branches. Caesar records that the Belgae raided maritime areas of Britain and that some eventually settled there. Certainly there are tribal names in central southern England that would support that. However, archaeologists have long searched without success for patterns in the distribution of material culture that would allow the movements of these people to be mapped. Some scholars from the time of Arthur Evans onwards have favoured identifying the Belgae with communities in Kent and the extreme southeast of England who used distinctive styles of pottery and are known as the Aylesford–Swarling Culture. The problem, however, is that nothing amongst the material culture of these areas pre-dates Caesar's visits to Britain in the mid 1st century BC. Others see the term Belgae or Belgic as having little or no meaning in the British context. The term is, however, widely and rather loosely used to refer to those tribes living in southeastern England in the 1st century BC who had close contact with the continental mainland and who, after 57 BC, traded with Roman–Gaulish communities then inside the empire.

Belgic pottery [Ar]. General term, now almost obsolete, sometimes applied to the range of late Iron Age wheel-turned pottery vessels found in southeastern England, especially Aylesford–Swarling pottery, even though this is too late to be directly related to Belgic settlement from the continent.

Belisarius [Na]. Roman general who campaigned against Persia in AD 527 and AD 540, captured Vandal Africa in AD 533–4, and began the reconquest of Ostogothic Italy in AD 535. Died AD 565.

bell [Ar]. A hollow metal dome-shaped object that when struck makes a clear musical note. Two main types can be recognized in Europe. The first, and oldest type, is made from a sheet of metal cut to a pattern and then bent into an open-ended rectangular or oval form, riveted together, with a clapper suspended in the centre. The second type, of medieval and later date, is made by casting the whole form in a single mould with a clapper being added to a cast spigot inside the bell. In China bells very rarely have internal clappers but are instead struck on the outside with a mallet.

Bell, Gertrude Margaret Lowthian (1868–1926) [Bi]. British archaeologist, diplomat, and traveller who specialized in the ancient history of the Near East. Born in County Durham, she was educated at Queen's College, Harley Street, and Lady Margaret Hall, Oxford, where she read history. She travelled widely from 1899 onwards, visiting friends in Jerusalem, learning Arabic, and in 1900 making a first expedition into the desert. In the following years she made valuable maps and plans of archaeological sites, including some of the earliest work in the An Nafud Desert. During WW1 she was attached to Military Intelligence in Cairo, bringing detailed knowledge of the region and its inhabitants. In 1917 she became Assistant Political Officer in Baghdad and was mentioned in dispatches four times. After the war she became Oriental Secretary to the High Commission

on Baghdad working to install Faisal, leader of
the Arab Revolt, as king of Iraq. During this
time she was Honorary Director of Antiquities
in Iraq, and in March 1926, shortly before her
death, she persuaded the Iraqi government to
make available one of the finest buildings in
Baghdad as a National Museum.

[Bio.: H. V. F. Winstone, 1978, *Gertrude Bell*. London:
Quartet Books]

bellarmine [Ar]. A capacious round-bellied
jug or pitcher bearing a grotesque human
mask. Originally created in the Netherlands
as a burlesque likeness of Cardinal Bellarmine, the idea spread widely and the term
later became applied to any jug bearing a
human mask.

bell barrow [MC]. A class of early Bronze Age
round barrow found in northwestern Europe
and comprising between one and four earth
and stone mounds set within a ditched enclosure. They are called bell barrows because, in
profile, the mounds resemble the campanile
form of medieval and later church bells—a
flattish top, slightly flaring sides, and a bevelled skirt around the bottom. The mounds,
which are separated from the surrounding
ditch by a BERM, cover one or more primary
burials and often have satellite and secondary
burials within the mound. The most common
type, the single bell barrow, ranges in size
from 10 m to over 60 m in diameter, most
being about 40 m across. Many of the primary
burials under bell barrows are accompanied
by rich grave goods. *Compare* BOWL BARROWS
and FANCY BARROWS.

bell beaker [Ar]. *See* BEAKER.

Belzoni, Giovanni Battista (1778–1823) [Bi].
An Italian popular entertainer and unprinci-
pled collector of Egyptian antiquities who
enriched many major European collections,
including those of the British Museum. Born
in Padua, Italy, he spent much of his early life
travelling around Europe looking for work,
appearing as a 'strong man' in theatrical performances. In Egypt he was given work developing irrigation schemes, but they were not
popular with the Pasha and Belzoni found
himself without money and employment. The
British Consul suggested that he should collect antiquities for him, and between 1817 and
1819 Belzoni systematically looted tombs
and monuments, causing many disputes with

local landowners and rival Italian and French
collectors. It is said that, in just two years,
Belzoni did as much damage to Egypt's archaeological heritage as time alone had done
over the previous 2000 years. Perhaps his best
discovery was the tomb of Seti I in the VALLEY
OF THE KINGS.

[Bio.: S. Mayes, 1961, *The Great Belzoni*. London: Putnam]

bema [Co]. The rostrum for public speaking
commonly found in a Greek agora.

benatura [Co]. A stoup or basin for holy water.

benchmark [Ge]. **1.** A surveyor's mark cut in a
wall, pillar, building, or similar position
which is used as a reference point for the calculation of altitudes and heights. In Britain
the Ordnance Survey established a series of
benchmarks in prominent positions that
were linked to its published mapping, although sadly these are no longer maintained.
Most archaeological excavations have a **temporary benchmark (TBM)** on site, either with
a notional value (e.g., zero) or an estimated
height transferred from a fixed point. **2.** A
published statement about the content, deliv-
ery, and assessment of academic subjects
taught in British universities; the Benchmark
Statement on Archaeology was published by
the Quality Assurance Agency in March 2000.

Benedictine [De]. Refers to a monastic order
of monks founded by St Benedict, the first in
western Europe. Introduced into England by
St Augustine in AD 597. Monks took vows of
poverty, obedience, and chastity and wore a
black habit. Each Benedictine monastery was
a self-sufficient community. *See* MONASTERY.

Benin [GE]. A kingdom in southern Nigeria
famous for bronze casting. Using the CIRE
PERDUE technique, metalworkers cast human
heads and relief plaques in a long series which
stylistic analyses suggest lasted perhaps from
the 15th to the 19th century AD.

Bennet, Crystal (1918–87) [Bi]. British archaeologist and historian specializing in the
ancient Near East. Born in Alderney in the
Channel Islands, she was educated at school
in Bristol and later at Bristol University where
she read English. During WW2 she worked at
the Ministry of Supply, after the war studying
at the Institute of Archaeology in London.
After excavating in Greece, she joined

Kathleen Kenyon at Jericho and Jerusalem. She became Assistant Director of the British School in Jerusalem, and Director from 1969 to 1980. Her specialism became the archaeology of Jordan, and in 1980 she was appointed Director of the newly created Institute of Archaeology in Amman, retiring in 1984.

[Obit.: *The Times*, 20 August 1987]

Bennett, Wendell Clark (1905–53) [Bi]. American archaeologist mainly working in Peru and Bolivia. He excavated a number of important sites including Tiahuanaco (Bolivia) in 1932, the Virú Valley survey (Peru) in 1946–7, and Huari (Peru) in 1950. He also made major studies of Peruvian ceramics.

[Obit.: *American Anthropologist*, 56 (1954), 269–73]

Benton, Sylvia (1887–1985) [Bi]. British archaeologist who specialized in Greek archaeology. Born in India, she was educated in England, read classics at Girton College, Oxford, and then trained as a teacher. After teaching for nearly twenty years, she turned to archaeology and studied for a B. Litt. at Oxford, which was awarded in 1928. Admitted as a student to the British School in Athens in 1927, she took part in various excavations, especially at Ithaca, both before and after WW2. She was elected a Fellow of the Society of Antiquaries in London in 1937 and published reports on her excavations in Greece and also work at Covesea, Scotland.

[Obit.: *Antiquaries Journal*, 66 (1986), 501]

Beorhtric [Na]. King of the West Saxons who was married to a daughter of Offa the Great and is believed to have been poisoned by his wife. Died AD 802.

Beowulf [Do]. Anglo-Saxon epic poem of the early 8th century AD or earlier, set among the Geats of Sweden. It is one of the longest and most complete examples of Anglo-Saxon verse, shedding much light on the nature and organization of society at the time.

Bering land bridge (Beringia) [Ge]. Land linking Alaska with Siberia in what is now the Bering Straits and Chukchi Sea but available for occupation during periods of low sea level. The land bridge was extensively available in the period 75 000 to 45 000 years ago; as a narrow periodically flooded isthmus 40 000 to 25 000 years ago; and again as a substantial landmass between 25 000 and 14 000 years ago. The land link between Asia and the Americas was finally broken about 12 000 BC, after which any contact between these regions must have been by boat. The Bering land bridge is regarded as the corridor which allowed the Americas to be colonized by people from eastern Asia, although the dating of such movements is a matter of continuing debate.

Berkeley Pattern [CP]. Coastally adapted Utian-speaking communities of the San Francisco Bay area of the American west coast between 2000 BC and AD 300. These groups lived in small villages, while exploiting the coastal marshlands for fish, shellfish, and edible plants. Burials typically include a few grave goods, although shaman graves have also been postulated.

berm [Co]. A ledge or level space between a bank, and its accompanying ditch or scarp. Also a narrow space separating an inner bank and ditch from an outer bank.

Bernal, García Ignacio (1910–92) [Bi]. Mexican archaeologist, well known for his work as Oaxacan sites such as Monte Albán and Dainzú, and for his excavations and restorations at Teotihuacán.

[Obit.: *Anthropological Newsletter*, 33.5 (1992), 4]

Bersu, Gerhard (1889–1964) [Bi]. A gifted German archaeologist with a wide-ranging interest in many aspects of Europe's ancient past. Born in Jauer, Silesia, his experience in the field began in 1907, when he assisted in excavations near Potsdam. In the following years he visited several European countries in an archaeological capacity. During WW1 he served in the Office for the Protection of Monuments and Collections on the western front and was later attached to the German Armistice and Peace delegations. In 1924 he began a long association with the Römisch-Germanischen Kommission (German Archaeological Institute) in Frankfurt-am-Main, becoming the second director in 1928 and the Director in 1931. Under his guidance the Institute took over new premises and became a centre for scholars from all over Europe to meet and discuss archaeological questions. In 1933 he was elected an Honorary Fellow of the Society of Antiquaries. In 1935 the Nazi government removed him from office and he began working overseas. He and his wife Maria moved to Britain and, at the invitation of the Prehistoric Society, he undertook a research excavation at Little Woodbury, Wiltshire, in 1938–9, introducing continental methods of excavation to the study of British prehistoric sites. During WW2 he was interned on the Isle of Man, but was allowed to continue his researches with the help of other internees, and between 1939 and 1945 he excavated a number of later prehistoric and Viking-age sites. After the war, in 1947, he was appointed to a Chair in the Royal Irish Academy in Dublin. Three years later he returned to Frankfurt to take up his former position at the German Archaeological Institute where he remained until retirement in 1956.

[Bio.: W. Krämer, 2000, *Gerhard Bersu. Ein deutscher Prähistoriker 1889–1964*. Frankfurt: Römisch-Germanische Kommission des Deutschen Archäologischen Instituts]

Bes [Di]. Egyptian god often depicted as an ugly dwarf, he was a domestic figure associated with childbirth and music. Shown sometimes with a lion's head, or in later periods in a soldier's tunic. Protector of the home, of children, and of women in childbirth. He became popular with the Phoenicians.

beta-ray backscatter [Te]. A non-destructive technique for gauging the chemical composition of the surface layers of materials such as pottery and glass. A sample is bombarded by a collimated beam of electrons from a weak radioactive beta source. The sample is arranged at 45 degrees to the beam with the backscatter particles counted using a Geiger counter. The whole system is portable and being non-destructive can be used on museum specimens in the field. The drawback is that the system is unable to identify specific elements responsible for the backscattering; it can only measure the presence of known elements of high atomic number within a matrix of low atomic number (for example, lead in glass).

betyl [Ar]. A sacred stone, often in the form of a block trimmed into a conical shape. *See also* OMPHALOS.

biconical [De]. A vessel is said to be biconical when the sides make a sharp, inward change of direction, as if two truncated cones were placed base to base.

biconical urn [Ar]. Style of early Bronze Age

pot found widely in northwestern Europe with a deep, largely plain, outwardly flared body above which is sharp carination, usually decorated and sometimes with an applied cordon, and an inwardly angled neck. The neck is usually decorated with impressed cord designs, and the rim is typically bevelled and lightly ornamented.

bier [Ar]. A movable wooden platform on which corpses are laid, sometimes together with grave goods, and eventually carried to a burial place.

biface [De]. General term referring to stone core-tool that is usually pointed at one end and flaked on both flat faces until thin and sharp-edged. Mainly found in PALAEOLITHIC tool industries, and the type-fossil of the ACHEULIAN, the tools range in size from about 10 cm to over 20 cm in length, and are believed to be multi-purpose tools for chopping, carcase dismemberment, and cutting.

bifacially worked [Ar]. An artefact that has been flaked on both sides.

bifid razor [Ar]. Type of tool current in the middle Bronze Age of Europe, having two ovate lobes of thin metal attached to a central tang. Typically 10–15 cm in length and with sharp edges to the main lobes, these tools are interpreted as razors for use in removing body hair.

billet-moulding [De]. A kind of moulding consisting of short, cylindrical pieces set in hollow mouldings at intervals about equal to their own length.

biome [Ge]. An ecological community of plants and animals established over a wide area.

biosphere [Ge]. All of the earth's living organisms interacting with the physical environment.

bioturbation [De]. Changes to the nature, form, and arrangement of archaeological deposits and sediments as a result of biological activity in the ground. This includes root action from plants and trees; animal activity at many different scales from large burrowing mammals through earthworms down to tiny insects and the mesofauna; and the effects of fungi, micro-organisms, and the degeneration of organic matter forming part of the deposit itself.

bipedalism [Ge]. The habit of walking on two feet. Apes can walk bipedally for short distances, but of the mammals only the hominids became fully adapted to bipedal walking.

bipolar technique [De]. The technique whereby a core is placed on an anvil and a flake is detached by striking it with a third implement. The flake is characterized by a double bulb of percussion, one at each of its ends or, more often on quartz flakes, by crushing at each end.

Birley, Eric (1906–95) [Bi]. British archaeologist who became the leading authority on the Roman army and Roman frontier control. Born in Lancashire, he was educated at Clifton College and Brasenose College, Oxford. While still a student he began working on excavations on Hadrian's Wall, and in 1928 joined R. G. Collingwood's survey of the Cumberland coast signalling stations. In 1930 he was appointed director of the Durham University Excavation Committee, and in 1931 became lecturer in Romano-British history and archaeology at Armstrong College in Newcastle-upon-Tyne, then part of Durham University. Throughout the 1930s he excavated at Roman sites on or around Hadrian's Wall. During WW2 he served in Military Intelligence Research, rising to the rank of lieutenant-colonel. Returning to Durham University after the war he was vice-master and then master of Hatfield College where he founded the School of Archaeology. He was appointed to the Chair of Romano-British History and Archaeology in 1956. He retired in 1971. He was elected a Fellow of the Society of Antiquaries in 1931, and a Fellow of the British Academy in 1969. His publications include *Roman Britain and the Roman army* (1953, Kendal: Titus Wilson) and *Roman frontier studies* (1969, Kendal: Titus Wilson).

[Obit.: *Daily Telegraph*, 17 November 1995]

Birnirk Cultures [CP]. Whale- and seal-hunting communities of the north Alaskan coast from Cape Nome to Point Barrow between about AD 500 and AD 1000. Contemporary with the Punuk and ancestral to the Thule. Birnirk communities took over areas previously used by Ipiutak folk.

Harpoon heads used by Birnirk Cultures show derivation from the Okvic–Old Baring Sea Traditions, while the small chipped stone tools suggest roots extending back to the Arctic Small Tool Tradition. Birnirk assemblages also contain many artefacts paralleled in the tool kits of modern Inuit.

biscuit firing [De]. The first of two firings given to glazed pottery of the post-medieval period and later. The biscuit firing creates a solid, evenly baked body to the vessel which is then glazed and fired a second time to fuse the glaze to the main fabric.

Biskupin, Znin, Poland [Si]. Early Iron Age fortified settlement in Biskupin Lake in the valley of the River Warta in central Poland. Discovered in 1933, the site has since been extensively excavated and physically restored by Jozef Kostrzewski and Zdzislaw Rajewski of Poznan University. Because the site is waterlogged, wood and other organic materials are extremely well preserved. Originally constructed on an island in the lake, an area 160 m by 200 m was enclosed by wooden stakes to act as a breakwater and then by a defensive BOX RAMPART. The entrance lay to the southwest and the way was protected by a gatetower. Inside, eleven streets were set out as CORDUROY TRACKS, more than 100 houses being ranged along these streets. All were built of horizontal logs jointed into uprights with wooden pegs. Each house had an anteroom and a main room with a hearth; a loft ran over the main part of the house, reached by a ladder. Two main phases have been recognized, beginning in the 7th or 8th century BC (Hallstatt C). In the first phase most of the timber used in construction work was oak, but in the second phase pine was more common.

[Sum.: W. Niewiarowski *et al.* 1992, Biskupin fortified settlement and its environment in the light of new environmental and archaeological studies. In B. Coles (ed.), *The wetland revolution in prehistory*. Exeter: WARP. 81–92]

bison (buffalo) [Sp]. Wild hump-backed shaggy-haired ox found in North America (*Bison bison*) and Europe (*Bison bonasus*). Bison are distinguished by their low horns, rounded forehead, and greater height of the forequarters compared with the hindquarters. They have a large hump on their shoulders and a thick mane covering the back of their heads, neck, and shoulders. Bison roamed the Great

Plains of North America and the North European Plain in large herds from Pleistocene times onwards, and were widely hunted by communities who lived almost exclusively from their flesh. In Europe bison were hunted to extinction before Neolithic times and now survive only in parts of Lithuania and the Caucasus. In North America bison were on the verge of extinction by the end of the 19th century AD, although protective legislation since 1910 has allowed their numbers to increase again.

bison jump [MC]. A steep cliff or other natural feature used to kill stampeding BUFFALO in North America. One of the best-known examples is HEAD-SMASHED-IN, Alberta, USA, which was used for over 7000 years.

bit [Ar]. A strong bar forming the mouthpiece on a bridle used to control a horse. The earliest domesticated horses were probably controlled by a simple halter. Organic bits with antler cheek pieces first appear in central Europe around 1700 BC, to be replaced later by bronze single-piece examples. The two- and three-piece bit was introduced during Iron Age times, some examples providing an outlet for craftsmanship of the highest order.

Bituitus [Na]. The son of Luernius and king of the Arverni, one of the principal tribes of Gaul in the 2nd century BC. He was defeated in 121 BC by the Roman forces. The Arvernian kings were apparently noted for their lavish feasts and displays of wealth.

bivallate [De]. An earthwork with two banks, each with a ditch.

bivalve mould [Ar]. In metalworking, a simple form of mould comprising two halves held in place by dowels whilst the molten metal is poured in. The mould is parted to release the cast object once the metal has cooled.

black and red ware [Ar]. Type of pottery found in many parts of India which is black on the inside and around the rim and red on the exterior surface. Generally dated to the Chalcolithic through to the Iron Age.

black-burnished ware [Ar]. A standard range of culinary vessel-forms manufactured in two different fabrics and widely imitated. BB1 (black-burnished ware Category 1), was black,

gritty, hand-made, mainly in Dorset, and widely distributed from c.AD 120 to the late 4th century AD. BB2 (black-burnished ware Category 2) was greyer and finer, with a silvery finish, wheel-thrown in the Thames Estuary area, and widely exported from c.AD 140 to the mid 3rd century AD.

Black Death [Ge]. A particularly severe outbreak of plague which crossed Europe between AD 1346 and 1350, probably a combination of bubonic and pneumonic plagues. Believed to have been carried by rats and fleas. It was brought to Britain from Europe in AD 1348. There were several major outbreaks from the mid 14th century through to the 17th century AD.

black-figure pottery [Ar]. *See* ATTIC BLACK-FIGURE WARE.

Black Rock period [CP]. Hunter-gatherer communities of the early Desert Archaic in the eastern and northern Great Basin of North America 4000 BC to AD 500. These communities appear to have been highly mobile, living in small family groups, and exploiting mountain sheep, deer, and rabbits, as well as available plant foods in this fairly arid region.

Blackwater Draw, Arizona, USA [Si]. A series of settlement sites along a shallow valley in the Llano Estacado with evidence of occupation from earliest Palaeo-Indian through to Archaic times. Finds include abundant Clovis and Folson points, and also well-made blades. The stone used to make these implements came from over 300 km away, and must therefore have been obtained through exchange or actually travelling out to the source.

[Rep.: F. Wendorf and J. Hester (eds.), 1975, *Late Pleistocene environments on the southern high plains*. New Mexico: Fort Bungwin Research Centre]

blade [De]. A long narrow stone flake. A blade must be at least twice as long as broad. Blades become much favoured in the Upper Palaeolithic, but are found in some earlier phases. Some blades are struck with soft punches. Blades are useful because of their long, sharp cutting edges.

blade core [Ar]. A flint or stone CORE from which BLADES have been struck. Such cores are typically conical or pyramidal in shape; to produce regular even blades a certain degree of preparation is needed as well as periodic rejuvenation. Both these activities produce their own distinctive DEBITAGE.

bladelet [Ar]. A small blade of the type used in the Upper Palaeolithic of Europe.

blade tool [Ar]. A tool made from a single thin narrow flake detached from a core. The controlled flaking technique is characteristic of the Upper Palaeolithic but it is also known from earlier cultures.

blank [Ar]. *See* CORE.

blanket bog [Ge]. Extensive layers of peat and wetland vegetation that spread out across mainly upland landscapes, covering them like a blanket. Most blanket bog is OMBROGENOUS BOG, formed because of high rainfall on soils with poor drainage. It is likely that the drainage problem was, in many cases, caused by human over-exploitation of the area through woodland clearance and land-use practices that caused an iron-pan to develop at the base of the soil profile. In upland areas of the British Isles, especially in Ireland, blanket bog begins to form in later Neolithic times, earlier in localized areas, with very extensive tracts developing in the later Bronze Age. Archaeologically, blanket bog is important as a record of local environment and also because it preserves areas of landscape that were abandoned by their inhabitants.

blanket peat [Ge]. *See* BLANKET BOG.

Blattspitzen industry [CP]. Early Upper Palaeolithic flint-working industries of central and eastern Europe characterized by oval bifacially worked implements, pointed at both ends.

Bleda [Na]. Brother of Attila and co-ruler of the Huns of the Danube area. Attila had Bleda murdered and assumed sole power in c.AD 445.

Blegen, Carl William (1887–1971) [Bi]. American archaeologist specializing in Greek prehistory. Born in Minneapolis, he was educated at Augsburg Seminary, the University of Minnesota, and Yale where he took his Ph.D. After working in Athens for some years, he became the Director of the American School of Classical Studies. During WW2 he served with the Office of Strategic Services in Washington and later became cultural relations attaché with the American embassy in Greece. In addition to his excavations at Korakou, Prosymna, and Pylos in Greece, he worked extensively at Troy, Turkey, as part of the Archaeological Expedition of the University of Cincinnati.

[Obit.: *Antiquaries Journal*, 52 (1972), 459]

blockhouse [MC]. **1.** Type of early Iron Age structure found in Shetland, rectangular in ground plan, three storeys high, heavily built, with a central passage at ground floor level, domestic accommodation to either side of the passage and on the first floor, and with a wall-walk and vantage point on the top floor. At the rear of the stone building was a small timber extension with a range of further accommodation. **2.** A small strongly built defensive structure used specifically to house guns and to protect the gunners and ammunition from attack. Usually built of stone, blockhouses were typically sited to command a river, harbour entrance, or anchorage, or as an outlying work to provide enfilading fire or protection to other defensive works. Accommodation within the blockhouse is confined to the short-term needs of the gunners or garrison. The basic design involves a tower dominating a bastion or gun platform, usually with a ditch or moat on its most vulnerable side. Built mainly between the late 13th and mid 16th centuries. Also known as gun towers.

bloomery [MC]. A furnace for smelting iron. Although bellows were used to force air into the furnace, it was not possible to make the iron hot enough to melt. Before it can be used, the spongy lump of iron removed from the furnace, called a **bloom**, has to be hammered at red heat in order to expel impurities and add a proportion of carbon.

Bluefish Caves, Yukon, Canada [Si]. Three small caves in the Old Crow Basin of the northern Yukon, possibly the earliest evidence of occupation in North America so far recovered. Discovered in 1975, and subsequently investigated by Jacques Cinq-Mars, the earliest layers at Bluefish Cave I yielded a few flint chips indicative of human activity in association with broken animal bones from Ice Age mammals such as the horse, bison, and caribou. The deposits are thought to date to between 15 000 and 12 000 BC.

[Rep.: J. Cinq-Mars, 1978, Bluefish Cave I: A late
Pleistocene eastern Beringian cave deposit in the northern Yukon. *Canadian Journal of Archaeology*, 3, 1–32]

bluestone [Ma]. *See* SPOTTED DOLERITE.

Boas, Franz (1858–1942) [Bi]. American anthropologist who worked at the American
Museum of Natural History and later at
Columbia University. He advocated detailed
regional studies based on empirical research
rather than a preoccupation with grand
evolutionary schemes. This school of
anthropology became known as 'historical
particularism'.

[Bio.: *American National Biography*, 3, 83–6]

Boat-axe Culture [CP]. A subgroup within the
Nordic SINGLE GRAVE CULTURE characterized
by the use of a slender type of stone BATTLE-AXE
shaped like an up-turned boat.

boat burial [MC]. *See* SHIP BURIAL.

Bodrogkeresztúr Culture [CP]. Local
Hungarian culture of the middle Copper Age
(early 3rd millennium BC) that succeeded
the Tiszapolgar Culture. There is marked
continuity between the two cultures in their
settlements and cemeteries. Cattle played
an important role in the domestic economy.
Copper tools of the period include shaft-hole
axe-adzes, chisels, and awls. Plain wares predominate in funerary deposits in contrast to
domestic sites, which yield pottery decorated
in 'stab-and-drag' (*Furchenstich*) technique,
with chequerboard and hatched patterns
filled with white paste. Succeeded by the
BADEN CULTURE.

Bodvoc [Na]. King of the DOBUNNI tribe in the
west of England in the early 1st century BC,
known from inscriptions on coins minted at
Bagendon, Gloucestershire.

Boethius, Anicius Manlius Severinus [Na].
Roman politician born *c.*AD 480. He became
senator and consul during the time of
Theodoric the Great but was suspected of
treason and imprisoned. During his time in
prison he wrote his well-known work: *On the
consolation of philosophy*. Executed in AD 524.

bog [Ge]. A general term often used rather
indiscriminately to describe permanent wetland in which communities of plants grow on

generally rather acid waterlogged ground.
See BLANKET BOG, TOPOGENOUS BOG, and
OMBRODGENOUS BOG. *Compare* FEN.

bog body [Ar]. A human corpse preserved in
waterlogged conditions such that skin and
hair often survive but most internal organs
and bones decay. Clothing also sometimes
survives in such circumstances. The best-
known example is TOLLUND MAN from
Denmark, but he is only one of many hundreds of bodies recovered in recent centuries
from wetlands all over northwestern Europe.

Boghaz Köy, Turkey [Si]. Capital of the HIT-
TITE empire set in a loop of the Halys River in
central Turkey. Excavations by Hugo Winkler
in 1906–12, Kirk Bittel during the 1930s, and
subsequent campaigns by German teams
show that the site was occupied since the
Copper Age, becoming the main city of the
Hittites, known then as Hattusas, about 1500
BC. At this time the city covered 180 ha and
comprised two main elements. At Büyükkale
was a walled inner town of 80 ha, the citadel.
Here were large administrative buildings, one
of which contained over 10 000 inscribed
clay tablets, an audience hall, and temples.
Upslope and to the south was a walled outer
city of about 100 ha. Three of the gates here
were decorated in reliefs showing warriors,
lions, and sphinxes. Four temples are known
inside, each set around a porticoed courtyard,
together with secular buildings and residential structures. Outside the walls are cemeteries, most of which contain cremation
burials, and the rock sanctuary of Yazilikaya.
After the collapse of the Hittite empire
around 1200 BC the site was abandoned until
the mid 1st millennium BC.

[Sum.: P. Neve, 1996, Housing in Hattuša the capital of
the Hitite Kingdom. In Y. Sey, *Housing and settlement
in Anatolia. A historical perspective*. Istambul: History
Foundation Publications. 99–115]

bog oak [Ar]. A fallen trunk tree, sometime
killed by waterlogging, but subsequently preserved in peat which formed around it and
enveloped it. The death of the trees and the
development of the bog are often connected.

Boian Culture [CP]. Neolithic culture of the
period 4100–3700 BC in northeast Bulgaria
and the lower Danube Valley of southeast
Romania, which forms part of a group of
related cultures including the MARITSA and

VADASTRA CULTURES which are regarded as contemporary with Level V at KARANOVO. Settlements of this period are bigger than those of the preceding Dudeşi and Vadastra I Cultures, some approaching small tells. Copper artefacts appear for the first time in late phases and there is evidence of trade networks through the Black Sea represented by imports of spondylus shell and Prut Valley flint. The pottery is decorated with geometric designs filled with white paste.

bolling [De]. The permanent base of a pollarded tree.

Bølling [CP]. **1.** Bølling Interstadial: a warm phase during the final stages of the last glaciation of mainland Europe (the Weichsel Glaciation), starting at about 10500 BC. **2.** Bølling Phase: a biostratigraphic subdivision of the FLANDRIAN STAGE in which conditions were warmer than in the preceding OLDEST DRYAS. Godwin's POLLEN ZONE Ib corresponds with the Bølling Phase in Britain, marked by the development of park tundra. The Bølling Phase spans the period from c.10500 BC down to c.10000 BC in northern Europe.

Bonampak, Chiapas, Mexico [Si]. A Maya ceremonial centre situated close to the Lacanha River dating to c.AD 450–800. The site is well known for its colourful frescos and murals which adorn the walls of palaces and temples. Dated to AD 792, these paintings depict a victory won by the ruler of this ceremonial centre. In one of the scenes he stands with his warriors on top of a stepped platform while stripped and bleeding captives sit on the steps below.

[Rep.: K. J. Ruppert, J. E. S. Thompson, and T. Proskouriakoff, 1955, *Bonampak, Chiapas, Mexico*. Washington: Carnegie Institution]

bonding-course [De]. A band of brickwork (or occasionally stone slabs) which alternates with wider sections of regular stonework. It normally runs through the entire thickness of the wall, presumably to give cohesion and stability to the mortared rubble core. A bonding course is also useful to level up courses during construction.

Boniface [Na]. Missionary born in Devon, England c.AD 680. Educated at Exeter and Winchester. In 716 he went to Frisia to convert the heathen. He was created bishop in AD 723

and archbishop in AD 732. He organized and reformed the new churches and the Frankish establishment. In AD 746 he was head of the eastern churches. He was killed by pagans at Dokkum, Friesland, in AD 755 and later made a saint.

boomerang [Ar]. A curved throwing stick, one form of which can be made to return to the thrower in flight. Several kinds of boomerang are traditionally used by Australian Aborigines for hunting and fighting. Archaeological examples from widely scattered findspots including Egypt, Holland, and Poland suggest the autonomous invention of this weapon.

bora ground (bora ring) [MC]. A kind of ceremonial site comprising a pair of earth-banked rings linked by a pathway. Found in New South Wales, Queensland, and Victoria in Australia.

Borax Lake Phase [CP]. Hunter-gatherer communities of the Archaic in the North Coast Ranges of California and the western USA dating to 5000 BC to AD 500. Their assemblages are dominated by chipped stone points, burins, MANOS, and METATES.

Bordes, François (1919–81) [Bi]. French prehistorian specializing in the Middle and Upper Palaeolithic periods. He became Professor of Archaeology in Bordeaux University where he established the Institut du Quaternaire. He excavated many sites, including the Palaeolithic deposits at Combe-General and Pech de l'Azé. He was an expert flint knapper and replicated early tools. He is probably best known for his classification of the Mousterian industries of southwest France in what became known as the *système Bordes*. He interpreted the variations between topological groups as reflecting chronological changes through time. He was famously challenged over this by Lewis Binford in the late 1960s who interpreted the data as reflecting functionally differentiated assemblages.

[Obit.: *Antiquity*, 55, 168–9]

Boreal Phase [Ge]. A biostratigraphic subdivision of the FLANDRIAN in which conditions were warmer and drier than in the preceding SUB-BOREAL. Godwin's POLLEN ZONES V and VI correspond with the Boreal in Britain, marked by the expansion of pine/birch forests and increasing amounts of mixed woodland; tree cover was continuous at lower altitudes. The Boreal generally spans the period from *c*.7700 BC down to *c*.5500 BC in northern Europe.

borough [De]. Settlement which obtained certain privileges relating to trade and the holding of markets, landholdings, and self-government, by means of a charter granted by the crown or a lord.

borrow pit [Co]. A small scoop or quarry-pit from which clay, earth, or mud is taken, usually for building purposes.

bosing [Te]. A low-tech technique for locating buried ditches and pits at sites with a solid underlying natural bedrock (e.g., chalk or limestone) and relatively thin stratigraphy. The procedure is to place a block of wood on the ground surface and then hit it hard with a sledge-hammer. A dull thud will be heard where there are disturbances in the bedrock while a sharper ring is emitted where undisturbed bedrock lies below the topsoil. By systematically working across a site and mapping the sounds, the distribution and extent of bedrock cut features can be worked out.

Bos primogenous [Sp]. *See* AUROCHS.

Botta, Paul-Émile (1802–70) [Bi]. French diplomat and antiquarian best known for his work in Iraq. While posted as French Consul to Mosul between 1840 and 1843 he excavated a number of sites, including Khorsabed which he believed to be the ancient city of NINEVEH. In 1843 he uncovered, for the first time, structures relating to the ASSYRIAN empire. He and others were struck by the magnificence of the art and decoration lavished on the buildings, especially the great winged bulls. With the recovery of loot his primary objective, Botta uncovered much of great importance in a short time. Many of the sculptures from Khorsabed are now in the Louvre in Paris.

[Bio.: F. H. McGovern and J. N. McGovern, 1986, Portrait of Paul Emile Botta. *Biblical Archaeologist*, 49.2]

Boucher de Crèvecoeur de Perthes, Jacques (1788–1868) [Bi]. A French customs officer and amateur antiquary whose discovery in the gravels of the Somme of chipped flints in association with the remains of extinct fauna led him to argue for the great antiquity of man. It took a considerable time for his theories to gain support, but they were slowly accepted by the French and British scientific communities. Boucher first set out his findings in his five-volume *De la création: essai sur l'origine et la progression des êtres* (1838–41) and later in his three-volume work *Antiquités celtiques et antediluviennes* (1847).

[Bio.: C. Cohen, 1989, *Boucher de Perthes: 1788–1868. Les origines Romantiques de la préhistoire.* Paris: Berlin]

Boudicca (Boadicea) [Na]. Female leader of the ICENI tribe of eastern England after the death of the client-king Prasutagus who had attempted to bequeath his kingdom jointly to his daughters and the Roman state. Roman officials ignored this claim and abused his queen, Boudicca, and her daughters. As a result, Boudicca led revolts against the Romans in AD 60–61 which included assaults on the settlements at Colchester (Camulodunum), St Albans (Verulamium), and London (Londinium). The Iceni forces were eventually defeated at the hands of the governor of Britannia, Suetonius Paulinus, and Boudicca reputedly poisoned herself.

bouleuterion [Co]. The council chamber of an ancient Greek city.

boustrophedon [De]. An archaic method of writing, found on some inscriptions, for instance in Gortyna in Crete, where the code of laws is written not in lines from left to right, but as an ox turns with the plough at the end of the furrow, so that having gone from left to right, it returns from right to left.

bout coupé [Ar]. A term used to describe well-made sub-triangular bifacially worked core tools of the Mousterian industry.

bow [Ar]. An offensive weapon used in hunting and war since early times. The earliest actual examples preserved in peat bogs date to the Mesolithic, but the presence of small projectile heads on sites extending back into the Middle Palaeolithic suggests that the bow is a much more ancient technology. There are essentially three kinds of bow: first, **simple bows** comprising a basic flexible wooden core with the draw-string fixed at either end and a hand-grip in the centre; second, **reinforced bows** where the wooden core is strengthened by sinew and bark; third, the **composite bow** made from various combinations of wood, bone, horn, and sinew. The composite bow is generally more compact and its development in the southern Russian steppe in the early 3rd millennium is generally associated with archers needing to fire arrows from horseback.

bowl [Ar]. A neckless metal, wooden, or ceramic vessel, which can be defined as having a height more than one-third of, but not greater than, its diameter.

bowl barrow [MC]. Simple kind of ROUND BARROW found widely over northwestern Europe from the Neolithic onwards, although especially common in the late 3rd and early 2nd millennia BC. Bowl barrows are distinguished by having a roughly hemispherical mound of turf, earth, and deposited bedrock over a centrally placed primary burial, either in a pit or in some kind of stone or wooden cist. SATELLITE and SECONDARY BURIALS are common within the mound. Bowl barrows are typically between 3 m and 40 m in diameter and anything up to 6 m high. Some are edged with stone kerbs, and a few examples had concentric rings of posts within the barrow mound as a constructional device. Many have surrounding ditches that provided a quarry for the mound-building material. Excavation often reveals that these monuments were constructed and enlarged over a considerable period of time. Certainly they were conspicuous features of the landscape for millennia, and in some cases remain so.

box flue tile [Ar]. *See* BOX TILE.

Boxgrove, West Sussex, UK [Si]. An ACHEULIAN site revealed in gravel pits east of Chichester near the south coast of England. Excavation by Mark Roberts between 1983 and 1996 revealed a buried chalk cliff, in front of which was a flat plain extending down to the coast perhaps a kilometre or so away. On the old beach surface, which dates to about 500 000 years ago, were flint-knapping areas and the remains of animal kills. In 1994 a tibia bone of the hominid species *Homo erectus* was found in the gravel quarry. Scientific studies of the specimen suggest it was a male who stood 1.8 m high and weighed about 80 kg.

[Rep.: M. B. Roberts and S. A. Parfitt, 1999, *Boxgrove: a middle Pleistocene hominid site at Eartham Quarry, Boxgrove, West Sussex*. London: English Heritage]

box rampart [De]. Style of rampart construction common amongst the late Bronze Age and early Iron Age hillforts of central and northern Europe. Two parallel lines of well-spaced paired upright timbers were joined together top and bottom, and linked longitudinally to create a wooden framework or series of boxes. These were then filled with rubble and soil to give strength and mass. The front face was vertical and either completely clad in timber or, where materials allowed, faced with dry-stone walling between the timber uprights. The rear face was sometimes ramped with soil, but mainly left vertical too. The top is never preserved archaeologically, but it is assumed that the front face was higher than the rear to create a breastwork and walkway along the top of the defences.

box tile [Ar]. A baked clay tile shaped like a rectangular box, open at both ends; often used for flues and occasionally for voussoirs.

Boyne Culture [CP]. Obsolete term formerly used to describe the later Neolithic communities of the Boyne Valley in the east of Ireland north of Dublin. *See* NEWGRANGE and KNOWTH.

bp/BP [Ab]. Before Present. A term widely used by QUATERNARY geologists and archaeologists with reference to radiocarbon ages and results from other radiometric dating techniques. The present is conventionally taken to be the calendar year AD 1950. Use of the lower-case form or the abbreviation RCYBP (Radiocarbon Years Before Present) is generally taken to mean the raw ages as calculated by the determining laboratory. These are not calendar years. Use of the upper-case form or the abbreviation CalBP (Calibrated Before Present) shows that the original determination has been calibrated to reflect calendar years. However, there is considerable variety in the way these abbreviations are used and anyone using dates cited in publications should check the rubric to see exactly how they are expressed.

bracer [Ar]. Rectangular or slightly oval plate of stone, usually up to 150 mm long, with perforations at either end for attachment to a strap. It is surmised that bracers were intended to protect an archer's inside wrist from the slap of the bowstring when an arrow is shot. They are characteristic of the BEAKER CULTURE throughout Europe and date to the later 3rd and early 2nd millennia BC. Also known as an 'archer's wrist guard'.

brachycephalic [De]. Descriptive term applied to human skulls where the cephalic index (greatest breadth expressed as a percentage of maximum length) is above 80 per cent. Individuals with such skulls may be said to be broad-headed. *Compare* DOLICHOCEPHALIC.

brandwirtschaft [De]. *See* SLASH AND BURN AGRICULTURE.

brass [Ma]. A yellow-coloured binary alloy of copper (typically 70–90 per cent) and zinc (typically 10–30 per cent). Brass is not common until post-medieval times, although it appears from Roman times onwards in small amounts.

breastwork [Co]. A low timber or stone wall projecting above the top of a rampart on the outside, sometimes an upward extension of the outer face, to provide a measure of protection and concealment for anyone standing on the rampart or moving along it.

breccia [Ge]. Conglomerate of rock and detritus consolidated by carbonate of lime into a hard bed. Often encountered in cave systems sealing earlier deposits.

Breton arrowhead [Ar]. A type of well-made BARBED AND TANGED ARROWHEAD, highly symmetrical in form, with graceful slightly concave or convex sides and flared barbs. The tang is the same length as the barbs. Characteristic of the early Bronze Age in northern France and southern Britain.

Breton dagger [Ar]. *See* ARMORICO-BRITISH DAGGER.

Breuil, Abbé Henri (1877–1961) [Bi]. French Catholic priest and antiquarian who specialized in the Upper Palaeolithic of northern Europe. Ordained as a priest in 1900, he never took up parish duties, as he was allowed to spend his time doing archaeology. A fine draughtsman, he devoted great energy to recording cave paintings and rock art. He worked out a sequence of four distinctive art styles and related these to ideas of sympathetic magic whereby the paintings represented an attempt to ensure success during hunting. He visited many European countries, including England, Romania, Spain, Portugal, and Italy. He worked in North Africa, visited China twice, studied rock art in Ethiopia, and spent the period 1942–5 in South Africa collecting flint tools and studying rock art.

[Bio.: A. H. Brodwick, 1963, *The Abbé Breuil, prehistorian. A biography*. London: Hutchinson]

brick [Ar]. A kind of building material consisting of a block of dried or baked clay, often with some kind of tempering agent such as stone, sand, or straw. There are many different shapes, sizes, and styles of bricks, and most are culturally or chronologically distinctive.

brick-relief [De]. A technique of sculpture in which subjects are left in bas-relief on a brick-built surface or wall.

brickworks [MC]. An establishment where bricks are manufactured in some quantity. Such a factory usually includes clay-pits, clay-preparation and cleaning floors, mounding sheds, drying racks, kilns, and storage yards for maintaining a stock of finished products. The kilns are generally more substantial than in a pottery, but products other than bricks may be made as well (for example, ceramic ROOF FURNITURE).

Brigantes [CP]. Large late Iron Age tribe living in the northeast of England in the later 1st millennium BC and continuing into the first few centuries AD as a Roman *civitas*. Their main OPPIDUM seems to have been at STANWICK, North Yorkshire. In the mid 1st century AD the leader of the Brigantes was Venutius. He was anti-Roman, although his wife Cartimandua was pro-Roman. In AD 69 Vespasian tried to establish Roman rule in northern England and the Brigantes rose in open revolt. Cartimandua sought safety outside her kingdom. An energetic governor, Petillius Cerialis, campaigned vigorously against Venutius between AD 71 and 74, and completed the conquest of the area soon afterwards.

briquetage [Ma]. Thick-walled very coarse ceramic material used for the manufacture of evaporation vessels in saltmaking from the mid 2nd millennium BC through to medieval times in northern Europe. The forms and fabrics of briquetage vessels are fairly distinctive and allow trade patterns and distribution networks to be established, especially for Iron Age times. Also known as **very coarse pottery (VCP)**. *See also* SALTERNS.

bristlecone pine calibration [Ge]. *See* CALIBRATION.

British Academy [Or]. Established by royal charter in 1902, the Academy is an independent learned society, the United Kingdom's national academy for the humanities and the social sciences. It aims to represent the interests of scholarship nationally and internationally, give recognition to excellence, promote and support advanced learning, further international collaboration and exchanges, promote public understanding of research, and publish the results of research. The Academy is a self-governing body of Fellows elected in recognition of their distinction as scholars in some branch of the humanities or social sciences. Fellows may use the distinction FBA. Archaeology is one of the eighteen discipline-based sections in which the Academy is organized. In addition to support for research through grants to archaeological fieldwork projects and other kinds of investigation, the Academy also supports the British schools and institutes overseas (e.g., the British School in Athens, the British School in Rome).

British Council [Or]. The United Kingdom's international organization for education and cultural relations. Established in 1934, its purpose is to promote and enhance the UK's reputation in the world as a valued partner. This is achieved by creating opportunities in education, English language teaching, the arts, science, governance, and information through a network of over 200 offices in more than 110 countries.

broach-spire [De]. A spire rising from the tower without any parapet.

broad rig [MC]. *See* RIG AND FURROW.

Broadward Complex [CP]. A localized metal-working tradition within the EWART PARK PHASE of the British late Bronze Age. Found mainly in the Welsh Marches, the Thames Valley, and parts of central southern England, it is exemplified by hoards of weapons such as that found in July 1867 at Broadward, Shropshire, which contained more than 70 items. Large barbed spearheads are particularly distinctive, as well as short tongue chapes, tubular ferrules, tanged chisels, and palstaves.

broch [MC]. A kind of dry-stone-built circular tower up to 30 m in diameter and 15 m high found widely across the Western Isles and adjacent areas of the Scottish mainland. The walls were hollow, doubled-skinned, up to 3 m wide, with chambers inside. In some cases the central court was roofed over, in others there were lean-to structures against the wall faces of the tower. They date to the late 1st millennium BC and early 1st millennium AD and appear to have been the fortified and imposing residences of local lords and chiefs. Some brochs are surrounded by clusters of small houses and yards rather in the form of a small dependent village. The best-preserved broch is the Broch of Mousa on Shetland.

Broken K Pueblo, Arizona, USA [Si]. A large single-storey masonry pueblo east of Snowflake, investigated in the late 1960s by James N. Hill using approaches and methods exemplary of the New Archaeology of the time.

The pueblo has 95 rooms, dating mainly to the 13th century AD. Three types of room were distinguished on the basis of plan, location, and content. The largest rooms had fire-pits and corn grinders and were probably the main domestic areas. Smaller rooms without fire-pits were for storage. The third kind of room was rather rare and sunk below ground level. They contained benches and wall niches and were interpreted as ceremonial places.

Pottery from the site suggested that two social or residential groups lived at the site.

[Rep.: J. N. Hill, 1970, *Broken K Pueblo: Prehistoric social organization in the American southwest*. Tucson: University of Arizona]

bronze [Ma]. An alloy of copper (typically about 90 per cent) and tin (typically about 10 per cent). It has many advantages over pure copper, notably a lower melting point, better casting properties, and a greater hardness when cold. The big disadvantage was that tin is relatively scarce compared to copper and thus long-distance trading links were necessary in order to secure supplies. The earliest use of bronze in Europe was probably in the lower Danube or Carpathian region during the second half of the 3rd millennium BC, influenced by metalworking traditions still further to the east in the Caucasus.

Bronze Age [CP]. One of the primary subdivisions of prehistoric time, established by the THREE AGE SYSTEM as the period succeeding the Neolithic which saw the introduction of BRONZE for tools and weapons. The Bronze Age has different start dates and different durations in different parts of the Old World.

brooch [Ar]. A piece of decorative metalwork attached to a garment by a pin either as a fastening or as an ornament. In pre-Roman contexts such brooches were mainly FIBULAE, but from the 1st century BC onwards far more elaborate and imaginative types appear. *See* SAUCER BROOCH, RADIATE BROOCH, EQUAL-ARMED BROOCH, CRUCIFORM BROOCH, CROSS BOW BROOCH.

Browne, Sir Thomas (1605–82) [Bi]. Physician and author, renowned for an encyclopedic knowledge of contemporary scientific and antiquarian theory. Knighted in AD 1671, as the leading citizen of Norwich. His *Hydriotaphia* (1658), a discussion of past burial customs, includes the first published description of Anglo-Saxon cremation urns.

[Bio.: J. Bennett, 1962, *Sir Thomas Browne: a man of achievement in literature*. Cambridge: CUP]

bucchero [Ar]. A type of fine grey-coloured ETRUSCAN pottery with a dark grey shiny surface produced between the 8th and 4th centuries BC.

Buchis [Di]. Egyptian god, the sacred bull of Montu, worshipped at Hermonthis, Armant.

bucket [Ar]. From later Bronze Age times through to the early medieval period, metal buckets of various kinds were important accoutrements and probably status objects throughout Europe. The earliest examples are of situla shape, made of sheet bronze, and date to the 8th century BC, imitating vessels found in the Mediterranean world still earlier. The association of buckets and also sheet-metal cauldrons with flesh-hooks suggests that they had a central role in feasting ceremonies where the chief would apportion particular cuts of meat from the communal cooking vessel according to rank, status, or privilege. Wooden buckets with elaborate or-

namental metal fittings are known through Iron Age times and outside the Roman world in northern Europe through the early 1st millennium AD. They reappear again very visibly over much of northwest Europe in the mid 1st millennium AD when examples are deposited in PAGAN SAXON graves.

bucket urn [Ar]. Type of large middle Bronze Age pot found within the overall repertoire of the DEVEREL–RIMBURY ceramic tradition of southern Britain in the period 1500 BC through to 1200 BC. Usually over 60 cm high, bucket urns are shaped like modern buckets with straight slightly sloping sides, wider at the top than the bottom. They are fairly plain with occasional applied cordons decorated with finger-tip impressions. Found on domestic sites where they were presumably used as storage vessels and as containers for cremations they are often found as SECONDARY BURIALS in earlier ROUND BARROWS.

Buckland, William (1784–1856) [Bi]. Early 19th-century antiquary who was a leading exponent of the Catastrophist school of thought which denied the antiquity of man and upheld the biblical account of the Flood. Buckland perpetuated this view despite having excavated the so-called 'Red Lady' in a cave at Paviland on the Gower Peninsula of South Wales in 1823. A Fellow of Corpus Christi College, Oxford, he became Professor of Mineralogy and first reader in geology at Oxford in 1813. Subsequently he became Canon of Christ Church and in 1845 Dean of Westminster.

[Bio.: E. O. Gordon, 1894, *The life and correspondence of William Buckland*. London: John Murray]

budares [Ar]. Large ceramic griddles used to toast manioc flour in Central and South America.

Bug Culture (Bug–Dniester Culture) [CP]. Widespread communities living in the valleys of the Rivers Bug and Dniester in the Ukraine who adopted the use of pottery around 5500 BC within a hunter-gatherer economy. Settlements appear to be short-lived camps beside rivers and lakes. The subsistence base revolved around red deer, wild pigs and cattle, roe deer, birds, shellfish, and fish, with some evidence for plant gathering. Some imported pottery of LBK and CRIŜS type suggests contacts with the agricultural communities to the west, but there is no evidence for agriculture amongst Bug Culture groups.

Bükk Culture [CP]. A regional variant of the LINEARBANDKERAMIC CULTURE centred on the Bükk Mountains of northeastern Hungary. Bükk pottery is very finely made with multiple parallel lines in spiral and curvilinear patterns. Sherds of the ware have been found as far afield as southern Poland. A large number of caves in the heartland of the Bükk Mountains were used at this time, suggesting perhaps a seasonal focus to transhumance and the exploitation of stone from the mountains for making axes.

bulb of percussion [De]. The cone-like shape of the fracture surface of a stone flake which indicates the place where the hammer struck.

Bulgars [CP]. Originally Asiatic nomads who inhabited the shores of the Black Sea at the end of the 5th century AD but after AD 679 they crossed the Danube and founded a state in the old province of Moesia.

bulla (pl. bullae) [Ar]. A hollow clay ball which contained tokens representing goods despatched or exchanged and was thus part of a system of accounts in early Mesopotamia.

bureaucracy [De]. A type of organization marked by a clear hierarchy of authority, the existence of written rules of procedure, and staffed by full-time, salaried officials. Often held to be one of the characteristics of an early state or civilization.

burgage [De]. Property which usually included a house and yard in an ancient borough. Often with a narrow street frontage and a long narrow strip of land behind. Held for a fixed money rent by a burgess who had special privileges and duties.

Burgundians [CP]. Germanic people of the middle Rhine who were settled near Geneva in the early decades of the 5th century AD where they established a kingdom in the Rhone Valley. The expansion of the Franks in the 6th century AD led to the annexation of Burgundy, but the Burgundians enjoyed periods of comparative autonomy. After the break-up of the Frankish empire in the 9th century AD Burgundy formed an independent kingdom until AD 1032.

burgus [MC]. A small fortified position or watch-tower usually controlling a main routeway.

burh (borough) [MC]. A fortified enclosure. Saxon burhs of the 9th century AD onwards in southern Britain were towns or boroughs defended by a substantial earthwork. Most were constructed by King ALFRED and his successors as protection against the Danes.

burial site [Ge]. A place where human communities deliberately interred their dead, either as inhumations or cremations. Such sites may or may not be elaborated with markers or other kinds of monumental construction. Many different kinds of burial rites have been identified from archaeological evidence, but four forms of inhumation are especially recurrent through many periods over wide areas: **extended burial** where the corpse is stretched out, arms to the sides; **flexed burial** where the corpse is lying slightly to one side with knees slightly bent; **crouched burial** where the corpse is lying on its side with the legs brought up underneath, knees bent, as if asleep; and **contracted burial** where the corpse is lying on its side with the legs and arms against the chest coiled up into the foetal position. *See also* PRONE BURIAL and SUPINE BURIAL.

burial urn [De]. A ceramic vessel in which the cremated ashes of one or more individuals are placed. *See* COLLARED URN, BUCKET URN, GLOBULAR URN.

buried soil [De]. An ancient soil profile that has become sealed beneath younger material or some kind of structure so that there is marked vertical separation between the older soil profile and the more recent ground surface. Buried soils represent important sources of data for understanding the former environment and land use in an area. Where a significant area of buried soil survives, for example under a later barrow or rampart, there is abundant scope for investigating horizontal variations in land use and the study of ancient landscapes.

burin [Ar]. A pointed tool of flint or stone with a transverse (chisel) edge made by the removal of one or more flakes. Used for working bone, antler, and ivory, and perhaps for engraving. Common in Upper Palaeolithic and Mesolithic stone industries.

Burkitt, Miles Crawford (1890–1971) [Bi]. British prehistorian whose speciality was the Palaeolithic period throughout the Old World and who spent a lifetime teaching others and instilling students with enthusiasm for study and archaeology. Educated at Eton and Trinity College, Cambridge, he was a lecturer in the faculty of Archaeology and Anthropology at Cambridge University from 1926 until his retirement in 1958. During this time he published many books and papers, notably *Our early ancestors* (1926, Cambridge: CUP) and *The Old Stone Age* (1933, Cambridge: CUP). He travelled extensively in Spain, Russia, Africa, and Turkey and played an important role in opening up the study of the Stone Age in Africa. He studied the French and Spanish caves under the direction of Abbé Breuil, he was at various times President of the Prehistoric Society and Section H of the British Association, and he was elected a Fellow of the Society of Antiquaries in 1923.

[Obit.: *Antiquaries Journal*, 52 (1972), 443–4]

burnish [De]. The action of rubbing the outer walls of a partially dried, unfired pot with an instrument such as a pebble or a bone. This gives the surface of the pot a smooth, faintly lustrous appearance (i.e., burnished).

burnt mound [MC]. A substantial mound representing the accumulation of burnt or fire-crazed stones, ash, and charcoal, usually situated beside a river or lake. Within or adjacent to the mound there are usually hearths and some kind of trough or basin capable of holding water. They are found in many parts of the British Isles, being especially numerous in Ireland, and date mainly to the 2nd and 1st millennia BC. There is much debate about their function, some authorities maintaining that they are cooking sites, while others prefer to see them as sweat-houses or perhaps even retreats for ritual observance and taking hallucinogens.

Bush Barrow, Amesbury, Wiltshire, UK [Si]. A large early Bronze Age round barrow about 1 km southwest of Stonehenge on Salisbury Plain in southern England. The mound has a bush growing out of it, hence its name, and has done since at least the 18th century AD. The barrow was excavated by William Cunnington in 1808 and was found to contain the remains of a single inhumation, probably an adult male. Accompanying the burial was a rich collection of grave goods including: a gold belt fastener, a gold lozenge-shaped breastplate, a small gold lozenge, a stone macehead with bone handle mounts, two bronze daggers (one with its hilt decorated with gold pins), and a flanged axe. The burial is widely interpreted as that of a powerful local chief, and has been taken to exemplify the early phase of the WESSEX CULTURE.

[Sum.: P. Ashbee, 1960, *The Bronze Age round barrow in Britain*. London: Phoenix, 76–8]

but and ben [MC]. A two-roomed cottage, strictly speaking one with an outer and an inner room.

Buto [Di]. Egyptian god. *See* WADJET.

Butovo Culture [CP]. Mesolithic hunter-gatherer communities occupying the upper Volga catchment of the forest zone of western Russia from about 8000 BC down to 5000 BC, named after the type-site beside the Volga, northwest of Moscow. Most of the settlements of the Butovo Culture were beside rivers and lakes, and the rich material culture includes bone harpoon points, flint knives, tanged points, and scrapers. Hunting and fishing provided the subsistence base. The Butovo Culture is ancestral to the VOLGA-OKA CULTURES of the forest region.

butt beaker [Ar]. A tall beaker shaped like a butt or barrel and having a small, everted rim. The body is usually decorated with cordons, rouletting, latticing, etc. Mid 1st century BC through to 1st century AD in date. Some were made in Gallo-Belgica, others were locally made in Britain.

butts [MC]. Area used for archery practice.

B ware [Ar]. A range of ceramic amphorae originating at a range of source areas in the east Mediterranean. They date from the 1st to the early 7th century AD, although in Britain they date mainly to the later part of their currency. Divided into four subgroups, Bi–Biv. Bi are characteristic of sub-Roman sites in western Britain. *See* AMPHORA.

Bylany, Czech Republic [Si]. A substantial village of the early LINEARBANKKERAMIC in central Bohemia about 50 km east of Prague. Excavated by Bohumil Soudský in the late 1950s, the settlement is a very typical example of an LBK village. The distribution of features covered more than 6.5 ha, but twenty phases of occupation were recognized. The excavator suggested that at any one time there was one large longhouse (possibly a clubhouse) around which was a cluster of perhaps five or six normal dwellings. Wheat and barley were cultivated, and cattle were the main domesticated animal species present.

[Rep.: B. Soudský, 1962, The Neolithic site of Bylany. *Antiquity*, 36, 190–200]

byre [Co]. Building used to shelter cattle. Sometimes byres were separate buildings within a farmstead or agricultural settlement, in other cases the byre was integral with the farmhouse or dwelling. Examples of the latter from recent times include the longhouses of Ireland, Wales, and many other areas of maritime Europe.

Byzantine empire (Byzantium) [CP]. The Byzantine empire started with the first Christian emperor of the eastern Roman empire, Constantine, in AD 330. At that time Byzantium was inaugurated as the new capital of the eastern empire and renamed Constantinople. In AD 392 the emperor Theodosius proclaimed Christianity to be the official religion of the Roman empire and on his death in AD 395 the empire was split between his two sons, never to be reunited. The eastern empire was ruled from Constantinople and developed as the Byzantine empire. The greatest Byzantine emperor was probably Justinian the Great who ruled from AD 527 to 565. He introduced a new legal system and expanded the boundaries of the empire as far west as Spain, Italy, and Africa. He encouraged the arts, a unique blend of late Roman and Greek influences, and commissioned the building of the great basilica of Haghia Sophia in Constantinople.

Following the death of the Prophet Mohammed in AD 632, Arab armies took Egypt, Syria, and Palestine from the Byzantines, and Constantinople was itself besieged from AD 674 to 678. It survived, but the empire was further reduced at this time by the loss of North Africa and Italy. It was brought to the brink of civil war by the Iconoclastic Crisis before enjoying another brief golden age under Basil II (AD 976–1025). But the empire's troubles increased as invaders made further incursions into Byzantine territory. In the 11th century the Seljuk Turks took large parts of Asia Minor and overran Anatolia, menacing Christian pilgrims on their way to Jerusalem. Reluctantly the emperor, Alexius I, sought help from the Christian west and the First Crusade was organized to help the Byzantines recapture the Holy Land from Muslim forces. The result was victory for the Crusaders, but they were not so lucky in the Second and Third Crusades. The Fourth Crusade, launched in 1202, was partly inspired by the Vatican's jealousy of Byzantium's trading power. It soon became an excuse to plunder Constantinople itself, the Crusaders ruling the city from 1204 through to 1261. The rise of the Ottoman empire during the 14th century finally put an end to the Byzantines, the fall of Constantinople itself being in April 1453.

cacao [Sp]. Seed pod from an evergreen tree (*Theobroma cacao*) native to the tropical lowlands of South and Central America from which chocolate is made. Cacao attained importance as a luxury commodity among Maya, Teotihuacán, and Aztec nobility.

cache [De]. A collection of items similar to a hoard, but more likely to have been intended for recovery. *See also* HOARD.

Cadbury, Somerset, UK [Si]. *See* SOUTH CADBURY, SOMERSET, UK.

Cadw [Or]. Government agency responsible for archaeology and related matters in Wales. Established in 1984 and based in Cardiff, its overall duties and functions are similar to those of ENGLISH HERITAGE.

Caenozoic Era [CP]. The latest era of the earth's geological history from about 2 million years ago back to about 65 million years ago which includes the TERTIARY and QUATERNARY PERIODS. Preceded by the Mesozoic.

Caereni [CP]. The late Iron Age tribe living in the far northwest of Scotland at the time of the Roman conquest, but completely unaffected by it. The traditional settlement pattern of BROCHS and DUNS spanned the later 1st millennium BC through to the mid 1st millennium AD.

Caesar, Julius [Na]. Roman general and statesman born *c*.100 BC who came to prominence as a member of the First Triumvirate in 60 BC along with Pompey and Crassus. From 58 BC to 51 BC he was engaged in military campaigns in Gaul, Germany, and Britain. In 49 BC he refused to disband his army and instead crossed the Rubicon and marched on Rome, thereby signalling the outbreak of civil war. Between 49 BC and 44 BC he progressively consolidated his power with campaigns in Egypt, Asia Minor, North Africa, and Spain. He was murdered on the Ides of March 44 BC. His commentaries on the Gallic Wars represent one of the principal literary sources relevant to the later prehistory of Celtic Europe.

Caesarea Maritima, Israel [Si]. An important coastal settlement situated on the Mediterranean coast between Tel Aviv and Haifa. As a result of extensive campaigns of investigation by Italian and Israeli archaeologists it is known that the predecessor of Caesarea was an anchorage equipped for coastal traffic by the Phoenicians when they captured the Sharon strip of the Palestine coast in the 3rd century BC. It was then called Strato's Tower. Herod the Great enlarged the city and rebuilt its harbour in a campaign of works starting in 22 BC, naming it Caesarea in honour of his patron Caesar Augustus when he inaugurated the town in 10 BC. An inscription that refers to Pontius Pilate is one of the best-known finds of this period. After Herod's death it became the Roman provincial capital of Judaea and was used as the headquarters for Vespasian's campaigns against Jewish revolts between AD 66 and AD 70. Over the next two centuries the town flourished and was a centre for both Christianity and Jewish thought and scholarship. The town was also important in the 12th and 13th centuries AD when it was used by Crusaders. Frequently changing hands between sides, it was redefended at this time.

[Sum.: R. L. Vann (ed.), 1992, *Caesarea papers: Straton's Tower, Herod's Harbour, and Roman and Byzantine Caesarea*. Ann Arbor MI: Journal of Roman Archaeology Supplementary Series 5]

Cahokia, Illinois, USA [Si]. An extensive Mississippian settlement and ceremonial centre of the period AD 700–1600 situated in an alluvium covered valley. Covering over 16 square kilometres, the site had an estimated population of about 38 000 souls at it height in the 11th and 12th centuries AD. However, the most striking feature of the site is the group of 45 or so mounds surviving out of an estimated original set of about 120. These mounds are of three types: platform, burial, and ridged. The largest is Monk's Mound, a platform mound built c.AD 900–1200: 316 m by 241 m, it rises in four terraces to a height of 33 m. On the top is a large building interpreted as a ceremonial centre and home for the ruler of the area. All around Cahokia there are numerous smaller settlements representing hamlets and farmsteads.

[Sum.: D. Young and M. Fowler, 2000, *Cahokia. The great native American metropolis*. Columbia: University of Illinois Press]

Cahuachi, Peru [Si]. One of the largest and most complicated settlements of the Nasca Culture which flourished in a desert area beside the Nasca River in southern Peru in the Early Intermediate Period, c.AD 1–700. The site comprises a series of about 40 artificially modified hills, and walled enclosures. Although the site is often considered an urban centre, excavations here by Helaine Silverman in 1987 revealed very little evidence of permanent occupation. Instead, the site may be seen as a pilgrimage centre. The mounds, constructed with thick mud-brick walls to contain construction material supported temples, shrines, and ceremonial structures.

[Sum.: H. Silverman, 1993, *Cahuachi in the ancient Nasca world*. Iowa City: University of Iowa Press]

Caiambé Phase [CP]. Cultural grouping found in the Lower and Middle Amazon and named after the type-site of Caiambé, Brazil, tentatively dated to the period c.AD 700–800. Characterized by pottery assigned to the Incised Rim Horizon of ceramic styles in the Amazon Basin.

Caimito Complex [CP]. Cultural groupings found in the Rio Ucayali area of Amazonia in the period c.AD 1200–1500, characterized by its varied ceramic assemblages which belong to the Polychrome Horizon in the Amazon Basin. Vessels include square-shaped open dishes, anthropomorphic urns, and pots with a square-shaped cross-section. The wares are well made and usually decorated with painted designs. Ethnohistorical records suggest that the Rio Ucayali region was colonized

by Cocama and Omagua tribes from the middle Amazon, the result of which is probably the Caimito Complex. The polychrome ceramic traditions continued until recent times among the Shipibo and Cashibo groups.

caique [Ar]. Traditionally, small wooden trading vessel, brightly painted and rigged for sail. Found around Greece and in the Aegean.

cairn [De]. A general term used to describe a deliberately constructed pile of stones or stone rubble, often forming a burial mound or BARROW, but sometimes the result of clearing fields in preparation for cultivation.

cairnfield [MC]. A group of clearance CAIRNS.

calabash [Ar]. A gourd used as a storage or drinking vessel.

calcareous [De]. Relating to the chemical compound calcium carbonate ($CaCO_3$), of which chalk and limestone are largely composed. Also refers to soils with a high calcium carbonate content which, in chemical terms, are usually alkaline.

calcite-gritted ware [De]. Pottery whose fabric embodies crushed calcite (either shell or mineral grit) as a tempering agent, used especially for kitchen wares such as storage jars, cooking pots, and bowls.

caldarium [Co]. Latin term for the hot room (moist heat) in a Roman bath-house. It usually contains or is adjacent to a hot plunge bath which produces a hot humid atmosphere.

Caledones [CP]. The late Iron Age tribe living in western Scotland (Strathclyde) at the time of the Roman conquest. Some of Agricola's campaigns of the late 1st century AD came up against and defeated the Caledones led by Calgacus. Despite this setback, the province continued to develop largely untouched by the Roman world.

calendar [De]. A formal system for measuring and documenting the passage of time. The basic unit of nearly all known calendars is the cyclical movement of the sun, giving the units known in the modern western world as days, and—rather less easy to gauge—the annual cycle or solar year. In ancient Egypt, for civil purposes, a solar calendar of 365 days to the year was used in which there were 12 months of 30 days and 5 intercalary days. For agricultural purposes, and for determining the timing of religious festivals, a second calendar was used, based on observations of the dog star Sirius (Sothis to the Egyptians). The annual heliacal rising (i.e. at the same time as the sun) usually preceded the Nile flood. The two calendars would coincide every 1460 years, a period known as the Sothic Cycle. The cycle of the moon provides a lunar month and this was used as the basis for the calendar in ancient Mesopotamia, where 12 months of 29.5 days were adjusted over 19 cycles to keep the calendar in step with solar years. How these basic units were divided, combined, and reconciled is culturally specific, and many different systems have been developed. All, however, fall into one of two main types.

Linear calendars start from a nominated moment and extend outwards from that time in an endless sequence of more or less equal-sized repetitive units. The western Christian calendar takes as its origin a notional point considered to be the Incarnation of Christ and extends linearly forwards (years AD from AD 1) and backwards (years BC from 1 BC). The reckoning system was established by Julius Caesar who adapted the Egyptian solar calendar to Roman usage, inserting extra days in the shorter months to make 365 days over 12 months with the insertion of an additional day into February every four years. The naming of the years was first established in Italy in the 6th century AD and based on the Julian calendar; it was later revised by Pope Gregory XIII in AD 1582 to provide the calendar used today, which is known as the Gregorian calendar (adopted by Act of Parliament in Britain in AD 1752). Other linear calendars were established in classical times and more recently, and include: a Roman calendar with a notional start date fixed as the founding of Rome in years AUC (*ab urbe condita*) which can be mapped onto the Gregorian calendar as starting in 753 BC; a Greek calendar with a notional start date fixed as the first Olympiad which maps onto the Gregorian calendar as 776 BC; and an Islamic calendar based on the flight of Mohammad from Mecca to Medina (the Hegira). Hegira year 1 (AH 1) maps onto the Gregorian calendar as AD 622 but Hegira years are lunar years with a mean length of 354.3 days.

Cyclical calendars use a floating starting position which is periodically returned to.

One of the most common is with reference to the reign of a king, queen, or other official so that dates are given as the regnal year of that person. When the person is replaced the calendar starts again for the next person. Ancient Chinese societies used a cyclical calendar of 60 years, designated by two ideographs in a series which covers the whole 60-year period before starting again. The Mayan calendar was based on a 52-year cycle (known as the calendar round) which combined a 260-day almanac and a 365-day year. The use of this system carried with it a belief that events, including disasters, repeated themselves with each turn of the cycle. *See also* TIME, LONG COUNT.

calibration (calibrated radiocarbon age/ calibrated date) [De]. When using RADIOCARBON DATES relating to archaeological materials from the last 10 000 years or so it is necessary to standardize or calibrate the laboratory determination (CONVENTIONAL RADIOCARBON AGE) to convert it into calendar years. This is especially important if radiocarbon determinations are to be compared with historically derived calendar dates, or dates determined by other means.

Laboratory determinations are given in radiocarbon years before present (RCYBP or BP), but radiocarbon years are not of equal length because of variations in the level of ^{14}C in the atmosphere in the past. Special corrections for the effects of certain factors that alter the background level of ^{14}C may also be necessary. Calibration is based on measurements of the ^{14}C levels in material of known age, principally samples of ancient wood taken from DENDROCHRONOLOGICALLY dated sequences. The earliest calibration curves, published in the mid 1970s, used samples from the bristlecone pine (*Pinus aristat*), an especially long-lived tree species that grows in the Sierra Nevada of California. During the 1980s and 1990s regional calibration curves were developed for different parts of the world based on local dendrochronological sequences. A number of excellent computer-based calibration programmes are available, including OxCal from the Radiocarbon Accelerator Unit in Oxford University, UK, and CALIB from the University of Washington in Seattle, USA. Both can be downloaded from the world wide web.

Calibrated radiocarbon ages are conventionally indicated by the abbreviations BC/AD or cal.BC/cal.AD. However, because the calibration process involves using the standard deviations provided by the laboratory for the original determination, the calibration of a specific determination will result in an age range, the width of which will depend on the size of the standard deviation, the level of certainty used (typically 66 per cent or 95 per cent based on one and two standard deviations respectively), and the nature of the calibration curve in the region covered by the initial determination. Thus, calibrated radiocarbon dates are usually given as a range, for example 2030–2125 BC, which if calibrated using a single place of standard deviation would mean that there was a 66 per cent probability that the actual date lies within that range. When citing dates it is standard practice to give the calibrated age, the original determination, and the laboratory code (e.g. 2472–2404 BC (3925 ± 35 RCYBP) OxA-5328). Within a book or academic paper all dates should be calibrated using the same procedures and the same calibration curve, and the parameters used should be summarized in the preface or some other convenient place. *See also* RADIOCARBON DATING, CONVENTIONAL RADIOCARBON AGE, and CORRECTED AGE.

Calico Mountains, California, USA [Si]. Possible Lower Palaeolithic site comprising lithic debris including flakes and blades from alluvial fan deposits on a former lake. Uranium-thorium dates suggest that the deposits formed *c.*200 000 years ago. If correct, and if the lithic debris is of human manufacture, then this would be the earliest evidence of settlement in the New World.

[Sum.: L. W. Patterson *et al.*, 1987, Analysis of lithic flakes at the Calico site, California. *Journal of Field Archaeology*, 14, 91–106]

Caliphs [De]. The successors of Mohammed as rulers and religious leaders of the Islamic world, the most powerful being those of the Umayyad and Abbasid dynasties.

Callanish, Lewis, UK (Calanais) [Si]. A series of stone alignments and a stone circle on the southern part of the Isle of Lewis in the Outer Hebrides of western Scotland. This complicated site was partly covered in up to 1.5 m of peat until the late 19th century AD. Investigations by Gerald and Margaret Ponting and excavations by Patrick Ashmore in 1980 and 1981 have revealed a great deal

about the history of the site. Perhaps most surprising is that prior to the construction of the stone monuments the area had been farmed. In the early 3rd millennium BC a STONE CIRCLE comprising thirteen pillars of local gneiss was built with a single large pillar in the centre. The circle is approached from the north by a stone AVENUE, while single STONE ROWS lead away to the west, south, and east. Some time after the circle and the alignments were built a small PASSAGE GRAVE was constructed between the pillars of the circle and the central standing stone on the east side. It has been suggested that Callanish incorporated a series of lunar alignments looking down the stone avenue through the circle onto the southern horizon when, every 18.6 years, the moon dances low over the hills to the south, sets, and then gleams brightly throwing the stones of the stone circle into silhouette as it passes a notch in the horizon.

[Sum.: P. Ashmore, 1995, *Calanais. The standing stones.* Stornoway: Urras nan Tursachan]

cambium [Ma]. A viscid substance under the bark of trees in which the annual growth of wood and bark takes place.

Camden, William (1551–1623) [Bi]. British antiquary, historian, and traveller. Born in London the son of a painter, he attended St Paul's School and then proceeded to Oxford where he was a student at Broadgate Hall (later Pembroke College). About 1575 he became a master at Westminster School and remained there for the rest of his life. He was appointed headmaster in 1593. During his time at Oxford he made frequent excursions into the countryside to inspect antiquities of various sorts, encouraged by patrons such as Sir Philip Sydney and Fulke Greville. As a result he began making notes of his observations and discoveries, eventually becoming more familiar with the antiquities of the country than anyone else alive. This material was gathered together in his principal work, the *Britannia*, the first edition of which was published in 1586. It includes important early accounts of such major monuments as Stonehenge and Hadrian's Wall. His intension, expressed in the volume, was 'to restore antiquity to Britain'.

The *Britannia* was revised and enlarged several times during Camden's lifetime, and after his death it continued to be modernized by a series of editors and translators, the most famous of which are Gibson (1695) and Gough (1789). County maps by Christopher Saton and John Norden accompanied the editions from 1607 onwards. Camden published a range of other works too and developed a notable reputation as a historian. He was encouraged in his work by King James I who gave access to state papers. In 1622 he founded a Chair in Civil History at Oxford University. Camden was a respected herald, being Clarenceux King-of-Arms from 1597 until his death. He is buried in Westminster Abbey.

[Bio.: S. Piggott, 1976, William Camden and the Britannia. In S. Piggott, *Ruins in a landscape*. Edinburgh: Edinburgh University Press]

Camelot, UK. [Si]. *See* SOUTH CADBURY, SOMERSET, UK.

cameo [Ar]. A Roman glass object made of two or more layers of different coloured glass bonded together, into the top of which is cut a design. Normally, a lighter coloured glass is used for the upper layer, so that when cut by the engraver the darker under-layer shows through. The technique was used in the manufacture of substantial objects such as vases and decorative plaques, although the commonly found applications are small insets for finger-rings or jewellery.

camerae [MC]. A subsidiary farm of a preceptory of the Knights Templar or Knights Hospitallers, generally specializing in arable agriculture, pastoral farming, dairying, or fish-keeping. In architectural terms the camerae refers explicitly to the offices of the obedientiaries of the site. In addition to a chapel, a camerae would typically include a great hall and service buildings enclosed by a boundary wall, around which would be appurtenances such as fishponds, windmills, field systems, stock enclosures, and grazing land.

Camerton–Snowshill dagger [Ar]. A type of early Bronze Age dagger, named after finds from two later WESSEX CULTURE burials: Camerton in Somerset and Snowshill in Gloucestershire. Typically, Camerton–Snowshill daggers have an ogival shaped blade, midrib, and two or three large rivet holes for the attachment of the hilt.

camp [MC]. Loosely used term which refers to almost any kind of enclosure bounded by a

bank and ditch. The term was favoured by antiquaries of the 18th and 19th centuries AD.

Campanian ware [Ar]. A type of pottery produced from the 4th century through to the 1st century BC at three main centres in southern Italy: two near Capua and one at Cumae. After the 1st century BC its popularity was eclipsed by ARRETINE WARE. Campanian ware was traded widely in the central Mediterranean and is sometimes found in Gaul from the 3rd century BC; very occasional finds have been reported from Silchester, Hampshire, and Ower, Dorset, in southern England.

campanulate bowl [De]. A bowl or other kind of vessel, whether of pottery, metal, or some other material, shaped to the form of an inverted bell.

Camulodunum, Colchester, Essex, UK [Si]. *See* COLCHESTER.

Canaanites [CP]. Bronze Age communities occupying Palestine and the Levant during the 2nd millennium BC, related to the HYKSOS. Their economy was largely based around acting as 'middlemen' for trade between Egypt to the south and Mesopotamia and the Hittites to the north and east. Their main settlements include Ugarit on the Syrian coast. Relatively little is known about them except what can be found in biblical texts and from very limited excavations. They were, however, responsible for developing the first alphabetic writing system. It is clear that while their supreme god was El, the most prominent was Ba'al. The Canaanites suffered a series of setbacks in the late 2nd millennium BC with attacks from the SEA PEOPLES in the north while in the south they were displaced by the Israelites and the Philistines. Those living in the north were known to the Greeks as the Phoenicians, although they called themselves Canaanites through into the early 1st millennium BC.

canabae [De]. A Latin term for self-governing communities or settlements of non-Roman citizens within the Roman empire. Often, but not always, based on pre-Roman tribal boundaries, sometimes established on military land near a fortress or fort. *See also* CIVITAS.

canal [MC]. An artificial watercourse or extensively modified natural channel used for inland water transport and/or the control and diversion of water for drainage or irrigation. Most canals have a fairly even width and a roughly uniform depth. They tend to run along the contour of the land or have a very slight fall to them in order to promote the flow of water. From the 18th century AD, locks were used to allow canals to rise up slopes. Some canals were built to link inland waterways with the sea, or occasionally to join seaways.

Candlemas [Ge]. A traditional calendar festival in northern Europe celebrated in recent times on 2 February, the Christian feast of the purification of the Virgin Mary.

cannibalism [De]. The practice of eating human flesh, normally either out of dire need or for ceremonial purposes. The latter is more common, and usually related to a belief that eating parts of deceased relatives or enemies slain in battle allows their power to be passed on to the celebrants. The practice is not easy to prove from the archaeological record, although cutmarks on bone that relate to de-fleshing a corpse, the splitting of long bones, and the systematic opening of the skull to extract the brain are usually taken as strong indicators.

canopic jar [Ar]. A stone or pottery container used in ancient Egyptian burial practices from Old Kingdom times onwards for holding the entrails of an embalmed body. Four separate jars were usually provided to hold the liver, lungs, stomach, and intestines. From New Kingdom times onwards each jar was covered by a lid carved with a head representing one of the four sons of Horus, each also having a protecting goddess: the falconheaded Qebhsnuf (the intestines) watched over by Selket; the human-headed Imsety (the liver) watched over by Isis; the jackal-headed Duamutef (the stomach) watched over by Neith; and the baboon-headed Hapi (the lungs) watched over by Nephthys.

Cantii [CP]. The late Iron Age tribe living in southeastern England (Kent and East Sussex) at the time of Caesar's visits to Britain in 55 BC and 54 BC. They were the first tribe in Britain to issue their own coinage to serve as small change. Caesar's accounts tell of four kings amongst the Cantii, suggesting that they comprised a number of separate kingdoms united by tribal affinities. Their main centre appears to have been near to modern Canterbury, with an earlier centre at nearby Bigbury. After a brief period under the influence of the Atrebates in the early 1st century BC they came within Trinovantian/Catuvellaunian control under Cunobelin prior to the Roman conquest in AD 43.

cantonal capital [De]. *See* CIVITAS.

Cape Denbigh, Alaska, USA [Si]. Archaic Stage hunter-gatherer sites on the shore of Norton Sound, excavated by J. L. Giddings over several seasons starting in 1948. The most complete sequence was found at Iyatayet, a campsite occupied by caribou hunters, where three main horizons were recognized: the Denbigh Flint Complex was the earliest (*c*.3000–2500 BC), followed by the Norton (*c*.100 BC to AD 200), and this in turn was followed by the Nukleet or western Thule (12th to 18th centuries AD). The Denbigh Flint Complex assemblage recovered was important because it not only included burins and microblades, but also showed that these items were associated with stone harpoon heads, spearheads, and knives.

[Sum.: J. L. Giddings, 1964, *The archaeology of Cape Denbigh*. Providence RI: Brown University Press]

capital [Co]. The top element of a column above the drums or monolithic shaft. Comprises two elements, the moulded part or *echinus* and the flat slab above known as the *abacus*. In the classical world there were three Greek Orders applied to the design of capitals: Doric, Ionic, and Corinthian.

capitol [Ge]. The principal hill in Rome, site of the temple of Jupiter Optimus Maximus, that served as a citadel and religious centre.

Capsian Culture [CP]. Mesolithic communities occupying the Mediterranean coast of North Africa, named after the site of Gafsa, Tunisia. Capsian Culture replaced the Oranian in the region after about 8000 BC. Occupation sites are well represented as shell middens and ash heaps. The main tool types include blades, burins, scrapers, backed blades, microliths, and microburins. From around 5000 BC pottery and domesticated animals appear in Capsian contexts, sometimes referred to as the **Capsian Neolithic**. The culture lasted down to the 2nd millennium BC.

capstone [Co]. A more or less horizontal slab or block of stone forming the top of a burial CIST or the roof of a chambered tomb.

Caracalla [Na]. Roman emperor, AD 211–17.

Caratacus [Na]. British tribal leader, one of the sons of King Cunobelin, who was ruling at the time of the Roman conquest. Being a fierce opponent of Roman rule, he was forced out of his homeland in the southeast of England, after which he fled to become leader of the resistance. At first he was based in the territory of the Silures and then among the Ordovices in North Wales. He was defeated there in AD 51, but escaped and sought refuge in the court of Queen Cartimandua of the Brigantes. Being pro-Roman, she surrendered him to the Romans, but after making an impressive speech in Rome, he was, according to the writer TACITUS, pardoned.

Carausius [Na]. A naval commander from Menapia, who seized power in Britain and parts of northern France in AD 286, following successful campaigns against barbarian pirates in the English Channel and North Sea. After successfully resisting the legitimate emperor in the west, Carausius was murdered by Allectus in AD 293, following the loss of Boulogne to Constantius Chlorus.

caravanserai [MC]. A staging-post on a camel caravan route where rest and refreshment were available. Also known as a khan.

carbon 14 dating [Te]. *See* RADIOCARBON DATING and CALIBRATION.

carbonization [De]. The burning or scorching of organic materials, particularly plant remains such as seeds or grains, in conditions of insufficient oxygen for full combustion. This results in their long-term preservation in a fairly stable state. Charcoal is the most widely known example of carbonized material.

carcares [Co]. A Latin term for the chambers in an amphitheatre in which beasts or gladiators were kept before a contest.

Cardial Culture (Cardium Culture) [CP]. *See* IMPRESSED WARE CULTURE.

cardial ware (cardium ware) [Ar]. The earliest pottery of the western Mediterranean and parts of Atlantic Europe, named after its characteristic cockle shell (*Cardium*) decoration. Also known as impressed ware, this pottery is generally well made and includes other decorative motifs as well as lines made with the edge of shells. Where dated, this ware falls within the period *c*.5000–3500 BC. *See also* IMPRESSED WARE CULTURE.

cardinal directions [De]. The four principal directions outwards from any defined spot: north, south, east, and west.

cardo maximus [Co]. Latin term for the principal street in a fort or town, theoretically running north to south and at right angles to the *decumanus maximus*.

Carib [CP]. Occupants of the Lesser Antilles at the time of Columbus. Originating in northern Amazonia, the Carib displaced the former occupants of the islands, the Arawak, presumably by force. The Carib had an agricultural subsistence economy and were skilled potters. Their spiritual beliefs focused on warfare and the ritual consumption of human flesh. The word 'cannibal' is derived from the word 'carib'.

caribou [Sp]. North American reindeer (*Rangifer tarandus*) grouped into two subspecies, the barren ground caribou and woodland caribou. The former is only found in Arctic parts of North America and has long, slightly curved antlers. The woodland caribou roams the forest districts of Canada and has shorter, branched antlers. The caribou has never been domesticated, although it has been hunted continuously since Palaeo-Indian times and many communities subsisted almost exclusively from it.

carinated [De]. A term often applied to a specific type of metal or ceramic bowl or jar with a flat or reeded rim and an almost vertical upper wall above a sharp inward change of direction (the carination). Carinated bowls are distinctive of the early Neolithic in northwest Europe.

Carlingford Culture [CP]. Obsolete term originally developed by J. X. W. P. CORCORAN in the early 1960s for a series of middle Neolithic communities living in Northern Ireland, characterized especially by their use of horned cairns (COURT CAIRNS).

Carmelites [Ge]. A monastic order of friars established in the 13th century and known as the White Friars. Their houses were mainly, but not exclusively, in towns.

Carnac alignments, Morbihan, Brittany, France [Si]. A major group of Neolithic ceremonial and ritual monuments north of Carnac on the Gulf of Morbihan in southern Brittany. Four main groups of alignments run in a roughly southwest to northeast direction between the Quiberon peninsula to the west and the River Crac'h to the east. Each set of rows has between six and thirteen broadly parallel lines of upright stones and range in length from about 300 m at Kerlescan up to about 1 km at Ménec. The southwestern end of each group typically culminates in an oval or rectangular enclosure demarcated by stone pillars or a chambered tomb of some kind. The rows date mainly to the later Neolithic, the 3rd millennium BC, as shown by the fact that the Kermario alignments run over the top of a LONG BARROW. All four main groups of alignments lie in an area rich in other Neolithic sites, including numerous STANDING STONES and PASSAGE GRAVES. Further multiple stone alignments are known around Erdevaen about 8 km to the northeast of Carnac.

[Sum.: A. Burl, 1993, *From Carnac to Callannish*. London and New Haven: Yale University Press]

Carnonacae [CP]. The late Iron Age tribe living in the far northwest of Scotland (Ross and Cromarty) at the time of the Roman conquest, but completely unaffected by it. Sandwiched between the CAERENI to the north and the Creones to the south, the Carnonacae had a traditional settlement pattern of BROCHS and DUNS during the later 1st millennium BC through to the mid 1st millennium AD.

carnyx [Ar]. A bronze war-trumpet constructed with an animal head (usually a boar with the tongue forming a clapper) atop a long straight tube, at the base of which is a curved mouthpiece. Held upright in battle, its purpose was probably to produce noise and panic. In use by the 2nd century BC; some rather fine examples are illustrated on the GUNDESTRUP cauldron.

Carolingian empire [CP]. In archaeological and architectural usage this term relates to the period from about AD 750 through to AD 900, although the term itself stems from the reign of Charles the Great (Charlemagne) between AD 771 and AD 814 immediately following the period of the FRANKISH empire. The Carolingian empire witnessed a cultural renaissance. The enormous wealth gained through decades of successful campaigning was partly used for massive ecclesiastical patronage, especially the building of new churches, the founding of monasteries, and the production of manuscripts. There were also ecclesiastical reforms, the revival of Latin learning, and a return to classical values in the arts.

Carp's Tongue Complex [De]. A tradition of metalworking characteristic of southeast England during the EWART PARK PHASE of the British late Bronze Age (800–700 BC). Colin Burgess has argued that during this time metalworking underwent something of an industrial revolution with the widespread introduction of lead bronze and an increase in the repertoire of objects made. This may in part be due to influences and connections with continental Europe. Objects regarded as part of the Carp's Tongue Complex include the eponymous CARP'S TONGUE SWORD, bag-shaped chapes, triangular perforated knives, hog's back knives, socketed axes, end-winged axes, gouges, spearheads, and bugle-shaped objects of unknown purpose.

carp's tongue sword [Ar]. A type of bronze sword current in many parts of western Europe during the 8th century BC, probably originating in northwest France. Characterized by a broad slashing blade drawn down to an elongated narrower tip in order to combine the qualities needed for a slashing sword with a weapon for thrusting or stabbing in close combat.

carr [De]. A type of wetland with peaty soils, generally found in low-lying situations, with a distinctive woody vegetation cover consisting of trees and shrubs such as hazel, alder, and willow.

Carrowkeel ware [Ar]. A type of later Neolithic pottery found in Ireland during the 3rd millennium BC, named after material recovered from the passage graves at Carrowkeel in Co. Sligo, Ireland. The fabric of Carrowkeel ware is generally rather thick, coarse, and heavily gritted. The forms comprise mainly open round-bottomed bowls and hemispherical cups. Decoration is extensively applied, often all over the outer surface of the vessel and over the rim, and is typically 'stab and drag' or impressed. Some of motifs used resemble PASSAGE GRAVE ART.

carrying capacity [De]. The optimum number of people that an area of land can support. Tensions caused by an imbalance between the size of a population and the carrying capacity of their environment is often cited as a cause for social change in archaeological interpretations. This is because the carrying capacity of an area can be increased through changes in social organization to exploit it or technological innovation to increase output.

Cartailhac, Édouard Philippe Émile (1843–1921) [Bi]. French archaeologist and one of the founders of the tradition of prehistoric archaeology in his home country. Born in Marseilles he was educated in law and the natural sciences, soon discovering that the latter, and archaeology in particular, was his real interest. For twenty years he was editor of the journal *Matériaux pour l'histoire primitive et naturelle de l'homme*, founded by MORTILLET, and he wrote many books on French and Mediterranean prehistory. Although initially unconvinced of the antiquity of French and Spanish cave art, he changed his mind after visiting ALTAMIRA in the company of the Abbé BREUIL and subsequently did much to shift public opinion towards an acceptance of these works as Palaeolithic in date.

[Obit.: *Antiquaries Journal*, 2 (1922), 269]

cart burial [MC]. *See* WAGON BURIAL.

Carter, Howard (1873–1939) [Bi]. British archaeologist famous for his discovery of the tomb of Tutankhamen in Egypt. Born in Brompton, London, the last of eleven children, he spent his early years in Swaffham, Norfolk, although details of his schooling are uncertain. In 1891 he was offered employment at Didlington Hall, the country seat of William Amhurst Tyssen-Amherst, a well-known collector of Egyptian antiquities. It was this introduction to archaeology that set the course of the rest of Carter's life. From the early 1890s he was working as a draughtsman and copyist for Percy Newberry who was carrying out an archaeological survey of Egypt. In September 1891 he joined Newberry in Egypt and later went on to work with Sir Flinders Petrie at Amarna.

Through the mid 1890s Carter developed great proficiency as an excavator and site manager, as well as an illustrator and photographer. On 1 January 1900 he took up an appointment as chief inspector of antiquities in Upper Egypt and Nubia with an office in Luxor. His role was to safeguard the antiquities of the region and supervise all archaeological work carried out there. This he did efficiently, changing roles in 1904 to look after the monuments in Lower Egypt. Things here did not go so smoothly and after badly handling a tussle between some French tourists and Egyptian guards, and various brushes with officialdom, he resigned in 1905.

Over the next few years he supported himself as an artist and illustrator. In 1909, however, Carter joined Lord Carnarvon's expedition at Thebes, the pair working in the Theban necropolis and elsewhere down to WW1. During the war Carter worked as a civilian in the intelligence department of the War Office in Cairo. After the war he continued working for Lord Carnarvon, but the political situation so far as archaeological investigations in Egypt were concerned was getting worse, permits were increasingly difficult to get, and Carnarvon grew increasingly disenchanted. In 1922 it was understood that the partners would make one last try to reveal something really worthwhile. Working in the Valley of the Kings, Carter began clearing the area in front of the tomb of Ramesses VI, and in early November 1922 he discovered the sealed entrance to the tomb of Tutankhamen. Clearing and recording the tomb took until February 1932, during which time there was a great deal of squabbling and intrigue, and the death of Lord Carnarvon from blood poisoning in April 1923. Carter never full published the excavations, nor was he ever fully accepted by the establishment of the time. His health deteriorated in the late 1930s and he died of Hodgkin's disease.

[Bio.: T. G. H. James, 1992, *Howard Carter. The path to Tutankhamen*. London: Kegan Paul]

Cartesian dualism [Th]. One of the foundations of western analytical thought is the separation of subject from object, the Cartesian separation of the world, an idea that can be traced back to the French philosopher and mathematician René Descartes (AD

1596–1650). The implications for archaeology include an essential dualism between mind and body and between people and things.

Carthage, Tunisia [Si]. Ancient city and seaport on the coast of Tunisia northwest of modern Tunis. The site has been the subject of many extensive campaigns of investigation, most notably the UNESCO 'Save Carthage' campaign under the aegis of the Tunisian Institut National d'Archéologie et d'Art and the Conservateur du site de Carthage between 1972 and about 1980, which involved collaboration by archaeological teams from twelve countries. It is believed that the city was founded in 814 BC as a colony of the PHOENICIAN city of Tyre, but no archaeological remains have yet been found earlier than the later 8th century BC. There is no doubt, however, that the colony became very prosperous relatively quickly, overlooked the straits separating the eastern from the western Mediterranean and providing an ideal anchorage. When Tyre fell under the domination of Assyria, a Punic (western Phoenicians) trading empire was established based on the former Phoenician colonies in the western Mediterranean. From the 6th century BC wealth was generated by merchants acting as middlemen, trade monopolies over certain products, and access to the mineral wealth of southwestern Spain. The town itself expanded through the intensive exploitation of the rich agricultural land along the North African coast. The new empire was constantly at war with the Greeks and later the Romans. Three great Punic Wars raged in the 3rd and 2nd century BC. In 241 BC, at the end of the first Punic War, Carthage lost Scilly and Sardinia to Rome. From an enlarged domain that included southern Spain, however, the Carthaginian general Hannibal led his army across the Alps to attack Italy from the north in 218 BC. He was later recalled to Africa where he was defeated by Scipio Africanus at Zama in 202 BC. Carthage was finally destroyed by Roman forces under Scipio Aemilianus in 146 BC.

From 29 BC the city was rebuilt as a Roman colony (*colonia Iulia Concordia Karthago*) by Julius Caesar and his heir Octavius. The city again prospered and became a major trading port for grain and olive oil produced in North Africa. It eventually replaced Utica as the provincial capital of Roman North Africa, and by the 4th century AD was the second largest city in the western empire after Rome itself. In the 4th and early 5th centuries it was a major centre for the early Christian church as it was home to St Augustine. The VANDALS took Carthage in AD 439, retaining control until the BYZANTINE invasion of AD 533. Thereafter it became the capital of the Byzantine province of North Africa until the Arab conquest of AD 698.

[Sum.: S. Lancel, 1995, *Carthage: a history*. Oxford: Blackwell]

Carthusian order [Ge]. A European monastic order founded at Grande-Chartreuse by St Bruno in AD 1086 that emphasized a return to the eremitic form of monasticism, with each monk having his own cell and garden plot to cultivate. The cells were arranged around a cloister, but there was very little communal activity.

Cartimandua [Na]. Queen of the Brigantes tribe of northern England at about the time of the Roman conquest. She was pro-Roman and reputedly surrendered Caratacus to the Romans in AD 51. This caused a breach with her husband, Venutius, who thereafter led the native resistance to the Romans until the Brigantes were conquered under Petilius Cerialis and Agricola in the AD 70s.

cartouche [De]. An oval frame with a straight stroke tangential to one end that was used by Egyptian scribes and masons to enclose the hieroglyphs of a royal name.

cartulary [Ge]. A medieval document comprising a collection of charters and other deeds gathered together and copied into book form as a convenient archive. Many surviving examples relate to ecclesiastical houses and MONASTERIES.

carved stone balls [Ar]. Roughly spherical or slightly lobate artificially shaped carved stones dating to the later Neolithic and found only in Scotland. Where decorated, the motifs used are similar to those in MEGALITHIC ART. Unornamented stone balls are, however, found in other areas of the British Isles in 4th and 3rd millennia BC contexts.

carvel-built [De]. Term used to describe a technique of constructing plank-built water craft in which the strips of wood forming the skin of the hull are joined edge to edge rather than overlapping (CLINKER-BUILT). In general such construction involves first making a framework or shell over which the hull is formed. The oldest known plank-built boat in the world, the royal funeral boat of Cheops dated to about 2650 BC, was built in this way.

caryatid [Co]. The sculptured female figure used in place of a column to support an entablature or architrave. Some of the earliest known examples were used in the treasury at Delphi and date to the 6th century BC.

cashel [MC]. Irish term for a substantial fortified hilltop settlement or hillfort of the 1st millennium AD, often reflected in the name of the site. The most famous example is Cashel, Co. Tipperary, home to the Eoghanacht dynasties of the 4th and 5th centuries AD, led by Conall Corc. Later, St Patrick consecrated the hill and established the site as a bishopric.

Cashibocaña Phase [CP]. South American cultural grouping found in the Rio Ucayali area of Amazonia in the period c.AD 500–700. Defined by its ceramics which belong to the Polychrome Horizon of painted wares. Vessels include lidded urns, large plates, and anthropomorphic burial urns.

Casper, Wyoming, USA [Si]. Bison kill site dating to about 6000 BC. Plano hunters stampeded a herd of about 100 bison and trapped them in a steep-sided U-shaped arrangement of sand dunes from which they were unable to escape. Once trapped in this way, the hunters dispatched the beasts using spears.

[Rep.: G. C. Frison, 1974, *The Casper site*. New York: Academic Press]

Cassiodorus, Flavian Magnus Aurelius [Na]. Roman senator and apologist who retired from official life in AD 537 and later founded a monastery in southern Italy which did much to preserve the manuscripts of classical authors. Died c.AD 583.

Cassius Dio, Cocceianus [Na]. Roman writer who lived in the late second and early 3rd centuries AD. He refers to events in Britain from the conquest of AD 43 onwards, but his often lively narrative is not always considered entirely reliable except when he is writing about his own times.

Cassivellaunus [Na]. Leader of the native resistance to Caesar's second invasion of Britain in 54 BC. He was probably the king of the Catuvellauni, and perhaps a forebear of Tasciovanus and Cunobelinus.

caste [De]. A form of stratification in which an individual's social position is fixed at birth and cannot be changed. There is virtually no intermarriage between the members of different caste groups.

castellum aquae [MC]. A Latin term for a water cistern fed by an aqueduct and in turn feeding a network of distribution pipes.

casting [De]. The process whereby objects are made from a thermo-setting molten material poured into a former or mould of some kind. In metalworking, casting usually involves the use of a sand, clay, or stone mould into which molten metal is poured to produce an object. Some care has to be taken, however, because metal melted over a fire absorbs gases from the combustion of the fuel and any moulds used thus have to be designed to ensure that bubbles of gas are not trapped to spoil the casting.

casting flash (casting jet/casting seam) [De]. A thin irregular ridge of metal on the outer face of a casting, resulting from seepage of the molten metal into the joint between the separate components of the mould used in its manufacture. A casting jet is similar but is a small plug of metal that originally filled the gate or aperture used to fill the mould. During the final cleaning and finishing of a cast object the jet and flash are usually knocked off and filed smooth.

casting-on technique [De]. A method used in a secondary stage of making metal objects in which a clay mould is made around part of an existing object. Molten metal is then poured in and fuses onto the original object. Used in adding handles, legs, and hilts to complicated artefacts.

castle [MC]. A general term referring to a major fortified residence or military position of the medieval period in northern Europe. Some are as large as fortified villages. The earliest examples are of the later 1st millennium AD and were modelled on the fortified homesteads of the SLAVS. By the 10th century the principal residence in these places was set on a mound, and this established the style for the development of the MOTTE-AND-BAILEY CASTLE in central and northern France in the 11th century. *See also* ARTILLERY CASTLE, QUADRAN-GULAR CASTLE, RINGWORK, SHELL-KEEP CASTLE, and TOWER KEEP CASTLE.

Castor box [Ar]. A shallow vessel in colour-coated ware (NENE VALLEY WARE) with a fitting lid of Roman date. Usually both box and lid were rouletted.

Castor ware [Ar]. *See* NENE VALLEY WARE.

castro [MC]. Portuguese term for a fortified settlement, applied especially to the forts of the Celtic Iron Age in the peninsular northwest.

castrum [MC]. A Latin term for a fortified place.

catacomb [MC]. An underground cemetery comprising a complex of passageways, burial niches, and recessed chambers cut into the living rock. Established during imperial times in Rome, the catacombs later came to be closely associated with the burial places of Christian and Jewish communities. The name was first applied to the example in Rome and then extended in its meaning to include all similar structures.

Catacomb Grave Culture (Katakombnaja) [CP]. A major subdivision of the Bronze Age KURGAN CULTURE of southern Russia and the Ukrainian steppes that is characterized by the use of so-called catacomb graves. Dating to the period *c*.2600–2200 BC, these are not catacombs in the Roman sense, but rather buried deposits in a niche cut into the side of a shaft excavated into the ground. Following the deposition of the corpse and associated grave goods the shaft was refilled and a round barrow (KURGAN) built over the top.

catafalque [MC]. A decorated wooden plat-form on which a sarcophagus was temporar-ily placed before burial.

Çatal Hüyük, Turkey [Si]. A large Neolithic tell standing on the edge of the Konya Plain near Çumra in south central Turkey. Extensive ex-cavations have taken place in the East Mound

at the site, first by James Mellaart between 1961 and 1964 and more recently since 1993 by Ian Hodder and a large international team. The East Mound covers about 13.5 ha and has 20 m of stratified deposits dating to between 6400 BC and 5600 BC. From at least 6300 BC Çatal Hüyük seems to have been a village of mud-brick houses, each built to a fairly stan-dard plan with a kitchen living room and stor-age area spread over about 25 square metres. The houses were built against one another with no streets or courtyards in between, sug-gesting that access was through the roof. Built-in furniture includes benches and plat-forms. Some houses had painted and relief ornamentation on the walls that included bull motifs and stylized images of a human female, in some cases giving birth. Stylized bulls heads (bucrania) were on the walls of some rooms. Burials under the floor were common, those in the highly decorated houses often being accompanied by precious objects. Mellaart argued that the decorated houses were shrines, but this view is not shared by Hodder and later writers.

Economic evidence shows that cereals were cultivated and that cattle, perhaps locally do-mesticated, made up 90 per cent of the animal bone assemblage. Sheep and goats were hunted and may have been domesticated in the later levels. Woodworking, weaving, ob-sidian working, and perhaps some incipient metalworking in copper and lead are repre-sented. The inhabitants of the settlement had extensive trading links with western Asia. Bull horns and cattle motifs have such a prominent place that they must have been highly significant in the belief systems and ideology of the population, together with the so-called 'mother goddess'.

[Sum.: J. Mellaart, 1967, *Çatal Hoyuk, a Neolithic town in Anatolia*. London: Thames & Hudson. I. Hodder (ed.), 1996, *On the surface: Çatalhüyük 1993–95*. Cambridge: McDonald Institute for Archaeological Research]

catastrophe theory [Th]. A mathematical theory developed by René Thom that is con-cerned with modelling non-linear interac-tions within systems that can produce sudden and dramatic effects from apparently small changes in one variable. It is argued that there is only a limited number of ways in which such changes can take place. Colin Renfrew has taken what may be referred to as elemen-tary catastrophes as models with which to explore major changes in the archaeological record, for example the collapse of Mycenaean Greece and the end of the Roman empire.

catastrophic age profile [De]. Distribution of ages in an animal population as a result of death by natural causes.

catastrophism [Th]. Proposition that the geological processes, cited by 18th-century and later scholars as evidence for the great antiquity of the earth, had been accelerated by a series of great catastrophes. Such catastrophes included the great flood of Noah recorded in the Bible. Accepting catastrophism allowed the Mosaic chronology of Archbishop USSHER to be adhered to. *See also* DILUVIALISM.

catch-plate [De]. Curved metal plate which holds the pin of a brooch in place, similar to that employed in a modern safety-pin.

Cathay [CP]. Old name for China, derived from Khitai (or Khitan), the name of the northern tribe who founded the Liao Dynasty in Manchuria and northeast China in AD 916. The name was carried to Russia by traders, and by Muslims to the west by the 13th century AD.

cathedra [Co]. Latin term for the throne of a bishop in the early church, usually placed in the apse behind the high altar.

cathedral [MC]. A substantial church which contains a chair (*cathedra*) symbolizing the authority of a bishop. A place that contains a cathedral is known as a see (from the Latin *sedes*, 'a seat'), and constitutes the administrative and spiritual focus of a diocese which is the territory over which a bishop exercises pastoral authority. Until the 11th century AD there was no common plan or form to a cathedral, which was more of a concept than a physical structure. Sees were established within monasteries or in non-monastic churches such as some minsters. From the 11th century AD cathedral churches become more standardized, grander, and more fixed as institutions. The main church containing the *cathedra* was usually accompanied by subsidiary buildings set within a close, the whole being termed a cathedral. Associated with the church as a place of Christian worship there were (and in some cases still are) meeting rooms, educational facilities, and private accommodation for the bishop, dean, canons, and others.

cation-ratio dating (CR dating) [Te]. A technique for dating the rock varnish that develops over the petroglyphic component of rock art. The technique works by determining the ratio of calcium and potassium to titanium—$(Ca + K/Ti)$-concentrations within the rock varnish. Calcium and potassium ions are more mobile than titanium and so tend to be more readily leached from the surface. Thus the older the varnish the nearer the ratio gets to $1:1$. The ion concentrations are determined using chemical analysis, the calibration of the ratios being dependent on having comparative samples from historical graffiti or other petroglyphs of known age.

Caton-Thompson, Gertrude (1888–1985) [Bi]. A British traveller and archaeologist well known for her work in Egypt and Zimbabwe. She began studying archaeology in 1921 under the guidance of Sir Flinders Petrie at University College, London. Excavating with Petrie at Abydos, Egypt, she later went on to conduct her own excavations at the predynastic village of North Sapur, Hemmamiya. Turning her attention to Africa she discovered a series of previously unrecorded Neolithic cultures living in the southern Saharan margins around Fayum Lake, work published as *The desert Fayum* (1934, London: Royal Anthropological Institute). In 1929 she began the first scientific investigation of the ruins at the Great Zimbabwe, firmly establishing that they had been built by an indigenous African culture in the period AD 1270 to AD 1450. Together with Miss E. W. Gardner she excavated at the Saharan Kharga Oasis and went on with Freya Stark to excavate later prehistoric sites in southern Arabia just before WW2. This was the last of her fieldwork, although later publications include *The tombs and moon temple of Hureidha (Hadhramaut)* (1944, London: Society of Antiquaries) and *Kharga Oasis in prehistory* (1952, London: Athlone Press). She received an honorary doctorate from Cambridge University, and was an Honorary Fellow of Newham College, Cambridge. She was elected a Fellow of the Society of Antiquaries in 1939.

[Abio.: 1983, *Mixed memoirs*, London: Paradigm Publishing]

cattle [Sp]. The domesticated form of the AUROCHS (*Bos primigenius*) that was probably tamed in a number of different places independently, defined as *Bos taurus* but probably the same species as the wild form and separable only in terms of size. The earliest evidence for the domestication of cattle is from ÇATAL HÜYÜK, Turkey, and other sites in northern Greece. A number of different breeds have been recognized including *Bos longifrons* in Europe and southwest Asia, and *Bos indica* in India.

Catuvellauni [CP]. Pre-Roman Iron Age tribe living in the area north of the Thames in modern-day Hertfordshire and Buckinghamshire in the south midlands of England at the time of the Roman conquest. Their capital was at Verulamium (St Albans). They minted coins and were closely engaged in long-distance trade in the 1st century BC. At the time of Caesar's visit to Britain in 55 and 54 BC their chief was CASSIVELLAUNUS.

cauldron [Ar]. A large metal bowl with a rounded base used for cooking and serving food. Two types of bronze cauldrons are known from the later Bronze Age of northwest Europe: Class A with necks, usually ribbed, whose bodies are made from three sheets of bronze, one circular in form to made the bottom and the other two rectangular to make the sides; and Class B which lack necks and are made from numerous small rectangular sheets of bronze riveted together. Both types are fitted with a pair of free-moving ring-handles to allow them to be suspended over a fire or source of heat.

cauldron chains [Ar]. Pairs of connected short lengths of iron chain used to suspend a bronze CAULDRON over a source of heat.

causal relationship [Th]. A connection between events or happenings whereby one state of affairs (the effect) is brought about by another (the cause).

causeway [Co]. **1.** A raised footpath or road constructed across marshy or periodically flooded ground. **2.** Ground interrupting the course of a ditch.

causewayed enclosure (causewayed camp) [MC]. One of the main kinds of Neolithic enclosure found in southern and eastern Britain, closely related to a range of other forms of ditched enclosures in northwest Europe. The synonymous terms causewayed camp/causewayed enclosure were first used in the 1930s, since when they have found widespread acceptance in the archaeological literature. The characteristic feature of a causewayed enclosure is the presence of frequent breaks or causeways in the boundary ditch. Some of these are entrance gaps, but most are simply narrow blocks of unexcavated natural bedrock formed because the boundaries were dug as a series of pits rather than a continuous ditch. Dating mainly to the 4th millennium BC, causewayed enclosures range in size from about 1 ha through to over 10 ha. A number of different designs have been recognized on the basis of the boundary arrangements including: single, double, and multiple concentric circuits of ditches; and spiral ditches. They occur in many different situations in the landscape including river valleys and hilltops. About 70 examples had been discovered up until the end of the 20th century AD, the majority through aerial photography.

The ditch fills show evidence of recutting and many had a long life spanning more than 1000 years. The fills also contain what appear to be deliberately placed deposits of pottery, animal remains, and human bone. There is much debate about the function of causewayed enclosures, although it is now widely recognized that despite a common technique of construction they were not all built for the same purpose. Some appear to have been defended settlements while others appear to be ceremonial sites, perhaps associated with periodic fairs or gatherings.

cave [MC]. Liberally interpreted in archaeological usage to mean any kind of natural hollow, enlarged fissure, cavern, or chamber within a body of rock that could have been or was used by people in the past. Exceptionally shallow hollows and the spaces beneath rock ledges and overhangs tend to be called **rock-shelters**. The occupation of caves is mostly confined to the entrance areas where there is good light and ventilation; deeper recesses were, however, used, perhaps for ceremonial and ritual purposes.

cavea [Co]. Latin term for the seating surrounding an amphitheatre arena. In British amphitheatres, the banks underneath the seating were usually of earth or gravel and the seats were often timber, unlike the great amphitheatres of the Mediterranean world which were built throughout in stone.

cave art [De]. A general term used to refer to the ROCK ART of the Upper Palaeolithic of northern Europe, often regarded as some of the oldest representational art in the world. It is generally divided into MOBILIARY art and PARIETAL art. The subject matter is predominantly animals, especially large herbivores such as mammoth, horse, wild cattle, deer, and bison. There are some human forms depicted, and also what are regarded as abstract forms of unknown meaning. The parietal art is generally executed in a range of colours including reds, blacks, yellows, and browns derived from ochre and other naturally occurring mineral pigments.

cave earth [De]. A general term applied to deposits composed of naturally accumulated shattered rock and, where present, humanly produced occupation debris within cave systems.

Caverton Phase [CP]. A regional industrial phase of the British early Bronze Age in Scotland, contemporary with the ACTON PARK industries.

cavetto rim [De]. A rim, found especially on black-burnished cooking pots, which curves outwards from the vessel to form a concave, quarter-round profile.

cavetto zone [De]. A concave area of the face of a ceramic vessel between CARINATIONS. Typically below a rim or at the shoulder of a vessel.

Çayönü, Turkey [Si]. A small 3 ha early Neolithic settlement in the valley of a tributary of the River Tigris in the Diyarbakir district of eastern Turkey. Excavated intermittently between 1964 and 1981 by Robert Braidwood, the occupation of the site begins about 7300 BC. Five main phases were identified, all aceramic. In phases I and II there were the fragmentary walls of rectangular houses and round pit-ovens. The inhabitants of these phases were reliant on wild animals, but some traces of domesticated cereals were present. In phases IV and V domesticated sheep, goat, and pig were present alongside the domesticated cereals. Even in

the later phases, however, hunting still made an important contribution to the economy. The site is also important for the quality of its architecture even from the earliest levels and the fact that in the later phases there is evidence for the small-scale use of locally derived copper.

[Rep.: L. S. Braidwood and R. J. Braidwood (eds.), 1982, *Prehistoric village archaeology in south-eastern Turkey. The eighth-millennium BC site of Çayönü: its chipped and ground stone industries and faunal remains.* Oxford: British Archaeological Reports, International Series 138]

CBA   [Ab].   *See*   COUNCIL   FOR   BRITISH ARCHAEOLOGY.

Ceawlin [Na]. King of the west Saxons in the later 6th century AD, successor to Cynic. Ceawlin fought against the Kentish kingdom in c.AD 568 and during battles with his British neighbours he is credited with the capture of Cirencester, Gloucester, and Bath in AD 577. According to the *Anglo-Saxon Chronicle* he campaigned in the west midlands and in South Wales, and seems to have been responsible for the rapid growth of the Saxon kingdom of Wessex. Died c.AD 593.

cella [Co]. Latin term for the great hall of a temple in which stood the generally colossal cult statue of the deity. The inner shrine of a Roman temple, edged in many cases by a colonnade or AMBULATORY.

celt [Ar]. Obsolete but occasionally used term for a prehistoric axe-like tool or weapon. The word is said to be derived from the pseudo-Latin word 'celtis', and was current as early as the 18th century AD when it was applied mainly to hafted cutting or chopping implements of bronze.

Celt (Celtic/Celts) [CP]. **1.** The name given by classical authors such as Hecataeus and Herodotus to the proto-historic peoples occupying Spain, Gaul, and central Europe. These writers distinguished the Celts from neighbouring peoples by their appearance, customs, language, and political organization. They spoke of them as tall, fair, excitable, ostentatious, and fierce people. They are portrayed by themselves as having wavy swept-back hair, heavy moustaches on the men, and wearing a metal torc or neck-ring. Many authorities extend this fairly narrow, if slightly ambiguous, definition to include the pre-Roman inhabitants of Britain and parts of northern Europe, and even more fancifully to include those same communities living outside the roman Empire who survived down into the later 1st millennium BC and beyond— the so-called 'Celtic fringe'. In fact there is no archaeological evidence for such a widespread and enduring common culture. As a cultural label the term should be seen as a blanket description for a whole series of more or less autonomous groups superficially linked through common ancestries, kinship ties, and shared artistic tastes. **2.** A branch of the INDO-EUROPEAN language group, that is traditionally divided into two main sections: Q-Celtic (Goidelic) which is now represented by Irish, Manx, and Scots Gaelic; and P-Celtic (Brithonic) which is now represented by Welsh, Cornish, and Breton. *See also* CELTIC ART.

Celtic art [De]. A style of decorative art, widely regarded as one of the most impressive known from antiquity that developed around 500 BC in central and western Europe and found expression in the following centuries over a wide area from Spain and Ireland across to eastern Germany. Also known in its early stages as La Tène art. The development of the style in the 5th century BC owes much to the artistic genius of local craftsmen building on the tradition of HALLSTATT geometric and abstract art, coupled with influences resulting from material introduced through trade, especially the animal designs seen on SCYTHIAN artefacts from the steppes of eastern Europe and the plant motifs found in the classical world. The result of this combination was a bold curvilinear style with a fascinating blurring of the distinction between naturalistic and abstract with a strong sense of balance but not of symmetry. Such art is applied extensively on bronzework, horse-gear, weapons, and eating and drinking equipment. There are also notable examples carved in stone. A series of stages to the development of Celtic art was suggested by Paul Jacobsthal in 1944: successively, the Early; Waldalgesheim; Plastic; and Sword styles.

The Celtic art styles of the later 1st millennium BC continued to flourish in the northern and western extremes of its early distribution, outside the direct influence of the Roman empire: for example, southern Scandinavia, Ireland, and the west of Britain. Indeed, the styles and ideas survived to return after the Roman withdrawal, fertilizing the artistic revivals of Anglo-Saxon, Norse, and British art from the 5th century AD onwards.

Celtic fields [MC]. A general and misapplied term referring to the small square and rectangular fields usually bounded by lynchets, originating in the Bronze Age, but widespread in Romano-British times in the British Isles and northwest Europe.

cemetery [MC]. Any group of two or more separate or substantive graves.

central place theory [Th]. A set of ideas and principles developed by the German geographer W. Christaller in the 1930s to explain the spacing and function of settlement patterns. Under ideal circumstances, he argued, central places of the same size and form will become established at roughly equal spacings with secondary or lower-order centres in between, each of which in turn may be connected to smaller units. Despite certain limitations, the general principles appear to have application to ancient settlement patterns, especially those relating to societies in which a MARKET ECONOMY of some kind was operating.

centre–periphery relations [Th]. *See* CORE–PERIPHERY MODEL.

centurai [Ge]. Unit of 80 legionary soldiers, commanded by a centurion.

centuriation [De]. The Roman practice of formally dividing up the countryside (*territorium*) around newly established *coloniae* into square blocks as allotments for the occupants of the colony. The blocks are typically 776 yards along each side, the boundaries being formed by roads or substantial fences/hedges. Once established the regular grid pattern usually survives into much later times even though the land tenure system changes.

centurion [Ge]. An officer of the Roman army, a centurion commanded a group of 80 men. Centurions usually rose through the ranks of the legion and were thoroughly experienced and professional soldiers. The senior centurion in a legion commanded the First Cohort and was known as *primus pilus*.

century [Ge]. A period of 100 calendar years.

cephalic index [Ge]. A measure of the shape of the human skull obtained by expressing the maximum breadth of the skull as a percentage of the maximum length measured from a point just below the eyebrow ridges. A figure below 75 is considered DOLICHOCEPHALIC, between 75 and 80 is mesocephalic, and above 80 is BRACHYCEPHALIC. It has long been argued that related population groups can, in broad terms, be distinguished from one another using this measure and to a point this is true. It is recognized, however, that the cephalic index is a rather crude measure and that far more dimensions are required adequately to compare skull shapes.

ceramic [Ma]. The state that clay achieves when converted into pottery by firing to a temperature of not less than 500 °C. The term 'ceramics' is often used to refer to assemblages of pottery.

ceramic petrology [Te]. A technique for studying the composition, character, and construction of ceramic materials by treating them like pieces of rock (which really they are). Two main approaches are used: THIN SECTION analysis and HEAVY MINERAL ANALYSIS.

cereals [Ge]. A general term covering a range of BARLEY, WHEAT, OATS, and RYE.

ceremonial centre [MC]. In Mesoamerica, ceremonial centres represent one interpretation for the main form of urban site, especially in the Olmec and Maya civilizations. Each centre typically comprises monumental religious buildings and temples, administrative buildings, ball-courts, and residential compounds used by the nobility. In this model, most of the population lived in small scattered settlements in the hinterland and only came to the ceremonial centre for festivals and religious gatherings.

ceremonial site [Ge]. A broad term used to refer to constructions or natural features which were attributed special symbolic or cosmological meanings by the communities that built or used them. Mainly non-functional in the strictly utilitarian sense.

Cerny Culture [CP]. Early Neolithic epi-LINEARBANDKERAMIC communities occupying the Paris Basin and Loire Valley of northeast France during the later 5th millennium BC.

Named after the site of Cerny, Essonne, France. The culture is characterized by round-based vessels, some with lugs or handles, carrying impressed decoration made with combs or points. The Cerny Culture precedes the CHASSEY in the region.

cess pit [Co]. A hole dug into the ground to serve as a lavatory or for the disposal of human waste. Such pits are commonly encountered on sites of historical age and usually contain a rich assemblage of environmental indicators that can be directly related to the diet and health of those who used the pit. Seeds, pips, insect remains, plant matter, and small fragments of bone are common. Of special interest are the remains of internal parasites from humans and animals. In some cases complete preserved human coprolites have been recovered. Cess pits are far less common on prehistoric sites, perhaps because they are more difficult to recognize after long periods of decay.

C-Group [CP]. Cattle-herding communities living in lower Nubia during the late 3rd and early 2nd millennia BC, broadly contemporary with the KERMA CULTURE of upper Nubia. In late C-Group times there was extensive trade with Egypt.

chacmool [Ar]. A type of anthropomorphous altar found on Mesoamerican religious sites dating to the early 1st millennium AD. The top of the stone altar is adorned with a reclining human figure with hands resting on the lower abdomen. These altars were often set near the entrances to temples.

Chaco Canyon, New Mexico, USA [Si]. A wide alluvium-floored canyon, 15 km in length, with high steep sides in northwest New Mexico. Over 2400 archaeological sites have been recorded within the 82 square kilometres of the canyon floor and its immediate surroundings. These document a long history of settlement from Palaeo-Indian and Archaic times onwards. Most remarkable, however, and sometimes known as the 'chaco phenomenon' was a rapid rise in population density and social complexity which began about AD 900 and lasted for some 250 years. In this period people constructed at least twelve large pueblo-type villages or towns and many smaller settlements of the Ansazi Tradition. They built an extensive road network and water control systems. An elaborate trading network was established for the acquisition of materials and objects from afar.

The largest of the pueblo towns in the canyon is PUEBLO BONITO which covers 1.2 ha. Aerial photographs have revealed roads running out from Chaco Canyon to settlements up to 100 km away. Since no wheels were available at this time the roads must have been for walkers or runners, or perhaps they had a symbolic significance.

[Sum.: H. Frazier, 1986, *People of Chaco: A canyon and its culture*. Springfield: Illinois State Museum; S. H. Lekson *et al.*, 1988, The Chaco Canyon community. *Scientific American*, 259(1), 100–9]

chaîne opératoire [De]. Literally, operational sequence, the term was introduced by the French anthropologist André Leroi-Gourhan in 1966 to provide a theory of technical processes in which technical acts were also social acts. In it he emphasized the importance of the human body as an expression and a source of meaning, power, symbol, and action. The actions carried out in making something may, quite literally, speak louder than words or the message conveyed by the final product.

chain mail [De]. A type of protective armour made from interlinked metal rings.

chain tower [MC]. A small stone or timber structure built beside a river or harbour mouth to house the end of a defensive chain, or the mechanism to raise and lower a defensive chain. Such chains were laid bank to bank across a river or inlet so that in normal circumstances they rested on the riverbed or sea bed. At times of trouble they could be lifted to run more or less along the waterline, thus barring access to hostile ships. The towers were usually strongly built so that they could be defended against attacks from landing parties set ashore to unblock the navigation. Most chain towers date to the 15th and 16th centuries AD.

Chalcatzingo, Mexico [Si]. Pre-Classic Olmec frontier site in the Amatzinac Valley of eastern Morelos. Two natural igneous intrusions rising to over 300 m above the valley floor dominate the whole area and must have been sacred places throughout much of prehistory. At the base of the sheer sides of the central mountain are a series of Olmec bas reliefs

carved on boulders. The most elaborate shows a woman sitting on a throne, holding in her hand a ceremonial bar. She sits within the mouth of the Olmec earth monster, as though within a cave. Also at the foot of the central mountain there are platform mounds and terraces. Excavations by David C. Grove and Jorge Angulo in the 1960s show that the site was founded about 1500 BC and reached its peak during the Cantera Phase of the middle Formative, 700–500 BC.

Chalcatzingo had many Olmec features in addition to the rock carvings, including crypt burials, human sacrifice, and the use of cultivation terraces. There are no local antecedents for the Olmec elements at the site so some kind of population movement must be envisaged.

[Sum.: D. C. Grove, 1968, Chalcatzingo, Morelos, Mexico: A reappraisal of the Olmec rock carvings. *American Antiquity*, 33(4), 486–91; D. C. Grove *et al.*, 1976, Settlement and cultural development at Chalcatzingo. *Science*, 192, 1203–10]

Chalcolithic [CP]. General term elaborating the basic THREE AGE SYSTEM divisions that is used to refer to the Copper Age which, where archaeologically recognized, lies after the Neolithic and before the Bronze Age. Many areas do not have a Chalcolithic period.

Chaldeans [CP]. Semi-nomadic communities who moved into southern Mesopotamia in the early 1st millennium BC from the west, settling down as sedentary groups although still organized as tribal descent groups. Strongly associated with UR and the biblical stories of Abraham, the Chaldeans contributed to political and economic upheavals in Assyria and Babylonia when they first settled the area, but in the 8th century BC they strongly resisted the Assyrian occupation of Babylonia. The rulers of the neo-Babylonian empire in the mid 1st century BC are sometimes referred to as being of the Chaldean Dynasty, but there is no evidence that they were Chaldeans.

chaltoon [Co]. Bottle-shaped underground chamber found in Mesoamerica, variously used for storing food or water. Mainly constructed during the 1st millennium AD.

chamber tomb (chambered tomb) [MC]. A general term covering a wide range of generally stone-built tombs in which one or more cells or chambers were used to receive successive burials over a period of time. Chamber tombs of different kinds were built in many different parts of the world at various times and in a range of contexts.

champlevé enamelling [Ar]. A style of enamelling in which the enamel is melted into a series of incised hollows in the surface of a piece of metal. Initially developed in the later 1st millennium BC amongst Iron Age metalworkers, the technique was afterwards copied by Anglo-Saxon metalworkers for the production of escutcheons for hanging bowls and the roundels supporting the handles of bronze bowls.

Champollion, Jean François (1790–1832) [Bi]. French linguist and antiquarian who deciphered the texts on the Rosetta Stone. Born at Figeac in France, he was educated at the Académie de Grenoble and when only sixteen years old read a paper there in which he argued that the Coptic language was the ancient language of Egypt. In 1807 he went to Paris where he studied at the School of Oriental Languages and the Collège de France. From this time on he devoted himself to the study of ancient languages, returning to Grenoble in 1819 to become Professor of History at the Lyceum. In the early 1820s he used the Rosetta Stone texts to present a solution to Egyptian hieroglyphics, publishing his results in 1824 as *Précis du système hiéroglyphique des anciens Egyptiens, figuratif, idéographique et alphabétique*. Later in 1824 he went to study the Egyptian antiquities in the museums of Italy and on his return was appointed director of the Egyptian Museum at the Louvre. From 1828 to 1830 he carried out expeditions to Egypt, and in 1831 he was appointed to the Chair of Egyptology specially created for him at the Collège de France. However, his health was already failing and he died in Paris a year later.

[Bio.: L. Adkins and R. Adkins, 2001, *The keys to Egypt: the race to read the hieroglyphs*. London: Harper Collins]

Chancay [CP]. A cultural grouping settled on the north central coast of Peru in the period AD 1000–1500, characterized by a distinctive ceramic style, typically an elongated jar with a face painted on a small neck. Numerous large cemeteries are known from this culture and the pattern of grave goods suggests marked social stratification. Conquered by the Inca empire in the 16th century AD.

chancel [Co]. The part of a church to the east of the nave, often separated by a screen, containing the altar. The chancel was often the portion appropriated by singers and is sometimes called the choir.

Chan Chán, Peru [Si]. An extensive urban centre situated in the Moche Valley of the north coast of Peru. Capital of the Chimú polity, the site has a civic core covering 6 square kilometres and an additional 19 square kilometres of outlying buildings.

Investigations have revealed nine large rectangular compounds in the central area, each about 200 m by 600 m. These probably served as the administrative headquarters and ceremonial centres of each of the successive rulers of the Chimú. Within or adjacent to each compound was a truncated pyramid mound which served as a burial platform.

The poverty of settlement sites in the surrounding areas suggests that most of the population of the Moche Valley lived at Chan Chán, a resident population of perhaps 10 000 people.

[Rep.: M. E. Moseley and K. C. Day, 1982, *Chan Chán*. Albuquerque: University of New Mexico Press]

Chang'an, China [Si]. A series of early capital cities relating to the Western Han, Sui, and Tang dynasties built on adjacent sites in the vicinity of modern Xi'an in Shansi Province. Excavations in the area since the 1950s have revealed a long history of settlement starting in the 5th millennium BC. The Western Han site (202 BC–AD 8) has been located about 10 km northwest of Xi'an with massive defensive walls of rammed earth, the interior being divided into more than 160 smaller walled units. There were also the remains of two palaces, an armoury, a drainage system, and a regular street pattern. The Sui Dynasty (AD 581–618) city is to the southeast of the Han city and was planned and built in a single event. The same site was used in the Tang period (AD 618–907) when the city lay at the eastern end of the Silk Route, and was one of the great cities in the world during the late 1st millennium AD. Its walls enclosed a settlement of 84 square kilometres, subdivided into 108 wards and a regular street grid, fourteen streets running north to south and eleven running east to west.

[Sum.: N. S. Steinhardt, 1990, *Chinese imperial city planning*. Honolulu: University of Hawaii Press]

channel-rimmed jar [De]. A type of Romano-British cooking pot having a simple out-turned rim with one or more distinct grooves on it. Particularly common in Northamptonshire and north Bedfordshire in the mid to late 1st century.

Chanson de Roland [Do]. An Old French epic poem, in its present form dating from *c.*AD 1100, based at considerable remove on an account of the Frankish defeat of Roncevaux (AD 778). The poem is of interest for the representation of attitudes to chivalry in the 11th century AD. Its influence on later medieval writers was considerable but its value as an aid to understanding the events of the 8th century AD is minimal.

chantry [MC]. A chapel established by bequest within a church or as a separate structure in which a priest was paid to say masses and pray for the soul of the deceased. Mainly late medieval in date.

chape [Ar]. Lower terminal of a sword or dagger scabbard which is reinforced to prevent damage to the scabbard by the tip of the blade. *See also* WINGED CHAPE.

chapel of ease [MC]. Chapel serving the spiritual needs of a community within a subdivision of a parish.

chapterhouse [Co]. A part of a monastery, usually a large room off the cloister, used for meetings to transact the daily affairs of the community; the place where the chapter (i.e. the canons) met to discuss essentially secular matters.

characterization [De]. The process of identifying the nature and source of materials used in the production of artefacts, especially those in clay, metal, and stone.

Charentian [CP]. One of the principal subdivisions of the MOUSTERIAN, defined by François Bordes and colleagues as having a predominance of side scrapers, relatively few handaxes, and retouched blades. Two subdivisions of the Charentian were recognized: the Quina and the Ferrassie. Overall, the Charentian is found across Europe and Russia where it is associated with Neanderthal remains. It is believed to date to the period 200 000 to 170 000 years ago, contemporary with the penultimate glacial period in Europe.

chariot [Ar]. A light two-wheeled war vehicle usually carrying a warrior and a driver pulled by horses. Clumsy four-wheel prototypes drawn by four asses can be seen in the URUK period of Mesopotamia and are figured on the royal standard of UR. Lighter two-wheeled versions appear in the Near East in the 17th century BC associated with the HYKSOS, KASSITES, and HURRIANS. The MYCENAEANS adopted the chariot in Greece and from there such vehicles spread rapidly into other parts of Europe. In China, the earliest chariots date to the 13th century BC. The chariot revolutionized warfare by allowing the rapid movement of warriors from one part of a battlefield to another.

chariot burial [MC]. The high status that seems to attach to the ownership and use of a chariot is reflected in the fact that some warriors (perhaps leaders) were buried with their vehicles. Graves containing chariots have been found in the Shang Dynasty of China from the mid 13th century BC, from the 7th century BC in Cyprus, from around 500 BC in the Rhineland of central Europe, and from the 4th century BC in eastern England (ARRAS CULTURE). *See also* WAGON BURIAL.

Charlemagne [Na]. *See* CHARLES THE GREAT.

Charles I [Na]. King of England from AD 1625, of the House of Stuart. Born 1600, second son of James I, he married Henrietta Maria, daughter of Henry IV of France. He was executed in 1649 aged 48, having reigned 23 years.

Charles II [Na]. King of England from AD 1660, of the House of Stuart. Born 1630, eldest son of Charles I, he married Catherine, daughter of John IV of Portugal. He died in AD 1685 aged 54, having reigned 24 years.

Charles the Bald [Na]. Frankish leader, born AD 823, youngest son of **Louis the Pious**. King of the West Franks who outlived his brothers and many of their heirs to become emperor in AD 875. He died in AD 877.

Charles the Fat [Na]. Youngest son of Louis the German and king of the West Franks from AD 882. He was crowned emperor and during his reign there was the great siege of Paris by the Vikings in AD 885. He was deposed by a coup in AD 887 and died c.AD 887.

Charles the Great (Charlemagne) [Na]. Son of Pippin the Short, Charlemagne united the FRANKS to become their sole leader in AD 771. In AD 800 he was crowned emperor in Rome by the pope. Contemporary biographers describe him as a cultured and very able person. He re-established many of the traditions of the former Roman world, especially the western Christian church. Surviving images of him show him as the Christian successor to the Roman emperors, and this is also how he is depicted on his coins and in his palace at Aachen, Germany. As a military leader he extended the CAROLINGIAN EMPIRE to cover much of mainland western Europe except Spain and southern Italy. He died in AD 814 to be succeeded by his son Louis the Pious.

Charles the Simple [Na]. King of France who conceded the lower Seine to the Vikings in AD 911 and thus enabled the formation of the duchy of Normandy. Son of Louis II the Stammerer. Imprisoned by Duke Randolf of Burgundy in AD 923 and died in prison in c.AD 929.

charter [Ge]. A deed recording a grant.

charterhouse [MC]. A MONASTERY of the CARTHUSIAN ORDER, planned to provide a community of contemplative monks with facilities for worship, accommodation, and subsistence. In its structure, a charterhouse provided for solitude and contemplation with numerous individual cells arranged around the cloister.

chase [MC]. The FOREST of a king's subject.

chasing tool (chaser) [Ar]. A kind of punch used in metalworking to create REPOUSSÉ style ornament.

Chassey Culture [CP]. Neolithic communities of the early 4th millennium BC whose origins lay in the IMPRESSED WARE CULTURES of southern France but who eventually occupied much of central and southern France. Named after the type-site of Chassey, Côte d'Or,

France, an enclosed settlement dating to the period 4500–3800 BC. Settlements include cave sites, open sites, and enclosures. Characteristic pottery includes round-bottomed bowls, baggy bowls, and carinated bowls. Some of the pottery has 'Pan-pipe' shaped lugs. Footed dishes known as vase supports are also known in the northeastern part of the area occupied by Chassey communities, notably western France and the Paris Basin. Burials are known in pits, in cist graves, and in various kinds of chambered tombs.

Châteauneuf-les-Martigues, France [Si]. A large rock-shelter site northwest of Marseilles, Bouches-du-Rhône, southwestern France. Excavated by M. Escalon de Fonton in the 1950s, the sequence of deposits spans a long period from later Mesolithic through to the Neolithic. The lower levels contain Castelnovian Culture material, especially geometric microliths. This is followed about 5000 BC with IMPRESSED WARE CULTURE layers containing CARDIAL WARE and the remains of domesticated sheep. Early reports of domestic sheep in the 6th millennium BC have proved unfounded.

[Sum.: P. Phillips, 1975, *Early farmers of west Mediterranean Europe*. London: Hutchinson]

châtelaine [Ar]. A set of short lengths of chain attached to a woman's belt for carrying keys and small items of domestic equipment.

Châtelperronian [CP]. The earliest Upper Palaeolithic traditions in southern and western France beginning about 34000 years ago (PERIGORDIAN I), perhaps derived from earlier MOUSTERIAN traditions in the region. Named after finds from a cave site in Allier, central France. The characteristic implement is a type of flint knife with a straight blade and a curved blunted back.

Chaucer, Geoffrey [Na]. Poet and courtier. Born c.AD 1340, the son of a London vintner, he served in the entourage of the duchess of Lancaster and rose to prominence as a royal official, knight of the shire (1386), clerk of the king's works (1389–91), and in other administrative positions. Chaucer is known now for his writings, especially his *Canterbury Tales* (1387 and later). He died c.AD 1400.

Chavín Culture [CP]. Early Horizon communities living in the northern highlands and the northern and central sections of the coast of Peru in the period 900–250 BC. Recognition of the Chavín Culture is based on similarities in architectural styles (temples), iconography (especially the representation of the 'Staff God'), and ceramic forms between sites, and this is taken as evidence of interregional political and social integration, perhaps the articulation of chiefdom-style social organization. In such a system the chiefs of each community developed access to luxury goods and adopted common iconography as a way of expressing their power and standing. The focus of the Chavín Culture is the site of CHAVÍN DE HUANTÁR, Peru.

Chavín de Huantár, Peru [Si]. Ceremonial centre situated at 3200 m above sea level on a tributary of the Rio Maranon in the Cordillera Blanca. Dating to the period 900–500 BC, the site consists of a civic centre covering 6 ha with an attached residential area of 50 ha.

The main complex consists of a sunken paved courtyard 48 m square with low platforms on the north and south sides and a great terraced platform 75 m square and 13 m high, known as the Castillo, on the west side. Some small buildings stood on the summit of the Castillo, but over a third of the mound was hollow and may have served as a funerary place.

Numerous carved stones in the early Horizon style have been found in the central area, most notable among which is the Lanzón stela. This stela is 4.5 m high, in outline the shape of a knife, and the decoration depicts a grimacing fanged jaguar-man with an eccentric eye, long curved fingernails, and hair in the form of snakes.

[Sum.: R. L. Burger, 1992, *Chavín and the origins of Andean civilization*. London: Thames & Hudson]

Cheddar Gorge, Somerset, UK [Si]. This narrow gorge contains numerous caves and rock-shelters occupied during the Upper Palaeolithic, especially the period 25 000 to 12 000 years ago. The complete skeleton of an adult male was found in Gough's Cave in 1903 and it was initially believed to be the remains of a Palaeolithic person. It is now known to be the remains of an adult male dating to around 8000 BC, the early Mesolithic.

[Sum.: R. Jacobi, 1982, Ice Age cave-dwellers 12 000–9000 BC. In M. Aston and I. Burrow (eds.), *The archaeology of Somerset*. Taunton: Somerset County Council, 11–13]

Cheddar point [Ar]. Type of later Upper Palaeolithic flint tool found in the British Isles, named after examples found in the Cheddar Gorge, Somerset, England. Made on a relatively narrow flint blade, both ends are worked to produce an elongated trapezoidal form with the long side of the blade left unworked and the shorter side blunted. Possibly used as knife blades.

Cheddar ware [Ar]. A regional type of late Saxon pottery (Saxo-Norman pottery) dating to the period AD 850 to AD 1150 manufactured in central Somerset, England.

cheekpiece [Ar]. Component of a horse bridle comprising a crescentic section of brow tine from a red deer's antler, perforated with a central hole or slot for the soft mouthpiece of rope or leather, with perforations above and below for a bifurcate rein. Early examples are found in the early Bronze Age of the Carpathian Basin dating to the mid 2nd millennium BC; they appear soon afterwards in northern and western Europe, although generally less heavily decorated than their southern counterparts.

cheese press [Ar]. A type of small, flat-bottomed ceramic dish with holes and concentric ridges in the bottom, sometimes with a flat matching lid. Presumed to have been used for making a moist cottage-type cheese.

Chelsea sword [Ar]. Early type of bronze sword found in southern Britain, having a leaf-shaped blade, flat section, and hilt tang. These were local copies of various imported weapons of Hallstatt A type from mainland Europe by PENARD PERIOD smiths.

Ch'en Dynasty [CP]. Last of the southern Chinese dynasties of the period of division between north and south, spanning the period AD 557 to AD 588. Conquered by the Sui Dynasty which reunited the empire, the Ch'en was a brief and undistinguished period.

chenes [De]. An architectural style of the Lowland Maya of central Yucatan current during the later 1st millennium AD. Characterized by the use of elaborately decorated pre-cut veneer slabs, a preference for earth-monster motifs, and the construction of towerless single-storey buildings. Good examples can be seen at Hochob, Mexico.

chert [Ma]. A flint-like material, usually black or dark brown in colour, a form of very finely crystalline mineral silica occurring as nodules in carboniferous limestone. Although it has a conchoidal fracture like flint it is not so fine-textured and does not lend itself to such fine working.

Chester-type ware [Ar]. A regional type of late Saxon pottery (Saxo-Norman pottery) dating to the period AD 850 to AD 1150 manufactured in northwest England.

chevaux-de-frise [Co]. A kind of defensive work comprising a series of closely set wooden spikes or upright stones that served to impede a cavalry charge or hamper the use of hand weapons such as slings and swords. Mainly found outside the ramparts of Iron Age HILLFORTS in northern Europe.

chevron [De]. Motif comprising a series of connected W-shapes. Often used in the decoration of pottery and metalwork.

Chichén Itzá, Mexico [Si]. A long-lived settlement and ceremonial centre situated on the dry limestone plain of the Yucatán. There are two main phases of construction. Old Chichén was built in Maya style and dates from the 7th century AD. Several of the natural waterholes or *cenote* within the area of the settlement became sacred places into which offerings were regularly deposited.

During the 9th century AD a new and much larger ceremonial centre developed north of the old settlement. This change is traditionally associated with the arrival of the Toltecs, and certainly some of the new structures were constructed in Toltec style. However, recent work suggests that the development of the site was not simply the result of invaders, but a more gradual process.

In AD 918 Itzá people came to the area and began building new structures in the Puuc style. These included what are known as the High Priest's Grave, the inner structure of the Castillo (see below), and the Caracol which is the only round building on the site and was probably an observatory.

Toltec influence at the site coincides with the banishment of the deity Quetzalcóatl from Tula in AD 987 and it may be that Chichén Itzá became a cult centre for Quetzalcóatl after this time; representations of the feathered serpent abound in the latest buildings.

At the centre of the site is a large stepped pyramid 25 m high known as El Castillo. A pathway leads from the base of the pyramid to the Sacred Cenote at the north end of the site. Other major buildings include the Temple of the Warriors, the Venus Platform, the Platform of the Skulls (*tzompantli*), the Platform of the Eagles, the Court of a Thousand Columns, two ball-courts, a sweat bath, and a market area.

Use of the site was relatively short-lived, and by the mid 13th century Chichén Itzá had become largely abandoned, as power shifted away to a new centre at Mayapan.

[Rep.: A. M. Tozzer, 1957, *Chichén Itzá and its cenote of sacrifice*. Harvard: Peabody Museum]

Chichimec [CP]. A general term used to refer to simple village farmers living on the northern fringes of Mesoamerica around the turn of the 1st millennium AD. The Chichimec were regarded as barbarians by the more sophisticated people of central Mexico, and were portrayed as fierce warring people. Between AD 1175 and 1425 some of these peoples moved south into the Basin of Mexico, the best known of which were the Aztecs. Chichimec is also a language group.

chiefdom [Ge]. A form of social organization characterized by the existence of a chief who exercises central authority at the head of a social hierarchy in which an individual's status is determined by birth and nearness by kinship to the chief. The chief occupies a central role socially, politically, and economically. Characteristically, the chief operates some kind of redistributive system wherein food and/or goods from separate sectors of the chiefdom are brought together and then dispersed according to fixed social rules.

Childe, Gordon Vere (1892–1957) [Bi]. Celebrated prehistorian who worked widely in Europe and who is particularly associated with the definition and application of the concept of 'culture' in archaeological analysis. Born in North Sydney, Australia, he graduated in Latin, Greek, and philosophy from Sydney University in 1913, developing at the same time good linguistic skills. Growing up alongside the rise of the Australian Labour Party he became a militant socialist. Between

1914 and 1916 Childe studied for a B. Litt. at Queen's College, Oxford, becoming a close friend of Rajani Palme Dutt who was later a leading figure in the British Communist Party. In 1916 Childe returned to Australia and became involved in the anti-conscription movement and Labour politics while supporting himself teaching in a Queensland secondary school and for a time at Sydney University.

After briefly working as a publicity officer in London he abandoned political work in 1922 and resumed his interest in European prehistory, although in 1926 he published his only political book *How Labour governs* (Melbourne: Melbourne University Press). From 1925 he was appointed librarian at the Royal Anthropological Institute, a post which allowed him to continue his researches and especially his travels in eastern Europe. Several books were published in this period including *The dawn of European civilization* (1925, London: Routledge) and *The Ayrians* (1926, New York: A. A. Knopf). In 1927 he joined with archaeologists from the Hungarian National Museum and Cambridge University in excavating the Hungarian Bronze Age site of Toszeg. In the same year he was appointed Abercromby Professor of Prehistoric Archaeology at Edinburgh University. By the end of the 1920s he had attained the greatest achievement of his early works, the linking of the idea of an archaeological culture as a device for tracing the history of a particular people with the idea of diffusionism as a means for the spread of ideas and people. Throughout the 1930s and early 1940s he applied these ideas locally within the British Isles and to the wider European scene, publishing such key works as *The Danube in prehistory* (1929, Oxford: Clarendon Press), *Prehistory of Scotland* (1935, London: Kegan Paul), and *Prehistoric communities of the British Isles* (1940, London: Chambers). His pursuit of Marxism took him to the Soviet Union for the first time in 1935.

He left Edinburgh in 1946 to became the Director of the Institute of Archaeology at London University, a position he retained until his retirement in 1956. He returned to Australia, seemingly disillusioned in his own ability to devise new ways of carrying forward the Marxist analysis of prehistory. After presenting some lectures and visiting friends, he committed suicide, falling 300 m from Govett's Leap in the Blue Mountains of New South Wales on the morning of 19 October 1957.

[Bio.: B. Trigger, 1980, *Gordon Childe*. London: Thames & Hudson]

chilli pepper [Sp]. A small hot-tasting red pod (*Capsicum annum*), native to Mexico, the south Andes, and lowland South America. Domesticated in central America by 6000 BC, and coastal Peru by *c*.400 BC.

chimaera [Ge]. A mythological fire-breathing monster with a lion's head, dragon's hind quarters, and a goat's middle. Allegedly once a visitant to Lycia in Asia Minor. The image was often used in forging trading connections between the Middle East and the Far East as it suggested familiarity with oriental decorative motifs.

Chimú empire [CP]. A regional tradition of the Late Intermediate Period (AD 1000–1500) in the Moche Valley of Peru. The site of CHAN CHÁN, founded in AD 800, became the capital of the Chimú empire. From about AD 1200 the Chimú started taking over other coastal valleys so that at their peak they controlled all the area between Tumbrey in the north and Chancay in the south, a territory over 1000 km from end to end. The Chimú were conquered by the Incas in AD 1465.

chinampa [De]. A form of intensive agriculture widely used in the Basin of Mexico during the early 1st millennium AD, often referred to as 'floating gardens'. Chinampa were constructed by cultivating large mats of floating plants in deep water and them moving them to where cultivation plots were required on mud flats and swampy areas where several were stacked one on another to create a thick foundation layer. Canals were dug around three or four sides to facilitate drainage and provide mud and silt which was then spread on top of the mats. Waste from nearby settlements was added to the raised beds to give additional fertility. Each chinampa was about 10 m by 110 m and they were usually constructed on a regular grid pattern. Chinampas were used to grow staple root, vegetable, grain, and fruit crops and were kept in production all year round. It has been reported that, in AD 1519, 10 000 ha of chinampa supported about 100 000 people.

Chindadn point [Ar]. Small bifacially worked stone teardrop-shaped projectile points typical of the period 12 000–10 000 BC in central Alaska where they characterize the Nenana Complex.

Ch'in Dynasty [CP]. The first imperial dynasty ruling all China, named after the kingdom of Ch'in from which it derived. Its duration was brief, 221–206 BC, but the achievement of a united empire became the objective of all subsequent regimes.

chipping-floor [De]. A workshop area used for the manufacture or maintenance of flint or stone tools, recognized archaeologically by a spread of working waste, broken or part-made implements, and discarded raw material.

chi-rho [De]. Emblem composed of Greek letters chi (X), and rho (P), the first two letters of Christ's name in that language. Common in early Christian art and epigraphy.

chisel-ended arrowhead [Ar]. A type of arrow tip, usually of flint or stone, that has a sharp straight cutting edge at right angles to the axis of the arrow shaft, rather than a point. Such arrowheads are believed to have been used for shooting birds. *See also* TRANSVERSE ARROWHEAD.

chiton [Ar]. An ancient Greek garment of linen or wool worn next to the skin by women and men. In the Ionian style the chiton was made of fine linen and fastened on the shoulders and down the upper arms to form sleeves. It was held at the waist by a girdle whence it fell in close folds to the feet.

Chitty, Lily ('Lal') Frances (1893–1979) [Bi]. British antiquarian and amateur archaeologist best known for her work on prehistoric sites in the west of England and the Welsh Marches. Born in Lewdown, Devon, her family moved to Shropshire while she was still young and here she was educated at home. During WW1 she trained as a secretary. In the 1920s she met a number of well-established archaeologists and through them developed and pursued an interest in the subject, especially in recording and documenting finds from the area she grew to know so well in the central Welsh Marches. This was done in many ways: providing the Shropshire cards for the British

Association Bronze Implement Catalogue was one, drawing the maps for Cyril Fox's *The personality of Britain* was another. She was elected a Fellow of the Society of Antiquaries in 1939 and later was made an OBE.

[Bio.: W. F. Grimes, 1972, Lily Frances Chitty. In F. Lynch and C. Burgess (eds.), *Prehistoric man in Wales and the west*. Bath: Adams & Dart, 1–3]

chopper (chopping tool) [Ar]. A stone tool with a working edge formed by flakes removed from two directions. Mainly confined to Lower Palaeolithic industries, but also found in later periods. Chopping tools in the form of bifacial core tools with a sinuous, transverse edge caused by alternate flaking are characteristic of Asian Palaeolithic industries of the mid Pleistocene.

Choris Stage [CP]. Hunter-gatherer culture within the Norton Tradition of coastal Alaska dating to the period 1000 and 500 BC. Characterized by fibre-tempered pottery decorated with linear stamping on the exterior surface, lanceolate stone projectile points, and oil lamps. Most of the communities of this stage seem to have been fairly isolated groups and there is much local variation. Use was made of marine and terrestrial resources.

Chou Dynasty [CP]. *See* ZHOU DYNASTY.

chringa (tjurunga) [Ar]. A ceremonial board of wood or stone used by Australian Aborigines which bears secret sacred designs. Usually the designs are painted or engraved.

chronological types [De]. Artefacts defined by form that are sufficiently distinctive to act as time markers. Useful in CROSS-DATING.

chronology [De]. An ordered sequence of related events, episodes, or defined blocks of time. A **relative chronology** exists where items in the sequence are related to one another but not to absolute dates, such as may be established through stratigraphy, typology, artefact correlations, or cross-dating. An **absolute chronology** exists where the items in the sequence are each independently dated in calendar years using techniques such as RADIOCARBON DATING or DENDROCHRONOLOGY.

chronometric dating [Te]. Dating method that provides an actual age in years for a defined piece of material or event. Because all such dates are, in statistical terms, estimates, the results are usually reported with a measure of probability, typically expressed as a standard deviation.

chryselephantine [De]. A high-quality Greek statue built up on a wooden core and covered with plates of gold for the clothing and ivory for the uncovered parts of the body. The two most famous examples are the cult statue of Athena that stood in the Parthenon in Athens and the statute of Zeus at Olympia. Both date to the 5th century BC.

chthonian [Di]. Literally meaning 'belonging to the earth', a term used to describe a god or goddess of the earth or the underworld. Also extended to mean the divine creative force, and the source of fertility in the crops, animals, and humans. The term is also used for underground deities connected with death. In ancient Greece, belief in the Olympian gods, under the sky god Zeus, succeeded the old belief in chthonian powers.

church [De]. A building belonging to an established religious organization and used for collective Christian worship, the performance of ceremonies, pilgrimage, and the veneration of relics. Early churches were hidden in catacombs or in caves, but from the 4th century onwards they were specially built structures often modelled on the basilican halls of late Roman public buildings. The plan and layout of all churches is partly related to liturgical needs and ceremonial functions, and partly to symbolic and spiritual factors. Thus the majority are rectangular or cross-shaped in plan, orientated broadly east to west, with the main focus at the east end.

Cimmerians [CP]. Bronze Age nomadic communities occupying the Russian steppes north of the Black Sea during the later 2nd millennium BC, well known in the archaeological literature for their horse-riding skills. The Cimmerians were driven out of their traditional homelands by the SCYTHIANS in the 8th century BC, retreating through the Caucasus to cause havoc in Anatolia and the Near East. Their relatives the THRACIANS retreated into the Balkans where they had rather more success in establishing themselves north of the Aegean.

cinerarium [Ar]. A Roman container for cremated remains, often in the shape of a box and usually made of marble. The name of the deceased was typically inscribed in a panel on one side while the other faces were decorated with garlands.

cinerary urn [Ar]. A ceramic vessel used to contain the cremated remains of one or more individuals for burial. Such urns were not always specially made for the purpose; many are in fact ordinary domestic vessels selected for the purpose and ending up, in archaeological terms, in a burial context.

cinnabar [Ma]. Mercury sulphide (HgS) occurring as a red ore that was used in ancient times as a colouring agent.

Circumpolar cultures [CP]. A general term used to refer to a range of hunter-gatherer cultures living in the extreme northern latitudes of Eurasia. Based around hunting reindeer, elk, and seal, these communities remained hunter-gatherers long after groups to the south adopted farming. Trade between the hunters and the farmers took place, however, especially in amber. Some circumpolar communities acquired pottery-making through these contacts. Rock art is found in some areas, mainly depicting hunting scenes as well as equipment such as skis, sledges, and skin boats. Also known as the Arctic Stone Age cultures.

circus [MC]. Latin term for a kind of oval racetrack used in the classical world for chariot racing. There were several examples in Rome itself, the best known and earliest of which is the Circus Maximus (600 m by 150 m). The race-track itself comprised a central wall (*spina*) with a turning point marked by a column at each end (*metae*). Seating for spectators was provided on banks along either side. Known in the Greek world as a **hippodrome**.

Cirencester, Gloucestershire, UK [Si]. Roman and medieval town in the heart of the Cotswolds in central southern England, 5 km northeast of the head of the Thames. Excavations since the late 1950s by Graham Webster, John Watcher, Alan McWhirr, Timothy Darvill, and Neil Holbrook among others have revealed something of the size and complexity of the town. Founded as a Roman military settlement in the later 1st century AD its initial role was probably in relation to the nearby tribal centre of the Dobunni at Bagendon and as a station on the first major frontier created across southeastern England after the conquest—the Fosse Way frontier. By the 2nd century, however, a civilian settlement had been established which was to become the *civitas* capital of this agriculturally rich region: Corinium Dobunnorum. By the 4th century the town was the second largest in the province of Britannia, next to London, and perhaps the seat of a regional governor. Walls were added to the town's defences in the 3rd century AD. There were temples, a fine forum and basilica, and a theatre inside the town, with extensive cemeteries and a large amphitheatre immediately outside the walls. Occupation continued through Anglo-Saxon times, Cirencester becoming one of the main market towns of the Cotswolds in the medieval period.

[Sum.: T. Darvill and C. Gerrard, 1994, *Cirencester: town and landscape*. Cirencester: Cotswold Archaeological Trust]

cire perdue [De]. *See* LOST-WAX CASTING TECHNIQUE.

cist [Co]. Stone-lined burial pit, sometimes sealed below a barrow mound, within which cremation or inhumation burials were placed. The stone walls frequently supported a flat cover-slab.

Cistercian order [Ge]. Monastic order of monks founded at Citeaux in Burgundy in AD 1098, although later found in other parts of Europe. The order came to Britain in AD 1128. The monks wore white habits and renounced wealth and grandeur, colonizing isolated areas and gaining a living from land previously uncultivated. They made extensive use of lay brethren to help run their establishments, especially dependent granges, many of which were devoted to sheep farming.

Cistercian ware [Ar]. A type of brown coloured pottery made in the north midlands of England in the late 15th and 16th centuries AD.

cistern [MC]. Large underground water storage facility.

citadel [MC]. A strongly fortified structure, especially within a city. *See* ACROPOLIS.

citizen [Ge]. A member of a politically or administratively defined community, having both rights and duties associated with that membership.

city-state [De]. In archaeology this term is used to refer to a social and political unit which consisted of a major urban centre and its hinterland, and which had achieved a high degree of autonomy and a clear identity. The hinterland might contain other cities or large settlements. A city-state had its own government and was not subject to any outside authority.

civitas (pl. *civitates*) [De]. A Roman local government administrative unit based on the citizenship of its occupants, usually based on pre-Roman tribal groupings. They were ruled from a *civitas* capital (also known as cantonal capitals) which, in Britain, were towns deliberately founded for the purpose. A *civitas* thus comprised the citizens and magistrates of a town together with the people occupying the surrounding associated territory.

clack mill (click mill) [MC]. A name applied to NORSE mills built in Scotland and elsewhere. A horizontal water wheel drove a pair of grindstones on the floor above. A peg in the upper stone knocked against a chute sprinkling grain into a hole in the top of the stones, thus making a distinctive clicking sound with each revolution.

Clactonian [CP]. A Lower Palaeolithic flake-based flintworking industry named after the assemblage recovered from the type-site of Clacton-on-Sea, Essex, England. Probably of Hoxnian age, 300 000 to 200 000 years ago. Apart from the tip of a wooden spear recovered from Clacton-on-Sea, the industry is characterized by a range of stone tools including trimmed flint flakes and chipped pebbles, some of which have been classified as chopper tools. Handaxes are generally absent from the assemblages, leading to some speculation that in fact the assemblages are complementary to broadly contemporary early ACHEULIAN assemblages.

clamp-kiln [MC]. *See* KILN.

clan [Ge]. A kin group stretching more broadly than the family, found in many pre-industrial societies.

clapper bridge [MC]. A simple stone bridge made by setting stone blocks at intervals across a river to act as supports for a series of stone slabs laid end to end across the top. Most surviving examples are found in the south-west of England, the best known being Tarr Steps on Exmoor, although they were formerly far more widespread. Often claimed as prehistoric because of their simplicity and rather primitive appearance, most clapper bridges in fact date to the period between the 14th and 19th centuries AD.

Clark, Sir John Grahame Douglas (1907–95) [Bi]. Distinguished British prehistorian who specialized in the Mesolithic period and is well known for his work on world prehistory and developments in the field of palaeoeconomy. Born in Bromley, Kent, he was educated at Marlborough and Peterhouse, Cambridge, where he remained for the rest of his career. He became a Bye-Fellow in 1933 and a Fellow in 1950, breaking off his academic work only during WW2 to serve in the RAF Volunteer Reserve where he worked on photographic interpretation. In 1952 he was appointed Disney Professor of Archaeology and in 1956 he became head of the Department of Archaeology and Anthropology. He was Master of Peterhouse from 1973 to 1980. Throughout his academic career and beyond into retirement there were a number of key strands to his work. First and foremost was an interest in the Mesolithic of northern Europe, starting with his first book, published at the age of 25, *The Mesolithic Age in Britain* (1932, Cambridge: CUP). His excavations at STAR CARR between 1949 and 1951 remain one of the most important pieces of work relating to the early Mesolithic. Beyond this his interests included world prehistory, a topic which displayed another of his talents, the ability to write for wide audiences and the general public. *Prehistoric England* (1940, London: Batsford) went through five editions, *World prehistory* (1961, Cambridge: CUP) through three. And beyond this still was his interest in economic prehistory and the need to take a social perspective, well exemplified in his *Prehistoric Europe: the economic basis* (1952, London: Methuen). Of course these were not his only interests. For 35 years he was the editor of the *Proceedings of the Prehistoric Society* and from 1958 to 1962 he was President of the Prehistoric Society. He served on numerous other committees and boards. He was elected a Fellow of the British Academy in 1951, appointed CBE in 1971, and knighted in 1992. In 1978 he was awarded the Gold Medal of the Society of Antiquaries.

[Obit.: *Proceedings of the British Academy*, 94, 357–87]

Clarke, David Leonard (1937–76) [Bi]. British prehistorian who was one of the principal exponents of the so-called NEW ARCHAEOLOGY. Educated at Dulwich College, he had two years of obligatory National Service before going to university. These he spend with the Royal Signals Corps at Essen in Germany. He went up to Peterhouse, Cambridge, in October 1957, graduating in archaeology and anthropology with first-class honours three years later. He was promptly accepted back as a Ph.D. student, his chosen subject being beaker pottery in the British Isles.

In 1964 he finished his dissertation and was appointed to a William Stone Research Fellowship. Two years later he was elected a Fellow of the college and Director of Studies in Archaeology and Anthropology. Part of his time was devoted to preparing his work on beakers for publication as the *Beaker pottery in Great Britain and Ireland* (1970, Cambridge: CUP). Alongside this, however, he was also working on a study of what archaeology was and what it should be. Drawing on many diverse disciplines he began to formulate a new way of thinking about and exploring the past. The results of this were published as *Analytical archaeology* (1968, London: Methuen), in which he argued that archaeology should become a science by developing its own explicit methodologies and theory based on SYSTEMS THEORY. This book was probably the single most important archaeological text published in Britain in the 1960s, and one that caused great controversy in ushering in the new archaeology on the European side of the Atlantic. A number of colleagues and students quickly picked up on the ideas and their implications, as shown by the papers in Clarke's edited book *Models in archaeology* (1972, London: Methuen). This was followed up in 1973 with an article in *Antiquity* entitled 'Archaeology–the loss of innocence' which took the ideas to a far wider audience and drew heavy criticism from more traditionally minded archaeologists.

Although hopeful of being given the Disney Chair of Archaeology in 1975, the electors chose Glyn Daniel instead. In 1976, Clarke was given an untenured assistant lectureship.

That same year he spent some time in hospital; he died at home the day after being discharged when a blood clot, formed by weeks of inactivity, detached itself and lodged in his lung.

[Bio.: N. Hammond, 1979, David Clarke: a biographical sketch. In *Analytical archaeologist. Collected papers of David L. Clarke*. London: Academic Press, 1–10]

class 1. [De]. Identifiable division or order within a society based on formally or informally recognized characteristics, for example social classes based on the nature of the work a person does. The possible existence of class divisions may be explored archaeologically through the distribution and associations of objects relating to the creation and projection of identity. **2.** [Th]. A grouping of material based on shared characteristics; one of the divisions used in a classification. Following the lead provided by the biological sciences, a class in archaeology may be regarded as more specific than a 'category' and less particular than a 'type'. Vessels are said to belong to the same class if they are of the same general form and usable for the same purpose; monuments are regarded as being of the same class if their form and function appear very similar, allowing for regional or chronological variations that can be defined at the level of type.

Classic [CP]. The fourth of five general cultural stages proposed by G. Willey and P. Phillips in 1958 as a framework for the study of ancient communities in the Americas. The Classic embraced communities with urban settlements and is thus confined in its application to Mesoamerica and the central and northern west coast of South America, where such societies were present in the period from about AD 250 through to about AD 900 depending on region. The Classic was therefore a time of high populations and elaborate social organization, the peak of social, artistic, and religious endeavour in Pre-Contact society, a succession of connected complex societies or states. The succeeding stage is known as the Post-Classic.

classical [Ge]. **1.** A term derived from the Latin word *classicus*, meaning of 'of the highest class' and used to indicate a high point in the development of a particular society or civilization. **2.** In art history the term refers to Greek art of the 5th and 4th centuries BC: the CLASSICAL PERIOD.

classical archaeology [De]. A branch of archaeology that focuses on the great civilizations of the Old World, especially Greece and Rome during the later 1st millennium BC and early 1st millennium AD.

classical period [CP]. Broadly the period from the Persian Wars through to the unification of Greece under Philip II and the world empire of Alexander the Great (i.e. the 5th and 4th centuries BC).

classical temple [MC]. A substantial ceremonial building constructed in Graeco-Roman styles of architecture for the worship or veneration of the gods and goddesses of the Graeco-Roman pantheon. Such temples comprise a platform or podium on which stood a CELLA fronted by a pronaos or vestibule with a colonnaded portico. The portico is usually approached by a stepped face to the podium. The cella may be surrounded by a colonnade forming the outside edge of the temple structure. Such temples are typically set within a sacred precinct or temenos. Widely constructed in the central Mediterranean region, examples were built throughout the Roman empire during the late 1st and early 2nd millennia BC.

classification [Th]. The ordering of archaeological data into groups (e.g. categories, classes, types) using various ordering systems. **Monothetic classification** is based on all the defined attributes being present all the time before something is accepted as part of a defined group. **Polythetic classification** allows overlapping subsets of attributes to be used in defining membership of a defined class.

classis Britannica [De]. Literally Latin for 'the British fleet'; the Roman navy fleet based at Boulogne and perhaps other ports on the channel coast that patrolled the English Channel from the 1st through to the 4th century AD and which was active in transporting supplies and military personnel and equipment along and across the Channel.

clast [De]. A geological term used to describe an individual component within a body of sediment that is applied in archaeology especially with reference to components of a deposit that have been introduced (clastic inclusions). Thus archaeological objects are clasts within a sediment matrix and tempering agents are large clasts within a clay matrix.

Claudian(us), Claudius [Na]. An Alexandrine Greek poet who came to Rome before AD 395 and whose Latin eulogies in honour of courtiers led to his position as court poet to HONORIUS and propagandist of STILICHO. His political poems provide evidence for events about the year AD 400. Died c.AD 404.

Claudius [Na]. Roman emperor, AD 41–54.

Clava tomb (Clava cairn) [MC]. A small group of early Bronze Age chambered tombs clustered around the Moray Firth in northeastern Scotland dating mainly to the late 3rd and early 2nd millennia BC. Two main types have been recognized amongst the 50 or so examples known: passage graves (Balnuaran type) with central chambers set in round mounds; and ring cairns (Gask type) with a doughnut-shaped stone bank surrounding a central open area. Both kinds are often set in the centre of a STONE CIRCLE.

clavicula [Co]. A Latin term for an outward curved extension of the rampart and ditch at one side of the gateway into a Roman fort or camp to provide additional defence for the entrance.

claw beaker [Ar]. A type of glass drinking vessel common in the 6th and 7th centuries in early Anglo-Saxon and FRANKISH graves in northern France, the Low Countries, and eastern England. It is basically a simple conical beaker embellished with a series of claw-like protrusions, probably made in Germany. The glass itself is sometimes tinted brown, blue, or yellow.

clay [Ma]. **1.** Extremely fine particles, less than 0.002 mm across forming constituent components of natural and anthropogenic sediments and deposits. **2.** The plastic raw material from which pottery, daub, bricks, and other forms of terracotta are made comprising mainly clay-sized particles of the principal clay minerals kaolinite, illite, and montmorillonite. Potting clay is a relatively abundant and widespread resource, although the quality and characteristics of different

outcrops vary greatly, the best being highly sought-after. **3.** A general term describing the texture and feel of a sediment: soft, sticky, and plastic when wet, hard when dry.

clay tablet [Ar]. Roughly rectangular slab of fine clay smoothed on one surface which was then used by scribes in the early civilizations of the Near East to cut or impress symbols and hieroglyphs.

clearance cairn [MC]. *See* CAIRN.

clearances [De]. A term generally used to refer to episodes of depopulation caused by a landlord or other authority turning communities off the land by incentive, coercion, or force. In Britain the Highland Clearances of the 18th and 19th centuries AD had a tremendous impact on the rural economy and the structure of the Scottish landscape, as sheep replaced people.

cleaver [Ar]. Roughly U-shaped stone tool with a transverse cutting edge. ACHULIAN bifacial cleavers resemble truncated handaxes with a straight or oblique edge instead of a point. On flake cleavers the cutting edge is generally formed by the intersection of the primary flake surface and a transverse flake seat on the upper surface.

clerestory [Co]. A lighting storey or range of windows in the highest part of the nave, chancel, or aisle of a church.

clientship [De]. A system of patronage, in which services are available to specific individuals in positions of influence or power. Those 'patrons' tie others to them by means of the rewards they control.

cliff castle [MC]. A coastal promontory adapted as an enclosure by the construction of one or more ramparts across the neck of the spur in order to separate it from the mainland and make it defensible. The promontories chosen usually end in steep cliffs on the seaward side. Numerous examples are known around the western coasts of the British Isles where they mainly seem to date to the later 1st millennium BC and early 1st millennium AD. Some appear to have been used as small settlements, others may have had a predominantly ritual or ceremonial purpose, perhaps connected with the sea.

clinker-built [De]. Term used to describe a technique of constructing water craft in which the strips of wood forming the skin of the hull are joined so that they overlap downwards rather than edge to edge (*compare* CARVEL-BUILT). The gaps between the overlapping strips are caulked with rope or tar. The technique is typical of boat-building in northern Europe and early examples including the Halsnoy boat where the planks were sewn together are dated to around 350 BC. Viking ships from the 8th and 9th centuries AD onwards were clinker-built.

clock time [Ge]. Time as measured by a clock, assessed in terms of days, hours, minutes, and seconds. Before the invention of clocks, time-reckoning was based on events of the natural world, such as the rising and setting of the sun.

cloisonné [De]. A decorative technique involving a metal filament bent into a desired design form and then superimposed on an enamel surface. Commonly used by Romano-British craftsmen.

cloister [Co]. The central articulating feature of a MONASTERY, usually set out in the form of a square. In the centre was a courtyard or open garth kept clear of structures, although sometimes arranged as a garden or burial ground. Around the garth was a continuous covered passage or cloister walkway. The outside wall of the walkway was sometimes an open arcade, although in later times they were often glazed. The walkway served to link and give access to all the main buildings and facilities of the complex. The church was usually on the north side of the cloister, the CHAPTERHOUSE, dormitory, halls, refectory, and abbot's lodgings being arranged on the other sides. The cloister walk sometimes includes washing facilities, places for study, and wall cupboards for books and records. In Carthusian houses the individual cells occupied by members of the community open from the cloister walk.

close [De]. A small area of enclosed ground.

closed association [De]. A group of artefacts and a structure of some kind within a single deposit that shows no signs of disturbance since its formation and which is sealed by another archaeological layer or deposit. Examples include the contents of a backfilled storage pit sealed by a metalled surface or a grave covered by a round barrow.

clothes-line enclosure [MC]. A class of early and middle Iron Age settlement found in many parts of the British Isles which comprises a small rectangular or sub-rectangular space bounded by an earthwork (usually a bank and ditch) one side of which is formed by an existing LINEAR BOUNDARY. In this way the enclosure appears to hang from the linear boundary—hence the name. In some cases a series of three or four such enclosures may hang from the linear boundary over a distance of 1–2 km.

Clovis [Na]. Son of Childeric and king of the Franks in the late 5th and early 6th centuries AD who undertook a series of conquests which extended his kingdom over much of central and eastern Gaul. In AD 507 he defeated the Visigoths and annexed the southwest of Gaul. He died *c*.AD 511.

Clovis, New Mexico, USA [Si]. A town in eastern New Mexico which gives its name to the Clovis Culture because numerous Clovis points have been found nearby at kill sites associated with the remains of butchered mammoth.

[Rep.: J. L. Cotter, 1938, The occurrence of flints and extinct animals in pluvial deposits near Clovis, New Mexico, Part VI: Report on the Field Season of 1937. *Proceedings of the Philadelphia Academy of Natural Science*, 90, 113–17; J. Warnica, 1966, New discoveries at the Clovis Site. *American Antiquity*, 31, 345–57]

Clovis Culture [CP]. Early Palaeo-Indian culture dating to the period 9500–9000 BC and represented widely over the central and southern Plains area of North America. Clovis Culture communities are well known as big game hunters, especially fond of mammoth and bison. They also took smaller game such as deer and rabbits, and used plant resources too. They are mainly recognized archaeologically by a distinctive chipped stone industry which includes Clovis points. The Clovis Culture is sometimes referred to as the Llano.

Clovis point [Ar]. Bifacially worked stone or flint point with an elongated symmetrical outline, parallel sides, an even point, and a hollow base caused by the removal of a fluted flake, dated to *c*.9500–9000 BC. Type-artefact of the Clovis Culture, although examples have been found over most of the USA, parts of southern Canada, and in central America.

Cluniacs [Ge]. A Roman Catholic monastic order established in AD 910 of which the abbey of Cluny near Maçon, France, was the parent house. All the daughter houses spread across Europe owed allegiance to Cluny. This order became extremely powerful and wealthy, its buildings ornate, and its services elaborate. By the 16th century AD there were about 2000 Cluniac houses across Europe.

Clyde cairn [MC]. A regional group of middle Neolithic LONG BARROWS defined in 1969 by Jack Scott and found widely scattered across southwestern Scotland, especially around the Clyde Valley. Scott argued that the Clyde cairns developed out of small simple megalithic structures which he called 'protomegaliths', in many cases being the physical elaboration of these early structures on the same site. The Clyde cairns are characterized by rectangular and trapezoidal mounds, stone-built chambers comprising linear groups of cells at the higher and wider end of the mound, concave or recessed forecourts, and a façade of large stones set around the back of the forecourt, usually diminishing in height outwards from the entrance to the chambers. Collective inhumation is the usual burial rite, although cremations are sometimes present. Grave goods are rare.

Clyde–Carlingford Culture [CP]. Now obsolete term coined by Gordon Childe in the 1930s and developed by Stuart Piggott in the 1950s to refer to the middle Neolithic communities living around the North Channel in southwestern Scotland, northern Ireland, and the Isle of Man. One of the main claims for the identity of this grouping was the form and distribution of long barrows—the so-called **Clyde–Carlingford tombs**—with deeply concave forecourts, orthostatic façades, and linear arrangement to the chambers which lead into the cairn from the back of the forecourt. Investigations in Scotland by Jack Scott and in Ireland by Ruaidhri de Valéra and others during the 1950s and 1960s showed that the similarities noted by Childe and Piggott were rather superficial and that the structures in southwest Scotland should be considered CLYDE CAIRNS while those in Ireland were part of a more widespread tradition of long barrow

construction in Ireland where examples are known as COURT CAIRNS. *See also* CARLINGFORD CULTURE.

coarse ware (coarse pottery) [De]. A general descriptive term applied to those components of a ceramic assemblage that can be regarded as everyday transportation, storage, food preparation, and cooking vessels. Such wares tend to contrast with fine-quality tablewares and special ceremonial vessels in their quality of finish, method of manufacture, and general appearance. Coarse wares usually represent more than two-thirds of any domestic assemblage.

coastal fish weir [MC]. A pair of walls arranged in a V-shaped pattern within the intertidal zone of a gently sloping foreshore with the pointed end at the seaward end. Built of stone or hurdlework, the walls may be up to 200 m long. A narrow gap of about 1 m is left at the point where the walls meet and here a net or fish-trap will be placed when the structure is in use. Built from prehistoric times onwards, these weirs work in a simple but highly effective way. At high tide the weirs flood, but as the tide goes out any fish within the area defined by the weirs are naturally channelled towards the traps placed at the junction of the two walls. When the tide is fully out the owner of the weir simply walks down the foreshore and takes the catch from the traps.

coatepantli [Co]. A type of elaborately decorated wall found at sites in Mesoamerica to separate ceremonial buildings from other structures. The decoration typically comprises a serpent motif.

Côa Valley, Portugal [Si]. An extensive series of open-air Palaeolithic rock-art panels in the deeply incised valley of the River Côa, a tributary of the Douro, in northern Portugal. The first panels were discovered in 1992 during surveys for an environmental impact assessment in connection with the proposed construction of a major dam and hydroelectric power plant which would mean flooding the valley. Between 1992 and 1995 several thousand panels were discovered as well as four rock-shelters and possible settlement sites dating to the Upper Palaeolithic. Following international pressure, the Portuguese government stopped the dam-building proposals in 1995 and declared the valley a national archaeological park. Several different styles are represented in the way the images were executed, including incised lines, pecking, and scraping. Most of the panels include motifs of animals, principally aurochs, horse, ibex, and red deer. Most are found on vertical rock faces with an aspect towards the river. Several different periods are represented, and the earliest are believed to span the SOLUTREAN, GRAVETTIAN, and MAG-DALENIAN; some images, however, extend down into the local Iron Age of the later 1st millennium BC.

[Sum.: A. F. de Carvalho, J. Zilhão and T. Aubry, 1996, *Côa Valley. Rock art and prehistory*. Lisbon: Ministério da Cultura]

coaxial field system [MC]. *See* FIELD SYSTEM.

cob [Ma]. Wet clay mixed with straw used in constructing walls, ovens, and other similar kinds of structure. To achieve the desired shape or form, cob was packed between wooden shuttering and allowed to dry.

cobble [De]. Medium to large-sized particles of more than 64 mm and less than 256 mm across forming constituent components of GRAVEL, including both natural and anthropogenic gravel. One of the principal size divisions of gravel which in ascending scale comprise: granular, pebble, cobble, and boulder gravel.

coca [Sp]. Small shrub of the order Linaceae (*Erythroxylon coca*), the dried leaves contain the alkaloid cocaine and can be chewed as a stimulant. Native to wide areas of South America below about 1200 m above sea level. Domesticated by *c*.2500 BC.

cockpit [MC]. A place of entertainment common in later medieval and post-medieval times comprising a small round arena in which cockfights were held, surrounded by a viewing area for spectators. Some examples are covered by a building, but as earthworks cockpits are usually circular depressions up to 40 m in diameter and 2–3 m deep. In Britain the sport was made illegal in AD 1849.

Cody Phase [CP]. One of a number of cultural subdivisions of the Archaic Stage hunter-gatherer communities occupying the Great Plains of North America, broadly dating to the period 7000–6000 BC. Characterized by ex-

quisitely made chipped stone points and a distinctive kind of off-angled knife.

Coedès, George (1886–1969) [Bi]. French archaeologist well known for his work in southeast Asia. He spent most of his career in French Indochina and Siam, during which time he discovered and explored in some detail the Srivijaya empire of Indonesia. Amongst more than 300 publications, he is best known for his synthesis of the early states in Indonesia first published in French in 1944 and later translated into English as *The Indianized states of southeast Asia* (1969, Honolulu: East-West Centre). In 1946, after seventeen years in Hanoi, he went to Paris where he was appointed Professor of Southeast Asian History at L'École des Langues Orientales. There he stayed and retained the position of curator of the Musée d'Ennery, until his death. Coedès' personal library, a collection of more than 6000 volumes, is now housed with the Australian National University in Canberra.

[Bio.: A. Nugent, 1996, Asia's French connection: George Coedès and the Coedès collection. *National Library of Australia News*, 6(4), 6–8]

coffer [Co]. The sunken panels used in decorating marble ceilings in important Greek and Roman buildings.

coffin [Ar]. A wooden box used to contain a human corpse prior to burial and usually deposited in the grave or cremated with the body. Many different kinds of coffin can be recognized from archaeological evidence, including plank-built examples (sometimes represented only by the nails that pinned the planks together) and MONOXYLOUS COFFINS made from one piece of timber. Coffins are culturally highly distinctive.

Cogidubnus [Na]. Client king of the Atrebatic people in the early years of Roman rule, he styled himself Tiberius Claudius Cogidubnus after the Emperor Claudius. Cogidubnus remained loyal to Rome throughout his life and may have been rewarded with the Fishbourne palace.

cognition [Th]. Human thought processes involving perception, reasoning, and remembering.

cognitive archaeology [Th]. A branch of archaeology that is primarily concerned with the study of past ways of thinking and symbolic structures from patterns in material culture.

cognitive processualism [Th]. A school of archaeological thinking that combines a broad processual approach with the integration of cognitive and symbolic factors and the recognition that ideology is an active organizational force in any society.

cohort [De]. A unit of the Roman army. A legionary cohort usually consisted of 480 men, although the First Cohort was of double strength. Auxiliary cohorts were units 500 or 1000 strong which were either wholly infantry (*cohors peditata*) or consisted of both infantry and some mounted troops (*cohors equitata*).

coil pot [Ar]. A type of ceramic vessel made using a technique whereby the pot is formed gradually by adding to a spiral of thin, sausage-like coils of clay, which are smoothed out afterwards to form the walls of the pot.

coin (coinage) [Ar]. A metal token, usually a disc, with specific weight and value, usually stamped with designs and inscriptions. The earliest known coins in the world were minted by the kingdom of LYDIA in the Near East in the 7th century BC. The coins, made of electrum, were simply pieces of metal of standardized weight stamped with designs and later inscriptions to identify the issuing authority. It is not exactly certain how they were initially used, but it was probably for high-level ceremonial exchange rather than everyday trade. After Cyrus the Great gained control of Lydia in the 6th century BC the ACHAEMENID Persians adopted a gold coinage that typically had a portrait of their king on one side and a punch mark on the other. The Greek cities of Asia Minor also copied the Lydian idea for coins in the 7th century, after which the idea spread widely throughout Greece. The first Roman coins were struck in the early 3rd century BC, initially in precious metals but by the later 3rd century in bronze as the *as* and the *denarius* in silver. The 4th-century BC staters of Phillip II and Alexander III of Macedon provided the prototypes for coins in Europe which developed their own sequence based on the use of CELTIC ART and local designs.

In the Far East, coinage developed in India in the 5th century BC through contacts with Persian/Achaemenid coinage by Mauryans and Kushans. In China shells and other small items were used as money down to the Zhou Dynasty and beyond, but from the 3rd century BC onwards round coins with a central square hole began to circulate.

coin balance [Ar]. Small lightweight scales used by merchants for checking the weight of coins offered in exchange. This was important because the value of a coin was in part determined by its metal content. Because precious metals such as gold and silver were used in making coins in order to retain their value, a good trade could be made by clipping off small amounts of metal from many coins to produce forged coins or other items.

Colchester, Essex, UK [Si]. The Roman city was established as the first *colonia* in Britain in AD 49. Situated beside the River Colne in southern Essex, the site has been investigated through many excavations by Mortimer Wheeler, Christopher Hakes, Philip Crummy, and others since the 1920s. It is now known that the site lies adjacent to and partly overlapping the extensive late Iron Age tribal *oppidum* of the CATUVELLAUNI, known as Camulodunum, who occupied the region down to the Roman conquest. A military fortress was built adjacent to Camulodunum in AD 44, probably occupied by the 20th Legion. In AD 49 the emperor Claudius visited the newly conquered province and established the town of Colonia Claudia Victricensis, with a colossal temple dedicated to him. The city was modelled on classical lines and was the embodiment of Roman colonial power in the newly annexed province. The town was extensively damaged during the Boudiccan revolts of AD 60, but was rebuilt. Walls were added in the 2nd century AD, one of the most impressive gates being the Balkerne gate on the west side of the town.

[Sum.: P. Crummy, 1997, *City of victory*. Colchester: Colchester Archaeological Trust]

collagen [Ge]. The major protein of bone constituting about 20 per cent by weight in fresh bone. The organic component of bone used in radiocarbon dating.

collared urn [Ar]. A type of early and middle Bronze Age CINERARY URN found extremely widely in the British Isles. Although there are a range of forms, the basic characteristics include a small flat base, a conical body, and a heavy overhanging rim or collar which is usually ornamented with incised or impressed decoration. Two main body forms are represented: bi-partite vessels and tri-partite vessels. The origin of these vessels is probably to be found in the Fengate wares of the British late Neolithic PETERBOROUGH series. Collared urns appear around 2000 BC and are replaced by other styles of urn with continental affinities before 1500 BC. Ian Longworth provided a two-fold typological division that reflected something of the chronological development of the tradition as a whole: the 'primary series' and the 'secondary series'.

collective burial (collective tomb) [De]. A deposit containing multiple burials within a single context, often the result of successive deposition over a long period of time.

college [MC]. In medieval and early post-medieval times a college was an establishment built to house a community of secular clergy sharing a degree of common life that was less strictly controlled than that within a monastery. Colleges were often founded under patronage but financed through the income of the priests and canons within them that derived from tithes or other kinds of income from the manors and villages they served. Many colleges included an educational element to their work, and it is this which has survived down into modern times. The monastic roots of ancient colleges can be seen in their arrangement around a cloister or quadrangle, the presence of a church or chapel, and the existence of extensive accommodation and domestic offices.

Collingwood, Robin George (1889–1943) [Bi]. British philosopher and archaeologist best known for his work on Roman Britain. Born in the Lake District, he was educated at Rugby before going up to Oxford to read Moderations and Greats at Pembroke College. From that time on, his life had two parallel tracks. Pembroke College elected him as a Fellow and Tutor to teach philosophy. His work in this area was considerable, including studies into the nature of history. This formed the subject of his inaugural lecture to the University of Oxford on 28 October 1935 and was later published as *The historical imagination* (1935, Oxford: Clarendon Press); later works

on the subject include *The idea of history* (1946, Oxford: Clarendon Press) and *Essays in the philosophy of history* (1965, Austin: University of Texas Press). Meanwhile, Professor F. J. HAVERFIELD picked out Collingwood's artistic and archaeological interests and scholarly gifts and persuaded him to help illustrate articles on the Roman forts of northern Britain. Numerous further studies of archaeological remains followed and Collingwood developed deep expert knowledge not only of the inscriptions and topography that underpinned his early work, but the whole archaeology of the province in Roman times such as can be seen in his publications *Archaeology of Roman Britain* (1930, London: Methuen) and *Roman Britain and the English settlement* (1945, Oxford: OUP).

[Abio.: 1939, *Autobiography*, Oxford: OUP (reprinted by Penguin, 1944)]

colluvium [Ge]. General term for the accumulations of sediment carried by gravity down hill slopes, including material in the process of down-slope movement on hill sides, material trapped by barriers on hill slopes (included that behind fences, walls, or in lynchets), and deposits that build up at the foot of steep slopes and cliffs, generally in the form of fans and wedges. Old ground surfaces are often sealed beneath deposits of colluvium and can be especially important for archaeological preservation where the mechanisms that have given rise to the liberation of mobile sediments at the top of a slope (e.g. deforestation, cultivation) post-date the active use of the ground surface at the bottom.

colonia (pl. *coloniae*) [MC]. The Latin name for the highest rank of a Roman chartered town. A *colonia's* inhabitants were Roman citizens who governed themselves according to a constitution modelled on that of Rome itself. In provinces like Britain, *coloniae* were founded by granting land to legionary veterans. In the later Roman period, the title might be awarded as an honour to some particularly important settlement. York, for example, was made a *colonia*, probably in the early 3rd century AD in recognition of its pre-eminent position in the north of England.

colonialism [Th]. The process whereby western nations established their rule in parts of the world away from their home territories.

Colonial Phase [CP]. A general term referring to the period *c.*AD 550–900 in North America, being one of the five main cultural-historical stages defined for the archaeology of south-western parts of the USA. Succeeding the Pioneer Phase and preceding the Sedentary Phase, the Colonial Phase is characterized by the expansion of agriculturalist communities whose origins lay in the Pioneer Phase. Increasingly sophisticated irrigation was developed so that two harvests a year could be taken.

colour chart [Ge]. *See* MUNSELL COLOUR CHART.

colour-coated ware [De]. Pottery which has been dipped into a slip rich in iron compounds. The colour of the slip varies (usually red, brown, dark green, or blackish), but is generally darker than the main fabric, and occasionally the surface has a metallic lustre. These wares, although produced earlier, became very popular in the Roman world in the 3rd and 4th centuries AD.

Colt Hoare, Sir Richard *See* HOARE SIR RICHARD COLT.

Columbanus, St [Na]. Irish monk who established monasteries in Francia and in AD 612 at Bobbio in northern Italy. He died *c.*AD 615.

column [Co]. An architectural feature which is both structural and decorative: a cylindrical pillar of wood or stone composed of three parts, a base, a shaft, and a capital. In large stone examples the shaft may be made in several segments or **drums** pinned together.

comb [Ar]. A toothed strip or block of wood, bone, stone, or metal. Such implements have a wide distribution across time and space, and a wide range of functions that include: hairdressing, carding wool, compacting the weft during weaving, and decorating pottery.

comb-impressed decoration (comb-stamping/combed ornamentation) [De]. On a pot, a repetitive series of decorative stabbing marks made with a toothed implement. *See also* COMBING.

combing [De]. On a pot, decoration made with a comb, which is drawn across the vessel to form linear, diagonal, or wavy patterns.

comes [De]. A Latin term, usually translated as 'count'; a *comes* was a title used for a commander of the Roman field army in the 4th century AD. Theodosius, who was sent to Britain after the Barbarian Conspiracy of AD 367 had the title of *comes*. The commander of the 'Saxon Shore' forts is referred to as a *comes* in the *Notitia Dignitatum*, although the officer in charge of frontier troops was more usually known as a *dux*, or duke.

comitatenses [De]. Latin term for the soldiers of the *comitatus*, or imperial field army, probably created during the reign of Constantine. They were largely heavily armed cavalry and since they were not tied to a particular province, as the legions had been, they gave the emperor a new flexibility in his military activities.

comites [De]. Latin term meaning 'companions', referring to those who accompanied the emperors on their travels. In the military reorganization of the early 4th century AD, the name was given to high military and civil officials. *See also* COMES.

comitium [MC]. Latin term for a building in the centre of a Roman town (often near the forum) used for voting and political meetings.

commandery [MC]. **1.** A small monastic house of the military orders. **2.** A military establishment constructed as the base from which newly conquered areas were administered during the Han Dynasty in China.

Commodus [Na]. Roman emperor, AD 180–92.

common bean [Sp]. A leguminous plant of the order Leguminosae (*Phaseolus vulgaris*) with edible seeds in a long pod. Native over wide areas in Central and South America. Domesticated from *c.*5000 BC and introduced to Europe in AD 1597.

common-sense beliefs [Ge]. Widely shared beliefs about the social or natural worlds held by lay members of society.

community [De]. A general term in archaeology that is applied to the tangible remains of a group of people who together occupy a settlement or region at any one particular period.

competition [Ge]. A concept taken from ecology and applied in archaeology with reference to the struggle of different species to occupy the most advantageous locations in a given territory.

competitive tendering [Ge]. The process, widely used in the commissioning of archaeological work, whereby a detailed specification of works is circulated to a number of potential contractors (typically three or four) each of whom bids for the work by providing a tender document that includes such matters as a price for the job, a timetable, and an explanation of how it will be carried out. The person commissioning the work is free to select between the tenders supplied, although certain public bodies may be forced to select the cheapest on grounds of principle. Many private organizations select on the basis of quality, reliability, projected speed of operations, and track record rather than price.

complex [Ge]. A rather general term used in archaeology to refer to a chronological subdivision of broad groups of defined artefact types such as stone tools or pottery. A recurrent configuration of elements or entities within a larger system.

component [Ge]. In North American archaeology this term refers to a culturally homogenous stratigraphic unit within a site. Defined by W. C. McKern in 1939 as 'the manifestation of a given archaeological focus at a specific site'. Thus a site with one period of occupation will have just one component; a site occupied five times will have five components. A component is site-specific and broadly equates with the concept of a 'phase' in European archaeology.

composite bow [Ar]. *See* BOW.

composite order [De]. In architecture, a combination of the Corinthian capital's rows of acanthus leaves with the volutes, slightly reduced in size, of the Ionic Order. A late development within the classical world.

composite tool [De]. A tool which combines different materials such as a bone harpoon with stone points and barbs set in it, or a wooden arrow with a shaped stone point at the tip.

computer simulation [Te]. *See* SIMULATION.

concentric stone circle [MC]. A type of late Neolithic STONE CIRCLE found in northwestern Europe in which two or more rings of pillars are set inside one another with a common centre. The most famous example is STONEHENGE, WILTSHIRE, UK, where in Phase 3 there are four concentric rings that focus on the altar stone.

conchoidal fracture [De]. A term that describes the way in which flint and other silica-based isotropic materials behave when hit by a hard object or are subject to great pressure. Because the material has the same physical properties in all directions, ripples radiate outwards from the point of percussion or applied pressure, appearing fairly clearly on the ventral surface of a detached flake or blade, generally resembling the surface of a mussel shell.

cone beaker [Ar]. Type of Anglo-Saxon glass drinking vessel made in the form of an elongated cone. Mainly 5th to 7th century AD.

coneygree [MC]. *See* WARREN.

conjoining [De]. *See* REFITTING.

conjunctive approach [Th]. A methodological alternative to traditional normative archaeology developed by Walter Taylor in the 1940s in which the full range of a culture system should be taken into account when considering explanatory models.

conservation [Th]. **1.** A philosophy underpinning approaches to the management of environmental and archaeological resources which promotes a positive relationship between change and preservation. As such it is an anthropocentric philosophy in which it is accepted that the environment is instrumental in the fulfilment of human desires, and the importance of the environment can be justified in terms of what it can provide for humans. All resources should therefore be used for the greatest good of the greatest number of people, and that where resources are scarce some should be held back for future generations. Although conservation is often seen only in terms of preservation, protection, and trying to prevent change, this is a rather narrow view of a philosophy that emphasizes the dynamic rather than the static. **2.** The practice of arresting the physical, chemical, or biological decay of objects and materials when they change environments (e.g. being taken out of the ground) or when the environments to which they have stabilized themselves change.

conservation archaeology [Ge]. A term popularized by Michael Schiffer and George Gumerman through a book with the title *Conservation archaeology* (1977, London and New York: Academic Press), which explores approaches to the utilization of cultural remains to their fullest scientific and historic extent and for greatest public benefit. *See also* ARCHAEOLOGICAL RESOURCE MANAGEMENT.

Constans [Na]. Roman emperor, AD 337–50.

Constantine I [Na]. Roman emperor, AD 306.

Constantine II [Na]. Roman emperor, AD 337–40.

Constantine III (Flavius Claudius) [Na]. Roman emperor who was proclaimed by the army in Britain in AD 407 and who crossed to Gaul where he founded an independent Gallic empire based on the southern French town of Arles. His usurpation was legitimized in 409 by Honorius who was hard pressed by the Visigoths. However, Alaric's death allowed the Roman authorities to defeat and kill Constantine and disperse his followers. He died c.AD 411.

Constantinople, Turkey [Si]. *See* BYZANTIUM.

Constantius [Na]. Roman emperor, AD 305–6.

construction trench [Co]. The linear hole that is dug to provide a solid footing for a wall. Such trenches are as wide as the wall will eventually be and are usually excavated to the point where a solid and stable substrate exists. The full width of the trench is then typically filled with a rubble footing onto the centre of which the wall is set. Once the construction of the wall has taken it above ground level the open parts of the construction trench on either side are backfilled, often with building debris and rubbish from the general vicinity. Such trenches are important to identify in archaeological excavations because they show the level within the stratigraphy at

which construction of a wall or structure began. Also known as a foundation trench or a bedding trench. *See also* ROBBER TRENCH.

context [Ge]. **1.** A generic term for the smallest identifiable stratigraphic unit recognized in an excavation. Contexts may be **positive** in the sense of an accumulation or deposit of some kind, or **negative** where they represent a cut or the removal of something. In single-context excavation all finds, samples, and records are directly linked to the contexts identified during the excavation process. **2.** The position of an archaeological find in time and space, established by measuring and assessing its associations, matrix, and provenance. The assessment includes the study of what has happened to the find since it was buried in the ground. **3.** The physical and cultural circumstances surrounding the deposition of archaeological material and the formation of archaeological deposits.

context sheet [Eq]. A form widely used in single-context excavations for recording and describing each recognized stratigraphic unit.

contextual archaeology [Th]. An approach to archaeological interpretation proposed by Ian Hodder in the mid 1980s in which emphasis is placed on methods of identifying and studying contexts in order to understand meaning. This involves two lines of enquiry. The first is to consider the environmental and behaviour context of action; understanding an object, for example, by placing it in relation to the larger functioning whole from which it is drawn. Second, it involves looking at the networks of associations that objects were placed within in the past and attempting to read meaning from such groupings as if the objects were words in text. The analogy here is that words on their own mean relatively little; it is only when they are put together in structured ways that the overall meaning becomes clear.

contour fort [De]. A HILLFORT that is constructed in such a way that its ramparts precisely follow the natural contours of the landform on which it is built.

contract [Ge]. A legally binding agreement between two or more parties in which there is an acceptance by one party of an offer made by the other party, there is evidence that the acceptance is intentional, and there is some kind of consideration or benefit that one party must confer on the other in return for the benefit received. Archaeological work is increasingly regulated by contracts which variously take the form of 'standard form contracts' for regular and routine work; 'design and execute contracts' in which the contractor devises a programme of work, agrees it with the other parties, and then carries it out; and 'fixed-price contracts' where a contractor agrees to carry out an agreed piece of work for an agreed sum.

contract archaeologist [Ge]. A professional archaeologist whose work programme comprises a series of archaeological projects carried out on behalf of third parties according to the terms of legally binding contracts. Such contracts are usually won through the process of COMPETITIVE TENDERING.

contracted burial [De]. *See* BURIAL SITE.

contradiction [Ge]. A term used by Karl Marx to refer to mutually antagonistic tendencies in a society.

control [Ge]. A statistical or experimental means of holding some variables constant in order to examine the causal influence of others.

contubernium (pl. *contubernia*) [Ge]. A Roman tent party—a group of eight men who shared a tent while the legion was on campaign, and two rooms when in barracks.

conventional radiocarbon age [Ge]. The laboratory determination of the antiquity of organic materials estimated by RADIOCARBON DATING. The conventional radiocarbon age is the standard way for reporting determinations and should take the form, as a minimum, of an age estimate in years before the present (BP), a standard deviation, and the laboratory code for the sample tested (e.g. 4678 ± 70 BP HAR-000). It is often useful to indicate what kind of material provided the source sample (e.g. charcoal, wood, bone, or shell). There are a number of assumptions implicit in the citation of a conventional radiocarbon age, for example that the Libby half-life for ^{14}C of 5568 years was used; that AD 1950 is the reference year zero; that 0.95 NBS oxalic acid provided the modern reference

standard; and that radiocarbon years BP are the units used to express the age. *See also* CALIBRATION and CORRECTED AGE.

convergence [Ge]. The production of similar final states from originally different starting points or conditions. For example, the more economically stable a society becomes, the more it resembles other industrialized countries.

Cook, Captain James (1728–79) [Bi]. British navigator, explorer, and ethnographer whose records of first contacts between Europeans and aboriginal communities in the Pacific region are an important source of information for archaeologists. Born in Marton, Yorkshire, he joined the navy in 1755, becoming master of the *Mercury* in 1759. Between 1769 and his death in 1779 he made three voyages of exploration to the Pacific, especially Polynesia, Melanesia, and Australia. Although Cook was not always the first to discover these islands he was one of the most thorough explorers in terms of describing and recording what he saw. He died in some kind of skirmish with native tribes on 14 February 1779 in the Hawaiian Islands.

[Bio.: J. C. Beaglehole, 1974, *The life of Captain James Cook*. Stanford: Stanford University Press]

cooking pot [De]. A term usually used for jars or bowls which are known from soot encrustation to have been used for cooking.

coolamon [Ar]. Australian aboriginal carrying dish made of wood or bark.

copal [Ma]. Incense made from resin used extensively during religious ceremonies in Mesoamerica from Maya times through to the present day.

Copán, Honduras [Si]. Large Lowland Maya city believed to have been one of the most important intellectual and artistic centres of Maya culture. Situated above a tributary of the Río Motagua, Copán has been the subject of an international research programme in recent decades. The site was founded by the Olmec who came to the area to exploit jade. The principal temples rest on an artificial acropolis. Among them is the Temple of the Hieroglyphic Stairway, constructed in the 8th century AD with a stairway, every one of whose 63 steps is embellished on the risers with a text of over 2500 glyphs. The ball-court at Copán is the most perfect in Mesoamerica.

[Rep.: G. Willey, R. Leventhal, and W. Fash, 1978, Maya settlement in the Copán Valley. *Archaeology*, 34, 32–43; W. Fash, 1991, *Scribes, warriors and kings: the city of Copán and the ancient Maya*. London: Thames & Hudson]

copper [Ma]. One of the first metals (Cu) to be exploited by human communities. In its native form it can be worked without prior treatment. It was later extracted from a range of ores: carbonates (including MALACHITE and azurite); oxides (including cuprite and melaconite); and sulphides (including chalcanthite). Shaping could be done by hammering, casting, or a combination of the two. Copper provides the main constituent for a number of alloys, the most widely used being BRONZE. The development of copper metallurgy happened independently in several parts of the world: in western Asia around 6000 BC; in Europe around 4000 BC; in the Longshan Culture of China around 2500 BC; in South America around 1500 BC in Peru, Bolivia, and Ecuador; AD 100 in central America; and in North America amongst the Old Copper Cultures of the Great Lakes region around 3000 BC.

Copper Age [CP]. *See* CHALCOLITHIC.

coppice woodland [MC]. Woodland consisting of deciduous trees cut periodically to near ground level, usually in strict rotation, to provide straight poles for fences, hurdles, and other purposes.

coprolites [Ma]. Human or animal excrement (faeces) preserved usually by desiccation, fossilization, or in waterlogged conditions. *See also* CESS PIT.

coprology [Ge]. The study of preserved human and animal faeces.

Coptic [Ge]. The language of ancient Egypt written in Greek letters with the addition of a few characters from the Demotic script. In art the term applies to forms and designs developed by Egyptians after the introduction of Christianity. The influence of both the art and the language has persisted to this day through the Coptic church.

coracle [Ar]. Traditional, highly manoeuvrable, keel-less bowl-shaped light water craft used for fishing and transport on the rivers of western Britain and Ireland. Comprising a wickerwork or lath frame over which greased cloth, leather, or hide is stretched, coracles are generally built to carry one person, the exact shape being particular to the area in which they are made: the majority, however, are roughly oval in outline with one end slightly flattened and one end taken to a rounded point.

coral [Ma]. A hard red, pink, or white calcareous substance secreted by a variety of marine polyps for support and to provide habitations. In ancient times it was collected from the Mediterranean and the Indian Ocean and extensively through the Old World for use in decorating metal jewellery such as brooches.

corbel [Co]. A stone block or timber projecting from a wall to provide the seating for a beam or rafter supporting an upper floor, balcony, or projection. Usually found in groups and often ornamented.

corbelled roof (corbelled vault) [De]. A roof constructed using stone slabs that progressively overlap each other to create a false vault or dome, the top being finished with a single capstone which spans the remaining hole. The technique was very widely used in the construction of PASSAGE GRAVES in Atlantic Europe during the 5th to 3rd millennia BC and in the construction of the Mycenaean tholos tombs in the 3rd and 2nd millennia BC.

Corcoran, John Xavier Willington Patrick (1927–75) [Bi]. British prehistorian and authority on Neolithic chambered tombs in northwest Europe. Born in Cheshire, he attended school in Birkenhead before studying archaeology at Manchester University. He presented a Ph.D. thesis on the Carlingford Culture of Ireland and developed a great interest in the archaeology of western Britain. He became Staff Tutor in Archaeology in the Department of Extra-Mural Studies in the University of London in 1957, before being appointed to a lectureship in archaeology in the newly formed Department of Archaeology in the University of Glasgow in 1961. In 1971 he was made Senior Lecturer. He published many works on the Neolithic period and the Iron Age of northern Britain but is best known for his papers showing that many Neolithic chambered tombs were multi-period constructions. He was elected a Fellow of the Society of Antiquaries in 1958. He died from a heart attack at the age of 48.

[Obit.: *Current Archaeology*, 5.2, 37]

cordate (cordate handaxe) [Ar]. A general term used to describe the regular heart-shaped, flat profiled form of the bifaces characteristic of the MOUSTERIAN in western Europe.

Corded Ware Culture [CP]. General term applied to a wide range of late Neolithic and early Bronze Age communities in central and northern Europe who used cord-impressed decoration on their pottery, especially beakers and round-bodied amphorae, during the later 3rd millennium BC. Their material culture often includes perforated stone battleaxes and single grave burial under a small round barrow or KURGAN. Once believed to represent a series of pan-European migrations from the steppe region of southern Russia, and credited with the spread of INDO-EUROPEAN languages, it is now recognized that the tradition of making and using corded ware is the result of many local developments that shared certain common ideas. Corded Ware Culture communities are now seen as sedentary agriculturalists. In Scandinavia the Corded Ware Culture is known as the SINGLE GRAVE CULTURE.

cordiform handaxes [Ar]. *See* CORDATE.

cordon [De]. A thin raised band of clay which is applied horizontally around the exterior body of a pottery vessel prior to firing, either for ornament or to aid grip.

cordoned urns [Ar]. A type of middle Bronze Age pottery found mainly in the northern parts of the British Isles during the 2nd millennium BC, probably derived from COLLARED URNS. Cordoned urns are generally tall straight-sided vessels with a flat base, slightly flaring body and a simple rim. Their name derives from the fact that the outer face is decorated with applied cordons which often define regions of the surface which are ornamented with incised decoration.

cord-ornamented pottery [De]. Ceramic vessels whose outer faces are decorated with motifs created by pressing twisted cord into the soft clay surface before the pot was fired.

Sometimes short individual motifs are represented (also called 'maggot impressions') where a length of cord has been wrapped around a small stick and then used as a stamp. In other cases long pieces of cord have been closely coiled around the pot and then pressed into the surface.

cord rig [MC]. The archaeological remains resulting from a technique of spade cultivation practised from later prehistoric through to medieval times in the uplands of northern England and southern Scotland. Cord rig is recognized in the field as a corrugated ground surface comprising numerous narrow parallel ridges of soil up to 1 m across and 0.15 m high, separated by slight furrows. It generally occurs in small plots up to 0.5 ha in extent, and is most easily identified from aerial photographs. Cord rig has been recognized running underneath, and thus pre-dating, HADRIAN'S WALL, in Northumberland.

corduroy tracks [MC]. Wooden trackways made from short logs laid parallel to each other side to side, thus forming a continuous corrugated surface.

core [Ar]. **1.** The piece of stone which a stone-knapper works so as to produce flakes, blades, or core tools. **2.** [Ge]. An intact solid cylinder-shaped sample of sediment, stone, or wood collected with a coring device or hollow drill. Deep-sea cores and ice cores provide important records of climatic change and sediment accumulation. Cores taken from archaeological sites provide a quick guide to the main stratigraphic subdivisions. Cores from peat bogs can be sampled for pollen analysis. Cores taken from substantial timbers are used in dendrochronology.

core–periphery model [Th]. The economic and political relationship existing between one more highly developed country or region (the 'centre') and the less developed countries or regions in contact with it (the 'periphery'). *See also* WORLD SYSTEM.

core rejuvenation flake (core tablet) [Ar]. A roughly round slightly wedge-shaped flake of flint with the remains of flake beds around the outside edge. Such flakes are the product of extending the life of a core that has become uneven or difficult to work but which still has the potential to yield further blades.

core tools [De]. Artefacts manufactured by modifying (usually by flaking) a single block of flint or stone to reach the desired shape. Typical core tools include axes, choppers, and adzes.

core tool and scraper tradition [CP]. A stone tool industry found widely across Australia and Tasmania dating to the late Pleistocene and early Holocene. Characterized by hand-held steep-edged flake scrapers, chopping tools, and horseshoe cores.

Corieltauvi (Coritani) [CP]. The late Iron Age tribe living in between the rivers Trent and Nene in central England at the time of the Roman conquest in AD 43. Once known in the archaeological literature as the Coritani, their name has been corrected in the light of new epigraphic evidence. The tribe issued coinage from about 70 BC with the first name of a king, Vep, appearing about 10 BC. Some connection with the Roman empire prior to the conquest is represented by imported materials at major sites such as Old Sleaford and Dragonby, Lincolnshire.

Corinthian Order (Corinthian Style) [De]. Greek architectural style characterized by columns with a diameter-to-height ratio of 1:10, and an enlarged capital (uppermost part) decorated with sculptured foliage, often acanthus leaves. This style was extensively used by the Romans. The Corinthian Order capital differed from the Ionic in being elaborately decorated with two or three tiers of carved acanthus leaves below small volutes. The considerable advantage over the Ionic lies in the four concave sides of the abacus, which give it, in plan, a cushion shape. Supported at the sharply pointed four corners by pairs of small volutes, this abacus solves the problem involved in the form of the Ionic capital, where the front and side views are different.

Coritani [CP]. *See* CORIELTAUVI.

corn-drier (corn-drying oven) [MC]. A common form of structure found on Romano-British sites comprising a T- or Y-shaped channel with signs of burning and a hearth area at one end. The channels are often lined with stone or chalk and are clearly flues along which warm air passed before being dispersed beyond the junction of the channel. Careful examination of the areas round about suggest that these features are the subsurface elements of an above-ground timber structure, and because cereal grain has been found in the flues they are often reported as corn-driers. Recent experimental work by Peter Reynolds and others has suggested, however, that they were in fact MALTING FLOORS.

cornice [Co]. The uppermost projecting element of a classical building, immediately below the roof line.

cornice rim [De]. On rough-cast and other beakers, a projecting rim, decoratively moulded, as in an architectural cornice.

Cornish urn (Cornish handled urn) [Ar]. Type of middle Bronze Age pottery vessels found in the extreme southwest of Britain and dating to the 2nd millennium BC. Generally rather barrel-shaped in profile and often with a highly decorated upper body, these large vessels commonly have strap handles. The decoration includes herringbone and lattice patterns, in the main executed in twisted cord and impressed techniques. Related to Trevisker ware in southwestern England.

Cornovii [CP]. The late Iron Age tribe living in the northern part of the Welsh Marches of western England and Wales at the time of the Roman conquest in AD 43. Their tribal capital was possibly at the Wrekin, Shropshire, some 6 km east of Wroxeter (Viroconium) where the *civitas capital* was established in the later 1st century AD. The settlement pattern of the area is dominated by substantial hillforts in the late 1st millennium BC and there seems to have been little contact with the tribes living further to the southeast.

corrected age [Ge]. A CONVENTIONAL RADIO-CARBON AGE that has been corrected for specific factors that can influence the recorded level of ^{14}C in a sample, for example the reservoir effect (marine reservoir); industrial effect; or atomic bomb effect.

corrugated [De]. A ripple effect in the wall of a vessel, resembling a series of grooves and cordons.

Cortaillod Culture [CP]. Early Neolithic communities occupying much of Switzerland during the 4th millennium BC, named after the lake village of Cortaillod beside Lake

Neuchâtel. Many settlements of the Cortaillod Culture were situated beside lakes or on the edge of wetland, with the result that remains are often well preserved. The houses were timber-framed with clay walls and thatched roofs. Their material culture included numerous birch-bark utensils and containers, fibre nets and ropes, and dark burnished round-based pottery. The subsistence base focused on mixed farming supplemented by hunting, fishing, and collecting wild foodstuffs including fruits and nuts. The Cortaillod Culture was succeeded by the Pfyn Culture in eastern Switzerland and the Horgen Culture in western Switzerland.

cortex [Ge]. The natural weathered crust found around the outside of a flint nodule.

cosmology [Th]. The world view and belief system of a community based upon their understanding of order in the universe.

costrel [De]. A type of medieval ceramic flask. The most common types are roughly round in shape with a slight neck into which a stopper was pushed. These were made from the mid 1st millennium AD and occur in Merovingian, Carolingian, and later contexts. Rather less common are those shaped like a barrel on its side with a small neck and handles on the top and small stud-like feet on the bottom. The body is often rilled to imitate a barrel. These tend to be later, 13th to 16th century AD in date and were probably made in France.

Cotswold–Severn long barrow (Cotswold–Severn tomb) [MC]. A regional type of middle Neolithic LONG BARROW found on the north Wessex Downs, Cotswold Hills, South Wales coast, and Brecon Beacons in the west of England and eastern Wales. Dating to the 4th millennium BC, these long barrows have rectangular or trapezoidal mounds, shallow forecourts at the higher and wider ends of the mounds, and in some cases an elaborated façade of large upright slabs. Two patterns of chamber location are represented: terminal chambers in a simple linear pattern with cells opening off a central passage; and lateral chambers where short passages lead into the body of the mound from the side to give access to a simple polygonal or rectangular chamber. The material used in constructing the mounds was derived from flanking quarries. In the areas where these barrows occur

the stone is suitable for dry-stone walling and the outer cairn walls of the barrows themselves are typically well constructed. Burial is by inhumation; grave goods are rare and mainly confined to personal objects. Excavations by Alan Saville at Hazleton, Gloucestershire, in the early 1980s showed that here at least bodies were first placed in the outer part of the entrance passage and that as the corpse decayed and room was needed for new burials parts were gradually moved further and further into the tomb. Also known as Severn–Cotswold long barrows.

cottage [MC]. A small house of medieval and later date occupied on a permanent basis by a single family. Found in villages, hamlets, and as isolated structures in the open countryside, these dwellings are mainly associated with peasants and landless labourers.

cotton [Sp]. Bushy plant (*Gossypinum hirsutum*) with seeds covered in a soft white fibrous substance (lint) that can be made into thread. Native to Mesoamerica and parts of South America. Domesticated by *c*.4300 BC.

Council for British Archaeology (CBA) [Or]. A membership organization founded in 1944 to represent archaeological opinion in Britain, both professional and amateur. It is an independent charity which works to advance the study and practice of archaeology in Great Britain and Northern Ireland. It seeks to educate and inform the public and to publish the results of research. It operates through its council, which embraces archaeological bodies of all kinds and provides a unique forum for British archaeologists to discuss matters of mutual interest. There are thirteen regional groups of the CBA, including the Council for Scottish Archaeology and CBA Wales.

counter-intuitive thinking [Th]. Thinking which suggests ideas contrary to common-sense assumptions.

counterscarp [Co]. The outer face or slope of the ditch of a fortification.

counterscarp bank [Co]. A small linear mound or bank immediately outside the counterscarp of a hillfort or defensive work.

countersunk handle [De]. A rounded handle partly sunk into the side of a vessel.

courery [MC]. A small subsidiary settlement associated with a CHARTERHOUSE, mainly occupied by lay brothers and worked as a farm to provide food and wealth both for itself and the monastery to which it was connected. Facilities for worship and domestic life were provided within the settlement. In general, coureries were situated fairly close to their mother charterhouse.

court cairn (court tomb) [MC]. A generic name popularized by Ruaidhri De Valéra in the early 1960s referring to a series of LONG BARROWS found especially in northern and central Ireland. The class is characterized by sites with a trapezoidal mound delimited by a stone kerb. Most contain a single oval court at one end with access from the back of the court into chambers which contained human burials. A few examples have a court and chambers at both ends of the mound (double court tombs) while a few contain subsidiary chambers in the back or the sides of the mound. Mainly 4th and early 3rd millennium BC in date. Burials were generally by inhumation, although some cremated remains have been found at excavated sites. Also known as horned cairns.

courtyard house [MC]. Type of late Iron Age house found in Cornwall in the southwest of England dating to the later 1st millennium BC and early 1st millennium AD. Such houses have a cellular plan with a central precinct off which there are two or more chambers. The outer wall is generally curvilinear and irregular in plan. Entry to the central precinct is gained through a single narrow doorway; from the precinct there is access to some but not all of the attached chambers, many of which are interconnecting and can only be entered via another internal room. Courtyard houses are found singly or in village clusters.

courtyard inn [MC]. A traditional style of inn, often originally a coaching inn, where the main buildings are set back from the street and are arranged around an open courtyard.

courtyard villa (courtyard house) [MC]. A type of Roman VILLA found in many parts of the empire distinguished by its characteristic ground plan in which there is a central rectangular courtyard entered by a front gateway, with ranges of rooms on at least one side and sometimes on all four sides. The sides not formed by ranges of rooms are marked by a wall. The courtyard itself can be paved or, more often, planted as a small garden. Some courtyard villas developed out of earlier WINGED CORRIDOR VILLAS through the addition of extra ranges. In general, courtyard villas were amongst the grandest villas and were presumably occupied by the more wealthy landowners.

coved [De]. Provided with a concave moulding.

cover sand [De]. Layers of sand deposited by wind action across areas of countryside to provide a cover deposit over any exposed ground surface or vegetation. The source of the sand is most often coastal dune systems or glacial outwash deposits. Substantial accumulations will sometimes occur with the result that old ground surfaces and any cultural material on them is buried and well sealed. Also known as blow sand layers.

Covesea Phase [CP]. A regional industrial tradition of the EWART PARK PHASE of the British later Bronze Age represented in Scotland and characterized by finds from the Covesea Cave, Grampian.

Coxcatlán Phase [CP]. Third phase of settlement represented in the Tehuacán Valley of Mexico and dating to the period 5000–3400 BC. Characterized by small dry-season camps and larger wet-season camps. Wild and semi-domesticated plants coupled with hunted small game made up the main diet. Maize first appears during this phase, and small gardens were made.

Crambeck ware [Ar]. A type of pottery made at Crambeck, North Yorkshire, which was widely distributed across the north of England and North Wales in the second half of the 4th century AD. Common types include cream-coloured mortaria and parchment wares, imitation Samian forms, and a range of lead-grey kitchen wares.

cranial capacity [De]. Volume of the brain expressed in cubic centimetres.

crannog [MC]. An artificial island usually constructed on a natural shoal or shallow within a lake or wetland by timber piling and laying down brushwood. Clay or plank floors for structures and surfaces are put on the foundation. A causeway typically joins the crannog to the mainland. Such sites are widely found in Ireland and western Scotland and date to between the 4th millennium BC and the 1st millennium AD. *See also* LAKE VILLAGES.

crater [Ar]. A large vessel used during classical times on festive occasions for containing wine or a mixture of wine and water.

Crawford, Osbert Guy Stanhope (1886–1957) [Bi]. British archaeologist who is best known as the founder of the journal *Antiquity* and for his work with aerial photographs. Born in Bombay, India, his mother died soon after he was born and he was brought up in London and later Newbury, Berkshire, by his father's sisters. He was educated at Marlborough College and then went up to Keble College, Oxford, where he started reading Greats but after discovering an interest in archaeology gave this up in favour of a geography diploma. It is clear that he enjoyed neither school nor university. His first tentative steps into archaeological fieldwork with the Wellcome Expedition to the Sudan was cut short by WW1. After a period in the infantry he was attached to the Third Army as a photographer and he then realized a long-standing ambition to work in the Royal Flying Corps. Here he became an observer but was shot down early in 1918. After the war he undertook various short-term jobs in field archaeology.

In 1920 he was appointed as the first Archaeology Officer in the Ordnance Survey. This suited him well, not least because it meant carving out a job for himself in an organization where nothing similar had previously existed. Continuing his work with aerial photography he also worked on the revision of archaeological features depicted on published maps. The aerial photographs that he took or acquired from others in the 1920s and 1930s have since proved to be some of the most valuable records of archaeological sites currently available. One innovation was the production of period maps showing archaeological distributions, one of the first being the *Map of Roman Britain*. Much of this work had to be done single-handedly as he had no assistants, and in the face of unsympathetic official outlooks. In 1927 he founded the international journal *Antiquity*, which he edited

through to his death in 1957. One of his best-known works, a series of aerial photographs of Wessex taken as part of a joint project with Alexander KEILLER, was published in 1928 (*Wessex from the air*. Oxford: Clarendon Press); other publications include *Man and his past* (1921, London: Milford), *Long barrows of the Cotswolds* (1925, Gloucester: John Bellows), and *Archaeology in the field* (1953, London: Phoenix). He was made CBE in 1950 and received several other awards and honours.

[Abio.: 1955, *Said and done*, London: Weidenfeld & Nicolson]

creationism [Th]. The attribution of all matter and biological species to separate acts of creation rather than evolution. Such theories were current during the early centuries of antiquarian and archaeological research, and many reputations were staked and much energy was spent refuting them.

cremation [De]. The practice of burning the dead, variously on a specially constructed above-ground pyre, in a crematorium pit or trench, or occasionally by burning the house in which they lived. There are also many variations in the way that the cremated remains are disposed of. Archaeologically, the most common tradition was to gather up the ashes, place them in a pottery vessel of some kind, and bury the vessel in a pit that may or may not have been covered with a barrow of some kind. However, there are many ways of disposing of cremated remains that leave little or no archaeological evidence and these were probably the most usual in the past.

cremation cemetery [MC]. An area used for the burial or scattering of cremated human remains. In some cases such cemeteries are represented by scatters of cremation-filled pits. *See also* URNFIELD.

cremation urn [Ar]. *See* CINERARY URN.

crenellated [De]. The provision of regular spaces along the top of a wall or parapet through which missiles could be fired.

Creswellian [CP]. British later Upper Palaeolithic cultures of the period 10 000 BC down to 8000 BC, named after the type-site of Creswell Crags, Derbyshire, in central England. The characteristic tools of these cultures are large trapezes, obliquely blunted blades, and small backed blades. They occupied caves as well as open sites, their technologies and perhaps their culture being linked to the Tjongerian and FEDERMESSER industries of the Low Countries and northern Germany; these areas were accessible via what Bryony Coles has termed Doggerland—the dry bed of the North Sea.

Creswell point [Ar]. Type of later Upper Palaeolithic flint tool found in the British Isles, named after examples found at Creswell Crags, Derbyshire, England. Made on a relatively narrow flint blade, one end is worked to produce a slightly elongated trapezoidal form with the long side of the blade left unworked and the shorter side blunted. Possibly used as knife blades.

Crickley Hill, Gloucestershire, UK [Si]. A multi-period hilltop enclosure used intermittently from about 4000 BC onwards. The hilltop is a triangular-shaped spur of some 3.8 ha, and has seemingly not been ploughed since prehistoric times. Extensive excavations were carried out on the site between 1969 and 1993 by Philip Dixon. The earliest main phase of occupation was a causewayed enclosure. After being rebuilt several times this was completely remodelled as a defended enclosure in its latest phase. The site was abandoned in the middle Neolithic, after being attacked and razed. A LONG MOUND was built over the top of the infilled enclosure boundaries. There is some slight evidence for Beaker occupation on the hilltop, but the site was not reoccupied until the construction of an Iron Age hillfort in the 7th century BC. Several phases of rebuilding have been recorded at this structure, each associated with the destruction of the existing fortifications. The site was again abandoned in the 3rd century BC, and was not subsequently re-occupied on a large scale again.

[Sum.: P. Dixon, 1979, A Neolithic and Iron Age site on a hill top in Southern England. *Scientific American*, 241(5), 142–50]

Criss Culture [CP]. See KÖRÖS CULTURE and STARCEVO CULTURE.

critical archaeology [Th]. A theoretical approach to archaeology that assumes that archaeologists have an active impact on their society.

critical theory [Th]. A school of thought derived in part from a disenchantment with classical Marxism and the development of Western Marxism within what became known as the 'Frankfurt School'. Associated with Adorno, Habermas, and Marcuse amongst others, critical theorists aim to uncover the inner workings of a society which they suggest lie concealed from view by a veneer of ideology.

critique [Th]. Not a methodology or body of theory as such but more an attitude which focuses on the social construction of knowledge and is thus very relevant to a self-reflective discipline such as archaeology. At its simplest, critique refers to the questioning element of liberal and academic debate focusing on the open criticism of the opinions and work of others. Critique is also a powerful tradition within western philosophy that focuses on the rational reconstruction of the conditions which make language, cognition, and action possible. As such, critique aims to subject everything to scrutiny, attempting to unveil and debunk while reflecting on the constraints to which people succumb in the process of constructing knowledge.

CRM [Ab]. *See* CULTURAL RESOURCE MANAGEMENT.

croft [MC]. A private field; a small close associated with cottages and usually adjacent to them.

Cro-Magnon Man [De]. A general and rarely used term that refers in a collective way to modern humans, *Homo sapiens sapiens*, of the period 35 000 to 10 000 years ago. The name comes from the type-site of Cro-Magnon in France where, in AD 1868, fossil human remains with AURIGNACIAN material culture were discovered.

Cromerian stage [CP]. A group of deposits representing a geostratigraphic stage within the PLEISTOCENE series of the British QUATERNARY system, named after the site of West Runton near Cromer, Norfolk, and dating to the period 700 000 to 450 000 years ago. The Cromerian is usually interpreted as an interglacial warm period, some Cromerian deposits being stratified below ANGLIAN glacial deposits.

cromlech [MC]. An obsolete term formerly used to describe MEGALITHIC TOMBS. It is derived from the Welsh *crom* meaning 'bent' and *llech* meaning 'flagstone'.

cropmark [De]. In studies of aerial photographs, cropmarks are patterns or variations in the colour or growth rates of cereals or other planted crops (including peas, grass, etc.) that are visible from the air, or on a photographic image taken from the air, and which are usually caused by the differential effects on plant ecology of below-ground disturbances or soil enrichment of some kind. Often these relate to archaeological features such as buried ditches and pits and thus provide a proxy indicator of what lies within or beneath the ground. In especially favourable conditions cropmarks can be seen from ground level.

crosier [Ar]. An elaborately decorated crook-like symbol of office used by bishops and archbishops in the Christian church. Usually considered to be the enshrined staff of the founder of a church or monastery.

crossbow [Ar]. A weapon invented in China in the 3rd or 2nd century BC in which a normal BOW is mounted on a block of wood so that it can be used horizontally and single-handedly. The system was much improved in the 1st century BC with the development of a cocking piece and ratchet so that the string can be drawn with ease and released via a trigger. The crossbow proved ideal for the mounted archers of the nomadic steppe tribes as it could be discharged from the saddle and had a longer range and greater power than conventional bows.

cross bow brooch [Ar]. A plain bow-brooch, often without headplate, attributed to the 4th or early 5th century. Derived from late Roman forms, the cross bow brooch seems to be the ancestor of the more elaborately decorated brooches of the migration period.

cross-cultural [De]. Pertaining to diverse cultures; systematic comparison between several societies.

cross-dating [Th]. The use of commonly recurring objects to date cultures or deposits of unknown date by reference to the occurrence of the same kinds of object in securely dated contexts elsewhere. This method was used in the early 19th century especially to tie the artefact typologies of northern and central Europe into the historically dated civilizations of the eastern Mediterranean.

cross-hall [Co]. Covered assembly area in the headquarters building of a fort.

cross-hatching [De]. *See* LATTICE DECORATION.

crossing [Co]. That part of a cruciform church in which the transepts cross the nave.

cross-ridge dyke [MC]. A bank and ditch, sometimes a ditch between two banks, crossing a ridge or spur of high ground. Such features are often of the later Bronze Age and Iron Age in northwest Europe.

crouched burial [MC]. *See* BURIAL SITE.

crown glass [Ma]. The main method of making sheets of glass in the 18th century AD was to fix a ball of semi-molten glass to the end of a rod and spin it into a disc up to 1.5 m across. This left the characteristic thickened ring where the disc was broken from the rod.

crucible [Ar]. A small clay bowl used for re-melting smelted metal so that it can be poured into a mould.

cruciform brooch [Ar]. A bow-brooch with a small headplate and long footplate. From the headplate protrude three knobs; the footplate is normally shaped into an animal head with eyes and nostrils. Found in Jutland and Holstein from the late 4th century. During the 5th and 6th centuries AD cruciform brooches spread across the North Sea to Britain.

cruck construction [De]. A technique widely used in medieval times for making timber-frame buildings such as houses and barns. The main feature of such buildings is the use of a series of frames made in the shape of an inverted 'V' along the length of the building, each frame, or 'cruck', being made from a pair of large timbers (known as blades) usually cut from the same tree. The base of each cruck is often set on a base pad or low wall. The crucks take the full weight of the roof and also serve to support the walls of the building.

crutch-head pin [Ar]. A type of bronze dress fastener characterized by a simple shaft with a short cross-piece set in the form of a T. Some examples have decoration on the upper part of the shank and head. Dating to the 15th century BC they are found in southern Britain in association with WESSEX CULTURE II graves and on the continent in Rienecke A2 contexts.

cryoturbation [Ge]. Disturbances and the rearrangement of clasts within soils and subsoils as a result of freeze–thaw processes in periglacial conditions. Convection currents and pressure caused by ice crystals in subsoils that refreeze after a seasonal thaw act to rotate stones and soil particles, with the result that they show marked structuring. Such structures, for example ice-wedges, pingos, stripes, stone rings, and involutions, can be misidentified as archaeological features.

cubiculum [Co]. **1.** Latin term for the bedroom in a Roman house. **2.** Latin term for a chamber in a CATACOMB that was used for rites and ceremonies connected with the dead.

Cucenteni Culture (Cucuteni Culture) [CP]. Romanian version of the Neolithic TRIPOLYE CULTURE, named for a type-site west of the River Prut.

Cú Chulainn [Na]. Hero figure whose exploits feature largely and in great detail in the ULSTER CYCLE. A supernatural figure, he is the defender of his tribe, a mortal endowed with superhuman powers. He is possibly the son of the god Lug. His name means 'the hound of Culann'.

Cuello, Belize [Si]. Small Maya farming settlement in northern Belize important as the earliest known site of the Northern Maya. Excavated by Norman Hammond in the period 1975–93, some fourteen major phases were recognized beginning in the middle Pre-Classic, *c.*1200 BC, and ending around AD 300 during the early Classic.

The Swasey/Bladen Phase of the site has red and orange mottled ceramics, associated with tiny cobs of corn, and root crops such as cocoyam and manioc. There is some evidence for early Maya architecture in the form of plastered platforms which would have supported perishable superstructures.

[Rep.: N. Hammond, 1991, *Cuello: An early Maya community in Belize*. Cambridge: CUP]

cuidadela [Co]. A royal compound belonging to a king of the Inca empire, which also served as a mausoleum after his death.

cuirass [Ar]. A piece of armour designed to protect the torso. It comprised both breast and back armour, sometimes shaped to the contours of the chest and back muscles (muscled cuirass). Variously made of laminated linen, leather, sheet-bronze, or iron, or scales of horn, hide, or metal.

cult [De]. A fragmentary religious grouping, to which individuals are loosely affiliated, but which lacks any permanent structure.

cult statue [Ar]. The statue of a god or goddess. Such statues were housed with great dignity in temples.

cultivation [De]. The manipulative production and reproduction of plants as sources of food and raw materials for human benefit. The object of attention is usually the fruit, seed, leaf, or fibrous stem of a plant, sometimes several of these for different purposes.

cultural anthropology [Ge]. One of the four fields of anthropology, focusing on the description and analysis of the forms and styles of social life of past and present human societies. Its subdiscipline, ethnography, systematically describes contemporary societies and cultures.

cultural area [Ge]. In North American archaeology this term refers to broad tracts of land which roughly correspond to ethnographically defined cultural areas recognized by early anthropological work.

cultural ecology [Th]. An approach developed by Julian Steward in the 1930s that focused on the dynamic interactions between human societies and their environments. Within this approach, culture is seen as the primary adaptive mechanism used by human societies to deal with, understand, give meaning to, and generally cope with their environment.

cultural evolution [Th]. A theory similar to that of biological evolution, which argues that human cultures change gradually throughout time, as a result of a number of cultural processes.

cultural materialism [Th]. The theory of cultural causation in which technology, economics, and environment are considered the independent variables.

cultural pluralism [Th]. The coexistence of several subcultures within a given society on equal terms.

cultural process [Th]. A deductive approach to archaeological research that is designed to study the changes and interactions in cultural systems and the processes by which human cultures change throughout time. Processual archaeologists use both descriptive and explanatory models.

cultural relativism [Th]. The position that there is no universal standard to measure cultures by, and that all cultures are equally valid and must be understood in their own terms.

cultural resource management [Ge]. In the USA this term refers to the legally mandated protection of archaeological sites situated on public lands that are threatened with destruction through development of any sort. Extensive laws have been enacted to protect sites on federal lands, but states and some cities have similar legislation. *See* ARCHAEO-LOGICAL RESOURCE MANAGEMENT.

cultural selection [Th]. The process that leads to the acceptance of some cultural traits and innovations that make a culture more adaptive to its environment; somewhat akin to natural selection in biological evolution.

cultural system [Th]. A perspective that thinks of culture and its environment as a number of linked systems in which change occurs through a series of minor, linked variations in one or more of these systems.

cultural tradition [Th]. In archaeology, a distinctive tool kit or technology that lasts a long time—longer than the duration of one culture—at one locality or several localities.

cultural transforms [Th]. *See* FORMATION PROCESSES.

cultural universals [Th]. Values or modes of behaviour shared by all human cultures.

culture [Ge]. Probably one of the most used terms in contemporary archaeology, and broadly derived from anthropology and sociology. The anthropologist E. B. Tylor set the scene in the late 19th century by defining culture as 'that complex whole which includes knowledge, belief, art, law, morals, custom and any other capabilities and habits acquired by man as a member of society'. Thus in a general sense culture is a commonly preferred learned form of behaviour which has been adopted by a given society and which includes distinctive and complicated systems of technology, social organization, thought, cosmology, and ideology. Culture is something that articulates a human society with its environment and, for Leslie White, writing in the late 1950s, could be seen in adaptive functional terms as 'an extrasomatic, temporal continuum of things and events dependent upon symbolling. . . . A mechanism whose function is to make life secure and continuous for groups and individuals of the human species'.

In the purely archaeological sense, the idea of a culture was firmly established in the late 1920s by Gordon Childe whose Marxist perspectives shine through in his proposition that 'we find certain types of remains—pots, implements, ornaments, burial rites and house forms—constantly recurring together. Such a complex of associated traits we shall term a "cultural group" or just a "culture". We assume that such a complex is the material expression of what today we would call a "people".' Thus, for archaeologists, a culture is usually taken to be a constantly recurring assemblage of artefacts which are assumed to be representative of a particular set of activities carried out at a particular time and place. As such, archaeological cultures are defined by archaeologists rather than the original participants.

culture history (cultural-historical approach) [Th]. An approach to archaeological data that orders structures and artefacts into a basic sequence of events in time and space, usually as a generalized description of human achievement under broad period-based headings. Widely regarded as a rather traditional approach to archaeological investigation, the culture history view has been criticized by PROCESSUAL ARCHAEOLOGISTS and POST-PROCESSUAL ARCHAEOLOGISTS for the fact that explanations in terms of migration or invasion are not explanations or understandings at all but merely descriptions of events.

Nonetheless, the development of a robust culture history remains the object of some archaeological work, especially the geographical and chronological mapping of cultures and cultural influences.

culturology [Ge]. The study of culture.

culverhouse [MC]. *See* DOVECOT.

culvert [MC]. A drainage channel, often underground.

Cumancaya Phase [CP]. South American cultural grouping found in the Rio Ucayali area of Amazonia in the period *c*.AD 800–1000. Defined by its ceramics which belong to the Polychrome Horizon of painted wares.

Cumbrian club [Ar]. A term given by L. CHITTY to a distinctive type of large polished stone axe of middle Neolithic date made in the Lake District of northwest England. Also known as a 'Cumbrian-type' stone axe. The main features of a Cumbrian club are its large size (150–380 mm long), broad-butted form, long, narrow proportions, its maximum width more or less in the middle of its length, and a distinct 'waisting' of constriction towards the butt end. All known examples are made of Langdale tuff (Group VI), examples being traded out from the Lake District to most other parts of the British Isles. The large size of these implements suggests they are ceremonial, prestige, or display objects.

cuneiform [De]. The term used to describe early writing in the Middle East (Sumerian, Akkadian and related languages) in which wedge-shaped impressions are left on a clay tablet. It was used from the 3rd through to the 1st millennia BC and is thought to have derived from older Sumerian pictographic script.

Cunnington, Maud (1869–1951) [Bi]. British prehistorian who married into the last of three generations of archaeologists who devoted their time to the exploration of Wiltshire's ancient past. For over 40 years Maud and her husband Benjamin excavated hillforts, barrows, and other sites in central Wiltshire, notably All Cannings Cross (1920–2), Woodhenge (1926–8), and The Sanctuary (1930). In 1931 she was elected the President of Wiltshire Archaeological and Natural History Society, the first woman to hold the post; in 1948 she was made a Companion of the Order of the British Empire in the birthday honours list 'for services to archaeology'.

[Obit.: *Wiltshire Archaeological and Natural History Magazine*, 54, 104–6]

Cunnington, William (1754–1810) [Bi]. British antiquary and pioneer excavator who worked for Sir Richard Colt Hoare in Wiltshire, England. Born in Northamptonshire, he was sent to Wiltshire to an apprenticeship at a clothier's near Warminster. In the early 1770s he was living in Heytesbury, and by the mid 1780s he seems to have developed his own business. During this time he seems to have developed an interest in the wealth of archaeological monuments of the area, and made friends with other antiquarians in the region. His first barrow opening appears to have been a small bowl barrow south of the Knook Long Barrow in or around 1800. Most of his archaeological work thereafter involved excavating round barrows, including Bush Barrow near Stonehenge.

[Bio.: R. H. Cunnington, 1975, *From antiquary to archaeologist: A biography of William Cunnington 1754–1810*. Princes Risborough: Shire Publications]

Cunobelin (Cunobelinus) [Na]. King of the Catuvellauni of southeast England in the first half of the 1st century AD. At his death in about AD 40, he was the most powerful native leader in southern Britain. One of his claims to fame is the minting of coins which appeared in considerable numbers during his reign. His burial place is thought to be the Lexden Tumulus in Colchester. A romanticized version of his life is the subject of Shakespeare's play, *Cymbeline*.

cup and ring mark [De]. Type of ROCK ART motif found widely in the British Isles and elsewhere comprising a central cup-mark or CUPULE around which are one or more concentric grooves.

cup-mark [Ar]. *See* CUPULE.

cupule [Ar]. Small cup-shaped marks deliberately pecked out of a rock surface. Their purpose and symbolism is not known, although there are some suggestions that in Scandinavia at least they are female signs.

Also known as pits, dots, and cup-marks in rock-art studies.

curation [Ge]. The professional care of monuments, objects or other archaeological materials on behalf of a general or specific public or organization.

curia [MC]. Roman senate house or council chamber of the governing body of a *civitas peregrina*, or of a community of high status.

curling stone [Ar]. A heavy piece of shaped granite used in the Scottish game of curling.

currach [Ar]. A skin-covered timber-framed boat of a type in use until recently on the west coast of Ireland and believed to have a long ancestry running back into prehistoric times.

currency bar [Ar]. A type of standardized iron bar romantically believed to have been used as a form of currency before the introduction of coinage, but more likely to be ingots or blanks relating to the circulation of raw material. In Britain three main types are known: sword-shaped, spit-shaped, and ploughshare-shaped. On the continent rhomboid ingots may have had a similar role.

cursive [De]. Term used to describe rounded forms of script used in everyday informal writing, usually on papyrus, paper, or wax.

cursus (pl. cursūs) [MC]. A kind of Neolithic ceremonial monument comprising a rectangular enclosure defined by a bank with external ditches. The longest example is the pair of end-to-end joined cursūs known as the Dorset Cursus on Cranborne Chase, Dorset, which together run for more than 10 km across the grain of the landscape. More typically, cursūs are between 500 m and 3 km long and up to 80 m wide. Dating mainly to the 3rd millennium BC, their purpose is not known, although they are widely believed to have been ceremonial pathways that, when used for processions, structured the participants' vision of the surrounding landscape and the monuments within it. William Stukeley was the first to recognize this class of monument back in the 18th century AD, but his belief that they were racecourses is not correct.

cursus publicus [Ge]. The Latin term for the posting system of the Roman empire. Inns and change points for horses and vehicles were maintained along principal roads by local authorities in order to facilitate the smooth running of the system.

curtain wall [Co]. Wall of a fortification.

curvilinear decoration [De]. *See* CELTIC ART.

cushion stone [Ar]. A flat-faced smooth stone used as a small anvil in metalworking. The earliest cushion stones from northern Europe are those from BEAKER graves.

custumal [Ge]. A written statement of the customs of the manor, the services owed by tenants, and the rights and obligations of the lord.

Cuvier, Baron Georges Leopold (1769–1832) [Bi]. Pioneer French geologist and exponent of the CATASTROPHIST theory. He acquired a great reputation as a naturalist, and is widely acclaimed as the founder of vertebrate palaeontology. He developed the theory that there had in fact been three separate creations, each of which had ended in a cataclysm such as a great flood, in order to explain the fossils visible in the rock sequences he examined. In a sense such thinking paved the way for the comprehension of very big geological eras.

[Bio.: D. Outram, 1984, *George Cuvier: vocation, science and authority in post-revolutionary France*. Manchester: Manchester University Press]

Cuzco, Peru [Si]. Capital of the Inca empire. The name Cuzco means 'navel' in Quechua, the holy place or Hauatanay on the southwest side of the town being the point at which the four quarters of the empire met.

Founded *c*.AD 1200 by Manco Capac, progenitor of the Inca dynasty, and rebuilt by Pachacuti at the time of Inca expansion after AD 1438, the city is built in the form of a puma and is divided into upper and lower halves. The enormous fortress of Sacsayhuamán lies at the northwest end and forms the head of the animal. The site was mainly a ceremonial and political centre rather than a major residential area. The Haucaypata has a large U-shaped plaza in the centre of the site, surrounded by public buildings.

[Rep.: J. H. Rowe, 1944, *An introduction to the archaeology of Cuzco*. Cambridge MA: Harvard University Press]

cyclopean (cyclopean masonry/cyclopean architecture) [De]. A style of construction often applied to walls built not of ashlar masonry however big the blocks, but of large boulders of a size which called for giants to handle them, and with interstices filled up with small stones. Typical of early Mycenaean walls.

cylinder seal [Ar]. A small stone cylinder incised with reversed designs so that when it was rolled over a soft surface the design appeared in relief. These seals were used in ancient Mesopotamia among other things to mark property and to legalize documents.

cylindrical hammer technique [De]. Removal of shallow flakes in the manufacture of handaxes and other tools, by using an implement of a softer material (wood or bone) than the tool itself. Characteristic of the ACHEULIAN and later cultures, often used as a means of distinguishing the Acheulean from the ABBEVILLIAN.

Cynric [Na]. King of the West Saxons in the mid 6th century AD. He is said to have defeated the British near Salisbury in AD 552 and set up an English kingdom. He died c.AD 560.

dado [Ge]. Continuous border round the lower part of a wall decorated with painted plaster.

Dales ware [Ar]. Coarse shell-gritted hand-made cooking pots, probably made near the confluence of the rivers Trent and Humber from the mid 2nd century AD onwards. The fabric is hard and coarse with a smooth but unpolished surface, grey, black, or brown in colour. The body of the clay contains small fragments of white shell. Sandy wheel-thrown imitations, Dales-type cooking pots, were made in Lincolnshire, the Humber Basin, and probably around York at the same time.

Dálriada [CP]. A small kingdom in western Scotland founded by Fergus and his brothers when they moved from Ireland in the later 5th century. It covers the region previously occupied by the DAMNONII who may well have been absorbed into the new kingdom. The kingdom was ruled from Dunadd in the Crianan Moss, Argyll, and developed a strong presence in the region. The Celtic church established an early monastery on Iona which provided a base for the conversion of northern Britain to Christianity. *See* SCOTS.

Dalton point [Ar]. Bifacially worked chipped stone projectile point, a variant of the Clovis point, with a hollow base rather like a fishtail in outline. Characteristic of the DALTON TRADITION of the Archaic in southeastern North America, dating to the period 8500–7000 BC.

Dalton Tradition [CP]. Early Archaic hunter-gatherer cultural groupings resident in the southeastern part of North America in the period 8500–7000 BC. Characterized by a lithic assemblage containing DALTON POINTS, known sites include short-term living places or base camps with middens, a possible cemetery at Sloan, Arkansas, and kill sites or butchery places where a very limited range of tools such as points, knives, choppers, and hammerstones are found.

damage assessment [Ge]. An examination by professional archaeologists of the results of acts of destruction or violation which have occurred to call into question the continued well-being of elements of the archaeological resource.

Damascus, Syria [Si]. A rich oasis city that is still the modern capital of Syria. Occupied from at least the 3rd millennium BC, much of the prehistoric and Roman town lies beneath the modern city and thus is not easily accessible for excavation. However, historical accounts show something of its long history. Egyptian texts and biblical references show that it was an important international trading centre from the 16th century BC. The Aramaens conquered the town in the 2nd millennium BC, the Israelites in the 19th century BC, and the Assyrians in the 8th century BC. By 85 BC it had become the capital of the Nabatean kingdom, and by 64 BC it was a Roman city of both commercial and strategic importance. In the mid 1st millennium AD it became a major Byzantine garrison. In 635 it was captured by Arab forces and chosen as their capital by the Ummayads who were the first Islamic dynasty spanning the period AD 611 to AD 750. The Great Mosque of the caliph Al-Walid was built between AD 706 and AD 714, in the ruins of a Roman temple, and still stands today.

[Sum.: W. T. Pitard, 1987, *Ancient Damascus: a historical study of the Syrian city-state from the earliest times until its fall to the Assyrians in 732 BCE*. Winona Lake, IND: Eisenbrauns]

Damnonii [CP]. Late Iron Age tribe living in southwestern Scotland at the time of the Roman conquest and for some time before.

Danebury, Hampshire, UK [Si]. A developed hillfort of the middle Iron Age on the chalk downlands of central southern England. Extensively excavated by Barry Cunliffe between 1969 and 1989, the site was first occupied in the 6th century BC, when the defences consisted of a single bank and ditch with two opposed entrances. Inside a road ran between the entrances and divided the occupation area into sectors: dwellings were set around the edges while the central area was used for storage. A series of square shrines occupied the highest spot in the middle of the fort. In the early 4th century a further line of ramparts was added outside the first, the southwest gateway was closed, and the east gate was strengthened. The site seems to have been abandoned during the 1st century BC, thereafter being used only as a temporary refuge. Investigations in the surrounding landscape have revealed that the hillfort was surrounded by other kinds of settlement and enclosure.

[Sum.: B. Cunliffe, 1983, *Danebury*. London: Batsford and English Heritage]

Danegeld [Ge]. A tax on land levied in England between AD 991 and AD 1084 in order to buy off Danish Vikings.

Danelaw [Ge]. Name given in the 10th century AD to the area which had been conquered and settled by the Danish Vikings and in which the kings of England allowed considerable autonomy to the Scandinavian settlers. In AD 878 the West Saxon king Alfred and the Danish leader Guthrum concluded a treaty which divided England into Saxon and Danish areas. In the Middle Ages the Danelaw in northern and eastern England had different administrative and fiscal arrangements from the Saxon areas to the south.

Danger Cave, Utah, USA [Si]. A deeply stratified cave site in the Great Basin of midwest North America. The deposits contained evidence of intermittent occupation from about 9000 BC through to the second millennium AD. The excavator of the site, Jesse Jennings, argued that the sequence represented in the cave illustrated the development of a single culture living in a desert environment: the Desert Culture. In this he was greatly influenced by the anthropological work of Julian Steward, and indeed used aspects of the lifestyle of the Shoshoni Indians living in the Great Basin at the time of European contact to flesh out his reconstructions of earlier communities.

The continuity inherent in Jennings' model is not now very widely accepted, although the site remains an important sequence for understanding the early occupation of the Great Basin.

[Rep.: J. D. Jennings, 1957, *Danger Cave*. Salt Lake City: University of Utah]

Daniel, Glyn Edmund (1914–86) [Bi]. British prehistorian and academic, well known for popularizing archaeology on television and radio in the 1950s and 1960s. Born in Barry, South Wales, he was educated first at University College, Cardiff, where he started reading geology before transferring to St John's College, Cambridge, where he read archaeology and anthropology. He put his archaeological training to good use during WW2, serving in the central photographic interpretation unit of the RAF. He returned to St John's in 1945 and stayed there until he retired in 1981. In 1974 he was elected Disney Professor. His academic specialisms focused on the Neolithic tombs of northwest Europe, his doctoral dissertation being published in 1950 as *The prehistoric chamber tombs of England and Wales* (Cambridge: CUP). He was also interested in the history of archaeology and archaeological thought and published several books on the subject, including *The idea of prehistory* (1962, London: C. A. Watts). He appeared on television with Sir Mortimer Wheeler in *Animal, Vegetable, Mineral?*, and helped popularize the subject further by editing more than 100 volumes in the Ancient Peoples and Places series, and between 1958 and 1985 he was the editor of the journal *Antiquity*. He was also interested in food and drink, a joy which he shared in his book *The hungry archaeologist in France* (1963, London: Faber and Faber), and in detective novels: he wrote two, both published by Penguin, one under the pseudonym Dilwyn Rees.

[Abio.: 1986, *Some small harvest*. London: Thames & Hudson]

Danilo Culture [CP]. Neolithic communities of the Dalmatian coast of Croatia and Bosnia of the period 4700 BC down to 3900 BC. The culture developed from the local IMPRESSED WARE CULTURE, its distinctive pottery being decorated with incised geometric shapes emphasized by the use of white and red filler added after firing. Occupation sites include caves and open sites. Danilo groups seem to have had trade links, as the ceramic assemblages include Ripoli ware from Italy.

Danubian Culture [CP]. *See* LINEAR POTTERY CULTURE.

Dark Ages [CP]. A term sometimes used to refer to periods immediately after the collapse of civilizations or when archaeological evidence suggests a phase of relatively little activity compared with what had been evident in previous times. Examples include the Dark Ages in Greece (*c*.1100–800 BC) after the Mycenaean collapse, and the British Dark Ages spanning the period AD 410–900 after the Roman collapse. The term is not very helpful, as it suggests that little is known about the period. The 'darkness' referred mainly to the paucity of evidence for the period, a paucity now partly remedied and more apparent than real.

Dart, Raymond Arthur (1893–1988) [Bi]. South African anthropologist best known for his discovery of the first Australopithecine fossil in 1924. Born in Brisbane, he trained as a doctor at Sydney University Medical School before serving in WW1 with the Australian army medical corps. After the war he went to London to pursue his research in brain anatomy at University College. At the age of 30 he was appointed Professor of Anatomy at the fledgling Medical School in the University of Witwatersrand, Johannesburg, a post he remained in until his retirement. In 1924 he was shown a fossil skull from Taungs near Kimberley and realized that it was an extremely early hominid of a type previously unrecognized. He named it *Australopithecus*, much to the dismay of those in the academic world who realized that the word was a cocktail of Greek and Latin. Although the place of *Australopithecus* in hominid evolution at the time of its discovery was hotly contested, Dart lived to see his views confirmed by finds at Olduvai and elsewhere. In 1966 he was made United Steelworkers of America Professor of Anthropology at the Institute for the Achievement of Human Potential in Philadelphia, USA.

[Obit.: *Antiquaries Journal*, 69 (1989), 404–5]

Darwin, Charles Robert (1809–82) [Bi]. British biologist and naturalist who developed and expounded the theory of evolution by natural selection and the survival of the fittest. After two years as a medical student in Edinburgh he earned a BA degree at Cambridge University in 1831. Here he met Adam Sedgwick and John Henslow, the latter of whom recommended him for the post of naturalist on the expedition ship *The Beagle*. Darwin used the trip, between 1831 and 1836, to make observations on biology and geology that would last him his entire career. Between 1846 and 1854 he spent much time researching the classification, variation, and origins of animal species. After the naturalist Alfred Russel Wallace sent Darwin a manuscript outlining similar evolutionary thinking, he published his abstract *On the origin of species* (1859, London), documenting his evidence for the operation of biological evolution. He later became interested in the early history of humans and developed his thinking on human evolution as *The descent of man and selection in relation to sex* (1871, London). His interest in soils and their formation led him to consider the work and role of the earthworm, published as *The formation of vegetable mould through the action of worms* (1888, London), which provided one of the first scientific considerations of how archaeological remains are buried.

[Bio.: J. Bowlby, 1991, *Charles Darwin: a biography*. London: Pimlico]

data recovery [Ge]. Systematic collection of information about aspects of the archaeological resource for future analysis.

dating [Te]. *See* ABSOLUTE DATING, RELATIVE DATING.

datum [Ge]. The base-point used as the main reference station in setting out a grid for recording archaeological excavations or field survey data. The horizontal position of the datum is usually determined in latitude and longitude and with reference to the local mapping grid. The vertical dimension is conventionally given as a height above sea level, often calculated from the national standard. In remote areas the use of GPS equipment allows the rapid determination of accurate locational details for a site datum. *See also* ORDNANCE DATUM.

daub [Ma]. Clay variously admixed with straw or dung and worked to a smooth consistency that is then used as a wall-covering or to make ovens and domestic fixtures. *See also* WATTLE AND DAUB.

David I (The Saint) [Na]. King of Scotland from AD 1124. Born *c*.1085, sixth son of Malcolm III and Margaret. Married Matilda, daughter of Waltheof, earl of Huntingdon. Died AD 1153, aged *c*.68, having reigned 29 years.

David II [Na]. King of Scotland from AD 1329 of the House of Bruce. Born 1324, son of Robert I and Elizabeth. Married Joanna, daughter of Drummond, widow of Sir John Logie (divorced). Died in AD 1371 aged 46, having reigned 41 years.

Davis, Edwin Hamilton (1811–88) [Bi]. American antiquary who, in collaboration with E. G. Squier, did much to describe and document the Ohio mounds and earthen enclosures. Davis was a physician living at Chillicothe, Ohio, who did his archaeology in his spare time.

[Bio.: *American National Biography*, 6, 185–6]

Dead Sea Scrolls [Do]. A series of more than 800 documents dating to the 1st and 2nd centuries BC and the 1st century AD which were found in 1947 in caves at Qumran near the Dead Sea in Israel. Written on parchment and papyrus, these documents were preserved because of the extreme aridity of the region. They are the religious writings of a Jewish sect known as the Essenes, and seem to have been hidden in the caves during the Roman subjugation of the Jewish Revolt in AD 68. The collection includes versions of all the Old Testament texts as well as sectarian works.

[Sum.: R. Eisenman and M. Wise, 1992, *The Dead Sea Scrolls uncovered*. Shaftesbury: Element]

debitage [Ar]. A general term for the waste flakes, chips, and spalls produced during the manufacture and maintenance of flint and stone tools. *See* FLAKE.

Decantae [CP]. The late Iron Age tribe living in northeastern Scotland in the region of the Black Isle north of the Moray Firth at the time of the Roman conquest. Little is known about their settlements or material culture, although it is in this area that Agricola fought many campaigns during attempts to bring the far north of the British Isles into the Roman empire.

Deceangli [CP]. The late Iron Age tribe living in north Wales and the northern part of the Welsh Marches at the time of the Roman conquest.

Déchelette, Joseph (1861–1914) [Bi]. French prehistorian and synthesizer of archaeological knowledge. He was born into a silk-weaving family and became interested in archaeology through his uncle, Gabriel Bulliot, who was excavating at Mont Beauvray. Joseph later took over his uncle's work and published the results in 1901. At the age of 37, however, he gave up his part in the family business and devoted himself to archaeology. He was the author of the first three volumes of the *Manuel d'archéologie préhistorique, celtique et gallo-romaine* (1908–13, Paris: Picard) which cover the prehistory and protohistory of France and adjacent areas of Europe. Déchellette was killed in action in the early days of WW1 and so never completed the third volume of his work, a task that was done by Albert Grenier. In 1915 he was posthumously awarded the Prix Lambert by the French Academy.

[Bio.: *Antiquity*, 36 (1962), 245–6]

declination [De]. The angular distance of a celestial body from the celestial equator. The equator has a declination of 0 degrees, the North Pole one of 90 degrees north. Declination is the only accurate means of expressing the position of the Sun or Moon at any particular time and is calculated from the combination of latitude, azimuth, and horizon height.

decoy pond [MC]. A specially designed pond used for attracting and trapping ducks. Of various types but usually with narrowing channels at each corner into which the ducks could be driven or lured.

decumanus maximus [Co]. Latin term for the principal street of a Roman town, theoretically running east–west, and at right angles to the *cardo maximus*.

dedicatory deposit [De]. A deliberately placed object, hoard, or burial of an animal or human, connected with the initiation or completion of a substantial project such as the construction of a house or temple.

deductivism [Th]. Reasoning from the general to the specific. The process involves the evaluation of generalizations by generating hypotheses which can be tested using appropriate data. Deductive research is cumulative and involves the constant refining of hypotheses. *See also* SCIENTIFIC METHOD. *Compare* INDUCTIVISM.

deep-sea core [Ge]. A narrow column of sediments taken by drilling into the sea-bed with a piston-corer. Such cores can provide a more or less complete record of climatic changes through the QUATERNARY. The superimposed layers of detritus include sediments and the fossil skeletons of sea creatures. In some cases these remains alone can provide indicators of climate and water salinity on the basis of their preferred habitats. They also store information about water chemistry that can be obtained using, for example, OXYGEN ISOTOPE ANALYSIS.

deer park [MC]. An extensive tract of land enclosed by a substantial pale, which is set aside and equipped for the management and hunting of deer and other wild animals to provide a constant and sustainable supply of foods throughout the year and sport for the owners. Deer parks also provided a protected area for woodland management and grazing. They were first constructed by the Norman aristocracy in France and Britain in the 11th century AD, but they became increasingly popular in many parts of northern Europe during the succeeding centuries, reaching a peak in the 13th and 14th centuries. Many were later replaced by ornamental parks and landscaped estates as wealthy owners moved their residences into the parks, but some continued to be used in the traditional way down to the 18th century AD.

defixiones [Ar]. A Latin term for prayers or curses inscribed on lead sheets and other material and deposited at a shrine.

degeneration [Th]. The theory of the 'fall of man' from some original divine or innocent state; also called degradation.

Delhi, India [Si]. Situated on the banks of the Yamuna River at the western end of the Ganga Valley the modern capital of India has under and around it much of the ancient past. The earliest occupation appears to be the town of Indrapratha, home of the *Mahabharata* hero King Yudhishthira in the early 1st millennium BC, now under the Purana Qila (the Old Fort). By the 3rd century BC it was an important point on the trade routes between China and the west. The Tomara Rajputs made it their capital in AD 736, calling the town Dhillika. It was captured by Moslem forces in AD 1193 and Qutb-ud-din Aybak established his sultanate there in AD 1206. With the advent of the Mughal empire in AD 1526 Delhi alternated with Agra as the capital, each successive ruler asserting himself with new architectural designs. The Qal'a-i-Kuhna-Masjid mosque was built in AD 1541 and is one of the oldest buildings of the Mughal period.

[Sum.: R. E. Frykenberg (ed.), 1993, *Delhi through the ages: essays in urban history, culture and society*. Oxford and Delhi: OUP]

Delphi, Greece [Si]. Situated on the steep slopes of Mount Parnassus in the centre of Greece, Delphi was home to the famous oracle and the principal shrine of APOLLO. The site seems to have acted as a religious focus for the different Greek city-states who organized games and festivals there. The Pythian Games in particular became a great national festival and over the years a series of twenty elaborate temple-like structures were built along the sacred way to house valuable offerings. Above, on a terrace cut into the mountainside and supported by an unusual masonry wall, stood the temple of Apollo with, at its centre, the omphalos stone symbolically marking the centre of the earth. A rock fissure in the temple emanated sounds that were supposed to inspire the Pythian priestess to give answers to questions posed to her. Damaged by an earthquake in *c*.350 BC the site was rebuilt and a theatre and stadium added. After about 300 BC interest in the oracle waned, and in Roman times there was further deterioration. Nero plundered the site, and finally Theodosius closed it down as being anti-Christian in 390 AD.

[Sum.: V. Pendazos and M. Sarla, 1984, *Delphi*. Athens: Yiannikos-Kaldis]

demesne [Ge]. The manorial home farm, land usually retained by the lord for his own use, on which tenants were expected to work in part-return for their tenancies.

Demetae [CP]. The late Iron Age tribe living in the extreme southwest of Wales, in Pembrokeshire and Carmarthen, at the time of the Roman conquest. Settlement here was dense with moderate-sized communities living in RATHS and small enclosed farmsteads. By the 2nd century AD Roman pottery and building styles had penetrated the area, although some settlements continued through from the 1st century BC into the first few centuries AD completely unhampered.

demic diffusion [Th]. A model developed by Ammerman and Cavalli-Sforza in the 1970s to account for the spread of the Neolithic package of ideas and material culture across Europe based on two factors: a rising population and random patterns of local migration. The two together create a 'wave of advance' that differs from colonization because the movements are not intentional, while standing apart from diffusion in the normal archaeological usage because movements of population are certainly involved.

democracy [Ge]. A political system that allows the citizens to participate in political decision-making, or to elect representatives to government bodies.

demography [Ge]. The study of populations. *See* PALEODEMOGRAPHY.

Denali Complex [CP]. One of a number of broadly contemporary Paleo-Arctic Tradition cultures living in the extreme northwest of North America in the period 8000–5000 BC. Known mainly from chipped stone industries which include microblades, small wedge-shaped cores for making them, leaf-shaped points, scrapers, and gravers.

denarius [Ar]. Roman silver coin in standard use from the 3rd century BC through to *c*.AD 242.

Denbigh Flint Complex [CP]. One of a number of broadly contemporary, regionally specific, cultural groupings within the Arctic Small Tool Tradition of the far north of North America, dating to the period 2000–800 BC. The Denbigh Flint Complex is found in Alaska, its name being derived from the site of a temporary caribou hunting camp discovered at Iyatayet Creek by Cape Denbigh on Norton Sound. Although widely applied, the Complex is really only recognizable in the Denbigh region itself. The lithic assemblages are characterized by microblades, small burins, graving tools, and numerous side and end blades carefully pointed at both ends.

dendrochronology [Te]. A highly accurate dating method that in favourable circumstances provides both absolute and relative dates. The idea of dendrochronology was developed in the early 20th century by Andrew Ellicott Douglass, an astronomer at the Lowell Observatory in Flagstaff, Arizona, as a result of his work on the effects of sunspots on terrestrial climate. Also known as tree-ring dating, the method is based on the fact that living trees add an annual growth ring to their trunk and branches. The size and character of the ring varies from year to year according to weather patterns and general climatic conditions: in dry years the ring is thin while in wet years it is relatively thick. Trees of the same species of similar age and living in the same region will show similar patterns of tree-ring growth. By analysing trees whose growth periods overlap it is possible to construct a master tree-ring profile for a region. When a piece of timber of unknown date is found in the same area its rings can be matched with the master sequence and its date established. Even where sequences cannot be tied down to absolute ages it is possible to construct 'floating' sequences so that timbers can be dated in relative terms; when the master sequence is eventually tied down these dates will become absolute dates.

A number of master curves have been or are being constructed for different parts of the world. One of the longest and most spectacular is the Belfast curve for the British Isles which spans the period back to about 5500 BC. The method has much to commend it, and for recent centuries, where large timbers survive in standing buildings, it is already widely used. For earlier times the key issue is the preservation of suitable timber: ideally a timber with more than 50 years' growth represented is needed to achieve firm dating.

Dendrochronology is also the basis for the construction of calibration curves for the conversion of radiocarbon ages to calendar years. *See* CALIBRATION.

Dennis, George (1814–98) [Bi]. Amateur British antiquary whose career as a civil servant and in the diplomatic service afforded him irregular opportunities to pursue antiquarian survey and excavation in Italy. His principal work, *Cities and cemeteries of Etruria*, was published in 1848 and served to establish the Etruscans as a significant pre-Roman civilization.

[Bio.: T. W. Potter, 1998, Dennis of Etruria: a celebration. *Antiquity*, 72, 916–21]

denticulate [Ar]. **1.** A term used to describe a flint or stone tool with one edge worked into a series of notches to give a toothed or serrated cutting blade. **2.** Term used by François Bordes for one of the defined MOUSTERIAN assemblages in southwest France which had few scrapers but high proportions of notched and denticulate blades.

dentils [De]. The line of teeth-like blocks of stone, suggesting the rafter ends of a flat roof, found, for example, under the cornice of a building of Ionic or Corinthian order.

deoxyribonucleic acid (DNA) [Ge]. Genes, the organizers of inheritance, are composed of DNA, thread-like molecules which carry the hereditary instructions needed to build an organism and make it work. Genes are copied or replicated with every new generation of living cells and thus preserve the blueprint for that form of life. For archaeology this opens up tremendous potential to address problems that could hardly be contemplated in the 1970s. What have been called studies of 'the archaeology of the human body' allow populations to be explored in terms the sex, hair colour, skin type, blood group, and family connections of individuals from whom DNA can be recovered. Major issues about patterns of colonization and relationships between human populations can also potentially be explored, although issues relating to early hominid development are way beyond the range of preserved DNA which so far has been recovered from preserved remains back to about 40 000 years ago. Already DNA studies of North American populations suggest three waves of migration between 15 000 and 9000 years ago.

dependent variable [Ge]. A variable or factor causally influenced by another (the independent variable).

Derbyshire ware [Ar]. A distinctive type of pottery produced in Derbyshire from the mid 2nd century AD through to the 4th century AD. It is hard and gritty with a surface that is sometimes described as being like 'petrified gooseflesh'. Colour varies from grey and light-brown to red. The surface texture is due to the presence of silica particles in the local clay. All vessels are jars, mostly with a lid-seating on the rim.

descriptive types [De]. Categories of material based on the physical or external properties of an artefact.

Desert Archaic (Western Archaic) [CP]. General term referring to the early Archaic Stage cultural groupings of the Great Basin and western parts of North America during the period 7500–2000 BC. These communities were mainly hunter-gatherers who exploited a wide range of habitats with commensurate diversity in their subsistence base reflected in the use of a range of waterfowl, shore-birds, rabbits, antelopes, and mountain sheep. The material culture includes baskets, mats, and many items of organic materials. Chipped stone artefacts including arrowheads and knives were carried around, but heavier items such as grinding stones may have been left at convenient stations on the main migratory routes.

Desert Culture [CP]. Obsolete term sometimes used to refer to the groups occupying the Great Basin of western North America. *See* DANGER CAVE, UTAH, and DESERT ARCHAIC.

deserted medieval village (DMV) [MC]. The abandoned remains of a nucleated rural settlement abandoned sometime between the 12th century AD and the 19th century AD. Such sites often survive as earthworks or, in marginal areas, as ruinous structures. In the larger examples it is possible to define the church, manor house, dwellings, yards, streets, and many other features of the village, while smaller examples may have comprised only farmsteads and dwellings. In most cases fields, tracks, and droves are also preserved as earthworks around the village itself. There are many reasons why such settlements became deserted, amongst them the oft-cited explanation of plague and especially the BLACK DEATH. The majority, however, appear to have been deserted for economic reasons: because of rural depopulation, through changes in landholding brought about by ENCLOSURE, and because of the creation of landscaped parks from the 17th century onwards, when wealthy landowners sometimes physically moved whole settlements.

deterrence [Ge]. The prevention of military conflict on the basis of ensuring that any aggressor believes they would suffer too many losses or have a fruitless task to make the initiation of hostilities worthwhile. The construction of large defences and access to the latest military hardware are both means of deterrence seen widely in the archaeological record.

De Valera, Ruaidhri (1917–78) [Bi]. Distinguished Irish archaeologist, best known for his work on Neolithic tombs in Ireland. Born in Dublin the fourth son of Irish president Eamon de Valera, he was educated at Blackrock College and University College, Dublin, where he obtained a Ph.D. with a thesis on court tombs. His first professional appointment was with the Ordnance Survey of Ireland. In 1957 he was appointed Professor of Archaeology at University College, Dublin, and thereafter developed his department into the largest school of archaeology in Ireland. Amongst his many publications are the first four volumes of *The survey of the megalithic tombs of Ireland*, which he wrote with Seán Ó Nualláin.

[Obit.: *Irish Times*, 31 October 1978]

developed passage grave [MC]. A type of later Neolithic burial monument found in clusters along the Atlantic coastlands of Northwest Europe, notably in central Ireland, north Wales, and Orkney. Dating mainly to the 3rd millennium BC, these structures represent enlarged or developed versions of the earlier SIMPLE PASSAGE GRAVES. They typically comprise a large round mound of earth and stone more than 35 m in diameter, within which there is one or more stone-built chambers accessible from the outside of the mound via a long narrow passage. The chambers are usually square, rectangular, or polygonal in plan and often show structural compartmentalization with side cells opening from the main chamber. Burials either by inhumation or cremation were made in the side cells. The walls of the passage and chamber often carry PASSAGE GRAVE ART, as do the stones forming the kerb around the outside of the mound in some examples. Decorated stones brought from elsewhere are sometimes broken up and used in the construction of developed passage graves. In a number of examples the passages are aligned such that the rising or setting mid-winter sun shines into the central chamber for a few days each year. The largest and best-known examples are those in central Ireland, such as NEWGRANGE and KNOWTH. *See also* PASSAGE GRAVE and MULTIPLE PASSAGE GRAVE.

development control [Ge]. Most forms of property development and material changes to land use need approval from a local or national government body responsible for spatial planning. This process is known as development control. The determination of applications and the granting of permission increasingly includes consideration of the archaeological implications of proposals. Where permission for development is granted, a condition can be imposed through the planning system which requires the developer to undertake, at their own expense, an agreed mitigation strategy that may variously involve the preservation or excavation of archaeological remains, or a combination of the two. As such, this approach provides a variant on the widely applied principle of environmental protection in which 'the polluter pays' for any damage done to the environment.

Devensian Stage [Ge]. A group of deposits representing a geostratigraphic stage within the PLEISTOCENE series of the British QUATERNARY system, dating to the period betwen 120 000 and 10 000 years ago. The Devensian is interpreted as the last full glacial series within the Pleistocene, with deposits being stratified above IPSWICHIAN interglacial deposits and below FLANDRIAN series deposits of the HOLOCENE. The Devensian is equated with the Weichselian glacial maximum in northwest Europe. The Alpine equivalent is the WÜRM (although the equivalence is not exact); the North American equivalent the Wisconsin. The later part of the Devensian embraces POLLEN ZONES I–III as defined by Godwin in 1940, and the DRYAS climatic phases.

Deverel–Rimbury Culture [CP]. Term used to describe the late Bronze Age communities of southern England after type-site burial monuments at Deverel and Rimbury in Dorset. The culture is characterized by globular, barrel-shaped, and bucket-shaped ceramic urns, extensive field systems, and settlements with round houses. Burials are usually cremations placed in urns or in simple pits dug into the ground, and typically cluster around earlier round barrows. Metalwork dates the culture to the period between 1400 BC and 1200 BC.

dewpond [MC]. A specially constructed pond with a water-tight lining of puddled clay mixed with straw. These ponds were built to maintain a supply of water on permeable rocks such as chalk or limestone.

diachronic [De]. Pertaining to events or phenomena as they change or exist over time.

diadem [Ar]. A plain or decorated headband of man-made or natural materials.

Diaguita [CP]. A broad cultural grouping of the Andes region of South America dating to the period AD 900–1600. Two main subdivisions are recognized on the basis of ceramic styles: the Argentinian on the east side of the Andes and the Chilean to the west.

The Argentinian Diaguita succeeds the Aguada Culture and is recognized by pottery decorated with stylized motifs of reptiles, birds, and humans. Polychrome decorated funerary urns are found associated with the burial of children, adults being interred in stone-lined pits.

Chilian Diaguita is characterized by delicately decorated ceramics with duck-shaped vessels and bird effigy jars. Both groups share many traits such as funerary practices, the use of bronze, petroglyphs, and possibly their language, although the extent of interaction is not known.

dialectics [Th]. Georg Hegel's philosophy of change through the resolution of opposites. In this the central tendency or thesis is opposed by its opposite or antithesis. When the tensions are resolved as a synthesis this in turn becomes the thesis which generates a new antithesis, and so on. Thus dialectics provides an interpretation of change which emphasizes the clash of opposing influences or groups as the motor of social transformation.

diamicton [De]. A sediment or soil comprising a matrix of sand, silt, and clay particles in which there are clasts of larger material. Defined in this way, diamictons include many deposits formerly classified as tills, and include also many alluvial and colluvial deposits.

diatoms [Sp]. Single-celled algae, different species of which live in different kinds of water. They secrete silicious skeletons that are morphologically distinct to species. **Diatom**

analysis involves sampling sediments from deep-sea cores or lake sediments and then analysing the species representation at different levels to provide a picture of the changing environment.

diffusion (diffusionism) [Th]. The spread of ideas, items of material culture, or cultural traits from one culture or society to another. Diffusion does not necessarily imply a movement of people, for ideas can move through trade and other forms of contact. What it does imply is that ideas and inventions tend to radiate out from one source area into surrounding regions. Prior to radiocarbon dating there was a general assumption that, within the Old World, most of the main developments and key innovations took place in the Near East, the Middle East, Egypt, and the Mycenaean world of Greece and the Aegean, and ideas spread out from there. Taken at its extreme, in what is sometimes known as **hyperdiffusionism**, major inventions happened only once, and a few key areas provided the inspiration for most major technical and social developments later imparted to the rest of the world: such things as agriculture, writing, urban settlement, metallurgy, and so on. It is now recognized, however, that many things were independently developed under different social conditions at different times. Moreover, radiocarbon dating has shown that the movement of ideas is far more complicated than originally thought and that it is inappropriate to think in terms of simple one-way movements outwards from supposedly 'higher civilizations'.

digging stick [Ar]. A straight stick, the end of which is often hardened by charring, which can be used to lever and dig out edible roots and plants or to break up the earth prior to planting.

diluvialism [Th]. View of early prehistory current in the 18th and 19th centuries AD which denied the antiquity of man witnessed by the discovery of fossil hominid remains and instead believed that the creation story set out in the Bible was literally true and that Noah's Flood and other events recorded in the Bible were facts of prehistory. According to these theories, fossilized human remains were the remains of those who perished in the Great Flood.

Diocletian [Na]. A Dalmatian soldier elected emperor of Rome by the army in AD 284. With the aid of a military junta he reconstructed the Roman empire after the disasters of the 260s and 270s. He reorganized the civil and army administration to take account of the increasing complexities of government. In AD 305 he resigned his position to his deputy for a period of retirement. He died c.AD 316.

Diodorus Siculus [Na]. Greek historian who wrote a book called *World history* sometime between 60 BC and 30 BC. This account included descriptions of the Celts and the Gauls which were largely based on descriptions provided by earlier writers including Posidonius.

diolchos [De]. Literally, the 'dray(way) across', used for the portage of ships across the Isthmus of Corinth. Invented by Periander in the 7th century BC, the technique involved hauling ships on a carriage running in grooves cut on a stone track across the Isthmus, thus avoiding the dangers of a long sea journey round the southern promontories of the Peloponnese.

direct historical approach [Th]. A methodology developed in the USA during the 1930s by W. D. Strong and others whereby knowledge relating to historical periods is extended back into earlier times. This involves taking a site for which there are historical accounts relating to recent periods of occupation and then excavating it to establish continuity back into prehistoric times. The historical data then becomes the basis of ANALOGY and HOMOLOGY for the study of the prehistoric communities at the site itself and other sites in the region. The main problem with the approach is of course that in many parts of the world there is no direct continuity between historically documented communities and the prehistoric occupants of the region.

dirk [Ar]. Extra-long dagger, typically with a blade more than 200 mm long, but not so long as a RAPIER.

disarticulated burial [De]. A human burial in which the skeletal material has become disordered and jumbled. This is often the result of EXCARNATION, disinterment, or the movement of body parts after decomposition of the corpse.

disc barrow [MC]. A type of FANCY BARROW characterized by one or more small low round mounds each covering a central burial and set within a circular or oval ditched enclosure. Mainly found in southern England and dating to the early 2nd millennium BC. Closely associated with the WESSEX CULTURE.

discourse [Th]. The context, environment, and conditions within which a defined knowledge is produced and made accessible to others. Discourse is not simply the content of what is said or shown (a printed text, lecture, museum display, TV programme, and so on), it also includes the conceptual, social, and historical conditions behind the statements made. Discourse brings in people, buildings, institutions, rules, values, desires, concepts, machines, instruments, and anything else that could have played a part in the construction of knowledge. The idea of discourse also carries with it the notion of inclusion and exclusion; statements are arranged according to systems whereby some people are admitted, others excluded, and contributions from some people are endorsed as legitimate candidates for assessment, while others are judged as not worthy of comment.

dish [Ar]. A shallow vessel, which can be defined as having a height less than one-third, but greater than one-seventh, of its diameter.

Dissolution [CP]. Following the Reformation in England, Henry VIII closed all the religious houses in the later 1530s AD; their property was redistributed or sold by the crown. Chantries, religious fraternities, and colleges were abolished in the later 1540s.

distal [De]. Remote from the point of origin, the place furthest away from the point of contact or connection with the source or host. In flint working the distal end of a flake is the one opposite the striking platform. *See also* PROXIMAL.

distance-decay model [Th]. A mathematically constructed function that expresses the inverse relationship between the quantity of a particular material, or the number of examples of an artefact type, and the distance from its source. The examination of different patterns of distance decay allows insights into early exchange practices, for example the use of regional markets as redistribution centres for bulk supplies of goods, or the use of river routes and seaways to facilitate the long-distance movement of goods that move very slowly over land.

divergence [Th]. The production of varied final conditions from originally similar states.

division of labour [Th]. The specialization of work tasks, by means of which different occupations are combined within a production system. All societies have at least some rudimentary form of division of labour, especially between the tasks allocated to men and those performed by women. With the development of industrialism, however, the division of labour becomes vastly more complex than in any prior type of production system.

DMV [Ab]. *See* DESERTED MEDIEVAL VILLAGE.

DNA [Ab]. *See* DEOXYRIBONUCLEIC ACID.

Dobunni [CP]. The late Iron Age tribe living in the west of England in the Cotswolds and in the upper Thames Valley to the east of the Severn and in the Forest of Dean and Worcester to the west. The capital of the region, at least from the early 1st century AD onwards, was at Bagindon near Cirencester, although other centres must also have been important in such a large area. Developed hillforts and enclosed *oppida* were the high-level units of the settlement system, around which were numerous smaller enclosures and open settlements. The Dobunni issued coins from about 35 BC: the succession of rulers recorded on these include Bodvoc (15–10 BC), Anted (10 BC–AD 10), Comux (AD 10–15), Eisu (AD 15–30), and Catti (AD 15–43).

dog [Sp]. Four-legged flesh-eating mammal (*Canis*), ultimately descended from the wolf, now represented as domestic and wild species with many different breeds. Dogs were probably the earliest species to be domesticated and were at first mainly used in hunting. In America, dogs probably accompanied the first human communities colonizing the continent. In North America domestic examples are known from before 10 000 BC, and in Peru domesticated examples date from about 600 BC. In Central America dog was an important source of food.

dog-tooth ornament [De]. An ornament consisting of a series of pyramidal flowers of four petals, typical of 13th century AD work.

dolichocephalic [De]. Term to describe cases where the cephalic index (greatest breadth expressed as a percentage of maximum length) of a human skull is below 75 per cent. *See also* BRACHYCEPHALIC.

dolmen [MC]. A traditional French term for any kind of megalithic chambered tomb. Formerly used occasionally in England but now obsolete except in the name PORTAL DOLMEN.

Domesday Book [Do]. A survey of landholdings made after the Norman conquest. At a council held in Gloucester at Christmas AD 1085 it was decided to record the number of HIDES of land existing in each English shire and assess the amount and value of acreage and livestock possessed by individual landowners. The resulting survey is arranged under tenurial rather than territorial headings. More than 13 000 pre-existing VILLS are recorded. It provides a fundamentally important source for historians and archaeologists investigating the early medieval period.

domestication [Ge]. A general term used to refer to the biological manipulation of the production and reproduction of plants and animals by early agriculturalists. This appears to have been achieved through selective breeding so that desirable traits might be encouraged. As a result, dependence on hunting and gathering was reduced.

Dominicans [Ge]. A religious order of friars, known as Black Friars, introduced in the early 13th century AD and concerned to maintain the faith and convert the infidel.

Domitian [Na]. Roman emperor AD 81–96.

Donald III (Bán) [Na]. King of Scotland from AD 1093. Born *c.*1033, second son of Duncan I. He was deposed in May 1094, restored in November 1094, and deposed again in October 1097, having reigned three years.

donjon [Co]. The innermost stronghold or keep of a medieval castle.

Dorchester Culture [CP]. One of the six or so secondary Neolithic Cultures of the British

Isles identified by Stuart Piggott in 1954 on the basis of finds from excavations at Dorchester-on-Thames, Oxfordshire. Since 1954 the main elements of the Dorchester Culture—henges, mini-henges, post circles, cremation cemeteries, and burials under round barrows—have all been shown to be common and widespread features of the 3rd millennium BC in the British Isles, thus rendering the term obsolete.

Dorians [CP]. Traditionally the Dorians are portrayed as a group of prehistoric tribes who moved southwards towards the end of the 2nd millennium BC to take over the whole of Greece, many of the islands of the Aegean, Crete, and parts of Asia Minor. They are sometimes credited with overthrowing the Mycenaeans. Archaeologically, however, there is little or no evidence for the Dorians, and while it is recognized that their language went on to become a dialect spoken in the Peloponnese and southern Aegean islands, and that they probably made a contribution to the emergence of classical Greek culture, their origins and exact role remain uncertain.

Doric Order [De]. Greek architectural style characterized by fluted columns with a diameter-to-height ratio of one to eight and an unelaborated capital. *See also* CORINTHIAN ORDER and IONIC ORDER.

dorsal surface [De]. Relating to the back or upper surface. In describing a struck flint or stone blade or flake it refers to the outer face furthest away from the core, usually with a ridged appearance and perhaps traces of old flake beds in it. *Compare* VENTRAL.

Dorset Tradition [CP]. Arctic cultures found in western Greenland, around the northern Hudson Bay area, and the islands of northern parts of North America, dating to the period 550 BC to AD 1100. Seemingly developing from the Pre-Dorset Tradition of the Arctic Small Tool Tradition, Dorset Tradition communities lived mainly on the coast. They were hunters and their subsistence economy was based mainly on sea mammals, especially seals, and other resources derived from the shoreline. However, terrestrial mammals such as caribou and even polar bears were also exploited, along with many smaller species.

Their material culture included bone hunting equipment, including toggling harpoons, lances and spears. Chipped and polished stone was also used for edged tools and weapons. Small stone lamps were used. Houses were rectangular semi-subterranean structures.

Dorset art styles were well established and elaborate. The repertoire includes lifelike portraits of actual people, and Dorset carvers were adept at working antler, bone, ivory, soapstones, and wood. Over half of their carvings were of human beings or polar bears. Few decorated objects were utilitarian pieces: most were masks, figurines, and plaques that were used in funerary rituals and in shamanistic and magical ceremonies.

Skeletal remains show that Dorset Tradition communities were the ancestors of modern Inuit, and it may be that when some of the Inuit legends refer to 'Tunnit' folk, giants with enormous strength, and people without dog sleds or bows and arrows, they are talking about Dorset Tradition societies.

double axe [Ar]. A shaft-hole axe with a symmetrically set cutting blade at either end, found in stone, copper, and bronze in prehistoric Europe. In MINOAN Crete the double axe was an extremely common religious symbol. Votive double axes are frequently found in shrines and sanctuaries. The significance of the double axe may derive from its use as a sacrificial implement.

double house [MC]. A kind of monastic house created to house a community of men and women in separate but adjacent accommodation. In plan such houses typically comprise one or two churches and domestic buildings arranged around two self-contained cloisters. Such houses originated in Merovingian Gaul and began to be built from the 7th century AD onwards. *See also* MONASTERY.

Douglas, James (1753–1819) [Bi]. British antiquarian well known for his fieldwork in Kent and Sussex which included the examination of a very large number of Anglo-Saxon burial mounds. Douglas's career included a period in industry and in the Austrian and British armies, and in 1780 he took holy orders. His publications include *Nenia Britannica* which records his exploits in Sussex and Kent.

[Bio.: R. Jessup, 1975, *Man of many talents: an informal biography of James Douglas*. Chichester: Phillimore]

Douglass, Andrew Ellicott (1867–1962) [Bi]. American astronomer at the University of

Arizona in Tucson who was responsible for developing the technique of DENDROCHRONOLOGY as a dating method. He began his work on living trees around 1901, before searching for ancient timber from archaeological sites. By 1929 he had developed two lengthy sequences for the American southwest.

[Bio.: G. E. Webb, 1983, *Tree rings and telescopes: the scientific career of A. E. Douglass.* Tuscon: University of Arizona Press]

dovecote [MC]. Small detached round or square building containing nesting boxes for the breeding and accommodation of doves or pigeons. Of greatly varying ground plan, dovecotes were important economic resources during medieval and later times as they provided sustainable supplies of meat, eggs, feathers, and manure. Also known as a columbarium.

down-the-line exchange model [Th]. A pattern of exchange practices where the recipient of a supply of goods keeps a proportion and passes the rest on (trades, sells, gives as gifts, etc.) to the next group who do the same. The pattern repeats but the volume of material gets less with every transfer. If the volume of material is plotted on a graph against distance from source, such a pattern of exchange will appear as an exponential decay curve; plotted on a logarithmic scale the fall-off appears as a straight line. *See also* DISTANCE-DECAY MODEL.

Dowris Phase [CP]. The latest industrial phase of the later Bronze Age in Ireland, named after a large hoard of bronzes found at Dowris in the 1820s AD. The hoard itself dates to the 8th century BC. The Dowris Phase is one of the regional traditions within the more broadly defined EWART PARK PHASE.

drachma [Ar]. A unit of silver coinage in the Greek world issued in multiple such as the *didrachm* (2), the *tetradrachm* (4), and the *deckadrachm* (10).

Drag [Ab]. *See* DRAGENDOFF FORM.

Dragendoff form [De]. A system for classifying the shapes of TERRA SIGILLATA vessels developed by the German archaeologist Hans Dragendorff (1870–1941) which he published in 1895–6. The scheme has since been expanded, but the basic structure remains.

Drakenstein urn [Ar]. Type of middle/late Bronze Age ceramic vessel found in the Low Countries. The pots are barrel-shaped with impressed cordon decoration on the upper part of the body and occasionally with zig-zag decoration. The shape and decoration of these vessels suggest some contact with the DEVEREL–RIMBURY WARES of southern England. *See also* HILVERSUM URNS.

dreaming track (songline) [De]. A route taken by a DREAMING or ancestral being, along which a series of events occurred which are part of Australian Aboriginal oral tradition and are marked by a series of sites and associated songs and stories.

dreamtime (dreaming) [De]. The ancestral past and the era of creation that existed before human beings and yet which also extends into the present, according to Australian Aboriginal beliefs. The time when ancestral beings, some human and some animal, travelled the country creating the form of the landscape and initiating the patterns and cycles of life.

Dressel form [De]. A system for classifying the shape of ceramic amphorae developed by H. Dressel (1845–1920) which was published in 1899. The system is still in use, although continually being expanded as new varieties are found. *See* AMPHORA.

dromos [Co]. The long horizontal passage, bordered by stone walls, cut into a small hill and giving access to a THOLOS, or beehive tomb, in Mycenaean Greece.

drove road (droveway) [MC]. Long-distance routeway, not maintained, used for herding cattle to market. Not subject to tolls.

Druids [CP]. Term used by classical writers to refer to a sector of Celtic society whose principal function was the performance of religious rites. Their training reputedly involved many years of study, and according to Caesar the Druids exercised legal as well as religious authority. Though the Celtic priesthood doubtless has a considerable antiquity, there is no direct evidence to link the Druids of prehistoric times with Stonehenge; this was a fanciful association generated by William Stukeley in the 18th century AD. The modern-day Druids, of which there are several hundred orders, are also a recreation of recent centuries, the first modern order being the Ancient Order of Druids founded in AD 1716.

Dryas [CP]. A series of cold climatic phases at the end of the DEVENSIAN period when there was a return to almost full glacial conditions. These broadly coincide with the post-glacial POLLEN ZONES established by Godwin. The Oldest Dryas (Dryas I/Pollen Zone Ia) dates to c.16000 to 15000 years ago; the Older Dryas (Dryas II/Pollen Zone Ic) dates to c.12300–11800 years ago; and the Younger Dryas (Dryas III/Pollen Zone III) dates to c.11000–10000 years ago.

Dry Creek, Alaska, USA [Si]. Late Pleistocene deposits containing two archaeologically relevant layers, situated in the Nenana River Valley in the northern foothills of the Alaska Range in North America. Important as evidence for the colonization of America.

Dry Creek I dates to about 9200 BC and contains cobble and flake tools, broken blades, thin bifacial knives, and points. It may be ancestral to Palaeo-Arctic Traditions and in particular to the Nenana Complex.

Dry Creek II dates to about 8700 BC and includes microblades and related technology which sits comfortably with local Palaeo-Arctic Tradition assemblages.

[Rep.: W. R. Powers and T. D. Hamilton, 1978, Dry Creek: a late Pleistocene human occupation in central Alaska. In A. L. Bryan (ed.), *Early Man in America from a circum-Pacific perspective*. Edmonton: University of Alberta, 72–7]

Dryopithecus [Sp]. A group of apes known only through fossils of the Miocene period.

dry-stone walling [Ma]. Walls constructed of stone without the use of mortar. This was the main technique of construction in Europe throughout prehistory and in some regions the tradition continues today. Extremely high-quality and solid walls can be built with the careful selection and bedding of the stones.

D-shaped barrow [MC]. A class of chambered tombs dating to the 3rd millennium found in central and northern parts of the British Isles where the stone-built chamber is set within an earthen mound or stone cairn with a D-shaped outline. The chamber opens from the flat face. In the north of Scotland these are also known as heel-shaped cairns.

Duamutef [Di]. Egyptian god, one of the FOUR SONS OF HORUS. Dog-headed models of his head were often used as stoppers for the CANOPIC JAR containing the stomach.

duces (dux) [Ge]. Latin term for 'leaders', sometimes used in the Roman army to refer to soldiers with duties beyond their normal rank. In the 4th century AD frontier forces were often commanded by *duces*. The *dux Britanniarum*, duke of the Britons, possibly based in York, commanded the frontier troops on Hadrian's Wall in the 4th century AD. The name survived into the Middle Ages as an expression of nobility (hence 'duke'), sometimes superior to that of the more normal *comites* ('counts').

duck decoy [MC]. *See* DECOY POND.

Dufour bladelets [Ar]. Small bladelets with semi-abrupt alternating retouching along one or both sides.

Dugdale, William (1605–83) [Bi]. British antiquary who is best known for the publication in 1656 of one of the earliest regional histories, *Antiquities of Warwickshire*. Dugdale was also a Royalist and an authority on heraldry; in 1677 he was appointed Garter King of Arms and knighted.

[Bio.: J. Broadway, 1999, *William Dugdale and the significance of county history in early Stuart England*. Stratford: Dugdale Society]

dugout canoe [Ar]. A simple form of canoe made from a single tree, the hollow in which is created by burning or chopping out the unwanted wood.

Dumnonii [CP]. The late Iron Age tribe living in the far southwest of England, Cornwall and Devon, at the time of the Roman conquest. Settlements of the immediate pre-Roman period continue through into the 1st and 2nd centuries AD, the whole area pursuing traditional patterns of life that include maintaining contacts with northern France and south Wales to south and north respectively.

dump construction rampart [Co]. *See* FÉCAMP RAMPARTS.

dun [MC]. A kind of small fort or fortified dwelling place found in the west of Britain and Ireland, dating to the late 1st millennium

BC and 1st millennium AD. Usually comprising a stone wall around a large house and associated agricultural structures. In early Irish literature duns are high-status dwellings; the term is also applied to promontory forts.

Duncan I [Na]. King of Scotland from AD 1034. Son of Bethoc, daughter of Malcolm II, and Coinan. Married a cousin of Siward, earl of Northumbria. Died AD 1040, having reigned five years.

Duncan II [Na]. King of Scotland in 1094. Born c.1060, elder son of Malcolm III and Ingibiorg. Married Octreda of Dunbar. Killed in AD 1094, aged c.34, having reigned six months.

dupondius [Ar]. Roman coin worth one eighth of a DENARIUS.

Durotriges [CP]. The late Iron Age tribe that formed a close-knit confederacy of smaller units occupying Wessex and the south coast of England west of the Solent. During the period from 100 to 60 BC the Durotriges were heavily involved in cross-channel trade with northern France through Poole harbour and Hengistbury. After 60 BC, however, trading patterns changed and the Durotriges were no longer so closely involved. Their coinage was impoverished, and they do not seem to have developed *oppidum*-style settlements. Hillforts still dominated the settlement pattern up until the conquest and when the Romans did arrive the tribe fought piecemeal.

Durrington Walls, Durrington, Wiltshire, UK [Si]. A late Neolithic henge enclosure in the valley of the River Avon northwest of Stonehenge dated to the middle part of the 3rd millennium BC. Excavated by Geoffrey Wainwright in 1966–8 showed that it comprised a large sub-oval banked enclosure over 450 m across with an external bank and internal ditch. There were two opposed entrances, the one to the southeast providing access to the river. Inside, the excavations revealed a series of massive circular banked timber structures represented by postholes. The two examined had both been rebuilt several times over the same spot. The excavator suggests that these were large roofed structures, but other interpretations are possible. Finds included much grooved ware pottery. The animal bones indicate that many pigs were consumed on the site and it has been suggested that feasting was one of the main activities carried out at the largest of the two structures investigated.

[Rep.: G. J. Wainwright and I. Longworth, 1971, *Durrington Walls: excavations 1966–1968*. London: Society of Antiquaries]

dux [De]. *See* DUCES.

dyke [MC]. A linear earthwork comprising a bank or ditch, or both.

dynasty [Ge]. A line of rulers whose right to power is inherited.

dysser [MC]. A kind of stone-built burial chamber characteristic of the TRB Culture where the chamber is generally surmounted by a capstone and enclosed within a low earthen mound surrounded by a stone kerb. In later phases of the TRB Culture, dysser are superseded by passage graves.

EA [Ab]. *See* ENVIRONMENTAL IMPACT ASSESSMENT.

Ea (Enki) [Di]. Sumerian god of sweet water, purification, and wisdom. Together with ANU and ENLIL he held the chief power over Sumer. He was the god that created the world and has power over humanity.

EAA [Ab]. *See* EUROPEAN ASSOCIATION OF ARCHAEOLOGISTS.

Eadred [Na]. King of the English from AD 946. He extended his control over the Danelaw and was responsible for the expulsion of Erik Bloodaxe, last Danish king of York. He was the son of Edward the Elder. Died *c*.AD 955.

ealdorman [De]. Elder or patriarch, used in the Anglo-Saxon kingdoms to refer to a viceroy of the king, official, noble, or sometimes ecclesiastic. Replaced by jarl ('earl') during the Danish occupation and gradually relegated to the title of an official in local government.

ear flare [Ar]. A large circular ear ornament, flared like the bell of a trumpet, which was often made of jade. The ear flare was an elaborate form of EAR SPOOL.

ear spool [Ar]. An ornament worn in the ear lobe, sometimes of such weight that the ear might be stretched to shoulder-length.

early Archaic [CP]. *See* ARCHAIC.

early dynastic period [CP]. **1.** In Egypt covering the first and second dynasties and broadly dated to *c*.2789–2658 BC. **2.** In Mesopotamia the Jemdet Nasr period through to the AKKADIAN period, broadly *c*.2900–2330 BC. The period is traditionally divided into three blocks, each of about 200 years: EDI–EDIII. The royal tombs of UR belong to EDIII.

early Horizon [CP]. General term referring to the third of seven broad chronological phases recognized in Peruvian archaeology, succeeding the INITIAL PERIOD and preceding the EARLY INTERMEDIATE PERIOD, dating to *c*.900–1 BC. Embraces the currency of the CHAVÍN CULTURE.

early Intermediate Period [CP]. General term referring to the fourth of seven broad chronological phases recognized in Peruvian archaeology, succeeding the EARLY HORIZON and preceding the MIDDLE HORIZON, dating to AD 1–600. A period when a number of distinctive local cultures emerged, including the MOCHICA and NASCA.

early style [De]. The first subdivision of European pre-Roman Celtic art in Jacobsthal's scheme. Distinguished by three main elements: plant and allied motifs derived from Greek prototypes; geometric designs developed from local Hallstatt antecedents; and exotic orientalizing elements received either directly or indirectly from southern influences.

early Tutishcainyo Phase [CP]. South American cultural grouping found in the Rio Ucayali area of Amazonia in the period *c*.2000–1500 BC. Defined by its ceramics which belong to the Zoned Hachure Horizon Style. Pots of this phase often have complicated profiles with body flanges with step-fret, rectilinear, and curvilinear scroll design decoration. Simple geometric designs incised into the surface of the vessel are also common. Evidence of sweet manioc production is often associated with sites of this phase.

early Woodland [CP]. A subdivision of the WOODLAND STAGE defined for the archaeology of the eastern parts of North America which succeeds the Archaic around 1000 BC. The transition from late Archaic to Woodland saw three major innovations: the development of pottery manufacture; the deliberate cultivation of native plants (especially gourds, squashes, sunflowers, and tobacco); and burial under funerary mounds. The most distinctive early Woodland cultures belong to the ADENA COMPLEX.

earthen long barrow [MC]. *See* LONG BARROW.

earth lodge [MC]. Type of structure found in the midwest and eastern regions of the USA comprising a timber building with an earth covering. The shape and size of these buildings differ greatly, but archaeologically they are represented by hard-packed earthen floors and postholes.

earthworks [De]. A general term describing any group of banks, ditches, mounds, scoops, hollows, platforms, or other structures of earth and stone.

Eastern Fluted Point Tradition [CP]. Palaeo-Indian hunter-gatherer cultures living in the eastern parts of North America (from Nova Scotia to Florida) in the period around 8600 BC. Characterized by a series of chipped stone fluted points, most of which were probably knife blades. Those groups living in the more northerly regions were mainly caribou hunters, but those in more southerly regions would have used forest game and wild plant foods. At least seven styles of fluted point are known in the northeastern part of the area, some with constricted blades, some with pentagonal shapes, some long and narrow, others almost triangular in outline. Some show similarities with the western CLOVIS and FOLSOM points and they are assumed to be of approximately the same age.

Eastern Woodland Cultures [CP]. *See* WOODLAND.

Eastern Zhou [CP]. *See* ZHOU.

Eastgate points [Ar]. Type of projectile head developed *c.*AD 500 as an arrowhead during the late Archaic Stage in the Great Basin and western interior of North America.

East Midland burnished ware [Ar]. Type of Roman pottery dating to the 3rd and 4th centuries AD and found mainly in the northeast midlands of England. The pots produced were grey-brown in colour and were dominated by bowls and jars.

Eayam Phase (Charles Phase) [CP]. Cultural grouping of the Archaic Stage on the northwest coast of North America between 2500 and 1200 BC. Characterized by chipped stone points with tangs or stems, and chipped and partly ground slate points and knives. Terrestrial and marine resources were being exploited by these communities.

Ebbsfleet ware [Ar]. *See* PETERBOROUGH WARE.

ecclesia [Ge]. The assembly of the whole male citizen body which gave its decisive vote on policies put before it by the Boule or Council at Athens and elsewhere. Later the term came to mean the Christian church.

ecofact [Ge]. Strictly, natural materials that have been used by humans, for example the remains of plants and animals that were eaten by a given community. More generally taken as material recovered from archaeological sites, or other sealed deposits, which is relevant to the study of ancient environments and ecology. Examples include: animal bones, seeds, snail shells, waterlogged wood, and pollen.

eco-functionalism [Th]. The proposition that human culture is an adaptation to the environment, and thus culture functions to maintain humans and the environment in a sustainable balance.

ecology [Ge]. The study of animals and plants in relation to their environment. Human ecology deals with human communities in relation to their environment. In archaeology, the **ecological approach** involves starting with the natural environment and examining the place of human communities within it. Such an approach has most utility for the Palaeolithic and Mesolithic periods.

economic archaeology [Ge]. *See* PALAEO-ECONOMY.

economic interdependence [Th]. Refers to the fact that, in the division of labour, individuals depend on others to produce all or most of the goods they need to sustain their lives.

economy [Th]. The aspect of a social system that functions to order technological procedures socially and to control them in the interests of social units, whether individuals or collectives.

ecosystem [Th]. The set of relationships between living and non-living things in nature, or a specific natural community, including the interactions of climate, soils, rivers, and all forms of animals and plants. An environmental system maintained by the regulation of vertical food chains and patterns of energy flow.

Edgar [Na]. King of Scotland from AD 1097. Born c.1074, second son of Malcolm III and Margaret. Died in AD 1107 aged c.32, having reigned nine years.

Edjo [Di]. See WADJET.

EDM [Ab]. See ELECTRONIC DISTANCE MEASURE.

Edmund 'Ironside' [Na]. King of England for a few weeks in AD 1016 and famous for his military prowess against the Danish invaders. He was the son of Aethelred II. His death in 1016 is believed to have been through sickness.

Edmund the Magnificent [Na]. King of southern England from AD 924. Expanded his kingdom at the expense of the Danish settlers. Son of Edward the Elder. Died c.AD 946.

Edward I (Longshanks) [Na]. English king from AD 1272, of the House of Anjou (Plantagenets). Born AD 1239, eldest son of Henry III. Married (1) Eleanor, daughter of Ferdinand III, king of Castile and (2) Margaret, daughter of Philip III of France. Died in AD 1307 aged 68, having reigned 34 years.

Edward II [Na]. English king from AD 1307, of the House of Anjou (Plantagenets). Born AD 1284, eldest surviving son of Edward I and Eleanor. Married Isabella, daughter of Philip IV of France. Deposed January 1327, and killed September AD 1327 aged 43, having reigned nineteen years.

Edward III [Na]. English king from AD 1327, of the House of Anjou (Plantagenets). Born AD 1312, eldest son of Edward II. Married Philippa, daughter of William, count of Hainault. Died in AD 1377, aged 64, having reigned 50 years.

Edward IV [Na]. English king from AD 1461, of the house of York. Born AD 1442, eldest son of Richard of York, who was the grandson of Edmund, fifth son of Edward III, and the son of Anne, great-granddaughter of Lionel, third son of Edward III. Married Elizabeth Woodville, daughter of Richard, Lord River, and widow of Sir John Grey. Acceded March AD 1461, deposed October AD 1470, restored April AD 1471. Died in AD 1483, aged 40, having reigned 21 years.

Edward V [Na]. English king of the house of York. Born AD 1470, eldest son of Edward IV. Deposed June AD 1483, died probably July–September AD 1483, aged 12, having reigned 2 months (April–June).

Edward VI [Na]. English king from AD 1547, of the House of Tudor. Born AD 1537, son of Henry VIII and Jane Seymour. Died AD 1553, aged 15, having reigned six years.

Edward the Confessor [Na]. King of England from AD 1042, Edward had close links with Normandy and suffered from the unrest of some of his nobles, especially Earl Godwin of Wessex. He was noted for his piety and was later canonized. He was the son of Aethelred II. Died in AD 1066.

Edward the Elder [Na]. King of the southern English from c.AD 899. He pursued a policy of cooperation with the Danes of the Midlands and of military action when advantageous. By his death in AD 924 he had extended the English kingdom as far as the River Humber. Son of King Alfred of Wessex.

Edwin [Na]. King of Northumbria from AD 617. He encouraged the conversion of his kingdom to Christianity. He was killed in battle by Penda, king of Mercia, in AD 633.

Effigy Mound Culture [CP]. Localized grouping of middle Woodland Stage communities in the upper Mississippi area west of Lake Michigan in Wisconsin and the midwest of North America during the early first millennium AD. Characterized by the construction of low monumental burial mounds. These mounds were often set out in the shape of animals (mainly birds) and the burials placed in significant positions such as at the head, heart, or hips of the symbolic creature.

eggshell ware [Ar]. Small, delicate beakers, bowls, or jars, usually in white or cream, but occasionally black. The name refers to the sides of the vessels which are typically 2 mm or less thick. Imported to Britain in the 1st century AD and imitated locally.

Egyptology [Ge]. The study of Egypt's ancient past, especially its history, belief systems, monuments, and cultural life.

EIA [Ab]. *See* ENVIRONMETAL IMPACT ASSESSMENT.

Eileithya [Di]. Egyptian god. *See* NEKHEBET.

Einhard [Na]. Aristocrat educated in the monastery of Fulda and later a friend and adviser of Charlemagne. After Charlemagne's death in AD 814 he was made abbot of a series of religious houses. Between AD 829 and AD 836 he wrote his *Life of Charlemagne* which remains the main source of much of what is known about the Frankish empire. Einhard died in AD 840.

einkorn [Sp]. *See* WHEAT.

Elamites [CP]. A small kingdom centred in southern Iran in the 3rd millennium BC with its capital at SUSA. Its development paralleled the rise of state organizations in Mesopotamia, with writing (proto-Elamite) appearing around 3000 BC. The Elamites often appear in Mesopotamian texts as enemies, and indeed it was Elamite incursions that brought down the third dynasty in Ur in the late 3rd millennium BC. The sculpture and metalwork of Elamite craft workers was of the highest quality, and the kingdom reached its peak under Untash-gal who extended its borders by invading KASSITE Babylonia. He built a new royal city at Choga Zanbil. Around 640 BC the Elamite kingdom fell to the Assyrians when Ashurbanipal sacked Susa.

electronic distance measure (EDM) [Eq]. A surveying instrument that utilizes an infrared or laser beam to measure the distance from the source point to a defined target point. Simple hand-held EDMs are widely available; more sophisticated versions are usually incorporated in a TOTAL STATION.

electron microscope [Eq]. *See* SCANNING ELECTRON MICROSCOPE.

electron probe microanalysis [Te]. A physical technique for determining the chemical composition of stone, ceramics, pigments, glass, metal, and surface treatments of various kinds. A highly focused electron beam bombards a small point (typically 1 μm in diameter) on a polished sample, exciting electrons which emit secondary x-rays. The wavelengths of these secondary x-rays are characteristic of the elements that emitted them, and the concentrations of elements can be calculated from the intensities of each wavelength represented in the energy spectrum.

electrum [Ma]. A binary alloy of gold and silver, used especially in making decorative vessels.

Elgin, Lord (1766–1841) [Bi]. Seventh earl of Elgin who was a British diplomat, explorer, and amateur antiquarian. He was the British ambassador to Turkey between 1799 and 1803, during which time he obtained permission to remove the marble metopes from the PARTHENON in Athens (Greece was a Turkish province at the time). This was done in 1801, the marbles then being taken to London where they have been on display in the British Museum since 1816. *See also* REPATRIATION.

[Bio.: *Dictionary of National Biography*, 3, 130–1]

elite [De]. *See* STRATIFIED SOCIETY.

Elizabeth I [Na]. English queen from AD 1558, of the House of Tudor. Born AD 1533, daughter of Henry VIII and Anne Boleyn. Died in AD 1603, aged 69, having reigned 44 years.

Elko points [Ar]. Large, roughly triangular-shaped chipped stone points with concave, straight, or slightly concave bases. Two main forms are known: those with corner notches on the base and those with 'ears' on the base. Dated to the period 1300 BC to AD 700 among Desert Archaic Stage communities of the Great Basin and western interior of North America.

Elliot Smith, Sir Grafton (1871–1937) [Bi]. Distinguished British anatomist who developed a general interest in the history of mankind. Following studies of Egyptian mummies he came to the view that the complicated process of mummification was only discovered once and that it must have spread out to all other parts of the world from Egypt. This led to his obsession with DIFFUSIONISM.

[Bio.: *Dictionary of National Biography*, 1931–46, 816–17]

elm decline [Ge]. An episode in the vegetational sequence of many parts of the British Isles and other parts of northern Europe, as revealed by pollen diagrams relating to the period around 3000 BC. At the elm decline the relative abundance of this species decreased considerably, sometimes in isolation and sometimes as part of a general reduction in tree cover. Before the application of radiocarbon dating to pollen sequences this was thought to be a widespread and broadly synchronous event which, in the 1940s, J. Iversen linked to the impact of early farmers on the post-glacial forest maxima. It is now clear that this event post-dated the first impact of farming, that it was not quite as synchronous as first thought, and moreover that in some areas at least it was probably brought about by the ancient equivalent of Dutch Elm Disease.

El Mirador, Guatemala [Si]. Large settlement site of the Mayan Lowlands dating to the late Formative (Pre-Classic) period. Construction began about 150 BC and the site was abandoned about AD 150. Covering over 16 square kilometres, the site consisted of two groups of monumental buildings about 1 km apart, connected by a causeway which may have had an astronomical alignment. The western acropolis was enclosed by a stone wall on the south and east sides, and by steep slopes on the north and west. It contained buildings with civic and religious functions, and residences for the elite. The estimated population is 80 000 at its prime.

[Rep.: R. T. Matheney, 1987, El Mirador: An early Maya metropolis uncovered. *National Geographic*, 172, 316–39]

El Riego Phase [CP]. Second phase of settlement represented in the Tehuacán Valley of Mexico and dating to the period 7000–5000 BC. Characterized by numerous small camps and relatively few larger wet-season camps situated in the lush river valleys. Deer hunting was a major subsistence activity, especially during the dry season. Trapping small game and gathering seeds and cactus leaves also contributed to the diet. During this phase there is some evidence of steps being made towards agriculture: squash, amaranth, chilli pepper, and avocado may have been planted.

Elsloo, Holland [Si]. A LINEARBANDKERAMIC village and cemetery beside the River Maas in Limburg, the Netherlands, excavated by P. J. R. Modderman between 1958 and 1966. These extensive excavations revealed more than 80 houses represented in arrangements of postholes, and Modderman organized these into six main phases, each with between eleven and seventeen houses in use at any one time. The associated cemetery is the largest of its kind known, with 113 graves, 40 of which were cremations. Grave goods include pottery drinking cups usually near the head, stone adze blades, flint blades, and in one case a quernstone. The cremation burials generally had fewer grave goods than the inhumations.

[Sum.: P. Modderman, 1975, Elsloo, a Neolithic farming community in the Netherlands. In R. Bruce-Mitford (ed.), *Recent archaeological excavations in Europe*. London: Routledge. 260–87]

embanked stone circle [MC]. A type of STONE CIRCLE in which the pillars of the main ring are set within or on top of a low stone or earth bank. Such circles fall into the middle period of Aubrey Burl's three phases in the development of stone circles, broadly 2670–1975 BC.

embodiment [Th]. A humanistic perspective that seeks to widen interpretation to include all dimensions of social existence and experience by rooting any understanding of it in the way that experience is developed through the senses of the body and cognition of the self in intellectual, physical, aesthetic, and affective terms.

emic [Ge]. Pertaining to the view from within. Developed within the mind of an individual or a culture; meanings developed in terms of native categories.

emir (amir) [De]. Arabic word meaning 'commander' and used to refer to the virtually independent rulers of conquered territories.

emmer [Sp]. *See* WHEAT.

empirical investigation [Th]. A factual enquiry carried out by simply recording what is observed or discovered.

empiricism [Th]. The theory that all knowledge derives from the senses, and that the data will speak for themselves without the benefit of any explicit theoretical perspective.

In the traditional view of empiricism it is believed that the mind of the observer plays no role whatsoever in forming knowledge, and that it somehow comes about as more and more 'facts' are discovered. Following the work of Kant and others, this view was modified to allow some role to be given to the mind in forming knowledge, though the problem has always been how to relate the two adequately. In POSITIVISM this is solved by the idea of INDUCTIVISM: the ability to infer general knowledge from particular sensory data. Empiricism of various forms is the dominant EPISTEMOLOGY in archaeology; empirical data, achieved mainly through controlled observation, provide the basis of knowledge and are generally kept separate from the distortions of subjectivity and any interpretations made.

empiricist [De]. A person who espouses empiricism, but the word is increasingly used as a term of abuse in referring to theoretically challenged archaeologists.

emporium (pl. emporia) [De]. A centre of commerce characterized by a wide range of goods, often from far afield.

enamel [Ma]. A kind of opaque or semi-opaque glassy material used for decorating metalwork by fusing the coating to the surface of the metal.

Encanto Phase [CP]. Cultural grouping represented by sites on the central Peruvian coast of South America and dating to 3600–2500 BC. Excavated sites appear to be temporary settlements, and have yielded abundant evidence for the use of shellfish and other marine resources. Small quantities of deer bones have been found, and also gourds, wild legumes, and fruit remains. Grass seeds and seed-processing equipment is also common. There is some evidence for the cultivation of squash from sites of this phase, the first signs of agriculture in coastal regions.

Encinitas Tradition [CP]. General term, now largely obsolete, referring to a series of Archaic Stage hunter-gatherer cultures living on the southern coast of California in the period 6000–1000 BC, broadly corresponding to the Southern Californian early period and its three phases the EX, EY AND EZ defined by Chester King. Many of these communities engaged in extensive use of gathered plant foods, especially seeds. While settlements contain abundant shellfish remains, evidence for the hunting of mammals and other kinds of fish is rare.

enclosed cremation cemetery [MC]. A type of burial ground generally dating to the later 3rd and 2nd millennia BC in northwest Europe which comprises deposits of burnt bone interred in pits within a well-defined area that is enclosed within a roughly circular or oval earthwork. Also known as embanked cemeteries. *See also* URNFIELDS.

enclosed oppidum [MC]. A nucleated settlement of the later Iron Age in southern Britain and northern France, usually covering in excess of 10 ha, whose boundaries are marked by large earthworks comprising a bank and outer ditch. Enclosed *oppida* appear to have been economic, political, and religious centres with a considerable resident population. The enclosures might have been for defence, but more likely they were built to assist these sites in having a distinctively urban feel.

enclosed urnfield [MC]. *See* URNFIELD.

enclosure [MC]. One of the most frequently encountered forms of archaeological site: an area of land which is bounded and defined by some kind of earthwork, fence, wall, or defensive work. There is enormous variety in the shape, size, and scale of enclosures, as well as in their situation, context, and date. They do, however, seem to represent an extremely widespread human instinct to create boundaries around many of the spaces that they use.

enclosure [Ge]. The process whereby open land or common land was parcelled up into privately owned blocks or fields. In Britain this started in the 16th century AD, gathering pace during the 17th and 18th centuries, and is known as the **Enclosure Movement**. This mainly meant re-allocating the rights that people had to cultivation plots and common grazing so that compact farms were created. From the early 18th century this required a private Act of Parliament.

encrusted urn [Ar]. A style of pottery current in many parts of the British Isles in the first half of the 2nd millennium BC, with a bucket-shaped profile and thick, rather coarse, fabric. It is distinctive in having heavy applied decoration in horizontal and vertical bands around the upper portion of the body.

enculturation [Th]. The processes of becoming knowledgeable and competent in one's culture. In contrast to socialization, which usually applies to the childhood years, enculturation continues throughout a person's life.

endocranial cast [De]. Cast made of the interior of the skull, principally to show the marks left by the cortex area of the brain.

endogamy [De]. A system in which an individual may only marry another person from within the same kin group, clan, or tribe.

end scraper [Ar]. Narrow blade tool with a convex working edge at one or both ends.

eneolithic [CP]. General term representing a development of Three Age System terminology to cover a Copper Age in southeastern parts of Europe between the conventional Neolithic and the Bronze Age. *See also* CHALCOLITHIC.

engaged column [Co]. A half-column (divided longitudinally), standing out on the surface of a wall.

English Heritage [Or]. The popular name for the government agency responsible for archaeology and related matters in England. Created in 1983, its full title is the Historic Buildings and Monuments Commission for England (HBMCE). Its general duties are to: secure the preservation of ancient monuments and historic buildings situated in England; promote the preservation and enhancement of the character and appearance of conservation areas situated in England; and promote the public's enjoyment of, and advance their knowledge of, ancient monuments and historic buildings situated in England and their preservation. In addition English Heritage looks after guardianship monuments, administers the management and consent procedures for SCHEDULED monuments, and provides support for archaeological advisers in local authorities. Their work in archaeology also includes grant aid for archaeological projects, a network of regional science advisers, the maintenance of the National Monuments Record, and the running of laboratories and specialist facilities to support archaeological recording and investigation. *See also* CADW, HISTORIC SCOTLAND.

Enki [Di]. Sumerian god. *See* EA.

enlightenment [CP]. The period from the last part of the 17th century through the 18th century when many important philosophical and scientific developments took place, some of which stimulated a new interest in the past. *See* ANTIQUARIANISM.

Enlil [Di]. Sumerian god of the sky and storms, son of An. Patron of Nippur, and the most important god in the pantheon until ousted by MARDUK.

entablature [Co]. A term to cover all the horizontal stonework resting on a row of columns, including the architrave (the lowest member), the frieze, and the cornice at the top.

entrance grave [MC]. A class of chambered tomb of late Neolithic date found only in western Cornwall, the Isles of Scilly, and southeastern Ireland. Distinguished by a small round mound edged with a kerb of large boulders, and a rectangular chamber occupying most of the central part of the mound. Also known as Scilly-Tramore tombs or Scillonian tombs.

Entremont, France [Si]. A large Celto-Ligurian OPPIDUM near Aix-en-Provence in the south of France. It was the capital of the Saluvii tribe until destroyed by the Romans in 124 BC. Originally constructed in the 3rd century BC, Entremont was roughly triangular in plan and enclosed by a stone wall with rectangular projecting towers. Within the enclosure were houses, a regular street plan, a drainage network, and, near the centre, an important sanctuary. Finds include human heads and torsos carved in the round and four-sided limestone pillars with severed heads carved in relief. The occupants of the site were well connected to the classical world, as shown by a wide range of imports to the site. Especially important was eating and drinking equipment, the use of which is demonstrated by the discarded amphorae containers in which luxury food and drink would have arrived.

[Rep.: F. Benoît, 1975, The Celtic oppidum of Entremont, Provence. In R. Bruce-Mitford (ed.), *Recent archaeological excavations in Europe*. London: Routledge. 227–59]

entrepot [MC]. A trading town or city, often a port, strategically situated for the redistribution of goods from a variety of sources.

environment [Ge]. The total surroundings in which a human society finds itself; all the factors that in any way affect its mode of life.

environmental archaeology [Ge]. A branch of archaeology concerned especially with documenting and understanding the physical environment in which particular cultural systems operated. The focus of such work is sometimes synchronic in trying to reconstruct a picture of land use at or around a site at a particular phase in its history, at other times diachronic in trying to understand the changing nature of vegetation cover or animal populations in a given landscape. Increasingly, interest has moved towards the matter of context, the dynamics of relationships between people and their environment, and the symbolic meanings that earlier populations attached to particular plants, animals, or sectors of the landscape they occupied.

environmental ecology [Ge]. A concern with preserving the integrity of the physical environment in the face of the impact of modern industry and technology. Archaeology is sometimes included in such quests as the remains of the past are included within the physical environment (i.e., HISTORIC ENVIRONMENT) of the present.

Environmental Impact Assessment (EIA) [Me]. A process that since the mid 1970s has been developed and increasingly applied to large and medium-sized development proposals whereby technical studies are undertaken in order to predict the likely impact that the scheme will have on the local, regional, and global environment. The aim is to better inform the decision-making process, allow alternative proposals to be compared, and, where appropriate, promote the development of acceptable mitigation measures. EIA was first applied widely in the USA; it was made a legal requirement for certain types of scheme in Europe following a European Community Directive issued in 1985. Archaeological remains are one of the resources that can be included in the scope of an EIA where it is believed that such things might be significantly affected by a proposed project. Also known as Environmental Assessment (EA).

eolith [Ar]. Obsolete term, formerly used for a naturally shaped or fractured stone fancifully considered to be created by humans. The origin of eoliths was once the subject of long-running debate connected to recognizing and accepting the great antiquity of the human species.

Epet [Di]. Egyptian god. *See* APET.

Ephesus, Turkey [Si]. Once a major seaport on the west coast of Turkey in the delta area of the River Cayster, this site is now 8 km inland. It is one of the richest and most splendid sites in the world. Excavations by John Turle Wood for the British Museum in the 1860s located the temple of Artemis, and later work by Austrian archaeologists uncovered a good deal of its early history. First occupied in Mycenaean times, tradition describes how the settlement was founded from Athens by King Androklos. Supreme prosperity arrived under Hellenistic and Roman rulers. The centre-piece is the temple of Artemis (Diana to the Romans and perhaps equivalent to the Anatolian god Cybele), one of the SEVEN WONDERS OF THE WORLD, but later destroyed by Alexander the Great in 356 BC. From the Greco-Roman town there are many public buildings, including seven gymnasia, administrative buildings, baths, and the agora. The theatre, from the HELLENISTIC period, could seat 24000 people and was the setting for St Paul's address set down in the Acts of the Apostles (Chapter 19). The Archaic Greek temple is also important as its foundation deposit includes a hoard of early electrum coins.

[Sum.: G. E. Bean, 1989, *Aegean Turkey*. London: Murray]

epigraphy [De]. The study of inscriptions.

epi-palaeolithic [CP]. Cultures of Palaeolithic tradition surviving into early post-glacial times.

epiphysis [De]. The articular end of a long bone, which fuses at adulthood.

epistemology [Th]. The branch of philosophy which deals with the character of knowledge, and how we know what we know; the study of what constitutes knowledge, its construction, its limits, its veracity, and its validation. An epistemology is a theory of knowledge, of which there are many, and for centuries it has been a central theme of philosophy. Since the NEW ARCHAEOLOGY of the 1960s it has also been a matter of considerable interest for archaeologists: what constitutes a knowledge of the past when all that connects the past and the present is material culture. A recent interest of POST-PROCESSUAL and SOCIAL ARCHAEOLOGY is the importance of the social reproduction of knowledge through DISCOURSE.

equal-armed brooch [Ar]. Bow-brooch with a flat headplate (generally semi-circular with some radiating knobs) and a long, lozenge-shaped footplate. A variety of types have been distinguished, decorated with precious stones or chip-carving and distributed from the Crimea to Spain from the 4th to the 7th centuries AD.

equinox [Ge]. The time when daylight and darkness are of equal length, around 21 March (vernal equinox) and 23 September (autumnal equinox). At such times the sun rises due east and sets due west. The position of the rising or setting sun at the time of the equinox can sometimes be recognized as a significant alignment within the structure of prehistoric monuments.

equites [De]. Term used by Caesar to describe a sector of Celtic society who were presumably horse-warriors or horse-riding soldiers of some kind.

Erbenheim sword [Ar]. Heavy bronze flange-hilted sword with a leaf-shaped blade for slashing rather than thrusting. Originating in the early URNFIELD TRADITIONS of central Europe, examples were exported to surrounding areas, some arriving in Britain, for example, in the Penard Phase of the later Bronze Age, the 12th century BC.

Ernutet [Di]. Egyptian god. *See* RENENUTET.

Ertebølle Culture [CP]. Late Mesolithic communities of the west Baltic coastal regions, named after a series of massive shell middens at Ertebølle, Jutland, Denmark, dated to c.3900–3250 BC. The later phases of the culture are marked by the appearance of pottery, especially large S-shaped pointed-base jars, and ground stone implements, both the result of contacts with farming communities to the south.

escutcheon [Ar]. Small metal ornamental plate or badge forming an emblem or cover plate attached to a larger object or structure.

Eskimo [CP]. A widely used but increasingly obsolete general term for the aboriginal peoples of the Arctic regions of North America. A French transliteration of an Algonquin word meaning 'raw-fish eaters'. The people themselves use the term 'Inuit' to describe themselves and this is preferred.

essentialism [Th]. The idea that there are certain attitudes or emotions that are biologically inherent to human beings in general or to males or females differently. Essentialist claims are often backed up with biological arguments, and are in some cases derived from sociobiology or humanism. Essentialist views, not all supportable, abound in archaeology: the most common is that males go hunting because of their killer urges while females gather plant produce.

ethnicity [Th]. The ascription, or claim, to belong to a particular cultural group on the basis of genetics, language, or other cultural manifestations. Definitions of what constitutes an ethnic group have varied over time and place, but have long been a central concern in archaeology. ETHNOARCHAEOLOGICAL studies have shown that while material culture may in some cases indicate sharp boundaries between groups, this is not always the case. Nor do such boundaries necessarily relate to contacts or movements: ethnicity is malleable and contingent on context. *See also* CULTURE.

ethnoarchaeology [Ge]. A branch of archaeology that uses ethnographical data to inform the examination and interpretation of the archaeological record. In some cases this involves the study of living communities by selectively looking at the archaeologically recoverable material culture: a sort of living archaeology that gained popularity as part of the NEW ARCHAEOLOGY of the 1960s and 1970s. Ethnoarchaeologists carry out a kind of ethnography to examine and document the relationships between human behaviour and the resultant patterns of artefacts and food remains, in some cases contributing to or developing MIDDLE RANGE THEORY.

ethnocentrism [Ge]. **1.** The belief that one's own values and views held true in all times and places. **2.** The tendency to look at other cultures through the eyes of one's own culture, believing that one's own culture is morally superior, and thereby misrepresenting others.

ethnography [Ge]. The descriptive documentation and analysis of a contemporary culture.

ethnohistory [Ge]. The reconstruction of the history of societies (usually non-literate) based upon information gleaned from oral traditions, written materials from outsiders, linguistic and archaeological data, or any other form of pertinent information. A study of the past using non-western, indigenous historical records, and especially oral traditions.

ethnology [Ge]. A term often used in Britain to describe those working particularly on material culture; a cross-cultural study of aspects of various cultures, usually based on theory to understand how cultures work and why they change; the theoretical analysis of culture in comparative perspective. In its wider sense it is also concerned with the classification of peoples in terms of their racial and cultural characteristics, and the explanation of these by reference to their history or prehistory. In western Europe the term is used in a way that is much closer to what in the USA would fall within the field of anthropology.

ethnomethodology [Ge]. The study of how people make sense of what others say and do in the course of day-to-day social interaction. Ethnomethodology is concerned with the means by which human beings sustain meaningful interchanges with one another.

ethnoscience [Th]. An attempt at cultural description from a totally EMIC standpoint, thus eliminating all the ethnographer's own categories.

ethology [Ge]. The study of animal behaviour in natural habitats.

etic [Ge]. Pertaining to a view from the outside. In science this view might come from the observer: the analytic view, presumably replicable by any trained observer.

Etruscans [CP]. Successors to the VILLANOVANS in north central Italy (modern Tuscany) during the early 1st millennium BC, they had become a recognizable society by the 8th century—a loosely knit but powerful confederacy of city-states. They developed long-distance trade contacts to Greece, Carthage, and across the Alps into central Europe. Their cities were substantial and wealthy: for example, Populonia, Vetulonia, and Tarquinia. Their influence extended over wide areas, including Aleria, the Po Valley, and parts of Campania. The area is rich in natural resources, including gold, copper and iron, and this led to a strong and influential craft base. The Etruscan language still causes problems because although it is written in an eastern Greek alphabet many aspects of its syntax and vocabulary are uncertain. But the Etruscans were under constant pressure from communities to the north, and increasingly from Rome in the south. Between the 4th and 2nd centuries Rome conquered all of Etruria, but despite their political extinction, the Etruscans contributed much to Roman civilization in such matters as infrastructure, political and social organization, art, architecture, theatre, and engineering skills.

Eugenius [Na]. A teacher of rhetoric in Rome who was befriended by Arbogastes, a commander-in-chief of Frankish origin who was suspected of having murdered Valentinian II. Eugenius was proclaimed western emperor by Arbogastes in AD 392 but was defeated and killed by Theodosius the Great in AD 394.

European Association of Archaeologists (EAA) [Or]. A membership-based association recognized by the Council of Europe that is open to all archaeologists and others with related interests. Established in 1994, the aims are to promote the development of archaeological research and the exchange of archaeological information, the management and interpretation of the European archaeological heritage, proper ethical and scientific standards for archaeological work and the interests of professional archaeologists in Europe. The association publishes the *European Journal of Archaeology*.

European Foundation for Heritage Skills [Or]. A non-profit-making non-governmental organization set up in 1996 as an initiative by the Council of Europe to help improve ways of preserving the existing heritage of Europe. This covers not only the great monuments, but also major rural and industrial buildings and sites, as well as the less tangible heritage of popular traditions. It works in three areas: in-service training, information exchange and networking, and development.

eustatic adjustment (eustasy) [Pr]. World-wide alterations in sea level, independent of any ISOSTATIC ADJUSTMENT of the land. The main implications for archaeology come in the PLEISTOCENE and HOLOCENE when water released from melting ice-sheets caused sea levels to rise during interglacials and the post-glacial.

evaluation (evaluation excavation/field evaluation) [Te]. The process of determining the nature, extent, quality of survival, and preservational characteristics of a known or suspected archaeological site. This is usually achieved by one or more of a variety of field techniques such as sampling with test-pits or trenches, geophysical surveys, geochemical prospection, and fieldwalking. It may also involve desk-based research using aerial photographs, historic maps, place-name evidence, and so on. Such studies typically follow from an archaeological ASSESSMENT of some kind. They might be undertaken in the context of preparing for the investigation of the site for purely research purposes (when they are sometimes referred to as trial-trenching), but increasingly such evaluations are undertaken in the context of ARCHAEOLOGICAL RESOURCE MANAGEMENT. Here such work is done in advance of development, sometimes as part of an ENVIRONMENTAL IMPACT ASSESSMENT in order to provide a local planning authority with relevant information to assist in determining a planning application. In the UK the need for evaluation is set out in the planning guidance issued by central government (*see* PLANNING POLICY GUIDANCE). Also known as archaeological evaluation or field evaluation.

Evans, Arthur John (1851–1941) [Bi]. British archaeologist, son of JOHN EVANS, and best known for his work on Crete. Born at Nash Mills, he was educated at Harrow and Brasenose College, Oxford. After leaving university in 1875 he spent some time travelling in the Balkans as a journalist. In 1884, however, he returned to Oxford and took up the post of Keeper of the Ashmolean Museum. His first interests were in coins and seals, and it was the early Greek seals that led him to

Knossos, on Crete, which he purchased in 1896. In 1899 he began excavations there at his own expense and for 35 years thoroughly researched not only the site but the whole MINOAN civilization that it related to. He termed what he found 'Minoan' after the legendary King Minos. He then used the family fortune to reconstruct much of the two-storey royal palace and the frescoes on its walls.

[Bio.: J. Evans, 1943, *Time and chance: the story of Arthur Evans and his forebears*. London: Longmans]

Evans, Clifford (1920–81) [Bi]. American archaeologist who, together with his wife Bettey Meggers, pioneered Amazonian archaeology, establishing the main cultural–historical sequence and chronology. Affiliated with the Smithsonian Institution from 1951 onwards, they carried out research in Ecuador, Venezuela, British Guiana, and Brazil.

[Obit.: *American Antiquity*, 47 (1982), 545–50]

Evans, Joan (1893–1977) [Bi]. British author, scholar, art historian, and antiquarian, daughter of Sir John Evans and half-sister to Sir Arthur Evans. After a haphazard early education she went up to St Hugh's College, Oxford, in 1914 where she remained as a don until 1922. During the 1920s she spend much time in France writing about its history and art, producing a new book more or less every year. She was President of the Society of Antiquaries between 1959 and 1964, the first woman to hold the post. Her many publications include *Romanesque architecture of the Order of Cluny* (1938, Cambridge: CUP), and *A history of the Society of Antiquaries* (1956, Oxford: Society of Antiquaries). She was made a DBE in 1976.

[Obit.: *Antiquaries Journal*, 58 (1978), 9–12]

Evans, Sir John (1823–1908) [Bi]. British businessman and antiquary, probably one of the greatest and last of his generation, whose work in the late 19th century focused on recording and documenting many different kinds of artefacts. Brought up in Market Bosworth, he trained in Germany to join the family paper-making firm of Dickinsons. His interests in archaeology developed at an early age; he joined the Numismatic Society when he was 26 and was elected a Fellow of the Society of Antiquaries when he was 29. In 1864 he published *Coins of the ancient Britons* (London: Longworth), and joined international debates on the age and human origin of early flint tools. His two greatest works, *Ancient stone implements of Great Britain* (1871; 2nd edition, 1897, London: Longmans) and *Ancient bronze implements, weapons, and ornaments of Great Britain and Ireland* (1881, London: Longmans), remain important sources to this day.

[Bio.: J. Evans, 1943, *Time and chance: the story of Arthur Evans and his forebears*. London: Longmans]

everted rim [De]. A rim which turns sharply outwards and upwards from the shoulder of the vessel.

evolution [Th]. The development through time of biological organisms by means of the adaptation of species to the demands of the physical environment. Such change generally involves an increase in complexity and functional improvement. Its greatest exponent was CHARLES DARWIN, whose *Origin of species* appeared in AD 1859 setting out the principles of evolution based on random mutation and natural selection. These principles have been carried over into archaeological thinking where they can be seen in terms of social evolution and the progressive climb from 'savagery' to 'civilization'. At the small scale, it is applied to the typology of artefacts which can often be arranged in a developmental sequence. At a large scale, society as a whole is sometimes viewed as a unilinear progression through a series of pre-defined stages.

Ewart Park Phase [CP]. Industrial phase of the British later Bronze Age, named after a hoard of metalwork found at Ewart Park, Northumberland. Dating to 800–700 BC, the Ewart Park Phase succeeds the Wilberton Phase and precedes the Llyn Fawr Phase that equates with Hallstatt C. During the Ewart Park Phase lead-alloyed metal becomes very widespread and scrap hoards and founder's hoards proliferate. Horse harness and vehicle fittings begin to appear. Regional traditions abound, including the Carp's Tongue Complex in southeastern England, the Llantwit-Stogursey Tradition of south Wales, the Broadward Complex of the Welsh Marches, the Heathery Burn Tradition of northern England, the Duddington, Covesea, and Ballimore traditions in Scotland, and the Dowris Phase in Ireland.

Ex, Ey, Ez Phases [CP]. Series of Archaic Stage communities living on the coast of southern California in North America during the period 6000–1000 BC. Through this period the sea level in the area was rising and accordingly subsistence economies were changing. In the Ex phase exploitation of shell-fish and gathered plant food predominated, but in later phases deer and sea mammals became an increasingly common part of the diet. These changes coincided with a transition from crude percussion-flaked lanceolate projectile heads to side-notched and stemmed heads. Bone gouges and multi-part barbed fish-hooks also come into use. Houses of these phases include some sunken-floor buildings.

excarnation [Ge]. The exposure of human corpses to the elements to facilitate the decomposition of the flesh before the bones are gathered up for burial or disposal.

excavation [Te]. One of the principal means by which archaeological data is captured and recorded, excavation involves the systematic exposure of deposits that are then taken apart. There are a number of different techniques of excavation, such as OPEN AREA EXCAVATION, PLANUM METHOD, QUADRANT METHOD, and WHEELER METHOD, each having its own strengths and weaknesses. Selecting a method that suits the kind of site under investigation and the questions being asked is an important preliminary to any excavation project. A widely held principle, however, is that excavation should proceed by removing the layers and deposits within the site in the reverse order to which they were laid down in the first place. The different methods also carry with them implications for the way things are recorded, although plans, sections, photographs, notebooks, finds indexes, context records, and sample logs will be found in almost all of them. Not all studies can be done on site (desirable though that is), and samples of material and finds have to be cross-referenced to the deposits from which they came so that they can be examined later in the laboratory. Excavation is destructive, and it is costly in time and resources. New technology such as digital recording systems is playing an increasing role on fieldwork projects, and frees the archaeologists to spend more time interpreting what they are finding as they go along.

excavation unit [Or]. *See* UNIT.

exchange [Th]. Transfer of goods, services, or information between individuals or groups of individuals. Such transfers may not necessarily involve payments or reciprocation with equivalence. The term is often used by prehistorians wishing to avoid the modern connotations of the word 'trade'.

exchange system [Ge]. A regular pattern in the way that goods and services are exchanged between individuals and communities.

excised decoration [De]. A technique for decorating pottery, in particular where strips or shapes are cut out from the vessel walls before firing and while the pot is still soft. The resulting voids are often filled with coloured paste to provide a contrast with the colour of the main body of the pot.

exedra [Co]. A curved marble wall, often used as a base for one or more statues, and provided with a marble bench which offered dignified and sheltered casual seating in public places.

exogamy [Ge]. A rule requiring marriage outside one's own social or cultural unit. *Compare* ENDOGAMY.

experimental archaeology [Ge]. A branch of archaeological investigation in which carefully controlled experiments are undertaken in order to provide data and insights that aid in the interpretation of the archaeological record. These experiments vary widely in their nature and purpose. Some, such as the creation and monitoring of experimental earthworks to see how they decay, are long-lived and massive in scale. Others, such as the reproduction of ancient tools to learn about the processes of manufacture, may take a matter of hours or days.

explanation [Th]. The development of a closed loop of interpretation in which a particular factor or a series of factors are deemed to be responsible for, or causally related to, a set of observed conditions. Explanation with reference to established laws is the main means of interpretation within the physical sciences; in the social sciences there is greater interest in developing an UNDERSTANDING of something rather than an explanation of it.

exponential growth [De]. A geometric, rather than a linear, rate of progression, producing a very fast rise in the numbers of a population experiencing such growth.

extended burial [De]. *See* BURIAL SITE.

extended family [Ge]. A family group consisting of more than two generations of relatives living either within the same household or very close to one another.

fabric [De]. In pottery studies the term is used to refer to the material from which a vessel is made, as it appears in its finished state. Fabric is usually described in terms of its texture, colour, surface treatments, core, visible constituents and hardness.

fabrica [MC]. A Latin term for a workshop.

fabricator [Ar]. A stone or bone tool used in the process of manufacturing other kinds of stone tools. The term is most often applied to a style of Mesolithic tool known in northwest Europe and believed to have been used in retouch flaking. It is a flint bar, D-shaped in cross-section, with rounded and usually rather worn ends.

façade [Co]. Front of a structure, often elaborated and visually impressive. In some prehistoric monuments, for example chambered tombs, it is not always clear what those who built and used them considered was the front; assumptions are therefore made by archaeologists.

face urn [Ar]. A jar with a human face, usually in appliqué technique, formed on the shoulder. The function of these vessels was often funerary. There are also flagons with faces moulded on the neck.

facies [Ge]. A part of a bigger unit or style that can be distinguished in some way on the basis of appearance or composition. Although the term was originally developed in the field of geology, it has increasing application in archaeology with reference to chronological or regional variants of bigger traditions or industries.

Faereyinga Saga [Do]. Icelandic saga, written about AD 1200, which gives a traditional and highly personalized account of the 9th-century AD settlement of the Faroe Islands.

faience [Ma]. Blue-coloured artificial glass-like material made from baked siliceous clay. Faience was used for the manufacture of a variety of ornaments and pieces of jewellery during prehistoric and later times. Beads of various shapes and sizes were used to form necklaces during the early Bronze Age in many parts of Europe. Faience was long believed to have been imported from the eastern Mediterranean, but there is now evidence to suggest that it was manufactured in Europe as well.

Fairmount Phase [CP]. Chronological subdivision of the Mississippian of the Eastern Woodlands of North America, dating to around AD 900.

false colour infrared photography [Te]. *See* INFRARED PHOTOGRAPHY.

false portal (false entrance) [Co]. A kind of dummy doorway or blind entrance in the side of a structure, either for symbolic reasons, to achieve architectural balance, or to foil would-be robbers.

false relief [De]. A form of decoration applied especially to pottery where two parallel rows of triangles are excised or impressed into the wall of the vessel so that the space between them gives the visual impression of being raised even though actually it is the same height as the rest of the vessel's surface.

fancy barrow [MC]. A general term used to describe a range of early Bronze Age round barrows in the British Isles that depart in their shape and form from the traditional common styles of BOWL BARROW and BELL BARROW. Fancy barrows usually comprise between one and five round mounds set within a ditched enclosure that often has a small outer bank and a larger inner bank flanking the ditch. The mounds are generally small, so-called saucer and disc forms, and there is a large berm between the mound and its surrounding ditch. Fancy barrows are typical of the early 2nd millennium BC and many in southern England are associated with the WESSEX CULTURE. In upland areas where ditches are more difficult to dig the area defined by the enclosure is instead defined by a low platform with the barrow mound set on the top of the platform.

farmery [Co]. The infirmary of a monastery.

farmstead [MC]. A single dwelling house with its adjoining agricultural appurtenances, including yards and buildings. Sometimes home to more than one family.

Farnham pottery [Ar]. *See* ALICE HOLT WARE.

Fatyanovo Culture (Fat'janovo Culture) [CP]. Late Copper Age and early Bronze Age communities of the 2nd millennium BC in the upper Volga region of Russia, named after a cemetery site excavated near Yaroslavl, Moscow Region. The extent of the culture covers the former VOLGA–OKA CULTURE area, but a northern variant known as the Yaroslav–Kalinin group and a southern variant known as the Moscow group have been recognized. Burials were in fairly deep-cut flat graves as single individuals, the main grave goods including globular jars, stone battleaxes with distinctive drooping blades, copper trinkets, and sometimes clay models of wheels. Part of the SINGLE GRAVE tradition.

faunal analysis [Ge]. *See* ARCHAEOZOOLOGY.

Fauresmith [CP]. A stoneworking industry found in south and east Africa related to the late ACHEULIAN, characterized by small pointed and neatly made handaxes, and named after a site in the Orange Free State. At Saldanha, Cape Province, Fauresmith artefacts were contemporary with fossil remains of *Homo neanderthalis*.

Faussett, Bryan (1720–76) [Bi]. British antiquary well known for excavations into Anglo-Saxon burial grounds between 1757 and 1773, mainly in Kent. His work was published in 1856 under the title *Inventorium sepulchrale*. A

Fellow of All Souls College, Oxford, Faussett was a cleric by profession and had livings in Shropshire and Kent.

[Bio.: *Dictionary of National Biography*, 6, 1114]

Fécamp rampart [De]. A type of earthwork forming the defences of late Iron Age hillforts in northern France and southern Britain, named after Le Camp du Canada at Fécamp, Pays de Caux, and introduced into Britain in the 1st century AD. It comprises a large mound of earth and stone forming a formidable bank outside of which is a wide flat-bottomed ditch.

Feddersen Wierde, Germany [Si]. A TERP settlement on the North Sea coast of Germany, extensively excavated by W. Haarnagel between 1955 and 1963. Occupied between the 1st and 5th centuries AD, the site was found to be more or less circular in plan, internally organized in radial segments running off from a central open area. An industrial zone provided evidence for leatherworking and bone working; the remainder of the settlement comprised farmsteads. The buildings were all of timber: aisled houses with wattle walls that incorporated a byre at one end and living areas for a family at the other. There was some evidence for foreign trade, but the settlement seems to have been fairly self-supporting. The site was abandoned around 450 AD.

[Rep.: W. Haarnagel, 1979, *Die Grabungen Feddersen Wierde*. Wiessbachen: F. Steiner]

federal archaeologist [Ge]. American term used to describe a professional archaeologist employed by a federal agency.

Federmesser [CP]. A toolmaking tradition of the late glacial period used by peoples living on the north European Plain in the period *c*.9800 BC through to *c*.8800 BC. Based on the use of small backed blades. Such pieces occur within the CRESWELLIAN in the British Isles.

feedback (feedback system) [Th]. A concept in the archaeological application of systems theory reflecting the continually changing relationship between cultural variables and their environment. A system in which the result of a signal, or series of signals, is another signal which in turn modifies and directs the next.

Fell's Cave, Chile [Si]. Early cave occupation site in Patagonia near the Straits of Magellan west of Palli Aike in the far south of South America. Excavated by Junius Bird in the 1930s, the cave had a deep layer of debris below which were the remains of an ancient roof-fall, and below this again further refuse. The lower deposit belonged to the early Magellan Complex and included an assemblage which comprised fishtail points, associated with late Pleistocene fauna such as native horse, sloth, and guanaco. Further excavations in the late 1950s by José Emperaire and Annette Laming-Emperaine confirmed Bird's record of the stratigraphy and provided dates which assign the lower deposits to the period before 9000 BC. Fell's Cave is thus important as one of the earliest pieces of evidence for the human occupation of southern South America.

[Rep.: J. Emperaire, A. Laming-Emperaire, and H. Reichlen, 1963, La Grotte Fell et autres sites de la région volcanique de la Patagonie chilienne. *Journal de la Société des Américanistes*, 52, 167–252; J. Bird, 1938, Before Magellan. *Natural History*, 41(1), 16–28]

feminist archaeology [Th]. An approach to archaeological interpretation that provides a critique of androcentric notions and biases, and foregrounds the experiences of women in the past. The belief that women have suffered from oppression in western society carries with it the implication that archaeologists need to examine gender roles and inequalities within the archaeological profession. *See also* GENDER ARCHAEOLOGY.

fen [Ge]. A marshy wetland characterized by alkaline conditions such as occur between fresh water and dry land along lake margins, in river cut-offs, or extensive wet shallows bordering river estuaries. Fens present an early stage in the progressive colonization of shallow water, the carr stage being next when trees start to establish themselves. The preservation of archaeological remains in fen areas is generally good.

Fengate, Cambridgeshire, UK [Si]. Multiperiod prehistoric settlements on the edge of the Fenlands in eastern England. Excavations by Francis Pryor and colleagues since 1971 have revealed a long sequence of occupation starting in the middle Neolithic and extending through into early Roman times. In the 4th millennium BC there was a small square Neolithic house, and a pit-grave all well spaced out across the landscape and representing the first major colonization of the area. During the 3rd millennium, however, the area started to fill up, with the establishment of a small field system and more extensive settlement. This process continued through the 2nd and 1st millennia BC, with the appearance soon after 1000 BC of a series of structures on a timber platform in a marshy area at what is now Flag Fen. A series of post alignments run across the wetland near the platform and during the later Bronze Age and early Iron Age acted to trap material moving about in the shallow water round the island, making a rich assemblage in archaeological terms. One of the activities happening within and around Flag Fen was the deposition into the water of metal objects, perhaps as some kind of offerings. Settlement in the area continued through the Iron Age and early Roman period, but from the 3rd century AD the water level rose, flooding the landscape and causing the people to move to drier ground.

[Sum.: F. Pryor, 1991, *Flag Fen*. London: Batsford and English Heritage]

Fengate ware [Ar]. *See* PETERBOROUGH WARE.

feretory [Co]. A shrine to contain the relics of a saint.

Fertile Crescent [De]. A term invented in 1916 by James Breasted, first director of the Oriental Institute, Chicago. What he referred to was the roughly crescent-shaped area of land between Egypt, through the Levant, into southern Anatolia and on to Mesopotamia and the Zagros Mountains. Conditions here were favourable for the development of farming, and it is here that many of the earliest farming sites have indeed been found. The term is less heavily used today, however, because early farming sites have also been found outside the Crescent and in more marginal landscapes.

feudalism [De]. A strictly hierarchical political and economic system in which land is granted in return for military or labour services.

fibula [Ar]. A Latin word for a common type of brooch or fastener similar in operation to a modern-day safety-pin, made of bronze or iron and consisting of a bow, pin, and catch plate. The earliest examples date to around

1300 BC, although their origins are controversial. There are two main kinds of *fibula*. The **single-piece** *fibula* belongs mainly to southern Europe and probably started with the 'violin bow' in Mycenaean Greece. The **multi-part** *fibula* is most common in northern Europe where the pin is almost always made separately from the bow and catch plate. The emergence of *fibulae* implies changes in the materials used in making clothes and the way such clothes were worn. *See also* BROOCH.

ficron handaxe [Ar]. François Bordes used this term to refer to roughly worked pointed bifaces of Middle Palaeolithic type. More generally it is applied as a morphological term to describe long pointed bifaces with slightly curved sides and a well-made tip.

field barn [MC]. An agricultural storage building that is situated amongst the fields it serves rather than within the farmstead. This kind of structure is most common when cultivated land is situated well away from settlement areas.

field evaluation [Te]. *See* EVALUATION.

field notes [Ge]. Records of observations or interpretations made during fieldwork or direct engagement with the archaeological resource. May include written notes, photographs, drawings, tape-recordings, video film, etc.

field school [Or]. A formal training programme in archaeological methods run under the supervision of trained professionals, usually as part of a major research project. Also known as a training excavation, but many field schools cover surveying, geophysical surveys, finds processing, and a range of other work that complements the excavations themselves.

field survey [Te]. A general term used to describe the discovery, mapping, and non-destructive investigation of archaeological remains in open country. The discovery of sites may involve walk-over surveys and systematic sampling of various kinds using direct observations, FIELDWALKING, SHOVEL PIT TESTING, and the ground-checking of information from aerial surveys and remote sensing. Mapping work will be done using one of a

range of surveying techniques from simple sketching through to detailed measured drawings of earthworks and structures using a TOTAL STATION or GPS. Non-destructive investigations mainly draw on geophysical surveys, geochemical studies, and detailed surface collection where sites lie under disturbed ground.

field system [MC]. At their most simple, field systems are groupings of plots established in order to graze animals and cultivate crops in a controlled way. Each plot or field is usually surrounded by a fence, hedge, or wall, the latter as often as not derived from stones collected up from clearing stones from the plot in order to facilitate cultivation. The creation of a field system implies an investment in the land, and in addition to the fields themselves there may well be infrastructure facilities such as wells, threshing floors, animal houses, folds and pens, shelters and tool stores, barns, and maybe even dwellings for those working the land. Connecting the plots will be tracks and droves of various kinds.

The arrangement of a field system, its organization, and the nature of the components within it say a lot about its origins and how it worked. In general there are two kinds of arrangement, although either can occur as an 'open field system' where there are few if any walls, banks, or hedges dividing the plots or as a 'closed field system' where the boundary works between and around plots are substantial. Closed field systems are especially common where livestock form part of the regime.

Regular field systems have a common plan and fairly tight structure to them. Most were set out as a single operation, or at least planned in a way that could be expanded on a modular basis later if need be. The field plots are usually fairly uniform in size and shape, square and rectangular fields being common. One particular variant of the regular field system is the so-called co-axial field system where a framework comprising the long parallel boundaries forming the axis of the system are set out and then these strips, which may be several kilometres long, are infilled with cross-walls to create the field plots. Such systems began to be made during the Bronze Age in Europe, some of the best preserved being those identified by Andrew Fleming and John Collis on Dartmoor, England.

By contrast, **irregular field systems** are rarely planned: rather they develop piecemeal (irregular aggregate field systems) either by the periodic addition of new plots or the modification of what was originally a regular system. Irregular field systems tend to have curved or crooked boundaries between the plots, fields of uneven shape and size, and a high proportion of fields that can only be accessed from other fields rather than from a trackway or drove.

fieldwalking [Te]. A powerful archaeological technique to systematically sample the upper surface of cultivated or disturbed ground in an effort to locate or map the distribution and extent of archaeological sites. The basic assumption is made that the topsoil contains distinctive traces of archaeological activity—fingerprints of what has gone on in the past. In this sense the topsoil is treated as a single extensive open archaeological context. It includes material that has been deposited onto or into the topsoil from above, for example debitage from an episode of flint knapping by someone sitting on the ground. It also includes material from features underneath the topsoil that are exposed to the effects of cultivation or ground works and therefore mechanically brought into the ploughsoil. Cultivation will have mixed all these different sources of material together, and a proportion of what is in the soil will be visible on the surface.

There are two main ways of carrying out fieldwalking. The first is **line walking**, where linear transects are defined at fixed intervals and the fieldwalkers traverse each line collecting material that they see within their corridor of vision. Lines are usually divided into stints (often the stints are the same length as the gap between transects to make data processing easier) and the material recovered is bagged by line and stint. The second technique is **grid walking**, where the survey area is divided into squares and the walkers spend a fixed amount of time working in each square gathering everything they can see during the allotted search period. At the end of the allotted time the finds are bagged together and the team moves on to the next square. In both systems it is important that each sample unit (a line stint or a grid square) is treated equally, otherwise the results will be worthless. After the finds have been collected, cleaned, sorted, and identified, different categories can be mapped and patterns identified.

figurine [Ar]. A small model of a human or animal, usually of clay, stone, wood, or metal, whose purpose generally seems to be ceremonial, devotional, or some kind of offering to a deity.

filigree [De]. A technique used in the manufacture of jewellery in which gold, electrum, or silver wire is bent into shape and then soldered onto an area of metal that is to be decorated. The technique was first developed by Sumerian craftsmen in the 3rd millennium BC.

Filitosa, Corsica [Si]. A fortified promontory settlement in the southwestern part of the island excavated by R. Grosjean in the 1950s. The main feature of the site is a Bronze Age TORRE or tower. Circular in plan and constructed in dry-stone walling, it is set within a walled enclosure which also contains oval houses. It dates to the mid 2nd millennium BC, and incorporates fragments of statue menhirs showing men armed with bronze daggers and swords.

[Rep.: R. Grosjean, 1961, *Filitosa et son contexte archéologique dans la Vallée du Taravo*. Paris: Académie des Inscriptions et Belles-Lettres]

filler [Ge]. General term for material added to clay when preparing it for use in potting or brickmaking. Filler may comprise grog (broken pottery crushed up into a gritty consistency), sand, crushed rock, or organic material such as dung or straw. The selection of the right filler is important in relation to the intended use of the product; cooking pots, for example, are best made using filler that helps conduct heat through the walls of the vessel, while vessels in which milk or water is to be stored are more useful if the fabric is porous so that surface evaporation will have the effect of cooling the contents.

fillet [Co]. A flat and narrow moulding on the surface of a wall or between the flutes of an Ionic or Corinthian column.

fineware [De]. Good-quality pottery that has a fine textured fabric, relatively thin walls, and is usually tableware or for personal use. Fineware may be decorated, but above all stands out within the overall repertoire of material used by a community in being of superior quality.

finial [Ar]. An ornament at the top of a gable, canopy, pinnacle, or similar on a building or structure. Usually made of stone or ceramic. *See also* ROOF FURNITURE.

Fiorelli, Giuseppe (1823–96) [Bi]. Italian archaeologist who took over the excavations at Pompeii between 1860 and 1875 and was one of the first to apply the principles of stratigraphy and large-area excavation. By dividing the city into a series of regions, his work allowed a systematic appraisal. He also developed a method for taking casts of hollows in the hardened ash which revealed the imprints of people, animals, plants, and wooden objects such as furniture. His training schools provided a source for many later archaeologists.

[Bio.: R. A. Genovese, 1992, *Giuseppe Fiorelli e la tutela dei beni culturali dopo l'unità d'Italia*. Napoli: Edizioni Scientifiche Italiano]

firedog [Ar]. A metal frame with a low crosspiece supported at either end by an upright. The firedog sits next to a fire with logs resting on the crosspiece so that they burn properly. Very fine decorative examples are known from La Tène contexts in Europe, some with animal heads adorning the tops of the uprights.

First Intermediate period [CP]. **1.** In Egypt, the period between the Old Kingdom and the Middle Kingdom and representing the 7th to the 11th dynasties, *c.*2150–2100 BC. **2.** Period between the earlier and middle Stone Ages in Africa. Dated to about 40 000 years ago.

Fishbourne, Chichester, UK [Si]. Extensive Roman palace in West Sussex on the south coast of England. Excavations directed by Barry Cunliffe between 1961 and 1969 revealed that the site started as a coastal depot to serve the Roman invasion. Granaries and stores have been found. A substantial house with a bath-house followed soon after, and in *c.*AD 75 a far more extensive building covering 4 ha and lavishly decorated with mosaics and painted wall plaster was built. The central courtyard was laid out as a formal garden. It is possible that this palace was built by Cogidubnus, king of the Regni and a noted romanophile. The building continued to be modified and occupied down into the 4th century AD.

[Rep.: B. Cunliffe, 1971, *Excavations at Fishbourne 1961–1969*. London: Society of Antiquaries]

Fishtail points [Ar]. Distinctive bifacially worked chipped stone point with an outline rather like the shape of a fish; the basal tang or stem represents the tail of the fish. Widely found in South America in the period 11 000–8000 BC, this kind of implement has certain affinities with the Clovis points of North America and represents the Palaeo-Indian stage in South America.

fission/fusion [Th]. A mode of social organization where a community breaks apart into several separate units (fission) for some of the year before coming back together again (fusing) as a single whole for the rest of the time. Such patterns may be seen in hunter-gatherer groups who work to exploit particular resources in specialist groups, and in transhumant pastoralist societies where part of the community takes the animals to summer pastures well away from the main residence areas.

fission-track dating [Te]. A method of dating tephra, obsidian, or archaeological materials such as pottery that have been heated in the past. The method is based on the spontaneous nuclear fission of uranium 238 (^{238}U) and the fact that one manifestation of this is a pattern of linear atomic displacements (tracks) along the trajectory of released energized fission particles. The rate of fission in ^{238}U is constant, so by knowing the concentration and the number of fission tracks present the age of the material since it was last heated to remove all previous tracks can be determined.

five-stone ring [MC]. A small Bronze Age STONE CIRCLE of four upright stones and one recumbent stone. Mainly found in southwest Ireland.

flagon [Ar]. A vessel with a narrow neck, globular body, one or more handles and often a footring, used for holding liquids. Its production was usually confined to specialist manufacturers.

flake [Ar]. A piece of flint struck from a core which characteristically shows traces of the processes of removal: concentric fracture ripples and a bulb of percussion. Flakes with a length:breadth ratio of 2:1 or more are usually referred to as blades. In some cases flakes are the result of shaping a block of flint into a tool of some kind. When removed from a prepared core, however, they were usually used as blanks for making tools. **Primary flakes** (also called decortication flakes) are large, thick flakes struck off a nodule when removing the cortex and preparing it for working. **Secondary flakes** (also called reduction flakes) are large flakes struck off a piece to reduce its size or thickness. **Tertiary flakes** are small flakes struck off when shaping the detail of a piece to make a specific tool. **Retouching flakes** are tiny, extremely thin flakes pinched or pushed off a piece to finish it, to fine-shape part of the surface, sharpen it, or resharpen it. **Notching flakes** are produced when putting hafting notches in stone tools. *See also* PRESSURE FLAKING, PERCUSSION FLAKING.

flake scar (flake bed) [De]. A depression left on a core, flake, or tool where another flake was driven off.

flake tool [De]. A stone or flint tool made from a flake deliberately removed from a prepared core of some kind.

Flandrian Stage [CP]. A group of deposits representing a geostratigraphic stage within the HOLOCENE series of the British QUATERNARY system covering the period 10 000 years ago down to the present day. The Flandrian represents the period following the DEVENSIAN STAGE at the end of the PLEISTOCENE, and as such could be seen simply as the latest in a succession of interglacial warm periods. The Flandrian embraces POLLEN ZONES IV through to IX as set out by Harry Godwin in 1940, and the climatic phases from the PRE-BOREAL through to the SUB-ATLANTIC.

flange [De]. In pottery, a prominent continuous projection or ledge extending out from the body, neck, or rim of a vessel, intended to facilitate handling.

flanged axe [Ar]. An early to middle Bronze Age style of flat copper or bronze axe that has the side edges of both faces bent out to form flanges that secure the haft in place and reduce the lateral movement of the haft when the axe is being used.

flash lock [MC]. Contrivance for releasing the rush of water to enable a boat to proceed up or down stream.

flask [Ar]. A narrow-mouthed jar without handles.

flat grave [MC]. A burial consisting of a simple oval or rectangular pit containing an inhumed individual. The pit is infilled but not marked by a mound or any kind of upstanding earthwork.

flat rimmed ware [Ar]. A type of late Bronze Age pottery found in northern and northwestern parts of the British Isles having a rather coarse fabric, generally dark colour, and distinctive unornamented flat-topped rims.

flesh hook [Ar]. A type of implement found in late Bronze Age and Iron Age contexts in Europe which comprises a long bronze shank, sometimes heavily decorated and ornamented with attachments, one end of which is bent and worked to form between one and three sharpened hooks. They are often associated with bronze buckets and cauldrons and it is believed they were used as serving implements to distribute choice cuts of meat at a feast.

flexed burial [De]. *See* BURIAL SITE.

flint [Ma]. A hard brittle siliceous rock with conchoidal fracturing properties that is highly suitable for the manufacture of edged tools by flaking or knapping. Found as nodules or tablets in chalk and limestone (in the latter case as chert), or redeposited as pebbles in clay and gravels. Usually black, grey, or brown in colour.

flint mine [MC]. A place where natural outcrops or seams of underground flint were worked to obtain blocks of raw material for knapping and making into tools. The mining techniques vary a little between mining areas but mines basically consist of pits or shafts. Pits are generally used where the flint is shallow and relatively large and rather irregular holes can be opened to get it. Shafts involve considerably more effort, and examples more than 15 m deep are known. The shafts themselves are steep-sided and cylindrical in form, although most originally have had fixtures and fittings to allow the miners to get in and out, and to allow soil and water to be removed. When the desired band of flint is reached it is followed outwards from the shaft as a series of galleries that optimize the extractable flint by leaving only small pillars to support the roof. Most flint mines are of Neolithic date, and examples are known in many parts of Europe including Poland, Holland, Belgium, and southern and eastern England.

Flint Run Complex [CP]. North American later Palaeo-Indian hunter-gatherer communities living in the area of north Virginia in the period 9500–8000 BC, characterized by gradually developing projectile points.

flint scatter [MC]. A general term applied to collections of worked flint, stone, debitage, and associated raw material gathered up from the surface of ploughed fields or disturbed ground. Such collections range in size from a few dozen through to many thousands of pieces, and may have been collected from areas of any size from a few metres across to several hectares. As such they do not represent distinct kinds of archaeological site but rather the archaeological manifestation of many different kinds of activity; their unity is a product of the way material has been recovered rather than the processes by which it was created in the first place. Much work has been devoted to characterizing flint scatters in terms of what they represent. It is now clear that some are caused by the erosion of underlying features and deposits which relate to a vast range of activities including settlements, stoneworking sites, and middens. In other cases the scatters reflect episodes of activity in the past that involved little more than the deposition of material on the contemporary ground surface which has subsequently become incorporated into the topsoil through natural and anthropogenic formation processes. *See also* SURFACE SCATTERS.

floatation (flotation) [Te]. A method of extracting carbonized plant remains, shells, small bones, and insect remains from ancient soils and sediments. The process involves stirring the sediment into a large barrel of water so that the lighter material floats and can be scooped off or floated over a weir and into a fine-meshed sieve. More sophisticated floatation machines have a water supply inside the barrel, thus forcing water upwards through the descending sediment, so helping to push light material to the surface. Various chemicals can be added to prepare the samples by breaking the sediments down or by creating froth in the floatation machine so that organic residues get trapped in air bubbles and are taken to the surface more easily.

floating chronology [Ge]. A sequence of chronometrically dated material, for example tree-rings or varves, that is internally consistent but tied to precise dates.

Flood (The Great Flood) [Ge]. A natural catastrophe involving a massive flood is reported in a number of historical texts written in the Near East in the 2nd and 3rd millenna BC. These include Genesis from the Bible and texts in Ashurbanipal's library in Nineveh. It is not certain that all these floods are the same event; rather they may all relate to difficulties controlling the water systems in the low-lying alluvial plain of southern Mesopotamia.

flower vase [Ar]. *See* TRIPLE VASE.

flue arch [Co]. Underfloor arch in a hypocaust allowing hot air to pass from furnace to room, or from one heated room to another.

flue tile [Ar]. Open-ended, box-shaped tile built into the thickness of the walls of a room heated by hypocaust.

fluorine analysis [Te]. A method for roughly determining the age of human or animal bones, and for comparing the relative ages of two bones recovered from the same context. The technique works on the basis that fluorine percolating through deposits in groundwater slowly replaces the calcium in buried bones. The exact rate of replacement depends on the amount of fluorine present and is thus neither a universal standard nor even the same across a single site. The replacement is, however, irreversible, so that bones of very different date from the same general area can be distinguished. This technique led to confirmation that PILTDOWN man was a modern forgery.

fluted point [Ar]. A general term applied to a wide range of chipped stone points found in the New World which are united in being of symmetrical outline, carefully manufactured, and finished with the removal of a single long parallel sided flake or flute from one or both sides. Fluted points are well represented by Folsom and Clovis points from North America.

flutes [Co]. The vertical hollows cut into the sides of a column which emphasized its rotundity—a device necessary in the brilliant sunlight falling on white marble—and which took off glare from the marble by the easy graduations of light.

fluting [De]. Pattern of ornamentation often found on pottery which comprises a series of broad parallel corrugations, either horizontal, diagonal, or vertical, which have a wave-shaped cross-section.

Fluvialism [Th]. Proposition by early 19th-century AD geologists that, contrary to the DILUVIALISM theory, geological strata were the result of the orderly deposition of sediments over a prolonged period of time, comparable to processes observable at the present time in rivers, lakes, and sea. *See also* UNIFORMITARIANISM.

fluxgate gradiometer [Eq]. *See* GRADIOMETER.

fluxgate magnetometer [Eq]. *See* MAGNETOMETER.

flying buttress [Co]. An arched supporting pier outside a building which takes most of the weight of the roof, allowing the walls to be devoted to window-space rather than being used to support the roof.

foederati [CP]. Name applied to barbarian tribes living on the fringes of the Roman empire and who formed an alliance by treaty with Rome. Federates mainly enjoyed their own customs and maintained a generally high degree of autonomy.

fogu [MC]. *See* SOUTERRAIN.

foliated points [De]. Elliptical shaped points, thin in section and pointed at both ends. Reminiscent of Solutrean 'laurel leaves' but form part of the Mousterian assemblages of central Europe.

folles [Ar]. Copper coins common at the beginning of the 4th century.

Folsom, New Mexico, USA [Si]. Archaic Stage hunter-gatherer kill site or camp close to the edge of a former marsh discovered in 1926 and found to contain distinctive flint tools (Folsom points) in direct association with the remains of 23 carcasses of an extinct form of bison. The importance of the site is twofold, first in providing firm evidence for early settlement in North America, and second as the type-site for the Folsom Tradition.

[Sum.: D. J. Meltzer, 2000, Renewed investigations at the Folsom Palaeoindian type site. *Antiquity*, 74, 35–6]

Folsom point [Ar]. Bifacially worked chipped stone projectile points with a symmetrical ovoid outline, hollow base, finely worked edges, and a central flute on one or both sides. Believed to have been developed from the CLOVIS POINT, although no intermediate forms are known. Found widely over North America, and characteristic implement of the Folsom Tradition dating to the period 9500–8000 BC.

Folsom Tradition [CP]. North American Palaeo-Indian cultures occupying the Great Plains and adjacent areas of the west and southwest, and extending east of the Mississippi into the Great Lakes area and across to New Jersey, during the period 9000–8000 BC. Believed to have developed from the Clovis Culture, Folsom is characterized by its fluted projectile points (generally rather smaller than Clovis points).

Most known Folsom Tradition sites are kill sites where bison have been slaughtered and butchered. Some kill sites contain the remains of up to 50 beasts. A more substantial site at Hanson, Wyoming, has evidence of three hardstandings which may have been the sites of houses. In addition to bison remains, bones of mountain sheep, deer, marmot, and cotton-tail rabbit illustrate the diversity of species exploited by groups within this tradition.

Font-Robert points [De]. Tanged points with leaf-shaped blades of plano-convex section. Only worked extensively on one face. Dated to Perigordian Phase V in France.

food vessel [Ar]. Type of early Bronze Age pot found in northern Britain and Ireland from the period 1800 to 1200 BC. The name derives from an antiquarian suggestion that these pits were intended to hold food for the deceased's journey into the afterlife, just as BEAKERS were thought to hold drink. Heavily decorated, food vessels are either biconical or bowl-shaped, usually in fine fabrics. They are mainly associated with cremation burials, and in some cases represent part of a set of grave goods that also includes plano-convex knives and necklaces of jet beads.

footing [Co]. The lowest part of the foundations of a stone wall, typically loose rubble or gravel spread in the bottom of a construction trench that is a little wider than the wall built on top will eventually be.

footring [De]. A low pedestal-like ring formed on the base of a vessel to enable it to stand more securely.

foot survey [Te]. Archaeological reconnaissance on foot, often with a set interval between members of the survey team. Also known as a walk-over survey.

forces of production [Ge]. A term used by Marx to refer to the factors promoting economic growth in a society.

ford [MC]. A convenient accessible place along a river or stream where in normal conditions the water is sufficiently shallow for people and animals to walk across in safety. In some cases a ford was created by artificially raising the riverbed through the construction of a causeway or weir.

forensic archaeology [De]. An expanding branch of archaeological investigation in which the methods and approaches of archaeology are applied to legal problems and in connection with the work of courts of law. Most commonly this involves the reconstruction of a chronology and sequence of events from the deposits found within and around graves and burial sites for homicide cases and investigations into the violation of human rights.

forest [MC]. In medieval times land on which the king and a few other major lords had the right to keep deer and other game and could make Forest Laws to protect them. Thus, a forest was not necessarily a place of trees but rather a place of deer and game for hunting and sport.

forging [De]. In metalworking, the shaping of a piece of metal by heating, to soften it, and then hammering.

form [De]. The physical characteristics—size, shape, composition, etc.—of any archaeological find. Form is an essential part of attribute analysis.

formal analysis [Th]. The process of describing the overall shape of an item as objectively as possible and with as much detail as possible.

formation processes [Th]. A term developed by Michael Schiffer in the early 1970s to describe the way in which archaeological deposits come about and change through time down to the point where they are excavated. Some understanding of this is critical to being able to understand and explain what is found during archaeological excavations. Schiffer identified two groups of formation processes. N-transforms are caused by non-cultural processes such as wind, water, rodent activity, and chemical action. By contrast C-transforms are cultural transforms which are the links between what people do and what is left in the archaeological record. Both impact on structures, objects, their associated matrix, and their associations in predictable ways as they move from the past (systemic context) into the present (archaeological context).

Formative (Pre-Classic/Transitional) [CP]. The third of five general cultural stages proposed by G. Willey and P. Phillips in 1958 as a framework for the study of ancient communities in the Americas, broadly covering the period *c*.2500 BC through to AD 300. The Formative embraced communities with village agriculture and sedentary lifestyles and is therefore mainly confined in its application to southwestern parts of North America, Mesoamerica, and the central and northern west coast of South America. The term is now largely obsolete because regionally specific traditions with better chronological and cultural resolution have been defined in most areas. During the Formative Stage, the foundations are laid for the emergence of a range of complicated social traditions or civilizations and nearly all the main traits that characterize these later civilizations were established: astronomical observations, calendrical systems, monumental architecture, hieroglyphic writing, craft specialization, planned settlements, and elaborate defined ceremonial and religious centres.

The main value of the concept of the Formative Stage is the recognition that no matter when it happened, the same basic pattern of development can be seen: sparsely scattered hamlet-type agricultural settlements increasing in their density in the landscape, coupled with the emergence of larger more important centres. Traditionally, the Formative is followed by the CLASSIC STAGE.

Formiga Phase [CP]. South American farming cultures found in the Marajo area of Amazonia and tentatively dated to c.AD 700–800. Characterized by their ceramic assemblages which belong to the Polychrome Horizon Style of the Amazon basin.

fort (fortlet/fortress) [MC]. A military construction that combines accommodation for troops, their transport, and their equipment with a defensible stronghold. In general, the design of a fort will reflect the style of warfare anticipated, and the kind of defence that might be mounted. Amongst the most widespread set of forts known through archaeological investigation are those built by the Roman army. Indeed, these provided models for later armies to copy and adapt. Roman forts were either temporary (also called marching camps), built of earth and wood with tents rather than buildings, or permanent/long-term, in which case they were built in stone and wood with considerable investment in the fortifications, infrastructure, and accommodation. Those used by cavalry units would have an annexe for stabling the horses if there was insufficient room within the main fort. The basic layout of Roman forts followed set patterns and all were built to the so-called 'playing-card' shape. Three main sizes can be recognized: **fortlets** of less than 1 ha; **forts** of between 1 ha and 4 ha to accommodate between 500 and 1000 troops; and **fortresses** which generally cover between 17 ha and 20 ha and were designed to accommodate a whole legion. The Roman term for a fort is *castellum*.

fort-vici [MC]. An extra-mural civilian settlement attached to or adjacent to a military fort or fortress providing accommodation and facilities for traders and merchants who provided goods and services to the moneyed troops. Such settlements are totally parasitic on the fort.

forum [MC]. Centrally situated market square, meeting place, and administrative centre in a Roman city.

fossa [Co]. A Latin term for a ditch.

fossil soil [Co]. *See* BURIED SOIL.

founder's barrow [De]. A term popularized by Leslie Grinsell to refer to the first barrow to be established in a barrow cemetery, often the biggest and most distinguished. In some early Bronze Age cemeteries the founder's barrow is in fact a Neolithic structure around which the later monuments cluster.

founder's hoard [De]. A collection of Bronze Age metalwork deposited together as a HOARD but which comprises the tools, equipment, and stock-in-trade of a bronze-worker. In addition to scrap metal and ingots there are typically moulds, punches, hammers, sets, gouges, an anvil, and a polishing stone.

Fountains Abbey, North Yorkshire, UK [Si]. One of the noblest and most extensive monastic sites in Europe, situated in Skelldale in northeast England. It was established in AD 1132 by Cistercian monks who took over a remote valley and transformed it into one of the largest producers of wool in the north. At the height of its fortunes in the 15th century there were about 120 monks and perhaps 400 lay brethren and servants. At the centre is a great church, begun in the 1150s AD, with an eleven-bay nave. The seven westernmost bays were for lay brothers while those to the east of the choir were for monks. At the east end of the church is the Chapel of Nine Altars, built in the 13th century to accommodate the growing number of monks. The west range comprises at first-floor level the lay brothers' long dormitory, 91 m long, with their latrine block at the end, built over the River Skell. Beneath the dormitory is a vaulted undercroft, used for storage and as the lay brothers' refectory. The monks' refectory lies at right-angles to the south range, a typical Cistercian arrangement. One of the last additions to Fountains Abbey is Abbot Huby's great bell-tower, built in the late 15th century. Externally it is decorated with statues of saints and painted biblical texts.

[Sum.: G. Coppack, 1993, *Fountains Abbey*. London: Batsford and English Heritage]

four-poster [MC]. **1.** A small Bronze Age STONE CIRCLE of four upright stones at the corners of a rough rectangle. Mainly found in central Scotland. **2.** Type of Iron Age structure represented archaeologically by a square-shaped setting of four substantial postholes. Believed to be the supports for an above-ground granary.

Four Sons of Horus [Di]. Egyptian gods, the protective genii who guarded the canopic jars.

Fourth World [Ge]. A collective name for indigenous peoples (e.g., Aborigines) in countries where an alien majority has now become the established government.

Fox, Sir Cyril Fred (1882–1967) [Bi]. British archaeologist and scholar specializing in the prehistory of the British Isles and the application of geographical models to archaeological data. Born in Chippenham, Wiltshire, and educated at Christ's Hospital he was destined for a career in market gardening. By a happy coincidence he was appointed superintendent of the University Field Laboratories in Cambridge. Here he became interested in archaeology and was admitted to Magdalene College to read for the tripos, but Professor H. M. Chadwick was so impressed by Fox that he arranged for him to proceed straight to a Ph.D. His thesis was on the archaeology of the Cambridge region. It was highly successful and innovatory, and was eventually published. In 1923 Fox became assistant curator of the University Museum of Archaeology and Ethnography, but a year later he moved to the dual post of Keeper of Archaeology in the National Museum of Wales and Lecturer in Archaeology at University College, Cardiff. In 1926 he succeeded to the directorship of the Museum where he remained until his retirement in 1948. During his time in Wales he carried out a great deal of fieldwork, including the excavation of several Bronze Age barrows and the surveying of Offa's Dyke. In building geographical models he noted the ways in which Britain was connected to mainland Europe via a series of seaways that were used over many millennia and he also proposed a division of Britain into a Highland Zone and a Lowland Zone as a way of characterizing key differences in the nature of the archaeological evidence, but also in the kinds of society that might have existed in the regions in the past. His numerous publications include *The personality of Britain* (1932, Cardiff: National Museum of Wales) and *Life and death in the Bronze Age* (1959, London: Routledge). He was knighted in 1935.

[Obit.: *Antiquaries Journal*, 47 (1967), 337]

Frankhthi Cave, Greece [Si]. A deeply stratified cave deposit on the Peloponnesian coast of the Argolid in southern Greece. Excavated by T. W. Jacobson between 1967 and 1979. The lowest levels dated to the period 20 000–8000 BC, the Upper Palaeolithic, and included the remains of wild ass, red deer, and a variety of fish. The upper levels date to the Mesolithic and Neolithic, and it was during the Mesolithic, around 7000 BC, that obsidian from Melos first appears in the sequence, demonstrating long-distance boat journeys across the Aegean. An abrupt change in subsistence patterns around 6000 BC saw the introduction of domesticated sheep and goat, with, a little later, cultivated barley, and finally pottery.

[Sum.: T. W. Jacobsen, 1976, 17 000 years of Greek prehistory. *Scientific American*, 234, 76–87]

Franks [CP]. A Germanic people who until the 5th century AD occupied an area to the east of the Rhine but who later expanded, first into Belgium and northern France. Later, under the leadership of King Clovis, they began another phase of expansion until the time of Charlemagne in the 8th century, when the Frankish empire consisted of most of western Europe. Many traditional Roman manufacturing industries were preserved by the Franks, but they also introduced Germanic craftsmanship into the arts and building technology.

Fredegar [Na]. The name given in the 16th century AD to an anonymous compiler of a major Frankish chronicle of events from the end of the Roman empire until the establishment of the Carolingians.

freestone [Ma]. Limestone of even, fine-grained texture.

Fremont Culture [CP]. Localized Archaic Stage cultural grouping in the eastern Nevada, western Colorado, and southern Idaho area of the Great Basin of North America in the period AD 400–1300.

Characterized by numerous small scattered

communities whose subsistence base included maize cultivation. Agriculture, and also the production of pottery, was probably adopted from Anasazi communities to the south. Pit-houses were built by Fremont communities throughout the period, although in later times some above-ground masonry pueblo-style houses were constructed too. Material culture included leather moccasins, pottery vessels with incised decoration, and clay figurines.

A number of regional variations of the Fremont Culture have been defined, sometimes subsumed under the term 'Sevier': Parowan Fremont (AD 900–1250) in southwest Utah; Sevier Fremont (AD 870–1250) in central west Utah and eastern Nevada; Great Salt Lake Fremont (AD 400–1350) around the Great Salt Lake and as far as the Rocky Mountains of Idaho; Unita Bay Fremont (AD 650–950) in northeastern Utah; and San Raphael Fremont (AD 700–1250) in eastern Utah and western Colorado.

Frere, John (1740–1807) [Bi]. British antiquary whose main contribution to the development of archaeological thought was his discovery of Acheulian handaxes and associated remains at Hoxne in Suffolk. He recognized the great antiquity of these finds, but his ideas were in advance of his time and his conclusions were ignored. The finds are reported in *Archaeologia* for 1800, along with the arguments for the early dating of the material. Frere was a Fellow of the Royal Society.

[Bio.: *Dictionary of National Biography*, 7, 707–8]

fresco [Co]. A watercolour painting on a wall or ceiling completed before the plaster is dry.

friary [MC]. *See* MONASTERY.

frieze [Co]. **1.** A band of decoration on a wall or vessel, which may be painted or in bas-relief. **2.** That member in the entablature of an order which occurs between the architrave and the cornice. **3.** Horizontal band above an architrave, sometimes carved with sculpture.

frigidarium [Co]. A Latin term used to describe an unheated room in a bath-house containing a cold bath and sometimes a labrum or emplacement for a cold shower.

frilling [De]. A crust decoration found on most tazzae.

Frisians [CP]. Peoples who inhabited the Dutch coastal plain (Frisia) and low-lying areas of northern Holland and northwest Germany in the late 1st millennium BC and early 1st millennium AD. According to the Roman author Procopius they were involved in the Anglo-Saxon colonization of Britain in the 5th century AD, but have left little record of their activities there. During the 8th century AD Frisia was annexed into the Frankish kingdom.

Frontius, Sextus Julius [Na]. Governor of Britain between AD 73 or 74 and 77 or 78. His period of office was marked by the establishment of a legionary fortress at Caerleon and campaigns which conquered and pacified the Silures of south Wales.

frontlet [De]. The upper skull and antlers of a deer or stag.

frying pan [Ar]. The name given to a type of shallow pottery bowl with a decorated base that is found in the early Bronze Age of the Cyclades in Greece. The handle consists of two divergent knobs or legs. The decoration includes spirals, female sexual symbols, and sometimes representations of boats. The function of these vessels is not known—suggestions include drums, mirrors, and lids—but they are certainly not for frying.

FSA [Ab]. Fellow of the SOCIETY OF ANTIQUARIES OF LONDON.

FSA (Scot) [Ab]. Fellow of the SOCIETY OF ANTIQUARIES OF SCOTLAND.

Fuegian Tradition [CP]. Archaic Stage communities living on the southern coast and offshore islands of southern Chile in South America in the period 4000 BC to historic times. Characterized by subsistence economies based on marine resources.

fulacht fiadh [MC]. An Irish term for a burnt mound or traditional cooking place. *See* BURNT MOUND.

fulling [De]. One of the finishing processes in the manufacture of woollen cloth. Pieces of the woven cloth were churned around in a soapy liquid which had the effect of felting the fibres together and making the cloth stronger, warmer, and more weather-proof.

When this process began to be industrialized, from Roman times onwards, the place where it was done was known as a **fulling mill**.

fumed [De]. A term which has been somewhat misleadingly used to describe the dark surface of vessels, in particular black-burnished ware, which has been exposed to a reducing atmosphere during the later stages of manufacture.

functionalism [Th]. An approach that explains social phenomena in terms of their integrative relationships and contributions to the maintenance of society, or to the needs of individuals, rather than in terms of causation. Implicit to such thinking is the notion that a social institution within a society has a function in fulfilling some or all of the needs of another part of the social organism. Thus, in a manner analogous to examining the human body, the form of one part can be explained by its functional relationship to other parts.

functional type [Th]. Type based on cultural use or function rather than on outward form or chronological position.

fundamentalism [Th]. A belief in returning to the literal meanings of scriptural texts.

Funnel-necked Beaker Culture [CP]. *See* TRICHTERBECKER CULTURE.

furrowing [De]. Decoration made by drawing the fingers or a tool across the body of a vessel, resulting in either a series of horizontal grooves or random groups of striations.

fürstengräber [MC]. A distinctive tradition of rich graves beneath round barrows (tumuli) of the early La Tène period in the Rhineland. The graves typically contain a range of exotic grave goods including items imported from southern Europe, as well as fine examples of local craftsmanship. The German word literally means 'chieftain's grave'.

fusion [Th]. *See* FISSION.

G

gablet [Co]. A small gable.

Gaiseric [Na]. King of the Vandals and the Alans from AD 428. In AD 429 he led his people from Spain into Africa. He resisted attempts by eastern emperors to overthrow him, and with the fleet he built at Carthage his navy dominated the western Mediterranean. In AD 455 he sacked Rome. Gaiseric died c.AD 477.

Gaius (Caligula) [Na]. Roman emperor AD 37–41.

Galerius [Na]. Roman emperor AD 305–11.

gallery grave [MC]. General and rather obsolete term applied to those kinds of chambered tombs in northern and western Europe in which there is no marked distinction between the entrance passage and the burial chamber. The latter commonly leads off the access passage or is integral to it. Gallery graves are commonly contained within a broadly rectangular mound, the ends of which may be elaborated to create a forecourt area which presumably served as a focus of ritual. *See ALLÉE COUVERTE*, SIMPLE PASSAGE GRAVE, ENTRANCE GRAVE, LONG BARROW.

Gallienus [Na]. Roman emperor AD 253–68.

Gallinazo Culture [CP]. Cultural grouping in and between the Moche Valley and the Viru Valley on the north Peruvian coast which flourished in the period c.200 BC–AD 200, the local Early intermediate Horizon. Characterized by huge pyramid mounds, villages, and a distinctive ceramic style which included oxidized red wares but is best represented as black-on-orange negative resist decorated ware. Some ceramic styles and technologies are possibly related to the Recuay style in the Peruvian highlands.

Gallo-Belgic [CP]. Term used to describe the latest Iron Age culture of Gaul, particularly north and east of the Seine and Marne, before the Roman conquest.

Gallo-Belgic ware [Ar]. Vessels imported from Gaul in the late 1st century BC and early 1st century AD, usually in black or silver-grey fabrics (TERRA NIGRA), or white fabric coated with red slip (TERRA RUBRA), or a dense white or cream fabric like pipeclay. Close British imitations of these fabrics and forms are known, and further copying of the forms was widespread. The imported vessels often have the name of the potter stamped on the inner surface of the base, a practice imitated in Britain but usually with illegible markings.

Gamblian [CP]. Last major pluvial period of the Pleistocene in Africa.

Gamio, Manuel (1883–1960) [Bi]. Mexican archaeologist, at one time a student of Franz Boas, well known for his systematic approach to the study of regions and stratigraphy. In 1911 he established a ceramic sequence for the Valley of Mexico based on excavations at Azcapotzalco, Mexico.

[Obit.: *American Anthropologist*, 64 (1962), 356–9]

garderobe [Co]. A medieval privy.

Garni, Armenia [Si]. Fortress founded in the 3rd century BC as a summer residence for the Armenian kings of the Yervandid and Artashesid dynasties. Situated on a naturally defended hilltop above the Azat River. The strongly walled enclosure contains a Greco-Roman temple, probably built by King Trdat III (287–330 BC), a bath-house of the 3rd century BC, and the ruins of a two-storey royal palace. Of later date is a round church built in AD 897. An earthquake in AD 1679 damaged the site very badly but reconstruction work between 1969 and 1975 has restored the temple to its former glory.

[Sum.: H. L. Petrosyan, 1988, *Garnin IX–XIV darerum.* Erevan: Haykakan]

Garrod, Dorothy Annie Elizabeth (1892–1968) [Bi]. British archaeologist and scholar noted for her work on the Palaeolithic and the first woman to hold an Oxbridge Chair. Born in Oxford she was privately educated before going up to Newnham College, Cambridge, and later Oxford University. In 1925–6 she excavated in Gibraltar, and in 1928 she directed an expedition to South Kurdistan. While a Research Fellow at Newnham between 1929 and 1932 she excavated at Mount Carmel, Israel, where she and Dorothy Bate revealed a long sequence of Lower Palaeolithic and later deposits in the Tabun, El Wad, and Es Skhul caves. In 1934 she was a Leverhulme Research Fellow, and in 1936 President of Section H of the British Association. In 1939 she was appointed to the Disney Chair of Archaeology in Cambridge University, a post she held until 1952, although between 1942 and 1945 she served as section officer in the Women's Auxiliary Air Force. In 1965 she was created CBE. Amongst her numerous publication are *The upper Palaeolithic age in Britain* (1926, Cambridge: CUP) and *The Stone Age of Mount Carmel* with D. M. A. Bate (1937, Oxford: Clarendon Press).

Bio.: P. J. Smith, 2000, Dorothy Garrod, first woman Professor at Cambridge. *Antiquity*, 74, 131–6.

Gaviota Phase [CP]. Cultural groupings of the period *c.*1900–1750 BC along the coast of Peru, many of them occupying small villages near productive shell-fish beds. Some inland sites were also occupied at this time, including the ceremonial centre at Chuquitanta, Peru.

Geb [Di]. Egyptian god, the earth god, represented as a man. A member of the Ennead of Heliopolis, husband of Nut.

gender archaeology [Th]. Approaches to interpretation that examine the social construction of gender and its representation in the archaeological record. In particular, attention is given to the activities, the relative positions of power and authority, the autonomy, and the symbolic meanings that were attached to males and females in different societies. Developing from this is an interest in how gender relations interact with other social categories such as class, age, ethnicity, religion, and kin. *See also* FEMINIST ARCHAEOLOGY.

general systems theory [Th]. *See* SYSTEMS THEORY.

genius [Di]. Latin term for the guardian spirit or deity of a particular place.

genius cucullatus [Di]. Hooded deity.

geoarchaeology [Ge]. An approach to the study of archaeological issues using the methods and concepts of the earth sciences. Attention is focused on the physical context of archaeological remains, especially in relation to geomorphological processes, site formation, post-depositional transformations, and the relationships between cultural and natural processes.

Geoffrey of Monmouth [Na]. Early British romantic historian born *c.*AD 1100 whose partly fantastic *History of the Kings of Britain*, completed in *c.*1135, enjoyed great popularity and introduced many of the legends of King Arthur to a wider audience. In 1152 Geoffrey was made Bishop of St Asaph, Wales. Died *c.*AD 1155.

geoglyphs [De]. Images and motifs set on the land surface using rocks, soil, or cuts into the ground surface. The NASCA LINES are large-scale examples of such things, as are the various hill figures of England.

Geographic Information System (GIS) [Eq]. A combined database and mapping system for the capture, storage, and manipulation of geographic data. Typically such data comprises a combination of location, attribute, and topological information about places and areas. Extremely useful in archaeology for plotting and analysing site distributions against environmental and other background data derived from remote sensing, digitized maps, and other sources.

geomagnetic reversal [Ge]. *See* ARCHAEOMAGNETIC DATING.

geometric microliths [Ar]. Small blade tools of geometric form usually having a point or transverse edge. Almost certainly hafted, possibly forming composite tools and weapons. Characteristic of the Mesolithic but they do begin to appear by the end of the Upper Palaeolithic.

Geometric period [CP]. The post-Mycenaean period when, with the Dorian invasions, the Iron Age was fully established throughout Greece and the country had settled again after a period of turmoil and population movement. A sub-Mycenaean, followed by a proto-Geometric period, is transitional to the Geometric period proper, which in Athens runs from about 900 BC to 700 BC. The period is characterized by its well-shaped pottery, later incorporating animal and human figures.

geophysical prospection (geophysical survey) [Te]. A general term referring to fieldwork projects where one or more techniques of geophysical survey are used to discover and define potential archaeological sites. *See* MAGNETOMETER, RESISTIVITY SURVEY, GROUND PROBING RADAR.

George I (Elector of Hanover) [Na]. British monarch from AD 1714, of the House of Hanover. Born 1660, son of Sophia (daughter of Frederick, elector palatine, and Elizabeth Stuart, daughter of James I) and Ernest Augustus, elector of Hanover. Married Sophia Dorothea, daughter of George William, duke of Lüneburg-Celle. Died AD 1727, aged 67, having reigned twelve years.

George II [Na]. British monarch from AD 1727, of the House of Hanover. Born 1683, son of George I. Married Caroline, daughter of John Frederick, margrave of Brandenburg-Anspach. Died AD 1760, aged 76, having reigned 33 years.

George III [Na]. British monarch from AD 1760, of the House of Hanover. Born 1738, son of Frederick, eldest son of George II. Married Charlotte, daughter of Charles Louis, duke of Mechlenburg-Strelitz. Died AD 1820 aged 81, having reigned 59 years.

George IV [Na]. British monarch from AD 1820, of the House of Hanover. Born 1762, eldest son of George III. Married Caroline, daughter of Charles, duke of Brunswick-Wolfenbüttel. Died AD 1830 aged 67, having reigned ten years.

Georgian [CP]. In England the Georgian period is approximately 1714–1810. Architec-

tural styles of the period were derived from classical and Renaissance Italian architecture.

Gepids [CP]. Germanic tribe who occupied the middle Danube area and who led a revolt against Attila's sons during the 450s AD. During the 6th century AD the Gepids fought a series of wars against their neighbours the Lombards which ended in their decisive defeat. The surviving Gepids were swallowed up by the Avars after 568.

Ghirshman, Roman (1895–1979) [Bi]. A Ukrainian-French scholar and archaeologist who did much to develop archaeological work in Iran and Afghanistan. Before WW2 he worked at Tello in southern Iraq with D. Genouillac before moving on to carry out important excavations at Giyan and Sialk in western Iran. Just before the war he worked at historic period sites in eastern Iran and in Afghanistan. After WW2 and through to 1963 he was director of the French excavations at Susa in Mesopotamia, with some work also at Choga Zanbil nearby.

[Bio.: *Iranica Antiqua*, 15–17 (1980–2)]

ghost wall [Co]. *See* ROBBER TRENCH.

Gibbon, Edward (1737–94) [Bi]. British politician and historian whose chief academic work focused on the history of Rome. His most famous publication, *Decline and fall of the Roman Empire*, appeared between 1776 and 1788 and remains a much-cited orthodox study of the Roman world and its achievements. In later life Gibbon lived in retirement in Lausanne, Switzerland.

[Bio.: *Dictionary of National Biography*, 7, 1129–35]

Gilbertine [Ge]. The only monastic order to originate in England. A double order of canons and nuns founded in AD 1131 by Gilbert of Sempringham in Lincolnshire. Gilbert attempted to make his order similar to that of the Cistercians.

Gildas [Na]. British monk who lived during the 6th century AD, probably in south Wales and Brittany where he is revered as a saint. He was called by Alcuin the 'wisest of the Britons', and his *Fall of Britain* completed c.AD 540 is an important source of information about Britain during the early 6th century. Gildas died c.AD 571.

Gilgamesh, The Epic of [Do]. The oldest substantial poem that has survived from antiquity, an Assyrian recension dating from the 7th century BC found on clay tablets in the ruins of the Royal Library of Ashurbanipal at NINEVEH. The subject of the epic is man's conquest of his environment and his quest for the secret of immortality. The hero is Gilgamesh, the lord of Uruk, and his friend the beastman Enkidu.

gilt (gilding) [Ge]. The application of a thin layer of gold paint or gold leaf over a base-metal, stone, plaster, wooden, or clay former or ornamental feature.

Gimbutas, Marija (1921–94) [Bi]. Lithuanian archaeologist well known for her encyclopedic knowledge of eastern European prehistory. Born and brought up in Vilnius, she took an MA degree at Vilnius University, before travelling to Tübingen, Germany, under difficult conditions in the later years of WW2. She took her Ph.D. in Tübingen in 1946, but emigrated to the USA in 1955. Initially undertaking rather routine translation work at Harvard University she found time to research and write and soon produced important books on the archaeology of eastern Europe such as the monumental *The prehistory of Eastern Europe, vol. I: Mesolithic, Neolithic, and Copper Age cultures in Russia and the Baltic areas* (1956, Cambridge Mass.: American School of Prehistoric Research). These established her as the foremost figure in the field and in 1964 earned her a full professorship at the University of California at Los Angeles where she worked until her retirement in 1990. There followed an enormously productive period during the 1960s and 1970s with surveys and excavations in Yugoslavia, Greece, and Italy. She brought together linguistic and folklore evidence alongside the archaeological material, focusing increasingly on the origins of Indo-European languages and their associations with Copper Age cultures of southeastern Europe. In exploring these questions she developed a series of ideas about the existence of a European mother goddess cult which she outlined in her book *Gods and goddesses of old Europe* (1974, London: Thames and Hudson) and which has found much favour with some sections of the feminist movement although not universally accepted.

[Obit.: The *Independent*, 23 February 1994]

girth beaker [Ar]. A vertical-sided beaker, with horizontal bands of corrugations, cordons, or latticing. Of mid 1st century AD date. Some were Gallo-Belgic and others locally made in Britain. *See also* BUTT BEAKER.

girth groove [De]. In pottery making, a continuous horizontal groove around the belly of a vessel.

GIS [Ab]. *See* GEOGRAPHIC INFORMATION SYSTEM.

Giza, Egypt [Si]. Egyptian sacred site and cemetery on the west bank of the Nile opposite modern Cairo. The centre-piece of the site is a group of three pyramids that date from the 4th Dynasty, the mid 3rd millennium BC. The most important is that of Cheops which differs from most other pyramids in having a great number of chambers and passages within it. The second pyramid is that of Chephren. The third is that of Mycerinus. Round about these great monuments are the working quarters of those who built them. Nearby is the Great Sphinx guarding the entrance to the Nile Valley.

[Sum.: G. A. Reisner, 1955, *A history of the Giza necropolis*. Cambridge MA: Harvard University Press]

Glacial Kame Culture [CP]. Late Archaic cultural grouping found around Michigan, Ohio, Indiana, and southern Ontario in the period *c.*1500–1000 BC. Characterized by mortuary rituals which involved interring the dead in natural hills of glacial gravel. Grave goods of copper ornaments and marine shells were sometimes included and attest long-distance trade links.

glacis rampart [De]. A bank and ditch, constructed to present an unbroken slope from the crest of the bank to the bottom of the ditch. Such defences were often used by the builders of hillforts in the middle Iron Age period in northern Europe.

gladius (pl. *gladii*) [Ar]. Latin term for a short sword used by Roman legionaries.

glandes [Ar]. A Latin term for the acorn shaped shot, often of lead, for a ballista or sling.

glass [Ma]. An artificial material produced by fusing silica sand with an alkali such as potash or sodium. It was probably developed from faience in the Near East during the 3rd millennium BC, but was not used for anything larger than beads until Hellenistic and Roman times.

Glastonbury ware [Ar]. A type of middle Iron Age pottery manufactured at a number of centres in the southwest of England. A wide range of forms are known, principal amongst which are globular bowls, jars, and shouldered bowls. Incised decoration in curvilinear motifs and so-called tram-line pattern is common.

glaze [Ma]. A transparent or semi-transparent vitreous or glassy layer fused on to the surface of a pot. This term is not correctly used to describe any other type of shiny surface.

glebe [De]. Land held by the parson for the support of himself and his church.

Glen Mayer Culture [CP]. Early Iroquois cultural grouping in southwestern Ontario after about AD 1000, representing a continuation of the middle Woodland hunter-gatherer lifestyles with the addition of maize agriculture.

Settlements appear to have been seasonal, with summer camps related to maize growing and fishing, while for the rest of the year communities dispersed to hunt. The summer villages were occupied by communities of between 100 and 400 people, the various families living in multi-family dwellings with hearths arranged down the centre.

Glevum ware [Ar]. *See* SEVERN VALLEY WARE.

gleying [De]. The process whereby the iron in soils and sediments is bacterially reduced under anaerobic conditions and concentrated in a restricted horizon within the soil profile. Gleying usually occurs where there is a high water table or where an iron pan forms low down in the soil profile and prevents runoff, with the result that the upper horizons remain wet. Gleyed soils are typically green, blue, or grey in colour.

Glob, Peter Vilhelm (1911–85) [Bi]. Danish archaeologist well known for his work on bog bodies and the Danish Bronze Age. He was Director General of Museums and Antiquities in Denmark. He published many papers and

books, amongst them *The bog people* (1969, London: Faber and Faber) and *The mound people* (1974, London: Faber and Faber).

[Obit.: *The Times*, 27 July 1985]

Global Positioning System (GPS) [Eq]. A means of accurately locating the position of any point on the surface of the earth by using a network of geostationary orbiting satellites to coordinate in three dimensions the position of a mobile receiver. Various grades of equipment are available, from the hand-held systems to survey-grade instruments that can take and log several readings per second. For archaeology the system offers tremendous potential, especially in areas where there are few topographic reference points and limited or no mapping. The availability of satellite cover is the main constraint, and for optimum operation it is sometimes necessary to work strange hours to get the best configurations for the task in hand.

Globular Amphora Culture [CP]. Late Neolithic communities of the later second millennium BC occupying the Vistula, Oder, and Bug river systems in north central Europe. They are distinguished by their bulbous pots with a narrow neck and perforated lugs or small handles for suspension. Cord impressed decoration is usual. Burial is in single graves, usually with a stone-lined cist. Grave goods include their distinctive pots and also axes made from banded flint obtained from the Holy Cross Mountains. The Globular Amphora Culture is contemporary with the CORDED WARE CULTURE and the SINGLE GRAVE CULTURE.

globular urn [Ar]. A type of middle Bronze Age pottery found widely in southern England and forming part of the range of vessels within the DEVEREL–RIMBURY tradition. Characterized by a flat base, expanded body, and vertical neck, globular urns are generally large and made from fairly coarse fabrics. Decoration is usually confined to the upper body and neck and is typically incised or made with impressed cord. Some examples have lugs or applied decoration at the junction between the body and the neck.

glyph [De]. A carved figure, character, or picture, incised, painted, or in relief. The system of picture writing is known as hieroglyphics.

goat [Sp]. A hardy short-haired mammal with horns and in the male a beard (*Capra*). The bezoar of the mountains of southwest Asia (*Capra hircus aegagrus*) was the wild ancestor of the domestic goat, early examples of which have been found dating from the 8th millennium BC in the Near East. *See also* SHEEP.

Gododdin [Do]. A poem composed in north Britain in the early 7th century, celebrating an unsuccessful attempt to drive out the English from Northumbria.

gold [Ma]. A yellow malleable ductile high-density metallic element (Au) that is resistant to chemical reaction. It was the most highly prized metal used in antiquity and, along with copper, was one of the earliest to be worked.

gorget [Ar]. A piece of armour for protecting the throat region.

Gorgon [Na]. In Greek mythology the Gorgons are three monstrous sisters, Stheno, Euryale, and Medusa. Of these only Medusa is mortal and she was killed by Perseus with the help of Athena. They are commonly depicted with rotund faces and snakes for hair, sometimes bearded and with wings. Their staring eyes were said to turn men into stone, and hence gorgon faces in art evidently acquired an apotropaic significance.

Gorodtsov, Vasily Alekseevich (1860–1945) [Bi] Russian archaeologist who developed a chronology for the Bronze Age of Russia. A retired infantry officer, he began excavating in the 1890s with financial support from the Countess Uvarova. In the early 1900s he became director of the Moscow Historical Museum and one of the founders of the Moscow Archaeological Institute. He excavated at a number of Palaeolithic sites including Gontsy, Il'skaya I, and Timonovka, and published several syntheses of Russian prehistory. He trained many professional archaeologists and was an exponent of a formalist approach to archaeology, studying the morphology of artefacts and seeking to arrange them into chronological sequences.

[Bio.: L. Klejn, 1999. Vasily Alekseevich Gorodcov. In T. Murray (ed.), *Encyclopedia of archaeology. The Great Archaeologists*. Oxford: ABC-CLIO. 247–62]

Gothic [De]. Architectural style characterized by pointed arches and the vault, succeeding the Norman or Romanesque style at the end of the 12th century AD. Subdivided into three periods: early (13th century AD), characterized by the lancet window without tracery; the decorated Gothic (*c*.1290–1350), in which windows have first geometrical, then flowing, tracery; and the perpendicular (*c*.1350–1530), where tracery has strong vertical lines. The Gothic style was followed by the Tudor style, but was later revived as neo-Gothic or Gothic during the 19th century AD.

Goths [CP]. Germanic peoples originating in the Baltic area in the 4th century AD and divided into two groups, the Ostrogoths and the Visigoths. In the 5th century AD the Visigoths occupied southern Gaul and Spain while the Ostrogoths occupied Italy. Both were strong barbarian kingdoms. The Ostrogoths succumbed to attacks by the eastern empire; the Visigoths were swallowed up by the expansion of the Arabs in the early 8th century AD.

gourd [Sp]. A half-hardy trailing plant (*Lagenaria siceraria*) which produces a large bulbous fruit. There are various kinds of gourd, including the marrow and the pumpkin. The rind of the bottle gourd is hard and when dried can be used to make water containers or musical instruments. Thought to be of African origin, but also found widely in the Americas, southern Asia, and the Pacific Islands. How gourds arrived in the New World is a puzzling problem, but they are present in South America by *c*.7000 BC. One possibility is that some fruits arrived by floating across the Atlantic. Certainly gourds remain viable after immersion in salt water for several weeks.

GPS [Ab]. *See* GLOBAL POSITIONING SYSTEM.

gradiometer [Eq]. A type of geophysical instrument used for magnetic surveys in which a pair of MAGNETOMETERS are normally mounted one above the other on a single support staff. Various kinds are available, but the most commonly used in archaeology is the fluxgate gradiometer with the direction-responsive sensors between 0.5 m and 2.0 m apart. This measures the gradient in a magnetic field and will detect shallowly buried features and structures. The use of dual sensors overcomes many of the problems associated with single-sensor instruments, for example variations in the strength of the Earth's magnetic field and deep-seated geological anomalies. By systematically scanning an area on a grid system and logging the readings at close intervals it is possible to build up detailed plots showing the shape and form of the archaeological anomalies. These can be used to propose the nature and extent of buried features.

graffito [De]. Writing scratched on tile, pottery, plaster, etc.

grange [MC]. A farm that is owned by a monastic house but run by lay brothers.

granulation [De]. A technique used in the manufacture of jewellery whereby grains of gold, electrum, or silver, are soldered onto metalwork.

grape cup [Ar]. Type of miniature cup or accessory vessel found in early Bronze Age (WESSEX II) graves in southern England. Generally less than 15 cm across, grape cups are characterized by having a narrow base, narrow mouth, and an expanded rather bulbous body covered in small applied balls of clay so that they look like a small bunch of grapes. *See* INCENSE CUP.

grass-tempered ware [Ar]. Pottery embodying chopped grass or straw in its fabric as a tempering agent. Grass-tempered wares are well represented amongst pagan Saxon communities of the immediate post-Roman period in southern and eastern England; indeed the presence of such pottery is the basis upon which sites of the period are recognized.

Gratianus, Flavius [Na]. Roman emperor from AD 367. He spent much of his time devoted to the defence of the Rhine frontier and in AD 375 he pulled out of the imperial election to let his brother Valentinian II win while he remained in Gaul. In AD 383 he was overthrown by Magnus Maximum and killed while trying to escape southwards.

Grave Creek Mound, West Virginia, USA [Si]. Adena Culture burial mound in the Ohio Valley, probably the largest humanly produced ancient mound in the Americas. The mound is about 21 m high with a basal diameter of 73 m. It contains an estimated 54 500 metric tons of soil (70 000 cubic metres). Around the mound was a moat 10 m wide and 1.5 m deep. It is a mortuary mound over a high-status burial, constructed in the 3rd or 2nd century BC.

[Rep.: T. Hennings, 1984, Investigations at Grave Creek Mound 1975–76: sequence for mound and moat construction. *West Virginia Archaeologist*, 36.2, 349]

grave goods [De]. Objects placed with the deceased at the time of burial and left with the body in the grave when it is covered and left. Archaeologically, disentangling the origins and meanings of the things included in graves can be tricky. Some objects are clearly dress fittings and personal items worn by or on the clothing of the deceased and raise the question of how the person was dressed and what in. Other things are also personal items, but it is not always clear that they belong to the deceased; they may have been placed as gifts by the mourners. These and related problems make the task of determining rank and status on the basis of grave finds fraught with difficulties.

gravel [De]. Medium to large particles of more than 2 mm across forming constituent components of natural and anthropogenic sediments and deposits. Gravel is often subdivided into: granular, pebble, cobble, and boulder gravel.

graver [Ar]. A stone or metal chisel-like tool with a sharp narrow blade that can be used to score incisions and grooves in wood, bone, or any other relatively soft material.

Gravettian [CP]. A major Upper Palaeolithic industry identified in Europe on the basis of distinctive flintworking technology that includes backed blades, scrapers, points, and, in some areas, burins. It is named after the site of La Gravette in the Dordogne region of France. Geographically, the tradition has been recorded from Spain in the west to Russia in the east. Chronologically, Gravettian industries span the period *c.*27 000 to 19 000 years ago. In France the Gravettian is known as the Upper Perigordian.

gravity model [Th]. The proposition that the degree of interaction between cultures is directly proportional to their proximity to each other.

Great Interglacial [Ge]. A traditional, although now rather obsolete, term for the Mindel/Riss phase of the middle Pleistocene in central Europe; the Elster-Saale or Hoxnian stage in northern Europe and Britain respectively.

Great Serpent Mound, Ohio, USA [Si]. Adena Culture ceremonial site in the Ohio Valley, the focus of which is a gigantic earthen mound in the form of a serpent with an egg or frog in its jaw and a tightly coiled tail. Overall, the serpent is 382 m long from the tip of the upper jaw to the end of the tail, 6 m wide and up to 1.5 m high. The serpent itself does not appear to have been a funerary monument, although a burial mound stands nearby.

[Sum.: R. Fletcher *et al.*, 1996, Serpent mound: a fort or ancient icon? *Midcontinental Journal of Archaeology*, 21.1, 105–43]

Great Wall of China, China [Si]. A massive monument extending for more than 6000 km from Shanhaiguan on Bohai Bay in the east to Jiayuguan at the edge of the desert in Gansu Province in the west. It is actually composed of a series of sections built by individual Zhou states in the mid 1st millennium BC and later; it is neither a continuous wall nor a single wall. In places there are as many as three parallel walls. Most of what is visible today is the Ming wall of the period AD 1368–1644 which links together many of the earlier stretches. Its purpose was to separate the agricultural communities to the south from incursions by the nomadic steppe populations who lived to the north of the wall.

[Sum.: A. Waldron, 1990, *The Great Wall of China*. Cambridge: CUP]

Great Zimbabwe, Zimbabwe, Africa [Si]. A late Iron Age town of 720 ha with impressive stone walls near Masvingo in southeastern Zimbabwe. Shona speakers occupied Zimbabwe Hill from about AD 1000 and later began building the stone walls. Between about AD 1100 and 1500, Great Zimbabwe was the capital of the vast Shona empire that stretched from the Zambezi River to the northern Transvaal of South Africa and eastern Botswana. Between 12 000 and 20 000 people lived within and around it. Social organization in the Shona was based on distinctions between commoners and a ruling class. The great size of the structures at the Great Zimbabwe was a symbol of the power and wealth of those who lived there. The Shona kings accumulated much wealth and prestige by controlling trade between the

southern Africa interior and the East African coast. They also had connections further afield and Chinese stone and glassware have been recovered from the site.

[Sum.: P. S. Garlake, 1973, *Great Zimbabwe*. London: Thames & Hudson]

greave [Ar]. A piece of leg armour designed to protect the lower leg. It originally covered the shin only, but in medieval Europe there was also a closed greave which protected both the shin and the calf.

Greek colonies [Ge]. Planted towns established during the 8th century BC as part of a complex and extensive trading network in the western Mediterranean. The colonies included: Malaga, Hemeroscopeum, Emporion, Massilia, Nicaed, Alatia, Ischia, Paestum, Metapontum, Taras, Sybaris, Croton, Messina, Rhegium, Naxos, Megara, Syracuse, Gela, and Acragas.

Greek Dark Ages [CP]. Period *c.*1100–800 BC. *See* DARK AGES.

green [MC]. Communal space, often within a village, subject to regulated or stinted grazing rights which belonged to the inhabitants, especially if they had a property fronting on to it. Only community buildings such as the church or smithy could be erected on the green and the village stocks and public well might also be found there. Village greens seem to have made a comparatively late appearance in the landscape, dating to the 12th century AD onwards.

Green River Culture [CP]. Late Archaic Stage communities occupying the area around the confluence of the Green River and the Ohio River at Evansville, Indiana, in the period *c.*3000–2000 BC. Large stable communities flourished over long periods, building up huge shell middens as a result of exploiting freshwater molluscs. A rich range of vegetable foods were also utilized, especially hickory nuts and acorns which could be easily stored. Burials are known. Males were commonly interred with axes, woodworking tools, fish-hooks, awls, and stoneworking punches. Females wore bone beads and were often buried with nutcracking stones. Traded goods were also present, including copper objects from the Lake Superior area. Warfare may have been widespread to judge from the number of burials with evidence of wounds.

Greenwell, William (1829–1918) [Bi]. British antiquary whose career as a minor canon of Durham cathedral allowed him to carry out an extensive programme of field investigations, mainly involving the excavation of barrows in England. His first barrow opening was at Chollerton, Northumberland, in December 1847, after which he went on to examine more than 230 over a period of 40 years or so. Much of his work was published in collaboration with G. Rolleston in *British barrows* (1887, Oxford: Clarendon Press).

[Obit.: *Proceedings of the Society of Antiquaries of London*, 30 (1917–18), 200–4]

Gregory, Tony (1948–91) [Bi]. British archaeologist well known for popularizing archaeology for children and for work liaising with metal-detector users. Born in Stapleford, Nottinghamshire, he attended the local grammar school before going up to Peterhouse, Cambridge, to study archaeology. After graduating he joined the Norwich Castle Museum and from there went to the Norfolk Archaeological Unit where he spent most of his career. Liaison with the public was one of his main tasks and while working with metal-detector users he managed to recover the Thetford Treasure after it had been hidden by the original finder. His many television programmes included the highly successful children's series *Now, Then*.

[Obit.: *The Times*, 1 July 1991]

Gregory I (the Great) [Na]. A Roman patrician who in c.AD 575 left an official career to become a monk. He became involved in church administration and in 590 was made Pope. He is famous for reputedly introducing the 'Gregorian' chant, and his correspondence contains a wealth of information about the later 6th century in Italy. In 596 he sent missionaries to convert the English to Christianity. Pope Gregory I died c.AD 604.

grey literature [De]. Archaeological reports with limited distribution, usually client reports prepared by archaeological contractors.

griddle [Ar]. Flat ceramic plate used for baking manioc as the final stage in the process of detoxifying it for human consumption. Such griddles are especially common in the north-eastern part of South America. The presence of such griddles is also a sign that manioc is being cultivated.

Grimes, William Francis (1905–88) [Bi]. British archaeologist and prehistorian who was the first archaeologist to be employed full-time on rescue archaeology. Peter, as he was invariably known, was born in South Wales and educated at the University of Wales where he read classics before going on to a master's degree on the Legionary Fortress at Holt in Denbighshire. He joined the National Museum of Wales as Assistant Keeper of Archaeology in 1926, remaining there until 1938 when he left to join the Ordnance Survey Archaeology Section. This continued to be his official post until 1945, but at the outbreak of WW2 he was seconded to the Ministry of Defence to record and excavate archaeological sites threatened with destruction because of wartime defence requirements. In 1956 he became director of the Institute of Archaeology in the University of London, and over the following decade and a half guided the Institute through many changes and developments. His many publications include *The prehistory of Wales* (1951, Cardiff: National Museum of Wales), *Excavations on defence sites 1939–45* (1960, London: HMSO), and *The excavation of Roman and medieval London* (1968, London: Methuen).

[Obit.: *The Times*, 28 December 1988]

Grimes Graves, Norfolk, UK [Si]. An extensive series of later Neolithic flint mines on the Breckland of East Anglia in eastern England. Surveys and limited excavations since the late 19th century AD have revealed more than 350 shafts over an area in excess of 7 ha. The high-quality flint available at the site lies in three bands—topstone, wall-stone, and floorstone—but it was only the deeper floorstone that seems to have interested the miners and they excavated shafts up to 12 m down into the chalk to get it. Use of the site spanned at least 1000 years and it is suggested that at any one time there might have been just a few shafts in operation.

[Rep.: R. Mercer, 1981, *Grimes Graves, Norfolk. Excavations 1971–72*, volume 1. London: Department of the Environment]

Grimston ware [Ar]. A type of early and middle Neolithic pottery found in the northeast of England, named after the site of Hanging

Grimston in what was formerly the East Riding of Yorkshire. Characterized by fine fabrics, good-quality finish, and round-bottomed forms with a carinated profile. In 1974 Isobel Smith suggested that such pots were part of a far wider distribution of carinated vessels found right across the British Isles and she proposed the term Grimston–Lyles Hill ware. These vessels represent the earliest style of pottery found in the British Neolithic, although the term **shouldered bowl** is now preferred to Grimston–Lyles Hill.

grinding stone [Ar]. Any stone, usually with at least one flat surface, used for grinding foodstuffs, medicines, cosmetics, or colorants.

Grinsell, Leslie Valentine (1907–95) [Bi]. British prehistorian who specialized in the archaeology of barrows and pursued a relentless programme of field survey and recording throughout southern England. Born and brought up in London, he joined Barclay's Bank as a clerk after leaving school. In 1925 his parents moved to Brighton and within a few months he discovered the Sussex Downs and started a lifelong interest in barrows, especially finding and recording them. By the outbreak of WW2 he had surveyed and published reports on the barrows of ten counties in meticulous detail, using his skills as a bank clerk to tabulate the descriptions. During WW2 he was a pilot officer in the photographic branch of the RAF which took him to Egypt and gave him the opportunity to visit the tombs there. After WW2 he returned to the bank briefly, taking up a position to work on the Victoria County History of Wiltshire in 1947. After completing the gazetteer for Wiltshire he joined the Bristol City Museum as Keeper of Archaeology in 1952, remaining there until he retired in 1972. Throughout his time at Bristol, and after his retirement when he continued to live in the city, he carried on with his surveys of barrows and by 1993 was proud to have completed studies on all the counties in southern England. He was treasurer of the Prehistoric Society between 1947 and 1970, and had many other interests—folklore, music, place-name studies, Egyptology, and coins. He was appointed OBE in 1972. His many publications include *The ancient burial mounds of England* (1953, London: Methuen) and *Barrow, pyramid and tomb* (1975, London: Thames and Hudson).

[Abio.: 1989, *An archaeological autobiography*. Gloucester: Alan Sutton]

Grobiņa, Latvia [Si]. Early medieval barrow cemeteries with prehistoric antecedents on the north bank of the River Ālande some 10 km inland from Liepāja on the Baltic coast. Surveys and excavations between 1984 and 1989 by Juris Urtāns and Valerij Petrenko have revealed that the earliest traces of occupation comprise a grave of the late Neolithic Corded Ware Culture stratified below burials of the 5th to the 13th centuries AD in the Atkalni I cemetery.

The largest and most impressive cemetery is the barrow cemetery at Priediens (also called Pastorāts or Priedulāji) on the eastern outskirts of modern Grobiņa. Recent surveys show that there are at least 2000 round barrows ranging in size from 3 to 15 m across and 0.1–1.4 m high. Excavations over the last century or more reveal the presence of single and double burials, cremations and inhumations. The grave goods are very rich and include swords, spearheads, helmets, belts, brooches, neck-rings, suspension plates, chains, bracelets, necklaces, combs, keys, and pottery. A unique stone stele was found in one of the mounds, similar in form and decoration to the picture-stones of Gotland. A broadly contemporary area of settlement in the form of 'dark-earth' deposits is known along a 2 km stretch of the north bank of the Ālande.

[Rep.: V. Petrenko and J Urtāns, 1995, *The archaeological monuments of Grobiņa*. Riga and Stockholm: Latvian Cultural Foundation and the Museum of National Antiquities]

grog [Ma]. Broken and crushed fragments of pottery, brick, or other fired ceramic materials recycled as a tempering agent in other ceramic products.

groma [Ar]. A Roman surveying instrument comprising four arms fixed at intervals of 90 degrees around a central post. Plumb-lines hanging from each arm allowed right angles and lines to be accurately set out during road-building and the construction of street plans and structures.

groove and splinter technique [De]. A technique of working bone and antler widely used in Upper Palaeolithic and Mesolithic times in northern Europe, but found in other contexts too, in which long thin strips of bone are produced by cutting slots or grooves longitudinally along the bone and then levering out the sections between the slots causing them to splinter at the end where they break off.

grooved ware [Ar]. Type of later Neolithic pottery found widely in the British Isles, formerly known as RINYO-CLACTON WARE. Dating to the middle and later 3rd millennium BC, the typical forms comprise flat-based, straight-walled, tub-shaped, and bucket-shaped vessels. Some are plain, but many are elaborately decorated with surface grooving and applied cordons. Grooved ware pottery is found on settlement sites and in later passage graves, but is also well represented at HENGES and HENGE ENCLOSURES.

Ground penetrating radar (GPR) [Eq]. A method of remote sensing by geophysical survey that can be used to provide a three-dimensional view of a buried site. The method works by systematically traversing a survey area with a portable radar that is directed downwards into the ground. A short pulse or wave of electromagnetic radiation is transmitted from the system into the ground. A receiver then records the reflected energy returned from interfaces between materials with differing conductivity or dielectric constants. The travel times of the reflections are also recorded and converted into depth measurements to provide a geo-electric depth section. By piecing together readings from across the survey area its is possible to produce, in visual form, vertically or horizontally sliced cutaways through the subsurface deposits. The reflections detected by the radar relate to changes of material at the interface of deposits and can thus be used to differentiate refilled pits and ditches, graves, buried paths and roads, air-filled chambers, and wood, metal, and stone artefacts.

ground stone tool [De]. A stone tool given a smooth final form by grinding it against another, more abrasive rock.

group [De]. Artefacts are said to form a group if they are found in association in circumstances implying that they were made, used, discarded, or deposited at about the same point in time.

grubenhaus [Co]. A form of building constructed in many parts of northern Europe (especially Britain) during the period between the 5th and the 7th centuries AD. Distinctive in having a subrectangular pit underneath the floor with a gabled roof supported at either end by a principal post.

guanaco (huanaco) [Sp]. A camelid (*Auchenia huanaco*) related to the LLAMA, with a coat of soft pale-brown hair used as wool. Native to the high Andean grasslands. Domesticated by c.5000 BC as a food source.

guard chambers [Co]. Small rooms or cells located just inside the entrances to fortified enclosures such as hillforts and castles where guards or look-outs defending the gate could rest, shelter, or hide.

guava [Sp]. Small tree (*Psidium guava*) bearing an edible pale yellow fruit with pink acid-sweet juicy flesh. Native to tropical and subtropical South America. Domesticated by c.3000 BC.

gui [Ar]. An early Chinese handled bronze bowl which often bore writing as well as complex designs.

Guilá Naquitz, Mexico [Si]. A rock-shelter in the eastern part of the Valley of Oaxaca which was discovered in 1964 and subsequently excavated from 1966 onwards by an interdisciplinary team led by Kent Flannery. The site is one of the most completely investigated rock-shelters in Mesoamerica and was found to contain a good sequence of Archaic Stage deposits spanning the period c.8750–6670 BC and therefore contemporary with the Ajuereado Phase of the Tehuacán Valley.

The later deposits in the shelter, dating to the period after 7400 BC, show some evidence of incipient agriculture.

[Rep.: K. Flannery (ed.), 1986, *Guila Naquitz: Archaic foraging and early agriculture in Oaxaca, Mexico.* New York. Academic Press]

guilloche [De]. A plaited or cable motif used as a decorative device in a range of applications comprising two or more interwoven strands or bands, sometimes continuous and sometimes broken.

guinea pig [Sp]. Small rodent with a sturdy body and vestigial tail (*Cavia porcellus*). Native to the lowland valleys of the Andean zone of

South America. Domesticated as a food source by *c.*2000 BC, although prior to this they had been tamed and managed for several millennia. Following domestication their body size increased and they became widely dispersed over much of South America, reaching Ecuador by about AD 700.

Guitarrero Cave, Peru [Si]. Occupied cave at the base of the Cordillera Negra in northern Peru excavated by Thomas Lynch in 1968. Two main horizons have been recognized, both within the Archaic Stage.

Guitarrero I dates to about 10 000 BC and includes a lithic assemblage comprising flaked tools of the Ayacucho Complex and Tagua-Tagua Complex. Stemmed points were also found. Human bones, including a mandible, represent the earliest human remains found to date in South America.

Guitarrero II dates to the period 8500–5700 BC and contained bone and wood artefacts as well as basketry and woven textiles. The lithic assemblage included willow-leaf projectile points. Domesticated beans from Guitarrero II represent the earliest known examples to date. Throughout both main phases the cave was probably a wet-season camp occupied as part of a transhumance regime by hunter-gatherer communities.

[Rep.: F. T. Lynch, 1980, *Guitarrero cave: early man in the Andes*. New York: Academic Press]

Gumelniţa Culture [CP]. Late Neolithic and Copper Age communities of the period 3800 BC to 3000 BC in the eastern Balkans and lower Danube. Contemporary with VINČA D and level VI at KARANOVO. Their settlements were often of TELLS situated in low-lying areas, as at the type-site itself. Others are flat sites enclosed by a square-shaped earthwork. In all cases the houses are characteristically rectangular rooms in plan, sometimes with an anteroom at one end. They are close-set with passageways between. Pottery includes a variety of coarse-gritted fabrics as well as fine graphite-painted wares. Ceramic anthropomorphic figurines are also represented. Metal objects include copper chisels and axe-hammers. There is evidence for emerging social differentiation, particularly visible in the diversity of grave goods and the fact that in cemeteries such as that at Varna some graves contain exceptionally high levels of wealth in terms of the artefacts represented.

Gundestrup, Denmark [Si]. A peat bog in Jutland where in 1891 a remarkable silver cauldron was discovered. The vessel was found dismantled into its constituent pieces: twelve separate sections of sheet silver, a round plate, and two tubular fittings. When restored it was found to be 69 cm in diameter and 40 cm high. The wall sections are decorated in raised relief and show scenes representing ritual or mythological events. The figures on the outer face were originally covered in gold leaf with eyes of red or blue glass. Various attempts have been made to interpret the scenes as having been drawn from Scandinavian mythology, but the likelihood is that the vessel was made elsewhere, perhaps in Thrace or perhaps still further east in the area of the Black Sea.

[Sum.: A. Bergquist and T. Taylor, 1987, The origin of the Gundestrup cauldron. *Antiquity*, 61, 10–24]

Gundlingen swords [Ar]. A type of bronze sword typical of the Hallstatt C period in central Europe with a long leaf-shaped blade, broad shallow butt and pommel tang. Examples were taken or traded out of their homeland area, some reaching Britain around 700 BC.

Gunther Pattern [CP]. Late Archaic Stage hunter-gatherer communities living in the Humboldt Bay, Eel River, and Mad River areas of the Pacific coastland of northwestern North America in the period *c.*150 BC to recent times. These communities specialized in riverside and coastal locations, relying heavily on seasonal salmon runs and other predictable marine resources. Hunting was also carried out in adjacent uplands. Lithic assemblages of the period include distinctive projectile points of triangular outline with pronounced basal barbs and a central tang. Long-distance trade allowed the acquisition of obsidian from sources over 400 km away. Cemeteries suggest some ranking among Gunther communities.

Günz [CP]. The earliest of the four main episodes of PLEISTOCENE glaciation that are traditionally recognized in the Alpine sequence, starting before 700 000 years ago. Comparable to the Nebraskan of the North American sequence; earlier than the CROMERIAN stage of the British sequence.

gymnasium [MC]. A Greek sports ground and centre for education. Typically includes spacious courts for exercise and games, washing-rooms, and classrooms with stone benches for sedentary periods.

gypsum [Ma]. A hydrated calcium sulphate mineral found occasionally in pure deposits but also available as a primary or secondary mineral in limestone, shale, marl, and clay. Extensively used in the building industry since late prehistoric times in many parts of the world, when mixed with water and sand gypsum makes a fine-textured paste that dries hard and smooth. Used as a coating for walls, architectural surfaces, and in making casts, moulds, and sculpture.

gyrus [Co]. Latin term for a circular horse-training ring.

H

habitat [Ge]. The place where an animal or plant lives; its immediate surroundings.

habitation sites [Ge]. Places where people lived, whether permanently or temporarily. They may be constructed dwellings, or possibly a cave or rock-shelter. Habitation sites need not be defended or otherwise enclosed, although many are. Many will be directly associated with other kinds of sites, for example burial grounds and field systems.

haematite [Ma]. A common iron oxide extensively used for colouring purposes—red, brown, or black—especially in pottery production.

Hacilar, Turkey [Si]. A small Neolithic settlement in the Taurus Mountains of southwest Turkey, excavated by James Mellaart in the 1950s. The earliest levels, dated to the 7th millennium BC, were aceramic and comprised small rectangular houses made from mud brick. These levels did, however, include domesticated crops (wheat, barley, and lentils). Bones of sheep and cattle were found, but they are not certainly domesticated. After a period of abandonment the site was re-occupied in the early 6th millennium BC. This new settlement had substantial rectangular houses, made of mud brick or timber and daub on stone foundations. They were finished internally in plaster; some were painted. Mortars, querns, and braziers were fitted into the floors. The kitchen area was separate and there was an upper level for storage. The occupants of this late Neolithic village used monochrome red and brown pottery. Figurines were also made. The upper levels (V to I) were Chalcolithic, around 5000 BC, and by this time the village had been fortified by the construction of a defensive wall.

[Sum.: J. Mellaart, 1961, Hacilar: a Neolithic village site. *Scientific American*, 205(2), 86–97]

Hadrian [Na]. Roman emperor AD 117–38.

Hadrian's Wall, Northumberland and Cumbria, UK [Si]. The most famous and most thoroughly explored frontier system created by the Roman army. The main wall runs coast to coast across northern England for 117 km from the Wallsend in Newcastle on the east to Carlisle on the Solway Firth in the west, with a continuation of the line as a series of forts and signal stations along the Cumbria coast. Construction of the wall began in AD 122 on the instructions of the Emperor Hadrian while on a visit to the province; it was completed in about AD 133. Various kinds of construction are represented along its length, but the basic idea was a stone wall punctuated at intervals of a Roman mile by small forts (milecastles) with turrets in between. Larger forts lay at intervals. There was a ditch on the north side, and a military zone on the south defined by an earthwork called the *vallum*, which is actually a ditch. The purpose of the wall was to control the movement of people in and out of the empire, and to counter localized threats and uprisings. Hadrian's Wall was abandoned between about AD 140 and AD 165 when the frontier moved north to the Antonine Wall, but otherwise it remained in place throughout the Roman occupation of Britain.

[Sum.: D. J. Breeze and B. Dobson, 1987, *Hadrian's Wall*. Harmondsworth: Penguin]

haft [Ar]. The handle section of an implement such as an adze or an awl.

Hakataya Tradition [CP]. A general term referring to a series of regionally distinct Archaic Stage cultures living around the Colorado River basin in southwestern North America in the period after c.AD 500. Sometimes known as the Patayan Tradition, these groups adopted agriculture and pottery-making from the Hohokam Culture of Arizona.

halberd [Ar]. Axe-like weapon where a pointed metal blade, similar to a dagger blade, is mounted at right-angles on the distal end of a wooden haft. Sometimes the blade is slightly curved. Halberds are especially characteristic of the early Bronze Age in Europe.

halberd pendant [Ar]. Small hanging ornament of metal or stone modelled in the shape of a halberd blade.

half-life [Ge]. The time taken for one half of a radioactive isotope to decay into a stable element. Different isotopes have different half-lives, ranging from a few seconds to many thousands of years. The most visible application in archaeology is in relation to radiocarbon dating and other radiometric dating techniques.

hall [Co]. **1.** Chief room of a house, mainly used for ceremonial and domestic life. With the decline in communal life since the Middle Ages, the term has been transferred to denote a lobby entrance. **2.** A large single-roomed building used for domestic accommodation and ceremonial or communal purposes.

Hallstatt, Gmunden, Austria [Si]. Prehistoric cemeteries and salt mines in the heart of the Salzkammergut 50 km southwest of Salzburg in the Austrian Alps. Excavations since the 19th century have revealed a wealth of material round the town of Salzbertal beside and above Lake Hallstatt. An extensive cemetery excavated between 1846 and 1863 by Johann Ramsauer contained 980 graves, and later excavations found more, bringing the total to over 1100. Most belong to the 7th and 6th centuries BC, and represent the whole community of men and women of all ages as well as children and infants. The wealth of the prehistoric community at Hallstatt was evidently based upon salt mining, and there are abundant traces of the early workings. Finds from the mines included leather knapsacks and clothing which had been well preserved as a result of saline conditions. No settlements of these mining communities have been found to date.

[Sum.: F. R. Hodson, 1990, *Hallstatt, the Ramsauer graves.* Bonn: Habelt]

Hallstatt Culture [CP]. Late Bronze Age and early Iron Age culture of central Europe named after the type-site at HALLSTATT, Austria. In the German system of classification the Hallstatt cultural sequence is subdivided into four units, A–D, of which A (12th and 11th centuries BC) and B (10th to 8th centuries BC) are regarded as Bronze Age cultures, and equate to the older and younger Urnfield cultures, while C and D were Iron Age cultures, dating to the 7th and 6th centuries BC.

Although the Hallstatt Culture developed from the preceding URNFIELD CULTURES there were a number of marked changes. First was the introduction of ironworking technology. Second, inhumation replaced cremation as the principal burial mode. And, third, Hallstatt society appears to have been highly differentiated, with wealthy chieftains buried in richly furnished graves that included amongst their grave goods material imported from the Mediterranean world.

hamlet [MC]. A cluster of houses and other buildings smaller than a village.

hammerhead mortarium [Ar]. A MORTARIUM with a rim and flange that form a single unit, shaped like the head of a hammer, its centre meeting the body of the vessel at right angles.

hammerstone [Ar]. In flintworking, the block of hard stone used to detach flakes from a core. Typically a conveniently shaped pebble or rounded stone is used; battering and cracking on the ends usually betray their use as hammerstones. *See also* MAUL.

Han [CP]. Chinese dynasty spanning the period 206 BC to AD 220 with an interregnum between AD 9 and AD 25 which separated the early (western) period from the later (eastern) period. The Han Dynasty was the first centralized state in China after the unification of the separate kingdoms by Qin in 221 BC. During the Han Dynasty trade routes to the west were opened and the court instituted monopolies on iron and salt. Some aristocratic burials of the period are extremely rich.

handaxe [Ar]. Characteristic stone core-tool of the Palaeolithic period consisting of a large core of flint or other stone, typically 8–30 cm in overall length, worked on both sides to form a point at one end and a rounded butt at the other. It was probably held in the hand and used as an all-purpose tool for clubbing, skinning, piercing, chopping, and digging.

Hap [Di]. Egyptian god. *See* APIS.

Hap'y [Di]. Egyptian god, god of the Nile inundation, represented as a man with breasts, a clump of papyrus on his head, and carrying heavily laden offering tables.

Harald Finehair [Na]. King of Vestfold (Oslo Fjord) who from the late 890s AD made himself master of the whole of Norway. The consolidation of his rule induced many Norwegians to emigrate, especially to Iceland. Harald died *c*.AD 930.

Harald Hardradi [Na]. King of Norway from AD 1047 and known as Hardrari which can be translated as 'hard ruler'. He invaded England in 1066 and was killed by King Harold Godwinson at Stamford Bridge, Yorkshire, the same year.

Harald Harefoot [Na]. King of northern England from AD 1035 and of all England from AD 1037. He was the son of King Knut by his mistress Aelgifu of Northampton. Harald died in AD 1040.

Harappa, India [Si]. A major city of the INDUS VALLEY civilization beside the River Ravi in the Punjab of west Pakistan. The site was first discovered in the 1820s by Sir Alexander Burnes and Charles Masson, but the importance of the site was not recognized until much later. The city is known to cover at least 100 ha and spans a long period of occupation in five main phases from about 3200 BC through to 1500 BC. On the west side of the site is an imposing high area surrounded by brick walls, designated as the citadel by Sir Mortimer Wheeler, but in fact it is just one of a number of major structures, many of which were made from a distinctive style of ceramic brick. Residential accommodation occupies a larger zone to the east. Two cemeteries are known from the period 2500 BC to 1500 BC, mainly supine inhumations in wooden coffins.

[Rep.: G. L. Possehl (ed.), 1992, *Harappan civilization: a contemporary perspective.* New Delhi: Oxford and I. B. H. Publishing]

Hardaway points [Ar]. Bifacially worked chipped stone projectile point with a triangu-

lar outline, a slightly hollow base, and a side notch towards the base on either side. Named after the construction company that used the site on which many examples were found by Joffre Coe in the 1950s, Hardaway points are thought to represent a stylistic variation within the larger DALTON TRADITION dating to the period *c*.8500–7000 BC.

Harder Phase [CP]. Archaic Stage cultural grouping in the Snake River area of eastern Washington and the plateau region of North America dating to the period *c*.500 BC to AD 1300. Villages of large pit-houses up to 6 m across are known along the river valleys, and salmon fishing as well as the hunting of elk, deer, antelope, and mountain sheep provided the mainstays of the diet. Spears were used in the early Harder Phase, but later the bow and arrow was adopted. Small corner-notched points were used as arrow tips. Domestic dogs were kept.

hard-hammer flintworking [Ge]. A method of flintworking where flakes are detached from a core using a stone tool. In general, hard-hammer-struck flakes are short and have a very marked bulb of percussion.

Haroeris [Di]. Egyptian god. *See* HORUS.

Harpocrates [Di]. Egyptian god. *See* HOR-PA-KHRED.

harpoon [Ar]. A type of spear adapted for hunting fish, seals, whales, etc., which features prominent barbs to prevent the point of the harpoon being dislodged, and also a line for retrieving the prey.

Harris matrix [Eq]. A graphical representation of the relationships between stratigraphic units, based on principles of archaeological stratigraphy. Also known as a Harris–Winchester matrix.

Harrison, Richard Martin (1935–92) [Bi]. British archaeologist who worked mainly on Roman and later sites in Turkey. Born in Windsor and educated at Sherborne School and Lincoln College, Oxford, he joined the British Institute in Ankara immediately after graduating. Here he started his surveys of Lycia and developed a life-long interest in Anatolia. After a spell at the British School in Rome and a short time teaching at Bryn Mawr he returned to Lincoln College as a research student. In 1964 he was appointed to a lectureship at the University of Newcastle-upon-Tyne and remained there until 1985, becoming Professor of Archaeology and head of department. In 1985 he moved back to Oxford as Professor of the Archaeology of the Roman Empire and Fellow of All Soul's College.

[Obit.: *The Times*, 16 September 1992]

Harsomtus [Di]. Egyptian god. *See* HOR-SMA-TAWY.

Harthacnut [Na]. King of Denmark from AD 1035. Son of King Knut of England but prevented from making good his claim to his father's English throne until shortly after the death of his brother HARALD HAREFOOT.

Hathor [Di]. Egyptian goddess, of Dendera and elsewhere. Cow goddess, or shown as a woman with cow's horns or a cow's face. Early forms in Old Kingdom times showed her as a woman with the horns of an antelope. Spoken of as 'the Golden One', she was worshipped at Memphis, Luxor, Cusae, and in Sinai. She was associated with the dead as Hathor of the West, and identified by the Greeks with Aphrodite. Her name means House of Horus and she was closely associated with HORUS as his wife and the mother of his son HOR-SMA-TAWY (sometimes called Ihy). The **Seven Hathors** were the goddesses, or fates, who decided the future of the newly born.

Hatshepsut [Na]. A queen of Egypt who reigned as a pharaoh of the 18th Dynasty between *c.*1479 BC and 1457 BC after the death of her husband.

Hatvan Culture [CP]. Hungarian Bronze Age culture, local successor to the Nagyrév Culture. Burial was mainly by cremation, and settlements, which were sometimes tells and often fortified, contain long rectangular houses of timber and daub construction.

Haua Fteah, Libya [Si]. A large cave in northern Libya containing the longest and most complete sequence of deposits in North Africa. Excavated by Charles McBurney between 1951 and 1955 the lowest levels were never reached. The oldest material recovered was the local Amudian, a pre-AURIGNACIAN blade industry, stratigraphically sealed by

Mousterian levels dated to about 60000 years ago. Above these were deposits of the Dabban industry dating to about 40000 years ago. This in turn was followed by eastern Oranian at 16000–14000 years ago and higher still Libyco-Capsian. Pottery, together with domestic sheep and/or goats, was present by around 5000 BC.

[Rep.: C. B. M. McBurney, 1967, *The Haua Fteah (Cyrenaica) and the Stone Age of the southeast Mediterranean*. Cambridge: CUP]

Haut Moyen Age (High Middle Ages) [De]. A European continental term for the early medieval period up to about AD 1100.

Havana Hopewell [CP]. *See* HOPEWELLIAN CULTURE.

Haven, Samuel Foster (1806–81) [Bi]. American antiquary and librarian of the American Antiquarian Society. In 1856 he published a remarkable book, *Archaeology of the United States* (Washington DC: Smithsonian Institute), which distilled all that was known about the prehistory of North America at that time. In it, he argued that the native American Indians were of high antiquity and that their ancestors had been responsible for constructing and using the great earthen mounds and platforms known in central and eastern parts of North America.

[Bio.: C. Deane, 1885, *Memoir of Samuel F. Haven*. Cambridge MA: John Wilson]

Haverfield, Francis John (1860–1919) [Bi]. British archaeologist and internationally known Roman historian. Born in Shipston-on-Stour, he was educated at Winchester and later went up to New College, Oxford, and obtained a first-class degree in Moderations. In 1884 he went to Lancing College as a sixth-form master, developing an interest in Roman epigraphy in his leisure. In 1892 he was invited to return to Oxford and spent the next fifteen years as a senior student at Christ Church. Roman Britain became an increasing passion, and during vacations he travelled widely, visiting or directing excavations. In 1907 he was appointed Camden Professor of Ancient History with an official fellowship at Brasenose College. He was regularly in touch with many scholars abroad and when WW1 broke out it troubled him greatly. After a cerebral haemorrhage in 1915 he died suddenly in 1919. Amongst his many publications were

The Romanization of Roman Britain (1905 London: British Academy) and the posthumous *The Roman occupation of Britain* (1924, Oxford: Clarendon Press).

[Obit.: *Proceedings of the British Academy*, 9 (1919–20), 475–91]

Hawkes, Charles Francis Christopher (1905–92) [Bi]. British pioneer in the study of European prehistory. Educated at Winchester and New College, Oxford, where he read Greats. He graduated in 1928 and the same year he was appointed to a post in the Department of British and Medieval Antiquities in the British Museum. His interest in excavation and in the Iron Age in particular had already been kindled through involvement with excavations at St Catherine's Hill, Winchester, in 1925–8. During WW2 he took up duties in the Ministry of Aircraft Production, returning to the British Museum briefly in 1945. A year later he was appointed as the first holder of the Chair of European Archaeology at Oxford, and was elected a Fellow of Keble College. He remained in the post until his retirement in 1972. While there he worked to develop a truly international view of prehistory. He also promoted the interests of scientific archaeology, was one of the founding fathers of the establishment of the Research Laboratory for Archaeology and the History of Art at Oxford, and invented the term 'archaeometry'. He worked closely with both his wives, first JACQUETTA HAWKES (née Hopkins) and later Sonia (née Chadwick).

[Obit.: *The Times*, 31 March 1992]

Hawkes, Jacquetta (1910–96) [Bi]. British archaeologist, author, and popularizer of archaeology. Born in Cambridge, daughter of biochemist and Nobel Prize winner Sir Frederick Gowland Hopkins, she was educated at Purse School and, after declaring an interest in archaeology at the age of nine, became the first woman to study the full degree course in archaeology and anthropology at Cambridge while registered at Newnham College. At the end of her second year she went to excavate at Colchester where she met CHRISTOPHER HAWKES; they were married in 1933. Before WW2 she worked in Palestine and on several projects with Christopher. During WW2 she became a civil servant working as assistant principal at the Post-War Reconstruction Secretariat and later at the Ministry of

Education. During this time she became interested in more imaginative writing and following an affair with the poet W. J. Turner published a book of poetry, *Symbols and speculations* (1949, London: Cresset Press). She became the Secretary of the UK National Committee for UNESCO and at the first UNESCO conference in Mexico City in 1947 she fell in love with J. B. Priestley. Leaving the civil service in 1949 to devote herself to writing, she divorced Christopher Hawkes, and married Priestley in 1953. Her book *A land* (1953, Newton Abbot: David and Charles), published the same year, remains an important study of landscape change and character. Later life also brought interests in many causes and she became, amongst other things, archaeological adviser to the Festival of Britain, a governor of the British Film Institute, and a vice-president of the Council for British Archaeology.

[Obit.: *The Independent*, 20 March 1996]

HBMCE [Ab]. *See* ENGLISH HERITAGE.

headland [Ge]. Area at the end of a furlong or other strip of ploughed ground on which the plough could be turned. Could be cultivated or left as pasture to serve as access to the field.

Head-Smashed-In Buffalo Jump, Alberta, Canada [Si]. A series of almost sheer sandstone cliffs surrounding a creek cutting into a shallow basin in a great plain, this site is the oldest, largest, longest-lived, and best-preserved buffalo jump in North America. Over 500 small stone cairns up to 0.3 m high and extending for up to 8 km from the cliffs mark the edges of drive-lanes along which animals were stampeded.

The remains of thousands of beasts have been found at the base of the cliffs, some dating back to 5400 BC. The jump was still used in AD 1797 when Peter Fidler of the Hudson Bay Trading Company visited the area. Near the kill site at the base of the cliffs was a campsite and an area for processing carcasses.

[Rep.: J. Brink *et al.*, 1986, *Final report of the 1984 season at Head-Smashed-In Buffalo Jump, Alberta*. Edmonton: Alberta Culture]

Heathery Burn Tradition [CP]. A regional metalworking tradition covering the north of England, within the EWART PARK PHASE of the British late Bronze Age. Named after the discovery of a hoard of bronzes in the Heathery

Burn Cave, Co. Durham, the tradition is characterized by three-ribbed and plain forms of socketed axe, late palstaves, socketed gouges and chisels, tanged chisels, knives with ribbed tangs, swords, plain rings, pegged spearheads, bronze buckets, tongs, horse-harness fitments, and the metal parts for wheeled vehicles.

heavy mineral analysis [Te]. A technique based on petrological methods for characterizing and tracing the origins of pottery or stone. By crushing samples and mixing them with a high-viscosity fluid various particles will separate out, amongst them the so-called heavy minerals, such as garnet, epidote, tourmaline, and zircon, which have a relatively high specific gravity. These are also the minerals that are most variable in their occurrence and which can sometimes be matched by suites from source areas. The technique was used very successfully to examine the production of Roman black burnished wares.

Hedeby, Germany [Si]. A substantial trading settlement covering 25 ha on the Schlei estuary at the southern end of the Jutland peninsula in northwest Germany. Defended by a rampart on the landward side, excavations over many seasons have revealed wooden buildings, well preserved in waterlogged conditions, and evidence of industrial as well as commercial activity. The main use of the site was between about 800 AD and 1050 AD.

[Sum.: T. Ramskou, 1962, *Hedeby: Vikingetidens internationale handelsby.* Copenhagen: Munksgaard]

hedgerow dating [Te]. A rough and ready way of approximating the age of living hedges on the basis that over the course of time one new species per century successfully colonizes the boundary—a proposition that has become known as **Hooper's hedgerow hypothesis**. The average number of species in a 30 m length of reasonably well-managed hedge gives the approximate age of the hedge in centuries.

Heekeren, H. R. van (1902–74) [Bi]. Dutch archaeologist who spent much time in Indonesia, conducting excavations on Sulawesi and Java. Amongst his numerous publications are *The Stone Age of Indonesia* (1957. 's-Gravenhage: M. Nijhoff), and *The Bronze–Iron Age of Indonesia* (1958. 's-Gravenhage: M. Nijhoff).

[Obit.: *Antiquity*, 50 (1976), 91]

Heka [Di]. Egyptian god of magic. Also connected with the fertility of the land, especially at Esna.

Heket (Heqet) [Di]. Egyptian frog goddess who was widely worshipped in Egypt, particularly at Antinopolis. Associated with water and the rapids in rivers, she often appears in connection with KHNM. One of the deities connected with childbirth.

Heliopolitan Ennead [Di]. The company of gods and goddesses closely associated with the cosmological system and creation myths taught by the priests of Heliopolis in ancient Egypt. These deities include: Nun (the father of the gods); Atum (the spirit that lived inside Nun prior to the creation); Ra (the sun god and creator); Khepri (a transformer god); Shu (a man created by Ra without recourse to a woman); Tefnut (sister of Shu); Anhur (the sky bearer); Geb (the physical foundation of the world); Nut (sky goddess); Osiris (god of the dead); Isis (wife of Osiris and mother of Horus); Set (evil brother of Osiris); Nephthys (goddess of the dead); Horus (solar god of the sky who also appears in various other guises as: Haroeris (sky god), Behdety (sky god), Harakhtes (god of the horizon), Harmakhis (god of the horizon), and Harsiesis); Hathor (sky goddess, daughter of Ra); Anubis (god of the underworld); Apuaut (he who opens the way); Thoth (messenger god); and Seshat (main wife of Thoth).

Helladic [CP]. General term applied to the Greek Bronze Age on the Greek mainland: equivalent to the term Cycladic referring to the island of Melos and others in the Cyclades and Minoan referring to Crete. Following the scheme developed by Wace and Blegan, the Helladic period is subdivided into early (*c.*3000–2000 BC), middle (*c.*2000–1550 BC), and late (*c.*1550–1050 BC) phases. These are often abbreviated to EH, MH, LH, and further split into numbered subphases, for example MHI. It was during the late Helladic period that the Mycenaean civilization developed, first at Mycenae, then at other centres in Greece, before spreading throughout the Aegean.

Hellenistic period [CP]. A general term to refer to the time between the unification of Macedonia and the Greek states by Phillip II of Macedon in 336 BC and the arrival of the

Roman empire in the late 1st century BC. During this time the Hellenistic world comprised Greece and the various kingdoms taken from the Persian empire in earlier centuries. Hellenistic art can be applied to post-classical material outside these strict geographical limits; indeed Hellenistic cultural influence continued to be a powerful force in the Roman and Parthian empires during the early centuries AD.

Hell Gap points [Ar]. Bifacially worked chipped stone projectile points of the PLANO Tradition with a broad pointed top set on a straight-sided trapezoidal body. The base is narrow and straight. Used by later Palaeo-Indian cultures of the North America Plains in the period around 7500 BC. Experiments show that these points were probably spearheads and fully capable of penetrating the hide and rib cage of large beasts such as bison.

Helots [CP]. The original inhabitants of Laconia and Messeania, enslaved by the Spartans after their conquest of these territories.

Helton Phase [CP]. Archaic Stage hunter-gather communities living in the eastern woodlands of North America in the period c.4000–3000 BC. Villages housing up to 150 people have been found, the houses having sunken earth floors and post and wattle construction walls on two sides, the ends being covered with skins or mats. Occupants made extensive use of shallow lakes and slow-moving water for fishing. They also used acorns, hickory, walnuts, pecans, and hazelnuts. Grass seeds were also exploited and processed in stone mortars. The hunters also took deer, small mammals and waterfowl such as ducks and geese. A cemetery is known at Koster, Illinois, in which the bodies had been smothered in red ochre.

Hembury ware [Ar]. Style of plain early and middle Neolithic pottery found in southwestern England during the 4th millennium BC. Named after the Neolithic enclosure site of Hembury in Devon, Hembury ware is characterized by round-bottomed vessels with straight sides or S-profiled bodies.

Hemigkofen sword [Ar]. A style of bronze sword with a leaf-shaped blade and flanged hilt developed in central Europe during the

Hallstatt A period and traded to other parts of northern Europe. They appear in Britain, especially in the Thames Valley, during the Penard Phase.

henge [MC]. A distinctive class of late Neolithic enclosure found throughout the British Isles and dating mainly to the 3rd millennium BC. Roughly circular in plan, henges are bounded by a bank, usually with an internal ditch. They usually have either a single entrance (Class I), two diametrically opposed entrances (Class II), or, exceptionally, four entrances (also Class II). Some examples have a second ditch outside the bank (Class IA/IIA). Single henges as well as groups of three or four examples near together are known. Henges frequently contain a scatter of pits, occasional burials, circular settings of posts, or stone circles. The largest example is at AVEBURY, Wiltshire, in southern England. Also known as classic henges.

henge enclosure [MC]. A term popularized by Anthony Harding to describe the large and rather irregular henges found in small numbers on the chalklands of southern England, especially Durrington Walls, Wiltshire, and Mount Pleasant, Dorset. All are situated in relatively low-lying positions, mainly in river valleys. In contrast to the classic henges they typically yield large amounts of domestic debris including pottery, animal bone, and flintwork. They may have been occupation sites or ceremonial centres or a combination of both. All date to the 3rd millennium BC.

hengiform monument [MC]. A very small henge-like structure, typically less than 15 m across, with a ditch and often some traces of an outer bank. Examples with one or two entrances are known. Some were constructed as a series of pits rather than with a continuous ditch. In the central area there are often pits and cremation burials. They are found throughout the British Isles in much the same areas as classic henges; indeed hengiforms are frequently associated with clusters of contemporary late Neolithic monuments such as cursūs, pit circles, timber circles, and classic henges.

Hengist [Na]. Jutish mercenary leader who according to the *Anglo-Saxon Chronicle* was invited by Vortigern to settle southeast England together with his brother Horsa. There is much uncertainty about whether Hengist ever came to Kent and if so when. Hengist is believed to have died c.AD 488.

Hengistbury Head, Dorset, UK [Si]. A substantial promontory sandwiched between Christchurch Harbour and Bournemouth Bay on the coast of central southern England that was a major trading port in later prehistoric times. Excavations by J. P. Bushe-Fox in 1911–12, St George Gray in 1918–24, and Barry Cunliffe between 1979 and 1984 have revealed something of the complexity of the site which is defended by a pair of substantial ramparts cutting off the headland. Between about 300 BC and AD 100 Hengistbury was the focus of cross-channel trade between Britain and France. The headland had been occupied much earlier too, with an Upper Palaeolithic (Creswellian) open-air settlement on the hill in the centre of the Head which, when it was occupied in about 10 500 BC, would have overlooked a big river valley where the English Channel now lies.

[Rep.: B. Cunliffe, 1987, *Hengistbury Head, Dorset*, volume 1. *The prehistoric and Roman settlement 3500 BC–AD 500*. Oxford. Oxford University Committee for Archaeology]

Henry I (Beauclerk) [Na]. English king from AD 1100, of the House of Normandy. Born 1068, fourth son of William I. Married (1) Edith or Matilda, daughter of Malcolm III of Scotland; (2) Adela, daughter of Godfrey, count of Louvain. Died in AD 1135, aged 67, having reigned 35 years.

Henry II (Curtmantle) [Na]. English king from AD 1154, of the House of Anjou (Plantagenets). Born 1133, son of Matilda, daughter of Henry I, and Geoffrey, count of Anjou. Married Eleanor, daughter of William, duke of Aquitaine, and divorced queen of Louis VII of France. Died in AD 1189 aged 56, having reigned eighteen years.

Henry III [Na]. English king from AD 1216, of the House of Anjou (Plantagenets). Born 1207, son of John and Isabella of Angoulême. Married Eleanor, daughter of Raymond, count of Provence. Died AD 1272 aged 65, having reigned 56 years.

Henry IV [Na]. English king from AD 1399, of the House of Lancaster. Born 1366, son of John of Gaunt, fourth son of Edward III

and Blanche, daughter of Henry, duke of Lancaster. Married (1) Mary, daughter of Humphrey, earl of Hereford; (2) Joan, daughter of Charles, king of Navarre, and widow of John, duke of Brittany. Died in AD 1413 aged 47, having reigned thirteen years.

Henry V [Na]. English king from AD 1413, of the House of Lancaster. Born 1387, eldest surviving son of Henry IV and Mary. Married Catherine, daughter of Charles VI of France. Died AD 1422 aged 34, having reigned nine years.

Henry VI [Na]. English king from AD 1422, of the House of Lancaster. Born 1421, son of Henry V. Married Margaret, daughter of René, duke of Anjou and count of Provence. Deposed March 1461, restored October 1470. Deposed again April 1471, and killed May 1471 aged 49, having reigned 39 years.

Henry VII [Na]. English king from AD 1485, of the House of Tudor. Born 1457, son of Margaret Beaufort, great-granddaughter of John of Gaunt, fourth son of Edward III, and Edmund Tudor, earl of Richmond. Married Elizabeth, daughter of Edward IV. Died AD 1509 aged 52, having reigned 23 years.

Henry VIII [Na]. English king from AD 1509 of the House of Tudor. Born 1491, second son of Henry VII. Married (1) Catherine, daughter of Ferdinand II, king of Aragon, and widow of his elder brother Arthur (divorced); (2) Anne, daughter of Sir Thomas Boleyn (executed); (3) Jane, daughter of Sir John Seymour (died in childbirth); (4) Anne, daughter of John, duke of Cleves (divorced); (5) Catherine Howard, niece of the duke of Norfolk (executed); (6) Catherine, daughter of Sir Thomas Parr and widow of Lord Latimer. Died in AD 1547 aged 55, having reigned 37 years.

Henslow, John Stevens (1796–1861) [Bi]. British botanist and geologist, founder of the Cambridge Philosophical Society and successively Cambridge Professor of Mineralogy (1822–7) and Botany (1827–61). Through the work of his most famous pupil, Charles Darwin, Henslow indirectly influenced archaeologists; his own entry into the study was less fortunate, for he believed the Anglo-Saxon urns from Kingston-on-Soar to be prehistoric.

[Bio.: L. Jenyns, 1862, *Memoir of the Rev. John Steven Henslow*. London: John van Voorst]

Herculaneum, Italy [Si]. A small but wealthy Roman city on the Bay of Naples in Campania which, like Pompeii, was overwhelmed during the eruption of Vesuvius in AD 79. Unlike the material that buried Pompeii, the debris that sealed Herculaneum was a slurry of up to 20 m of liquid mud that solidified as a tufa-like substance. Excavations began here in 1738, at first based around digging shafts and tunnels to expose the remains in underground passages, which could be visited by the intrepid. From the 19th century more conventional excavations have taken place, although not on the scale of those in Pompeii. Little is known about the origins of Herculaneum, but the Roman town has the appearance of a quieter and less commercial place, probably based on fishing, and the streets are not so rutted and dirty. The preservation is arguably better, especially internal and external structures in timber.

[Sum.: M. Brion, 1960, *Pompeii and Herculaneum*. London: Elek].

here [Ge]. Anglo-Saxon noun often translated 'army' but not necessarily implying large numbers of men. Defined in the 8th century AD as a band of men greater than 35 in number, it is the normal term used in the *Anglo-Saxon Chronicle* to refer to the Danish armies of the 9th century.

Herishef [Di]. Egyptian ram-headed god from Heracleopolis, protector of foreigners. Equivalent to the Greek Arsaphes.

heritage [Th]. A widely used term that has come to stand in a very general way for everything that is inherited, including structures, objects, images, ideas, sentiments, and practices. Not all of this need be very old, although some of it is. Distinctions are sometimes made between the cultural heritage and the natural heritage. All heritage, however, is constructed in the sense that people or communities have selectively assembled, defined, and validated those things that they wish to consider components of the heritage. Scale is often important here and the appropriation of a heritage is often linked to the creation of global, national, or local identity. Once defined, in whatever way, the material that is taken as being the heritage is often commodified and exploited for educational, economic, or political gain, or simply as diverting entertainment.

herm [Co]. A square-section pillar, tapering out from ground level, typically about 2 m high, and surmounted by the sculptured head of a deity. They are found widely in the Greek world, for example in the agora, and were also popular in the gardens of private houses in Roman times.

Hermanaric [Na]. Gothic chieftain in southern Russia whose kingdom was swamped by the movement of Huns and Alans westwards in the 370s AD. Hermanaric's defeat and suicide in AD 376 began the migration of Visigoths into the empire, and his memory was revered as the last of the old rulers of the Goths.

hermeneutics [Th]. The art, skill, theory, and philosophy of interpretation and understanding, especially in relation to reading texts. Originally developed in the 19th century by the German historian W. Dilthey and others, it revolved around perceived distinctions between natural and social phenomena, and hence the natural and social sciences with their approaches to the creation of knowledge: explanation (*erklaren*) and understanding (*verstehen*), respectively. Further development by Martin Heidegger introduced the concept of pre-understanding to the way people situate themselves in the world. This was taken up by H. Gadamer to constitute the basis of a **hermeneutic circle**. This tried to encapsulate the act of understanding or interpretation by recognizing that the relationship between a person and the perceived world in which they exist is always historically located and set within a tradition that is credited with authority. More recently still, Anthony Giddens has suggested a double hermeneutic circle in the sense that the responses that an individual gets from their engagement with the world within the framework of underlying pre-knowledge itself loops back to modify that pre-knowledge for future engagements. In archaeology this has three main areas of application. The first is in terms of exploring ancient material culture, explicitly recognizing the pre-knowledge that has gone into its development and deployment. The second is in relation to the archaeological process and the way that research unfolds in a kind of spiral action in which the knowledge created by one phase of enquiry becomes the pre-knowledge for the next. The third is in relation to the way that here in the present archaeologists give means to material culture that was produced in the past.

Hermes [Di]. Egyptian god. *See* THOTH.

hermitage [MC]. A settlement housing a religious individual or group seeking solitude and isolation. It generally includes a small chapel or oratory, one or more cells, and a domestic range. Larger examples are arranged around a courtyard or cloister. A hermitage is a kind of monastery, although its inmates led a more isolated and austere life. Some hermitages would serve just a single hermit, while other were occupied by a community of hermits—what Charles Thomas has called an 'eremitic monastery'.

Hernmark Phase [CP]. South American farming cultures found in lowland Bolivia and tentatively dated to *c.*AD 500–1000. Characterized by their ceramic assemblages which belong to the Polychrome Horizon Style with broad and narrow painted bands that may have affinities with ceramics in the Amazon basin.

Herodotus [Na]. Greek historian and traveller of the 5th century BC, born *c.*490 BC, whose principal work records the struggles between the Greeks and the Persians. Accounts of the campaigns of the 6th-century Achaemenid kings Cyrus, Cambyses, and Darius are followed by a description of the Ionic revolt, and of the attempts of Xerxes to exact retribution from the Greeks. Persian successes at Artemisium and Thermopylae finally led to the crucial sea-battle at Salamis in 480 BC, in which the Greeks under Thermistocles were victorious. Herodotus travelled widely in search of historical material, and in digressions from his central theme he gives accounts—some rather garbled—of barbarian tribes far beyond the Greek world. Died *c.*425 BC.

herringbone [De]. Descriptive of a style of construction in which stonework or tiles are set in a zig-zag pattern.

Heuneburg, Baden-Württemberg, Germany [Si]. Hallstatt-period hillfort of about 3 ha overlooking the River Danube in southern Germany. Extensive excavations directed by Kurt Bittel between 1950 and 1958 and by Egon Gersbach between 1963 and 1979 have revealed that the hilltop had first been occu-

pied in the Bronze Age, but abandoned during the early Iron Age (Hallstatt C). During the 7th century BC it was re-occupied and from this period (Hallstatt D1) there are five main building phases. In the early 7th century BC the defences comprised a traditional timber-framed box rampart with a wall of timber back and front. This was replaced around 550 BC by a remarkable defensive system in a distinctively Greek style of construction. A wall was built of mud brick on a limestone foundation, punctuated by projecting bastions to allow crossfiring against anyone attacking the wall. Inside were rectangular houses of timber construction. This evidence of Greek influence is also reflected in the finds from the second phase, which include ATTIC BLACK-FIGURE WARE, wine amphorae imported from the Greek colony at Massalia, and coral. There was also extensive evidence for local manufacturing and trade. Throughout its life the Heuneburg seems to have been the seat of power for a local chiefdom, the power and wealth of which at least partly depended on the control of long-distance trade with the Mediterranean world. About 2 km east of the fort is a rich cemetery at SPECKHAU, centred on the Hohmichele.

[Sum.: W. Kimmig, 1983, *Die Heuneburg an der oberen Donau* (2nd edition). Stuttgart: K. Theiss]

heuristic [Th]. A set of activities that are designed to throw up fresh ideas, new ways of looking at things, or alternative explanations of observed phenomena, as a prelude to the formulation of new propositions and theories. Some EXPERIMENTAL ARCHAEOLOGY and a great deal of ETHNOARCHAEOLOGY is heuristic.

hiberna [De]. Latin term for the winter quarters of a military force.

hide [De]. An early medieval measure of land area, which at the Domesday Survey in AD 1086 in England can be taken to average about 120 acres (48.5 ha), but there are wide disparities between regions. How it was measured in early medieval times is more difficult: it was either a unit of productivity, of extent, or of tax liability. A hide contained 4 virgates. The term is often encountered when working with early medieval documents in relation to archaeologically derived settlement patterns.

hierarchical society [De]. *See* STRATIFIED SOCIETY.

hieroglyphics [De]. From the Greek literally meaning 'sacred signs', the term is used to describe ancient Egyptian writing and also other scripts, for example Mayan, with pictographic or ideographic symbols.

Higgs, Eric (1908–76) [Bi]. Distinguished British prehistorian, well known for his work on early farming and as the founder of the palaeoeconomic school of archaeology. Born in Shropshire, he did not take up archaeology until he was 47. Before that he took a degree in agricultural economics at London University before living for a while as a professional card player, construction worker, and hill farmer. In 1954 he entered the two-year postgraduate programme in archaeology at Cambridge and the combined influences of Charles McBurney and Grahame Clark got him hooked on archaeology. In 1956 he was appointed a research assistant in the Department of Archaeology and Anthropology at Cambridge, becoming senior assistant in 1963 and assistant director of research in 1968. He remained in post until his death. Amongst his many field programmes was his work on Palaeolithic sites in the Epirus region of Greece between 1962 and 1967. Higgs wrote and edited many books, notably *Science in archaeology* edited with Don Brothwell (1963; revised 1969, London: Thames and Hudson), and *The archaeology of early man* with John Coles (1969, London: Faber and Faber).

[Obit.: *The Times*, 28 September 1976]

high cross [MC]. A large monumental stone cross typical of the later 1st millennium AD and early 2nd millennium AD in northwest Europe. They are generally free-standing, with a shaft that is square or nearly square in cross-section, standing on a base or plinth (socle), and frequently carved with decorative panels. Two types of cross-head have been recognized: free-armed, which characterizes the earlier (pre-Viking) crosses; and the ringed or infilled cross-head which characterizes the Viking and later examples. The role of these monuments varied from place to place. Some were cenotaphs, while others were meeting places with a role in the ritual geography of religious communities.

Highland Zone [Ge]. A term popularized in archaeological circles in Britain by CYRIL FOX from the 1930s onwards to refer to the upland regions of the north and west of the British Isles that are characterized by rather different kinds of archaeology to those found in the south and east. This is partly a product of geography, but this, Fox argued, had an effect on the human populations who absorbed new ideas rather than allowed them to be imposed and where populations fused rather than experienced replacement. *See also* LOWLAND ZONE.

Hildebrand, Bror Emil (1806–84) [Bi]. Swedish antiquarian who studied in Copenhagen as a pupil of Thomsen and in 1830 introduced the THREE AGE SYSTEM into Sweden through the classification of the archaeological collections at Lund and Stockholm. Hildebrand became King's Antiquary in 1837.

[Bio.: G. O. Montelius, 1915, *Bror Emil Hildebrand Minnesteckning*. Stockholm]

Hiller borer [Eq]. *See* AUGER.

hill figure [MC]. GEOGLYPHS found mainly on the chalk downlands of southern England. Usually made by cutting away the turf and topsoil to reveal the white bedrock surface beneath, although in some cases trenches have been dug and chalk rubble rammed into place to form the outline. The most ancient example so far confirmed is the White Horse at Uffington, Oxfordshire, which was first cut in the late Bronze Age (*c*.1000 BC), but other examples, including the Cerne Giant, Dorset, and the Long Man of Wilmington, Sussex, are generally considered to be old. Comparatively recent examples include the figure of George III near Weymouth, Dorset.

hillfort [MC]. A general term used to describe a fortification on a hilltop, the best known of which are the later prehistoric examples mainly of later Bronze Age and Iron Age date, the 1st millennium BC, in Europe. Usually situated in a prominent and defensible position, hillforts were fortified with one or more lines of stone walls or earthen ramparts and ditches and elaborate defences. Their construction often relates to the kind of warfare common in the region in which they lie at the time of their occupation. Many were permanently occupied, although some were temporary refuges in times of trouble.

hilltop enclosure [MC]. A type of HILLFORT dating to the mid 1st millennium BC in southern England which is characterized by its large size, relatively insubstantial defences, and position spread across large promontories and gently sloping hills. Because they fit within the first phase of hillfort construction, and are broadly contemporary with small compact highly fortified sites, they are interpreted as temporary refuges for both people and livestock.

hillwash [Ge]. Sediment that has accumulated in valley bottoms.

Hilversum Culture [CP]. Middle Bronze Age groups living in north Belgium and southern Holland. Characterized by the use of cremation burial under round barrows set in round barrow cemeteries. In such burials the urns used to contain the ashes of the deceased were also quite distinctive and are known as **Hilversum urns**. Because similar urns and burial traditions were also found within the DEVEREL–RIMBURY CULTURE of southern England, some authorities have suggested the movement of populations from Britain to the Low Countries.

hinge fracture [De]. A kind of fracture that occurs around the distal end of a flint flake during flint knapping when the core is mis-struck or there are flaws in the flint. Characteristically a hinge-fractured flake has a rounded distal end with small burrs at the tip of the ventral surface.

hippo sandals [Ar]. Iron shoes worn by draft animals during Roman times for temporary protection of their hooves or to aid grip in wet conditions.

hippodrome [MC]. A course for horse and chariot racing, similar in form to the STADIUM, but larger. The hippodrome was the model for the Roman CIRCUS which also involved chariot racing.

historic [Ge]. Referring to the period after the advent of written historical records in a given geographical region. Historic Native American sites date to the time after the arrival of Europeans.

historical archaeology [Ge]. A branch of archaeology based on the text-aided study of archaeological questions. It involves combining archaeological and historical methods, sources, and perspectives, and naturally focuses on relatively recent periods. It is sometimes called historic sites archaeology.

historical materialism [Th]. Marx's interpretation of social change through history which is determined primarily by economic forces.

Historic Buildings and Monuments Commission for England (HBMCE) [Ge]. *See* ENGLISH HERITAGE.

historic environment [De]. All the physical evidence for past human activity, and its associations, that people can see, feel, find, and understand in the present world. It is the habitat that the human race has created through conflict and cooperation and the consequences of human interaction with nature.

historicism [Th]. A general and increasingly ambiguous term meaning a number of different things to different people. At its heart, however, is the idea that a society and its culture exist mainly in their dynamic and developmental character. In this it gives emphasis to non-rational behaviour, all-round creativity, and doubts many of the beliefs inherent to a progressive view of change.

historicity [Th]. The use of an understanding of history as a basis for trying to change it.

Historic Preservation Act [Le]. The legislation in the USA enacted in 1966 to establish the National Register of Historic Places and the National Trust for Historic Preservation.

Historic Scotland [Or]. The government agency responsible for archaeology and the conservation of the historic environment in Scotland. Its duties and responsibilities are very similar to those of ENGLISH HERITAGE.

Historic Sites Act [Le]. The principal legislation in the USA enacted in 1935 declaring a national policy to identify and protect important archaeological and historical sites on federal land.

history [Th]. Traditionally, the study of the past using mainly documentary sources created by or about the society under scrutiny. Inevitably such investigations concentrated on societies where writing had been adopted. *See also* PREHISTORY, PROTO-HISTORIC.

Hittites [CP]. A group of tribes whose origins are uncertain but who emerged as a unified state in the early 2nd millennium BC and expanded to control Anatolia, Syria, and surrounding areas. Their history has three main phases, representing cycles of integration, expansion, and collapse. The Old Kingdom (c.1750–1450 BC) had its capital at Kussara (Hattusas) and later at Boghaz Köy. Mursilis I expanded control by overrunning north Syria in about 1600 BC and pushing as far as Babylon. Under the Empire (c.1450–1200 BC) a stable state was built up covering most of Anatolia and north Syria, displacing the kingdom of the Mitanni, and successfully challenging both Assyria and Egypt. The end of the Empire came suddenly in about 1200 BC when it was overwhelmed by invaders, the identity of whom is uncertain but who were probably part of the general movements of people in the period of unrest in the Mediterranean at the time. During the third phase (c.1200–720 BC) areas such as north Syria continued as neo-Hittite city-states, but in the early 1st millennium BC the Hittite empire came under ASSYRIAN rule after the defeat of the Hittite army by Sargon II c.720 BC. The Hittite language is one of the earliest recorded Indo-European languages; the Hittites also developed a means of smelting iron, a secret they guarded fairly well until their downfall.

hlǣw [MC]. Anglo-Saxon term for a round barrow. Leslie Grinsell argues that the term was used almost exclusively to refer to barrows created and used by the pagan Saxons.

hoard [Ar]. The term applied to a deliberate deposit of complete and/or broken objects buried in the ground at one time for subsequent recovery or as a symbolic act. Hoards of metal objects are especially common during the European Bronze Age, and several different types have been recognized: for example, merchant's hoards, founder's hoards, personal hoards, weapon hoards, and votive hoards.

Hoare, Sir Richard Colt (1758–1838) [Bi]. British antiquary and traveller who engaged William Cunnington to carry out a number of excavations in the county of Wiltshire. He was born to abundant wealth in a family of bankers, being educated at private schools before joining the family business. He lived at Stourhead, a large estate with land in Wiltshire, Dorset, and Somerset, which he took over at the age of 25. After some years of foreign travel he took more interest in the local area and this brought him face to face with the rich antiquities of Salisbury Plain. These he started to research, eventually opening no fewer than 468 barrows in the process, and between 1812 and 1821 he privately published two substantial volumes entitled *The ancient history of Wiltshire* (reprinted 1975, Wakefield: EP Publishing). The opening line of the first volume, 'We speak from facts, not theory' echoes much of the INDUCTIVIST thinking of early 19th-century antiquarianism.

[Bio.: K. Woodbridge, 1970, *Landscape and antiquity*. Oxford: Clarendon Press]

Hofheim-type flagon [Ar]. A single or double-handled flagon with a cylindrical neck and outcurved rim, triangular in section; named after types from the mid 1st century AD military site at Hofheim, Germany.

hog-backed grave cover [Ar]. The distinctive stones used to cover graves during the 10th century AD in northern England and southern Scotland. They are characterized by rectangular blocks of stone with a flat bottom and pitched top. The upper surfaces are usually decorated with interlaced designs. They may have been made in imitation of houses or buildings.

Hogg, Alexander Hubert Arthur (1908–89) [Bi]. British archaeologist, known to his friends as Bob, well known for his fieldwork and studies of hillforts in the west of Britain. Born in London and educated at Highgate School he went up to Sidney Sussex College, Cambridge, in 1927 where he took a first in civil engineering with part 1 of the maths tripos. His first job was with MacAlpine's as an assistant engineer, but he was sacked soon afterwards. He subsequently worked on the construction of the dry dock at Southampton and the St Albans by-pass before moving to the Road Research Laboratory at Oxford. In 1936 he was appointed lecturer in civil engineering at King's College in the University of Newcastle-upon-Tyne. After service in the Royal Naval Dockyard in Rosyth during WW2 he returned to Cambridge in 1945 and in 1947 took up a lectureship there. Throughout his career since leaving Cambridge he pursued an interest in archaeology, at first studying barrows and burial sites and later hillforts. His interest grew, and in 1949 he applied for and got the post of secretary to the Royal Commission on Ancient and Historical Monuments in Wales and Monmouthshire. Here he stayed for the rest of his working life, establishing high standards of survey and recording.

[Bio.: S. Briggs, 1981, A. H. A. Hogg—an appreciation. In G. Guilbert (ed.), *Hillfort studies—essays for A. H. A. Hogg.* Leicester: Leicester University Press, 15–18]

Hogup Cave, Utah, USA [Si]. Archaic Stage hunter-gatherer site 120 km northwest of Salt Lake City in the Great Basin of North America. Deposits within the cave accumulated over thousands of years to reach a thickness of 4.2 m. Best represented is material from 9000 BC to AD 500, the Bonneville, Wendover, and Black Rock phases of the Desert Archaic. Excavations by C. M. Alkens during the 1960s revealed that the hunter-gatherers using Hogup Cave relied heavily on plant foods, especially pickleweed. They also hunted deer, pronghorn antelope, wild sheep, and bison. The cave deposits yielded the remains of a total of 32 species of animals and 34 species of birds. Spear-throwers, together with stone-tipped and wooden spears, were used in hunting, as well as snaring and netting.

[Rep.: C. M. Alkens, 1970, *Hogup Cave.* Salt Lake City: University of Utah]

Hohokam Culture [CP]. Late Archaic Stage agricultural communities occupying the drainage basins of the Salt and Gila Rivers in the Arizona desert of North America during the period *c.*300 BC to AD 1400. Characterized by small villages of rectangular pit-houses, cremation of the dead, and plain grey or brown pottery, sometimes painted red on buff. Influences from Mesoamerica can be seen throughout the life of these cultures, but especially after about AD 500 when maize cultivation makes an appearance and elaborate patterns of canals are constructed for irrigation. At the same time, platform mounds and ball courts begin to be built, and material culture expands to include copper bells, mosaic mirrors, and a range of imported luxury goods. The end of the Hohokam Culture seems to arise from the absorption of these communities into broader cultural groupings.

hollow-scraper [Ar]. Blade or flake tool with a notch worked into the side or the end showing signs of being worked.

hollow way [MC]. A road or track running in a natural or man-made hollow deepened through wear caused by prolonged usage or the raising of the ground on each side.

Holmes, William Henry (1846–1933) [Bi]. American geologist and antiquarian who began his professional career as a geological illustrator. In the late 1880s and early 1890s he carried out a survey of the Palaeolithic material in North America and concluded (wrongly, as it later transpired) that the supposed Palaeolithic material was the refuse of Indian toolmakers. His draughtsmanship and systematic survey methods allowed him to produce detailed classifications of aboriginal pottery in the eastern USA (published in 1903) and studies of ancient ruins in Mexico. He later became head of the Bureau of American Ethnology.

[Bio.: D. J. Meltzer and R. C. Dunnell (eds.), 1992, *The archaeology of William Henry Holmes.* Washington, DC: Smithsonian Institution]

Holocene [Ge]. The later of two chrono-stratigraphic units or epochs forming the QUATERNARY PERIOD (the earlier one is the PLEISTOCENE) dating from 10 000 years ago down to the present day. The series of deposits represented are simply the latest major INTER-GLACIAL stage following the DEVENSIAN stage at the end of the Pleistocene, known in Britain as the FLANDRIAN although in other areas (rather confusingly) as the Holocene.

Holstein [Ge]. An group of QUATERNARY interglacial deposits in northwestern Europe; they are stratified above the Elster and precede the SAALE. They date to the period after 300 000 years ago and are no more recent than 20 000 years ago.

Holt ware [Ar]. Pottery made at the legionary works depot at Holt, Denbighshire, in the late 1st and early 2nd centuries AD. Of light-red and buff fabric, often imitating Samian forms, and found mostly in Chester and adjacent areas.

Homer [Na]. Greek poet, believed to have been blind, writing in the mid 1st millennium BC, who is credited with two important works with direct archaeological relevance because of their subject matter: *The Iliad* relates the events of 51 days in the last year of the siege of Troy by the Greeks; and *The Odyssey* describes the wanderings of Ulysses on his way back from the Trojan War and the vengeance he exacted on the suitors of his wife Penelope. The first printed editions of Homer's works appeared in AD 1488.

Homeric hymns [Ge]. Songs in praise of gods, such as *The hymn to Apollo*. Not composed by Homer, or even belonging to his time, but carefully written in the Homeric epic style by later poets, perhaps in the 5th or 4th centuries BC.

hominid [Sp]. General term for the family of mammals represented by the single genus *Homo*, and today by one species: *Homo sapiens*. The term is a contraction of HOMINOIDEA, and is used to describe all the species within the family of man and its evolutionary predecessors. Hominids probably reached their greatest diversity around 2 million years ago when there were probably five contemporary species of Australopithecines and *Homo*.

Hominoidea [Sp]. The superfamily including hominids and pongids.

Homo [Sp]. The genus to which humans belong. *See* HOMO HABILIS, HOMO ERECTUS, HOMO SAPIENS, HOMO NEANDERTHALENSIS.

Homo erectus [Sp]. An early and long-lived human species (the name means 'upright man') that appeared about 1.8 million years ago and survived until at least 250 000 years ago. It is the first human species found outside Africa and appears to have colonized Asia, Indonesia, and Europe around 1 million years ago. The ancestry of *Homo erectus* is uncertain. The species may have derived directly from the Australopithecines, but differed from them in a number of ways: *homo erectus* was heavier and taller, had a more linear body form, better bipedal movement, less sexual dimorphism, and a larger brain. *Homo erectus* was also the first hominid to have a projecting nose. Alternatively, *Homo habilis* may stand on the evolutionary line between the gracile Australopithecines and *Homo erectus*. The stone and flint industries associated with *Homo erectus* are almost exclusively ACHEULIAN.

It is possible that following the dispersion of the species around the globe there were significant regional developments within the species, leading, for example, to recognizably related species such as *HOMO NEANDERTHALENSIS*.

Homo habilis [Sp]. An early human species (the name means 'handy man') that lived in Africa between 2 million and 1.5 million years ago. The species was identified from fossils found at Olduvai Gorge in 1964 by Louis Leakey, John Napier, and Philip Tobias. It has since also been identified at Koobi Fora. It is probably *Homo habilis* that is responsible for the Oldowan industries and that the species developed directly from the gracile Australopithecines (*Australopithecus afarensis* and *Australopithecus africanus*). *Homo habilis* appears to have been contemporary with the more robust Australopithecines (*A. robustus/paranthropus*), and perhaps also early *Homo erectus*.

homology [Th]. A special form of analogy in which two temporally separate things or social phenomena are similar to each other because of historical and/or genetic connections.

Homo neanderthalensis [Sp]. An early species of *Homo* that is believed to have developed from *Homo erectus* in Eurasia around 200 000 years ago and continued until around 30 000 years ago. *See* NEANDERTHAL MAN.

Homo sapiens [Sp]. Modern humans. Although it is generally believed that this species emerged about 40 000 years ago, claims of exceptionally early finds dating back to between 130 000 and 70 000 years ago have been made for fossils found in Africa and the Levant. The toolmaking traditions of the Upper Palaeolithic outside Africa are associated with modern humans, and these date back to about 40 000 years ago too. The main controversy surrounding the origin of *Homo sapiens* is whether they are all descendants of early examples in Africa or whether there was local multi-regional development from *Homo erectus*. In the **multiregional hypothesis**, advocated by Milford Wolpoff, Alan Thorne, and others, it is believed that major population groups established in Africa, Europe, Asia, and Indonesia all developed in parallel, with some gene flows between regions, and with no one region developing modern humans any earlier than any of the others. The **out of Africa model**, also known as the African replacement hypothesis, is championed by Chris Stringer, Rebecca Cann, Alan Wilson, and others and suggests that regional groups of *Homo erectus* developed independent evolutionary trajectories, leading, for example, to the appearance of *Homo neanderthalensis*, but that these were overtaken and eventually replaced modern humans, who had evolved from *Homo erectus* in Africa and spread rapidly to other areas.

honey jar [Ar]. A double-handled, often bulbous jar with a wide mouth. There is no firm evidence that such jars held honey.

Honorius, Flavius [Na]. Emperor of the western Roman empire from AD 395 and widely recognized as one of the least effective holders of that title. During his reign Britain, Spain, and parts of Gaul were lost to the empire and Rome itself was captured by Alaric. Honorius was the son of Theodosius the Great.

hood-moulding [Co]. A projecting moulding on the face of a wall above an arch, usually following the form of the arch.

Hopewell, Ohio, USA [Si]. A farm formerly belonging to Captain M. C. Hopewell near the town of Chillicothe, Ohio, containing an extensive mound complex which gives its name to the middle Woodland Stage Hopewellian Culture. Excavated in the 1890s by W. K. Moorehead, the site was found to comprise a rectangular enclosure covering 45 ha, within which were 38 mounds.

In the central mound was the burial of a tall young man and a young woman. She was buried with thousands of pearl beads, and copper buttons. She wore copper bracelets. Both individuals wore copper ear spools, copper breastplates, and necklaces of grizzly bear teeth. Rather strange was the presence of artificial copper noses. A cremated male buried in Mound 11 may have been a master obsidian worker. A male in Mound 17 was buried with 3000 sheets of mica and 90 kg of galena.

[Rep.: W. K. Moorehead, 1922, *The Hopewell mound group of Ohio*. Chicago: Field Museum of History]

Hopewellian Culture [CP]. Middle Woodland Stage communities occupying the Ohio Valley and much of the eastern woodlands and midwest of North America in the period *c.*200 BC

to AD 400. Named after the owner of a farm in Ross County, Ohio, Hopewellian Culture developed out of the Adena Complex of the eastern woodlands to become one of the most remarkable cultural traditions in North America.

Characteristic Hopewellian material culture includes pottery with deeply incised or rocker-stamped decoration, broad-bladed chipped stone points, and small stone platform-pipes for smoking tobacco. These pipes were often carved in zoomorphic forms.

Settlements were semi-permanent or permanent hamlets and villages, often in river valleys and at intervals of about 20 km. Houses were rectangular or oval in plan, built with wood forming a frame, over which mats and animal skins would be stretched. The subsistence base mainly depended on hunting and gathering. Small mammals, turkeys, fish, and shellfish were important foods, as too were hickory nuts. Some maize may have been cultivated, but was probably not a major component of diet.

The Hopewellian is best known for its ceremonial centres, of which the largest were those built in the Ohio Valley. Each centre typically comprises one or more earthwork enclosures containing burial mounds. Both cremation and inhumation burials are known, although inhumation appears to have been reserved for the elite. The burial rites involved placing the dead person in a charnel house made of wooden posts, burning it, and then constructing a mound over the top. The elite were often buried in log-lined tombs within the charnel houses, accompanied by a selection of rich grave goods.

Extensive trading links known as the HOPEWELL INTERACTION SPHERE are reflected in the range of imported goods and raw materials. The Hopewellian Culture had many local styles and regional variations (e.g. Havana Hopewellian, Illinois Hopewellian, Marksville Hopewellian), the differences sometimes being greater than the similarities. Throughout, however, artistic expression and craftsmanship were of a high level and many fine artefacts were created or acquired by Hopewellian communities.

Hopewell   Interaction   Sphere [Ge]. Hopewellian communities living in and around the Ohio and Mississippi valleys acquired a very wide range of exotic goods and raw materials from all over North America.

Native copper from around the Great Lakes to the north, silver from near Cobalt, Ontario, obsidian from the Yellowstone area of Wyoming, meteoric iron from a number of different meteor falls, marine shells, shark and alligator teeth from Florida, grizzly bear teeth from the Rocky Mountains, and mica, quartz crystal, and chlorite from the Appalachians. How these items and materials were acquired is not exactly known. Expeditions to remote sources may have been responsible in some cases, but the majority probably arrived through 'down-the-line' exchange between villages, the trade being controlled by some kind of elite or local 'big men'.

hoplite [Ge]. In Greek military orders, an infantry soldier whose armour included helmet, breastplate, shield, and greaves, with sword and spear as standard equipment.

horizon [Ge]. In American archaeology this term refers to patterns of locally distinct phases or cultures that are linked together into bigger groups through recurrent cultural patterns and/or distinctive artefacts. Stone tools or pottery types provide typical features defining widespread horizons. The term was introduced by G. Willey and P. Phillips in 1955.

horizon control [De]. American term referring to the process of locating and recording artefacts, ecofacts, and features in two-dimensional, horizontal space.

horizon style [Ge]. The concept behind this term was introduced to Andean archaeology by Max Uhle in 1913 and later formalized by A. L. Kroeber in 1944. In essence, an horizon style is a widespread but chronologically restricted cultural continuum represented by the wide distribution of a recognizable art style. Such horizon styles may cross-cut local sequences and provide the means of relating sequences between regions.

horizontal loom [Ar]. A structure on which woven cloth is manufactured, comprising a frame set horizontally across vertical supports. The warp threads were tied across the frame from front to back so that they could be wound out as weaving proceeded. The warp was usually arranged so that alternate threads could be raised and lowered, thus allowing the weaver to pass a shuttle containing the weft thread from side to side across the warp. The horizontal loom was developed later than the UPRIGHT LOOM and provided the basis for the development of mechanical looms during later medieval and post-medieval times.

horns of consecration [Ar]. A religious or ceremonial symbol found extensively in Minoan contexts, probably based on the horns of bulls. The term was coined by Sir Arthur Evans while working at Knossos. Horns of consecration are often represented as a stone slab, the upper part of which has been shaped into two points.

hornwork [Co]. An outwork of an earthwork enclosure, such as a hillfort, often consisting of a single bank thrown out to protect an entrance.

Hor-Pa-Khred [Di]. Egyptian god, Horus the younger or child, son of Isis and Osiris. Shown as a small boy with the side-lock of youth, holding one finger to his mouth. Equivalent to the Greek Harpocrates.

horreum [MC]. Latin term for a granary. Archaeologically such buildings are recognized by the raised floors which are usually supported on a series of closely spaced parallel walls.

Horsa [Na]. Jutish mercenary who, along with his brother Hengist, was apparently invited to settle in southeastern England by Vortigern. Horsa was killed in battle in *c*.AD 455.

horse [Sp]. A solid-hoofed plant-eating quadruped (*Equus caballus*) found wild in many parts of the world during late PLEISTOCENE and post-Pleistocene times. It is well represented in rock art of the Upper Palaeolithic in Europe. It is far from clear when the horse was first domesticated, but the first evidence of possible manipulation is in the TRIPOLYE CULTURE of the steppes in southern Russia and the Ukraine dating to the 4th millennium BC. The earliest horse harness fittings are antler cheek-pieces, also of the 4th millennium BC, and date from the Sredny-Stog Culture of the Ukraine. The use of horses for riding and as a draught animal to pull chariots and carts spread quickly through the Middle East, and can be recognized in northern Europe from about 2500 BC.

Horsham Culture [CP]. A late Mesolithic culture found in southern England and named after a small town in Sussex. Rather distinctive of the culture are the hollow-based points, sometimes referred to as Horsham points. The term is not widely used.

Hor-Sma-Tawy [Di]. Egyptian god, Horus-Uniter-of-the-Two-Lands, son of Hathor and Horus. Equivalent to the Greek Harsomtus.

Horus [Di]. Egyptian falcon god of Edfu, where he is called Horus the Behdetite. He is usually depicted as a hawk-headed man. The royal god par excellence, since the ruler of the day was considered to be Horus incarnate. Became identified with Hor-Pa-Khred, son of Isis and Osiris.

Hoskins, William George (1908–92) [Bi]. Renowned British local historian who did much to integrate archaeology with local studies and the understanding of the landscape. Born and brought up in Exeter, he was educated at Hele's School and the University College of the South West (now Exeter University). Youthful explorations of Devon and especially the Exe Valley started his interest in landscapes which he took with him to Bradford Technical College where he taught for a short time and where he saw the contrasting landscape of Yorkshire. In 1931 he was appointed assistant lecturer in commerce at University College, Leicester (now Leicester University). During WW2 he worked at the Board of Trade, and immediately after the war Leicester established a full department of local history with Hoskins as its head. In 1951 he moved to Oxford as a reader in economic history. He greatly disliked being at Oxford, although it was while there that he published his best-known book *The making of the English landscape* (1955, London: Hodder and Stoughton) at the head of a series he edited dealing with the landscape history of English counties. In 1965 he returned to Leicester University as Hatton Professor of English History, retiring in 1968. In his later years he developed a keep interest in popularizing his particular brand of landscape history, and between 1976 and 1978 made a number of programmes for television which made him a household name.

[Obit.: *The Times*, 15 January 1992]

Hotchkiss Phase [CP]. Archaic Stage, coastally adapted communities of the San Francisco Bay area of the American west coast between AD 600 and recent times. These groups lived in small villages, exploiting the coastal marshlands for fish and shellfish, while also using a wide range of edible plants, especially acorns. Small side-notched points were probably arrow tips; barbed bone spears were used in fishing. Burials were usually by cremation, any grave goods, mainly ornaments and beads, being burnt too. Hotchkiss communities are regarded as ancestral to the Wintum, Miwok, and Yokuts who occupied central California at the time of European contact.

hour-glass perforation [De]. A term used to describe the kind of hole made through a piece of stone or similarly hard material where drilling has started on two opposite faces and continued from both sides until they meet in the middle.

household unit (household cluster) [De]. An arbitrary archaeological unit defining artefact patterns reflecting the activities that take place in and around a house, usually assumed to be the products of one household.

house platform [Co]. A flat area created on sloping ground to form the foundation on which a structure of some kind, often a dwelling, is built. Such platforms are usually made by a combination of cutting back into the slope at the back and making a terrace in the front.

Hoxnian Stage [CP]. A group of deposits representing a geo-stratigraphic stage within the PLEISTOCENE series of the British QUATERNARY system, named after the site of Hoxne, Suffolk, and dating to the period 300 000 to 200 000 years ago. The Hoxnian is usually interpreted as an interglacial warm period, some Hoxnian deposits being stratified above ANGLIAN glacial deposits and below WOLSTONIAN glacial deposits. However, there is some evidence that the Hoxnian material may represent more than one interglacial. CLACTONIAN and ACHEULIAN flintwork is found in Hoxnian gravels, and at Swanscombe, Kent, part of the skull of a *Homo erectus* has been found.

huaca [Ar]. A general term from South America used to refer to places that the Inca believed to be sacred and to have magical powers. Derived from the Quechua word for shrine, huaca can take almost any form from a natural rock or cave down to a portable amulet.

Huánaco Pampa, Peru [Si]. A large Inca city covering two square kilometres in the north central highlands of Peru. Probably a provincial capital, the city was set out in sectors around a central plaza some 550 m by 350 m.

Functionally specialized sectors include high-status residence areas, food preparation zones, a military garrison, and a compound with restricted access which might have been occupied by 'chosen women'. Hundreds of storage buildings were constructed on the hillside above the site.

Excavations by Craig Morris suggest that the site was occupied mainly by people brought in to give their labour to the empire. In rooms adjacent to the plaza, excavations revealed much pottery from storage vessels as well as food preparation and serving vessels. The plaza was possibly used for large-scale communal feasting organized by the chiefs and suggesting that the Inca state derived its authority through the liberal ceremonial redistribution of food, drink, and goods.

[Sum.: C. Morris and D. E. Thompson, 1985, *Huánaco Pampa: An Andean city and its hinterland*. London: Thames & Hudson]

hulled barley [Sp]. *See* BARLEY.

humanism [De]. A philosophy or ethical system that centres on the concept of the dignity, freedom, and value of human beings. The belief that there is an essential human condition that emerges regardless of historical circumstance and that this can be used as the basis for developing an understanding of the past.

Humbolt Series points [Ar]. Bifacially worked chipped stone points of lanceolate outline manufactured by Archaic Stage communities on the Great Plains and western interior of North America in the period *c*.3000 BC to AD 700. There are numerous variations in style and in size, but most have a hollow base and none have side notches.

hundred [Ge]. An administrative division of a SHIRE and the forerunner of the modern district in England. Particularly important in

Saxon times but gradually declined as other forms of administration developed. A court was held monthly within the hundred at a fixed open-air location. It was presided over by the hundred reeve, representing the king, and consisted of freeholders who considered minor criminal and civil cases. It could also levy taxes. Manorial and shire courts gradually took over the functions of the hundred court, but as a unit of administration it formally survived until the Local Government Act of 1894. In origin, a hundred was either a hundred hides or a hundred families.

hunebed [MC]. The Dutch name for the Neolithic PASSAGE GRAVES found in the northern part of the Netherlands. These tombs are associated with TRICHTERBECKER C material.

Huns [CP]. Nomadic people from Asia forming one of the barbarian tribes which destroyed the Gothic kingdoms of southern Russia in the last quarter of the 4th century AD. United briefly in the 440s AD and early 450s by Attila, the Huns invaded Gaul and Italy but were driven back to their homelands in Hungary and soon afterwards split up into small tribal units, amalgamating with other nomadic peoples.

Hunsrück-Eifel Culture [CP]. Early Iron Age culture of the middle Rhineland named after two regions flanking the Moselle. The culture is known mainly through its burials which in the early La Tène period included a number of outstanding princely burials. Characteristic pottery of the culture includes the pear-shaped pedestal vases, the appearance of which coincides with that of the potter's wheel.

Huntcliff ware [Ar]. A distinctive variety of calcite-gritted pottery limited to a range of distinctive forms, made in east Yorkshire from the 1st century AD through to the 4th century AD. The fabric is black or dark brown, and the dishes and jar bodies were hand-made. During the late 4th century an extremely common form was a thick-walled cooking pot with a heavy curved rim, often with a groove on the inside of the lip.

hunt cup [Ar]. A popular style of Roman colour-coated beaker with a decorative scene, usually depicting dogs hunting stags or hares, executed in BARBOTINE.

hunter-gatherers [Ge]. A general term used to refer to societies whose mode of subsistence is gained from hunting animals, fishing, and gathering edible plants. Most commonly associated with the Palaeolithic and Mesolithic periods and a simple BAND level of social organization, it is a way of life that should not be pigeonholed as a stage in social development and must certainly not be seen as in any sense 'primitive'. As American anthropologist Marshal Sahlins pointed out, many hunter-gatherer societies represent the original affluent society because only a small proportion of their time was spent obtaining food and the basic needs of life. At one time all of the inhabited world was occupied by hunter-gatherer groups, something which no subsequent economic mode has achieved. In that sense agricultural and industrial societies have, at various times, established themselves on the edge of the hunter-gatherers' world.

Hupa-Iya Phase [CP]. South American farming cultures found in the Rio Ucayali area of Amazonia and tentatively dated to c.200–1 BC. Characterized by their ceramic assemblages which belong to the Incised Rim Horizon Style of the Amazon basin. At the site of Yarinachocha, Peru, incised rim and plastic ornament decoration are found together in the Hupa-Iya Phase, in association with the first tangible evidence for bitter manioc processing. Spindle-whorls also appear in the archaeological record at this time.

Hurrians [CP]. Communities from the mountainous regions of the Caucasus who settled in northern Mesopotamia in the 3rd millennium BC to form a series of small kingdoms. Their language was non-Semitic and non-Sumerian and in origin may have been related to the Jura-Araxes Culture. By the 2nd millennium BC they had been absorbed into the local Mesopotamian cultures.

hut circle [MC]. A circular or oval depression in the ground with traces of a low wall around it representing the stone foundation of a round house whose superstructure was of timber and thatch. Found in large numbers in upland regions of the British Isles, most date to the 2nd millennium BC.

Hutton, James (1726–97) [Bi]. British traveller and pioneer geologist. He argued the UNIFORMITARIAN view of geological processes, notably in his *Theory of Earth*, published in 1785.

[Bio.: J. Playfair, 1997, *James Hutton and Joseph Black: Biographies*. Edinburgh: RSE Scotland Foundation]

hüyük [MC]. The Turkish term for a TELL.

hydria [Ar]. Greek three-handled pitcher for containing water. Typically these vessels have a low pedestal base, cylindrical neck, and the handles are mounted horizontally on the shoulder and vertically between shoulder and rim.

Hyksos [CP]. The name given by the Egyptians to warrior groups who infiltrated Egypt at the end of the Middle Kingdom to dominate the Nile Valley in the second intermediate period between 1640 and 1570 BC and to form the 15th Dynasty. Their capital was at Avaris in the Nile Delta. Their expulsion in c.1567 BC under Amosis, the founder of the 18th Dynasty, heralded the start of the New Kingdom in Egypt. The Hyksos are not easily recognized in the archaeological record, although in Palestine they seem to have built defensive ramparts faced with smooth hard plaster. They seem to have been ruled by a military aristocracy and were responsible for the introduction of the horse and chariot to Egypt, and perhaps also the upright loom, the olive and the pomegranate.

hypocaust system [MC]. Roman central heating system, incorporating either a low basement chamber over which a fireproof floor was supported on small pillars, or a system of underfloor channels. Both systems provided for the circulation of warm air from an external furnace, with the air finally escaping through flues of BOX TILE embedded in the walls.

hypogeum [MC]. A kind of rock-cut chambered tomb with a series of interlinking cells or rooms, mainly used for inhumation burial.

hypothesis [Ge]. A statement of plausible connections between specific defined elements or variables, put forward as a basis for empirical testing. In archaeology this usually means putting forward a set of ideas or predictions about how the archaeological record should look if a particular model or explanation holds true.

hypothetico-deductive reasoning [Th]. A critical element of the NEW ARCHAEOLOGY of the late 1960s and 1970s which allowed the translation of the SCIENTIFIC METHOD into archaeological work. Under its rubric, a HYPOTHESIS is set up, predictions are deduced from the hypothesis, and these are then tested against empirically derived data.

Iberians [CP]. A series of cultural groupings that occupied the coastal regions of eastern and southeastern Spain during the 1st millennium BC. Their origins are unclear, although may involve some movements from North Africa. Their language was non-Indo-European and while their script is based on Greek characters there are additional syllabic signs. Some regional groups can be seen within the Iberian Culture, but there are widely shared elements of material culture, especially in jewellery and statues. The Iberians disappear in the early 1st millennium AD following the Romanization of Spain, partly through fusion with the peoples of the interior and partly no doubt through the displacement of their distinctive language by Latin.

ICAHM [Ab]. *See* INTERNATIONAL COMMITTEE ON ARCHAEOLOGICAL HERITAGE MANAGEMENT.

Ice Age [Ge]. *See* PLEISTOCENE.

ice-free corridor [Ge]. A narrow strip of land along the east side of the Rocky Mountains in North America which escaped glaciation during the later Pleistocene and allowed human and animal populations from the north access to the continental interior.

ice house [MC]. Building used for the storage of ice needed to keep food fresh before the advent of modern refrigeration. Particularly common during the 18th and 19th centuries AD. Usually consists of the small chamber either partly or wholly underground.

Icehouse Bottom, Tennessee, USA [Si]. Archaic Stage settlement dating to about *c*.7500 BC on a river terrace in the Little Tennessee Valley. Excavated by Jefferson Chapman in the early 1970s; interpreted as the base camp for hunter-gatherer bands who

exploited the surrounding territory. The situation of Icehouse Bottom was ideal for a base camp because of abundant supplies of animal and plant foods, and the presence of fine chert for toolmaking.

Evidence suggested that several bands used the camp at once, each family group living in a small skin, bark, or matting hut. Twenty-nine hearths were found as the only remaining evidence of these structures. White-tailed deer, black bear, elk, fox, opossum, raccoon, squirrel, rabbit, turkey, and pigeon were hunted for food. They also fished, and gathered hickory nuts and acorns.

[Rep.: J. Chapman, 1973, *The Icehouse Bottom site 40MR23*. Knoxville: Department of Anthropology, University of Tennessee]

Iceni [CP]. Late Iron Age tribe living in East Anglia and the borders of the Fens in the east of England. During the 1st century BC they minted their own coins and traded widely with their neighbours the TRINOVANTES and CATUVELLAUNI to the south. Little is known about their settlements, and their capital has not been identified. The ruling elite was, however, wealthy, and displayed it in the form of gold and electrum torcs and arm-rings. Horse harness and chariot fittings are also of high quality. At the time of the Roman conquest they were in alliance with the Romans, but shortly afterwards they revolted under their energetic and successful war leader Queen BOUDICCA.

ICOMOS [Ab]. *See* INTERNATIONAL COUNCIL ON MONUMENTS AND SITES.

icon [Ar]. A kind of portrait of a sacred person with a formal pose and exaggerated spiritual expression which spread through the Christian world from the mid 6th century AD onwards. Usually icons are painted on wood and housed in jewelled and highly ornate mounts. Some became so powerful as objects of devotion as to cause a rift in the Christian church, known as the iconoclastic dispute, where icons were banned in the Byzantine empire from AD 726, although the Latin church continued to allow their use. They remain a central component of the material culture of the Orthodox church.

iconography [De]. A system of illustrations, usually of a symbolic and metaphorical nature, concerning a particular subject.

iconostatis [Co]. The tall continuous screen in an Orthodox church which cuts off the sanctuary with the altar from the nave, and usually from the sight of the people, until the central door is opened at the crisis of the Eucharist: icons of Our Lord, the Holy Mother, the patron saint of the church, and of others are set up on the iconostasis, as its name states, and are used as an avenue of worship.

Ida [Na]. English warlord of the mid 5th century AD, who settled on the coast of Northumberland, c.AD 547, built a fortress on the rock of Bamburgh, and founded the royal House of Bernicia, the northern region of Northumbria, which grew rapidly in power after his death (c.AD 559).

ideal type [Th]. A 'pure type', constructed by emphasizing certain traits of a given social entity which do not necessarily exist anywhere in reality.

idealism [Th]. The theoretical position that phenomena and events exist only in so far as they are perceived as ideas. The idealist believes that thoughts are prior to actions, and that the mental or cognitive world is more important than the material world. In COLLINGWOOD'S notion of historical idealism the key to interpretation of the past was empathetically to rethink the thoughts of past peoples.

identity [Th]. 1. The use of material culture to aid understanding of the definition and status of individuals and groups in the past. Such studies include the recognition of gender, rank, status, or place within society at the individual level, but may also look more widely at the relationships between contemporary cultures and the extent to which material culture is used to signal differences between social groups. 2. The way in which archaeolog-

ical remains are widely used in order to promote and support particular views of contemporary personal, local, regional, and national identity, especially through the application of ARCHAEOLOGICAL RESOURCE MANAGEMENT, the deployment of public funds, and state legislation. In this sense archaeology is an extremely powerful political tool, and has been for many generations.

ideology [Ge]. The belief system, true or untrue, shared by members of a society or a subgroup within a society. Adherence to the belief system is an obligation of membership of the society or subculture. There are many ways in which ideologies can be identified. They may refer to a set of ideas held by a group of people, to ideas about social reality which are false (false consciousness), or to ideas, knowledges, or practices which result in the reproduction of social relationships characterized by inequality or contradiction. Following Marx, ideology serves to legitimate or mask the real state of social relations. It is thus a key concept in exploring patterning in the archaeological record on a number of different scales, and has become a major theme in the field of SOCIAL ARCHAEOLOGY.

idiographic [De]. 1. Term used to describe a form of writing in which the signs or characters represent ideas. Ideographic writing may use either crude pictures copied from nature (pictograph) or symbols derived from pictures which express objects or ideas. 2. Particularistic; unique; specific as opposed to general.

Ierne See AVIENUS.

IFA [Ab]. See INSTITUTE OF FIELD ARCHAEOLOGISTS.

Ihy [Di]. Egyptian god of music, shown as a boy with the side-lock of youth and carrying a sistrum. Son of Horus and Hathor.

Illinois Hopewellian [CP]. See HOPEWELLIAN CULTURE.

illuvial horizon [De]. Part of a soil profile where minerals, humus, or plant nutrients have been deposited after being washed down from above.

imbrex [Ar]. A Latin term used to describe a semi-cylindrical tile used to cover the flanges of two adjoining TEGULAE. A roof-ridge tile, semi-circular in cross-section.

imbrication [De]. A term applied to the overlapping arrangement of ORTHOSTATS forming the side walls of some Neolithic CLYDE–CARLINGFORD tombs in the west of Britain. Starting from the front of the chamber each pair of orthostats overlaps with the pair in front on the outside.

Imhotep [Di]. Egyptian god, chief minister of Djoser of the 3rd Dynasty. Architect of the Step Pyramid at Sakkara, and later deified and worshipped as a god of medicine. He is shown as a man holding a roll of papyrus. Equated by the Greeks with Asklepios and Imouthes.

imitation Samian [Ar]. Vessels whose form, and sometimes finish and decoration, imitated Samian ware. *See* TERRA SIGILLATA.

immunis [De]. A Latin term used to describe a legionary with special skills who was exempted from routine duties; the special status of *immunes* was not officially recognized until the time of Hadrian.

Imouthes [Di]. Egyptian god. *See* IMHOTEP.

impasto [Ar]. A type of pottery made during the VILLANOVAN period in northern Italy. Generally made from unrefined clay fired to a dark brown or black colour. Forms include biconical urns and models of small houses or huts which were used to contain cremations.

imperium [De]. Latin word for a command, which grew to signify the right to give orders, and so to mean supreme power, normally equivalent in the later Roman period to 'empire'. *Imperator*, originally 'commander-in-chief', became a title used by the emperors, and came to signify 'emperor'. The Latin writers of the Dark Ages could use *imperium* of a single kingdom, but the word retained the connotation of a kingdom supreme among others.

impluvium [Co]. The tank placed in the ATRIUM of a Roman house to receive the rain which fell through the opening in the centre—the *compluvium*.

impost [Co]. A moulded stone at the top of a pilaster flanking an opening. The member of a pillar or pier from which the arch springs.

A **discontinuous impost** is where the arch mouldings simply die out in the splayed jambs.

impressed decoration [De]. A general term referring to ornamentation on ceramic vessels made by pressing objects or materials into the vessel walls while the clay is still soft. Common forms of impression include the serrated edges of sea shells, the ends of bones or sticks, fingernails, thumbnails, pieces of stick, notched combs, twisted cord, knotted cord, or string (also known as whipped cord), etc. **Stamped decoration** is a special form of impressed decoration, more common from the 1st millennium BC onwards than in earlier times.

impressed ware [Ar]. **1.** Distinctive pottery used by the first farmers of the western Mediterranean from the east coast of Italy to southern Spain in the period 5000–3500 BC. The pottery is usually dark-surfaced and is extensively decorated with impressions made with the serrated edge of cardium shells. Such ceramics are sometimes referred to as CARDIAL WARES. Other methods of decoration include impressions made with the fingers, sticks, and other tools. The pottery forms are generally simple and include bowls and open-mouthed storage vessels. Stentinello ware in Sicily and Ghar Dalam ware in Malta represent specialized versions of impressed ware. **2.** Early style of ceramics found in North Africa, perhaps originating in the Sahara or Sudan region. **3.** The term is sometimes used in a very general sense with reference to the highly decorated wares of the later Neolithic in the British Isles and northern Europe; the predominance of various kinds of cord impressions on these wares means that they are better referred to as part of the very widespread **corded ware** tradition of the 3rd and early 2nd millennium BC.

Impressed Ware Culture [CP]. The early Neolithic communities of the Mediterranean coast of Europe, named after the practice of ornamenting pottery with impressions of cardium shells and other items (IMPRESSED WARE). Though there is evidence for the introduction of agriculture, hunting and fishing remained an important aspect of the culture, and its stone and flint industries retained some characteristic Mesolithic types. Generally dated to the period 5000–3500 BC.

Early sites tend to be in caves and rock-shelters or, on the coast, associated with shell middens. Sheep are the main domesticated animal species. In the later stages open settlements become common and in Italy these are enclosed by ditch systems (the so-called *villaggi trincerati*). Other types of pottery are found alongside the impressed wares at this stage, including fine red painted ware in Italy.

Imseti [Di]. Egyptian god, one of the four sons of HORUS. Human-headed; a model of his head was often used as the stopper of the canopic jar containing the liver.

Inanna [Di]. Sumerian deity, the queen of heaven, who was the daughter of Nanna and the goddess of love and war, and also of storehouses and rain. Closely associated with Warka and roughly equivalent to the AKKADIAN Ishtar.

Inca (Inka) [CP]. A late Horizon cultural grouping centred on its capital at Cuzco, Peru, which in the early 15th century AD began expanding outwards through conquest and alliance to form the Inca empire. At its peak in the early 16th century, this empire stretched from northern Ecuador to south-central Chile, a distance of more than 4000 km.

The period of Inca expansion began around AD 1410 under the semi-mythical emperor, or Sapa Inca, Viracocha, and was continued by his son Yupanqui (who assumed the name Pachakuti or 'Cataclysm'), who defeated a series of neighbouring rival states and kingdoms including the Chanca, the Colla, and the Lupaqa. Pachakuti's son Topa defeated the Chimu in AD 1463, thereby removing the last serious obstacle to Inca dominance of the Andes. Topa became emperor in AD 1471 and proceeded to enlarge the Inca domain still further. Topa's successor Huayna Capac took more territory in the upper Amazon region and built a second capital at Quito.

The Inca empire was called 'Tawantinsuyu' by the Inca people, meaning the land of the four quarters. Each quarter was a large province which radiated out from Cuzco. The four provinces (Antisuyu, Collasuyu, Chinchasuyu, and Cuntisuyu) were each subdivided into smaller regions, the boundaries of which broadly followed those of the conquered kingdoms.

At the head of the empire was the Sapa Inca who was believed to be descended from the sun god Inti. When a Sapa Inca died his body was mummified and thereafter became the focus of a cult. High-ranking officials in the Inca empire were recruited from royal lineages. Although the Incas generally left the social and political hierarchy of conquered kingdoms in place they required the rulers' sons to go to Cuzco to learn the Inca language, Quechua. Surprisingly, this was only a spoken language as the Inca did not use writing.

Sacred objects from conquered provinces were also taken to Cuzco to reside in the temple of the sun god or in some specially constructed shrine.

Over 30 000 km of paved roads linked Cuzco with the provincial centres, facilitating the movement of troops and the transportation of luxury goods. It has been estimated that there were between six and twelve million subjects within the Inca empire, so administration was a major task.

Agricultural land was divided into three divisions: that belonging to the temples, to the state (i.e. Sapa Inca), and to the landowning commoners known as *aylluses*. Every *ayllu* had to spend time working on the state-owned land and temple land as labour tribute or *mita*. Food produced for the state was kept in great storehouses and used to feed the army, officials, and those engaged on state projects. The main crops were potatoes, maize, and other grain crops. Specialist craftsmen produced ceramics and metalwork. All luxury goods were produced and distributed by the state.

The Inca did not build cities. The population was essentially rural with numerous small villages and towns housing less than 1000 people. The capital, Cuzco, was occupied only by members of the Sapa Inca's court and priests. The architecture of Inca centres is impressive, as is the quality of the building work done.

The Inca empire came to an end in the mid 16th century. Internecine strife and a civil war between Atahuallpa and Huascar, the sons of Huayna Capac, between AD 1525 and 1532 weakened the empire considerably. Atahuallpa won the civil war but within weeks was captured at Cajamarca by a party of just 168 Spanish conquistadors led by Francisco Pizarro, and within a year Cuzco and the whole empire had been taken over by the Spanish.

incense burner [Ar]. Stone or ceramic vessel of various shapes and sizes in which resins and other materials were slowly burnt in order to give off smoke and fumes, usually for ritual or ceremonial purposes. In Mesoamerica incense burning was widespread from the Formative Stage through into the Classic. Pine resin, the Maya word for which is 'copal', was widely traded as incense.

incense cup [Ar]. General term for miniature cups or accessory vessels found in early Bronze Age (WESSEX II) graves in southern England. There are various types, including ALDBOURNE CUPS, GRAPE CUPS, and SLASHED CUPS. The name was fancifully given in the 19th century; the actual function of the cups is not known.

Inchtuthill, UK [Si]. A Roman legionary fort established in the Tay Valley of eastern Scotland, extensively excavated by Shephard Frere between 1952 and 1965. Built by Agricola during his northern campaigns during the early 80s AD, the fort covers about 20 ha and was constructed mainly of earth and timber. The internal buildings include 64 barrack blocks, a commandant's house, officers' quarters, and a hospital. About AD 87 the fort was systematically dismantled as part of a calculated withdrawal from the region. Many of the contents of the fort were broken and buried in pits. One pit contained more than a million used nails.

[Rep.: L. Pitts and S. Frere, 1985, *Inchtuthill: the Roman legionary fortress excavations 1952–65*. London: Society for the Promotion of Roman Studies]

incised decoration [De]. A method of ornamenting ceramic vessels by cutting the soft clay walls with a sharp instrument such as a pointed stick, knife blade, or piece of flint.

indented [De]. Refers to the sides of a vessel which have been regularly pushed in to form a series of oval concavities; described also as thumb-indented, dimpled, and folded.

independent invention [Ge]. *See* AUTONOMOUS INVENTION.

independent variable [Ge]. A variable or factor which causally affects another (the dependent variable).

Indian Knoll, Kentucky, USA [Si]. An extensive Archaic Stage shell midden, living floors, and cemetery dating to *c*.2500–2000 BC. As a whole the site covers about 1 ha with some of the shell middens over 1.5 m high. Excavations by William Webb during the Great Depression revealed a cemetery of over 1100 burials representing all age groups from newborn infants to elderly adults. Grave goods associated with some internments suggest social ranking, perhaps through differentiated kinship groups. Grave goods associated with males included axes and groundhog incisors for woodworking, fish-hooks, antler flint-retouchers, awls, and items which may have been from medicine bags. Items found exclusively in female graves included nutcracking stones, bone beads, pestles, and stone gravers. About 4 per cent of the graves contained objects that had come from distant sources: copper ornaments and marine shell ornaments.

[W. S. Webb, 1946, Indian Knoll site, Oh 2, Ohio County, Kentucky. *University of Kentucky Reports in Archaeology and Anthropology*, 4(3), 115–365]

Indian land [Le]. The lands of an Indian tribe or a specific Indian individual which are either held in trust by the United States government or subject to a restriction against alienation imposed by the United States government. The term may in some cases exclude subsurface interests.

Indian tribe [Le]. Any band, nation, or other organized group or community, including an Alaska native village or regional or village corporation as defined in, or established pursuant to, the Alaska Native Claims Settlement Act.

indigenous [Ge]. Native to the land, the original inhabitants. *See also* ABORIGINES.

indirect percussion [Ge]. *See* PERCUSSION FLAKING.

Indo-European [De]. Term applied to a large group of cognate languages, including the majority of European language groups—Italic, Germanic, Celtic, Baltic, Slavonic, and Greek—as well as Indo-Iranian (Persian and Hindi) and Sanskrit. Many attempts have been made to model and explain the dispersal of Indo-European languages, a problem fraught with difficulties because of having to correlate linguistic groups with material culture, ethnic communities, and cultural groups.

Following earlier work by Gordon Childe and others, Marija Gimbutas has articulated and elaborated the long-held traditional view which situates the homeland of a proto-Indo-European language in the Euro-Asiatic steppe of south Russia and western Asia. From here it spread into Europe with the single-grave, corded ware, and globular amphorae groups during the 2nd millennium BC. A similar argument was elaborated still further by Jim Mallory in 1989, confirming the area north of the Black Sea as the Indo-European homeland and seeking its spread around 4000 BC, late in the Neolithic or early Copper Age of the region. However, the precise origins, timing, and social context of the language spread has been disputed by Colin Renfrew who forcefully argues for an origin in Anatolia and northern Greece and a much earlier spread, starting in the 7th millennium BC, linked to the dispersal of farming technologies and the classic Neolithic lifestyle.

inductivism [Th]. Reasoning by which one proceeds from specific observations to make general conclusions. Thus in archaeology inductivist research starts with the observation or analysis of data and moves on to the development of general statements and conclusions from them. This approach contrasts with DEDUCTIVISM and hypothesis-driven research.

Indus Valley civilization [CP]. An extensive civilization that developed on the plains of the Indus Valley of Pakistan and northwestern India in the middle of the 3rd millennium BC and lasted for about five centuries. Also known as the Harappan civilization. The discovery of the Indus civilization was a piece of pure archaeological research that began in the late 19th century AD with work by Sir John Marshall and with the discovery of some seal-stamps at HARAPPA. Unlike many other great civilizations, no hint of its former existence came through in the later historical texts from the Indian subcontinent.

The origins of the Indus civilization are poorly known. Certainly there are some connections with the AKKADIAN period in Mesopotamia, but the extent of any influence is impossible to gauge. There does, however, appear to be a period of rapid cultural change in the Indus Valley about 2600 BC with the emergence of major cities such as Mohenjo-daro, Harappa, Ganweriwala, and perhaps

also Chanhu-daro, Lothal, Dholavira, and Kalibangan. A form of writing developed, still not deciphered, and there was agricultural intensification with concentration on barley and wheat. The peoples of the Indus were also cattle-keepers on a grand scale, with cattle bones representing more than 50 per cent of the material in any assemblage; there is also abundant cattle imagery in art. Long-distance trade both east and west is well attested, as well as internal commerce in artefacts and foodstuffs. Metal was worked and there was an early use of the fast wheel for potting. The central theme of Indus religion is the combined male/female deity symbolized by animal horns and broad curving plant motifs. There is some speculation that some of the beliefs and imagery represent a proto-Shiva or early form of Buddhism, but this is highly speculative. There is an interest in water and cleanliness. How and why the civilization came to an end is unknown. The major settlements were simply abandoned around 2000 BC, with no archaeological evidence for natural disasters or invasions by other peoples.

industrial archaeology [Ge]. A term coined by Donald Dudley in the 1950s to describe an emergent branch of archaeology that at the time was explicitly concerned with the archaeology of industry, with a particular focus on the surviving monuments and structures of the Industrial Revolution and later. Since then its scope has broadened to cover an interest in the industry and communications of any period in the past. Because of its interests there is a substantial input from related subjects such as engineering, architecture, building craftsmen, and experts in particular fields of craft or production (e.g., mining, metalworking, shipbuilding, and weaving). Although it shares many methods of fieldwork with other areas of archaeology its overall aims remain grounded in description and investigation and there is relatively little use of general archaeological theory to develop insights into the meaning and wider social implications of the material remains.

industrial effect [Ge]. Dilution of the atmospheric ^{14}C concentration caused by the burning of coal and oil. Also called the fossil-fuel or Suess effect.

industry [De]. A descriptive term applied to sets of assemblages of the same material, especially stone and flint tool assemblages, that share features of their manufacture and have common products. An industry in this sense is taken to imply production within a single society.

Ine [Na]. King of the West Saxons from AD 688, and a vigorous upholder of his kingdom's rights, who issued a code of laws (the first of the West Saxons to do so). In AD 726 he abdicated to go on pilgrimage to Rome, where he died sometime later.

inevitable variation [Th]. The notion that cultures change and vary with time cumulatively, but that the reasons for these changes cannot easily be understood.

infant mortality rate [Ge]. The number of infants who die during the first year of life, usually measured in terms of the number of deaths per thousand live births.

infrared absorption spectrometry [Te]. A technique of physical analysis used to determine the mineralogy or chemical composition of artefacts and organic materials such as amber. A sample is bombarded by infrared radiation, causing the atoms in the sample to vibrate at frequencies characteristic of the material present. That part of the radiation spectrum vibrating at the same frequency as an interatomic bond in the sample is absorbed, the rest is transmitted. Thus measurement of the extent of absorption at each wavelength in the range 2.5–16μm provides information on the interatomic bonds associated with the specimen and this can be used to identify the mineral phases and chemical compounds, both organic and inorganic, that are present.

infrared photography [Te]. A useful technique for recording detail in objects, sites, and landscapes is to use film that is sensitive to the infrared spectrum so that it effectively responds to radiated heat rather than reflected light. Monochrome infrared film provides a wide range of grey tones. **False colour infrared photography** uses different colours to emphasize the contrast between features revealed through infrared photography. The colours bear no relation to the natural colours of the matter photographed.

ingot [Ar]. A shaped mass of smelted but unworked metal. The shape and size of ingots are determined by custom rather than function, although their weight may be related to the capacity of the means by which they were commonly moved about. Where ingots from a particular source are of standard size and weight they can thus be used as currency for trade. *See* OX-HIDE INGOT, CURRENCY BAR.

inhumation [De]. The name given to the burial custom by which the body was laid unburned in a grave (*compare* CREMATION). Inhumation is common in the archaeological record of many periods and many areas, and is often taken as a key cultural trait that is ideologically based.

Initial Period [CP]. General term representing one of the seven main chronological subdivisions used in Andean archaeology in South America, referring to the period *c.*1800–900 BC. At this time settlement appears to have shifted its focus from the coast to inland riverine situations, pottery was introduced, and both agriculture and animal husbandry began to be practised. Monumental architecture appeared in coastal Peru. The Initial Period was a time of cultural heterogeneity, predating the Formative Stage.

Inka [CP]. *See* INCA.

inn [MC]. An establishment which provided food, drink, stabling and, usually, accommodation for travellers. Inns commonly stand along main highways and in market towns.

inorganic materials [De]. Material objects that are not part of the animal or vegetable kingdom.

inscribed [De]. Term used to describe marks or lines forming a design, motif, image, or pattern of some kind that can been cut into stone, metal, bone, wood, ceramic, or other fairly soft material.

inscription [Ar]. A set of words or pictographic images cut into the surface of a block of stone, ceramic panel, metal plate, or some other kind of durable material in order to record some kind of event or dedication.

insect analysis [Te]. The recovery of insect remains from anaerobic and semi-anaerobic deposits can be very revealing about the climate, local environment, and the health and welfare of local populations. The most common find is the hard exterior skeleton of beetles, but other fragments of insects themselves, their eggs and lava can also be recovered. Remains are usually collected by froth FLOATATION in the laboratory and studied using comparative reference material. Their preferences and habitats can be modelled by observing modern insect populations.

in situ [Ge]. In its original position.

instinct [De]. A fixed pattern of behaviour which has genetic origins and which appears in all normal animals within a given species.

Institute of Field Archaeologists (IFA) [Or]. The main UK-based association for archaeologists working in all sectors of the discipline which firmly establishes archaeology as a self-regulating profession. The IFA came into being on 21 December 1982 as the culmination of some ten years of discussion in Britain on the need for a professional institute. The objects of the Institute are to advance the practice of archaeology and allied disciplines; to define and maintain proper standards and ethics in training and education in field archaeology, in the execution and supervision of work, and in the conservation of the archaeological heritage; and to disseminate information about field archaeologists and their areas of interest. Central to its operation is an agreed code of conduct, which, together with other by-laws, all members agree to abide by. Membership is available at a number of levels depending on the level of education, training, and experience. Entry level is generally that of Practitioner, above which is an Associate Member, and then a Member, as a person's experience and career builds up. Membership carries the right to use the appropriate distinction—PIFA, AIFA, and MIFA respectively. Associate membership for students and those starting out in the profession is also available. Joining the Institute, or changing levels of membership, is attained by submitting for review and validation a portfolio or work and evidence of training and experience.

insula (pl. *insulae*) [Co]. Literally an 'island', being the Latin term for the space between the streets in an urban street grid. A rectangular block of buildings surrounded by streets.

intaglio [Ar]. **1.** The process of cutting a design into the surface of a small hard stone or gem. **2.** The object so created, usually used as a seal or as a stone to be set in a ring.

Integration Period [CP]. General term developed by Betty Meggers to refer to the period *c*.AD 500–1500 in Ecuadorian archaeology, although it is also applied in other adjacent areas of South America where it is sometimes known as the Late Period. The Integration Period is characterized by great cultural uniformity, the development of urban centres, class-based social stratification, and intensive agriculture. The culmination of the period is the absorption of Ecuador into the Inca empire.

interaction [Ge]. A general term used in archaeology to refer to any close contacts established between communities or regions that is evidenced in the archaeological record through material culture. Where fairly extensive contact is made over a wide area the term **interaction sphere** may be appropriate.

interest groups [Ge]. Groups organized to pursue specific interests in the political arena, operating primarily by lobbying the members of legislative bodies.

interglacial [Ge]. A warm period between two major phases of glaciation. During an interglacial, which may have a duration of more than 100 000 years, ice sheets diminish in size, climates warm up, sea levels rise, and there are changes to the nature and extent of the wild flora and fauna.

Intermediate Period [CP]. General term used in Peruvian archaeology to denote phases of change. Two distinct intermediate periods can be recognized.

The early Intermediate Period covers the period *c*.200 BC to AD 600 and is characterized by the rise of the first city-states.

The late Intermediate Period refers to the period *c*.AD 1000–1476 and therefore covers the fragmented units which appeared after the decline of Tiahuanaco and Huari.

International Committee on Archaeological Heritage Management (ICAHM) [Or]. A specialist committee of ICOMOS established in 1985 to provide an international forum for the exchange of experience and expertise between those concerned with archaeological heritage management, to promote international cooperation, and to advise on the development of ICOMOS policies and programmes in this field. In 1988 a *Charter for the Protection and Management of the Archaeological Heritage* (Stockholm: ICAHM) was agreed and published.

International Council on Monuments and Sites (ICOMOS) [Or]. A non-governmental representative body composed of specialists professionally concerned with conservation from more than 60 member nations. Established in 1965, ICOMOS has set up international committees consisting of leading experts on wood, stone, cultural tourism, historic towns, vernacular architecture, rock art, earth structures, training, photogrammetry, historic gardens, stained glass, and archaeological heritage management. These committees are in touch with the latest technical developments and through them ICOMOS provides specialist advice to governments and organizations around the world. ICOMOS also has national committees in its member countries and these provide local membership schemes for individuals. Internationally, ICOMOS provides advice to UNESCO on nominations for cultural sites to be added to the World Heritage List through its World Heritage coordinator. It also debates, agrees, and publishes international charters setting down relevant core principles. *See also* ICAHM.

interpluvial [Ge]. Period when the rainfall was less than it is at present.

interpretation [Th]. The stage in research at which the results of archaeological analyses are synthesized and there is an attempt to explain their meaning or consolidate a knowledgeable understanding of the results. *See* DISCOURSE.

interpretive archaeology [Th]. An approach to archaeology that builds out of POST-PROCESSUAL thinking as a simple reaction to PROCESSUAL ARCHAEOLOGY and instead sees interpretation as a creative process with a number of key characteristics: in the foreground is the person and work of the interpreter; archaeology is a material practice in the present which makes knowledge and narratives from the material traces of the past; archaeology is social practice which is to do with mean-

ings and making sense of things; the interpretive process is an ongoing one in which there can be no final or definitive account of the past; that interpretations are less concerned with explanations than with making sense of things that were probably never certain in the first place; that interpretation is multivocal in the sense that different interpretations of the same thing are possible; and that there can be plurality of interpretation in which each strand is suited to the different purposes, needs, and desires of a different constituency.

interrupted ditch enclosure [MC]. *See* CAUSEWAYED ENCLOSURE.

interstadial [Ge]. A short warmer and milder interlude within a glacial phase of insufficient duration to allow major changes in sea level or vegetation patterns. *Compare* INTERGLACIAL.

intervallum [Co]. A Latin term used to describe a space between the rear of the rampart and the *VIA SAGULARIS*. More generally, it is the space between a rampart of a fort or camp and the building-lines or tent-lines within.

intrados [De]. The interior curve of an arch.

intramural [De]. Located within the confines of a settlement; outside such a site is **extramural**.

Inuit [Ge]. An indigenous word meaning 'the people', which is the term much preferred by communities living in the high latitudes of North America instead of 'Eskimo' or 'Esquimaux'.

invasion hypothesis [Th]. The idea that cultural change is brought about by the conquest of one group by another. In some cases this is certainly true, but from the 1920s through to the 1960s especially the idea of invasion was closely connected with that of DIFFUSIONISM to the extent that the arrival in an area of almost any new kind of material culture was associated with folk-movements and waves of invaders. Such a view is no longer accepted and invasions need to be demonstrated rather than assumed.

inverse retouch [De]. Retouching done by a direct or indirect percussion technique, working from the top of the flake so that chips are removed from its smooth underside.

Ionic Order [De]. In Greek architecture, a style characterized by columns with a diameter-to-height ratio of between 1 : 8 and 1 : 10. It was a development in architectural form that perhaps originated in Asia Minor to create an order more decorative and elaborate than the austere and earlier Doric. Its columns have bases ornamented with a variety of mouldings, and are more slender, with deeper flutes and no sharp or vulnerable edges as in the Doric Order. Capitals have a pair of spiral volutes extending out on either side, front and back, over a ring of egg-and-tongue moulding round the top of the column. There are no triglyphs.

Ipiutak Culture [CP]. Communities representing the most recent variant of the NORTON TRADITION of coastal Alaska in the period c.AD 1–500, and later in some areas of north Alaska. This group lacks the stone lamps, pottery and ground slate tools of the Norton Tradition, but has a highly developed art and uses similar projectile points and other kinds of stone tools. At the type-site of Ipiutak on Point Hope, Alaska, the ruins of over 600 rectangular houses arranged in four rows along ridges in the beach have been found. Some of the dead were buried in log coffins set in pits in the ground, others were placed on the ground surface and covered in logs or wooden frames. Carved ivory pieces included realistic and fantastic animals, human heads and skulls, snow goggles, and grotesque masks. Ipiutak carving was not restricted to grave goods but was applied to everyday items too.

Ipswichian Stage [Ge]. A group of deposits representing a geostratigraphic stage within the PLEISTOCENE series of the British QUATERNARY system, represented by a series of lacustrine muds, river terraces, and estuarine and marine sediments overlying WOLSTONIAN sands and gravels, and sealed by DEVENSIAN deposits containing material indicating cold conditions. Traditionally, Ipswichian deposits are taken to represent a single warm phase, the last interglacial, dating to the period 150 000 years ago down to 115 000 years ago. There may in fact be considerable variation within the period. Archaeologically, Mousterian artefacts of the Middle Palaeolithic are found in Ipswichian deposits.

Equivalent to the Riss-Würm in the Alpine sequence, the Sangamon in North America, and the Eemian in northern Europe.

Ipswich ware [Ar]. Type of middle Saxon pottery made between the 7th and 9th centuries AD around Ipswich, Suffolk, where the remains of kilns have been found. Outputs include cooking pots and decorated pitchers that were distributed around East Anglia, and stamped pitchers that were traded still more widely to York and beyond.

Irene [Na]. Byzantine empress born about AD 752 who became the wife of Leo IV (d. AD 780), and guardian of their son, Constantine VI. She favoured the use of icons in church and proved high-handed in her advocacy. In AD 797 she had her son blinded and proclaimed herself empress. Removed by a coup in AD 802, she died in exile a year or so later.

Irish bowl (Irish food vessel) [Ar]. Type of early Bronze Age ceramic vessel found in Ireland and the west of Scotland, mainly accompanying inhumation burials. These vessels have a small flat base, and a BICONICAL form to the body with elaborated and sometimes perforated lugs on the carination, and an internally bevelled rim. The upper part of the body, neck, and rim is usually decorated with impressed cord or other motifs. The bowls date to the early 2nd millennium BC.

iron [Ma]. A hard grey-coloured metal (Fe), widely available in the form of ores such as laterites, haematites, siderites, and pyrites, as well as in the form of bog iron created through precipitation. The earliest ironworking in Eurasia appears to have been amongst the HITTITES in the mid 2nd millennium BC, knowledge of the technology only becoming more widely available after the collapse of the Hittite empire at the end of 2nd millennium BC. Although iron was probably the most widely used metal ever from the early first millennium BC onwards, the fact that it is prone to rapid corrosion in most buried environments means that it is archaeologically rather under-represented.

Meteoric iron, containing a high percentage of nickel, is found naturally and, since its heavenly origin was widely recognized, it was highly prized for its reputed magical properties. Such iron was used in making the sacred crook of Osiris held by the pharaohs of Egypt.

Iron Age [CP]. The third of the principal periods of the THREE AGE SYSTEM. The working of iron was introduced, probably from Asia Minor, into southeastern Europe around 1000 BC, and into central Europe by the 8th–7th centuries BC. The European Iron Age has conventionally been divided into two phases, named after type-sites at HALLSTATT in Austria and LA TÈNE in Switzerland. In areas conquered by the Romans the 'Iron Age' is succeeded by the 'Roman' period. Contemporary cultures outside the empire are described as being of the 'Roman Iron Age'. From about 400 AD these periods are succeeded by the migration period.

irregular aggregate field system [MC]. *See* FIELD SYSTEM.

irregular enclosed field system [MC]. *See* FIELD SYSTEM.

irregular open field system [MC]. *See* FIELD SYSTEM.

Isaac, Glynn Llywelyn (1937–85) [Bi]. South African archaeologist who after taking first degrees at Cape Town University in 1958 and Cambridge (UK) in 1961 researched his Ph.D. at Peterhouse, Cambridge, completed in 1969. He is well known for his work in Africa and especially that on early man. He was Warden of Prehistoric Sites in Kenya (1961–2) and Deputy Director of the Centre for Prehistory and Palaeontology at the National Museums of Kenya (1963–5). In 1966 he joined the anthropology faculty at the University of California, Berkeley. He was co-director of the Koobi Fora project in East Africa with Richard Leakey. In 1983 he was appointed Professor of Anthropology at Harvard University, where, at the time of his death, he was developing a series of new research projects.

[Obit.: *Antiquity*, 60 (1986), 55–6]

Ishtar or Inanna [Di]. The Sumerian goddess of the planet Venus. Like her classical counterpart she was credited with jurisdiction over love and procreation.

Isis (Aset) [Di]. Egyptian moon goddess and one of the great goddesses in the HELIPOLITAN ENNEAD. She was mistress of magic, wife of Osiris, and mother of Horus. With Nephthys, Neith, and Selket, she was one of the four protector goddesses of the dead: she watched over the canopic jar containing the liver. She is often depicted as a woman with a moon-disc on her brow. In the late period Philae was her cult centre.

Islam [Ge]. A religion founded by Muhammad in AD 622 (1 AH), spreading rapidly to many parts of the Near East, Middle East, and Far East during the later 1st millennium AD, reaching China, for example, by the 8th century AD. **Islamic civilization** covers a vast area from the North African shores of the Atlantic to the western periphery of the Pacific and from central Asia to sub-Saharan Africa. It is bound together by the shared heritage of Islam and its associated intellectual traditions.

Archaeologically, Islam and the civilization it engendered includes many different peoples of various religious and cultural traditions and a tremendous variety of regional assemblages, aesthetic tastes, and social practices.

isostasy [Ge]. The tendency for the earth's crust to maintain a state of near equilibrium so that, for example, during a glacial period the weight of the terrestrial ice-caps cause the land beneath to sink. When the ice melts the land rises again through the process known as **isostatic adjustment**. As a result there are alterations in the height of the land relative to the sea. *Compare* EUSTASY.

Israelites [CP]. In origin a semi-nomadic branch of the SEMITES that developed from the Khabiru-Hebrews who, according to biblical sources, escaped from Egypt under Moses and established themselves in Palestine under Joshua during the 13th century BC. By the 10th century they had conquered the CANAANITES and the PHILISTINES to become a powerful kingdom with a capital at Jerusalem. Soon afterwards the single kingdom split into two parts, Judah and Israel, and remained so until Judah was destroyed by the Assyrians in 722 BC and Israel was taken by the Babylonians in 587 BC.

Itacoatiara Phase [CP]. South American farming cultures found in the Lower and Middle Amazon areas of Amazonia and tentatively dated to *c*.AD 1300–1500. Characterized by their ceramic assemblages which belong to the Incised and Punctuate Horizon Style of the Amazon basin. At the type-site of Itacoatiara, Brazil, fine-line incision and punctuate bands of decoration were arranged alternately on the exteriors of tall vessels and on the interiors of shallow open bowls.

iudex [De]. Latin term for a judge, the name given by Roman writers to the chief of the VISIGOTHS.

ivory [Ma]. Animal tusk, usually from the elephant, walrus, or narwhal. In Palaeolithic times, tusk from mammoth was also used.

iwan [Co]. A vaulted, open-fronted hall or reception room facing onto a courtyard in a Persian palace.

Iyatayet, Cape Denbigh, Alaska [Si]. *See* CAPE DENBIGH, ALASKA.

J

jacal [Ma]. American term used in southwestern parts of the US for the wattle and daub construction of walls.

jack bean [Sp]. A leguminous plant (*Canavalia plagiosperma*) with edible seeds in a long pod. Native to South America and Mesoamerica. Domesticated by *c*.3000 BC in Mesoamerica.

Jacobstahl, Paul Ferdinand (1880–1957) [Bi]. German archaeologist and scholar specializing in Celtic art. Born and brought up in Berlin, educated at Luisenstädtisches Gymnasium, and at the Universities of Berlin, Gottingen, and Bonn. He was appointed to a lectureship in Gottingen University in 1908, and in 1912 he was made Professor of Classical Archaeology in Marburg University. Forced to leave Germany in 1935 he found a home in Britain and was appointed Reader in Celtic Archaeology in the University of Oxford.

[Obit.: *Revue Archéologique*, 1958 (Tome II), 103–4]

jade [Ma]. A hard semi-precious stone that comes in a range of colours from reddish brown through greens to white. Outcrops in East Asia were used from Neolithic times onwards for the manufacture of ornamental and ritual objects. Sources in the Alps of southern Europe were also exploited from early times, and objects such as axes, pendants, and bracelets were traded over vast distances. A JADEITE AXE deposited in about 3807 BC beside the Sweet Track in Somerset, England, was more than 1200 km from it source.

jadeite axes [Ar]. Thin highly polished unperforated implements, probably for ceremonial use. Examples date mainly from the 4th and 3rd millennia BC in northwest Europe.

jamb [Co]. **1.** The side of a door or window. **2.** A wing of a building. **3.** In heraldry, the leg of an animal.

James I (VI of Scotland) [Na]. King of the House of Stuart from 1603. Born 1566, son of Mary, queen of Scots and granddaughter of Margaret Tudor, elder daughter of Henry VII, and Henry Stewart, Lord Darnley. Married Anne, daughter of Frederick II of Denmark. Died in 1625 aged 58, having reigned 22 years.

James I [Na]. King of Scotland of the House of Stewart from 1404. Born 1394, son of Robert III. Married Joan Beaufort, daughter of John, earl of Somerset. Assassinated in 1437, aged 42, having reigned 30 years.

James II [Na]. King of Scotland of the House of Stewart from 1437. Born 1430, son of James I. Married Mary, daughter of Arnold, duke of Guelders. Killed accidentally in 1460 aged 29, having reigned 23 years.

James II (VII of Scotland) [Na]. King of the House of Stuart. Born 1633, second son of Charles I. Married (1) Lady Anne Hyde, daughter of Edward, earl of Clarendon; (2) Mary, daughter of Alphonso, duke of Modena. His reign ended in flight from the kingdom in December 1688. This was followed by an interregnum from December 1688 to February 1689. Died 1701 aged 67, having reigned three years.

James III [Na]. King of Scotland of the House of Stewart from 1460. Born 1452, son of James II. Married Margaret, daughter of Christian I of Denmark. Assassinated in 1488, aged 36, having reigned 27 years.

James IV [Na]. King of Scotland of the House of Stewart from 1488. Born 1473, son of James III. Married Margaret Tudor, daughter of Henry VII of England. Killed in battle in 1513 aged 40, having reigned 25 years.

James V [Na]. King of Scotland of the House of Stewart from 1513. Born 1512, son of James IV.

Married (1) Madeleine, daughter of Francis I of France; (2) Mary of Lorraine, daughter of the duc de Guise. Died in 1542 aged 30, having reigned 29 years.

Jamestown, Virginia, USA [Si]. The first permanent English settlement in America, founded in AD 1607 by 105 settlers, on the James River about 24 km inland from Chesapeake Bay. Originally, the town was the capital of Virginia. The early settlers lived off fishing, small-scale farming of maize, squash, and pumpkin, and trading with local aboriginal Indian communities. Some staples were imported from England. At first houses were timber-framed with wattle-and-daub walls and thatched roofs. Later, baked clay bricks were used for walling. Pottery and glassmaking also became local industries. The town had its troubles, however, with attacks by Indians, famine, fire, and civil strife. It was built in an unhealthy location and, once established, many of the planters preferred to live on their estates. Jamestown went into decline in the 18th century after Williamsburg became the capital of the colony. The US National Park Service took over the site in 1934, and in 1954–6 a major programme of excavations was carried out by J. L. Cotter in anticipation of the 350th anniversary of the site's foundation.

[Rep.: J. L. Cotter, 1958, *Archaeological excavations at Jamestown, Virginia*. Washington, DC: US Department of the Interior]

Jane [Na]. English queen of the House of Tudor in 1553. Born 1537, daughter of Frances, daughter of Mary Tudor, the younger sister of Henry VIII, and Henry Grey, duke of Suffolk. Married Lord Guildford Dudley, son of the duke of Northumberland. Deposed July 1553, and executed February 1554 aged 16, having reigned nine days.

Japura Phase [CP]. South American farming cultures found in the Lower and Middle Amazon areas of Amazonia and tentatively dated to *c*.AD 500–700. Characterized by their ceramic assemblages which belong to the Incised Rim Horizon Style of the Amazon basin.

jar [De]. A vessel with a constriction at the neck whose width is usually less than its height. It is convenient also to distinguish wide-mouthed, medium-mouthed, and nar-

row-mouthed jars. This term in general excludes FLAGONS and BEAKERS.

Jarmo, Iran [Si]. A Neolithic village site in the foothills of the Zagros Mountains near Kirkuk in northwest Iraq. Excavated by Robert Braidwood between 1948 and 1955, the site is important because of its early evidence for food production. Sixteen main levels were defined within the 7 m thick stratigraphy, the first eleven of which lacked pottery. The earliest levels date to the 7th millennium BC and reveal the presence of mud-brick houses. Cereals at the site include wheat and barley, and there was equipment present for processing the grain. Field pea, lentil, and blue vetchling were also present. Goat was domesticated from the earliest levels, but pig was undergoing domestication when the settlement began. Hunting and gathering remained important throughout the sequence with pig, sheep, and gazelle being exploited together with pistachio and acorns.

[Sum.: R. J. Braidwood, 1960, The agricultural revolution. *Scientific American*, 203(3), 130–48]

Jastorf Culture [CP]. Early Iron Age communities in the southern Baltic region who were amongst the first to use iron on the north European Plain. Dating to the late HALLSTATT.

Jataka [Ge]. Buddhist stories of Indian origin included in the sacred literature but in fact entertaining tales of supernatural adventures.

Jauarí Phase [CP]. South American cultures of the Intermediate Stage found in the Lower and Middle Amazon areas of Amazonia and tentatively dated to *c*.1200–700 BC. Characterized by their ceramic assemblages which belong to the Zone Hachured Horizon Style of the Amazon basin. Pottery from Jauarí itself comes from a midden surrounding a pile-built house and is dated to about 1000 BC.

Java Man [De]. Name given to early hominid remains found in AD 1891 by Eugène Dubois at Trinil in Java. Dating to between 1 million and 500 000 years ago the fossils are now known to be those of *Homo erectus*.

javelin head [Ar]. A kind of large flint projectile point used during the Neolithic in the British Isles. Usually lozenge-shaped in outline with slightly convex curves on the leading edges. Finely made, and sometimes polished and ground on the large flat sides, presumably to reduce the weight and produce a thinner blade.

Jazdzewski, Konrad (1908–85) [Bi]. Polish archaeologist and leading prehistorian. Born in Silesia he was educated at Poznan University between 1926 and 1930, attaining his doctorate in 1935. He held various academic posts in Poznan and Warsaw, and in 1939 was nominated to the Chair in Prehistory at Wilna University but was prevented from taking it up because of the outbreak of war. After WW2 he served as Director of the Museum of Archaeology and Ethnography in Łódź, where he stayed until his retirement in 1979. Simultaneously he was associate professor and in 1959 full professor in Łódź University. During this time he excavated a number of important sites including Brześć Kujawski and Łeg Piekarski. He was elected an Honorary Fellow of the Society of Antiquaries in March 1976.

[Obit.: *Antiquaries Journal*, 66 (1986), 499]

Jefferson, Thomas (1743–1826) [Bi]. Born in Shadwell, Virginia, USA, Jefferson trained as a lawyer but was also a committed amateur archaeologist. He was Governor of Virginia between 1779 and 1781 before becoming a member of the House of Congress. In 1784, he excavated a burial mound on his estate in Virginia in order to establish its age and cultural affinities. The work was carried out very scientifically, with careful observation and an understanding of stratigraphy; it was reported in 1801 in *Notes on the state of Virginia* (London: John Stockdale). In 1799, when he was President of the American Philosophical Society, he circulated a letter to members enjoining them to make accurate plans, drawings, and descriptions of ancient remains. Jefferson was the third President of the USA, in office 1801–9. In retirement he founded the University of Virginia.

[Bio.: K. Lehmann-Hartleben, 1943, Thomas Jefferson, archaeologist. *American Journal of Archaeology*, 47, 161–3]

Jelling, Vejle, Denmark [Si]. A Viking royal site of the 10th century AD in East Jutland. The complex is dominated by two large mounds, the biggest barrows in Denmark, 78 m in diameter and 11 m high. They are believed to have contained the burials of the last pagan monarchs: Gorm, who died in AD 950, and his queen Thyra. However, excavations by Ejnar Dyggve in 1941–7 revealed that the southern mound contained no burial, prompting speculation that Gorm and Thyra were buried together in the northern barrow, the chamber of which had been cleared in 1821 and 1861. Between the barrows stands a Romanesque church outside which is a very fine SYMBOL STONE bearing the oldest crucifixion scene yet known in Denmark. A second stone has a magnificent lion drawn on it. Both the stones carry runic inscriptions telling of the exploits and Christian conversion of Gorm the Old and Harald Bluetooth. There are also the remains of a large stone-edged monument in the shape of a ship in the churchyard.

[Rep.: E. Dyggve, 1948, The royal barrows at Jelling. *Antiquity*, 22, 190–7]

Jemdet Nasr [Si]. A settlement near Kish at the northern end of the Mesopotamian alluvial plain. Excavations by Stephen Langdon in the 1920s revealed a series of deposits containing a distinctive style of painted pottery (black and red paint over buff fabric) that has come to define the Jemdet Nasr Phase in the southern Mesopotamian sequence and dates to the late 4th millennium BC. It is equivalent to URUK III and has evidence for writing, the use of fine sculpture, increasing trade, and craft specialization. Jemdet Nasr was occupied from late Uruk through to early Dynastic I times and serves to demonstrate the essential continuity of the period. A substantial structure uncovered at Jemdet Nasr may prove to be the earliest known palace in southern Mesopotamia.

[Rep.: E. J. H. Mackay, 1931, *Report on excavations at Jemdet Nasr, Iraq*. Chicago: Field Museum of Natural History]

Jenness, Diamond (1886–1969) [Bi]. Canadian ethnographer and archaeologist who worked extensively in the Arctic. In 1925 he first described the DORSET TRADITION.

[Obit.: *American Anthropologist* 73 (1971), 248–51]

Jericho, Palestine [Si]. A massive tell mound in the Jordan Valley of Israel, just north of Wadi el-Mafjar. Excavated at various intervals since the 19th century AD, notably by J. Garstang in 1930–6 and Kathleen Kenyon in 1952–8, the site shows a long and uninterrupted sequence from the Natufian through to the late Bronze Age. The Natufian levels date to about 8000 BC and seem to represent a hunter-gatherer campsite, although Kenyon discovered a rectangular stone platform that may have been some kind of shrine. These are followed by the Pre-Pottery Neolithic A levels (PPNA) at about 7500 BC: a settlement of 4 ha was enclosed by a fortification wall that includes a large tower against its inner face. It is one of the earliest permanent settlements known. The houses are round and of mud brick. Subsistence here included cereal cultivation and hunting animals. The succeeding PPNB, dated to c.6500 BC, had rectangular houses with plastered floors. An increased range of crops was cultivated, and it is possible than domesticated sheep were exploited. Evidence of an ancestor cult was found in the form of plastered skulls with cowrie shell eyes. There was a break in occupation after the PPNB, but the site was reoccupied in late Neolithic and Chalcolithic times. This was the Proto-Urban phase dating to about 3200 BC, and it is from here the site begins takes on a distinctively city-like character, the earliest in Palestine. The middle Bronze Age town was defended by a GLACIS and occupied by the Hyksos; it was destroyed by the Egyptians in 1580 BC. The Late Bronze Age town of about 1400 BC has been correlated with the city destroyed, in Biblical accounts, by Joshua and the ISRAELITES.

[Rep.: K. M. Kenyon, 1957, *Digging up Jericho*. London: Ernest Benn; K. M. Kenyon, 1981, *Excavations at Jericho*, volume III. London: British School of Archaeology in Jerusalem]

Jermanovice points [Ar]. Laurel-leaf points, flaked completely on one side but bifacially only on the lower part of the blade and on the bulb of percussion. Characteristic of the Upper Palaeolithic Jermanovice Culture in Poland.

Jerome, Eusebius Hieronymus [Na]. Church Father and saint, born in Dalmatia c.AD 348 and already following an official career when he entered religious life. The life of asceticism appealed to him and he travelled in the eastern deserts. A short stay in Rome (AD 382–5) led to a commission to correct the variant texts of the Bible then current, and the years from 389 to his death were spent in theology and commentary writing. His principal works are the revised Latin translation of the Bible, the Vulgate, and his *Chronicle* which provides a key source for the events of the years around

AD 400, but his correspondence preserves much curious detail. Died c.AD 420.

Jerusalem, Israel [Si]. A major city in the Judean Hills that has been occupied continuously for many millennia and which contains some of the most sacred sites in the world for at least three of today's major religions. Excavations in the city have gone on almost continuously since the work of Charles Warren in 1867–70, rather little of the city's early history remaining visible because of the succession of destructive episodes in its more recent past.

The first major constructions on the site were the stone walls of the Late Bronze Age citadel, a Jebusite town that stood on the ridge of Ophel. Jerusalem was captured by the Israelites under King David in c.996 BC and they covered Ophel with their town. Solomon added the temple immediately to the north and a palace nearby. The city fell to the Babylonians in c.587 BC and was extensively destroyed. It was rebuilt about 540 BC under Persian patronage. The present plan of the city dates back to the time of Herod the Great, around 37–35 BC, who constructed his palace and a massive new temple mount over earlier structures. The city was again razed by Titus in AD 70. In AD 130, during the reign of Hadrian, it became a Roman *colonia* and was rebuilt. At this time the Jews were forbidden entry to the city.

In AD 330 Jerusalem was transformed into a Christian city, with a major phase of church-building patronized by the Byzantine emperors. The Church of the Holy Sepulchre was built by Constantine the Great; other churches include the Eleona Church and the Church of the Ascension on the Mount of Olives. In AD 638 the city fell into Muslim hands and, except for a brief period of domination by the Crusaders in 1099–1187, has remained so ever since. Muslims believe that Muhammad began his night journey to heaven from the city. The place where this happened is now under the Dome of the Rock, built in AD 685–92, and by far the most striking Islamic building in the city.

[Rep.: K. M. Kenyon, 1974, *Digging up Jerusalem*. London: Ernest Benn]

Jesse window [Ar]. A style of 12th-century AD church window which portrays the genealogy of Christ. At the base a vine issues from a reclining figure of Jesse to form a series of oval spaces. Each space contains the figure of a king with a prophet by his side. The end of the series shows the Holy Mother with Christ above her surrounded by the end branches of the vine.

jet [Ma]. A kind of fossil wood found in geologically young shales and related rocks. It is hard, dense, and black in colour. It will take a strong polish which together with its workability made it ideal for jewellery. Jet was exploited by many cultures that had access to outcrops from prehistoric times onwards. In Britain the main source of jet is around Whitby. *See also* SHALE.

jettied [De]. Term to describe a style of timber-framed house found in Europe from the 13th century AD, especially in towns, where each successive storey overhangs the one below to provide larger rooms towards the top of the building.

jetton [Ar]. A kind of token with an engraved design that could be used as a gaming piece or in private commercial transactions.

Jobey, George (1918–92) [Bi]. British archaeologist and specialist in the Roman period of northern Britain. Born in Tynemouth, Northumberland, he was educated at the Municipal High School and Durham University. During WW2 he served in North Africa and the Italian campaigns with the Durham Light Infantry and was awarded the DSO. In 1944 he was badly wounded and invalided home, returning to his old school as history master. In 1947 he became staff tutor responsible for military education in the extra-mural studies of what was later to become Newcastle University. Over the next few years his interests shifted to archaeology, a subject he had taken some classes in at university, and he built up a skilled team of excavators. In 1972 he was transferred to the Department of Archaeology in Newcastle University, in 1974 being promoted to a readership, and in 1981 he was given a personal Chair in Prehistoric Archaeology. Throughout the 1960s and 1970s he surveyed and excavated settlements of the later prehistoric and Roman periods around his native Northumberland.

[Obit.: *Daily Telegraph*, 21 January 1992]

Jogassian Culture [CP]. Provincial late HALL-STATT culture of northeastern France, named after the cemetery site at Les Jogasses in the Marne, which itself continued in use into the ensuing early LA TÈNE phase of the Marne Culture.

John (Balliol) [Na]. King of Scotland of the House of Balliol from 1292. Born *c*.1250, son of Dervorguilla, great-great-granddaughter of David I, and John de Balliol. Married Isabella, daughter of John, earl of Surrey. Abdicated 1296 and died 1313 aged *c*.63, having reigned three years.

John (Lackland) [Na]. English king of the House of Anjou (Plantagenets) from 1199. Born 1167, fifth son of Henry II. Married (1) Isabella or Avisa, daughter of William, earl of Gloucester (divorced); (2) Isabella, daughter of Aymer, count of Angoulême. Died in 1216 aged 48, having reigned seventeen years.

Jomon [CP]. The earliest postglacial period in Japan, characterized by hunter-gatherer communities, conventionally divided into six main periods between 10 000 and 300 BC. The oldest is the Incipient (10 000–7500 BC), followed by the Earlier (7500–5000 BC). From the Early Jomon (5000–3500 BC) there are settled villages and an increasing use of marine resources resulting in a well-known series of midden sites. During the Middle Jomon (3500–2500 BC) widespread trading networks develop, and ritual structures become more common. In the Late Jomon (2500–1000 BC) settlement systems collapse in the Chubu and Kanto regions. In the Final Jomon (1000–300 BC) there is increasing development of deep-sea fisheries, the development of rice agriculture by the north Kyushu groups, and the beginning of pottery production.

Jómsvikinga Saga [Do]. Icelandic saga, written down *c*.AD 1200, which tells of the foundation of a fortified camp on the southern coast of the Baltic by a Dane from Funen. In the camp, Jómsborg, lives a military elite under strict discipline. The saga owes much to a 12th-century nascent chivalry, but perhaps enshrines the memory of garrison camps like those of Svein Forkbeard in Denmark.

Jorvik [Si]. *See* YORK.

jug [De]. A flagon or handled jar with a spout.

Julia Domna [Na]. Wife of the Emperor Septimius Severus and a Syrian by origin, Julia Domna was a woman of great character and personality who wielded considerable political authority during both her husband's reign and that of her son, Caracalla. In statuary Julia Domna is often represented as Ceres. She is known to have taken a great interest in eastern religions.

Julian[us], Flavius Claudius [Na]. Roman emperor, of the royal House of Constantine, born c.AD 332, proclaimed emperor in AD 355, who fought for four years against the Franks and Alamanni (AD 356–9). In AD 363, he invaded Persia and won some successes, but was killed in battle. Unlike the other 4th-century emperors, Julian was a pagan. He tried to promote pagan observances and was later nicknamed 'the Apostate'.

Julius Caesar [Na]. *See* CAESAR.

Jupiter [Di]. Roman god of light—the sun and the moon—and of celestial phenomena such as the wind, rain, thunder, tempest, and lightning. From his Etruscan origins he was equipped with three thunderbolts that could be used to warn or punish mortals.

Justinian[us], Flavius Petrus Sabbatius [Na]. Roman emperor, born in c.AD 482, the nephew of the emperor Justin whom he succeeded in AD 527. Responsible for the reconquest of much of the western Mediterranean—Africa, Italy, and part of Spain—for major reforms of Roman law, and for the great church of St Sophia at Constantinople. Died c.AD 565.

Jutes [CP]. Germanic people, believed to have occupied the northern part of the Danish peninsula (Jutland) at the beginning of the migration period. Some of them are traditionally said to have taken part in the invasion of Britain, and have been traced to Kent and southern England.

Juvenal [Na]. Famous as the author of *The Sixteen Satires*, Juvenal was born in about AD 55 in Spain. He saw military service as the commander of an auxiliary unit in Britain under Agricola. He then spent most of his life in Rome cultivating social contacts. The *Satires* were published in the early second century AD.

Juxtlahuaca Cave, Guerrero, Mexico [Si]. A deep cave extending nearly 2 km into the hills of Guerrero east of Chilpancingo near the village of Colotipa. Important because of the polychrome paintings in some of the inner passages approximately 1.2 km from the entrance which were discovered by art historian Gillett Griffin and retired Italian businessman Carlo Gay. The paintings are believed to date to about 1000 BC, the oldest documented in the Americas, and were done in the Olmec style, although the site lies well outside the heartland of Olmec influence. Among the images is a tall bearded figure in a red and yellow striped tunic, limbs clad in jaguar pelts, brandishing a trident-like object over a second, black-faced figure interpreted as a captive. Other motifs include the feathered serpent, jaguars, and crosses resembling St Andrew's cross. Throughout Mesoamerica, caves and caverns were held to be entrances into the underworld; this site may have been connected with secret rites celebrated by Olmec living on the edge of their domain.

[Rep.: A. K. Romne, 1973, *The Mixtecans of Juxtlahuaca, Mexico*. Huntington, NY: R. E. Krieger]

Kabáh, Mexico [Si]. Maya ceremonial centre of the late Classic period in Yucatán. The best-known structure in the centre is the Codz Poop palace, a range of buildings whose façade is covered with long-nosed masks. Little is known about the history of the site although its main occupation seems to have been in the 8th to 10th centuries AD, after which it was abandoned. A paved causeway or *sacbe* linked the site to the nearby city of Uxmal.

[Sum.: G. de la Barrera y Alvárez, 1950, *Chichén Itzá, Uxmal y Babah en el arte Maya*. Mexico: Secretaría de Educacion Publica]

kabal [Ar]. A simple turntable used in pottery manufacture in the New World.

Kachemak Tradition [CP]. Early Arctic coastal communities living on Kodiak Island, the Alaska Peninsula and Cook Inlet in North America in the period 500 BC to AD 1100. Descendants of the Ocean Bay Tradition, but more sedentary with extensive living sites marked by middens which include hearths and storage pits. Hunting included birds, whales, fish, and shellfish. The material culture of these groups is rich and includes both ground and chipped stone tools, bone points and harpoons, and fishing equipment. Personal ornaments are also abundant. Skulls interpreted as trophy heads occur, with features modelled in clay and inset with artificial bone eyes.

Kageran [Ge]. Formerly the first pluvial period dated to the lower Pleistocene. Now more or less abandoned or incorporated with the KAMASIAN.

Kalambo Falls, Tanzania [Si]. An in-situ Lower Palaeolithic site and a series of later deposits beside a small lake basin behind the lip of the 220 m high Kalambo Falls on the Kalambo River on the border between Tanzania and Zambia. Discovered in 1953, the area has been extensively surveyed and excavated by J. Desmond Clark and a large team of international collaborators.

The earliest deposits are the remains of dry-season encampment by Acheulian communities around 200 000 years ago. An arc of stones may be the remains of a windbreak, while two grass-filled hollows may be sleeping places. Bone was not preserved at the site, but pieces of wood appear to show deliberate shaping and burning. Pollen shows that plants favouring a rather cooler and damper climate than prevails in the area today were present in the late Acheulean. These in-situ deposits are amongst the very few such Lower Palaeolithic sites in the world. The area was also occupied around 100 000 years ago with Sangoan and later Lupemban industry flintwork recovered from later deposits.

[Rep.: J. D. Clark, 1969–74, *Kalambo Falls prehistoric sites*. Cambridge: CUP, 2 vols.]

Kamasian [Ge]. Second pluvial period in Africa, dated to the middle Pleistocene.

Kaminaljuyù, Guatemala [Si]. A large Maya ceremonial centre and settlement in the southern highlands on the western outskirts of Guatemala City. Originating in the Formative stage (early Pre-Classic), the most important occupation dates to the Miraflores Phase (*c*.100 BC to AD 100). From this period there are over 200 mounds of mud brick, some of several phases. Tombs were sometimes dug into the mounds, many with luxury grave goods and evidence for the sacrifice and ritual burial of the retainers of the deceased. Mound E-III-3 is typical and consists of several superimposed temple pyramids which in its final form rose to a height of 18 m. Each successive building operation took place to house the remains of an exalted person, whose burial place was constructed in the top of the pyramid as a pit formed from a series of stepped rectangles of decreasing size. The corpse was deposited in the lowest, smallest part of the pit, grave goods being set on the steps rising up all around.

After about AD 200 there is a hiatus in the use of parts of the site, before a phase of regeneration and reconstruction in the Classic Stage accompanied by an influx of Teotihucán material. At this time the site seems to have controlled obsidian production on the Pacific slopes and contact between central Mexico and Teotihuacán. A group of temple pyramids and a ball-court were constructed near the centre of the site, and rich tombs continued to be built. Its wealth and importance may be related to the local production of cacao and cotton.

[Rep.: A. V. Kidder, J. L. Jennings, and E. M. Stook, 1946, *Excavations at Kaminaljuyú, Guatemala*. Washington: Carnegie Institution]

Kanjeran [Ge]. Third pluvial period in Africa, dated to the later part of the middle Pleistocene.

kantharos (catharus) [Ar]. A type of drinking cup popular in the classical world from the 6th to the 3rd centuries. Distinctive whether in metal or ceramic in having two vertical handles which often project above the rim. Early examples are often stemmed.

Karanovo, Bulgaria [Si]. Large tell in the Azmak Valley near Nova Zagora, whose deposits span the early Neolithic through to the middle Bronze Age and provide not only a full account of the cultural history of southern Bulgaria but also an important sequence connecting central Europe with southeastern Europe. Excavated by V. Mikov and G. Georgiev in the late 1930s, more than 12 m of deposit were investigated and grouped into seven levels. Levels I and II represent the early Neolithic, part of the STARČEVO group of cultures, with square houses built of wattle and daub. Level III has VESELINOVO associations with dark burnished and carinated pottery. Level IV is characterized as Kalojanovec culture and seems to reflect a local tradition. Level V has Marica Culture material including graphite painted wares and excised pottery. Together, levels IV and V are contemporary with the late Neolithic VINČA CULTURES of the western Balkans. The very thick level VI is the GUMELNIŢA horizon with graphite painted wares and the evidence for an emergent copper metallurgy. In this period the tradition for small square houses was changed, and rather larger rectangular structures, many with more than one room, were built, most of them internally plastered and painted. After a stratigraphic hiatus the final level (VII) belongs to the early Bronze Age.

[Rep.: S. Hiller, 1988, *Tell Karanovo 1987*. Saltsburg: Institut für Alte Geschichte und Altertumskunde der Universität Saltzburg]

Karari industry [CP]. A Lower Palaeolithic stoneworking industry found in northern Kenya and surrounding areas and within the OLDOWAN tradition. Dates to between 1.5 and 1.25 million years ago. It includes bifaces and a greater range of tool types than its predecessors.

Karasuk Culture [CP]. Bronze Age communities who succeeded the ANDRONOVO CULTURE in southern Siberia and Kazakhstan in the later 2nd millennium BC. Karasuk communities were farmers who specialized in sheep husbandry. Settlements include pit-houses; cemeteries include stone cists covered by low mounds set in a square stone enclosure. Metalwork was well developed, the most distinctive products being a kind of bronze knife or dagger with a curved profile and a decorated handle. Their art includes the extensive use of realistic animal images, a style that perhaps later contributed to the Scytho-Siberian animal art style. Remains of Karasuk Culture bridles mark the beginning of horse-riding on the Siberian steppe.

Kassites [CP]. Originally one of the Elamite tribes living in the Zagros mountainous district east of Babylon. In the early 2nd millennia BC they infiltrated part of Babylonia, founding a dynasty based on Babylon after the HITTITE raid of 1595 BC. This empire lasted for nearly 500 years but has been studied very little. During that time Kassites became integrated with the Babylonian population, their kings taking on Semitic names. Some Kassite deities were introduced into the Babylonian pantheon, and it is probable that their sacred animal, the horse, was introduced into Mesopotamia. Horse-breeding and riding were established skills among the Kassites. The Kassite rule ended in *c*.1157 BC with the conquest of Babylonia by ASSYRIA.

Kayenta [CP]. Regional variant of the ANASAZI TRADITION which flourished in northwest Arizona. Mainly recognized through distinctive ceramics and architectural styles.

keep [Co]. Central stronghold of a medieval castle.

Keiller, Alexander (1890–1955) [Bi]. British archaeologist best known for his excavations at Windmill and Avebury and his pioneer flights recording the archaeology of Wessex from the air. Born in Dundee, Scotland, he was a member of the wealthy Keiller family, well known amongst other things for their marmalade and preserves. Educated at Eton, at the age of nine he became sole heir to the company and his family's fortune, and devoted the rest of his life to spending it. He became interested in aircraft and went flying intermittently from 1909 onwards, becoming a pilot in the Royal Naval Air Service in WW1. After meeting and becoming firm friends with O. G. S. Crawford, the two undertook what have become historic flights across the Wessex landscape recording archaeological sites using a captured German Service Type F.KI camera purchased from the Disposals Board and a De Havilland Company DH9 aeroplane. The work was published in 1924 as *Wessex from the air* (Oxford: OUP).

One of the sites they photographed was Windmill Hill in Wiltshire, and in 1925, after it was threatened by the construction of radio masts, Keiller bought it and began excavating it. He subsequently bought further land in the area, including much of Avebury and the adjoining West Kennet Avenue. Though much of the work was done in conjunction with the Office of Works, the whole cost of undertaking it was met by Keiller. To provide a base for operations he established the Morvan Institute of Archaeological Research (named after the Keiller estate in Aberdeenshire) in a small building near Avebury Manor which is now the site museum. The excavations took place between 1925 and 1939, with restoration works thereafter to open the site for public viewing. In 1943 he transferred the whole Avebury Estate to the National Trust.

Keiller was not only interested in archaeology, however. Before WW1 he owned a car manufacturing company which in 1919 went bankrupt, but he was passionately interested in motorcars and owned a string of rather fast ones. He was an expert skier and was president of the British Ski Jumping Club in 1932.

During his life he had four wives, a string of mistresses, but no heirs. Keiller was elected a Fellow of the Society of Antiquaries in 1927 and of the Geological Society in 1928.

[Bio.: L. J. Murray, 1999, *A zest for life. The story of Alexander Keiller*. Wootton Bassett: Morven Books]

Keith, Sir Arthur (1866–1955) [Bi]. British anatomist and anthropologist, best known in archaeology for his numerous reports on human skeletons mainly from excavations of prehistoric sites. Born in Aberdeen, he studied medicine at Aberdeen University, where he took first-class honours in 1888. He then studied at Leipzig and University College, London. In 1894 he was admitted MD of the University of Aberdeen. In the same year he was appointed Senior Demonstrator of Anatomy at the London Hospital Medical College, a post he held for twelve years. In 1908 he was appointed Conservator and Arnott Demonstrator at the Royal College of Surgeons, and in 1917 he became Fullerton Professor of Physiology at the Royal Institution. Throughout, his main interest lay in applying his knowledge of anatomy, physiology, and pathology to anthropological material. His work in this field was so conspicuous that he was selected President of the Anthropological Institute in 1912. In 1913 he was elected a Fellow of the Royal Society and in 1921 his services to science were recognized with a knighthood.

[Obit.: *The Times*, 8 January 1955]

Keller, Ferdinand (1800–81) [Bi]. Swiss archaeologist and prehistorian who was ordained as a priest but subsequently became Director of the Zurich Museum and pioneered the investigation of the Swiss 'lake-dwellings'. With other researchers he recognized that these settlements were not of one period, but showed a progression from Stone Age to Iron Age, providing further corroboration of the THREE AGE SYSTEM.

[Obit.: *Proceedings of the Society of Antiquaries of London*, 9 (1881–3), 122]

Kells, Co. Meath, Ireland [Si]. A monastery was founded at Kells in *c*.AD 804 as a refuge for Columban monks from Iona which had been attacked by the Vikings two years earlier. They brought with them a lavishly ornamented book which later become known as the **Book of Kells**. It is one of the earliest surviving illuminated manuscripts in Europe and contains gospels, prefaces, summaries, and concordances, and a large portion relating to 11th-century legal documents relating to the abbey of Kells. It is written on vellum. In AD 1152 the monastery was made a bishopric, but the community did not survive the Middle Ages and all that remains of the monastery is a ROUND TOWER more than 30 m high. The Book of Kells is now in Trinity College, Dublin.

[Sum.: L. Judge, 1993, *The story of Kells*. Kells: Kells Publishing Company]

Keltaminar Culture [CP]. Neolithic communities occupying the area east of the Caspian Sea through to the upper Tobal River catchment in southern Russia, Kazakhstan, and Uzbekistan in the 4th and 3rd millennia BC. In the early stages these communities relied on hunting and gathering for their subsistence base, but later they became involved with stock-breeding and animal husbandry. The flint industry was essentially of Mesolithic derivation, microlith-based. Pottery consists of large bag-shaped vessels with pointed bases, the outer surfaces being decorated with short incisions arranged in rows and sometimes forming patterns. Succeeded by the AFANASIEVO CULTURE.

Kemble, John Mitchell (1807–57) [Bi]. British philologist and historian whose studies concentrated attention on Anglo-Saxon language and history. His publications included a major edition of the poem *Beowulf* (1833) and a significant paper in 1856 in which he drew attention to the similarities in material from England and from Hanover.

[Bio.: R. A. Wiley, 1979, Anglo-Saxon Kemble: the life and works of John Mitchell Kemble, 1807–1857. *Anglo-Saxon studies in archaeology and history* (Oxford: British Archaeological Reports British Series 72), 165–273]

Kendrick, Sir Thomas Downing (1895–1979) [Bi]. British archaeologist who became Director of the British Museum. Born in Birmingham he was educated at Charterhouse and Oriel College, Oxford. In WW1 he served in the Warwickshire Regiment and was severely wounded while fighting in France. He returned to Oriel in 1919 and read anthropology. He began a study of the archaeology of the Channel Islands, but in 1922 joined the Department of British and Medieval Antiquities in the British Museum, becoming Assistant Keeper in 1928, Keeper in 1938, and

in 1950 was appointed Director and Principal Librarian, a post he held until his retirement in 1959. Kendrick had infectious enthusiasm, as shown by his numerous publications that include: *The Axe Age* (1925, London: Methuen) and *Late Saxon and Viking art* (1949, London: Methuen). He was elected a Fellow of the British Academy in 1941 and a Fellow of the Society of Antiquaries in 1934. In 1951 he was knighted.

[Obit.: *The Times*, 23 November 1979]

Kennewick, Washington, USA [Si]. The burial of a single adult male on land controlled by the US Army Corps of Engineers that has caused considerable legal and ethical turmoil over questions of ownership, cultural affinity, and the needs and desirability of scientific analysis. Known as the Kennewick Man, the skeleton was found in 1996 by spectators at a boat race after the remains eroded from an embankment. Upon examination it was found that, rather unusually, a stone projectile point was embedded in the pelvis. A radiocarbon determination dates the remains to about 7300–7600 BC (8410 ± 60 BP, UCR-3476). Initially, the Army Corps of Engineers proposed that the remains were culturally affiliated to the local Umatilla tribe and agreed repatriation. However, competing claims were brought forward, amongst them a claim by a group of scientists who want to study the remains. In September 2000 that USA's Department of the Interior determined its view that the remains were those of a Native American and were covered by NAGPRA. Five claimants were identified in the ruling and at the end of 2000 the remains were still in storage in a museum in Seattle. While the first part of the judgement is widely accepted, considerable concern has been expressed over the generality of the wide-ranging cultural attribution which many believe runs contrary to both the spirit of NAGPRA and the potential for the scientific investigation of early people and their societies.

[Sum.: S. Hutt, 2000, Meriwether Lewis and Kennewick Man: two travellers in reluctant pursuit of a eulogy. In D. F. Craib (ed.), *Topics in cultural resource law*. Washington: Society for American Archaeology, 59–68]

Kenniff Cave, Australia [Si]. A rock-shelter situated in the sandstone hills of eastern central Queensland which contains one of the longest and most complete cultural sequences in Australia. Excavations by John

Mulvaney in 1962 revealed deposits spanning the period 17000 BC through to 550 BC. The stone tools from the lowest levels through to about 3000 BC comprised steep-edge flake scrapers and cores. Between 3000 BC and 550 BC there was an extensive assemblage of Australian Small Tool Tradition. Pieces of ochre were scatted right through the sequence. The walls of the cave carry images of stencilled hands and other images including boomerangs, shields, and spear-throwers.

[Rep.: D. J. Mulvaney and E. B. Joyce, 1965, Archaeological and geomorphological investigations at Mt Moffatt Station, Queensland, Australia. *Proceedings of the Prehistoric Society*, 31, 147–212]

Kensington Stone, Minnesota, USA [Si]. A stone slab found in the late 19th century with an inscription in RUNES purporting to record the arrival of VIKINGS. Always controversial, it is now dismissed as a fake.

[Rev.: G. Daniel, 1958, The Minnesota petroglyph. *Antiquity*, 32, 264–7]

Kenyon, Kathleen (1906–78) [Bi]. British archaeologist who pioneered the application of stratigraphic excavation in the Near East. Born in London, daughter of Sir Fredrick Kenyon who was Director of the British Museum. Educated at St Paul's Girls' School and Somerville College, Oxford, where she read modern history and obtained a third-class degree in 1928. She took an active interest in the university's Archaeology Society and was the first woman to be elected President. After travelling to Zimbabwe with an expedition organized by the British Association she joined the team of archaeologists working for Mortimer Wheeler at Verulamium. In 1931 she joined J. W. Crowfoot's expedition to Samaria, almost single-handedly introducing British excavation methods to the region. Returning to work in Britain at Leicester and elsewhere in the late 1930s she was drawn into Wheeler's plans for the Institute of Archaeology in London, of which she was Secretary between 1935 and 1948, and Acting Director 1942–6. After WW2 she was appointed to a lectureship in Palestinian Archaeology at the Institute, but the political situation in the Near East prevented her from immediate involvement in fieldwork. Instead she excavated at Sabratha, Libya, from 1948 until 1951. In 1951 she became Honorary Director of the British School in Jerusalem and in 1952 she began a pro-gramme of excavations at Jericho in the Jordan Valley, followed in 1961 by excavations in Jerusalem. In 1962 she left the Institute of Archaeology to become Principal of St Hugh's College, Oxford, where she remained until retirement in 1973. Although not always popular amongst her peers, her excavations and surveys fundamentally changed understandings of the prehistory of Palestine and the Near East. Her translation of the Wheeler box method of excavation to the Near East made such an impact that it is often referred to as the Wheeler–Kenyon method. In 1973 she was appointed DBE.

[Obit.: *The Times*, 25 August 1978]

kerb [Co]. A ring of stone slabs or boulders (**kerbstones**) defining and revetting the edge of a cairn or barrow.

Kerma kingdom [CP]. An independent Nubian kingdom or city-state of the early 2nd millennium BC, based at the site of Kerma near the third cataract of the River Nile in modern Sudan. One of the states of KUSH, the Kerma kingdom reached its height around 1700 BC following a contraction of the Egyptian civilization during the 13th Dynasty. Heavily involved in long-distance trade, the Kerma kingdom accumulated considerable wealth. Kerma rulers were buried under huge barrows up to 80 m across. The Kerma kingdom ended with the Egyptian reconquest of Nubia during the 18th Dynasty.

kernos [Ar]. A ceramic jar with an integral series of small cups in its lip. Found in the eastern Mediterranean and dating mainly to the Bronze Age, the function of such vessels is uncertain.

kero [Ar]. A large wooden beaker with either straight or concave flaring sides. They are usually decorated with incised geometric patterns during INCA times, but later have scenes painted in lacquer. Similar vessels are known in pottery from earlier (TIAHUANACO) times.

Khan [Ge]. Turkish title for a prince or ruler.

Khent-amenty [Di]. Egyptian god, ancient jackal-headed god of Abydos, late identified with Osiris.

Khephri (Khephre) [Di]. Egyptian god, the scarab-beetle god, associated with Ra as the young sun god.

Khmer [CP]. Linguistically linked ethnic groups occupying Cambodia, southern Vietnam, and adjacent parts of Thailand, who developed an extensive but relatively short-lived empire around the turn of the 1st millennium AD, dominating their traditional areas and also Thailand and southern Laos. Their beginnings can be traced back to the 3rd millennium BC when rice cultivators moved down the Mekong into Cambodia. By 1500 BC they had developed bronze casting, and from 500 BC iron was being used. During the later 1st millennium BC the population grew, chiefdoms developed, and steps were taken to cope better with the environment. As the Khmer empire grew, water controls in the form of ditches around settlements and channels linking the fields to allow water distribution in the dry season and drainage in the wet season spread. The capital is at Angkor which during this period became a very wealthy city. Destroyed by the Thais about AD 1400.

Khonsu (Khons) [Di]. Egyptian god, one of the triad of Thebes, child of Mut and Amun. A moon god, shown as a young man with the side-lock of youth, a staff in his hand and the horns and disc of the moon on his head. Has several forms: worshipped at Karnak as Khonsu Neferhotep; and has an aspect as expeller of demons.

Khum [Di]. Egyptian god, ram-headed god of the Cataract Region. He was the consort of Anuket and Satet. A creator god, he was thought to have fashioned man on his potter's turntable. Worshipped at Elephantine, Esna, Silsileh, and in Nubia.

kick [De]. The raised centre of a base which rises to a hollow peak.

Kidder, Alfred Vincent (1885–1963) [Bi]. American archaeologist trained at Harvard and widely travelled in Europe and the Near East, renowned for his application of stratigraphic principles to excavation and the use of interdisciplinary techniques. Above all, he helped move archaeology from an antiquarian pursuit into a scientific discipline. From 1916 Kidder excavated at Pecos, New Mexico, a pueblo site near Santa Fe which was, at the time, the largest excavation that had taken place in North America. The work provided an important artefact sequence and classification which helped build a chronol-

ogy for the American southwest which still stands today. Kidder also carried out a series of excavations and surveys at Maya sites on behalf of the Carnegie Institution. In 1927 Kidder initiated the Pecos Conference to bring archaeologists together to exchange information and agree basic standards.

[Bio.: R. B. Woodbury, 1973, *Alfred Kidder.* New York: Columbia University Press]

Killke [CP]. Style of ceramics dating to the late Intermediate Period and found in the Cuzco area of Peru. First recognized by J. H. Rowe, Killke pottery is characterized by globular forms, white or buff slip coating, and simple geometric decoration, usually in black or black on red.

kill site [Ge]. Place where one or more animals were killed and butchered by hunters. They are represented archaeologically by animal bones, weapons, and butchery tools, and sometimes traps or other devices constructed or used by the hunters to enhance their chances of success.

kiln [MC]. A kind of oven, purpose-built for firing pottery, bricks, or other kinds of ceramic materials. At its most simple, a **clamp kiln** need comprise no more than a pile of fuel on which is placed the material to be fired, the whole being covered with a layer of turf or sods before the fuel is lit from below and allowed to burn through. In the **updraught kiln** a firebox contains the source of heat which can be stoked and replenished as necessary, the hot gases and smoke from the fire being drawn through a chamber in which the material to be fired has been stacked. The chamber may be above or to one side of the firebox.

Kimberley point [Ar]. Bifacially worked stone and flint projectile tips found mainly in the Kimberley region of Western Australia and traded widely in northern and central Australia. Fashioned using pressure flaking, Kimberley points sometimes have serrated edges. They were being made at European contact, and have been made since, using materials such as glass and porcelain. The antiquity of form is not, however, known.

Kimmeridge Shale [Ma]. A soft, fine-grained rock quarried in Dorset in the Iron Age and the Roman period. Manufactured articles include parts of furniture.

kin [Ge]. A period of time in the Maya LONG COUNT equal to a single day.

Kingdoms [CP]. The three Kingdoms of ancient Egypt represent peaks in the development of early Egyptian society, separated by phases of disorder and decline. The Old Kingdom spans the 3rd to 6th Dynasties (*c*.2658–2150 BC); the Middle Kingdom spans the 12th to 13th Dynasties (*c*.2100–1750 BC); and the New Kingdom spans the 18th to 20th Dynasties (*c*.1550–1070 BC).

kin-group [De]. A group of people related by blood rather than, for example, age or gender. *See also* KINSHIP.

kinship [Ge]. In anthropology, relationships between people that are based on real or imagined descent or, sometimes, on marriage. Kinship ties impose mutual obligations on all members of a kin group; these ties were at the core of most prehistoric societies.

kitchen midden [MC]. *See* SHELL MIDDEN.

kiva [Co]. A subterranean or semi-subterranean room, usually circular in plan, used for ceremonial purposes and meetings among the pueblo cultures of the southwestern USA.

knapping [Ge]. A general term used to describe the process of working flint or stone either by percussion (direct or indirect) or by pressure.

Knapton ware [Ar]. Type of crude hand-made pottery dating to the 4th century AD. Manufactured and circulated in the Humberside area of northeastern England.

knarr (Knörr) [De]. Scandinavian name for the heavy cargo ships used by merchants and by the settlers of the Atlantic islands.

knife [Ar]. *See also* BACKED BLADE.

knight jug [Ar]. Style of medieval jug with a tubular spout and representations of horses and knights decorating the body, dating to the 14th century AD and later in Europe.

Knighton Heath Period [CP]. A phase of the British early Bronze Age spanning the period 1400–1200 BC which was defined by Colin Burgess in the late 1970s. Coming immediately after the BEDD BRANWEN PERIOD and the later part of the WESSEX CULTURE little remained of the tradition of prestigious burial and complex ritual which had existed for thousands of years. DEVEREL–RIMBURY ceramics dominate during the period, flat cremation cemeteries being the norm. Regional styles including the Ardleigh Urns in East Anglia and Trevisker Urns in Cornwall represent local variations. In metalworking the period coincides with the end of the ACTON PARK PHASE and the beginning of the TAUNTON PHASE which connects British metalwork into the wider European scene far more securely. The Knighton Heath period is succeeded by the PENARD PERIOD.

Knights Hospitallers [Ge]. The Hospital of St John of Jerusalem was founded in the late 11th century, originally to care for pilgrims to Jerusalem. The calling of the brothers was principally to care for the sick, but as time went on the emphasis shifted to a military role: that of fighting for the faith. In AD 1187 the knights were driven out of Jerusalem by Saladin and moved to Acre and then Cyprus. They retreated further to Rhodes in 1308, absorbing the KNIGHTS TEMPLAR in 1312. In 1522 the knights were expelled from Rhodes by the Turks and sought a new base to continue their fight for Christendom. Charles V of Spain gave them Malta and in AD 1530 they settled there, drawing on the wealth generated by properties all over Europe. The knights became more and more of an anachronism and surrendered without a blow when faced by the revolutionary fervour of the French in AD 1798.

Knights Templar [Ge]. An international military order, originally founded to protect pilgrims after the recapture of Jerusalem in AD 1099. After scandals in 1307–8 the Knights Templar were severely constrained and in 1312 all their possessions were passed to the Knights Hospitallers.

Knossos, Crete, Greece [Si]. Minoan palace famed in antiquity as the home of the legendary King Minos, and location of the labyrinth with its monstrous bull-headed Minotaur. Situated in north central Crete, 5 km from the coast, the site was known in the 19th century AD and a variety of archaeologists including Heinrich Schliemann excavated there. It was the work of Sir Arthur Evans between 1900 and 1929 which really opened the site up. The earliest occupation extends back to about 6000 BC with an aceramic Neolithic exploiting the agricultural potential of the fertile and well-watered valley. By 1900 BC the Neolithic settlement had expanded considerably and even as early as 2400 BC had within it some substantial structures and the first signs of a densely occupied town. The main elements of the palace had been built by about 1900 BC, although it continued to expand and change. At the centre lay a great court, flanked on the west by a second court. Near the west wing were storehouses. Artefacts recovered from here and elsewhere in the palace showed extensive trading with Egypt and the Near East.

Around 1700 BC Crete was devastated by a massive earthquake and the palace was destroyed. The builders of the second palace levelled the earlier structure, removing many deposits in the process. This new structure flourished between 1700 and 1450 BC, a time when Crete reached its zenith of cultural sophistication and power. The complexity of the internal arrangement of the second palace is clearly the origin of the labyrinth myth, although in fact there is some order to the structure. The prime functions of the palace were economic and religious, and this is reflected in the remains found which include eighteen storerooms, seals and Linear A and Linear B writing tablets, and cult equipment. The Knossos throne room has a magnificent throne flanked by wall paintings showing griffins and projects an image of divine power. Around 1450 BC the town that had grown up around the palace was destroyed, the palace itself surviving until around 1375 BC. Its final destruction is linked to a Minoan rebellion again Mycenaean overlordship.

[Rep.: J. D. S. Pendlebury, 1974, *A handbook to the Palace of Minos, Knossos, with its dependencies* (2nd edition). London: Macdonald and Janes]

Knoviz Culture [CP]. A regional group of the central European URNFIELD CULTURE found in Bohemia, Bavaria, and parts of Thuringia between 1400 and 900 BC.

Knowth, Co. Meath, Ireland [Si]. Large passage grave cemetery on the north side of the River Boyne in central Ireland. Extensively excavated and restored by George Eogan from 1961 onwards, the site is one of three such cemeteries in what is known as the Bend of the Boyne between Drogheda and Slane. In the 4th millennium BC the cemetery is dominated by simple passage graves, eighteen of which have been recorded, but around 3200 BC work started on the construction of a large DEVELOPED PASSAGE GRAVE over 60 m in diameter. It covers two chambers, each approached by a passage, one opening into each side of the mound. The mound is surrounded by a kerb of decorated slabs, while further stones bearing PASSAGE GRAVE ART lie in the chambers and along the sides of the approach passages. *See also* NEWGRANGE and DOWTH.

[Sum.: G. Eogan, 1986, *Knowth*. London: Thames & Hudson]

Knut (Canute) [Na]. Younger son of Svein Forkbeard, king of Denmark. After 1016 king of England (through his father's conquest) and from 1018 king of Denmark, on the death of his elder brother. After 1030 he also became king of Norway, but his powerful North Sea empire collapsed at his death in AD 1035.

Kodiak Tradition [CP]. Early Arctic coastally based hunter-gatherer communities living on Kodiak Island and the adjacent mainland of Alaska in the period 4000 BC through to historic times. Characterized by the extensive use of chipped basalt and polished slate in the production of tools and weapons. The subsistence economy, probably derived from OCEAN BAY TRADITIONS, was based on hunting sea mammals, salmon fishing, and caribou hunting.

Koldewey, Robert (1855–1925) [Bi]. German archaeologist and classicist, best known for his excavations at Babylon between 1899 and 1914. His excavations at Babylon were of a high quality for the time, and the results were published promptly in 1914 as *The excavations at Babylon* (London: Macmillan).

[Bio.: W. Andrae, 1952, *Babylon: die versunkene Weltstadt und ihr Ausgraber Robert Koldeway*. Berlin: W. de Gruyter]

Köln-Lindenthal, Germany [Si]. Early Neolithic LBK village on the middle terrace of the River Rhine on the outskirts of Cologne. The excavations between 1929 and 1934 by W. Buttler were a pioneer attempt to apply open area excavation to a settlement site. At the time the site was interpreted as having a series of timber barns and pit-houses; these can now be reinterpreted as timber long houses and borrow pits. Dating to the period *c*.4300–4100 BC it is also now clear that for much of its life the village lay within a series of enclosures. Seven main periods can be recognized in the occupation of the site, each with an average of 21 houses at any one time. Buttler believed that these phases represent periodic revising of the area as part of a SLASH AND BURN AGRICULTURAL system, but this is no longer accepted.

[Rep.: W. Buttler and G. Haberey, 1936, *Die bandkeramische Ansiedlung bei Köln Lindenthal*, Leipzig]

Koobi Fora, Kenya [Si]. Area of badland landscape in northern Kenya that has yielded an important sequence of early hominid remains and artefacts, although not in good association. The area was discovered by Richard Leakey in 1968, and investigated in subsequent years. There are two cultural traditions represented. The earliest dates to around 1.8 or 2 million years ago, with material of a similar kind to the Oldowan from Olduvai Bed I. Higher in the sequence is Karari industry material dated to 1.5 million years ago and matching well the Bed II finds from Olduvai. In addition to the stone tools there are fossil hominid remains representing at least 150 individuals: four species of *Australopithecus* together with *Homo habilis* and *Homo erectus* are present.

[Rep.: M. G. and R. E. Leakey, 1978, *The fossil hominids and an introduction to their context, 1968–74*. Oxford: Clarendon Press]

kore (kourus) (pl. korai, kouroi) [De]. Conventionally applied to the clothed female and the nude male sculptured figures of the Archaic, pre-Persian War period in Greece: they stand erect with the weight distributed between the feet, of which the left is slightly forward, but no motion is suggested; on their faces is often the 'archaic smile'. The best of these beautiful korai, or maidens, are in the Acropolis Museum at Athens, and of the male figures in the National Museum, where the steady progress of the sculptor's art from the purely static figure to the dynamic is readily seen and enjoyed.

Körös Culture [CP]. Hungarian version of the early Neolithic STARČEVO CULTURE, named for a tributary of the river Tisza, known in Romania as the CRIŞ. One distinguishing trait of the Körös Culture is the use of footed vessels and the relative lack of painted wares. Sometimes referred to as the Starčevo–Körös Culture.

Kossinna, Gustaf (1858–1931) [Bi]. German linguist and prehistorian well known for his nationalistic views on the use of archaeological research. Born in Tilsit, East Prussia, he attended the universities of Göttingen, Leipzig, Berlin, and Strasbourg. He then became a librarian and worked in the library of the University of Berlin from 1892. During this time he read widely on archaeology and published numerous papers on material culture in relation to German territory. Rather strangely, in 1904, he was appointed Professor of German Prehistory in the University of Berlin. Through much of his work he viewed Germany as the centre for numerous developments which spread outwards from there into the wider world. Such views about the central European archaeological record contributed to the ideological base of Nazism during the 1920s and 1930s.

[Not.: B. Arnold, 1990, The past as propaganda: totalitarian archaeology in Nazi Germany. *Antiquity*, 64, 464–78]

Koster, Illinois, USA [Si]. Archaic Stage site spanning the period 7500 BC through to AD 1200 in fourteen distinct cultural horizons represented by over 10.5 m of stratigraphy. Excavated under the direction of Stuart Struever and James Brown in the 1970s, the site is important for its contributions to understanding the changing relationships between the occupants and their environment. The earliest levels show periodic visits by Palaeo-Indian groups. In Horizon 11, there was an Archaic settlement dating to about 6500 BC, a seasonal camp with temporary dwellings covering an area of 0.3 ha. By Horizon 8, *c*.5600–5000 BC, the settlement had become more substantial and more permanent with timber houses. By Horizon 6, *c*.3900–2800 BC the village had expanded to cover 2 ha with perhaps 150 inhabitants. Overall, evidence was recovered for a number of key transitions in subsistence, economy and settlement type: the emergence of sedentism, the development of broadly based subsistence regimes, and the origins of wild-plant cultivation.

[S. Struever and F. Holton, 1979, *Koster: Americans in search of the prehistoric past*. New York: Anchor Press]

Kotosh, Peru [Si]. A major ceremonial centre situated at 1950 m above sea level on the eastern slopes of the central Andes above modern Huanuco. Dating from the late Pre-Ceramic period through to the early Horizon, roughly 3000–1000 BC, the site has four main phases. The earliest (Mito phase) is Pre-Ceramic, but includes the Temple of the Crossed Hands. Square in plan, this temple has a single entrance with a niche on each side facing inwards. Below each niche, modelled in mud plaster, is a pair of crossed human forearms, some of which are larger than the others suggesting perhaps a male/female duality. Around the interior of the temple is a low stone bench; there is a fire-pit in the centre of the floor. The second phase (Waira-Jirca) is associated with ceramics of the Zone Hachure Horizon Style and dates to c.1800–1150 BC. The third phase (Kotash) dates to c.1000–900 BC. During this time the temple was rebuilt following the demolition of its predecessor. New pottery forms are present, including stirrup-spout vessels. Maize was probably being cultivated at this time. The fourth phase (CHAVÍN), is again recognizable by new pottery styles.

[Rep.: S. Izumi and T. Sono, 1963, *Andes 2: excavations at Kotosh, Peru, 1960*. Tokyo: kand o kawa]

Kow Swamp, Australia [Si]. An early burial ground close to the Murray River, Victoria, southern Australia, excavated by Alan Thorne from 1968 to 1972. Dating to between 11 000 BC and 7000 BC the 40 individual burials represent a range of practices while the skeletal material represents an anatomically robust population that lies outside the extremes of the range of recent Aboriginal populations. Some stone tools consisting of quartz flakes and bipolar cores are typical of the period but shed little light on the origins and associations of the population. On the basis of the finds from Kow Swamp, however, Thorne suggests a dual origin for Australia's Aboriginal population. Overall, the Kow Swamp collection is the largest single late Pleistocene population so far recovered: the remains themselves were returned to the local Aboriginal community for reburial.

[Rep.: A. G. Thorne and P. G. Macumber, 1972, Discoveries of Late Pleistocene man at Kow Swamp, Australia. *Nature*, 238, 316–19; D. J. Mulvaney, 1991, Past regained, future lost: the Kow Swamp Pleistocene burials. *Antiquity*, 65, 12–21]

krater [Ar]. A large Greek pottery vessel for mixing wine. Usually with a low footring base and a pair of handles, but shapes otherwise vary, the volute krater, for example, having handles mounted on the shoulder and projecting above the height of the rim.

kremlin [MC]. The fortified citadel of medieval Russian and Slav towns. The best known is the Moscow Kremlin which dates to the 14th century AD. Within it lies a range of palaces and cathedrals, and state buildings in a range of architectural styles spanning the 14th to the 18th centuries. More modern buildings were added in Soviet times to house the country's administration.

Kroeber, Alfred Louis (1876–1960) [Bi]. American anthropologist and archaeologist who advocated the efficiency of seriation as a means of understanding artefact sequences. He formally defined the idea of the HORIZON STYLE. He carried out fieldwork on Californian shell mounds and in Peru he excavated sites at Cahuachi and Estaqueria in the Nasca region.

[Bio.: J. H. Rowe, 1962, Alfred Louis Kroeber, 1876–1960. *American Antiquity*, 27(3), 395–415]

kshemenitsa [MC]. A term used in eastern Europe, of Russian derivation, to refer to a flint scatter of Palaeolithic or Mesolithic date which represents the remains of an open settlement site.

Kuban Culture [CP]. Copper Age communities of the north Caucasus region, especially the Kuban Valley of western Caucasia. Burials were made under KURGANS and were generally rather rich. Battle-axes are common, and there are metal Pontic hammerhead pins.

k'uei [Ar]. Bronze handled bowl designed to contain food. Common in the Zhou Dynasty of China.

Kujavian (Kujavish) grave [MC]. Class of middle Neolithic (TRB CULTURE) burial monuments found in the lower Vistula region of Poland dating to the later 4th millennium BC. Each tomb consists of a triangular or trapezoidal mound, sometimes more than 100 m long and usually surrounded by a stone kerb, covering up to three flat graves containing single inhumations.

Kulli Culture [CP]. Chalcolithic communities occupying southern Baluchistan in the early 3rd millennium BC. Distinguished by their pottery which is wheel-made, buff in colour, and with black painted decoration showing elongated zebu cattle, felines, goats, or spiky trees between zones of geometric ornament. Terracotta bull and female figurines are plentiful. Burial is by cremation; settlements comprise small tells with mud-brick architecture and are associated with evidence of water control and developed agriculture. In the late Kulli Culture there are clear signs of links to the INDUS VALLEY CIVILIZATION and also to early dynastic Mesopotamia.

Kunda Culture [CP]. Mesolithic hunter-gatherer communities of the east Baltic forest zone extending eastwards into northern Russia dating to the period *c*.7000–5000 BC. Most Kunda settlements are located near the edge of the forests beside rivers, lakes, or marshes. Elk was extensively hunted, perhaps helped by trained domestic hunting-dogs. On the coast seal hunting is represented. Pike and other fish were taken from the rivers. There is a rich bone and antler industry, especially in relation to fishing gear. Tools were decorated with simple geometric designs, lacking the complexity of the contemporary MAGLE-MOSIAN communities to the southwest. The Kunda Culture is succeeded by the NARVA CULTURE who use pottery and show some traces of food production.

kurgan [MC]. A Russian term for a mound or barrow covering a burial in a pit-grave, mortuary house, or catacomb-grave. Comparable with the ROUND BARROW of northern Europe, the earliest kurgans date to the 4th millennium BC. Kurgans carry on being built, with fluctuations in popularity, down into SCYTHIAN times and can also be found amongst the Sarmatians of the steppe zone.

Kurgan Culture [CP]. A general and long-lived grouping of successive cultures, proposed by M. Gimbutas as central to the development and spread of populations and material culture in the steppe regions of southern Russian and the Ukraine, and links beyond into eastern and central Europe. The main phases of the Kurgan Culture are differentiated on the basis of the different kinds of graves under the barrows. Thus: pit-graves (Yamnaya), broadly dating to the period *c*.2400–1800 BC; catacomb-graves (Katakombnaya) dating to *c*.2300–1800 BC; and timber-graves (Scrubnaya) dating to *c*.1600–900 BC. The earliest of these focuses on the lower Volga region and is characterized by its contracted inhumation burials which are commonly sprinkled with red ochre. The diffusion westwards of this culture is sometimes equated with the appearance in eastern Europe of corded ware and globular amphorae, and the introduction of Indo-European-speaking peoples.

Kush [CP]. An Egyptian word for Upper Nubia in general and for any independent state that established itself there during periods of Egyptian weakness.

kylix [Ar]. A Greek, shallow pottery cup with pedestal base and two opposed handles, mounted horizontally.

labret [Ar]. A kind of lip stud, usually decorated, and inserted into a ready-made incision in the lower lip. Made of almost any hard material such as stone, bone, metal, or ceramic, they were very popular in Mesoamerica. Examples have been found in almost all parts of the Americas.

labrum [Ar]. A Latin term used to describe a large, shallow basin on a pedestal, usually carved from marble, granite, or a fine-grained stone, and found in the CALDARIUM (and sometimes the FRIGIDARIUM or TEPIDARIUM) of a Roman bath-house. It held hot water.

labyrinth [Co]. A complicated and elaborate arrangement of passages or pathways in which it is easy to get lost and difficult to find the way out. The best-known labyrinth is the legendary example in Crete that was inhabited by the Minotaur who was eventually killed by Theseus with a little help and a ball of string from King Midas' daughter Ariadne. Egyptian labyrinths are also known and the tradition of creating mazes as open-topped labyrinths was widespread in the ancient world. They probably represent dancing grounds on which were performed intricate dances representing the passage of the soul from life to death and back again. There was a curious revival of the tradition of making mazes in the Middle Ages, sponsored by the church; several French and Italian cathedrals have them set into the floor. The hedge-mazes found in gardens are only indirectly related to these early forms; they derive from the Italian geometrical style of gardening which spread through Europe in the 16th century AD. *See also* KNOSSOS.

Laconian ware [Ar]. A type of pottery manufactured at Sparta in Greece in the 6th century BC, including BLACK-FIGURE WARE and black glossed ware. Exported widely to other parts of Greece, the Greek colonies, and Etruria.

laconicum [Co]. A Latin term for a room in a bath-house (usually circular in plan during the 1st century AD) with a hot dry atmosphere.

lacquer [Ge]. A gummy sap obtained from the lac tree (*Rhus vernicifera*), which, when spread over the surface of an artefact and left to dry, will form an impermeable layer. Originally grey in colour, the sap hardens in moist air to a jet black, but this can be modified through the addition of dyes such as cinnabar, or arsenic sulphates.

lacquer ware [Ar]. Ornate wooden domestic and funerary vessels common in China from the Shang Dynasty (14th century BC) onwards, manufactured by repeatedly coating a wooden or fabric pre-form with lacquer in order to build up a rich shiny surface.

laeti [De]. Latin term used in the later Roman empire to refer to barbarians who were settled by the Roman authorities as farmers in areas that had previously been deserted because of intrusive raids. In taking the land they also took an obligation, inherited by their descendants, to perform Roman military service.

lagena [De]. A large, two-handled flagon, at least 0.5 m high, to be distinguished from an amphora.

Lagoa Santa, Brazil [Si]. A series of late Pleistocene occupation sites in Minas Geiras, many of which have lithic industries in association with extinct animal species such as mastodon, sloth, and horse. Human remains may also be present, although controversy surrounds their association with the other materials. Hundreds of rock paintings dating to between 5000 BC and 1000 BC are also represented.

The rock-shelter of Lapa Vermelha IV was excavated by A. Laming-Emperarie in the 1970s and has a 13 m deep stratigraphy which includes deposits dating back to before 12 000 BC. Small quartz flakes were recovered. The Cerca Grande Complex contains deposits dating to between 8000 and 6000 BC. Small flakes of rock crystal as well as axes, bone projectile points, and burials are known. The nearby cemetery of Santana do Riacho contained over 50 flexed inhumations.

[Rep.: W. R. Hurt, 1960, The cultural complexes from the Lagoa Santa Region, Brazil. *American Antiquity*, 62, 569–85]

Lagozza Culture [CP]. Later Neolithic culture of the late 4th and 3rd millennia BC in northern Italy, named after the type-site lake village in the Po Valley. The culture is characterized by plain dark pottery, sometimes burnished, that appears mainly in carinated forms. These wares are generally seen as related to the western series of round-based Neolithic wares that includes CHASSEY and CORTAILLOD types. Lagozza Culture communities were mixed farmers, concentrating on cereals and dairy produce, although well-preserved waterlogged deposits reveal that wild fruits and nuts were important too. A few copper artefacts from Lagozza sites suggest the incipient development of metallurgy in the area, and are the earliest in northern Italy. Burial traditions are poorly known, but include some crouched inhumations in cists.

Lake Forest Tradition [CP]. Late Archaic Stage woodland-dwelling hunter-gatherer cultures living mainly around the northeastern shores of the Great Lakes and the St Lawrence River in North America in the period *c.*3200 to 1000 BC. Their subsistence economy focused on the exploitation of heavy fish runs and seal colonies, although other animals and plants were used as well. These communities had great seasonal movement, mainly living in small bands moving about within well-defined territories, but coming together at defined base camps from time to time. There are two well-defined variants of the Lake Forest Tradition: the OLD COPPER CULTURE and the LAURENTIAN.

Lake Mungo, New South Wales, Australia [Si]. An early occupation site beside the former Willandra Lakes in the arid region of New South Wales. Surveys by J. M. Bowler in 1968 and 1969 revealed midden deposits associated with stone tools belonging to the Australian core tool and scraper tradition dating to between 23 000 and 30 000 years ago. Fossilized skeletal material representing three individuals was found, some of it suggesting deliberate cremation. The Willandra Lakes started to dry up about 15 000 years ago and with growing aridity the area became increasingly deserted.

[Sum.: J. M. R. Bowler, R. Jones and A. G. Thorne, 1970, Pleistocene human remains from Australia: a living site and human cremation from Lake Mungo, western New South Wales. *World Archaeology*, 2(1), 39–60]

lake village [MC]. A settlement which was originally built on dry land at the edge of a lake or on an island, but which was subsequently inundated by rising water levels. Such settlements are found in many parts of the world at different times, but the most famous are undoubtedly those found in Switzerland and northern Italy, also known as PILE DWELLINGS.

Lambeth sword [Ar]. Type of late Bronze Age straight-sided bronze sword with a flat midsection and rectangular hilt-tang found in southern Britain in the 12th and 11th centuries BC (Penard Phase). Local indigenous copies of the Rosnoën swords made in northern France.

La Milpa, Belize [Si]. Major Lowland Maya site situated at 180 m above sea level on an upland area between the Río Bravo escarpment and the Río Azul. The site was first explored by Sir Eric Thompson in 1938 but only rarely studied between that time and 1992, when a major new survey and investigation programme began under the direction of Norman Hammond.

The focus of the site occupies an area some 680 m by 250 m and is dominated by the Great Plaza. At *c.*165 m by 120 m this plaza is one of the largest public spaces built by the Maya. It is dominated by four large temple pyramids, the highest of which rises 24 m above the plaza floor. To the south are two reservoirs, and beyond them a second group of buildings comprising three open plazas and a series of open courtyards. There are also two ballcourts, an acropolis, and a royal residence.

Eighteen stelae are known at La Milpa, most of them set on the eastern side of the Great

Plaza in front of the pyramids. They were erected over a period of nearly four centuries between AD 406 and 780, possibly longer. In Contact Period times, *c.*AD 1500–1650, some of these monuments may have been moved by pilgrims who also deposited incense-burners in front of some of them.

Around the ceremonial core of the site there is extensive evidence of occupation with perhaps as many as 130 courtyards. Small-scale excavations suggest a sequence of occupation from late Pre-Classic times through to the Post-Classic.

[Rep.: G. Tourtellot III, A. Clarke, and N. Hammond, 1993, Mapping La Milpa: a Maya city in northwestern Belize. *Antiquity*, 67, 96–108]

laminating [De]. A process for the production of a high-quality metal tool or weapon by repeatedly forging out a blank form, folding the metal over, and forging it again so that qualities of malleability and hardness can be combined. *See also* PATTERN-WELDING.

Lammas [Ge]. A traditional calendar festival in northern Europe that in recent times is taken as 1 August. It marked the end of the hay harvest when stock could be let into the meadows to graze. Also the beginning of the grain harvest.

lamp [Ar]. A vessel of some kind to provide a reservoir for oil or other fuel to feed a light-giving flame via a wick. The simplest forms, known from the Palaeolithic onwards, are small hollowed-out stone basins. From classical times ceramic lamps with a special spout or pinched lip to take the wick were extremely common.

lamp-filler [Ar]. A globular, narrow-mouthed jar with a projecting spout of very narrow bore. It was perhaps used for filling lamps or as an infant/invalid feeding cup.

lamp-holder [Ar]. A shallow, flat-bottomed, asymmetric dish, shaped like the mouth of a jug, usually with a handle, found throughout the Roman world; thought to have been used as a container for an oil lamp.

lancehead [Ar]. A projectile point of stone, bone, wood, or metal that is larger than an arrowhead but smaller than a spearhead. Lanceheads would have been used to tip light spears or javelins.

lanceolate [De]. Anything which is lance-like or lozenge-shaped, tapering at both ends.

lancet [Co]. A tall narrow window with a pointed top.

landnam [De]. A Danish term, literally meaning 'taking land', usually applied to the process of forest clearance in preparation for farming. The term was introduced to the archaeological literature by J. Iversen in 1941 when describing the results of his investigations of pollen profiles in Denmark. He found charcoal layers associated with falls in the proportion of forest tree pollen, a rise in non-tree pollen, and in some cases cereal and cultivation-weed pollen at the same horizon. Iversen proposed that these changes were the kind of indicators that would be expected as a reflection of forest clearance for cultivation. The fact that these clearance episodes were not all of the same date, and that some pollen profiles had more than one phase of clearance, led to the suggestion that some kind of shifting cultivation was happening in the early and middle Neolithic of northern Europe. This is now generally rejected, although the term remains a useful one, recognizing that much early Neolithic clearance was highly localized.

Landnámabók [Do]. A 12th century AD compilation of traditions about the colonizers of Iceland: *The Book of Settlements*.

landscape [De]. Initially introduced into English with reference to paintings and particular ways of seeing the world from the Dutch *landskap*, the idea of the landscape has gradually expanded to embrace what is perhaps better described as the countryside. The historical depth to the landscape has in a sense been recognized since the time of the first antiquarian investigations; the contribution that the past makes to the present shape, feel, and form of the landscape, and our appreciation of it, is something that came into sharp focus through the work of W. G. HOSKINS during the 1950s and 1960s. More specifically, landscape is seen as the social construction of space, containing a bundle of practices, meanings, attitudes, and values. As such, it is a term appropriate to a humanistic understanding of the environment.

landscape archaeology [De]. A major branch of study within archaeology that draws on archaeological, historical geography, human geography, ecology, anthropology, and place-name studies. A number of different approaches have been, and continue to be, used which fall into two main areas. First is the largely **descriptive** work of mapping and plotting archaeological features over wide areas and then trying to work out their sequence and patterns of contemporaneity. Such work usually produces a series of extremely useful phase plans or snapshot images of the physical arrangement of the landscape at a point in time. Second is the **interpretative** work that focuses on the social use of space by past communities, together with their comprehension and engagement with the world. The application of PHENOMENOLOGY here has proved illuminating. The greatest significance of all landscape archaeology is the way it has replaced the focus on single tightly defined sites with an interest in much bigger areas that are more closely matched with the physical scale at which human societies operate.

Lane Fox, Augustus (1827–1900) [Bi]. *See* PITT RIVERS.

langi tombs [MC]. Large square and rectangular earthen monuments found on the island of Tonga, and dating to the Tui Tonga Dynasty. Most have terraced sides faced with slabs of cut coral limestone and some have internal burial chambers also of coral limestone. Traditionally, these monuments are the burial places of the Tongan ruling aristocracy, but none have been excavated.

L'Anse aux Meadows, Newfoundland [Si]. An early 11th-century AD settlement on a low marine terrace overlooking Epaves Bay in North Newfoundland, important as the only certain example of a Viking settlement in North America. Excavations by Helge Ingstad and Anne Stine discovered eight sod-walled longhouses, at least one of which was in multiple occupation. The settlement also had a work-shed, a smithy set a little way from the main focus, a possible bath-house, and four turf boat-sheds. Norse artefacts, including a spindle whorl and a needle hone, were found. The site is ideally situated to exploit coastal grazing for cattle and also as a base for exploration of the St Lawrence Valley.

[Sum.: A. Ingstad, 1977, *The discovery of a Norse settlement in America*. Oslo: Universiteforlaget]

lapis lazuli [Ma]. A kind of semi-precious stone with an intense blue colour sometimes flecked with gold. The main source used in the ancient world was in the mountains of Badakhshan, northern Afghanistan, from where it was traded extremely widely, especially to Egypt. Lapis lazuli was used as inlay in the manufacture of ornaments, jewellery, seals, etc. Tepe Hissar and Shahr-i Sokhta seem to have functioned as trading centres for the working and distribution of lapis lazuli.

Lapiths [CP]. A mythical people in Thessaly who, under King Pirithous, fought and conquered the Cebtaurs. This conflict was frequently used to represent the triumph of civilization over barbarism and of Greeks over Persians, as on the metopes of the PARTHENON.

Larco Hoyle, Rafael (1901–66) [Bi]. Peruvian landowner, businessman, and amateur archaeologist who did much to help scholars working on the north Peruvian coastal plain. His own contribution was to define the Cupisnique and Salinar cultures and subdivide the MOCHICA into a number of phases. During his life he amassed the finest private archaeological collection in Peru.

[Bio.: K. Berrin, 1997, The Spirit of R. Larco Hoyle: an introduction. In K. Berrin (ed), *The Spirit of ancient Peru*. New York: Thames & Hudson]

larnax [Ar]. A closed box often used as a container for human remains. In Minoan–Mycenaean times it took the form of a ceramic coffin imitating a wooden chest. In Hellenistic times it was a kind of terracotta sarcophagus that enjoyed a brief period of popularity during the 6th and 5th centuries BC. Some were painted in imitation of contemporary vase styles. A small gold larnax containing the ashes of a male was found in the so-called royal tomb at Vergina, Greece.

Larnian (Larnian Culture) [CP]. A term once generally applied to the later Mesolithic of Ireland, and especially the communities living in coastal regions of northern Ireland. Following investigations at Newferry and elsewhere, however, it is clear that its use is inappropriate as a general cultural label, and instead Peter Woodman suggests using it only with reference to a particular technique of flintworking that involves direct percussion for the production of broad blade industries.

Lartet, Edouard (1801–73) [Bi]. French scholar and archaeologist best known for his work on the Palaeolithic. Initially he was a magistrate working in the south of France but he gave up law to study palaeontology and from there to examine cave deposits containing the remains of early human communities. From 1863 onwards he worked in collaboration with his British friend Henry Christy, the two of them carrying out the first systematic studies of French caves in the Dordogne, including Laugerie-Haute, Le Moustier, and La Madelaine. Realizing that several different phases were represented in these sites they divided the excavated material into a series of stages: an early group with two subdivisions based on associations with cave bear and later with woolly mammoth and rhinoceros bones; and a late phase with two subdivisions characterized by associations with reindeer bones and later aurochs. These two main phases have become the Middle and Upper Palaeolithic respectively. They also discovered mobiliary art in a proper archaeological context, so helping the arguments in favour of the cave art of France being truly ancient.

[Bio.: E. T. Hamy, 1872, *Édouard Lartet: sa vie et ses travaux.* Brussels]

Lascaux, France [Si]. A Palaeolithic cave site on a hillside above Montignac in the Dordogne region of southern France, containing what are probably the most famous cave paintings in the world. The cave was discovered in September 1940; it was cleared out and opened to the public in 1948, sadly without proper excavation. The level of tourist interest was such, however, that in 1963 it was closed to the public because of fears about the long-term survival of the paintings. A facsimile of the cave has been created nearby (Lascaux II), and this opened in 1983.

Little is known about the Lascaux cave and its original use; even the original entrance remains unknown. It seems unlikely, however, that it was an occupation site; rather it is seen as a place that was periodically visited for the purposes related to the paintings themselves. Stylistically the images relate to the Upper Palaeolithic and were made between 20 000 and 15 000 years ago, the MAGDALENIAN. There are about 600 paintings in the cave, including images of bulls, horses, and deer, and a range

of other motifs. What appears to be a bird-headed man with a wounded bison and a rhinoceros is usually interpreted as a shaman. In addition there are nearly 1500 engravings, again of both animals and motifs. Some of the tools and equipment used by the artists, for example lamps, mixing pallets, mortars and pestles, and engraving tools have been found in the caves. Wooden scaffolding must originally have been used to reach some of the high ceilings and upper parts of the walls.

[Sum.: A. Leroi-Gourhan and J. Allain, 1979, *Lascaux inconnu.* Paris: Editions du CNRS]

latchlifter [Ar]. An early kind of key, found in Roman and early medieval contexts, it is simply a bent piece of iron rod with an expanded end that could be pushed through a hole in a wooden door to raise a catch-bar on the inside.

late Archaic [CP]. General term referring to the most recent phase of the Archaic Stage as defined in North American archaeology. The late Archaic embraces a wide range of traditions and cultures and begins and ends at different times in different areas: in the eastern woodlands of North America it spans the period 5000–700 BC, whereas in the Plains and Great Basin it relates to the period from about 1000 BC down to AD 200.

late Glacial [CP]. The later part of the DEVENSIAN STAGE when the glaciers and main ice-sheets were retreating. Chronoclimatic and vegetation zones provide subdivisions of this series of changes, while the main cultural groupings include Ahrensburgian, CRESSWELLIAN, FEDERMESSER, and Hamburgian.

late Horizon [CP]. General term referring to the most recent of the seven main phases recognized in Andean archaeology: the period *c.*AD 1450–1533 when the Inca empire expanded to control most of the Andean region.

late Intermediate Period [CP]. General term referring to the fifth of the seven main chronological phases recognized in Andean archaeology, broadly the period *c.*AD 1000 to 1450. It follows the collapse of middle Horizon empires such as the Tiahuanaco and Huari, during which distinctive regional cultures emerged along the coast and in highland areas. The most extensive of these was the CHIMÚ CULTURE. The various polities that developed during the late Intermediate Period were subsequently conquered by the Inca empire.

La Tène, Switzerland [Si]. Iron Age site on the shores of Lake Neuchatel in western Switzerland, discovered in 1857 when the water level in the lake was unusually low. This revealed timber piles and a wide range of iron objects, especially weapons. Subsequent excavations by Emile Vouga between 1880 and 1885 and William Wabre and Paul Vouga between 1907 and 1917 have resulted in the recovery of a vast collection of objects, human skeletal material, and further evidence for timber structures, but no certain evidence for the purpose or nature of the site. While some scholars see La Tène as a settlement, others interpret it a timber platform on the edge of the lake, approached via timber causeways, from which votive deposits and perhaps burials were made. In support of this is the relative poverty of domestic debris from the site and the abundance of high-quality iron and bronze weapons and personal ornaments including: 166+ swords and scabbards, 269+ spearheads, 29 shields, 382+ brooches, and 158 belt clasps. In addition there is a bronze cauldron, dart wheels, wooden buckets, and tools for metalworking, woodworking, and leatherworking.

[Rep.: J. M. de Navarro, 1972, *Finds from the site of La Tène, I: Scabbards and the swords found in them*. Oxford: OUP]

La Tène art [De]. A style of ornamentation and decoration current from the 5th to the 1st centuries BC in western Europe showing influences from Scythian and Mediterranean art but also local originality, using bold abstract curvilinear designs with infilled zones. In those parts of northwest Europe untroubled by Roman invasions, La Tène art styles continued to develop through into the mid 1st millennium AD and beyond. Also known as Celtic art.

La Tène Culture [CP]. Term applied to the second period of the Iron Age in Europe, following the HALLSTATT: on Paul REINECKE'S scheme, broadly the period 450 BC to 50 BC. The culture is defined on the basis of finds from the site of La Tène in Switzerland, and is conventionally divided into three main phases: La Tène I, c.480–220 BC; La Tène II, c.220–120 BC; and La Tène III, c.120 BC down to the Roman conquest. Elements of the La Tène

first appeared in southern Britain during the late Iron Age.

late period [CP]. In Egypt covering the 26th to the 30th Dynasties, c.664–332 BC, plus the second period of Persian occupation in the 31st Dynasty.

latera praetorii [Co]. Latin term for the areas on each side of the headquarters building in a fortress or of the general's tent in a camp; the central range in a camp or fort.

laterite [Ma]. Ferruginous rock formed in situ by the weathering of basic rocks under wet tropical conditions. When eroded and redeposited it is called detrital laterite.

later Woodland [CP]. A subdivision of the Woodland Stage defined for the archaeology of the eastern parts of North America which succeeds the middle Woodland around AD 400. The transition from middle Woodland to late Woodland saw the development of a complex patchwork of chiefdoms of different sizes throughout the eastern woodlands of the USA down to European contact. These were hunter-gatherer societies which indulged in limited farming based on cultivated gardens and small plots. The most distinctive late Woodland culture was the MISSISSIPPIAN.

late Stone Age [CP]. The final stage of the stoneworking industries in sub-Saharan Africa dating to the period from about 30 000 years ago down into historical times.

late Tutishcainyo Phase [CP]. South American farming cultures found in the Rio Ucayali area of Amazonia and tentatively dated to c.1500–1000 BC. Characterized by their ceramic assemblages which belong to the Zone Hachure Horizon Style of the Amazon Basin.

Lathrap, Donald Ward (1927–90) [Bi]. American archaeologist working mainly in South America. He showed that Amazonian regions were the focus of complex societies rather earlier than had previously been thought, and argued for the pre-eminence of the Amazon Basin and Pacific Coast cultures.

[Obit.: *Anthropology Newsletter*, 31(8), 5]

Latians [CP]. Iron Age communities of southern Latium, the area south of Rome in central

Italy, in the early 1st millennium BC. The Latians are thought to have developed from the Pianello regional variant of the URNFIELD CULTURE, and certainly cremation burials in Latian contexts were widespread in the Alban Mountains and around Rome itself. The Latians were the ancestors of the Romans and were responsible for the construction of houses on the Palatine Hill during the 9th century BC.

latifundia [MC]. Large planned agricultural estates geared to efficient production and high profits through the use of cheap, often slave labour. Although strictly a Roman term, its use extends to agricultural estates in general where production is at an industrial level.

latrine [Co]. Latin term for lavatory.

lattice decoration [De]. Ornamentation formed by a criss-cross of diagonal lines, described as acute-angled if the angle to the horizontal is more than 45 degrees and obtuse-angled if less than this; also known as **cross-hatching**.

Laura rock art, Queensland, Australia [Si]. A complex of Aboriginal rock paintings and peckings in caves and rock-shelters around Laura on Cape York. The motifs represented include paintings and engravings of animals, tracks, and abstract symbols. Charcoal from occupation layers in the Early Man Rock-Shelter which cover the paintings and peckings has been radiocarbon dated to the period c.13 000 BC to 10 000 BC, making this amongst the earliest examples of rock art in Australia. The shelter was used down into recent times and the latest images present were probably executed in the 1930s AD.

[Sum.: A. Rosenfeld, D. Horton, and J. Winter, 1981, *Early man in north Queensland: art and archaeology in the Laura area*. Camberra: Australian National University]

laurel-leaf point [Ar]. An elegantly worked long thin leaf-shaped flint implement up to 35 cm long, characteristic of the SOLUTREAN tradition. The high-quality finish is usually achieved with careful invasive retouch.

Laurentian Tradition [CP]. Late Archaic cultures representing various hunter-gatherer communities living in the St Lawrence Valley of North America in the period c.3200–1400 BC and forming a subdivision of the LAKE FOR-

EST TRADITION. Characterized by distinctive broad-bladed and side-notched Otter Creek points, scraper types, slate points and knives, ground stone gouges, and stone fishing-line weights. Polished stone ATLATL weights, known as 'bannerstones', are also known. A number of phases or local variations have been recognized: Vergennes (3200–3000 BC), Brewerton, and Vosburg.

Lausitz Culture (Lusatian Culture) [CP]. Late Bronze Age communities forming a regional variant of the URNFIELD CULTURE living between the Elbe and the Oder and eastwards into Poland in the mid 2nd and early 1st millennia BC. Characterized by its fine bronze work and dark pottery, the latter sometimes graphite-burnished and decorated with applied bosses and fluting. A few fortified settlements are known from the Lausitz Culture, including the well-preserved site of Biskupin in Poland. Burials show a combination of cremations either in flat cemeteries (urnfields) or under round barrows. In northern areas of its range this culture may have persisted down into the Hallstatt Iron Age.

La Venta, Chiapas, Mexico [Si]. Major Olmec religious centre on an island in the marshy lowlands of Tabasco Province near the Tonala River. Overall, the site was used from about 1000 BC down to 600 BC, but it reached its greatest size during the Middle Formative Stage (c.850–750 BC) after the abandonment of San Lorenzo in c.900 BC. La Venta is dominated by a large clay pyramid, about 33 m high and 128 m in diameter at the base, built in the form of a fluted cone. Its form may imitate volcanic cones such as can be seen in the Tuxtla Mountains only 100 km to the west. Round about, spread over an area covering 5 square km, there are numerous platforms, mounds, pyramids, and plazas. All the major structures are aligned broadly north–south. Some of the platforms are thought to have supported houses for the elite, constructed in perishable materials and long since gone.

Carved stone stelae (many probably broken at the death of those they celebrate), altars, colossal stone heads, and three massive mosaic pavements in serpentine set in the form of a jaguar mask represent monumental works of the very highest quality. The mosaics are each 4.5 m by 6 m and include 485 separate serpentine tiles. They are all the more impressive because the stone used is not native to the area and had to be imported from over 100 km away.

The well-known Jade Group of objects, comprising sixteen human figure statuettes and six celts, were found arranged in a kind of circular gathering. Household refuse is scarce, but prestige goods including magnetite mirrors, sting-ray spines, and worked jade illustrate the high status of the site.

[Rep.: P. Drucker, R. F. Heizer, and R. J. Squier, 1959, *Excavations at La Venta, Tabasco, 1955*. Washington DC: Bureau of American Ethnology]

Layard, Sir Austen Henry (1817–94) [Bi]. British antiquarian whose expeditions and self-taught archaeological methods led to the investigation of sites in the Near East. Born in London and trained as a lawyer, Layard and a friend, Edward Mitford, set out to ride from England to Ceylon in 1839. During this journey Layard became fascinated by archaeology and became an unpaid diplomatic attaché in Constantinople so that he could continue and expand his interests. Between 1845 and 1847 he excavated at NIMRUD (thinking it was Nineveh), and while his methods were brutal compared with modern standards they were typical of the day and resulted in the discovery of a lot of structural evidence as well as artefacts. His book, *Nineveh and its remains*, published in 1849 sold well and allowed him to make good contacts. He resumed excavations the same year, and upon his return to England in 1851 prepared a second volume, *Discoveries and ruins of Nineveh and Babylon*, which appeared in 1853. It included a provisional chronology for the Assyrian kings and a description of their state. Layard subsequently became a politician and then British ambassador in Madrid and later Constantinople.

[Bio.: G. Waterfield, 1963, *Layard of Nineveh*. London: John Murray]

layer [Ge]. *See* CONTEXT.

Lazón [CP]. *See* CHAVÍN.

lazy bed [MC]. A method of manual cultivation in which land is dug over with a spade to form low ridges of between 0.5 m and 2.5 m wide and with narrow furrows in between to assist drainage. Common in upland areas from the early 1st millennium AD onwards.

LBK [Ab]. *See* LINEARBANDKERAMIC.

lead [Ma]. A soft, heavy, silvery-coloured metal (Pb) with a low melting point that was alloyed with copper and tin to form lead-bronze for much of later prehistory. In classical times lead was commonly used on its own for making pipes, roofing plates, and coffins, amongst other things.

lead isotope analysis [Te]. The measurement of stable isotopes of lead using a mass spectrometer in order to characterize particular samples and associate them with known lead sources. Four isotopes are commonly used— ^{206}Pb, ^{207}Pb, ^{208}Pb, and ^{204}Pb—the first three of which are the ultimate decay products of the radioactive series associated with ^{238}U, ^{235}U, and ^{232}Th respectively, and will therefore vary considerably in their concentration according to the geological age of the lead ores. The main lead sources in Greece, England, and Spain, for example, can each be distinguished from one another on the basis of their isotopic ratios.

Leakey, Louis Seymour Bazett (1903–72) [Bi]. A Kenyan-born archaeologist and palaeontologist who spent most of his life working on the recovery and analysis of early hominid remains from East Africa. Born and brought up at Kabete, Kenya, into a family of missionaries, his boyhood was spent with local children through whom he came to learn about and love Africa. In 1919 he went to Weymouth College and then to St John's College, Cambridge, where he read modern languages for the first two years followed by the archaeology and anthropology tripos. Between graduating in 1926 and 1935 he led four expeditions to East Africa and established the sequence of early cultures in Kenya and northern Tanzania. He took his Ph.D. in 1930 and was elected a research Fellow for six years in his old college.

In addition to archaeology, Leakey was a great lover of animals and heavily involved in the politics of Kenya. At the outbreak of WW2 he was in charge of the Criminal Investigation Department in Nairobi, and in 1945 he was made curator of the Coryndon Memorial Museum in Nairobi, a post he held until 1961. In 1942 Leakey and his wife **Mary Leakey** (1913–96) discovered the Acheulian site of Olorgesailie in the Rift Valley, but it is the site of Olduvai for which they are best remembered. In the first season, 1959, Mary Leakey found the skull of Zinjanthropus

(*Australopithecus*) and the following season their son Jonathan discovered the first remains of *Homo habilis*. Through this work over a period of more than a decade Leakey and his family revolutionized understandings of the Lower Palaeolithic, and promoted the study of African archaeology in its world context.

At his death the Kenyan authorities established a museum and research institute now called the Louis Leakey Memorial Institute for African Prehistory. He is buried beside his parents overlooking the Rift Valley.

[Bio.: S. Cole, 1975, *Leakey's luck*. London: Harcourt; Mary Leakey, Obit.: *The Times*, 10 December 1996]

leat [Co]. Artificial channel created to supply water from a natural source to a mill or other installation.

leather-hard [De]. The state of a pottery vessel after it has been air-dried, before firing. The clay is stiff enough for the vessel to be picked up without distortion, yet soft enough to respond to pressure for burnishing, attaching handles, and other finishing processes.

Leeds, Thurlow (1877–1955) [Bi]. British archaeologist and Anglo-Saxon scholar. Born near Peterborough he was educated at Uppingham before going up to Magdalene College, Cambridge, to study the classics tripos. From 1900 to 1903 he was a cadet in the Federated Malay States service and spent some time in China learning Chinese. His health broke down in the Far East and he returned home to recuperate. A chance encounter with Arthur Evans in 1908 brought him an appointment as Assistant Keeper at the Ashmolean Museum in Oxford, a kind of work that delighted him. He went on to become Keeper of the Department of Antiquities and in 1928 Keeper of the Museum. While working at the Ashmolean, Leeds carried out fieldwork in the Oxford area and published numerous books and articles about the Anglo-Saxon period especially, including *The archaeology of Anglo-Saxon settlements* (1913, Oxford: Clarendon Press) and *Early Anglo-Saxon art and archaeology* (1936, Oxford: Clarendon Press).

[Obit.: *The Times*, 18 August 1955]

legion [De]. The main unit of the Roman imperial army. In the early Republican period a legion comprised about 3000 troops, all with property qualifications, but this had increased to 5000–6000 soldiers together with a number of mounted men and officers by the mid 1st century BC. Later, from the time of Diocletian onwards, the number of legions was increased but the size of each decreased. Each legion was based in a legionary fortress, a larger and more permanent version of the FORT. Each was given a number and a standard in the form of an eagle. A legion was typically divided into ten cohorts, each cohort being divided into six centuries.

legionary [De]. A Roman soldier; a member of a LEGION.

legionary wares [De]. Distinctive types of pottery in use by the legions in Britain especially in the mid 1st century AD, when local products were found to be inadequate. These wares were peculiar to each legion and have been identified at Wroxeter, Lincoln, York, and Caerleon, but there has only been one production centre identified, at Holt, Chester, where there was a works depot for tile-making.

legitimacy [Ge]. The belief that a particular political order is just and valid.

legitimation crisis [Ge]. The failure of a political order to generate a sufficient level of commitment and involvement on the part of its citizens to be able properly to govern.

Leisner, Georg (1879–1957) [Bi]. German archaeologist and prehistorian who, together with his wife **Vera Leisner** (1885–1972), devoted his life to making a comprehensive survey and analysis of the Neolithic chambered tombs of Iberia. Their massive undertaking was published in a series of volumes under the title *Die megalithgräber der Iberischen Halbinsel* (1942–65, Berlin).

[Obit.: (Georg) *Ampurias*, 19–20 (1957–8), 294–5 (Vera) *Madrider Mitteilungen*, 14 (1975)]

leister [Ar]. A kind of two-pronged fork-like spear used in fishing, with a pair of bone or antler heads set with their barbs pointing inwards and backwards. Usually represented archaeologically by the barbed points, which when found separately are indistinguishable from harpoon tips. Common in Mesolithic and riverside or coastal Neolithic assemblages. The name is taken from the term for contemporary Eskimo fish-spears.

lekythos [Ar]. A Greek vessel with a slender, cylindrical body and narrow neck, and a handle between the shoulder and neck. Used to contain perfumed oil.

Leland, John (*c*.1506–52) [Bi]. British antiquary and traveller who held the post of librarian to Henry VII before being appointed King's Antiquary in 1533. Between 1534 and 1543 he travelled throughout England collecting material for a major history, but became insane in 1550. Because of this his work was never published, but his notes were preserved and published as Leland's *Itineraries* in 1710. They provide important source material for archaeological studies of all periods.

[Bio.: *Dictionary of National Biography*, 11, 892–6]

Le Moustier, France [Si]. A pair of rockshelters about 15 km from Les Eyzies beside the Vezère River in the Dordogne, the type-site for the MOUSTERIAN industries of the Middle Palaeolithic. Excavations by Edouard Lartet and Henry Christy in the 1860s established the basic stratigraphy of the site and its contents. A skeleton believed to be of *Homo neanderthalis* type was found in the lower shelter in 1908, but has never been fully examined.

[Sum.: J. Coles and E. Higgs, 1969, *The archaeology of early man*. London: Faber and Faber, 272–3]

Lengyel Culture [CP]. Late Neolithic (post-LBK) communities of the 4th millennium BC living in western Hungary, parts of Austria, Slovakia, the Czech Republic, and Poland. Named after the type-site near Szekszard in western Hungary excavated by M. Wozinszky in the 1880s and found to comprise a settlement and adjoining cemetery of 90 inhumations. Many regional variations of the Lengyel have been identified, but they are also linked to the TISZA CULTURE of the Hungarian Plain and these connections may be responsible for the introduction of painted pottery and the occasional use of copper items. There are also links with the RÖSSEN CULTURE.

Two branches of the Lengyel are commonly recognized: the **Painted Lengyel** defined by the presence of white, red, and yellow crusted wares dating to the early 4th millennium; and the **Unpainted Lengyel** defined by the presence of knobbed and incised pottery dating to the second half of the 4th millennium BC.

The culture is characterized by pottery in a variety of forms including bowls, small amphorae, biconical vessels, and pedestalled bowls. Settlements include open sites as well as some large ditched enclosures such as Hluboke Mašůky. All have trapezoidal timber-framed houses. Burials are mainly contracted inhumations in flat cemeteries or within settlements.

Lepenski Vir, Yugoslavia [Si]. A small Mesolithic and Neolithic settlement on the banks of the Danube above the Iron Gates in Serbia. The site was discovered in 1960 and extensively excavated by D. Srejović between 1965 and 1971. Three levels have been identified, the first two being Mesolithic and spanning the period 6000–4000 BC. Here the occupants lived in trapezoidal houses with plastered floors. A total of 25 houses were excavated from these levels, all of them with their wide ends facing the river. Their economy was based on fishing, and as such the site and the community it represents is quite remarkable because of the cultural elaboration achieved. Amongst their material culture were a series of stone heads showing human faces but with 'fishy' features. The third level is a STARČEVO CULTURE village with rectangular houses but none of the architectural niceties of the earlier phases. Domesticated pigs, cattle, sheep, and goats are represented in this phase.

[Sum.: D. Srejović, 1972, *Europe's first monumental sculpture: new discoveries at Lepenski Vir*. London: Thames & Hudson]

Lepsius, Karl Richard (1810–84) [Bi]. German antiquary and philologist who specialized in early Egyptian texts. Born in Naumburg-am-Saale, he studied classics, philology, and archaeology at the universities of Leipzig, Göttingen, and Berlin, followed by three years in Paris. Between 1836 and 1842 he visited all the main European collections of Egyptian antiquities, making copies of the inscriptions and texts. Chronology and funerary texts became his speciality and with financial support from Frederick William IV of Prussia he organized an expedition to Egypt and Nubia to record inscriptions, the results of which were published in twelve large volumes between 1849 and 1859 as *Denkmäler aus Ägypten und Äthiopien*. In 1865 he was appointed Keeper of the Egyptian collection in Berlin and Director of the National Library in 1873.

[Bio.: G. Ebers, 1887, *Richard Lepsius: a biography*. New York: W. S. Grottsberger]

Leptis Magna, Libya [Si]. The principal city in Roman North Africa which is well preserved because after its decline in the 7th century AD it became covered in sand. The site has a long and complicated history during which the city has been in the hands of many different cultures. Its foundation as a settlement in the 7th century BC was by colonists from Phoenicia. It was then successively Carthaginian (until 146 BC), Numidian (until 46 BC) and then Roman. The town was the birthplace of the Emperor Septimus Severus in AD 193, and Roman domination brought great wealth and prosperity to the city and its region. Invasions by the Vandals in the 5th century and Arab forces in the 7th century caused its final decline.

[Sum.: K. D. Matthews and A. W. Cook, 1957, *Cities in the sand: Leptis Magna and Sabratha in Roman Africa.* Oxford: OUP]

Lerma point [Ar]. Type of chipped stone projectile point of leaf-shaped outline dating to before *c.*7000 BC and found mainly in Mexico and Central America.

Leroi-Gourhan, André Georges Léandre (1911–86) [Bi]. French archaeologist and scholar, best known for his work on Palaeolithic cave art. Born in Paris he spent his student years learning Russian and Chinese before turning to ethnography and archaeology. He was involved in setting up the Musée de l'Homme and was director of *Gallia Préhistoire* from 1962 onwards. Following periods at the University of Yonne and the Sorbonne, he became Professor at the Collège de France in 1969. His work on Palaeolithic cave art introduced the idea that the motifs were carefully arranged in purposefully constructed scenes.

[Obit.: *Antiquity*, 55 (1986), 136]

Levallois technique [De]. A distinctive type of flint knapping found occasionally in the Lower Palaeolithic but most associated with the MOUSTERIAN industries of the Middle Palaeolithic. In the Levant the technique is also used in the Upper Palaeolithic. The technique is named after finds made during the 19th century at Levallois-Perret in the suburbs of Paris, and involves the careful preparation of substantial core prior to the removal of the intended flake. Preparation involved establishing a striking platform, trimming the edge of the core to the desired shape and working the surface to create a slightly domed form by flaking inwards from the outer edges

towards the centre. The finished core before the flake is removed is often known as a 'tortoise core' because of its faceted domed back and flat underside. When the desired flake is detached from the core the flake itself (known as a Levallois flake) shows the scars of the preparatory work on the dorsal surface while the ventral face is smooth. Because of the wide range of cultural contexts in which this technique was used the idea of a Levallois Culture is now obsolete.

Levantine art [De]. A general term to describe the rock art found in rock-shelters in eastern Spain and believed to be of Mesolithic and Neolithic date. The images are dominated by red painted figures of deer, ibex, and humans, some in hunting scenes.

levigate [De]. In pottery making, a method of purifying clay by sedimentation. The clay is thoroughly mixed with water and then left to stand. The coarser particles will sink to the bottom while the water and any organic impurities will rise to the top and can be poured off. In the middle there will be a layer of especially fine textured clay.

Lhwyd, Edward (1660–1709) [Bi]. British antiquary and Celtic scholar, he was Keeper of the Ashmolean Museum, Oxford, 1690–1709, and a Fellow of the Royal Society. He travelled extensively in Wales to collect material for a new edition of Camden's *Britannia* and published *Archaeologia Britannica* in 1707. Some of his drawings and paintings of the sites he visited provide important details about their construction that have now vanished.

[Bio.: F. Emery, 1958, Edward Lhwyd and the 1695 *Britannia. Antiquity*, 32, 179–82]

Lialovo Culture (Lyalovo Culture) [CP]. Early Neolithic forest zone communities forming part of the Volga-Oka Cultures of the 4th millennium BC in the upper Volga and Oka rivers and their tributaries around Moscow in western Russia. In origin, the Lialovo Culture results from local later Mesolithic groups adopting the use of pottery and characteristically Neolithic stone artefacts from groups further to the south. The basic economy of hunting, fishing, and food gathering, and the settlement pattern that focused on lake margins and river valley locations, remained unchanged. Lialovo pottery vessels are bag-shaped with pointed bases. They are heavily decorated using the pit and comb technique, usually with horizontal rows of pits or patterns made using pits and comb impressions. Three main phases have been recognized on the basis of decorative patterns: early styles which almost exclusively use round pits as motifs; the middle style using comb impressions and pits together; and the late style which is predominantly decorated using comb impressions. It is possible, however, that these different styles of decoration represent spatial variations between contemporary groups rather than successive phases.

Libby, Willard Frank (1908–80) [Bi]. American chemist and atomic physicist. Born in Colorado, USA, he took a bachelor's degree and doctorate in chemistry at the University of California (Berkeley) and also studied at Princeton. After ten years teaching at Berkeley he joined the Manhattan Project which developed the first atomic bomb. After the war Libby taught at the Institute for Nuclear Studies in the University of Chicago, and served on the Atomic Energy Commission. From 1959 to 1962 he was Professor of Chemistry in the University of California, and from 1962 Director of the Institute of Geophysics.

Libby is best known in archaeology for developing RADIOCARBON DATING, for which, at the age of 52, he received the 1960 Nobel Prize for Chemistry.

[Bio.: R. Burleigh, 1981, W. F. Libby and the development of radiocarbon dating. *Antiquity*, 55, 96–8]

lid-seated vessel [De]. A pot in which the rim is ledged, dished, or grooved internally to keep a lid in place.

life expectancy [Ge]. The number of further years that people of a given age can, on average, expect to live.

life histories [Ge]. Studies of the lives of individuals, often based on both self-reporting and documents such as letters. Also applied to archaeological objects where the aim is to examine their progress from creation to eventual recovery through the archaeological process.

life span [Ge]. The maximum length of life that is biologically possible for a member of a given species.

Lightfoot, Joseph (1828–89) [Bi]. Fellow of Trinity College, Cambridge, and Lady Margaret Professor of Divinity, who in 1879 became bishop of Durham. An exponent of the Mosaic cosmogony, he amplified Archbishop Ussher's calculations by arguing that the creation took place at 9 o'clock on the morning of 23 October in the year 4004 BC. The proximity of this date to the traditional start of the Michaelmas term has often been remarked upon.

[Bio: J. A. T. Robinson, 1981, *Joseph Barber Lightfoot*. Durham: Dean and Chapter of Durham Cathedral]

lima bean [Sp]. A leguminous plant (*Phaseolus acutifolius*) with edible seeds in a long pod. Native of South America. Domesticated from *c*.4000 BC.

limace [Ar]. A type of blade tool retouched along both sides to form a slug-shaped object.

Lima Culture [CP]. Early Intermediate Period communities living in the central coastal region of Peru.

lime [Ma]. *See* QUICKLIME.

limekiln [MC]. An industrial-scale structure in which calcium carbonate in the form of limestone or, exceptionally, sea shells, is burnt at temperatures of around 900°C to convert it to QUICKLIME. Most limekilns are simple structures with a chamber to contain the material to be burnt mixed with fuel such as wood, charcoal, or coal above a stoke-hole which allows more fuel to be added if necessary and a means of extracting the finished quicklime. Limekilns are often constructed into a hillside so that they can be filled or charged by tipping material into the chamber through a hole in the top, which also serves as a flue. Limekilns of Roman and later date are well known in almost any areas where suitable stone for making quicklime occurs naturally.

limes [De]. The term commonly used for the frontier zone of the Roman empire which is generally believed to have been under direct military control. The term is especially often used for the frontier between the Rhine and the Danube in central Germany and between the Danube and the Black Sea in Dobrudja.

limitanei [De]. A Latin term used to describe the troops stationed on the frontiers of the

Roman empire in the 4th century AD, as opposed to the higher status *comitatenses* of the mobile field army.

limpet scoop [Ar]. A small stone tool usually fashioned from an elongated pebble with one end bevelled off to form a rough blade. Limpet scoops are used while harvesting seafood to remove limpets and other crustacea from the rocks to which they cling.

linchpin [Ar]. A metal spike, sometimes enlarged or elaborated at one end, that is passed through a hole in the end of a fixed axle on a cart or chariot in order to stop the wheel falling off.

Lindisfarne, Northumberland, UK [Si]. An early monastic site on a small rocky island accessible by a causeway only at low tide off the exposed north coast of Northumberland. In AD 634 King Oswald gave the island to the monastery of Iona. A year later St Aiden and monks from Iona established the monastery on Lindisfarne which soon became the centre of Celtic Christianity in the kingdom of Northumbria with associated houses at Jarrow, York, and Hexham. Its most famous bishop was St Cuthbert who lived there from about AD 685 until AD 687. From around AD 700, after the Celtic church had acknowledged the supremacy of the Roman church, Lindisfarne became the focus of a cultural renaissance in the region. This is especially well seen in the art of the period and in the beautifully made illuminated manuscripts, of which the best surviving example is the Lindisfarne Gospel dating to about AD 700. The monastery flourished until AD 793 when it became the target of the first Viking raids on Northumbria's east coast. The church and monastic buildings on Lindisfarne today date from the Norman period when a Benedictine monastery was established on the island.

[Sum.: D. O'Sullivan and R. Young, 1995, *Lindisfarne*. London: Batsford and English Heritage]

Lindow Man, Cheshire, UK [Si]. A bog body found in Lindow Moss in the wetlands of northwest England in 1984. On examination it proved to be the body of a young man around 25 years of age who before being dumped in a shallow pool in the mire had been violently hit on the head twice, garrotted, and had his throat cut. Radiocarbon dates place these events in the 1st or 2nd century

AD, and they are probably to be interpreted as a ritual sacrifice.

[Rep.: I. M. Stead, J. B. Bourke, and D. Brothwell, 1986, *Lindow Man. The body in the bog*. London: British Museum Publications]

lineage [De]. A kin-group defined through a number of generations by a specific line of descent, either through the male side (patrilineal) or the female side (matrilineal).

Linear A [De]. A syllabary script written with a sharp point on clay tablets recovered from middle Minoan III and late Minoan I levels (broadly 2000–1500 BC) in Crete and some of the Cycladic islands. The name was given by Arthur EVANS in order to distinguish it from earlier hieroglyphic texts and the later Linear B script. Linear A has not yet been deciphered.

Linear B [De]. A second type of syllabary script written on clay tablets, but later in date than LINEAR A, being found in late Minoan II contexts in Crete and Mycenaean IIIA–B contexts in mainland Greece (broadly 1500–1100 BC). This script was brilliantly deciphered by Michael VENTRIS in 1952 who recognized it as an early form of Greek. Most of the tablets known are accounts and inventories.

Linearbandkeramic (LBK) [CP]. The earliest Neolithic cultures in central and northern Europe, communities that rapidly established themselves on the loess lands of the major river valleys from the Czech Republic to the North Sea coast during the 5th millennium BC. A second rapid expansion northwards around the rim of the Carpathian Basin and into Poland and the Dnieper region of the Ukraine took place in the early 4th millennium BC. Some limited outwards expansion from these areas can be seen in, for example, central France and the Paris Basin, but it was the post-LBK communities who were responsible for moving off light loess-based agricultural lands. It is thought that the LBK developed initially from the KÖRÖS CULTURE of the northern Balkans.

The LBK is named after its distinctive decoration applied to round-bottomed bowls and jars: incised and sometimes painted wares with linear designs that include curvilinear, zig-zag, and meander patterns. Later styles include stroke-ornamented and punched ornament in the form of small pits. Other elements of material culture include stone shoelast adzes and a microlithic stone industry.

Settlements of the LBK are highly distinctive and very similar throughout the spread of the culture. They are mainly situated on the edge of river floodplains and are dominated by clusters of rectangular houses—small villages. The houses are typically 8 m wide and up to 40 m long. Some are simply dwellings, others are dwellings with a barn attached, still others have three components in the form of a central dwelling with a barn at one end and a byre at the other. All were timber-framed, represented archaeologically as sets of postholes and slots. Round about are borrow pits for taking clay to make wattle and daub walls. The villages were long-lasting, and while it used to be thought that LBK farmers practised slash and burn farming so that they returned to the same village at intervals of perhaps a century or so, this is no longer accepted and it seems that most villages represent the simple process of periodic house replacement so that there were always perhaps 5–10 structures standing at any one time. Richard Bradley has argued that the houses were left to collapse naturally when no longer required and that the decayed remains of these longhouses provided the inspiration for the construction of LONG BARROWS by later communities in more northerly parts of Europe. Some LBK villages were open sites, but others such as KÖLN-LINDENTHAL in Germany were set within ditched enclosures.

The LBK economy was based on cattle husbandry and the cultivation of cereals, mainly wheat and barley. Cemeteries are relatively few, but where excavated comprise inhumations and cremations in flat graves, some with grave goods. Also known as Bandkeramik, Linear Pottery Culture, or Danubian I Culture.

linear boundary (dyke) [MC]. A kind of earthwork found in the British Isles that comprises one or more lines of banks and ditches that run across country for anything from a few hundred metres to more than 100 km. Their date and purpose vary greatly, the earliest being built in the Bronze Age, the latest during the early post-Roman period. In many cases they were probably constructed as territorial boundary markers.

Linear Pottery Culture [CP]. *See* LINEARBAND-KERAMIK.

lintel [De]. Wooden beam or stone slab lying horizontally above a doorway or window opening in order to discharge the weight of the structure above.

liquid scintillation counter [Eq]. Instrument for the measurement of carbon-14 in ancient samples which works by recording the disintegration rate of the remaining ^{14}C over a period of time, normally using liquid benzene prepared from sample carbon. *See also* RADIO-CARBON DATING.

Lisburn dirk [Ar]. Type of bronze weapon rather like a rapier, with a straight-sided blade and notched butt for attachment to the hilt. Dating to the PENARD PHASE of the middle to late Bronze Age and found mainly in Ireland.

Lithic [CP]. The earliest of five general cultural stages proposed by G. Willey and P. Phillips in 1958 as a framework for the study of ancient communities in the Americas. The Lithic embraced the whole New World and referred to the earliest, essentially Pleistocene, cultural manifestations. The term is now obsolete as more regionally specific traditions have been defined, for example the Palaeo-Indians, or Arctic Tradition of North America.

lithics [Ge]. General term applied to all collections of stone tools, working debris, and raw materials recovered during an archaeological project.

Little Bighorn, Wyoming, USA [Si]. A battlefield on the north side of the Little Bighorn River now known as Custer Ridge. In June 1876 the US Seventh Cavalry was defeated by a large force of Cheyenne and Sioux Indians there. The cavalry force was led by Lt. Col. Custer. The battle lasted less than an hour and left 210 men of the US cavalry dead. Recent archaeological investigations have attempted to reconstruct the progress of the battle from the distribution of spent cartridge shells from the Springfield carbines and Colt revolvers used by the US cavalry.

[Rep.: R. A. Fox Jr, 1993, *Archaeology, history and Custer's last battle: the Little Big Horn reexamined*. Norman: University of Oklahoma Press]

Little Woodbury Complex (Little Woodbury Culture) [CP]. Middle Iron Age communities living in central southern England in the 3rd and 2nd centuries BC. The culture was named by Frank Hodson in 1964 on the basis of material from Gerhard BERSU's 1938–9 excavations at Little Woodbury near Salisbury, Wiltshire, but is not widely used.

living floor [Ge]. Scatter of stone tools, animal bones, and other artefacts suggestive of an occupation area.

Livy (Titus Livius) [Na]. Roman historian born around 60 BC whose major work documents the history of Rome in 142 books. Of particular relevance to archaeologists of protohistoric Europe are his accounts of the sack of Rome at the hands of the Gauls and of subsequent Roman campaigns in Gaul and against the Cumbri. Livy died around AD 12.

llama [Sp]. Domesticated camelid (*Lama glama*; native species are guaraco and vicuña) found on the high grassland Andean plains of South America. Domesticated by *c.*5000 BC. Used as a food source and as a beast of burden. Capable of carrying loads of up to about 60 kg.

Llano [CP]. Largely obsolete term for the earliest Palaeo-Indian big game hunting communities in North America between 10 000 and 9000 BC.

Llantwit-Stogursey Industry [CP]. One of the regional industries within the Ewart Park Phase of the British late Bronze Age found in South Wales and the Bristol Channel area. It is named after hoards discovered at Llantwit Major in South Glamorgan and Stogursey in Somerset. Amongst its distinctive products are three-ribbed South Wales-style socketed axes.

Llyn Fawr Phase [CP]. The final industrial tradition of the British Bronze Age, contemporary with the continental Hallstatt C and thus truly transitional between the Bronze Age and the Iron Age. Named after a large hoard of metalwork from Llyn Fawr in Mid Glamorgan in South Wales discovered between 1911 and 1913. Imported metalwork includes Gündlingen swords which influenced the development of local styles such as the Thames sword. Other products of the period include winged chapes, cauldrons, razors, horse harness mounts, massive SOMPTING axes, and a vast array of pins. Iron is used to make spearheads and sickles, amongst other things.

loess [Ge]. Deposits of fine rock dust, sand, and related sediments carried by the wind in arid conditions, for example during glacial periods, from exposed glacial moraines and outwash deposits. In Europe these deposits are found widely across the southern steppes and in the major river systems across central and western Europe. In Neolithic times they were extensively used by early farmers who found the light stone-free soils to be fertile, well drained, and easy to cultivate.

logboat [Ar]. A wooden vessel made by hollowing out a substantial tree-trunk. In many cases such vessels were used with no further elaboration, in others the dug-out trunk formed the hull of a more substantial vessel built up from it. The earliest known date from the Mesolithic period in Scandinavia and northern Russia, where several examples are painted or carved with the forms of animals. Care must be taken in identifying logboats because tree-trunks were also hollowed out in prehistoric times to make troughs and coffins. Also called by the less satisfactory term dug-out canoe.

Lollius Urbicus [Na]. As governor of Britain from AD 138 or AD 139 to perhaps AD 144 he was responsible for the construction of the ANTONINE WALL in Scotland.

Lombards (Lombard) [CP]. Germanic people who migrated southwards to occupy the Hungarian plains during the 6th century. Pressure from the Avars caused them to move westwards, and in AD 568 they invaded Italy and established a kingdom in the Po Valley, with virtually independent duchies in the south. The northern kingdom was annexed by Charlemagne but the duchies survived until the Norman conquest of the mid 11th century AD.

London, UK [Si]. The capital city of England since medieval times, and of the UK in recent centuries, straddling the River Thames in the southeastern part of the British Isles. Although prehistoric settlements are known in the area later occupied by London, the major settlement on the site was the creation of a Roman town (Londinium) in the mid 1st century AD. In AD 66 the town was sacked by the Boudiccan rebellion. After its rebuilding it grew steadily, with a timber bridge across the Thames to Southwark by AD 70. The main town lay on the north side of the river, but was not walled until the later 2nd century when a fort seems to have been added to the north side. In its southwest quarter were a series of high-status and monumental structures including a temple erected in AD 294–5, a Mithraic temple, a large bath-house, and the governor's palace. Outside the walls were large cemeteries.

Although there is little evidence for occupation in the 5th and 6th centuries, London was chosen as the seat for the bishopric of the East Saxons in AD 604, and it was probably at this time that the cathedral of St Paul was founded. By the mid 7th century there was a port at London, and by the 9th century a substantial town was re-established to the west of modern-day Wallbrook, walled by c.1050.

The main consequence for London of the Norman invasion was the construction by WILLIAM I of the White Tower in what is now the Tower of London. West of the city there was also much activity around Westminster where an abbey existed from at least the 8th century and which later became the focus for a royal palace and the seat of power. Throughout the medieval period the city was prosperous with churches, monastic houses, merchants, traders, and industrial quarters all developing. The Civil War did not affect London greatly, but in 1666 the Great Fire of London caused much loss of property, as about one-third of the walled area was razed to the ground. The post-Fire reconstruction took many years but included great achievements such as Christopher Wren's masterpiece of architecture at St Paul's Cathedral.

[Sum.: E. Harwood and A. Saint, 1991, *London*. London: HMSO]

London ware [Ar]. A type of pottery with a relatively fine burnished grey or black fabric, often imitating various forms of Samian bowls, and often decorated with inscribed lines, impressed stamps, rouletting and compass-scribed circles. Made in the Thames Estuary area, Suffolk, Hertfordshire, and the Nene Valley in the late 1st and 2nd centuries AD, and widely distributed during this period.

long barrow [MC]. A class of middle Neolithic burial monument found extensively across the British Isles and related to other contemporary tomb-building traditions in other parts of northwestern Europe, especially northern France. The essential features of a long barrow are: the long rectangular or trapezoidal mound of soil and stone sometimes edged with a peristalith, a dry-stone wall, or timber posts; flanking ditches or quarry pits from which the material to construct the mound was obtained; chambers within the mound built either of orthostats or timber; and some kind of elaboration to the higher and broader end of the mound in the form of a concave forecourt or façade. Much literature on the period distinguishes between so-called **earthen long barrows** in the southern and eastern parts of the country and the stone **chambered tombs** of the north and west. Both are part of the same tradition of long-barrow building, although not all chambered tombs are long barrows (some are PASSAGE GRAVES, PORTAL DOLMENS, etc.).

The chambers within long barrows are located in one of two areas: terminal chambers that open into the mound form the wider higher end of the barrow, from the back of the forecourt or centre of the façade; or lateral chambers that open into the side of the mound. In all cases the chambers represent a small proportion of the overall structure, prompting speculation that the barrows may also have served as territorial markers. The burials are usually disarticulated inhumations, the corpses having been placed in the entrance areas to the chambers and then, bit by bit, moved further into the mound as they decayed and space was needed for the introduction of new burials.

All dated long barrows were built and used during the mid 4th millennium BC; many show signs of abandonment and in some cases deliberate blocking after about 3000 BC. A number of regional groupings can be recognized on the basis of concentrations in the distribution and the use of particular architectural details, including: Cotswold–Severn tombs, Clyde tombs, Carlingford tombs, Wessex long barrows, Yorkshire long barrows, Medway tombs, East Anglian and Midland group; and East Scottish group.

long count [Ge]. A calendrical system for measuring absolute time devised in Mesoamerica during the Formative (Pre-Classic) period. The day forms the basic unit (*kin*), thereafter multiplying up into larger units progressing by 20s: *uinal* (20 days), *tun* (360 days), *katun* (7200 days), and *baktun* (144 000 days). Dates are expressed as units in a five-place notation starting with the largest units. Thus 8.2.4.5.1 means 8 *baktunob*, 2 *katunob*, 4 *tunob*, 5 *uinalob*, and 1 *kin*. The Maya began their counting at a time equivalent to 3114 BC, perhaps marking some mythical event in Maya history. They inscribed their dates in the notation given above as hieroglyphs in which bars represented units of five and dots units of one. The long count system was replaced after AD 900 by a short count system in which the *katun* replaced the *baktun* as the largest unit.

long mortuary enclosure [MC]. A term proposed by Richard ATKINSON in 1950 to describe a class of rectangular ditched enclosures found first at Dorchester-on-Thames in Oxfordshire and later known sporadically throughout England and Scotland. They date to the middle Neolithic, broadly the later part of the 4th millennium BC, and appear to be ceremonial structures, perhaps the precursors of CURSUS monuments. Although Atkinson originally thought they might be the places where corpses were excarnated, prior to their bones being interred within LONG BARROWS, this is no longer accepted.

long mound [MC]. See BANK BARROW.

loom [Ar]. A frame used in weaving cloth. See WARP-WEIGHTED LOOM, UPRIGHT LOOM, HORIZONTAL LOOM.

loomweight [Ar]. A perforated stone or ceramic block weighing around 1 kg that was used for stretching the threads forming the warp or the weft on a loom. In many cases the loomweights and pin-beaters are all the physical evidence that remains for weaving at an excavated settlement.

looped handles [De]. Small sharply curving handles, fixed to the body of a vessel without being countersunk.

looped spearhead [De]. A type of bronze spearhead common in the middle Bronze Age of Europe which has a pair of small loops cast into the outside of the hafting socket near the base. It is assumed that these loops were to assist in securing the shaft to the spearhead itself.

LOOT [Ab]. Acronym for the 'Listing Of Outlaw Treachery'. See LOOT CLEARINGHOUSE.

LOOT Clearinghouse [Ge]. An archival database of information on past archaeological incidents and cases which is maintained by the Archaeological Assistance Division of the American National Park Service in Washington DC.

lorica hamata [Ar]. Latin term for a type of body armour worn by Roman legionaries, consisting of a shirt made of iron chain mail.

lorica segmentata [Ar]. Latin term for a type of body armour worn by Roman legionaries, consisting of a cuirass made from iron strips hinged together.

lorica squamata [Ar]. Latin term for a type of body armour worn by Roman legionaries, consisting of a cuirass made from shaped scales of iron and bronze riveted together.

Los Millares Culture [CP]. Copper Age communities of the 3rd millennium BC in southeastern Spain. Named after the type-site of Los Millares in the Almeria Province, excavated on several occasions since 1892, most recently by Almagro and Fernando Molina in the late 1970s and 1980s. The major settlements of the culture were enclosed villages, at Los Millares itself bounded by a stone wall with semicircular projecting bastions and an area of 5 ha. Inside, the citadel occupies the tip of the promontory and is defended by three walls. Three smaller forts lie outside the main structure. Cemeteries comprise collective burials in passage graves. Grave goods found in the tombs include pottery, stone tools, copper tools and weapons, and a variety of so-called idols made in stone, bone, or ceramic. Objects of ivory and ostrich-eggshell imported from Africa are also known. Beaker pottery is present in the later phases of the culture. At one time it was thought that the Los Millares Culture developed as a result of colonization from the Aegean, but a local origin is now favoured, with the development of local elites controlling the water supplies to the arid lands in this part of Spain, and also sources of metal.

lost-wax casting technique (cire perdue) [De]. A method of casting intricate metal shapes by first modelling the required form in wax, then surrounding the wax with clay, firing it and draining out the melted wax. This leaves a high-quality mould for a single casting.

lot system [Te]. A system of archaeological record-keeping in which all artefacts and ecofacts that are found together in a single horizontally or vertically defined unit are combined into one group (i.e. lot) for the purposes of collection, analysis, and storage.

Louis the German [Na]. Third son of Louis the Pious born *c.*AD 805, king of the East Franks from AD 840 until his death in AD 876.

Lower Palaeolithic [CP]. *See* PALAEOLITHIC.

Lowland Zone [De]. A term popularized in archaeological circles in Britain by Cyril FOX from the 1930s onwards to refer to the lowland regions of the south and east of the British Isles that are characterized by rather different kinds of archaeology from those found in the north and west. This is partly a product of geography, but this, Fox argued, had an effect on the human populations who had many miles imposed on them because of their proximity to the European mainland and who tended to be replaced as a result of migrations and colonization. *See also* HIGH-LAND ZONE.

low-relief [De]. *See* BAS-RELIEF.

Lubāna Plain, Latvia [Si]. Mesolithic and Neolithic settlements dating to the period 9000–2000 BC around Lubāna Lake on the borders of the Balvi, Madona, and Rēzekne districts of eastern Latvia. Investigations directed by I. Loze and F. Zagorskis between 1963 and 1982 revealed 23 separate settlement areas, some 13 of which were sampled by excavation. Hunting and fishing provided the subsistence base of the settlements of the Kunda Culture and Narva Culture horizons. Finds include preserved parts of fish-traps and nets as well as artefacts in flint, slate, bone, horn, and wood. From the later Neolithic, Corded Ware Culture and Lubāna pottery horizons *c.* late 3rd millennium BC, crop cultivation, and cattle breeding took over. Houses included piled structures with stone hearths set in marshy ground. Throughout the Neolithic, the Lubāna Plain was a centre of amber working and exchange.

[Rep.: I. Loze, 1979, *Akmens laïkmets Lubāna klānos*. Riga]

Lubbock, John (1834–1913) [Bi]. British banker, politician, and antiquary, later Lord Avebury, best known to archaeologists as the author of *Prehistoric Times* (1865, London). Lubbock became interested in archaeology at an early age and as a close friend of Charles Darwin was an early advocate of evolutionary thinking in his approaches to archaeological material. He published *Prehistoric Times* at the age of 35, introducing two new archaeological terms—Palaeolithic and Neolithic—as subdivisions of the Stone Age. The book went through seven editions, the last in 1913, and was enormously popular. It drew on ethnography to help interpret the archaeological material, and it also touched on one of Lubbock's other interests, the preservation of archaeological remains. Lubbock was the architect of the first ancient monuments legislation in Britain, finally succeeding in getting the Ancient Monuments Protection Act onto the statute book in 1882 after nearly a decade of negotiations. Outside of his archaeological life, Lubbock was a successful banker and a hard-working Liberal MP. Amongst his other successes in parliament was the introduction of a bill to establish bank holidays.

[Bio.: A. Grant Duff, 1924, *The life-work of Lord Avebury (Sir John Lubbuck) 1834–1913*. London: Watts & Co]

Lucretius [Na]. Roman poet, born *c.*94 BC, whose only surviving work, *De Rerum Natura*, is a didactic poem expounding the Epicurean philosophy of man and the universe. Died *c.*55 BC.

ludus [Co]. Latin term for a training or exercise area, such as a military amphitheatre.

lug (lug handle) [De]. A small solid clay protuberance integral with the wall of a pot to aid handling. Contrasts with the STRAP HANDLE which is formed by a projecting loop.

Lulach [Na]. King of Scotland. Born *c.*AD 1032, son of Gillacomgan, mormaer of Moray, and Gruoch (and stepson of Macbeth). Died in AD 1058 aged *c.*26, having reigned 7 months (August–March).

Lumbini, India [Si]. Birthplace of the Buddha in northeast India. Some archaeological work has taken place in the area and the presence of northern black polished ware pottery of the 1st millennium BC confirms the antiquity of the site. The emperor Asoka, head of the

Mauryan empire, visited the site in 249 BC and set up a commemorative pillar which still exists.

[Sum.: B. K. Rijal, 1996, *100 years of archaeological research in Lumbini, Kapilavastu and Devadaha*. Kathmandu: S. K. International]

luminescence dating [Te]. *See* THERMOLUMI-NESCENCE DATING.

lunula [Ar]. Crescentic necklets of sheet gold, so named because of their resemblance to the shape of a crescent moon. Generally decorated with fine incisions or REPOUSSÉ work. Mainly of early Bronze Age date and found widely across northern Europe, especially in Scotland and Ireland.

lur (pl. lurer) [Ar]. A type of musical instrument known from the late Bronze Age contexts in northern Europe in the form of a long horn of bronze with a double curve in it and a distinctive funnel-shaped distal end. Their manufacture was extremely complicated as they were made in several sections using the LOST-WAX CASTING TECHNIQUE. They are often found in peat bogs, usually in pairs, suggesting that they were votive deposits.

Luristan Culture [CP]. Communities living in and around the Zagros Mountains between Iran and Iraq in the late 2nd and early 1st millennia BC, distinctive for their bronze-working industry. Their origins are obscure, but they may have originated in the Caucasus away to the east; they seem to have been ancestral to the MEDES and PERSIANS. Their bronze work is characterized by ornamentation that includes the free use of animal and demonic human forms applied to such products as weapons, horse fittings, and jewellery.

Lusatian Culture [CP]. *See* LAUSITZ CULTURE.

lustral basin [Co]. A sunken room entered down a short flight of steps found in Minoan palaces. Arthur EVANS believed that they were used for ritual purification, but they could simply be bathrooms.

Luxor, Egypt [Si]. The modern town on the east bank of the Nile in Upper Egypt which covers the site of ancient Thebes. In the southern part of the town is the great temple of Luxor, built by Amenhotep III and Rameses II. It was connected to the second great religious complex at Karnak in the northern part of the city by a ceremonial way. Karnak was the most important religious centre in Egypt during the New Kingdom, although its roots extend back much further. Covering more than 120 ha, the site is dominated by the central temple to AMEN, around which are temples to Mut and another to Montu.

[Sum.: N. Strudwick and H. Strudwick, 1999, *Thebes in Egypt: a guide to the tombs and temples of ancient Luxor*. London: British Museum]

Lycians [CP]. The inhabitants of a small kingdom on the southern coast of Turkey that flourished in the early 1st millennium BC. Their capital was at Xanthos but little is known about them or their culture. They spoke an Indo-European language. They are mentioned in historical texts as being pirates, and are believed to have been one of the groups that come together as the SEA PEOPLES. Their kingdom was absorbed into the Achaemenid empire in the 6th century BC.

Lydians [CP]. The inhabitants of a small kingdom in western Turkey that flourished in the early 1st millennium BC. The capital at Sardis became rich as a result of exploiting gold in the nearby Pactolus River, and by the 7th century BC it was an important trading post en route between the Aegean and the oriental civilizations in India and China. Overrun by the CIMMERIANS for a while in the mid 7th century BC, the Lydians bounced back to become strong again. In addition to being very fine masons and architects, they were also the first people to create a coin-based currency. This innovation was subsequently adopted by both the Greeks and the Persians. Lydia flourished until the mid 6th century when, during the reign of King Croesus, they were overcome by the Achemenids. Sardis later became the western capital of the Persian empire, linked to SUSA by a royal road.

Lyell, Sir Charles (1797–1875) [Bi]. Geologist, traveller, and leading early proponent of *uniformitarianism*. Lyell's works, notably his *Principles of Geology* published between 1830 and 1833, were very largely responsible for the discrediting of the diluvialist and catastrophist theories about the antiquity of the human species based on the biblical chronology.

[Bio.: J. North, 1965, *Sir Charles Lyell: interpreter of the principles of geology*. London: Barker]

Lyles Hill ware [Ar]. *See* GRIMSTON WARE.

lynchet [Co]. A field scarp, usually produced by ploughing, in the form of a small-scale terracing effect visible particularly in ancient field systems where there has been an accumulation of soil against an obstruction such as a field boundary. *See also* STRIP LYNCHETS.

Lyngby axe [Ar]. A kind of axe made from an antler stem and tine, the end of which has been bevelled to form a sharp edge. Of early Mesolithic date and possibly used as a pole-axe.

Lyon ware [Ar]. Fine colour-coated cups and beakers with rough-cast appliqué or rusticated decoration. Made at Lyon in France, and imported to other parts of the Roman empire (mainly for military markets) from *c*.AD 43 through to *c*.AD 70.

Maat [Di]. The ancient Egyptian goddess of truth and order, whose symbol was the ostrich feather. She represented order, balance, correct attitudes and thinking, morality, and justice. She was a goddess of the underworld, sitting in judgement over the souls of the dead in the Judgment Hall of Osiris. The power of Maat was said to regulate the seasons, the movement of the stars, and the relations between men and the gods. Maat is a very ancient goddess and was found in the boat of Ra as it rose above the waters of the abyss of Nu on the first day.

Macbeth [Na]. King of Scotland from AD 1040. Born c.1005, son of a daughter of Malcolm II and Finlaec, mormaer of Moray. Married Gruoch, granddaughter of Kenneth III. Killed in AD 1057, aged c.52, having reigned seventeen years.

mace [Ar]. A club-like instrument with a perforated stone or metal head attached to a wooden or metal haft that was used as a weapon or ceremonial item. In medieval times, maces were made of iron and used for breaking defensive armour with a crushing blow.

macehead [Ar]. The stone or metal top of a MACE, usually perforated. In 1968 Fiona Roe published a classification of British late Neolithic stone maceheads, recognizing five main groups: ovoid; Maesmore group; flint nodule type; Thames pestle; and Orkney pestle.

macellum [Co]. A Latin term for a marketplace for perishable foods, especially meat, consisting of shops around a colonnaded court. The central building was usually either round or octagonal. Some more sophisticated examples have individual architectural features associated with them, for example a porticoed and enclosed rectangular courtyard, with one or two colonnaded pavilions in the central area.

MacEnery, Father J. (1796–1841) [Bi]. A Roman Catholic priest known for his excavations at Kent's Cavern, England, between 1825 and his death in 1841. Here he discovered Palaeolithic flint tools alongside the bones of extinct animals in an undisturbed stratum. He concluded that man and these ancient animals must have coexisted, but these views found little acceptance at the time; indeed Dean Buckland argued very strongly against MacEnery's interpretations claiming instead that 'ancient Britons' had cut ovens in the stalagmite layer that sealed the Palaeolithic layers and that the implements had penetrated the stalagmite only through these holes. Unfortunately, MacEnery died without publishing his results, a task completed by William Pengelly in 1869.

[Bio.: J. J. Walsh, 1926, *These splendid priests*. New York: J. H. Sears]

Machalilla Culture [CP]. Formative Stage farming culture thriving in coastal Ecuador during the later 2nd and early 1st millennia BC. Machalilla ceramics, in contrast to earlier Valdivian wares, are painted (red banded and black on white), and figurines are rare and crudely made. Wattle-and-daub fragments in middens indicate something of the nature of their houses, but no foundations have been defined. These communities appear to be the earliest maize cultivators in this part of South America. Successors to the Valdivia Culture; succeeded by the Chorrera Culture.

machicolation [De]. *See* MURDER HOLE.

Machu Picchu, Peru [Si]. Small Inca centre perched high on a rocky ridge between two peaks at an elevation of 2340 m above sea level overlooking a loop of the River Urubamba. The so-called lost city of the Incas (Vilcabamba), Machu Picchu was rediscovered in 1911 by Hiram Bingham, Professor of Archaeology at Yale University.

Defended by a stone wall, Machu Picchu has only one entrance. A stair leads up the hill to the site, and roadways connect it to Cuzco. The construction of the temples and other buildings involved creating level platforms on the hilltop. A sequence of small plazas lies along the ridge, the steep flanking slopes being terraced for houses and cultivation. One of the most extraordinary buildings is a circular astronomical observatory. Houses were rectangular in plan, high gabled, with thatch roofs and trapezoidal doors.

A programme of radiocarbon dating carried out in the late 1980s suggests two main phases to the site: the first, non-Inca, in the 7th century AD, and the second spanning the period AD 1200–1450. Some earlier dates of around 1000 BC suggest, however, that the Incas were not the first people to build on the ridge.

[Sum.: H. Bingham, 1930, *Machu Picchu—a citadel of the Incas*. New Haven: Yale University Press; R. Berger *et al.*, 1988, Radiocarbon dating Machu Picchu, Peru. *Antiquity*, 62, 707–10]

MacNeish, Richard Stockton 'Scotty' (1918–2001) [Bi]. American archaeologist who pioneered research on the evolution of agriculture and who studied the earliest human migrations into the New World. Born in New York he was a schoolboy boxer of note, taking his degrees at the University of Chicago and completing his BA in 1940 and his Ph.D. in 1949. He joined the National Museum of Canada as an archaeologist in 1949, remaining there until 1964 when the Tehuacán Project in Mexico was already well under way. This project examined the long-term cultural and environmental history of the Tehuacán Valley and was the first post-Pleistocene sequence for any region important in New World archaeology. It documented changes in subsistence patterns and the development of agriculture and village life which underpinned the rise of Olmec, Zapotec, and Maya civilizations. In 1964 he founded the Department of Archaeology in the University of Calgary, Canada, the first such freestanding department in the Americas. He continued this tradition and commitment to archaeology as a distinct discipline by spending the period 1982 to 1986 at the newly established Department of Archaeology in Boston University, the first such department in the USA. Between 1968 and 1983 he was director of the Robert S. Peabody Foundation for Archaeology in Andover, Massachusetts, but resigned after a disagreement with the governing body there about the allocation of funds. In the mid 1980s he established the Andover Foundation for Archaeological Research which served as a vehicle for receiving grants and running his projects for the rest of his life. Always a field archaeologist, he calculated that he spent 5683 days in the field during four decades of active research. He was awarded many honours and prizes for his work, including membership of the United States Academy of Sciences. Tragically, he died following a car crash in Belize where he was taking a working holiday to examine the sites of Lamanai and Caracol.

[Obit.: *Antiquity*, 75 (2001), 9–11]

macroband [Ge]. A group of several, usually related, families who set up seasonal hunter-gatherer camps. Well established through anthropological research, such social units are often used as a model for prehistoric societies. There may be more than one camp in the region exploited by a given macroband, the group itself moving from one area to another to exploit seasonal food resources. At some times of the year, the macroband splits into microbands. *See also* FISSION/FUSION.

macrobotanical remains [De]. Plant remains recovered from archaeological contexts that can be seen with the naked eye. These tend to be seeds and wood fragments, but nuts and other fruits may also be represented.

Maes Howe, Orkney, UK [Si]. Neolithic DEVELOPED PASSAGE GRAVE on Mainland in the Orkney Islands, Scotland. Constructed around 2750 BC the site has been partially investigated on several occasions, the first systematic excavations being those by Gordon Childe in 1954–5; later work includes a section through the surrounding ditch by Colin Renfrew in 1973–4, and a trench on the platform immediately outside the entrance by Colin Richards in 1991. Prior to all these, however, the central chamber had been entered and sacked by Vikings in the 12th century AD. They made runic inscriptions on the walls and claimed, amongst other things, to have carried off a great treasure.

The main mound is 7.3 m high and 35 m in diameter. A passage 12 m long leads into the mound from the southwest side and gives access to a very well-constructed vaulted chamber about 4.5 m square. This chamber has small square cells set into three of its walls above the floor level. Internal buttresses in each of the corners support the corbelled roof. The mound stands on a platform constructed over the remains of earlier structures, possibly houses, and is surrounded by a bank and ditch.

[Rep.: C. Renfrew, 1979, *Investigations in Orkney*. London: Society of Antiquaries. 31–8]

Maes Howe Group [CP]. A regional group of DEVELOPED PASSAGE GRAVES defined by Audrey Henshall. Centred on Orkney in the far north of Scotland, the group is named after the type-site of MAES HOWE. About twelve examples are known, characterized by their large rectangular chambers, small side cells leading off the main chamber, restricted entrances to the side cells, and long narrow approach passages.

Magdalenian [CP]. Late Upper Palaeolithic hunter-gatherer communities occupying much of northern and western Europe during the period 16 000–10 000 BC. The classic Magdalenian is concentrated in southern France and northern Spain, but it can also be recognized extending northwards into Britain and eastwards into the North European Plain in Germany, Poland, and as far as the Sudost River in Russia. The name is taken from the type-site rock-shelter of La Madeleine in the Dordogne Valley of southwest France. The Magdalenian stone industry is characterized by small geometrically shaped implements, especially triangles and semilunar blades, that were probably set into bone or antler handles for use, burins, scrapers, borers, backed bladelets, and shouldered and leaf-shaped projectile points. Bone was used extensively to make wedges, adzes, hammers, spear heads with link shafts, barbed points and harpoons, eyed needles, and jewellery. Their economy was based on reindeer hunting and fishing, and there is evidence of occupied caves as well as open sites. Some of the finest cave art in France and northern Spain can be attributed to these communities, as can a great many decorated bone and

ivory pieces. The Magdalenian followed the SOLUTREAN and AURIGNACIAN and was succeeded by the simplified AZILIAN. Magdalenian culture disappeared as the cool, near-glacial climate of the late DEVENSIAN warmed and the animal herds the communities depended upon became scarce.

Maglemosian Culture [CP]. Early Mesolithic communities occupying the North European Plain from Scandinavia to the northern Balkans in the period *c*.9000 BC to 5000 BC. This extremely widespread culture was named after the finds from a bog at Mullerup, in the Magle Mose, on the island of Zealand in Denmark, where evidence of the industry was first recognized. The name Magle Mose means 'big bog' in Danish. The material culture of these communities is well known because a number of excavated sites lay in waterlogged areas and were well preserved. Their tools and equipment included microliths, woodworking tools such as chipped axes and adzes, picks, barbed points, bone and antler spearheads, and fishing equipment such as spears and fish-hooks. Wooden bows, paddles, and dugout canoes have been found. Some Maglemosian material culture was artistically designed, with decoration on tools and wooden canoes. Ornaments such as pendants, bead necklaces, and amulets are also known. Their way of life was adapted to a forest, riverside, or lakeside environment, with fishing and the hunting of red deer the main sources of food and materials. Domesticated dogs are known.

magnetic dating [Te]. *See* ARCHAEOMAGNETIC DATING.

magnetic susceptibility [Te]. A technique that measures the degree to which a body of soil or sediment becomes magnetized when exposed to a magnetic field of known strength. All soils have some potentially magnetizable components, the nature of the ferrous mineralization and particle size being a major influencing factor. This allows apparently similar sediments to be distinguished from one another according to the degree of susceptibility. Especially useful for archaeology is the fact that the introduction of humic, organic, and burnt material, such as might be associated with settlements or areas of human occupation, tend to increase the susceptibility of soils. In archaeological prospection, systematically sampling an area of landscape may allow areas of high and low magnetic susceptibility to be recognized and thus settlement areas and activity sites to be identified. Within an individual site the technique can be used to characterize deposits and variations within them, thus allowing the position of houses, industrial areas, and middens to be recognized, and patterns formed by the recurrent use of certain spaces to be mapped.

magnetometer [Eq]. A portable device for measuring localized anomalies in the intensity and direction of the earth's magnetic field as a result of variations caused by changes in subsurface geology or as a result of human activity that changed the magnetic properties of the ground. Burning and the heating of sediments is the most significant factor, especially in detecting the presence of magnetically enhanced sediments in ditch fills, pit fills, and around structures. Ferruginous artefacts and deposits can also be located. A number of different kinds of magnetometer have been adopted for archaeological use. A **proton magnetometer** utilizes a sealed container full of water or alcohol in which is suspended a metal coil. When a current is passed through the coil the protons of hydrogen atoms in the liquid align themselves to its magnetic field. When the current is cut off, the protons realign themselves according to the local natural magnetic field, its strength being indicated by the frequency of their gyration on realignment. This frequency is transmitted back from the coil to the instrument where it is measured and logged. An **alkali vapour magnetometer** is a highly sensitive magnetometer that works at the atomic rather than the nuclear level. Developed by the University Museum of Pennsylvania University and Varian Associates in the 1960s it has the advantage of producing a continuous signal. Depending on the elements used, these instruments are also known as optically pumped magnetometers, optical absorption magnetometers, rubidium magnetometers, or caesium magnetometers. The last mentioned has become the most popular and in these the sensor is a glass cell containing caesium vapour at low pressure. Both the proton magnetometer and the alkali vapour magnetometer measure the total magnetic field so that systematic surveys across an area using close-set transects or a grid pattern will allow a map of magnetic anomalies to be built up.

The resolution of the resultant plot, and the scale of the anomalies found will depend on the size of the sampling interval, the sensitivity of the equipment, and the magnetic characteristics of the area being surveyed. An instrument in which a pair of sensors is used, either one above the other or side by side, is known as a GRADIOMETER.

Magnus Maximus [Na]. Roman emperor. A Spanish soldier who commanded the army in Britain and who led his troops into Gaul where he overthrew the Emperor Gratian. Theodosius the Great recognized his claim to Gaul, Spain, and Britain, but resisted Maximus' attempt to control Italy, and led an army which defeated him; Maximus was executed in AD 388. Thinly disguised as 'Prince Macsen', his memory remained a potent force in Welsh court circles until the 13th century AD.

Magosian [CP]. A obsolete term formerly applied to stone industries found in eastern and southern Africa, dated to the period 10 000 BC down to 6000 BC, and named after the type-site of Magosi in Uganda. Characteristic tools include small points, microliths, and small blades. An advanced Levallois technique was employed for the production of flakes for the manufacture of other tools, together with a punch technique for the production of microlithic artefacts. Projectile points were produced by pressure flaking. However, the assemblage from the type-site has been shown to be mixed and so can no longer be regarded as representative.

Magyars [CP]. Barbarian people, perhaps Finnish in origin, who migrated into southern Europe, and in the early 10th century AD occupied Hungary, from where their horsemen raided into France, Italy, Germany, and even Spain. Defeated at the battle of Lechfeld in AD 955, they settled down in Hungary and established a civilized Christian kingdom which survived into modern times.

Maiden Castle, Dorset, UK [Si]. One of the largest Iron Age hillforts in Britain, situated on the chalk downlands south of Dorchester in southern England. Excavated by Sir Mortimer WHEELER in 1934–7 and more recently by Niall Sharples in 1985–6, the hilltop has a long and complicated history starting in the middle Neolithic with the construction of a causewayed enclosure around 4000 BC. This was followed around 3400 BC by the building of a long mound partly over the infilled ditches of the earlier camp. The site was not heavily used during Bronze Age times, but occupation resumed around 500 BC with the construction of a hillfort. This fort was remodelled several times by the 3rd century, extending to 20 ha with three or four concentric ramparts and ditches and massive heavily defended entrances to the east and west. Maiden Castle was at that time a permanent settlement with stone and wooden houses linked by surfaced trackways. During the Roman conquest, the fort was sacked by Vespasian's legions. The Romans established a new centre for the Durotriges at Durnovaria (Dorchester), and the hillfort was abandoned until the 4th century AD when a Romano-Celtic temple was built there.

[Rep.: N. Sharples, 1991, *Maiden Castle excavations 1985–86*. London: English Heritage]

Maikop, Russia (Maykop) [Si]. Exceptionally rich kurgan grave of the early Kuban Culture dating to the mid 3rd millennium BC situated in the Kuban Valley of the northern Caucasus. The barrow, which is 10 m high and over 200 m in circumference, was excavated in 1897 and found to contain a timber mortuary house over a stone pavement, divided into three sections. The central section contained the burial of an adult male sprinkled with ochre and laid under a canopy with gold and silver supports. In each of the two flanking compartments was the burial of a woman. Overall, the burial is interpreted as that of a king, prince, or very important person accompanied by his wife or wives. Grave goods included tools and weapons of copper, gold ornaments, gold vessels, and silver vases engraved with animal scenes. The metalwork shows links with Mesopotamia and southwest Asia. Two of the vessels are decorated with engraved figures of mountains, streams, animals, and birds which Professor Farmakovsky has interpreted as a view of the landscape of the king's realm.

[Sum.: A. M. Tallgren, 1933, The Dolmens of north Caucasia. *Antiquity*, 7, 190–202]

Maikop Culture [CP]. Copper Age communities occupying the Caucasus mountain region of southern Russia in the later 3rd millennium BC, named after the rich grave at MAIKOP, Russia. Maikop settlements comprise

groups of up to ten houses, were usually built in defensible positions, and were sometimes enclosed by stone walls or timber palisades. Cist graves under small barrows were the usual burial tradition.

maize [Sp]. A stout annual cereal plant (*Zea mays*, sometimes called Indian corn) growing up to 1.8 m tall and yielding large grains set in rows on a cob. Teosinte, the wild ancestor of maize, is found in Mesoamerica from Mexico to Honduras, and perhaps further south still. The transition from wild grass to a maize cob appears to have happened in about a century or less, although it took far longer for large succulent cobs to evolve. First domesticated by *c*.3500 BC in Mesoamerica, maize makes its first appearance in the COXCATLÁN PHASE of the Tehuacán Valley sequence dated to before *c*.5000 BC. In North America it was the hardy low-yielding chapalote form of maize that was first cultivated in the southwest in the period *c*.1500–1000 BC, but this was soon replaced by the far more productive form maiz de ocho which is adapted to dry conditions but highly productive.

maker's marks [De]. Manufacturing marks etched or stamped onto mass-produced ceramics, glassware, and metals.

malachite [Ma]. Hydrous copper carbonate ($Cu_2(OH)_2CO_3$) representing a minor but widespread copper ore, green in colour. Probably first exploited as a cosmetic and ointment for the eyes, to cut down the glare of the sun and to discourage flies. The extensive deposits in Sinai were much exploited in antiquity. It was also used for oils and watercolours and encrusted on other materials as ornament.

malachology [Ge]. The study of molluscs. *See* MOLLUSCAN ANALYSIS.

Malambo Culture [CP]. Early farming communities occupying the north coast of Colombia in the 1st millennium BC and early 1st millennium AD, named after the type-site of Malambo south of Barranquilla on the Gulf Coast of Colombia. Characterized by pottery with distinctive incised, punctuated, and adorno (appliqué) modelled decoration.

Malcolm II [Na]. King of Scotland from AD 1016. Born *c*.954, son of Kenneth II. He acceded to Alba 1005, secured Lothian *c*.1016, and obtained Strathclyde for his grandson Duncan *c.*1016, thus forming the kingdom of Scotland. Died in AD 1034 aged *c.*80, having reigned eighteen years.

Malcolm III (Canmore) [Na]. King of Scotland from AD 1058. Born *c.*1031, elder son of Duncan I, he married (1) Ingibiorg (2) Margaret (St Margaret), granddaughter of Edmund II of England. He was killed in battle in AD 1093 at the age of *c.*62, having reigned 35 years.

Malcolm IV (The Maiden) [Na]. King of Scotland from AD 1153. He was born *c.*1141, son of Henry, earl of Huntingdon, second son of David I. He died in AD 1165 aged *c.*24, having reigned twelve years.

Mallowan, Sir Max Edgar Lucien (1904–78) [Bi]. British archaeologist well known for his work in the Middle East and one of the last of the 'old-school' archaeologists. A graduate of New College, Oxford, his archaeological career began as an assistant to C. L. WOOLLEY at Ur in 1925. Following this his career focused on the investigation of sites in northern Mesopotamia including Nineveh, Arpachiyah, Chagar, Bazar, Tell Brak, and Nimrud through the 1930s, 40s, and 50s. He was elected a Fellow of the Society of Antiquaries in 1933. After wartime service with the RAF he became Director of the British School of Archaeology in Baghdad and also presided over the British Institute of Persian Studies. In 1947 he was appointed to the Chair of Western Asiatic Archaeology in the University of London, a position he held until his death. Knighted in 1968, Sir Max was a Fellow of All Souls, Oxford, from 1962 until 1971 and Emeritus Fellow in 1976. In 1930 Mallowan married the writer Agatha Christie who thereafter used the experience of being involved with archaeological fieldwork in her detective stories, as for example in *Murder in Mesopotamia* (1936, London: Fontana) where the victim is modelled on Lady Woolley.

[Abio.: 1976. *Mallowan's Memoirs*. London: Collins]

Mal'ta, Siberia, Russia [Si]. Upper Palaeolithic open-air site on the Belaya River near Lake Baikal in south-central Siberia. Excavated by M. M. Gerasimonov, G. P. Sosnovsij, and others between 1928–37 and 1956–8. The Upper Palaeolithic level is dated to the beginning of the last glacial maximum around 24000 years ago. There are traces of a dwelling, partly constructed with limestone slabs, and the burial of a child possibly of mongoloid affinities. Associated artefacts include prismatic cores, retouched blades, end scrapers, a number of decorated objects, and human and animal figurines made of bone and ivory. A more recent, Mesolithic, horizon lay under the topsoil on the third terrace.

[Sum.: M. M. Gerasimov, 1964, The Palaeolithic site at Malta. Excavations of 1956–57. In H. N. Michael (ed.), *The archaeology and geomorphology of northern Asia. Selected works, vol. 3,* Toronto: Arctic Institute of North America/University of Toronto Press]

Malthusianism [Th]. A doctrine about population dynamics developed by Revd. Thomas Malthus, according to which population increase comes up against 'natural limits' which trigger famine and war and have the effect of reducing overall population levels.

malting floor (malting kiln) [Co]. A large well-ventilated room where barley grain could be spread out in order to sprout before being used to made beer. In some cases underfloor heating is provided to hasten the process. *See also* CORN DRIER.

Malvernian ware [Ar]. A pottery industry based around the Malvern Hills in west central England. The earliest production dates to the middle Bronze Age, but from the mid 1st millennium BC onwards the industry produced a range of very coarse, handmade, simple jars. They were distributed over considerable distances, particularly in the Marches, South Wales, and Gloucestershire.

mammisi (birth-house) [MC]. A distinct religious building within larger temple sites and cult centres of the Graeco-Roman period in Egypt which is connected with the mythological birth of the god to whom the temple or sanctuary is dedicated.

mammoth [Sp]. A type of elephant (*Mammuthus (Elephas) primigenius*) now extinct but widespread throughout middle and higher latitudes in the Northern Hemisphere during the Pleistocene and early Holocene. Distinguished by its long hair, thick woolly under-fur, and long tusks which curved upwards and outwards, mammoth were probably the largest animals hunted by Palaeolithic (including Palaeo-Indian) hunters, although exactly how they were captured and killed is not known. The woolly mammoth became extinct *c*.10 000 BC.

Mamóm [Ar]. Style of pottery made in Lowland Maya villages in late Formative (late Pre-Classic) times, characteristically monochrome with a waxy feel to the surface, made in a limited range of styles, but most commonly as flat-bottomed bowls.

Manacapurú Phase [CP]. South American farming cultures found in the Lower and Middle Amazon areas of Amazonia and tentatively dated to *c*.AD 400–500. Characterized by their ceramic assemblages which belong to the Incised Rim Horizon Style of the Amazon Basin. Some of the settlements of this phase are extremely large: the midden at the type-site of Manacapurú, Brazil, is approximately 2 km long by 400 m wide.

Management of Archaeological Projects (MAP2) [Do]. A scheme or model that outlines a set of principles for the planning, organization, and running of medium and large-scale archaeological projects. Published first by English Heritage in 1989, an elaborated and expanded document was issued in 1991 that has become known as MAP2. Based on the requirements of large-scale archaeological excavations and the subsequent programme of post-excavation analysis, the suggested system involves a continuous loop of four steps: proposal; decision; data-collection; and review. This cycle applies sequentially through five main stages in the life of a project: planning; fieldwork; assessment of potential for analysis; analysis and report preparation; and dissemination.

management plan [Ge]. A fully researched, structured, and formally approved scheme or strategy for the long-term maintenance of an archaeological site or land unit containing archaeological remains. Such plans may deal only with archaeological matters or be more broadly based with archaeology as one component. A management plan usually includes a summary of what is known of the site, its importance, the issues that relate to its future well-being, and a series of actions for immediate, medium-term, and long-term implementations. Different philosophies underpin the aims of management plans, for example conservation only, exploitation through public

access and presentation, or excavation and research. Typical issues covered by a management plan include: appropriate land use, tree-growth, animal activity, fencing, public access, litter and amenity, movement through and within the area (footpaths, roads, tracks, etc.), signboarding, interpretation, and further archaeological research.

Manching, Bayern, Germany [Si]. Late Iron Age *oppidum* originally adjacent to the Danube near Ingolstadt, Bavaria, Germany, established during the La Tène period, *c*.200 BC. Excavations by Werner Krämer during the 1950s showed that Manching was one of the largest *oppida* in Europe which may have been a regional market. The defences were elaborate, consisting of timber and stone walls 7 km in length, enclosing 350 ha, with four main gateways. Internally the settlement was well organized, probably pre-planned, with wide streets and regular rows of rectangular buildings in front of zones containing pits and working areas. Other areas were enclosed for granaries or horse stalls. The site was divided into work areas for particular crafts, such as wood, leather, and ironworking. Coins were minted and used on the site. There is evidence of a violent end to the settlement *c*.50 BC, although some occupation may have continued later in the northern part of the site.

[Sum.: W. Krämer, 1960, The *oppidum* of Manching. *Antiquity*, 34, 191–200. Rep.: W. Krämer and F. Schubert, 1970, *Die Ausgrabungen in Manching 1955–1961. Einführung und Fundstellenbüersicht*. Stuttgart: Franz Steiner Verlag]

Manchu Dynasty [CP]. The last imperial dynasty of China, AD 1644–1912. The Manchus were originally a nomadic people centred on the northern province of Kirin, Manchuria. They acquired much technical knowledge from the Chinese, to whom they were subject in the Ming Dynasty. They established their own kingdom in the 17th century AD and were able to invade and assume the government of China in AD 1644.

Manes [Ge]. The Roman spirits of the dead to whom dedications were often made on tombstones using the formula D.M. standing for *Dis Manibus*.

Manetho [Na]. An Egyptian historian who lived during the reign of Ptolemy Philadelphus (285–246 BC) and who wrote a history of his country. Although the original full text is lost, extracts appear in the works of later authors. Especially important are his listings of Egyptian pharaohs which he must have taken from available sources such as the PALERMO STONE and which provide the basis on which the main successive dynasties are identified.

manifest functions [Ge]. The functions of an aspect or type of social activity which are known to, and intended by, the individuals involved in a given situation of social life.

manioc [Sp]. Cassava plant (*Manihot esculenta*) with starchy tuberous roots. Native to the tropical lowlands of South America and Mesoamerica and the principal staple crop of early agricultural groups in northeastern South America. Although rich in carbohydrates, manioc is poor in protein and so a manioc-based diet must include supplemental protein from fish or meat.

There are two varieties of manioc: sweet and bitter. Both contain poisonous prussic acid: in the sweet variety the acid is concentrated in the skin and can be removed by peeling the tuber. In the bitter form the prussic acid is more pervasive and the tuber must be peeled, grated, washed, and squeezed before being eaten. The manioc flour produced by this process is usually toasted on large ceramic griddles called *budares*. These are archaeologically recognizable as evidence for manioc cultivation. Sweet manioc can be used to make a sweet beer. Manioc cultivation may have begun in the lowland tropical forests of the Orinoco Basin of Venezuela by *c.*5000 BC before spreading to Colombia, Ecuador, and southwards into Amazonia, western Ecuador and eastern Peru. It had appeared in the Maya Lowlands by about 1000 BC.

mano [Ar]. In American archaeology a cylindrically shaped grinding stone used in the hand, often in conjunction with a *metate*—a bottom or nether-stone. Used for grinding vegetable material such as maize, seeds, nuts, and pigments, the *mano* dates to the Archaic Indian period. The word comes from Spanish *mano de piedra* ('hand stone'). Their form varies considerably, from a barely modified cobble to a long cylinder similar to a rolling pin. *See also* METATE.

manor [MC]. The basic social, political, and economic unit of the manorial system, found in parts of northern Europe, Britain especially, from the 9th century AD. At its heart was a self-sufficient landed estate, or fief, that was under the control of a lord who enjoyed a variety of rights over it and the peasants (serfs) who worked on it. The lord of the manor exercised his rights through a manor court. Some of the tenants also owed a variety of dues and/or labour services on the demesne depending on their tenure. A manor could be part of, co-extensive with, or spread over several vills. In Britain manors ceased to have any general legal significance after AD 1925.

manor house [MC]. The main residence of the lord of the MANOR, typically comprising a substantial house, together with associated agricultural buildings and administrative offices. In England the manor house was often located near the main church serving the manor.

mansio [MC]. A Latin term for an inn of the *cursus publicus*. A small town (posting-station), or an inn, especially for government officials. They were typically spaced one day's journey apart; many were defended or enclosed by a rampart, with a gatehouse, guardrooms for the road police, and a canteen or *taberna*. Between *mansiones* there were rest houses, *mutationes*, with stables for changing horses and a small *taberna* for refreshing the riders.

Manteño Culture [CP]. Integration period chiefdom centred on Manta, Ecuador, from about AD 500 down to the Spanish conquest. The Manteño Culture is notable for its towns, mass-produced pottery, copper tools, and stone sculptures which often took the form of U-shaped seats supported by figures. T-shaped copper axes were common, but too thin to have been functional: they were probably some form of money or standardized unit of exchange.

manuport [De]. An unmodified stone carried to its findspot from elsewhere by human agency. Examples include seashells found inland or water-rolled pebbles away from any river.

Maoris [CP]. Native peoples of New Zealand who probably arrived from central Polynesia in the 12th century AD according to available radiocarbon dates.

MAP2   246

MAP2 [Ab]. *See* MANAGEMENT OF ARCHAEOLOGI-
CAL PROJECTS.

marae [MC]. Polynesian temples, comprising
walled and paved courtyards containing
altar-like ahu before which ceremonies took
place. Marae are among the most important
remains on Easter Island, the Hawaiian
Islands (especially Heiau), and the Tuamoto,
Society, Cook, Austral, and Marquesas Islands.
Ancestral forms probably go back to Early
Eastern Polynesian settlement around AD 500,
but are especially characteristic of the period
AD 1200–1800.

Marajoara Culture [CP]. South American
farming communities found in the Marajo
area of Amazonia and tentatively dated to *c*.AD
1000–1400. Characterized by their ceramic assemblages which belong to the Polychrome
Horizon Style of the Amazon Basin. *Tangas*,
pottery pubic covers, have been found
together with labrets, clay stools, spindle
whorls, and figurines of seated humans.
Burial mounds were built, and often contain
secondary burials in anthropomorphic polychrome urns. Marajoara settlements comprise large artificially constructed earthen
mounds, often 50 m by 35 m by 6 m high.
Multi-family houses were built on these
mounds which raised the houses well above
any seasonal floodwaters.

marble [Ma]. A granular limestone or
dolomite composed of calcium-magnesium
carbonate that has become recrystallized
under the influence of heat, pressure, and
aqueous solutions. This dense fine-textured
stone can be polished and was used for sculpture and decoration in many civilizations of
the Old World from Egyptian times onwards.

marching camp [MC]. A temporary Roman
fort set up by the army while on the move
for overnight stops and short stop-overs.
Surveyors laid out a suitable and reasonably
flat rectangular site, and tent positions were
planned and marked, usually surmounted by
a palisade of stakes. These distinctive enclosures may be identified by aerial survey.

Marcomanni [CP]. 'Border Men', a Germanic
people, from the 1st century BC, established
in Bohemia. Major wars were fought against
them from 166 BC to 180 BC, but they remained a threat to the Danube frontier, and
in the 6th century AD they annexed Bavaria.

Marcus Aurelius [Na]. Roman emperor, AD
161–80.

Marduk [Di]. Babylonian god, also called **Bel**,
originally a god of thunderstorms, who in the
13–12th centuries BC ousted Enlil as the most
prominent deity in the Sumerian pantheon.
He became the ruler of the gods, rather than
just their head, which represented a shift in
the relationship between the gods that paralleled the rise in power of the Mesopotamian
kings.

Margaret (The Maid of Norway) [Na]. Queen
of Scotland from AD 1286. She was born in
1283, daughter of Margaret (daughter of
Alexander III) and Eric II of Norway. She died
in AD 1290 aged seven, having reigned four
years.

Margary, Ivan Donald (1897–1976) [Bi].
British farmer, businessman, and archaeologist best known for his work on Roman roads.
After a period of war service with the Royal
Sussex Regiment he went up to Exeter College,
Oxford, graduating in 1921 with a degree in
chemistry. His life was spent in Sussex, farming first at Chartham Park and later at Yew
Lodge, East Grinstead. Alongside farming he
pursued an interest in archaeology, especially
in documenting and mapping the road network of Roman Britain. This was published in
a two-volume corpus *Roman roads in Britain*
(1955, London: John Baker), which was an immediate success and went through two successive editions during his life. Margary was a
wealthy and shrewd farmer and businessman
who applied his resources generously and
widely during his lifetime, including: helping
with the acquisition of Avebury for the
National Trust; funding rebuilding works at
Exeter College; and establishing the Margary
Room in the Barbidan House Museum in
Lewes and the *camerone* in the British School
at Rome.

[Obit.: *The Times*, 27 February 1976]

Mari, Iran [Si]. Mesopotamian city situated
on the right bank of the River Euphrates on
the border between modern Syria and Iraq
that flourished during the Old Babylonian
period as a principal commercial centre on
the trade route between Syria and Babylonia.

Extensively excavated by French archaeologists André Parrot from 1933 and Jean-Claude Margueron from 1979. The earliest deposits date to the Jemdet Nasr period (*c*.3200–2900 BC). The early dynastic remains include a number of substantial mud-brick buildings identified as temples and palaces. One of the most extensive palaces is Zimri-Lim, dated to the early 2nd millennium BC. The complex covers over 2.5 ha and contains over 300 rooms, including stables, storerooms, archives, and bitumen-lined bathrooms. One surviving mural depicts the ruler of Mari in the presence of various deities, including Ishtar in the form of the goddess of war. The most important discovery in the palace was the archive of some 23 000 Old Babylonian cuneiform tablets dating from *c*.1810 to 1760 BC. The cache includes scientific and economic texts, as well as several thousand items of diplomatic correspondence, including a vital set of letters between the ruler of northern Mesopotamia, Shamshi-Adad, and his son, Yasmah-Adad, the ruler of Mari. The palace was never rebuilt after its destruction at the hands of the Babylonian ruler Hammurabi in *c*.1759 BC.

[Rep.: K. Kohlmeyer, 1985, Mari (Tell Hariri). In H. Weiss (ed.), *Elba to Damascus: art and archaeology in ancient Syria*. Washington DC: Smithsonian Institution. 134–48 and 194–7]

Mariette, François Auguste Ferdinand (1821–81) [Bi]. French Egyptologist well known for his excavations at many major Egyptian sites. Born in Boulogne-sur-Mer, on leaving school he went to work in his father's office of the Marine Department. He left soon afterwards, however, first to take a post as drawing master at a private school in Stratford-upon-Avon in England, and then to be a teacher at the College of Art in Boulogne. He was an active journalist and essayist and was very interested in art. He was first introduced to Egyptology by his cousin Nestor Lhote, and became hooked. He learnt hieroglyphics and Coptic and spent his vacations in the Louvre Museum studying its collections. In 1849 he was offered a post at the Louvre which he gladly accepted. The following year he began a series of expeditions to Egypt, initially to collect manuscripts but this soon turned into excavations at Saqqara where he found the burials of the Apis bulls and the jewels belonging to Ramesses II. His ambition was to establish a museum of antiquities in Cairo, and

in 1858 Said Pasha the viceroy of the Ottoman emperor agreed to the plans. He founded the Egyptian Antiquities Service and what was to become the Cairo Museum (National Museum of Egyptian Antiquities). Later excavations included work at Giza, Abydos, Thebes, Edfu, and Elephantine. He was buried in a sarcophagus in front of the Cairo Museum.

[Bio.: G. Lambert, 1997, *Auguste Mariette, ou, L'Egypte sauvée des sables*. Paris: J. C. Lattes]

Marinatos, Spyridon Nikolaou (1901–74) [Bi]. Greek archaeologist well known for his excavations at Akrotiri on the island of Thera. Born at Lixouri on the island of Cephalonia, he studied archaeology and philology at Athens, Berlin, and Halle universities. His archaeological career began when he was made caretaker of antiquities on Crete, eventually spending twenty years there and becoming Director of the Archaeological Museum of Herakleion. In 1937 he became Director of the Archaeology Division of the Education Ministry, and in 1939 he was given the Chair of Archaeology at the University of Athens. In the same year he proposed the idea that the collapse of Minoan civilization in the Aegean was caused by the eruption of Thera in *c*.1500 BC. Later, in 1966, he discovered the buried Bronze Age port city at Akrotiri on Thera and spent most of the later part of his life excavating it. Marinatos also discovered the site of the battle of Thermopylae (480 BC) and the burial ground associated with the battle of Marathon (490 BC). Amongst his many publications is *Crete and Mycenae* (1959, London: Thames and Hudson). In 1955 he was elected a member of the Athens Academy. When the military junta seized power in Greece in 1967 he was appointed Inspector-General of the Archaeological Services, duties he was relieved of after the second military coup. Marinatos was killed in an accident during the excavations at Akrotiri and is buried in the site.

[Obit.: *The Times*, 3 October 1974]

maritime archaeology (marine archaeology) [Ge]. A subdiscipline of archaeology that focuses on the scientific investigation of the relics of past ships and seafaring. Although some of the evidence on which this is based comes from dry-land sites, the majority is below water within the intertidal zone and beyond.

Maritime Archaic [CP]. Archaic Stage hunter-gatherer communities occupying the north-eastern Atlantic seaboard of North America, especially New England and the maritime provinces of Canada, Newfoundland and Labrador from about 7000 BC down to historic times. The subsistence base of these communities was seasonal and combined the exploitation of caribou, elk, moose, and other land resources in the winter with sea mammals and fish in the summer. At the site of Port aux Choix, Newfoundland, over 100 graves were excavated. The burials were found to have been covered in red ochre and variously interred with elaborate barbed bone points, harpoons, and bone, antler, or ivory daggers. Their skin clothes were adorned with shell beads. After 4000 BC the Maritime Archaic declines as PRE-DORSET and DORSET TRADITION groups move southwards.

Maritsa Culture [CP]. Late Neolithic communities of the eastern Balkans in the period c.4000–3700 BC. Characterized by their distinctive dark-coloured ceramics with incised decoration which is filled with a white filler after the pot has been fired. Contemporary with Level V at KARANOVO and broadly contemporary with VINČA C.

mark [De]. In ROCK ART studies, any drawing, painting, engraving, or other modification of nature which is the product of some human action.

market [MC]. A defined place where people periodically gather together at predetermined times for the purchase and sale of goods, livestock, services, or commodities of various kinds within the structure of a MARKET ECONOMY. From Greco-Roman times onwards such activities usually took place in fairly elaborate surroundings, often in the centre of towns and cities. Throughout medieval Europe settlements were constructed around market-places which took on other social functions too.

market economy [Ge]. An economic system based on a mode of exchange in which the price of a commodity is fixed by the relative proportions of supply and demand. The process of buyer–seller exchange requires a degree of social control, for instance to guarantee access to goods and the security of traders. This is often achieved through the institutionalization of markets through regulation of the time and place where they take place. The prices are fixed independently, usually through negotiation, although participation in a market may require the payment of taxes to those who control the market.

market house (market hall) [MC]. A building designed for use as a market, usually in the centre of a settlement within or adjacent to a market-place. Many market houses were built on pillared arcades with an open area at ground-floor level and a large room or hall above.

market-place [MC]. *See* MARKET.

Marksville Hopewellian Culture [CP]. *See* HOPEWELLIAN CULTURE.

Marnian Culture [CP]. Name traditionally given to the Iron Age communities occupying a large area of northeastern France centred on the Marne valley in the later 1st millennium BC. They used a distinctive form of burial rite that in some cases involved depositing a chariot in the grave. There were close connections between the Marne region groups and the Arras Culture of eastern Yorkshire.

Marshall, Sir John Hubert (1876–1958) [Bi]. British archaeologist known for his work in India as Director-General of Archaeological Survey in India. Born in Chester and educated at Dulwich and King's College, Cambridge, Marshall received an excellent training in classical archaeology. Between 1898 and 1901 he was based at the British School in Athens, taking part in excavations at Knossos and various other sites on Crete. In 1902 he was appointed Director-General of Archaeology in India and from then until 1934 he set about reorganizing the department, recruiting Indians to work for the Survey, creating scholarship and training programmes, listing and recording ancient remains, and expanding the provision of museums. In addition he excavated many sites, notably Mohenjodaro, reported in a three-volume work entitled *Mohenjodaro and the Indus civilization* (1931, London: A Probsthain); Sanchi in central India with its fascinating group of Buddhist monuments; and Taxila in the Punjab which is closely associated with Alexander the Great's campaigns in the east, the Buddhist emperor Asoka, the Parthian king Gondofares, and

Apolonius of Tyana. He was knighted in 1914 and was awarded many honorary degrees, medals, and prizes. In 1936 he was elected a Fellow of the British Academy.

[Obit.: *The Times*, 18 August 1958]

Marshalltown trowel [Eq]. Excavation tool with a short flat metal blade fixed to a wooden handle by a cranked tang. In North America, Marshalltown trowels are widely regarded as the finest quality for archaeological use.

Martello tower [MC]. A type of gun tower designed solely as a defence against ships armed with guns attacking the southeast coast of England during the Napoleonic Wars. Built in the period 1805 to 1812, the 105 freestanding towers are set at intervals along the coast from Seaford, Sussex, to Aldeburgh, Suffolk. The towers are squat, built of stone or rendered brick, circular in form, with two floors and a roof-top gun platform designed to carry a single large cannon capable of all-round traversing. A moat was sometimes constructed around the tower for additional protection from land forces.

Martialis Marcus Valerius [Na]. Roman historian from Spain where he was born about AD 40. He spent much of his time in Rome where he published twelve books of epigrams before returning to die in Spain in about AD 104.

Martin Down style enclosure [MC]. A type of later Bronze Age ditched enclosure found in southern Britain and dating to the early 1st millennium BC. Characteristically rectangular in plan and generally less than 0.3 ha in extent, these enclosures are often situated on valley sides and low-lying ground where they are associated with settlement and animal husbandry. The example at Martin Down in Cranborne Chase, Dorset, provides the type-site.

Martinmas [Ge]. A traditional calendar festival in northern Europe celebrated in recent times on 11 November. Martinmas or All Hallows marked the time when stock were excluded from the fields in tillage and when the sowing of winter corn was expected to be complete.

Marxism [Th]. A body of thought deriving its main elements from Marx's political and economic theories, notably the idea that change in a society is seen as the result of contradictions arising between the forces of production (technology) and the relations of production (social organization). Such contradictions are seen to emerge as a struggle between distinct social classes. Using these theories Marx predicted the overthrow of capitalism and common ownership of the means of production in a classless society.

Marxist archaeology [Th]. An approach to archaeological interpretation and explanation that draws on the work of Karl Marx and Friedrich Engels to explore materialist models of social change and the central questions of social relations. Understanding who has power, and how that power is exercised, are seen as vital elements in explaining social change. Marxists regard each human society as defined and shaped by its 'mode of production', which comprises both the 'forces of production' (i.e. science, technology, and all other human and natural resources), and the 'relations of production' (i.e. the ways in which people relate to one another in order to facilitate the production and distribution of goods). Social organization and change are seen in terms of conflicts between segments of society: for example, those based on class, sex, or age. Among western archaeologists one of the first to draw heavily on Marxist theory was Gordon Childe who emphasized the forces of production as being fundamental influences on prehistoric economies, societies, and ideologies. In many of his early works he effectively challenged the fascist German-based views of prehistory current at the time.

Mary [Na]. Queen of Scotland of the House of Stewart. Born 1542, daughter of James V and Mary of Guise. She married (1) the dauphin, afterwards Francis II of France, (2) Henry Stewart, Lord Darnley, (3) James Hepburn, earl of Bothwell. She abdicated in 1567 and was held prisoner in England from 1568, where she was executed in 1587, having reigned 24 years.

Mary I [Na]. English queen from AD 1553, of the House of Tudor. Born 1516, the daughter of Henry VIII and Catherine of Aragon, she married Philip II of Spain. She died in AD 1558 aged 42, having reigned five years.

Mary II [Na]. Queen of England from AD 1689, of the House of Stuart. Born 1662, elder daughter of James II and Anne Hyde. Ruled with her husband the Dutch Protestant William III (of Orange). As daughter of the Catholic James II, she was invited to succeed after the expulsion of her father and the revolution of AD 1688. She died in AD 1694 aged 32, having reigned five years.

Mary Rose [Si]. A Tudor warship, flagship of Henry VIII's fleet which sank in the Solent off Portsmouth on its maiden voyage on the warm sunny afternoon of Sunday 19 July 1545. The site of the wreck was discovered in 1966 by Alexander McKee and Margaret Rule who carefully excavated and recorded it in what became one of the largest underwater archaeology projects ever undertaken. The remains of the hull of the ship were finally raised on 11 October 1982 with live television coverage. Since then it has been undergoing conservation treatment in a specially constructed museum in Portsmouth, Hampshire, UK. The finds from the ship, including the skeletons of many of the 700 hands that went down with her, provide a unique microcosm of material culture relating to navy life in mid 16th-century AD Britain.

[Sum.: M. Rule, 1982, *The Mary Rose: the excavation and raising of Henry VIII's flagship.* London: Conway Maritime Press]

Masada, Palestine [Si]. A great naturally fortified settlement on a plateau at the edge of the Judaean desert west of the Dead Sea in modern Palestine. Excavated by Yigael Yadin in 1963–5, the site is of great historic as well as archaeological interest. It was occupied from at least the Chalcolithic period (c.4000 BC) onwards but it flourished particularly during the Iron Age. The first major fortifications were erected by the Hasmonean king Alexander Jannaeus who ruled in the period 101–3 BC. However, Herod the Great was the chief builder of Masada. His constructions between 37 and 31 BC included two ornate palaces (one of them on three levels), heavy walls, and aqueducts, which brought water to cisterns holding nearly 200 000 gallons. After Herod's death in 4 BC, Masada was captured by the Romans, but in AD 66 Jewish Zealots took it by surprise and occupied it. In AD 73 the site achieved lasting fame as the stronghold in which almost a thousand Zealots committed mass suicide rather than surrender to the 10th Roman Legion who had besieged the hilltop.

[Sum.: Y. Yadin, 1966, *Masada: Herod's fortress and the Zealots' last stand.* London: Weidenfeld and Nicolson]

Masicito Phase [CP]. South American farming cultures found in lowland Bolivia and tentatively dated to c.AD 1000–1200. Characterized by their ceramic assemblages which belong to the Polychrome Horizon Style of Amazonia.

Massiliote Periplus [Na]. *See* AVIENUS.

mass spectrometer [Eq]. A machine for measuring the atomic weight or mass of an element and hence useful for distinguishing between different elements and different isotopes of the same element. *See also* ACCELERATOR MASS SPECTROMETRY.

mastaba [MC]. A flat-topped, bench-like Egyptian tomb structure under which rulers, high-ranking officials, and priests were buried, mainly of the early dynastic and Old Kingdom. The term comes from the Arabic word for 'bench'. Early examples tend to be low rectangular buildings with a flat roof and vertical or slightly inclined walls that enclosed a shaft leading to an underground burial chamber. Later versions were reinforced with stone and were more elaborate. They often contained a chapel and a statue of the deceased, and had several rooms. The pyramids were a direct development from the mastaba.

MAT [Ab]. Mousterian of Acheulian Tradition. *See* MOUSTERIAN.

matchlock [Ar]. A type of musket developed in the 15th century AD which used an attached burning taper to light the gunpowder.

Matera ware [Ar]. A type of middle Neolithic pottery found at many sites in southern Italy, notably the ditched villages of Murgecchia and Murgia Timone. Characteristically a dark burnished fabric represented as curved bowls and straight-necked jars, decorated with rectilinear geometric designs scratched into the walls after firing and filled with an inlay of red ochre. A quite different ware comprising a thin, buff-coloured pottery painted with broad bands of scarlet, is sometimes included within the range of Matera ware products.

material culture [Ge]. A term used to describe the objects produced by human beings, including buildings, structures, monuments, tools, weapons, utensils, furniture, art, and indeed any physical item created by a society. As such, material culture is the main source of information about the past from which archaeologists can make inferences. A distinction is often made between those aspects of CULTURE that appear as physical objects and those aspects that are non-material.

materialist conception of history [Th]. The view developed by Marx, according to which 'material' or economic factors have a prime role in determining historical change.

matriarchal [De]. Family authority resting with the woman's family. Thus **matriarchy**, rule by women.

matrilineal inheritance [Ge]. The inheritance of property or titles through the female line only. Also known as matriliny or matrilineality.

matrilocal family [Ge]. A family system in which the husband is expected to live near to the wife's parents.

matrix [Ge]. **1.** The material or sediment in which cultural debris is contained; the surrounding deposit in which archaeological finds are situated. **2.** See HARRIS MATRIX. **3.** The main metal component of an ALLOY.

Matt [Di]. See MAAT.

mattock [Ar]. A digging tool comprising a flat blade set transversely to a wooden handle. The oldest examples are Mesolithic in date and were presumably used for digging holes and grubbing up edible roots and tubers. Later examples were extensively used for breaking up ground for agriculture. Also called a **hoe**.

Maudslay, Alfred Percival (1850–1931) [Bi]. English soldier and scholar who was one of the first people to visit and make a scientific record of the great Maya sites of central America. Inspired by accounts of the ruins, he visited Guatemala and the neighbouring republics in the 1880s and 1890s. During this work he took photographs and made casts, plans, and drawings at such sites as Quiriua, Palenque, and Chichén Itzá. He was the first archaeologist to see the important ruins of Yaxchilan. Between 1889 and 1902 he pub-

lished eight volumes of photographs and drawings of Maya monuments and cities, accompanied by a text, as *Biologia Centrali-Americana. Appendix: archaeology* (London). Maudslay's work is important because it was accurate and objective; his records remain a valuable source of information.

[Obit.: *American Anthropologist*, 33 (1931), 403–11]

maul [Ar]. A type of massive, heavy, stone hammer used for battering rock surfaces.

Mauryan empire [CP]. An ancient Indian state dating to the later 1st millennium BC, centred on Pataliputra (modern Patna) near the junction of the Son and Ganges rivers. After Alexander the Great's death in 323 BC, Candra Gupta founded a dynasty that encompassed most of the subcontinent except for the Tamil south, driving the Greeks out of India and establishing the Mauryan empire as an efficient and highly organized autocracy. The empire was characterized by a differentiated economy based on food-gathering tribes, pastoralists, various kinds of peasant cultivators, and traders. There was a standing army and a kind of civil service. The Buddhist Mauryan emperor Ashoka who reigned between *c.*265 and 238 BC is known for the stones erected throughout his realm bearing edicts; these are among the oldest deciphered original texts known in India. The Mauryan empire subsequently declined and was deposed by Sunga in 187 BC.

mausoleum [MC]. An above-ground storage structure for the dead which often comprised large and impressive sepulchral monuments. The original mausoleum was the gigantic tomb of Mausolus, ruler of Caria in southwest Asia Minor, built at Halicarnassus *c.*353–350 BC. It was considered one of the SEVEN WONDERS OF THE ANCIENT WORLD. The term later came to be used for any tomb built on a monumental scale.

Mawangdui, China [Si]. A group of early Han Dynasty tombs near Chang-Sha (Changsha City) in Hunan Province. Excavated in 1972–4, the three tombs each take the form of a massive compartmented timber box at the bottom of a deep stepped shaft. The shaft was filled in with rammed earth, and a mound was raised over it. Tomb 2 is probably the earliest and belonged to the first marquis of Dai who died in

186 BC, a high official of the Han administration.

Tomb 3 is probably the burial place of the marquis's son who died in 168 BC. Its contents were better preserved than those in Tomb 2, comprising silk paintings, three rare musical instruments, and an extraordinary collection of manuscripts, some on silk and some on bamboo slips. The writings deal with such subjects as contemporary philosophical themes, early historical events, military information, astronomical and calendrical matters, geography, and medicine.

Tomb 1 is that of the marquis's wife who died shortly after 168 BC. The earthen mound was 16 m in height. The contents of this tomb were very well preserved. The body and internal organs of its occupant showed it to have been a 50-year-old female of short stature. Details from the autopsy of the cadaver showed a variety of ills leading up to her death, including coronary arteriosclerosis, pulmonary tuberculosis, and gallstones. The body had been wrapped in silk and laid inside four richly decorated nested coffins. More than 180 dishes, toilet boxes, and other lacquered articles, silk clothing, offerings of food, musical instruments, small wooden figures of servants and musicians, and a complete inventory of the grave goods written on bamboo slips serve to depict extreme wealth.

In construction and contents these three tombs are rather different from other Han princely burials in northern China and reflect the lingering traditions and material culture of the Chu kingdom, which had fallen to the Qin less than a century earlier.

[Sum.: Q. Hao, 1981, The Han tombs at Mawangdui, Changsha: underground home of an aristocratic family. In Q. Hao (ed.), *Out of China's earth*. London: Muller. 87–125]

Maximian [Na]. Co-emperor of the Roman empire, AD 286–305.

Maya [CP]. A regionally distinct cultural grouping, united by material culture and language, occupying eastern Mesoamerica from the Formative Stage down to the present day. During the Classic Stage from about AD 300 to AD 900 the Maya emerged as the most sophisticated civilization in pre-Columbian America.

The origin of the Maya is a matter that has attracted much research but little clarifica-

tion. The ancestral lands were probably the Guatemalan–Chiapas highlands where, during the Early Formative, maize farming became widespread before communities began moving westwards into the adjacent lowland areas of Yucatán. Among the earliest villages known in the lowlands is Cuello, Belize, established about 1200 BC. Within three or four centuries, a network of small chiefdoms established itself across what is now Guatemala, Belize, southeastern Mexico, and the western parts of Honduras and El Salvador. Various models of what happened next, and how these chiefdoms became states, have been advanced. A common theme to many of these models is the problem of population pressure. Some areas, for example the Usumacinta and Belize River basins, were rich agricultural areas and here the population rose, with the result that agricultural land became scarce and warfare between local chiefdoms increased. The need for military leaders and for authoritative individuals to allocate land led to the emergence of an elite. Trade was also important, and there is some evidence for contact with the Olmec to the north.

After AD 800, Maya villages seem to have become more closely connected with one another through internal trade and exchange systems, most clearly seen in the distribution of Mamóm style pottery. At the same time, ceremonial centres begin to develop, leading to a two-tier settlement hierarchy. At Nakbe, Guatemala, a ceremonial centre seems to have developed on the site of a former village, perhaps indicating the centralization of local power. By 400 BC there were several ceremonial centres in both the lowlands and the highlands, each site including pyramids, temples, platforms, and stelae.

Population continued to grow during the late Formative (late Pre-Classic), and the transition from chiefdom to state seems to have happened around AD 250 in lowland areas. The two-level settlement hierarchy developed into a four-level system comprising villages, small ceremonial centres, large ceremonial centres, and regional centres. Large and small ceremonial centres were regularly spaced at intervals of 13–26 km.

An elaborate calendrical system was evolved, not least to identify appropriate days for holding ritual and ceremonial events. The LONG COUNT calendar provides a valuable tool for dating Maya sites and objects.

Although irrigation was known it was not

extensively used, and the economic basis of the Maya state was intensive but broadly based agriculture. In particular it focused on utilizing raised fields to grow maize, beans, squash, chilli peppers, and root crops. Settlement was mainly dispersed, with small hamlets of up to five houses arranged around a courtyard. Some of the large and regional ceremonial centres also acted as settlements and recent investigations around Tikal, for example, show that the ceremonial centre was the religious and administrative core of a city of perhaps 70000 inhabitants.

The Maya elite was engaged in exchange practices, building on the networks established during late Formative times. The commodities acquired included salt and grinding stones as well as raw materials such as obsidian, shell, and chert for the production of fine objects. Jade was the most precious material known to the Maya and was widely traded from its restricted sources in the Motagua Valley.

The ceremonial centres included temples, pyramids, ball-courts, palaces, and plazas, usually linked by causeways or wide paved roads. The massive monumental structures were intricately carved and decorated with scenes showing how the hereditary dynasties of the kings united with the gods.

After about AD 800, many of the Classic Maya centres fall into decline and population decreases: the so-called Classic Maya Collapse. Many causes for this have been put forward, including epidemic disease, earthquakes, drought, agricultural collapse, the severing of trade routes, a peasant revolution, and invasion. No one single cause adequately accounts for the process, and social and political factors may in fact have been the most important, especially the fall of Teotihuacán in Mexico before AD 750, and the power struggles and political unrest that must have ensued. Maya culture remained, albeit in slightly different form, flourishing in northern parts of Yucatán down to AD 1000 when Toltec invasions caused further changes. The Maya remained the indigenous people of Mesoamerica at the time of Spanish conquest, and there are about 6 million Maya living today.

Mayapán, Mexico [Si]. Capital of the Maya-dominated state in northern Yucatán, established by the Cocom dynasty of the Itzá after the Classic Maya Collapse and the final aban-

donment of Chichén Itzá in the 13th century AD.

Mayapán is enclosed by a stone wall, a testimony to the unrest at the time, and covers about 6.5 square kilometres. There are over 2000 dwellings within the walls, and its population may have been as high as 12000. Most lived in thatched houses of no great pretention.

Mayapán's temples, including the centrally placed Temple of Kukulcan, and palaces were poor imitations of those at earlier centres, perhaps a sign of cultural decline or growing disinterest by the population in impressive public architecture.

Mayapán was destroyed by its own inhabitants around AD 1450 during a rebellion against the Cocom rulers who dominated the territory.

[Rep.: H. E. D. Pollock, R. L. Roys, T. Proskouriaroff, and A. L. Smith, 1962, *Mayapán, Yucatan, Mexico*. Washington DC: Carnegie Institution]

Maykop, Russia [Si]. *See* MAIKOP, RUSSIA.

maypole [MC]. A tall wooden post, typically 6–10 m high, erected on a village green or convenient public open space in southern Britain in early spring, that provides the centrepiece for formal communal dancing and celebrations. The dances were traditions 'rounds' where the participants form a circle. Traces of the stone sockets in which maypoles were placed can be seen on some village greens. References to maypoles extend back to the 14th century AD; the tradition of dancing round the maypole with plaited ribbons was introduced by Professor Ruskin in AD 1889.

Mazapan ware [Ar]. A type of pottery that developed out of Coyotlatelco styles and first appeared in association with major architecture at Tula, Mexico, in the Post-Classic Toltec phase (9th–12th century AD). The orange-on-buff and red-on-buff ware was decorated by straight or wavy parallel lines produced by multiple brushes.

maze [MC]. *See* LABYRINTH.

MBA [Ab]. Middle Bronze Age.

McBurney, Charles Brian Montagu (1914–79) [Bi]. Prehistorian best known for his work on the Palaeolithic. American by birth, he was brought to England when he was eleven and privately educated there. Although his family lost their farm in Stockbridge, Massachusetts, in the Great Depression, McBurney went up to King's College, Cambridge, in 1933 to study archaeology, becoming a British citizen in 1940. He remained at Cambridge as a university lecturer in archaeology and was given a personal Chair in 1977. He worked at numerous sites in North Africa, Britain, and central Asia, and his publications include *The Stone Age of Northern Africa* (1960, Harmondsworth: Penguin) and *The Hauna Fteah (Cyrenaica) and the Stone Age of the south-east Mediterranean* (1967, Cambridge: CUP).

[Obit.: *The Times*, 17 December 1979]

McKean Complex [CP]. Middle Archaic communities living on the Great Plains of North America who manufactured and used a distinctive chipped stone point known as the MCKEAN POINT in the period *c.*2900–1000 BC. Named after its type-site in northeast Wyoming, the McKean Complex is not, however, universally recognized, as many specialists feel it subsumes a wide range of cultural groupings. The importance of the complex is that these communities developed a hunter-gatherer adaptation that involved the careful scheduling of economic activities through the year to coincide with the seasonal abundance of plants and animals.

McKean points [Ar]. Bifacially worked chipped stone projectile points characteristic of the McKean Complex of the middle Archaic Stage in the Great Plains of North America during the period *c.*2900–1000 BC. Lanceolate in outline with curved sides and a hollow base these points were probably spearheads used in bison hunting.

meadow [Ge]. **1.** An area of grassland used for making hay. **2.** An area of low-lying marshy ground usually beside a river or stream that is seasonally flooded but when dry enough used for grazing cattle. *See also* WATER MEADOW.

Meadowcroft, Pennsylvania, USA [Si]. A rock-shelter near the town of Avella in southwestern Pennsylvania investigated by James Adovasio between 1973 and 1977. The very extensive sequence of deposits in the shelter divides into eleven main strata. Dated by over 70 radiocarbon determinations, these strata span the period from the late glacial (before 30 000 BC) down to historic times. The earliest artefacts come from Stratum IIa and belong to what is believed to be a pre-Clovis Palaeo-Indian tradition with small blades, a bifacially worked flake knife which the excavator called 'Mungai' and a lancolate projectile point. This material is not typical of eastern Palaeo-Indian assemblages and eight radiocarbon determinations date it to the period between 17 000 and 11 000 years ago. These dates have been disputed by the geologist C. Vance Haynes on the basis of possible contamination, while others have questioned such an early dating because the environmental evidence for the same strata does not match with the kind of tundra conditions which would be expected at this time. At present, however, the Meadowcroft is the best candidate for early occupation of North America.

Later deposits include Archaic and Woodland Stage occupation, all with acceptable radiocarbon dates and associated cultural material.

[Sum.: J. M. Adovasio, 1978, Meadowcroft Rockshelter, 1977: An overview. *American Antiquity*, 43(4), 632–51; R. C. Carlisle and J. M. Adovasio (eds.), 1982, *Meadowcroft: Collected papers on the archaeology of Meadowcroft Rockshelter and the Cross Creek Drainage*. Minneapolis: Society of American Archaeologists]

Meadowood Phase [CP]. Woodland Stage hunter-gatherer communities flourishing in New York State and surrounding areas of the Atlantic seaboard of North America in the period *c.*700 BC to 300 BC. These groups seem to have had large semi-permanent base camps around which plant food was cultivated to tide them over periods of poor hunting. Adena and Hopewellian exchange networks extended into Meadowood areas with resulting cultural influences.

Burial grounds were set on low natural hills. Bodies were usually cremated and deposited in ochre-covered shrouds. The grave pits themselves were lined with bark, and traded goods, luxury items and projectile points were deposited with the dead.

mealing bin [Co]. A small adobe or stone-lined pit in which was placed a *metate*, used for grinding maize.

meander [De]. A running linear design consisting of a single line or band twisting regularly. Variations include the spiral meander in the form of a coil, and the square meander as a rectilinear form of the same thing.

meaningful activities [De]. Human action which is carried out for definite reasons, and with specific purposes in mind. The vast bulk of human behaviour is composed of meaningful activities, this being one of the main characteristics which separates human conduct from the movements, objects, and events of the natural world.

means of production [De]. The facilities whereby material goods are created within a given society, including not only the technology but also the social relations between those involved.

Medes [CP]. Communities speaking Indo-European languages who occupied northwest Iran from the late 2nd millennium BC through to the mid 1st millennium BC. Their origins are rather obscure, but they appear to have arrived in the region via the Zagros Mountains at about the same time as the PERSIANS, to whom they may have been related. At first the Medes were the more powerful of the two peoples. During the early 1st millennium BC they played an active part in the complicated politics of the region. Although initially dominated by the late Assyrian rulers, they seized the opportunities presented by the collapse of Elam to destroy Assyria in 614–612 BC, under their ruler Cyaxarea. They then created their own empire, taking in most of Iran, northern Mesopotamia, and eastern and central Asia Minor. They inherited much of the kingdom of Urartu. Their capital was at Ecbatana (modern Hamadan), and major settlements have been excavated at Godin Tepe, Bab Jan, and Nush-I Jan.

The Persian king Cyrus the Great overran the Medes in the mid 6th century BC, although they remained ruling partners in the Achaemenid empire he set up. The Medes and the Persians were subsequently united by marriage connections. The Medes are well illustrated in the friezes of Persepolis, and are traditionally credited with the invention of trousers.

medieval frontier work [MC]. *See* LINEAR BOUNDARY.

medieval period [CP]. Also known as the Middle Ages. When used in Britain, the term

defines the period between about AD 800 and *c.*AD 1500, though in practice it is often divided into a pre-conquest or early medieval period (AD 800–1066) and a post-conquest, later medieval or high medieval period (AD 1066–1500).

Medway tomb [CP]. A regional style of Neolithic LONG BARROW found in the area around the River Medway in north Kent. Characterized by rectangular mounds with peristaliths and simple square chambers at one end of the mound. About ten examples are known in the group, of which the most fully explored is The Chestnuts at Addington excavated by John Alexander in 1957.

meeting house [MC]. A non-conformist place of worship. The term was (and still is) used particularly by Independents and Quakers.

megafauna [De]. General term for the large-bodied big-game animals that flourished during the Pleistocene and its immediate aftermath. The main megafauna species in the Northern Hemisphere included: mammoth, mastodon, bison, giant sloth, and sabre-tooth tiger.

megafauna extinction [Ge]. All over the world the early Holocene period saw the decline and extinction of MEGAFAUNA. The causes of this are a matter of some debate. Changing environmental and climatic conditions must have played a part, but so too did the activities of hunter-gatherer populations. With reference to North America, where 32 genera of mammals became extinct, Paul Martin has argued that the CLOVIS CULTURE big-game hunters were responsible for the megafauna extinction because of wasteful hunting methods.

megalith [Ar]. Literally, a big stone. Often applied as a general term to monuments of Neolithic and early Bronze Age date in northwest Europe which incorporate such stones into their construction: for example, chambered tombs, stone circles, and alignments as well as individual standing stones or menhirs. Also used as an abbreviated form of megalithic tomb.

megalithic architecture [De]. A rather obsolete term once applied to the design of Neolithic long barrows, other types of chambered tombs, and related monuments that utilized megaliths in their construction. As variations in the form of the structures have been recognized and explored, less attention has been given to the techniques used in their construction.

megalithic art [Ge]. General term for the styles of ROCK ART found on component stones of PASSAGE GRAVES and DEVELOPED PASSAGE GRAVES in northwest Europe, especially northern Spain, Brittany, Ireland, Wales, England, and Scotland. Some of the stones were decorated while part of the tomb, but others were clearly decorated prior to being used during the construction of the monument. Typical motifs include: spirals, lozenges, zig-zags, concentric circles, axe motifs, oxen, human breasts, and crook symbols.

megalithic tomb [MC]. A general term applied to chambered tombs in which massive blocks of stone (*see* MEGALITH) were used to create the walls and roof of passages and chambers. The term is often used generically for all kinds of stone-built chambered tombs, or loosely when the exact type of tomb is not known. *See* LONG BARROW, PASSAGE GRAVE, PORTAL DOLMEN.

megalithic yard [Ge]. A unit of measurement proposed by Professor Alexander Thom in 1962 as being the yardstick used in setting out STONE CIRCLES and other similar structures characteristic of the later Neolithic and early Bronze Age in northwest Europe. Equal to 0.829 m or 2.72 feet, Thom deduced the existence of a standard measure from the systematic metrical analysis of over 40 stones circles. While it is generally accepted that some standard measurement was used in the construction of stone circles, few agree that such a specific standard measurement could have been adopted throughout Atlantic Europe.

megaloceros [Sp]. An extinct kind of large deer (*Megaloceros giganteus*), also known as the giant deer and, rather erroneously, as the Irish elk. Found widely across northern Europe and western Asia during Pleistocene times it stood up to 1.8 m high at the shoulders. The males had huge palmated antlers with a span of up to 3 m. It became extinct around 10 000 years ago.

Megalopolis [Ge]. The 'city of all cities' in an-

cient Greece; used in modern times to refer to very large conurbations.

megaron (pl. megara) [MC]. Form of tripartite rectangular hall or building particularly associated with Mycenaean citadels, in which a rectangular room is approached through a forecourt and vestibule forming an extension of one end. The principal room commonly contained a central hearth surrounded by four columns and a dais to one side.

Megiddo, Israel [Si]. A large tell (Tell el-Mutesellim) formed over a natural hill within the southern Jezree Valley of Israel, about 35 km southeast of Haifa. Excavations by J. Schumacker in 1903–5 identified the site with the Biblical town of Megiddo, and this and subsequent investigations by Clarence Fisher and Yigael Yadin in 1925–39 revealed at least 25 major phases of occupation, beginning with sporadic occupation during the Neolithic and Chalcolithic. The site became a substantial town during the early Bronze Age, the early 4th millennium BC. It quickly became a fortified centre through its strategic position on the land route from Egypt to Mesopotamia. Megiddo was captured by the Egyptian king Thutmose III in about 1503 BC, and was subsequently transformed into an Egyptian garrison during the 15th and 14th centuries BC.

During the late 2nd millennium and early 1st millennium BC the site was sacked many times. In the 13th century BC it was in Canaanite hands and at this time a rock-cut shaft and a 65 m long passage were built to give access to a spring inside the walls. In the 9th century BC it was in the hands of the Israelites and from this period there is a palace, shrine, and stable buildings. The site became important for Phoenician trade too, and among a number of notable finds there is a hoard of 400 Phoenician ivories.

The town was destroyed at the end of the 8th century BC, and, although rebuilt under Persian domination, it declined into insignificance during the Hellenistic period.

[Rep.: G. Loud, 1948, *Megiddo II. Seasons of 1935–9*. Chicago: University of Chicago Press]

Meldon Bridge Period [CP]. A phase of the British late Neolithic spanning the period 3000–2750 BC which was defined by Colin Burgess in the late 1970s using Meldon Bridge in Peebleshire, Scotland, as the type-site.

Following the middle Neolithic, the start of the Meldon Bridge period is marked by the development of PETERBOROUGH WARE and GROOVED WARE. It is followed by the MOUNT PLEASANT PERIOD. During the Meldon Bridge period major new types of monuments such as HENGES, HENGE ENCLOSURES, CURSŪS, PALISADED ENCLOSURES, DEVELOPED PASSAGE GRAVES, and STONE CIRCLES began to develop. In some areas single graves became more common. The later part of this period also sees the first use of copper in the British Isles, initially in Ireland with items imported to other areas. This has been defined by Colin Burgess as metalworking Stage I (Castletown Roche industries) and Stage II (Knocknague/Lough Ravel industries).

Melkarth (Melkart) [Di]. Phoenician god, chief deity of Tyre and its colonies Carthage and Gadir. Represented in Solomon's temple in Jerusalem and sometimes equated with Heracles.

melon bead [Ar]. Type of Roman glass bead made in the shape of a melon.

melting pot [De]. Refers to the idea that ethnic differences can be combined to create new patterns of behaviour drawing on diverse cultural sources.

Memphis, Egypt [Si]. Ancient capital of Egypt during the OLD KINGDOM, and thereafter one of the most important cities of the Near East, situated at the point where the Nile begins to divide its waters at the head of the Delta, 24km south of Cairo. Traditionally, the city was believed to have been founded by MENES, first ruler of the 1st Dynasty in the early 3rd millennium BC. The site itself was seen as the seat of the creator god PTAH.

During the NEW KINGDOM, Memphis became the second, or northern, capital of Egypt, parallel to THEBES in the south. Despite the increased importance of the god AMON in Thebes, Ptah remained one of the principal gods of the pantheon. The Great Temple at Memphis was added to or rebuilt by virtually every king of the 18th Dynasty; chapels were constructed by Thutmose I and Thutmose IV, and by Amenhotep III. Amenhotep III's son Akhenaton built a temple to Aton in Memphis.

Memphis continued to be important in later times, not least because of its geographical position, and in 322 BC Alexander the Great used Memphis as his headquarters while making plans for his new city of Alexandria.

West of the city there are very extensive cemeteries, including the pyramid fields of Abu Ruwaysh, GIZA, Zawayet e-Aryan, Abu Si, Saqqara, and Dahshur.

[Sum.: H. S. Smith and D. G. Jeffreys, 1986, A survey of Memphis, Egypt. *Antiquity*, 60, 88–95]

Menes [Na]. The first ruler to unify Upper and Lower Egypt in the early 3rd millennium BC, traditionally regarded as the first king of the 1st Dynasty and the founder of MEMPHIS. The name Menes was recorded in the 3rd century BC by the Egyptian historian Manetho; the 5th-century BC Greek historian Herodotus referred to him as Min. According to Manetho, Menes reigned for 62 years and was killed by a hippopotamus.

menhir [MC]. A term derived from the two Breton words meaning 'long stone' and colloquially used in northern France and the southwest of Britain for large freestanding slabs or blocks of stone. Some menhirs carry rock art, and in Brittany some were broken up and re-used as the orthostats or roof-slabs of passage graves. *See* STANDING STONE.

Menhyt [Di]. Egyptian lion-headed goddess, consort of Khnum at Esna.

Menlow Phase [CP]. Archaic Stage hunter-gatherer communities living in the Plateau area of northeastern California in North America in the period c.4000–3000 BC. Permanent villages are known, from which groups would venture out on foraging missions to occupy small temporary camps for short periods. The Menlow diet included bison, deer, antelope, mountain sheep, rabbit, and a range of other small mammals. They also processed and consumed nuts, to judge from the presence of pestles and mortars.

merchant's hoard [De]. A collection of Bronze Age metalwork deposited together, possibly either for ceremonial reasons or to hide it in times of danger, comprising mainly new or recently manufactured objects ready to be traded.

Mercia [Ge]. An Anglo-Saxon kingdom covering central England, bordered on the north by NORTHUMBRIA and on the south by WESSEX.

The name is thought to mean 'border folk', and indeed it is the most westerly Anglo-Saxon kingdom. Its western edge is defined by OFFA'S DYKE. The kingdom was established in the 7th century AD with a succession of rulers including Aethelbald, Offa, and Coenwulf leading it to its high point in the 8th and 9th century AD.

mere [MC]. **1.** A boundary between two fields which might be marked by merestones or a mere path. **2.** A pond.

Merewether, John (1797–1850) [Bi]. Dean of Hereford and excavator of numerous prehistoric sites in southern England during the first half of the 19th century. One of the Dean's most ambitious schemes was in 1849 when, with finance from the Royal Archaeological Institute, he drove a tunnel into the south side of Silbury Hill near Avebury. Throughout his work his field technique was characteristic of 19th-century clerical excavators. He is reputed to have opened 35 barrows on the Marlborough Downs between 18 July and the 14 August 1849.

[Bio.: *Dictionary of National Biography*, 13, 275–6]

Merimde Culture [CP]. Neolithic communities living in the western Nile Delta of Egypt in the 5th millennium BC, named after the typesite of Merimde Beni Salama. The Merimde Culture overlaps with the AMRATIAN CULTURE of Upper Egypt.

Meroitic [CP]. An early state that controlled the Nile Valley from near the first cataract in Egypt southwards to at least Sennar on the Blue Nile from about 750 BC through to around AD 350. Also known as the state of **Kush**, the capital of these communities was at Meroe on the east bank of the Nile some 200 km north of Khartoum in the Sudan. The Meroitic rulers modelled themselves and the administration of their state on Egypt; indeed the Meroitic king Piankhi conquered Egypt to found the 25th Dynasty in the 8th century BC.

Merovingians [CP]. Royal family of the Frankish rulers from Childeric in the mid 5th century AD through to the middle of the 8th century AD. The name derives from an obscure mid- 5th-century individual named Merovech, possibly the father of Childeric. Archaeologically the term is widely applied to material found in the region from the western Rhineland through to the Atlantic coast of France. The Merovingian world embraced a number of semi-autonomous kingdoms including Austrasia in the Rhineland, Neustria in central northern France, and Burundia in central France.

Mertseger [Di]. Egyptian goddess, 'She-who-lives-silence', the goddess of the Theban Peak and serpent goddess of the West Bank at Thebes, worshipped by the local workmen.

Mesoamerica [Ge]. An area which extends from central Honduras and Costa Rica through Mexico to Tamaulipas and Sinaloa that was first defined in 1943 by Paul Kirchoff as a geographical and cultural entity.

Mesolithic [CP]. Literally the middle Stone Age, the period between the Palaeolithic and the Neolithic, often characterized by a microlithic flint industry. The transition from hunting, fishing, and fruit gathering to cereal cultivation and animal domestication has long been regarded as diagnostic of the Mesolithic and the Neolithic periods respectively. The change is now seen as a less abrupt and radical development in temperate Europe than it used to be.

messuage [MC]. A dwelling house or homestead and the land occupied by it. The capital messuage of an estate is the chief or most important house.

metal detector [Eq]. An electronic device used specifically for the detection of buried metal objects. Hand-held metal detectors began to be manufactured in large numbers during the mid 1970s and sold to create the basis of a hobby interest in finding old things. Human interest in discovering ancient things coupled with an extensive and lucrative market in ancient artefacts led to a great deal of damage to archaeological sites and to hostility between metal detector users and archaeologists. While a good deal of work is well conducted and the finds properly logged and reported there remains a criminal element who loot protected sites and sell what they find.

metalling [Co]. The hard-packed surface of a road, track, or street, usually comprising layers of rammed gravel and stone and often showing signs of repair and patching. In some cases cobblestones or paving blocks may be laid down to provide a very robust metalling.

metallurgical analysis [De]. The study of metals and the metalworking process through the examination of finished products, manufacturing waste, tools and equipment connected with manufacture, and the raw materials used.

metallurgy [De]. Metalworking in all its aspects; the art of working metals.

metate [Ar]. American term for the base or lower grinding stone of a two-part mill for preparing plant food. The upper, movable stone is a MANO. Found in many shapes and sizes, and made from any coarse-grained rock that will work well as an abrasive surface.

methodology [De]. A general term applied to the procedures and approaches used to carry out a piece of archaeological research whether it is an excavation, survey, artefact study, or any other kind of analysis. Inherent to the methodology will be a series of underlying assumptions, theories, principles, and philosophies relating to the conceptualization of the material under study and the categories that will be used to define, describe, analyse, and talk about it. A methodology is usually written down as a **method statement** relating to a particular enquiry.

metope [Co]. The plain panel alternating with the decorated cover-plate for the roof beam-ends (the triglyphs) in the Doric frieze. In classical times a sculptured relief decorated the plain space, the series of metopes around the temple illustrating a single theme, e.g. Greeks versus Amazons, Lapiths versus Centaurs, or the Labours of Hercules.

metrical analysis [De]. Taking a set of defined measurements from items of interest and then using the measurements as an aid to classification and analysis.

metroon [De]. A Greek sanctuary dedicated to the Mother of the Gods.

Metsamor, Armenia [Si]. A multi-phase prehistoric settlement in the Ararat Valley. Excavations since 1965 show the presence of superimposed Eneolithic, Bronze Age, and Iron Age occupation. In its early phases it was an urban-type settlement of 10.5 ha with a citadel surrounded by a sturdy Cyclopean wall and ziggurat observatory situated on a low ridge. By the middle Bronze Age (late 3rd to middle 2nd millennia BC) the size and architectural sophistication of the site had increased considerably and by the 10th century BC it covered 100 ha. About 500 m southeast of the citadel was a cemetery with barrows and stone tombs. Finds suggest trading links with Egypt and Babylon in the mid 2nd millennium BC.

[Sum.: R. Dezelus, 1993, *Metsamor: foyer metallurgique et culturel de la préhistoire armenienne 3000–600 av.* Vienne: Edition Mechithariste]

mica-dusted pottery [De]. Pottery coated with a slip containing mica particles to give a golden or bronze-like sheen. Also called mica-gilt pottery.

Michaelmas [Ge]. Traditional calendar festival in northern Europe recently celebrated on 29 September marking the end of the harvest and thus the end of the agricultural year.

Michelsberg Culture [CP]. Middle Neolithic communities occupying the area from Belgium through to the Alps in the period 4500–4000 BC. Named after a hilltop camp in the Rhineland. The Michelsberg Culture succeeded the Rössen Culture and is characterized by distinctive pottery forms including tulip beakers, round-based flasks with tall, conical necks, and vessels with finger-impressed ornament around their rims. The culture has strong affinities with the Western Chassey and the middle Neolithic cultures of southern England, as well as with the TRB cultures of northern Europe. Michelsberg sites include ditched enclosed settlements and flint mines.

microblade [Ar]. A very small, narrow blade.

microburin [Ar]. Residual product in the fabrication of a MICROLITH by notching a blade on one side and then snapping it. The smaller piece is the residual or microburin, the longer section of blade forms the blank from which a microlith can be made. Microburins have no functional purpose.

microlith [Ar]. Very small implement, commonly of flint, regarded as characteristic of the Mesolithic period in Europe. Typically microliths are between 10 mm and 50 mm long and shaped into either a point or a barb. They were mostly used in composite tools such as harpoons, arrows, or knives.

microwear [De]. *See* USE-WEAR ANALYSIS.

midden [MC]. Any heap of rubbish or occupation debris adjacent to a dwelling or other site. *See also* SHELL MIDDEN.

Middle Ages [CP]. *See* MEDIEVAL PERIOD.

middle Archaic [CP]. General term to define the middle of three subdivisions of the Archaic Stage in the North American cultural sequence. Broadly the period 6500–4500 BC.

middle Horizon [CP]. General term referring to the fifth of the seven main chronological phases recognized in Andean archaeology, broadly the period AD 600 to 1000. It is characterized by the florescence of powerful regional states such as the Tiahuanaco and Huari.

Middle Kingdom [CP]. **1.** In Egypt covering the 12th and 13th Dynasties, *c*.2100–1750 BC, the period of Egyptian history following the reunification of Upper and Lower Egypt by the 11th Dynasty king Mentahopte II, ushering in more than two centuries of stability and prosperity. **2.** A translation of the Chinese *Chung Kuo*, now the Chinese name for the country known in the west as China. It was anciently used to designate the part of the Chou feudal realm that was governed by the king of Chou; later it came to mean that part of China whose inhabitants were true Chinese. Thus the southern kingdoms of Ch'u, Wu, and Yüeh were not seen as parts of the Middle Kingdom, and doubts were expressed about whether the western Ch'in should be so regarded.

Middle Missouri Tradition [CP]. Village-based farming communities living in the Missouri River drainage, especially in the states of North and South Dakota, in the period *c*.AD 1000–1500. The subsistence base relied on a special strain of cold-resisting quick-maturing maize, although some hunting and gathering was also practised. Dwellings were square or rectangular in plan, often semi-subterranean, arranged in enclosed villages of between six and twenty houses, set on promontories overlooking a river. These were defensive positions

and conflict and warfare seems to have been common. There is skeletal evidence of massacres and scalping. Pottery includes a distinctive grit-tempered ware, often in globular or wide-mouthed forms. Woodland and Mississippian influences are evident in the pottery assemblages. The Middle Missouri Tradition disappeared after about AD 1500 but historic tribes such as the Mandan, Arikara, and Hidatsa are thought to be their descendants.

Middle Period [CP]. Chronological subdivision proposed by Roy Carlson for the early hunter-gatherer traditions in the northwest coast of North America, broadly covering the period 3500 BC to AD 500. During the Middle Period the cultural diversity that prevailed in the preceding Early Period gave way to greater homogeneity. This can be explained in terms of a more stable environment and through the development of extensive exchange networks.

middle range theory [De]. A term developed in sociology by Robert K. Merton in the late 1940s as a way of connecting high-level social theory with empirically observable patterns. Similarly, in archaeology, it has become a way of seeking accurate means for identifying and measuring specified properties of past cultural systems. The emphasis is on trying to understand how the archaeological record was formed, what survives, why things survive, and how the record can be interpreted. As such it stands between high-level social theory (e.g. HERMENEUTICS) and low-level general laws or principles (e.g. STRATIGRAPHY). It may also be seen as a bridging argument that connects what is observed in the archaeological record with reasonable interpretations of those observations.

middle Stone Age [CP]. *See* MESOLITHIC.

middle Woodland [CP]. Chronological subdivision of the Woodland Stage in North America, broadly the period between *c*.200 BC and AD 400. During this time most of the area was dominated by the HOPEWELLIAN CULTURE, although to the southeast there lived a variety of hunter-gatherer societies who also engaged in some limited plant cultivation.

Midland Tradition [CP]. Late Palaeo-Indian hunter-gatherer communities who flourished in the period *c*.8700–8400 BC on the plains of North America. Characterized by distinctive hollow-based projectile points of similar outline to FOLSOM POINTS but lacking the central flute.

midrib [De]. A thickening along the central part of a bronze blade to strengthen it.

Midwestern Taxonomic System (McKern Classification) [Th]. A cultural-historical classification for eastern parts of North America developed by W. C. McKern and colleagues during the 1930s. Based on artefact classifications, the system was at first simply a taxonomy with no direct relationship to time or space. A hierarchy of traits reflected in specific items and assemblages was created, the smallest unit being a **component** (a site or a layer within a site), gradually building up through **focus**, **aspect**, **phase**, and **pattern**, to **base** which represented the most generalized grouping of cultural traits. In time, however, the system became sufficiently elaborate that its taxonomic categories acquired chronological and spatial definition.

MIFA [Ab]. *See* INSTITUTE OF FIELD ARCHAEOLOGISTS.

Migdale–Marnock Industry (Migdale–Killaha Industry) [CP]. An early industrial stage (Stage IV) of the British early Bronze Age spanning the later 2nd millennium BC and part of Burgess's MOUNT PLEASANT PERIOD. Named after hoards from two Scottish hoards: Migdale in Highland and Marnock in Grampian. The industry is characterized by the use of copper, bronze, and gold in the production of pins, awls, tubular beads, basket-shaped earrings, rings, bracelets, narrow-butted flat axes, riveted flat daggers and hollow cones. The industry overlaps with the early stages of the WESSEX CULTURE, and has links to the early Únětice/Reinecke A1 metalworking traditions on the continent.

migration [Ge]. The process by which, over a period of time, people living in one area gradually move into another region perhaps some distance away. Such movements occur mainly through the physical transfer of small groups (families and extended families) at a time, the incomers making their new homes in the midst of the existing occupants of the area, although as the migrants become the domi-

nant social group various social tensions may build up.

migrationism [Th]. A general theory of social change and a way of accounting for the introduction of novel material culture to a region, very popular in archaeological interpretation during the 1960s and 1970s, and contrasting with the INVASION HYPOTHESIS of earlier decades.

migration period [CP]. The age of folk movements in northern Europe. Though Germanic migrations outside the Roman empire began in the 2nd century AD, the term is usually confined to the period of the great movements in the 5th and 6th centuries AD. In northern Europe the migration period is conventionally followed by the age of the Vikings, the last of the Germanic migrations.

Milagro Culture [CP]. Small chiefdom communities living in the Guayas River basin of Ecuador, South America, in the integration period, *c*.AD 500 to the Spanish conquest. Milagro people built their houses on small mounds above seasonal flooding, while larger platforms up to 100 m long and 10 m high were used for the construction of temples and chiefs' residences. Mounds of intermediate size were used for burials, some of which were placed in tubes formed by knocking the bottoms out of a number of ceramic urns and stacking them one on top of another. Intensive agriculture was practised using water management systems. Milagro craftsmen were very skilled metalworkers and copper money axes were common.

Milavče Culture [CP]. Bronze Age communities of the early 2nd millennium BC in southwest Bohemia, named after the type-site of Milaveč, Domalžice, Czech Republic. Postdating the TUMULUS CULTURE in the region, the dead were cremated but the ashes were gathered together and covered by a barrow. Pre-dating the local URNFIELD CULTURE.

Mildenhall treasure [Ge]. A massive hoard of late Roman silverware found in a field at West Row near Mildenhall, Suffolk, England, in AD 1942. The hoard contains 34 pieces including a large dish depicting the head of Oceanus surrounded by friezes of sea deities and others revelling; two smaller platters with Bacchic scenes; a niello dish with geometric designs;

bowls; ladles; and spoons. Some of the objects carry Christian inscriptions. The whole group is traditionally regarded as the household valuables of a wealthy Roman family who buried it in the 4th or early 5th century AD to save it from Saxon raiders. However, in 1997 Richard Hobbs and Paul Ashbee rehearsed a range of doubts over the integrity of the find, suggesting that it might have arrived in Britain during the 20th century from a findspot elsewhere in the Roman empire.

Mildenhall ware [Ar]. A style of middle Neolithic pottery found over much of central eastern England and East Anglia during the 4th millennium BC. Characterized by round-bottomed bowls with fairly elaborate decoration. Deep S-profiled forms with rolled or thickened rims predominate.

milecastle (milefort) [MC]. A small Roman fort site at intervals of approximately one Roman mile along one of the major defended frontiers of the empire. On HADRIAN'S WALL the milecastles are typically rectangular in plan with a gateway through the wall and a watchtower overlooking it. Small barrack blocks provided accommodation for about 30 soldiers. A second gate provided access into the land south of the wall.

milestone [MC]. Blocks or pillars of stone set up beside major roads to show distances from that point to major settlements along the road. In the Greco-Roman world such stones began to be erected from about 250 BC.

mill [MC]. An industrial-scale structure purpose-built for grinding corn. Examples are known from the Roman period onwards and are generally classified according to the main power source used: WINDMILLS, WATERMILLS, and TIDEMILLS.

millefiori glass [De]. Decorative glass formed by cutting slices from bundles of thin multi-coloured glass rods, fused together (the word literally means 'a thousand flowers'). The slices were then set into a background mount of metal or enamel. The technique seems to have been developed by Anglo-Saxon crafts-people.

millenarianism [Ge]. Beliefs held by the members of certain types of religious movement, according to which cataclysmic changes will

occur in the near future, heralding the arrival of a new epoch.

Miller Culture [CP]. Southward expansion of the HOPEWELLIAN CULTURE of North America into the Mississippi.

Milling Stone Cultures [CP]. A collective name for Archaic Stage communities of 6th millennium BC date living in southern California and whose economic base relied heavily on the collection and processing of plants.

milliprobe [Te]. *See* X-RAY MILLIPROBE ANALYSIS.

mill pond [Co]. Pond created as a reservoir in order to provide a regular supply of water to a WATERMILL or TIDEMILL.

mill race [Co]. *See* LEAT.

millstone [Ar]. Large circular slab of coarse rock up to 1 m in diameter and typically 0.2–0.3 m thick used for grinding grain in a MILL. One face is roughened by means of a pattern of lines cut into the surface while the other face may be slightly domed. Millstones were used in pairs (an upper and lower stone), a central hole in each taking the spindle that keeps them concentric and in the case of the upper stone attaches to the power source that turns it.

milpa [Ge]. South American term (literally meaning 'cornfields') for slash and burn agriculture. Trees are cut down in December, brush and scrub being continually cleared in ensuing months, and the dried vegetation is burnt the following April. This process leaves behind a layer of nutrient-rich ash and charcoal on the ground surface. Using a digging stick to make holes, seeds of maize, beans, squash or peppers are planted in the ash. If the rains come on time in May the seeds will be well watered and produce a good crop. Fertility depends on the quality and thickness of the ash layer. Few milpa plots allow more than two years cultivation, often with up to twenty years left fallow in between for trees to regenerate and provide the fuel to supply the next layer of ash.

Mimbres Culture [CP]. Pueblo-based farming communities living along the Mimbres River in southwest New Mexico, North America, in the period c.AD 1000–1130. Mimbres is probably best known for its very fine ceramics which include magnificent ceremonial bowls adorned with painted geometric and pictorial designs. Examples are often found inverted over the head of the deceased in burial deposits, ritually broken by making a small hole in the centre of the base. Mimbres communities lived in single-storey pueblos of up to 150 rooms. Ceremonial rooms included large rectangular subterranean kivas rather like those of the earlier MOGOLLON TRADITION. There is little evidence of long-distance exchange; society seems to have been nucleated, essentially egalitarian, and inward-looking.

mimi figures [De]. A style of motif used in the ROCK ART of Arnhem land in northern Australia based on thin, stick-like representations of human beings. They are earlier than the X-ray style and are disclaimed by contemporary populations who attribute them to mimi spirits.

Min [Di]. Egyptian god of the desert, thunder, storms, and of fertility. Depicted with an erect phallus and holding aloft a flail, Min was an early god of Coptos, later associated with Amun at Luxor. The Feast of Min was an important festival.

Mindel [CP]. Second major glacial stage of the Pleistocene in the Alps, recognized as a group of moraines and related river terrace deposits. Dated to between 450 000 and 300 000 years ago.

Mindel-Riss [CP]. A major interglacial stage of the Pleistocene in the Alps, between the Mindel and Riss glaciations. Dated to between 300 000 and 200 000 years ago. Equivalent to the HOXNIAN in the British sequence.

mine [MC]. Any kind of excavation into the ground for the purpose of extracting some kind of raw material such as stone, metal ore, coal, or flint. The simplest mines are basically pits sunk into the ground to find or follow outcrops of the desired material; these can be described as **open-cast mines**. Lines of shallow extraction pits following surface outcrops of metal ore are known as **rakes**. Deeper, rather cylindrical holes may be described as **simple shaft mines**. Examples where the shaft is expanded at the bottom to maximize the area available for extracting a particular layer of material are known as **bell pits**. Shafts that provide access to a series of galleries that follow seams of material underground are known as **galleried shaft mines**. Pits that run horizontally into a hill slope or cliff following material into the slope are known as **adits** or **drift mines**. The techniques of mining developed steadily from Neolithic times onwards in most parts of the world, the use of fire-setting and stone mauls being the commonest way of extracting hard rocks until hardened iron or steel tools became available in later medieval times. The use of drills and explosives appears from the 18th century AD. In prehistoric times, soft rock such as gravel or chalk was excavated using bone and antler tools and stone and flint axes. The archaeology of mines and mining is often rather complicated because as well as the underground elements (which are often well preserved) there will be surface structures including spoil heaps, processing areas, working floors, a range of shelters and facilities, drainage works, and perhaps aqueducts, leats, reservoirs, and other water management works where water power was used or where material removed from the mine itself needed to be washed.

Ming Dynasty [CP]. The penultimate Chinese imperial dynasty dating to the period AD 1368 through to AD 1644. It was established after the expulsion of the Mongols by Chu Yüan-Chang, an illiterate mercenary who had begun life as a refugee from famine, then became a Buddhist monk, a bandit, and a rebel leader. The Ming first had a century of effective power and strong government, but declined in the 16th century and succumbed to an internal rebellion and subsequent Manchu invasion in the middle of the 17th century AD. Celebrated for the development of porcelain, and in literature for the rise of the Chinese novel, they also produced memorable and impressive architecture of which the Ming tombs and the Imperial Palace at Peking are superb examples.

miniature cups [De]. A generic term for a range of small ceramic vessels accompanying Bronze Age cremation burials in the British Isles during the 2nd millennium BC. See ALDBOURNE CUP, PYGMY CUPS, GRAPE CUP, INCENSE CUP.

mini-hillfort [MC]. See SPRINGFIELD STYLE ENCLOSURE.

minim [Ar]. Type of small Roman coin of low value that first appeared in the 3rd century AD and continued to be minted through into the 4th century AD. The word is simply a Latinized equivalent of 'the smallest'; it is not known what the coins were called in Roman times.

minimissimus [Ar]. Type of extremely small Roman coin of low value, generally about 4 mm across, issued in the 3rd and 4th centuries AD. The word is simply a Latinized equivalent of 'the very smallest'; it is not known what the coins were called in Roman times.

Minns, Sir Ellis Hovell (1874–1953) [Bi]. British archaeologist whose studies focused on eastern Europe. After school at Charterhouse he studied for the classical tripos at Pembroke College, Cambridge, opting for Slavonic and learning Russian. After a period in Paris he spent 1898 to 1901 working in the library of the Imperial Archaeological Commission in St Petersburg, mastering the literature on Russian archaeology. Returning to Cambridge he was appointed to a lectureship in the Department of Classics, a post he held until 1927 when he was appointed Disney Professor in the Department of Archaeology and Anthropology. Amongst his many publications are *Scythians and Greeks* (1913, Cambridge: CUP) and *The art of the northern Nomads* (1944, London: H. Milford).

[Bio.: G. Clark, 1989, *Prehistory at Cambridge and beyond*. Cambridge: CUP, 30–4]

Minoan [CP]. A term developed by Sir Arthur EVANS for the Bronze Age civilization of Crete and surrounding areas, being an adaptation of the name of the legendary King Minos of Crete. The Minoan civilization emerged in the early 3rd millennium BC and is traditionally divided into three main phases, each with subdivisions: early Minoan (EM) 3000–2000 BC; middle Minoan (MM) 2000–1550 BC; and late Minoan (LM) 1550–1050 BC. Evans also subdivided each phase into three subdivisions denoted by Roman numbers (e.g. EM-III), onto which still finer subdivisions denoted by letters and arabic numbers have been added. An alternative scheme proposed by Nicholas Platon takes account of the architectural development of the civilization: Pre-Palatial (= EMI-III), Proto-Palatial (= MMI-II), Neo-Palatial (= MMIII–LMIIIA1), and Post-Palatial (LMIIIA2–IIIC).

During the middle Minoan period, urbanism became apparent, towns appeared, and the great palaces were built. At this time the Minoan civilization can be characterized as a palace-based redistributive economy in which food products, raw materials, and manufactured goods were collected together and redistributed from the palaces.

By the beginning of the late Minoan period Crete controlled the southern Aegean and the islands therein. In the mid 15th century BC the Greek-speaking MYCENAEANS took control of Crete and the Aegean until their empire too collapsed around 1200 BC.

The Minoan civilization was the earliest European civilization known. Its people used LINEAR A writing and developed a high level of architectural and artistic skill. Religious belief systems are not fully understood, but seem to have included a much represented female deity, the sacred double-axe sign, and the horns of consecration. Sacred cave and hilltop sanctuaries are known. Bulls appear widely in sporting/ceremonial contexts.

minster [MC]. A type of church, usually of royal or magnate foundation in the later 1st millennium AD, that was served by more than one priest exercising pastoral responsibility over a large area. Some early minsters were effectively small monastic communities.

Minyan ware [Ar]. A term give by Heinrich Schliemann to the type of fine, smooth, grey or yellow-coloured pottery, made on the wheel, found widely from about 2000 BC in Thessaly and Macedonia to the Argolid and considerably at Troy. Ancestral to MYCENAEAN pottery. The makers and users of Minyan pottery were probably not the same as the Late Bronze Age communities associated with the fabulously rich King Minyas whose exploits are chronicled by epic and lyric poets in classical times.

Miocene [CP]. The epoch preceding the PLIOCENE and dated to between 25 million and 5 million years ago. It was during the late Miocene that the earliest hominid species begin to appear in the fossil record.

Mississippian Tradition [CP]. Late Woodland Stage chiefdom-based farming cultures living in the southeastern parts of North America in the period *c*.AD 700–1500. The origins of the tradition are a matter of some debate, there being evidence of continuity from the Hopewellian Culture as well as some evidence for the diffusion or adoption of cultural traits from Mexico and Mesoamerica.

The standard plan of Mississippian settlements comprises platform mounds supporting temples and residences for the elite arranged around an open plaza and surrounded by numerous dwellings. Most settlements were situated on the floodplains of major rivers, but there were also some shifting farmsteads in adjacent uplands. Mississippian communities used shell-tempered pottery, including painted and effigy bowls, and a bow with arrows tipped by triangular chipped stone points. Maize and squash were cultivated in river valleys, and after AD 1200 beans were grown too. Hunting and fishing were also sources of food, as was the harvesting of wild food such as nuts.

Their religious system appears to have been devoted to maintaining the fertility of the land, centring on a god with solar attributes and associated with fire. Ceremonies at the mound-top temples were connected with the supernatural, expressions of ancestral obligation, success in food production, and burial rites for social leaders. Society was stratified and local chiefs appear to have been rulers of autonomous groups. Thus the Mississippian embraces a wide range of essentially localized groups: the Middle Mississippian, Fort Ancient, South Appalachian Mississippian, Plaquemine Mississippian, Caddoan Mississippian, and the Oneota. In the later phases, increasing competition for land seems to have provoked an increasing warfare, the fortification of settlements, and the practice of beheading and scalping.

mi'ta [Ge]. A tax or duty exacted from citizens of the Inca empire by the state, payable in the form of labour.

Mitanni [CP]. A short-lived HURRIAN kingdom of the mid 2nd millennium BC in the uplands between the Tigris and the Euphrates. The capital of Wassukkanni has not yet been identified, but Mitanni traded on near equal terms with Egypt and the Hittite empire for more than a century. The kingdom was overthrown by the Hittites in *c*.1370 BC.

Mithraeum [MC]. A temple dedicated to the god MITHRAS.

Mithras [Di]. A Near Eastern god found in the Persian world and Asia Minor who also assumed considerable importance in the Roman world, especially amongst soldiers and in military circles. Mithras is portrayed as a young man wearing a Phrygian cap, usually crouched on the back of a bull which he is killing by a thrust to the neck with a short sword. David Ulansey has convincingly identified Mithras with Perseus and shown how the tauroctony embodies cosmic symbolism relating to a secret knowledge of the precession of the heavens and Mithras himself as the ruler of the cosmos (*kosmokrator*). Mithraism was a mystery cult that flourished alongside early Christianity and showed many similarities to it. As in all mystery cults the rites were kept secret such that the truth and benefits came only to initiated believers who had to pass through a series of seven grades of initiation. The disciple also underwent baptism, took part in the re-enactment of a sacred meal, and bore the seal of his discipleship on his body.

mitigation strategy [Ge]. The programme of works developed to conserve, protect, record, and/or investigate archaeological structures and deposits that are threatened by wholesale or partial destruction through some kind of construction work, quarrying, or natural erosion. Such proposals may, for example, include the use of particular foundation designs to minimize the impact of construction on buried deposits, or the use of open space to allow the in situ preservation of significant remains. Equally, a mitigation strategy may comprise rescue excavation and site-recording operations in advance of destruction.

Mixtec [CP]. Pre-Classic chiefdom-based communities sharing cultural and linguistic affinities, centred on Oaxaca in Mexico during the period AD 700–1500. Mixtec craftsmen excelled in metalworking and stoneworking, as well as in sculpture, the painting of pottery, and the manufacture of folding books made of bark paper or deerskin. These codices recount the exploits of Mixtec rulers using a mixture of pictographs and phonetic symbols.

Mladeč points (Lautch points) [Ar]. Large elongated oval or lozenge-shaped bone, antler, or ivory points from the cave of the same name in the Czech Republic, characteristic of the Aurignacian in central Europe.

Mnevis [Di]. Egyptian god, sacred bull of Re at Heliopolis.

moai [MC]. Colossal stylized stone human figures found on Easter Island. About 1000 examples are known, all made from volcanic tuff quarried at Rano Raraku on the island. They were made between AD 600 and AD 1500, each being up to 10 m high and weighing up to 82 tonnes. Some originally wore a cylindrical red stone head-dress and had white coral eyes fitted. They are regarded as ancestral figures.

moat [Co]. A deliberately constructed ditch or cutting filled with water that surrounds a structure or settlement. Moats are usually constructed to provide a measure of defence, drainage of the central area, and/or a supply of aquatic food resources such as fish and fowl.

moated manor (moated farmstead) [MC]. A style of small settlement, generally of high status, comprising a manor or substantial farmstead set on an island bounded by a water-filled moat. This tradition developed in many parts of northwest Europe in the 12th century AD, perhaps copying the use of moats on earlier castles. Great numbers have been defined in England, Ireland, and northern France, the peak of moat building being between AD 1250 and 1350.

moated site [MC]. A type of proto-historic and early historic site found in Thailand and Cambodia. Many seem to have been well-established settlements or industrial areas before one or more concentric rings of moats were added during a period of expansion around AD 300–500. Many seem to have dominated clusters of smaller, non-moated sites in the vicinity. By about AD 650 many of the larger settlements of the Mon states in central Thailand were moated. Rectangular moats are characteristics of the Khmer sites of the 11th to 13th centuries AD in Thailand.

mobiliary art (chattel art) [De]. A general term used to cover all portable decorated objects, especially those of Palaeolithic date.

Mochica Culture (Moche Culture) [CP]. Early Intermediate Period state-based society centred on the northern coast of Peru in South America during the period AD 200–700. The site of Moche in the Moche Valley was the capital of the Mochica state and comprised two huge adobe platforms, an immense plaza, and an extensive residential area. Mochic society was stratified and militaristic. The Mochica state expanded through conquest, new territories being linked to the core area by a network of roads and paths. Fortified garrisons were established in some valleys. The construction of Moche was probably achieved through draft labour rendered to the state. Burial monuments are known, the higher levels of society being interred in platform mounds. Mochica pottery includes stirrup-spouted funerary vessels on which there are painted depictions of gods, ceremonies, and scenes from everyday life. The Mochica state seems to have lasted until c.AD 700 when it was absorbed into the Huari empire.

model [De]. A generalized picture, analogy, or simplified explanation of reality; a theoretical reconstruction of a set of phenomena, devised to visualize them or understand them better. Archaeological models can be descriptive or explanatory and vary greatly in their complexity and the degree to which they can be tested with archaeological data.

Mogollon Tradition [CP]. Later prehistoric farming communities living in Arizona and New Mexico, North America, in the period c.AD 250–1450. Characterized by distinctive red-on-brown and polished red ceramics, early Mogollon settlements were small villages with few houses and large associated ceremonial complexes. Many were sites on low hills. After c.AD 700 settlements were more commonly on low-lying fertile ground. Pit-houses with a rectangular outline and entry ramp were typical and some of the ceremonial structures had entrances in their flat roofs. Maize, beans, and squash was cultivated, although there was always some reliance on hunting and gathering. By the end of the Mogollon Tradition multi-roomed houses constructed above ground were common, some with hundreds of rooms presaging the Pueblo traditions.

Mohenjodaro, Pakistan [Si]. Early city on the west bank of the River Indus in the Sind region of Pakistan. During the later 3rd and early 2nd millennia BC it was one of the twin capitals of the Indus Valley civilization. Excavated by John Marshall in the 1920s, Ernest Mackay in the 1930s, and more recently by Mortimer Wheeler in 1950, George Dales in 1964, and since 1979 a team of architects and archaeologists led by Michael Jansen, the city was set out on a formal grid pattern. Broad streets separated the blocks, each of which was provided with drains and densely built over with structures made of mud brick. Most of the buildings excavated appear to be dwelling houses mainly in the form of ranges of rooms opening from a central courtyard. A block in the middle of the west side stood higher than the rest and seems to have formed a citadel. The citadel is fortified with mud-brick walls and contains within it a ceremonial structure known as the Great Bath, the Granary, the Assembly Hall, and the College. The exact purpose of these structures is not, however, known. The site was abandoned around 1950 BC, seemingly after a massacre of the population, as many skeletons were found lying in houses and in the streets.

[Rep.: M. Jansen and G. Urban (eds.), 1985, *Mohenjo Daro: report of the Aachen University mission, 1979–1985*. Leiden: Brill]

Moh scale [Ge]. A general measure of hardness represented as a scale running between 1 (soft) and 10 (hard) in which each step is represented by a distinctive mineral: 1 = talc; 2 = gypsum; 3 = calcite; 4 = fluorspar; 5 = apatite; 6 = felspar; 7 = quartz; 8 = topaz; 9 = corundum; 10 = diamond. If a sample of material (e.g. pottery) can be scratched with one of these minerals then it is softer than that mineral; through a process of trial and error a sample's position on the scale can be determined.

Moi fort [MC]. Type of circular earth-walled enclosures of the later 2nd millennium BC found in the foothills of the middle Mekong Valley in east central Cambodia. Also known as **Cham forts**.

MOLAS [Ab]. *See* MUSEUM OF LONDON ARCHAEOLOGICAL SERVICE.

molluscan analysis [Te]. Shells from marine, estuarine, freshwater, and land molluscs are well preserved in calcareous archaeological deposits and naturally accumulating sediments. By sampling such deposits and sediments the shells can be recovered and identified to species to reveal a great deal of information about economy and environment. In the case of shell middens, the molluscs mainly accumulate as a result of human discard patterns and thus mainly relate to the economy and eating habits of the community responsible. Other situations, for example buried soils, ditch and pit fills, slopewash deposits, blown sand and loess, old water courses, and alluvium, are important for their environmental evidence because most species prefer to live in particular habitats and rarely move far from home. A typical sample for analysis comprises 1 kg of sediment wet-sieved using a 0.5 mm mesh. Land Mollusca species can be broadly subdivided into: shade-loving woodland species; open-country grassland, arable, and scree-loving species; catholic species capable of living in a wide range of habitats; and marshland species who live in damp marshy conditions. Freshwater Mollusca can be divided into: slum species that live in small bodies of water, poorly aerated and subject to periodic drying; catholic species found in almost all freshwater contexts; ditch species that prefer plant-rich slow streams; and moving-water species that prefer large bodies of well-oxygenated water. Where accumulating sediments are available it is possible to take samples from different horizons and thus chart changes in local environment through time.

monastery [MC]. A monastery (from the Greek 'to live alone') is a more or less self-contained settlement constructed to house a community of monks or canons. The idea of a monastic lifestyle based around a religious community may have originated in prehistoric times, but finds its first expression in the Christian context in the eastern roman empire during the 4th century AD. Two types emerged, the **cenobitic monastery** where a groups of monks lived a communal life, presided over by an abbot, with a shared routine of worship, work, and meals, and the **eremitic monastery** where monks lived in isolation in separate cells but assembled each Saturday and Sunday for common worship and to obtain supplies for the following week. The eastern monastic tradition, centred on BYZANTIUM, was diverse, with no formal orders. As the influence of the church and the practice of monasticism moved westwards and northwards, however, specific orders began to develop alongside the early autonomous communities.

One of the earliest orders was that of the Benedictines, established by St Benedict towards the end of the 5th century AD, followed later by the Cluniacs in the 10th century, and the Carthusians and the Cistercians in the 11th century. In the early days monastic monks were generally lay people, with only sufficient priests amongst them to maintain the services to a proper level. Most priests were seculars, living in the world and working amongst ordinary people. Later, the proportion of priests in monasteries increased and a number of orders of canons appeared, including the Augustinians in the mid 11th century, the Premonstratensians in the early 12th century, and the Gilbertines in the mid 12th century. Another group of monasteries grew up around friars who although taking the triple vow of poverty, chastity, and obedience were mendicants who moved about the country using any house of their own order as a base. These included the Franciscans founded in AD 1210, the Dominicans founded in AD 1216, the Carmelites in the 1220s, and the Austin friars in the 1230s.

The physical arrangement of monasteries varied greatly through time and according to the needs of the communities who built and occupied them. Early examples tend to be small, with a church, domestic buildings usually arranged around a cloister, and a cemetery. Some later examples are extremely large and complicated structures involving not only the main monastic centre but various outlying farms and agricultural facilities (e.g. granges, coureries) that provided the wealth to maintain the community. By the high Middle Ages in Europe monasteries were some of the wealthiest and most landed institutions in existence.

Monasteries are known by a range of terms depending on the character of what they did and the religious order or rule under which they lived. Thus early monasteries may be associated with cathedrals, colleges, and minsters. Double houses include both men and women, often in different cloisters. Friaries were occupied by friars, abbeys were headed by abbots, priories by priors. Charterhouses were monasteries of the CARTHUSIAN order; preceptories were monasteries maintained by the military orders, the Knights Templars and the Knights Hospitallers; and hermitages and cells were small-scale monastic sites in the eremitic tradition.

monastic grange [MC]. A consolidated block of monastic demense land, anything from 30 ha to more than 2000 ha in extent, and usually some distance away from the monastery that owns it. Granges were worked as estate farms more or less independently of the manorial system with its communal agriculture and servile labour. At the heart of the grange were farm buildings, paddocks, gardens, granaries, industrial areas and workshops, and a chapel. Granges were especially characteristic of the holdings of Cistercian abbeys, but the system was imitated by other orders including the Premonstratensians, Gilbertines, and some of the older-established orders such as the Benedictines and the Cluniacs. Some monastic granges had particular functions, for example as agrarian farms, sheep farms (bercaries), cattle ranches (vaccaries), horse studs, or industrial workings.

Mondsee Culture [CP]. Early Copper Age communities of upper Austria, the first people in the area to smelt local copper ores. Characterized by PILE DWELLINGS and for pottery decorated with white inlaid circles and stellar designs.

Mongols [CP]. A confederacy of nomadic tribes who gave their name to the steppe region of northern China—Mongolia. In the early 13th century AD, under their leader Chingis Khan, the Mongols conquered the north China Chin Dynasty. Later, under Chingis and his successors they also conquered the southern dynasty, the Sung, and united China under their own regime known to the Chinese as the Yüan Dynasty (AD 1278–1385). The Mongols also conqered central Asia, Persia, parts of Russia, and most of modern Turkey. They invaded Hungary and eastern Germany, but their advance was halted by news of the death of Chingis Khan. They were expelled from China by the founder of the MING DYNASTY, Chu Yüan-chang.

Monk's Mound, Illinois, USA [Si]. *See* CAHOKIA.

monogamy [Ge]. A form of marriage in which each married partner is allowed only one spouse at any given time.

monogenesis [Ge]. The theory that all humans are one species with a common ancestor.

monogram [Ge]. A set of letters combined into one.

monolith [MC]. A single, large, isolated stone, often shaped and usually standing upright. Synonymous with MENHIR in the Neolithic of northwest Europe.

monotheism [Th]. Belief in a single god.

monoxylous coffin [Ar]. A type of wooden burial case made from a single piece of wood, usually by hollowing out a section of tree trunk.

Mont Beuvray, France [Si]. A major Celtic *oppidum* identified as the ancient site of Bibracte near Bourges in central France. The site was originally the tribal capital of the Aedui and is known from Caesar's account of the conquest of Gaul where he recounts fierce resistance in the area. From 125 BC, however, the Aedui were allies of Rome and in the winter of 52 BC Caesar stayed at Bibracte following the battle of Alesia.

Archaeologically the site is dominated by its defences which comprise a rampart nearly 5 km long built in the MURUS GALLICUS style. Extensive excavations were carried out by J. G. Bulliot and J. Déchelette in the early 19th century, and since 1984 an international team of scholars has been working at the site under the aegis of the Ministry of Culture and Communications. Together these investigations have revealed an intensive occupation and evidence for extensive trade between the Aedui and the classical world. Site position is important as it controlled the passage of goods through the Saône and Loire valleys. Within the site its vast area was divided into quarters, each with its own distinct function. Near the entrances were industrial sectors with ironworking, bronze working, and many other crafts. At the heart of the site was a general market area with a space set aside for meetings and ceremonial events. The residential areas were well set out with wide paved streets between the houses. Some of the houses in the wealthiest sector of the site were modelled on Roman styles. The *oppidum* was replaced in the later 1st century BC by the town of Augustodunum, modern Atun.

[Sum.: J. P. Guillaumet, 1991, Bibracte: an *oppidum* of the Aedui people. In S. Moscati *et al.* (eds.), *The Celts*. London: Thames & Hudson, 519]

Monte Albán, Mexico [Si]. Zapotec capital set on a steep bluff in the middle of the Valley of Oaxaca which rose to prominence after about 400 BC. Four main phases in the development and occupation of the site have been recognized. In Period I (500–200 BC) the slopes of the hill were levelled off to form over 2000 terraces. An acropolis protected by stone walls lay at the centre. Inside was a stone platform surrounded by 140 carved stone slabs depicting contorted human figures. These were executed in Olmec style. In Period II (200 BC–AD 300) the first palaces were built, along with ball-courts, temples, and an arrow-shaped building in the main plaza. During this period there appears to have been extensive contact with Maya Lowland centres and the increasingly powerful Teotihuacán.

At its peak in Period III (AD 300–750), Monte Albán had an estimated population of 25–30000. Public buildings, terraces, and residences covered over 40 square kilometres. Period IV (AD 700–1000) was a time of decline as the main plaza was abandoned. Zapotec influence disappeared, although the site was partially reoccupied by the Mixtec.

[Rep.: R. Blanton, 1978, *Monte Alban: settlement patterns of the ancient Zapotec capital*. New York: Academic Press]

Montelius, Gustaf Oscar Augustin (1843–1921) [Bi]. Foremost Swedish prehistorian well known for his typological studies of Bronze Age artefacts. Born in Stockholm, Montelius lived all his life in the same house in the town. He studied at Uppsala University from 1861, first studying natural science but later switching to history and the Scandinavian languages. In 1869 he was awarded a Ph.D. in history with a thesis in archaeology. By 1863 he was employed on a part-time basis at the Museum of National Antiquities in Stockholm, moving to a permanent position in 1868. Between 1907 and 1913 he was state antiquarian and head of the Central Board of Antiquities and the Museum of National Antiquities.

Montelius's greatest achievement was in his work on the prehistoric chronology of northern Europe. In this he divided European prehistory into a series of numbered periods, three relating to the Neolithic, and six to the Bronze Age. Initially his analysis was done on the basis of artefact typology. However, he extended the principle of cross-dating, pioneered by Petrie for Egypt and the Aegean, to northern and western Europe, thus providing a chronological framework for his Bronze Age sequence. He was an exponent of the *ex oriente lux* theory that innovation in barbarian Europe was generated by impulses diffused from the more advanced civilizations of the Near East, as set out clearly in his book *Der Orient und Europe* (1899, Stockholm).

[Bio.: B. Gräslund, 1999, Gustaf Oscar Augustin Montelius (1843–1921). In T. Murray (ed.), *Encyclopedia of archaeology I: the great archaeologists.* Oxford: ABC-Clio, 155–64]

Monte Verde, Chile [Si]. Palaeo-Indian encampment in south central Chile with controversial evidence of earlier occupation. Excavated by Tim Dillehay, the site has two main layers. The upper one comprises the remains of twelve wooden structures, abundant plant remains (including wild potatoes), and the bones of butchered mastodon and guanaco. The houses, with external hearths, were of plank construction and are thought to have been covered with hides. Projectile points which resemble the El Jobo points of Venezuela have been found. This layer is sealed by a deposit of peat which has been dated to 11 700–9800 BC. A second, lower layer, yielded broken stones and charcoal which have been claimed as evidence of occupation extending back to 30 000 years ago. At present, these finds are unverified as being related to human settlement. Both layers at the site make important contributions to the debate about the spread of early settlement in the Americas.

[Rep.: T. Dillehay, 1989, *Monte Verde: A late Pleistocene settlement in Chile,* vol. I. *Palaeoenvironment and site context.* Washington: Smithsonian Institution]

Monticello, Virginia, USA [Si]. Earthen mound situated beside the Rivanna River excavated by Thomas Jefferson in 1782 and important as the first documented archaeological excavation in North America. Jefferson's investigation had the aim of shedding light on a then current controversy about who the 'mound builders' of the Mississippi area were: ancestors of the aboriginal Indians, Toltec Indians from Mexico, or even cultures from further afield (the Welsh and a variety of 'lost races' were seriously suggested). Jefferson confirmed that the mounds were repositories for the dead and that associated with the burials were artefacts similar to items of Indian origin.

[Rep.: T. Jefferson, 1797, *Notes on the State of Virginia.* London: Stockdale]

Montu (Mont) [Di]. Egyptian war god of Thebes, originally from Armant (Hermonthis), depicted as a hawk-headed man.

monument [De]. In common usage the term is taken to mean any large artificial structure of archaeological interest. In England, Wales, and Scotland, however, there is also a legal usage. The *Ancient Monuments and Archaeological Areas Act 1979* defines a monument as being: 'any building, structure or work above or below the surface of the land, any cave or excavation; any site comprising the remains of any such building, structure or work or any cave or excavation; and any site comprising, or comprising the remains of, any vehicle, vessel, aircraft or other movable structure or part thereof . . .' (S61(7)). *See also* ANCIENT MONUMENT.

monumental arch (triumphal arch) [De]. A large freestanding masonry structure, sometimes straddling a main road or thoroughfare, built in the form of a short length of wall pierced by one or more gateways. The faces of the arch are often decorated or ornamented with carvings and sculpture. Such arches were erected in the Roman world and later to celebrate and commemorate great events such as victory in battle.

monumental mound [MC]. A large conical-shaped mound of earth and stone dating to the 2nd or 3rd millennium BC, often carefully constructed with internal revetments, surrounded by a substantial quarry ditch, and in some cases an outer bank. The whole structure is generally more than 150 m in diameter, and most are associated with HENGE ENCLOSURES. The largest example in Britain in SILBURY HILL, Wiltshire.

Monuments Protection Programme (MPP) [Ge]. An initiative established by ENGLISH HERITAGE in 1986 to provide a systematic review of all recorded MONUMENTS in England with a view to identifying those of national importance and providing them with statutory protection through SCHEDULING or other appropriate mechanism.

moot [MC]. Communal meeting place specifically identified and set aside for courts and other bodies who dealt with the administration and organization of the countryside in Saxon and medieval times. They were located within the area of jurisdiction, usually a hundred, wapentake, or shire, at a convenient conspicuous or well-known place which might be marked by a natural feature such as a hill or large tree, or at a monument such as an earthen mound or standing stone. Some moots were established on existing barrows or within hillforts; in other cases a mound or structure was built for the purpose. Initially moots were held in the open air but through time many moved to halls and meeting houses within villages or urban centres. *See also* THING.

Morgan, Lewis Henry (1818–81) [Bi]. A lawyer practising in New York who developed a special interest in the social organization and origins of the American Indians and the light this threw on the general problem of cultural origins. Much of his work was influenced by the writings of Engels and Tönnies; he lived with and was adopted into the Iroquois tribe. In 1877, Morgan published a book entitled *Ancient society* (New York: Henry Holt) in which he proposed three main evolutionary stages in the development of human societies: savagery, barbarism (in seven substages), and civilization. This scheme proved popular for a while, although was soon abandoned as being too simplistic.

[Bio.: T. R. Trautmann, 1987, *Lewis Henry Morgan and the invention of kinship.* Berkeley: University of California Press]

Morris, Ronald Wilson Boyd (1902–92) [Bi]. British lawyer and amateur archaeologist well known for his work on British rock art. After graduating in law from the University of Glasgow he followed his father into the Scottish legal profession, joining one of the oldest law practices in Glasgow where he later became senior partner. Although well beyond call-up age in 1939, he saw active service with the Royal Navy Volunteer Reserve. After his retirement from legal practice in 1963 he turned to archaeology and the study of rock art in northern Britain. He published numerous articles and books including *The prehistoric rock art of Galloway and the Isle of Man* (1979, Poole: Blandford Press). He was elected a Fellow of the Society of Antiquaries in 1971.

[Obit.: *Society of Antiquaries Annual Report and Proceedings 1992–1993*, 54]

Morrow Mountain points [Ar]. Middle Archaic bifacially worked chipped stone projectile points found in eastern parts of North America and dating to the period *c*.6000–4000 BC. Characteristically, the points are triangular in outline with slightly flared sides towards the base, and a small rounded tang on the base.

mortar [Ma]. A fairly deep bowl-like vessel, usually of stone but sometimes of wood or metal, used in conjunction with the PESTLE for crushing foodstuffs by placing them in the mortar and pounding them with the pestle.

mortarium [Ar]. A stout mixing bowl with a strong lip and a pouring spout, dusted on the inside with hard grit (trituration grits) to improve its ability to shred foodstuffs rubbed around it and to strengthen it against wear during the pounding of foodstuffs.

Mortillet, Gabriel de (1821–98) [Bi]. French prehistorian best known for his work on the classification of Palaeolithic material. A pupil of Edouard Lartet (1801–73), he took the criteria of classification used in palaeontology and applied them to archaeological materials, especially tool types. He extended the geological system of periods and epochs into the recent past, characterizing each by a series of archaeological 'type-fossils' and naming them after a 'type-site'. In 1864 he founded one of the earliest archaeological journals, entitled *Matériaux pour l'histoire positive et philosophique de l'homme*. By 1869 his scheme for European prehistory was fairly well elaborated and included: the Thenasian (for the now obsolete Eolithic), Chellean, Mousterian, Solutrean, Aurignacian, Magdalenian, and Robenhausian. Many of these remain in use as cultural-historical labels for bodies of material, but whereas de Mortillet saw each as a block of time they are now seen as geographically as well as chronologically defined entities.

[Bio.: G. Junghans, 1987, *G. de Mortillet (1821–1898). Eine biographie: materiellen zur Darstellung seiner Ideen und Beitrage zur Erforschung von Ursprung und Geschichte des Menschen.* Bonn: Habelt]

Mortlake ware [Ar]. *See* PETERBOROUGH WARE.

mortuary enclosure [MC]. *See* LONG MORTUARY ENCLOSURE.

mortuary house [Co]. A simple timber structure in which one or more corpses was placed, perhaps with some grave goods. As such it performed the role of sepulchre and in some cases it remained freestanding and was allowed to decay naturally. In most instances, however, an earthen mound (barrow) was raised over the structure. Mortuary houses were probably constructed as replicas of actual dwellings; in some cases the deceased were in fact buried in their own homes that were burnt or covered in a mound.

mosaic [De]. A wall or floor decoration made up of many cubes of clay, stone, or glass blocks (*tesserae*) of different colours. Mosaics may be either **geometric**, composed of linear patterns or motifs, or **figured** with representations of deities, mythological characters, animals, and recognizable objects. Mosaics became extremely popular in the Graeco-Roman world. The earliest dated mosaic from Britain comes from the legionary fortress bath-house at Exeter dated to AD 55–60, closely followed by those in the Fishbourne Roman palace. The great age of mosaics in Britain, however, is the early 4th century AD. Mosaics were also a feature of the Byzantine empire, some of the finest mid 1st millennium AD examples being those at Ravenna, Italy.

mosaicist [Ge]. A person who makes MOSAICS.

mosque [MC]. An Islamic place of worship found widely distributed in the Islamic world from the 7th century AD. The earliest examples were simple enclosures imitating the courtyard of the Prophet Mohammad's house at Medina. Later congregational examples have an essentially common architecture: large areas that are partly open and partly covered where the congregation meets for prayer; a niche (*mihrab*) at the centre of the end wall in the direction of Mecca, sometimes with a screen (*maqsura*) across the front; to the right of the *mihrab* is a stepped pulpit (*minbar*); one or more minarets (*manar*) outside the main structure from which the faithful are called to prayer by the muezzin (*mu'adhdhin*); and facilities for washing. Schools and libraries may also be part of the complex.

motif [De]. In ROCK ART studies, a recurrent visual image which has a particular arrangement of components; an element in a (usually) complex design. It may be non-representational or pictorial.

motte [Co]. Earth mound marking the site of a small medieval castle.

motte and bailey castle [MC]. A widespread type of early medieval military stronghold comprising an artificially constructed earthen MOTTE, surrounded by a ditch, with an adjoining separately defined enclosure known as a bailey. The basic idea seems to have developed in the Rhineland during the 10th century AD and was adopted by the Normans a century later during their conquests of England, Wales, Ireland, and elsewhere. Motte and bailey castles were built for offensive operations as well as for defence, and are found in urban areas and rural settings. Motte and bailey castles were superseded by other kinds of defensive work in the 12th century AD, but some were made permanent by the replacement of wooden components with stone structures, as at Windsor Castle, Berkshire, England.

motto beaker [Ar]. A beaker made in Gaul or the Rhineland decorated with white-painted scrolls and words forming phrases such as: *da mihi vinum* (give me wine); *valete* or *vivas* (good health); *nolite sitire* (thirst not); and *bibe* (drink up).

mouflon [Sp]. A species of wild sheep found in southwest Asia and the eastern Mediterranean (*Ovis orientalis*), domesticated from about 9000 BC. *See also* SHEEP.

mould **1.** [Ar]. The hollow former into which molten material (typically metal) is poured or soft plastic material is pressed to harden into a required predetermined shape. The simplest type of mould is a one-piece open former in which the casting emerges with one flat unshaped face. Two- and three-piece moulds for use in metalworking were available from middle Bronze Age times onwards. Moulds were also used for making figurines and occasionally for making pottery (e.g. relief-decorated Samian ware). **2.** [De]. In American archaeology this term is used to refer to the topsoil.

mound builders [Ge]. Obsolete term to describe a range of North American cultures and traditions living in the eastern woodlands that constructed platform mounds for ceremonial and burial purposes. *See* ADENA CULTURE; HOPEWELLIAN CULTURE; MISSISSIPPIAN TRADITION.

Moundville, Alabama, USA [Si]. Mississippian ceremonial centre and settlement beside the Black Warrior River, important as the largest such site known. The centre flourished between AD 1250 and 1500 when it covered more than 120 ha. At the centre was a rectangular plaza of 32 ha, around which were twenty large platform mounds. The largest (mound B) was over 17 m high. Public buildings, a sweat-house and charnel structure, and houses for the elite also surrounded the plaza. Higher-status people lived and were buried east of the plaza. Others, perhaps as many as 3000 at any one time, lived in the vicinity of the ceremonial centre, the three sides of the site away from the river being protected by a palisade.

Over 3000 burials have been found on the site, the high-status individuals being buried in the mounds while everyone else was buried in the major village areas.

Moundville was the major ceremonial centre at the heart of a three-tiered settlement pattern of the kind that is typical of an established chiefdom. Ten minor ceremonial centres in the surrounding area each comprised only a single mound, while of still lower status were numerous villages and farmsteads.

[Rep.: C. Peebles, 1979, *Excavations at Moundville 1905–1951*. Ann Arbor: University of Michigan, Museum of Anthropology]

mount [Co]. A mound constructed as a viewing platform within part of a garden, or in order to overlook a garden, in the 16th or 17th century AD.

Mount Pleasant Period [CP]. A phase of the British late Neolithic spanning the period 2750–2000 BC which was defined by Colin Burgess in the late 1970s using the henge enclosure of Mount Pleasant, Dorset, as the type-site. The Mount Pleasant period follows the MELDON BRIDGE PERIOD and preceded the OVERTON PERIOD. It is characterized by the appearance of BEAKER pottery in Britain and the continued development of metalworking through Stages III (Frankford industries), IV (Migdale-Marnoch/Migdale-Killaha industries), and V (Ballyvalley–Aylesford industries). Stage IV involves the early use of bronze as well as copper and gold, and shows some links to the early ÚNĚTICE (Reinecke A1) industries on the continent.

Mousterian [CP]. A Middle Palaeolithic stoneworking industry associated with Neanderthal communities. Named after the type-site of Le Moustier in the Dordogne Valley, France, Mousterian industries are found over most of the unglaciated parts of Eurasia as well as the Near East and Africa, dating to the period *c*.200 000 to 30 000 years ago. Stone tools of the tradition include triangular points made on flakes, racloirs, triangular bifacial handaxes, and burins and awls made on blades. The LEVALLOIS TECHNIQUE of working flint was extensively used. Several variations of the Mousterian have been recognized: the Mousterian of Acheulian Tradition (MAT) named by François Bordes and relating to southwest France, the earlier elements of which (type A assemblages) are dominated by handaxes, backed knives, denticulates, and scrapers, while the later elements (type B assemblages) have fewer handaxes but a higher proportion of burins and awls; the Charentian with an abundance of side scrapers; and a central European variant with leaf-shaped points.

Movius, Hallam Leonard (1908–87) [Bi]. American prehistorian well known for his work on the Palaeolithic of Europe and the Near East. Born in Massachusetts, he graduated from Harvard in anthropology and archaeology in 1930. Something of an athlete at college, he planned to follow a business career but this fell by the wayside after he joined an archaeological expedition to Czechoslovakia immediately after graduating. On his return he enrolled in the Harvard Graduate School and studied in the Department of Anthropology. Between 1931 and 1937 he worked with Dorothy Garrod in Palestine and Hugh Hencken in Ireland. During WW2 he served with the United States Air Force in the Mediterranean, afterwards returning to the Harvard and Peabody Museum where he eventually became professor. During the 1940s and 1950s his interest focused on the French Palaeolithic and especially the great cave sites of the Dordogne Valley. He excavated at La Colombière and Abri Pataud. He received many awards and honours for his work, and the French government named the new museum at Abri Pataud after him. He was elected a Fellow of the Society of Antiquaries of London in 1944. His many publications include the substantial *Early man and Pleistocene stratigraphy in southern and eastern Asia* (1944, Cambridge MA: Peabody Museum).

[Obit.: *Antiquaries Journal*, 68 (1988), 396]

Muckelroy, Keith (1951–80) [Bi]. British archaeologist who did much to establish underwater archaeology in the British Isles. After graduating in history and archaeology from Cambridge he decided to take up underwater archaeology. In 1974 he became a research assistant at the Institute for Maritime Archaeology at St Andrews University, before returning to Cambridge in 1977 as a postgraduate to research cross-Channel trade in the later Bronze Age. In March 1980 he was appointed to the staff of the National Maritime Museum at Greenwich, but died later that year, at the age of only 29, in a tragic accident while carrying out underwater research in Loch Tay, Scotland. His publications include the widely acclaimed volume *Maritime archaeology* (1978, Cambridge: CUP).

[Obit.: *The Times*, 13 September 1980]

mud brick [Ma]. Sun-dried blocks of clay mixed with straw or dung used in building houses and other structures common in parts of the world with a hot dry climate. Buildings constructed with mud brick have a surprisingly long life (30–50 years) if the walls and roof are kept dry. Known as ADOBE in the Americas.

muff glass (cylinder glass) [Ma]. A flat piece of window glass made by blowing a bubble of glass. The bubble was swung to and fro on the blow-pipe as it was being blown so that it became a long cylindrical bubble. The ends were cut off the cylinder which was then split along the middle and allowed to uncurl on a flat surface in an oven to produce a flat sheet of glass.

muller [Ar]. A small grinding stone, often for use with pigments but also grains, ores, and drugs.

Müller, Sophus Otto (1846–1934) [Bi]. Danish archaeologist well known for his work developing excavation technique. Born in Copenhagen, he enrolled at Copenhagen University in 1864 to study classics and attend lectures by Jen WORSAAE. During the 1870s he worked for a short time as a teacher but gradually became more closely involved with the collections in the Copenhagen Museum and in 1871 he accompanied Worsaae on visits to Germany, Austria, and Switzerland. In 1878, after further travels, he was employed as a scientific assistant to his father in the Department of Numismatics in the museum. He became curator of the Royal Museum in 1885, and in 1892, when the museum was reorganized as the National Museum, he became co-director with responsibility for the prehistoric collections. He remained here until retirement in 1921. Throughout his professional life Müller carried out a lot of fieldwork and considerably developed the techniques of stratigraphic excavation, especially in respect of recognizing superimposed burials within round barrows. He also developed a more socially sensitive view of early communities by recognizing the existence of local and regional cultures rather than the very broad chronological horizons that were the concern of Montelius and others.

[Bio.: M. L. Stig Sørenson, 1999, Sophus Otto Müller (1846–1933). In T. Murray (ed.), *Encyclopedia of archaeology I. The great archaeologists*. Oxford: ABC-Clio, 193–210]

mullion [Ar]. A vertical post or bar dividing a window into two or more lights.

multilinear cultural evolution [Th]. A theory of cultural evolution that sees each human culture evolving in its own way by adaptation to diverse environments: different 'pathways' of evolutionary development followed by different societies. Sometimes divided into four broad stages of evolving social organization: band, tribe, chiefdom, and state-organized society.

multiple ditch system [MC]. A class of enclosure complex associated with extensive linear ditch systems on the chalk ridges of southern Britain, dated to the later Iron Age. Sites of this class cover large areas, typically between 25 ha and 60 ha, the boundaries being marked by discontinuous single or multiple ditches. They seem to have been settlements as well as the contexts for a range of agricultural, political, and ceremonial activities. One of the most fully investigated is Blagdon Copse at Hurstbourne Tarrant, Hampshire.

multiple enclosure fort [MC]. A class of later prehistoric enclosure found in the southwest of Britain, usually on sloping ground. The defining characteristics are the series of two or more broadly concentric earthworks bounding the site. The central areas are generally small, between 0.4 ha and 3.5 ha, although some have a range of annexes and appended structures. They usually have a single entrance and where excavated show evidence for domestic occupation. They were probably farmsteads occupied by pastoralist communities. Also known as hillslope enclosures.

multiple passage grave [MC]. A type of Neolithic PASSAGE GRAVE found along the Atlantic coastlands of northwest Europe which comprises two or more chambers set within a single mound. Dating mainly to the 4th and 3rd millennia BC, these structures are mainly elaborations of the SIMPLE PASSAGE GRAVE tradition, although a few are so large as to be regarded as variations of the DEVELOPED PASSAGE GRAVE tradition. Multiple passage graves typically comprise a large round or rectangular mound of earth and stone, within which there is a series of stone-built chambers each being accessible for the outside of the mound via a narrow passage. The chambers are usually round, square, rectangular, or polygonal in plan. In some cases the passages open only from one side of the mound, in other cases the openings are on opposite sides, or, more rarely, from all around the circumference of the mound. Burials either by inhumation or cremation were made in the chambers. One of the best-known examples is at BARNENEZ in Brittany.

multiregional hypothesis [Th]. *See* HOMO SAPIENS.

multivalency [De]. In studies of material culture, the ability of a single item to represent more than one thing at once.

multivallate hillfort [MC]. A hillfort or enclosure that has more than one rampart or defensive circuit.

multivariate analysis [De]. A statistical study of the relationships between three or more variables.

multivocality [Th]. Literally, 'many voices'; an approach to archaeological reasoning, explanation, and understanding that accepts a high degree of relativism and thus encourages the contemporaneous articulation of numerous different narratives or parallel discourses. Thus different groups will adopt different positions in relation to their interpretation of the past, and the meanings that they attach to physical remains. While respecting the right of any group or individual to develop and expound a particular interpretation of some aspect of the past there is some debate as to whether all such parallel positions should be treated as equally acceptable, especially where a particular position is being overtly used, or misused, as a political tool. Ian Hodder has argued (2000) that the misuse of the past can only be evaluated socially and ethically, while most archaeologists, however relativist, would accept that archaeological interpretation should be grounded in, and somehow answerable to, data of some kind.

mummification [De]. The technique of preserving a human or animal body according to rites practised in ancient Egypt. The viscera and brain were extracted from the corpse and preserved in a series of four CANOPIC JARS. The body was then treated with natron (sodium carbonate) to dry it out before it was wrapped tightly in bandages. Jewellery, religious texts, and unguents of various kinds were bound into the bandaging and covering shroud. All stages of the ritual, which could take months, were accompanied by elaborate ceremonies, culminating in the Opening of the Mouth Ceremony which symbolically restored the completed mummy to life.

The term 'mummification' has been extended to refer to corpses wrapped in bandages and naturally preserved by desiccation, as for example in the Peruvian deserts and remote Andean caves.

mummy [Ar]. The body of a person or animal that has been subject to MUMMIFICATION. Human mummies were usually enclosed within a wooden or gold case before being buried.

municipium [MC]. A self-governing chartered city of the second grade; a chartered settlement of Roman citizens or of people enjoying 'Latin rights'. *Municipia* are ranked next in dignity to COLONIAE, but the status was normally conferred on an already existing community.

Munsell colour chart [Ge]. A set of standard colour swatches developed for the Geological Survey of America that provides an objective for describing soil colour or, in archaeological finds analysis, the colour of ceramic fabrics. Three factors are assessed: **hue**–the spectrum is divided into ten main colours, each of which is subdivided into ten variants; the **value**–the darkness or lightness of the colour rated from 1 to 10; and the **chroma**–the greyness or purity of the colour rated on a scale from 1 to 10. A typical Munsell colour reference might therefore read: 5YR4/6. Anyone with a set of charts can look up the relevant swatch and see the original colour.

murder hole (machicolation) [Co]. An opening in the ceiling of an enclosed gateway or the parapet of a wallwalk through which missiles or burning oil could be thrown onto attackers below.

Murray, Margaret (1863–1963) [Bi]. British archaeologist well known for her work in Egypt. Born in Calcutta, Murray spent most of her childhood and adolescence in India. In 1893 she enrolled for a course of study at University College London under Flinders Petrie, and here she was introduced to Egyptology. In 1899 she was appointed junior lecturer in Egyptology at University College and in 1902 joined Petrie's expedition to Egypt. During WW1 college duties made work in Egypt impractical and she turned her attention to other matters, the results of which were later published as *The witch cult in western Europe* (1921, Oxford: OUP). After the war she continued work in Egypt, being made a Fellow of University College in 1922 and an Assistant Professor in 1924. Publications from this period include *Egyptian sculpture* (1930, London: Duckworth) and *The splendour that was Egypt* (1949, London: Sidgwick and Jackson). Having retired from her post, Murray spent WW2 working for an organization that sent lecturers to army outposts in the UK.

[Abio.: 1963, *My first hundred years*, London: Kimber]

murus gallicus [Co]. Latin term for a Gallic wall or rampart. It is distinguished by its stone-faced construction with timber and rubble core, in which the timbers were placed in horizontal layers, criss-crossing laterally and longitudinally, with the lateral beams inserted flush into the stone revetment front and rear.

museum [Ge]. Following the creation of the first public museum, the Ashmolean in Oxford, which opened its doors on 6 June 1683, many thousands of similar institutions have been opened worldwide. Over the centuries their functions and role have changed, although at their heart is the preservation and display of collections. So far as archaeology goes there are three main roles or responsibilities that are fulfilled by museums today: the long-term management and curation of archaeological materials and associated archives; the presentation of a selection of this material to a range of audiences through displays and other interpretative means; and the researching and investigation of both the archaeological dimensions of the material and also its cultural nature as one of the agents that help to create a contemporary picture of the past.

The means by which museums have acquired some of their collections have come under intense scrutiny and debate in recent years, especially in relation to archaeological objects and heritage materials. Most of the world's great museums built their collections through campaigns that literally mined the cultural resources of countries around the world. In 1970 UNESCO agreed an international 'Convention of the means of prohibiting and preventing the illicit import, export and transfer of ownership of cultural property' that has been endorsed by many countries. More recently a new body of legislation known as the UNIDROIT Convention has been drafted by the International Institute for the Unification of Private Law, and in November 1986 the International Council of Museums (ICOM) adopted a code of professional ethics that includes the need to consider the connection between illicitly acquired material and the destructive means by which such material is usually acquired. In the USA, the Native American Graves Protection and Repatriation Act adopted in 1986 mandates the return of all human remains and associated funerary objects to lineal descendants of the tribe from which the material was collected.

Museum of London Archaeological Service (MOLAS) [Or]. One of the three largest archaeological contractors working in Britain, based in London but working throughout the southeast of England and occasionally beyond. The Museum of London first became involved in major archaeological fieldwork in 1974, following the formation of the Department of Urban Archaeology (DUA). The name was changed to the Museum of London Archaeology Service in December 1991.

Mut [Di]. Egyptian goddess, consort of Amun in the Theban triad. Originally a vulture goddess but later depicted as a woman wearing a vulture crown. Later associated with Sekhet and also represented as a lioness. Her temple was situated at Asheru, a suburb of Thebes, now in the precinct of the main temple at Karnak.

mutation [Ge]. A process of random genetic change introducing an alteration in the physical characteristics of an animal or plant. In a tiny proportion of cases mutation produces characteristics which allow new species to flourish, but the vast majority of mutant organisms fail to survive.

Mycenae, Greece [Si]. Bronze Age acropolis, ancient capital of Greece, and type-site of the Mycenaean civilization, situated in the Argolid overlooking the Plain of Argos in the eastern Peloponnese of southern Greece. First excavated by Heinrich Schliemann in 1874, and more recently by, amongst others, Christos Tsountas, Alan Wace, George Mylonas, William Taylour, and Spiridon Iavokides, the site is extensive and long-lived. The hilltop was first occupied in the early Neolithic period at about 6500 BC, with small-scale settlement continuing through into the Middle Bronze Age. It was at the very end of the Middle Helladic period and during the early part of the Late Helladic, around 1650 BC, that the city really rose to prominence. From the 14th century the city was surrounded by massive walls of CYCLOPEAN construction, and was entered by the monumental Lion Gate built in the mid 13th century BC on the northwest side. On the top of the hill in the centre was a palace and a megaron, with houses all around on the lower slopes. Outside the defences there were further areas of housing.

Just inside the Lion Gate in the western quarter of the citadel were the royal SHAFT GRAVES in what has become known as Circle A. Excavated by Schliemann in 1874, this consisted of six tombs dating to the Middle Helladic period, all richly furnished with weapons, drinking vessels, jewellery, face-masks, and pottery. STELAE carved with images of chariots, hunting scenes, and spirals marked the position of each tomb. Grave IV was the richest in the circle and contained the burials of two women and three men. These and other rich burials were considered by Schliemann to be members of the legendary House of Atreus recorded by Homer; indeed he believed one of the gold masks he found was that of Agamemnon, 'king of men' who led the Achaean expedition to war against Troy. It is now known that Circle A pre-dates the Late Helladic prominence of Mycenae and the burials in it are thus too early for Schliemann's interpretation.

A second royal grave circle, Circle B, was discovered and excavated by J. Papadimitriou and George Mylonas in 1952, outside the citadel walls to the west. It was found to be slightly earlier than Circle A, dating to the 16th century BC, and with sixteen graves, slightly less richly appointed than those of Circle A. Later members of the royal family of Mycenae, those associated with the use of the citadel, were buried in the THOLOS tombs to the west of the settlement.

The city seems to have suffered a severe earthquake around 1250 BC with further evidence of disruption around 1200 BC. At this point the palace-organized economy seems to have ceased, though parts of the citadel continued to be occupied until about 1050 BC.

[Sum.: S. Iavokides, 1977, The present state of research at the Citadel of Mycenae. *Bulletin of the Institute of Archaeology*, 14, 99–141]

Mycenaean [CP]. A Greek Bronze Age civilization, at first limited to the mainland but later spreading throughout Greece and across the Aegean after the fall of the Minoan empire. Centred on the city of MYCENAE, the Mycenaeans called themselves ACHAEANS, their achievements being remembered in legendary form by the classical Greeks of the later 1st millennium BC.

The origins of the Mycenaeans remain the subject of much research, but they can be recognized in Greece from about 2000 BC onwards. Influenced by the MINOANS and the development of extensive trading links, the Mycenaean civilization was well established by the 16th century BC and by about 1450 BC was powerful enough to take over Crete and the Aegean. Trade with the eastern Mediterranean was especially strong, but links also extended northwards into continental Europe, bringing, for example, Baltic amber into southern Greece.

The Mycenaeans used LINEAR B writing and occupied walled citadels containing palaces centred on a MEGARON. Like Linear B, much of their material culture derived in adapted form from Minoan sources. In other ways they differed from the Minoans in being more warlike, having defended settlements, and a strong emphasis on weapons as grave goods.

Mycenaean power was relatively shortlived. Local unrest increased in the late 13th century BC, exemplified by the Trojan Wars. The civilization went into abrupt decline soon after 1200 BC. Many sites were abandoned, others decreased in size, and the palace bureaucracy collapsed. Many theories have been advanced to explain this decline, including natural catastrophes, invasions, and environmental disasters.

Mykerinus (Mycerinus/Men-kau-re) [Na]. Egyptian pharaoh of the 4th Dynasty who erected the third of the great pyramids at GIZA.

Mylonas, George (1898–1988) [Bi]. Greek archaeologist best known for his excavations at Mycenae. Born at Smyrna, he studied archaeology at Athens University. After serving in the Greek army against the Turks in 1922 he went to America where, from 1928 onwards, he held a number of university teaching posts. In 1957 he was elected president of the Archaeological Institute of America. He excavated at a number of sites in Greece, including Ayios Kosman, Eleusis, and Olynthus, but he is best remembered for his work at Mycenae where he became director of excavations in 1958 after earlier collaboration with J. Papadimitriou on the outer grave circle. Between 1979 and 1988 he was Secretary General of the Archaeological Society of Athens. He was elected an Honorary Fellow of the Society of Antiquaries in 1978. His numerous publications include *He neolithike epoche en Eleusis* (1928, Athens, reprinted 1975), and *Ancient Mycenae: the capital city of Agamemnon* (1957, London: Routledge and Kegan Paul).

[Obit.: *Antiquaries Journal*, 68 (1988), 389–90]

Myres, Sir John Linton (1869–1954) [Bi]. British classicist and ancient historian well known for his study of ancient Greece. Born in Preston, educated at Winchester and New College, Oxford, he graduated with a firstclass degree from the Classical School. Between 1892 and 1895 he travelled extensively in Greece before returning to Oxford with a studentship at Christ Church. In 1907 he moved to Liverpool University as Gladstone Professor of Greek, while at the same time lecturing in ancient geography. In 1910 he returned to Oxford as Wykeham Professor of Ancient History and took up the Fellowship at New College attached to it. Here he remained until 1939, although during WW1 he attained the rank of lieutenant-commander and later commander in the Royal Navy Volunteer Reserve. He was awarded the Greek Order of King George I of the first class. He excavated in Cyprus and compiled a catalogue of the Cyprus Museum. Amongst his numerous publications were *Who were the Greeks?* (1930, Berkeley: University of California Press), and *Herodotus: father of history* (1953, Oxford: Clarendon Press). He was knighted in 1943.

[Obit.: *The Times*, 8 March 1954]

myth [De]. A narrative organizing data such as beliefs about transcendental powers, the origins of the universe, social institutions, or the history of the people. Viewed in functional terms myths serve to record and present the moral system whereby contemporary attitudes and actions are ordered and validated.

mythology [Ge]. The study of religious or heroic legends and tales that seem incredible and which were created by particular communities as MYTHS. One constant rule of mythology is that whatever happens amongst the gods or other mythical beings was in one sense or another a reflection of events on earth: as Emile Durkheim emphasized, god is another name for society, for humans make their god in their own image. Thus recorded myths and legends, perhaps preserved in literature or folklore, have an immediate interest to archaeology in trying to unravel the nature and meaning of ancient events and traditions.

Nabataeans [CP]. A nomadic population speaking a Semitic language occupying the region of Tayma and Madain Salih, first attested in the annals of the Assyrian King Ashurbanipal in the mid 7th century BC. By the early 6th century BC they had established a kingdom south and east of Edom, ancient Midian, on a trade route between the Red Sea and the Mediterranean. The Nabataeans infiltrated Edom and forced the Edomites into southern Palestine. They made PETRA, Jordan, their capital c.312 BC, but they also controlled Bosra, Damascus, and many other towns at the height of their power.

A notable achievement of Nabataean technology was their elaborate network for water collection, storage, and distribution in their cities, as well as for agricultural use throughout the kingdom. Nabataean fineware pottery, both plain and painted, was locally produced and is amongst the finest ceramics produced in the Middle East up to that time. Their mining, processing, and manufacturing of iron, copper, bronze, lead, gold, and silver objects were on a par with the rest of the Roman world.

The Aramaic-speaking Nabataeans created a new writing form, a running cursive or semi-ligatured script which was used for both lapidary inscriptions and graffiti. This later evolved into the Arabic writing still in use today.

In 64–63 BC the Nabataean kingdom was conquered by the Romans under Pompey, but it remained independent while paying imperial taxes. The kingdom was finally annexed by the Romans under Trajan in AD 106 to become *Provincia Arabia Petraea*.

NAGPRA [Ab]. *See* NATIVE AMERICAN GRAVES PROTECTION AND REPATRIATION ACT.

Nagyrév Culture [CP]. First phase of the Hungarian Bronze Age dating to the later 3rd millennium BC, the local successor of the Vucedol-Zok group and precursor of HATVAN and Fuzesabony cultures. Most settlements of this period are TELLS surrounded by enclosing banks and ditches. Timber-framed houses are used at some sites, but mud-brick structures with internal partitions are also known. The main style of pottery is the one- or two-handled cup with a tall funnel neck that is made in a black burnished ware. Burials are mainly in urned cremations and grave goods are rare.

Nahua [CP]. General term for a succession of societies occupying central Mexico, the latest of which were AZTECS.

Nahuatl [Ge]. The native language spoken by Toltec, Aztec, and other Mesoamerican communities, still spoken in the Basin of Mexico. One of the Uto-Aztecan languages found over a large part of northwest and central America. Loan-words from Nahuatl to English include: tomato and chocolate.

nail [Ar]. **1.** A metal spike for fixing things to wood (including other pieces of wood). **2.** Round metal cylinder with an expanded flat top set in the street of trading ports for merchants to use when doing business. Some of the best preserved are in Bristol, UK.

Nakbe, El Peten, Guatemala [Si]. Maya urban and ceremonial centre of the Formative (middle Pre-Classic) Stage, dating to the period 600–400 BC. The site comprises 80 or more structures in two main clusters of platforms and mounds, including a pyramid some 50 m high. A carved limestone stela depicting two rulers or deities facing one another is probably the oldest known stela in the Maya Lowland. The site is also important because the ceremonial centre appears to overlie an earlier village established about 1000 BC. It thus provides a glimpse of the transition from tribal villages to centralized chiefdoms. Nakbe was eclipsed by El Mirador some 13 km away to the northwest in the Classic stage.

[Rep.: I. Graham, 1967, *Archaeological explorations in El Peten, Guatemala*. New Orleans: Tulane University]

naked barley [Sp]. *See* BARLEY.

Nakhon Pathom, Thailand [Si]. Large proto-historic and early historic site in the lower Chao Phraya Valley of central Thailand. Local tradition records that it is the oldest city in Thailand and is said to have been visited by the Buddha. The town, which covers an area of nearly 4 km by 2 km is thought to have been the capital of the Dvaravati state. Artefacts dating from the 6th century AD onwards have been found. The Phra Pathom, the highest stupa in Thailand, rises to 116 m. The rectangular moat may have been added around AD 1000 during the period of Khmer control of the region.

[Sum.: G. Coedès, 1966, *The making of South East Asia*. Berkeley: University of California Press]

Namatianus, Rutilius Claudius [Na]. Roman official under Honorius who left Rome (probably in AD 417) to look after his ancestral Gallic estates, apparently near Toulouse, then threatened by the impending Visigothic settlement in Aquitaine. His autobiographical poem *De reditu suo* ('On his return') describes the devastation of Italy. His account contrasts with the prevailing fatality of the Christian historians, for he was a pagan and believed in the mission of Rome and its old gods, whom he saw as undermined by Christianity as much as by barbarian invaders.

Nanna (Nannar) [Di]. Sumerian god connected with the moon and with fertility. His principal city was UR. Equivalent to the Akkadian god Sin.

Napo Phase [CP]. South American farming cultures found in the Rio Pastaza and Rio Napo areas of Amazonia and tentatively dated to *c*.AD 1000–1200. Characterized by their ceramic assemblages which belong to the Incised and Punctuate Horizon Style of Amazonia.

NAR [Ab]. *See* NATIONAL ARCHAEOLOGICAL RECORD.

narrative [Th]. The creation of a historical narrative is, for many, the ultimate aim of archaeological research—developing a rounded knowledge about the past, or some aspect of it, which combines the particulars of the archaeological record with events, people, societies, and a plot. The creation of such narratives is a major theme of interest in POST-PROCESSUAL ARCHAEOLOGY. Narrative is a basic human means of making sense of the world, and narratives form a basic component of self-identity. The development of a narrative is itself a creative and intellectual process. Not surprisingly, narratives feature prominently in nationalist and heritage appropriations of the archaeological past for they provide a means of externalizing particular ways of seeing the world and projecting understandings of meaning and significance to others.

Narrow Point Tradition [CP]. Late Archaic hunter-gatherer communities living in southern New England, North America, in the period *c*.2700–2000 BC, within the more broadly constituted Mast Forest late Archaic. Narrow Point Tradition communities are characterized by chipped stone projectile points of long narrow outline.

Narses [Na]. General of Justinian, at first an assistant of Belisarius in Italy (AD 538), and from AD 550 to AD 554 commanding general in Italy, which he conquered in AD 554. Until his death in AD 567 he acted as regent and administered the Italian reconstruction.

narthex [Co]. The comparatively narrow vestibule of an early Christian church which stretched along the whole width of the church at the west end. It was often adorned with mosaics or frescoes and three doors opened from the narthex into the church proper. When open these enabled catechumens and penitents (whose place was in the narthex) to hear the service in the church.

Narva Culture [CP]. Neolithic communities of the 4th and 3rd millennia BC living in the eastern Baltic littoral and beyond into Lithuania, Latvia, Estonia, parts of Poland and Belarus. Descendants of the KUNDA CULTURE they share much in common with their forebears, including a dependence on hunting and fishing. The material culture of the Narva Culture includes pointed-base pottery in straight-sided and S-profile forms.

NASA [Ab]. *See* NATIONAL ASSOCIATION OF STATE ARCHAEOLOGISTS.

Nasca Culture [CP]. Early Intermediate Period farming communities which flourished in the valleys of Peru's southern coast c.AD 200–700. The most characteristic artefacts are the distinctive ceramics decorated in polychrome style in continuation of the local Paracas style. Up to sixteen colours were used, fixed during firing. Favoured motifs include the stylized biomorphs, such as the cat demon, and bodiless heads. On stylistic grounds nine main phases to the Nasca ceramic industry have been defined. In the early phases most communities lived in small villages adjacent to arable land. Later, many of these villages were abandoned as the population moved to nucleated centres, some of them defended.

Throughout, the dead were interred in extensive cemeteries, typically as cloth-wrapped mummies deposited in circular chambers approached from the surface by a shaft. The site of Cahuachi, Peru, was a ceremonial centre which also seems to have been used in all phases. Nasca Culture communities also made fine woven textiles, although their greatest artistic achievement is represented by the NASCA LINES.

Nasca lines, Peru [Si]. A series of large-scale geoglyphs: straight lines, geometric shapes, and representational motifs on the surface of the desert plain in the Nasca region of southern Peru. The straight lines range in size from 500 m to 8 km in length and are up to 50 m wide. The other motifs are up to 1.7 km long. All were created by clearing the ground surface of stones to reveal a light-coloured soil beneath. Because of their size, all the images are best appreciated from the air.

Many of the straight lines radiate out from low hills or ridges. The representational motifs include giant animals such as spiders, humming birds, monkeys, and fish. They are similar to images depicted on Early Intermediate Stage Nasca Culture ceramics and textiles, and on this basis the markings are believed to date to the period AD 200–700. Various interpretations have been put forward: ceremonial pathways leading to sacred places; depictions of constellations in the night sky. There is no basis for Erich von Daniken's claim that the lines were set out to guide extraterrestrial astronauts to their landing strips.

[Sum.: H. Silverman and D. Browne, 1991, New evidence for the date of the Nazca lines. *Antiquity*, 65, 208–20]

natatio [Co]. A Latin term used to describe a swimming-pool usually found in the PALAESTRA of a large bath-house.

Natchez [CP]. Late Woodland chiefdom-based farming communities flourishing in the lower Mississippi Basin of North America from about AD 1150 down to European contact. Possibly descended from the Mississippian, the Natchez had two administrative levels. The upper level comprised the supreme chief (Great Sun) and a war chief (Tattooed Serpent) who ruled the whole tribe. Below these were a series of local chiefs who each ruled one of the nine regions into which the Natchez were divided. The two high-level chiefs lived in the Grand Village which comprised a few cabins and a temple built atop an earthen mound. The rest of the population lived in isolated hamlets and farmsteads.

Socially, the Natchez were organized into moieties, halves associated with cardinal directions. Individuals from one moiety married partners from the other.

National Archaeological Record (NAR) [Ge]. *See* NATIONAL MONUMENTS RECORD.

National Association of State Archaeologists (NASA) [Or]. A representative association of official state archaeologists working in the USA, limited to one delegate per state. Their aim is to communicate among themselves, share good practice, facilitate the conservation of cultural resources, and deal in a collective way with problems within the archaeological profession.

National Historic Preservation Act [Le]. An Act that came into force in the USA in 1966, and which has been variously amended since, which establishes a programme for the preservation of historic properties throughout the United States. It covers the National Register of Historic Places and National Historic Landmarks; the creation of State Historic Preservation Officers; the need for federal agencies to take into account the impact on archaeological and historical resources of any projects they undertake or support (known as a Section 106 review); the establishment of a preservation programme by each federal agency; and the establishment of an Advisory Council on Historic Preservation.

nationalism [De]. A set of beliefs and symbols expressing identification with a given national community.

National Monuments Record (NMR) [Ge]. In England, and similarly in other parts of the United Kingdom, the state agency responsible for the historic environment and maintaining a computerized database of recorded archaeological sites and remains. The English record has a number of elements, reflecting the historical development of the system. The **National Archaeological Record (NAR)** was developed from records initially created and held by the Ordnance Survey but transferred to the NMR in c.1980. These are basically descriptions and plans of archaeological sites with bibliographic links to associated reports and publications and additional material from surveys by the RCHME. Tied to the NAR are a series of indexes, including the Excavations Index which lists archaeological interventions and their results. The **National Buildings Record** was developed from a range of architectural records and surveys and includes details on all the protected buildings (listed buildings) in England. Finally, the **National Library of Aerial Photographs** is a collection of more than two million images (vertical and oblique) mainly taken since AD 1945, together with plots of areas that have been the subject of detailed study. A National Mapping Programme is undertaking a preliminary analysis of these pictures and the creation of a basic record of the archaeological features visible on them.

nation-state [Ge]. Particular type of state, characteristic of post-medieval and modern times, in which a government has sovereign power within a defined territorial area, and the mass of the population are citizens who know themselves to be part of a single nation. Nation-states are closely associated with the rise of nationalism, although nationalist loyalties do not always conform to the boundaries of specific states that exist today. Nation-states developed as part of an emerging nation-state system, originating in Europe, but in current times spanning the whole globe. *Compare* CITY-STATE.

Native American [Ge]. A general term for the past and aboriginal inhabitants of North America, thus distinguishing them from European and other settlers and their descendants.

Native American Graves Protection and Repatriation Act (NAGPRA) [Le]. A major piece of legislation that became law in the USA on 16 November 1990 and which provides a series of rights by which native groups can influence the deposition and treatment of human remains and associated artefacts.

Specifically, section 3 of the Act relates to any human remains and objects excavated or discovered on federal or tribal lands, giving ownership or control of that material to the lineal descendants of the Native American where that can be determined, or the Indian tribe on whose tribal land the material was discovered, or the tribe with the closest cultural affiliation with such remains or objects and which states a claim for such remains. Section 5 requires each federal agency and museum which has holdings or collections of Native American remains and funerary objects to compile an inventory of the material and identify the geographical and cultural affiliation of it. Section 7 provides for the expeditious repatriation of Native American human remains and objects held by federal agencies and museums at the request of a known lineal descendant or tribe that formerly owned or controlled the material. Section 8 establishes a review committee to monitor the inventory and identification process and to adjudicate in cases of competing claims.

NAGPRA and its operation has been the focus of much debate during the first decade of its implementation, some archaeologists claiming that it overly restricts access to human remains and cultural material for scientific study.

Natsushima, Japan [Si]. An initial Jomon period shell midden near Tokyo, Japan. Dated to c.7500–7300 BC the main occupation layer included deep conical bowls with cord-mark decoration, the bones of domestic dogs, bone and stone arrowheads, grinding stones, partially ground pebble axes, bone fish-hooks, and eyed needles.

[Rep.: S. Sugihara, 1957, *Kanagawa-ken Natsushima ni okeru Jomon bunka shoto no kaizuka*. Tokyo: Meiji Daigaku Bungaku Kenkyujo]

Natufian Culture [CP]. Epipalaeolithic communities of the Levant in the period 10 500 BC to 8 000 BC, named after the site of Wadi en-Natuf in Palestine. Natufian groups seem to have been settled or semi-settled hunter-gatherers and occupied a range of sites including caves. Some larger settlements, including the first phase at JERICHO, include what appear to be permanent architectural constructions, food-storage facilities and fixed food-processing equipment such as seed pounders. Cemeteries suggest a degree of social differentiation. Material culture includes geometric microliths, bone points and speartips, fish-hooks, and a range of items such as sickle-blades, pestles and mortars, and grindstones that suggest the harvesting of cereals. There is, however, no evidence for the deliberate planting of crops, nor is there any evidence for the domestication of livestock.

natural selection [Ge]. The principle that the organisms which are best adapted to their environments will live to reproduce the most viable offspring. The primary mechanism of evolutionary change.

natural type [De]. An archaeological type coinciding with an actual category recognized by the original toolmaker.

Navan, Co. Armagh, Northern Ireland [Si]. A hilltop enclosure west of Armagh city, the ancient Emain Macha, and the first capital of Ulster. Excavations carried out by Dudley Waterman between 1961 and 1971 show that the site has a long history stretching back to the Neolithic. The main use of the hill begins in the 3rd century BC with the construction of a massive enclosure 230 m across and with a ditch 4.5 m deep. Inside were a series of circular structures and monuments of which the most substantial was an earthen mound 50 m in diameter and 6 m high (site B). In its early life this comprised a ditched enclosure in which a series of periodically renewed figure-of-eight timber post-built structures were built. Finds from the site included the skull of a Barbary ape which is taken to illustrate the wide trading links that the site had by the middle Iron Age. The figure-of-eight structures were replaced by a single massive timber structure with concentric rings of postholes about 95 BC, the whole thing being rapidly filled with stones and then burnt before being encased in its mound of earth and stone.

The Navan fort passes into history as the ancient seat of the kings of Ulster and perhaps the setting for the epic tales of Cu Chulainn. When Emain Macha was finally abandoned is uncertain, but it seems likely to coincide with the establishment of a very early church nearby at Armagh, where St Patrick established the ecclesiastical capital of Ireland.

[Rep.: D. Waterman (ed. C. Lynn), 1997, *Excavations at Navan Fort 1961–71*. Belfast: Stationery Office]

nave [Co]. The western part of a Christian church, extending westwards from the CHANCEL whose maintenance was traditionally the responsibility of the parishioners.

nave band [Ar]. A circular frame or disc arranged to revolve on an axle and used to facilitate the motion of a vehicle.

naveta [MC]. A type of chambered tomb found on the Balearic Islands and dating to the period 1500 BC through to 800 BC. The tombs are characterized by their elongated U-shaped plan, a corbelled roof, and a flat or slightly concave façade. The gallery-shaped burial chamber is approached by a corridor through the thickness of the wall, and there is occasionally a porthole slab partially blocking it.

Nazca Culture [CP]. *See* NASCA CULTURE.

NBR [Ab]. National Buildings Record. *See* NATIONAL MONUMENTS RECORD.

Neanderthal man [Sp]. An extinct hominid species *Homo sapiens neanderthalensis*, first recognized from fossil remains found in the Feldhofer Cave in the Neander Valley, near Dusseldorf, Germany, in AD 1856.

Anatomically, Neanderthals were somewhat shorter but much more robust than *Homo sapiens sapiens*. They had distinctive cranial features that included prominent brow ridges, low, sloping foreheads, a chinless and heavy forward-jutting jaw, and extremely large front teeth. Their brain size was comparable to that of *Homo sapiens sapiens*, averaging about 1600 cc. Neanderthal skeletal remains have been found over a wide area of Asia, Europe, and Africa, and are regularly associated with Middle Palaeolithic flint industries that are characterized as the Mousterian. Dates for the skeletal remains and associated industries suggest that the species thrived between about 230 000 and 30 000 years ago. There has been much debate about both the origin and the fate of the Neanderthals. Their origins amongst the European *Homo erectus* now, however, seem fairly certain, both in terms of the traits revealed by the fossil human remains and the development of the lithic industries. Some scholars believe that the Neanderthal line leads to modern humans, but Chris Stringer and Clive Gamble have persuasively argued that the Neanderthal species was a dead end and that it was replaced by modern humans who evolved in Africa and were better organized and better equipped. *See also* HOMO SAPIENS.

Nea Nikomidhia, Greece [Si]. An early Neolithic tell settlement in Macedonia, northern Greece, excavated by Robert Rodden between 1961 and 1964. The period over which the site was occupied was relatively short, 6200 to 5300 BC, and so it provides a snapshot of life in one of the earliest Neolithic settlements in Greece. The houses were constructed in the style of those further east: square-plan single-roomed structures made from timber and mud. A large structure in the centre of the mound contained terracotta female figurines and is thought to have been a shrine. Plain and painted pottery was found, together with frogs carved from greenstone, flint blades, and many ground stone axes. The earliest domesticated cattle date from about 6000 BC, and were associated with cultivated einkorn, emmer, and barley.

[Rep.: K. A. Wardle, 1996, *Nea Nikomedeia: the excavation of an early Neolithic village in northern Greece, 1961–1964*. London: The British School at Athens]

nearest-neighbour analysis [Te]. A technique for examining the spatial distribution of two-dimensionally recorded points, for example settlement sites within a river catchment. Assuming that all the points to be examined are contemporary and that all relevant examples are known, a series of statistics can be calculated by measuring the linear distance between sites. This can very easily be done using a GIS system. A nearest-neighbour index (usually denoted by the symbol R), is calculated from the ratio of the average observed distance from each point in the pattern to its nearest neighbour, to the average distance expected if the pattern were randomly distributed, which depends solely on the density of the pattern being studied. The index R varies from 0.00 for a totally clustered pattern through 1.00 for a random distribution to a maximum of 2.15 for a completely regularly spaced pattern.

Nebuchadnezzar   (Nebuchadrezzar, Nebuchodonosor) [Na]. The most famous of the kings of Babylon, the second of that name, ruling from *c*.605 BC through to 562 BC. His father, Nabopolassar, ejected the Assyrians to restore Babylon's independence and to found the Neo-Babylonian kingdom. During his father's reign Nebuchadnezzar defeated the Egyptian Pharaoh Necho at Carchemish in 605 BC, thus giving him control over a wide area of western Asia. It was also the start of intensified conflict between Babylonia and Egypt that eventually led to the defeat of Nebuchadnezzar's army three years later. This defeat may have stimulated further trouble for Nebuchadnezzar in the form of a revolt in Judaea which was finally crushed in 597 BC when Zedekiah was installed as a puppet king. Further revolts over the following decade led Nebuchadnezzar to lay siege to Jerusalem, finally destroying it in 586 BC. Nebuchadnezzar was responsible for building a great palace and the hanging gardens in Babylon, one of the SEVEN WONDERS OF THE WORLD.

necked bowl [De]. Bowl or jar with a rim curving outwards from its shoulder to form a neck of concave quarter-round profile. Sometimes referred to as a cavetto rim or neck.

necklace [Ar]. A chain, band, or cord, often ornamented with beads, pearls, jewels, etc., worn around the neck.

necropolis [MC]. An area of tombs, temples, and pathways which together amount to a 'city of the dead'.

needle [Ar]. A thin, pointed implement normally of bone or metal used for sewing. There is a hole at the blunt end for threading the sewing material through the needle, which is then used to carry it through the fabric being joined or embroidered.

needle-case [Ar]. A container in which needles are held.

Nefertiti [Na]. An Egyptian queen, the chief wife of Akhenaten, who appears to have played a prominent role in public life and has tentatively been identified with the pharaoh Smenkhare who briefly succeeded Akhenaten.

Nefertun [Di]. Egyptian god, third member of the triad of Memphis. Represented either as a man with a lotus on his head or as a child wearing the side-lock of youth and sitting on a lotus.

negative painting [De]. A style of painting where the central image or motif is left blank and paint is applied all around it to colour or emphasize the surroundings. In pottery-making negative decoration was often achieved by covering the design area with a paint-resistant substance (e.g., wax, gum, clay) and then dipping the whole pot into paint or dye before it was fired. Alternatively, the pot might be either smoked or dipped into a black wash. The dark coating is unable to reach those areas of the surface protected by the resistant substance, and when the latter is removed, the pattern stands out in the original colour against the black background.

negotiation [Ge]. The way in which people match their understanding of the world, their aspirations, and their interpretation of their place in it with social reality and what their senses tell them.

Neith [Di]. Egyptian goddess, the city deity of Sais in the Delta, but worshipped throughout Egypt. A very ancient creator goddess, depicted as a woman wearing the Red Crown of Lower Egypt and clasping a bow and arrows in her hand. She, like Isis, Nephthys, and Selket, became one of the four guardian goddesses of the dead, and watched over the sarcophagus and the canopic jar containing the stomach. She was also credited with the invention of weaving. The Greeks identified her with Athena.

Nekhbet [Di]. Egyptian goddess, the vulture goddess of el-Kab (Nekheb) and the titulary goddess of Upper Egypt. Shown either as a vulture hovering over the king or as a woman wearing the White Crown of Upper Egypt. The Greeks identified her with Eileithya.

Nemrut Dağ, Anatolia [Si]. Mountain-top sanctuary of the 1st century BC situated 250 km northeast of Gaziantep in the Taurus Mountains of eastern Turkey. The site was examined by Karl Humann and Otto Puchstein

in 1890 and Friedrich-Karl Dorner between 1939 and 1963 and is one of a number of dynastic shrines built by the Commagene rulers before their kingdom was absorbed into the Roman empire around AD 72. The principal feature of Nemrut Dağ is the colossal stone sculptures and mausoleum erected by Antiochus I (c.69–34 BC). The fragmentary Greek inscriptions indicate that the statuary represented the Achaemenid and Seleucid rulers whom Antiochus claimed as his ancestors, as well as a variety of syncretic gods including Apollo-Mithras and Zeus-Oromasdes. The burial chamber of Antiochus has never been located.

[Rep.: D. H. Sanders (ed.), 1996, *Nemrud Dagi: the hierothesion of Antiochus I of Commagene. Results of the American excavations.* Winona Lake IND: Eisenbrauns]

Nenana Complex [CP]. Palaeo-Indian hunter-gatherer communities of south-central Alaska in the period c.10 000–8000 BC. Characterized by small bifacially worked chipped stone projectile points and the absence of microblade technology. Nenana sites, probably related to big-game hunting, lie along river valleys in well-drained situations close to water and offering good look-out points.

Nene Valley ware [Ar]. Type of Roman pottery manufactured at various sites immediately west of Peterborough in the lower Nene Valley from where it was widely distributed in Roman Britain from the mid to late 2nd century AD to the late 4th century AD. In particular, there are brown or black colour-coated tablewares including the HUNT CUP with trailed decoration en BARBOTINE. Also known by the rather obsolete term Castor ware.

neo- [Ge]. A prefix meaning 'new' or 'different from'. As a hyphenated prefix it often refers to the reappearance of a culture or tradition after a period of decline or abandonment, as in 'neo-classical'.

neo-Assyrian [CP]. The Assyrian empire can be divided into three main periods, the last of which dates to the Iron Age and is known as the neo-Assyrian. After a period of mediocrity between about 860 BC and 740 BC, Tiglath-Pileser III began the creation of the Assyrian empire, well reflected in the scriptures of the Old Testament and amongst whose rulers are Sargon (721–705 BC), Sennacherib

(704–681 BC), Esarhaddon (690–699 BC), and Ashurbanipal (668–627 BC). At its largest, the neo-Assyrian empire ran from Elam to Egypt. It was destroyed in 612 BC by an alliance of the Babylonians and the Medes.

neo-classical [De]. Architectural and decorative style dominant in the 18th century, developed from classical forms discovered in Italy and Greece.

neo-evolutionism [Th]. A school of thought based on the idea that human behaviour and cultural change are characterized by distinct patterns and mechanisms that can be explained by evolutionary change. Whereas 19th-century evolutionists were prepared to accept that cultural change might have resulted from deliberate human attempts to change their environment for the better, neo-evolutionists are fundamentally deterministic, arguing that humans have always sought to maintain traditional ways of life, with the dominant roles in cultural change being played by such uncontrollable factors as economics, demography, or technology. From the 1940s onwards, neo-evolutionary ethnologists such as Leslie White and Julian Steward argued that, in different environments, very different cultures might arise from identical social processes. This was taken up by archaeologists during the 1960s, but under the glare of the mature processual archaeology of the 1970s and 1980s appeared rather simplistic.

neo-Gothic [De]. The Gothic revival movement in architecture began in the mid 18th century AD but reached a peak in Victorian times.

Neolithic [CP]. A period of prehistory originally defined by the occurrence of polished stone tools and pottery. Now used most frequently in connection with the beginnings of farming. Literally the New Stone Age, as opposed to the Palaeolithic or older Stone Age. The appearance of characteristic polished flint and stone types, including axes, adzes, and arrowheads, is generally also associated with the introduction of cereal cultivation and animal domestication, and in Europe with the earliest manufacture of pottery. The radical nature of these innovations has probably been exaggerated in the past by the use of the term 'Neolithic Revolution'. The appearance of Neolithic culture is dated vari-

ously from around 8000 BC in the Middle East to the 5th and 4th millennia BC in Atlantic Europe.

Neolithic Revolution [Ge]. A term popularized by Gordon CHILDE in the 1940s to reflect the huge impact on life that was made by the development and spread of farming which he saw as one of two critical moments in early history (the other he called the Urban Revolution).

Nephri [Di]. Egyptian god, spirit of the corn.

nephrite [Ma]. One of two kinds of jade (the other is JADEITE), being a semi-precious stone widely used for making ornaments and jewellery. Technically an iron calcium magnesium silicate of the amphibole mineral group, nephrite is generally a whitish to dark green colour, although it can be blue or black. Sources of nephrite material are known in China, Siberia, Pakistan, New Zealand, the Philippines, New Guinea, Australia, Poland, the Swiss Alps, Italy, Sicily, and North and South America.

Nephthys [Di]. Egyptian goddess, sister of Osiris, Isis, and Seth, wife also of Seth, and a member of the Heliopolitan Ennead. She, like Neith, Isis, and Selket, was a guardian goddess of the dead and watched over the canopic jar containing the lungs. She was also said, according to some legends, to be the mother of Anubis.

Nero [Na]. Roman emperor AD 54–68, stepson and heir of the emperor Claudius. He became infamous for his personal debaucheries and extravagances and, on doubtful evidence, for his burning of Rome and persecutions of Christians.

Nerva [Na]. Roman emperor AD 96–8, the first of a succession of rulers traditionally known as the Five Good Emperors. A member of a distinguished senatorial family, Nerva was distantly related by marriage to the Julio-Claudian house and had been twice consul (AD 71 and 90) when, on the assassination of the emperor Domitian, he became emperor.

net sinker [Ar]. A piece of perforated stone or terracotta used to keep a gill net vertical in the water. Also known as a net weight.

netting needle [AR]. A needle for making and mending nets, often forked at both ends, and with a hollow centre in which the thread or twine being used can be conveniently wound.

neutral soil [De]. A soil in which the surface layer is neither acid nor alkaline in reaction, typically with a pH value around 7.

neutron activation analysis [Te]. A method used to determine the chemical composition of various substances such as flint, obsidian, pottery, and metal found in archaeological contexts. It is generally non-destructive as it involves exciting the atomic nuclei rather than their electrons. The specimen is irradiated inside a nuclear reactor so that the neutrons will interact with nuclei in the sample to form radioactive isotopes that emit gamma rays as they decay. The energy spectrum of the emitted rays is detected by a scintillation or semiconductor counter. Constituent elements are identified by the characteristic energy spectrum of emitted rays while their intensity provides a measure of concentration. The time between the neutron activation of the sample and the measurement of the resultant gamma rays depends on the half-lives of the radioactive isotopes which range from seconds through to thousands of years. Generally a few weeks is allowed before measurement takes place.

Neutron activation analysis has an advantage over X-ray fluorescence spectrometry because it analyses the whole specimen as opposed to the surface only. However, care must be taken that the neutron dose is not so great as to make the specimen radioactive and therefore unsafe for handling. The technique is used less frequently than it might be because of the increasingly limited availability of suitable nuclear reactors.

New Albion, California or Oregon, USA [Si]. The site of the first English settlement on the west coast of North America established by Sir Francis Drake in AD 1579 during his circumnavigation of the world aboard the *Golden Hind*. Controversy surrounds the location of the settlement. Traditionally, it was believed to lie near San Francisco in California, but Bob Ward, an English amateur historian, has shown that a site on the east side of Whale Cove, Oregon, is more likely. Geophysical surveys have revealed traces of a stockaded enclosure.

[Sum.: J. Harlow, 1996, Drake's American colony is found. *The Sunday Times*, 28 January 1996, 1.8]

New Archaeology [Ge]. A movement that began in America in the 1960s, aimed at making archaeology more scientific, with explicit theory and rigorous methodologies. At the heart of the thinking was a positivist belief in the principles of the scientific method (especially hypothesis testing or hypothetico-deductive reasoning). In the USA many of these ideas were set out by Lewis Binford in his book *New Perspectives in Archaeology* published in 1968. In it he stressed: the need to use new technologies such as the computer for statistical and matrix analyses of data; the concept of the ecosystem for the understanding of the economic and subsistence bases of prehistoric societies; an evolutionary view of culture; the use of models of cultures that could be viewed as systems; incorporating an evolutionary approach to culture change; and a close relationship between archaeology and anthropology. In Britain David CLARKE'S book *Analytical Archaeology*, also published in 1968, took up similar themes, emphasizing particularly the application of systems theory to archaeological modelling.

Although the proponents of the New Archaeology were heavily criticized by more traditionally minded scholars, especially for their use of jargon and for dehumanizing the discipline, the basic principles became widely accepted. The product of studies that implemented and developed the ideas set down under the rubric of the New Archaeology is what is now often referred to as PROCESSUAL ARCHAEOLOGY.

New Forest pottery [Ar]. Type of Roman pottery made in the New Forest area of southern England in the 3rd and 4th centuries AD. The most distinctive fabric is very hard, almost a STONEWARE, in a purple colour-coat with a metallic lustre. It is used especially for the production of indented BEAKERS. There are other wares in grey and white in a wide range of vessels, some with a very local distribution.

Newgrange, Co. Meath, Ireland [Si]. The best known of the three large developed passage graves in the Bend of the Boyne between Slane and Drogheda in eastern Ireland, about 50 km north of Dublin. The site was excavated by Michael O'Kelly between 1962 and 1975, and restored under his direction thereafter. The focus of the site is a vast circular cairn c.80 m across and 12 m high, retained at the base by a kerb of 97 boulders, some decorated in the style of British ROCK ART known as megalithic art. It was built about 3200 BC. A passage, 19 m in length, leads into the mound from the southeast side and gives access to a cruciform chamber roofed by a lofty corbelled vault. The orthostats of the passage support roof slabs, but at the very front of the passage is a unique 'roof-box' which allows light to shine into the tomb through a slot above the roof of the outer passage. This happens at sunrise around the time of the winter solstice, the first rays of the sun illuminating the rear wall of the chamber for about 17 minutes.

The passage grave was originally within a STONE CIRCLE, twelve pillars of which still survive. By the later Neolithic the tomb had fallen out of use and the sides were already beginning to slump by the time BEAKER-using groups arrived in the area. The present reconstruction with vertical quartz-clad walls has proved highly controversial; many authorities believe that the surface of the barrow was originally far less steep and covered in quartz boulders.

[Sum.: M. O'Kelly, 1982, *Newgrange. Archaeology, art and legend*. London: Thames & Hudson]

New Kingdom [CP]. The Egyptian period following the expulsion of Asiatic Hyksos rulers and the subsequent reunification ties including Thuthmoses I–IV, Akhenaten, Tutankhamun, and Ramesses I–XI. Broadly the 18th to the 20th Dynasties, c.1550–1070 BC. To this period belongs much of the monumental architecture of Egypt.

New Stone Age [CP]. *See* NEOLITHIC.

New World [Ge]. General term for the Americas following their discovery by Europeans in the 16th century AD, thus setting them in contradistinction to the Old World of Africa, Europe, and Asia.

Niah Cave, Sarawak [Si]. Within the Gunung Subis limestone massif of north Borneo is a series of caves that have been used for burial and settlement over many millennia. The most important, known as the Great Cave, was extensively excavated by Barbara and Tom Harrison intermittently between 1954 and 1967. They showed that the site contained a long series of deposits starting in the Middle Palaeolithic with a pebble and flake industry. What is claimed to be an early *Homo sapiens* skull dating to perhaps 40 000 years ago was also found, although the association between the bones and the charcoal that yielded the radiocarbon date is not secure. Higher deposits in the cave include flexed inhumations from the period 12 000–15 000 BC, and extended burials in wooden coffins or on mats from the 1st and 2nd millennia BC. The most recent burials in the cave are jar burials and cremations from the period 1500 BC through to about AD 1000. Distinctive styles of local pottery appear around 2500 BC along with Neolithic polished stone axes. A new multidisciplinary programme of excavations by Graeme Barker and David Gilbertson started in 2000 with the aim of reinvestigating this important sequence.

[Sum.: G. Barker *et al.*, 2000, The Niah Caves project. *Sarawak Museum Journal*, NS 76, 111–49]

Nicaea Council [Ge]. Church council held in the city of Nicaea (Iznik, Turkey) in AD 325, at which Arianism was denounced and the Nicene Creed was formulated.

Niedermendig lava [Ma]. Lava from the Niedermendig–Andernach–Eifel region of the Rhineland widely used in making querns and grinding stones from the later Neolithic onwards. The quality of the stone is such that it was traded widely in northern Europe.

niello [Ma]. A bluish-black paste produced by heating powdered sulphides of copper and silver. Niello was extensively used to decorate inlaid Mycenaean daggers of the 2nd millennium BC, and also by Germanic and Anglo-Saxon metalworkers in the 1st millennium AD.

Nike [Di]. Goddess of victory, portrayed in Greek art as a winged figure descending to award victory. The earliest Nike statue was found in Delos. The most famous are the Winged Victory of Paeonius in the Olympia Museum, dated 425 BC, and the Victory of Samothrace in the Louvre dated to about 320 BC.

Nile [Di]. Egyptian god. *See* HA'PY.

Nilsson, Sven (1787–1883) [Bi]. Swedish contemporary of WORSAAE and Professor of Zoology at Lund, who recognized, with qualifications, the validity of the Danish technological model and proposed, on the basis of comparative studies, a socio-economic model of development from savagery through pastoralism and agriculturalism to civilization. His principal work, *Skandinaviska Nordens Urinvanare*, published in 1834, was later translated into English by John Lubbock under the title *The primitive inhabitants of Scandinavia* (1868).

[Bio.: J. Hegardt, 1999, Sven Nilsson. In T. Murray (ed.), *Encyclopedia of archaeology. I. The Great Archaeologists*. Oxford: ABC-Clio. 65–78]

NIMBY [Ab]. Abbreviated form of the principle 'Not In My Back Yard' underlying much environmental protest when confronted with proposed new but unwelcome development.

Nimrud, Iraq [Si]. Situated beside the Tigris River, south of modern Mosul in Mesopotamia, the ancient city of Nimrud has been the subject of several excavation programmes, starting with the work of Sir Henry Layard in the mid 19th century (who wrongly believed he was excavating NINEVEH).

Although large, Nimrud does not have the great antiquity of many other cities in Mesopotamia. It was established by Shalmaneser I of Assyria in the mid 13th century BC. In 883 BC, under Ashurnasirpal II, it became the Assyrian capital (Kalhu/Calah), a role it retained until 710 BC when the capital moved first to Khosrsabad and subsequently to Nineveh. In its heyday, the city was enclosed by a wall some 8 km in circumference, enclosing at one corner a citadel that contained a ziggurat, temples, and palaces. The palaces have yielded the richest finds: enormous stone winged bulls, reliefs, and exquisite carved ivories that once adorned the royal furniture. Many of the sculptures were brought back to England by Layard and are now in the British Museum.

[Sum.: M. E. L. Mallowan, 1966, *Nimrud and its remains*. London: Collins]

Nineveh, Iraq [Si]. Large walled city that was a capital of the ASSYRIAN empire from the end of the 8th century BC. Situated across the Tigris from Mosul, Nineveh has seen a steady stream of excavations since the early work by Emile Botta in AD 1842. These show that the site was occupied from at least the 6th millennium BC with pottery from the Hasuna phase onwards. Destroyed by the Medes late in the 7th century

BC some occupation continued until its rise to prominence in 705 BC when Sennacherib established the Assyrian capital here. Today the site is dominated by two large mounds that relate to the rebuilding of the city by Sennacherib: Kuyunjik (the citadel) and Nebi Yunus (the arsenal). A great palace was built, its walls covered in splendid reliefs. Many of these, together with a great archive of cuneiform tablets that constituted the two libraries of Sennacherib and his grandson were taken to the Louvre in France and the British Museum in the UK during the 19th century. Around the city was a substantial wall, 12 km in circumference, parts of which still stand.

[Sum.: A. H. Layard, 1970, *Nineveh and its remains* (edited by H. W. F. Saggs, with a new introduction). New York: Praeger]

nitrogen dating (nitrogen analysis) [Te]. A relative dating technique that can be applied to bone. It is based on the gradual reduction of nitrogen in bone as collagen is broken down into amino acids and leached away. Nitrogen is a fairly major constituent of bone (about 4 per cent) and as bone collagen decomposes it gradually releases the nitrogen at a fairly uniform rate. The exact rate of decay depends on the burial environment, but the relative ages of samples from the same environment can be compared by measuring the remaining nitrogen content.

NLAP [Ab]. National Library of Aerial Photographs. *See* NATIONAL MONUMENTS RECORD.

NMR [Ab]. *See* NATIONAL MONUMENTS RECORD.

Noailles graver (Noailles burin) [Ar]. Small gravers or burins made from thin, flat blades, truncated and retouched to give several chisel-like blades on the same tool. Named after the cave of Noailles, Corrèze, in France and dating to the Perigordian at around 27 000 years ago.

nomads [Ge]. Herding societies whose seasonal movements are primarily dependent on the search for fresh pastures, although exceptionally they may also be involved with limited cultivation.

nome [Ge]. An administrative district in ancient Egypt.

nomothetic [Th]. Describing approaches based on producing generalizations, common principles, or laws relating to human behaviour.

non-conformist chapel [MC]. A building used for worship and meetings by Protestants outside the established church, including the Old Dissent groups (Quakers/Society of Friends; Baptists; Presbyterians; Congregationalists; Independents; or Unitarians) and the New Dissent groups that developed after AD 1750 (Moravians; Methodists; Wesleyans; and Primitive Methodists).

non-verbal communication [Th]. Communication between individuals based on facial expression, bodily gesture, or the deployment of material culture such as clothing, ornaments, objects, and structures. The last area is important for archaeology as these items are potentially recoverable from the archaeological record.

Norman architecture [De]. Distinctive style of architecture characterized by the Romanesque or round-headed arch, often highly decorated and of several orders, constructed of cut stones of approximately equal size set radially.

Normans [CP]. The occupants of the duchy of Normandy in northwest France, descendants of the Franks and 10th-century Norse settlers. From AD 1063 onwards they expanded their lands considerably with the conquest of Sicily, southern Italy, and, in AD 1066, Britain. These military feats were consolidated by a tightly controlled army and a feudal aristocracy. Strong forts were constructed both as defensible positions and statements of power. The Normans were the driving force behind the Crusades of the 11th century onwards, and they promoted the French language and Romanesque styles of architecture. By about AD 1200 Norman conquerors had been absorbed into the cultures they came to control, although their presence continued to be felt down into the Middle Ages.

normative theories [Th]. A view of human culture based upon the identification of abstract rules and general conditions that can then be applied to a particular culture in order to explain or understand its workings or material culture. Such an approach provides a widely used framework for studying archaeological cultures throughout time.

Norse [CP]. A general term used to describe the people and cultural traditions of communities living in, or migrating out from, Norway during the later 1st and early 2nd millennia AD. The term is sometimes misused to refer to all Scandinavian peoples of this period. *See also* VIKINGS.

Northampton ware [Ar]. Type of late Saxon pottery found in the midlands of England from the period *c*.AD 850 to 1150.

Northern Archaic Tradition [CP]. Archaic Stage hunter-gatherer communities postdating the Palaeo-Indian groups in the far north of North America, flourishing in the period from 4000 BC down to modern times. Northern Archaic communities used projectile points reminiscent of those used on the Great Plains. Among other things, they hunted caribou and waterfowl. Lithic assemblages include side-notched asymmetrical projectile points, unifacial knives, and end scrapers.

northern black polished ware [Ar]. A type of pottery found in the lower Ganges and Punjab regions of India and Pakistan that dates to the period between 500 BC and 100 BC. Distinctive in being a very fine grey coloured ware with a lustrous black surface that was created using an alkali flux applied to the surface of the vessel before it was fired in a reducing atmosphere.

Northumbria [Ge]. A Saxon kingdom occupying the northeastern part of England. Established in the 7th century AD by the amalgamation of the earlier kingdoms of Bernicia and Deira. Following the conversion of King Edwin to Christianity in AD 626, a number of monasteries were established in the kingdom, including Jarrow and Monkwearmouth. From the later 7th century Northumbria was an important and influential kingdom, especially through its schools, arts, monumental sculpture, and production of illuminated manuscripts.

Northwest Coast Culture [CP]. Archaic Stage hunter-gatherer communities occupying large tracts of what is now British Columbia, the Yukon and southern Alaska in the north-west of North America from about 5500 BC down to recent times. Characterized by bone harpoons. Roy Carlson divided the culture into three subphases: early period (5500–4000 BC), middle period (4000 BC–AD 500), and the late period AD 500 down to the last century.

Norton Tradition [CP]. Archaic Stage hunter-gatherer communities centred on the coastal regions of Alaska in the period c.1000 BC to AD 800. The Norton Tradition succeeds after a short hiatus the Arctic Small Tool Tradition of the same area, but was probably not descended directly from it. Rather, Norton Tradition communities probably originated among contemporary cultures living in Siberia. Norton groups were heavily reliant on both coastal and terrestrial resources: caribou, small mammals, fish, and sea mammals.

Many Norton settlements lay beside major salmon streams. Their houses mainly comprise square semi-subterranean dwellings with short sloping entrances, central hearths, and pole and sod roofs. Material culture includes the earliest pottery in Alaska: check-stamped ware showing affinities with broadly contemporary Asian wares. Stone lamps were also introduced.

Chronological subdivisions of the Norton Tradition include the Choris Stage (1000–500 BC), Norton Stage (500 BC–AD 800), and the Ipiutak Stage (AD 1–800).

nosed scraper [Ar]. *See* END SCRAPER.

Notitia Dignitatum [Do]. A document usually dated to about AD 395 (although only existing today as 15th-century AD and later copies). It is a list of the principal civilian and military officials of the Roman empire. Details are given of the stations within each military command and their garrison. It is, therefore, an invaluable document for the study of the late Roman army.

Notker (the Stammerer) [Na]. Author of a credulous treatise about Charlemagne, identified as a monk of St Gall, Switzerland, born c.AD 840, who was writing in the 880s and died c.AD 912.

Novantae [CP]. Late Iron Age tribe occupying southwestern Scotland at the time of the Roman conquest.

Novgorod, Russia [Si]. An ancient city situated on the River Valhow about 160 km south of St Petersburg. Excavations have been carried out in the town since the first systematic work by Artemi Artsikhovsky in 1932, and have uncovered a remarkable series of deposits which preserve in waterlogged conditions a sequence of wooden buildings and streets from the 10th century AD up to the 18th century. The site was first occupied in the 9th century when it developed as a trading post. The kremlin was established in the 11th century and is one of the earliest to have stone defences. By the 14th century it had come to control a vast territory extending from the Arctic Ocean to beyond the Ural Mountains. In addition to the well-preserved buildings and structures, excavations have revealed a wealth of unusual material including industrial areas for the manufacture of textiles, bone objects, leatherwork, and glass working. A collection of more than 700 letters written on birch bark between the 11th and 15th centuries have been found and provide a valuable insight into the life of this trading city and the administration of its hinterland.

[Rep.: M. Brisbane (ed.), 1992, *The archaeology of Novgorod, Russia*. Lincoln: Society for Medieval Archaeology]

nuclear family [De]. A family group consisting of wife, husband (or one of these) and dependent children.

Nueva Esperanza Phase [CP]. South American farming cultures found in the Rio Ucayali area of Amazonia and tentatively dated to c.AD 700–900. Characterized by their ceramic assemblages which belong to the Polychrome Horizon Style of Amazonia.

numerus [De]. A Latin term for a body of troops, a unit of lower grade than *auxilia*.

Nun [Di]. Egyptian god, the primeval ocean from which the earth emerged, personified as a god. He had a female counterpart, Nunet.

Nunamiut [CP]. Contemporary indigenous hunter-gatherer peoples living in Alaska who were the subject of detailed ethno-archaeological studies by Lewis Binford. Nunamiut communities gain over 80 per cent of their subsistence from caribou hunting, relying on stored food for 8.5 months of the year. Fresh meat is available for only two months or so.

Nunet [Di]. Egyptian goddess, female counterpart of Nun.

nunnery [MC]. A settlement built to sustain a community of religious women, comprising a church and domestic accommodation arranged around a cloister. *See also* MONASTERY.

nuraghe (pl. nuraghi) [MC]. A class of stone fortress built on the island of Sardinia between the early 2nd millennium BC and the late 1st millennium BC. The early examples are simple stone towers with internal chambers. Over time, however, they become larger and more complicated in their design so that later examples tend to have multiple towers with elaborate internal rooms and a warren of passages. These later examples form one component of fairly extensive defended settlements. The nuraghi of Sardinia are very similar in form and date to the torri of Corsica and the talayots of the Balearic Islands.

The Sardinian fortifications also give the name to the **Nuraghe Culture** which is associated with a flourishing bronze-working industry using locally available ores. Amongst the diverse range of products are figurines. Stone chambered tombs also feature in Naraghe Culture, as do sacred wells.

Nut [Di]. Egyptian goddess, a member of the Heliopolitan Ennead, daughter of Shut and Tefnut and wife of Geb, the earth god. She personified the vault of heaven, and representations show her as a woman standing bent over with the tips of her fingers brushing the ground. Sometimes she was represented as a cow, straddling the earth. In both cases her body is spangled with stars. She was said to swallow the sun each night and to give birth to it each morning. According to one legend, she gave birth to her five children, Osiris, Isis, Seth, Nephthys, and Horus the Elder, on the five epagomental days of the year.

Nyerup, Rasmus (1759–1829) [Bi]. Secretary of the Danish Royal Committee for the Preservation and Collection of National Antiquities, the purpose of which was the establishment of the Danish National Museum of Antiquities.

[Not.: O. Klindt-Jensen, 1975, *A history of Scandinavian archaeology*. London: Thames & Hudson. 46–8]

nymphaeum [MC]. Generally, any place consecrated to nymphs, especially natural places such as a spring, river, mountain, or tree. In classical times it often took the form of an elaborately decorated semi-circular fountain-house with niches in the walls containing sculpture.

Oakley, Kenneth Page (1911–81) [Bi]. British anthropologist and specialist in the Palaeolithic period. Born in Amersham he was educated at Halloner's Grammar School and University College, London, where he studied geology both at undergraduate and postgraduate level. In 1934 he took a post with the Geological Survey but this was short-lived because a year later he was appointed to an assistant keepership at the British Museum (Natural History). Here he spent the rest of his working life except for a brief period back in the Geological Survey on war service. From the late 1930s he began working on Palaeolithic and Pleistocene sites in the Thames Valley. Early hominid fossils fascinated him and soon after the war he spent much time developing ways of dating early remains. This later led to considerable involvement with radiocarbon dating. Amongst his best-known publications are *Man the tool-maker* (1949, London: British Museum (Natural History)), and *Frameworks for dating fossil man* (1964, London). He was elected a Fellow of the Society of Antiquaries in 1953 and a Fellow of the British Academy in 1957.

[Obit.: *The Times*, 5 November 1981]

oar [Ar]. A wooden pole with a blade at one end that is used to propel a boat along through leverage against the water. Oars differ from paddles in being secured to the side of the boat itself and being used in pairs. In northern Europe they probably appear in the later Bronze Age to judge from representations on model boats and rock art.

oasis [Ge]. Localized fertile areas within a desert.

oasis theory [Th]. A general theory explaining the development of agriculture and the Neolithic way of life that was first put forward by Pumpelly in 1908, reiterated by Newberry in 1924, and popularized by Gordon CHILDE, in the 1920s. Simply stated, the argument runs that as the climate got warmer and drier in the early post-glacial period people, plants, and animals became concentrated in relatively few and increasingly restricted fertile areas. The symbiosis that developed included the 'domestication' of plants and animals through the manipulation of their production and reproduction. The model has largely been abandoned, however, because there is little evidence of major desiccation in the required period.

oats [Sp]. A group of cereals domesticated in the Near East during the 5th or 6th millennia BC. Most domesticated oats are hexaploid types with six sets of chromosomes derived from the wild red oats (*Avena sterilis*) found around the Mediterranean. The main cultivated varieties include the common oats (*Avena sativa*) found in cool climates; the cultivated red oats (*Avena byzantina*) found in warmer climates; and the large-seeded naked oats (*Avena nuda*) found mainly in southwest Asia. Other wild hexaploid species include the common wild oats (*Avena fatua*) and the winter wild oat (*Avena ludoviciana*). The use of oats was not widely adopted in northern Europe until the Iron Age.

OAU [Ab]. *See* OXFORD ARCHAEOLOGICAL UNIT.

Oaxaca, Mexico [Si]. A highland plateau and valley at about 1550 m above sea level in the southern part of the Sierra Madre of Mexico. Surveys and excavations directed by Kent Flannery, Richard MACNEISH, and others provide a detailed picture of cultural development in the area.

Archaic Stage remains have been found at the cave site of Guila Naquitz and Cueva Blanca, the former providing abundant evidence of over a dozen species of plants being exploited by communities living in the area between c.8700 and 7000 BC. Incipient agriculture was being practised from about 7400 BC. By 1500 BC Formative Stage villages were being built. Houses were of wattle and daub, rectangular in plan, and arranged around an open area of plaza which may have served as a dancing ground or a place for public rituals.

In the Rosario Phase, 700–500 BC, the town of SAN JOSÉ MOGOTÉ had grown to fifteen times the size of the next largest centre and acted as a ceremonial centre for perhaps fifteen or twenty villages. This was the first stage in the development of chiefdom and eventually state-based society in the area, centred on MONTE ALBÁN which was successively used by Zapotec and Mixtec.

[Rep.: K. Flannery, J. Marcus, and S. Kowalewski, 1981, The Pre-Ceramic and Formative of the Valley of Oaxaca. In J. A. Sabloff (ed.), *Supplement to the Handbook of Middle American Indians*. Austin: University of Texas Press, 48–93]

Obanian Culture [CP]. Late Mesolithic communities living in the western isles of Scotland during the 4th millennium BC, named after a series of sites investigated on the island of Oban, Argyll. Settlements include shell middens and rock-shelters and suggest a marine-based economy. Artefacts include barbed spears and stone limpet scoops.

obelisk [MC]. From the Greek word meaning 'spit' or 'dagger', the term was applied to the long narrow shafts of stone, usually granite, with pyramidal-shaped tops set upright in pairs before the entrance to Egyptian temples. Old Kingdom examples are squat and closely relate to the PYRAMIDS. Later examples are taller and more slender. One of the best-known examples outside Egypt is Cleopatra's Needle on the Embankment in London. It once formed a pair with the obelisk now in Central Park, New York, and both were originally set before the temple at Heliopolis dedicated to Tuthmosis III, and also bear an inscription of Ramesses II.

objectivity [Th]. The idea that things exist, or that statements about things are true, in absolute terms and independently of human existence or belief. Such a view stands in opposition to subjectivism, which holds that knowledge and truth are not independent of human existence. In many ways the debate between PROCESSUAL and POST-PROCESSUAL ARCHAEOLOGY has at its heart this polarization between objectivist and subjectivist approaches.

oblique aerial photograph [De]. Photographic image taken from an aircraft or similar high-level elevated platform where the camera direction is at an angle to the ground beneath. Such photographs do not need special equipment, and using carefully chosen views and good lighting can provide a good impression of a complicated set of remains. However, oblique aerial photographs distort perspective and cannot easily be used for plotting and mapping visible features without rectification. *See also* VERTICAL AERIAL PHOTOGRAPH.

obliquely blunted point [Ar]. Type of early Mesolithic MICROLITH found very extensively in northern Europe and elsewhere, essentially a narrow flint blade that has been backed or blunted along one edge towards the tip.

obsidian [Ma]. A naturally occurring black volcanic glass extensively used in the production of edged tools. It fractures at the molecular level and produces some of the sharpest edges known on stone tools. One of the largest exploitation sites is on the Cycladic island of Melos but other sources are known at Lipari, Sicily, on Sardinia, in central and eastern Turkey, and in Hungary. Obsidian was exported widely around the eastern Mediterranean. In the Americas obsidian is found in Mexico. It also occurs in southeast Asia and in the Pacific, including important sources in Melanesia; obsidian from Talasea was traded from at least 17 000 BC. There are also many sources in New Zealand.

obsidian dating (obsidian hydration dating) [Te]. A method that is able to determine the age of an obsidian tool in terms of when it was made. When obsidian is chipped a thin layer of hydrated rock slowly builds up on the fresh surface. The thickness of the hydration layer can be measured as the basis for an estimate of how long ago the surface was exposed. The technique can be used back to about 25 000 years ago, but there are always difficulties using the technique because the rate of hydration varies in relation to the chemical composition of the obsidian and the local environment in which it is preserved.

oca [Sp]. Tuberous plant (*Oxalis tuberosus*) native to Andean South America. Domesticated as a root crop by *c*.AD 1500.

occupation debris (occupation layer) [De]. A general term used to describe any set of deposits that are believed to represent in situ settlement at a site, especially quantities of domestic refuse such as, for example, broken pottery, discarded tools, faunal remains, and ash and charcoal from hearth sweeping.

Ocean Bay Tradition [CP]. Archaic Stage marine-mammal-hunting communities, descendants of the Palaeo-Arctic traditions, living on Kodiak Island and the Alaska Peninsula in the period *c*.4000–2500 BC, predating the emergence of sedentary coastal populations. Barbed stone harpoon points of polished slate and stone lamps are known. Hunted food sources include sea otter, seal, sea lion, and porpoise. The spears used in hunting were lightly coated in aconite poison from the monkshood plant to increase efficiency.

Oc Eo, Vietnam [Si]. An early trading port in the Mekong Delta in Cochin China, South Vietnam, excavated by L. Malleret in the 1940s, and thought to be the main port of the Funan kingdom. The town, which dates to the early 1st millennium AD, had substantial defences comprising five ramparts and four moats. The area enclosed covers 450 ha. Inside there are buildings of stone as well as timber structures on piles. The scale of trade is represented by the finds of objects of Mediterranean origin, including a gold coin of Antonius Pius dated AD 152 and Sassanid seals. Indian material also includes seals of 3rd-century AD date, beads, and jewellery. There are also Chinese bronzes. Local craft production included the manufacture of glass and stone beads, and extensive tin, bronze, and gold working. The town was linked to the coast and its hinterland by a series of canals that can be traced on aerial photographs.

[Sum.: L. Malleret, 1959–63, *L'archéologie du Delta du Mekong*. Paris, 4 vols.]

OCH Group [Ab]. *See* ORKNEY–CROMARTY–HEBRIDEAN GROUP.

ochre [Ma]. Naturally occurring soft oxides of iron in either yellow or red forms. Ochres were much used as colouring materials in pre-historic and later times for cave art, decorating pottery, and probably colouring parts of the human body. Red ochre was certainly used in a ceremonial context to colour corpses before burial from Palaeolithic times onwards.

ochre-coloured pottery [Ar]. A type of thick red-coloured pottery with an ochre wash on the surface found at sites in the upper Ganges Valley of India and Pakistan. Dating to the later 2nd millennium BC, it bridges the period between the late HARAPPAN CULTURES and the INDUS VALLEY CIVILIZATION.

oculists' stamp [Ar]. Small rectangular tables of stone, Roman in date, with inscriptions neatly cut in retrograde on the sides for marking cakes of eye ointment with the author of its prescription.

oculus [Co]. **1.** A decorative motif used on pottery and in rock art comprising a pair of circles or spirals resembling a pair of eyes. Such designs are widely found in western Europe in the 3rd millennium BC, especially in Spanish Copper Age ceramics, and in PASSAGE GRAVE ART. **2.** A round window or opening in the top of a dome.

OD [Ab]. *See* ORDNANCE DATUM.

odeum [MC]. A small building in form and plan like a theatre with semi-circular seating. Some were roofed. Chiefly used for musical contests, concerts, and meetings.

Odoacer [Na]. Skirian officer elected Roman emperor in AD 476 in opposition to Romulus and his father Orestes. He ruled Italy until defeated and killed by Theodoric the Great in AD 493.

Offa's Dyke, England [Si]. A very substantial linear earthwork believed to have been built by King OFFA of Mercia in the 8th century AD as a frontier between his kingdom and the lands to the west. The earthwork comprises a large bank to the east and a ditch to the west. It runs for more than 192 km from Treuddy in the north to Chepstow in the south, close to the modern border of England and Wales. Studies by Sir Cyril Fox and others, however, show that it is not a single earthwork but rather a series of constructions joined together and in some places running roughly parallel to each other.

[Rep.: C. Fox, 1955, *Offa's Dyke*. London: British Academy]

Offa the Great [Na]. English king of Mercia from AD 757. During his reign the Mercian kingdom achieved its greatest extent. He was responsible for a massive border defence along the western frontier of his kingdom (OFFA'S DYKE), and at an international level he established close links between Mercia and the Carolingian empire. His daughter married one of Charlemagne's sons. Died AD 796.

offset [De]. Point at which the thickness of a wall is reduced, forming a horizontal 'step' in one or both faces. The offset provides a ledge on which to support a floor.

offset planning [Te]. A method of creating a scaled representation of part of an excavation site or larger area. A baseline is established through the feature or area of interest and then measurements are taken at right angles to a series of target points. On the plan the baseline is marked out to scale and then the target points are plotted from it. Once the target points are fixed on the drawing they can be joined up to outline the structures or items being planned.

off-site archaeology [Th]. A model of regional archaeological structure proposed by Robert Foley in 1978 that questions the idea that human behaviour is spatially confined to what archaeologists refer to as 'sites'. His basic hypothesis, widely accepted, is that due to a number of factors the archaeological record is spatially continuous and that its structure may be described in terms of variable artefact density across a landscape.

ogam [De]. See OGHAM.

ogee [De]. A double curve, one concave the other convex.

ogham [De]. A form of writing in which twenty or so letters or sounds are represented by groups of strokes, no more than five in number, either vertical or diagonal and either above or below or through a baseline. Many inscriptions are written along the edge of a stone using the corner angle as the baseline. Widely found in the western parts of the British Isles, it may have originated in Ireland or South Wales as a secret script in the 3rd century AD. Its use dates to the period from the 3rd century AD through to the 9th century AD when it is found on SYMBOL STONES. Claims

have been made for the presence of ogham inscriptions in North America, but these are treated with extreme scepticism.

oinochoe [Ar]. A type of jug made from precious metal, bronze, or clay. In Greek times it was used to dispense wine during a symposium and is often depicted in conjunction with a phiale during the pouring of libations at an altar.

O'Kelly, Michael Joseph (1916–82) [Bi]. Irish archaeologist who specialized in the prehistory of Ireland. Born and brought up in County Limerick, he studied archaeology at University College, Cork. In 1944 he was appointed curator of the Cork Museum, and in 1946 succeeded S. P. O'Ríordáin to the Chair of Archaeology in University College, Cork. Amongst his numerous excavations the best known is that undertaken with his wife Claire at Newgrange, County Meath, between 1962 and 1975. O'Kelly served on the councils of many learned societies and advisory boards in Britain and Ireland. He was elected a Fellow of the Society of Antiquaries in 1947.

[Obit.: *The Times*, 27 October 1982]

Okvic Culture [CP]. Archaic Stage marine-mammal-hunting communities flourishing around the coasts of the Bering Straits in North America and Siberia between about 200 BC and AD 500, either predating or, more likely, contemporary with the Old Bering Sea Culture in the same area. The two cultures were very similar except in art styles: the Old Bering Sea Culture preferred ornate, plastic, and curvilinear styles while the Okvic Culture used a flat angular style of ornamentation.

Old Bering Sea Culture [CP]. Archaic Stage marine-mammal-hunting communities flourishing around the coasts of the Bering Straits in North America and Siberia between about 200 BC and AD 500. Representing the early stages of the Thule Tradition, the material culture includes pottery influenced by developments in Siberia. Stone tools tend to be polished slate rather than chipped stone, and include lanceolate knives, projectile heads, and the *ulu* transverse-bladed knife.

Weapons of these groups were decorated with incised designs and spirit images in the belief that their beauty, which honoured the animal spirits, would draw game to the hunter. Feathers and wings transformed the weapons into swift birds of prey. Stylistic variation suggests that the carvings were the symbols of individuals rather than groups. Kayaks and *umiaks* (large skin boats) appear in the archaeological record, as do a wide range of bone tools dominated by ivory harpoon heads, bird darts, fish spears, snow goggles, blubber scrapers, needles, awls, mattocks, snow shovels made from the shoulder-blades of walrus, and harpoon-mounted ice picks for winter seal hunting.

Houses were rectangular with an entrance tunnel that dipped lower than the floor of the living space in order to trap cold air. Yupid Eskimo hunters of southwest Alaska continued these traditions down to the present century. The Old Bering Sea Culture was the predecessor of the Punuk Culture that developed on the St Lawrence islands after AD 500.

Oldbury-type beads [Ar]. Type of late Iron Age bead found in southeastern England, hexagonal in outline with white spirals in a blue ground mass.

Old Copper Culture [CP]. Late Archaic Stage hunter-gatherer communities linked not so much through cultural affinity as by the exploitation of native copper ores around the shores of the Great Lakes of North America in the period *c*.3000–2500 BC. These communities used cold hammered and annealed native copper for the production of edged tools and ornaments. Among the items made were copper points as substitutes for chipped stone projectile points, axe and adze blades, gouges, wedges for splitting wood, fish hooks, beads, bracelets, and headdress pieces. Most of the copper artefacts were used within a radius of about 500 km of the sources, but interest in such items gradually expanded and items were exchanged widely with surrounding groups.

Old Cordilleran Culture [CP]. Late Pleistocene hunter-gatherer communities living in the highlands of the Pacific Cordilleran Mountains of North America in the period *c*.9000–5000 BC.

Older Dryas Phase [CP]. A biostratigraphic subdivision of the late DEVENSIAN STAGE in which sub-Arctic conditions prevailed; the second of three subdivisions of the North Atlantic cold-climatic phase known as the DRYAS. Godwin's POLLEN ZONE Ic corresponds

with the Older Dryas in Britain, marked by tundra vegetation. The Older Dryas spans the period from *c*.10 000 BC down to *c*.9800 BC in northern Europe.

Oldest Dryas Phase [CP]. A biostratigraphic subdivision of the late DEVENSIAN STAGE in which Arctic conditions prevailed; the earliest of three subdivisions of the North Atlantic cold-climatic phase known as the DRYAS. Godwin's POLLEN ZONE Ia corresponds with the Oldest Dryas in Britain, marked by tundra vegetation. The Oldest Dryas spans the period from *c*.13 000 BC down to *c*.10 500 BC in northern Europe.

Old Kingdom [CP]. The period preceding the MIDDLE KINGDOM during which the 3rd to 6th Dynasty kings ruled over Egypt and were buried in colossal stone pyramids. Broadly the period *c*.2658–2150 BC.

Oldowan [CP]. An early phase in the development of hominid societies recognized on the basis of stone toolmaking industries from Bed I sites in the Olduvai Gorge, Tanzania, and other African sites. Consisting of simple chipped pebbles made by removing flakes from alternate faces of a naturally rounded pebble or cobble. Known as 'choppers', these tools show signs of use for cutting and scraping, but were probably opportunistically made as the need arose. Oldowan industries have been dated to the period 2 million to 1.6 million years ago and are provisionally associated with *Homo habilis*.

Old Sarum, Salisbury, Wiltshire [Si]. Multiphase hilltop settlement overlooking the river Avon about 2 km north of modern-day Salisbury. Excavations and studies of the historical accounts of the site suggest at least four main phases to its use, starting in the 2nd century BC with the construction of a HILLFORT enclosing the entire hilltop. Occupation continued through into the Roman period when it lay at the junction of two major roads. The second main phase of use began immediately after the Norman conquest when William I constructed a motte and bailey castle in the middle of the earlier hillfort. A cathedral consecrated in AD 1092 was built adjacent to the castle, together creating an important political and ecclesiastical centre. During the 12th century AD, the castle was elaborated and the cathedral expanded. An outer curtain wall was built to enclose the settlement, which by this time was a prosperous trading centre too. The final phase dates to the 1220s when under the guidance of Bishop Poore the cathedral and the settlement were moved to the present site of Salisbury and the existing buildings and structures demolished.

[Sum.: RCHME, 1980, *City of Salisbury*, vol. 1. London: HMSO]

Old Stone Age [CP]. *See* PALAEOLITHIC.

Olduvai Gorge, Tanzania [Si]. An ancient lake basin on the edge of the Serengeti Plain in northern Tanzania containing a long sequence of sediments that contain one of the longest sequences of cultural remains currently known in the world. Excavated and surveyed by Louis and Mary Leakey intermittently between 1931 and the late 1960s, these deposits contain stone tools, faunal assemblages, and hominid fossils spanning the period 1.9 million years ago through to about 10 000 BC. The earliest hominid fossils are those of *Homo habilis* and *Australopithecus boisei* associated with beds I and II and with the OLDOWAN stone tool industries. From about 1.6 million years ago the tool industries change to Acheulian and Developed Oldowan, the earliest fossils of *Homo erectus* being from about 1.25 million years ago and extending through beds III and IV.

[Rep.: M. D. Leakey, 1971, *Olduvai Gorge, excavations in Beds I and II, 1960–1963*. Cambridge: CUP]

Old World [De]. General term used to refer to Europe, western Asia, the Near East, and North Africa.

olive [Sp]. An evergreen tree (*Olea*) that produces a small oval oil-producing fruit. Grown around the Mediterranean from the 3rd millennium BC onwards, the cultivated variety (*Olea europaea*) is believed to derive from a wild species native to Afghanistan, although wild species are known further west.

olla [De]. An obsolete term, formerly used for cooking pots and jars.

Olmec [CP]. Chiefdom-based civilization, the earliest in Mesoamerica, comprised of numerous small polities that flourished around the Gulf of Mexico in central Mexico from about 1200 to 600 BC. The origins of Olmec culture are not clear, some scholars preferring a local development involving the transformation of tribal farmers, while others advocate a migration from Guerrero or Oaxaca. High agricultural production was a key to their success, and Olmec communities mainly settled beside slow-flowing rivers which during times of flood produce fertile alluvial soils.

San Lorenzo, occupied 1200–900 BC, seems to have been the main Olmec settlement, supported by two other centres, Tenochtitlán (not the same as the Aztec capital of the same name) and Potrero Nuevo. All the Olmec ceremonial centres comprised complexes of platforms supporting ceremonial courts, house mounds, stone monuments (including carved stone heads, altars, and large free-standing sculptures), and large conical pyramids. The large stone heads are particularly distinctive, up to 3 m tall, and thought to be representations of chiefs and the elite of Olmec society. The labour to build these sites was found from among the agricultural population living in widely scattered hamlets in the lowland areas of the country.

Trade was important and again focused on the ceremonial sites: obsidian, magnetite, serpentine, and mica were among the materials acquired through exchange. More local exchange networks must also have existed, and together with the long-distance network served to spread the Olmec way of life and the sophisticated cosmology that went with it over wide areas. Olmec priests had developed a 260-day calendar and a set of beliefs which involved a were-jaguar (a mythical being that changes from a jaguar to a human being) and a flaming serpent. The Olmec style of art is visible mostly in sculpture and is realistic in its representation of natural and supernatural forms. Craftsmanship of a very high order is represented in objects of shell and jadeite.

By soon after 600 BC Olmec culture was waning and the exchange systems had decreased in their intensity. The settlement pattern expanded and previously sparsely settled areas were infilled, especially in the Valley of Mexico. The development of the Olmec did, however, set the stage for the appearance of other advanced civilizations in the area in succeeding centuries.

Olszanica, Poland [Si]. An LBK village dated to the late 5th millennium BC situated on a loess-covered plateau near Cracow in southern

Poland. Excavations by Sarunas Milisauskas in the early 1970s revealed thirteen longhouses of varying sizes. The largest, house 6, was over 40 m long and was interpreted as the residence of a high-status family. Obsidian and Bükk pottery from Hungary was found.

[Sum.: S. Milisauskas, 1986, *Early Neolithic settlement and society at Olszanica*. Ann Arbor: University of Michigan]

Olympia, Greece [Si]. Ancient sanctuary of Zeus and his consort Hera at Elis in the Peloponnese, Greece. Excavations in 1829 by a French expedition uncovered remains of the temple of Zeus in which once stood the chryselephantine statue of the god regarded as one of the seven wonders of the ancient world. Within the temenos were the remains of a temple to Hera and several other buildings. Athletic events undertaken as part of the festival of Zeus provide the context for the origin of the Olympic Games. The first Olympiad was held in 776 BC, although tradition places the origins still earlier in the 9th century BC. The games took place every four years in an unbroken sequence between 776 BC and AD 393 when Theodosius I abolished them.

[Sum.: A. Yalohris, 1987, *Olympia: the museum and the Sanctuary*. Athens: Ekdotike Athenon]

ombrogenous bog [Ge]. An area of peat growth within wetland caused by high rainfall. Ombrogenous mires, often called bogs, are usually acid because the rainfall that sustains them is itself acid, and are found in mainly upland areas in the form of blanket bog. *See also* TOPOGENOUS BOG.

omphalos [Ar]. A sacred conical or spherical stone symbolically representing the navel of the earth. Found in Mycenaean contexts in Greece, as at Delphi.

omphalos-based jars [De]. Ceramic vessels with a prominent hollow dome raised into the base of the pot.

Onnophris [Di]. Egyptian god, *see* OSIRIS.

Onnuris [Di]. Egyptian god, warrior god shown wearing high plumes and drawing a sword. Worshipped particularly at Abydos and Sebennytos.

ontology [Th]. A branch of philosophy concerned with what exists, its nature, character, and meaning. Much Anglo-American archaeo-logical thought in the late 20th century focused on EPISTEMOLOGY and methodology, but since the early 1990s some archaeologists have turned to consider instead the very character of archaeological materials. Such archaeological ontology considers the character of material culture and social practice, and asks what archaeologists are really attempting to interpret or explain.

open area excavation [Te]. The examination of archaeological sites using large trenches, typically more than 10 m by 10 m but in some cases extending to several hectares, with no predefined baulks or sections. In rural situations the topsoil or overburden is usually sampled and then machine-stripped to reveal areas of natural bedrock containing discrete or intercutting features and deposits. These are excavated. In deeply stratified urban areas the overburden is removed and excavation begins at the highest definable stratigraphic unit. In Britain open area excavation is closely linked with the use of single context recording.

open field system [De]. Agricultural arrangements by which land was managed by common agreement by a local community. The arable land of a township or parish was divided into a multitude of small strips, each of perhaps half an acre or less. Each tenant's strips were scattered and lay intermixed with those of others. For convenience, open field strips were aggregated into groups known as furlongs, themselves grouped into fields. From late medieval times a good deal of piecemeal consolidation of holdings took place, to provide fewer but larger pieces of land. The more landholders there were, however, the more difficult it was to arrange. Crop rotation, pasturing of animals, and other matters of common interest were decided by the local landholders at the manor courts. *See also* RIDGE AND FURROW.

open lineage family [De]. A family system traditional in Europe, in which domestic relationships are closely intertwined with the local community.

open mould [Ar]. A single-piece mould comprising a stone, ceramic, or sand matrix, used in casting copper or bronze objects where the top is left uncovered.

open system [Th]. In archaeology, cultural systems are regarded as being open because they interchange matter, energy, and information with their environment and other cultural systems.

open work [De]. A decorative technique in which gaps or interstices are left around a pattern, sometimes to be filled in with a different material.

Opet [Di]. Egyptian god, *see* APET.

opistodomos [Co]. Literally, 'the room at the back'.

oppidum (pl. *oppida*) [MC]. The term used by CAESAR to describe fortified tribal centres encountered by him in Gaul in 58–51 BC which did not merit categorization as cities (*urbes*). In archaeological usage it is applied more generally to fortified sites and large permanent settlements of the late pre-Roman Iron Age in Europe. These served as centres for administration, trade, craft production, and religion. The word is sometimes, rather misleadingly, applied to any sizable or significant HILLFORT.

optical emission spectrometry [Te]. A method of chemical analysis used to determine the composition of archaeological materials, especially metal, glass, pottery, and stone. A small sample (5–10 mg) of the material to be analysed is volatilized or vaporized either in a laser beam or in an electric arc to excite the electrons in the sample and cause them to emit light. The wavelengths of the light emitted in this way are related to the chemical composition of the material being studied. Thus by analysing the spectrum of the light it is possible to calculate the range of elements present and their concentrations.

opus sectile [De]. Latin term to describe a Roman construction technique in which pieces of coloured stone are cut to geometric shapes and set together to form a paved floor or wall covering.

opus signinum [Ma]. Latin term for a kind of Roman hydraulic concrete partly composed of crushed brick that was used for covering walls and floors.

oracle bones [Ar]. Cattle shoulder-blades and tortoise shells used in Chinese divination

rituals during the Shang and early Chou periods. The cracks resulting from the application of a heated point formed the basis of the divination. It has been suggested that as some of the cracks came to mean good or bad omens or to have specific meanings they were recorded and thus became the origin of the Chinese idiographic script. Some from Anyang Shang dating to the late 2nd millennium BC are inscribed with the earliest form of the Chinese script.

oral tradition [Ge]. Historical traditions, often genealogies, passed down from generation to generation by word of mouth.

oratory [MC]. Place for private prayer. From the Latin *orare*, to pray.

orchestra [Co]. The large circular space used for dancing in Greek religious events, later incorporated into the design of Greek theatres as the area between the stage and tiered seating.

Ordnance Datum (OD) [Ge]. All mapping created by the Ordnance Survey within the British Isles shows heights above mean sea level. Until 1921 the datum used to calculate these heights (known as the Old British Datum) was in the Victoria Docks, Liverpool, and was based on observations in March 1844. Since 1921 a new datum has been used (the New British Datum) which is based on the mean sea level at Newlyn Tidal Observatory in Cornwall, and is derived from measurements made between May 1915 and April 1921.

Ordovices [CP]. The late Iron Age and early 1st-millennium AD tribal grouping occupying the central mountainous area and narrow coastal plain of west Wales, south of the Gangani and north of the Demetae. Very little is known about their settlements or material culture.

ore [De]. The mineral matrix in which metals occur in nature. Oxide ores occur on the weathered surfaces of ore-rich lodes and are the easiest to work. Sulphide ores come from the unweathered parent ores and are generally more difficult to work.

organic analogy [Th]. The comparison of society with an organism.

organic materials [De]. Substances such as bone, wood, horn, or hide that were once living organisms.

organization [Ge]. A large group of individuals, involving a definite set of authority relations. Many types of organization exist in industrial societies, influencing most aspects of everyday life. While not all organizations are bureaucratic, there are quite close links between the development of organizations and bureaucratic tendencies.

oriel [De]. A large polygonal recess built out from the upper storey of a building, being supported from the ground by columns or piers or on corbels in the wall. Some oriels are partly or wholly glazed and are known as oriel windows. Oriels developed in the 15th century AD.

orientation [De]. The direction of an object from a given position. Sometimes used in place of 'alignment', but this is careless usage. All objects and structures will have an orientation whether or not anything is aligned on them.

Orient Tradition [CP]. Terminal Archaic Stage hunter-gatherer communities living in the New York region of the eastern seaboard of North America in the period from about 1320 to 700 BC. Descended from the Susquehanna Tradition, these communities are characterized by the use of long narrow projectile points with fish-tail bases. Oval and rectangular soapstone bowls were used, especially in large base camps and appear to have been highly prized. Most of the settlements were along rivers and around the coast. Cremation was the local burial tradition.

Orkney–Cromarty–Hebridean Group [MC]. A regional tradition of middle and late Neolithic PASSAGE GRAVES found in the Northern and Western Isles of Scotland. There is considerable variety among the 300 or so known examples, but most comprise round mounds with centrally placed chambers. In early examples the chambers are small and relatively simple in form, but later they become larger and have more complicated arrangements with side cells and, in the case of the STALLED CAIRNS of Orkney, many subdivisions. Some 'double-decker' chambers with two levels are also known.

ornament horizon [CP]. A period of the European middle Bronze Age marked by the widespread occurrence of bronze and gold personal ornaments such as rings, torcs, bracelets, and pins alongside the more well-established range of tools and weapons. In southern Britain the ornament horizon coincides with the TAUNTON PHASE. The smiths in this tradition were especially influenced by types current in Montelius II and III phases in northern Germany.

Orosius, Paulus [Na]. Spanish churchman who fled from the VANDALS to Africa in AD 414, and became an adherent of St Augustine. His *Historiae adversus paganos*, a tract tracing events from the Creation to AD 417, relies heavily on earlier writers, but adds details of his own knowledge from contemporary history.

Orpheus [Di]. Greek god, hero of Thrace and in origin perhaps a Thracian king. Son of Apollo he owed his fame to his amazing musical talent. He sang and played the lyre with such art that the savage beasts came running to listen to him. His skills were well used during the voyage of the Argonauts.

orrery [Ar]. A model showing the movement of the planets around the sun.

orthostat [Co]. Large upstanding stone used in constructing the walls of the chambers and passages in many kinds of MEGALITHIC TOMB during the Neolithic in Europe. The orthostats directly or indirectly support the roof structure.

Oshara Tradition [CP]. Archaic Stage hunter-gatherer tradition centred on north-central New Mexico, the San Juan Basin, and the Rio Grande in southwestern North America and flourishing in the period 5500 BC to AD 600.

Osiris [Di]. Egyptian god, one of the great gods of Egypt, a member of the Heliopolitan Ennead. Judge of the dead and king of the underworld. God of resurrection. His main place of worship was at Abydos, but he was universally revered. He may have had his origins in a king of Egypt who was later deified. The murder of Osiris by his brother Seth, Isis's quest for the body, the struggle of his son Borus to avenge his father's death on Seth, and the eventual resurrection of Osiris, has become one of the greatest legends of Egypt. Osiris was called Unnefer (Greek: Onnophris), the permanently happy one. He had festivals at Abydos, and an annual miracle play. Episodes from his mysteries were re-enacted at many Egyptian temples, and the late period temples of Dendera, Edfu, and Philae all have chapels dedicated to Osiris.

OSL [Ab]. *See* THERMOLUMINESCENCE DATING.

ossuary [Ar]. A receptacle for storing the bones of the dead, usually in an unburnt state.

ossuary cave [MC]. A natural cave used as a charnel house for the multiple deposition and storage of human bones.

osteoarchaeology [Ge]. A branch of archaeology that deals with the study and analysis of human and animal anatomy, especially skeletal remains, in the context of archaeological deposits.

Ostia, Italy [Si]. The main port of Rome situated west of the city at the mouth of the River Tiber. Extensive excavations have taken place in recent times and show that the port was established in the 4th century BC with a fort and stone defences. The demands of Rome's growing population, especially for corn imports, soon forced the port to grow and in the early 1st century BC it covered at least 64 ha and was defended by substantial walls.

Silting and changes to the coastline were always a problem, however, and in AD 42 additional breakwaters and new docks were built under the Emperor Claudius a short distance back from the mouth of the Tiber itself. Later, Trajan constructed a hexagonal inner harbour capable of taking 100 ships at a time, connected to the Tiber by a canal, and surrounded by warehouses and port facilities. The Square of Corporations contained offices for merchants and traders from all over the Mediterranean world, and the port also contained tenement houses, baths, temples, and a synagogue. The site was largely abandoned as a major port in the 5th century AD.

[Sum.: A. Gallina Zevi and A. Claridge (eds.), 1996, *Roman Ostia*. London: British School at Rome]

ostrakon [Ar]. **1.** A fragment of soft stone or pottery bearing jottings or a writing exercise. **2.** In classical Greek times a potsherd used as a voting paper. One particular ceremony was the practice of *ostrakismos* where each citizen could write the name of someone whom they wished to see banished on a potsherd. If sufficient votes were cast against the person they would be banished for ten years.

Ostrogoths [CP]. *See* GOTHS.

Otley-type ware [Ar]. Type of late Saxon wheel-thrown pottery of the period *c*.AD 850–1150 found in Yorkshire and the north midlands of England.

otoliths [Ge]. Small calcareous concretions found in the middle ear of fish. Because of their durability they survive well in archaeological deposits and can be recovered by wet sieving. Their importance lies in the fact that their shape and form allows them to be recognized to species and they can also provide information about the size, age, and sometimes even the season in which the fish was caught.

Otomani Culture [CP]. Eastern European culture, centred upon northeastern Hungary and northwest Romania during the early and middle Bronze Age, broadly 1600–1300 BC. Settlements were generally fortified and set on low hills. Others lay on promontories, by rivers, or in marshland. Otomani pottery is distinguished by its elaborately fluted and bossed ornament, and the classical phase of the culture is associated with exotic metalwork hoards like those of Hajdusamson and Tufalau. Cemeteries are not well known, but those that have been explored suggest inurned cremation was the main burial rite.

Otter Creek points [Ar]. Archaic Stage large bifacially worked chipped stone projectile points with a side notch found in northeastern parts of North America and dating to the period *c*.4500–2600 BC.

Otto the Great [Na]. Son of Henry the Fowler made Saxon king of Germany in AD 936, and emperor from AD 962. In AD 955 he defeated the MAGYARS at the Lechfeld. Died *c*.AD 973.

outer bailey [Co]. *See* QUADRANGULAR CASTLE.

outhouse [Co]. A small building detached from the main house.

outlier [Co]. **1.** An example of something (e.g. a site or object) found a long way detached from the main distribution of similar things.

2. A standing stone outside and some distance apart from a STONE CIRCLE.

out of Africa model [Th]. *See* HOMO SAPIENS.

oval barrow [MC]. Class of middle and late Neolithic burial found in the British Isles in the 4th and 3rd millennia BC. The barrow mound is oval in plan, typically less than 45 m long, and made from earth and stones. In some cases there is a kerb or peristalith around the edge of the mound, while internal subdivisions of the mound seem to reflect building techniques. Flanking ditches are common and provided a source of material for building the mound. In some cases the ditches completely encircle the mound. Early examples cover a platform or simple timber mortuary structure containing disarticulated multiple inhumations. Later examples usually cover a centrally placed grave with one or two flexed inhumations. Grave goods are rare, but include personal ornaments that were probably introduced with the corpses.

ovate (ovate handaxe) [Ar]. A type of ACHEULIAN bifacially worked handaxe with an oval or elliptical shape. Most are relatively thin in cross-section, and have either a flat or deliberately twisted profile.

oven [Co]. A closed structure used for cooking, distinct from a hearth. Ovens are generally constructed of clay or stone. In simple examples a fire is lit inside the chamber and is then cleared out before the food is put in to cook in the residual heat. In more sophisticated examples there is a separate firebox and cooking chamber so that the heat can be maintained and varied during the cooking process.

overhanging rim urn [Ar]. *See* COLLARED URN.

Overton Period [CP]. A phase of the British early Bronze Age spanning the period 2000–1650 BC which was defined by Colin Burgess in the late 1970s. Coming immediately after the MOUNT PLEASANT PERIOD, the Overton Period sees the emergence of what are often regarded as traditional Bronze Age burial practices: cremations in cinerary urns and inhumations and cremations accompanied by food vessels. The period also saw the final stages of the use of BEAKER pottery. It is

named after the barrow cemetery at West Overton near Avebury in Wiltshire.

The richly furnished early WESSEX CULTURE burials dominated by inhumations and associations with ARMORICO-BRITISH DAGGERS belong to the Overton Period, including the Bush Barrow burial from near Stonehenge in Wiltshire. Metallurgy during the Overton Period fits within Burgess's Stage VI, the Falkland industrial phase which shows influences from the classic Únětice/Reinecke A2 metalworking on the continent. The Overton Period is succeeded by the BEDD BRANWEN PERIOD.

ovicaprids [De]. *See* SHEEP.

Owasco Tradition [CP]. Late Woodland Stage Iroquoian farmer-hunter communities living in and around New York State in northwestern North America in the period AD 1000–1300. Settlements comprise small villages of up to ten square or rectangular houses. By AD 1200 earthworks and palisades protect some settlements as warfare becomes more common among Iroquoian groups. Maize, beans, and squash were cultivated. Burials were generally made in cemeteries and under mounds, the deceased being interred fully clothed with few if any grave goods. Towards the end of the period, however, skeletons riddled with arrowheads are present and human bones are also found on village middens.

ox (pl. oxen) [Sp]. Technically, a castrated male of the cattle species (*Bos taurus*), but the name is more widely applied to any large, usually horned, bovine animal used for draught.

Oxford, England [Si]. Medieval market town and bridging point of the rivers Thames and Cherwell in the upper Thames Valley east of the Cotswold Hills. The urban origins of the town lie in the 8th century AD. Edward the Elder fortified the settlement in the 10th century AD, and may have been responsible for laying out much of the street pattern. Through the 10th and 11th centuries it was a prosperous market centre, despite being sacked by the Danes in 1009 AD. This prosperity continued after the Norman conquest, Robert d'Oilly building a MOTTE AND BAILEY CASTLE there in 1071. By the end of the 12th century the university was beginning to be felt as a new presence. However, as the university expanded through the 13th and 14th centuries the town went into decline, with the end of large-scale river-borne trade and a string of civil disorders and plagues playing a role too. After the Restoration the city regained its former status and began a new phase of post-medieval expansion.

[Sum.: T. Hassall, 1986, The archaeology of Oxford City. In G. Briggs *et al.* (eds.), *The archaeology of the Oxford region.* Oxford: Oxford University Department of External Studies, 115–34]

Oxford Archaeological Unit (OAU) [Or]. One of the three largest archaeological contractors in the UK, undertaking rescue projects and research programmes in Britain and other European countries. Founded in 1973, the unit carries out a wide range of work from small-scale planning advice and field evaluations through to strategic surveys, major excavations, environmental impact assessments, and educational displays. In 2000 there was a core staff of 150 based at its headquarters in Oxford.

Oxfordshire wares [Ar]. Pottery made mostly in the vicinity of Oxford in a variety of fabrics. Vessels include distinctive types of mortaria, PARCHMENT WARE, and red colour-coated ware in the Samian tradition. This centrally placed industry became one of the largest and most important in Britain during the 4th century AD.

ox-hide ingot [Ar]. Type of ingot either of copper or tin circulating in the Mediterranean in the early Bronze Age. It was shaped like a stretched ox-hide: roughly rectangular with a projection at each corner. The copper examples weigh about 27 kg each and probably come from mines in Cyprus. More than 200 of them were found together with a wealth of other traded objects in a shipwreck dating to the 14th century BC near Kaş off the south coast of Turkey.

oxidized ware [De]. A ceramic fabric in which iron oxide in the clay has absorbed as much oxygen as possible during firing. It is produced when vessels are fired with an ample and continuous supply of oxygen, usually resulting in a white, buff, orange, or red colour. Pottery can be partly oxidized (indicated by colour differences between the surface and core of the fabric), or unevenly oxidized (indicated by colour differences on the surface of a vessel).

ox-scapula shovel [Ar]. The shoulder-blade of an ox or large cow which has been used to shovel up broken rock and soil. Discarded and broken examples of such shovels are well represented at Neolithic and early Bronze Age sites in the British Isles, usually in association with ANTLER PICKS and antler rakes which, together perhaps with baskets, leather ropes, and wooden levers, comprising the main tool kit of those responsible for earthmoving.

oxygen isotope analysis [Te]. A method of determining patterns of climatic change over long periods using the ratio of the stable oxygen isotopes ^{18}O to ^{16}O as an indicator of the amount of water locked up in ice-sheets and thus of global temperature. Sea water contains many isotopes of oxygen, the most common being ^{18}O to ^{16}O. During cold periods the glaciers grow, water is drawn up into them, and the proportion of ^{18}O increases. When the ice-caps melt during periods of warm climate the proportion of ^{18}O decreases. There are two ways of obtaining data about the ^{16}O to ^{18}O ratio, both using measurements made using a mass spectrometer. The first is to use cores from the polar ice-caps which preserve layers of snow ultimately made from sea water. The second is to use the skeletons of foraminifera preserved in ocean-bottom ooze because these marine fossils had the same ^{16}O to ^{18}O ratio as the sea water during the time they were alive. Using this data a series of at least eleven cycles of cooling and warming climatic conditions have been recognized in the northern hemisphere during the PLEISTOCENE.

Ozette, Washington, USA [Si]. Makah Indian village situated on the western tip of the Olympic Peninsula on the coast of Washington State. The site was occupied from the 16th century AD down to the 20th century AD.

Once described as a hunter-gatherer 'Pompeii' because of its excellent preservation, excavations directed by Stephen Samuels and Richard Daugherty provide a vivid insight into the cultures of the Northwest Coast Tradition. The quality of survival arises because of a series of mudslides which periodically overwhelmed the settlement, thereby sealing it.

The most catastrophic inundation came about AD 1550 (stratigraphic unit IV), covering at least four timber houses and entombing no less than thirteen dogs in the process. The longhouses had been constructed of cedar planks. They were found to contain abundant artefacts of wood and other organic material. Baskets full of tools or stored food were found. Finely carved bone objects were represented including a replica whale fin with shells set in it.

The Makah were renowned whale hunters and stratigraphic unit V yielded the remains of at least 67 animals, mainly humpbacks and greys. Evidence of social stratification was evident in the disposition of artefacts and food waste within the houses. Each house was probably home to several nuclear families, each with its own hearth, but the family living in the northeastern corner of the house lived a demonstrably different way of life.

[Rep.: S. R. Samuels (ed.), 1991–4, *Ozette archaeological project research reports*. Seattle: Washington State University, 2 vols.]

Ozieri Culture [CP]. Late Neolithic and Copper Age communities of Sardinia in the western Mediterranean in the late 4th and 3rd millennia BC. Open villages, caves, and rock-cut tombs are known. The pottery is of very high quality with polished and burnished surfaces. Decoration includes incised motifs such as zig-zags, hatched triangles, arcs, festoons, and stars. The carinated forms suggest some connections with CHASSEY or LAGOZZA pottery, but the decoration is quite different. Marble figurines and a few copper and silver objects are also known. Beaker ceramics reached Sardinia from southern France during the later Ozieri Culture.

pa [MC]. A Maori defended settlement either comprising an enclosure bounded by a bank and ditch or, in swampy areas, an enclosure defended by one or more palisades. Mostly found in the North Island of New Zealand.

Pacacocha Culture [CP]. South American farming cultures found in the Rio Ucayali area of Amazonia and tentatively dated to *c*.AD 400–500. Characterized by their ceramic assemblages which belong to the Polychrome Horizon Style of Amazonia.

Pacal [Na]. Ruler of Palenque, Mexico, between AD 615 and 682 during which time the town became an important centre of the Maya Lowlands. When Pacal died he was buried in a subterranean crypt over which was constructed the Temple of the Inscriptions.

Pachacamac, Peru [Si]. Large ceremonial centre of the middle Horizon situated in the Lurin Valley south of Lima. Excavated by Max Uhle, the site appears to have been a major pilgrimage centre focused on the oracle of Pachacamac, possibly part of the Huari empire although possibly the centre of its own polity.

Pottery from the graves associated with early temples on the site define three main styles in the local polychrome technique known as the Pachacamac technique. When the Inca conquered the site they added their own Temple of the Sun to the existing structures. Numerous richly appointed female mummies were found associated with this temple, some showing evidence of death by strangulation.

[Rep.: M. Uhle, 1903, *Pachacamac*. Philadelphia: University of Pennsylvania; M. Rostworowski de Diez Canseco, 1992, *Pachacamac y El Señor de los Milagros*. Lima: Instituto de Estudios Peruanos]

Pacific Eskimo Cultures [CP]. General term covering the descendants of Palaeo-Arctic communities occupying the coastal fringes of western and northern Alaska, lands fringing the Arctic Ocean, around Hudson Bay, the north Labrador Coast, and parts of Greenland from about 3000 BC. These groups are commonly believed to be the ancestors of modern Inuit communities. They made use of resources found in the sea, on the coast, and on the tundra.

One of their most distinctive innovations was a bone toggling harpoon. This was a harpoon with a detachable head that could twist sideways (toggle) in the flesh of animals that were shot. They probably used dog traction and had boats.

packhorse bridge [MC]. Strongly arched stone bridge over streams and small rivers along routes used by packhorses for transporting goods and materials during medieval times in Britain and other parts of northern Europe.

paddies [MC]. Fields for the intensive cultivation of rice, flooded naturally or by irrigation.

paddle and anvil method [De]. A method of smoothing and finishing the walls of hand-made pottery vessels where a small stone or wooden 'anvil' is held against the inner wall of the vessel while a flat or curved wooden 'paddle' is used to beat the outer surface into shape.

padstone [Co]. A flat slab of stone placed on the ground to provide a support for a wooden upright forming part of the structure of a timber-framed building. A group of padstones is often the only archaeological trace remaining of such buildings. Originally padstones served the twin purposes of spreading the weight of the structure taken to earth through the upright while also raising the timber off the ground a little to inhibit its decay.

pagan [De]. In Roman times a *pagus* was the smallest unit of land in a country district; pagans were those who followed the beliefs and religions of the countryside rather than the officially recognized cults. When Christianity was adopted as the official religion in the Roman empire, pagans were those who continued local traditions and were thus represented as heathens.

Pagan, Burma [Si]. Extensive city in northern Burma situated near the confluence of the Irrawaddy and Chindwin rivers adjacent to the irrigated rice-growing plain of Kyauskse, founded in AD 849 through the amalgamation of many small villages. Originally called Arimaddanapura, the city became the capital of the Burman kingdom. The rulers of the Pagan Dynasty in the period AD 1044 to 1287 built more than 5000 Buddhist temples in the area. Pagan was captured by the Mongols in AD 1287.

[Sum.: M. Aung Thwin, 1985, *Pagan: the origins of modern Burma*. Honolulu: University of Hawaii Press]

pagan Saxons [CP]. Anglo-Saxon individuals and communities who were not Christian and who followed native religions and beliefs. Archaeologically, pagan Saxons are identified from the north–south orientation of their graves, the range of grave goods buried with the dead including weapons with men and jewellery with women, buckets, hanging bowls, toilet sets, girdle hangers, and pots. Broadly dating to the period AD 450–650.

pagoda [MC]. A Buddhist temple tower of several storeys, common in East Asia.

Paiján points [Ar]. Bifacially worked chipped stone points of triangular outline with a small stem or tang at the base. Characteristic of the Archaic Stage Paiján Tradition of South America in the period 9000–7000 BC.

Paiján Tradition [CP]. Pre-Ceramic (Archaic) Stage hunter-gatherer communities flourishing in north and central Peru in the period *c.*9000–7000 BC. Characterized by PAIJÁN POINTS. Paiján tradition communities may have been among the first in the region to exploit marine resources on a significant scale. Snails and lizards also seem to have been used as food sources at the site of Pampa de Fosiles 13, Peru.

paint [Ma]. **1.** In pottery making, a mineral or organic compound applied decoratively or figuratively to the surface of a ceramic vessel before firing so as to produce a colour contrast with the underlying fabric or background slip. **2.** Organic or mineral-based material in liquid form that can be applied to a surface to impart colour to it.

painted grey ware [Ar]. Fineware frequently decorated with simple designs in red or black paint including circles and pothooks. Characteristic of the Ganges civilization of northern India. Later 2nd and early 1st millennia BC in date, perhaps associated with the spread of ironworking.

Pakht [Di]. Egyptian god of Memphis, and head of the triad of Memphis. Represented as a mummified man standing inside a shrine, holding his staff or measuring rod, and wearing an amulet. He was one of the great creator gods, who created the world by thought and speech. He was also associated with craftsmen as their patron god, and, as Ptah-Sokar, with the dead. The Greeks equated him with Hephaestus.

palace [MC]. A substantial administrative, economic, social, religious, and cultural centre providing official residences for royalty, royal priests, and their retainers. Typically, palaces were constructed using imposing architectural traditions and were lavishly decorated.

palaeo- [Ge]. Adjectival prefix denoting that something is old or ancient; for example, palaeo-channel—an old river channel. From the Greek *palaeos* meaning 'ancient'.

Palaeo-Arctic Tradition (Paleo-Arctic Tradition) [CP]. General term covering a heterogeneous collection of communities living in the Arctic region of North America and Siberia from *c.*8000 to 5000 BC. Recognized by distinctive microlithic blade-based assemblages of chipped stone tools, wedge-shaped cores, bifacial knives, scrapers, and occasional fluted projectile points.

The subsistence base was mainly hunting and gathering: the main resources exploited included bison, horse, elk, and caribou. Many Palaeo-Arctic sites will have been lost to rising sea levels during the Holocene.

palaeobotanist [De]. A person who studies ancient plant remains from archaeological sites or environmental sequences.

palaeobotany [Ge]. The study of ancient plant remains, mainly using charred, water-logged, or desiccated seeds, plant fibre, leaves, wood, or fruit. The impressions left by plant remains in clay or other plastic materials can also be useful.

palaeodemography [Ge]. The study of past populations in terms of their size, distribution, birth rates, death rates, life expectancy, and age and sex distributions.

palaeoecology [Ge]. The study of human communities in their environment and especially the effects that people had on the physical environment and vice versa.

palaeoeconomy [Ge]. A school of archaeological thought developed in the 1960s by Eric HIGGS and his colleagues based in Cambridge which focused on the long-term determinants of human behaviour resulting from the relationships between people and their environment: 'the study of man's roles in the prehistoric ecosystems of which he was a member', as Higgs and his colleague Michael Jarman themselves put it.

palaeoenvironment [Ge]. An ancient or past environment.

Palaeo-Indian (Paleo-Indian) [CP]. A general term relating to the earliest inhabitants of the Americas, pre-ARCHAIC hunter-gatherer communities, in the period before *c*.8000 BC. The Palaeo-Indian Stage covers a series of regional or chronologically specific traditions and cultures including the CLOVIS CULTURE, the FOLSOM TRADITION, the EASTERN FLUTED POINT TRADITION, and the SAN DIEGUITO COMPLEX which are mainly defined by their clipped stone industries. The Palaeo-Indian Stage is broadly contemporary with the Dyukhtai Culture and Sumnagin Culture of Siberia with which it may have had some relations prior to the disappearance of the BERING LAND BRIDGE at *c*.10 000 BC.

Palaeolithic [CP]. Literally, the Old Stone Age, spanning the three and a half million years of human evolution from the advanced hominids to the end of the last Pleistocene

glaciation around 11 000 years ago. Generally sub-divided into the LOWER, MIDDLE, and UPPER PALAEOLITHIC phases.

Palaeolithic art [De]. *See* ROCK ART.

palaeomagnetic dating [Te]. A dating technique developed in the field of geology that dates rocks on the basis of polar reversals. Such reversals occur when the magnetic pole moves to the opposite side of the globe; this has happened many times during the history of the planet. By taking a sample of in situ rock and comparing its modern orientation with that preserved in the rock itself as a reflection of polar orientation at the time of its formation, something of its age can be established by reference to a master chronology of global reversals. For archaeology the main use of this technique is for deposits containing early hominids. Reversals in the period 1.65 to 1.0 million years ago, for example, have helped to date beds II and III at OLDUVAI in Tanzania.

palaeopathology [Ge]. The study of diseases, nutrition, dental state, and traumatic injuries in early populations, prehistoric and historic, through the analysis of preserved biological material including skeletal remains, body parts, and body waste (e.g. coprolites). Documentary and artefactual evidence can also be useful.

palaeopedology [Ge]. The study of the origins and character of ancient soils (PALAEOSOLS), especially those below later monuments, structures, or deposits that serve to seal and preserve them.

palaeoserology [Ge]. The study of ancient population groupings through the analysis of blood groups. Samples are derived from human remains preserved by freezing or desiccation, although spongy bone tissue can also be used in some cases.

palaeosol [De]. An ancient soil profile preserved within or beneath a stratified sequence of deposits or the structure of a monument, such as the old ground surface beneath a round barrow or rampart.

palaestra [MC]. **1.** A Roman building smaller than a gymnasium, often built as a colonnade round a central court, for the training of boxers, wrestlers, and participants in gymnastic contests. **2.** Exercise hall of a Roman public bath-house where patrons might amuse themselves with games and sports or work up a sweat before bathing.

palafitta [MC]. Italian name for prehistoric lakeside villages constructed on wooden piles. *See* PILE DWELLING.

Palaikastro, Crete [Si]. A substantial Minoan settlement and port on the extreme eastern side of Crete. Extensively excavated by J. MacGillivray and colleagues in the 1980s and 1990s, the settlement is dominated by its elegant main street flanked on either side with prosperous town houses. Other blocks of large and airy houses lay nearby. The wealth of the town derived from the excellent agricultural land round about and is clearly visible in the architecture and the design of the wide streets with drains running along them. Surprisingly, no palace has ever been identified at the site.

[Sum.: J. A. MacGillivray *et al.*, 1991, Excavations at Palaikastro, 1990. *Papers of the British School at Athens*, 86, 121–47]

pale [Co]. Boundary fence, especially of a park, usually comprising a stout wooden fence or hedge set on a low bank with a ditch in the inside.

Palenque, Chiapas, Mexico [Si]. A Maya ceremonial centre and settlement on the edge of the Chiapas Mountains. This site is the most westerly such centre and reached its height in the late Classic as Teotihuacán was declining.

Those constructing the numerous temples and structures on the site took little regard of the local topography. In the centre is a palace complex with a unique four-storey tower. The palace is linked via a subterranean vaulted passage or aqueduct to the eastern terraces on which stand the temples of the Foliated Cross, the Cross, and the Sun. Palenque was abandoned after AD 810.

Excavations by Alberto Ruz in 1949–52 in the Temple of the Inscriptions revealed the burial of PACAL, ruler of Palenque from AD 615 to 682. Pacal's skeleton lay in a single-piece stone sarcophagus covered with a slab of limestone 3.8 m long. A jade mosaic mask, ear spools, a necklace, rings and numerous other ornaments had been placed with the body. Two jade figurines lay beside Pacal, one representing the sun god. Red cinnabar had been sprinkled over the body and grave goods.

[Sum.: L. Ruz, 1953, The pyramid tomb of a prince of Palenque. *Illustrated London News*, 223, 321–3]

paleo- [Ge]. *See* PALAEO-.

Palermo Stone [Ar]. A slab of black basalt on which an inscription cut around 2400 BC recorded the rulers of the first five Egyptian dynasties. The last king to be mentioned is Neferirkara, the third king of the 5th Dynasty. Only six fragments now survive, the largest of which has been in Palermo Museum since 1877 (four others are in the Cairo Museum and one is in the Petrie Collection of University College, London).

palette [Ar]. A slab of stone or wood for grinding and mixing substances such as paint or cosmetics.

palimpsest [De]. From the Greek work *palimpsestos* meaning a papyrus or other kind of writing material on which two or more sets of writing had been superimposed in such a way that, because of imperfect erasure, some of the earlier text could be read through the later over-writing. In archaeology the term is often applied to landscapes in which traces of earlier arrangements can be seen amongst and below the modern pattern.

palisade [Co]. A stake-built or post-built defensive barrier, often on top of an embankment or rampart.

palisaded enclosure [MC]. Class of large late Neolithic enclosure found in the British Isles which comprises a distinctive boundary built using massive tree trunks set close together in a palisade slot or at intervals in separate postholes with planking between. There is often an elaborated entrance with an outer parallel-sided palisaded passage. The largest examples are more than 17 ha in extent, though most are between 0.5 ha and 2 ha. Alex Gibson has suggested three phases to the development of these enclosures: the earliest using widely spaced timber uprights, the middle phase having close-set postholes, and the latest examples using a continuous palisade slot. Also known as stockaded enclosures.

palisaded hilltop enclosure [MC]. A small defended occupation site of the early Iron Age in the British Isles. They are usually situated on spurs, promontories, or hilltops and cover less than 0.4 ha. The boundary works comprise either single or double lines of rock-cut trenches which held substantial timber palisades. Inside there are usually the remains of one or two timber round houses, pits, and animal shelters.

Palladian [Ge]. A school of architectural design named after Andrea Palladio, its originator. Derived from late 16th-century Venice and adopting the principle of combining architecture and sculpture, the style became most popular in the early 18th century.

palm cup [Ar]. Style of Saxon glass vessel in the form of a hemispherical bowl with a wide everted rim. Dated to the period AD 400–700.

palmette [Ge]. A stylized palm frond often used as a decorative motif in various ways in Greek and Roman art. In early Celtic art there is a similar motif, adapted from Greek models, resembling a fragmented frond leaf.

Palo Blanco [CP]. Seventh main phase of activity in the Tehuacán Valley of Mexico, dating to the period AD 150–700. This was the period when the first towns appear in the valley.

palstave [Ar]. Form of axe current in the middle Bronze Age in Europe, distinguished by having the blade separated from the heel by a stop ridge and a heel which usually has more or less developed side flanges. The stop ridge and flanges served to prevent lateral movement and stop the haft from splitting during use. Palstaves may have side loops to aid binding or for carrying in bundles.

palynology. *See* POLLEN ANALYSIS.

pan [Ar]. Any broad shallow vessel of metal or ceramic. Mainly used in cooking, but sometimes found only in ritual contexts.

Pan [Di]. Greek god who was eventually brought into the retinue of Dionysus, son of Hermes, who was born with the legs, horns, and beard of a goat. He was considered to be the protector of flocks and agriculture, particularly the vine and the olive. Pan taught the art of bee-keeping.

Pan Shan [CP]. A subdivision of the YANGSHAO Neolithic culture of China known mainly from cemeteries excavated in the hills of the upper Yellow River Basin in Kanso Province. Distinctive ceramics include large globular urns decorated with bold spirals and curvilinear designs painted in red and black.

pantheon 1. [MC]. A temple dedicated to a range of gods. **2.** [De] A group of related gods or deities.

Pantheon [Si]. A classical Roman temple built in the heart of Rome, Italy, by Agrippa in 27–25 BC, rebuilt by Domitian, and finally reconstructed *c*.AD 118–25 by Hadrian. The Hadrianic temple consists of a massive domed rotunda lit by a central aperture open to the sky. The building owes its survival to the fact that it was converted into a Christian church in AD 608.

[Sum.: W. L. MacDonald, 1976, *The Pantheon: design, meaning and progeny*. London: Allan Lane]

pantocrator [De]. Literally, 'the Almighty', nearly always the subject of a mosaic or fresco dominating the interior of a church from its central position at the height of the dome.

papyrology [Ge]. The study of ancient writing on PAPYRUS.

papyrus 1. [Sp]. A type of reed (*Cyperus papyrus*) found around the Mediterranean with a distinct flower, once growing abundantly in the marshy districts of Lower Egypt. **2.** [Ma]. A cheap and serviceable writing material made from the stems of papyrus reeds split, beaten, and pasted together in two layers at right angles. Papyrus was the main writing medium in widespread use in Egypt from the 5th Dynasty (Old Kingdom) through to early Christian times and was also adopted in the Greek and Roman worlds. Papyrus was suitable for writing on, using an ink-like liquid and was normally stored in rolls.

Paracas Culture [CP]. Early Horizon farming communities living on the southern coast of Peru in the period 1000–500 BC. Heavily influenced by the Chavín Culture, the Paracas Culture is mainly known from burials and ceremonial sites. Ceramics are often decorated with incised geometric or representational motifs, and painted after firing with resin-based paints. Woven textiles of very high quality are known, some used as wrapping for mummies. Tapestries were woven and embroidered with depictions of mythical creatures. The Paracas Culture was antecedent to the Nasca Culture.

paradigm [Ge]. A term used and popularized by Thomas Kuhn to refer to a common set of philosophies and methods shared by a scientific community within which basic assumptions and orientations are left uncriticized. When competing approaches successfully challenge and replace an existing position there is said to be a 'paradigm shift', as for example between Newtonian and Einsteinian physics. A number of successive paradigms can be seen in archaeology–for example, FUNCTIONALISM, PROCESSUALISM, POST-PROCESSUALISM–although there is considerable debate as to whether each represents a true paradigm shift.

parallax [Ge]. The apparent movement of an object when seen from different positions. The effect of parallax can easily be seen by looking at a nearby object with first the left and then the right eye. Taking account of parallax is important in archaeology when planning features on site, drawing objects, and making observations relating to alignment and intervisibility.

parallel evolution [De]. The evolution of the same trait or characteristic independently in more than one culture or place although not necessarily at the same time.

Paranthropus. *See* AUSTRALOPITHECUS.

parapet [Co]. An outer wall protecting soldiers moving along a walkway around the top of a fort or town defences.

parchment [Ma]. A long-lasting thin flexible writing material made from cleaned and stretched animal skins, usually sheep or goat skins.

parchment ware [Ar]. A range of tableware, mostly bowls, in pale fabrics with simple red-brown painted decoration that was popular in Britain in the 3rd and 4th centuries AD.

Paredão Phase [CP]. South American farming cultures found in the Lower and Middle Amazon areas of Amazonia and tentatively dated to *c*.300–100 BC. Characterized by their ceramic assemblages which belong to the Incised Rim Horizon Style of Amazonia. At the type-site of Paredão on the River Negro, Brazil, excavations in a midden revealed manioc roasting plates, spindle whorls, pottery beads, and large ceramic cinerary urns decorated with zoomorphic relief models. The urns contained disarticulated human bones.

Parian marble [Ma]. Marble from quarries on the island of Paros, Greece, which is white in colour, close-grained, and peculiarly suitable for sculpture: it was widely used by the leading sculptors throughout the Mediterranean world.

parietal [De]. Pertaining to a wall; parietal art is art on walls. Generally extended to include related surfaces such as floors and ceilings. *See* ROCK ART.

paring chisel [Ar]. A type of tool made of stone or, more usually, metal with a shaped narrow blade that can be used carefully to remove thin strips or shavings of wood when fashioning a joint or shaping a block.

parish church [MC]. An ecclesiastical building used by secular communities in Britain from about AD 1000 onwards and forming the religious focus of the smallest administrative unit defined at the time, the parish. Parish churches were essentially rectangular structures aligned broadly east–west. They were designed for congregational worship and thus have two main parts: the **nave** at the west end which provided accommodation for the laity, and the **chancel** which was the domain of the priest and contained the principal altar at the far east end. Aisles provided space for additional altars and chapels. The font used for baptism was traditionally adjacent to the main entrance on the south side of the nave. During medieval times the size of the parish church and the nature and extent of its decoration were largely dependent on the wealth of the local community. The church itself is usually surrounded by its graveyard, in which might be found a lychgate, cross, anchorage, bell tower, school, and a priest's house.

Parisi [CP]. Iron Age tribal group occupying north-eastern England around the Humber estuary. Communities in this area were in close contact with northern France in the later 5th century BC and this gives rise to the ARRAS CULTURE. There is little sign of continued contact with the continent in later centuries and the Parisi developed their own traditions down to the Roman conquest. The tribal capital is not certainly identified, but may be the large hillfort at Barwick-in-Elmet which later came to contain the *civitas* capital of Aldborough.

Parisian ware [Ar]. A thin, dark grey, highly burnished ware decorated with impressed stamps and found mainly in Yorkshire and Lincolnshire, dating to the late 1st and the 2nd centuries AD.

park [MC]. In Anglo-Saxon times a park was simply any piece of land within a fence. In medieval times a park was an area for growing timber and/or keeping beasts of the chase such as deer. From the 16th century AD through to the 19th century many landscape parks were created around the country mansions and palaces of the landowning classes. These were chiefly designed and landscaped to look attractive according to prevailing tastes at the time of their creation, although many were still used to graze deer and cattle. Most recently, parks have become public open spaces for recreation and leisure.

parkland [De]. A traditional style of land use, also known as wood pasture, that was widely developed in later medieval times in Britain and parts of northern Europe comprising areas of open grassland studded with single established trees or deliberately planted clumps. These landscapes were browsed by deer and cattle with the result that the trees have a distinctive flat base to their foliage caused by maximum reach of the grazing animals. Parkland was economically important both for grazing and the production of substantial timber.

paroiko [De]. The dependent peasants of a Byzantine monastic economy.

parrot beak jug [Ar]. Type of glazed ceramic jug found in Britain and northern Europe in the 14th and 15th centuries AD, distinctive in having a rather stylized polychrome image of a large-beaked bird on the side.

Parthenon, Athens, Greece [Si]. The principal temple situated in the centre of the ACROPOLIS in Athens and visible from many places within the city. The temple has a long and chequered history, and in the late 20th

century AD was the subject of a major conservation and restoration programme. The temple is dedicated to the maiden Greek goddess Athena and was probably begun in limestone at the end of the 6th century BC. It was replanned in marble after the battle of Marathon in 490 BC, but it was not constructed in its final form until 447–432 BC when it became the centre-piece of Pericles' scheme for the Acropolis. The architects were Ictinus and Callicrates who worked under the supervision of the sculptor Phidias. Pentelic marble is the main material used in its construction, the design and form of the buildings being widely regarded as the highest achievement in the DORIC ORDER of architecture. In 438 BC a great statue of Athena in gold and ivory was dedicated in the shrine, where it remained until its transportation to Constantinople in AD 426.

After the classical period the temple was converted first to a church and then a mosque. It survived well until Turkish occupying forces used it as powder magazine; it exploded in 1687 after being hit by Venetian fire. Some of the finely sculptured marble friezes were acquired from the Turkish authorities by Lord Elgin and taken to London, where from 1816 they have been displayed in the British Museum.

[Sum.: R. A. McNeil, 1991, Archaeology and the destruction of the later Athenian acropolis. *Antiquity*, 65, 49–63]

Parthians [CP]. A semi-nomadic steppe people who established themselves in northern Iran about 250 BC under Arsaces. Between 160 and 140 BC Mithridates I extended the Parthian state into an empire which survived 350 years or so. Geographically it covered all of modern Iran and Iraq and most of Afghanistan. Its original capital was at Arsak but later moved to Ctesiphon on the middle Tigris. The Parthians were in constant conflict with the Seleucids and, later, the ROMANS. In the west the Parthians were known as superb horsemen, their art and architecture showing an interesting blend of eastern and western styles. The Parthian state was overthrown by the SASSANIANS in AD 224.

participant observation [Ge]. A method of research widely used in sociology and anthropology in which the researcher takes part in the activities of a group or community being studied.

particle size analysis [Te]. The description and characterization of sediments or soils by quantitatively establishing the size distribution of the constituent particles. A combination of sieving and measuring is usually used to distinguish (in increasing order of size) the proportions of clay, silt, sand, gravel, stones, pebbles, cobbles, and boulders. Microscopic methods are also used in some cases to examine the finer material. Various systems of classification are available, one of the most common being the Wentworth–Udden scale developed in geology. Although particle size distributions are not diagnostic of particular formation processes, they can be enormously helpful in differentiating deposits.

passage grave [MC]. Form of megalithic tomb in which a burial chamber set in the centre of a BARROW is approached by means of a narrow passage. The barrow is usually round in plan, but other shapes are known. Most passage graves have a single chamber, but again variations are known and some have up to ten chambers opening into a single barrow from different parts of the outer perimeter. There is also much variation in the shape and size of the chamber, round, square, rectangular, and polygonal forms being the most common. Some chambers have side cells opening off them. Passage graves are found in western France, Spain, the western parts of the British Isles, and Scandinavia. Various subtypes are known, including: SIMPLE PASSAGE GRAVES; DEVELOPED PASSAGE GRAVES; MULTIPLE PASSAGE GRAVES. The earliest passage graves date to about 4500 BC in Brittany; the tradition continues down to about 2000 BC in some areas.

passage grave art [De]. A series of motifs including spirals, lozenges, and lines pecked or incised onto stones forming the walls and kerbs of PASSAGE GRAVES in the west of Britain, Ireland, France, and Spain. *See also* ROCK ART.

Pastaza Phase [CP]. South American farming cultures found in the Rio Pastaza and Rio Napo areas of Amazonia and tentatively dated to *c*.1500–1000 BC. Characterized by their ceramic assemblages which belong to the Zoned Hachure Horizon Style of Amazonia.

paste [De]. The prepared clay from which pots are thrown. In the finished vessel the term is often used to refer to the body of a vessel, as distinct from the outer surface.

Pasteurs des Plateaux [CP]. Late Neolithic and Copper Age cultures of the upland regions of Languedoc, France, dating to around 2000 BC.

pastoralism [De]. A rather ill-defined and loosely applied term referring to an economy in which the bulk of the food supply is derived from animal herding, usually in the form of secondary products such as milk, yoghurt, cheese, and blood. Some pastoralism communities are nomadic and can be highly mobile. In modern times such communities have tended to live in extreme environments and may not therefore be representative of the kinds of pastoralism that existed in the past.

Patch Grove ware [Ar]. Kind of pottery with a rough grey core and an orange or brown surface, found mainly in northwest Kent and Surrey, usually in the form of wide-mouthed storage jars and with notched decoration on the shoulder. It is in a native British tradition that lasted into the 2nd century AD.

patera [Ar]. **1.** A rounded saucepan-like bowl, often of bronze, with a long handle, probably used for pouring libations. **2.** A shallow round disc-like vessel believed to have been for ceremonial use in Roman worship. **3.** A projecting ornament, square or round.

patina (patination) [De]. Changes to the outer surface of an artefact that make its colour, texture, feel, or composition different from the main body of the piece, usually as a result of chemical, physical, or biological alteration through contact with the surrounding environment. On flint, patination often appears as a bluish milky-white layer on the surface. This is caused by alkaline conditions slowly affecting the surface of the flint when exposed to the atmosphere or rainwater. The term is also used to refer to the green crust that forms as a result of corrosion on the surface of bronze objects. Under normal circumstances patina takes time to form and is therefore often taken as a reliable indicator of antiquity.

patriarchate [De]. An area of ecclesiastical administration under the jurisdiction of one of the four principal sees of the eastern church: Antioch, Jerusalem, Alexandria, and Constantinople.

patriarchy [De]. Rule by men.

Patrick, St [Na]. Saint and bishop. Born around 373 AD, perhaps in Dumbarton, and captured by the Scotti in AD 389. After six years of slavery he went to study under St Martin of Tours before sailing back to Ireland in AD 405. Here he converted Ulster to Christianity and founded a missionary centre near Armagh; he was buried here following his death in c.AD 463. Later, when the Irish and Roman churches were in conflict, he was made Ireland's patron saint.

patrilineal inheritance [Ge]. The inheritance of property or titles through the male line only. Also known as patriliny or patrilineality.

patrilocal family [Ge]. A family system in which the wife is expected to live near the husband's parents.

pattern-moulding [De]. A technique of manufacturing glass vessels in which blobs of molten glass are blown into elaborate moulds which are shaped and have the desired decoration cut into them. Large numbers of identical vessels can be produced in this way.

pattern-welding [De]. A technique used to produce strong and attractive-looking flexible iron blades for swords and other ornate weapons from the early post-Roman period onwards. Strips of metal and wire in different colours were WELDED together and then hammered to produce the patterned effect. Some of the finest examples are those produced by Frankish and Anglo-Saxon smiths. Good examples are also known amongst Viking arms.

patu [Ar]. A Polynesian short club-like weapon, made of a variety of materials including wood and whalebone (paroa).

Paulinus of Pelia [Na]. Gallo-Roman aristocrat born c.AD 377, the son of a proconsul with estates in Aquitaine. In AD 414 he accepted office under the brief imperial usurpation of Attalus. After Attalus' downfall, Paulinus was dispossessed and saved his life only by an appeal to the king of the Alans; thereafter he lived in exile in Marseilles. His poem *Echaristicon* ('Thanksgiving'), is a pessimistic account of the disasters of the early 5th century. He died c.AD 440.

Paviland Cave, Gower, Wales [Si]. A limestone cave also known as Goat's Hole on the Gower Peninsula of South Wales excavated in 1822 by Dr William Buckland. Deposits in the cave contain a rich Upper Palaeolithic assemblage of faunal remains and flint tools dating to the period c.36000 through to 8000 BC. However, the site is most famous for the human burial whose bones had been stained red with ochre and which was accompanied by a series of ivory objects. Buckland named this burial 'The Red Lady' of Paviland, although it is now known that it is the remains of a young adult male of about 24000 years ago.

[Rep.: S. Aldhouse-Green (ed.), 2000, *Paviland cave and the 'Red Lady': a definitive report*. Bristol: Western Academic and Specialist Press]

Pazyryk, Russia [Si]. An extensive site in the high Altai mountain region of central Asia used as a burial ground in the later 1st millennium BC by nomadic communities related to the SCYTHIANS. Excavations by Russian archaeologists have revealed burials dating from the 5th to the 3rd centuries BC, many of them in large pits covered in low cairns (KURGANS). Some are well preserved because they have remained frozen since deposition. Four-wheeled wagons were included in some cases, as were horses with bridles, saddles, and saddlecloths. The men had been tattooed and all the bodies had been embalmed. It is thought that these burials belong to the leaders of mobile groups.

[Sum.: S. I. Ruelenko, 1970, *Frozen tombs of Siberia: the Pazyryk burials of Iron Age horsemen*. London: Dent]

Peak group [MC]. A regional group of SIMPLE PASSAGE GRAVES in the Derbyshire Dales of central England.

peak sanctuary [MC]. Type of MINOAN cult centre lacking in monument architecture where votive offerings were made.

peanut [Sp]. A leguminous plant (*Archis hypogaea*) bearing pods that ripen underground and contain edible seeds. Native to the lowlands of South America below about 2000 m above sea level. Domesticated by c.2500 BC.

peasants [Ge]. People who produce food from the land, using traditional farming methods, and who comprise an agricultural class dependent on subsistence farming.

peat [Ge]. A body of sedimentary material, usually dark brown or black in colour, comprising the partially decomposed remains of plants and organic matter that is preserved in anaerobic conditions within an essentially waterlogged environment. Peat deposits provide important sources of PALAEOENVIRONMENTAL materials, especially macrobotanical remains, pollen, beetles, gastropods, and sometimes human and animal remains too. Peat can be radiocarbon dated. It is also cut and dried as a source of fuel.

pebble [De]. **1.** A small rounded block of stone that has usually been smoothed and shaped by water action. **2.** A size subdivision of sediment components which ranges between 4 mm and 64 mm in diameter on the Wentworth–Udden system.

pebble tools (pebble choppers) [Ar]. Early and technologically speaking most primitive kinds of tool comprising a natural nodule or pebble that has been modified by striking off a few flakes to produce an irregular working edge. The earliest known examples date to around 2.6 million years ago and are associated with AUSTRALOPITHECUS.

Pecel Culture [CP]. *See* BADEN CULTURE.

pecking [De]. A method of shaping the surface of natural stones to fashion tools, modify the form of the stone, or create patterns or designs of various sorts. It involves hitting the surface of the stone to be fashioned in a controlled way using a harder stone of appropriate size (a hammerstone), thereby crushing the surface of softer stone to a powder and so removing small portions at each blow.

Pecos Classification [Th]. A cultural sequence for prehistoric material from the southwestern parts of North America devised in 1927 at the first Pecos Conference. Eight stages in the sequence were identified: BASKETMAKER I–III and PUEBLO I–V. Architecture and ceramics provide the basic elements in defining the stages.

pectoral [Ar]. A decorative and/or protective plate which covers the chest.

pedestal [Co]. **1.** A free-standing raised plinth or bollard. **2.** In pottery making it is a raised section in the bottom of a kiln chamber either to support a raised oven floor or (in single-chambered kilns) to aid the stacking of the pottery and the circulation of hot air around it.

pedestal beakers [Ar]. Type of drinking cup with a distinct base section or foot forming an integral part of the lower body; some are Gallo-Belgic, others are locally made in Britain.

pedestalling [De]. In excavation this involves leaving finds and excavated objects in situ on a column of soil until all the surrounding stratigraphic unit has been removed. Rarely used.

pediment [Co]. A triangular-shaped recess located above the ENTABLATURE on the gable ends of classical temples and similar buildings. The recess is often filled with sculpture. *See also* TYMPANUM.

pedology [Ge]. Study and analysis of soils, in particular their origins, development, character, and distribution.

pedoturbation [De]. The disturbance of soils, and by implication any cultural material they contain, by physical, chemical, or biological agents. In the long term such disturbance will result in homogenization of the main elements of the SOIL PROFILE. *See also* BIOTURBATION.

Pedra Furada, Brazil [Si]. Large rock-shelter in the sandstone hills of the Sierra Talhadra in the Piauí region of eastern Brazil. Excavated by Niede Guidon in the 1970s and 1980s, the site yielded a long sequence from Palaeo-Indian times onwards. The walls of the rock-shelter are adorned with paintings, fragments of which have been found in stratified layers dating to about 10 000 BC. Earlier levels dating to before 39 200 years ago have yielded quartzitic artefacts.

[Sum.: N. Guidon and G. Delibrias, 1985, Carbon-14 dates point to man in the Americas 32 000 years ago. *Nature*, 321, 769–71; R. G. Bednarik, 1989, On the Pleistocene settlement of South America. *Antiquity*, 63, 101–11]

peer group [De]. A friendship group composed of individuals of similar age and social status.

peer review [De]. The process used by publishers and editors of academic journals to provide a chance for scholars to examine and critique a paper or monograph before it is published to help ensure its integrity and veracity.

pegged spearhead [De]. A variety of socketed spearhead common in the European late Bronze Age in which the shaft is secured to the metal head by means of a metal or wooden peg set at right angles to the main axis of the shaft passing through a pair of opposed holes in the metal casing of the socket.

Pekin Man [Sp]. Obsolete term once used to describe the hominid remains from Choukoutien in China which are now classified as being of *Homo erectus*.

Pelasgians [CP]. The name in Greek literature for the pre-Hellenic peoples living in central and northern Greece at the time of the immigration of the first true Greeks about 2000 BC. The Pelasgians were widely dispersed in these mass movements, and Herodotus mentions pockets of the Pelasgian language surviving to his own day in Chalcidice and near Cyzicus on the Sea of Marmora. The Athenians claimed a Pelasgian ancestry and in doing so believed that they were the autochthonous inhabitants of Attica. The name of their city and goddess is indeed pre-Hellenic: more probably, a Pelasgian element survived and was absorbed when Attica was occupied by Greeks in the early immigration. The Dorian invasion had little effect on Athens, which was the only citadel of Mycenaean times to survive into the Hellenistic period.

pele tower [MC]. A type of small roughly built barn-like house of oblong plan and between two and four storeys high found in the borderlands of England and Scotland and mainly dating to the period between the 14th and 16th centuries AD. Pele towers are characterized by thick dry-stone-built walls, external stairs, and the presence of a barmkin or enclosed yard round about. Originally they were built as defensive refuges for occupation in times of trouble.

pemmican [Ma]. A mixture of pounded meat and fat made by hunter-gatherer groups in North America in recent times, and presumably in the ancient past as well. Pemmican was manufactured from meat dried after a major kill. It is easily transportable and able to be eaten on the move.

pen [Co]. An enclosure within which animals are kept.

penannular [De]. In the shape of a ring, but with a break at one point. Often used to describe brooches and torcs as well as arrangements of posts, slots, and ditches forming the walls of round houses and enclosures.

penannular brooch [Ar]. A common type of metal dress fastening found especially in post-Roman and later times down to the 10th century AD in northwest Europe. Developed out of earlier Iron Age and Roman brooch forms, penannular brooches comprise an open hoop with two terminals and a pin backing the hoop. The terminals in particular were often ornamented, some very elaborately.

Penard Period [CP]. Industrial phase of the British Bronze Age immediately following the KNIGHTON HEATH PERIOD. Named after a hoard of bronze tools and weapons found in a quarry at Penard, West Glamorgan, in South Wales in 1827, the tradition spans the period 1200 BC through to 1000 BC. During this time there was much experimentation in metalworking, stimulated by contact with URNFIELD smiths in northern and central Europe. Imports in the period include early styles of sword and perhaps shields. Inventions include cylinder sickles and leaf-shaped pegged spearheads. Sheet metal became more extensively worked than in earlier phases and there was increasing use of clay moulds and more lead-rich alloys.

pendant [Ar]. Ornament designed to be worn, frequently around the neck, on a strap or chain.

Pendlebury, John Devitt Stringfellow (1904–41) [Bi]. British archaeologist specializing in the prehistory of Egypt and the Aegean. Born in London he was educated at Winchester and Pembroke College, Cambridge, displaying an interest in Egyptology from an early age. In 1927 he became a student at the British School in Athens and the following year married fellow student Hilda White. In the late 1920s he excavated at Tell-el-Amarna, Egypt, and from 1928 to 1934 was curator at Knossos for the British School in

Athens. During this time he excavated the post-Minoan refuge city of Karphi in eastern Crete. His best-known book, *The archaeology of Crete*, was published in 1939. In 1940 he was appointed as an extra British vice-consul in Crete. When Greece came into WW2 he was given the rank of captain and liaison officer to the British Military Mission in Crete with the task of preparing for guerrilla warfare in the event of the island being invaded. He was killed during the German invasion of Crete in May 1941.

[Obit.: *Annual of the British School in Athens*, 41 (1946), 5–8]

Pengelly, William (1812–94) [Bi]. English schoolteacher and amateur geologist who excavated at Kent's Cavern, Devon, in the 1840s and 1850s, and at Windmill Hill Cave, Brixham, Devon, in 1858–9. Both excavations confirmed the association of early stone tools with the bones of extinct animals below layers of naturally formed stalagmite, and thus played a critical role in establishing the antiquity of man.

[Bio.: *Dictionary of National Biography*, 15, 739–40]

penknife point [Ar]. Type of late Upper Palaeolithic flint tool found in northwest Europe. Made on fairly broad blades, these tools are characterized by a straight unworked edge along one side, a curved distal end, and a lightly retouched edge parallel to the unworked side.

Pentelic marble [Ma]. Named from its source on the mountains bordering the Attic plain in Greece. Eminently suitable for fine buildings both in ancient and modern times. All the finer Athenian buildings of Pericles are made of Pentelic marble, the particles of iron in it giving the famous golden tinge of colour.

Peoples of the Sea [CP]. *See* SEA PEOPLES.

peplos [Ar]. A type of Greek woman's garment, made of wool, long and sleeveless, being fastened on each shoulder with a pin, and having a deep fold hanging free from neck to waist. In the Panathenaic festival every four years a new peplos embroidered by Athenian women was carried in procession to the Acropolis and presented to Athena.

perambulation [Ge]. The custom of walking, inspecting, and redefining boundaries, particularly those of a parish. This sometimes results in documents giving a verbal description of the boundaries and the features along it. The earliest perambulations in England are of Saxon date.

percussion flaking [De]. A stoneworking technology applied to isotropic materials such as fine stone and flint where a stone, bone, or wooden hammer is used to detach flakes in a controlled way in order to shape the material being worked. Direct striking of the core with a hammerstone tends to give thick bulbous flakes; with a cylindrical (bone or wooden) hammer the flakes produced are thinner and flatter. **Indirect percussion**, also known as punch flaking, necessitated the use of a bone or wooden punch between the hammer and the core, controlling the precision of flaking.

peribolos [Co]. The wall of a sanctuary or TEMENOS.

periglacial [Ge]. Arctic conditions in the regions surrounding an ice-sheet. Although such conditions are now confined to high latitudes, during the PLEISTOCENE they were far more extensive.

Perigordian [CP]. French Upper Palaeolithic sequence of flint industries based on the topological analysis of tools and assemblages that is taken to represent a continuous tradition spanning the CHÂTELPERRONIAN and GRAVETTIAN. The scheme was advocated by D. Peyrony in the 1930s but is not widely accepted.

period [De]. **1.** In archaeology it is taken to be a unit defining a major block of time. Such a period may contain several phases and pertain to a wide area. **2.** In geology, 'periods' are second-order time units according to the American Commission on Stratigraphic Nomenclature's internationally agreed scheme set out in 1949. The chronostratigraphic units making up each period are known as systems: thus the QUATERNARY SYSTEM embraces the Pleistocene and the Holocene.

periphery [De]. The term refers to countries which have a marginal role in the world economy, and are thus dependent on societies in a 'core area' producing materials for trading relationships.

peristalith [Co]. A member of the ring of upright stones on the edge of a cairn.

peristyle court [De]. An enclosed area surrounded by columns, central to a villa using a courtyard plan. Also refers to the row, or rows, of columns round a temple.

permafrost [De]. More or less permanently frozen ground represented as a zone up to 3 m deep the surface of which undergoes seasonal freezing and thawing. Common in PERIGLACIAL conditions, the effects of permafrost in the creation of geomorphological features such as ice-wedges, involutions, and pingos have important implications for archaeology because they are sometimes confused with anthropogenic features.

perpendicular style [De]. A style of architecture found in Britain in the late 14th century AD through to the 16th century AD in which there is a strong emphasis on the vertical elements of construction and decoration. Pointed arches common in earlier centuries are flattened and arches and windows become framed by rectangular outlines. Towers of great height are added to ecclesiastical buildings and ceilings and roofs are often richly decorated.

Persepolis, Iran [Si]. Capital of the Achaemenid empire from its foundation in 518 BC by Darius through to its destruction by Alexander the Great in 331 BC. The site was built on a terrace in the mountainside and comprised a series of palaces and colonnaded halls. Monumental stairways are flanked by reliefs showing Median and Persian nobles, tribute bearers from all quarters of the empire, and the enthroned rulers themselves.

[Rep.: E. F. Schmidt, 1953–7, *Persepolis*. Chicago. Chicago University Press. 3 volumes]

Persians [CP]. Originally from what is now Turkestan, the Persian peoples settled in the province of Parsa during the 2nd millennium BC. They twice built great empires through the Middle East, first under the ACHAEMENID family between 558 and 331 BC and later under the SASSANIANS in AD 224 to AD 651. Persia is the ancient name for modern Iran.

personal distance [De]. The physical space that individuals maintain between themselves and others.

pest house [MC]. Early equivalent of the isolation hospital in post-medieval Britain. Managed by the parish and usually in an isolated situation for persons suffering from any infectious diseases.

pestle [Ar]. A club-shaped tool used for crushing or pounding material in a MORTAR.

Peterborough Culture [CP]. Late Neolithic communities in the southern and eastern parts of the British Isles characterized by the use of PETERBOROUGH WARE. Also termed Secondary Neolithic Culture, the term has become obsolete.

Peterborough ware [Ar]. A family of elaborately decorated Neolithic ceramics found in southern and eastern parts of the British Isles. Dating to the period 3000 to 2000 BC, Isobel Smith divided Peterborough wares into three successive styles – Ebbsfleet, Mortlake, and Fengate – on the basis of their occurrence in the ditch fills at Windmill Hill. It is now recognized that these three groups overlap rather more than originally thought, and that they are best seen as part of the broad group of impressed wares found over much of northern Europe in the 3rd millennium BC. The decoration on Peterborough ware consists of pits, 'maggot impressions' made by impressing tightly rolled cord, and the impressions made by pressing the ends of bird bones into the soft clay before firing. Some of the later vessels are the first in Britain to be made with flat bases.

petit-tranchet arrowhead [Ar]. A style of later Mesolithic flint arrow tip in northwest Europe in which a blade is broken into trapezoidal pieces with the broken edges forming the divergent long sides with the naturally sharp blade edges at either end. The broader end is mounted as the leading edge. Also known as transverse or chisel-shaped arrowheads.

petit-tranchet derivative arrowhead (PTD arrowhead) [Ar]. Diverse series of later Neolithic flint arrowhead forms found in Britain and believed to derive from the development of petit-tranchet arrowhead forms. The group was defined and classified in 1934 by Grahame Clarke and includes a range of triangular and trapezoidal pieces; some were perhaps for use in hunting birds.

Petra, Jordan [Si]. An ancient city set deep in a valley on the western side of the limestone plateau of Jordan that owed its origins to good supplies of spring water, an important position on trading routes between the Dead Sea and the Red Sea, and the presence of abundant natural caves that could be turned into dwellings and storehouses. Petra was the name given by Greek and Roman traders; it was known as Rekem or Arkem in Hebrew and Sela by the Crusaders.

Petra was successively the capital of the Edomite and NABATAEAN kingdoms, which established it as a trading centre in the 1st millennium BC. Roads were built into the valley (the Sik) and the high cliffs on either side were decorated with emblems of the god Durares. At the head of the Sik in the transverse gorge of Wadi al Jarra is the façade of a massive temple, Khazneh al Faraún, sculptured into the rose-red rock. Throughout Petra every available rock surface has been worked into a vertical face and in many cases sculptured into the façade of a temple, shrine, palace, or dwelling. Behind each façade is a large chamber hewn into the rock and entered through a tall rectangular doorway. In Roman times a large rock-cut amphitheatre with 33 rows of seats was added, as well as a temple known as Kasr al Bint Faraún. Later on the Crusaders fortified Petra and held it until the Moslem conquest drove the Franks out of the Middle East. Petra was then completely abandoned and its location lost.

[Sum.: I. Browning, 1989, *Petra* (3rd edition). London: Chatto and Windus]

Petrie, Sir William Matthew Flinders (1853–1942) [Bi]. English archaeologist who specialized in Egyptology. Born in Charlton, Kent, Flinders was educated at home by his parents and through what he could pick up himself. At an early age he developed an interest in antiquities through visits to the British Museum, and in surveying structures and earthworks under the tutelage of his father who was a civil engineer. In 1877 he published *Inductive metrology* and in 1880 he produced an excellent survey of STONEHENGE, Wiltshire. These early publications stand at the head of a prodigious and wide-ranging bibliography. In 1880 he went to Egypt to survey the Great Pyramid at Giza, in 1883 becoming unpaid joint secretary and field director of the recently formed Egypt Exploration Fund, working first at Tanis. Petrie was responsible for advances in excavation technique and artefact analysis, devising a system of sequence dating of artefacts independent of period labels. Equally important was his recognition of Mycenaean and 'proto-Greek' pottery in Egypt and Egyptian imports in the Aegean, which formed the basis for cross-dating between the regions. In 1897 he married Hilda Isabel, by whom he had two children. He was elected an FRS in 1902 and a Fellow of the British Academy in 1904; he was knighted in 1923. From 1892 to 1933 he was Professor of Egyptology in the University of London. After 1926, dissatisfied with conditions in Egypt, he worked in Palestine until his death in Jerusalem in July 1942.

[Bio.: M. Drower, 1985, *Flinders Petrie*. London: Gollancz]

petroform [De]. Arrangements of rock or boulders on the ground surface that when viewed from afar or from the air make up the outline of an animal, mythological figure, or other kind of distinctive shape.

petroglyph [De]. *See* ROCK ART.

petrology [Ge]. The study of rocks and their mineralogy through the examination of thin sections under a petrological microscope in either plain or polarized light. The thin sections comprise slices of rock samples 0.003 mm thick which have been fixed to glass microscope slides for easy handling. One of the first applications of this technique to archaeological problems was by H. H. Thomas when in 1923 he demonstrated that the bluestones at Stonehenge originated in the SPOTTED DOLERITES of the Prescelly Mountains of southwest Wales. Since then many studies of stone and pottery (which is actually only fired rock) from archaeological contexts have led to the recognition of source areas and allowed distributions to be plotted.

Pevensey ware [Ar]. The products of a small local factory near Pevensey, Sussex, which made imitations of OXFORDSHIRE and NEW FOREST type pottery in a very hard orange-red fabric and a deep red colour coat.

pewter [Ma]. A grey-coloured metal alloy based on tin with lead, copper, antimony, and various other metals. Used from Roman times onwards mainly for domestic utensils.

PFB [Ab]. *See* PROTRUDING FOOT BEAKER.

pH [De]. A measure of soil acidity or alkalinity calculated as the logarithm of the reciprocal of the hydrogen-ion concentration in moles per litre of a solution. The pH scale runs between 0 (highly acid) and 14 (highly alkaline): a value of 7 is neutral. The survival of archaeological materials is highly dependent on soil acidity, calcareous materials such as bone and shell being well preserved in alkaline soils but lost in acidic soils.

phalerae [De]. Bronze roundels used to decorate saddle cloths and straps on horse gear from the later Bronze Age onwards. Some were worn by Roman soldiers on their breast armour.

phallic [De]. Relating to or resembling a phallus or penis. Often seen in the design or ornamentation of ancient objects; speculatively suggested for almost any tall narrow form or structure by those so inclined.

pharaoh [Ge]. The title taken by the rulers of ancient Egypt who assumed the duel duties of king and god. Each line of pharaohs formed a DYNASTY, 31 in all. The title originates from the Egyptian term for 'great house'.

pharos [MC]. A Latin term for an early kind of lighthouse. Built of stone and/or wood these were simply towers situated in prominent coastal positions in order to display beacon lights to guide ships at sea. The most famous is the Pharos at Alexandria, one of the Seven Wonders of the Ancient World. The only remaining example known in Britain is at Dover, Kent.

phase 1. [Ge]. In North American archaeology this term refers to the common incidence of a component at a number of sites within a defined geographical area and specific time period. Originally defined by Alfred Kidder in 1946, the term was modified to more or less its modern application by G. Willey and P. Phillips in 1958: 'an archaeological unit possessing traits sufficiently characteristic to distinguish it from all other units similarly conceived, whether of the same or other cultures or civilizations, spatially limited to the order of magnitude of a locality or region and chronologically limited to a relatively brief interval of time'. Distinctive traits recognized through items of material culture or the content of assemblages are therefore used to define phases. Subphases may be identified as more sites belonging to a phase illustrate details of geographical or temporal variation. A phase is thus broadly equivalent to the concept of a CULTURE in European archaeology. **2.** [De]. In describing the development of a particular site or building, groups of broadly contemporary features are represented as a single entity even though in reality this approach conflates time and a whole succession of actions relating to the use of individual elements over widely differing durations.

phenomenology [Th]. A set of theoretical approaches that attempt to understand the way in which people experience the world they create and inhabit; the study of human experience and consciousness in everyday life. The starting point is the idea of 'being' in the world, that is being situated in a physical and social space. Writing in the early 20th century, Edmund Husserl believed he could create a presuppositionless analysis of human experience, but this was challenged by Martin Heidegger who maintained that any observer was situated within the world being observed.

Philistines [CP]. Mobile communities of the eastern Mediterranean in the late 2nd millennium BC, perhaps of Aegean or European origin, one of the SEA PEOPLES. After unsuccessfully attacking Egypt in c.1200 BC they drove the CANAANITES from the coastal plain of Palestine and settled there. One of their main cities was Ashkelon, but imported Aegean and Cypriot material of the period is found widely in the region. The Philistines were eventually subsumed by the ISRAELITES around 1000 BC.

Phillips, Charles William (1901–85) [Bi]. British archaeologist with both a distinguished amateur and professional career in the subject. Following a degree in history at Cambridge in 1922 he was appointed Librarian and Fellow of Selwyn College. All his spare time was devoted to field archaeology, especially in Lincolnshire and the Fens. Immediately before the outbreak of war in 1939 he was put in charge of excavations at SUTTON HOO, Suffolk. During the war he was at the Central Photographic Interpretation Unit in Medmenham where he became an authority on aerial photography. In 1945 he was appointed to his first professional post in archaeology as Archaeology Officer at the

Ordnance Survey, a position he held until his retirement in 1965.

[Abio.: C. W. Phillips, 1987, *My life in archaeology.* Gloucester: Alan Sutton]

Phoenicians [CP]. A Semitic people from the eastern Mediterranean renowned as traders in later prehistory, erroneously credited with many wondrous exploits around the world. Descendants of the CANAANITES, their early history is obscure. By the later 2nd millennium BC, however, they occupied the narrow coastal plain of Lebanon and Syria with important settlements at Tyre, Sidon, and Byblos. Under Hiram I of Tyre (970–936 BC) the Phoenicians enjoyed a golden age; soon afterwards a series of colonies was established as part of a complex and extensive trading network in the western Mediterranean. The colonies included: Gades, Gibraltar, Tingis, Carthago Nova, Ebusius, Cherchell, Algiers, Hippo, Carthage, Utica, Sabrata, Lepcis Magna, Malta, Nora, Caralis, Sulicis, Tharros, and Olbia. After their incorporation into the Babylonian empire in 574 BC they continued their role as merchants, traders, and middlemen. They were the leading seafarers of the 1st millennium BC, sailing into the Atlantic and reputedly circumnavigating Africa. It is often claimed that they came to Britain, but this has never been substantiated. Towards the end of the 1st millennium BC they were absorbed into the Hellenistic and Roman world. The Phoenicians are believed to have developed the first alphabetic script around 1500 BC; the Greek, Roman, Arabic, and Hebrew alphabets all derive from the Phoenician one.

phosphate (phosphorus) [Ma]. Phosphates are naturally present in all soils at varying levels. Anthropogenically derived phosphates have their sources in a wide range of organic materials with the result that in occupation areas, burials, food-processing areas, latrine areas and animal compounds and droveways the phosphate levels in the soil can be considerably enhanced. Once in the soil, phosphate is generally fixed in an insoluble form to inorganic aluminium, calcium, and iron components, or associates with organic molecules to form insoluble complexes. Fixed in this way it can survive for long periods. In archaeology, identifying concentrations of phosphates through PHOSPHATE ANALYSIS is extremely useful for the recognition and definition of settlement sites, and mapping the different levels of activity within a site. Phosphates can also be used to identify the presence of burials in ground where all physical traces have vanished.

phosphate analysis (phosphate survey) [Te]. The systematic collection of soil samples from a defined study area (e.g. the floor of an ancient house, a field system, or a whole river valley) which are then analysed to determine their phosphate content. Phosphate levels can then be mapped either as absolute values or as deviations from the natural background level to identify significant concentrations. Because of fluctuations in the local background level throughout a region, and also variations within the soil profile, sampling deposits for phosphate studies has to be done with extreme care.

photogrammetry [Te]. The creation of scaled maps and plans based on features visible on one or more photographs of known scale and orientation. In some cases the photographs have to be rectified or adjusted to take account of distortions. The ideal is to use STEREOSCOPIC PAIRS of photographs.

photomicrograph [Ge]. A photograph taken of anything that can be viewed under magnification through a microscope. Photomicrographs are usually taken with cameras fitted via an attachment to the normal eyepiece of the microscope or, more commonly, through attachment to a special facility in the image path through the instrument.

Phrygians [CP]. Originally living in Thrace, the early history of these communities is poorly understood, but they moved into west and central Turkey after the downfall of the HITTITE empire in the 12th century BC. The Phrygians established a short-lived empire under Midas, with a capital at Gordium, in the period c.750–680 BC. Religious and ceremonial centres comprising elaborately carved rock faces were established, while burials were placed under large round barrows. Many of the ceramic styles used were related to contemporary Greek pottery. The Phrygian empire was destroyed by the CIMMERIAN invasion at the end of the 8th century BC, though Phrygian traditions continued into classical times.

Phylakopi, Melos, Greece [Si]. An extensive Bronze Age settlement on the northern coast of the Cycladic island of Melos in the southern Aegean, Greece. The site has been excavated on several occasions since the late 19th century AD, most recently by Colin Renfrew in 1974–7. Three successive phases were represented: Phylakopi I–III, of early, middle, and late Cycladic date respectively. The first phase relates to the Grotta-Pelos culture, the first town being Phylokopi II built around 2000 BC, with a substantial perimeter wall. The town was destroyed in the 18th century BC, but was rebuilt and flourished again in its third phase down to the mid 14th century BC. The later phase had close ties with Minoan Crete and later with MYCENAEAN Greece. The administrative centre and cult centre have been identified. The shrines excavated in 1974–7 had a complicated history starting towards the end of the third city (about 1360 BC), and thus extending the life of the site as a cult centre. It is also notable that the shrines contained both male and female figurines.

[Rep.: C. Renfrew, 1985, *The archaeology of cult. The sanctuary at Phylakopi*. London: British School at Athens and Thames & Hudson]

physical anthropology [Ge]. The biological aspects of anthropology including the study of fossil human beings, genetics, primates, and blood groups.

phytolith [Ge]. Small hard rock-like bodies formed in the spaces between the living cells of a plant through the structured accumulation of silica brought into the cells with water. The identification of phytoliths from different plants preserved in archaeological material can provide an indication of the local vegetation.

Picardy pin [Ar]. Style of bronze pin common in northern France and southern England during the Ornament Horizon of the middle Bronze Age. Picardy pins are distinctive in having a tapering shaft that is considerably thickened at the head end, a swollen neck, and an elaborated domed or mushroom-shaped head. They often have some incised decoration near the head and may be pierced through the swollen neck.

pick [Ar]. Long narrow core tool, sometimes slightly curved in profile, truncated at one end and pointed at the other. Typical of the Sangoan in Africa.

Picosa Culture [CP]. Archaic Stage hunter-gatherer communities living in the southwestern parts of North America in the period 7000 BC to AD 200. The Picosa Culture was recognized by Cynthia Irwin-Williams on the basis of a series of general or 'integrative' traits, and subdivided into four chronologically or spatially separable traditions on the basis of a series of 'isolative' traits. The four subdivisions of the Picosa Culture (whose name is a compound of the first two letters from each of the first three subdivisions) are: Pinto (7000 BC to AD 500), Cochise (7000–200 BC), San Pedro (1500–200 BC), Southeastern (not fully dated), and Oshara (5500 BC to AD 600).

Picti (Picts) [CP]. Literally, 'the painted people', a term used by the Romans during the late 3rd century to refer to those communities living north of the Antonine Wall in the northern parts of the British Isles. The name these groups used for themselves was Cruithni and they probably had an ancestry extending well back into the later Iron Age. They were enemies of Rome, and appear to have survived as a kingdom down to the 9th century AD when they became incorporated into the kingdom of Scotland. Amongst the material culture of the Picts were distinctive SYMBOL STONES carrying incised or carved relief images of animals, human figures, and other symbols. Later examples are ornamented with crosses and sometimes bear OGHAM inscriptions.

pictograph [De]. **1.** A single character within a picture-writing system such as HIEROGLYPHICS or CUNEIFORM. **2.** A symbol or other marking painted on rock. *See* ROCK ART.

Picts [CP]. *See* PICTI.

pie crust [De]. *See* FRILLING.

pie dish [Ar]. A term sometimes used for a dish with a flat rim, usually in Romano-British BLACK-BURNISHED WARE, and often decorated with a lattice pattern on the side and loops on the outside of the base. There is no evidence that it was used as the name suggests.

piece mould [Ar]. In metalworking, a clay mould, made of a number of separate pieces fitting together, for casting intricately shaped objects.

Piedmont Tradition [CP]. Late Archaic Stage hunter-gatherer communities flourishing in northeastern North America in the period 4000–1000 BC. Characterized by distinctive stemmed points.

Piette, Edouard (1827–1906) [Bi]. French antiquarian responsible for excavations at Palaeolithic and Mesolithic sites in southwest France through the 1880s and 1890s. Excavations at Mas d'Azil in 1887 allowed the definition of the AZILIAN culture which bridged the gap between the local Palaeolithic and Mesolithic phases. He proposed subdividing the French Palaeolithic into the Amygdalithic, Niphetic, and Glyptic phases, but the scheme was never widely used. He was also one of the first scholars to support the authenticity and antiquity of the cave art at ALTAMIRA.

[Bio.: Anon, 1906, *Edouard Piette: ancien magistrat, officier de l'instruction publique*. Paris]

PIFA [Ab]. Practitioner of the Institute of Field Archaeologists. *See* INSTITUTE OF FIELD ARCHAEOLOGISTS.

pig 1. [Ar]. An ingot of metal, especially lead or iron, taken from a smelting furnace. **2.** [Sp]. An omnivorous hoofed bristly mammal, descendant of the wild boar (*Sus scrofa scrofa*) and native to virtually the whole of Europe and southern Asia. Pigs were first domesticated in the Near East in the 7th millennium BC. Modern domestic pigs (*Sus scrofa vittatus*) mainly derive from examples native to southeastern Asia which were introduced to Europe in the 18th century AD.

pig fibula pin [Ar]. Bone pin made from the fibula of a pig with a long narrow triangular outline and a perforation at the thicker wider top end. Scandinavian in origin this simple style is found widely across northern Europe in the later 1st millennium AD. Possibly used as netting needles or dress pins.

Piggott, Stuart (1910–96) [Bi]. British prehistorian well known for his studies of the European Neolithic. Born in Petersfield he was educated at Churcher's College and later at St John's College, Oxford. After five years with the Royal Commission on the Ancient and Historical Monuments of Wales starting in 1929, he went on to become assistant director of excavations at Avebury, Wiltshire. During WW2 he served in the army and from 1942 to 1945 was in India where, in the company of Mortimer Wheeler, he greatly advanced archaeological research, later publishing a book on *Prehistoric India* (1950). Upon returning to England he went to St John's College, Oxford, to take a B. Litt.; his thesis was on the noted 18th-century antiquary WILLIAM STUKELEY. In 1946 he was appointed to the Abercromby Chair of Archaeology in the University of Edinburgh, where he stayed until his retirement in 1977. In 1953 he excavated at Stonehenge, Wiltshire, and in 1955 at the West Kennet long barrow, Wiltshire. His publications include *The Neolithic cultures of the British Isles* (1954) and *Ancient Europe* (1965). The latter remains a key textbook on the prehistory of Europe and illustrates very well Piggott's ability to synthesize large bodies of material into an informative narrative. He was elected a Fellow of the British Academy in 1953 and made a CBE in 1972. Piggott continued his academic studies after his retirement, from his home in West Challow, Oxfordshire. In this period he published important texts such as *The first wheeled vehicles* (1983) and *Ancient Britons and the antiquarian imagination* (1989). He was also productive outside archaeology with a volume of poems published as *Fire amongst the ruins 1942–1945* (1947) and contributions to other works.

[Obit.: *Proceedings of the British Academy*, 97 (1988), 413–42]

pike [Ar]. Medieval weapon comprising a long narrow lance-like head and a shaft between 3 m and 6 m long.

pilae [Co]. Pillars of brick (or stone) typically 20–40 cm square and up to 0.8 m high supporting the floor of a room with a hypocaust below.

pila muralia [Ar]. Latin term for a double-pointed wooden stake carried by Roman soldiers for use in fortifying the ramparts of temporary camps.

pilaster [Co]. **1.** Column or pillar incorporated into a wall. **2.** In pottery kilns, integral short piers, buttresses, or column-like projections of varying shape, protruding from the kiln wall on the inside of the combustion chamber, and usually intended to support the raised oven floor of the kiln.

pile dwelling [MC]. Type of settlement found in Switzerland, southwest Germany, and northern Italy characterized by clusters of large wooden stakes found projecting from the muddy floors of established lakes, and associated with Neolithic pottery and a wealth of organic material that was preserved in the waterlogged conditions. When first found in the mid 19th century it was believed that these represented the remains of villages constructed on piles above open water. It has recently been shown, however, that since Neolithic times the water in the lakes has risen to its present level. Originally these structures were built on marshy land around lake shores. The earliest are of the 3rd millennium BC Jura and CHASSEY CULTURES, but later examples of the CORTAILLOD and LAGOZZA cultures are also known. The latest belong to the later Bronze Age (URNFIELD) period.

pilgrim [Ge]. A person who undertakes a long and arduous journey in order to worship at the shrine of a particular saint and to earn both spiritual and physical salvation. The greater the hardship and danger endured in making the journey (**pilgrimage**), the greater the eventual rewards were deemed to be.

pilgrim bottle [Ar]. Ceramic barrel-shaped or cylindrical container, usually with a flattened shape and two suspension lugs, carried by pilgrims to contain their supply of water or wine. Also called costrels.

pilgrims' badge (pilgrim's sign) [Ar]. A small metal plaque available at the major shrines visited by pilgrims and worn by successful pilgrims as a souvenir and proof of their journey. Amongst the most distinctive are the scallopshell badges from the shrine of St James in SANTIAGO DE COMPOSTELLA.

pillar [Co]. Tall slender vertical stone, masonry, or wooden structural or decorative component of a building which physically or visually supports some kind of superstructure such as a roof, balcony, floor, or gable. See also COLUMN.

pillar crypt [Co]. A subterranean room in a MINOAN house or palace which contains one or two stone pillars. Although the pillars are clearly structural, the fact that some carried sacred symbols led Arthur Evans to wonder whether they were also cult centres or shrines of some kind.

pillared hypocaust [MC]. A Roman-style underfloor heating system in which the floor is supported on PILAE so that hot air can circulate under the roof and into the channels provided in the walls.

pillar-moulded bowl [Ar]. Style of Roman glass bowl made by casting molten glass in a mould. Early examples are usually brightly coloured, but after the 1st century AD most are a bluish-green colour.

pillar stone (pillar) [Co]. Slab or block of stone forming one of the upright components of a STONE CIRCLE.

pillow mound [Co]. Rectangular or circular earthwork, usually flat-topped, with a shallow surrounding ditch constructed as a habitation and breeding place for rabbits or hares. Within the mound there may be stone tunnels and chambers, the tunnels leading to openings in the side of the mound where nets would be placed to catch any animals flushed out by a ferret. One or more pillow mounds may be found within a WARREN. Medieval and post-medieval.

pillow stone [MC]. A rounded stone slab placed under the head of a body in a grave. Some examples dating to the later 1st millennium AD in northern Europe have RUNIC inscriptions on them.

Piltdown, Sussex, England [Si]. A gravel pit at Barkham Manor near Lewes on the south coast of central southern England between 1908 and 1915 Mr Charles Dawson found what were claimed to be skull fragments of modern type with a jaw of more apelike appearance. Those keen to promote a link between apes and humans saw the finds as the 'missing link', but even by 1935 serious doubts were cast on the integrity of the finds and it later emerged that the whole thing was a hoax. Pieces of crania from a modern human and the jaw from an orang-utan had been artificially aged and 'planted' together in a deposit alongside a variety of other animal remains.

[Sum.: R. Millar, 1998, *The Piltdown mystery: the story behind the world's greatest archaeological hoax*. London: S. B. Publishers]

pipe clay

PIM [Ab]. *See* PULSED INDUCTION METER.

pin [Ar]. At its simplest, a pin comprises no more than a thin strip of metal or bone, the shaft or shank, with a point at one end and a head at the other. Mainly used to secure clothing together. Many elaborate styles were developed, however, usually by ornamenting and expanding the head in some way.

pin beater [Ar]. A thin rod of wood or bone (occasionally stone) with tapering ends used to compact the weft threads on an upright loom by pushing down between each of the warp threads one at a time. *See also* WEAVING COMB.

pinch method [Ge]. Simple technique of making pots by crudely shaping a ball of clay and then, by forcing the thumb into the centre, gradually pinching out the walls to an even thickness and the desired shape.

pinched neck (pinched rim, pinched lip) [De]. Type of flagon top pinched out with a finger and thumb action into the form of a figure-of-eight in order to facilitate pouring from the finished vessel.

pinfold [MC]. A small enclosure in which stray cattle were placed and only released to their owner on payment of a fine.

pingo [Ge]. A mound of soil and glacial moraine that forms under PERIGLACIAL conditions with a block of ice at the core. When the ice eventually melts the overburden collapses to form a natural, more or less circular rampart. Some can look deceptively like archaeological monuments.

pintadera [Ar]. A small ceramic object comprising a patterned face with a knob behind to hold it. The face is presumed to have been used as a stamp, perhaps for applying pigments to the skin or to garments in a repeat pattern. They date to the late Neolithic of central Europe, although similar things are also known in the Americas from quite separate origins.

Pinto Basin Tradition (San Dieguito–Pinto Tradition) [CP]. Archaic Stage hunter-gatherer communities of the Southern Basin and southern Californian desert of western North America flourishing in the period 5000–1900 BC. Pinto appears to have developed from Palaeo-Indian San Dieguito roots. Characterized by nomadic populations using distinctive Pinto points.

Pinto point [Ar]. Bifacially worked chipped stone projectile point characteristic of the Pinto Basin Phase of western North America 5000–1900 BC. Triangular in outline, Pinto points are shouldered towards the bottom of the long side to produce a straight stem; they have a hollow base.

Pioneer Phase [CP]. A general term referring to the second of the five main cultural historical stages defined for the archaeology of southwestern parts of North America: broadly the period *c*.100 BC–AD 600, succeeding the Archaic and preceding the Colonial. The Pioneer Phase represents the earliest agriculturalist communities. The period is characterized by the gradual introduction of maize and other tropical cultigens, gradually transforming the resident hunter-gatherer populations into sedentary agricultural communities. The several different environments in the area produced adaptations with recognizable subdivisions, one of the most notable of which is the Hohokam of the southern Arizona desert which dates from the very end of the 1st millennium BC. The first Hohokam Phase includes the cultivation of crops using irrigation canals, the first use of ceramics in the area, and sub-rectangular pit-houses in small villages.

pipe [Ar]. Stone or ceramic holder for use in smoking tobacco. The main elements are the bowl and a connecting tube through which smoke can be drawn into the mouth. Pipes first appear in the archaeological record on Archaic Stage sites in Illinois, North America, from around 1500 BC onwards. They become common in the eastern woodlands by 500 BC. It is possible that organic pipes were used before this time, but tobacco is a native plant of South America and so must have been taken northwards in the same way as other crops. Some stone pipes, for example those made by Middle and Late Woodland communities, were extremely elaborate in their design and decoration.

pipe clay [Ma]. Relatively pure clay containing little or no iron which is usually fired to a white or pale cream colour. In recent times it was commonly used in making tobacco pipes.

pipe-clay figurine [Ar]. Small statuettes modelled or cast in fine white pipe clay.

pipkin [Ar]. Style of medieval ceramic vessel in the form of a saucepan with a single hollow handle probably made to take a wooden extension.

Pirri point [Ar]. A type of roughly symmetrical unifacially worked leaf-shaped point in flint or stone, up to 7 cm long, found widely distributed across inland Australia from South Australia to the Northern Territory. During manufacture the bulb of percussion is sometimes removed in order to produce a rounded and thinned butt. Part of the AUSTRALIAN SMALL TOOL TRADITION and conventionally dated to the period after 3000 BC.

piscina [Co]. **1.** Swimming-bath in a Roman public bath-house. **2.** A perforated stone basin for carrying away water used to wash the chalice and the hands of the priest following church ceremonies, often contained in a wall niche near the altar.

pisé [Ma]. Clay, earth, or gravel beaten down until it is solid and used as a building material for floors and walls.

pit [Co]. A relatively steep-sided hole dug into the ground surface. Pits are probably the single most common feature encountered during archaeological excavations and are known in many different shapes and sizes. Originally they were probably constructed for many different purposes, from the regular cylindrical or bell-shaped forms used for storing foodstuffs to the highly irregular borrow pits that served as quarries for clay or stone to build or refurbish an adjacent structure. Many others no doubt served as lavatories.

pit alignment [MC]. A linear arrangement of pits, typical of the middle and later Bronze Age in southern and central England, originally forming a boundary feature, probably in conjunction with the spoil dug from them raised up as a bank to one side.

pitched stone [Co]. Rubble foundations of floors or roads where the stones are packed on edge or slightly inclined.

pitcher [Ar]. A deep jar with a fairly open mouth and usually with a handle used for collecting, storing, or serving liquids. Some pitchers have spouts for pouring.

pitchfork [Ar]. A two- or three-pronged implement equipped with a long handle, made of wood or having a wooden shaft and metal head, used for pitching hay or straw usually in the course of turning it, moving it, or building a storage rick.

pitchstone [Ma]. Dark-coloured type of obsidian resembling pitch. Widely used by prehistoric stoneworkers wherever it outcrops.

pit circle [MC]. A class of middle and late Neolithic monument found in the British Isles comprising an arc or ring of shallow but fairly regular oval scoops. In overall diameter such circles are rarely more than 20 m across. Deposits comprising selected objects are sometimes found placed in the bottom of the scoops. Some pit circles are found within or adjacent to HENGE monuments. *See also* TIMBER CIRCLE.

pit-comb ware [Ar]. A style of rather coarse round-bottomed pottery decorated with small pits made in the outer surface of the vessel often in association with the marks left by impressing a bone comb into the clay. Such ware is found widely over the forest zone north and east of the Baltic and in CIRCUMPOLAR CULTURES through into northern Russia. It dates mainly to the 3rd and 4th millennia BC and is associated with late hunter-gatherer and incipient agriculture-using groups.

pit dwelling [De]. *See* PIT HOUSE.

pit firing [Ge]. A method of firing ceramic materials in a shallow pit or scoop containing an open fire.

Pit Grave Culture [CP]. *See* KURGAN CULTURE.

Pithecanthropus [Sp]. Name originally given to early hominid fossils from Java but now reclassified as the remains of *HOMO ERECTUS*.

pithos (pl. pithoi) [Ar]. A large ancient Greek storage jar used for containing oil, wine, grain, olives, and other kinds of produce.

pit house (pit dwelling) [MC]. A dwelling in which the floor level is below the surrounding ground level. In an archaeological context all that remains to be detected of such houses is a large scooped-out hollow. *See also* GRUBENHAUS.

Pitt Rivers, General Augustus Henry Lane Fox (1827–1900) [Bi]. British soldier, anthropologist, and archaeologist often regarded as the 'father of scientific archaeology'. Born on 14 April 1827 at Hope Hall near Bramham Park, North Yorkshire, little is known of his childhood. He was known by his father's surname of Lane Fox until 1880 when he assumed the name of Pitt Rivers. In 1841 he entered the Royal Military Academy at Sandhurst, followed by a commission in the Grenadier Guards where he developed a special interest in musketry. He married Alice Stanley in February 1853, by whom he had six sons and three daughters. In February 1854 he went to the Crimea where his efforts resulted in decorations and mention in dispatches. In May 1857 he was promoted to lieutenant-colonel by purchase; in October 1877 he was promoted to major-general, retiring in 1882 with the honorary rank of lieutenant-general. During his army career he developed an interest in archaeology and ethnography. After reading *The origin of species* on its publication in 1859, he developed a parallel theory of the evolution of culture. He was elected an FRS in 1876. The inheritance from his great-uncle (George Pitt, second Baron Rivers) of large estates in Dorset and Wiltshire in 1880 enabled him to expand the scope of his archaeological work and he spent the last twenty years of his life devoted to large-scale excavations of prehistoric and Romano-British sites. This work was done with a measure of technical competence unknown among his contemporaries. The results were published privately in a series of major volumes, *Excavations in Cranborne Chase* (1887–98). In 1882 he was appointed the first Inspector of Ancient Monuments for England to administer the recently passed Ancient Monuments Protection Act, 1882. He died at the family home of Rushmore on 4 May 1900.

[Bio.: M. Bowden, 1991, *Pitt Rivers*. Cambridge: CUP]

place-name [Ge]. The local name given to a particular location, topographic feature, settlement, or region. Studies of these names reveal a great deal about the early history and settlement of an area, as the form of the name will often indicate, for example, a Celtic, Latin, Germanic, or Norse origin. Place-

names can also help identify features in the landscape that no longer exist, for example deserted settlements, abandoned burial grounds, or former industrial sites.

plague pit [MC]. A large hole dug for the rapid disposal of human or animal corpses when the number requiring burial outstrips the capacity of normal procedures, as happens especially when populations are hit by plagues.

Plains Coalescent [CP]. A general term referring to the last of the five main cultural historical stages defined for the archaeology of the Great Plains of central North America: broadly the period *c*.AD 1400 down to European contact. Succeeding the Plains Village, Plains Coalescent is characterized by the movement of Plains Village Indians from the Central Plains to the middle Missouri area. The reason for the movement was probably a period of prolonged drought.

Plains later Archaic [CP]. A general term referring to the second of the five main cultural historical stages defined for the archaeology of the Great Plains of central North America: broadly the period *c*.1000 BC–AD 200. Succeeding the Archaic and preceding the Plains Woodland.

Plains Village [CP]. A general term referring to the fourth of the five main cultural historical stages defined for the archaeology of the Great Plains of central North America: broadly the period *c*.AD 800–1400. The Plains Village Tradition is characterized by a wide diversity of essentially semi-sedentary village-based groups broadly divisible into those of the Southern Plains, Central Plains, Oneota, and middle Missouri. The subsistence base of all these groups was mainly maize and other tropical cultigens, although bison was a significant part of the diet in eastern areas. Many of the settlements were defended, with enclosed clusters of rectangular or square houses. Many of the Plains Village communities were in regular contact with each other and in the southwest area there was widespread contact with Pueblo communities to the southwest. Horses were introduced from the southwest in historic times and led to greater mobility, but this was short-lived as the village tribes were gradually destroyed by European and American diseases, spirits, trade, war, and treaties.

Plains Woodland [CP]. A general term referring to the third of the five main cultural historical stages defined for the archaeology of the Great Plains of central North America: broadly the period c.AD 200–800, succeeding the Plains later Archaic and preceding the Plains Village. These Plains Woodland cultures were the western counterparts of the Hopewell Culture of the middle Woodland stage further east. However, Plains Woodland cultures retained a subsistence base which relied on hunting deer and small mammals and gathering wild plant foods.

Plainview points [Ar]. Bifacially worked chipped stone projectile points found in central areas of North America in the period around 8000 BC. Similar in form to CLOVIS points although lacking the distinctive flutes of Clovis and perhaps pre-dating them in some areas.

plan [Eq]. A small-scale map that records in the form of a drawing the disposition and arrangement of visible features and items within a site or excavation trench projected as a horizontal plane. As such, plans form one of the most important elements in documenting and recording the examination of archaeological deposits.

plane table [Eq]. A portable drawing board mounted horizontally on a tripod and used for surveying sites and earthworks by constructing a map directly onto paper or film attached to the board. With the board positioned directly above a survey station whose position is marked on the paper, an alidade is used to sight onto a target point. A line can then be drawn along the straight edge of the alidade and the distance from the survey station to the target point scaled off to fix its position. If measurement is not possible, then two survey stations a set distance apart can be used to TRIANGULATE the target point as the intersection of the two alidade-defined lines. Plane-table surveys have the distinct advantage that the surveyor can fill in detail by eye as the work progresses.

plank coffin [Ar]. Wooden box made from planks fixed together (rather than a hollowed trunk, for example) for the containment of a human corpse prior to and during burial. For Roman and later times plank coffins are usually recognized archaeologically from the pattern of nails found in the grave. Plank coffins made before the availability of nails can sometimes be recognized by the patterns of grave fill.

planned street system [De]. Term applied to areas of a town or settlement where the streets and lanes are arranged in regular patterns, usually following some sort of grid. Such regular systems usually suggest that the area was set out according to a single unified plan rather than as a result of uncontrolled piecemeal development.

planned town [Ge]. A town that is established according to a preconceived plan which is set out on the ground in a formal way in order to structure the pattern of property development and the layout of roads, public buildings, and open spaces. In some societies towns are planned according to cosmological principles, in others a simple rectangular grid is used.

planning frame [Eq]. A square or rectangular chassis, typically 1 m by 1 m internally, that is used on archaeological sites to assist with accurately planning features, objects, or structures. The chassis comprises rigid wooden, metal, or plastic sides that are drilled at regular intervals to allow a grid of criss-cross strings to be formed in the centre of the frame. Grids are typically 10 × 10 cm or 20 × 20 cm. Sophisticated planning frames may be equipped with extendable legs at each corner and a spirit level on two of the sides in order to level the frame and thus reduce PARALLAX. By laying the frame over an area that is to be planned or drawn, and locating the corners by off-sets or triangulation, the planner can carefully observe the material to be drawn in relation to the grid within the planning frame and transfer this to scaled squares on the drawing board.

Planning Policy Guidance (PPG) [Le]. Documents that set out the government's views and instructions on the way that each local planning authority in England should implement its responsibilities and duties in respect to town and country planning (spatial planning). Two such documents deal with archaeological matters: PPG15 issued in September 1994 entitled *Planning and the historic environment*, and PPG16 issued in November 1990 entitled *Archaeology and plan-*

ning. Both documents emphasize the interest and importance of various components of the historic environment and use the dual strands of the planning system to provide for the protection, conservation, and management of important sites, structures, and deposits and their setting. The role of **strategic planning** in balancing the needs of local communities and the preservation of archaeological remains is recognized, and the guidance recommends strong policies for protecting important sites. These policies will underpin what can be achieved through **development control** where the possible impact of individual proposals on archaeological materials is considered. Here the guidance provides an approach to the proper consideration of archaeological issues in which the prospective developer submits to the local authority the results of specialist studies (desk-based assessment and/or field evaluation or environmental impact assessment). The guidance places a responsibility on the local authority to have due regard to the preservation of archaeological deposits which are considered to be of national importance by making it a 'material consideration'. If planning permission for a development is granted, the authority may, if it wishes, impose an archaeological condition (a specimen is given in PPG16) whereby the developer must undertake an agreed programme of archaeological works (known as a mitigation strategy) at their own cost. Similar intentions are set out in planning guidance notes issued for Wales and Scotland.

plano-convex knife [Ar]. Type of later Neolithic and early Bronze Age flint tool found in the British Isles, particularly associated with burials in northeastern England. Plano-convex knives have a leaf-shaped outline and slightly elongated form, worked on large thick flakes with retouch around and sometimes all over the convex dorsal surface but a plain untouched ventral surface. Also known as a slug-knife.

Plano Cultures [CP]. Late Palaeo-Indian hunter-gatherer communities representing many different cultures found widely over the Great Plains of North America in the period 9000–6000 BC. Characterized by unfluted leaf-shaped projectile points which are generally known as PLANO POINTS. In general, these various communities were bison hunters, although they also took pronghorn ante-

lope, elk, deer, raccoon, and coyote. By the beginning of the Archaic Stage, however, Plano groups were developing a more broad-spectrum approach to subsistence.

Plano points [Ar]. General term covering all the unfluted styles of bifacially worked chipped stone projectile points from the Great Plains area of North America in the period 9000–6000 BC. These Palaeo-Indian points have been subdivided into numerous styles on the basis of size, shape, and other attributes and include, for example, Alberta, Cody, Fredrick, Eden, and Scottsbluff points.

planted town [Ge]. An urban settlement that was deliberately constructed to a pre-conceived plan. In some cases, for example Salisbury in England, started in AD 1219, they were established on a totally new site. In other cases they substantially enlarge an existing settlement. Some planted towns had a regular form with chequerboard, ladder pattern, or concentric street grids that determined their morphology; others were more irregular and were often built around a central open area or market-place.

plant impression [De]. The negative cast left by some part of a plant when it was deliberately or accidentally pressed into a plastic substance such as clay or plaster that has survived to be excavated.

planum method [Te]. *See* SPIT EXCAVATION.

plaster [Ma]. A soft pliable mixture of sand and lime or crushed gypsum, sometimes mixed with organic matter such as hair or chopped straw to improve strength and bonding, which is spread onto walls and ceilings in order to produce a hard smooth surface when dry. Fine plaster can also be moulded into decorative features and panels.

plastic style [De]. In JACOBSTHAL's scheme for the subdivision of pre-Roman Celtic art in Europe this relatively late style is characterized by an exuberant, three-dimensional quality seen especially in ornate bracelets or animal representations in ornamental metalwork.

plate [Ar]. A shallow vessel whose height is not greater than one-seventh of its diameter.

plate armour [Ar]. Protective armour in the form of sheet-iron fittings tailored to the shape of the body and strapped in position. This type of armour was current in the 15th–16th centuries AD in Europe.

platform [Co]. In earthworks, a space that has been artificially levelled to receive a building.

platform mound [Co]. Flat-topped mound constructed of earth and/or stone and rubbish, usually surmounted by a building, found on many sites of the Woodland Stage in North America. Some platform mounds supported residences, other were ceremonial.

plaza [Co]. An open square in ancient cities of the New World used as a focus for meetings and events.

Pleistocene [CP]. The earliest of two chronostratigraphic units or epochs forming the QUATERNARY PERIOD (the later one is the HOLOCENE), from about 2 million years ago to 10 000 years ago. Also known as the Great Ice Age, the Pleistocene includes six main stratigraphic stages representing an alternating pattern of stadials (i.e. glacial) and interstadials (i.e. interglacial). Although it is now recognized that these are overly simplistic in terms of the complicated stratigraphy that exists for the Pleistocene, they do at least provide a working model within which to view the activities of human communities. The last glacial phase of the Pleistocene, the DEVENSIAN, marks the end of the Pleistocene epoch; it is succeeded by the Holocene which contains just one main stratigraphic stage, the FLANDRIAN.

plinth [Co]. Projecting course at the foot of a wall or the stone base of an altar or similar ornamental or ceremonial structure.

Pliocene [Ge]. Last of the five epochs within the TERTIARY PERIOD, dating from about 14–2 million years ago.

ploshchadki [De]. Russian term for a style of constructing house floors in the Neolithic of southeast Europe which involved laying horizontal logs over which a layer of clay was deposited and then hardened by burning to produce a firm surface.

Plot, Robert (1640–96) [Bi]. British antiquary and first Keeper of the Ashmolean Museum, Oxford. His principal works were his *Natural history of Oxfordshire* (1677) and *Natural history of Staffordshire* (1686).

[Bio.: *Dictionary of National Biography*, 15, 1310–12]

plough [Ar]. An implement used in breaking up ground for cultivation which comprises one or more blades that are drawn through the soil, together with attachments for guiding it and providing the motive power. Ploughs are usually drawn along by animal traction (mainly oxen or horses), although people are occasionally used. There are two basic kinds of plough. The **ard** or scratch plough is essentially a single blade like a hoe set at an angle of about 60 degrees to the ground with a guiding handle behind and a beam in front for connection to a yoke and a pair of animals. An ard simply stirs the soil rather than turning it over. For effective cultivation an ard ideally needs to be used in two opposite directions, creating what is known as cross-ploughing. The earliest ards date to the 5th millennium BC in the Near East, and were available in Europe by the middle of the 4th millennium. By contrast, the **mouldboard plough** or heavy plough is wheeled and can be adjusted to control penetration into the ground. The shares comprise a cutting blade and a curved mould-board that physically inverts the soil profile. Such ploughs were not developed until the mid 1st millennium AD.

plough beam [Ar]. The wooden or metal bar that connects the blades, shares, and their mountings to the yoke, which in turn is attached to the harnesses fitted to the draught animals that provide the power. The plough beam has to be strong enough to transmit the power from the traction through to the blades and share cutting through the ground, but long enough for the draught animals not to be snagged by the ploughing mechanism itself.

ploughed out [De]. Term applied to earthworks and upstanding archaeological structures that because of repeated ploughing have been reduced in height and spread, and had some or all of their archaeological integrity damaged or destroyed through the mixing and de-stratification of deposits.

ploughland [De]. The area of ground that is subject to cultivation by ploughing.

plough marks [De]. Grooves or scars cut into the subsoil underlying a cultivated soil profile by the downward penetration of the blade or shear of an ard or mould-board plough. Prehistoric plough marks have been recorded underneath long barrows and round barrows; plough marks from modern cultivation can often be seen cutting into the top of archaeological deposits.

ploughshare [Ar]. The part of a plough that goes into the ground to disturb or turn the soil. These often become detached from the main mechanism of the plough while working and are subsequently lost. For this reason many ploughsoils, both ancient and modern, contain within them broken or lost ploughshares as a tell-tale sign of past or ongoing agricultural practices.

ploughshare-shaped currency bar [Ar]. Type of iron ingot found in the 1st and 2nd centuries BC in southern England, typically about 0.5 m long, an elongated triangle in outline, with turned-in corners at the wider end. Examples of this style of currency bar are mainly found in the Thames Valley and south midlands.

ploughsoil [Ge]. A soil profile in which the L, F, H, O, A, E, and B horizons have been mixed and homogenized through cultivation. In setting the depth of ploughing the general aim is to avoid breaking into the C horizon, although this is sometimes inevitable.

ploughwash [Ge]. Fine sediment that is liberated from vegetation-free cultivated soils and moved down slope either under gravity or, more usually, by being washed down during rain. The accumulation of such material at the bottom of slopes is COLLUVIUM and is also sometimes known as valley fill.

plumbate ware [Ar]. A type of fine pottery made in the Mexico–Guatemala border region in early POST-CLASSIC times. Widely traded, the ware has a shiny glaze-like surface that results from the special types of clay used.

plunge-bath [Co]. *See FRIGIDARIUM.*

pluralism [Th]. Diversity in interpretation. Because the world cannot be reduced to a series of simple conceptual categories there will always be a range of approaches, understandings, and interpretations. In this sense the world is polysemous and characterized by multiplicity. *See also* MULTIVOCALITY.

pluralist theories of democracy [Th]. Theories which emphasize the role of diverse and competing interest groups in preventing too much power being accumulated in the hands of political leaders.

plural society [De]. A society in which several ethnic groupings coexist, each living in communities or regions variously separate from the others.

pluvial [Ge]. Period when the rainfall was greater than it is at present as a result of climatic changes during the PLEISTOCENE. Mainly refers to tropical and subtropical regions outside the limits of the main ice-sheets.

pnyx [MC]. An ancient Greek open-air auditorium for public assemblies.

pochteca [De]. Term applied to professional merchants from Mexican states.

podium [Co]. **1.** The masonry platform on which a building is constructed. **2.** A raised platform or dais from which speeches or orations are made.

podzol [Ge]. A distinctive kind of soil with an almost black organic horizon overlying a rather loose, bleached, and weathered horizon from which all the iron, aluminium, and other weatherable minerals have gone. At the bottom of the profile there are likely to be deposits of iron and aluminium oxides, and occasionally humic material too. Podzols develop naturally in areas of high rainfall and moorland vegetation.

point [Ar]. General term referring to an artefact, usually of stone, bone, or wood, which served as the tip for a spear or arrow.

pointille [De]. A type of dotted decoration applied to metalwork with a small pointed punch.

point-pattern analysis [Te]. Form of spatial analysis in which a recorded distribution of points is compared with a random distribution, deviations from randomness being used to suggest concentrations and trends.

Point Peninsula Culture [CP]. Middle Woodland hunter-gatherer communities of the northwest area of North America during the first millennium AD. The population had a low density and lived in small mobile bands, each with its own territory. They exploited game, aquatic resources, and wild plant foods. Some may have cultivated native plants such as maize. In summer they would join together into larger groups at fishing stations and beside lakes or rivers for weddings, trading, ceremonies, and the burial of important individuals.

Polanyi, Karl (1886–1964) [Bi]. An Austrian economist and historian who fled the Nazis, first to England and then America. In 1944 he published *The great transformation* which dealt with 19th-century history and led to research on pre-industrial economics. Along with a number of colleagues he published *Trade and market in the early empires* in 1957 which included case studies from the Assyrian and Babylonian empires as well as 19th-century Africa and India. These provide valuable insights that have been drawn upon by archaeologists studying prehistoric trade and exchange systems.

[Bio.: S. C. Humphreys, 1969, *History, economics and anthropology: the work of Karl Polanyi*. Middletown, CONN: Wesleyan University Press]

Poldar Phase [Ge]. Scottish equivalent of the WILBURTON–WALLINGTON industrial phase of the British Bronze Age.

polis [Ge]. A city or city-state of ancient Greece, usually incorporating smaller towns and villages into the territory.

polissoir [Ar]. A block of coarse stone, sometimes as an earthfast boulder or natural outcrop, used for grinding and polishing stone axes in the final stages of production. Archaeologically they are distinctive in having bowl-shaped depressions on which the bodies of the axes were ground. Some also have V-section grooves in which the blades were finished.

polity [De]. Generally, a complex of decision-making roles that relate a society to the goals of its individual members through collective decisions. Colin Renfrew used the term in a particular archaeological context to refer to small-scale politically autonomous early states such as can be seen in MYCENAEAN Greece or ETRUSCAN Italy.

pollen [Ge]. Fine dust-like grains discharged from the male part of a plant with a tough outer layer called the exine surrounding the fertile gamete. Pollen grains are distinctive to species level or beyond in their shape and form and survive well for long periods. Fern spores also survive in a similar way.

pollen analysis [Te]. Studies of the plant life of a certain period using the remains of pollen grains found in the soils of the same period. The proportions of pollen grains representing different species will give an indication of the type and mix of flora. Analysis involves the extraction of preserved grains from the matrix in which they lie and then sampling residue by identifying a randomly selected fixed number (typically 200) in each sample.

pollen core [De]. A column of soil or peat extracted from the ground containing a continuous record of pollen grains representative of changing vegetation over a period of time.

pollen zone [Ge]. The post-glacial vegetational and climatic succession was subdivided into a series of zones, first by von Post in Sweden, and in 1940 by Harry Godwin for the British Isles. These zones are widely accepted and connected to biostratigraphic/climatic phases as a general phasing for the late DEVENSIAN and FLANDRIAN. As such they have come to be applied more widely than was originally intended. The nine main zones proposed by Godwin and linked to biostratigraphic zones are: Ia Oldest Dryas (13 000–10 500 BC) Tundra; Ib Bølling (10 500–10 000 BC) park tundra; Ic Older Dryas (10 000–9800 BC) tundra; II Allerød (9800–8800 BC) tundra, park tundra and birch forest; III Younger Dryas (8800–8300 BC) tundra; IV Pre-Boreal (8300–7700 BC) birch forest; V and VI Boreal (7700–5500 BC) pine/birch forest with increasing mixed forest; VII Atlantic (5500–3000 BC) mixed oak forest; VIII Sub-Boreal (3000–500 BC) mixed oak forest; IX Sub-Atlantic (500 BC+) spread of grasses and pine/beech woodland. In more recent studies, pollen analysts have tended to subdivide particular sequences into **pollen assemblage**

zones which are based on fluctuations seen in that specific sequence and therefore take better account of local variations in vegetation history.

polyandry [Ge]. A form of marriage in which a woman may have two or more husbands at the same time.

Polybius [Na]. Greek historian born around 200 BC who spent much of his life in Rome, and whose principal work, the *Histories*, documents the rise of Rome from the first Punic War to the mid 2nd century. Died *c*.118 BC.

polychrome [De]. Strictly, decoration using more than two colours, but in practice often applied to schemes involving two or more colours. Often applied to decorative schemes on ceramic materials.

polychrome jewellery [Ar]. General term used to refer to a wide range of highly colourful jewellery and ornaments found in cemeteries of the 5th to the 7th centuries AD in southeastern England and in continental FRANKISH burials.

polygamy [Ge]. A form of marriage in which a person may have two or more spouses simultaneously.

polytheism [Ge]. Belief in two or more gods.

pommel [Ar]. Protuberant knob on a sword hilt, frequently decorated with inlay or semiprecious stones.

Pompeian red ware [Ar]. A type of Roman colour-coated pottery made in France and exported to various parts of the Roman world in the late 1st century BC and 1st century AD. The name derived from the colour, Pompeian red, rather than its source.

Pompeii, Italy [Si]. Substantial Roman town of 65 ha on the Bay of Naples in Campania, southwestern Italy, 7 km from Naples. Discovered in 1748 and extensively excavated in the following years and down to the present day. The importance of the site lies in the fact that it was buried beneath volcanic ash and pumice in AD 79, perfectly fossilizing a functioning city. Excavations suggest that Pompeii's origins perhaps lie in a small fishing village established in the 10th century

BC. It came successively under ETRUSCAN and Greek influences, and in *c*.424 BC was occupied by the Samians. From 80 BC the town became a Roman colony in which many wealthy Roman citizens built summer residences. An earthquake in AD 62 caused serious damage, while the eruption of Vesuvius on 24 August AD 79 overwhelmed the whole town. Pompeii was a walled town with an amphitheatre, forum, basilica, several public baths, two theatres, and at least nine temples. Hotels, taverns, gambling houses, brothels, and a wide variety of shops and workshops have been uncovered, as well as private houses. Amongst the most emotive finds are the negative impressions of people and animals buried alive during the eruption. Pliny the Younger gives an eye-witness account of the eruption in *Epistulae* VI.16, 20.

[Sum.: M. Brion, 1960, *Pompeii and Herculaneum: the glory and the grief*. London: Paul Elek]

pond barrow [MC]. A class of early Bronze Age burial monument found in southern Britain which comprises a circular depression, very well and regularly formed, the spoil from which has been used to make an embanked rim. Within the enclosed central space there is generally a series of pits and/or a shaft, some of which contain burials. The shafts may be up to 30 m deep. Pond barrows range in diameter between 5 m and 30 m and are often found as components of ROUND BARROW CEMETERIES.

Pontic ware [Ar]. A type of pottery produced in Etruria during the ARCHAIC period that is characterized by black figures on a red ground. The style appears to imitate techniques used in Attica and other parts of Greece.

Pontnewydd Cave, Wales [Si]. A cave in the limestone hills flanking the Elwy Valley in North Wales excavated by Stephen Green between 1978 and 1980. Local igneous rock that is rather difficult to work was extensively used by the upper Acheulian communities in the area between about 230 000 and 170 000 years ago to make core tools such as handaxes, points, scrapers, and denticulates, some in the Levallois technique. Hominid remains with Neanderthal features representing at least three individuals were found. They date to about 180 000 years ago and are the earliest finds of this kind in northern Europe.

[Rep.: H. S. Green, 1984, *Pontnewydd Cave—A lower Palaeolithic hominid site in Wales*. Cardiff: National Museum of Wales]

poorhouse [MC]. A house set up by the parish authorities under the Elizabethan Poor Law to accommodate those poor people who could not be supported at home. Parish poorhouses were abolished by the Poor Law Amendment Act, 1834.

poppy head beaker [Ar]. A beaker shaped like the seed-head of a poppy plant in a grey or black fabric with a polished surface. It has an everted rim and the body is often decorated with panels of dots en BARBOTINE, or with ROULETTING. The largest sizes could be classified as jars.

population [Ge]. In sampling methods, the sum of all sampling units selected within a data universe.

porcelain [Ma]. A fine form of pottery which is fired to a very high temperature in order to vitrify the clay.

porch [Co]. Small covered space over the entrance into a building.

porphyry [Ma]. A type of granite that can be found in red, green, and black varieties, which was quarried in the eastern desert of Egypt for making sculptures and statues during Roman times. There is some evidence that the quarries were under the direct control of the emperors.

port [Ge]. **1.** Generally taken as a settlement situated on a river or coast whose occupants were engaged in water-borne trade, commerce, and industry, including fishing. **2.** In early medieval England a port was also a specialized kind of market town at which tolls could be collected and which was not necessarily on a river or the coast.

porta decumana [Co]. Latin name for the rear gate of a Roman fort or camp.

portal [Co]. A doorway or carriageway in a gate structure.

portal dolmen [MC]. A class of small stone-built chambered tomb of the early and middle Neolithic along the Atlantic seaboard of Europe. The characteristic feature is an H-shaped setting of three slabs taken to be the front of the structure, behind which are further smaller slabs forming the walls of the chamber. The portal setting and the back slabs support a massive capstone which is usually set on a tilt with the highest part over the portal setting and projecting slightly proud of it. A low cairn or platform surrounds the structure, but there is no evidence of covering mounds. Grave goods are scarce, and little is known of the original burial rites.

porta praetoria [Co]. Latin name for the front gate of a Roman fort or camp, approached by the *via praetoria* leading from the headquarters building, or from the general's tent.

porta principalis dextra [Co]. Latin name for the gate at the right-hand end of the main transverse street (*via principalis*) of a Roman fort or camp as viewed from the front of the headquarters building, or from the general's tent.

porta principalis sinistra [Co]. Latin name for the gate at the left-hand end of the transverse street (*via principalis*) of a Roman fort or camp as viewed from the front of the headquarters building, or from the general's tent.

Portchester ware [Ar]. Type of late Saxon pottery manufactured on the coast of central southern England.

port-hole slab [Co]. A distinctive kind of entrance to a burial chamber, often in a chambered tomb, comprising either a single stone or a pair of stones set side by side, in which a round or sometimes square access hole has been cut. Where a pair of stones is used each has a cut-out in one side which when placed together form the port-hole. Some of the best examples are known amongst COTSWOLD–SEVERN long barrows of western Britain and the dolmens of the northwest Caucasus in southern Russia.

portico [Co]. An entrance porch with a colonnade.

portway [De]. A road which led to a market town. *See* PORT.

Posidonius [Na]. Philosopher and historian, born *c*.135 BC in Apamea, Syria, but afterwards settling in Rhodes. His principal work, a *History*, occupied 52 books but is no longer extant. Fragments do, however, survive in the borrowings of later writers including Caesar, Strabo, Diodorus, and Athenaeus, whose observations on the Celts are largely based upon Posidonius' ethnography. Posidonius died in *c.*50 BC.

positive feedback [De]. A system's response to external stimuli leading to further changes that serve to reinforce the initial response, thereby creating and accelerating a cause and effect loop.

positive lynchet [Co]. The build-up of soil and sediment on the up-slope side of a wall or fenceline running across a hillside. Because the wall or fence serves to halt the down-slope movement of material, the accumulation may eventually bury it. Such a build-up is further exaggerated by the fact that on the down-slope side of the developing lynchet there is likely to be a loss of material from the soil profile. This is known as the **negative lynchet**. Ultimately, the effect of lyncheting is to create a series of flat steps or cultivation terraces up the side of a hill.

positivism [Th]. The school of philosophy developed by Auguste Comte in the 19th century stating that reality can be apprehended objectively and that data (facts) should be separated from the theories that explain them (interpretations). Following this logic, explanation in the social sciences can and should be as objective and empirical as in the natural sciences, and any interpretative statements made should be testable in some way. This finds expression in archaeology as PROCESSUAL or NEW ARCHAEOLOGY where an essentially EMPIRICIST approach is adopted. Here the aim is to explain observed phenomena with reference to a set of general relationships rather than a series of laws, as might be expected in the natural sciences. Archaeology places an emphasis on empirical data as the primary means of testing the explanations offered because such data are regarded as objectively recovered through archaeological fieldwork. Quantitative and mathematical techniques are liberally applied within positivist archaeology. In seeking explanations, positivist archaeology differs very considerably from POST-PROCESSUAL ARCHAEOLOGY which attempts understanding.

post and panel [De]. A term applied to the construction of the kerbs in some classes of MEGALITHIC TOMBS in which upright stones (PERISTALITHS) are set at intervals with blocks of dry-stone walling between.

post circle [MC]. *See* TIMBER CIRCLE.

Post-Classic [CP]. The last of five general cultural stages proposed by G. Willey and P. Phillips in 1958 as a framework for the study of ancient communities in the Americas. The Post-Classic, which directly follows the CLASSIC, embraces communities that can be identified with an imperialistic state organization. Its application is therefore highly restricted within Mesoamerica and the central and west coasts of South America, where such societies were present in the period from about AD 900 down to the Spanish conquest in the 16th century. During this time the high civilizations of earlier periods declined and changed as in a cyclical pattern of conquest and collapse. Many of the societies that lived in this period were strongly militaristic and warfare was widespread. The principal Post-Classic groups of the period include the Inca, Toltec, and Aztec.

Post-Deverel–Rimbury ware [Ar]. Various styles of pottery circulating in southern England from the first half of the 1st millennium BC, superseding the previously common and widespread DEVEREL–RIMBURY traditions. Post-Deverel–Rimbury wares include a fine-ware component comprising mainly thin-walled plain jars, bowls, and cups, together with a wide range of coarsewares including large storage vessels. From the 8th century onwards there is an increase in the amount of decoration applied, especially incised lines, fingertip impressions, and slight cordons.

postern [Co]. Minor gate or door in the defensive wall of a town or fortification.

post-excavation [De]. Describing the set of tasks, analysis, and operations carried out following the fieldwork stage of an archaeological project in order to bring about an understanding of the material, the publication of the results, and the deposition of the records and original material in a formal archive of some kind for future reference.

post-glacial [Ge]. General term for the period after the end of the Pleistocene Ice Age, from about 9000 BC through to the present.

posthole [Co]. A rock or earth-cut socket which at one time held an upright timber post. Commonly found on excavations, such holes usually comprise several distinct elements. The **post pit** is the original hole dug to receive the post; once the post is inserted and positioned it is usually fixed in place by the insertion of **post packing** round about. Stones are often used to make a strong setting. Because timber posts rarely survive archaeologically the centre of a posthole is usually a negative impression of the post that once stood there, and this is known as the **post pipe**.

posting station [Ge]. Small Roman town on a main road where travelling officials could find an inn (MANSIO).

post-medieval [CP]. Term describing the period after the medieval. In the British Isles this is often taken to be the period after the dissolution of the monasteries around AD 1540. Some take the post-medieval period down to the end of the 20th century AD, but others prefer to interpose a 'modern' period between about AD 1750 and the present day.

postmill [MC]. The earliest type of windmill, consisting of a timber body containing the machinery and carrying sails which was mounted on a single timber post around which the body of the mill could be turned into the wind. Many postmills were set upon specially constructed artificial mounds or made use of existing round barrows.

post packing [De]. *See* POSTHOLE.

post-pipe [De]. *See* POSTHOLE.

post-processual archaeology [Th]. A term first used by Ian Hodder in 1985 to refer to a series of theoretical approaches deployed in archaeological thinking that share little except being critical of PROCESSUAL ARCHAEOLOGY while emphasizing social factors in the way human societies operate. Post-processual archaeology is not so much a coherent body of thought as a reaction against positivist approaches and their explicit use of models taken from the natural sciences. Post-

processual archaeology incorporates many different approaches derived from MARXISM, HERMENEUTICS, POST-STRUCTURALISM, and constructivism, but is perhaps united in an interest in social ontology—the character of social reality. Here attempts have been made to provide archaeology with more sophisticated conceptions of past society and the tools to explore ancient societies through archaeological materials. Understandings of human behaviour must be sought in the societies themselves in order to identify specific and often rather idiosyncratic responses to particular conditions. Appropriate lines of enquiry thus include the investigation of social power, structure, contradiction, social change, and gender. A key concept here is that of agency—people are knowledgeable agents and thus attention should be paid to questions of intention, meaning, and the signification of action in order to understand past social phenomena. Also known as interpretive archaeology.

post-structuralism [Th]. A relativist philosophy based on the ideas and works of a number of French scholars working in the 1960s, notably Derrida, Lacan, Foucault, Barthes, and Kristeva, to develop earlier thinking by Hegel, Nietzsche, Husserl, Heidegger, Freud, and Marx. The approach challenges the STRUCTURALIST notion that there are fixed relationships between signs and meanings, between the signifier and the signified, arguing instead that meaning is contextualized within the individual and highly nuanced. A general trend of post-structuralist method, often termed deconstruction, is to unsettle any allegedly firm, detached, or neutral conclusions on the basis that claims of truth are internal to any particular discourse. In doing so it opens up alternative readings and meanings.

pot [Ar]. *See* POTTERY.

potash-lime glass [Ma]. A type of glass developed in northern Europe in the later 1st millennium AD in which potash was used as the flux in place of soda.

potassium–argon dating [Te]. An absolute dating technique similar to radiocarbon dating but applicable to much older deposits. It is used to determine the age of volcanic rock strata containing or sealing archaeological objects rather than to date the artefacts themselves. The technique works by measuring the ratio of radioactive potassium-40 to the stable gas argon-40 in volcanic rocks. Over time ^{40}K decays to become ^{40}Ar at a known rate, its halflife being 13 000 million years. In volcanic rocks any argon present will have escaped when the rock was last molten but will start to accumulate again when it solidifies. Thus by carefully measuring the amount of ^{40}K and ^{40}Ar present in a sample it is possible to work out how long ago it was that the rock solidified. Because of the long half-life of ^{40}K the amount of argon present in samples less than 1 million years old is insufficient to measure, but the technique is very useful for work on early hominid deposits associated with volcanic layers.

potato [Sp]. A leafy plant (*Solanum tuberosum*) which produces a starchy edible tuber. Native to the Lake Titicaca area of the southern Peruvian Andes. Domesticated by *c.*8000 BC in some areas (late Pre-Ceramic stage), but not until *c.*AD 500 in northern coastal Peru. Introduced into Europe in the 16th century AD and into Britain by Sir Walter Raleigh about AD 1585. Over a thousand different varieties of potatoes are known.

pot boiler [Ar]. The term used to describe small stones that have been heated in a fire and then dropped into vessels containing some kind of liquid in order to heat it up. Such stones are characteristically cracked or crazed on the surface from repeated heating and then quenching. *See also* BURNT MOUNDS.

potin [Ma]. A bronze alloy with high tin content.

potin coin [Ar]. Type of British or Gaulish coin made from POTIN from the early 1st century BC onwards. Potin coins are unusual in that they are cast rather than struck. The earliest examples are the first kinds of coin made in Britain and are found mostly in southeastern counties. Derek Allen has traced the origins of the potin coin series back to the bronze coinage of Massalia some time in the 2nd century BC, the prototypes for the British series probably coming via Gaul. Also called Kentish cast bronze coins.

potlatch [Ge]. A ceremonial feast in which the conspicuous consumption of food played a major part. Practised among coastal communities on the northwest coast of North America from perhaps 3500 BC down to historic times, the potlatch was in effect a redistribution system for large accumulated surpluses of foodstuffs in which a few wealthy and powerful individuals controlled the redistribution as a way of gaining prestige.

pot-lid fracture [De]. A kind of thermal fracturing that naturally detaches flint flakes from parent blocks. Pot-lids are small rounded flakes, sometimes with traces of rippling on the ventral surface; a rounded pit is the negative impression left on the parent block by the detachment of the flake.

potsherd [De]. A fragment of a clay vessel. *See also* SHARD.

potter's stamp [Ge]. A small block that the potter impresses into the base of a vessel he/she has made while still soft in order to give it a personalized mark. Some potter's stamps give the potter's name in the Latin or Greek alphabet; other stamps are so-called 'illiterate' and comprise only lines and signs. Especially common on SAMIAN, ARRETINE, and GALLO-BELGIC wares.

potter's wheel [Ar]. A flat-topped horizontal turntable that can be rotated to assist a potter in shaping a ceramic vessel. Slow-turning wheels or tournettes were used from the 5th or 6th millennia BC in the Near East to help true up hand-made vessels. From the early 4th millennium BC, however, fast wheels began to be introduced. Using a fast wheel a potter could centre a piece of clay while the wheel was spinning and then fashion the desired form of the vessel. The technique is still used today. Fast wheels may be powered by simply kicking a stone or wooden fly-wheel attached to the bottom of a spindle connected to the wheel-head (so-called 'kick-wheel') by using a treadle, or in more recent times by attaching an independent power source. Fast wheels began to be used in MINOAN Crete about 2500 BC, and were used in Britain by about 100 BC. Potter's wheels were not used in the Americas until after European colonization.

pottery [Ma]. Clay that has been fashioned into a desired shape and then dried to reduce its water content before being fired or baked to fix its form. At temperatures of about

400 °C water begins to be lost from the molecules forming the clay and at this point
the clay cannot be returned to a plastic state
through rehydration. At around 1000 °C the
clay molecules begin to fuse, and at higher
temperatures still the minerals vitrify into a
solid mass.

Pottery is made in many different ways
either by hand or using a POTTER'S WHEEL.
Because of the widespread availability of usable clay, pottery was independently invented
in many parts of the world at different times.

pound [MC]. In medieval and later times in
Britain, an enclosure into which stray animals
that damaged crops or contravened manor
court regulations could be corralled. A fee had
to be paid to extract stock impounded in this
way.

Poverty Point, Louisiana, USA [Si]. Late
Archaic Stage ceremonial or communal gathering place on the Macon Ridge overlooking
the Mississippi floodplain near the
confluence of six rivers. The site comprises a
large earthwork some 1.8 km across and is
composed of six individual embankments. It
is semi-circular in plan, each of the six concentric earthworks being arranged in five
segments. The open side of the earthwork enclosure is closed by the line of the river. The
concentric earthworks are set 40 m apart,
each being capped with midden deposits up
to 1 m thick. It has been estimated that about
3 million work-hours would be needed to construct these earthworks, but their purpose is
not known.

In the centre is a massive plaza in and
around which were found numerous pieces
of burnt clay of unknown function. Several
mounds are also present at the site, the largest
21 m high and 183 m across.

[Rep.: J. A. Ford and C. H. Webb, 1956, *Poverty Point: A late
Archaic site in Louisiana*. New York: American Museum of
Natural History; J. L. Gibson, 1974, Poverty Point, the
first native American chiefdom. *Archaeology*, 27, 96–105]

Poverty Point Culture [CP]. Late Archaic
Stage hunting–gathering–farming communities flourishing in and around the lower
Mississippi Basin in the period 1700–700 BC.
Named after the type-site at Poverty Point,
Mississippi. Distinctive material culture includes clay balls, an elaborate microlithic industry, occasional clay figurines, and baked
clay vessels. Extensive trade networks are

suggested by the presence of steatite vessels
and the limited use of copper among other
luxuries. The subsistence base was dependent on hunting, the exploitation of riverine
resources, and some cultivation of native
plants.

Powell, John Wesley (1834–1902) [Bi].
American geologist, antiquarian and ethnographer well known as the first American
to traverse the Grand Canyon by boat. In
1879 the Smithsonian Institute's Bureau of
Ethnology was founded thanks to the lobbying of Powell, and he became its first Director.

[Bio.: D. D. Fowler and C. S. Fowler, 1969, John Wesley
Powell, anthropologist. *Utah Historical Quarterly*, 37(2),
152–72]

Powell, Thomas George Eyre (1916–75) [Bi].
British archaeologist with a special interest
in Neolithic chambered tombs and Celtic
culture. He was known by his nickname—
'Terence'—given him by his contemporaries
studying archaeology at Cambridge in the
mid 1930s. He was appointed to the Rankin
lectureship in Prehistoric Archaeology in
the School of Archaeological and Oriental
Studies in Liverpool University in 1948. From
1971 until his death he was Rankin Professor
of European Archaeology. Powell served as
President of the Prehistoric Society from 1970
until 1974. He was elected an FSA in March
1948.

[Obit.: *The Times*, 17 July 1975]

power [Th]. Generalized symbolic capacity to
make and make stick binding decisions on
behalf of a collectivity.

power elite [De]. Small networks of individuals who, according to the interpretation of
C. Wright Mills, hold concentrated power in
modern societies.

Pownall, Thomas (1722–1805) [Bi]. British
politician and amateur antiquarian interested in the representation of the past. Born in
Lincolnshire and educated in classics and philosophy at Trinity College, Cambridge, he obtained a post at the Board of Trade in 1743. In
1753 he was appointed personal assistant to
the Governor of New York, and in 1755 was
made Lieutenant-Governor of New Jersey.
Upon returning to England in 1760 he became
MP for Tregony in Cornwall. During the 1770s
and 1780s he published a series of articles in

Archaeologia and two books: *A treatise on the study of antiquities* (1782) and *An antiquarian romance* (1795). In these he explored the idea that the past can be reconstructed through the universal laws of human nature. Other themes that emerge from his writings include a concern for accuracy in recording antiquities, domestication, and the importance of separating fact from opinion. In this Pownall was one of the first to apply the ideas of the European Enlightenment to the field of archaeology.

[Bio.: B. Orme, 1974, Governor Pownall. *Antiquity*, 48, 116–24]

pozzolana [Ma]. A kind of waterproof and very strong concrete made using volcanic ash from Pozzuoli in central Italy. This kind of concrete hardens under water and was extensively used in the Roman world when making large outdoor structures such as jetties, harbour works, and water channels.

PPNA/PPNB [Ab]. *See* PRE-POTTERY NEOLITHIC.

praetentura [Co]. Latin term for the front division of a fort or camp, lying forward of the *via principalis*.

praetorium [Co]. Latin term for the general's tent in a camp, the residence of the commander in a fort or fortress, or the principal posting station of the *CURSUS PUBLICUS*.

Pre-Boreal Phase [Ge]. A biostratigraphic subdivision of the FLANDRIAN in which conditions were warmer and drier than in the preceding YOUNGER DRYAS. Godwin's POLLEN ZONE IV corresponds with the Pre-Boreal in Britain, marked by the development of birch forests in formerly tundra regions. The Pre-Boreal generally spans the period from *c*.8300 BC down to *c*.7700 BC in northern Europe.

preceptory [MC]. A monastery of the military orders of the Knights Templars and Knights Hospitallers (also known as the Knights of St John of Jerusalem). Preceptories included provisions for worship and communal living, but were founded to raise revenues to fund the 12th- and 13th-century AD crusades to the Holy Land. In the 15th century the Hospitallers directed their revenues towards defending Rhodes from the Turks. Each preceptory provided services and collected dues and voluntary contributions from their districts. In addition, the Templars' preceptories functioned as recruiting and training barracks for the knights. Those of the Hospitallers provided hospices which offered hospitality to pilgrims and travellers and distributed alms to the poor. Lazarine preceptories had leper hospitals attached.

Pre-Ceramic Stage [CP]. The earliest of seven main subdivisions of Andean prehistory, spanning the period 9000–1800 BC, embraces the time from the earliest human presence in the region down to the first use of ceramics. The Pre-Ceramic stage is usually divided into six subperiods. Subperiods I (before 9000 BC) and II (9500–8000 BC) are characterized by a hunting subsistence base. Subperiod III (8000–6000 BC is seen as transitional from just hunting to hunter-gatherer subsistence. Subperiod IV (6000–4000 BC) sees cyclical seasonal migrations. In subperiod V (4000–2500 BC) sedentary occupation sites first appear, as do monumental structures. In subperiod VI (2500–1800 BC) larger settlements are known and the first agriculture and ceremonial centres appear. The early Pre-Ceramic (I and II) is equivalent to the Palaeo-Indian Stage identified elsewhere in the Americas.

precision [Ge]. In archaeological science, precision is the degree to which random errors effect a set of measurements; high precision means that the overall random error is small and that replicated measurements will provide closely similar results. A random error in this sense is one which, when averaged, tends to zero as the number of measurements averaged is increased. High precision does not, therefore, mean that the measurements will necessarily be close to the true value; systematic errors may give low accuracy. In other words, precise results are not necessarily accurate results and vice versa. *Compare* ACCURACY.

Pre-Classic [CP]. *See* FORMATIVE.

predictive sampling [Te]. The use of existing models or literature searches to create a background knowledge about the location and extent of target populations. Such locations are then checked to determine presence or absence.

Pre-Dorset Culture [CP]. Archaic Stage hunter-gatherer communities living in northern areas of North America in the period

1700–900 BC. There is much debate about the relationship of Pre-Dorset Cultures to the Arctic Small Tool Tradition and other related groups. Although the question has not been solved, the matter of seasonality may underlie some of the apparent differences. Pre-Dorset groups relied heavily on seals for their subsistence, hunting them at their winter breathing holes. Musk ox, caribou, polar bears, and other smaller animals were hunted with harpoons and bows and arrows. Fish, especially Arctic char were caught in weirs and traps and taken using fish spears. Pre-Dorset communities used bone and ivory needles to make tailored clothing. They kept dogs, perhaps for hunting. Camps are generally coastal. Summer dwellings seem to have been tents weighted down by stones around the periphery. Winter dwellings may have been built from stone blocks like the familiar igloos of more recent times. Heat and light were provided by soapstone lamps burning seal fat. The Pre-Dorset culture evolved into the Dorset culture around 800–500 BC, continuity being evident in the tool kits, although Dorset assemblages generally include more ground stone items.

pre-dynastic [CP]. The period before the establishment of ruling dynasties and the emergence of a unified state in ancient Egypt c.3000 BC. The first ruler of all Egypt was MENES who forged a kingdom out of the previously incompatible elements of the people occupying Upper and Lower Egypt.

prefecture [De]. A unit of civic administration in early state societies such as the Tang and Sung dynasties of China.

prehistoric (prehistory) [De]. Generally referring to the time before written history assists understanding of the past. The term 'prehistory' was first introduced into the English language in 1851 by Daniel WILSON in the title of his book *The prehistoric annals of Scotland* (London: Macmillan). The French term *préhistorique* was in use from the 1830s to refer to the time before the appearance of writing.

prehistoric site [De]. An archaeological site dating to the period before literary, historical, archival, or recorded oral documentation for the period of use or the material culture it contains.

Prehistoric Society [Or]. Membership organization founded in 1935 devoted entirely to the study of prehistory. The society aims to advance education and promote interest in all branches of prehistory and allied subjects, and to promote the conservation of the archaeological heritage for the benefit of the public. Publications include the *Proceedings of the Prehistoric Society*.

prehistory [De]. *See* PREHISTORIC.

prepared core [De]. A nodule of flint, chert, obsidian, or other flakable stone that is deliberately shaped in order to allow the easy production of flakes or blades of a desired shape or size.

pre-pottery Neolithic (PPNA, PPNB, PPNC) [CP]. A term developed by Kathleen Kenyon during her excavations at Jericho, Israel, and subsequently widely used to refer to the earliest phase of the Neolithic in the Near East when agriculture was practised but pottery was not produced. Kenyon divided the early Jericho pre-pottery Neolithic into two phases: PPNA, broadly 8500–7600 BC, and PPNB, 7600–6000 BC. During the later of these, domesticated animals began to appear. Excavations at 'Ain Ghazal, Jordan, suggests that a third and final pre-pottery Neolithic can be defined, PPNC, at about 6200–5900 BC.

presbytery [Co]. The part of the church reserved for the officiating priests, mainly comprising the choir and other eastern portions of the building.

pressure flaking [De]. A method of stone-tool production in which small, narrow flakes or blades are removed from a core using pressure applied to it at the correct place, using the tip of an antler or a bone or wooden point. Pressure-removed flakes or blades show no obvious BULB OF PERCUSSION.

prestige [De]. The respect accorded to an individual or group by virtue of their status.

primary burial [De]. The first burial (inhumation or cremation) deposited before the construction of a covering barrow or monumental structure. *See also* SECONDARY BURIAL.

primary context [De]. An archaeological layer or deposit that is undisturbed and thus contains well-associated artefacts.

primary fill [De]. The first material to accumulate in the bottom of a pit or ditch after it has been constructed. In general such material comprises fine particulate deposits that result from the initial weathering of the sides and upper part of the feature together with any material deliberately thrown or placed in the bottom of it. Archaeologically it is generally accepted that any artefacts in the primary fill of a feature date to approximately the time of its construction or earlier.

Primary Neolithic [CP]. The term used by Stuart Piggott in 1954 to describe the earliest Neolithic of the British Isles, represented by the Windmill Hill Culture which was thought to represent intrusive farming groups. Although the term is sometimes used to refer to early farming groups in other areas too, it is essentially obsolete. *See also* SECONDARY NEOLITHIC.

primary silt [Ge]. *See* PRIMARY FILL.

principia [Co]. A Latin term for the headquarters building of a Roman FORT or FORTRESS, consisting of a courtyard surrounded by porticos on three sides, behind which lay ranges of rooms, and a cross-hall (*basilica principiorum*) on the fourth.

priory [MC]. *See* MONASTERY.

prismatic core [Ar]. A roughly rectangular block of flint prepared for the effective removal of long narrow blades by creating a striking platform at either end so that blades could be removed in alternate directions.

privy [MC]. A lavatory or earth closet in a shed or enclosure detached from the main dwelling, often situated at the end of the garden. Such facilities may have seating for up to four people at a time.

probe [Eq]. Thin metal rod used in PROBING.

probing [Te]. Method of exploring buried layers or structures using a thin metal probe pushed or hammered into the ground in the hope of making contact with the target object. Very useful for finding buried stones, ditches, and the extent of metalled surfaces below soft overburden.

processional door [Co]. The doors by which a monastic procession left the church (east) and re-entered it (west).

processual archaeology [Th]. Essentially, the NEW ARCHAEOLOGY of the late 1960s and 1970s, processual archaeology is grounded in a POSITIVIST view of the past and takes an essentially anthropological view of ancient societies. Drawing on earlier work in the field of biology, SYSTEMS THEORY became a dominant model in processual views of the past. In this, societies are seen as a series of subsystems interacting with each other and the environment in which the system is set. What interested processual archaeologists were the processes that prompted and thus explained change whether they were natural (e.g. climatic) or anthropogenic (e.g. population growth; agricultural intensification; accelerated trade). The overall aim was to move away from simply describing archaeological evidence towards trying to provide robust explanations for the patterns in it.

Procopius [Na]. Greek historian born around AD 500 who served with Belisarius in Persia, Africa, and Italy in the period AD 527–40. Prefect of Constantinople in 562. His *History of the Wars of Justinian* (completed before *c*.AD 551) contains much of what is known of the period and preserves many details of events outside its main theme. A parallel work, *The Secret History*, retraces the same ground, but as a continuous and violent attack on Justinian's policies. Procopius died in the mid 560s.

procurator [De]. A Roman civil administrator with responsibilities ranging from estate management to the governorship of minor provinces.

profane [De]. That which belongs to the mundane or everyday world, as opposed to the religious world.

professional archaeologist [Ge]. An individual who earns their living through working in the field of archaeology.

projectile point [Ar]. Stone, bone, or metal point made to strengthen the tip of a spear or arrow. Usually made of a material different from that of the shaft.

project management [Ge]. A project can be seen as a initiative or activity characterized by having a clearly defined aim which is linked to a set of objectives and fixed timescales, and is executed by a team of people. Project management is a collection of loosely connected techniques which are used to plan, implement, run, and bring projects to a successful conclusion.

promontory fort [MC]. A fortified enclosure constructed on a raised block of land that forms a promontory of some kind projecting out from a hillside or cliff line. The main defences cut off the neck of the promontory, the remainder of the perimeter having natural defensive capabilities.

pronaos [Co]. A small porch through which the cella of a Greek temple was entered and the cult statue approached.

prondnik [Ar]. An asymmetrical bifacially worked scraping tool found in Middle Palaeolithic assemblages in central Europe.

prone burial [De]. A burial in which the corpse has been deposited facing downwards into the ground. *See also* SUPINE BURIAL.

prophylactic [Ge]. Literally, 'intended to guard against (evil)'. Used, for example, to describe the eyes painted on either side of the handles of a wine-cup.

propylon (pl. propylaea) [Co]. In Greece, a dignified entrance between columns to a sanctuary, temple, agora, or a major building within an enclosure: an idea from Minoan architecture adapted by the Mycenaeans and retained in the classical period.

proskenion [Co]. The front of the low building which supported the stage in the developed Greek theatre.

proto- [De]. Prefix denoting the early development stage of some phenomenon.

Proto-Classic period [CP]. General term used in Maya areas to denote the period between the Pre-Classic and the Classic, that is *c*.50 BC–AD 250.

proto-geometric [De]. A style of Greek pottery, derived from sub-Mycenaean forms, common towards the end of the second millennium BC, which itself develops by the 9th century BC into the full geometric style in which zig-zag and meander designs are characteristic.

proto-historic [Ge]. **1.** Referring to a period when prehistoric communities in one area are in contact with groups in an adjacent area that use writing to create documents and texts that mention their neighbours. **2.** Referring to the period when a society begins to use writing to create records, documents, and texts about itself and the things it does.

proto-Neolithic [De]. The early stages in the adoption of characteristic Neolithic traits such as animal and plant domestication and the manufacture of pottery.

proton gradiometer [Eq]. *See* GRADIOMETER.

protruding foot beaker [Ar]. Type of late Neolithic ceramic vessel found in the Netherlands and lower Rhine Valley with a characteristic splayed neck, S-shaped profile, and everted flat base. Such pots are typically ornamented with cord impressed decoration mixed with comb impressions and herringbone-style incisions. These vessels probably provide the origins of the more widely distributed BELL BEAKER vessels.

provenance (provenience) [Ge]. The place where an object was found or recovered in modern times; the findspot.

proximal [De]. The place or end of something that is closest to its origin. Thus the proximal end of a bone is the end attached to the body.

prytaneion (prytaneum) [MC]. A Greek town hall in which a fire was always kept burning on the altar of Hestia as a sign of the city's continuity with its past.

pseudo-archaeology [Ge]. A broad spectrum of largely unconnected topics and approaches which misapply, misinterpret, and misrepresent archaeological material in a non-scientific and often speculative way. Such topics include the search for lost continents such as 'Atlantis', the idea that astronauts from other worlds visited earth in the past, and the existence of connections between sites that are represented as force fields or 'ley lines'.

Ptah [Di]. God of MEMPHIS in ancient Egypt, patron of crafts, guardian of artists and artisans, and often represented as a MUMMY.

PTD [Ab]. *See* PETIT-TRANCHET DERIVATIVE ARROWHEAD.

Ptolemy [Na]. The name used by all the kings who ruled Egypt in the period 304 BC to 30 BC. The founder of the dynasty was Ptolemy Lagus who was a general of Alexander the Great and who established himself in Egypt following the death of Alexander and the break-up of the Macedonian empire in 323 BC. Although Egypt was essentially a HELLENISTIC state during the Ptolemy period, many traditional forms of art and architecture were maintained and hieroglyphics were still used.

public archaeology [Ge]. *See* ARCHAEOLOGICAL RESOURCE MANAGEMENT.

pueblo [MC]. A Spanish word used to describe a type of stone or brick-built multi-roomed dwelling found in the southwest USA. Pueblos usually occur as a complex agglomeration of individual houses and other structures, sometimes on several levels. Many of the rooms were entered via a trap-door in the roof.

Pueblo Bonito, New Mexico, USA [Si]. An Anasazi pueblo village in the Chaco Canyon, probably the largest such pueblo known in the area. Excavated by George Pepper and Richard Wetherill in 1897–9, and again by Neil Judd on behalf of the National Geographic Society in 1921–7, the site comprises over 300 ground-floor rooms and 32 kivas covering an area of 1.2 ha.

Bonito was a planned settlement, set out in the form of a giant D with the back of the structure around the curve of the D so that it was built against the mesa cliff. The structure rises to four or five storeys and there are over 800 rooms in all.

At the focus of the pueblo was a large plaza in which was a great kiva flanked by rectangular rooms, possibly storerooms for food and ritual paraphernalia.

Two main phases of construction have been recognized: the earliest in the 10th century AD (Pueblo II), the second in the later 11th century AD (Pueblo III). The site seems to have been abandoned by AD 1200.

[Rep.: N. M. Judd, 1964, *The architecture of Pueblo Bonito*. Washington DC: Smithsonian Institution]

Pueblo Cultures [CP]. A general term used to describe culturally homogeneous but linguistically diverse agricultural communities of the Anasazi, Hohokam, and Mogollon cultures of southwestern parts of North America in the period after about AD 1400. The key feature of the Pueblo Tradition was the use of large settlements with multi-roomed, sometimes multi-storied houses, and some masonry construction.

At the 1927 Pecos Conference, five main stages to the Pueblo Tradition were identified. Pueblo I (AD 700–900) was represented by increased diversity of house types, improved ceramics, and the appearance of kivas. In Pueblo II (AD 900–1150) surface dwellings became the norm, pottery decoration changed, and multiroomed complexes began to appear. Pueblo III (AD 1100–1300) is marked by greater nucleation of the population in fewer but larger settlements, including cliff dwellings such as at Monte Verde. Pueblo IV (AD 1300–1600) saw the virtual abandonment of small villages and the concentration of population along the Rio Grande. Pueblo V (AD 1600–present) is the period of European contact.

pulsed induction meter [Eq]. A kind of metal detector used in geophysical surveying to detect primary metals and, under favourable conditions, shallowly buried features. A magnetic field is generated by a transmitted pulse in order to induce a magnetic moment in the soil and its contents. The magnetic moment continues to increase in magnitude while the field is maintained. When the magnetic field is removed at the end of the transmitted pulse, a small magnetic moment remains and the subsequent decay of this so-called magnetic viscosity induces a voltage in a receiver coil. The voltage induced is broadly proportional to the magnetic susceptibility of the soil and any materials in it at the point sampled. The technique is not very widely used.

pumpkin [Sp]. A trailing and climbing plant (*Cucurbita pepo*) with large lobed leaves and tendrils that produces a large rounded yellow-coloured fruit with a thick rind and edible flesh. Native to Southern Mexico and Guatemala. Domesticated by *c.*8000 BC. Introduced into Europe in the 16th century AD.

punch [Ar]. In flintworking a punch is generally a wooden or bone rod that directs the force applied to the top of the punch with a hammer to the desired point on the flint core in a very controlled way. In metalworking various types of punch are used. In cold working punches are mainly used to mark metal either in setting out designs or for the creation of decoration. In hot working a punch is generally a metal tool, round in cross-section and longitudinally tapered, which is used to make or enlarge holes in heated bars or sheets during forging.

punctuated equilibrium [Th]. A theory of social change which focuses on periods of continuity and relative stability (equilibrium) broken by phases of rapid change which upset the equilibrium. Thus such change need not be progressive or for the better in a purely developmental sense.

punctuating [De]. A type of decorative scheme, usually on ceramics, created by using a pointed implement to create small pits or holes in the surface.

Punuk Culture [CP]. Whale-hunting descendants of the Old Bering Sea Tradition of the Bering Strait area of North America flourishing in the period c.AD 500–1300.

purlin [Co]. A horizontal beam running along the length of a roof to support the rafters or roof-boards. The purlin is supported at the ends by gables and at various points along its length by crucks or frames.

Purron [CP]. Fifth main phase of activity in the Tehuacán Valley of Mexico, dating to the period 2300–1500 BC. Poorly represented archaeologically, although this is the time when pottery first appears.

putlog holes [Co]. Openings left in a wall for the insertion of scaffolding.

Putnam, Fredrick Ward (1839–1915) [Bi]. Distinguished American archaeologist, sometimes known as the 'father of American archaeology'. Born and raised in Salem, Massachusetts, Putnam was privately educated. After pursuing various interests in natural history he became, in 1868, Director of the Peabody Academy of Sciences in Salem. Here he remained until taking the post of curator of the Peabody Museum from 1875 to 1909. During this time he also became

Professor of American Archaeology and Ethnology at Harvard University from 1887 to 1909. Under Putnam, the Peabody Museum became a leading centre for research into early man in America. His main interests lay in two areas: the mounds of the Ohio Valley and the study of early man, and he carried out excavations at Madisonville and the Great Serpent Mound, both in Ohio.

[Bio.: A. M. Tozzer, 1935, Fredrick Ward Putnam. *National Academy of Sciences Biographical Memoirs*, 16.4]

Puuc style [De]. A florid style of architecture prevalent in, and named after, the Puuc region in the north-central Maya area of Mexico. Puuc buildings have facings of thin squares of limestone veneer over a cement and rubble core. Key features include boot-shaped vault stones, decorated cornices, round columns in doorways, engaged or half-columns in long rows, and the use of stone mosaics on the upper façades of buildings. Uxmal has one of the best collections of Puuc architecture.

puzzle jug [Ar]. A type of ceramic jug or pitcher from the 15th and 16th centuries AD in Europe, which is pierced in several places and is supposed to provide a challenge for the user in terms of which hole the contents will flow out of.

pygmy cup [Ar]. Small ceramic vessel in a range of shapes, but typically less than 50 mm high, found in early Bronze Age burials in northwestern Europe, usually in association with an urn of some kind. Also called incense cups and accessory vessels.

pylon [Co]. A monumental gateway at the entrance to Egyptian temples and palaces. Built of stone and usually decorated with relief figures and hieroglyphic inscriptions.

pyramid [MC]. Strictly speaking, a square-based structure with four triangular sides tapering to a point, as represented in the large stone examples found in Egypt. The term is also used for step-sided structures of pyramidal form found in Egypt and elsewhere in the world. In Egypt pyramids were used as monumental tombs, whereas in Mesopotamia, Mesoamerica, and South America they were temple platforms. The Egyptian pyramids developed out of simple mud-brick MASTABA tombs of the ARCHAIC PERIOD. During the OLD KINGDOM such tombs became more elaborate and bigger, and were increasingly built from stone. The earliest pyramid is the Step Pyramid of Sakkara. The largest and best-known pyramids are at Giza and were built by Cheops, Chephren, and Mykerinus in the 4th Dynasty. The Great Pyramid of Cheops has a base-side length of 230.4 m and was originally 146.6 m high. It is estimated that more than 2.5 million separate blocks of stone were used in its construction. Elaborate rituals accompanied the burial of a pharaoh in his pyramid, witnessed by the presence of elaborate temples connected to the pyramid itself.

pyramidal loomweight [Ar]. Style of stone or ceramic loomweight dating to the later Bronze Age in the British Isles. It has a flattish base and sloping sides with a single suspension hole towards the top. These loomweights were replaced in the Iron Age by triangular loomweights.

pyxis [Ar]. A type of vessel or box used in Greek times to hold trinkets, typically cylindrical in shape with a flat shoulder and lid.

Qadan [CP]. Mesolithic Stage communities living in Nubia in the upper Nile Valley prior to 9000 BC, at a time of relatively high water levels in the Nile, characterized by a diverse stone tool industry that is taken to represent increasing degrees of specialization and locally differentiated regional groupings. There is some evidence of conflict between the groups. The Qadan economy was based on fishing, hunting, and the extensive use of wild grain.

Qilakitsoq, Greenland [Si]. Burial ground beneath an overhanging rock on the west coast of Greenland where the mummified remains of eight people were excavated in 1972. The bodies, all women and children between the ages of six months and 50 years, had been buried in two graves between AD 1425 and 1525. The quality of preservation was high because of mummification through natural freeze-drying, with the clothing largely intact and the remains of the last meal in the stomach of one. Five of the adults had facial tattoos. All the bodies belonged to the archaeologically defined THULE Culture.

[Rep.: J. P. Hart Hansen, J. Meldgaard and J. Nordqvist, 1985, The mummies of Qilakitsoq. *National Geographic*, 167(2), 190–207]

Qin [CP]. Eastern ZHOU state centred on the Wei River Valley of Shaanxi Province in China; also the name of the dynasty founded after the Qin state had been conquered and absorbed into the rest of China, broadly the period 221–206 BC. The first emperor of the dynasty was Qin Shihuangdi with his capital at Xianyang near Chang'an. He was buried in a large mounded tomb near Xian City which is believed to contain a scale model of the palace, rivers of mercury, and cocked crossbows ready to deter plunderers. A terracotta army of over 7000 life-sized soldiers made at his instigation and buried in three large pits

near the tomb was discovered in 1974. The name 'China' derives from the name of the Qin Dynasty which was the first dynasty to unite under single rule most of the area later regarded as the state of China.

Qing [CP]. Manchu Dynasty that ruled China from AD 1644 to 1911.

Quadi [CP]. Germanic tribe, associated in the 2nd century AD and later with the MARCOMANNI, and a constant threat to the Roman frontier of the Danube. During the 5th century AD some Quadi joined the VANDALS and ALANS in the conquest of Spain.

quadrangular castle [MC]. Strongly fortified residence of stone or brick build around a square or rectangular courtyard known as a 'ward'. The outer walls formed the defensive line of 'enceinte' and towers would usually be placed at the corners and sometimes in intermediate positions too. Some very strongly fortified castles of this class have an additional wall set a short distance out from the main enceinte and concentric with it, the area between the two walls being termed the outer ward. Moats, either wet or dry, often encircle the walls. Accommodation within the castle was provided in the towers or in buildings set against the walls and opening into the ward. Quadrangular castles were the strongly defended residences of the king or a lord, situated for offensive as well as defensive operations, and often acting as an administrative centre. Most were built in the 14th century AD, although they continued to be built and used through into the early 15th century. Amongst the best examples in Britain are Bodiam, Sussex, and Castle Bolton, Yorkshire.

quadrant excavation (quadrant method) [Me]. A system of excavating circular or near-circular archaeological sites and features such as round barrows, ring cairns, pits, or round houses where the entity to be examined is divided into four equal sectors or quadrants. The removal of two alternate quadrants provides a complete transverse section along each of the major axes and thus allows good control over the stratigraphy. Variations in the method include leaving cross baulks along the main axes and staggering the baulks so that complete sections are retained while the central area is excavated.

quadrat [De]. A rectangular area defined for data collection or analysis within a sampling scheme.

Quanterness, Orkney, Scotland [Si]. Developed passage grave on the Orkney island of Mainland extensively excavated by Colin Renfrew in 1972–4. The mound was circular in plan, 30 m in diameter, and up to 3.2 m high. In the centre was a rectangular chamber 6.1 m by 1.6 m, with a corbel-vaulted roof and six side cells opening from it. The chamber was approached by a narrow passage from the east. Within the excavated part of the chamber were the disarticulated remains of 157 individuals; multiplied up to take account of the areas not excavated, there may have been as many as 400 individuals represented in the tomb. Renfrew suggests that the tomb was used by a small egalitarian community, perhaps an extended family, over a period of up to 1000 years.

[Rep.: C. Renfrew, 1979, *Investigations in Orkney*. London: Society of Antiquaries]

quantification [Ge]. The measurement of key defined attributes and dimensions of an object, assemblage, or site in order to characterize it and allow comparisons to be made with other similarly quantified material. Comparisons are often based on statistical analysis of the populations under study.

quarry [MC]. Extraction pits, worked exposures, mines, and other kinds of working areas where natural substances and raw materials such as stone, flint, or metal ores were obtained.

quarter stater [Ar]. Small denomination coin of the later Iron Age in Europe.

quartz [Ma]. Opaque white crystalline silicate stone found in many parts of the world and variously used for toolmaking and in ceremonial contexts. In Atlantic Europe white quartz pebbles were used as talismans, perhaps representing the soul of a person, from the early Neolithic through into early Christian times. White quartz is frequently found deposited around STONE CIRCLES and PASSAGE GRAVES.

Quartzite is a metamorphic rock consisting mainly of quartz which was also used for making tools and weapons, as it is hard and has conchoidal fracturing properties just like flint.

Quaternary system [CP]. A major chronostratigraphic subdivision; the latest of the two PERIODS forming the Cenozoic era (the other is the TERTIARY), itself composed of two epochs, the PLEISTOCENE and the HOLOCENE. These terms can be applied to groups of deposits (geostratigraphic subdivisions) as the Quaternary 'system' embracing Pleistocene or Holocene 'series'. The Quaternary system, beginning about 2.4 million years ago, comprises a number of elements that were once seen as a succession of glacial and INTERGLACIAL episodes. Deep-sea cores and the analysis of deep-ocean sediments now show this view to be overly simplistic.

quatrefoil [De]. Leaf shape comprising four elements or petals radiating from a common centre.

Quechua [Ge]. Language of the Incas, called by them Runa Simi, and still spoken in several dialects in the Andean regions of Peru and Bolivia.

Queen Anne style architecture [De]. Relating mainly to the period 1702–14, this style was characterized by the use of red brick, sash windows, and hipped roofs disguised behind parapets. The style was revived in the Victorian period.

queen post [Co]. Type of timber roof structure in which a pair of uprights (queen posts) rest on a horizontally set tie-beam to support a horizontally set collar connected to the purlins and rafters of the main roof.

queer archaeology (queer theory) [Th]. An approach to the recovery, interpretation, and presentation of archaeological data and knowledge in a way that actively and explicitly challenges the heteronormativity of scientific practice by seeking to take the perspective of anyone who feels marginalized sexually, intellectually, or culturally. It is not a system of theory to explain something; rather it is an alternative to normative archaeological discourse.

quenching [De]. In metalworking, the plunging of a red-hot iron implement into cold water or brine to harden it.

Quentovic, Boulogne-sur-Mer, France [Si]. Important trading port, inland from modern-day Etaples on the north French coast, that flourished in the early medieval period. The Quentovic mint began in the early 7th century AD and in the following two centuries was one of the most important in the CAROLINGIAN empire. Quentovic was attacked by Vikings several times and by the 11th century it was abandoned in favour of more easily fortified sites nearby.

[Rep.: D Hill *et al.*, 1990, Quentovic defined. *Antiquity*, 64, 51–8]

quern [Ar]. A hand-operated device used for grinding corn to produce flour. Querns consist of two coarse stones (quernstones), usually granite, sandstone, or a conglomerate, set one above the other and rubbed together with the corn in between. The lower stone is usually fixed and stationary while the upper stone is moved either in a rotary motion (ROTARY QUERN) or by a push–pull motion (SADDLE QUERN). Mechanical querns operated with the help of animal, water, or wind power are referred to as MILLS. *See also* METATE.

quernstone [Ar]. *See* QUERN.

Quetzalcóatl [Di]. Widely recognized deity known in many parts of Mesoamerica in Olmec, Toltec, Maya, Teotihuacan, and Aztec times. Usually depicted as the feathered serpent, but god of many things including the wind, the morning star, and the evening star. In Aztec cosmology Quetzalcóatl was the creator god of learning and patron of the arts, agriculture, and science. In Aztec legend Quetzalcóatl or a historical figure closely associated with him was banished from Mexico in *c*.AD 987, but in leaving he promised to return. This promise became so bound up in Aztec mythology that in AD 1519 when Cortez and his Spanish conquistadors arrived in Mexico he was regarded for a time as the returning deity.

quicklime [Ma]. A white caustic alkaline substance (calcium oxide) used in making mortar. It is made by heating or burning limestone in a LIMEKILN.

Quimbaya Culture [CP]. Late prehistoric communities flourishing in western Columbia, South America, in the period AD 300–1600. Quimbaya ceramics are sometimes decorated with incised lines and negative painting. These communities are also known for their fine goldwork.

quinoa [Sp]. Herb (*Chenopodium quinoa*) which attains a height of 1.5 m. The small green clustered flowers are succeeded by small fruits each containing a single seed. The seeds are boiled to make a kind of gruel called carapulque. Native to the Pacific slopes of the Andes over about 2400 m above sea level in South America. Possibly locally domesticated by *c*.6000 BC, but in general, not widely domesticated until *c*.AD 500.

quinquereme [Ar]. A Roman or Hellenistic warship which was larger and more powerful than its predecessor, the trireme.

quipu [Ar]. A thick cord from which was suspended a series of knotted strings, sometimes of different colours. This was used by the Inca as a mnemonic device to keep imperial records, the position, size, colour, and position of each knot having a special meaning. A special hereditary group of state functionaries, the *quipucamayocs*, memorized the history, myths, and statistical information symbolized by the knots and recited them to state officials.

quoin [Co]. Large dressed stones forming the angle of a building, usually carefully placed and set by skilled masons, while the general walling between was raised by less skilled or experienced craftsmen.

quoit [MC]. Local Cornish name for a PORTAL DOLMEN.

quoit beads (quoit-shaped beads) [Ar]. Doughnut-shaped type of early Bronze Age FAIENCE bead.

quoit brooch [Ar]. Ornate circular Anglo-Saxon brooch of the early 5th century AD, distinctive in being essentially a penannular brooch to which has been added a wide decorative plate with a round hole in the middle.

quoit-headed pin [Ar]. Middle Bronze Age pin typical of the Ornament Horizon in north-west Europe (British Taunton Phase) comprising a thin shank with a point at one end and a large, rather ostentatious, ring cast onto the shank at the other.

Quynh-van, Vietnam [Si]. A substantial early Neolithic shell midden on the coast of northern Vietnam south of the Red River delta near Vinh. The midden is over 5 m thick and dates to about 3000 BC, perhaps a late variant of the local Hoabinhian Culture. A flaked stone industry, cordimpressed pottery, ceramic net weights, and grinding stones have been found in the midden, together with contracted burials. The faunal remains include wild deer, cattle, pig, dog, and elephant, all presumably hunted.

[Sum.: K. Taylor, 1983, *The birth of Vietnam*. Berkeley: University of California Press]

Ra (Re) [Di]. The supreme god of ancient Egypt who takes the form of the sun and is closely connected with the king. Head of the Ennead of Heliopolis. His dead form is represented as a ram-headed man in a shrine. Ra was often syncretized with other gods to give them a solar aspect and to enhance their importance, as with Amun-Ra, Sobek-Ra, or Ra-Harakhte (Horus-of-the-horizon).

rabbit warren [MC]. *See* WARREN.

rabotage [Te]. Excavation technique in which the surface of a deposit is carefully scraped with a trowel, knife, or sharp spade to reveal features and cuts represented by differences in texture, colour, or composition. The technique is especially useful in silty and sandy soils. *See also* SPIT.

race [Ge]. Differences in human physical stock regarded as the basis for categorizing large-scale human groups. Although a concern of much antiquarian investigation during the 19th century, it is not a major focus of modern archaeological research.

racloir [Ar]. Type of side scraper distinctive of MOUSTERIAN assemblages. Such tools probably functioned as both a knife and a scraper.

racquet pin [Ar]. Style of bronze pin shaped like a tennis racquet with a flat oval piece attached to a thin pointed shaft. Products of the early Bronze Age industrial traditions in the British Isles.

radiate [Ar]. Type of Roman imperial coinage on which the emperor is depicted wearing a radiate or solar crown, typical of the 3rd century AD. *See also* BARBAROUS RADIATE.

radiate brooch [Ar]. General term referring to bow-brooches with a semi-circular headplate decorated with a row of radiating knobs. Two major types are the radiate brooch with a straight-sided footplate (found in Frankish territories) and that with a lozenge-shaped footplate (found in Lombardic contexts).

radiocarbon dating [Te]. A technique for determining the absolute date of organic matter developed by Willard LIBBY in 1949 and based on the fact that all living organisms contain a small but constant proportion of the radioactive isotope of carbon, ^{14}C. When the organism dies the ^{14}C is no longer replenished from the environment and what is present at the time of death decays at a constant rate. The half-life of ^{14}C was calculated by Libby as being 5568 years. By measuring the radioactivity of the carbon remaining in a specimen its age can be calculated; radiocarbon determinations (usually expressed as an age BP or as RCYBP) have to be calibrated using curves derived from tree-ring chronologies to give calendar dates (usually expressed as BC/AD or cal.BC/cal.AD). Radiocarbon dating is useful back to about 70 000 years ago.

radiography [Te]. *See* X-RADIOGRAPHY.

radiometric dating [Ge]. Blanket term used to refer to methods of providing absolute dates for archaeological materials based on the decay of radioactive isotopes. *See* RADIOCARBON DATING; URANIUM SERIES DATING; and POTASSIUM–ARGON DATING.

RAE [Ab]. *See* RESEARCH ASSESSMENT EXERCISE.

Raedwald [Na]. King of the East Angles, who accepted Christianity at the prompting of AETHELBERHT of Kent, though continuing to worship his old gods. He was recognized as Bretwalda, 'high king', of the English. It is likely, though not certain, that the great ship-burial of Sutton Hoo, Suffolk, was the tomb of Raedwald. He died *c*.AD 625.

Raetian mortarium [Ar]. Orange mortarium usually with lug handles, an angular cut-out spout and a glossy red-brown slip applied only on the top of the flange, rim, and the internal concave moulding. The tradition stemmed ultimately from the continent, with factories known in Raetia. Most examples in Britain were locally made in kilns such as those at Holt, Wilderspool, Carlisle, and southwest Scotland.

RAI [Ab]. *See* ROYAL ARCHAEOLOGICAL INSTITUTE.

raised beach [Ge]. An ancient shore-line formed at a time when the sea level was higher than it is today. As the sea level went down the former beach was left behind and may in some cases be far inland of the present shore.

raised granary [MC]. Wooden, brick, or stone-built structure used for storing grain or other crops built on stilts or legs of some kind to raise it off the ground. This allows the grain to be kept drier through the circulation of air below the floor and to be better protected from vermin. In England, medieval raised granaries were supported on mushroom-shaped **staddle stones**.

Rajagriha, Pakistan [Si]. Ancient city of the Ganges civilization, capital of the Magadha kingdom, now under the modern city of Rajgir. Early remains include a stone rampart of the 6th century BC. In later times the city was frequently visited by the Buddha and a series of elliptical structures may represent the remains of his Jivikarama monastery.

[Sum.: M. H. Kuraishi, 1951, *Rajgir*. Delhi: Department of Archaeology]

Ramapithecus [Sp]. Miocene-period hominid species dating to between *c.*15–6 million years ago generally believed to be ancestral to the AUSTRALOPITHECUS of *c.*5–1.5 million years ago and thus at the head of the sequence of hominid evolution that results in *Homo sapiens*. Ramapithecus was a small ape-like hominid that spent more time in the trees than on the ground; fossil remains have been found as far apart as Fort Ternan, Kenya, and the Siwalik Hills, India.

Ramesses–(Ramses) [Di]. The name used by two pharaohs of the 19th Dynasty and nine in the 20th Dynasty of ancient Egypt. Ramses II,

who reigned between *c.*1290 and 1224 BC, devoted much time to protecting Egypt's boundaries against Hittite invasions, and also carried out much building work, including the construction of the fine temples at ABU SIMBEL. Ramses III defeated invasions by the SEA PEOPLES and in *c.*1170 BC the Libyans.

rampart [Co]. Technically an elongated bank or wall forming the defensive boundary of an enclosure. Most ramparts are associated with external ditches that provide an extra component of the defensive structure. The construction of ramparts varies considerably from simple mounds of earth and stone (dump ramparts) to elaborate structures involving timber frameworks (box ramparts and timber-laced ramparts), and stone revetted walls. Sometimes a stone rampart may be deliberately burnt to increase its strength and stability (vitrified ramparts). The size of many prehistoric and later ramparts means that they frequently preserve substantial areas of old ground surface that reflect local conditions in the period up to the time the rampart was built.

Ramses [Di]. *See* RAMESSES.

Rams Hill, Oxfordshire, England [Si]. A multi-period enclosure site on the Berkshire Downs of south Oxfordshire overlooking the Vale of the White Horse and the middle Thames Valley. Extensively excavated between 1972 and 1975 by Richard Bradley and Ann Ellison, the site has four main structural phases and is critical for understanding the early development of hillforts in southern Britain. The earliest phase dates to the early 12th century BC and comprised a stone-faced dump rampart inside a chalk-cut ditch that defined a roughly oval-shaped enclosure of about 1 ha. There were probably two or three entrances. In phase 2, the late 12th century BC, a timber-laced rampart was constructed to replace the earlier defences. In the third phase, around the beginning of the 10th century BC, a double palisade was built on top of the former, by this time mainly silted-up, ditch. In the final phase, dated to the 7th century BC, a much larger enclosure of 3.5 ha was built around the hilltop in the style of early hillforts.

[Rep.: R. Bradley and A. Ellison, 1975, *Ram's Hill: a Bronze Age defended enclosure and its landscape*. Oxford: British Archaeological Reports British Series 19]

ranch boundary [MC]. *See* LINEAR BOUNDARY.

random sampling [Te]. A method of selecting examples to study in which every case in the target population has an equal chance of being chosen. This is usually achieved by using a random number table or number generator to select cases to examine.

ranging rod [Eq]. A wooden or metal pole with a point at one end, marked up in equal-sized units (usually feet or half-metres) painted in contrasting colours. Essentially a piece of surveying equipment, ranging rods are often used by archaeologists to provide scale in photographs of features and structures.

rank-size analysis [Th]. A form of regional analysis that attempts to determine whether any settlement or defined place varies from a predicted linear pattern of rank in relation to size.

rapier [Ar]. An offensive weapon typical of the European middle Bronze Age with a relatively narrow blade typically 40–50 cm long and a simple butt onto which a hilt could be riveted. Essentially an elongated dagger used for thrusting.

rath [MC]. *See* RINGWORK.

Ravenna, Italy [Si]. Ancient city of the Adriatic coast of northern Italy well known for its wealth and position in the late Roman and Byzantine world. In 402 AD the official royal residence of the western exarchate of the Byzantine empire was moved from Milan to Ravenna, the city rising to great importance during the reign of Theodoric (AD 498–526). During this time many new churches and public buildings were constructed, drawing on the architectural styles of the Middle East as well as traditional western Roman forms. Major buildings include the tomb of Galla Placidia of about AD 450, and the basilicas of St Apollinare Nuovo and St Apollinare in Classe. Especially notable are the numerous mosaics on the floors and walls of these buildings.

[Sum.: G. B. Montanari, 1983, *Ravenna e il porto di classe. Venti anni di ricerche archeologiche tra Ravenna e classe.* Bologna: Bologna University Press]

Rawlinson, Lt. Col. Sir Henry Creswicke (1810–95) [Bi]. British army officer, diplomat, and amateur archaeologist who was instrumental in deciphering the CUNEIFORM languages of western Asia. Born in Oxford, he demonstrated a remarkable command of languages and he was appointed an officer cadet in the East India Company in 1827. In 1833 he was one of a party of British officers sent to help reorganize the shah of Persia's army. Posted to Kurdistan, he set about trying to decipher King Darius's trilingual inscription on the Great Rock of Bisitun. First producing a translation of the Persian text, by 1857 he also had a version of the Babylonian text. In 1843 was appointed British consul in Baghdad and this allowed extra time for his studies, especially work on cuneiform tablets found at Assyrian cities such as Nimrud and Nineveh. Although Rawlinson produced some academic papers detailing his work, in later life he moved into politics, becoming an MP and later a minister to the Iranian court.

[Bio.: G. Rawlinson, 1898, *A memoir of Major-General Sir H. C. Rawlinson.* London: Longman Green]

razor [Ar]. A type of tool known from the European Bronze Age which comprises a thin bronze blade, often double-edged, which is believed to have been used for removing facial or body hair. A number of different styles can be recognized including bi-fid, horseshoe, Hallstatt, Scandinavian Terramara, quadrangular, and crescentic forms.

RCAHMS [Ab]. *See* ROYAL COMMISSIONS.

RCAHMW [Ab]. *See* ROYAL COMMISSIONS.

RCHM (RCHM(E)/RCHME) [Ab]. *See* ROYAL COMMISSIONS.

RCYBP [Ab]. Radiocarbon years before present. *See* RADIOCARBON DATING and CONVENTIONAL RADIOCARBON AGE.

Re [Di]. *See* RA.

reamer [Ar]. A blacksmith's tool in the form of a tapered square-sectioned rod that is used to expand a hole in a piece of thin or soft metal by rotating the reamer in the hole while pushing down on the top.

reaping hook [Ar]. Iron tool in the form of a long slightly curved knife, usually with a single blade on the inner face of the curve, used for harvesting cereals, grass, or reeds.

reave [Co]. Local name found on Dartmoor in southwestern England for low banks and walls, perhaps once capped with hedges, forming the boundaries of Bronze Age field systems. Such boundaries are typically 0.5–1.0 m high and up to 2 m across.

Recarred [Na]. Visigoth king, who succeeded his father Leovigild in 586 and in the next year was baptized a Christian. In 589 he summoned a council at Toledo which marked the end of official **Arianism** in Spain. Died c.AD 601.

reciprocity [De]. In archaeology this refers to exchanges between individuals or communities who are symmetrically placed, that is they are exchanging things more or less as equals: a sort of gift exchange. One gift does not have to be followed by another at once, but an obligation is created every time a gift is given and this needs to be reciprocated. Anthropologist Marshall Sahlins suggests that amongst close kin gifts are freely given with no expectation of return (positive reciprocity); within a wider kin network gifts are given and there is a general expectation of return in roughly equal measure (balanced reciprocity); while outside the kin group gifts are given to strangers or other communities with the hope that you exchange partner will return something better (negative reciprocity).

reconstruction [De]. Literally, to construct again; in the archaeological context this is taken to mean the rebuilding of something using non-original materials but to a design or pattern that is well established. This applies to structures and artefacts. Thus in the case of a ruined Roman villa it may be appropriate to reconstruct the main walls of the building to a certain height, using the original foundations and re-using the stone present in the excavated collapsed remains of the original wall. It would not be appropriate, however, to reconstruct the roof of that same building because it is not known exactly what it was like. When carrying out reconstruction it is normal to discretely mark the boundary between the original construction and the reconstruction for future reference. The main aim of reconstruction is usually a combination of preservation and presentation.

A variation on conventional reconstruction is experimental reconstruction within the context of EXPERIMENTAL ARCHAEOLOGY. Here, all available archaeological evidence is used to propose the nature of the original structure which is then reconstructed to see whether it could in fact have been like that and what the alternatives might be.

recorded site [Ge]. An archaeological site or monument which has been identified, located, and documented by a professional archaeologist or other trained individual, details of which have been lodged with a recognized archaeological record or inventory of some kind.

recording system [Te]. A systematic and structured set of procedures for creating a record of archaeological excavations or fieldwork. These will generally provide for descriptive accounts of the stratigraphic units examined (context records/feature records, etc.), together with a means of linking these to the finds recovered and samples taken (finds index, samples index, etc.); photographic and video records; drawings, plans, and sections; audio tapes and spoken commentaries; and the daybooks and logs maintained by the director, supervisors, and key specialists. Most large excavation units have established recording systems which variously use manual and computerized logging of data and information.

recreation [De]. Literally, to create again something that once existed or is believed to have existed but which no longer survives. In archaeology this usually involves making what is essentially a replica of something based on research and the examination of similar examples elsewhere. Most recreations involve the application of imagination, some far more than others. All, however, reflect the contemporary understanding of what it is they are trying to recreate.

recumbent stone circle [MC]. Type of STONE CIRCLE of Aubrey Burl's late period characterized by the presence of a large recumbent slab set between a pair of flanking pillars which are usually the tallest stones in the ring. The pillars are graded in height, gradually reducing in size with distance away from the recumbent. This type of stone circle dates to the later Neolithic and early Bronze Age and is concentrated in eastern Scotland and south-west Ireland.

red deer [Sp]. Large four-hoofed grazing mammal (*Cervus elaphus*) native to northern Europe and extensively hunted during late Upper Palaeolithic, Mesolithic, and Neolithic times. The antlers of the males are shed and replenished annually and during prehistoric and later times were widely collected and taken from hunted animals for use in toolmaking.

red-figure ware [Ar]. Style of Attic pottery characteristic of the 5th and 4th centuries BC, being introduced in the last quarter of the 6th, in which the scene is depicted in the red fabric of the ware itself, and the background is infilled in black.

Red God [Di]. Egyptian god. *See* SETH.

red hill [MC]. Local name found in East Anglia, England, for mounds of burnt clay, ash, and broken ceramic materials resulting from coastal salt production during later prehistoric and Roman times. *See* SALTERN.

redistribution systems [Ge]. The dispersal of trade goods from a central place throughout a society, a complex process that was a critical part of the evolution of civilization.

Red Lady of Paviland [Si]. *See* PAVILAND CAVE.

red polished ware [Ar]. Type of pottery produced in south Asia in the early 1st millennium AD characterized by a red or orange slip that is burnished to produce a glossy surface. Such wares are found along coastal regions of northwest India as well as inland further south. They have sometimes been confused with imported Roman ceramics, but the forms are very different.

reduced ware [Ar]. A fabric in which the iron oxide in the clay is in a low state of oxidation. It is produced when the final stages of heating and cooling are carried out without oxygen, which is removed from the solid compounds, resulting in a grey or black colour. Pottery can be partly reduced (indicated by colour differences between the surface and the core of the fabric) or unevenly reduced (indicated by colour differences on the surface of a vessel).

reductionism [Th]. The general principle that complicated phenomena can be explained by conceptually reducing them to a set of simple variables. This is often linked to essentialist or socio-biological approaches.

reeding [De]. The regular horizontal grooving on the flange of some types of mortaria and on the rim of some types of bowl.

refectory [Co]. The hall or room in which meals were taken in a monastic establishment.

refitting [Te]. The reassembly of conjoining stone or flint debitage and cores to reconstruct ancient lithic technologies and core reduction strategies.

reflex bow [Ar]. A small but powerful bow made such that, until strung, the ends of the bow project forwards rather than backwards.

Regency style [De]. Decorative or architectural style current from about AD 1810 to 1839. Succeeded by Victorian architecture.

region [De]. A geographically defined area in which ecological adaptations are basically similar.

Register of Professional Archaeologists (ROPA) [Or]. Established in 1998 as the successor to the SOCIETY OF PROFESSIONAL ARCHAEOLOGISTS, ROPA is the professional archaeological institute in America. Its aim is to establish, support, and maintain professional and ethical standards in all aspects of archaeological work. It offers a certification process whereby professional archaeologists, students, teachers, amateur archaeologists, and all those interested in archaeological education and research can become registered archaeologists. In doing so they agree to abide by a set of ethical codes and research standards. Registration allows the use of the distinction RPA.

regular enclosed field system [MC]. *See* FIELD SYSTEM.

regular open field system [MC]. *See* FIELD SYSTEM.

Reiche, Maria (1903–98) [Bi]. Self-taught archaeologist who for more than 50 years studied the enigmatic Nasca lines of the Peruvian desert. Born in Dresden, Reiche read mathematics and geography at Hamburg and Dresden universities before moving to Peru in 1932 to become governess to the German consul's children at Cuzco. After years of studying the Nasca lines, she concluded that they represented a giant calendar linked to the movements of the sun, moon, and constellations. In 1993 she was awarded the Order of the Sun by the Peruvian government.

[Obit.: *The Times*, 13 June 1998]

reihengraberfeld [MC]. A classic form of graveyard dating to the 5th through to the 7th centuries AD in France, West Germany, and the Low Countries in which burials were made in individual trenches in neat rows. Such cemeteries are often found some distance from a settlement beside a river on a south-facing slope. In such cemeteries men were traditionally buried with one or more weapons and women with their brooches, hairpins, and items of dress.

reindeer [Sp]. Large four-hoofed mammal (*Rangifer tarandus*) that generally roams in large herds over the Arctic and tundra regions of the northern hemisphere. Archaeological evidence from the Middle Palaeolithic through to modern times shows that hunting communities reliant on this species as a source of food and materials are part of an extremely long-lived tradition. Reindeer were also used domestically to draw sledges and as a source of milk.

Reinecke, Paul (1872–1958) [Bi]. German prehistorian whose periodization of the European Bronze and Iron Ages published between 1902 and 1911 still provide the basic classificatory schemes for a substantial body of material. Largely on the basis of typology he divided the early and middle Bronze Age into four divisions: Reinecke A to D. He also recognized the essential continuity of the late Bronze Age through into the Iron Age of central Europe and applied the term HALLSTATT to this period. The Hallstatt was likewise subdivided into four phases A to D. Subsequent revisions to the essential sequence now suggest a degree of overlap between Reinecke D and Hallstatt A.

[Obit.: *Revue Archéologique de L'est et du Centre-est*, 10 (1959), 160–4]

Reisner, George Andrew (1867–1942) [Bi]. American Egyptologist best known for his well-recorded excavations. Born in Indianapolis, he attended Harvard University to study law but soon transferred to study Semitic languages. He won a scholarship that allowed him to travel to Berlin, and here he met the Egyptologist Kurt Sethe who fired his interest in the topic. On returning to Harvard he took up a lectureship in the School of Semitic Languages. In 1897 he was invited to join an international team compiling a catalogue of material in the Cairo Museum, and from this time on he spent much of his time in Egypt. In 1910 he became curator of the Department of Egyptian Art at the Boston Museum, and by this time he had already started excavations in Egypt. He was a methodical excavator who prided himself on the records he kept. His early work focused on Qift, Deir el-Ballas, and Naga ed Deir. Later he worked at Giza to explore the enclosure of the Third Pyramid, his most sensational discovery being the burial of Queen Hetepheres, mother of Cheops. He directed an archaeological survey of Nubia in 1907 when the first Aswan Dam was raised, and from 1916 to 1923 he explored the pyramids of Meroe in the Sudan. He died in Cairo after suffering from increasing blindness over many years.

[Bio.: *American National Biography*, 18, 328–9]

relative dating [Te]. Determining the age of a specimen relative to its position in a stratigraphic or topological sequence based on the principles of superposition or artefact ordering.

relativism [Th]. **1.** The claim that there is no knowledge independent of an individual, and that all knowledge is created within a cultural system. It therefore follows that there can be no absolute or independent means of judging between different knowledge claims, including science. However, such relativism is self-refuting since what it states about knowledge must equally apply to that claim itself. In contrast, a relativist position which stops with the argument that knowledge is constructed and is temporally and spatially located does not necessarily have these problems. Relativism is a charge often directed against post-processual archaeologists; it is a primary concern of the constructivist philosophy of science. **2.** The belief that all accounts of the past are equally valid in their own terms, there being no neutral or objective way to judge between them. **3.** The view that other cultures are no better or worse than any other, they are simply different.

relic 1. [Ar]. A personal memorial of a holy person, either a piece of clothing or some other item associated with a saint, or a part of the saint's body, preserved and revered as an inspiration to piety. Relics might be displayed to pilgrims, and were collected by them and kept safe in reliquaries (suitably shaped caskets), which were frequently ornately decorated. It was widely believed that spiritual value could be transmitted through the relics of a person who in life was blessed with miraculous powers. Accordingly, relics had an economic as well as a religious importance since important pieces would attract numerous pilgrims. **2.** [Ge]. A synonym for the more technical term 'artefact'.

relict cultural landscape [Ge]. At its simplest such a landscape can be seen as a piece of natural or artificial scenery containing remains relating to a particular form, stage, or type of intellectual development or civilization which exists now in the same pattern or arrangement as in some previous age. In defining such areas such questions as the scale of what is represented and the integrity of the elements that survive need to be addressed.

relieving-arch [Co]. An arch built as part of a solid wall to take the weight of the construction above by diverting it away from weak points such as doors and windows lower down.

reliquary [Ar]. A specially constructed case or box in which RELICS were stored or exhibited. Because of the importance and significance of the relics themselves many reliquaries are extremely ornate and constructed with the lavish use of rare and precious materials.

remnant magnetism [Te]. *See* ARCHAEOMAGNETIC DATING.

remote sensing [Te]. General term referring to a group of techniques used for the detection of hidden archaeological features. *See* AERIAL PHOTOGRAPHY, GEOPHYSICAL SURVEY.

rendering [Ge]. A coating of clay, plaster, or a lime–sand mix applied to an external stone,

brick, or timber wall face to create a relatively smooth surface and make it weatherproof.

rendzina soil [Ge]. A relatively thin soil consisting of an almost black calcareous mull humus formed entirely of worm casts lying on relatively unaltered calcareous rock. Erosion caused by the movement of groundwater widens cracks in the underlying bedrock to allow plant roots to penetrate into the subsoil and strata beneath.

Renenutet (Ernutet) [Di]. Egyptian serpent goddess who was the protectress of the harvest and of agriculture in general.

repatriation [Th]. As a result of the 19th- and early 20th-century propensity to collect ancient objects from all over the world and take them into established collections in Europe and America there is a great deal of material which has become detached from its cultural context, and there is now increasing pressure to return it to its country or culture of origin. Human remains taken for scientific study are amongst the most sensitive, and significant collections such as those held by the University of Nebraska in America and Edinburgh University in Scotland have already been returned to the indigenous communities from whom they were taken. The British Museum has returned to the Egyptian authorities a fragment of the beard of the great Sphinx of Giza. In 1980 France returned to Iraq fragments of Babylonian codes, and in 1978 Holland returned Hindu and Buddhist sculptures to Indonesia. Great controversy, however, surrounds claims for the repatriation of some objects, most notably the Elgin Marbles, originally from the Parthenon on the Acropolis in Athens, but since 1816 displayed in the British Museum in London.

replication [Th]. The act of repeating an experiment or set of observations to determine if the same result or pattern occurs.

repoussé [De]. Type of decoration used on cold sheet bronze or gold produced by hammering from the back surface against a pattern mould to create a relief effect. *See also* CHASING TOOL.

reredorter [Ge]. The latrines of a monastic establishment.

RESCUE [Or]. A pressure group and membership organization representing a Trust for British Archaeology formed in 1971 by amateur and professional archaeologists as an expression of their concern at the massive erosion of Britain's archaeological heritage. The aim was to increase public awareness of the accelerating destruction of the archaeological heritage and campaign for better funding and infrastructure for archaeological investigations. In these matters the organization achieved considerable success and by 1973/4 the government had increased fourfold the budget available for rescue archaeology in England.

rescue archaeology [Ge]. A term coined in the 1960s in Britain for field archaeology carried out on sites under threat of destruction; synonymous with the American SALVAGE ARCHAEOLOGY. In Britain the term is closely associated with the large increase in the loss of archaeological sites as a result of increased development in the 1960s and 1970s, especially the motorway construction programme and urban regeneration.

Research Assessment Exercise [Ge]. Periodic review of research achievement by academic discipline in UK universities. The first such assessment took place in 1985, since when there have been successive reviews in 1992, 1996, and 2001. Each submission is peer-graded on a scale from 1 (low) to 5* (high).

research design (project design) [Ge]. A detailed proposal relating to a defined piece of archaeological endeavour which includes: a definition of a problem, subject, or hypothesis for investigation; the background and context to the investigation; the proposed means and methods of the investigation; the work plan and timetable; details of the proposed investigators, management arrangements, and quality control procedures; a table of costs. *See also* MANAGEMENT OF ARCHAEOLOGICAL PROJECTS.

reservoir effect [De]. Distortions in the radiocarbon age of samples derived from environments where samples from a particular carbon reservoir may not be in complete equilibrium with the atmosphere, so that their normalized isotope ratio is not the same as that of contemporaneous terrestrial wood. The most common example of the effect

occurs with marine shells because the surface ocean waters where they grow have a significant contribution from older deep-ocean waters. The magnitude of the correction necessary for marine shell ages will depend on the geographical location: for mid-latitude samples the gap is probably about 400 years while for higher latitudes the correction may rise to more than 1000 years. In all cases the correction is subtracted from the conventional radiocarbon age. Also known as the marine effect or the environmental effect.

resistivity survey [Te]. A kind of geophysical survey used to locate buried features by mapping differences in the way that soils conduct an electric current. Using a **resistivity meter** a controlled electric current is passed through the soil between four electrodes. One pair of electrodes carries the current while the second pair measures the voltage passed through the ground; the resistance (in ohms) is determined and recorded. In general, fine densely packed damp silty material offers little resistance to current passed through it but stony deposits and those with abundant spaces in the matrix are highly resistant. Different arrays of electrodes allow different depths to be targeted, and by moving the electrodes in a systematic pattern a detailed map of subsurface soil conditions can be built up. Rubble-filled ditches and pits, walls, courtyard surfaces, and roads are the easiest features to identify with resistivity. Limitations in the technique include the problem of filtering out natural from anthropogenic anomalies, and ensuring that the survey is conducted under fairly uniform soil conditions (neither too wet nor too dry).

resource stress model [Th]. A model of hunter-gatherer behaviour explained by Canadian archaeologist Brian Hayden in which the biggest determinant of social change is the modification of behaviour patterns to overcome stress caused by food shortages or other related phenomena. Thus, although hunter-gatherer communities would normally cope with resource stress by deploying little-used techniques, on occasion they develop wholly new and more efficient ways of obtaining food.

Resseta Culture [CP]. Late Upper Palaeolithic communities of the forest zone of western

Russia, characterized by lakeside and riverside settlements and a rich material culture.

restoration [De]. Literally, the act of restoring something that already exists to a former position or state. In archaeology this typically means dismantling a structure or taking an artefact apart, cleaning the component parts, replacing or strengthening broken or weak elements, and then reassembling the whole in its original order or form. It is often a matter of degree as to whether an operation is really restoration or reconstruction, although the extremes are easy to see. The aim of restoration is mainly conservation through the protection and preservation of the remains.

retaining kerb [Co]. A ring of boulders or stone slabs set around the outer edge of a cairn or barrow to define its limits and serve to revet and support the edge of the mound or cairn.

retaining wall [Co]. *See* REVETMENT.

retentura [Co]. Latin term for the rear division of a fort or camp, lying behind the central range.

retouch [De]. In knapping flint, stone, or obsidian, the final edge-working carried out during the production of an implement. Whether on a core tool, flake, or blade, retouch usually comprises fine flaking and chipping to shape, blunt, or sharpen a particular edge. Several different styles are recognized, including invasive retouch which is achieved by working from the edge of the implement towards the centre. Also known as SECONDARY WORKING.

retting [Ge]. The process of softening and rotting fibrous plant stems such as hemp and flax by soaking them in water or by exposing them to moisture until much of the non-vascular plant material has decayed. The stems can then be beaten to detach the fibres from the woody core. The facility used for retting, usually a hole in the ground capable of holding water, is known as a **retting pit**.

revetment [Co]. Facing of hard and solid material given to a body of softer or less stable material in order to retain and support it and prevent collapse: a revetment wall along the face of an earth bank, for example.

Rhenish ware [Ar]. Pottery from Gaul and the Rhineland imported into Britain during the late 2nd century AD and later. It has a thin red paste and a black metallic colour coat; some of the vessels are decorated with scrolls or sometimes words in fine white paint. The commonest form is an indented rouletted beaker. Close imitations appear to have been made in Britain in the Nene Valley.

Rhodian amphora [Ar]. *See* AMPHORA.

rhyton [Ar]. A deep jar-like vessel with a single handle, often made of precious materials and of elaborate form, common in the MINOAN, MYCENAEAN, and Classical worlds. They were used for pouring liquid libations or offerings to the gods or spirits of the dead. Some examples have a hole at the lowest point which can be covered with a finger or hand until the appropriate moment in a ceremony; releasing the cover will allow the contents to flow out.

ribbon torc [Ar]. Gold neck ornament current in the middle Bronze Age of northwestern Europe (1200–900 BC) comprising a circlet of twisted metal with simple hooks and balls at the terminals to fasten the ends together when worn.

ricasso [De]. The blunting of the cutting edges of a sword just below the hilt so that its user can grip the weapon without fear of being cut. Some swords have a notch (ricasso notch) below the hilt to prevent the blades of other swords running down onto the hilt.

rice [Sp]. A cereal plant of the genus *Oryza* known in two cultivated species. Asian rice (*Oryza sativa*) is the most widespread and is native to southeast Asia. It was cultivated from at least 3500 BC in the Indus Valley and in China from Neolithic times (5th millennium BC) in the lower Yangtze region. Rice must have been introduced to Japan as a cultigen as it is not part of the native flora. African rice (*Oryza glaberrina*) seems to have been domesticated in West Africa, but little is known of its early history and use.

Richard I [Na]. English king, also known as Richard Coeur de Lion (Richard the Lion Heart), of the House of Anjou (Plantagenets). Born 1157, third son of Henry II. Married Berengaria, daughter of Sancho VI, king of

Navarre. Died aged 42, having reigned nine years between 1189 and 1199.

Richard II [Na]. English king of the House of Anjou (Plantagenets). Born 1367, son of Edward (the Black Prince), eldest son of Edward III. Married (1) Anne, daughter of Emperor Charles IV (2) Isabelle, daughter of Charles VI of France. Deposed September 1399, killed February 1400 aged 33, having reigned 22 years between 1377 and 1399.

Richard III [Na]. English king of the House of York. Born 1452, fourth son of Richard of York and brother of Edward IV. Married Anne Neville, daughter of Richard, earl of Warwick and widow of Edward, prince of Wales, son of Henry VI. Killed in battle aged 32, having reigned two years between 1483 and 1485.

Richmond, Sir Ian Archibald (1902–65) [Bi]. British archaeologist who specialized in the Roman period. Born in Rochdale, Lancashire, he was educated at Ruthin School and Corpus Christi College, Oxford, before spending two years (1924–6) at the British School in Rome. Here he developed an interest in Roman military architecture and the methods of the Roman army. This was to form the theme of his research throughout his life. He also gained practical archaeological experience working for Mortimer Wheeler at Segontium in Wales. From 1926 to 1930 he was a lecturer in classical archaeology at the Queen's University, Belfast. In 1930, however, he returned to Italy as Director of the British School in Rome. Two years later he had to retire because of ill health and for nearly three years he was without a post. In 1935 he was appointed to a lectureship in Romano-British history in the University of Durham where he remained with only a brief break for National Service until 1956. He was given a personal Chair in 1950, and during his 21 years at Durham carried out numerous excavations along Hadrian's Wall and other sites in the vicinity. In 1956 he was translated to Oxford as the first holder of the Chair in the Archaeology of the Roman Empire. He was knighted in 1964. During his life he published many books and articles, notably *Roman Britain* (Penguin, 1955) and, together with R. G. Collingwood, *The archaeology of Roman Britain* (Methuen, 1930 with several revisions). He also held many offices in learned societies, including that of President of the Society of Antiquaries of London from April 1964 until his death.

[Obit.: *The Times*, 6 October 1965]

ridge and furrow [MC]. The archaeological manifestation of a system of strip cultivation that was widely used in England during medieval times. Fields (typically two or three in each settlement) were divided into groups of strips (furlongs) that were each ploughed separately (lands) by turning the soil towards the centre. This had the effect of creating raised areas separated by troughs or furrows, the whole having a marked S-shaped form in plan with headlands for turning the plough at either end. When cultivation ceased, the corrugated effect was fossilized in the landscape, especially if the land was put down to grass. Some of the best-preserved ridge and furrow is to be found in the south midland counties of England, especially Oxfordshire, Bedfordshire, Warwickshire, and Northamptonshire. The width of the ridges preferred seems to vary between regions, while dates for ridge and furrow range from the immediate post-Roman period through to the 17th century AD.

ridge tile [Ar]. Stone or ceramic tile used along the ridgeline of a roof, usually shaped to sit over the ridge itself to provide a water-tight seal with the roof sections on either side.

ridgeway [MC]. An ancient and traditional pathway and communications route running along the top of a prominent ridge. The paths were not constructed as such and usually exploited a wide corridor. Some were later used as Roman roads and medieval droveways. In Britain the best-known ridgeways are: the Berkshire Ridgeway running eastwards from Avebury, the Icknield Way in the Chilterns, and the Pilgrim's Way on the North Downs of Kent.

Ridley, Cressida (1917–98) [Bi]. British archaeologist specializing in Greek prehistory. The granddaughter of British Liberal prime minister H. H. Asquith, Ridley (née Bonham-Carter) took up archaeology late in life, influenced by childhood experiences in and around her home at Stockton in Wiltshire. In 1961 she started as a student in the Institute of Archaeology in London, graduating two years later top of her class with a postgraduate diploma. She had a scholarship at the British

School in Athens before working at a number of sites in Greece, starting work in the Haliakmon Valley in northern Greece in 1971. Her most famous excavations were at Servia, a Neolithic settlement threatened with destruction by the building of a hydroelectric scheme.

[Obit.: *The Times*, 8 June 1998]

riemchen [Ar]. German term for a type of ceramic brick commonly used in late URUK-period structures in Mesopotamia. Such bricks are long and thin with a square cross-section.

rig and furrow [MC]. A kind of RIDGE AND FURROW cultivation found in upland areas where spades appear to have been used rather than ploughs. *See also* CORD RIG and RUN RIG.

Riley, Derrick (1915–93) [Bi]. British archaeologist and pioneer of aerial archaeology. Born in Matlock, Derbyshire, he was brought up in Norfolk and educated at King's School, Ely, and Haileybury College. On leaving school he joined United Steel in Scunthorpe as a trainee manager, and it was at this time that he began his archaeological fieldwork with investigations at Risley Warren. During the war he served with the RAF in Bomber Command, flying missions in Whitleys, Wellingtons, and Mosquitoes. He was awarded the DFC for a daring raid on the Kiel Canal. After his tours of duty he was put to training pilots at Stanton Harcourt in Oxfordshire and it was here that he developed an interest in archaeological reconnaissance. After the war he returned to United Steel, but continued his archaeological interests with surveys and excavations. From 1970 he renewed his interest in aerial photography and in 1975 obtained a private pilot's licence. Taking early retirement in 1977 he devoted himself full-time to archaeology and recorded many prehistoric and later sites, especially around Sheffield and the Peak District. He published many books and articles documenting his work, including *Early landscapes from the air* (1981, Sheffield: Sheffield University). He received an honorary doctorate from the University of Sheffield.

[Obit.: *The Times*, 28 August 1993]

Rillaton Barrow, Cornwall, England [Si]. A large Bronze Age round barrow some 25 m in diameter situated on Bodmin Moor in southwest England. Excavated in 1837, an inhuma-

tion burial was found to have been deposited in a large centrally placed stone cist over 2 m long and nearly 1 m wide. Grave goods included a bronze dagger, pottery, and a unique biconical gold cup with a beaten plate handle attached with rivets. The cup has the form of a late Neolithic BEAKER, its surface ribbed in the style of corded decoration, but probably dates to the period 1650–1400 BC. Following its discovery the cup had an unusual history, as it was given to King William IV and was later used for many years by George V to hold his collar studs. It was eventually presented to the British Museum in 1936.

[Sum.: C. Hawkes, 1983, The Rillaton gold cup. *Antiquity*, 57, 124–6]

rilling [De]. Technique of ornamentation on pottery comprising a series of parallel channels, generally horizontal, either square-cut or forming a series of conjoined arcs in section. Fine, close-set horizontal lines formed by scribing (with a comb, for example) on the body of a pottery vessel.

ring cairn (ring barrow) [MC]. A prehistoric ritual monument comprising a circular bank of earth or stones up to about 20 m in diameter surrounding a hollow central area. The bank may be kerbed on the inside and sometimes on the outside too, with small uprights or laid boulders. Within the central area there will be burials and pits with ash-rich fills, hearths, and sometimes small low cairns. Ring cairns with stone banks are mainly found in western and upland areas of the British Isles but examples with earth banks occur in southern and eastern areas. They date to the later Neolithic and Bronze Age, broadly 2000 BC through to 1000 BC.

ring ditch [Co]. A bedrock cut ditch or trench of circular or penannular plan, usually identified through aerial photography either as soil marks or cropmarks. When excavated, ring ditches are usually found to be the ploughed-out remains of a round barrow where the barrow mound has completely disappeared leaving only the infilled former quarry ditch.

ringfort [MC]. A small circular enclosure or fort, also known as a rath. Typically between 30 m and 50 m in diameter they are bounded by one or more concentric earthworks comprising a bank and outer ditch. Found widely across Ireland, southwest Wales, and central

Scandinavia. Within the enclosure there are usually house foundations and traces of stock pens. Such ringworks date from the early 1st millennium BC through to the 11th century AD and were mainly farms, although some were occupied by families of significantly higher status. *See also* CASHEL, ROUND.

ring-headed pin [Ar]. Bronze or iron dress-fitting comprising a slender shaft typically 5–10 cm in length with a point at one end, while the other end has been bent round onto itself to form a loop or ring. Found in middle and later Iron Age contexts in the British Isles.

ring neck [De]. A flagon neck with mouldings forming a series of superimposed horizontal rings; not to be confused with a SCREW NECK.

ringwork [MC]. Early form of medieval castle originating in Germany in the 10th century AD and at first little more than a fortified manor. Introduced to England immediately before the Norman conquest, numerous examples were built in the later 11th and early 12th century. More elaborate examples comprise a ringwork and bailey where the ringwork takes the place of the more usual motte and the bailey provides a military stronghold.

Rinyo-Clacton Culture [CP]. Late Neolithic Culture of the British Isles defined by Stuart PIGGOTT in 1954 on the basis of a distinctive type of highly decorated pottery found at sites as far apart as Clacton, Essex, and Rinyo, Orkney. Bone tools and associations with HENGES and ritual pits were also considered part of the distinctive material culture. Investigations since 1954 show that the elements Piggott selected as representative are in fact the widely spread components of what is a more highly regionalized pattern of social groupings.

Rinyo-Clacton ware [Ar]. Obsolete term for a style of British late Neolithic pottery now referred to as GROOVED WARE.

Rio Bec [De]. One of three main styles of architecture current during Maya times in northern Yucatan, Mexico. Characterized by the extensive use of uncut stone and stucco, emphasizing appearance rather than function.

Rio Palacios Phase [CP]. South American farming cultures found in lowland Bolivia and tentatively dated to *c*.AD 1500+.

Characterized by their ceramic assemblages which belong to the Incised and Punctuate Horizon Style of Amazonia.

rippled decoration (ripple burnishing) [De]. A method of burnishing pottery in which the whole surface is worked into ripples, in extreme cases approaching FLUTING.

ripple-flaking [De]. A style of secondary flaking applied to flint and stone tools in which a series of small elongated flakes are removed from the surface of the tool being manufactured in such a way that each new flake scar cuts into the edge of the last one to produce a corrugated or rippled surface.

Riss Stage [CP]. Third, penultimate, major glacial period of the PLEISTOCENE Ice Age in the Alpine sequence, broadly dated to the period 200 000 to 170 000 years ago.

ritual (ritual deposit) [De]. A favourite but deplorable term commonly used by archaeologists looking to explain unfamiliar patterns in material culture that seem to have no functional explanation. Ritual strictly refers to practices connected with magical, supernatural, or religious experiences and beliefs, ritual deposits being the result of material culture deployed as part of such practices. It is now widely recognized, however, that in non-capitalist, non-westernized societies there is no formal boundary between what is ritual and secular, between the sacred and the profane.

river fishery [MC]. A stretch of flowing water set aside for catching fish by the use of wickerwork or basketry traps attached to artificial structures placed on the bed of the river or stream. In many cases a weir or platform provides the foundation for the traps, and may extend across the full width of the water course. Alternatively, traps may be secured to stakes driven into the bed of the water course or be weighted down to rest on the river bed. There may be associated structures such as fish houses and processing areas on the adjacent banks. Occasionally water courses may be artificially created to provide fisheries. Widely found in many parts of the world at different times, river fisheries occur in both tidal and freshwater catchments. Early examples of wicker fish traps go back to Mesolithic times in northern Europe.

Riverine Archaic [CP]. Late Archaic Stage hunter-gatherer communities living in the eastern states of North America, particularly in the Mississippi and Missouri basins. One of a series of regional adaptations to different environments, Riverine Archaic people took advantage of the wide range of resources available in the deciduous forests and river valleys of this region. They hunted and trapped small mammals such as deer, turkey, and wildfowl and took turtles, fish, and mussels from the rivers. They gathered nuts (e.g. hickory nuts, black walnuts, acorns, pecans, and hazelnuts) and seeds (e.g. from marsh elder and pigweed). Settlements sometimes comprised small villages of up to six post-built houses providing home to a nuclear family. Burials were typically flexed inhumations in pits, heads turned to the right. The corpses had been sprinkled with red ochre.

river terrace [Ge]. A platform of land formed beside a river flowing across a plain where, for some reason, the river channel has deepened and cut down to create a new flood-plain at a lower level. River terraces are often made of fluvially eroded material laid down during the creation of the flood-plain. This material sometimes includes archaeological material and faunal remains which date from any time earlier than the creation of the deposit in which they are incorporated. In this way some river terraces can be roughly dated by reference to the latest material present in the assemblages. Large river valleys usually have more than one set of terraces forming a complicated series of platforms.

rivet [Ar]. Small metal rod passed through two or more overlapping pieces of material (usually metal) that need to be joined together, the ends of which are hammered over to spread and flatten the rod and draw the material together. Riveting is one of the earliest methods of fastening metal together and was first used in metalworking during the early Bronze Age in Europe.

Rivet, Albert Lionel Frederick (1915–93) [Bi]. British archaeologist specializing in the Roman empire. Educated at Oriel College, Oxford, his archaeological interests were aroused intellectually by R. G. Collingwood at Oxford and practically by working for Mortimer Wheeler at Maiden Castle in Dorset in the mid 1930s. Briefly working as a school-master, in 1938 Rivet enlisted as a private soldier before service with the Royal Signals where he eventually rose to the rank of major and undertook service in East Africa. After the war he was a bookseller in Cambridge for five years before taking up a post as an archaeological officer with the Ordnance Survey. Working there for thirteen years, he was responsible for producing the third edition of the *Map of Roman Britain* (1956, Ordnance Survey); it was also during this period that he wrote *Town and country in Roman Britain* (1958, London: Hutchinson). In 1964 he was appointed to a lectureship in classics at Keele University, and it was from this time that he started publishing on the place-names which led to a magisterial volume written in association with Colin Smith entitled *The placenames of Roman Britain* (1979, London: Batsford). He was awarded a personal Chair at Keele University in 1974 and was elected a Fellow of the British Academy in 1981. He served on numerous committees and editorial boards for academic societies, and published widely.

[Obit.: *The Times*, 22 September 1993]

Rixheim sword [Ar]. Distinctive type of early bronze sword from the URNFIELD period of central Europe, having a narrow blade and a tang for the attachment of a hilt using four or six rivets. Such swords were traded to many other parts of Europe and prompted the development of local imitations. In the British Isles they appear during the Penard Industrial Phase, around 1000 BC.

Rixheim–Monza sword [Ar]. Variant on the early bronze Rixheim sword from southern areas of central Europe where a hooked tang or a rod tang was cast above the blade to provide the means of attaching and securing the hilt.

robbed [De]. A term used to describe a structure from which building materials have been removed for reuse. A **robber trench** is the hole dug to extract usable building materials from an existing structure, usually by simply chasing the walls down to their foundation courses. The plan of many substantial Roman and medieval buildings is now represented archaeologically only by their footings and robber trenches.

Robert I [Na]. King of Scotland of the House of Bruce, also known as Robert the Bruce. Born

1274, son of Robert Bruce and Marjorie, countess of Carrick, and great-grandson of the second daughter of David, earl of Huntingdon, brother of William I. Married (1) Isabella, daughter of Donald, earl of Mar (2) Elizabeth, daughter of Richard, earl of Ulster. Died aged 54, having reigned 23 years between 1306 and 1329.

Robert II [Na]. King of Scotland of the House of Stewart. Born 1316, son of Marjorie, daughter of Robert I, and Walter, High Steward of Scotland. Married (1) Elizabeth, daughter of Sir Robert Mure of Rowallan (2) Euphemia, daughter of Hugh, earl of Ross. Died aged 74, having reigned nineteen years.

Robert III [Na]. King of Scotland of the House of Stewart. Born c.1337, son of Robert II and Elizabeth. Married Annabella, daughter of Sir John Drummond of Stobhall. Died aged c.69, having reigned sixteen years between 1390 and 1406.

rock art [De]. At a general level, any artificially created mark that is cut, engraved, incised, etched, gouged, ground or pecked into, or applied with paint, wax, or other substance (organic or mineral) onto, a rock surface. Within this broad field, the term **petroglyph** is applied to marks made by carving, incising, engraving, pecking, or grinding the rock surface, while the term **pictograph** refers to marks made by painting organic and mineral pigments onto the surface.

The individual marks in rock art are often referred to as **motifs**; groups of motifs in close juxtaposition as **panels**; and places where one or more panels have been identified as **sites**. It is recognized, however, that in making these identifications and using such terminology a structure is being imposed that may not have been known or relevant to the people who made the rock art in the first place. Indeed, use of the very term 'art' carries with it a series of assumptions from modern western culture about the nature of the various marks that can be observed.

Rock art is extremely widely spread around the world and appears to have been made since Lower Palaeolithic times for a variety of purposes such as during religious rites, depicting historical or mythological events and narratives, as decoration, or to mark territories and routeways. Dating rock art is often extremely difficult because of its general open and exposed positions and lack of associations. Interpreting the motifs used is also difficult. The most widespread motif is the simple cup or hollow either singly or in groups. Some rock art contains motifs that are symbols, shapes and lines, in other cases people, animals, objects, events, and structures are depicted.

Many different kinds of rock surface have been used in the creation of rock art, but a number of key situations are widely recognized: **parietal** panels are those on the walls of a natural structure such as a cave or rock-shelter; **open-air** panels are those on natural earthfast boulders and rock outcrops that lie unprotected in essentially open countryside; **monument-based** panels are those found on the faces of stones incorporated into the fabric or structure of deliberately constructed monuments—some of these pieces may have been open-air rock art before being lifted and used in monument building; and **mobiliary rock art** where panels occur on the surface of stones that have been relocated from their source and may have been moved several times in the past—essentially portable pieces of rock art.

rock-cut tomb [MC]. A tomb constructed by excavating a chamber in the natural rock. Such tombs may be entered directly from a cliff face or by a shaft running vertically or at an angle down from the ground surface above. Such tombs are found in many parts of the world from the Neolithic through into medieval times.

rock-shelter [MC]. A naturally formed hollow or shallow cave in the face of a cliff or rock outcrop that has been used as shelter for a small settlement or encampment.

rod [Ar]. Term applied to a type of Mesolithic microlith found especially in northwestern Europe. Rods are rounded forms of microliths retouched along the edges.

roddon [De]. Local Fenland name for the ghost of a former river channel.

rolled [De]. A term used to describe the battered and abraded condition of flint or stone tools that have been incorporated into terrace gravels or glacial tills after being moved about by fluvial or glacial action.

roller stamping [Ge]. Impressed decoration applied by a roller in a repetitive sequence. It usually comprises three or more small panels of design, with different patterns, which have been cut into the roller; not to be confused with stamped wares which have no regular sequence of pattern but a haphazard arrangement due to the use of one or more independent dies.

Roman (Roman empire) [CP]. One of the largest ancient empire states known, the Roman empire began in central Italy in the middle of the 1st millennium BC. In the wake of collapsing ETRUSCAN cultures Rome expanded through a mixture of force and diplomacy so that by 250 BC it controlled the whole of peninsular Italy. This expansion inevitably led to conflicts with existing powers around the Mediterranean, especially Carthage, and Rome's struggle to control the western Mediterranean, the Punic Wars, lasted more than a century, Carthage finally being captured in 146 BC.

Until the mid 1st century BC the Roman world was a republic, governed from its centre by a senate and two annually elected consuls. Julius Caesar's assassination in 44 BC was followed by the development of imperial rule, headed by the first emperor, Augustus. Further expansion followed, and by the 2nd century AD the empire was at its largest, extending for more than 4000 km east to west and 3700 km north to south. Its population was more than 50 million, most living in self-governing provinces. The army amounted to more than 300 000 soldiers, mainly concentrated around the fringes of the empire to defend its borders.

The main source of wealth was agriculture, although a vast and extensive trading economy based on luxury goods as well as staples developed around the Mediterranean, along the Atlantic seaways to the west, and eastwards into the Black Sea and beyond to India and China.

Culturally, the empire always had an eastern part in which Greek was the dominant language and a western part where Latin was dominant. The dividing line ran along the Adriatic coast of Dalmatia. Politically these two regions began to pull apart from the 3rd century AD onwards, and in the 4th century they were more formally divided. In the 5th century Rome's control over the western empire collapsed as barbarian groups broke down its borders; the eastern empire continued to flourish from its capital in Constantinople, eventually becoming the Christian Greek world of Byzantium.

Roman barrow [MC]. A substantial circular mound of earth and stone up to 50 m across, usually with steep sides and a slightly flattened top, covering one or more burials. The burials are variously cremations or inhumations, the barrows themselves occurring singly or in groups of up to ten. Their location near to Roman towns and cities in areas where ROUND BARROWS were used for burial during prehistoric times suggests that these Roman structures may in part reflect the continuation of local traditions.

Roman camp [MC]. *See* CAMP.

Romanesque [De]. A style of architecture based on that of Rome in the 5th century AD which spread northwestwards across Europe during the period AD 600–1200. While it developed differently in different areas, the most common features are widely found, notably the broad round-headed arches and openings (doors, windows, etc.).

Roman fort [MC]. *See* FORT.

Roman fortlet [MC]. *See* FORTLET.

Roman fortress [MC]. *See* FORTRESS.

Romanization [Ge]. The process by which non-Roman communities became part of the Roman empire following annexation. In some areas this seems to have taken place easily through negotiation and acculturation while elsewhere it involved the full weight of the military machine.

Romano-Celtic temple [MC]. A square, circular, rectangular, or polygonal religious building, known as a cella, which is set apart from its secular surroundings by being situated within a temenos or precinct. An ambulatory or covered walkway may surround the central cella. Statues of the deity to whom the temple is dedicated will be positioned in the cella, and the whole structure may be orientated towards significant celestial events. Such temples were often built on the site of earlier religious or ceremonial structures and many continued to be used in modified form into early Christian times.

Romano-Saxon ware [Ar]. This term is used both of wheel-made Roman pottery in coarse or colour-coated fabrics with stamped or bossed decoration resembling that on many hand-made Saxon vessels, and of hand-made Saxon pottery imitating Roman forms. It is found mainly in eastern England. The former class belongs to the late 3rd and 4th centuries and is not to be confused with stamped ware of earlier periods such as LONDON and PARISIAN wares.

Roman Society [Or]. More formally known as the Society for the Promotion of Roman Studies, this membership organization was founded in 1911 to deal with the archaeology, art, literature, and history of Italy and the Roman empire down to the year AD 700. The society publishes the *Journal of Roman Studies* and *Britannia*.

Rome, Italy [Si]. Below the modern streets of the capital of Italy lie the remains of one of the greatest and most influential centres in the ancient world. Legend holds that Rome was founded in 754 BC by the twins Romulus and Remus who were abandoned by their parents but suckled by a she-wolf, but archaeology shows that the story begins rather before this and can be divided into five main phases.

The early settlement began in the 10th or 9th century BC when a series of farmsteads and villages developed on the famous seven hills (Capitoline, Palatine, Aventine, Caelian, Esquiline, Viminal, and Quirinal) overlooking the River Tiber. The areas between the hills were poorly drained and were used as burial grounds.

In the 7th century BC the existing settlements were brought together as an Etruscan city by rulers from the north. New and substantial buildings were erected and the low-lying marshland was drained and used for the construction of public buildings and the city centre. The city became an important religious and trading centre.

In the 6th century the Romans rose in revolt against their Etruscan rulers and expelled them from the city. In place of the monarchy they set up a republic with power vested in a senate and two annually elected consuls. The city quickly grew and by the 4th century needed its own water supplies to be brought via the Aqua Appia, the first of many aqueducts feeding the city.

Julius Caesar's assassination in 44 BC was followed by the development of imperial rule, headed by the first emperor, Augustus. By this time Rome was the largest city in the ancient world with a population of around 1 million people. Augustus and his successors embarked on ambitious building programmes and the expansion of the empire to support it. By the later 3rd century AD the empire had reached its peak and from that time began to decline. Defence became important and one of the most conspicuous monuments even today are the massive walls started by the emperor Aurelian around AD 271. Rome declined in importance during the 4th century AD, and was sacked by the Goths in AD 410.

Rome retained its pre-eminence as a religious centre and Papal State into the Middle Ages and beyond, while classical Roman traditions lived on in art and architecture.

[Sum.: A. Claridge, 1998, *Rome. An Oxford archaeological guide*. Oxford: OUP]

Ronaldsway Culture [CP]. Late Neolithic culture of the Isle of Man named after a substantial assemblage of material recorded during the wartime excavation of a sunken-floor structure at Ronaldsway Airport in the south part of the island. Characterized by deep baggy jars, stone axes with roughened butts, and distinctive types of flint tools, the Ronaldsway Neolithic dates to the 3rd millennium BC and is found exclusively on the Isle of Man. Contacts with surrounding areas are represented by shared monument types such as mini-henges, stone circles, passage graves, and entrance graves, but the culture has its own unique structures too, including the deposition of earthfast jars.

rongorongo [Ge]. The ancient script of Easter Island in the Pacific Ocean. The script has about 120 pictographic symbols but has not been deciphered and no outside source is known.

roof furniture [Ar]. Wooden, stone, or ceramic items used as decorative and functional features of a roof. They include **finials** on the gables, **antefixes** to act as stoppers for hollow tiles emerging at the eaves, **chimney pots**, **louvres**, and **smoke turrets** to ventilate fires inside the building and let fumes escape, and **ridge tiles** along the highest point.

Roonka Flat, Australia [Si]. A multi-phase Aboriginal open-air occupation site and burial ground on an elevated terrace of the Murray River in South Australia. The earliest use of the site dates back to about 16 000 BC with fairly extensive evidence of occupation and two burials. Later, between 5000 and 2000 BC, the area was mainly used as a burial ground. Finally, from 2000 BC down to the 19th century AD, it was again used for settlement as well as burial. More than 100 burials are known from excavations, including flat graves with either dorsal or flexed burials and shaft graves in which the body was placed upright but later crumpled as the shaft filled with debris. Grave goods were found in the shaft graves, including animal remains, ochre, bone and shell ornaments, and, in the late phases, stone and bone tools.

[Sum.: G. L. Pretty, 1977, The cultural chronology of the Roonka Flat. A preliminary consideration. In R. V. S. Wright (ed.), *Stone tools as cultural markers: change, evolution and complexity*. Canberra: Australian Institute of Aboriginal Studies, 288–331]

ROPA [Ab]. *See* REGISTER OF PROFESSIONAL ARCHAEOLOGISTS.

Rosegate series points [Ar]. Bifacially worked chipped stone projectile points characteristic of Archaic communities living in the Great Basin of North America in the period AD 700–1300. Distinguished by having a triangular outline, small corner notches and a basal tang. Once known as Rose Spring and East Gate types, they are now recognized as part of a single series.

Rosetta Stone [Ar]. An inscribed basalt stela discovered at Rosetta at the western mouth of the Nile in Egypt in July 1799 during Napoleon's occupation of the country. The inscription is an honorific decree by Ptolemy V passed on the 27 March 196 BC which has parallel texts in Greek, Demotic, and Egyptian hieroglyphs. It provided the key to the decipherment of the ancient Egyptian hieroglyphic script by the French scholar Jean François Champollion in the early 1820s. The Rosetta Stone is now in the British Museum in London.

rose window [Co]. Large round window found in cathedrals and churches in Europe from the 12th century AD onwards. Often highly ornate with STAINED GLASS.

Roskilde Fjord, Denmark [Si]. Between AD 1000 and 1050 the communities living around the Roskilde Fjord deliberately scuppered a large number of wooden ships to create a barrier across the mouth of the fjord and thereby help protect their settlements from raiders. In 1962 the National Museum of Denmark mounted an ambitious underwater excavation to recover waterlogged remains of these Viking vessels. A coffer-dam was built and a large number of timbers raised and subsequently preserved. A number of reconstructed ships are now displayed in the Roskilde Ship Museum, including: a knarr (long-distance sea-going cargo vessel propelled by a sail), an oar-propelled merchant ship, a warship similar in form to those depicted on the Bayeux tapestry, a ferry or fishing boat 12 m long, and a Viking longship of the type that would have been crewed by 40–50 men.

[Sum.: O. Olsen, 1990, *Five Viking ships from Roskilde Fjord*. Roskilde: Viking Ship Museum]

Rosnoen sword [Ar]. Early style of bronze sword based on the Rixheim swords of central Europe but produced locally in France and Britain. Characterized by a relatively short slender blade and fairly parallel sides, with a short tapering point. At the top of the blade is a perforated tang for the attachment of the hilt using four rivets.

Rössen Culture [CP]. Middle Neolithic culture of central Europe, named after an inhumation cemetery of 70 graves near Merseburg in central Germany. The Rössen Culture is the successor to the LBK in the upper Danube and Rhineland, dating to the early 4th millennium BC. Settlements may be enclosed and houses were generally trapezoidal rather than long and rectangular in plan as in the LBK. Pottery includes round-bottomed and pedestalled bowls with characteristic ornament in incised or 'stabbed' technique.

Rostovtzeff, Michael (1870–1952) [Bi]. Ukrainian archaeologist and scholar specializing in the history of Greece and Rome and the early history of southern Russia. Born in Kiev, he was a schoolboy in the classical gymnasium in Kiev. In 1895 he received from the University of St Petersburg a grant to study abroad for three years, during which time he became interested in excavations and archaeological studies. In 1903 he was made professor of Ancient History in St Petersburg Imperial University and in the University for Women. He held these Chairs for fifteen years. The Bolshevist revolution forced him to flee Russia and he spent two years in Oxford. He also devoted his energies to helping found the Russian Liberation Committee in London. In 1920 he accepted the Chair of Ancient History in Wisconsin University and in 1925 was appointed to the parallel Chair in Yale University. In 1928, with support from the French Academy of Inscriptions and Letters, he took over excavations at Dura-Europeas on the Euphrates. He published more than 600 papers, reviews, books, and essays.

[Obit.: *The Times*, 22 October 1952]

rotary quern [Ar]. Type of QUERN developed in late prehistoric times with a thick round stationary lower stone in which there is a socket for a spindle, and a hemispherical (beehive-shaped) rotating upper stone that sits over the lower stone. The two stones are held in register by the central spindle which also serves as a chute down which grain can be poured, so that it is taken between the stones near the centre of the quern and gradually moves outwards as it become finer in texture. A socket in the upper stone allows the insertion of a handle to make turning the quern easier. *See also* BEEHIVE QUERN.

Rouffignac, France [Si]. A large cave system in the Dordogne of southern France with occupation deposits in the entrance area dating to the period between 9000 and 8000 BC, the SAUVETERRIAN. In 1947 speleologists reported MAGDALENIAN cave paintings and engraved drawings of animals inside the cave, and in 1956 further panels were discovered. The images are dominated by over 100 illustrations of mammoths, which have caused some controversy because mammoths were believed to have been extinct in the area before the end of the Pleistocene.

[Rep.: L. R. Nougier and R. Romain, 1958, *The cave of Rouffignac*. London: G. Newnes]

rough-cast ware [Ar]. Pottery decoration consisting of small particles of dried clay or gritty material dusted over the surface of a vessel, generally under a slip coating.

rough-out [Ar]. Product of the first stage in the production of a flint or stone axe where a block of raw material has been selected and crudely shaped by removing unwanted peripheral material. At this stage the suitability of the raw material for the intended finished product can be seen fairly clearly and the piece was discarded if deemed to be unusable. Some blocks break during the roughing-out process as natural flaws reveal themselves. Selected rough-outs can be taken on to the next stage of fine flaking, grinding, and polishing, as appropriate, this work usually being carried out away from the main quarry sites associated with working areas where the roughing-out is done.

rouletting [De]. Incised decoration made by a toothed wheel or roller (roulette) applied while the vessel is turning on the potter's wheel.

round [MC]. An embanked univallate enclosure with an external ditch and a single entrance. Inside are buildings and structures representing a single farmstead or small hamlet belonging to an agricultural community. They are similar to the raths and RINGFORTS of western Britain and Ireland, although the term 'round' generally only applies to examples in Devon and Cornwall in the southwest of England. Rounds generally date to the later 1st millennium BC and continue to be built and used through to the mid 1st millennium AD.

round barrow [MC]. Probably the most widespread and numerous class of archaeological monument in Europe, and found in other parts of the world too. At the most basic a round barrow is simply a roughly hemispherical mound of soil, stone, and redeposited bedrock heaped over a central burial. Depending on the nature of the bedrock, such mounds may be predominantly stone (cairns) or earth. The basic pattern is elaborated by the range of constructional features and devices. Some examples have a surrounding ditch which acted both to delimit the monument and as a quarry for material with which to make the mound. Kerbs are found round some mounds, while others have a gap or berm between the mound and the surrounding ditch. Compositionally some mounds are carefully made with alternating layers of turf, soil, and stone forming successive envelopes, and in a few cases there are concentric rings of posts set in the original ground surface and giving structure to the mound. Stones are used instead of posts in some western areas of the British Isles. The central burial may be an inhumation, usually in a pit or cist, or a cremation either in a pit or contained within an urn or jar. As well as a central primary burial, many round barrows contain satellite burials added during the construction of the barrow mound. Secondary burials are often added to the mound, in some cases many centuries later.

The simplest round barrows are generally referred to as bowl barrows because of their shape, variations and more complicated forms being termed FANCY BARROWS. In the British Isles the majority of round barrows are of Bronze Age date, but the tradition as a whole begins in the early Neolithic around 4000 BC and continues intermittently until late in the 1st millennium BC.

round barrow cemetery [MC]. Clusters of five or more prehistoric round barrows, typically including bowl barrows and a range of FANCY BARROWS. The spacing and number of barrows varies considerably, but some of the largest such cemeteries are those around Stonehenge in England and can include more than 30 separate barrows spread over an area more than 300 m across. Such cemeteries are said to be either **linear**, when there is a marked axis to the spread of barrows; **nuclear**, when the barrows form a tight cluster; or **dispersed**, when the individual barrows are spread out and lacking any obvious pattern to their arrangement. In many cases a round barrow cemetery develops around what Leslie Grinsell called a 'founder's barrow', usually a particularly large barrow or a Neolithic barrow that provides a focus for later activity. Few barrow cemeteries have been excavated, but where investigations have taken place there is usually abundant evidence for flat graves between and around the barrows. Such groups of burials accumulate over long periods of time, typically many centuries.

roundel [Ar]. Circular panel containing a design, for example on a mosaic.

round house [MC]. General term applied to roughly circular houses typical of the later 2nd and 1st millennia BC in northwest Europe, especially the British Isles. Such houses may be of timber construction or have stone foundations with a timber superstructure. In general the doorways open in a

southeasterly direction and they have central hearths. Those which functioned as dwellings would have been home to an extended family. Although the timber superstructures and thatched roofs are often regarded as a fire hazard, experiments show that these buildings can have a long life and that with a fire burning inside a layer of carbon dioxide gas builds up under the roof and serves to extinguish any stray sparks rising up towards the thatch. *See* STONE HUT CIRCLES.

round tower [MC]. Tall narrow circular stone towers with conical roofs built within Irish monasteries, probably as places of refuge, from the 9th century AD onwards. A small number of examples were built in western Scotland and the Isle of Man. Typically such towers had several storeys, each lit by a small window. The doors were set high off the ground, making them eminently defensible. Some were later used as campaniles; others may have been built for this purpose.

Royal Anthropological Institute of Great Britain and Ireland [Or]. Membership organization established in 1843 to promote the study of the science of man. It is one of the few institutions in Britain which still attempts to cater for all the different interests of anthropology.

Royal Archaeological Institute [Or]. Membership organization established in 1844 as a national archaeological society. Its interests span all aspects of the archaeological, architectural, and landscape history of the British Isles. It publishes the *Archaeological Journal*.

Royal Commissions [Or]. Royal Commissions on ancient and historical monuments were established for England (Royal Commission on the Historical Monuments of England), Wales (Royal Commission on Ancient and Historical Monuments in Wales), and Scotland (Royal Commission on the Ancient and Historical Monuments of Scotland) in the early years of the 20th century to create definitive records of the archaeological sites and monuments in their respective areas. This was mainly achieved by publishing highly detailed county inventories. The functions of the Royal Commissions have developed considerably since their inception. The most recent Royal Warrants for each Commission, given in 1992, require that they provide for the survey and recording of ancient and historical monuments and constructions by compiling, maintaining, and curating a national record of the archaeological and historical environment. In 2000 the English Royal Commission was closed down and its duties and responsibilities transferred to English Heritage.

Royal Society [Or]. The UK's national academy of science, founded in AD 1660, the Royal Society is one of the oldest scientific societies in Europe. Covering all scientific disciplines, the Society has 1300 peer-elected Fellows and represents the interests of top-quality science and technology in its interactions with government, the public, and the media. Fellowship of the Society carries the distinction FRS.

RSC [Ab]. *See* RECUMBENT STONE CIRCLE.

rubber [Ar]. A small bun-shaped block of coarse stone used as the upper stone in a SADDLE QUERN or for grinding and crushing seeds or plant material in a bone basin or mortar.

rubbing stone [MC]. Substantial upright stone block or slab, sometimes roughly shaped to a square or rectangular cross-section, set upright in the middle of fields from late medieval times onwards for livestock, especially cattle, to rub themselves again.

rubbish pit [Co]. One of the great archaeological misnomers. Pits were very rarely dug for the purpose of rubbish disposal; rather pits initially used for storage or ceremonial purposes were later used as convenient places for burning rubbish. It is this secondary use which is encountered archaeologically when such structures are excavated.

Rudna Glava, Yugoslavia [Si]. Early copper-mining area in the limestone hills of the Saska Valley in the upland Majdapek area of eastern Serbia. Excavations by B. Jovanovi between 1968 and 1982 revealed more than 25 shafts following veins of malachite 20 m or more into the ground. The technique used seems to have been to build platforms on the steep hillside and from these to follow the almost vertical veins down into the ground. Sealed deposits of miners' lamps, antler picks, and stone mauls have been found in abandoned shafts. Pottery of the VINČA CULTURE has also been found in the backfilled shafts, emphasizing the antiquity of these operations back into the early 4th millennium BC.

[Sum.: B. Jovanovi, 1979, The technology of primary copper mining in south-east Europe. *Proceedings of the Prehistoric Society*, 45, 103–10]

ruin [De]. A dilapidated, devastated, decayed, partly destroyed, fallen-down, or tumbled structure or construction. Usually as applied to buildings or architectural features.

runes [De]. An angular script consisting of simple strokes devised by Germanic peoples through contact with Mediterranean alphabets in the 3rd century AD. Runes were used throughout northern Europe up to the Middle Ages as a result of Viking expansion, most commonly in dedications on jewellery and on free-standing memorial stones.

rune stone [MC]. General term for an upright block of slate or stone carrying a runic inscription. Found in northern and western parts of the British Isles and Scandinavia, but few remain in situ.

runner bean [Sp]. A leguminous plant (*Phaseolus coccineus*) with kidney-shaped edible seeds in a long thin pod. Native of Mesoamerica. Domesticated from perhaps 3000 BC.

run rig [MC]. A kind of RIDGE AND FURROW cultivation used in northern and western parts of the British Isles, especially in Scotland. Here agriculture was based on a farmstead rather than the village so that the area of cultivated land was usually smaller. Near the farm was 'infield' that was regularly cultivated. Beyond was 'outfield' that received no manuring and would be ploughed annually for a short time (typically five years) before being allowed to revert to grassland. All the arable was divided into ridged strips as in lowland England.

Russian Chronicle [Do]. Local annals, compiled in the early 12th century AD, which preserved detailed accounts of Swedish trade and settlement in Russia.

rusticated ware [Ar]. Type of pottery, mainly jars, and usually in a grey fabric. During manufacture, very plastic clay was applied to the exterior of the vessel after throwing, and worked up with the fingers into rough knobs, parallel ridges, or spidery encrustations. Of the 1st and 2nd centuries AD, with some still being made in the 3rd century AD in East Anglia.

rye [Sp]. A group of cereals of the genus *Secale* which occur in wild form in the Near East. Cultivated rye (*Secale cereale*) has been recognized in Anatolia from the 7th millennium BC, but it only became common in central and northern Europe from the Iron Age onwards.

SAA [Ab]. *See* SOCIETY FOR AMERICAN ARCHAEOLOGY.

Saale [Ge]. A widely dispersed group of terminal moraines marking the maximum southern extent of the Pleistocene ice-sheets in northern Europe and Russia. There are several phases to the deposition of the Saale within the broad period 200 000 to 1 200 000 years ago, each representing retreats of the ice-sheets. The oldest, represented as the most eroded deposits, are known as the Drenthe moraines, or in Russia the Dnieper moraines. The more recent, well defined and less eroded, are the Warthe moraines, or in Russia the Moscow moraines.

Saalian [CP]. Penultimate cold stage of the north European Ice Age climatic sequence, broadly 200 000 to 170 000 years ago; following the HOLSTEINIAN and preceding the Eemian. Equivalent to the RISS of the Alpine sequence, the Illinosian in North America, and the Wolstonian in Britain.

Sabratha, Libya [Si]. Phoenician and Roman port on the North African coast in modern-day Libya, excavated by Kathleen Kenyon between 1948 and 1951. Founded by the Phoenicians in the 5th century BC, it quickly became a major trading port. It was annexed to the Roman world in 46 BC, later becoming one of the three cities of the Roman Tripolitania, alongside Oea and Leptis Magna. The port was an important part of the sea-routes of the western Mediterranean, but also served to connect the sea-borne trade to the overland routes used by the trans-Saharan caravans. The city enjoyed great prosperity during the early empire, and in the 2nd century AD was made a *colonia*. A number of bath buildings and the Antonine-period theatre survive from this period. Sacked by the Austuriani in AD 363 and the Vandals in the 5th century, eventually the city enjoyed a second period of prosperity as part of the Byzantine empire in the 6th century AD. New walls were constructed, albeit enclosing smaller areas than in earlier times. Occupation of the site ended about AD 643 when the city was taken by Arab forces.

[Rep.: P. M. Kendrick, 1986, *Excavations at Sabratha 1948–1951. A report on the excavations conducted by Dame Kathleen Kenyon and John Ward-Perkins*. London: Society for the Promotion of Roman Studies]

sacellum [Co]. Latin word meaning the shrine in the headquarters building of a Roman fort.

sacramentary [Ar]. Book containing the prayers and order of ceremony used at (Catholic) church services.

sacred [De]. An object or structure that prompts or inspires attitudes of awe or reverence among believers in a given set of religious ideas.

sacrifice [Ge]. The slaughter of an animal or person or the surrender of a possession as an offering to a deity. Many societies in different parts of the world and at different times practised sacrifice, often according to regularized astronomical or calendrical events relating to dangerous or critical moments. Although generally seen as ceremonial in context, sacrifice may have functional ends institutionalized in the practice itself, for example the regulation of population and the creation of an instrument of political terror.

Sacsayhuaman, Peru [Si]. Inca ceremonial centre and fortress situated on a hill on the outskirts of modern Cuzco. Set out some time after AD 1438 in the shape of a puma's head, the site was originally planned as a Temple of the Sun to stand at the head of a site which would have extended over what is now Cuzco.

A round tower was built on the top of the hill, and three parallel zig-zag walls of cut and fitted polygonal stones run along the northern side of the hill creating terraces 550 m long. In the interior there were also storage structures and dwellings, a reservoir, and a water supply system. The site was used as a fortress against the Spanish in the 16th century AD, but after the conquest the round tower was demolished.

[Rep.: V. R. Lee, 1987, *The building of Sacsayhuaman*. Berkeley CA: Institute of Andean Studies]

saddle quern [Ar]. Two-part prehistoric handmill operated by moving an upper stone (rubber) backwards and forwards across the material to be ground which is spread across a rough-topped lower stone.

sæx [Ar]. In Old English a sæx was a single-edged knife or cleaver; examples are commonly found in Saxon and Anglo-Saxon graves. Continental versions have a curving back while English types (late 6th century AD and later) are straight-backed with an angle near the point.

saga [Ge]. Old Norse word meaning a story (originally in prose) of quasi-legendary events; colloquially, a long tale. Used chiefly to describe the historical stories current in Iceland in the Middle Ages.

saggers [Ar]. Large cylindrical fired ceramic vessels, with or without holes in the sides, used to contain unfired pots (especially glazed ware) or other kinds of ceramic products (e.g. clay pipes) to protect them during firing. Items were stacked in the sagger either on props or in a bed of sand. The filled saggers were then stacked up in the kiln, separating the items to be fired and thus guaranteeing less wastage.

sago [Sp]. Palm (*Metroxylon sagu*) native to Indonesia and Samoa which stores large amounts of starch in its trunk prior to flowering. The starch can be washed out of the chopped pith of felled trees and then cooked as a kind of porridge or in cakes. The antiquity of its exploitation is unknown, but it was widely used in Indonesia and Melanesia.

Saintonge ware [Ar]. Type of pottery manufactured in the Saintes region of western France from the 13th century AD through to modern times. The best-known vessels in this ware are tall jugs with polychrome glazed decoration dating to the 14th century. They are found widely across northern Europe, especially in England, and were probably traded alongside French wine. The jugs were only one of the types of vessel manufactured at centres such as La Chapelle des Pots, where kilns and workshops have been excavated.

saite [CP]. Twenty-sixth dynasty of Egypt dating to about 672–525 BC, during which time Sais in the Nile Delta was used as the capital.

Saladoid Culture [CP]. Early Horizon farming communities living in the Orinoco Basin of South America in the period from 6000 BC to 800 BC, before moving to the coast of Venezuela and beyond into the Caribbean islands around AD 50. Maize and manioc were cultivated, the former perhaps being the trigger to population expansion and movements. Saladoid Culture levels are recognized by the presence of distinctive ceramic styles, especially white-on-red painted wares. Some incised patterns and adornos are also present, suggesting connections with the Barrancoid styles.

Salamis, Cyprus [Si]. Situated on the east coast of Cyprus near modern Famagusta, this was an extensive major prehistoric and classical trading port. A Mycenaean settlement is known at Enkomi a short distance inland which may have been the precursor of the coastal port; legend records that Salamis was founded by Teucer, son of Telamon the king of the Greek island of Salamis, at the end of the Trojan War. The earliest deposits so far uncovered date to the 11th century BC, and the city was certainly thriving from the 6th century BC onwards when it was the most powerful city in Cyprus. A vast burial ground to the west of the town dates from this period and includes many richly furnished burial chambers. During the 5th century BC the town was the focus of resistance to the Persians, and the ships of Salamis aided Alexander at the siege of Tyre. After a turbulent period between 300 BC and the mid 1st century BC, Cato was sent to annex Cyprus to Rome in 58 BC. A Christian community was founded at Salamis by St Paul and St Barnabas in AD 45–6; St Barnabas, a native of the city, was martyred there. Salamis thrived during the Roman period but suffered badly from an earthquake in the reign of

Vespasian and during the Jewish revolt of AD 116. Further earthquakes in AD 332 and AD 342 completed its ruin. Constantius II rebuilt it and in his honour the new Christian city was renamed Constantia. Salamis was exposed to the full brunt of the Arab incursions of AD 647; despite several restorations it was finally abandoned in the Middle Ages.

[Rep.: V. Karageorghis, 1969, *Salamis in Cyprus*. London: Thames & Hudson]

Salcuta [CP]. Late Neolithic and Copper Age communities in southwestern Romania named after the eponymous tell site in Oltenia and derived from the VĂDASTRA CULTURE. Few settlements were true tell sites, the majority being short-lived open occupations. Copper objects are rare, but include axes, tools, and ornaments.

Salian [CP]. Meaning 'salty', the name given to Frankish communities who from about AD 350 settled in Holland and Belgium along the coastal plain and whose royal family, the Merovingians, subsequently became masters of Gaul.

Salin, Bernhard (1861–1931) [Bi]. Swedish archaeologist and the successor of Oscar MONTELIUS in the State Historical Museum, whose penetrating analysis of animal ornament of the 5th to 8th centuries AD was published as *Die altgermanishe Thierornamentik* (1914). It provided the basis of the chronology of migration period metalwork.

[Obit.: *Fornännen*, 28 (1933), 1–46]

Salin styles [De]. General term used to describe a series of art styles of the 5th to 7th centuries on northern Europe after they were first described by Bernhard Salin in his work *Die altgermanische Thierornamentik* published in 1914. Originally derived from Roman naturalistic animal ornament, the Salin styles are characterized by anthropomorphic designs transformed by German craftsmen into an evolving range of surreal and abstract expressions. Although mainly found on metal work, they also find their way into the stone carvings and manuscript illuminations of Christian craftsmen. Salin style I is of the 5th and 6th centuries AD and features crouching quadrupeds, usually totally disjointed and with the various parts intermixed in a close-knit pattern. This style is the counterpart of Müller's migration style. Salin style II is 6th and early 7th century in date and has the same beasts elongated into ribbon and tendril designs which are intertwined and interlaced together. In England the animals are etched in double outline and the bodies infilled with dots. This style is well represented on the gold objects from SUTTON HOO. Salin style III emerged in the late 7th and 8th centuries and has a more naturalistic emphasis, but introduces a ferocious gripping beast to many designs. This is what eventually gives way to Viking art styles.

saltern [MC]. A place where salt was produced by evaporating the water from brine to leave crystalline salt blocks. In northern Europe most salterns are situated on the coast and comprise a series of large open tanks that could be flooded with a controlled amount of seawater at high tide before being closed off to allow natural evaporation to concentrate the solution. When the brine in the open tanks was sufficiently salt-rich it would be taken to smaller tanks that could be heated by fires underneath in order to be further concentrated. In later prehistoric and Romano-British times, highly concentrated salt water would be placed in ceramic containers (briquetage) for final reduction and drying in purpose-built hearths. Inland, salterns are also found around saline springs such as in Cheshire, England.

Archaeologically salterns can be identified by the earthwork remains of the preliminary evaporation tanks and the extensive areas of burning associated with the reducing hearths. In Essex, England, these areas of burning have become known as 'red hills'.

salt-glazed stoneware [De]. In the 14th century AD it was found that the addition of salt to the kiln gases during the firing of stoneware meant that the salt volatilized and the resultant sodium chloride vapour fluxed with the silicas in the body of the vessels to form a soda-glass glaze. As a further refinement, a brown-coloured surface could be achieved by coating the vessels in a thin iron wash before firing. A patent was granted for the manufacture of such salt-glazed wares in England in 1671.

saltus [Co]. **1.** An area of pasture. **2.** Term sometimes used of a demesne in imperial ownership.

salvage archaeology [Ge]. North American term for the kind of systematic investigations, often partial, precipitated by development pressure or the need to rescue remains prior to their destruction. Based on the premiss that some work is better than none, salvage archaeology is the main source of archaeological information in areas where remains are constantly under threat. Because salvage archaeology is threat-led, it is only rarely possible to be selective about what is examined, and time constraints often mean that many of the more refined techniques of data recovery cannot be deployed. Known as RESCUE ARCHAEOLOGY in Britain.

salvage excavation [Ge]. North American term for the kind of archaeological excavations carried out in the context of salvage archaeology.

Salvian [Na]. Priest and writer. Born in Trier about AD 400, he became a monk at Lerins in AD 425 and presbyter in Marseilles about AD 439. He saw the barbarians, who by then had made his native province a German kingdom, as instruments of divine wrath and in his *De gubernatione dei* written in AD 440, presented this theological viewpoint, revealing incidentally much about provincial life in the 5th century AD. He died about AD 470.

Salzman, Louis Francis (1878–1971) [Bi]. British historian and editor of the VICTORIA COUNTY HISTORY of England. Born in Brighton, Salzman was educated at Haileybury and Pembroke College, Cambridge, where he studied medicine. Endowed with a small income at an early age he settled in Hailsham and abandoned medicine for historical research. During WWI he taught in a school and after the war moved to Cambridge and undertook coaching and supervision for the history tripos. In 1935 he succeeded Dr William Page as the editor of the Victoria County History of England. He retained this post until his retirement in 1949, steering what had already become a great endeavour through some difficult times and with slender funds. Under his management the 100th volume was issued in 1938. He published numerous other books, including *English industries in the Middle Ages* (1913, London: Constable) and the pioneering *Building in England down to 1540* (1952, Oxford: OUP). He retained an interest in Sussex throughout his life, being elected president of the Sussex Archaeological Society in 1954 and 1955, and helping with excavations at Pevensey Castle, Alfriston Saxon Cemetery, and Robertsbridge Abbey. In 1965 he was awarded an honorary D.Litt. by the University of Sussex.

[Obit.: *The Times*, 6 April 1971]

SAM [Ab]. Scheduled Ancient Monument. *See* SCHEDULING.

sambaqui [MC]. Local name for Archaic Stage shell middens on the Brazilian coast of South America. Some examples date from about 4000 BC, although the floruit of the culture is the period 3500 BC down to 2000 BC. One especially distinctive element of material culture is the well-finished polished stone effigies of birds and fish. Each effigy has a hollow on the back surface and it has been suggested that they were used in the ritual taking of snuff.

Sami (Saami) [CP]. Indigenous communities traditionally practising reindeer pastoralism in northern Scandinavia, north Russia, and Greenland. Formerly known by the general name of Lapps.

Samian ware [Ar]. *See* TERRA SIGILLATA.

sampling [Ge]. The process of taking a defined and quantified proportion of a larger population of target items as being representative of the population as a whole. A number of sampling schemes are commonly used in archaeology including: SIMPLE RANDOM SAMPLING, STRATIFIED SAMPLING, and SYSTEMATIC SAMPLING.

San Agustín Culture [CP]. A regional chiefdom of farming communities living in the highlands of south Columbia in South America in the period 500 BC–AD 500. Over 30 sites are known, mostly dispersed hamlets, although some ceremonial centres have been recognized. Agriculture was intensive and involved terracing and small-scale irrigation systems in the highlands. The ceremonial sites include earth mounds up to 30 m across, used for burials. Each mound contained galleries and tomb-chambers built of stone slabs. The dead were placed in carved stone sarcophagi. Sculpture was also characteristic of the San Agustín Culture, mainly anthropogenic forms carved on boulders, in cliff faces, or as free-standing pillars. The heads of these sculptures often have grimacing faces whose mouths reveal crossed fangs.

sanction [Ge]. A mode of reward or punishment that reinforces socially or politically expected forms of behaviour or conduct.

Sanctuary (The), Avebury, Wiltshire, UK [Si]. *See* AVEBURY.

sand [De]. Fine to medium-sized particles of between 2 mm and 0.06 mm across forming constituent components of natural and anthropogenic sediments and deposits.

Sandhills ware [Ar]. Style of middle Neolithic pottery found in Ireland and dated to between 3500 and 2500 BC. In 1961 Humphrey Case noted that the recurrent features of the style were the presence of round-bottomed inturned bowls, the upper part of the vessel decorated from a very large repertoire, partiality having been shown towards impressions of twisted cord. Lugs are common and the fabrics generally rather sandy. Included within his category of Sandhills ware were four substyles: Sandhills Western, Goodland Bowls, Dundrum Bowls, and Murlough Bowls. More recently, Alison Sheridan has questioned the integrity of the Sandhills ware group, preferring instead a series of regional sequences with parallel developments in coarseware and fineware.

San Dieguito Complex [CP]. Late Palaeo-Indian communities occupying southern California in the period 9000–8000 BC. They post-date local Clovis sites, and are characterized by the presence of leaf-shaped points/knives, choppers, scrapers, and hammerstones. The exploitation of coastland and marshland seems to have been important to these groups.

Sangoan Culture [CP]. Middle Palaeolithic, post-ACHULIAN, stoneworking industry found in equatorial and southeastern Africa, named after the type-site of Sango Bay on Lake Victoria, Uganda. The industry is characterized by light tools that include triangular-sectioned picks, scrapers, and core axes. However, few in situ assemblages have been found and the industry is extremely heterogeneous. Once seen as a technological response to wooded environments in the period

around 100 000 years ago, it is now seen as relating to communities exploiting dry relatively tree-free landscapes.

San José Mogoté, Mexico [Si]. Early farming village and ceremonial centre of the Formative (Pre-Classic) Stage situated in the Valley of Oaxaca. Investigated by Kent Flannery in the 1970s, the site appears to have developed after 1300 BC. Evidence of Olmec influence becomes apparent after *c*.900 BC when the settlement had grown to cover 20 ha or more and probably served as the ceremonial centre for up to twenty surrounding villages. A carved stone monument of this period depicts a sacrificed captive whose heart seems to have been torn out. Finds suggest that the occupants were involved in the manufacture and exchange of magnetite mirrors and shell ornaments. By about 400 BC, San José Mogoté seems to have been overshadowed by the new ceremonial centre of Monte Albán.

[Sum.: J. Marcus and K. Flannery, 1996, *Zapotec civilization. How urban society evolved in Mexico's Oaxaca Valley*. London: Thames & Hudson]

Sankalia, Hasmukh D (1908–89) [Bi]. Indian archaeologist who built the Department of Archaeology at Deccan College. Born into a middle-class family in Bombay he studied Sanskrit for his first degree at Bombay University and Indian history and culture for his MA degree. In 1932 he completed a thesis on the ancient Buddhist educational establishment at Nalanda before spending some time in London where he took a doctorate in 1936 on the dynastic history of ancient monuments in Gujarat. During this time he worked for Sir Mortimer Wheeler at Maiden Castle where he learnt the techniques of excavation. He was selected as professor of proto-Indian and ancient Indian history at Deccan College in Poona in 1939. Sankalia chaired the Department of Archaeology at Deccan until his retirement in 1973, building the reputation of the department and developing numerous programmes of survey and excavation in the region.

[Obit.: *American Anthropologist*, 92 (1990), 1006–10]

San Lorenzo, Mexico [Si]. Large early Formative Stage Olmec village and ceremonial centre situated on a raised natural plateau in the open country of the Rio Chiquito in the Gulf Coast lowlands of Veracruz. It was occupied from about 1200 BC down to 900 BC and was probably the main centre of Olmec civilization in its early stages.

The main axis of the site is north–south, and the main structures were built on an artificially modified salt dome. At the centre is a large platform mound surrounded by up to 60 smaller mounds and what may be the earliest ball-court in Mesoamerica. A unique feature of the site is its system of stone drains. It is estimated that over 1000 people lived at San Lorenzo. There is some evidence for an abrupt end to the Olmec occupation c.900 BC, perhaps because the population was torn between having to farm large tracts of surrounding countryside and building monumental public buildings. When the site was abandoned many of the carved stone heads were defaced and the structures dismantled. It seems likely that La Venta took over as the regional centre.

[Sum.: M. D. Coe, 1968, San Lorenzo and the Olmec Civilization. In E. P. Benson (ed.), *Proceedings, Dumbarton Oaks conference on the Olmec*. Washington DC: Dumbarton Oaks, 41–78]

San Pedro Culture [CP]. Archaic Stage hunter-gatherer communities, a subdivision of the Cochise Tradition, living in the southwestern areas of North America in the period 1500–200 BC. Characterized by the use of large projectile points with corner or side notches and straight or convex bases. Some settlements of this culture include oval pit-houses suggestive of a degree of permanence. Some groups may have been cultivating maize and other crops.

Sanskrit [Ge]. An early INDO-EUROPEAN language, still used in India as the literary language of Hindu religious texts. In 1786 Sir William Jones recognized the similarities between Sanskrit and Greek and Latin, thereby allowing the possibility of extremely widespread early language families.

Santa Maria [CP]. Seventh main phase of activity in the Tehuacán Valley of Mexico, dating to the period 1000 BC to AD 150. Characterized by small hamlets and villages.

Santa Rosa Culture [CP]. Southward expansion of the Hopewell Culture recognized as a distinct grouping in Florida. *See* HOPEWELL CULTURE.

Santa Rosa Island, California, USA [Si]. Possible Pleistocene kill site dating to c.30 000

years ago where it is claimed that dwarf mammoths, which were native to the island, were slaughtered by human groups. However, there is no certain association between the artefacts recovered and the mammoth bones.

[Sum.: C. V. J. Haynes, 1966, Elephant hunting in Northern America. *Scientific American*, 214(6), 104–12]

Santarem Phase [CP]. South American farming cultures found in the Lower and Middle Amazon areas of Brazil and tentatively dated to c.AD 1500 and later. Characterized by their ceramic assemblages which belong to the Incised and Punctuate Horizon Style of Amazonia. Vessels in this style from Santarem itself were festooned with adornos in the form of humans, crocodiles, jaguars, monkeys, birds, and frogs. Such adornment would have precluded much everyday use and instead these wares are interpreted as funerary vessels.

Santiago de Compostela, Galicia, Spain [Si]. This ancient city a little inland from the Atlantic coast of northern Spain was built around its great cathedral dedicated to St James the Great, son of Zebedee. A sanctuary was built on the site of the present cathedral in AD 813 to house St James's relics but this was destroyed by Almansor in AD 997. The present fabric was begun during the reign of King Alfonso VI in the 11th century AD. It was consecrated in AD 1105 and finished in AD 1128. Although many alterations have been made since, the basic plan of the church in the form of a Latin cross and the Romanesque arches in the nave are still prominent. The cathedral became one of the most popular centres of pilgrimage in northwest Europe.

[Sum.: M. Stokstad, 1978, *Santiago de Compostela: in the age of the great pilgrimages*. Norman: University of Oklahoma Press]

Saqqara, Egypt [Si]. Major necropolis adjacent to modern Abusir in southern Egypt. Burials started in the 2nd Dynasty, including many royal tombs. Over time the tombs became bigger and more elaborate, eventually being hewn from the solid rock. In the 3rd Dynasty two pharaohs, Sekhemkhet and Djoser, each built massive stepped pyramids surrounded by walled enclosures.

[Sum.: J. P. Laier, 1976, *Saqqara: the royal cemetery of Memphis*. London: Thames & Hudson]

Saracens [CP]. Originally the Arab tribes of Syria but later extended to refer to all Arabs, especially those of Spain, Italy, and Palestine.

Sarapis [Di]. Egyptian god, a late god introduced into Egypt in the reign of Ptolemy I, and a hybrid, having the characteristics of the Egyptian Osiris and the Greek Zeus and intended to appeal to both Greeks and Egyptians. Never popular with Egyptians but his worship spread from Alexandria around the Mediterranean. Represented as a bearded man.

sarcophagus [Ar]. Stone coffin, frequently highly decorated, in which mummified or wrapped bodies were placed for burial. Less commonly, lead, wood, or terracotta were used. The term comes originally from a Greek word meaning 'flesh-eating' and in strict usage refers to a limestone credited with the power of destroying flesh without trace.

Sargon [Na]. The founder of the AKKADIAN empire in the 24th century BC, the first successful empire-builder in Mesopotamia. Born around 2330 BC he was originally associated with Kish, but subsequently founded a new capital at Agade. Died around 2280 BC.

Sarka style [De]. Late variant of the LBK ceramics in western Bohemia around 4000–3900 BC. Sarka vessels were painted with black spirals on buff fabric before firing.

sarsen [Ma]. Hard crystalline sandstone found as boulders scattered across the chalk downland of central southern England, seemingly the remnants of now-eroded geological strata that once covered the chalk. Sarsen slabs were extensively used in the construction of Neolithic and Bronze Age monuments.

Sarup, Fyn, Denmark [Si]. An extensive series of Neolithic enclosures in Funen, excavated between 1971 and 1984 by Neils Andersen. The earliest and largest enclosure covers 8.5 ha and is known as Sarup I. It belongs to the Fuchsberg Phase of the Danish early to middle Neolithic (FUNNEL NECKED BEAKER CULTURE) around 3400 BC. This enclosure comprised a palisade fence, a fenced enclosure built onto the outside of the palisade, a fenced entrance passage, and two parallel rows of interrupted ditches. The material found in front of the palisade fence, in the ditches, and within the interior suggested to the excavator

that the site was used for ritual, ceremonial, and funerary purposes by a fairly large group of people. Sarup II, dating to around 3250 BC, was a similar structure but smaller (3.5 ha) and of slighter construction. It was a ceremonial site serving a population that lived on a number of small settlements in the Sarup region.

[Rep.: N. H. Andersen, 1997, *Sarup, vol. 1: The Sarup enclosures.* Moesgaard: Jysk Arkaeologisk Selskab]

Šašal, Jaroslav (1924–88) [Bi]. Slovenian scholar and archaeologist. Born in Ljubljana he was a student of Professor Klemene at Ljubljana University and taught himself in the archaeology department from 1951 to 1962. In 1962 he was appointed to the Slovenian Academy in Ljubljana, having special responsibility for Roman epigraphy. He published many reports and papers, including a magnificent archaeological gazetteer of Slovenia in 1975, to earn himself an international reputation. He undertook excavations at Emona, the forerunner of modern Ljubljana.

[Obit.: *Antiquaries Journal,* 68 (1989), 390]

Sassanian period [CP]. A Persian dynasty that ruled an empire extending from India to Syria from about AD 224, when Ardashir Papakan revolted against the PARTHIANS, until about AD 651, when the empire was brought to an end by Islamic forces. At its largest the empire extended from Transcaucasia and central Asia in the north to the Indus and southern Arabia in the east and south. In the west the Sassanian rulers were frequently in conflict with the Roman world. Sassanian cities were rich in impressive architecture deployed in palaces, temples, and fortifications. The vast territory was controlled by a relatively centralized political and military system.

satellite burials [Co]. Inhumation or cremation burials added to the structure of a barrow mound (long barrow or, more commonly, a round barrow) during the course of its construction. Satellite burials are thus broadly contemporary with the mound-building event, stratigraphically later than the primary burial(s) and earlier than any secondary burials.

satellite sensor imagery [Te]. A method of recording sites from the air using infrared radiation that is beyond the practical spectral response of photographic film. Useful for tracing prehistoric agricultural systems that have disturbed the topsoil over wide areas.

Satet (Satis) [Di]. Egyptian goddess of the Cataract and consort of Khnum. Shown as a woman wearing the white crown and horns. A goddess of fertility and the Inundation. Worshipped at Elephantine, Seheil, Esna, as well as throughout Nubia.

sati [Ge]. Originally an Indian word to describe the practice of a widow accompanying her husband to the grave. Archaeologists sometimes use the term to describe situations where a female burial is found alongside a male burial in the same grave.

Satis [Di]. Egyptian goddess. *See* SATET.

sauceboat [Ar]. Ceramic or metal elongated vessel with a wide spout at one end and a handle at the other, characteristic of Greece and the Cyclades in the mid–late 3rd millennium BC, probably used for drinking rather than pouring.

saucepan pot [Ar]. Coarse, cylindrical flat-bottomed cooking vessel shaped like a saucepan without a handle, current in central southern England in the mid–late IRON AGE.

saucer barrows [MC]. Type of Bronze Age round barrow found in southern Britain, named as such by Sir Richard Colt HOARE in the mid 19th century AD because of their shape and cross-section. Saucer barrows are circular, up to 40 m across, with an outer bank and ditch defining an enclosed space, in the centre of which is a low well-spread mound covering a centrally placed primary burial. Double central mounds are sometimes present. One of the range of Bronze Age round barrows that are sometimes known as FANCY BARROWS.

saucer brooch [Ar]. Circular brooch, concave in section, like a modern lapel badge, generally decorated in chip-carving. Distributed in the north German lowlands and in England, and dated to the 5th and 6th centuries AD.

Sauveterrian [CP]. Early Mesolithic communities of France and neighbouring parts of northern Europe dating to about 7000 BC. Named after the finds from two rock-shelters

at Sauveterre-la-Lémance, Lot-et-Garonne, France. Sauveterrian flint assemblages are characterized by a lack of wood-working tools and the abundance of geometric microliths.

Savernake ware [Ar]. Output from a substantial Roman pottery industry focused in northwest Wiltshire, especially the area now known as Savernake Forest. A number of kilns have been excavated and together suggest a nucleated industry comprising many separate workshops. The pottery itself is typically light grey in colour, flint-tempered, with clay pellets and grog visible in the fabric. Typical products include jars, bowls, flagons, butt beakers, and platters. Output starts at about the time of the Roman conquest or a little before and continues through into the later 2nd century AD.

Savory, Hubert Newman (1911–2001) [Bi]. British archaeologist specializing in the prehistory of Wales. He joined the National Museum of Wales in 1939 as Assistant Keeper. During WW2 he was involved in military intelligence because of his expertise in cartography and aerial photography. In 1955 he became Keeper of the Department of Archaeology at the National Museum of Wales, a post he held until his retirement in 1976. In addition to publishing several catalogues of prehistoric material held by the National Museum of Wales, he excavated several sites, including the Neolithic tomb at Penywyrlod, Powys, and the Iron Age hillfort of Dinorben, Clwyd.

[Obit.: *The Times*, 12 March 2001]

saw-pit [MC]. Long narrow trench or pit, usually lined with planks, over which large tree-trunks could be placed in such a way that they could be sawn into sections using a long rip-saw with one end worked by someone standing in the pit underneath the trunk while the other end was worked by someone standing on top of the trunk.

Saxo-Norman pottery [Ar]. General term for pottery produced in the period *c.*AD 850 through to AD 1150. During this time the use of the fast wheel became widespread and numerous local and regional industries emerged. The most distinctive pottery of the period is THETFORD WARE, STAMFORD WARE, and WINCHESTER WARE.

Saxons [CP]. Germanic people whose homeland was in the north German coastal plain, especially between the rivers Elbe and Weser. During the 5th century AD groups from these communities migrated to Britain either by invitation or invasion and in due course founded kingdoms which can generally be recognized by the fact that their names have the suffix 'sex' (e.g. Wessex). Those who remained in Saxony were absorbed into the Frankish kingdom during the 8th century AD.

Saxon Shore [Ge]. A term applied to the coast of southeast England from the Wash round to Southampton which from about AD 200 onwards was subject to raids by Saxon pirates. The name derives from the Latin term *litus saxonicum* which occurs in a late Roman history. The Saxon Shore was defended by a series of stone forts from the early 3rd century onwards.

Saxon Shore forts [MC]. A series of substantial stone-built forts along the southeast coast of England, usually at the entrance to large estuaries which served as harbours for attached naval units. The forts were created in response to repeated raids by Saxon pirates. Each fort had massive stone defences strengthened by projecting bastions and characterized by narrow gateways. A comprehensive coastal command developed with appropriate communications and administration. From north to south the Saxon Shore forts that have been recognized comprise: Brancaster (Norfolk); Burgh (Suffolk); Walton Castle (Suffolk); Bradwell upon Sea (Essex); Reculver (Kent); Richborough (Kent); Lympne (Kent); Pevensey (East Sussex); Porchester (Hampshire); Bitterne (Hampshire); and Carisbrooke (Isle of Wight). *See* SAXON SHORE.

SBAC [Ab]. *See* SCIENCE-BASED ARCHAEOLOGY COMMITTEE.

scabbard [Ar]. Leather, wooden, metal, or woven case in which a sword or rapier is kept when not in use. Most scabbards are provided with fittings so that they can be hung from a belt or sash; those for use by mounted cavalry will have a chape on the distal end that allows the scabbard to be held in place by the rider's foot while the sword is drawn.

scalar retouch [De]. Fine flaking on the surfaces and edges of flint or stone artefacts that

produces a finish that resembles the scales of a fish.

scalene triangles [Ar]. *See* MICROLITH.

scanning electron microscope (SEM) [Eq]. High-powered indirect microscope that produces an image by bombarding a sample with a beam of high-energy electrons. The electrons emitted from the sample are then scanned to form a magnified image which allows the examination of the structure, relief, and morphology of materials at between 20× and 50 000× magnification. In addition to its great magnification, the SEM also has a great depth of field. Most SEMs also have a facility to analyse the X-rays given off by the target as a result of its bombardment and, as each element in the periodic table produces its own X-ray spectrum, this can be used to determine the elemental content of the sample.

scapula shovel [Ar]. A scraping or scooping tool made from the shoulder-blade of a large mammal such as a cow, ox, or horse, commonly used by Neolithic communities in northern Europe during earthmoving or quarrying.

scar [De]. In describing flint or stone tools or cores a scar is the negative impression left after the removal of a flake or blade.

scarab [Ar]. A stone image of the sacred dung beetle of the Egyptians, an insect with black wings of the genus *Scarabeus*. Amulets and other pieces of ornament in which there was a gem engraved with a scarab were often worn in ancient Egypt as symbols of fertility. Many beautifully carved examples have been found in tombs and were used as replacements for the heart during the embalming process.

scarcement [Co]. A narrow ledge formed where a wall is set back from an underlying wall or structure.

scarlet ware [Ar]. A type of pottery found in the early Dynastic period in Mesopotamia in the period 2900–2370 BC, characterized by a set of geometrical designs in black on a buff-coloured ground, separated by large areas painted in red. Later examples of the tradition become progressively more elaborate and include animal and human figures in red outlined in black.

scarp [De]. An abrupt slope, natural or artificial.

SCAUM [Ab]. *See* STANDING CONFERENCE OF ARCHAEOLOGICAL UNIT MANAGERS.

sceatta [Ar]. Small silver coin minted during the period AD 690 until AD 790 in southern English and Frisian kingdoms. They are distinctive in being made from pellets hammered between a pair of dies. The earliest sceattas are those from Frisia in the last decades of the 7th century AD; these were imitated from about AD 690 by the kings of Kent and issued in a series of designs collectively known as the primary series. A secondary series came slightly later during the middle Saxon period and were issued by a number of kings and bishops. Secondary-series sceattas are found widely over England southeast of a notional line between the Humber and the Exe.

SCFA [Ab]. *See* SUBJECT COMMITTEE FOR ARCHAEOLOGY.

Scheduling [Le]. In the British Isles the legal protection of archaeological sites involves the selection of nationally important examples which are then added to an official list or Schedule. The process is known as Scheduling; monuments protected in this way are known as Scheduled Monuments or, incorrectly, Scheduled Ancient Monuments (SAMs). To be protected in this way a monument must be judged to be of national importance according to the following criteria: period; rarity; documentation; group value; survival/condition; fragility/vulnerability; diversity; and potential. There is no appeal against the Scheduling process which defines an area of land containing the archaeological site known as the Scheduled Area. Protection takes the form of controlling works within the Scheduled Area; before any works are carried out within a Scheduled Area, Scheduled Monument Consent (SMC) from the Secretary of State is required. Damaging a Scheduled Monument or undertaking works without consent is a criminal offence.

Schliemann, Heinrich (1822–90) [Bi]. Businessman turned archaeologist who set out to unravel the reality behind Homer's epic poetry. Born the son of a Protestant clergyman in Neubucklow, Mecklenburg-Schwerin, Germany, Schliemann attended the *Realschule* in Neustrelitz. After a five-year apprenticeship in a small grocer's shop he set sail for Columbia in November 1841, but was shipwrecked off the coast of Holland. He worked as a clerk in the office of the consul-general of Prussia in Amsterdam where he learnt numerous languages. In 1846 he was sent to St Petersburg where he became a remarkably successful dealer in commodities. He applied his business skills and ability with languages, eventually amassing a considerable personal fortune that allowed him to retire at the age of 46 in order to devote himself to the archaeology of the eastern Mediterranean. In 1868 a trip to Italy, Greece, and the Troas changed his life. He published an account of his observations and it earned him a doctorate in 1869. He became convinced by the authenticity of the places described by Homer, and set out to find them. He excavated at Troy over a series of four campaigns between 1871 and 1890; in 1874–6 he excavated at Mycenae where he discovered the shaft graves and revealed the wealth of the Aegean Bronze Age; in 1880 he dug at Orchomenos in Boetia, and in 1884–5 he worked at Tiryns. His discovery of 'King Priam's treasure' at Troy in May 1873 caused a sensation, helped perhaps by pictures of his second wife, Sophia, wearing some of the ornaments and jewellery. Subsequent studies have shown that some of Schliemann's claims are contaminated by untruths and that the 'treasure' was in fact a composite of finds from several spots. Nonetheless, his achievement is considerable, not least in attracting media attention and making archaeology a subject of public interest.

[Bio.: D. Traill, 1995, *Schliemann of Troy*. London: John Murray]

Schlumberger, Daniel (1905–72) [Bi]. French archaeologist specializing in the ancient Near East. Born in Mulhouse, he attended university in Strasbourg and Paris. Between 1929 and 1941 he was first Assistant Inspector and then Inspector of Antiquities for the French High Commission in the Levant. During this time he carried out excavations at Qasr-al-Khayr-al-Gharbi in the Syrian desert, and established an international reputation. In 1945 he went to Kabul as Director of the Délégation Archéologique Française in Afghanistan, where again he carried out a great deal of fieldwork, including the discovery of a Greek city dating back to the time of

Alexander the Great at Ay Khanum on the River Oxus close to the Russian border. In 1963 he returned to France to take up a Chair in Strasbourg University, but in 1969 he went back to the Near East to take charge of the Institut Français d'Archéologie in Beirut. At the time of his death he was on study leave at the University of Princeton, New Jersey.

[Obit.: *The Times*, 25 October 1972]

schola [MC]. A building used for religious observance and relaxation by members of a corporation or guild.

science-based archaeology [De]. The use of methods from the physical, medical, natural, and biological sciences to answer archaeological questions.

Science-Based Archaeology Committee (SBAC) [Or]. An advisory committee of the Natural Environment Research Council in Britain. Founded in 1978 to encourage and support research into the development and extension of scientific methods in archaeology. In 1998 the Committee changed its name to the Science-Based Archaeological Strategy Group.

scientific method [Th]. Grossly simplified, this means making an observation, developing an idea to explain the observation, turning the idea into a theoretical proposition or hypothesis, and then testing the theory against further observations made in a way that is replicable. Many archaeologists wish to adhere to such a method to ensure objectivity in their work. Essentially positivist in outlook, the quest for explanation is sometimes labelled critical rationalism. In archaeology, as in other social sciences, there are several inherent problems in applying the scientific method. One is the interdependency of the test observations with the theoretical assumptions of the hypothesis. Another is that because every piece of data collection involves unique circumstances it is almost impossible to replicate observations. For many archaeologists any use of the scientific method as an objective route to knowledge about the past is extremely implausible.

Scillian entrance grave (Scilly–Tramore Entrance Grave) [MC]. Type of late Neolithic tomb dating to the late 3rd and early 2nd mil-

lennia BC found in the extreme southwest of England, the Isles of Scilly, and a few restricted areas of coastland around the Irish Sea. Typically a Scillian entrance grave comprises a small round cairn up to 10 m in diameter, delimited by a kerb of orthostats, and containing a rectangular chamber opening from the outer kerb. The chamber is usually roofed with a small number of large stone slabs. Cremation is the usual burial rite and grave goods are rare.

scooped enclosure [MC]. A type of later prehistoric settlement found in northern England and southern Scotland. Each consists of a series of scoops and platforms lying within a stone enclosure wall or bank, generally situated on hillslopes above the valley floor in non-defensive positions. The size of the enclosures varies, some being homesteads with a single enclosed scoop and a slight platform through to large examples with perhaps ten scoops and floors separated by unexcavated ridges.

Scots (Scotti) [CP]. A tribal grouping living in the northwestern part of the British Isles whose early history and movements remain obscure. It is widely believed that from at least the mid 4th century AD the Scots were mainly living in what is now northeastern Ireland, although some scholars argue for an early presence in western parts of modern-day Scotland even by this time. Certainly the Scots are mentioned by Roman writers as being one of the tribes who joined together in attacking the northern frontiers of the Roman province of Britannia. By the 5th century there were certainly Scots in the kingdom of DÁLRIADA centred on Argyll, and they appear to have united with Pictland in c.AD 849. The king-lists give the names of the kings of the Picts and Scots together down to Malcolm III (d. 1095); the common ancestor they give is Fergus mac Erc who is reported elsewhere as leading the colonization of Dalriada from Ireland. By the 11th century Scots Gaelic was used throughout Scotland, except for the Hebrides and the Northern Isles which remained under Norse control.

scramasax [Ar]. An iron weapon comprising a sharp blade with a single cutting edge and an angled back typical of the 7th through to the 10th centuries AD. Over time they become increasingly elaborate with fine inlays in a variety of metals and some very distinctive pommels.

scraper [Ar]. A distinctive kind of flint or stone tool comprising a roughly round or horse-shoe-shaped flake which has been shaped deliberately with an extreme oblique angle to provide a working edge around some or all of the circumference. Where the working is confined to the distal end of the flake the resultant tool is often referred to as an **end scraper**; when working is confined to the sides of the flake it is referred to as a **side scraper**. USE-WARE ANALYSIS suggests that scrapers had a range of functions in woodworking, boneworking, and in removing unwanted fat from the insides of animal skins without damaging the hide.

screen [Co]. In medieval architecture in Europe, a partition separating the hall from the service space; sometimes applied to the space so cut off. Also applied to low dividing partitions in a church.

screening [Te]. American term for sieving where soil or archaeological deposits are passed through a mesh screen in order to recover small objects and ecofacts in a systematic and quantifiable way. *See also* WET SIEVING.

SCUPHA [Ab]. Standing Committee of University Professors and Heads of Archaeology. *See* SUBJECT COMMITTEE FOR ARCHAEOLOGY.

Scythians (Scyths) [CP]. Nomadic communities occupying the Eurasiatic steppes who, according to Herodotus, attacked the Cimmerians, living north and east of the Black Sea, causing them to withdraw south across the Volga and the Caucasian passes into Anatolia. The Scythians allegedly pressed on southeast into Media, where their raids are recorded in Assyrian cuneiform records of the late 8th century BC. The Scythians are noted for their vigorous art style, which was one of the formative influences on the development of CELTIC ART in Europe. Archaeological investigations suggest that the Scythians were essentially a settled agricultural population ruled by a horse-riding warrior aristocracy. Scythian burials such as those under mounds at Pazyryk, Russia, are very elaborate and contain many artefacts decorated with fantastic animal motifs. Scythian groups remained in southern Russia until absorbed by the Goths and other immigrants in the 2nd and 3rd centuries AD. In early modern times the term 'Scythian' was used more widely to refer to all later prehistoric cultures of eastern Europe.

Seahenge, Norfolk, UK [Si]. Prehistoric ceremonial monument discovered in spring 1998 as a result of coastal erosion. Excavated in July 1999 amid calls to preserve the remains in situ. Extremely well preserved, the structure comprises a ring of 55 closely set oak posts, slightly oval in plan 7m by 6m across, with an entrance opening to the southwest. In the centre was the stump of an upturned oak tree with its trunk embedded in the ground and root-plate uppermost. The remains of the honeysuckle fibre ropes used to drag it into position survived around the trunk. DENDROCHRONOLOGY has shown that the tree was 167 years old when felled in the spring of 2050 BC. Originally, the site lay well inland from the coast on fairly open dry land.
[Sum.: F. Pryor, 2001, *Seahenge*, London: Harper Collins]

sea level [De]. The mean height of water in the sea between highest and lowest tides. There are long-term variations in sea level as a result of two processes: changes in the volume of water held in the oceans, which is known as eustatic sea level change; and movements in the relative height of the land surface as a result of deformations in the earth's crust, which is known as isostatic change.

Sea Peoples [CP]. A collective term referring to various maritime groups in the eastern Mediterranean. Some were probably of Aegean origin, some possibly central European warriors recruited as mercenaries by Mycenaean princes during a period of great political turmoil in the Mediterranean during the period from the mid 13th century BC through to the late 12th century BC. They seem to have been responsible for the destruction of cities such as Ugarit and Alalakh. Historical records in Egypt refer to raiders who were repulsed in the late 13th century BC by the pharaoh Merneptah, and again in the early 12th century by Ramesses III. *See also* PHILISTINES.

secondary burial [De]. A burial, cremation, or inhumation that is dug into a pre-existing barrow or grave any time after its initial construction.

secondary context [De]. Archaeological material (including not only the more visible finds and environmental material but also context matrix and other components) that has moved from where it was first deposited as a result of subsequent human activity or natural phenomena. Secondary contexts may well include residual material from a number of PRIMARY CONTEXTS.

secondary flaking [De]. *See* RETOUCH.

Secondary Neolithic [CP]. General term, now discredited, developed by Stuart PIGGOTT in 1954 to refer to the late Neolithic cultures of the British Isles which he believed to be the result of local indigenous Mesolithic traditions merging with those of the primary immigrant Neolithic communities. Piggott's Secondary Neolithic was characterized by cultures using PETERBOROUGH WARE and RINYO-CLACTON WARE.

Secondary Products Revolution [Th]. An explanatory model published in 1981 by Andrew Sherratt to account for a series of changes in the later Neolithic material culture and subsistence base in central and northern Europe. Sherratt took the changes to indicate a fundamental shift away from flood-plain agriculture towards a reliance on domestic livestock, especially their 'secondary' products such as traction power for wheeled vehicles and ploughs, wool, and milk.

secondary working [De]. *See* RETOUCH.

Second Intermediate Period [CP]. In Egypt covering the 14th to the 17th dynasties, *c.*1750–1500 BC.

sect [Ge]. Religious movement which breaks away from orthodoxy.

section [Te]. The vertical side wall of an excavation trench, or standing vertical face cutting through selected deposits or features within an excavation trench, to allow the study and recording of stratigraphic sequences. Such faces are frequently drawn (SECTION DRAWING) and photographed. Attempts have also been made to take casts or peels of standing sections for future reference.

Section 106 review [Le]. *See* NATIONAL HISTORIC PRESERVATION ACT.

section drawing [Ge]. A detailed scale drawing representing the archaeological deposits observed in a standing SECTION. Some section drawings aim to be faithful representations of what is visible in terms of differently textured deposits and stones without any interpretation as to the identified limits of defined deposits or contexts. Others aim to depict the recognized boundaries between contexts and provide generalized descriptions of the nature of the deposits themselves.

secular cathedral [MC]. *See* CATHEDRAL.

sedentary lifestyle [De]. A residential pattern based around a single main settlement rather than involving moving camp at regular intervals.

Sedentary Phase [CP]. The fourth of five main periods defined in the cultural sequence of southwestern parts of North America, broadly the period AD 100–1200. Succeeding the Colonial and preceding the Classical, the Sedentary Phase is characterized by the expansion of agricultural communities, building on advances in irrigation made during the Colonial Phase. There were important introductions from northwest Mexico, including ball-courts, platform mounds, painted and effigy ceramics, legged vessels, and shell ornaments. Religious concepts associated with crop fertility were also introduced. House plans became more rectangular with the long axis at right angles to the entrance which was typically situated half-way along one side. A distinctive red-on-buff pottery was developed, the decoration comprising geometric patterns or figure patterns reflecting hunting activities or other aspects of everyday life. The Sedentary Phase embraces a range of local and regional cultures, including PUEBLO CULTURE.

sediment [Ge]. An accumulation of fragmentary particulate matter derived from the erosion, decay, or weathering of natural deposits or man-made structures.

segmental arch [De]. A rounded arch, the arc of which is less than a semi-circle.

segmental bowl [Ar]. Bowl of which the body forms part of the segment of a sphere.

segmentary society [De]. A social system comprising numerous relatively small autonomous groups who generally regulate their own affairs but who periodically come together to form larger groups and who, in some senses, may collectively appear to be a single large community. Segmentary societies tend to be agricultural societies living in small discrete areas of a larger identifiable territory.

segmented cist [MC]. A style of chamber construction found amongst long barrows in northwest Europe in which the chamber is divided into a series of compartments by the use of septal slabs and jambs.

Seine–Oise–Marne Culture (SOM) [CP]. Late Neolithic culture of the Paris Basin dating to the period 3400–2800 BC, characterized by a variety of tomb types including passage graves similar to those of Brittany, as well as local forms like simple stone-lined trench graves and underground gallery graves (*allées couvertes*), some with access through a circular 'porthole' in a blocking stone. Collective burial was practised. Grave goods include plain, flat-based, pots; leaf-shaped, tanged, and transverse arrowheads; a variety of stone ornamental pendants, amulets, and buttons; and occasional beads of copper.

Sekhmet [Di]. Egyptian lion goddess worshipped at Memphis as the consort of Ptah, and with shrines throughout Egypt. She was regarded as a manifestation of the Eye of Re, and acted as a destroyer of mankind. She represented the harmful powers of the sun. Her name means 'the Powerful One' and she was known as the Lady of the Messengers of Death. Associated with pestilence, she also became the patron goddess of healing, and her priests became doctors.

selective excavation [De]. Archaeological excavation of parts of a site using sampling methods or carefully placed trenches that do not uncover the entire site.

Selket [Di]. Egyptian scorpion goddess. Like Isis, Nephthys, and Neith, a goddess who guarded the dead. She watched over the canopic jar containing the intestines. Equivalent to the Greek Selkis.

Selkis [Di]. Egyptian goddess. *See* SELKET.

SEM [Ab]. *See* SCANNING ELECTRON MICROSCOPE.

semantics [Th]. The study of the imputed relations between signs and the designata: the meaning of signs such as may be found in material culture and its disposition.

Semenov, Sergei Aristarkhovich (1898–1978) [Bi]. Soviet archaeologist who pioneered the technique of microscopic analysis of wear patterns on archaeological artefacts to determine their function and uses. His seminal work on the subject, *Prehistoric technology*, was first published in Moscow in 1957; it was later translated into English and published in Britain in 1964.

[Obit.: *Soviet Archaeology*, 1979 (4), 314–5]

semiotics [Ge]. The study of the ways in which non-linguistic phenomena can generate meaning. In archaeology this is especially important because of its focus on material culture which is well known as a means of simultaneously carrying a wide range of meanings.

Semitic (Semites) [CP]. A general term that applies to a group of related languages rather than a set of recognizable communities. Semitic languages are characterized by the importance of consonants where three are typically used to form the root of a word. Arabic and Hebrew are the two most significant surviving Semitic languages.

Sennacherib [Na]. King of Assyria between approximately 704 BC and 681 BC. In 689 BC he conquered BABYLON, but much of his military power was devoted to maintaining his kingdom. One of his main achievements was the construction of an enlarged palace at NINEVEH.

septal stone [Co]. A stone slab set on edge to form a raised kerb between compartments within the chambers of Neolithic long barrows. Some especially large septal slabs have circular holes cut in them, known as 'PORTHOLES', to allow access between compartments.

Septimius Severus [Na]. Roman emperor AD 193–211.

sequence dating [Th]. A method developed by Sir FLINDERS PETRIE to provide a relative chronology for predynastic Egyptian ceramics but later applied more widely. The basic idea was to create a sequence of pottery types based on a typology of form correlated with stratigraphic relationships. Stages in the sequence were assigned numbers, 'sequence dates', so that when similar pottery was found at another site it could be correlated with the sequence and assigned a sequence date.

seraglio [MC]. The complex of buildings and courtyards which makes up the palace of a Sultan.

seriation [Th]. A method used to place artefacts in approximate chronological order based on the recognition of small-scale incremental changes in form or style. It is assumed that single artefacts or assemblages that are most similar are closest to one another in time and space. Sequences based on seriation can be tied to absolute chronologies if one or more of the artefacts can be dated.

Serpent Mound, Ohio, USA [Si]. *See* GREAT SERPENT MOUND.

Seshat [Di]. Egyptian goddess of writing and keeper of the royal annals, shown as a woman with horns reversed on her head over a star. She assisted the king to lay out the foundations of temples.

Seshmu [Di]. Egyptian god of perfumes, known from the Old Kingdom onwards. In the *Book of the Dead*, Seshmu is said to be a torturer.

Sesklo, Thessaly, Greece [Si]. Neolithic tell near Volos in the Plain of Thessaly in northern Greece excavated between 1956 and 1970 by D. R. Theocharis. Nine main phases to the settlement were recognized, beginning with a Pre-Pottery Neolithic that included domesticated animals and cereal remains. The early Neolithic phases (EN I–III) yielded very few traces of structures, and it is only because EN III was destroyed by fire that any remains of mud-brick houses were preserved. The main phase of settlement dates to the middle Neolithic (MN I–III), the 6th millennium BC, and comprises closely grouped houses of mud brick set on stone foundations. Each house has a domed oven in the centre. The site gives its name to a distinctive style of pottery comprising a fine white slipped fabric decorated with painted red geometric designs. The Classic Sesklo levels are succeeded by a late Neolithic horizon (Dimini) and a Chalcolithic horizon (Rachmani).

[Rep.: M. Wijnen, 1982, *The early Neolithic I settlement at Sesklo: An early farming community in Thessaly, Greece*. Leiden: Universitaire Pers Leiden]

sestertius [Ar]. Roman coin worth one quarter of a denarius.

Seth (Set or **Sutekh)** [Di]. Egyptian god, member of the Heliopolitan Ennead as son of Nut and Geb, brother of Osiris, Isis, and Nephthys, and husband of Nephthys. Represented as an animal with a long, graceful, greyhound-like body, long, stiff, forked tail, and square-topped ears unlike any of the canine family. His animals were the pig, the donkey, the hippopotamus, and the desert oryx. He was known as the Red God, god of the desert and thunderstorms; and above all as the murderer of Osiris. He was a very ancient god, not originally regarded as wicked, who gradually fell into disrepute during Egypt's long history. However, even as late as the 19th Dynasty, Sety I claimed him as his god, and he was a favourite with the kings of that period. The Greeks identified him with Typhon; and by Christian times, he had sunk in rank to an evil spirit or demon rather than a god.

Sethos (Seti, Sety) [Na]. Pharoah of Egypt at the beginning of the 19th Dynasty, 1304–1291 BC.

settlement [Ge]. An area of habitation comprising dwellings and associated private and communal facilities, perhaps surrounded by associated closes, fields, paddocks, approach ways, and other features, which together constitute a living space for the inhabitants of the settlement.

settlement archaeology [De]. The study of the internal structure, arrangement, distribution, and relationships of ancient settlements in the context of their environmental setting and landscape position.

settlement pattern [Ge]. Distribution of settlement sites in the landscape.

settlement system [Ge]. The arrangement of contemporary settlement sites in relationship to each other in terms of economic, political, and social structuring and order.

Seven Wonders of the World [Ge]. More properly the Seven Wonders of the Ancient World, these monuments were listed by the Greek writer Antipater in the 2nd century BC as being the most impressive buildings and works of art in the world at the time. Most of the sites have been destroyed or damaged by earthquakes and wars since Antipater set down his list. The Seven Wonders are: the statue of Zeus at Olympia, Greece, dated to about 450 BC; the tomb of Mausolus at Halicarnassus, Greece, dated to about 353 BC; the Colossus of Rhodes, Greece; the temple of Diana (Artemis) at Ephesus, Turkey, dating to the 4th century BC; the Pharos at Alexandria, Egypt, built in the 3rd century BC; the pyramids of Giza, Egypt; and the Hanging Gardens of Babylon, Iran, dating to about 626–539 BC. All except the pyramids of Egypt have been destroyed, although sculpture from the temple of Diana and the tomb of Mausolus are preserved in the British Museum in London.

Severn–Cotswold tombs [MC]. *See* LONG BARROW.

Severn Valley ware [Ar]. Burnished wares mainly in the form of bowls, jars, and tankards in a colour range from creamy-buff to orange-red made at various centres along the Severn. Kiln sites are known at Malvern and Shepton Mallet, Somerset. It was at one time known as Glevum ware, since it was first recognized at Gloucester. It is found all over the Severn Valley and small quantities reached the western part of Hadrian's Wall.

sex [Ge]. The biological and anatomical differences distinguishing females from males.

shaft [Co]. **1.** A straight-sided narrow deep hole cut into the ground. **2.** A slender column.

shaft furnace [MC]. A tall slender structure in the form of an upright tube or chimney open at the top with a combustion area or hearth at the bottom. There is an arrangement at the base of the furnace to control the flow of air into the hearth, usually by using natural draught or bellows. The draw created by the chimney section of the hearth allows a strong flow of air and very high temperatures to be achieved. *See also* BOWL FURNACE.

shaft-hole axe [Ar]. An axehead of metal or stone with a hole throughout for hafting.

shaft tomb (shaft grave) [MC]. A distinctive type of burial monument characterized by a deep narrow shaft running down into the ground with burials deposited either in the bottom of the shaft itself or in a small chamber opening from the base of the shaft. Found widely in many parts of the world at different times, the best known are those dating to the later 17th through to the 16th centuries BC at MYCENAE. Here the dead were placed in cists, either individually or in groups, at the bottom of an oblong shaft up to 4 m deep. The position of the grave is sometimes indicated at the surface by a stone marker or stele.

Shakimu [CP]. South American farming cultures found in the Rio Ucayali area of Amazonia and tentatively dated to *c.*600–200 BC. Characterized by their ceramic assemblages which belong to the Incised Rim Horizon Style of Amazonia.

shale [Ma]. Fine soft rock, also known as Channel coal and jet, that splits easily and can be worked into ornaments and trinkets. In northern Europe during prehistoric times dark-coloured black and grey shales were sought after and used for making pendants, rings, bracelets, etc. Sources include Kimmeridge, Dorset, and Whitby, North Yorkshire. Kimmeridge shale was also widely used in Romano-British times for ornaments and inlays.

shaman [De]. An individual believed to have special magical powers; a sorcerer or witch doctor. A medicine man in 'primitive' societies, often with supernatural powers, who was capable of healing or harming.

shambles [MC]. Originally a medieval market in which the stalls were let out for the sale of fish and meat. Later a shambles consisted of specially constructed buildings with stalls either side of a central channel into which blood and unsalable animal remains were swept.

Shang (Yin) [CP]. The earliest named Chinese dynasty known from historical records and confirmed archaeologically. Spanning the 16th to the 11th centuries BC, this Bronze Age power ruled the North China Plain. Traditionally preceded by the Xia period, the Shang is divided into a number of phases including the Erlitou, the Erligang, and the Anyang (1300–1030 BC). Historical records of the dynasty comprise oracle bones discovered around 1900 AD at the site of its last capital near modern-day Anyang. During the Shang period several settlements rose to prominence as cities, amongst them the capitals at Cheng Chou and Anyang in Honan Province near the middle Yellow River. Buildings were mainly of timber on rammed earth foundations. City defences were also of rammed earth. Burial was typically by inhumation in pit graves with the corpse extended and face down. The royal tombs at Anyang were richly furnished. The Shang period also saw the invention of the Chinese ideographic script and the discovery and development to a very high order of artistic and technical skill in bronze casting.

Shanidar, Iraq [Si]. A high-altitude cave site in the Zagros Mountains of northern Iraq excavated between 1950 and 1960 by Ralph Solecki. Thick deposits in the cave span many periods, the earliest of which dates to the MOUSTERIAN. It is from these levels that several Neanderthal skeletons dating to between 60 000 and 44 000 years ago have come, some thought to have been killed by rock falls. One Neanderthal was buried in a pit with flowers laid on the body and represented archaeologically by clusters of pollen. Another burial seems to have had his arm amputated at the elbow and lived for some time afterwards. Later deposits in the cave include Upper Palaeolithic levels dating to the Baradostian (c.33 000–27 000 years ago), and at the top of the sequence, around 10 000 BC, ZARZIAN Culture levels with some evidence of early farming in the region.

[Rep.: R. S. Solecki, 1971, *Shanidar—the first flower people*. New York: Knopf]

shard (sherd/potsherd) [De]. A piece of a broken pot or ceramic or glass vessel.

shawabti [Ar]. A wooden, stone, terracotta or faience statuette buried with the dead in ancient Egypt in order that it might perform any duties required of it by the deceased in the afterlife.

sheep [Sp]. A ruminant mammal (*Ovis*) with a thick woolly coat usually living in groups as flocks and known for their timidity. Wild sheep are now almost extinct, surviving only as wild populations in remote mountain regions of the Near East and Asia, and distinguished by horn-shape, build, and pelage. Amongst domestic sheep, six main groups are recognized: **Mouflon** (*Ovis musimon*) originally from Sardinia and Corsica where they are regarded as feral domestic sheep, recently introduced into the mountains of mainland Europe; **Urials** (*Ovis orientalis*) found in the mountains of Turkey, Iran, Afghanistan, southern Russia, Pakistan, and northern India; **Argalis** (*Ovis ammon*) very large sheep found in the Himalayas, Mongolia, and western Siberia; **Snow sheep** large-sized sheep found in Siberia; **Dall sheep** found in Alaska and the northern Rocky Mountains; and **Bighorns** found in the mountains of western parts of North America.

The domestication of sheep appears to have taken place in the Near East before 7000 BC. At ALI KOSH in the southern Zagros Mountains of Iran, an assemblage dating to about 7000 BC that includes hornless sheep is taken as clear evidence of flock manipulation. Sheep seem to appear in Europe already domesticated around 6000 BC in the Aegean and not long afterwards in the western Mediterranean. When alive, sheep can be separated from goats (*Capra*) by differences in scent glands, the lack of a 'beard' on sheep, distinctive horn types in the two species, and genetically in terms of the number of chromosomes present. Archaeologically, however, sheep and goats are difficult to tell apart from skeletal remains alone, the key differences being in the horn cores, metapodials, and phalanges. For this reason, many archaeological reports refer to identifications as being sheep/goat or ovicaprid.

sheepwalk [Ge]. Open expanse of ground used as sheep pasture.

sheila-na-gig (sheela-na-gig) [Co]. Stone relief panel of early medieval date, often incorporated into the fabric of churches and public buildings in the British Isles. All depict a grotesque female figure with exaggerated genitalia. Believed to be Irish in origin and intended as a symbolically protective device to ward off evil and ensure fertility.

sheiling [MC]. A small house or hut, often within an enclosure, found in upland regions and which served as temporary summer accommodation for herders and their families involved in TRANSHUMANCE. In Wales, sheilings are known as hafods.

shell-gritted ware [De]. Pottery made from a fabric tempered with crushed marine shell or fossil shell.

shell-keep castle [MC]. Round or sub-circular stone structure constructed on top of an earthen mound or motte at the focus of a more extensive defensive system that provides a fortified residence and military stronghold. Built in northern Europe from the mid 13th century AD onwards, many replaced earlier motte and bailey castles. The shell keep is typically 15 m to 25 m in diameter with thick walls and perhaps a single tower. Adjoining the keep will be one or more baileys providing an outer defensive circuit and accommodation for troops and servants. One of the best examples in England is Windsor Castle, Berkshire.

shell midden [MC]. An extensive rubbish heap consisting largely of shells discarded after the removal of the soft edible body portion, the result of many years of exploitation of marine resources as a main or supplementary food source. Shell middens are found in many different parts of the world from many different cultures.

sherd [De]. *See* SHARD.

shield [Ar]. A piece of armour carried in the hand or on the arm, usually the left, to protect against and ward off blows from offensive weapons.

Shield Archaic [CP]. Archaic Stage hunting communities living in eastern Canada from about 6000 BC. Few details of these cultures are known, although they were probably caribou hunters. They probably descended from Palaeo-Indian groups in the area. They used Agate Basin points in the Plano tradition of the Northern Plains. They are thought to be ancestral to the Algonquian-speaking Indians of the region who were still living in the area at the time of European contact in the 17th century AD.

shield boss [Ar]. A strengthened outward-projecting cover at the centre of a shield behind which is the handle or grip used to hold the shield. The purpose of the boss is therefore to protect the hand of the person using the shield. Shield bosses are often of metal, even where the main structure of the shield is wood or leather. They are often decorated or ornamented. The shape and form of shield bosses are often chronologically and culturally specific.

shield-pattern palstave [Ar]. Style of bronze palstave characteristic of the Acton Park

Industrial Phase of the British Bronze Age (*c*.1500–1250 BC) with a raised triangular-shaped area cast into the body of the palstave immediately below the stop ridge.

shifting cultivation [De]. *See* SLASH AND BURN AGRICULTURE.

ship burial (boat burial) [MC]. A burial deposited inside a boat or ship that is taken out of the water and put in a pit in the ground. Such burials are sometimes covered by barrows, as in Mound 1 at SUTTON HOO, Suffolk. Ship burials are a distinctive feature of Viking communities in northwest Europe, but are found in other cultures too.

Shipibo Phase [CP]. South American farming cultures found in the Rio Ucayali area of Amazonia and tentatively dated to *c*.AD 1500 and later. Characterized by their ceramic assemblages which belong to the Polychrome Horizon Style of Amazonia.

Shirataki, Japan [Si]. A group of Upper Palaeolithic sites on the terraces of the Yubetsu River in the Hokkaido region of Japan. Excavations in the 1950s and 1960s revealed two main groups of material. The oldest dates to between 18 000 and 13 000 years ago and includes large blades, burins, scrapers, and some bifacial points made on obsidian. The younger group dating to the period 13 000 through to 10 000 years ago has more bifacial points and microblades, the latter made in a distinctive technique, known as the Yubetsu technique, in which a large biface is made into a core in the form of a long carinated scraper.

[Rep.: T. Naganuma *et al.*, 1999, Excavation report on the Shirataki site group in Shirataki Village, Manbetsu District. *Journal of the Japanese Archaeological Association*, 8, 101–16]

shire [Ge]. An administrative and political subdivision of the Saxon kingdoms which developed into the principal division of England as a whole during the later 1st millennium AD. Initially established as military districts from which an army could be raised, the ealdorman as the leader of a shire soon had other responsibilities including tax collection and presiding over a shire court or MOOT. By the mid 10th century AD subdivisions of the shires were also widely recognized: **hundreds** in the midlands and south and

wapentakes in the north where Scandinavian influence was strongest. It is suspected, however, that these smaller units (roughly equal to 100 HIDES of land) were in fact much older as defined territories than the shires they formed part of; in some cases the hundreds may originate in late Roman administrative units.

shoe-last adze [Ar]. Long thin chisel-shaped ground-stone tool with a D-shaped cross-section. Common in LBK assemblages of central Europe during the early Neolithic where they were probably used as a sort of hoe.

shooting butt [MC]. An earthen bank used to support a target for archery practice or, more recently, for shooting practice using a firearm such as a rifle or pistol.

short-necked beakers [Ar]. *See* BEAKER.

shot-gun survey [Sl]. Use of intuitive knowledge (real or imagined) to direct survey areas or sample points to places that are likely to yield good results.

shouldered point [Ar]. A general type of flint or stone tool manufactured on a blade with a notch on one side to create an asymmetrical outline. Such points may be wholly or partly flaked on one or both sides. They occur in the assemblages of many cultures, but are especially common in the Upper Palaeolithic industries of Europe.

shovel pit testing [Te]. An extensive survey technique to sample the content of topsoil within a defined area by taking a fixed volume of soil (usually a shovelful) out of the ground and sieving/screening it to separate out and quantify the artefact population. Widely used in the field evaluation of large areas in order to identify buried sites and define their approximate extent.

shovel scraping [Te]. Use of a sharpened shovel to carve thin slices from the floor of an excavation unit.

shrine [MC]. A small sacred place associated with a particular deity or dedicated to a particular person or event. A shrine may be constructed as part of a religious or ceremonial structure, but many exist within domestic buildings or in isolation to mark the special character of a particular place.

shroud [Ar]. A sheet-like garment or covering used to wrap a corpse prior to burial.

shrunken medieval village [MC]. *See* DESERTED MEDIEVAL VILLAGE.

Shu [Di]. Egyptian god of the air, son of Atum. He and Tefnut were the first pair of the Heliopolitan Ennead. Shu was represented as a man with arms raised above his head holding up Nut, the sky goddess, and separating her from Geb, the earth god. He was the personification of the 'breath of life' which gives life to all creatures.

Sibyl [Ge]. Perhaps originally a single prophetess who wandered from centre to centre, but later there are recognized individuals taking the role of the Sibyl at Delphi, Claros, Dodona, Cumae, etc. That the Sibyl was important at Delphi is proved by the preservation of an outcrop of rock, left unworked in its natural state, in the midst of an area of fine building and statues, just because in early times the Sibyl had given her utterances from that improvised platform.

sickle [Ar]. A kind of knife designed for reaping corn. Early examples comprise flint blades mounted in a wooden or bone haft.

sickle gloss [De]. A distinctive shine found along the cutting edges of flint and stone tools that have been used for cutting cereals or grasses. The polish results from the abrasive action of silica present in the stems of wild and cultivated cereals.

side-notched point [De]. Bifacially worked chipped stone projectile head with shallow and wide notches worked into both side edges near the base. These notches were presumably to assist attachment to the shaft on which the point was set. Side-notched points are especially characteristic of the NORTHERN ARCHAIC TRADITIONS of North America.

side-scan sonar [Te]. A remote sensing tool used in underwater archaeology to provide a plot of the features on the sea-bed. An acoustic emitter sending out sound waves in a fan-shaped beam is towed behind a vessel. The sound waves reflected from the sea-bed are detected by a transducer on the vessel and recorded on a rotating drum. The time taken by the sound to reach the transducer depends on the distance travelled and thus a three-dimensional plot of the sea-bed surface can be produced.

side scraper [Ar]. Scraper made by retouching one or more edges of a flint flake.

Sidonius Apollinaris [Na]. Gallo-Roman aristocrat from Lyon, born about AD 430, son-in-law of the emperor Avitus, and holder of official posts in Rome. Elected bishop of Clermont-Ferrand in the Auvergne in 469, he coordinated resistance to the Visigoths. After the annexation of the Auvergne by the Goths in 475, Sidonius was imprisoned, but in 476 was restored to his bishopric. His surviving works include poems and letters which throw light on society in 5th-century Gaul. He died AD 479.

sieva bean [Sp]. A leguminous plant (*Phaseolus acutifolius*) with edible seeds in a long pod. Native of Mesoamerica. Domesticated from perhaps 3000 BC.

sigillata [Ar]. *See* TERRA SIGILLATA.

signal station [MC]. In Roman times a signal station was a distinctive military installation comprising a rectangular tower of stone or timber situated within a small enclosure. The tower was used for observation of the surrounding area and as a platform from which signals could be passed from tower to tower using fires or smoke.

sike [Co]. A drainage ditch, sometimes forming part of a meadow.

Silbury Hill, Avebury, UK [Si]. Reputedly the largest prehistoric man-made mound in Europe. Its present shape is a truncated cone with a base area of 2.1 ha and a height of 40 m. The flat top is 30 m in diameter. The chalk to build this mound was quarried from a ditch which runs round the monument, but which is now partly silted up. It has been excavated on numerous occasions, but most recently under the direction of Richard Atkinson between 1968 and 1970, work sponsored by the BBC. These excavations revealed that the construction of the hill took place in three stages.

Silbury I (*c*.2800 BC) consisted of a flat circular area about 20 m across which was enclosed by a low wattle fence. In the centre was a clay mound covered in soil and turves until it reached the fence. Over this was more earth

and stone to form a mound 36 m in diameter and 5.5 m high. Silbury II involved the enlargement of the first mound with chalk from the surrounding quarry to form a structure 73 m in diameter. In the final phase, Silbury III (?*c*.2200 BC), the mound was again extended to give a diameter of 160 m. The new mound seems to have been built in a series of stages producing the effect of a stepped cone. Each stage was constructed with a series of buttress-like dumps of chalk contained within retaining walls. The total volume of chalk in the mound is estimated at 350 000 cubic metres. What the purpose of the monument was is not known, as no burial has ever been discovered within it. It is partly intervisible with AVEBURY and a number of other contemporary sites in the area.

The top of the hill was occupied in medieval times, presumably because of its defensive potential.

[Rep.: A. Whittle, 1997, *Sacred mound, holy rings*. Oxford: Oxbow Books]

Silchester, Hampshire, UK [Si]. A major Roman city (*Calleva Atrebatum*) of some 43 ha which is remarkable because it was not occupied in the post-Roman period and now survives in open countryside. Extensive excavations during the late 19th century, together with more recent campaigns directed by George Boon in the 1950s and 1960s, and Michael Fulford since 1974, provide a detailed picture of the development of the site.

Occupation started in the late 1st century BC when a series of earthworks defined an *oppidum* site of the ATREBATES. Following the Roman conquest the settlement was made into the cantonal capital of the region and was enclosed within a series of perimeter walls defining an irregular octagon in plan. Internally a regular street grid was laid out with the usual range of central administrative buildings such as the forum and basilica. Some areas within the walled town appear to have been occupied as urban farms, while elsewhere there were well-appointed town houses. Several temples are known inside the town, and there is an amphitheatre to the northeast. There is a possible early Christian church of the 4th century AD. The site was abandoned in the later 5th or early 6th century AD.

[Rep.: M. Fulford and J. Timby, 2000, *Late Iron Age and Roman Silchester*. London: Society for the Promotion of Roman Studies]

Silk Route [Ge]. A rather generalized overland trading route of considerable antiquity that linked China with the Mediterranean. Dating from at least the 2nd century BC, if not earlier, the route is best known as the main conduit of silk, but other materials passed along it too. Starting in Chang'an (capital of the Han Dynasty) in China the route passed through the Gansu corridor and Wuwei into the Tarim Basin at Dunhuang. Here it branched into two main tracks across the nearly 2000 km of desert (the Gobi and the Taklimakan) and the Pamirs before converging at Merv to continue on westward via Ecbatana and Ctesiphon to Palmyra and the Mediterranean coast. The cities along the Silk Route (such as Kuqa, Khotan, Jiaohe, and Gaochang) became immensely prosperous at the height of usage in Roman and later times down to the 11th century AD. Marco Polo followed the Silk Route in the 13th century to reach the court of Yuan emperor Kubilai Khan.

silt [De]. Fine particles of between 0.06 and 0.002 mm across forming constituent components of natural and anthropogenic sediments and deposits.

Silures [CP]. Tribal grouping recorded as occupying much of Wales and the Welsh Marches in the west of Britain at the time of the Roman conquest. They are often associated with the prolonged resistance to the Roman forces led by Caratacus.

silver [Ma]. Soft lustrous greyish-white malleable metal (Ag) usually mixed with harder metals for the manufacture of coin, plate, and ornaments, etc. In antiquity most silver came from lead ore (galena) which usually contains silver oxide as an impurity. Silver was removed by the process of cupellation in which the lead is oxidized leaving the silver unaltered.

simple passage grave [MC]. A type of early and middle Neolithic burial monument found widely along the Atlantic coastlands of northwest Europe. It typically comprises a round mound of earth and stone up to about 35 m in diameter, within which there is one or more stone-built chambers accessible from the outside of the mound via a short narrow passage. The chambers are usually round, square or polygonal in plan and lack any structural compartmentalization. Burials by either inhumation or cremation were made within the chambers.

simple random sampling [Te]. A type of probabilistic sampling where the points to be sampled within a defined area or population are each assigned a unique number, the cases selected for analysis being determined using a table of random numbers.

simulation [Te]. The formulation of dynamic models or schemes that can be implemented by experiment or by being run within a computer.

Sinanthropus [Sp]. An early name for PEKIN MAN, now reclassified as *Homo erectus*.

Single Grave Culture [CP]. General term used to refer to a series of late Neolithic communities of the 3rd millennium BC living in Scandinavia, northern Germany, and the Low Countries that share the practice of single burial under barrows, the deceased usually being accompanied by a battle-axe, amber beads, and pottery vessels. *See* BATTLE-AXE CULTURE; CORDED WARE CULTURE; and GLOBULAR AMPHORA CULTURE.

Sipán, Peru [Si]. Burial ground of the early Intermediate Period situated in the Lambayeque Valley on the northern coast. The site was first discovered by looters in 1987, and subsequently excavated by Walter Alva.

The burial ground contains an unknown number of tombs belonging to Moche Culture royal and high-status people. One of the most spectacular tombs excavated so far (the tomb of the Lord of Sapán) was that of a warrior-priest buried about AD 290 while in his mid 30s. His body lay in a wooden box with a range of grave goods including a necklace of gold beads, feather ornaments, and fabric banners. His lower face was encased in a gold mask. In his right hand was a gold rattle, while in his left was a copper knife. Round about were the remains of two 20-year-old women (wives or concubines?), two 40-year-old men, and a dog. In the entrance lay the remains a 20-year-old man, dubbed the 'guardian', who wore a gilded helmet and carried a copper shield but whose feet had been cut off prior to burial.

[Sum.: W. Alva, 1988, Discovering the New World's richest unlooted tomb. *National Geographic*, 174, 510–50]

Sitagrio, Greece [Si]. Neolithic tell mound in the Plain of Drama, eastern Macedonia, excavated under the direction of Marija Gimbutas and Colin Renfrew in 1968–9 in order to explore the chronological and social relationships between the Aegean and the Balkans. More than 10 m of stratified deposits are represented on the site, resolving themselves into six major phases and spanning a period of perhaps 3000 years. The earliest, I–III, roughly correspond to the middle and later Neolithic of Bulgaria (KARANOVO III onwards) and date to about 4500 BC. Sitagroi III included material of Gumelniţa type. The later levels at Sitagroi (IV, Va, and Vb) correspond to the Bulgarian early Bronze Age (Ezero Phase). Sitagroi IV includes material comparable with that from Troy I. Together the Sitagrio sequence supports the claim for the autonomous development of metalworking in southeast Europe, separate from developments in Anatolia.

[Rep.: C. Renfrew, M. Gimbutas, and E. Elster, 1987, *Excavations at Sitagroi: a prehistoric village in northeast Greece 1*. Los Angeles: University of California Institute of Archaeology]

site [De]. **1.** Any place where objects, features, or ecofacts manufactured or modified by human beings are found. A site can range from a living site to a quarry site, and it can be defined in functional and other ways. **2.** A term used to define places of archaeological interest. Typically, they are assumed to be places where human activity took place in the past, but the term also refers to places where archaeologists are working in the present (which may not necessarily be the place of activity in the past).

site catchment analysis [Te]. A systematic study of an arbitrarily defined area around a series of known sites so that the main features of such areas can be compared to check for patterning or regularity. Developed by Eric Higgs and Claudio Vita-Finzi during the late 1960s, the purpose of site catchment analysis was to reconstruct something of the economy of archaeological sites. The size of the areas of search may be based on the sources of material found at the site or on notional working areas such as the distance that could be travelled out from the focus during the course of a day's journey.

site exploitation territory [De]. The area around a particular site which would have been most intensively or frequently exploited for resources such as food.

site files [Ge]. American term referring to the forms and records filled out by an archaeologist to describe the location, cultural affiliations, physical features, state of preservation, and other basic information about a site.

site formation processes [Ge]. *See* FORMATION PROCESSES.

site inventory form [Ge]. A pro-forma document upon which basic information about an archaeological site or monument is recorded by a professional archaeologist or suitably trained individual, usually during the inventorization of the archaeology of an area or during surveys leading to the discovery of previously unrecorded sites. The categories of information typically recorded include: type of site, location, date or age, size, form, archaeological materials present, condition.

site report [De]. A text and supporting illustrations that describe the results of an archaeological excavation or survey.

sites and monuments record (SMR) [Ge]. British term used to describe the detailed records of the known archaeological investigations (sites or events), remains (monuments), findspots, buried deposits, and areas of archaeological potential of various kinds within the geographical jurisdiction of a local authority (usually a county, district, National Park, unitary authority, or region). Most SMRs involve a computerized database linked to a series of maps, increasingly through the application of GIS technology. The main purpose of SMRs is to underpin advice given through the planning process, but they are also important tools for research and education. In 2000, the SMRs in England held about 1 million separate records of archaeological items.

situla [Ar]. Literally, a bucket, the term is applied to various forms of sheet-bronze buckets of the late Bronze Age and Iron Age in Europe, whose function was most probably as containers of wine for ceremonial or festive occasions. Pottery vessels, too, are sometimes described misleadingly as 'situlate' in reference to their shape, when their derivation from metal prototypes is at best secondary and their relation in function obscure. An outstanding series of bronze buckets from northern Italy and around the head of the Adriatic, dating from the late 7th to the early 4th century BC, is ornamented with elaborate human and animal scenes in a style known as SITULA ART.

situla art [De]. Embossed or incised decoration of early Iron Age date in south-central Europe, the medium for which was usually a bronze shouldered bucket-shaped vessel (situla).

situlate [De]. Used to describe a form of vessels, with wide mouths, short everted necks, high shoulders, and straight sides tapering downwards, characteristic of the early Iron Age in Britain.

Skara Brae, Orkney, Scotland [Si]. A Neolithic settlement situated on the exposed west side of the Orkney island of Mainland in the far north of the British Isles. Excavated extensively by Gordon Childe in 1928–30 and more recently by David Clarke during the early 1970s, the site is a village of up to seven stone-built houses occupied at any one time, surrounded by a midden and debris resulting from many centuries of occupation. Occupation of the site appears to fall into two main phases, spanning the period 3100 BC to 2500 BC, and is characterized by the use of GROOVED WARE style pottery. Perhaps because of a shortage of wood, the occupants of Skara Brae used stone slabs to construct furniture (beds, dressers, etc.) as well as fittings and fixtures within their houses, thus providing an almost unique representation of things that are lost elsewhere. Although the economy of the site included a major contribution from fishing and the use of marine resources, sheep and cattle were kept and there was some small-scale cultivation of cereals.

[Sum.: D. V. Clarke, 1976, *The Neolithic village at Skara Brae, Orkney*. Edinburgh: HMSO]

skeletal analysis [Te]. The study of human remains using the approaches of physical anthropology to determine such matters as age, sex, cause of death, racial affinity, evidence of disease, and the presence of wounds or injuries. Increasingly, use is made of DNA analysis to provide details of the person's physical form and appearance.

skeuomorph [De]. In archaeological usage, a non-functional survival in shape or decoration which implies derivation from an earlier form or from a prototype in another material.

skewer pins [Ar]. Long thin bone pins, sometimes with elaborated heads, typical of the later Neolithic in the British Isles.

Skorba, Malta [Si]. Major Neolithic site on the limestone Bidnija Ridge in northwest Malta excavated in 1961–3 by David Trump on behalf of the National Museum of Malta. The uppermost levels comprised a small temple that started life as a three-apsed structure in the Ggantija Phase (3600–3000 BC) before being extended in the Tarxien Phase (3000–2600 BC). Underneath is a fairly extensive settlement of the Ghar Dalam Phase (c.5000 BC) of the Maltese Neolithic, comprising houses with stone foundations and mud-brick walls. Nearby was what might be a precursor of the temples: an oval-roomed building dating to between 4300 and 4000 BC.

[Rep.: D. H. Trump, 1966, *Skorba*. London: Society of Antiquaries]

skyphos [Ar]. A type of deep cup with two horizontal handles mounted near the rim, common in prehistoric Greece and believed to have been used as a drinking vessel.

slab construction [De]. In studies of ancient ceramics this term refers to vessels produced by first joining slabs of clay together and them shaping the resultant vessel into the desired form by smoothing or Hammer and Anvil working.

slag [Ma]. Partly vitrified non-metal residue and waste material left behind after the smelting of a metal ore or in glass-making.

slash and burn agriculture [De]. A farming technique in which patches of forest are cleared for agriculture by cutting and burning the undergrowth. The plots are used for a relatively short time before being abandoned in favour of freshly cleared areas. Alternative terms include the German **brandwirtschaft**, the Spanish American **roza**, and the North American **swidden**.

slashed cup [Ar]. Type of miniature cup or accessory vessel found in early Bronze Age (WESSEX II) graves in southern England. Generally less than 15 cm across, slashed cups are characterized by having a narrow base, narrow mouth, and an expanded body with vertical slots cut in the side. *See* INCENSE CUP.

slates [Ar]. Thin slabs of slate, sandstone, or limestone used for roofing.

slavery [Ge]. A form of social stratification in which some individuals are literally owned by others as their property.

Slavs [CP]. A general term referring to a series of ethnic groups, distinguished mainly on linguistic and place-name evidence, who during the early Middle Ages inhabited the area centred on what is now Poland. The origin of these communities is not fully understood, but they appear to derive from the indigenous Iron Age tribes of the Oder–Vistula area such as the Przeworsk, Zarubintsy, and Chernyakhov cultures. State-level political organization can be seen amongst the Slavs from the 9th century AD, with nodes of trade and commerce established in towns such as Novgorod, Russia, and Kiev, Ukraine. The basic settlement unit of all these communities was the 'gród' or stronghold.

sleeper beam [Co]. A horizontally set timber that rests on the ground or in a prepared slot forming the base of a wall or the lowest structural component of a timber frame in a building or structure. Commonly used in Roman and later times in northern Europe, sleeper beams are rarely found archaeologically, but can be identified from compaction or the slots in which they once lay.

sleeper wall [Co]. Low wall supporting a raised floor, especially in a granary.

sling [Ar]. A weapon for projecting stones or roughly spherical shot at high speed comprising two thongs attached to a pouch. By placing the shot in the pouch and whirling it round to gather velocity the slinger can release one of the thongs to hurl the shot a considerable distance and, with practice, a fair degree of accuracy.

sling-shot [Ar]. A roughly spherical stone, clay, or lead projectile for use with a SLING.

slip [Ma]. A fluid mixture of clay and water (with or without added colourants) into

which a vessel is dipped to produce a fine smooth surface.

slipped [De]. The surface finish obtained after a slip-covered vessel has been fired. When a slip is made darker than the paste of the vessel which it covers, the vessel is said to be colour-coated. *See also* COLOUR-COATED WARE.

slopewash [Ge]. A general term to refer to COLLUVIUM found at the base of a slope as a result of soil erosion and the down-slope movement of sediment and any associated artefactual material. Slopewash deposits may in some cases seal and thus protect early land surfaces.

slow wheel [Ar]. *See* POTTER'S WHEEL.

slug knife [Ar]. *See* PLANO-CONVEX KNIFE.

small find [Ge]. An object recovered during an excavation which because of its nature or position is individually recorded. The range of materials treated in this way will vary according to the nature of the deposits being examined and the range and quantity of material being recovered. On some excavations all finds are treated as small finds while on others it may be that, for example, pottery, bone, and building materials are treated as bulk finds and recorded only in their context of origin while coins, metal objects, and finely worked objects in other materials are treated as small finds.

smelting [De]. The process of extracting usable metal from an ore by heating to extreme temperatures in a hearth or furnace. Some metals may melt while being smelted and these can be run off or trapped in crucibles as ingots. But melting metals was not necessarily the aim; the main chemical reaction in smelting is that of reducing a metal oxide in the form of a bloom which can then be further worked by forging to drive off the remaining impurities. Archaeological remains of the smelting process include hearths and furnaces containing slag, tuyères, cinder, slag, and possibly ingot fragments.

Smith, Charles Roach (1807–90) [Bi]. British antiquary and recognized expert on the early history of London. Born and brought up on the Isle of Wight, Smith attended a number of local schools before being placed in the office of a solicitor at Newport. Soon tiring of this work, he became an apprentice to a chemist in Chichester, but after six years moving to the firm of Wilson Ashmore and Co. at Snow Hill in London. Later he set up on his own account at the corner of Founder's Court, Lothbury. From an early age he was interested in collecting Roman and prehistoric antiquities, and while living in London he spent 20 years watching and collecting from building sites and the dredging of the Thames. By the mid 1850s his collection was very sizable and recognized as being of great importance. After some negotiation he sold it to the British Museum for £2000; here it formed the basis of the British Museum's national collection of Romano-British antiquities. Smith belonged to many learned societies and was elected a Fellow of the Society of Antiquaries on 22 December 1836. He contributed many articles and papers to journals and magazines, and in conjunction with Thomas Wright founded the British Archaeological Association in 1843. In 1856 he published the records of Anglo-Saxon burials excavated in Kent by Bryan Faussett between 1757 and 1773 under the title *Inventorium sepulchrale*.

[Obit.: *Proceedings of the Society of Antiquaries of London*, 13 (1889–91), 310–12]

smith's hoard [De]. Term applied to collections of Bronze Age metalwork found in northern Europe that appear to represent the tools and stock-in-trade of a metalworker. Thus they typically contain broken tools and weapons cut up for recycling, ingots, moulds, and tools for working metal. It is speculated that these hoards were deposited or concealed by itinerant smiths for safety, but for whatever reason they were never able to recover them. Also known as **founder's hoards**.

smock mill [MC]. Type of windmill, of wooden construction, usually tapered and circular with a revolving cap for turning the sails into the wind.

smudge pits [MC]. Small oval pits with straight sides and flat bottoms found on numerous sites of the 2nd millennium AD in the mid west of North America. The fills typically contain carbonized plant remains and charcoal, especially in the lowermost levels. The uppermost fills generally comprise grey silts and loam. These pits were made famous because in 1967 they were used by Lewis Binford to illustrate the application of ethnographic analogy in archaeological reasoning and to show that they were probably used in the process of smoking hides.

snail shells [Ge]. *See* MOLLUSCAN ANALYSIS.

snake-thread glass [Ar]. Well-defined series of glasses of Roman date decorated with serpent-like lines or threads of glass which are either the same colour as or differently coloured from the body. The glasses were made both in the east, probably in Syria, and in the west, at Cologne and perhaps elsewhere.

Snaketown, Arizona, USA [Si]. Hohokam Culture village settlement of the Pioneer and early Sedentary stages (300 BC–AD 1100) situated in the lower Gila River valley. Excavations by Emil Haury in 1964–5 revealed that the site covered more than 1 square km with over 60 refuse mounds. In the centre is a plaza and ball-court, around which were numerous pit-houses. Cultivated areas around the village were watered through an extensive irrigation system. Maize, squash, and beans were grown. Pottery production and the manufacture of shell ornaments took place at the site. Links with Mesoamerican communities are attested by the presence of copper bells and figurines.

[Rep.: E. W. Haury, 1976, *The Hohokam, desert farmers and craftsmen: Excavations at Snaketown 1964–1965*. Tucson: University of Arizona Press]

Snefru [Na]. Egyptian ruler and founder of the 4th Dynasty. Well known for his building works, including the two pyramids at Dahshur.

Sobek (Sobek-re) [Di]. Egyptian god, the crocodile god of Kom Ombo and the Fayum. Shown either as a crocodile or as a crocodile-headed man. Worshipped wherever the River Nile presented difficulties, for example at Silsileh, in the cataracts, and in swampy areas. Equivalent of the Greek Suchos. *See also* RA.

social action [Th]. A concept borrowed from sociology and which originated in the work of Max Weber and the four-fold categorization of social action: Wertrationalität, Zweckrationalität, Traditional, and Affektuell. Social action can be conceived in terms of an actor/person behaving in such a way that his/her action is intended to influence the actions or behaviour of one or more other people. Thus in archaeology the creation of monuments or material culture can be seen, in these terms, in pre-capitalist societies orientated to the 'traditional' rationale in Weber's analysis.

social anthropology [Ge]. An offshoot of the general discipline of anthropology which emphasized social and cultural factors in explaining human behaviour and material culture. The British equivalent of cultural anthropology.

social archaeology [Th]. A subdiscipline of archaeology developed in the 1970s by Colin Renfrew and others which follows the contention, widely held in Anglo-American archaeology, that understanding the archaeological past must involve reconstructing past societies and social practices in their totality; that artefacts and other archaeological finds must be placed in a social context. Taking a lead from anthropological and sociological enquiries this means taking a 'top-down' view by focusing on the systems, institutions, and organization of society before attempting to look at the role of the individual and their actions.

social change [Ge]. One of the most difficult but equally one of the most fascinating problems addressed by modern archaeology. For most of the 19th century and the first half of the 20th century archaeologists followed an essentially evolutionary model which mapped human history in terms of progression from barbarism to civilization. From the 1960s, however, attention began to focus on tracking more localized trajectories of change using SYSTEMS THEORY and what have become characterized as PROCESSUAL approaches. Since the later 1980s attention has tended to focus on still smaller-scale views of change, as represented within the use of individual structures, monuments, and landscapes, for example.

social constructivism [Th]. The proposition that all knowledge, including so-called 'scientific knowledge' is not a neutral body of data independent of cultural norms and values, but is actually socially constructed in support of particular values and understandings.

Social Darwinism [Th]. View of social evolution emphasizing the importance of struggle

or warfare between groups or societies as the motor of development and social change.

socialization [Ge]. The patterns of child-rearing that serve to endorse behaviours and understandings of the world that are approved of by society.

social reproduction [Ge]. The processes which sustain or perpetuate characteristics of a given social structure or tradition over a period of time.

social system [Ge]. The organizational form of a given society which according to Anthony Giddens is constituted by processes involving the mutual orientation of actors toward one another such that each is both an individual and an object of orientation for other actors. This mutual orientation gives rise to mutual responses of a plurality of goal-directed actions in a symbolically defined environment.

Society for American Archaeology (SAA) [Or]. Founded on 28 December 1934 at the Hotel Roosevelt, Pittsburgh, Pennsylvania, when 31 individuals signed the constitution. The SAA has since come to represent professional and non-professional archaeologists in America and is one of the premier archaeological societies in the world. The society publishes the journals *American Antiquity* and *Latin American Antiquity*, and holds an annual conference.

Society for Medieval Archaeology [Or]. Membership society, one of the main period societies based in the UK, established in 1957 to further the study of the period from the 5th to the 16th centuries AD, primarily from the archaeological evidence, and to act as a forum for coordinating the efforts of archaeologists working on medieval matters. Although the primary focus of attention is Britain and Ireland this is set within a broader international perspective. Publications include *Medieval Archaeology*.

Society for Post-Medieval Archaeology [Or]. Membership society, one of the main period societies based in the UK, established in 1967 to promote the study of archaeological evidence of British and colonial history of the post-medieval period before the onset of industrialization. Publications include *Post-Medieval Archaeology*.

Society for the Promotion of Roman Studies [Or]. *See* ROMAN SOCIETY.

Society of Antiquaries of London [Or]. Founded in December 1707 for the encouragement, advancement, and furtherance of the study and knowledge of antiquities and history of Britain and other countries. The society is the second oldest of the Royal Societies in Britain, receiving its Royal Charter from King George II on 2 November 1751. With a fellowship of about 2000 elected by secret ballot of its existing Fellows, the society holds weekly meetings and maintains one of the largest specialist archaeological libraries in the world at its rooms in Burlington House, Piccadilly, London. Publications of the society include *Archaeologia*, *Antiquaries Journal*, and the *Reports of the Research Committee*. Fellowship of the society permits use of the distinction FSA.

Society of Antiquaries of Scotland [Or]. The society was instituted in 1780 to study the antiquities of Scotland, particularly through archaeological research. A library and offices are maintained at the National Museums of Scotland in Edinburgh. Publications include the *Proceedings of the Society of Antiquaries of Scotland* and *Research Reports*. Fellowship of the society permits use of the distinction FSA (Scot).

Society of Professional Archaeologists (SOPA) [Or]. Established in 1976, SOPA was an association of professional practitioners of archaeology in North America. There were two categories of affiliation: Certified Member, and Certification in one or more areas of emphasis without membership. Before Certification and/or Membership was granted an individual's qualifications were assessed. The basic responsibilities of SOPA were to define professionalism in archaeology, to provide a measure against which to evaluate archaeological recommendations and research, and to furnish a forum for a challenge to such recommendations and research. All Certified Professional Archaeologists, whether Members or not, agreed to adhere to a code of ethics and standards of research performance. SOPA published an annual *Directory of Certified Professional Archaeologists* and a *Newsletter*. After 22 years of operation, however, SOPA was wound up and trans-formed into the REGISTER OF PROFESSIONAL ARCHAEOLOGISTS.

sociobiology [Ge]. An approach which attempts to explain the behaviour of both animals and human beings in terms of biological principles.

sociocultural [Ge]. Combining social and cultural factors.

socketed axe [Ar]. A type of tool typical of the later stages of the European Bronze Age in which the body of the tool is hollow so that it can receive a shaped projection at the end of the haft in order to secure the haft to the metal axehead. Socketed axes were produced in multi-piece moulds.

socketed spearhead [Ar]. A type of spearhead typical of the middle and later stages of the European Bronze Age in which an elongated hollow was cast into the base of the blade to receive the shaped end of the wooden spear shaft. Some socketed spearheads are fixed to the shaft by means of a peg set at right angles through the metal walls of the spearhead and the wooden shaft within; others are secured by lashings fixed to loops cast into the base of the metal spearhead.

soffit [De]. The underside of an architectural feature such as an arch, lintel, vault, or stair meant to be seen from below.

soft-hammer flintworking [De]. Method of flaking stone or flint in which a relatively soft material such as antler, bone, or wood is used to strike flakes or blades from the core.

soil [Ge]. A general term describing the organic-rich surface layer that forms naturally on the top of most bedrock types as a result of the weathering of the parent material, the addition of water-borne, air-borne, and anthropogenically introduced extraneous material, and the build-up of organic matter through colonization by plants. The study of soils is known as pedology. *See also* SOIL PROFILE.

soil chemistry [De]. The study of the chemical composition and properties of soils and archaeological deposits in order to determine the nature and extent of activities within the area examined.

soil mark [De]. Trace of a levelled or buried feature revealed by differences in colour or texture of the soil, usually in ploughed land.

soil profile [De]. A vertical sequence of recognizable horizons resulting from the development of a SOIL over time. Different soils have slightly different profiles because of local conditions and processes. A typical profile would comprise the following horizons or zones: organic horizons (L, F, H, and O); mixed mineral and organic horizons (A); eluvial horizon (E); horizons of accumulation (B); rock undergoing alteration horizon (C). Soils that are periodically waterlogged may also have a gleyed horizon (G).

Sokar [Di]. Egyptian god of the dead at Memphis. Represented as a hawk-headed deity. Equivalent to the Greek Sokaris. *See also* PTAH.

soldering [De]. Method for joining two or more pieces of metal together using a fusible alloy that attaches to both parts and forms a solid bridge between or around then. First recognized during the middle Bronze Age.

solidus [Ar]. Roman gold coin, weighing 72 to the pound, minted from 309 as part of the reform of the currency after the economic collapse of the 3rd century. The prestige coin of the later empire, in which taxes and tribute were demanded, it was valued by barbarians as far as Scandinavia.

solifluction [Ge]. When, in periglacial conditions, the upper layer of a soil profile thaws and the soil itself becomes waterlogged and sludgey because the water cannot drain away. Solifluction occurs when the liquid soil flows down to the lowest point available. This can cause the disruption or displacement of archaeological deposits as well as the burial of landscapes underneath displaced material.

Solomon [Na]. King over the united kingdoms of Israel and Judah during the period 965–928 BC. During this time he undertook several campaigns of building works, including works at sites in Jerusalem.

sol lessivé [De]. Type of SOIL that typically develops under open vegetation conditions and arable regimes, normally in areas of relatively low annual rainfall where soils can dry out during the summer months. They are common in northern Europe and appear to have originated in the post-glacial brown forest soils which were stripped of their protective forest cover and lost nutrients by grazing and crop cultivation.

solstice [De]. Literally, the sun's standstill. The extreme positions of the sun at midsummer and midwinter when its eastern risings and western settings appear to take place in the same position on the horizon for three or four days in succession.

Solutrean [CP]. Upper Palaeolithic cultures of western Europe named after material recovered from the site of Solutré in the Sâone-et-Loire in central France. The flint industries of the Solutrean are characterized by bifacially chipped laurel-leaf points. Examples date from around 17 000 years ago and were first made using pressure flaking. By the later phases of the Solutrean pressure flaking was also used to produce slim leaf-shaped projectile heads and small single-shouldered points. Many of the decorated caves in southern France belong to this period.

SOM Culture [Ab]. *See* SEINE–OISE–MARNE CULTURE.

Sompting axes [Ar]. Type of SOCKETED AXE typical of the Hallstatt C phase in southern England (*c*.700–600 BC) at the transition between the late Bronze Age and the early Iron Age. Sompting axes are so named after seventeen of them were found together in a hoard with other objects at Sompting, West Sussex, in 1946. They are made in bronze, of large size, show certain influences from contemporary Armorican axes, and have a pronounced collar with surface decoration comprising raised ribs and pellets.

sondage [Te]. **1.** Small deep trench or test excavation sunk through the deposits of an archaeological site to allow a preliminary investigation of their character and stratigraphy. **2.** Rather derogatory term used critically to refer to an untidy, hastily dug, poorly understood, and badly recorded excavation.

SOPA [Ab]. *See* SOCIETY OF PROFESSIONAL ARCHAEOLOGISTS.

Sopater [Na]. Greek writer of the late 4th century BC who produced parodies and farces and who probably lived and wrote in Alexandria.

Sopdu [Di]. Egyptian god of the Delta and deserts. Shown as a falcon on a shrine or on a perch. Protector of the desert routes and of the eastern frontier.

sounding [De]. A deep test pit excavated down through an archaeological sequence into the underlying natural strata in order to provide a preview of the deposits. *See also* SONDAGE.

souterrain [MC]. A long narrow stone-walled subterranean gallery, usually with a slab roof, found in western parts of Britain and Brittany, and dating from the Iron Age through to the early Christian period. In Cornwall they are called 'fogous'. Some have small chambers off the main passage. A few examples are known below apparently contemporary houses and in a few cases seem to extend below the boundary features of surrounding enclosures. Interpretations vary, some authorities preferring to see them as cold storage places, some as refuges in times of trouble, and still others as underground cult places.

South Cadbury, Somerset, UK [Si]. Large Iron Age hillfort overlooking the Somerset lowlands excavated between 1966 and 1970 by Leslie Alcock. Although there was occupation on the hilltop in the Neolithic it was not until around 600 BC that the site was defended by substantial ramparts. Over a period of about five centuries the site was intensively occupied and remodelled several times over. The use of the fort carried on past the Roman invasion at least to about AD 70 when for some reason there appears to have been an attack and some of the inhabitants massacred. From around AD 470, however, the site saw renewed activity. The ramparts were refurbished and those living inside the fort had access to imported pottery from the Mediterranean. The excavator associates this phase with the legendary site of Camelot, a proposal first put forward by John Leyland in the 16th century. Whether or not it was Arthur's fortress, the defences were strong and inside the enclosure was a massive timber hall 19 m by 10 m divided by a single partition and accessed through a pair of doors in the long sides. This occupation lasted until about AD 557 and was the last major use of the hilltop, although

King Aethelred took his forces there in AD 1010 and AD 1017 when under Danish attack, and in medieval times a small church and a mint were built there.

[Rep.: J. Barrett and A. Woodward, 2000, *Cadbury Castle, Somerset: the later prehistoric and early historical archaeology*. London: English Heritage]

Southern Cult (Southeastern Ceremonial Complex) [Ge]. A recurrent series of motifs, designs, and artefacts, often death-related, which suggests shared beliefs or understandings among a variety of Mississippian cultures in the southeastern part of North America in the 13th century AD. The motifs include crosses, the feathered serpent, 'sun circles', swastikas, and skull and long-bone, and eye-and-hand symbols. Traditionally, the repertoire is believed to owe something to Mesoamerican influences, but local origins are now regarded as more likely. The chiefly elites appear to have been the main participants in the cult, and whatever ceremonies and activities were involved they are likely to have been orientated to supporting the power and authority of these individuals.

space [Th]. One of the two key dimensions fundamental to archaeological research (see also TIME) and seen in a variety of ways. **Physical space** is of interest to archaeologists because human action is variously distributed in spatial terms and thus has to be explained. Distribution maps and, at a smaller scale, excavation plans help with this. Further detail can be added through studies of land use and the environment. More relevant, however, is **social space**, the arrangement of the world created by its inhabitants and defined by them in terms of differential values, emotions, and attributed meanings. Social space is defined and manipulated using material culture, and people's experiences of it and engagement with it are structured using the same means. Social space is also structured in terms of power, gender, and social relations through the subdivision of space and the control of access to it. *See also* LANDSCAPE and TASKSCAPE.

spacer-plate [Ar]. In amber necklaces of the early Bronze Age, broad, flat, specialized beams or spacer-plates were used to keep separate the strands of a multi-strand necklace by means of their several internal perforations, and to enable the strands to bifurcate as the necklace widened from neck to chest.

spade marks [Ge]. Negative semi-circular impressions left in the ground as a result of systematically digging an area using a spade. The marks are best seen archaeologically when the tip of the spade penetrates and removes a slide of subsoil which is then replaced by mixed soil from above as the ground subsequently compacts.

spatial analysis [Te]. Studies of the way that finds or sites are geographically distributed either in relation to each other or to other features such as terrain. The aim of spatial analysis is to recognize and understand patterns and regularities, and this can be achieved using a variety of statistical and mathematical approaches such as NEAREST-NEIGHBOUR ANALYSIS or THIESSIAN POLYGONS.

spatial association [Th]. An assumed close relationship between two or more archaeological items (objects or structural elements) because of their physical proximity and/or location relative to other more securely relatable items. Thus, for example, a pit situated in the centre of a ring ditch can be said to be spatially associated with it even though there is no physical connection.

spatula [Ar]. A bone or stone tool comprising a broad thin blade. The use of such items can rarely be specified, but they seem to have been used for burnishing pottery and in leatherworking.

Spaulding, Albert Clinton (1914–1990) [Bi]. A graduate of the universities of Montana and Michigan in 1935 and 1937 respectively, Spaulding had a long career in academic archaeology at a number of institutions, latterly at the University of California, Santa Barbara, where he was Dean of the College of Letters and Science from 1967 to 1971. He is remembered for his contributions to the development of quantitative methods in archaeology and his advocacy of methodological rigour and processual archaeology.

[Obit.: *American Antiquity* 57, 197–201]

spearhead [Ar]. A pointed and sharp thrusting blade for mounting on the end of a long shaft for use as a weapon in hunting or warfare. Early examples in flint are usually leaf-shaped and seemingly mounted in a cleft in the spear shaft. Later examples in metal often have a socket cast into the blade so that the spear shaft can be firmly attached.

spear-thrower [Ar]. A device that increases the power with which a spear can be hurled. Most consist of a stick or narrow board with a grip at one end and a hook or attachment to hold the butt of the spear shaft at the other. The spear-thrower thus becomes an artificial extension of the thrower's arm, giving extra leverage and range.

specchia (pl. specchie) [MC]. A type of burial monument found during the Iron Age of Apulia, southern Italy. It is normally a stone cairn over a single crouched inhumation within a slab-built cist lined to the outer edge of the mound by a narrow passage. The name is also applied to some larger mounds of uncertain function.

Speckhau, Baden-Württemberg, Germany [Si]. Mortuary complex comprising about 35 burial mounds grouped around the Hohmichele, the second largest early Iron Age round barrow in Europe with a diameter of about 80 m and a preserved height of 13 m, associated with the HEUNEBURG hillfort. The Hohmichele was partially investigated by G. Riek in the 1930s and found to contain eight inhumations and five cremations. Two of the burials had wagons with them. All appeared to date to the 6th century BC. More recently, excavations directed by Bettina Arnold and Matthew L. Murray have investigated Mound 17. Before excavation this mound stood 3 m high and was about 20 m in diameter. Five individuals of above average status had been buried in the mound, starting in about 600 BC with the central cremation. A later warrior grave contained a bronze cauldron and a set of iron weapons. The last burial dated to about 450 BC.

[Sum.: G. Riek, 1962, *Der Hochmichele*. Berlin: De Gruyter; B. Arnold, M. L. Murray, and S. A. Schneider, 2000, Untersuchungen an einem hallstattzeitlichen Grabhügel der Hochmichele-Gruppe im 'Speckhau', Markung Heiligkreuztal, Gde. Altheim, Kreis Biberach. *Archäologische Ausgrabungen in Baden-Württemberg 1999*, 64–8]

spectrograph analysis [Te]. Chemical analysis that involves passing the light from a number of trace elements through a prism or diffraction grating that spreads out the wavelengths in a spectrum. This enables the emissions to be separated and different trace elements identified. A useful approach for studying metal objects and obsidian artefacts.

speculum [Ma]. An alloy of copper and tin.

spelt [Sp]. *See* WHEAT.

spheroids [Ar]. Chipped spherical missiles either thrown or slung, or possibly used as a form of bolas.

sphinx [Ar]. A mythical beast with the body of a lion and the head of a human being found widely in Egyptian, Hittite, and early Greek art. In ancient Egypt it typified the might of the pharaohs and the mysticism underlying their strength. The best-known example is the Great Sphinx of El Gizah, more than 80 m long and 20 m high, probably dating from the 4th Dynasty, about 2529 BC, and perhaps representing the pharaoh Khafra.

spindle whorl [Ar]. A small, perforated disc of stone or pottery which acts as a fly-wheel, maintaining the momentum of a spindle rotated by the spinner whilst he or she teases more fibres out of a fleece.

spit [De]. Originally a 'spade-depth of earth' but in modern archaeological excavation the term is applied to a defined thickness of deposit (typically between 1 cm and 10 cm) that is removed as a single operation. *See also* SPIT EXCAVATION.

spit excavation [Te]. A commonly used method of excavating archaeological deposits by removing arbitrarily defined slices or spits of even thickness. Finds can be assigned to the spit and if necessary subdivided spatially by using a grid or coordinate system. Also called the **plano system**, spit excavation is useful in extensive, thick, and poorly differentiated deposits, but where clear boundaries can be seen between exposed deposits most excavators prefer to proceed by removing the deposits in reverse stratigraphic order.

spit-shaped currency bar [Ar]. Wrought iron bars found in the middle and later Iron Age of central and midland parts of England that are typically parallel-sided strips of metal sometimes with the corners bent upwards at one end. They are assumed to be ingots of metal, although whether they ever had any value as currency as their name suggests is questionable.

Spitsyn, Aleksandr (1858–1931) [Bi]. Russian archaeologist and founder of the empirical school of archaeology in eastern Europe. Spitsyn was a member of the Imperial Archaeological Commission to record the cultural heritage of Russia. Later his interests focused on the role of archaeological research and he developed the position that the basic task of the archaeologist was to provide the most detailed and accurate descriptions of artefacts and sites possible, eschewing premature historical or sociological conclusions.

[Bio.: S. A. Zhebelev, 1948, Biography and bibliography of A. A. Spitsyn. *Soviet Archaeology*, 10 (1948), 9–52]

spondylus shell [Ma]. A type of mollusc (*Spondylus gaederopus*), found only in the Mediterranean and on the Black Sea coast, which was extensively used during the early Neolithic for the manufacture of ornaments such as bracelets and necklaces. They were widely traded, and some found their way into temperate Europe where they occur in LINEARBANDKERAMIK contexts.

sponge finger [Ar]. A type of stone object found in later Neolithic and early Bronze Age graves in northern and western Europe, often associated with BEAKER pots. Sponge fingers, shaped rather like the modern-day biscuits of the same name, are elongated stones with a D-shaped cross section and rounded ends that typically show signs of wear. They were perhaps used in pottery production or leatherworking as burnishers or spatulae.

spotted dolerite [Ma]. A distinctive blue/grey igneous rock with white spots that outcrops in the Prescelly Hills of Pembrokeshire. It was used for making axe-hammers and battle-axes in the late Neolithic, and blocks of it were taken to Stonehenge, Wiltshire, for use in the stone circles of the Phase 3 monument. Group XIII in the classification scheme set out by the Implement Petrology Committee of the COUNCIL FOR BRITISH ARCHAEOLOGY.

spouted strainer [Ar]. A type of bowl, usually biconical, having a projecting tubular spout with an internal strainer, probably used for wine.

springer [Ar]. The VOUSSOIR which rests on the cap above a JAMB and marks the beginning of an arch.

Springfield style enclosure [MC]. Type of middle to late Bronze Age settlement found in southern and eastern Britain named after an example excavated at Springfield, Essex. A Springfield enclosure is roughly circular in plan, usually situated on a low hill or spur, bounded by a single or double line of ramparts each comprising a ditch flanked on the inside by a bank or box rampart. Generally less than 1 ha in extent, these enclosures served not only as settlements but also as ritual foci and the setting for craft activities such as textile production and metalworking.

square barrow [MC]. A burial monument of later prehistoric date in the British Isles that comprises a circular mound of earth and re-deposited bedrock, anything between 6 m and 15 m across, which covers a central burial deposit and which is enclosed within a roughly square or rectangular quarry ditch. The central burial is usually an adult inhumation and is variously set on the old ground surface or in a burial pit. Grave goods, in some cases including complete or dismantled wheeled vehicles, usually accompany the interment. Most square barrows date to the La Tène I period in Britain, broadly the 6th and 5th centuries BC, and are mainly found in Humberside and the East Riding of Yorkshire. An increasing number, however, are being recognized in other parts of England. The square barrow tradition in England has been characterized as a key part of the Arras Culture which may have been introduced to eastern England by settlers from France.

square barrow cemetery [MC]. Groups of later prehistoric square barrows forming organized cemeteries. Large cemeteries of this kind may contain more than 500 individual barrows, as at Dane's Graves and Burton Fleming in the East Riding of Yorkshire.

square-mouthed pot [Ar]. Term applied to the type of pottery found in middle Neolithic contexts in northern Italy. The characteristic shape is produced by taking a round pot and, while still pliable, pinching the mouth to produce a squared-off top.

squash [Sp]. An annual herb (*Cucurbita mixta*) that grows as a trailing plant and produces large yellow-coloured fruits with edible flesh. Native to south Mexico and South America. Domesticated by *c*.3000 BC. Recorded in the eastern parts of North America by *c*.2000 BC.

Squier, Ephraim George (1821–88) [Bi]. A North American journalist by profession, Squier was also an amateur archaeologist who is best known for his work excavating and recording hundreds of prehistoric mounds in the Ohio and Mississippi valleys. In 1851 he published an account of his work done jointly with E. H. Davis: *Ancient monuments of the Mississippi Valley* (Washington DC: Smithsonian Institution). Squier also carried out excavations in central America, Peru, and Bolivia.

[Bio.: *American National Biography*, 20, 519–20]

St Acheul, Amiens, France [Si]. Exposed river terrace formations in the Somme Valley that have been the subject of interest for geologists and archaeologists since the late 19th century. One of the first to study the sequence was V. Commont. He defined three main terraces according to their height above the floor of the buried channel below the terrace exposure: the High Terrace at 45 m, the Middle Terrace at 30 m, and the Low Terrace at 10 m. Although it is now known that Commont's sequence is over-simplified, nonetheless it is a reasonable approximation and allows a general understanding of several Lower Palaeolithic industries. The 45 m terrace is especially important because it is associated with a faunal assemblage of CROMERIAN affinities, broadly 200 000 to 300 000 years ago. It is here also that pear-shaped bifacially worked handaxes that have come to characterize an Acheulean tradition now recognized throughout Africa and the Old World have been found in considerable quantity.

[Sum.: J. M. Coles and E. S. Higgs, 1969, *The archaeology of early man*. London: Faber and Faber]

stadial [Ge]. A short period of colder climate during a glacial period that is associated with the growth of glaciers and ice-sheets.

stadium [MC]. An ancient Greek open-air running track and sports ground, providing for spectators by raised earth banks. The stadium was shaped like a hairpin, one end curved and the other, the starting point, either open as at Athens and Delphi, or squared as at Olympia. In the Roman period, stone seating was normal. Occasionally, as at Nicopolis, a Roman stadium was rounded at both ends. The standard length was 600 feet which gave a straight course for the sprint race of about 200 yards. The two-grooved starting line is seen at Corinth (in the agora), Delphi, and Olympia; postholes indicate a separation of the runners at the start.

stage [Ge]. In American archaeology this term is used to denote a general level of cultural development which may be regional or continental in its applicability. Thus the main ·North American stages are: Palaeo-Indian, Archaic, Woodland, and Formative.

stained glass [Ma]. Essentially glass which has been coloured either through painting the surface with translucent material or, more commonly, adding elements to the glass during its production to give a permanent tint. From about the 12th century onwards pieces of cut and shaped coloured glass were joined together in lead frames to produce pictures of scenes, events, and motifs that were put into windows. Mainly used in ecclesiastical architecture, by the 14th century and on into the Renaissance, stained-glass windows were being treated much like a painter's canvas.

stakehole [Co]. The cavity left behind in the ground after the removal or decay of a stake or post, which would usually have been part of a structure or fence. The cavity becomes filled with soil of a slightly different colour or texture from that into which the stakehole was originally cut, thus allowing its detection by archaeologists. *See also* POSTHOLE.

St Albans points [Ar]. Bifacially worked chipped stone projectile points with corner notches, manufactured by early Archaic Stage communities in eastern parts of North America around 7500 BC.

stalled cairn [MC]. Type of middle Neolithic chambered tomb found only on Orkney in the far north of Scotland. Some seventeen or eighteen examples are known, all part of Audrey Henshall's family of Orkney–Cromarty–Hebridean passage graves. Each tomb has an elongated mound with a central stone-slab-built chamber subdivided into compartments with projecting side slabs. The largest is the Knowe of Ramsey where the chamber is 27 m long with fourteen compartments and an original roof height of over 3 m.

Stamford ware [Ar]. One of the earliest forms of glazed ceramics manufactured in Britain. Dating to the 9th to 13th centuries, Stamford ware was made in a number of small centres concentrated around Stamford in Lincolnshire. The main products were spouted pitchers and jugs that were much in demand in England and sometimes traded abroad.

stamnos [Ar]. Squat two-handled vase used for the storage of wine during classical times in Greece and in Etruria during the 4th century BC.

standard deviation [Ge]. A measure of the distribution around the mean of a group of defined values. Normally, the values of 68 per cent of cases fall within one standard deviation of the mean, 95 per cent between two, and 99 per cent within three standard deviations either side of the mean. Standard deviation is usually expressed as a plus-or-negative ($\pm$).

Standing Conference of Archaeological Unit Managers (SCAUM) [Or]. Representative organization formed in 1976 to promote the interests of archaeological contracting units working in the British Isles to government, government agencies, and the public.

standing stone [MC]. A block or slab of stone perhaps selected for its shape or mass that was set upright as a marker of some kind. In the British Isles and neighbouring areas of northwest Europe the majority of standing stones date to the Neolithic and Bronze Age period, part of a long-lived tradition of using stones in this way. As free-standing structures they seem to mark sacred places, alignments, and sometimes burial grounds. Many are connected with broadly contemporary monuments such as STONE CIRCLES, and a high proportion have evocative names. A few examples, such as Long Meg in Cumbria, have been adorned with ROCK ART, while in Brittany, where they are also known as **menhirs**, large examples were broken up in Neolithic times and used in the construction of SIMPLE PASSAGE GRAVES.

Stanwick, North Yorkshire, UK [Si]. Extensive Iron Age *oppidum* of 300 ha, extensively surveyed and excavated by Sir Mortimer Wheeler in 1951–2 and more recently by Colin Haselgrove between 1981 and 1986. The site is believed to have been the principal settlement of the BRIGANTES in the last few centuries BC, and up to and after the Roman conquest.

The massive defences were mainly built in the mid 1st century AD, perhaps incorporating elements of earlier small enclosures. The focus appears to have been around the present-day church, in The Tofts, and in the northern part of the site. Equally important is the fact that the northwest entrance into the main occupation area was elaborate and massive in a way that was perhaps more to impress than frighten. This, coupled with the presence of imported Roman goods (including wine amphorae and tableware) suggests that the rulers of the Brigantes at this time were both powerful and well connected in international trade.

The great defences of Stanwick were only used for a short time. By the late 1st century AD they had fallen into disuse and the internal settlements abandoned. Historically, this coincides with the Roman conquest of the region, although it is always difficult accurately to match historical events with archaeological evidence. It is believed, however, that in the mid 1st century AD the leader of the Brigantes was a man named Venutius. He was anti-Roman, although his wife Cartimandua was pro-Roman. In AD 69 the Emperor Vespasian tried to establish Roman rule in northern England and the Brigantes rose in open revolt. Cartimandua sought safety outside her kingdom. An energetic governor Petillius Cerialis campaigned vigorously against Venutius between AD 71 and 74, and completed the conquest of the area soon after.

[Rep.: C. Haselgrove, P. Turnbull, and R. L. Fitts, 1990, Stanwick, North Yorkshire, Part I: Recent research and previous archaeological investigations. *Archaeological Journal*, 147, 1–15]

Star Carr, North Yorkshire, UK [Si]. Mesolithic lakeside settlement in the Vale of Pickering, dating to the 8th millennium BC, extensively excavated by J. G. D. CLARK between 1949 and 1951. The site is exceptional because of the quality of preservation brought about by the prevailing damp conditions. The focus of the site was a brushwood platform on the lake edge which had seemingly been used as a summer camp by people probably based on

the coast at other times of the year. The finds included more that 180 barbed bone points, bone mattock heads, a wooden paddle, and a group of perforated red-deer frontlets which may have been worn as ceremonial masks or hunting camouflage.

[Rep.: P. Mellars and P. Dark, 1998, *Star Carr in context*. Cambridge and Oxford: McDonald Institute for Archaeological Research and Oxbow Books]

Starčevo, Yugoslavia [Si]. Extensive Neolithic settlement on the north bank of the Danube opposite present-day Belgrade. Following its discovery in the course of clay extraction for use in making bricks, the site has been excavated on a number of occasions, notably between 1928 and 1929 by Miodrag Grbic of the National Museum in Belgrade, and intermittently between 1932 and 1938 by V. J. Fewkes for the American School of Prehistoric Research. Six main horizons have been recognized at the site, dating to between about 6000 BC and 4500 BC. However, most of the deposits at the site itself relate almost exclusively to the later phases of the Starčevo Culture, the period 4900–4600 BC.

[Sum.: R. W. Ehrich, 1977, Starčevo revisited. In V. Markotic (ed.), *Ancient Europe and the Mediterranean*. Warminster: Aris and Phillips, 59–67]

Starčevo Culture [CP]. Early Neolithic culture of the Balkans, dating from the period 5500 to 4600 BC, named after a type-site on the Danube near Belgrade. Part of a widespread group of broadly contemporary groups including KARANOVO I, KÖROS, and CRIŞ. The presence of sickles and saddle querns is evidence of cereal cultivation, and there is also evidence for the domestication of sheep, goats, pigs, and cattle, though the economy was still supplemented by hunting and fishing. Pottery comprised principally coarse wares, commonly globular vessels with rusticated ornament, and other material remains include characteristic bone spatulae and clay figurines. Starčevo Culture settlements are generally situated on the upper terraces of river valleys or on the edges of plateaux. The settlements rarely form mounds and almost never form tells, perhaps indicating a degree of adaptation to the more temperate environment. Cattle bones also exceed those of sheep/goat in the northern regions, again suggesting local adaptations to environmental conditions. The culture was succeeded locally by the VINČA CULTURE.

stateless society [Ge]. A society which lacks formal institutions of government.

stater [Ar]. Coin of gold, silver, electrum, or bronze; the basic unit of currency in Britain from *c*.100 BC until replaced by Roman coinage. The same as a shekel in the Near East and a didrachm in Greece.

state society [Ge]. A society characterized by a strong centralized government, socio-economic class divisions, a market economy and large populations. Settlements are substantial and may be classified as cities with formal planning and monumental architecture. States represent the most complicated form of social and political organization so far recognized.

statue menhir [Ar]. A stone slab carved or modified to represent the human form, often in a highly stylized manner, found amongst the later prehistoric cultures of Europe. Both male and female forms are known. Some examples show details of clothes, weapons, and ornaments. There are a number of clusters of such monuments, although most probably developed independently of each other, in Spain, southern France, Corsica, Sardinia, Italy, and the Channel Islands. Originally, statue menhirs appear to have stood upright in the ground.

status [De]. The rank or position of an individual within a society, and the responsibilities and privileges that go with it. Status may be achieved (as a result of the actions and works of the individual) or ascribed (usually by birth into a particular family or group).

stave bow [Ar]. A simple form of bow made from a single piece of wood, such as yew.

stave construction [De]. A technique for constructing timber buildings in which longitudinally split logs were either set in the ground, curved side out, or fixed to a horizontal wooden sill beam to form a wall. The top of the upright staves would have been tied to the sill and to a wall plate by mortice and tenon joints; in some cases the staves were slotted together with tongue and groove joints. Corner posts may have been given extra strength by using whole unsplit logs. In many cases the interior wall surfaces were plastered to conceal the timberwork. The technique of construc-

tion was common in Scandinavia, especially for church building, from at least the 9th century, and was probably widely used in northern Europe during the late 1st millennium AD.

steatite [Ma]. A kind of greyish or greenish stone with a soapy feel and look about it, from the Greek word for tallow. Such stone is generally soft and can easily be worked to make figurines, vessels, seals, and other objects. Sometimes used in Minoan art for ornamental vases, and covered with gold foil.

steel [Ma]. An alloy of iron and carbon first made during the Iron Age by the carburization of wrought iron. For this, strips of iron were gently heated to around 800 °C together with charcoal. Carbon diffuses into the surface of the metal to make steel, but its penetration is limited, so only thin strips can be made in this way. To make a large tool or weapon it is possible to forge strips of steel together; from the later 1st millennium AD, however, this could be achieved by PATTERN-WELDING.

steelyard [Ar]. A device for weighing things, consisting of a balance arm with a scale pan for the goods to be weighed suspended from one end and a weight that could be moved along the arm at the other.

stela (pl. stelae) [Ar]. A freestanding inscribed, carved, or decorated stone slab set upright in the ground, usually commemorating a person or event. Often connected with ceremonial sites or burial places; a stone slab set up in a public place, with an inscription recording a victory, treaty, or a decree; also a grave-stone. Many beautiful funeral stelae, sculptured in relief, are to be seen in the National Museum, Athens.

Stephen [Na]. English king of the House of Normandy. Born not later than AD 1100, third son of Adela, daughter of William I, and Stephen. Crowned king in 1135. Between February and November 1141 he was held captive by adherents of Matilda, daughter of Henry I, who contested the crown until 1153. Died aged over 53, having reigned 18 years.

Stephens, John Lloyd (1805–52) [Bi]. A New York lawyer who became a traveller and amateur archaeologist, visiting and documenting abandoned Maya centres in the mid 19th century. His books became bestsellers and together with drawings by Frederick Catherwood aroused popular interest in what was at the time an unknown civilization.

[Obit.: *Pulman's Monthly Magazine of American History, Science and Art*, 1 (1853), 64–8]

step trenching [Te]. **1.** In deep excavations the side of the trenches may be stepped at intervals in order to maintain the stability of the trench walls and reduce the risk of collapse. An inevitable consequence is that an excavation that starts relatively large will provide only a limited view of the deepest levels. **2.** Where clearly defined cultural levels are recognized during an excavation, these may be exposed in step fashion to show the full sequence before being totally removed.

stereoscopic pairs [Ge]. Two vertical aerial photographs taken from slightly different positions but printed so that the scale is the same and the field of view significantly overlaps. By viewing the two overlapping areas using a stereoscope the human eyes can be tricked into seeing the view as if three-dimensionally.

Steward, Julian Haynes (1902–72) [Bi]. American anthropologist and ethnographer who developed the theoretical perspective known as 'cultural ecology' which was based on the idea that cultures do not simply interact with one another but also with their environment. He argued that regularities in these relationships could be used to explain cultural change. Between 1946 and 1950 he edited and published the very detailed *Handbook of South American Indians* (Washington DC: Smithsonian Institution). Other books include the 1955 publication *Theory of Culture Change* (Urbana: University of Illinois Press).

[Obit.: *American Anthropologist*, 75 (1973), 886–903]

stichbandkeramik [Ar]. *See* STROKE-ORNAMENTED WARE CULTURE.

Stilicho, General Flavius [Na]. A Vandal by birth, and therefore one of a number of barbarians who, in the late 4th century AD, rose through the ranks of the army to high office in the Roman administration. He married the niece of the Emperor Theodosius and, during the first part of the reign of the Emperor

Honorius, who succeeded in AD 395, he was the effective ruler in the west. Stilicho was probably the last Roman leader to make a serious attempt to defend Britain, but he was murdered in AD 409 as the result of a court intrigue.

stillbay [CP]. Now obsolete term used to describe rather poorly defined stone tool assemblages found in southern and eastern Africa that were comparable with material from the site of Stillbay on the Cape coast of South Africa.

Stirling, Matthew Williams (1896–1975) [Bi]. American archaeologist who carried out numerous investigations and surveys of Olmec sites in Mesoamerica, including: La Venta, San Lorenzo, Tres Zapotes, and Cerro de las Mesas.

[Obit.: *Anthropology Newsletter*, 16 (1975), 3]

stirrup jar [Ar]. A pottery vase of strange shape, characteristic of the Mycenaean period: the vase is spheroidal with a narrow foot, but gets its name from the double handle. This is somewhat in the shape of a stirrup and rises on either side of a false, narrow, central spout which is, in fact, a support for the horizontal top of the handle. The actual spout is also narrow and is set forward of the flat-arched handle.

stirrup-spout vessel [Ar]. A closed globular jar with a hollow loop of clay attached to the body of the vessel at both ends and a tubular spout set into it in a vertical plane. Common to many Peruvian cultures, especially the CHAVÍN.

St Joseph, John Kenneth Sinclair (1912–94) [Bi]. British archaeologist specializing in the development and application of aerial photography. Born and brought up in Bromsgrove, Worcestershire, St Joseph went up to Selwyn College, Cambridge, in 1931 taking a first degree in geology followed by a doctorate awarded in 1937. In 1939 he was elected a Fellow and college lecturer at Selwyn where he later served as dean, librarian, and vice-master. His interest in aerial photography was started by O. G. S. CRAWFORD, but it was during his wartime duties in the Ministry of Aircraft Production that he became fully aware of the potential of aerial reconnaissance for academic studies. Soon after the war he began a programme of interdisciplinary flying and photographic recording through borrowed access to RAF training flights, which by the time of his retirement in 1980 had amassed a collection of a third of a million pictures. In 1949 the university appointed him as its first Curator of Aerial Photography. In 1973 he was made Professor of Air Photographic Studies. He was appointed OBE in 1964 and CBE in 1979. St Joseph published many books and papers including *The uses of aerial photography* (1966) and *Roman Britain from the air* (with S. S. Frere, 1983). He also lectured widely, with breathtaking pictures as visual aids, but with an intonation that earned him the nickname 'Holy Jo'.

[Obit.: *The Times*, 26 March 1994]

stoa [MC]. A colonnaded market-hall in an ancient Greek city. Consisting of a long straight colonnade with a vertical wall and sometimes rooms at the back and a roof over. Examples appear from about 650 BC onwards.

stockade [Co]. An enclosure boundary or fence formed using upright posts or planks set in a slot in the ground and perhaps fixed together at a higher level for additional strength.

stockaded enclosure [MC]. *See* PALISADED ENCLOSURE.

stocks [MC]. Instrument of punishment in which the culprit was fastened by the ankles in a public place.

stoke-hole [Co]. Furnace area for a hypocaust.

Stokes, Margaret M'Nair (1832–1900) [Bi]. Irish archaeologist specializing in Celtic and early Christian art. Privately educated as the daughter of William Stokes, physician to the Queen in Ireland, it was not until middle age that she was able to indulge her taste for research. She became an Honorary Member of the Royal Irish Academy and of the Society of Antiquaries of Ireland. Her most notable and important publication was *The High crosses of Ireland* (1898).

[Bio.: *Biography of British women* (1993, London: Mansell), 381]

stone alignment [MC]. A single line, or two or more parallel lines, of upright stones set at intervals along a common axis or series of axes. The number and size of stones in known alignments varies, but the minimum number needed to form an alignment is three. Such structures are common from the later Neolithic and Bronze Age of the British Isles, northern France, and parts of Scandinavia. Amongst the most impressive is in CARNAC, France.

Stone Age [CP]. The most ancient of the three subdivisions of the ancient past in the THREE AGE SYSTEM. Characterized by the use of stone for the manufacture of tools and weapons.

stone axe [Ar]. A block of hard generally fine-grained stone fashioned by flaking and grinding into a roughly triangular or trapezoidal shape with an oval cross-section and a blade at the broader thicker end. Found widely throughout the world in essentially Neolithic contexts there are numerous typological and stylistic variations on this simple theme. In the European Neolithic many stone axes were probably used for felling trees and woodworking, although the term is generally applied to implements that on closer inspection turn out to have been wedges, adzes, chisels, and gouges. Some stone axes are so finely made, of such large size, or manufactured from such soft material that they must have had a ceremonial or symbolic function. Almost all stone axes would originally have been mounted in a wooded or bone haft.

stone axe factory [MC]. A place where the raw material for making stone axes was quarried and roughed out. Archaeologically such sites are represented by the remains of quarry pits, adits, and boulder reduction areas, together with abundant waste flakes and part-made broken implements. Several examples have been excavated in northwest Europe, including Langdale, England, and Plussulien, France.

stone balls [Ar]. Spherical stone objects up to 10 cm in diameter made by pecking and grinding blocks of stone or pebbles to achieve the desired shape and size. Some are faceted, and many carry decorative motifs similar to those found amongst British ROCK ART. They are believed to be of later Neolithic date, and the majority are found in eastern Scotland. Also known as **carved stone balls**.

stone circle [MC]. A setting of upright stone pillars forming a ring whose exact ground plan many vary between being almost exactly circular through to elliptical or egg-shaped. Upon excavation such circles are often found to be the final phase in the evolution of a monument that started as a TIMBER CIRCLE. Stone circles are widely scatted through the western parts of the British Isles, northern France, and parts of Scandinavia. They broadly date to the later Neolithic and early Bronze Age, but Aubrey Burl has identified three main phases to their construction. Early-period circles (3370–2670 BC) are moderately large, fairly regular in plan, have closely set stones, and a conspicuous entrance. Middle-period circles (2670–1975 BC) are generally very large, up to 100 m across, occur in a range of sometimes elegant shapes, have widely spaced stones, and occur in groups. Late-period circles (1975–1200 BC) are generally small rings of varying shapes and sizes although ovals predominate. Regional types such as recumbent circles and four-posters proliferate.

Stonehenge, Wiltshire, UK [Si]. Probably the most famous prehistoric ceremonial monument in Europe, situated on the chalk downs of Salisbury Plain in central southern England. Extensively excavated by William Gowland in 1901, William Hawley in 1919 to 1926, and more recently by Richard ATKINSON, Stuart PIGGOTT, and J. F. S. Stone intermittently between 1951 and 1964, the site as visible today has three main phases to its construction. **Phase 1** comprises the circular earthwork enclosure constructed around 2950 BC. There were at least three entrances, the main one being to the northeast. Inside the bank was a circle of 56 postholes (Aubrey Holes) that originally held wooden posts. **Phase 2** dates to the period 2900–2400 BC, the late Neolithic, and sees the ditch filling in through a combination of human actions and natural processes. The posts in the Aubrey Holes decayed or were removed and a series of timber settings were constructed in the northeastern entrance and in the central area. Towards the end of Phase 2 the site was used as a cremation cemetery. **Phase 3** dates to the period 2550–1600 BC, the end of the late Neolithic and the early Bronze Age. It is subdivided into a number of subphases and these represent the evolution of the stone structures in the centre of the site. The first such structure comprised two concentric circles of bluestones imported from southwest Wales set up around 2500 BC. Round about were the four station stones and

the heelstone and its twin outside the rings to the northeast to provide a sighting on the rising midsummer sun for those inside the circles. Beyond these stones was an embanked avenue leading across the landscape to the northeast. The bluestone circles were later removed and a new much larger set of circles constructed. Ultimately this comprised a series of four concentric rings of stones (from the centre out): a horseshoe of bluestones with the altar stone at its focus; a horseshoe setting of five trilithons; the circle of bluestones; and the outer sarsen circle with lintelled uprights. Observers standing at the site at sunrise on midsummer morning would have seen the light from the rising sun appear to shine up the avenue (which may also have had stones added to the bank at this time) and into the circles.

Altogether, the construction and use of Stonehenge spanned at least 1500 years, probably more. Stonehenge was not built primarily as an observatory or giant calculator but rather a place where people came to engage in ceremonies and events. The way they used the site, their movements within it, and the apparatus that controlled those movements changed from time to time while at the same time maintaining connections with the signals and celestial events that gave their actions meaning.

[Rep.: R. M. J. Cleal, K. Walker, and R. Montague, 1995, *Stonehenge in its landscape. Twentieth-century excavations*. London: English Heritage]

stone hut circle [MC]. A roughly round setting of upright stones, coursed slabs, or stone rubble which represents the foundations and in some cases the walls of a building that originally had a wooden and/or turf superstructure and roof. Traces of a doorway and flooring arrangement can be seen in some preserved examples, and more elaborate cases may have annexes and forecourts of various sorts. Dating mainly to the middle and later Bronze Age in the British Isles and adjacent areas of the Atlantic seaboard of northwest Europe, these structures were mostly dwellings, but some were used for storage and as animal shelters. The majority of preserved examples are to be seen in upland areas such as Dartmoor, England, or northeast Perthshire, Scotland.

stone row [MC]. *See* STONE ALIGNMENT.

Stonesfield slate [Ma]. A sandy oolitic limestone, occurring in the Great Oolite series, which splits readily into thin slabs suitable for roofing.

stoneware [De]. Pottery fired to a high temperature, usually over 1200 °C, at which the fabric of the vessel vitrifies. Stoneware seems to have been produced first at Siegburg in Germany about 1200 AD.

stop ridge [De]. A transverse ridge moulded into the surface of early bronze flanged axes and palstaves during the European Bronze Age in order to prevent the cleft wooden haft from splitting.

storage jars [Ar]. Large jars used for storing grain or other materials.

storage pits [Co]. Roughly cylindrical or conical pits dug through the topsoil into the underlying bedrock to depths of up to 3 m to provide underground storage space for cereal grain. Experiments show that if the tops are kept sealed they provide very effective storage and allow high germination rates where the grain is to be used as seed. In the British Isles such pits are especially common on sites dating to the 1st millennium BC; archaeologically they are important because they were often used as rubbish pits after their primary purpose had been fulfilled.

Strabo [Na]. Greek geographer and historian born about 64 BC whose extensive *Geography* includes descriptions of the Mediterranean world from Spain to Egypt and Asia Minor, together with accounts of barbarian Europe including Gaul and Britain. He died about AD 21.

strandloper [De]. General descriptive term referring to communities who have a subsistence base grounded in beachcombing and a hunter-based marine diet.

strangulated blade scraper [Ar]. Long blade tool with a retouched notch on one or both sides. Possibly used as a wood-working tool like a modern spokeshave. Characteristic of the AURIGNACIAN.

strap end [Ar]. Metal reinforcement (often decorated) which prevented wear and damage to the end of a strap.

strap handle [De]. On ceramic vessels a strap handle is one made from a strip of clay that is shaped by hand and then attached to the body of the pot at two points before firing.

strata [De]. *See* CONTEXT.

strategic planning (regional planning) [Ge]. The preparation and agreement of an overarching plan that sets out the policies and proposals that will be followed by a local government authority in respect of such matters as land use, property development, environmental protection, transportation, employment, and so on for a defined period (typically 5–10 years). Once approved, the policies set out in a strategic plan are binding on the authority and must be followed in the course of DEVELOPMENT CONTROL. In Britain, central government provides **regional planning guidance**, county councils prepare **structure plans**, and district councils prepare **local plans**. Where the roles of different tiers of local authorities have been merged, as with unitary authorities, then a **unitary plan** will be produced. Where special issues are important to a local area, for example minerals extraction, then a **subject plan** may be produced. Archaeology and the historic environment in general is included in such plans, usually under the general heading of environment.

stratification 1. [Ge]. The differentiation of the population on a prestige scale of kinship units in such a way that the distinctions among such units, or classes within them, become hereditary to an important degree. **2.** [Th]. *See* STRATIGRAPHY.

stratified sampling [Te]. A probabilistic sampling technique used to cluster and isolate sample units when regular spacing is inappropriate for cultural reasons. **Stratified random sampling** involves dividing the target population or study area into broad zones (e.g. cultivated land, river valley, mountain, etc.) and then randomly selecting sample units so as to give each zone a number of units proportional to its area. **Stratified systematic sampling** combines the definition of broad zones with the application of a fixed sampling scheme within each zone but the random selection of specific points within the fixed scheme.

stratified society [De]. A society in which competing groups have unequal access to power and/or resources, some groups being subordinate to others. The uppermost stratum is termed an elite.

stratigraphic association [Th]. A closely established relationship between two or more archaeological items (objects or structural elements) because they are physically linked by virtue of being within or attached to the same stratigraphically determined deposit or layer.

stratigraphic matrix [Eq]. *See* HARRIS MATRIX.

stratigraphic sequence [De]. A series of deposits that can be arranged in depositional order using the principles of STRATIGRAPHY.

stratigraphy [Th]. The study of the formation, composition, sequence, and deposits or formations. Stratigraphy provides the basic rules by which the context and relationships of archaeological materials are constructed and events put in sequence. The basic rules include the following. **Principle of superimposition**: layers or strata are overlain or buried by progressively younger deposits so that the oldest deposits are the deepest while the youngest are nearest the surface. This layering of soils one above another allows archaeologists to trace the development of a site and to place a range of archaeological remains (e.g. artefacts) within the layers into a time sequence. Natural erosion or man-made intrusion may interrupt this process, of course, and it should not be assumed that successive layers of approximately equal depth need correspond to equal periods of time, since varying intensities of building activity, flooding, etc., may result in quite different depths of debris. **Principle of intercutting**: a feature or deposit that cuts across or into an existing layer of strata must be more recent. **Principle of incorporation**: all material or debris contained within a layer or deposit must be the same age or older than the formation of the deposit. While it is possible that material from an older deposit can be incorporated in a younger deposit the opposite cannot be true. **Principle of correlation**: parallels may be drawn between deposits of the same character, containing the same range of materials, and occupying comparable stratigraphic positions within related sequences.

stratum [De]. A single deposit or cultural level.

stray find [De]. An archaeological object found by chance and with little or no associated archaeological context.

street grid [Ge]. Regular pattern of streets crossing at right angles.

St Remy ware [Ar]. Fine pottery, often with relief decoration, in a white fabric with a green or yellow (lead) glaze, made at St-Remy-en-Rollat, near Vichy. Small jars, bowls, and flagons were imported into Britain in the 1st century. Imitations were made in Britain up to the mid 2nd century.

strigil [Ar]. Thin narrow curved scraper of horn, bone, or metal used by Greek and Roman bathers in the hot rooms of their bath-houses to cleanse the skin.

strike-a-light [Ar]. A type of flint tool in the form of a rod or bar with a slightly pointed end that is often considered to have been used in conjunction with a piece of suitable stone (e.g. iron pyrites) for making sparks with which to start a fire.

striking platform [Ge]. Point on a flint core, at right angles to the intended line of the flake, which is struck to detach this flake.

string marks [De]. The marks on the base of a vessel caused by the potter detaching the pot from the wheel by means of a wire or string.

strip fields [MC]. Long, narrow fields, characteristic of the medieval and later OPEN FIELD SYSTEM of agriculture.

strip lynchet [MC]. Long, narrow strip fields set on hillsides and bounded by LYNCHETS.

Stroke-Ornamented Ware Culture [CP]. Middle Neolithic communities of central Europe, especially southern Poland, the Czech Republic, and parts of southern and central Germany, characterized by the use of pottery decorated with geometric designs executed in short incised lines. This style of pottery appears to have developed from the local LBK ceramics during the 5th and early 4th millennia BC. Some of the most common motifs used are zig-zags.

Strong, Donald Emrys (1927–73) [Bi]. British archaeologist whose main interests lay in the art and architecture of the Roman world. Born and brought up in Haverfordwest, Pembrokeshire, he gained an open scholarship to Brasenose College, Oxford, in 1948, reading Greats and taking a diploma in Classical Archaeology. He studied at the British School in Rome from 1952 and was awarded his D.Phil. in 1954. After a brief spell with the Inspectorate of Ancient Monuments of the Ministry of Works he joined the Department of Greek and Roman Antiquities in the British Museum in 1956. Here he published many papers and articles. In 1968 he was appointed to the Chair of the Archaeology of the Roman Provinces in the London Institute of Archaeology, a post he held until his death. He was president of the British Archaeological Association in 1972–3 and was a key figure in the founding of the Society for Libyan Studies and the Archaeology Abroad Service.

[Obit.: *Antiquaries Journal*, 54 (1974), 410–11]

Strong, William Duncan (1899–1962) [Bi]. American archaeologist best known for developing the DIRECT HISTORICAL APPROACH during the interwar years. This involved working backwards in time from the recorded historical past into prehistoric times to develop local sequences of continuity and discontinuity.

[Bio.: G. R. Willey, 1998, William Duncan Strong. In *Portraits in American archaeology*. Albuquerque: University of New Mexico Press, 74–96]

structural archaeology [Th]. Theoretical approach to the analysis of archaeological material based on STRUCTURALISM, stressing the idea that human actions are guided by beliefs and symbolic concepts that are themselves underpinned by ways of thinking about the world. The basis of such studies is therefore to uncover the structures of thought and to see how these influenced the codes and rules that find expression in material culture. Structural codes denote particular meanings to members of a society—meanings that can change according to the context and associations of their visibility.

structural-functionalism [Th]. The theoretical position that social parts are integrated and function to maintain the structural whole.

structuralism [Th]. A theoretical approach, derived originally from the study of language, concerned with the identification of structures in social or cultural systems. A philosophy holding that there are non-apparent, innate psycho-biological structures common to all human beings. Structuralism is a very influential approach and a body of cultural theory derived ultimately from work in linguistics. A major distinction is between language as it is spoken (*parole*) and language as the underlying system of signs (*langue*). Structuralism focuses on the latter, and makes a further distinction within the sign, between the signifier (for example, a word) and the signified (that which the sign refers to). The emphasis is on the system of signs, and their differences, rather than on the individual signs themselves. In anthropology, the approach was adopted by Lévi-Strauss, who analysed, among other things, native myths. He made heavy use of binary oppositions such as culture:nature, hot:cold, and raw:cooked to explain the way people saw the world. It is through this kind of analysis that structuralism is perhaps most widely known in archaeology, while a more pervasive influence has been through the linguistic or textual analogy, that cultural phenomena are structured as in a language. The major problem with structuralism is its privileging of structure over agency. There is the crucial, but often unanswered, question of the genesis and maintenance of structure, a question which STRUCTURATION and humanistic approaches attempt to address.

structuration [Th]. Structuration theory was developed by Anthony Giddens in the 1970s and has since had a significant influence on post-processual social archaeology. It is concerned to overcome the dualism of individual agency, meaning, and understanding, as against social structure. Its major thesis is the replacement of the dualism with a duality wherein social structure is both the medium and the outcome of the social practice by knowledgeable social agents. In his later work, Giddens emphasized how time and space are basic constituents embedded within social life: the limitations of individual presence are transcended by the stretching of social relations across time and space.

structure [Th]. At its most general this refers to the basic framework or form of society. Elements of a physical structure such as an artefact are often associated with function, hence functionalist and structural-functionalist theory treats society as analogous to an organism with each institutional part (religion, economy, etc.) functioning to maintain the whole. Such an approach is related to SYSTEMS THEORY, and both have generally received much application in processual archaeology. More particularly, structure refers to the *longue durée* in Braudel's temporal scheme, the fundamental baseline of a historical period, seen by the earlier *Annales* historians as essentially geographical or environmental in character. In spite of such refinement of the concept, it is perhaps overworked in the social sciences, 'structured' now being used to mean little more than organized, patterned, or non-random.

structured deposition [De]. Patterning in the way that artefacts are found when uncovered through excavation which allows the suggestion that behavioural regularities underlie the way in which they were put into the ground in the first place. Examples include the placement of a joint of meat as the final act before sealing a pit containing rubbish or the placing of ceramic vessels in the terminal of boundary ditches adjacent to entrances.

stucco [Ma]. Decorative plasterwork, especially used to create interior architectural elements.

stud [Co]. The common post or upright within a timber-framed wall.

studded pottery [De]. Ceramic vessels decorated by the addition of pellets of clay to its surface.

stud partition [Co]. A partition formed with vertical timber posts known as studs.

study [Co]. A small room traditionally contained within a corner turret although more recently situated in other parts of a house.

Stukeley, William (1687–1765). British antiquary, traveller and co-founder of the Society of Antiquaries of London. Born in Holbeach and brought up in the fenlands of Lincolnshire in eastern England, Stukeley learned medicine at Cambridge University (Bennet/Corpus Christi College) before study-ing at St Thomas's Hospital, London, under Dr Mead from 1709. Beginning in 1710 he took an annual tour on horseback across England, exploring gardens, architectural curiosities, and ancient sites. Between 1710 and 1717 he was in medical practice at Boston in his native Lincolnshire, but moved back to London in May 1717 and in January 1718 become the first secretary of the Society of Antiquaries of London. In 1722–4 his tours took him to Avebury and Stonehenge where he made very detailed records of what he saw. He later became a clergyman and was ordained into the Anglican church in 1729. Throughout his later life he became obsessed with the romantic idealization of the Druids and the religion of the ancient British. His published works included *Itinerarium curiosum* (1724), *Stonehenge* (1740), and *Avebury* (1743).

[Bio.: S. Piggott, 1985, *William Stukeley: an eighteenth century antiquary* (2nd edition). London: Thames and Hudson]

stupa [MC]. A South Asian Buddhist monument consisting of a hemispherical mound of earth, brick, or stone, containing burials or relics, often the focus of a monastery.

style [Ge]. A term borrowed from art history and used in archaeology to refer to groups of distinctive decorative motifs.

style zones [Ge]. An area within which artefacts or designs of a particular STYLE are commonly found. Often used to describe the areas within which distinctive kinds of pottery were circulating.

stylistic type [De]. Type based on stylistic distinctions.

stylobate [Ge]. A continuous foundation supporting a row or rows of columns.

stylus [Ar]. A writing implement consisting of a small rod with a pointed end for scratching letters on wax-covered tablets and a blunt end for obliterating them.

sub-assemblage [De]. Association of artefacts denoting a particular form of prehistoric activity practised by a group of people.

Sub-Atlantic Phase [Ge]. A biostratigraphic subdivision of the FLANDRIAN STAGE in which conditions were colder and wetter than in the preceding SUB-BOREAL. Godwin's POLLEN ZONE VIII corresponds to the start of the Sub-Atlantic in Britain and is marked in southern England at least by the appearance of beech and hornbeam. The Sub-Atlantic generally spans the period *c*.500 BC down to the present day in northern Europe.

Sub-Boreal Phase [Ge]. A biostratigraphic subdivision of the FLANDRIAN STAGE in which conditions were warm and dry compared with the preceding ATLANTIC period. Godwin's POLLEN ZONE VII corresponds with the Sub-Boreal in Britain, marked by the ELM DECLINE and the main human impact on the post-glacial forests in the later 5th and 4th millennia BC. The Sub-Boreal generally spans the period from *c*.3000 BC down to *c*.500 BC in northern Europe.

subculture [De]. A self-defining group within a society which holds different values and norms to those of the majority. This may be represented by specialized types of material culture or the differences in the way material culture is used.

Subject Committee for Archaeology (SCFA) [Or]. A representative body of the 30 or so university departments of archaeology in UK universities, which seeks to represent the collective interests of higher education archaeology to government agencies and other official bodies. Established as SCFA in March 2001, the organization is a direct descendant of the Standing Committee of University Professors and Heads of Archaeology that was founded in January 1986 under the chairmanship of Professor Rosemary Cramp in the face of continuing government cuts to higher education.

submarine archaeology [Ge]. *See* UNDERWATER ARCHAEOLOGY.

submerged forests [MC]. Areas of peat bed, sometimes with in situ broken or uprooted tree stumps, that are exposed in the inter-tidal zone at low water. These are the remains of terrestrial landscapes that have become inundated during periods of sea-level rise. Around the Atlantic coast of northwest Europe many submerged forests are of Mesolithic and Neolithic date.

subsistence economy [Ge]. That aspect of social life that revolves around securing food resources.

subsoil [Ge]. Material at the base of the SOIL PROFILE, usually slightly discoloured parent bedrock.

succession [Ge]. An ecological term referring to the replacement of one dominant type of species by another, in a particular environment.

Suchos [Di]. Egyptian god. *See* SOBEK.

sudatorium [Co]. Latin term for the hot dry-heat room in a Roman bath-suite.

Suebi [CP]. Germanic communities living to the east of the River Elbe from at least the 2nd century AD. In the invasion of AD 406, the Suebi crossed Gaul and founded a kingdom in Galicia, Spain, which survived until AD 585. The Franks, who annexed the lands to the east of the Rhine in the 6th century, continued to call these territories Suebia.

Suetonius Paulinus [Na]. Gaius Suetonius Paulinus was governor of Britain at the time of the Boudiccan revolt in *c*.AD 60. Having recently captured Anglesey, he retreated from North Wales and went on to defeat BOUDICCA. However, he was subsequently withdrawn from Britain because it was feared that he would abuse the Britons' surrender and punish future offenders too harshly.

Sui [CP]. Chinese dynasty dating to the period AD 581–618 when China was reunited as a single state. The imperial family, from north China, were of mixed Tartar and Chinese descent. The second ruler brought the dynasty to ruin by excessive extravagance and unsuccessful wars with Korea.

Sumer (Sumerian) [CP]. The earliest recognized civilization in the world, focused on southern Mesopotamia in what is now Iraq and Iran. The name is taken from inscriptions, and has been applied to the language represented on clay tablets. Sumer (Biblical Shinar) began in the early 4th millennium BC. The main stimulus to development was probably the need to organize farming groups previously living in the highlands of Iran to take advantage of the floods and droughts of the

Tigris–Euphrates Valley. As a result, craft specialization, administrative organization, and great advances in architecture and sculpture followed. The political unit was the city-state, in which the patron deity was the major power in all matters, promoted through the priesthood and temple organization. Secular leaders were required in times of war but had little power otherwise. The various city-states were united under a common culture and religion. Political unification did not come until about 2370 BC with the conquest by the Semites of Akkad.

sun disc [Ar]. Decorative circular plate of gold or bronze, typically less than 50 mm in diameter, found widely in Copper Age and Bronze Age contexts in northern Europe and believed to be some kind of dress fitting that symbolically represented the sun.

sunflower [Sp]. A tall annual herb (*Helianthus annuus*) which grows to a height of 1.8 m or more and has a very large showy golden-rayed flower which contains abundant small edible seeds. The seeds can also be pressed to obtain sunflower oil. Native to parts of the southeastern United States. Domesticated by *c*.1500 BC for its seeds, dye, and oil. Introduced into Europe in the 16th century AD.

Sung Dynasty [CP]. A Chinese dynasty ruling during the period AD 960 to 1288, with the northern Sung reigning from the foundation until AD 1121, when north China was overrun and conquered by the Chin Dynasty which was a regime of the Tartar tribe, the Juchen. The southern Sung continued to reign for another century and a half in Hangchou, Chekiang Province, over the whole of southern China, which in this age became highly developed and very wealthy. Porcelain manufacture developed, navigation was aided by the adaptation of the compass to marine uses, and there was extensive trade with southern Asia. The Sung were finally conquered by the Mongols under Kubilai Khan in AD 1280–8. The period is also famous for the development of landscape and other painting.

sunken-floor hut [MC]. *See* GRUBENHAUS.

superorganic [Ge]. The realm of culture or behaviour considered as a thing in and of itself, independent of human beings.

supine burial [De]. A burial which has been deposited with the corpse lying on its back, face upwards. *Compare* PRONE BURIAL.

supra-orbital torus [Ge]. A protruding bony brow-ridge, frequently found in early hominid skulls and most marked in male gorillas.

surface scatters [MC]. In America, surface scatters are sites that have geological or geographical context but no archaeological associations. This includes material incorporated in secondary contexts such as river gravels or colluvium. In Britain, surface scatters are spreads of humanly worked material, often struck flint, which is taken to represent one of two things: (1) material brought into the topsoil by cultivation and derived from disturbed archaeological features of some kind (e.g. pits, ditches); (2) material remains of activities which only have a topsoil dimension in the sense that the material was originally dropped or placed or abandoned on the ground surface and over the course of time it has become incorporated into the topsoil where it has remained ever since. *See also* FLINT SCATTERS.

surface survey [Te]. The collection of archaeological finds from disturbed ground surfaces (e.g. cultivated fields) with the objective of gathering representative samples in order to establish the types of activity within the area examined. Such surveys may be unsystematic: that is, the pattern of scanning is unstructured and simply involves scanning the route of a more or less precisely defined path. By contrast, systematic surface survey involves setting out a grid across the survey area and either walking each line as a series of stints of defined length and duration (line walking), or spending a set amount of time scanning the surface of each grid square (grid recovery). The material collected during surface surveys can be quantified under a series of classifications and TREND SURFACE ANALYSIS can be used to produce density plots for particular classes of material (flint tools, Roman pottery, etc.).

Surrey white ware [Ar]. Type of medieval pottery produced in Surrey from about 1300 AD onwards. Distinctive in having an off-white or buff-coloured fabric, often with a patchy green glaze. From the 15th century, however, thick green and yellow glazes were used. The term TUDOR GREEN ware is usually used to describe the products dating to the 16th century. The main forms produced were cooking pots, cauldrons, skillets, pipkins, jugs, jars, and pitchers.

Susa, Iran [Si]. Large tell mound representing the remains of a very substantial early city on the bank of the Karkeh River in the Khuzistan region of southwest Iran. Excavated more or less continuously since 1897 by a succession of French archaeologists, it has four main phases parallel to those of Mesopotamia: UBAID, URUK, JEMDET, NASR/early dynastic. Overall, however, the site shows an almost unbroken line of occupation from about 4000 BC down to early medieval times.

The site itself covers more than two square kilometres and comprises a number of separate components: the acropolis which seems to have been the focus of prehistoric settlement; the royal city which has produced important Elemite remains of the 2nd millennium BC; the Apadana with a large and impressive Achaemenid palace; and the artisans' town which is also of the Achaemenid period.

[Sum.: P. Harper *et al.* (eds.), 1992, *The royal city of Susa*. New York: Metropolitan Museum]

suspensura [Co]. A Latin term to describe the floor above a hypocaust, generally of concrete laid over a layer of tiles supported at each corner by *pilae*.

Susquehanna Culture [CP]. Late Archaic Stage hunter-gatherer communities living in eastern Pennsylvania and southern Maine, North America, in the period 1800–1200 BC, forming part of the more widely scattered Mast Forest Tradition. The Susquehanna Culture is characterized by broad triangular stemmed points. Post-dating the Narrow Point Cultures, Susquehanna groups appear to have used elaborate burial ceremonies involving cremations and possibly multiple burials in large pits.

Sutton Hoo, Suffolk, UK [Si]. Extensive Anglo-Saxon royal cemetery of the 6th and 7th centuries AD comprising more than fourteen barrows overlooking the valley of the River Deben in the southern part of East Anglia close to the Suffolk coast. Excavations in 1938–9 under the direction of Basil Brown and Charles Phillips investigated one of the largest mounds (Mound 1) which was found to contain the remains of a large boat 27 m long and originally propelled by 38 oars. In the chamber in the centre of the boat was a rich collection of outstanding objects from all over Europe and beyond and dating to the 4th to 7th centuries AD. Although no traces of a body were found, the site is widely interpreted as the pagan memorial to King Raedwald of Essex who died in AD 625. The grave goods include a sword, shield, and decorated helmet in Swedish style, a large gold belt buckle with intricate animal interlace decoration, and a purse and cloak clasps with decoration in multi-coloured glass. There are Merovingian gold coins and silver vessels from Byzantium. Researches by Martin Carver between 1983 and 1992 on the site and in the territory it commands have shown that the kingship signalled at the site is pagan in its ideology and Scandinavian in its allegiance.

[Sum.: M. Carver (ed.), 1992, *The age of Sutton Hoo*. Woodbridge: Boydell Press]

svears [De]. Term used to describe the 'inverted eyebrow' motif common on migration period pottery from north Germany, a sagging U-shaped series of incised lines.

Swanscombe, Kent, UK [Si]. A gravel pit in the lower Thames Valley which preserved a series of river terraces containing useful environmental evidence, abundant mollusc and faunal remains, and large assemblages of Lower Palaeolithic stone tools. The lower gravel beds have a CLACTONIAN assemblage dating to perhaps 420 000–360 000 years ago, while the middle gravels yield ACHEULIAN material of perhaps 200 000 years ago. Three fragments of a human skull (probably female) were found in 1935, 1936, and 1955 within the upper part of the middle gravels. First classified as Swanscombe Man it is now believed to be an early form of *Homo sapiens* with strong Neanderthal characteristics.

[Rep.: C. D. Overy (ed.), 1964, *The Swanscombe skull*. London: Royal Anthropological Society]

swan's neck pin [Ar]. Style of pin made of bronze or iron in the 1st millennium BC in the British Isles, distinctive in having three bends in the upper part to create an S-shaped head.

sweet potato [Sp]. Trailing perennial herb (*Ipomoea batatas*) which produces a fleshy edible tuber. Native to the tropical lowlands of

Mesoamerica and South America. Reported from sites in Peru as early as 8000 BC, probably domesticated by c.2000 BC, if not earlier. In the first millennium AD the sweet potato was taken to Polynesia and New Zealand, and after the Spanish settlement of the New World spread still further afield.

Sweet Track, Somerset, UK [Si]. A Neolithic timber trackway preserved in the low-lying peats of the Somerset levels, extensively excavated by John and Bryony Coles between 1970 and 1982. At least 1.8 km of trackway is known, leading from the dry land of Westhay Island down into the wetland and reed swamp of the levels. Built mainly of oak planks supported on stakes driven down into the peat, dendrochronology shows that the main structure was built in the winter of 3807 and the spring of 3806 BC. This makes the site Europe's oldest known trackway.

[Sum.: B. Coles and J. Coles, 1986, *Sweet track to Glastonbury*. London: Thames & Hudson]

swidden agriculture [De]. *See* SLASH AND BURN AGRICULTURE.

sword [Ar]. A bronze, iron, or steel weapon of war and prestige comprising a long thin blade for slashing, thrusting, or both. Swords are distinguished from daggers by their greater length and from rapiers by their wider and more substantial blades. Single-edged swords are relatively rare and better classified as sabres or falchions. Swords usually have substantial hilts cast with the blade and then elaborated with organic materials to provide extra grip. The earliest swords in Europe are of Bronze Age date and seem to have appeared in central Europe in the early 2nd millennium BC. They spread to Greece and the Aegean before 1650 BC and thereafter to the rest of Europe and western Asia. In China the earliest swords date to the 10th century BC.

syllabary [Ge]. A system of writing in which each symbol represents a syllable (consonant plus vowel). Early examples include LINEAR A and LINEAR B.

symbol [Ge]. One item used to stand for or represent another—as in the case of a flag which symbolizes a nation.

symbolic interactionism [Th]. A theoretical approach in sociology developed by George Herbert Mead, which places strong emphasis on the role of symbols and language as core elements of all human interaction.

symbolkeramik [Ar]. Type of Copper Age ceramic found in southern Spain. Characterized by incised stylized designs believed to have had symbolic meaning, as with the OCULUS motif.

symbol stone [MC]. Type of PICTISH monument found in Scotland in the form of roughly shaped pillars or boulders depicting animals and/or geometric patterns and objects. They date to between the 5th and 7th centuries AD and are clearly not Christian in their inspiration.

symposium [Ge]. A male drinking session traditionally held at the end of a Greek meal during classical times. Scenes of the symposium frequently appear as decoration on Greek pottery showing that the range of activities included not only drinking but also music, singing, dancing, games, and sexual intercourse.

synchronic [De]. Being of a single time or of limited time depth; non-historical. *See also* DIACHRONIC.

syncretism [De]. The fusion of two or more systems of belief and ritual.

synostosis [Ge]. The fusion of separate pieces of bone in human skeletons. The timing of this process in different bones is an important indicator of age. For example, the distal epiphyses of the radius has fused by about 20 years, the proximal epiphyses of the fibula by about 25 years.

synthesis [De]. A type of archaeological publication that attempts to pull together and interpret a broad range of data and information about a particular topic or geographical area.

systematics [Th]. In archaeology, procedures for creating sets of archaeological units derived from a logical system for a particular purpose.

systematic sampling [Te]. A form of probabilistic sampling in which the target is divided into equal-sized blocks (for example, a series of squares covering an archaeological site or survey region) and a sample taken at a predetermined point in each block (e.g. on the grid intersection or in the middle of each square). This method is useful for sampling unevenly distributed populations, but runs the risk of missing things that are regularly spaced.

systems-ecological approach [Th]. The combined application of the three interconnected models of systems theory, cultural ecology, and multi-lineal evolution to understand social change.

systems theory [Th]. A method of formal analysis in which the object of study is viewed as comprising a series of distinct but interconnected components or subsystems. Initially developed in the field of cybernetics, general systems theory, in particular that relating to so-called 'open systems' was brought into the social sciences in the 1960s. In archaeology it was used as a means of investigating social complexity and long-term change. In 1968, for example, David CLARKE published a simple systems model involving four subsystems (economy; religious pattern; social pattern; and material culture) connected together and through the medium of technology with the system environment. By developing an understanding of the connections between subsystems, and measuring the flows of matter and energy through the system, it was believed possible to identify the causes and consequences of both progressive change and major episodes of discontinuity.

Tacitus, Cornelius [Na]. Roman historian born *c*.AD 56, and the author of three major works that have become prime sources of information for the early history of Roman Britain: *The Histories*; *The Annals*; and a biography of his father-in-law, *The Agricola*, Agricola being governor of Britain between AD 78 and AD 84. Although he reveals little about himself in his writings, Tacitus is known to have been of senatorial rank and the civilian governor of western Anatolia. He died *c*.AD 120.

TAG [Ab]. *See* THEORETICAL ARCHAEOLOGY GROUP.

taiga [Ge]. Ecological zone that is slightly more temperate than TUNDRA, with a vegetation cover composed of stunted forest, mainly coniferous, on frozen subsoil. Probably much more extensive than tundra in periglacial Europe. Also known as boreal forest.

Taima-Taima, Venezuela [Si]. Late Pleistocene, pre-CLOVIS, deposits investigated by R. Gruhn and A. L. Bryan in 1976. Mastodon bones and stone tools were recovered and interpreted by the excavators as an occupation site dating to the period *c*.12 000–15 000 BC. The association between the bones and tools has, however, been called into question.

[Sum.: A. L. Bryan *et al.*, 1978, An El Jobo mastodon kill at Taima-Taima, Venezuela. *Science*, 200, 1275–7]

Tairona [CP]. Later prehistoric communities of the early 2nd millennium occupying northeastern Columbia. Some sites (e.g. Pueblito) are very large with up to 3000 houses as well as public architecture. Most villages have a central PLATFORM MOUND.

Taj Mahal, India [Si]. Overlooking the River Yamuna, the Taj Mahal is a classic example of Moghul architecture, with the Taj itself built as a mausoleum at the northern end of an extensive formal walled garden designed in the *charbagh* style and structured on the Islamic theme of 'paradise'. The whole site was built by Shah Jahan between AD 1632 and 1653 as the final resting place of his favourite wife Arjumand Bann Begum (also known as Mumtaz Mahal) who died in AD 1631 shortly after giving birth to their fourteenth child. Upon his death in AD 1666, Shah Jahan was buried alongside his wife in the Taj.

More than 20 000 workers were involved in its construction, and the marble and semi-precious stones that cover the wall faces were brought from Rajasthan, Persia, Russia, Afghanistan, Tibet, China, and the Indian Ocean. Essentially square in shape, the Taj has peaked arches cut into its sides, topped by a dome that rises to a height of 55 m. The whole is set on top of a square marble platform with a high minaret at each corner.

[Sum.: P. N. Oak, 1989, *Taj Mahal* (4th edition). Houston: A. Ghosh]

talayot [MC]. A massive tower built of dry-stone walling found in the Balearic Islands of the western Mediterranean, similar to the NURAGHE of Sardinia. Talayots (the local word for 'watch-towers') were built in a range of forms with circular, square, and stepped examples. Most have a central chamber and are of Bronze Age date, broadly 1500–500 BC. Many became the focus of a small village of dry-stone-built houses.

talent [Ar]. **1.** A unit of weight used in the classical Greek world and Near East, the equivalent of 60 minas, 25.86 kg in Athens. **2.** A coin which in Pericles' time in Athens was equivalent in value to 6000 drachmae at a time when a normal wage for a week's work was 3.5 drachmae.

tampo (tambo/tampu) [MC]. A rest-house found along Inca roads in South America.

These stations were spaced at intervals of about 3 km, with larger examples at intervals of about one day's travel. Tampo were used by official travellers and as posts for relay runners. Each tampo was equipped with rest-rooms and government stores; stationed at each were the runners (*chasqui*) responsible for carrying messages relay-fashion throughout the empire.

T'ang [CP]. Chinese dynasty of the period AD 618 to AD 907. The T'ang period falls into two parts, the first being from the foundation of the dynasty until the rebellion of An Lu-Shan in AD 756. During this time the empire was ruled successively by T'ai Tsung, the empress Wu, and the emperor Hsuan Tsung. In the second period, after the An Lu-Shan disaster, the court never regained full control of the administration of the provinces, military governors becoming increasingly powerful. The capital was at Chang'an, but the dynasty was destroyed by a series of internal rebellions from AD 874 onwards.

tang [De]. A narrow projection on the base of a stone, bone, or metal tool or weapon that was used to attach a handle or shaft of a different material.

tanged point [Ar]. A projectile point of flint or stone, typically of triangular or leaf-shaped form, with a small projection at the base for the secure attachment to a wooden shaft.

Tanis, Egypt [Si]. Substantial temple and cemetery area in the Nile Delta, excavated by Flinders Petrie in 1883–6 and Pierre Montet in 1929–51. Amongst the most significant discoveries were the rich and well-preserved royal tombs of the 21st and 22nd Dynasties (1070–715 BC) constructed in the precincts of the great temple dedicated to AMEN.

[Sum.: H. Stienlin and C. Ziegler, 1987, *Tanis: trésors des pharons*. Paris: Seuil]

Tanit [Di]. Local representation of the Phoenician goddess Asarte as worshipped at CARTHAGE, sometimes referred to as 'the face of Ba'al'. The symbol of Tanit is a truncated cone surmounted by a disc. In a precinct dedicated to her were buried jars containing the cremated remains of infants sacrificed to her.

tankard [Ar]. A single-handled drinking vessel with vertical or only slightly angled side walls.

tannery [MC]. An industrial area where animal hides (raw hides) are converted into leather by soaking in a liquid containing tannic acid or by the use of mineral salts. Archaeologically, tanneries of whatever scale are represented by one or more large pits or soaking vessels, together with such ancillary buildings or structures as were used for preparing and storing the hides and finished leather.

Tanum, Sweden [Si]. Coastal region of Bohuslän which contains a major concentration of Bronze Age rock art sites. The panels are mainly on glacially smoothed rock surfaces and include depictions of ships, ploughing scenes, warriors armed with spears and battle-axes, carts, and possibly sun discs. Ships with fighting warriors standing within them and numerous oars for propulsion are especially distinctive.

[Sum.: J. Coles, 1990, *Images of the past*. Uddevalla: Bohusläns Museum]

t'ao t'ieh (taotie) [Ar]. A monster-mask believed to represent a mythical animal figure with claws and horns that figures frequently in the decoration of Chinese bronzework of the SHANG and ZHOU Dynasties.

taphonomy [Ge]. Literally, 'the laws of burial', in archaeology it is the study of the processes by which animal bones and other remains are transformed by human and natural processes during their incorporation into archaeological deposits, their subsequent long-term preservation within those deposits, and their recovery by archaeologists. The aim is to separate out and understand those characteristics of an assemblage that reflect past social actions in contrast to any patterning that might be the product of selective preservation or sampling biases.

TAQ [Ab]. *See* TERMINUS ANTE QUEM.

Tara, Co. Meath, Ireland [Si]. A low hill on which lies an extensive series of later prehistoric, pre-Christian, and early Christian monuments and structures forming one of the royal seats of early Ireland. The earliest upstanding monument on the hilltop is the Neolithic passage grave known as the Duma na nGiall (the Mound of the Hostages). Built about 3000 BC, but reused in the earlier Bronze Age, it lies within an oval ditched enclosure, the Ráith na Ríg, some 300 m by 250 m, which also contains two conjoined ringforts, one a bivallate structure known as Forradh (the Royal Seat), the other a univallate example known as Cormac's House. A decorated stone known as the Lia Fail (the Stone of Destiny) now stands within the Forradh, although originally it stood on the Duma na nGiall. It was used in the inauguration of Irish kings from at least the 8th century AD, and was widely regarded as having magic powers.

Two small enclosures lie outside the Ráith na Ríg, one to the north, the other to the south. Northwards there is also a long rectangular structure defined by parallel ditches 250 m long and 30 m wide. It is known as the Banqueting Hall, and may have been used for this purpose in medieval times even though its origins are probably far earlier. West of the Banqueting Hall is a group of three further ringforts. As a whole the site shows evidence for occupation and use over a very long period.

[Sum.: C. Newman, 1997, *Tara: an archaeological survey*. Dublin: Royal Irish Academy].

Tarascan (Purépecha) [CP]. State-organized society of the late Post-Classic Stage centred on Michoacan Province in west Mexico in the early first millennium AD. Although contemporary with the Aztecs it was never part of the Aztec empire. Tarascans claimed a Chichimec ancestry and their language was unrelated to any other in Mesoamerica. The first Tarascan capital was Tzinzunzan, overlooking Lake Pátzcuaro. Here was a large ceremonial complex with a huge platform mound on which stood five pyramids. Their religion seems to have focused on sun worship and to have included the practice of human sacrifice. The Tarascan state survived into early historic times.

Tardenoisian [CP]. Term to describe final Mesolithic communities along the Atlantic fringe of northwest Europe from Spain through into southwest France, Belgium, and Britain dating to the period 6000–4000 BC. The culture is named after the site of Fère-en-Tardenois, Aisne, in France and post-dates the SAUVETERRIAN. Characterized by microliths of standard geometric form, especially trapezes, crescents, and triangles that were used as projectile points or barbs. The Tardenoisian shows marked influences from contemporary adjacent Neolithic cultures.

target population [Ge]. The entire group of items—sites, artefacts, features, etc.—that archaeologists are interested in studying or analysing. Since it is rare to get access to the entire target population (even where it is known), it is usually approximated through some kind of sample.

Tărtăria, Romania [Si]. Late Neolithic tell settlement extensively excavated by K. Horedt and N. Vlassa in 1961. The site has four main levels beginning with Criç occupation in Level I; Turdaç-Petreçti/Vinča culture in Level II; Petreçti-Turdaç in Level III; and a Copper Age Coţofeni-Petreçti horizon in Level IV. A pit cut from Level II contained a ritual assemblage including a cremation, fired clay and alabaster figurines, spondylus shell bracelets, and three fired clay tables bearing incised signs. The group as a whole has sometimes been interpreted as the equipment of a shaman, but it has caused considerable controversy because of suggested resemblances between the Tărtăria tables and symbols on tablets from Jemdetnasr and Uruk in Mesopotamia. The Mesopotamian examples are some 1000 years later (late 4th millennium BC) than those from Tărtăria and so the similarities are best regarded as coincidental.

[Rep.: E. Neustrupný, 1968, The Tartaria tablets: a chronological issue. *Antiquity*, 42, 31–5]

Tartars [CP]. Generic name for various nomadic communities who inhabited Mongolia in the later first and early second millennia BC which is also applied to early historic groups found in Siberia and eastern Russia.

Tarxien, Malta [Si]. A late Neolithic temple complex on the outskirts of modern Valetta comprising the remains of at least four structures extensively excavated by T. Zammit between 1915 and 1919. The earliest temple was built about 3300 BC in the Ggantija Phase, but little survived the remodelling of the site about 3000 BC when two temples (the South and East Temples) were built in the TARXIEN PHASE. Both have four apses, but the South Temple is the finest of the two, with elaborate spiral decoration on the walls and the lower part of a large statue originally about 2.75 m high still in position. A door in the right-hand rear apse of the South Temple leads into the fourth and latest temple on the site, the Central Temple. This example has six apses and a central niche. All the temples were abandoned about 2500 BC and for the following millennium the area was used as a cemetery for inurned cremations.

[Rep.: T. Zammit, 1930, *Prehistoric Malta: the Tarxien temples*. Oxford. OUP]

Tating ware [Ar]. Distinctive type of ceramic pitcher probably made in the Rhineland during the 8th century AD. Readily recognizable because it was decorated with applied tin foil. Tating ware was widely traded to sites along the North Sea and English Channel coasts and beyond.

taskscape [Th]. Term proposed in 1993 by Tim Ingold, which has since created wide interest and found considerable application, to refer to the entire ensemble of tasks or actions that a society, community, or individual performs. The idea of the taskscape recognizes that all tasks are interlocking, and that any one task is embedded in the way that other tasks are themselves seen and understood. Thus the very notion of a taskscape as a continuous or seamless spread of heterogeneous events and experiences stands in opposition to the widespread western practice of classifying activities into groups such as technological, subsistence, or ritual.

taula [MC]. A kind of stone-built ritual monument found on the Balearic Islands and dating to the Bronze Age. Taulas were made from two carefully fashioned stone slabs with one balanced on top of the other to form a T-shaped structure. The two stones were sometimes fixed together with a mortise and tenon joint. The largest taula is at Trepuco and is 4 m high.

Taunton Phase [CP]. An industrial tradition within the KNIGHTON HEATH PERIOD of the British middle Bronze Age that flourished in the period 1400–1200 BC and is named after a large hoard of metalwork found in the grounds of the Taunton workhouse, Somerset, in 1877. Comparable hoards have been found at Bishopsland, Co. Kildare in Ireland, and this stage is sometimes referred to as the **Taunton–Bishopsland Phase** in western parts of the British Isles. The Taunton Phase is characterized by local copying of imported continental objects, especially ornaments such as twisted torcs, armlets, lozenge-section penannulars, ribbed bracelets, cones, coiled finger-rings, and many

different kinds of pin. Tools and weapons also benefited from these wider influences, especially the introduction of the basal-looped spearhead with leaf-shaped blades. The presence of so many ornaments and the continental connections led M. A. Smith to suggest in 1959 that the Taunton material in Britain was part of a widespread north European phenomenon known as the ORNAMENT HORIZON that could be linked with phase III and IV of Montelius' scheme for Scandinavia, Reinecke D, and Hallstatt A1/A2 in central Europe. More recently, in 1980, Colin Burgess argued that Smith's dating should be revised backwards in time to connect at least in part with Montellius IIb–c, so that a longer period of European contact can be envisaged. Also known as the Barton-Bendish Phase or the Glentool Phase.

Tawantinsuyu [De]. The name which the Incas gave to their empire. It means the 'four inextricably linked quarters'.

Taweret (Taueret) [Di]. Egyptian goddess of childbirth who symbolized maternity and suckling. She is usually represented as a female hippopotamus with pendant mammae standing upright on her back legs and holding the hieroglyphic sign of protection, a plait of rolled papyrus. Also seen as an avenging deity. Equal to the Greek Thoeris.

taxonomy [Ge]. An ordered set of operations that results in the objective classification or labelling of objects, and other kinds of material culture, into discrete units or *taxa*. Such ordered classification is based on visible or scientifically determined similarities and carefully defined traits. Taxonomy provides the basis for the organization of most archaeological materials. *See also* TYPOLOGY.

Taylour, Lord William Desmond (1904–89) [Bi]. British archaeologist well known for his work in Greece. Born in Ireland and educated at Harrow, he was the second son of the fourth Marquess of Headfort. After careers in banking and interior design in New York, and war service in North Africa, he studied archaeology and anthropology at Trinity College, Cambridge, before completing a Ph.D. on Mycenaean pottery in Italy. His career as excavator started during the 1950s, and after ALAN WACE's death in 1957 he took over and completed the British expedition to Mycenae. He excavated at Hagios Stephanos in Laconia between 1959 and 1977.

[Obit.: *Antiquaries Journal*, 70 (1990), 526]

tazza (pl. tazzae) [Ar]. A cup-like vessel, usually in a light-coloured fabric, with a stem and foot, decorated with bands of frilling. The frequent occurrence of signs of burning on the inner surface of such vessels indicates their possible use as lamps. May have been used in religious rituals.

technology [Ge]. The application of knowledge to facilitate the obtaining and transformation of natural materials. Technology involves the creation of material instruments (such as machines) used in human interactions with nature.

tectonic movements [Ge]. Movements in the earth's crust, which result in such structural features as the folding or faulting of rocks and the uplift or sinking of part of the earth's surface.

Tefé Phase [CP]. South American farming cultures found in the Lower and Middle Amazon areas and tentatively dated to *c*.AD 1100–1300. Characterized by their ceramic assemblages which belong to the Polychrome Horizon Style of Amazonia.

Tefnut (Tefnet) [Di]. Egyptian lion-headed goddess representing the moisture in the air, clouds, dew, and rain. A primeval deity and a member of the Heliopolitan Ennead, perhaps a theological conception rather than a real person. The Greeks sometimes identified her with Artemis.

tegula [Ar]. A Latin term used to describe a flat rectangular roof tile with flanges running down its longer sides.

tegula mammata [Ar]. A Latin term used to describe a rectangular tile with conical projections or flanges at each corner on one side. They were fixed to the surface of walls with clamps in order to form cavities through which hot gases from the hypocaust circulated.

Tehuacán Valley, Mexico [Si]. A highland valley in the semi-arid Puebla region which was

the subject of detailed multi-disciplinary investigations directed by Richard MacNeish during the 1960s. Situated at over 1800 m above sea level, the valley is remarkable for preserving a long sequence of sites and deposits which chart the social and economic development of groups living in the valley from Archaic times through to historic times. This is especially important because it spans the period during which agriculture developed as well as the period when chiefdoms and states dominated the region.

Nine main phases have been defined in the valley: the Ajuereado (9500–7000 BC), the El Riego (7000–5000 BC), the Coxcatlán (5000–3400 BC), the Abejas (3400–2300 BC), the Purrón (2300–1500 BC), the Ajalpan (1500–830 BC), the Santa María (830 BC–AD 150), the Palo Blanco (AD 150–700), and the Venta Salada (AD 700–1540).

[Rep.: D. S. Byers (ed.), 1967–77, *The prehistory of the Tehuacán Valley*, 5 vols. Austin and London: University of Texas Press]

tell [MC]. Artificial mound or hill resulting from the accumulation of occupation debris over a long period of time. In the Near East and southeast Europe (especially northern Greece, Turkey, Bulgaria, and Romania) the use of mud brick lent itself to the building up of deep deposits as successive phases of settlement were constructed upon the ruins of their predecessors and then in turn levelled to provide a platform for succeeding structures. The terms *tal*, *tepe*, *depe*, and *hüyük* are local names for tell mounds in different parts of Anatolia and the Near East and are often reflected in modern place-names and archaeological sitenames.

Tello, Julio Cesar (1880–1947) [Bi]. One of the founding fathers of Peruvian archaeology, educated in science and medicine in Peru and in anthropology at Harvard University in the US. He excavated many important sites in Peru, including CHAVÍN, PARACAS, and PACHACAMAC. He argued that the Chavín was the first major civilization in the Andes, a view that was widely held until the 1990s. In 1945 he founded what later became the National Museum of Anthropology and Archaeology in Lima. Following his death in 1947 he was buried in the museum grounds.

[Obit.: *American Antiquity*, 14 (1948), 50–6]

temenos [Co]. **1.** In southern Iraq, an artificial raised platform. **2.** In the Greco-Roman world, a sacred enclosure, sanctuary, or sacred precinct at an established cult centre, sometimes incorporating many buildings. In Roman times it came to mean the enclosed area in which a temple stood: a temple precinct.

temper (tempering agent) [Ma]. A non-plastic additive to clay (e.g. sand, shell, crushed pot, or charcoal) to improve workability and assist uniform drying by preventing excessive shrinking. In pottery manufacture, temper is an additive to the raw clay such as sand or finely crushed stone which helps to prevent the pot shrinking or cracking during firing.

tempering [Ge]. A process for hardening iron blades, involving heating and rapid cooling.

temple [MC]. A specialized building devoted to the worship, or regarded as the dwelling place, of a god or other deity. Styles, construction, and layout vary greatly between cultures, but amongst many include some kind of ceremonial entrance; an open courtyard sometimes with elaborate colonnades or statuary around the edges; a focal building in the courtyard; and a central sanctuary within the focal building. In many cases the temple may be enclosed within a TEMENOS of some kind.

temple mound [MC]. An artificial mound of earth and stone on which was constructed a temple or shrine, found widely over Mesoamerica. The mounds are sometimes terraced or stepped. In some cases the mounds also served as tombs.

Temple Mound period [CP]. Largely obsolete term originally introduced by J. A. Ford and G. Willey to denote the period *c*.AD 700–1700 in the eastern woodlands of North America when a large number of PLATFORM MOUNDS were built. *See* MISSISSIPPIAN CULTURES.

templum-in-antis [MC]. In the classical world, the simplest form of temple in which 'the house of god' is the same in plan as an ordinary house: a rectangular room, with the long side walls extended to form the walls of a porch, and with two columns between the antae (or wall endings), to support the porch

roof and make a fine entry. A good example is the so-called Treasury of the Athenians at Delphi, Greece.

temporality [Th]. In contrast to the measurable and calculated notion of TIME or chronology, temporality is concerned with the secular or routinized way in which a sequence of events, a kind of history, is physically experienced by those who live through them or experience them. Thus the passing of time is treated not as a neutral dimension but rather as being constituted by social practices. The French historian Braudel suggested that different temporal scales could be recognized (events; cycles or conjunctures; and the *longue dureé*), while Ricoeur contended that historical narratives are 'allegories of temporality' that use a discursive mode to convey something of the experience of time.

tendril [De]. In early Celtic art a characteristic plant-derived motif incorporating a series of running loops or spirals.

Tenochtitlán, Mexico [Si]. Capital city of the Aztecs situated on the site now occupied by Mexico City. Tenochtitlán was founded in *c*.AD 1325 on an island in Lake Texcoco. The city itself was formally planned, with six main canals set on a north–south axis and two main canals running east–west. There were four main districts in the city, each containing between fifteen and twenty wards. Each ward had its own public buildings and was based on kinship groups.

At the centre of the city was a sacred precinct with numerous public buildings. At the focus was the Great Temple (*Templo Mayor*), a truncated pyramid 60 m high on which stood two temples: one dedicated to Huitzilopochtli the Aztecs' patron god, the other to Tlaloc the rain god. Legend records that at the dedication of the former some 20 000 human victims were sacrificed. There were more than twenty other pyramid-temples in the central area, including those dedicated to Tezcatlipoca and Xipe Totec, together with priests' quarters, seven *tzompantli* (racks for displaying the skulls of sacrificed victims), two ball-courts, arsenals, plazas, and other public buildings.

Surrounding the sacred precinct were the palaces of the rulers. Moctezuma II's palace included not only his luxury residence but also pleasure gardens, an aviary, a zoo, and apartments for human freaks. In the northern part of the city was a massive market complex known as Tlateloco. Tenochtitlán was taken by Hernan Cortés in AD 1519; it was subsequently razed by the Spanish when they came to construct their own city.

[Rep.: S. Linné, 1934, *Archaeological researches at Tenochtitlán, Mexico*. Stockholm: Ethnographic Museum of Sweden; Sum.: A. F. Molina Montes, 1980, The building of Tenochtitlán. *National Geographic*, 156(6), 753–65]

Teotihuacán, Mexico [Si]. City-state in the northeastern part of the Basin of Mexico which rose to prominence after AD 100 and reached its peak in the early Classic Stage, AD 450–650. The first major excavations in the city were undertaken by Leopoldo Batres in 1905, since when there have been numerous excavations and surveys including work by Ignacio Bernal, René Millon, and William T Saunders.

The name Teotihuacán means 'place of the gods' in Nahuatl, and from its inception as an urban centre the site was planned and formally laid out. At the focus was a complex of ceremonial structures arranged along the Street of the Dead, including two massive pyramids, one dedicated to the sun, the other to the moon. A cave discovered under the Pyramid of the Sun in 1971 may have been important as a sacred place where communication with the underworld was possible and therefore the place around which the city grew up.

The city was probably controlled by ritual leaders who also had secular powers. These leaders occupied a series of palaces while the rest of the population lived in large apartment-like compounds set around courtyards.

By the mid first millennium AD, Teotihuacán covered an area of 20 square kilometres and had an estimated population of 125 000–200 000, making it the largest city in the pre-industrial world. It is estimated to have contained about 80 per cent of the inhabitants of the Valley of Mexico. Moreover, its size and importance made it powerful and influential among the emergent states of Mesoamerica during Formative and Classic times. The city's power and position were both created and supported by the fact that it lay on a major trade route, it had control over a major obsidian source, it was favourably located for the development of intensive agriculture, and it may have had important ritual

or symbolic connections too. The influence exerted by Teotihuacán extended to the domination of other centres in the vicinity, at times culturally and stylistically through art and architectural styles, trade, and religious guidance, at other times through military domination. After AD 650 the population of Teotihuacán began to decline and by AD 750 the city had been destroyed. No satisfactory explanation for this collapse has been offered, although sacking by rival Chichimecs is one possibility.

[Sum.: R. F. Millon, 1967, Teotihuacán. *Scientific American*, 216(6), 38–48]

tepary bean [Sp]. A leguminous plant (*Phaseolus acutifolius*) with edible seeds in a long pod. Native of Mesoamerica. Domesticated from perhaps 3000 BC.

Tepeu [CP]. Maya Lowland Phase covering the period AD 600–900, most easily recognized through the presence of polychrome vases.

tephrochronology [Te]. Stratigraphic dating method based on the fact that during volcanic eruptions ejected material (tephra) is spread in the atmosphere over a wide area before falling to ground as ash, cinders, or dust. This material is incorporated into archaeological deposits and natural accumulations such as peat bogs as a more or less discrete layer that can be identified and sampled. As a relative dating technique layers of tephra provide isochronous horizons that allow separate sequences of deposits to be linked. Since tephra from certain major eruptions of known age is also chemically distinctive absolute dates can be assigned to layers containing that particular kind of tephra. The best known volcanic eruption that provides a dating horizon for archaeological sites is probably Mount Vesuvius in AD 79 which covered Pompeii, Herculaneum, and many other settlements in central Italy.

tepidarium [Co]. A Latin term used to describe a room of moderate moist heat lying between the FRIGIDARIUM and CALDARIUM.

terminus ante quem **(TAQ)** [Ge]. Literally, Latin for the 'time before which'. A datable layer or structure in an archaeological sequence gives a TAQ dating endpoint for the deposition of all layers and material stratigraphically below it.

terminus post quem (TPQ) [Ge]. Literally, Latin for the 'time after which'. A datable object provides a TPQ for the layer in which it is found, and all deposits stratigraphically above it, in the sense that the layer(s) must have been deposited some time after the date at which the object was manufactured.

ternary diagram [Ge]. A graph that allows three variables to be plotted simultaneously, usually taking the form of an equilateral triangle with one scale along each side.

terp (pl. terpen) [MC]. A type of artificial mound found in late prehistoric and migration periods of northwest Europe, especially along the Frisian coastlands, created by the continual remaking of clay floors and deposition of rubbish. Terpen, or Wierden, in Germany, supported small settlements and are typically found in areas regularly threatened by flooding. Excavation shows that terpen were densely populated with numerous buildings. The economic base of terp settlements appears to have been stock-raising and fishing.

Terra Amata, France [Si]. Open-air Palaeolithic settlement with Acheulian associations dating to about 380 000 years ago near modern-day Nice in southern France. Excavated by Henry De Lumley in 1966, the site overlooks the coast and was found to have eleven main levels of occupation suggesting period revisitation of the spot over many years, perhaps in the spring or early summer. The imprints of small wooden posts suggested that temporary huts had been erected with stones pinning the base of the walls to the ground. The huts were oval between 7 m and 15 m long and 4 m to 6 m wide. A small hearth was found in the centre of each successive hut.

[Sum.: H. De Lumley, 1969, A Palaeolithic camp site at Nice. *Scientific American*, 220, 42–50]

terrace [Co]. **1.** In archaeology a terrace is an artificially created more or less level platform cut into the side of a hill. Often they are made by digging back into the hillslope while throwing the resultant quarried material forward downslope to extend the width of the platform. Revetments are sometimes made on the downslope side to contain the redeposited material. The resultant terrace is usually planted with a crop such as cereals or vines.

2. In geology terraces are broadly horizontal deposits of gravels laid down by river systems at different times in the past. The gravels in these deposits sometimes contain archaeological material. *See also* RIVER TERRACE.

terrace way [MC]. A track cut into the side of a hill so that it runs along a TERRACE more or less at right angles to the prevailing slope so as to produce comparatively gentle gradients along the track itself.

terracotta [Ma]. Literally, 'baked earth'. Mainly used to refer to fired clay that remains porous, such as might be used in building materials or coarse pottery.

terramara [MC]. Descriptive term applying to a class of middle Bronze Age settlements in the Emilia region of northern Italy because they appear in the modern landscape as spreads of rich black organic soil. Terramara is often quarried by local farmers for use as fertilizer.

terra nigra [Ar]. Black or silver-grey coloured Gallo-Belgic tableware produced in Gaul during the 1st century BC through to the mid 1st century AD. Exported from Gaul to other nearby parts of the Roman empire for military and civilian use, and to communities outside the empire who presumably acquired it as a traded luxury item. Close imitations of fabrics and forms are known amongst copies made in Britain. The imported vessels usually have the name of the potter or workshop stamped on the inner surface of the base, a practice imitated in Britain but usually with illegible markings.

terra rubra [Ar]. As TERRA NIGRA, but red in colour.

terra sigillata [Ar]. Roman mass-produced pottery with a range of forms but characterized by its glossy red glaze-like slip. It was mould-made in both plain and decorated forms. Vessels usually bear the name stamp of individual potters or workshops. Two principal types are recognized: **Arretine** produced at Arezzo in northern Italy between 30 BC and AD 50; and **Samian** produced in several areas of Gaul from AD 20 through to the late 2nd century AD. The main centres for the production of Samian were La Graufesenque, Lezoux, and Lyon. Samian ware was classified by

H. Dragendorff in 1895–6 and is still referred to by its Drag. number. Both Arretine and Samian were exported throughout the western Roman empire on a vast scale and can be a very accurate chronological indicator. Derivative forms of *terra sigillata* include the late Roman Argonne and Marne wares, African red slip ware, and eastern red wares.

terret (terret ring) [Ar]. Metal loop or ring, one of a set serving as rein guides on a horse-drawn vehicle.

territorial *oppidum* [MC]. A kind of OPPIDUM found in southern Britain that dates to the late 1st century BC and early 1st century AD comprising a collection of farmsteads, field systems, and semi-urbanized nucleated settlements of various sorts scattered across a large area of ground, typically between 30 and 90 square kilometres, bounded by a series of substantial earthworks known as dykes. The dykes are usually discontinuous and sometimes have a strong rectilinear aspect. The boundaries often complement or supplement natural features such as escarpments, rivers, or bogs. The precise role and function of territorial *oppida* are matters of debate, but the most widely accepted interpretation is that they were tribal capitals or major focal points for trade, industry, and commerce in immediately pre-Roman Iron Age Britain and represent the later stage in the progression from pre-urban settlements to a fully urban system.

Tertiary [Ge]. A major geochronological subdivision; the earliest of the two PERIODS forming the Cenozoic era (the other is the QUATERNARY), itself composed of five epochs: the Palaeocene (65–54 million years BP); the Eocene (54–38 million years BP); the Oligocene (38–26 million years ago); the Miocene (26–27 million years BP); and the Pliocene (7–2 million years BP). The last two of these epochs represent the period when early hominids developed as a recognizable species.

Teshik-Tash, Uzbekistan [Si]. Small cave (the name means 'stone with an opening') high in the west Himalayas south of Samarkand, where excavations directed by A. P. Okladnikov in 1938–9 brought to light the skeleton of a Neanderthal boy aged about 8. Dating to about 440 000 years ago, the site shows evidence of careful ritual and cere-

mony in connection with the burial, as the horn cores of Siberian mountain goats had been driven into the ground around the grave pit. Five levels containing flint tools of MOUS-TERIAN tradition were found in the cave, together with bones of wild sheep and goats.

[Sum.: H. L. Movius, 1953, *The Mousterian cave of Teshik-Tash, southeastern Uzbekistan, central Asia*. Cambridge MA: American School of Prehistoric Research, Peabody Museum]

tessellated floor (pavement) [Co]. A floor surface comprising small cubes (TESSERAE) of stone, tile, or glass, either plain or patterned in various colours, set in mortar to form mosaic.

tessera [Ar]. Small cube of coloured stone, tile, or glass, which, set in mortar, form components of a mosaic decoration.

test pit [Ge]. An excavation unit used to sample or probe a site before large-scale excavation or to check surface surveys. Typically small square trenches or holes arranged in such a way as to sample a site. *See* SHOVEL PIT TESTING.

testudo [Ar]. A Latin word for a device used to maintain the temperature of a Roman bath. It consists of a water container of half-cylindrical section with one end opening into the bath; the flat base of the *testudo* was placed above a furnace flue forming its roof.

tetrapylon [De]. A four-arched crossing in a church or basilica.

Teutons [CP]. A north European tribe which attacked the Roman republic in 110 BC. The name has subsequently come to refer to members of a Teutonic nation, especially Germans.

text [Th]. In post-modernist thinking the idea of text implies far more than the written word: a text is an extended discourse produced in accordance with rules and procedures that make it not simply the work of its author but rather something that is interdependent with the mass of texts and statements which precede, accompany, and succeed it up to the point where it is being read by someone: what Kristeva has called 'intertextuality'. Seeing a text in this way denies any notion of univocity and instead regards it as an open work susceptible to multiple readings that are intimately linked to cultural and political positioning—multivocity. In archaeology this way of thinking about text has implications not only for the study of excavation reports and published works in general, but also for situations where material culture has been interpreted through textual analogy—the proposition that material culture is structured and operates like text.

textiles [Ma]. Woven cloth made from spun fibres of animal or plant source. Although textiles themselves only survive from the ancient past under special conditions, their presence may be recognized through impressions made on more durable materials (e.g. pottery) or inferred from the recovery of evidence for looms or spinning equipment. *See also* WEAVING.

texture [De]. In ceramic studies, the term used to describe the uniformity of the fabric used to made a vessel or object.

thatch [Ma]. Traditional style of roofing used in many parts of the world at different times whereby bundles of organic material such as reed, straw, heather, turf, or ling are tied together over a wooden frame with the long axis of the plant fibre parallel to the slope of the roof to provide good weather-proofing.

thatch weight [Ar]. Heavy stone or ceramic object, usually with a perforation or groove in it so that it can be attached to a rope or net, that is used to hold roofing thatch in place.

theatre [MC]. A structure in which dramatic or ceremonial performances could be staged in front of an audience. In their developed form theatres are relatively complicated and generally enclosed buildings, although still retaining much of the essential form of earlier designs. Examples are known in Greece from the 6th century BC. The D-shaped or U-shaped structures had three main elements: the **orchestra** or central floor used for processions and dancing; the **auditorium** which housed the audience either standing or seated in tiers; and the **skene**, a structure for the convenience of the performers which later became elaborated as a stage in front of a building that supported scenery. The largest theatres in the Greek world were those of Syracuse and Ephesus which held 20 000 spectators. The theatre at Epidaurus is probably the best preserved and most beautiful of all: it

seated 16 000 people and is still in use for an annual festival.

Thebes, Egypt [Si]. The capital of UPPER EGYPT from the time of the 11th Dynasty, situated on the east bank of the Nile with the necropolis opposite on the west bank. The main part of the town is clustered around the great temple of KARNAK dedicated to AMEN. Thebes reached its peak in the 17th to 19th Dynasties. After RAMESSES II, however, it was relegated to being one of several capitals. It was finally destroyed after several sieges and rebellions in the reign of Augustus. *See also* LUXOR.

[Sum.: N. Strudwick and H. Strudwick, 1999, *Thebes in Egypt: a guide to the tombs and temples of ancient Luxor.* London: British Museum]

themata [Ge]. Large units of the Byzantine armed forces found between the 7th and 10th centuries AD.

theodolite [Eq]. Optical surveying instrument designed accurately to measure angles. Used in archaeological fieldwork to set out grids and prepare measured surveys of structures or areas of land.

Theodoric the Great [Na]. Ostrogoth king born in AD 451 who, with Byzantine support, conquered Italy (489–93), and founded a Gothic kingdom. Long recognized as the greatest of barbarian kings, his realm for a time united Germans and Italians. He died in AD 526. During the reigns of his successors, Theodoric's kingdom was absorbed in the eastern empire.

Theodosius [Na]. Count Theodosius was sent by the emperor Valentinian I to restore order in Britain after the Barbarian Conspiracy of AD 367. His measures probably included rebuilding work on Hadrian's Wall, the construction of early-warning signal stations on the Yorkshire coast, and the addition of bastions to the walls of towns. Unlike many army commanders of this time, he was a provincial landowner rather than a career soldier. He was made emperor in AD 379 and reigned until his death in AD 395.

Theodosius II [Na]. Eastern Roman emperor, son of Arcadius, born *c*.AD 401, who as a child succeeded his father in AD 408. He was dominated by his sister and his wife until the AD 440s, and at all times by a series of powerful ministers. During his reign successes were achieved in wars against Persia (AD 421–2 and 441) and against John the Usurper (AD 425), but the easterners were unsuccessful against the Vandals (AD 441) and afterwards against Attila. The great walls of Constantinople (after AD 413) are named 'Theodosian' after him. He died c.AD 450.

Theoretical Archaeology Group (TAG) [Or]. The first public TAG conference was held at Sheffield University in December 1979 following the success of two seminars held for students and staff in the universities of Sheffield and Southampton. TAG meetings aim to act as a forum in which the nature and development of archaeological theory can be discussed in a wide-ranging way. A conference has been held annually in December since 1979, its venue moving between those universities in Britain with an interest in such matters.

theory [Ge]. In archaeology the term is generally applied in a wide sense to mean any kind of discourse that is abstract in nature. Less frequently it is used in a more technical sense to mean structured concepts, statements, or models that are intended to make understandable in some way a specified set of phenomena. A theory is thus a statement that accounts for causes or relationships between phenomena.

thermae [MC]. Public baths developed during the imperial Roman period as very large, beautiful, and elaborate bathing, fitness, and recreation centres. Large examples were built in Rome and in all the major cities of the empire; there were even small ones in some villages. The Thermae of Caracalla at Rome cover 11 ha, but there were nearly 1000 others in Rome in the latest period. In addition to the actual baths (seat rooms, hot wash-rooms, cooling-off rooms, and cold plunge baths), there were facilities for swimming sports and spectators, gymnastics and sports and games in the modern sense, massage, libraries, gardens, rest-rooms, fountains, sculpture, and exhibitions, with shops and refreshments available nearby in the colonnades on the outside of the vast building. The afternoons of Roman citizens were often spent in the thermae.

thermal fracture [De]. In studies of stone and flint artefacts a thermal fracture is a break line or crack caused by excessive heating or cooling. Frost can penetrate cracks in the CORTEX, and prise off a flake or 'pot-lid'. Frost fractures are flattish with minute cracks and a pitted surface. When flint is placed in a fire it will usually shatter, with fragments detaching themselves from the surface.

thermoluminescence dating (TL) [Te]. A dating technique applicable to pottery and other ceramic materials. It works on the principle that all matter is constantly bombarded by cosmic rays and radiation given off from the decay of radioactive elements in the ground and in objects themselves. Minerals that are bombarded in this way by radiation build up a store of energy within their crystalline structure which is released when heated. The longer or more intense the bombardment, the more energy is stored and thus the more there is to be released. When a piece of pottery is fired, all the previously stored energy is released and the build-up starts afresh. After excavation a sherd can be heated again and its stored energy released and measured. If the level and extent of bombardment to which the pottery has been exposed while buried is known (the dose rate), or can be estimated, then the age of a sample can be calculated in terms of the time that has elapsed since it was last heated. The range of the technique is potentially unlimited, but it has an accuracy of ±5–10 per cent.

thermo-remnant magnetism [Te]. *See* ARCHAEOMAGNETIC DATING.

Thetford ware [Ar]. Mass-produced wheel-turned late Saxon pottery manufactured in workshops near Thetford in Norfolk, England, from the late 9th century through to the early 12th century. The fabric is hard and sandy, grey to buff in colour. The products are mainly cooking pits and jars with limited rouletting and applied thumb-strip decoration.

Theudelinda [Na]. Queen of the successive Lombard kings Authari (AD 584–90) and Agiluf (AD 590–615), daughter of the duke of the Bavarians. As a Catholic she corresponded with Pope Gregory the Great and founded the monastery of St Columbanus at Bobbio. She died c.AD 628.

Thiessen polygons [Te]. A formal method for exploring settlement patterns based on notional polygons constructed around a series of distributed points by taking the calculated mid-line between each pair of adjacent points to form the lattice. They provide a general approximation of the extent, shape, and orientation of the spheres of influence or territory around recorded settlements or other nodes in the settlement pattern.

thimble [Ar]. Small clay, bone, or metal cap, usually with a closed end, that is worn over the tip of a finger to protect it and to push a needle when sewing.

thing [MC]. A Norse open-air assembly site at which periodic gatherings were held to promulgate laws, dispense justice, and declare leaders or kings. Some thing sites were established on earlier monuments such as round barrows, while others are marked by natural features such as trees or distinctive hills. The Tynwald on the Isle of Man, which is still used for its original purposes on 5 July each year, has a stepped profile so that the social order is physically represented. *See also* MOOT.

thin orange ware [Ar]. Thin-walled orange-coloured fineware manufactured in the Valley of Puebla and found widely traded through Mesoamerica following its introduction in the PRE-CLASSIC PERIOD. It is taken as evidence of the extent of central Mexican influence during the CLASSIC PERIOD. Potentially confusable with Post-Classic fine orange ware.

thin section [Ge]. Slice of rock, ceramic, or other material mounted on a microscope slide and then ground and polished to a consistent thickness of 0.03 mm so that under a petrological microscope it is possible to identify the minerals using plain or polarized transmitted light and see the basic structure of the material itself. In archaeology petrological examination has been widely used to characterize stone artefacts and ceramic materials which, when comparative raw materials are also available, can lead to the determination of sources.

Third Intermediate Period [CP]. In Egypt covering the 21st to the 23rd Dynasties, *c.*1070–712 BC.

Thoeris [Di]. Greek god. *See* TAWERET.

tholos (pl. tholoi) [MC]. A building with a circular chamber and a CORBELLED vault, often approached by a long CORRIDOR. In Aegean and classical archaeology such structures are mainly tombs with a beehive-shaped burial chamber, often built into a natural hillside, the chamber being approached along a stone-revetted open passage or dromos. In finer examples the inner face of the stonework is dressed, as for example in the Treasury of Atreus at MYCENAE where the space above the vault was covered with rubble to form an artificial mound. The term was sometimes applied more loosely to certain PASSAGE GRAVES in Atlantic Europe which had corbelled vaults, but this is now rarely used.

Thom, Alexander (1894–1985) [Bi]. Scottish engineer and amateur archaeologist who researched widely on the construction of prehistoric stone monuments in northwest Europe. Born in Argyllshire, he graduated in engineering from Glasgow University and after a spell in civil and aeronautical engineering he returned to the university as a lecturer in these subjects in 1921. He joined the Royal Air Force in 1938 and spent the war years developing and operating wind tunnels for testing early Spitfires. In 1945 he was elected Professor of Engineering and Science and Fellow of Brasenose College, Oxford, a post he held until his retirement in 1961. His interest in archaeology came after a visit to Callanish in August 1933, and he subsequently made very high-quality plans of more than 400 stone circles and rows, including the extremely large and complicated structures at Carnac in France. In publishing his work he developed the idea that prehistoric people used a standardized measuring stick, the 'Megalithic yard', which was 0.83 m in length. He also suggested that although stone circles varied greatly in plan, there were regular patterns to their outline and that proto-Pythagorean geometry had been applied. Such views remain controversial, although the quality of his surveys and the detail of his mathematical arguments command wide respect.

[Obit.: *Antiquity*, 60 (1986), 136–7]

Thompson, Sir John Eric Sidney (1898–1975) [Bi]. British archaeologist who worked extensively on the Maya of Mesoamerica. Educated at Winchester College, he left to join the army during WW1, fighting in France with the

Coldstream Guards. His family had Argentine connections and for some time after the war he worked as a gaucho on a cattle ranch in South America. A growing interest in archaeology took him to Cambridge in 1924 where he studied at Fitzwilliam House (now College). From 1926 through to 1935 he was on the staff of the Field Museum of Natural History in Chicago, during which time he carried out much of his fieldwork. He applied ethnology to his work of interpretation, and excavated a number of sites in British Honduras, including San Jose, Bushilha, and San Antonio near Lubaantun. He was the first to establish a detailed chronology for the Belize Valley and to make a distinction between ceremonial centres and urban areas. Perhaps his greatest work was in advancing the decipherment of Mayan hieroglyphic scripts and in linking the Mayan calendar to the Christian calendar. In 1935 Thompson joined the Carnegie Institution in Washington where he remained until his retirement in 1958.

[Obit.: *American Anthropologist*, 78 (1976), 317–20]

Thomsen, Christian Jürgensen (1788–1865) [Bi]. Son of a wealthy Danish merchant, he at first followed his father into business while developing an interest in antiquities. In 1816 Thomsen succeeded Rasmus Nyerup as Secretary of the Danish Royal Committee and became the first curator of the National Museum in Copenhagen at its opening in 1819. Bringing a businessman's mind to the development of the museum and its collections, his major contribution was the formulation and introduction of the THREE AGE SYSTEM. This he explained in his *Ledetraad til Nordisk Oldkyndighed*, published in 1836, as an effective but at that time conjectural method of dividing up prehistory into the successive ages of Stone, Bronze, and Iron. Coincident with a broadly evolutionary perspective, this model has formed the basic chronological scheme used in prehistoric studies down to the present day. Thomsen's 1836 book was translated into English by Lord Ellesmere and published as *A guide to northern antiquities* in 1848.

[Bio.: J. Jorgen, 1987, Christian Jürgensen Thomsen: an appreciation in the bicentennial of his birth. *Acta Archaeologica*, 58 (1987), 1–15]

Thoth [Di]. Egyptian god, a moon god, scribe of the gods, inventor of writing, and reckoner of the years. His chief place of worship was

Hermopolis Magna (El-Ashmunein) but he was highly regarded throughout Egypt. He was the god of learning and intellect, and patron deity of scribes. He was depicted as an ibis-headed man, and the ibis and the ape were sacred to him. The Greeks identified him with Hermes, the messenger of the gods. He had a famous book in which all the wisdom of the world was recorded. He also acted as scribe in the Hall of Judgement.

Thothmes [Na]. The name used by four Egyptian pharaohs of the 18th Dynasty of whom Thothmes III was the most influential. Around 1490 BC he secured Egypt's possessions in Palestine and Syria by constant campaigning.

Thracians [CP]. Bronze Age nomadic communities related to the CIMMERIANS who occupied parts of the Russian steppe north of the Black Sea during the later 2nd millennium BC. Well known for their horsemanship and the early use of wheeled vehicles, they were driven out of their traditional homelands by the SCYTHIANS in the 8th century BC, retreating through the Caucasus and then across to the Balkans where they established themselves in the eastern part of the Balkan peninsula north of the areas of Greek settlement. By the 5th century BC Thracia encompassed the land which is now Bulgaria and Romania. In the 4th century BC the Thracian leader Seuthes established a capital at Seuthopilis but by the 1st century AD Thracia had become a province of the Roman empire.

Three Age System [Th]. The system of classification pioneered by the Danish antiquarian C. J. THOMSEN in the early 19th century whereby artefacts of stone, bronze, and iron were recognized as characteristic of successive periods or phases in prehistory. This scheme, based essentially on the materials used in the manufacture of ancient artefacts, was used as a method of sorting the Danish archaeological collections and formed the basis upon which they were displayed in the Danish National Museum after 1836. With further subdivisions, including the partitioning of the age of stone into a Palaeolithic, Mesolithic, and Neolithic, the scheme remains the basis of prehistoric classification until the present day and underpins much cultural-historical periodization of the ancient past.

three-dimensional recording [Te]. Recording the position of objects, materials, and samples discovered or recovered during excavation in Cartesian space using two coordinates in the horizontal plain (X and Y) and one in the vertical plane (Z). These are typically calculated either with reference to a local site-specific grid or tied in to a more extensive geo-referencing system such as the Ordnance Survey National Grid in Great Britain.

threshing floor [Ge]. Hard roughly level surface, either covered or open, used for processing cereals, especially the separation of the grain from the husk or straw using flails to beat the harvested plants in order to fracture the husk and shake the grain free.

through-room [De]. A room occupying the full depth of a building.

Thule Tradition [CP]. Late prehistoric hunting communities dating to the period 700 BC through to modern times living around the Siberian and American coasts of the Chukchi Sea, and around the American shore of the Baring Sea. These groups were mainly whale-and seal-hunting communities. They are characterized by the presence of polished slate tools, sophisticated toggling harpoons, and an elaborate and intricate art style. The Thule Tradition embraces a series of geographically and regionally distinct cultural groups including Old Bering Sea Cultures, the Punuk Culture, and the Birnirk Cultures. Sometime around the beginning of the second millennium AD Thule people began migrating to the east so that by the 13th century AD they had settled throughout the coasts of the Canadian Arctic and Greenland. Here they replaced the Palaeo-Eskimo (i.e. pre-Dorset and Dorset cultures) with what might be termed Neo-Eskimo.

thumb-nail scrapers [Ar]. Round scrapers on small flakes or ends of blades; known to have been hafted in certain cases by traces of resin on specimens.

Tiahuanaco, Bolivia [Si]. Capital city of the Tiahuanaco empire, situated on the altiplano of the central Andes at 4000 m above sea level at the southern end of Lake Titicaca. Flourishing during the middle Horizon.

In the centre is a major ceremonial complex spread over an area 1000 m by 500 m. The largest temple platform is called the Akapana; each side measures 200 m long and it stood 15 m high. A lower, smaller platform, the Kalasasaya, 3 m high and 126 m by 118 m stood at its base. At the northwestern entrance to the Kalasasaya stood a massive carved monolith known as the Gateway of the Sun. Made from a single slab of andesite weighing at least 10 tons, this monolith is carved in the form of a doorway with niches on either side. Above the door is a representation of the most important local deity, the Staff Deity: a human wearing an elaborate headdress with appendages ending with the heads of animals and holding a staff in each hand.

The surrounding state was large and appears to have extended into southern Peru, northern Chile, most of Bolivia, and some of Argentina. There was a sharp boundary between Tiahuanaco and the adjacent Huari state. Tiahuanaco declined in the late first millennium AD and was abandoned by about AD 1000.

[Rep.: C. W. Bennett, 1934, Excavations at Tiahuanaco. *Anthropological Papers of the American Museum of Natural History*, 34, 359–494]

tidemill [MC]. A water-powered mill where seawater is used to fill a pond at high tide so that it can be released to power the waterwheels as the tide goes out.

Tikal, Guatemala [Si]. Large Classic Stage Maya ceremonial centre which at its height covered over 120 square kilometres. Excavations and surveys by Edwin Shook and William R. Coe between 1956 and 1970 showed how extensive the site was and identified a large number of house platforms. This in turn triggered the reinterpretation of other Maya centres.

At the centre of Tikal is a group of ceremonial structures including the Great Plaza with a temple at either end, and the associated North Acropolis which supported three large temples and two smaller ones. Around the site are a series of earthworks which may have been for defence.

[Sum.: W. R. Coe, 1975, Resurrecting the grandeur of Tikal. *National Geographic*, 148, 792–811]

tilery [MC]. Manufacturing site where ceramic tiles were made, usually involving a series of clay pits, forming sheds where the various kinds of tile were shaped, drying racks, kilns, and yards for storing finished products.

till [Ge]. Poorly sorted material carried by ice-sheets and glaciers and deposited directly by the ice. All grades of material are represented, from clay-sized particles up to substantial boulders, the lithology and origin of the material being a reflection of the surface geology over which the ice-sheet or glacier previously flowed. Also known as boulder clay. Archaeologically, till is one of the most difficult natural substrates to work on because there are many variations in the texture and composition of the till at all sorts of scales, many of which look like archaeological features such as pits and ditches, as well as the geomorphological effects of a previously glaciated environment such as frost cracking and cryoturbation.

timber circle [MC]. Archaeologically represented as the foundation sockets (postholes) for a large wooden structure comprising two or more concentric rings of timber uprights variously interpreted as the stanchions of a roofed building or as freestanding posts. Dated to the later Neolithic, broadly 3000–2000 BC, and found widely across the British Isles either as discrete monuments or situated within HENGES and HENGE ENCLOSURES.

timber-framing [De]. Method of constructing a building using a framework of timber.

timber-laced rampart [De]. A rampart reinforced by vertical and horizontal timbers tied together as a rigid framework.

time [Th]. As the indefinite continued progress of existence, time is one of the key dimensions used in archaeological research and is seen in two ways. Measured time, CHRONOLOGY, can be viewed as a series of blocks of defined duration that occur in sequence and which can be counted, like the ticking of a clock. Such time is an artificial social construction tied to observable events, often the movements of celestial bodies, and for convenience archaeologists frequently back-project modern notions of time (for example, years, centuries, and millennia in the western Christian calendar) onto earlier societies. In contrast, TEMPORALITY refers to the human experience of time in terms of the sequence of events which may not be entirely successive and which defy measurement.

time-geography [Th]. An approach to the study of human behaviour, pioneered by the Swedish geographer Torsten Hagerstrand, which emphasizes the movement of individuals simultaneously across time and space.

time-space convergence [Ge]. The process whereby distances become 'shortened in time' as the speed of modes of transportation increases.

tin [Ma]. Soft bright silvery-white malleable metal (Sn) with a low melting point that resists corrosion, occurring naturally in cassiterite and other ores. Used in alloys, especially as a constituent of bronze (along with copper and lead) from early Bronze Age times onwards. Tin ores are relatively scarce in the Old World, the main sources being Cornwall in Britain, northwest Spain, and Bohemia. Lesser sources may have been used in central Italy and eastern Turkey, along with highly localized outcrops now lost. As a result, tin was widely traded in antiquity.

ting [Ar]. A pottery or bronze vessel with three legs common in early China.

tip line [Ge]. The interface between two contrasting materials whose form and topography can be interpreted as evidence for the deliberate dumping or tipping of material, usually into a pit, ditch, or structure as fill. Material which is tipped into a pit, for example, tends to fan out from the point of origin until it reaches its natural angle of rest. In section, tip lines appear as sloping edges usually bounding wedge-shaped deposits.

Tiryns, Greece [Si]. A strongly fortified Mycenaean settlement and palace in southern Greece. The site was investigated by H. Schliemann intermittently between 1876 and 1885. Although the site was occupied during the early Bronze Age, the palace and an accompanying defensive wall were not built until about 1400 BC. The palace was of typical Mycenaean form with a central MEGARON opening onto a porticoed courtyard. Frescoes on the walls show MINOAN influences. Tiryns was destroyed about 1200 BC, subsequent occupation being on a small scale and rather poor compared with earlier times.

[Rep.: H. Schliemann, 1886, *Tiryns*. London: John Murray]

Tisza Culture [CP]. Late Neolithic culture of the early 4th millennium BC in eastern Hungary, northeast Yugoslavia, and northwest Romania, broadly contemporary with the Vinča-Pločnik Phase south of the Danube. Characteristic pottery forms include anthropomorphic vessels and vessels with incised basketry designs or painting applied after firing. Copper objects are known. Settlements include villages of up to 15 ha, usually situated near the confluence of important rivers. Cereal cultivation was an integral part of the economy and is demonstrated by the large number of storage jars, fired-clay bins, and granaries found at settlements. In addition, local domestication of wild aurochs is attested, allied to intensive cattle husbandry.

Tiszapolgár Culture [CP]. The oldest stage of the central European Copper Age (3300–3100 BC) named after a cemetery at Tiszapolgá-Basatanya in eastern Hungary. Settlements are generally short-lived and small, although a few occupied tells are known. Most distinctive are the burial sites which, unlike those of its southeast European neighbours, are separate from contemporary settlements and seem to have been established communally to serve several farmsteads. Pottery is almost exclusively undecorated, including tall pedestalled bowls. Copper tools include axe-hammers, chisels, and awls; flint was widely used too, some of it brought from north of the Carpathians.

tithe barn [Co]. A large barn in which the tithes of hay and grain were stored.

titulum [Co]. Short detached stretch of rampart (and ditch) protecting the gateway of a marching camp. Outlying length of bank and ditch blocking direct approach to the gate of a camp or fort.

Titus [Na]. Roman emperor, AD 79–81.

Tivacundo Phase [CP]. South American farming cultures found in the Rio Pastaza and Rio Napo areas of Amazonia and tentatively dated to *c*.AD 500–700. Characterized by their ceramic assemblages which belong to the Polychrome Horizon Style of Amazonia.

tjaele [Ge]. Also called permafrost. Conditions by which subsoil is permanently frozen under periglacial conditions.

Tlaloc [Di]. Mesoamerican god of water and rain. Typically represented as goggle-eyed with a scroll-edged mouth and often, but not always, wearing some kind of flat rectangular head-gear.

tlatoque [De]. Aztec ruler or petty king of a city-state. The tlatoque claimed descent from Quetzalcóatl through the Toltecs and thus believed in a divine right to rule.

TL dating [Ab]. *See* THERMOLUMINESCENCE DATING.

tobacco [Sp]. Narcotic plant (*Nicotina tabacum*) with leaves that can be smoked, chewed or, in powdered form, snorted. The plant is a coarse rank-growing annual up to 2 m tall. A native of South America where it was domesticated by *c*.AD 400. Soon afterwards it spread to many other parts of the New World. The tobacco plant was first brought to Europe in AD 1558 by the Spanish physician Francisco Fernandes.

toft [Co]. A plot on which a house stands or once stood.

tollhouse [MC]. A building constructed beside a turnpike road where tolls were collected from travellers passing through the turnpike and which provided accommodation for the toll collector.

Tollund, Denmark [Si]. Tollund Moss is a narrow bog set amongst high hills near Aarhus in Jutland. Here, in 1950, Professor P. V. Glob excavated the body of a man in a remarkable state of preservation: the clothing, skin, hair, and even the stomach contents had all survived. Dating to about 210 BC, the man had been naked except for a well-made leather cap and a belt around the waist. When examined it was found that he had been strangled or hanged and part of a braided leather rope still encircled his neck. Study of the stomach contents revealed that he had eaten his last meal 12–24 hours before his death and that it had consisted of a sort of gruel made up of various seeds, both wild and cultivated.

[Sum.: P. V. Glob, 1969, *The bog people*. London: Faber & Faber]

Toltec [CP]. Early state-organized society occupying central Mexico in the period AD 900–1100; the dominant culture of the early Post-Classic Mesoamerica. The origins of the Toltec are unclear, but they were probably one of the Chichimec groups which migrated southwards after the decline of Teotihuacán. The Toltec capital was established at Tula, Mexico, in *c*.AD 960 by the leader Topiltzin.

At its peak the Toltec state spread to include the Yucatán and areas which until that time had been relatively peripheral. Human sacrifice was a major feature of Toltec religion. Large carved statues characterized ceremonial centres of the period.

The Toltec state was not especially long-lived, and had crumbled away by the mid 13th century AD, perhaps triggered by a climatic deterioration. Numerous later Mesoamerican groups, notably the Aztecs, claimed descent from the Toltecs.

tomb [MC]. Structure built for the burial of the dead, either individually or collectively. Most tombs contain a strong reflection of the belief systems and ideologies of those who built them, and archaeologists regularly use indicators such as the size and sophistication of the structure to draw conclusions about the status and wealth of those buried within. It is also widely recognized that tombs were often much more than simply burial places of the dead; they also had a role amongst the living as territorial markers, ceremonial centres, and places of pilgrimage.

tombstone [Ar]. A stone monument marking the position of an essentially subterranean burial. Tombstones usually bear some kind of epitaph.

Tongglüshan, China [Si]. An early copper mine and smeltery, the earliest known in China, near the Yangtze River in Hubei Province. Native copper and malachite were extracted and worked from the Eastern Zhou period of the 8th century BC down to the Western Han period of the 1st century BC. The mines themselves extend over an area of about 2 square kilometres, while the systems of shafts and galleries reach depths of 50 m below ground level. The shafts and galleries were generally square in cross-section, lined with timber, and never more than 1.2 m across. A smelting area with at least seven furnaces has been examined. These furnaces pro-duced ingots of about 10 kg. Slag deposits estimated at more than 400 000 metric tons have been mapped and serve to illustrate the scale of the workings. It is thought that more than 10 000 metric tons of copper could have been produced from the mines.

[Sum.: Y. Zhu, 1981, Copper smelting technique at the ancient Tongglüshan mines, China. *Youse Jiashin*, 33(4), 63–7]

tongue chape [Ar]. Metal fitting of elongated form and roughly triangular outline manufactured in the WILBURTON Tradition. The chape fitted on the end of a scabbard to prevent the tip of the sword cutting through the leather.

tool kit [De]. In the study of stone or flint assemblages this term is used to describe an idealized or typical assemblage of artefacts used by an individual or group: for example, a hunting group or a woodworker.

topogenous bog [Ge]. Marsh, swamp, or fen that develops as a result of a high local groundwater table caused by local relief such as a poorly drained basin or underlying impervious rock strata. In general, topogenous bogs tend to be either alkaline or neutral and thus do not preserve organic materials especially well. *See also* OMBROGENOUS BOG.

topographic maps [De]. Maps that relate archaeological sites to the basic landform and key features of the natural landscape in which they are set.

topsoil [Ge]. A generic term referring to the uppermost horizons of a soil profile that generally contain high levels of organic material and the root systems of surface vegetation. From the top down these comprise: the L horizon of loose leaf litter; the F horizon of organic residues undergoing comminution by the soil fauna; the H horizon of completely humified material; and the A horizon composed of a mixture of organic material and mineral components variously worked by the actions of earthworms and other soil fauna. The mixture of mineral and organic matter produced by earthworm activity is known as mull humus.

torc [Ar]. A neck-ring of twisted metal, generally of bronze or gold, known in various forms from the early Bronze Age to the later Iron Age in Europe, and sometimes thought from representations in sculpture and metalwork to have had cultic or magical associations.

tor cairn [MC]. A kind of prehistoric ceremonial site found in western parts of the British Isles, especially southwestern England, comprising a circular bank of stones or a platform of loose stones constructed around a prominent natural outcrop of rock, usually a tor or a very large grounder. The overall diameter of tor cairns ranges from 12 m to over 30 m, and the height of the cairns from 0.5 m to about 4.0 m. There is usually an entrance into the enclosed area, and pits dug into the ground in the area between the central outcrop and the enclosure. Cultural debris including flint tools, pottery, quartz pebbles, and bronze weapons and ornaments have been found at tor cairns and allow them to be dated to the early second millennium BC, the early Bronze Age.

Torksey-type ware [Ar]. Type of late Saxon pottery found in central England and dating to the period AD 850 to 1150. Manufactured using a fast wheel at workshops in the area around Torksey, Lincolnshire.

torre (pl. torri) [MC]. Stone towers of Bronze Age date found mainly in the southern part of Corsica. Generally 10–15 m across and up to 7 m high, they have a single narrow entrance and a central corbelled chamber. Their function is uncertain but they are rather small to have been settlements or defensive structures. Superficially similar to the NURAGHI of Sardinia and the TALAYOTS of the Balearic Islands.

tortoise core [Ar]. A style of CORE typical of flintworking in the LEVALLOIS technique where the aim is to produce large oval flakes with a sharp edge all round. This results in a core that has one flattish face and a low domed back that, overall, resembles a tortoise.

torus moulding [De]. A bold convex moulding generally semi-circular in cross-section.

total archaeology [Th]. A term popularized by Christopher Taylor in 1974 to describe archaeological surveys that develop a diachronic understanding of an area (for example, a parish or county) but drawing on the fullest possible range of sources including field archaeology, the examination of historical sources and records, the study of place-names, the critical use of early maps and plans, and, where appropriate, the integration of folklore and local tradition. Such an approach was found to provide very detailed insights into the evolution of selected tracts of landscape, especially for the post-Roman period, and proved an important step in the development of more broadly based traditions of LANDSCAPE ARCHAEOLOGY.

totalitarianism [Ge]. A form of political administration in which power is concentrated in the hands of a dictator, who operates through a mixture of cultivating a devoted following and terrorizing those who do not agree with stated policies.

total station [Eq]. A multi-purpose electronic surveying instrument with a built-in EDM capable of measuring horizontal distances, slope distances, angles, vertical height differences, three-dimensional coordinates, and a number of other positional features useful in archaeology. Coupled to a digital data-logger the measurements, together with point codes and attribute information assigned by the surveyor, can be downloaded into a surveying, mapping database or a GIS programme.

totem (totemism) [Ge]. A totem is a guardian spirit of a particular unit of kinship or social organization such as a clan or tribe. A totem may be a species of plant, insect, animal, bird, or even a mythical entity. Totemism is the belief that a group has a particular relationship to its totem, usually seeing it as a sacred ancestor, and thus subject to special taboos and ritual observance.

tournette [Ar]. A pivoted platter which can be rotated manually to ease the manufacture of a pot, but which is not turned mechanically and so is not a potter's wheel.

tower house [MC]. Fortified private residence commonly built from the 15th century through to the 17th century in northwest Europe, especially the English/Scottish borders, and parts of Ireland. Typically these buildings are square or rectangular in plan and have four or five storeys. They are characterized by thick stone walls and a stone vaulted basement. Although less well fortified than a CASTLE, tower houses nonetheless often have battlements, a heavily protected entrance, and small windows doubling as archery-loops. They generally provided permanent residences for wealthy and/or aristocratic members of society.

tower keep castle [MC]. A strongly fortified residence of a king or lord in which the KEEP, which may be freestanding or surrounded by a defensive enclosure, is the principal defensive feature. Tower keep castles were sited for defensive or offensive operations, often being administrative centres as well as fortifications. They are found in both rural and urban situations in many parts of northwestern Europe, being constructed from the 11th century AD through to the 15th century.

tower mill [MC]. Type of windmill, usually built of brick or stone, with a circular or conical body with a revolving cap for turning the sails into the wind.

town house [MC]. A residential dwelling within an urban or semi-urban environment, generally with a small frontage onto a street or thoroughfare and a yard of some kind behind.

Towthorpe bowl [Ar]. Style of middle Neolithic pottery dating to the fourth millennium BC, found at sites widely scattered over northeastern England and named after finds from a round barrow at Towthorpe in North Yorkshire. The style is characterized by mainly plain bowls with rounded bases and thick outturned rims.

Toynbee, Jocelyn Mary Catherine (1897–1985) [Bi]. British classicist, archaeologist, and Roman art historian. Educated at Winchester High School and Newnham College, Cambridge, she had a short spell teaching at Cheltenham Ladies' College immediately after graduating. She spent the rest of her working life in universities: St Hugh's, Oxford; Reading; from 1927 to 1951 as Fellow and Director of Studies in Classics at Newnham; and from 1951 as Laurence Professor of Classical Archaeology in the University of Cambridge. Amongst her best-known publications are *Art in Roman Britain* (1962, London: Phaidon) and *Animals in Roman life and art* (1973, London: Thames and Hudson).

[Obit.: *Antiquaries Journal*, 66 (1986), 509]

TPQ [Ab]. *See* TERMINUS POST QUEM.

trace elements [Ge]. Elemental components of a material that upon analysis are found to comprise less than 0.1 per cent of the substance. The analysis of trace elements sometimes allows the characterization of otherwise rather homogenous materials such as obsidian, which in turn may lead to the identification of sources and the recognition of dispersal patterns.

tracery [De]. Ornamental work in the head of a window, screen, or panel formed by the curving and interlacing of bars of stone or wood grouped together over two or more windows or bays. In windows the tracery may be used as the glazing bars to hold pieces of glass in place.

trackway [MC]. A formalized communications route linking one or more settlements, or a settlement with related features such as fields or quarries, which is unsurfaced except where it crosses difficult terrain and requires reinforcement of the ground surface with vegetation or laid timbers.

trackway field system [MC]. One or more field plots, each defined by a ditch, hedge, or fixed boundary of some kind, which are linked together by a series of pathways or tracks running between the fields. In most cases it is probable that the tracks were first set out with the field plots aligned on them. The tracks not only connect the fields to adjacent settlements but also provide the main means of access from one field to another. Such arrangements are found in England and other parts of northwest Europe and have been dated to the 1st and 2nd millennia BC.

trade [Ge]. In archaeology this term tends to be used in its broadest sense to mean the transfer of goods between communities, recognizing that many different social mechanisms may be responsible for those movements. *See also* EXCHANGE.

trading centre [Ge]. Centrally situated focal point where a number of individuals or communities could come together for trading and exchange. Possibly also a HABITATION SITE.

trading network [Ge]. Network of economic exchange linking companies or countries.

tradition [Ge]. In American archaeology this term refers to styles of artefact, assemblages of tools or other items of material culture, architectural styles, economic practices, or artistic styles that last longer than a phase or the duration of a horizon. The idea of a tradition implies a degree of cultural continuity even if there are local or regional patterns in the archaeological material. The term was defined in its modern usage by G. Willey and P. Phillips in 1955, although the word had been widely used in a variety of ways before that time, and continues to be variously and less specifically applied. The ARCTIC SMALL TOOL TRADITION is a good example of the way the term applies: persistent technological or cultural patterns identified by characteristic artefact forms. These persistent forms outlast a single phase and can occur over a wide area.

traditional states [Ge]. State-based societies in which the main basis of production is agriculture or pastoralism. Traditional states are often referred to as 'early civilizations'.

trait [Ge]. A proposed observable distinguishing feature or characteristic of an artefact, structure, or some other element of material culture.

Trajan [Na]. Roman emperor AD 98–117.

Trajan's Column [Si]. A tall commemorative stone column erected in the centre of Trajan's Forum in Rome in honour of the emperor Trajan and dedicated to him on 18 May AD 113. Composed of eighteen massive drums of marble the whole structure stands 29.5 m high to the base of the statue plinth. The decoration is a continuous spiral frieze commemorating the emperor's triumphs in Dacia in AD 101–2 and 105–6. This provides an important source of information about the structure and workings of the Roman army on campaign.

[Sum.: F. Lepper and S. Frere, 1988, *Trajan's Column*. Gloucester: Sutton Publishing]

trajectory [De]. An idea borrowed from systems analysis to refer to a course of development representing medium- or long-term social change that can be mapped in archaeological terms by reference to changes in specific characteristics through a series of successive stages.

tranchet axe [Ar]. Tool having a straight cutting edge caused by the removal of a flake parallel to it.

transepted gallery grave [MC]. Now obsolete, this term was widely used during the early and mid 20th century to describe the chambers of certain types of Neolithic long barrow in northwest Europe where individual cells open off a central passage or chamber. Commonly found in the Cotswold–Severn long barrows of western England and Wales and also in similar barrows around the mouth of the Loire in western France.

transhumance [Ge]. Transferring livestock from one region to another according to the season of the year so that two complementary ecozones are exploited. Typically, transhumance systems utilize areas of lowland during the winter months and nearby uplands during the summer. Some or all of the population will move with the livestock, especially in the case of long-distance transhumance where the regions are perhaps 50 km or more apart.

transitional [De]. **1.** General term used to describe cultures or styles during a period of change from one distinctive form to another. **2.** In American archaeology see FORMATIVE. **3.** In European architecture, the style of ecclesiastical architecture intervening between the Romanesque and the Gothic.

transmission electron microscopy [Te]. A method for studying the surface and internal structure of a range of materials, including metals, ceramics, and stone, in far more detail than can be achieved with an optical microscope. The transmission electron microscope utilizes a high-energy electron beam generated by a heated filament which is focused onto a specimen by means of a condenser lens. The electron beam illuminates an area just a few microns in diameter. After transmission of the electron beam through the sample an appropriate magnified image of the specimen is formed by the objective lens that throws the image (magnified more than 100000 times) onto a fluorescent screen or photographic plate. The whole process is undertaken under high-vacuum conditions. The sample has to be extremely thin in order to allow the electron beam to pass through it; this is usually achieved by grinding with a fine powder and mounting it on a carbon film. Wear marks on the surface of materials can be examined by making a replica of the surface in plastic or carbon film and examining that under the microscope.

transom [Co]. A beam or beams dividing a window horizontally into two or more lights.

transverse arrowhead [Ar]. Style of flint or stone projectile tip of trapezoidal outline in which the wider straight end forms the leading edge. Typical of the later Mesolithic in northern Europe. Also known as a PETIT-TRANCHET ARROWHEAD.

travertine [Ge]. Calcareous bed laid down by water action, especially by springs.

TRB [Ab]. *See* TRICHTERBECKER CULTURE.

treasure trove [Le]. An ancient common-law doctrine in the British Isles whereby items of gold and silver (treasure) which are shown to have been hidden with intent to recover, but for which ownership is now unknown, pass to the crown. The finder of such items is, by custom, rewarded with the commercial value of the find. In 1996 the common law was replaced by *The Treasure Act 1996* which came into force in England, Wales, and Northern Ireland on 24 September 1997. This defined treasure as being: any object other than a coin provided that it contains at least 10 per cent of gold or silver and is more than 300 years old; all coins from the same find provided that they are more than 300 years old and contain more than 10 per cent gold or silver, but if less than 10 per cent gold or silver then there must be at least ten of them; associated objects. Such finds must be declared to the local coroner within fourteen days of discovery. Thereafter a lengthy process ensues whereby objects confirmed as treasure are offered to national or local museums, which, if they choose to take the material, must compensate the finder with the value of treasure as determined by an independent valuation panel. Since 1996 the number of items declared treasure has risen significantly.

tree hole [Co]. A hole or depression in the subsoil caused by root action from the long-term presence of a large tree or as a result of a substantial tree being toppled (e.g. by the wind), so that in falling it pulls out part of its root system and associated soil/subsoil, leaving a depression in the ground. Some tree holes recorded in excavations are of considerable antiquity.

tree-ring dating [Te]. *See* DENDROCHRONOL-OGY.

tree-trunk coffin [Ar]. A wooden coffin made by cutting a tree trunk longitudinally so that one part (usually the larger) is hollowed out while the other can be used as a lid. In the British Isles this kind of construction is typical of the early 2nd millennium BC. Also known as monoxylous coffins, they are often rather similar to dugout canoes.

trench [Ge]. In archaeology the term trench is used to refer to any area of ground that is subject to a formal excavation. Although originally archaeological trenches were often long narrow cuttings, since the 1950s there has been a trend towards the use of larger and more open areas.

trend surface analysis [Te]. A procedure for producing a generalized map from observed distributions by standardizing data represented at a number of sample points (for example, the percentage of a particular kind of pottery represented in a series of assemblages) and then drawing contour lines to show different levels of representation. Such a map will show the broad trends and also local variations in the distribution, in part at least overcoming irregularities in the distribution of sample points.

trepanation [Ge]. Surgical operation involving the removal of a disc of bone from the skull. First practised by Neolithic communities in Europe using flint blades, presumably for the relief of physical, mental, or spiritual ailments. Widely practised since prehistory in many parts of the world and still occasionally used today.

Tres Zapotes, Mexico [Si]. An Olmec ceremonial centre in the Tuxtla Mountains of southern Vera Cruz believed to have been occupied in the period 1000–600 BC. Excavations by Matthew Stirling from 1938 to 1946 have shown that Tres Zapotes came to prominence after La Venta was destroyed.

[Rep.: M. W. Sterling, 1940, *An initial series from Tres Zapotes, Vera Cruz, Mexico*. Washington DC: National Geographic Society]

triangular loomweight [Ar]. Block of baked clay weighing around 1 kg with a triangular outline and parallel sides cross-section with perforations through the corners for attachment to the warp threads on an upright loom during textile production. Generally later Bronze Age and Iron Age in date in the British Isles, these objects provide some of the earliest evidence of weaving.

triangulation [Te]. Method of fixing the position of a defined point in the horizontal plane by measuring its distance from two points whose position is already established (e.g. grid pegs) and calculating with trigonometry or plotting on paper the third point. When using the paper method the new point can be plotted by scaling the measured distance from each of the known points with a compass so that the new point is the position where the arcs intersect.

tribal archaeologist [Ge]. A professional archaeologist employed by an indigenous tribal population.

tribe [Ge]. A group of indigenous persons, families, or clans believed to be descended from a common ancestor and forming a close-knit community under a defined leader, chief, or ruling council. A larger group of bands unified by sodalities and governed by a council of representatives from the bands, kin groups, or sodalities within it.

tribunal [Co]. Raised platform for a commanding officer or magistrates.

Trichterbecker Culture (TRB) [CP]. Neolithic culture of the later fourth and third millennia BC in northern Europe, the first Neolithic culture in the region, named after its characteristic pottery style, the funnel-necked beaker, which has a globular body and outturned rim. Amphorae and flasks are also known in the ceramic repertoire. The origins of the TRB are thought to lie in the acculturation of local Mesolithic communities through contact with the Linear Pottery Cultures (LBK) to the south. TRB settlements are poorly known, but enclosures such as SARUP in Denmark are now being recognized more widely. Burials are well known and include single graves in DYSSER in Scandinavia, KUJA-VIAN graves in Poland, and in later periods PASSAGE GRAVES. Five main regional groups of the TRB have been identified: the western group in the Netherlands; the southern group in Germany; the southeastern group in the Czech Republic; the eastern group in Poland; and the northern group in Denmark. Ground stone axes and battle-axes are known. Copper tools were made during later periods of the TRB in the southeastern group and distributed from there to surrounding regions. The TRB is succeeded by the SINGLE GRAVE cultures.

triclinium [Co]. Latin term for a dining room, often with an arrangement of three couches in a horseshoe shape.

Trier, Rheinland-Pflax, Germany [Si]. The principal Roman city of northeast Gaul and important medieval administrative and trade centre situated in the Moselle Valley. The site was settled in the later 1st millennium BC by the local Treveri tribe who appear to have built a tribal sanctuary there. Following the Roman conquest of Gaul the site was selected by the emperor Augustus as the regional capital because of its favourable position in relation to the Rhine frontier as a supply base to the Roman army, for regional trade, and as an administrative centre for the three provinces of Gallia Belgica and two Germanies. By the 4th century AD Trier had become a spiritual and political capital for western Europe and later was the centre of an archbishopric.

[Sum.: E. M. Wrightman, 1970, *Roman Trier and the Treveri*. London: Hart-Davies]

triforium [Co]. The gallery or arcade, usually without windows and so a 'blind storey', above the main arcade and below the 'clerestory'.

trilithon [Co]. An arrangement of large stones comprising two uprights with a lintel across the top. The best-known examples are at STONEHENGE, England.

Trinovantes [CP]. Tribal grouping or petty kingdom of the last few centuries BC and 1st century AD in southeastern England, seemingly occupying the area north of the River Thames over what is now the southern part of East Anglia. The main tribal centre was probably the TERRITORIAL *OPPIDUM* at CAMULODUNUM, but many other settlements are also known, some showing signs of proto-urban structure and form. The Trinovantes were clearly in close contact with the Roman empire through trade and perhaps also alliances and personal contacts, as evidenced by the wealth of imported luxury goods, wines, and foodstuffs from the Mediterranean world.

tripartite urn [Ar]. Form of early Bronze Age collared urn found in the British Isles in which the body has three distinct components or sections: a trunco-conic or ogee body; a concave neck; and a collar which is usually angled but occasionally vertical.

Tripillja Culture [CP]. Late Neolithic culture of the Ukraine, named after a type-site (Tripillja or Tripolye) near Kiev. Settlements are of long, rectangular houses, sometimes arranged in radial plan, and characteristic assemblages include anthropomorphic clay figurines and painted pottery as well as small copper artefacts.

triple vase [Ar]. Vessel comprising three small jars, either attached to the top of a tubular ring-base which is often hollow, or joined together at the body. Such vessels have also been described as flower vases. Roman in date.

tripod [Ar]. **1.** A stand or support of some kind with three legs. **2.** Homer writes of bronze tripods as being large three-footed vessels like cauldrons. They were clearly of great value; Linear B tablets from Knossos show a careful count of these objects in the Minoan palace. In classical times beautifully decorated tripods, sometimes of gold, are presented as gifts to a god. Exactly what the significance of these items was is not, however, known.

tripod bowl [Ar]. Bowl with three legs, normally of the 1st century AD.

tripod pitcher [Ar]. A large jug-like vessel for containing liquids with three small legs projecting from the base for support when placed on a surface. Typical of the medieval period in northwest Europe.

Tripolye, Russia [Si]. *See* CUCUTENI CULTURE.

trireme [Ar]. The earliest type of Greek warship which used a battering ram in the prow as its main weapon. Named after the three banks of oars by which it was propelled, it was the standard warship of the 5th and 4th centuries BC.

trivet [Ar]. A ceramic, stone, or metal stand on which a cooking pot or kettle is stood for support or to protect an underlying surface.

trolling lure [Ar]. A fishing device which is towed behind a moving boat.

trowelling [Te]. Excavation technique in which a mason's pointed trowel is used to shave thin slices of material from the floor or face of an excavation unit. At the start of an excavation the entire TRENCH floor may be cleaned several times by trowelling in different directions in order to identify the position, extent, and nature of archaeological features and their relationships.

Troy, Turkey [Si]. Large TELL near Hissarlik on the Aegean coast of Asia Minor overlooking the Dardanelles, discovered by HEINRICH SCHLIEMANN in AD 1871 and proclaimed as the lost city of Troy referred to by HOMER in *The Illiad*. Schliemann excavated at the site between 1871 and 1890. The results from this and subsequent work, notably by Carl Blegen in the 1930s, allow the identification of seven successive cities, each with numerous subphases, spanning the period 3000 BC to 1000 BC.

Troy I dates to the period 3000 BC to 2500 BC and was a small settlement of 0.5 ha defended by a mud-brick wall set on stone foundations. Houses of the period had built-in cupboards and sleeping platforms. Tin-bronze was introduced during Troy I. Late in the 4th millennium the site was destroyed.

Troy II, dated to 2500 BC to 2300 BC, was larger and wealthier than its predecessor, but the buildings were still modest in scale. Most were of MEGARON form. It was from this phase of the site that Schliemann recovered a massive hoard of nearly 9000 objects that have become known as the Treasure of Priam.

Troy III–V dates to the period 2300 BC down to 1900 BC. During this time the citadel grew in size, but was not especially wealthy.

Troy VI, broadly 1900 BC to 1350 BC saw a new fortification built around a town of 2 ha. This was a wealthy town with evidence of trade with the MYCENAEAN centres of Greece. The defensive wall was of fine ashlar masonry with a pronounced batter. The destruction of the site around 1300 BC was probably the result of an earthquake.

Finally, Troy VII was probably the town that should be identified with Homer's Troy. It was destroyed in the mid 13th century BC, perhaps by Greeks fighting the Trojan War.

Around 700 BC the site was re-occupied by Greeks from Lemnos and, as Illium, became the capital of a league of cities in the coastal region of Anatolia formed in 306 BC. There were further prosperous times in the later Roman period before a period of decline and decay that led to the town's disappearance for many centuries.

[Sum.: C. Blegen, 1963, *Troy and the Trojans*. London: Thames & Hudson]

trunnion [De]. A cylindrical projection from the side of a cannon or mortar that when seated in a semi-circular notch cut into the framework or housing provides support while allowing the cannon to swivel in the vertical plane.

Tuart [Di]. Egyptian god. *See* TAWERET.

tuáth [Ge]. Unit of community in early Irish society, comprising king, aristocracy, and free commoners, but which also acquired a territorial connotation. The individual's rights existed only within his own tuáth, but this could be extended by affiliations of clientship between an entire tuáth and a more powerful overlord.

Tucannon Phase [CP]. Archaic Stage hunter-gatherer communities living along the Snake River in eastern Washington, North America, in the period 3000–500 BC. Tucannon assemblages are characterized by the presence of crudely chipped corner-notched or stemmed points, chipped knives, and edge-worked cobbles. Elk, deer, and antelope were hunted and salmon taken from the river. Hopper mortars and pestles suggest some systematic use of plant food.

Tudor green ware [Ar]. Style of pottery manufactured in southeastern England (mainly in Surrey) in the 16th century AD which has a distinctive rather thick green or yellow glaze over a light coloured body.

tufa [Ma]. Stone deposit of sponge-like texture formed as a result of the evaporation of water heavily charged with lime. Calcareous deposits left by springs, used as indicators of consistent rainfall in now arid areas.

tuff [Ma]. Soft volcanic deposits of fragmentary rock and dust bonded together after cooling. Sometimes used as a source of raw material.

Tula, Mexico [Si]. Capital of the Toltec state (Tollán), founded on the site of an existing settlement by the priest-ruler Topiltzin *c*.AD 960. The city flourished and by AD 1000 had expanded to cover 11 square kilometres with a population of perhaps 50 000.

The focus of the ceremonial centre within the site is the Temple of Quetzalcóatl which contains six Atlantean statues. Each nearly 5 m tall, they support the roof.

Tula was destroyed in the mid 12th century AD, probably by Chichimec groups.

[Sum.: R. A. Diehl, 1983, *Tula: The Toltec capital of central Mexico*. London: Thames & Hudson]

tumbaga [Ma]. Alloy of copper and gold used for making fine ornaments in pre-Columbian Middle and South America.

tumulus (pl. tumuli) [MC]. *See* ROUND BARROW.

Tumulus Culture [CP]. Term applied to a group of cultures of the middle Bronze Age of central and eastern Europe, broadly the early 2nd millennium BC, in which inhumation beneath a round barrow is the distinctive and predominant burial rite. Formerly regarded as the material manifestations of an intrusive population, the Tumulus Culture is now seen to have developed out of the ÚNĚTICE CULTURE and spread over a wide area from Hungary and Romania in the east through a heartland of southern Germany, to Alsace in the west. It is characterized by developed bronze types including palstaves, flange-hilted swords, dirks with rounded or trapezoidal butts, and a variety of pins and bracelets. These are found as grave goods in burials and in hoards. Pottery includes globular vessels with cylindrical necks, pedestalled bowls, and one-handled cups, sometimes with embossed ornament. The Tumulus Culture is succeeded by the URNFIELD CULTURE of the late Bronze Age.

tun [De]. Unit equal to 365 solar days used in the Classic Maya LONG COUNT system.

tundra [Ge]. PERIGLACIAL type of environment with a permanently frozen subsoil. Vegetation is restricted to mosses, small plants, shrubs, etc.

turf line [Ge]. A layer of organic-rich material forming the upper part of an in situ soil profile, the whole sealed beneath a deposit of mixed redeposited material, typically the matrix of a bank or mound. Although the term 'turf line' technically only refers to the uppermost horizon of a buried soil, it is more generally used in the archaeological literature to refer either to the whole buried soil or to a dark layer within an accumulation of some kind.

turkey [Sp]. Large game-bird of the Phasianidae family (*Meleagris gallopavo*) with dark plumage, native to North America from Canada down to Mexico. Widely hunted from Archaic times onwards, especially in the Great Plains and eastern woodlands. In their wild state turkeys have been hunted to extinction in North America, although there are many domestic breeds. Brought to Europe in the 16th century AD.

turma [De]. squadron of cavalry, usually of about 30 men, forming part of an *ALA*.

turnpike road [MC]. A toll road established and run by a private company, usually known as a Turnpike Trust. The 'turnpike' itself was the gate or tollbar, through which travellers could pass after payment of the toll.

turquoise [Ma]. Hydrated copper aluminium phosphate occurring naturally as a semiprecious stone, sky-blue to pale green in colour. Highly prized for use in making jewellery by many ancient cultures in western Asia, Egypt, Mesoamerica, and the American southwest. The main Asiatic source lies in Iran, from where it was widely traded, other sources being known in the Sinai Desert and the Eastern Desert of Egypt. In the Americas rich deposits are known in Nevada, Arizona, and New Mexico.

turret [Co]. Small tower projecting outwards from the face of a wall and usually higher than the wall itself. Widely used on defensive structures from later prehistoric times onwards.

Tutankhamen [Na]. One of the last pharaohs of the 18th Dynasty, probably the son of Amenophis IV, he was born around 1345 BC. In 1333 BC he became pharaoh at a young age, but reigned for only nine years until his death in 1323 BC. During this time the capital was returned to THEBES and the worship of AMEN

was re-established. Tutankhamen is well known because his tomb in the Valley of the Kings (KV 62) remained intact until it was discovered by HOWARD CARTER in 1922 and entered by Carter and Lord Carnarvon on 4 November that year. Although probably poorer than many of the great long-reigning pharaohs, the tomb nonetheless contained a remarkable treasure (now in the Cairo Museum) and provided much detailed information about the ritual of royal burial.

tutela [De]. Latin term for the gods who look after or guard a particular place or community.

tutulus 1. [Ar]. A circular bronze ornament worn at the waist by women during the Danish Bronze Age. **2.** [Co]. The Latin name for a short length of ditch dug to bar a direct line of approach to the entrance gate of a Roman fort or camp.

tuyère [Ar]. In metalworking, a tube or refractory material (typically ceramic or stone) linking the outlet from a pair of bellows to the central hearth of a furnace. Air from the bellows is forced through the tuyère in order to increase the heat in a furnace. For this reason, the inner part of the tuyère is often vitrified and may have fuel, slag, and other materials from within the furnace fused to it.

tweezers [Ar]. A pair of small pincers, usually of a pliable material such as metal or bone, for taking up or pulling small objects or plucking out hairs.

Tylor, Edward Burnett (1832–1917) [Bi]. English banker and businessman who became interested in anthropology as a result of a casual contact with Henry Christy. He became reader in anthropology at the University of Oxford in 1884 and Professor in 1896. His special area of study was ancient Mexico.

[Obit.: *American Anthropologist*, 19 (1917), 262–8]

tympanum (tympanum) [Co]. An enclosed space in the head of an arch or doorway; the vertical face, usually triangular in outline, at the rear of a pediment.

type [De]. A specific artefact, structure, or other definable element of material culture defined by the consistent clustering of attributes which serve to represent the *taxon* of which it is a member. **Ideal-types** are idealized specimens, all other examples differing from them to a greater or lesser extent. Ceramic vessels, for example, are said to be of the same type if they are identical in all significant features of form and fabric and not merely similar in general appearance.

type-assemblage [De]. A grouping of associated artefacts identified and characterized for comparison with other groups. The formulated grouping may or may not coincide with the actual patterns of tool association perceived by the original manufacturers.

type-series [De]. A set of objects of the same general class, but of different types, that are arranged in topological order in such as way as to suggest a chronological sequence.

type-site [De]. A place, usually an excavated site or the site of a major discovery, that gives its name to a culture, cultural period, tradition, or artefact type because it provided the first recognized, best studied, or most representative example.

Typhon [Di]. Egyptian god. *See* SETH.

typology [Te]. The classification of objects, structures, or specimens by subdividing observed populations into a theoretical sequence or series of groups (types) and subgroups (subtypes) according to consideration of their qualitative, quantitative, morphological, formal, technological, and functional attributes. Once established, typological sequences are often used as a surrogate chronology or culture history. The basic ideas underpinning typological studies were originally formulated in the field of biology. *See also* TAXONOMY.

Tyre, Lebanon [Si]. Early port and settlement situated on a coastal promontory south of Beirut. More or less continuous occupation down to the present day has limited the amount of excavation that has taken place, but the broad sequence is clear enough; its location was so desirable for long-distance trade that it was frequently captured and occupied by successive dominant powers in the eastern Mediterranean. In ancient times the main settlement was on a small offshore island. There was a double harbour linked by a canal so that ships could enter port in almost any conditions and this was flourishing under Egyptian protection from the 18th Dynasty. Later, as a Phoenician city it appears to have been the capital of the western Phoenician (Punic) world, at least until 572 BC when Tyre was taken by the BABYLONIANS under NEBUCHADNEZZAR after a thirteen-year-long siege. The site remained a powerful and important trading centre although it fell again to a siege by Alexander the Great in 332 BC. After this a causeway was built out to the mainland and it is this promontory that was occupied through Greek, Roman, and Byzantine times. It was an archbishopric during Christian times but fell to the Arabs in AD 636. The region around Tyre was well known in the ancient world for its purple dye (Tyrian purple) made from the *murex grandaris* mollusc.

[Sum.: M. E. Aubet, 1993, *Tyre and the Phoenician colonies in the west*. Cambridge: CUP]

Tzakol [CP]. Early Classic Stage Maya Lowland Phase characterized by the mass-produced but elegantly decorated polychrome pottery.

tzolkin [Ge]. A sacred almanac of 260 days forming part of the calendar used in Mayan cultures, called by the Nahuatl speakers *Tonalpohualli*. See also LONG COUNT.

Uaxactún, Guatemala [Si]. A Pre-Classic and Classic Stage Maya settlement situated in the northeastern Peten Province, flourishing between AD 328 and AD 889 according to the range of dates preserved on stelae. The site was extensively excavated by Oliver Ricketson in 1926–30 and A. Ledyard Smith in 1931–7, with more recent work by J. Antonio Valdés. Pottery from the site was used by Alfred Kidder as the basis of his seriation that provided the sequence for the Lowland Maya chronology. Although small, the site has two temple pyramids in the central area together with a small plaza and a palace.

[Rep.: L. A. Smith, 1950, *Uaxactún, Guatemala: Excavations of 1931–7.* Washington DC: Carnegie Institution]

Ubaid Culture [CP]. Communities who were the first occupants of the alluvial plain of southern Mesopotamia around 5000 BC and whose distinctive village settlements, buff-greenish pottery decorated with geometric designs, stone and metal tools, and agricultural economy lasted down to the beginnings of the URUK PERIOD around 4000 BC. The culture is named after the small tell of Al Ubaid, Iraq, partly excavated by SIR LEONARD WOOLLEY in 1922.

Uhle, Max (1856–1944) [Bi]. German philologist turned archaeologist whose explorations of South American archaeology began in Peru in the 1850s. Uhle was the first to produce a general chronology for Peruvian archaeology based on detailed stratigraphic associations and sequences. He excavated at Pachamac, Tiahuanaco, and Cuzco, as well as numerous smaller sites. In 1941 Uhle published *Aztecs of Mexico* (New York: Doubleday).

[Bio.: J. H. Rowe, 1954, Max Uhle, 1856–1944: A memoir of the father of Peruvian archaeology. *University of California Publications in American Archaeology and Ethnology*, 46(1), 10–134]

uinal [Ge]. A period of time equal to 20 solar days in the Mayan LONG COUNT.

Ulfila [Na]. Bishop to the Goths, who preached according to the doctrine of Arius (341–8). The subsequent conversion of the Goths to Arianism has been attributed to Ulfila's influence, but was probably the result of contacts in the Balkans after the Gothic entry to the empire in 376. Ulfila translated the Bible into the Gothic dialect.

ulluco [Sp]. A trailing perennial herb (*Ullucus tuberosum*) native to the Andes of South America bearing fleshy tubers. Domesticated locally by *c.*8000 BC.

Ulster Cycle [Ge]. Series of Irish tales relating the exploits of the king and warrior-heroes of Ulster in their struggle against other Irish kingdoms. The best known and longest of these tales is 'The Cattle Raid of Cooley', which concerns an expedition from Connaught to steal the famous bull of Cooley and the deeds of the champion of Ulster, Cúchulain, who, as a child prodigy, tragically chooses a valiant but short life.

ultima ratio regis [Ge]. 'The king's final argument', an inscription commonly found on Spanish royal cannon.

ultra-violet visible spectrophotometry (uv-vis) [Te]. A method for determining the chemical composition of materials. Based on the same principle as AAS, a beam of light is passed through a sample such that the amount of light absorbed is proportional to the concentration of the chemical under investigation. It can be used either to scan through a range of wavelengths from the ultra-violet to the visible or to analyse at one wavelength. Typical applications include the analysis of phosphates in soil extracts (where the phosphate is made to form a blue-coloured complex which absorbs in the visible region), the determination of iron and aluminium levels in soil, or the chemical composition of ancient glass.

Umayyads [CP]. First dynasty of Arab leaders, the descendants of a Meccan merchant who submitted to Muhammad. They seized power in AD 661 and maintained a system based on that of the nomadic desert tribes until split by internal feuds and the rise of the Persian ABBASIDS in AD 750.

umu ti [Co]. Kind of earth oven found in the South Island of New Zealand.

unchambered long barrow [MC]. *See* LONG BARROW.

undercroft [Co]. A vaulted subterranean room or basement usually wholly or partly under a larger building. Commonly used in medieval times as secure storage for goods and commodities by traders and merchants.

understanding [Th]. Different philosophical underpinnings to the way that archaeological problems are approached carry with them specific implications for the way in which the results or outcomes are presented. Positivist approaches, seen for example in PROCESSUAL ARCHAEOLOGY, favour the development of EXPLANATIONS. The relativist approaches axiomatic to most POST-PROCESSUAL ARCHAEOLOGY seek instead to develop understandings; the articulation of a set of perceived meanings or knowledge which together form a DISCOURSE that is situated within a particular set of circumstances. In this sense an understanding carries with it the idea of contradiction and an acceptance that what is being presented is neither the 'truth' nor a complete picture that everyone agrees with. *See also* MULTIVOCALITY.

underwater archaeology [Ge]. A subdiscipline involving the study and investigation of archaeological sites, deposits, and shipwrecks beneath the surface of the water in the seas, oceans, lakes, and rivers. *See also* MARITIME ARCHAEOLOGY; WETLAND ARCHAEOLOGY.

unenclosed Bronze Age urnfield [MC]. *See* URNFIELD.

unenclosed settlement [De]. Group of dwelling houses and associated structures and working areas that are not surrounded by a defensive or boundary work such as a fence or rampart. Unenclosed settlements are often closely associated with or directly connected to field systems and tend to be built where the need for defence against animals or other communities is minimal.

UNESCO [Ab]. United Nations Educational, Scientific and Cultural Organization. Established in 1946 for the purpose of advancing, through the educational, scientific, and cultural relations of the peoples of the world, the objectives of international peace and the common welfare of mankind.

Únětice Culture [CP]. A large group of early Bronze Age communities in central Europe, especially Bohemia, Bavaria, southeastern Germany, and western Poland dating to the second half of the 3rd millennium BC. Named after a cemetery of 60 graves excavated north of Prague in the Czech Republic. Also known as the **Aunjetitz Culture**. The early phase seems to have developed out of the local BELL BEAKER CULTURE and embraces a series of regional groups including Nitra (western Slovakia), Adlerberg (mid-Rhine), Straubing (Bavaria), Marschwitz (Oder Basin), and Unterwölbling (Austria). The later or 'classic' Únětice Culture dates to the end of the 3rd millennium BC. Burials are generally inhumations, sometimes within wooden mortuary houses under round barrows, and show marked social differentiation. The most lavish have been compared to the broadly contemporary WESSEX CULTURE burials of southern England. One of the distinguishing features of the culture is its use of tin-bronze metallurgy. Amongst the metal artefacts made were ogival and triangular daggers with metal hilts, flanged axes, halberds, spiral arm-rings, solid bronze bracelets, and a variety of pins. Settlements are less well documented than cemeteries, but have produced timber houses of long rectangular plan. To the east, the Únětice Culture overlaps the currency of the NAGYRÉV and HATVAN cultures, all within Montelius' Bronze Period I.

unguent flask (unguent bottle) [Ar]. A small narrow-necked vessel, usually in a rough fabric, used as a container for ointment or perfume. Because of what they contained, such vessels are often found long distances from source as evidence of trade and exchange.

unifacial flaking [De]. Style of working flint or stone flakes into tools or implements by limited retouch confined to one side of the flake only.

unifacial tool [De]. Artefact, usually of flint or stone, that has working on one side only.

uniformitarianism [Th]. A proposition, developed by James Hutton in the late 18th century and elaborated by Sir Charles Lyell in the early 19th century, which states that processes observed happening today can reasonably be assumed to have happened in a comparable way in the past too. Initially applied in the field of geology to show that geological deposits were laid down as part of a continuous and uniform process over a long period of time rather than as the result of a series of catastrophes, the same principle can to some extent be used to underpin experimental attempts to understand the formation of archaeological deposits such as ditch fills or the decay of stone cairns.

unilinear cultural evolution [Th]. A late 19th-century evolutionary theory that envisaged all human societies as evolving along a common track from simple hunting and gathering communities to literate civilizations. In this, all societies would pass through the same basic sequence of stages, although the speed of transition might vary. Reflections of such a way of thinking can be seen in the THREE AGE SYSTEM and in schemes grounded in anthropological theory which identify BAND, TRIBE, and CHIEFDOM as successive stages.

unit [Ge]. **1.** General term used in Britain to refer to an archaeological contracting company and sometimes mentioned in the name of the organization (e.g. Birmingham University Field Archaeology Unit, BUFA). **2.** A basic category used in describing the components in a STRATIGRAPHIC SEQUENCE or for grouping comparable artefacts together when describing and analysing them.

univallate [De]. An enclosure defined by a single bank and ditch. *Compare* MULTIVALLATE HILLFORT.

univallate hillfort [MC]. A defended enclosure common in the later Bronze Age and Iron Age of northwest Europe which is bounded by a single line of ramparts. Some strengthening may be visible around the entrance by the construction of outworks or an out-turned bank to create an entrance passage in front of the main gate. Early univallate hillforts often have timber-laced or box-framed banks to provide a strong but substantial inner element to the defences.

unlooped socketed spearhead [Ar]. A large metal projectile point typical of the later Bronze Age in Europe that was mounted on a wooden shaft by way of a socket cast into the base of the object, usually with a hole to allow a peg to pass through the socket walls and the shaft to ensure secure attachment. Such spearheads lack the loops of earlier designs which seem to have been used to tie the spearhead to the shaft.

Unnefer [Di]. Egyptian god. *See* OSIRIS.

Unstan ware [Ar]. Style of Neolithic pottery found in the northern part of the British Isles, especially the Hebrides, Western Isles, and Orkney, defined by Stuart Piggott in 1954 on the basis of an assemblage from the chambered tomb of Unstan on Orkney. Including both decorated and undecorated vessels, Unstan ware is diverse in the range of shapes and sizes represented. However, it can be typified by round-bottomed forms either as deep bowls and jars or as shallow bowls with a carinated profile produced by the application of a fillet or cordon of clay. The decoration is generally incised with oblique or horizontal lines, triangles, or a zone of hatched triangles. Dated examples of this ware fall within the period 3500–2800 BC, Unstan ware being slightly earlier than GROOVED WARE in the region.

Unu, Iraq [Si]. *See* URUK.

unurned cremation [De]. Cremation burial that is not contained within a ceramic urn or container. Typical of the early and middle Bronze Age of northern Europe, unurned cremations are usually deposited in small pits or scoops under a barrow or within a cremation cemetery.

Upchurch ware [Ar]. Romano-British pottery industry making polished and burnished black and grey wares (e.g. poppy head beakers) in the Upchurch Marshes of Kent in south-eastern England.

updraught kiln [MC]. Containing structure for firing or baking pottery or other ceramic artefacts in which the material to be fired is placed on a natural or raised floor in such a way that heat and fumes from a fire built adjacent or below the material is drawn up through and around it before passing out through a vent in the roof or superstructure.

Upper Egypt [De]. The part of Egypt represented by the Nile Valley stretching to the south of Lower Egypt as far as Aswan.

Upper Palaeolithic [CP]. The last of three broad subdivisions of the Old Stone Age or Palaeolithic widely applied in the Old World. Characterized by the presence of modern humans, HOMO *sapiens sapiens*, and associated tool types regionally distinct to particular parts of the world. Broadly the period from 40 000 through to 8500 years ago. PALAE-OLITHIC ART is mainly associated with Upper Palaeolithic cultures, especially in northwest Europe. In the British Isles the Upper Palaeolithic is traditionally divided into earlier (EUP) and later (LUP) phases, the former relating to the period prior to the DEVENSIAN glaciation, while the latter refers to cultural material dating to the later phases of the Devensian and the immediate post-glacial period. Preceded by the Middle Palaeolithic and succeeded by the MESOLITHIC.

upright loom [Ar]. A structure on which woven cloth is manufactured comprising two more or less vertical supports (often set in the ground) with a horizontal beam across the top. The warp threads are tied to the cross-beam so that they hang down, thus allowing the weaver to move a horizontal **shed rod** between alternating sets of the warp in order that a shed is opened up for the weft to be threaded through. The warp threads were tensioned by LOOMWEIGHTS (*see also* WARP-WEIGHTED LOOM). The upright loom was commonly used in antiquity, traces of them being known in Europe from the middle Bronze Age onwards.

Ur, Iraq [Si]. Large tell mound in southern Mesopotamia first identified in 1854 and later extensively investigated under the direction of Sir Leonard Woolley for the British Museum and the University of Pennsylvania in 1918–19 and 1922–34. The site was identified with the Biblical city of Ur of the CHALDEANS, birthplace and early home of Abraham. The earliest occupation dates to UBAID times in the 6th millennium BC. At this time the settlement covered about 10 ha and was already one of the most important towns in the region. In the 3rd millennium BC it grew to city size and status, covered 50 ha, and lay at the heart of the SUMERIAN civilization, by about 2100 BC becoming the ceremonial centre of the UR III empire which controlled much of Mesopotamia and the adjacent Zagros region. An associated royal cemetery with sixteen tombs was excavated in 1922 and illustrates the extreme wealth of the royal and elite burials, as well as showing the marked differentiation when compared with other contemporary burial grounds. The religious architecture of the period was especially impressive, including the ziggurat of NANNA the moon god. Abundant written texts and inscriptions provide a great deal of detail about the inhabitants and use of the site. Occupation continued during the 2nd and down to the end of the 1st millennium BC, and while it grew in size to reach a maximum of 60 ha as a result of participation in long-distance and local trade, it was never of the same importance as in earlier times. Ur ceased to exist in the 4th century BC, probably because the River Euphrates changed course.

[Sum.: C. L. Woolley and P. R. S. Moorey, 1982, *Ur of the Chaldees* (revised edition). London: Herbert]

uraeus [Ar]. The coiled serpent shown on the forehead of Egyptian kings as a symbol of authority.

uranium dating (uranium series dating) [Te]. Absolute dating method that uses the decay patterns of a series of radioactive isotopes of uranium, usually ^{238}U or ^{235}U. Dates are usually based on the measurement of one of the uranium isotopes and a relatively short-lived daughter isotope expressed as isotopic ratios. When uranium is precipitated as a trace constituent in surface outcropping minerals it begins producing daughter isotopes. In applying the technique for dating, samples are ideally chosen from chemically closed systems in which the isotopic ratio used to calculate the sample age was initially zero. The great value of uranium dating is that it can be applied to materials far more ancient than could be covered by radiocarbon dating, in exceptional cases back to 1 million years ago. The kinds of material that can be dated are also slightly different, and include coral, mollusc shells, marl, bone, teeth, caliche and calcretes, peat, wood, and detrital sediment.

Urartu kingdom [CP]. An extensive and generally decentralized state covering modern northwest Iran, northeast Turkey, and Armenia that emerged in the 11th century BC and lasted through most of the 1st millennium BC. The geographical focus of the kingdom was a series of sites around Lake Van, for example Toprakkale, Turkey, although important centres existed elsewhere too, for example at Karmir Blur, Armenia. The art and architectural styles of the Urartu kingdom show heavy influences from the contemporary Assyrian culture, and the Urartu was a major obstacle to the northward expansion of Assyria between 900 BC and 600 BC.

urban archaeology [Ge]. Subdiscipline involving the application of archaeological methods to the study of major towns, cities, and urban areas, and to the process of urbanization.

urban cemetery [MC]. A cemetery containing an essentially urban-living population, generally found within or outside but nearby a major urban area. Such cemeteries are often large and long-lived.

urbanism [De]. A term used by Louis Wirth to denote distinctive characteristics of urban social life, such as its impersonality, but more recently expanded to encompass physical features of urban existence such as can be recovered archaeologically, such as planning, the large size of settlement, and the presence of religious and political foci alongside residential areas.

urial [Sp]. A species of sheep (*Ovid vignei*) found wild in Iran, Turkestan, and the Himalayas, the ancestor of nearly all modern breeds of sheep.

Ur III empire [CP]. The period broadly 2100–2000 BC corresponding with the third dynasty of SUMERIAN kings listed on documents found at UR, principally Ur-nammu (2112–2095 BC) and Shulgi (2094–2047 BC).

During this time the dynasty controlled most of southern Mesopotamia and the adjacent highlands of the Zagros region with an extensive and elaborate bureaucracy exercising control over many aspects of economic life. The Ur III empire collapsed under military pressure from ELAMITE and AMORITE states.

urn [Ar]. A generic name applied to a vase or jar, generally with a rounded body, narrow neck, and a height greater than its maximum diameter, that was used (not necessarily exclusively) to contain the cremated remains of the dead. The name has become applied to some styles of prehistoric pottery (e.g. COLLARED URNS) because examples were found in burial contexts before they were widely recognized on contemporary settlement sites. Many prehistoric urns are simply domestic vessels of a style preferentially selected for use in burial rites; in later times ceramics were especially produced for use in burial and ceremonial situations.

urn cover [Ar]. A flat and relatively thin piece of stone, wood, or ceramic placed over the open top of an urn before, during, or after its deposition in a burial pit.

urned cremation [De]. A deposit of burnt human and/or animal bones gathered up from the pyre and placed inside a ceramic vessel manufactured or selected for use in burial (*see* URN). The urn is typically placed in a CIST, pit, or other specially designated resting place which may or may not be elaborated with a superstructure or barrow of some kind.

urnfield [MC]. A group or cemetery of inurned cremations buried in pits dug into the ground distinctive of the European late Bronze Age URNFIELD TRADITION, but also found in areas of northern Europe. The majority of cemeteries are open sites, in many cases constructed on or around earlier round barrows. A few, however, are contained within a ditched enclosure. These tend to be smaller examples of up to several dozen burials.

Urnfield Tradition [CP]. A series of related cultures distinctive of the European late Bronze Age, broadly 1200 BC through to 800 BC, distinguished by their cemeteries of cremated burials deposited as URNFIELDS. The appearance of urnfields marks a major transition in burial rites from the previous predominance of inhumations, often under round barrows, to a predominance of cremations. The Urnfield Tradition in central and eastern Europe is generally equated with the HALL-STATT sequence as defined by Paul REINECKE in the early years of the 20th century AD, and has been divided into five phases. Each is characterized by diagnostic pottery and metal types. By the end of the second millennium BC, the Urnfield Tradition had spread through Italy, northwestern Europe, and as far west as the Pyrenees. It is at this time that fortified hilltop settlements and sheet-bronze metalworking also spread widely across Europe, leading some authorities to equate these changes with the expansion of the CELTS. These links are no longer accepted.

Uruk (Warka), Iraq [Si]. This is the largest archaeological site in southern Iraq, situated east of the present course of the Euphrates. The Sumerians knew the site as Unu, the Akkadian speakers as Uruk. The Akkadian name appears in the Bible as Erech.

The site was first investigated by William Loftus in the mid 19th century AD, but it was not until 1912 that systematic excavations began, albeit sporadically at first, under the direction of Julius Jordan for the Deutsche Orient-Gesellschaft. As a result of this work it is now known that the site began in the 5th millennium BC, the Ubaid period, growing to urban proportions by the early 4th millennium BC. By the later 4th millennium BC, the late Uruk period, the city covered at least 100 ha and was the largest settlement in Sumer: the world's first city and housing the first urban society.

In the late 4th millennium BC Uruk encompassed two distinct centres: Eanna and Kullaba. Kullaba was probably dedicated to the sky god An and centred on the so-called White Temple which had gypsum plastered walls and comprised a long central room with an altar and offering table, flanked on both the long sides by smaller rooms. The temple itself stood on a platform or proto-ziggurat 13 m high. Some 500 m to the east was Eanna, dedicated to the city goddess Inanna. Here again temples and large ceremonial buildings abounded. Around 3000 BC the temples at both Kullaba and Eanna were remodelled, that at Eanna becoming and remaining the focus of Uruk's ritual and civic existence for nearly three millennia. Amongst the debris from the rebuilding of Eanna the excavators found thousands of fragmentary clay tablets bearing pictograms, probably an early form of SUMERIAN. Other rather unusual artefacts include fine sculpture and cylinder seals.

The city continued to expand to its maximum of about 400 ha in 2900 BC. At this time a massive defensive enclosure 10 km in length encircled the settlement. Evidence from surrounding villages suggests that at this time many of the communities previously living in the countryside moved into the town. This was the high point of its existence and it was at this period that rulers such as GILGAMESH governed the city, later to appear in epics as superhuman beings. The ziggurat that dominates the site today was built around 2000 BC by Ur-Nammu, but by that time the site was already in decline. Although Babylonian and Assyrian rulers maintained the Eanna temples down into the 6th century BC or beyond, the city had lost its position. The final occupants of the site were the PARTHIANS who built a small temple to Gareus around AD 100.

[Sum.: R. M. Boehmer, 1991, Uruk 1980–1990: a progress report. *Antiquity*, 65, 465–78]

Uruk period [CP]. The period between about 4200 BC and 3300 BC that marked the emergence of Mesopotamian state societies named after the long and important sequence at URUK, Iraq. During the Uruk period large existing settlements developed the hallmark characteristics of urban settlements, elaborate ritual centres within key cities, the development of writing systems, extensive administrative systems, the mass production of pottery and other goods, and sophisticated art. In the late Uruk period such patterns are seen outside southern Mesopotamia to the east and northwest, setting the scene for the development of the early dynastic phase of Sumerian civilization in the region.

use-wear analysis [Te]. Microscopic analysis of the surfaces and working edges of artefacts to detect signs of wear, damage, or residue caused by their use. The work is generally done using high-powered microscopes, and may involve replication studies to allow the comparison of traces of known cause with observed patterns on ancient material. The technique is mainly applied to flint and stone tools. Considerable success has been achieved in detecting evidence for sawing, cutting, and piercing.

Ussher, James (1581–1656) [Bi]. Scholar, professor of divinity, and vice-chancellor of Trinity College, Dublin, who subsequently became bishop of Meath and, in 1625, archbishop of Armagh. He is noted as a strict exponent of the Mosaic cosmogony. Taking biblical accounts of the period from the Creation to the time of classical civilizations literally, in AD 1650 he famously published a book entitled *Annales veteris et novi testamenti* in which he set out his calculation to show that the earth was created in 4004 BC. This was widely accepted and from 1701 was printed in the margins of the Authorized (King James) Version of the Bible. Later, Bishop Lightfoot asserted that it was in fact nine o'clock in the morning of 23 October 4004 BC when the world first came into existence.

[Bio.: R. B. Knox, 1967, *James Ussher, Archbishop of Armagh*. Cardiff: University of Wales Press]

usnu [Co]. A platform or earth mound represented at important INCA settlements. The Inca emperor stood on the usnu when holding court, and it may have been used for astronomical observations. Some usnu are associated with water channels to facilitate the making of liquid offerings.

Uto [Di]. A SUMERIAN god connected with the sun and frequently represented by his symbol, a winged sun disc, that later became a standard representation of royalty. Uto was the god of justice before whom legal contracts were sworn and whose name appears in various law codes. Equivalent to the AKKADIAN deity Shamash.

Uvarov, Count Aleksei Sergeevich (1828–84) [Bi]. Russian antiquarian and archaeologist. In 1864 he organized the Imperial Russian Archaeological Society and in 1869 he organized the first archaeological congress. During the 1850s he excavated at Chersonese and in 1877 excavated the Upper Palaeolithic site at Karacharovo on the Oka River.

[Not.: A. L. Mongait [TRANS. M. W. Thompson], 1961, *Archaeology in the USSR*. Harmondsworth: Penguin, 68]

UV-VIS [Ab]. *See* ULTRA-VIOLET VISIBLE SPECTROPHOTOMETRY.

Uxmal, Mexico [Si]. Late Classic and early Post-Classic Stage ceremonial centre flourishing in the Yucatan Peninsula in the period AD 800–1000. Best known for its impressive Puuc style architecture.

There are at least three main structures: the pyramid of the Magician, the Monjas, and the Governor's Palace. The Monjas comprises a huge patio surrounded on all four sides by a range of single-room cell blocks. Uxmal was connected by a causeway (*sacbe*) to the site of Kabáh.

[Rep.: J. K. Kowalski, 1987, *The house of the Governor: A Maya Palace at Uxmal, Yucatan, Mexico*. London: Norman]

Vădastra Culture [CP]. A middle to late Neolithic culture of southwestern Romania and northern Bulgaria, north of the VESELI-NOVO CULTURE, dating to the late 5th millennium BC and thus contemporary with stage A–B of the VINČA CULTURE of the western Balkans. Named after the type-site tell in the modern village of Vădastra, this culture had a full agricultural economy. Cattle bones from sites of the culture suggest that draught animals were used for traction. Distinctive styles of pottery were made in three main categories: poorly fired coarse tempered wares for storage; decorated bowls in a medium quality ware; and thin-walled rather fine pottery fired grey or black in colour decorated with narrow channelling or fluting.

Valdai Culture [CP]. Early Neolithic period (3500–3000 BC) communities occupying a broad region north of the Upper Volga and Western Dvina rivers in western Russia. Descended from local Mesolithic communities, the Valdai Cultures were hunters and fishers with a flint industry that included many archaic forms such as microlithic tools. Pottery with organic material used as a tempering agent was used, as well as pointed-based vessels with irregularly scattered thin comb impressions and incisions.

Valdivia Culture [CP]. FORMATIVE period culture dating to the later 4th millennium BC on the coast of Ecuador, South America, named after a site of the same name excavated by B. Meggars and C. Evans in the early 1960s. The culture is important in being amongst the earliest in the region to have a developed ceramics industry which used a variety of plastic techniques for decorative motifs. Artefacts suggest a marine-orientated subsistence pattern.

Valens [Na]. Roman emperor, elevated in AD 364 by his brother Valentinian I, the western

emperor, to rule the east. He was an Arian, and intolerant. He permitted the Visigoths to enter the empire, and was killed by them in AD 378 at Adrianople.

Valentinian I [Na]. Roman emperor, proclaimed by the army in AD 364. He placed his brother Valens in power in Constantinople and he himself took over Rome. Much of his reign was spent defending the northern frontiers. He died in AD 375.

Valentinian II [Na]. Roman emperor, a son of Valentinian I and his successor in Italy in AD 375. His reign was troubled by the usurpation of Magnus Maximus and the overthrow of Gratian in Gaul. He fled from Italy to escape Maximus. His restoration by Theodosius the Great was shortly followed by his death, perhaps murder, in AD 392, at Vienne.

Valentinian III [Na]. Western Roman emperor, nephew of HONORIUS and his eventual successor in AD 425. Most of his reign he was dominated by his mother Placida and by the commander in Gaul, AETIUS, whom he murdered in AD 454. He died in AD 455, a victim of retribution by Aetius' retainers.

Valley of the Kings, Egypt [Si]. Situated in the western desert on the west bank of the Nile opposite Thebes, the Valley of the Kings is a narrow steep-sided valley into the walls and floor of which were cut numerous tombs for the kings of the NEW KINGDOM from Tuthmosis I through to RAMESSES XI. Some members of the immediate royal family and high court officers were also buried here. To date some 62 tombs have been identified and numbered, each tomb having a corresponding temple on the banks of the Nile for the performance of the rituals necessary for the well-being of the dead person. The best-known tomb in the valley is that of TUTANKHAMUN, discovered in 1922. In addition to the tombs, excavations in the valley have revealed traces of huts occupied by workers.

[Sum.: J. Romer, 1988, *The Valley of the Kings*. London: O'Mara]

vallum [Co]. **1.** Roman term for a heaped rampart or bank. **2.** The vallum along the south side of HADRIAN'S WALL in northern England is a misnomer since its principal feature is a great ditch, perhaps marking a military zone along the frontier; the term has been applied to this feature since the time of Bede in the 7th century AD.

value-free interpretation [Th]. Within a scientifically constituted archaeology the idea of value-free interpretation means aspiring to the exclusion of value-laden terms and value judgements. While it is accepted that the selection of material for investigation involves value judgements about how interesting or relevant it may be on the basis of academic or professional values, the overall aim is to separate 'facts' from 'interpretation'. That this is either possible or desirable has been widely challenged. As an alternative it is argued that archaeologists should take full responsibility for their work and not try to detach themselves from issues of cultural politics or contemporary social articulations; archaeologists cannot justifiably claim to be concerned with neutral knowledge separable from the conditions within which it is produced and applied.

Vandals [CP]. Germanic people, perhaps originally from the Baltic region, who invaded Gaul in AD 406, and established a kingdom in Spain. The majority of Vandals later migrated to Africa where they founded a state which survived until the reconquest of the western Mediterranean under Justinian in AD 535. The Vandal empire was overrun by the Arabs late in the 7th century AD.

Vapheio cup [Ar]. A type of MYCENAEAN drinking vessel named after the find of two gold examples in a THOLOS burial at Vapheio near Sparta, southern Greece. A Vapheio cup has a flat base, straight flaring sides, and a single handle. The original gold examples were decorated in relief with scenes of bulls. Vapheio cups are found in middle MINOAN levels in Crete and were popular on the mainland in the late HELLADIC period.

variable [Ge]. A factor that can be assigned a measurable dimension of some kind that varies: for example, cost, life-span, age, length, height, or weight. A **dependent variable** is any measurable factor whose behaviour is controlled by another. An **independent variable** is any measurable factor that produces change or reaction in another.

Varna, Bulgaria [Si]. Late Neolithic/Copper Age cemetery near the Black Sea coast of eastern Bulgaria. The site was discovered in 1972 when drainage works cut through a rich grave. Subsequent excavations by I. Ivanov have uncovered more than 280 graves. Dating to the early 4th millennium BC, the significance of the site is that it is earliest floruit of gold metallurgy in the world. The cemetery comprises flat graves with individuals buried in shallow pits, males, females, adults, and children all being represented. A small proportion of the graves contained exceptionally rich grave goods, including gold sceptres, diadems, pendants, and earrings as well as copper artefacts, pottery, and flint tools. Analysis of the gold itself indicates two sources: the eastern Mediterranean and the Caucasus. Other exotic items include copper and graphite, spondylus and dentalium shells, carnelian, and marble. The range of grave goods represented suggests social ranking amongst local communities, and illustrates the very wide trading networks in which they must have participated.

[Sum.: C. Renfrew, 1978, Varna and the social context of early metallurgy. *Antiquity*, 52, 199–203]

varnished ware [Ar]. Pottery, usually small bowls, decorated with rough-cast scales or roundels, or rough-cast beakers in white fabric with greenish-brown shiny slip. Generally 1st century BC/AD in date and produced in central Gaul and on the Rhine.

Varus, Publius Quinctilius [Na]. Roman general, a favourite of Augustus, who after a successful career in Africa and Syria commanded the Rhine army, which was ambushed and destroyed in 9 AD somewhere near the middle Weser in Germany.

varve [Ge]. Laminated lake sediment showing alternating layers of coarse and fine mud laid down over the course of a single year as a result of seasonal fluctuations in the sediment load of water courses emptying into the lake. The kind of sediment depends on the proximity of glaciers and local climatic conditions. Varved sediments typically preserve excellent environmental sequences providing palaeoenvironmental contexts for local archaeological sites, including evidence for progressive changes in vegetation, forest fires, and the effects of human communities on soil erosion and run-off regimes within the catchment. Varves provide high-quality geochronological resolution to the environmental data through VARVE ANALYSIS.

varve analysis [Te]. The use of annual VARVE couplets as a geochronological measure to provide relative dates to specific horizons in lake sediments. Pioneered by the Swedish geologist Baron Gerard de Geer, a reasonably complete chronology for environmental changes during the early HOLOCENE has been established for Scandinavia.

vase support [Ar]. Classic ceramic form of the middle Neolithic CHASSEY CULTURE of northwestern France comprising a hollow cylindrical base supporting a dished upper surface. The outer faces are often highly ornamented with incised chevron, lattice, and chequerboard designs. Their exact function is not certain, but they are believed for be incense burners.

vault [Co]. A form of roofing in stone or brick using the principle of gravity to lock the materials together. The barrel vault is continuous and of semi-circular section, whilst in the rib vaulted roof the weight of the roof itself is carried by structural elements known as ribs.

vaulted [De]. Term to describe a space such as a room or courtyard covered by a vault.

VCH [Ab]. *See* VICTORIA COUNTY HISTORY.

VCP [Ab]. Very coarse pottery. *See* BRIQUETAGE.

Venetian window [De]. A window having three apertures, of which the central one is much larger than the lateral ones, separated from one another by slender piers.

Ventana Cave, Arizona, USA [Si]. A deeply stratified sequence of cave deposits representing a series of occupations and use from 10 000 BC down to about 5000 BC. Excavated by

Emil Haury in 1941, the earliest levels yielded projectile points of Clovis/Folsom types. A single grinding stone is suggestive of some interest in plant foods. Later levels include Desert Tradition finds.

[Rep.: E. W. Haury, 1950, *The stratigraphy and archaeology of Ventana Cave*. Tucson: University of Arizona Press]

ventral [De]. Relating to the front or lower surface. In describing a struck flint or stone blade or flake it refers to the face that was most recently attached to the core, usually with visible traces of ripples and the bulb of percussion. *Compare* DORSAL SURFACE.

Ventris, Michael (1922–56) [Bi]. British scholar who, in 1952, deciphered the LINEAR B script found in Mycenaean and Minoan contexts, showing that it was an early form of Greek. An architect by profession, he became interested in the problem of Linear B after hearing a lecture by Sir Arthur Evans. During WW2 he served as a navigator in the Royal Air Force, but after the war he resumed his spare-time study of ancient scripts, collaborating with John Chadwick in Oxford. In 1953 he published his conclusions in the *Journal of Hellenic Studies* and they were greeted with acclaim. He was made an OBE in 1955, received an honorary degree from the University of Uppsala, and was made an Honorary Research Associate of University College, London. Tragically, he was killed in a road accident in September 1956.

[Bio.: *Dictionary of National Biography* (1951–60), 1009–10]

Venus [Di]. Roman goddess occupying a modest position in the pantheon where, together with Feronia and Flora, she symbolized spring and fruitfulness. Equated with the Greece goddess APHRODITE.

Venus figurine [Ar]. Small stylized female statuettes sculptured in the round, of Upper Palaeolithic date, representing women with, in many cases, exaggerated sexual characteristics such as breasts, hips, and stomach. The faces are generally featureless and the arms and legs little emphasized. Found from southern France through to Siberia and made in stone, bone, ivory, steatite, and clay in GRAVETTIAN and related cultures.

Vercingetorix [Na]. Son of the Arvernian king Celtillus, Vercingetorix was proclaimed by general agreement the leader of the Gaulish rebellion against Caesar in 52 BC. After a series of campaigns, he was eventually defeated with the combined Gaulish forces at Alesia.

Verlade Phase [CP]. Provisionally defined almost entirely by ceramic styles found in lowland Bolivia and tentatively dated to c.AD 500–700.

Vermillion Accord [Le]. International agreement on the treatment of human remains (Full title: 'The Vermillion Accord on Human Remains') adopted by the World Archaeological Congress in 1989 at its inter-congress meeting in South Dakota, USA. The six items in the accord specify: respect for mortal remains of the dead; respect for the wishes of the dead where known or reasonably inferred; respect for the wishes of local communities, relatives, or guardians; respect for the scientific value of human remains; the need for negotiated agreements on the disposition of human remains; and the recognition of concerns held by various ethnic groups.

vernacular [De]. **1.** Term to describe buildings, particularly cottages or small houses, of a native, local, or traditional style. Generally built in locally available materials. **2.** Term to describe the writing, speech, architecture, art forms, etc. common among the indigenous people of a country or region.

vertical aerial photograph [De]. Photographic image taken from an aircraft or similar high-level elevated platform where the camera direction is at right angles to the ground beneath and the face of the film is more or less parallel to the ground surface. Vertical aerial photographs can be precisely scaled if the distance between the ground and the camera and the focal length of the camera's lens is known. Overlapping pairs of vertical aerial photographs allow stereoscopic viewing to create an optically realistic three-dimensional image. Compare OBLIQUE AERIAL PHOTOGRAPH.

Verwood ware [Ar]. Products of a medieval and later pottery industry based in the New Forest of southern England.

Veselinovo Culture [CP]. Middle Neolithic farming communities occupying southern Bulgaria, the lower Danube Valley, the Plain of Drama, and the Strumica Valley in the later 5th millennium BC, named after the type-site tell near Jambol in eastern Bulgaria. The culture is often recognized by its distinctive pottery: coarse wares and thick-walled finewares. The finewares are almost always undecorated and made in piriform and cylindrical beakers with flat bases or standing on cylindrical legs. Many of the pots were provided with curving handles with a round cross-section and a knobbed terminal. Clay figurines of humans and animals are also known. The Veselinovo Culture is represented in Level III at KARANOVO and is contemporary with stages A–B of the VINČA CULTURE.

vesicular ware [Ar]. *See* CALCITE-GRITTED WARE.

Vespasian [Na]. Roman emperor, AD 69–79.

vexillation [Ge]. Detachment of a Roman legion normally comprising 1000 men.

vexillation fortress [MC]. A term applied to large Roman forts of between 6.4 ha and 12.0 ha which were occupied on a temporary basis by campaigning forces of between 2500 and 4000 troops. Defined by a single rampart and one or more outer ditches such forts have a characteristically rectangular outline with rounded corners. Most contain evidence of internal buildings because although temporary in the overall scheme of things most were in fact occupied for several seasons. They are frequently recognized through aerial photography.

via decumana [Co]. In a Roman camp or fort, the road linking the gates in the long sides and passing in front of the *principia*.

via praetoria [Co]. In a Roman camp or fort, the street leading from the front of the headquarters building or general's tent to the front gate.

via principalis [Co]. In a Roman camp or fort, the main transverse street, passing in front of the headquarters building or general's tent.

via quintana [Co]. In a Roman camp or fort, the transverse street running behind the headquarters building and *latera praetorii*, parallel with the *via principalis*.

via sagularis [Co]. In a Roman camp or fort, the perimeter street running behind the rampart on the inside, sometimes termed the *intervallum* street.

Victoria [Na]. British monarch of the House of Hanover. Born 1819, daughter of Edward, fourth son of George III. Came to the throne in 1837. Married Prince Albert of Saxe-Coburg and Gotha in 1840. Died in 1901 aged 81; reigned 63 years.

Victoria County History [Or]. A programme of research established in 1899 to mark Queen Victoria's diamond jubilee aimed at a historical portrayal of the English counties. Although the originators of the work, G. L. Gomme and H. A. Doubleday, envisaged that the research would be completed and published in 160 volumes by 1905, work on the project continues to this day. Each set of county volumes comprises general volumes covering such matters as archaeology, architecture, and ecclesiastical history; and topographic volumes which describe each city, town, and parish in the county.

Victorian [Ge]. Term used to describe the period from about 1837 to 1901. Victorian architecture is characterized by extensive borrowing from and reworking of classical and particularly GOTHIC styles.

Victoria West technique [De]. A variant of the LEVALLOIS technique in which the blow to remove the flake is made on the side of the core. Produces short wide flakes, often transformed into flake cleavers in the African ACHEULIAN.

vicus (pl. *vici*) [MC]. A civilian settlement, urban area, or village which developed near a military establishment, often to provide services for it. It had the lowest legal status accorded to a built-up area in the Roman world and would therefore have been subordinate to a higher (military) authority.

viereckscanzen [MC]. A later prehistoric ritual or religious enclosure found in central and western Europe and characterized by a generally square or rectangular plan, an area of less than 1 ha defined by an earthen bank and steep-sided ditch, and a single entrance. Within the enclosure there may be one or more of the following: pit, shaft, well, standing stone, post-built structure, hearth, area of burning. Excavated examples range in date from URNFIELD contexts of the 12th century

BC through to the 1st century BC, some being superseded by Roman-style temples. Typical examples include Holzhausen, Germany, and Libenice, the Czech Republic. They are generally regarded as sacred enclosures or sanctuaries, but Matthew Murray has argued that in fact they functioned as feasting places.

Vikings [CP]. General term applied to Scandinavian communities from Denmark, Sweden, and Norway of the later 1st millennium AD who were great navigators, traders, and colonists. Widely regarded in the popular imagination as raiders well versed in rape and pillage, this seems to have been only part of the story. Their trading activities took them along the main river systems of eastern Europe to the Black Sea, Byzantium, and the Mediterranean. In the 8th and 9th centuries they raided the rivers and coasts of western Europe, including the Isle of Man and Ireland. In 865 their raids on eastern England led to the conquest of much of the eastern part of the country with a capital and major trading port at York (Jorvik). In the 10th century they briefly colonized Greenland and portions of the North American coast.

Viking (Vikingur) [De]. Scandinavian words used to describe the seafaring raiders from Norway, Sweden, and Denmark who ravaged the coasts of Europe from about 800 AD onwards. The etymology of the word 'Viking' is disputed but its use signified 'pirate'. The noun 'viking' means a pirate raid.

vill [MC]. A group of three or more early medieval houses forming a small discrete rural settlement which lacks the commercial, legal, and ecclesiastical services found in larger settlements. Widely scattered across midland and eastern England, dating to the 6th century AD through to the Norman conquest in the mid 11th century.

villa [MC]. In Roman times a villa was an independent rural settlement of some consequence, distinguished archaeologically by a central building with heated rooms, baths, mosaic pavements, or sophisticated architectural details such as columns. Around the central buildings there may be barns and agricultural facilities, since the villa was usually the social and economic focus of a substantial estate. In the Mediterranean world, from the 2nd century BC onwards, examples began to appear that showed less emphasis on farming and more on the function of a country house for the urban rich. Various architectural styles are represented, two of the most common being the WINGED CORRIDOR VILLA and the COURTYARD VILLA.

Villafranchian [CP]. Formerly classed as Upper PLIOCENE, now included in the Lower PLEISTOCENE.

village [MC]. In northern Europe, a cluster of farmhouses and cottages, larger than a hamlet, and sometimes including a church and other communal buildings and facilities. In most cases villages develop out of earlier VILLS in the 11th century AD and many are still occupied.

village green [Co]. *See* GREEN.

Villanovan Culture [CP]. Term applied loosely to the early Iron Age of Etruria and northern Italy, named after the type-cemetery near Bologna, excavated in 1853 and dated to the 9th–8th centuries BC. The origins of the culture can be traced in later Bronze Age Terramara and Apennine Cultures, with elements derived from the north Alpine Urnfield Culture, though not necessarily as a result of immigration. The classic Villanovan assemblages from around Bologna have been divided into four principal periods extending broadly from the 9th to the 5th centuries BC. The principal settlements were villages, cemeteries being of the URNFIELD type with decorated biconical urns and well-developed bronze objects used as grave goods, for example helmets, drinking vessels, *SITULAE*, and personal ornaments such as *FIBULAE*.

Vinča, Serbia [Si]. Substantial TELL beside the River Danube near Belgrade, extensively excavated by Miloje Vasić between 1908 and 1912. The deep stratigraphy, up to 10.5 m thick in places, showed occupation spanning the period from 5000 BC through to about 3500 BC. The lowest levels were of the STARČEVO CULTURE above which were all the recognized phases of the eponymous VINČA CULTURE.

[Sum.: D. Srejovic and N. Tasic (eds.), *Vinča and its world*. Belgrade: Serbian Academy of Sciences and Arts]

Vinča Culture [CP]. Middle and late Neolithic culture of southeastern Europe, named after a type-site on the Danube near Belgrade. The Vinča Culture succeeds the STARČEVO culture in the region. It is commonly subdivided into an earlier Vinča-Tordos phase of the late 5th millennium BC, and a later Vinča-Pločnik phase of the early 4th millennium BC; both are each further subdivided. Settlements are in some cases extensive open sites such as Selevac, Yugoslavia, while others, such as Vinča itself, are substantial TELL mounds with up to 8 m of occupation. Both kinds of settlement are characterized by single-roomed oblong buildings. Ceramic types include bowls and jars in dark burnished ware. Decoration includes channelling of the surface. Distinctive of the culture are the figurines of the Pristina style, and the appearance in later Vinča-Pločnik levels of copper artefacts.

Vindolanda, Northumberland, UK [Si]. Roman fort and associated civilian settlement established in the late 1st century AD, subsequently incorporated into the HADRIAN'S WALL frontier. Extensively excavated under the direction of Robin Birley between 1969 and 1989. Amongst the structures revealed are a military bath-house, mansion, houses, and a mausoleum. Localized waterlogging provides ideal conditions for the preservation of organic finds, the most notable group being over 1000 fragments of letters and official papers written in ink on thin pieces of wood.

[Sum.: R. Birley, 1977, *Vindolanda: a Roman frontier post on Hadrian's Wall*. London: Thames & Hudson]

vineyard [MC]. An area of land, often enclosed, which is set aside and equipped for the cultivation of vines. The grapes that are produced are used to provide a constant and sustainable supply of wine and there may be storage and processing equipment within or adjacent to the vineyard. Typical components of a vineyard that may be found archaeologically are terraces, revetments, growing beds, boundary walls, buildings, stakes, and rigging.

Vinland Map [Do]. Parchment map of the 'unknown world' now in Yale University Library. Published in 1965, but purportedly dating to *c*.AD 1440, showing the 'island' of Vinland where North America stands. The map is probably a forgery.

Visigoths [CP]. *See* GOTHS.

vitrification [De]. The formation of glassy material in a ceramic body resulting from firing at a high temperature, 800°C or more, depending on the clay constituents.

vitrified fort [MC]. Name applied to a group of Iron Age hillforts in Scotland which are distinctive in having timber-laced ramparts that have been fired, either deliberately or accidentally, causing the stone within the rampart core to fuse. Excavated examples date to the last few centuries BC.

Vix, Côte d'Or, France [Si]. A very large burial mound 42 m in diameter and 6 m high immediately outside the massive hillfort of Mont Lassois. Excavations by M. René Joffroy in 1953 revealed that the mound covered an extremely rich HALLSTATT D burial of the later 6th century BC. Within a rectangular wooden chamber was the body of a woman wearing a solid gold torc on a dismantled cart. The torc had been imported from the classical world, as had an Etruscan bronze vessel and an Attic black figure cup. The most notable object in the grave was a massive bronze KRATER 1.64 m high of Greek manufacture and thought to have been made either in Sparta or the Greek colony of TARENTUM in southern Italy. The decoration on this piece was elaborate and included an embossed frieze of foot soldiers and chariots around the neck. The burial was clearly that of an elite female and serves to indicate the powerful role that women played in Iron Age society.

[Sum.: J. V. S. Megaw, 1966, The Vix burial. *Antiquity*, 40, 38–44]

vizier [Ge]. In ancient Egypt, the prime minister or right-hand man to the king or pharaoh.

Volga-Oka Culture [CP]. A collective name sometimes applied to pottery-using hunter-gatherer communities in the forest zone of the central Russian Plain in the region enclosed by the Upper Volga, Oka, and Desna rivers during the 4th and 3rd millennia BC. This area was the homeland of the PIT-COMB WARE cultures, direct descendants of the local Mesolithic groups. The earliest of the Volga-Oka cultures was the LIALOVO CULTURE in the mid 4th millennium BC. Closely related was the BELEV CULTURE that developed in the later 4th millennium BC to the south of the Lialovo. Both had a settlement pattern that kept to the riverbanks, the shores of lakes, or sand-dunes. The accumulated layers at excavated sites on lake margins point to a rather settled way of life, but sites on sand-dunes appear to be transitory. No agriculture or animal husbandry was practised, subsistence economies being based on hunting and fishing. The pottery comprises characteristic baggy vessels with a pointed or rounded base, decorated with deeply impressed pits often arranged in horizontal zones divided by comb impressions. Regional and local variations in ceramic styles are evident. Superseded by the FATYANOVO CULTURE around 2000 BC.

volute [De]. The spiral-patterned element in the capital of the Ionic, Corinthian, and Composite Orders: derived from the voluted ram's horns, or of geometrical origin, or perhaps suggested by the perfect natural spiral of the seed-box of one of the commonest Greek clovers.

vomitorium [Co]. Access route to the tiered seating (*CAVEA*) in a Roman theatre or AMPHITHEATRE.

Vortigern [Na]. British prince who flourished in the mid 5th century AD after the withdrawal of the Roman administration. According to tradition Vortigern established federate Saxons in southeastern England, apparently to ward off attacks by the Picts and other pirates. The traditional account makes this the first settling of the heathen in Britain, and Vortigern is castigated for his policy by subsequent writers.

vosk [De]. Danish word for a disease in cattle resulting from deficiencies in the mineral content of their diet and causing progressive debility. Held to account for migrations away from marginal lands in Scandinavia.

votive [De]. Term used to describe the offering to a deity of a gift of some kind in order to appease, thank, or enhance the success of pleas, prayers, or supplications. In Mycenaean times a terracotta model, often of an animal, seems to have been used as a device to make the donor's prayer more likely to be remembered by the deity. In Greek and Roman societies a person or city might dedicate a statue, or a golden tripod, or some other valuable object to one or other deity with the result that a considerable collection of *objets d'art* accumulated around the temples. In other cultural contexts such objects accumulated in pits, shafts, bogs, lakes, or whatever places were sacred to the gods.

votive deposit [Ge]. A group of material deposited in circumstances that can be interpreted as being votive in intent.

voussoir [Ar]. Wedge-shaped stone, brick, or box tile forming one of the units of an arch.

V-perforation [De]. **1.** A hole made through a piece of bone, stone, or other hard material by grinding or drilling a conical depression from one side only of the material, work proceeding until the tip of the cutter emerges on the other side. See also HOUR-GLASS PERFORATION. **2.** In making buttons, V-perforations involve drilling two convergent holes until they meet at an angle within the body of the button. Especially common in the European early Bronze Age.

WAC [Ab]. *See* WORLD ARCHAEOLOGICAL CONGRESS.

Wace, Alan John Bayard (1879–1957) [Bi]. British archaeologist specializing in prehistoric Greece. He studied at Pembroke College, Cambridge, before becoming a Craven Student in 1903 and librarian at the British School in Rome two years later. After holding a fellowship at Pembroke College and a lectureship in ancient history and archaeology at St Andrews, he was appointed Director of the British School in Athens in 1914, a post he held until 1923. In 1924 he became deputy keeper in the Department of Textiles in London's Victoria and Albert Museum before returning to Cambridge in 1934 to become Laurence Professor of Classical Archaeology. Retiring early from Cambridge in 1944, he was appointed Professor of Classics and Archaeology in the University of Alexandria, a post he occupied until 1952. During his archaeological career he directed excavations at a number of sites in Greece, notably Loconia and Mycenae. At the time of his death he was working on material he had excavated outside the acropolis walls at Mycenae.

[Obit.: *The Times*, 11 November 1957].

Wadjet (Edjo/Uto) [Di]. Egyptian goddess of Lower Egypt, depicted as a cobra, or as a woman wearing the Red Crown of Lower Egypt, or as a cobra with the wings of a vulture. Her shrine was the House of Flame and her city Dep in the Delta. Equivalent to the Greek Buto.

wagon burial [MC]. A kind of aristocratic burial characteristic of the central European HALLSTATT CULTURE, in which individuals were buried with a four-wheeled funeral wagon under a tumulus. Excavated examples include the Hohmichele tomb beside the upper Danube, and the Vix burial beside the upper Seine. The tradition of vehicle burial continues into the LA TÈNE Iron Age, the four-wheeled wagon being superseded by the two-wheeled chariot or cart burial. In both variants the vehicle is sometimes intact, but most frequently dismantled before being placed in the grave. The horse teams, occasionally buried with the vehicle, are more commonly indicated only by the presence of harness and bridle fittings. Some wagon graves are richly furnished with personal items, weapons, and feasting equipment and provisions.

Wairau Bar, South Island, New Zealand [Si]. MAORI cemetery in the northern part of South Island investigated by Sir Roger Duff in the early 1940s. Dated to the 11th–12th centuries AD, Wairau Bar has yielded one of the richest artefact assemblages from any ancient site in New Zealand. About 26 burials were found, singly or in groups, many furnished with grave goods that included adzes, necklaces, fish-hooks, and moa eggs. The style of the artefacts suggests links with parts of eastern Polynesia.

[Sum.: R. Duff, 1950, Moas and man. *Antiquity*, 24, 72–83]

waisted axe [Ar]. Neolithic axehead (generally of flint or stone) typical of the later Neolithic in northern Europe with a generally triangular outline but having concave long sides so that the central part is narrower than either the butt or the blade.

Waldalgesheim style [De]. The second of four distinctive styles of pre-Roman Celtic art in Europe defined by Paul JACOBSTHAL in 1944. Named after a chieftain's grave found near Bonn in the Rhineland, the Waldalgesheim style was characterized by an individual use of classical non-representational forms, especially the free use of flowing curvilinear motifs, as on the torc and rings from the type-site.

Broadly dated to the later 4th and early 3rd centuries BC.

walkway [Co]. A path or constructed pedestrian link, sometimes elevated, linking two or more structures or occupation areas.

Wallington Phase [CP]. Industrial phase of the British later Bronze Age that was broadly contemporary with the WILBURTON PHASE (10th–8th centuries BC) but confined to the area north of River Humber and south of the Forth. Unlike industries further south, the Wallington Tradition is characterized by rather old-fashioned types made using old-fashioned technology. Metalwork of the industry includes palstaves, square-mouthed socketed axes with flat collars, dirks, rapiers, basal-looped spearheads, and tools such as hammers and chisels.

wall painting [Ge]. Mural or fresco added using coloured paints to a prepared plasterwork wall surface as decoration or to simulate other materials. Common in domestic and ceremonial architecture from the early Neolithic onwards. Especially common in the classical world, with much surviving from Roman times throughout the empire. In Europe wall painting was very common in the medieval period and is well represented in ecclesiastical contexts.

wall plaster [Ma]. Layer of well-mixed lime and sand, sand and cement, or lime putty applied as a more or less even coat on a wall or ceiling to provide a smooth hard surface. The recovery of wall plaster from archaeological levels is important not only for information on the smooth surface about the nature of the decor applied to the room, but also because the back face of the plaster will often preserve impressions that provide insights into the construction of the building (e.g. lathwork ceiling, timber-framed walls). Reassembling the wall plaster can also reveal the position and size of architectural features such as doorways, windows, and focal points within the room from which it derived.

wall-sided [De]. Term used to describe a ceramic vessel used as a bowl or mortarium whose side rises more or less vertically above a carination and which terminates in a plain or relatively plain rim.

wall-walk [Co]. Level platform for use by sentries or pedestrians along the top of a fortification.

ward [Co]. An open courtyard or bailey within a medieval castle, usually heavily defended with curtain walls, palisades, and/or earthworks. Some larger castles may have more than one ward, each being given over to slightly different uses and increasingly heavily defended the deeper into the castle it is situated.

ware [De]. Distinctive ceramic products made of the same materials from a single production site or area, e.g. NEW FOREST WARE, or vessels having the same basic characteristics or technique of manufacture, e.g. COLOUR-COATED WARE.

Wari empire [CP]. Communities occupying the central Andean highlands of Peru in the period AD 750 to AD 1000 that were bound together by extensive networks of political and economic control. At the centre of the system was the site of Wari itself in the Ayacucho Valley which was an urban centre that started as the capital of its region and rose to control surrounding areas. Provincial centres are known at Pikillaqta, Jincamocco, Cajamarca, and the unfinished site of Viracochapampa. Archaeologically, the most distinctive features of the Wari are its architecture and urban planning: great rectangular structures set out on a rigid grid plan that was subdivided into square or rectangular plots called 'patio groups'. Each patio comprised an open central area edged by long narrow rooms, sometimes two or three deep and up to three storeys high. Few doors allow access between patio groups, and it has been suggested that the intention of Wari architecture is in part to restrict movements within each enclosure. The Wari empire emerged during the EARLY INTERMEDIATE PERIOD as Huarpa cultures interacted with the nearby NASCA Culture at a time of intense interregional exchanges and widespread disruption to existing cultural traditions.

warming-house [Co]. Building or room in a monastic range in which there was a fire.

warp-weighted loom [Ar]. An apparatus on which textiles are manufactured that is arranged in such a way that the warp threads running lengthwise through the material are tensioned by means of weights (usually clay or stone) attached to one end while the other ends are secured to the loom itself. *See also* UPRIGHT LOOM.

warren [MC]. Area of land used for keeping and managing large communities of rabbits or hares for exploitation as a source of food and/or fur. Warrens usually include one or more PILLOW MOUNDS in which the animals were kept under controlled conditions. Vermin traps and a warrener's house are also common. Warrens were important economic resources in medieval times in northern Europe.

warrior burial [MC]. A grave containing the inhumed or cremated remains of an individual accompanied by an array of weapons and sometimes body armour such as a helmet, shield, or protective tunic. Warrior graves are common in the European Bronze Age, Iron Age, and later first millennium AD.

Wasserburg Buchau, Germany [Si]. Settlement of the late Bronze Age URNFIELD period situated on a low island in moorland surrounding the Federsee. Excavations by Hans Reinerth between 1921 and 1937 revealed two main phases of occupation. Both were enclosed by a pair of timber palisades defining a roughly oval area some 150 m by 120 m. Pine logs had been used to make the palisade, more than 15 000 posts being present in the outer perimeter alone. The earliest occupation comprised 37 single-roomed rectangular structures each 4 m by 5 m, together with one rather larger two-roomed building. The second phase was rather different and comprised nine multi-roomed buildings, each set out with three wings around a central courtyard, together with an assortment of outbuildings. The pottery assemblage places the site within the early first millennium BC, HALLSTATT A2, B1, and B3.

[Sum.: W. Kimmig, 1992, *Die 'Wasserburg Buchau'—eine spätbronzezeitliche Siedlung: forschungsgeschichte—Kleinfunde.* Stuttgart: Theiss]

waste [De]. A medieval term describing poor uncultivated land, often used for common grazing and as a source of fuel and building material. Waste belonged to the lord of the manor.

waste flake [De]. Flint, chert, obsidian, or stone flake created as a byproduct of shaping a core or working a core tool and discarded without further modification.

waster [Ar]. A complete or broken ceramic vessel spoilt or flawed in manufacture (e.g. cracked, blistered, sintered, distorted, discoloured). **Waster heaps** comprising accumulated masses of discarded wasters can often be found near pottery production centres. Wasters were sometimes crushed for recycling as GROG in coarse pottery or brick.

watchtower [Co]. A tall, generally narrow, stone or wooden structure topped by a viewing platform on which observers can stand in order to keep a lookout. Such towers may be freestanding or attached to the perimeter walls of a castle or settlement.

waterlogged [De]. In the archaeological context this refers to material that is permanently wet as a result of being below the level of the local water table or within a microenvironment such as might be created in the bottom of a ditch, pit, or well. Organic remains, especially wood, are generally well preserved through waterlogging because ANAEROBIC conditions prevail.

water meadow [MC]. A low-lying area of grassland adjacent to a river or stream that can be artificially flooded and drained to promote enhanced grazing for livestock or the production of grass for hay. Found in northwest Europe possibly from Roman times onwards, their construction and use became more common in medieval and later times, especially after the early 17th century when intricate systems of water management using sets of cut channels known as 'drowners' for flooding the meadow and 'drains' for reducing the water level were introduced. Weirs, sluices, and hatches were installed to control the flow of water. Some water meadows cover up to 60 ha. Once established a water meadow is capable of sustained operation over a long period. In southern England a few are still used today, although many more have fallen into disrepair.

watermill [MC]. An industrial monument in which a set of machinery dedicated to a particular purpose is powered by the motion obtained from a WATER WHEEL, the machinery itself being housed in a wooden or stone building.

water wheel [Co]. A wooden or metal wheel with paddles or buckets of some kind attached to the outside so that when set in a watercourse it will rotate as a result of pressure from the movement of the water. The energy captured by such wheels in the form of rotary motion is usually transmitted via a connecting rod to some kind of machinery. Three main kinds of vertically set waterwheel can be identified: the **undershot** wheel rotated by water passing below the wheel; the **overshot** wheel where water is fed onto the top of the wheel, filling buckets which unbalance the wheel causing it turn; and the **breastshot** wheel where water is fed onto the wheel at an intermediate level. Water wheels appear to have been first used in the Greco-Roman world during the 1st century BC. The Roman engineer Vitruvius writing between 20 BC and 11 BC describes what is essentially an undershot wheel set vertically with a horizontal drive shaft. The use of such water wheels appears to have spread fairly rapidly within the Roman world and beyond, being known in Gaul by AD 370. It is possible that such wheels were preceded by a primitive horizontally set wheel with a vertical shaft, but no certain early evidence for these has been found.

wattle and daub [Ge]. Interwoven hazel rods (wattle) coated with a mixture of clay, straw, dung, and other materials (daub) used structurally to form a wall or screen. It was used for, among other things, house walls, ovens, and simple pottery kilns. Often revealed archaeologically by the impressions of wattle-work in burnt daub. Early examples of wattle and daub construction date back to at least the Mesolithic.

Wealden house [MC]. Type of timber-framed building, usually a farmhouse, found widely over the southeast of England. Dating to the 15th century, Wealden houses have a distinctive open hall in the centre flanked at either end by multi-storeyed wings. In the most classic example the wings are jettied at the front while the central section is recessed.

weathering (weathered) [De]. The erosion of archaeological materials and deposits through natural fluvial and aeolian processes caused by wind, rainfall, groundwater changes, freezing and thawing, river action, ocean currents and tides, glacial action, gravity, and abrasion. Such processes may result in the physical loss, peneplaining, fragmentation, or reduction in the size of structures, deposits, or single artefacts; these are described as 'weathered'.

weaving [Ge]. The use of wool, cotton, silk, flax, or some other plant or animal fibre yarn or thread to produce textiles of various sorts by criss-crossing the yarns together in at least two directions. **Warp** threads are those which run up and down the length of a piece of textile, **weft** threads are those that run across the weave at right angles to the warp. Many different patterns are possible, producing different kinds of textile and styles of weave. Patterns can be introduced by using different coloured threads in a set order. The earliest evidence of weaving is that represented as textile and flexible basketry impressions on burnt clay from Pavlov in the Czech Republic which date to between 25 000 and 23 000 BC. The oldest woven cloth so far discovered is made from flax, dates to about 7000 BC, and comes from Çayönü, Turkey.

weaving comb [Ar]. Bone or wooden implement with a handle at one end and a toothed edge at the other. The tool is used during weaving to pack the weft together tightly; the prongs of the weaving comb fit between the warp threads, so allowing the weaver to exert considerable downward or lateral pressure on the accumulating weft. *See also* PIN BEATER.

wedge [Ar]. Stone, wood, or metal tool with parallel sides and tapering faces that meet as a straight blade at the thin end while the thicker end has a flat striking platform for direct percussion with a hammer or mallet. Wedges are traditionally used to split tree trunks to form planks or beams.

wedge tomb (wedge grave) [MC]. Irish megalithic tomb consisting of a rectangular, trapezoidal, or D-shaped cairn with a long narrow chamber opening into the cairn from the wider higher side. With no separate entrance passage, the chamber is typically constructed of orthostatic walls supporting massive capstones forming the roof. Generally the chamber decreases in height towards the back. There is a slight tendency for the tombs to face west. Burials are mainly multiple cremation; grave goods are rare. Dated examples cluster in the period 2300–1800 BC, the late Neolithic, although many were later re-used as burial places.

Wedlake, William James (1904–89) [Bi]. British amateur archaeologist who worked mainly in the southwest of England. His early life was spent on a farm at Camerton in Somerset where he developed a passionate interest in the countryside and the early history of Somerset. In the 1930s he took part in the excavations at the Meare Lake Village and later became foreman to St George Gray at Combe Beacon and Burrow Mump. During the pre-war excavations at Maiden Castle, Dorset, Wedlake was the foreman and assistant to Sir Mortimer Wheeler, and he later worked with Wheeler on many other sites in England and northern France. While working for the Admiralty in Bath from 1940 until his retirement in 1972, Wedlake excavated the Romano-British settlement at Camerton, and in 1947 founded the Camerton Club to carry out work around Bath. His last major excavation was the Romano-British temple at Nettleton, near Bath, Avon.

[Obit. *Antiquaries Journal*, 70 (1990), 527–8]

weeds of cultivation [Ge]. Distinctive species of plants that grow amongst cultivated cereal crops as a result of contamination either through seeds getting into the main crop before sowing, remaining in the ground after the soil has been cultivated, or being introduced to an emergent crop by windaction or animal transportation. The main species are cleavers (*Galium aparine*), charlock (*Sinapis arvensis*), members of the thistle family (*Cirsia*), fat hen (*Chenopodium album*), poppies (*Papaveraceae*), hedge mustard (*Sisymbrium officinale*), and, on acid soils, red shank (*Polygonum persicaria*) and pale persicara (*Polygonum lapathifolium*). The presence or absence of these species allows detailed insights to the nature and extent of crop processing and agricultural practices.

Weichselian [Ge]. Final glacial advance in northern Europe, named after a major north German ice-sheet present during the period 120 000 to 10 000 BC. The Weichselian glaciation corresponds to the WÜRM in the Alpine sequence, the DEVENSIAN in the British Isles, and the WISCONSIN in North America.

weight [Ar]. **1.** Stone, wooden, metal, or clay object that when suspended by a rope or cord acts to stretch, tension, or pull tight some kind of fabric or material (e.g. thatch weight; net weight). **2.** Stone, clay, or metal object of standard weight used in measurement on balances or scales of some kind.

welding [De]. A means of fusing together two or more pieces of iron or other kinds of metal with similar properties. In ancient times welding was achieved by pressing heated pieces of metal together at high temperature (i.e. white-hot but not melted), usually by hammering. This is commonly known as fire-welding; early examples include iron jewellery from late Helladic contexts in Greece. In more recent times welding is usually achieved by bringing the pieces of metal together in molten form by melting the contact zones using an electric arc or hot-burning gases. Fillers and fluxes may sometimes be used in this process. *See also* SOLDERING.

well [Co]. Pit or shaft, sometimes lined with stone or wood, dug from the ground surface to a point below the local water table so as to allow the bottom of the well to fill with water as a small reservoir accessible by lowering a bucket or receptacle down from above. Some wells are fitted with a cover, others with a protective wall around the top. Some are fitted with a winding mechanism to raise and lower the bucket, or a pump to raise the water by suction. Recesses in the top section of the well shaft were sometimes built as storage places for foodstuffs that are best stored in cool conditions. Wells are sometimes associated with special powers or as links to the underworld.

Welwyn burials [MC]. A group of richly furnished aristocratic graves dated to the La Tène III period (*c.*40–10 BC) found in a restricted area to the north of the River Thames around modern-day Welwyn, Buckinghamshire, England. The burials were usually cremations placed in the centre of a large pit or subterranean chamber, with no covering mound. Around the burial itself were placed many grave goods, mainly items connected with eating, drinking, or feasting: imported continental tableware, wine amphorae, bronze vases, strainers, and patellae, silver cups, glass dishes, fire-dogs, and hearth furniture. Personal items such as buckles, bracelets, beads, and gaming pieces are also found. Meat on the bone and weapons are conspicuous by their absence. More than a dozen examples have been discovered and excavated.

Wepwawet [Di]. Egyptian god known as the 'Opener of the Ways', depicted as a wolf god, a deity of the necropolis and avenger of Osiris. Principal places of worship were at Assiut and Abydos.

Wessex [Ge]. Variously defined region dominated by the chalk downlands of southern England and well known in the archaeological literature because of the wealth of well-preserved archaeological sites, many of which were subject to investigation early in the history of antiquarian and archaeological research. In Anglo-Saxon times Wessex was a large kingdom of the West Saxons covering the present counties of Dorset, Wiltshire, Hampshire, and Berkshire. It was probably the last such kingdom to be established, perhaps in the 6th century AD by Cerdic. By the 9th century it had expanded considerably in land area and influence under its most famous ruler ALFRED THE GREAT. Eventually, the royal house of Wessex became the nucleus for a unified kingdom of England. More recent perceptions of Wessex have been influenced by the writings of Thomas Hardy whose literary vision of Wessex focused on the more westerly part of the earlier kingdom, centred on his home town of Dorchester, Dorset.

Wessex Archaeology [Or]. One of the largest archaeological contractors in Britain, based at Salisbury, Wiltshire. Originally established in 1974 as the Trust for Wessex Archaeology, it was born out of the Wessex Archaeological Committee as one of the first regional rescue archaeology units in the country. Still a charity, the company is independent of ties to local or national government, and carries out archaeological investigations, surveys, and management projects throughout England.

Wessex Culture [CP]. Early Bronze Age culture of central southern England defined by Stuart PIGGOTT in 1938 on the basis of a series of well-known richly furnished burials under round barrows in the Wessex region of Dorset, Hampshire, Wiltshire, Berkshire, and surrounding areas. Later, in 1954, Arthur ApSimon proposed subdividing the Wessex Culture into two consecutive phases initially on the basis of the dagger typology: Wessex I

(c.2000–1650 BC) with richly furnished inhumation graves containing bronze triangular daggers (Bush Barrow type), axes, beads, and buttons of amber and shale, and gold dress fittings. The most famous example is the Bush Barrow burial near Stonehenge, Wiltshire. Wessex II (c.1650–1400 BC) was characterized by ogival daggers (Camerton–Snowshill type) together with cremation replacing inhumation and faience beads becoming more common. Goldwork is less common in Wessex II graves. Connections between both phases of the Wessex Culture and contemporary communities in northern France are widely accepted (e.g. with the Armorican Tumulus Culture), and these date to the European early Bronze Age, Reinecke A1 and A2. There has been much discussion of the possibility of long-distance links to the Aegean world, but most can be discounted on chronological grounds. Wessex I is closely associated with the construction and use of the later phases of Stonehenge, specifically Stonehenge 3. In recent decades the Wessex Culture has been seen as a limited social stratum within a broader cultural phenomenon rather than a distinct cultural grouping.

Western Neolithic [CP]. General and now little-used term applied to the early and middle Neolithic communities of western Europe, especially the CHASSEY, CORTAILLOD, LAGOZZA, WINDMILL HILL, and ALMERIA. Although each had different specific characteristics they were seen as having more in common amongst themselves that with the LBK and TRB cultures of central and eastern parts of Europe. In particular, the presence of megalithic tombs, long barrows, round-based pottery, and an absence of painted decoration was used to characterize the differences.

Western Style Neolithic pottery (Western Neolithic ware) [Ar]. Style of plain or little decorated early and middle Neolithic pottery found in the western parts of the British Isles, especially Ireland. In 1961 Humphrey Case defined Western Neolithic ware pottery as being round-based bowls, normally thin-walled, hard, generally dark-brown, and with a shouldered profile. Four substyles were recognized in Ireland: Dunmurry style; Ballymarlagh style, Limerick style, and the Lyles Hill style. The last mentioned was used by Isobel Smith in 1974 to help define a widespread class of early Neolithic pottery that she called the **Grimston-Lyles Hill** series; these vessels are now more commonly known as CARINATED bowls.

West Kennet, Wiltshire, England [Si]. A very large Cotswold-Severn-style long barrow with a chalk mound some 100 m long and up to 3 m high, perhaps constructed in two or more phases. Extensive excavations directed by Stuart PIGGOTT and Richard ATKINSON between 1955 and 1956 revealed that the mound was built from chalk quarried out of two flanking ditches originally 3 m deep and 7 m wide. The chamber, small in comparison to the mound, is of transepted plan and opens from the east end of the mound. Two pairs of cells open from the passage and there is a fifth cell at the far end of the passage. When first constructed the tomb was entered from a small forecourt which was later filled with stones. The burials lay scattered across the floors of all the cells within the chamber; at least 46 individuals in all, although many were incomplete disarticulated skeletons. Some pottery and personal ornaments were included with the burials. One of the burials had probably been shot with an arrow tipped by a leaf-shaped flint arrowhead. Radiocarbon dates suggest that the main period of use was between 3800 BC and 3400 BC. Sometime after 3000 BC the tomb fell out of use and was blocked up. Soil and stones were placed in the passage and chambers, and stones were piled up in the forecourt. A facade of large sarsen boulders was set up across the front making further access to the interior impossible.

[Rep. S. Piggott, 1963, *The West Kennet long barrow. Excavations 1955–56*. London: HMSO]

West Kennet Avenue, Avebury, Wiltshire, England [Si]. *See* AVEBURY.

Westropp, Hodder Michael (1820–85) [Bi]. Irish archaeologist born in Co. Cork as the son of a moderately wealthy landowner. Educated at Trinity College, Dublin, he was a flamboyant student who regarded himself as English because of family connections several generations earlier. While at Trinity he began work developing the Cycle of Development which was a framework for understanding the way that human societies developed under broadly similar conditions. In 1867 he published a *Handbook of archaeology*, the first such volume of its kind, and later produced works on Irish round towers. His most enduring contribution to scholarship was his definition and proposed introduction in 1872 of the term 'MESOLITHIC' as the technologically recognizable phase between the PALAEOLITHIC and the NEOLITHIC. It was not until 1893 and the work of J. A. Brown, however, that the term found its way into wider archaeological literature.

[Rev.: *Antiquity*, 57 (1983) 205–10]

wetland archaeology [De]. Archaeological work that focuses on essentially terrestrial areas that are permanently or periodically waterlogged, for example peat bogs, salt marshes, river and lake margins, and the inter-tidal zone around the shores of large lakes and oceans. Such areas generally have good preservation of organic materials such as timber, bone, and textiles. Work in areas that are permanently submerged below standing water of one sort or another is generally referred to as UNDERWATER ARCHAEOLOGY or MARITIME ARCHAEOLOGY.

wet sieving [Te]. Process of recovering finds and ecofacts from excavated archaeological deposits by passing them through one or more screens or sieves either suspended in water or washed through with running water, in some cases under pressure. The water acts to break down the finer sediments, removing them from the larger clasts and objects that are left on the sieve. The size of mesh used in the sieves varies from less than 1 mm up to 10 mm or more according to what kinds of material are being sought. In most modern excavations only a defined sample (e.g. 20 per cent) of stratified deposits are wet sieved. *See also* FLOATATION.

Whale Cove, Oregon, USA [Si]. *See* NEW ALBION, CALIFORNIA, USA.

Wharram Percy, North Yorkshire, England [Si]. Deserted medieval village covering about 16 ha in a small valley amid the rolling chalk downland of the Yorkshire Wolds of northeast England. Visible earthworks include roads, a fishpond, the foundation of a manor house, and 30 peasant houses set out in regular rows. Extensively excavated between 1950 and 1990 under the direction of John Hurst and Maurice Beresford, this site has made an important contribution to understanding the development and desertion of traditional medieval villages in England. The earliest occupation on the site appears to have been in Anglo-Saxon times, perhaps from the 8th century AD onwards. Over the ensuing centuries a regular pattern developed with timber longhouses each set in a yard or 'toft', the holdings being ranged along the main streets. There were two manor houses of more substantial construction, and a church established in the 12th century AD. Around the village there were open fields and paddocks. It was originally the centre of a large parish containing five villages, four of them now deserted. Wharram Percy itself was gradually abandoned in the 14th–15th centuries and was completely deserted by about AD 1500.

[Sum.: M. Beresford and J. Hurst, 1990, *Wharram Percy: deserted medieval village*. London: Batsford and English Heritage]

wheal [MC]. Colloquial name for a mine, common in Devon and Cornwall in the southwest of England.

wheat [Sp]. Domesticated cereal of the genus *Triticum* widely used as a crop by early farming communities in the Old World. Two wild forms of wheat are represented in the Near East: wild einkorn (*Triticum boeoticum*) and wild emmer (*Triticum dicoccoides*). Goat grass (*Aegilops*) is also present in the region and it is the hybridization of this with *Triticum* that accounts for most of the domesticated wheats, especially *Triticum monococcum* (einkorn), *Triticum dicoccum* (emmer), *Triticum aestivum* (bread wheat), *Triticum compactum* (club wheat), *Triticum spelta* (spelt wheat), and *Triticum durum* (macaroni wheat). Emmer, both wild and domesticated, appears on early Neolithic sites in the Near East from about 7000 BC.

wheel [Ar]. Wooden or metal disc attached at its central point to an axle or pivot in such a way that it can rotate freely to allow a vehicle or other mechanical device attached to the axle to move freely. Widely regarded as one of the single most important inventions ever made, the idea of a wheel seems to have cropped up in many cultures from early times. However, its application in pre-industrial societies is mainly confined to agriculturalist and pastoral societies in the Old World. One reason for this is that wheeled vehicles can only be used on relatively flat terrain or along constructed bearing surfaces such as roads and tracks. Another prerequisite is the availability of draught animals to pull wheeled vehicles.

The earliest evidence of wheels comes from Uruk, Iraq, where depictions of what appear to be sledges mounted on four wheels appear on pictograms of the early 4th millennium BC. From the later 4th millennium BC there are a series of depictions of wheeled vehicles on pottery or as ceramic models across a wide swathe from the Near East via central Europe to the Atlantic coastlands: from the TRB culture in southern Poland, the late Copper Age of Hungary, the Kura-Araxes Culture in Transcaucasia, the Pit Grave cultures of southern Russia, and the Corded Ware cultures of northwest Europe. In all cases these wheels appear to be solid wooden discs with a thickened hub. Actual examples of such wheels have been found dating to the mid 3rd millennium BC, for example at De Eese, the Netherlands. Later, multi-part discs were made, often with three elements secured together with cross-pieces on either side.

Spoked wheels appear from the mid 2nd millennium, first in the Transcaucasus region but soon afterwards within broadly the same areas that already use wheeled vehicles. By the 1st millennium BC iron tyres were being fixed to the outside of the rim of spoked wheels, proving to be a far more robust yet lightweight structure. Wheels were not used indigenously in the Americas, nor in Africa south of the Sahara.

Wheeler, Sir Robert Eric Mortimer (1890–1976) [Bi]. British archaeologist (Rik to his friends) well known for his excavations at Colchester, St Albans, Maiden Castle, and Stanwick, amongst many other pieces of fieldwork that made major contributions to the development of excavation and recording techniques. Born in Glasgow but brought up in Saltaire, Bradford, from the age of four, he was educated at Bradford Grammar School and University College, London, where he read classics. In 1913 he won the first Franks studentship and a year later married Tessa Verney. Between 1913 and 1915 he worked for the Royal Commission on the Historic Monuments of England before joining the Royal Field Artillery. He was posted to France in 1917 and as Major Wheeler had a week in the thick of Passchendaele before serving in Italy and then Germany. He was awarded the MC and was mentioned in despatches, his military experience bringing out his powers of leadership and dashing style. After the war he was appointed keeper of archaeology in the National

Museum of Wales but in 1926 he left Wales to become Director of the London Museum. Together with his wife he threw himself into transforming the collections in Lancaster House and raising money to establish an academy in which to train archaeologists. In 1937 he founded the Institute of Archaeology in London University, now the largest university department of archaeology in Britain, and was its first director. In the period from the early 1920s through to 1939 the Wheelers excavated many important sites including Lydney Roman Temple, Gloucestershire (1928–9), Roman and Belgic Verulamium, Hertfordshire (1930–3), and Maiden Castle, Dorset (1934–7). In this work Wheeler developed and introduced new approaches to stratigraphic excavation, including what later became known as the WHEELER SYSTEM. In 1936 a great partnership was broken when Tessa died.

Shocked by political events in 1938–9, Wheeler raised an anti-aircraft battery at Enfield which was later expanded into the 42nd Royal Artillery Regiment which joined the Eighth Army in North Africa. Wheeler was at El Alamein and in the long advance to Tunis. He also fought in Italy. In 1943 he accepted an appointment as Director-General of the Indian Archaeological Survey, requiring him to regenerate and structure a substantial organization, providing training and developing new publications for what was a demoralized group of staff when he took over. He was made a CIE in 1947, returning to London in 1948 to a part-time professorship in the University of London and a role as honorary secretary to the British Academy. He was knighted in 1952. Although he retired in 1968, he maintained an interest in all thing archaeological until his death. Wheeler was always interested in popularizing archaeology and, together with Glyn Daniel, was an early proponent of archaeology on television. In 1954 he was voted television personality of the year. Amongst many honorary positions and awards, Wheeler became a Fellow of the Society of Antiquaries in 1922, a Fellow of the Royal Society in 1968, a Fellow of the British Academy in 1970, Director of the Society of Antiquaries 1940–4 and 1949–54, President of the Society of Antiquaries 1954–9, Trustee of the British Museum 1963–73, and Chairman of the Ancient Monuments Board 1964–6).

[Abio.: 1955, *Still digging.* London: Michael Joseph. Bio.: J. Hawkes, 1982, *Mortimer Wheeler. Adventurer in archaeology.* London: Weidenfeld]

Wheeler system (Wheeler method) [Te]. A method of setting out archaeological excavation trenches in a pattern of regular square or rectangular boxes with baulks between, pioneered by Sir Mortimer Wheeler at sites in India and southern Britain. The boxes provided suitable subdivisions for the organization and control of labour, for the recording of finds, and, most importantly, so that following the excavation of each unit it was possible to record the stratigraphy in the sides of the baulks, and this developed both a vertical sequence for individual parts of the site and a means of correlating layers and deposits across the site in the horizontal plane. At the end of the excavation the baulks were removed to provide a single view of the lower levels of the whole area. Although useful, the small size of the boxes (typically 3 m by 3 m) and the fixed position of the baulks throughout the sequence are major encumbrances and this system has now largely been replaced by open-area excavation.

wheelhouse [MC]. Round stone-built structure, the interior of which is divided by short radial stone piers projecting from the wall but leaving the central area open. The piers presumably supported a wooden roof structure covered in turf or thatch. They are found mainly in northern Scotland and the outer isles especially the Hebrides, Orkney, and Shetland. Dated examples cluster in the early centuries of the 1st millennium AD and are thus broadly contemporary with BROCHS; a few examples may, however, be rather earlier, perhaps 3rd or 2nd century BC, and may thus pre-date the brocks in the neighbourhood.

wheel marks (wheel ruts) [De]. **1.** Pairs of parallel grooves or channels cut into a bearing surface such as a roadway or track as a result of the repeated passage of wheeled vehicles along a defined course. The distance between related pairs of wheel ruts provides a general indication of wheel spacing or axle width. **2.** On ceramic vessels, the spiral marks, usually on the inside of a vessel, caused by the potter's fingers cutting into the clay walls as the pot revolves on the wheel.

wheel-thrown [De]. Term used to describe ceramic vessels made using a potter's wheel. A lump of raw clay is centred on the wheel as it rotates, after which the potter can draw out and shape the walls of the vessel as the wheel continues to rotate. Decoration and surface finishes can also be added while the vessel is on the wheel. Recognizing wheel-thrown pots is not always easy in archaeological samples, the presence of WHEEL MARKS being one of the most diagnostic.

whetstone [Ar]. An abrasive stone, usually sandstone or siltstone of some kind, with one or more shaped faces that can be used for sharpening the blades of metal edged tools such as axes, swords, knives, awls, sickles, or chisels.

whirligig [De]. In early CELTIC art a motif comprising three or four conjoined spirals either radiating from, or swirling about, a common centre, of which one element may be eccentric, being larger or more complex than the others. The four-part version may appear as a curvilinear rendering of the swastika motif. As with similar motifs in Celtic art, it may be used in a series or as part of a larger design.

whistle [Ar]. **1.** Simple musical instrument comprising a hollow tube, often of bone or wood, down which air can be blown; one or more holes in the side of the tube can be covered and uncovered with the fingers to alter the flow of air and thus produce a range of different sounds. When the holes are placed at proportioned intervals, a simple chromatic scale can be produced. Some of the earliest examples known include the hollowed femur of a cave bear with three holes, one in the posterior surface and two in the anterior, from an Upper Palaeolithic context in the Istállóskö Cave, Hungary. It provides a musical range A^{iii}, B^{iii}, B^{iii}, E^{iii}. The basic design involving a hollowed bone provided with holes is represented throughout later prehistory by many examples from findspots scattered widely across Europe. **2.** A small tube in which there is a fixed constriction such that when blown a shrill sound is produced. The earliest examples, perhaps decoy whistles, are from Upper Palaeolithic occupation sites in France and parts of central Europe. All are made from reindeer phalanges pierced on one surface.

Whitby-type ware [Ar]. Middle Saxon style of pottery made using a slow-turning potter's wheel at workshops around Whitby in North Yorkshire, England.

White, Leslie Alvin (1900–75) [Bi]. American anthropologist well known for promoting evolutionary thinking in archaeology and anthropology. He viewed culture as a system and saw the development of societies as being related to the need to capture ever greater amounts of energy in order to sustain themselves. In this, White ignored the influence of environment and one culture on another, emphasizing instead the long-term nature of cultural development and the fact that if human groups did not stay ahead they were subsumed by other groups. As a result his perception of cultural change was materialistic and rather deterministic, but it was an approach that contributed much to the development of PROCESSUAL ARCHAEOLOGY. White published two important general accounts of his work: in 1949 as *The science of culture: a study of man and civilization* (New York: Strand), and in 1959 as *The evolution of culture* (New York: McGraw-Hill).

[Obit. *American Anthropologist*, 78 (1976), 612–29]

white-ground ware [De]. Style of Greek pottery common in the 5th century BC in which a white slip was applied to the surface of a vessel onto which was painted figurative decoration in a range of colours. The most common vessel form decorated in this way was the LEKYTHOS, often linked with funeral ceremonies.

white horses [MC]. *See* HILL FIGURE.

WHS [De]. William Hunt and Sons (now part of Spear and Jackson), manufacturers of high-quality robust steel mason's pointing trowels that have become the industry-standard tool for excavating in Britain. Experienced excavators often have a collection of prized trowels, the blades variously worn down from the preferred 4-inch starting size, that have served through many seasons so that each has a story to tell.

wickerwork [Ma]. Interwoven branches or withies formed as panels for screens and revetments, or shaped as fabrications such as baskets, traps, and containers.

Wilburton-Wallingford Phase [CP]. Industrial stage of the British late Bronze Age characterized technologically by the widespread introduction of copper–lead–tin alloys and typologically by styles of leaf-shaped slashing swords, socketed spearheads with a peg for securing them to their wooden shaft, horse-bits, and socketed axes. Broadly dated to 1000–

800 BC centuries BC, and named after a large hoard of bronzework found at Wilburton in Cambridgeshire in January 1882.

wild boar [Sp]. *See* PIG.

Wilfrid, Bishop [Na]. One-time bishop of York and spokesman of the Catholic church against Celtic observance at the Synod of Whitby in AD 664. Much of his career was spent in disputes with Northumbrian kings and with archbishops of Canterbury, and twice he visited Rome to plead his cause. Founder of the churches at Hexham and Ripon, and in AD 678 apostle to the Frisians. Born *c*.AD 634; died 709.

William I (The Conqueror) [Na]. English king of the House of Normandy. Born 1027/8, son of Robert I, duke of Normandy, he obtained the English crown by conquest following the Battle or Hastings in 1066 when Norman forces defeated Harold's army. Married Matilda, daughter of Baldwin, count of Flanders. Died in 1087 aged *c*.60; reigned twenty years.

William I (The Lion) [Na]. King of Scotland. Born *c*.1142, brother of Malcolm IV. Married Ermengarde, daughter of Richard, viscount of Beaumont. Died in 1214, aged *c*.72; reigned 49 years.

William II (Rufus) [Na]. English king of the House of Normandy. Born between 1056 and 1060, third son of William I; succeeded his father in England only. He was killed in 1100 while hunting in the New Forest aged *c*.40; reigned twelve years.

William III [Na]. King of England, Wales, Scotland, and Ireland from 1689; born of the House of Stuart in 1650; son of William II, prince of Orange, and Mary Stuart, daughter of Charles I. Married Mary, elder daughter of James II. Died in 1702 aged 51; reigned thirteen years.

William IV [Na]. British monarch of the House of Hanover from 1830. Born 1765, third son of George III. Married Adelaide, daughter of George, duke of Saxe-Meiningen. Died in 1837, aged 71; reigned seven years.

Williamsburg (Middle Plantation), Virginia, USA [Si]. British colonial settlement, at first called Middle Plantation, established in AD 1633 on a narrow peninsula between the York and James rivers. When it became the capital of Virginia in 1699, the town was renamed in honour of King William III.

At its peak, structures of stone and wood housed a population of 5000–6000. Public buildings included the Raleigh Tavern, the Capitol Building, and the College of William and Mary (founded 1693). When its tenure as state capital ended in 1780, the town went into decline.

Since 1928, however, excavations have been going on at the site and it now has one of the most extensive restoration projects in North America. As such it provides a picture of life in the 18th century AD.

[Rep.: A. L. Kocher and H. Dearstyne, 1949, *Colonial Williamsburg, its buildings and gardens. A study of Virginia's natural capital*. Williamsburg: Colonial Williamsburg]

Willibrord, Saint [Na]. British religious leader and missionary born *c*.657. Educated at Ripon and sent in 690 to the Frisians to complete Wilfrid's mission. With Frankish support he was made archbishop of the Frisians in *c*.695, and founded the bishopric of Utrecht, Holland. Died *c*.738.

willow-leaf point [Ar]. Long, thin bifacially worked flint points of the SOLUTREAN Tradition in the European Upper Palaeolithic.

Wilson, Daniel (1816–92) [Bi]. Scottish artist and antiquary who was the first English speaker to apply the Danish approach to prehistoric archaeology outside Scandinavia. Born in Edinburgh, he attended Edinburgh High School before being apprenticed to a steel engraver. Between 1837 and 1842 he worked in London as an engraver and popular writer, but returned to Edinburgh to run an artist's supplies and print shop. Although Wilson developed an interest in history and matters antiquarian from a relatively early age, it was not until he was invited to help turn the collections of the Society of Antiquaries of Scotland into a modern national museum that he turned from antiquarianism to archaeology. In reorganizing the collection he adopted the Danish model of ordering the artefacts according to the THREE AGE SYSTEM. Wilson's arrangement presented an evolutionary approach to viewing the artefacts, and this also came across in the catalogue that he wrote to go with the exhibition.

Later, in 1851, he published an extended version of the catalogue as *Archaeology and prehistoric annals of Scotland* (London: Macmillan). This was the first comprehensive treatment of early Scotland based on material culture and the first time that the term 'prehistoric' was used in English. Although Wilson received an honorary LLD from the University of St Andrews, he was unable to get an academic position in Scotland. In 1853, with help from friends in Edinburgh, he was appointed to the Chair of History and English Literature in University College, Toronto, Canada. Wilson enjoyed teaching in Canada and continued his interest in archaeology, but all the while expanded his interest in anthropology and ethnography. Throughout his life he was a talented landscape painter.

[Rev.: B. G. Trigger, 1992, Daniel Wilson and the Scottish Enlightenment. *Proceedings of the Society of Antiquaries of Scotland*, 122, 55–75]

Wilton [CP]. A series of later Stone Age microlithic industries found widely across southern Africa and dating to the period 6000 BC through to AD 500 or later. Named after a small rock-shelter near Alicedale in the eastern Cape Province of South Africa, the lithic industries include small convex scrapers, thumbnail scrapers, adzes, segmented blades, and crescent-shaped backed blades, but organic materials are also known, together with occupied caves and burials. Rock painting is well represented. The economy was based on the exploitation of a wide range of plant and vegetable species and marine, aquatic, and animal resources including melkhoutboom and antelope. Changes in the relative percentage of different classes of stone tools can be seen over the duration of the tradition, and a **Coastal Wilton** and **Interior Wilton** are widely recognized. After the early 1st millennium AD pottery began to be made and used in some areas and this is sometimes referred to as the **Post-Climax Wilton** or **Ceramic Wilton**.

Winchester, Hampshire, England [Si]. Large historic town in central southern England situated beside the River Itchen. At the time of the Roman conquest the site was already a major tribal centre, and was soon adopted as the capital of the new administrative area and named Venta Belgarum. Defences were constructed in AD 60–70 and the rectangular grid of streets was established at about the same time within the walls. By the 2nd century AD the town covered 58 ha. After the decline of Roman power Winchester continued to be occupied, and in the 7th century a substantial church was built: the Old Minster. There was a major revival in its fortunes in the later 9th century AD when it became a BURH with planned streets and a strong defensive system. The Old Minster was extended several times, and in the 970s the open-air tomb of St Swithin was incorporated into the structure. The town again rose to prominence to became the capital of the Anglo-Saxon kingdom of Wessex.

Winchester continued to thrive through later centuries as a regional centre, market, and the seat of a bishopric. Today it is the county town of Hampshire. In 1961 Winchester achieved a special significance in archaeological terms in being the first English town to have a permanent field unit established to carry out both rescue and research projects in and around the city. Headed by Martin Biddle, the Winchester Archaeological Unit has carried out numerous excavations and surveys, and continues to do so.

[Sum.: T. B. James, 1997, *Winchester*. London: Batsford and English Heritage].

Winchester ware [Ar]. Late Saxon (Saxo-Norman) style of earthenware pottery typical of the period AD 850 to 1150 and found widely in southern England and occasionally beyond. The ware is wheel-thrown in a hard sandy fabric usually with a yellowish-red or green-coloured glaze. The range of vessel types includes spouted pitchers, cups, bowls, jars, tripod pitchers, and bottles. The last-mentioned appear to be skeumorphic copies of leather prototypes. Winchester ware is often decorated with lines, rouletting, stamped osettes, cordons, or applied strips.

Winckelmann, Johann Joachim (1717–68) [Bi]. German scholar and antiquarian who made numerous contributions to the integration of archaeology and art history, emphasizing that classical texts were not the only source of information on ancient times. Born in Stendal, Prussia, he attended the local grammar school before a brief period in Berlin and from 1737 he studied theology at the University of Halle. From 1743 he was a private tutor and school teacher until in 1748 he found a position as librarian of the collection of Imperial Count Heinrich von Bünau near Dresden. Fascinated by the library and Dresden, it was here that he developed his interest in the history of art. In 1755 he moved to Rome where he remained for thirteen years, tirelessly searching for new knowledge and working in a variety of libraries. He is best known in archaeological circles for his work on the art of POMPEII and HERCULANEUM.

[Bio.: M. Kunze, 1999, Johann Joachim Winckelmann. In T. Murray (ed.), *Encyclopedia of archaeology I. The Great Archaeologists*. Oxford: ABC-Clio. 51–63]

Windermere Interstadial [Ge]. A warm phase of the DEVENSIAN glaciation in northwest Europe dated to between 12 000 and 9 000 BC. The Windermere Interstadial has been correlated with Godwin's POLLEN ZONE II.

windmill [MC]. An industrial monument in which a set of machinery dedicated to a particular purpose, usually grinding corn, is powered by the motion of a wheel to which a series of sails are attached so that it can be turned by the force of the wind, the machinery itself being housed in some kind of structure around or below the aerially mounted sails. In northern Europe windmills have been recorded from the 12th century AD onwards, and many remain in a form not unlike those common in the Middle Ages. By the 17th century windmills were a common sight in town and countryside. The earliest types were **postmills** where the whole structure revolves around a central wooden post rising from a ground frame comprising two intersecting beams known as cross-trees. These cross-trees were sometimes set in a round mound of earth and stone or rested on brick or stone piers. Above the ground frame was a superstructure containing the machinery that pivoted on the central post so that the whole thing could be turned to move the sails into an optimum position to take full advantage of the wind. From the 14th century **towermills** began to appear (also called smockmills) in which the greater part of the structure was stationary with only the cap at the top, carrying the sails, able to be rotated into the wind. Tower mills were therefore far more substantial, usually of timber on a brick or stone base, but occasionally having the whole tower of brick or stone. Archaeologically, early windmills of both main types are represented by low earth mounds or circular foundations.

Windmiller Culture [CP]. Archaic Stage hunter-gatherer communities living in and around the Sacramento Valley of California, North America, in the period 2300–500 BC. These groups shared an elaborate material culture characterized by ornamented tools and equipment. Most conspicuous are polished charm stones. Burials were accompanied by necklaces, pendants, and other objects. Hunting and fishing were important.

Windmill Hill, Wiltshire, England [Si]. One of the largest causewayed enclosures yet discovered in Britain. It has an area of about 8 ha, and its outer ditch has a diameter of approximately 360 m. The boundary earthworks comprise three roughly concentric rings of interrupted ditches which originally had internal banks. It is notable that the ditches do not lie around the top of the hill, but rather run down the northern slope. Windmill Hill was excavated on several occasions, most notably between 1925 and 1939 by Alexander Keiller, in 1957–8 by Isobel Smith, and in 1988 by Alasdair Whittle.

The earliest occupation dates to about 3800 BC when there was a small unenclosed site in a woodland clearing. It was probably about 3500 BC that the enclosure was built, all three ditch circuits being built at broadly the same time. Within the enclosure ditches there is a considerable quantity of domestic rubbish (pottery, bones, flintworking waste, etc.). There was clear evidence of recutting in the ditches, suggesting that they were periodically cleared out. There were also a number of burials (mostly infants) on the ditch floors, and human bones were found scattered throughout the ditch fills. The enclosure ditches were not redug after about 2500 BC, although debris from later occupation, presumably from a settlement in the vicinity, found its way into the upper silting of the ditches. The purpose of the enclosure has been much debated. Isobel Smith suggested that it was a seasonal rallying point for dispersed farming communities who gathered there for festivals and trade, a view that is widely supported.

[Rep.: A. Whittle, J. Pollard, and C. Grigson, 1999, *The harmony of symbols. The Windmill Hill causewayed enclosure*. Oxford: Oxbow Books]

Windmill Hill Culture [CP]. Middle Neolithic culture defined in 1954 by Stuart Piggott as typical of communities occupying central southern England. Based on the cultural assemblage recovered from the type-site of WINDMILL HILL, the culture was founded upon mixed farming, especially cattle husbandry and the cultivation of wheat and barley. In addition to causewayed enclosures the population built long barrows that also provided repositories for the dead. The pottery was well made and frequently decorated. Trading connections with other parts of the British Isles and near continent were well attested through evidence for exchanges of stone axes and pottery. Radiocarbon testing relating to Windmill Hill Culture sites date them to the period 3600–3000 BC, although the term Windmill Hill Culture itself is now almost obsolete.

Windover, Florida, USA [Si]. Middle Archaic Stage burial ground dating to the period 5000–6000 BC, in a peat bog near Cape Canaveral. The site, which had remarkable preservation because of the waterlogged conditions, was excavated by G. Doran in 1982. The burials were flexed. Seven types of woven textiles, probably of palmetto fibre, have been identified, including blankets, mats, and a bag deposited with the deceased. One twelve-year-old was buried with a range of grave goods including a stone biface, bone awls, a shark's tooth, and barbed bone points. A bottle gourd was recovered from one grave, the earliest example known in North America. Preserved brains were found in over 80 of the bodies; these are currently the subject of detailed investigations and DNA analysis.

[Sum.: R. C. Brown, 1994, *Florida's first people: 12 000 years of human history*. Sarasata: Pineapple Press]

wine [Ge]. Fermented grape juice prepared as an alcoholic drink and of considerable antiquity in the Old World. Grape seeds have been found in archaeological contexts from the LOWER PALAEOLITHIC onwards, although it is uncertain whether these early finds relate to the production of alcoholic drinks or were simply a food source. The earliest certain remains of wine recorded to date is the sediment in an amphora dated to about 3500 BC from Godin Tepe in Iran. Ceramic vessels developed for the storage and consumption of wine appear from Bronze Age times onwards in the eastern and central Mediterranean. The wild vine (*Vitis vinifera sylvestris*) was once widely distributed around the Mediterranean

and between the Black Sea and the Caspian Sea. It was in this last-mentioned area, in Armenia and southern Georgia, for example, that vines were probably first domesticated in the 4th millennium BC (*Vitis vinifera sativa*). Trade in wine developed rapidly from the mid 3rd millennium onwards, and it is the containers used to transport wine (mainly amphorae but later barrels as well) that allow reconstructions of the process to be made from archaeological evidence.

winged chape (wing-shaped chape) [Ar]. A metal cap covering the end of a sword scabbard that has one or more projecting ribs or wings so that a swordsman riding on horseback can hold the scabbard with the heel of his boot while drawing his sword singlehandedly. Winged chapes are especially characteristic of the European later Bronze Age (Hallstatt C) where they are a sure indicator of cavalry warfare.

winged corridor villa [MC]. Style of Roman house in which a corridor or verandah runs along the front of the building giving access to rooms in the main range and linking to a pair of flanking wings, one at either end. Good examples have been excavated in Britain at Great Staughton, Huntingdonshire, and Folkstone, Kent. Additions to the basic plan sometimes mean that winged corridor villas achieve an H-shaped plan, as at Hambleden, Buckinghamshire. Winged corridor villas are not confined to Britain, however, as they are also common in France, Belgium, and Germany.

Wisconsin Stage [Ge]. Final geostratigraphic stage of the Pleistocene in upper North America, dating to the period *c.*75 000 to 8000 BC. Five substages are generally recognized: the **Altonian** (75 000–25 000 BC), with loess sedimentation in a cold climate with some glacial advances; **Farmdalian** (25 000–22 500 BC), cool interstadial; **Woodfordian** (22 500–10 500 BC), with a major glacial advance and retreat in a cold climate; **Twocreekan** (10 500–9800 BC), interstadial with soil formation in a cool climate; **Greatlakean** (9800–8000 BC), with a minor glacial readvance followed by a general warming of the climate. PALAEO-INDIAN remains have been recorded in deposits relating to the last two substages.

Wolstonian Stage [Ge]. A group of deposits representing a geostratigraphic stage within the PLEISTOCENE series of the British QUATER-NARY system, named after the site of Wolston in Warwickshire where a fine sequence of deposits of this period has been recorded. The Wolstonian is usually interpreted as the penultimate cold stage in the Pleistocene sequence represented in the British Isles, broadly spanning the period 200 000 to 125 000 BC. Some Wolstonian deposits have been found stratified above HOXNIAN interglacial deposits and below IPSWICHIAN interglacial deposits. The Wolstonian is broadly equivalent to the RISS in the Alpine sequence and the Illinoisan in North America. ACHEULIAN artefacts have been found in Wolstonian deposits.

wood [MC]. Area of land covered in trees that are maintained as a managed resource for the production of timber, underwood, coppice wood, browsing, and pannage. In medieval Europe woods were an extremely valuable economic resource and their management provided a livelihood for many people. Archaeologically, woods contain many features relating to the economic exploitation of the woodland resources including charcoal-burning platforms, saw pits, internal subdividing banks, boundary works (woodbanks), and trackways.

woodbank [Co]. Earthwork bank with exterior ditch forming the boundary of a wood. The purpose of the woodbank was to keep browsing animals from straying into the wood when not required there, to prevent woodland animals escaping into surrounding agricultural land, and preventing woodland resources being medieval in date. The bank is often characterized by the gnarled vestiges of trees surviving on it.

Woodhenge, Durrington, Wiltshire, England [Si]. Classic late Neolithic class I henge monument constructed about 2500 BC, situated immediately outside DURRINGTON WALLS to the south. The monument comprises an earthwork enclosure 88 m across formed by a bank and internal ditch up to 12 m wide. There is a single entrance to the northeast. The site was fully excavated in 1926–8 under the direction of Maud Cunnington, after being discovered through aerial photography a short while before. Excavations in the interior revealed traces of a circular wooden building represented by six concentric circles

of postholes. The building is very similar to those found inside Durrington Walls, and one possibility is that Woodhenge was a shrine or temple adjacent to a settlement inside the larger henge enclosure. The long axis of the rings of postholes at Woodhenge points to the entrance of the henge enclosure and also aligns with the midsummer rising sun. Also in the interior was a child's grave and a possible stonehole. The finds from the site included quantities of grooved ware pottery. Following excavation, the site was restored for presentation by the then Ministry of Public Building and Works. As such it now represents a monument to early 20th century AD heritage presentation as much as it does an archaeologically meaningful site.

[Rep.: M. E. Cunnington, 1929, *Woodhenge*. Devizes: privately printed]

Woodland [CP]. A general term for cultural groups living in the wooded eastern parts of North America during the FORMATIVE. Woodland subsumes many local adaptations, but in general these were hunter-gatherer communities whose subsistence base was augmented with some cultivation. Woodland communities used pottery and had elaborate toolmaking and artistic traditions. Burials were usually made in established cemeteries, often within large earthen mounds. Trade networks were extensive. Starting about 1000 BC, Woodland comprises a series of distinctive cultures including ADENA, HOPEWELL, MISSISSIPPIAN, and Iroquoian. In some areas Woodland societies continued down to modern times. *See* EARLY WOODLAND, LATE WOODLAND.

Woolley, Sir Charles Leonard (1880–1960) [Bi]. British archaeologist with a background in classics educated at New College, Oxford. In 1905 he became assistant director at the Ashmolean Museum, learning archaeological methods at the Roman site of Corbridge in Northumberland. Later he transferred his interests to the Near and Middle East. Between 1911 and 1914, and again in 1919, he directed excavations on the HITTITE city of Carchemish in Syria, assisted by T. E. Lawrence. During WW1 he served as an intelligence officer before being captured by Turkish forces and spending two years as a prisoner of war. In 1922 he began a twelve-year project as the director of a joint British Museum/University Museum of Pennsylvania expedition to excavate UR and Eridu in southern Mesopotamia. Alongside his detailed technical publications, Woolley also provided popular accounts of his results, recognizing the importance of public relations and the high level of interest in archaeological matters amongst the general public.

[Abio.: 1953, *Spadework in archaeology*. New York: Philosophical Library. Bio.: H. V. Winstone, 1992, *Woolley of Ur, the life of Sir Leonard Woolley*. London: Heinemann]

woolly rhinoceros [Sp]. Large thick-skinned and hairy plant-eating ungulate (*Coelodonta antiquitatis*) with one or more horns on the nose and plated or folded hairy skin that was adapted to cold-climate regions. Now extinct, the species was present in the northern hemisphere during the RISS and WÜRM phases of the PLEISTOCENE, and was hunted by human communities. Woolly rhinos disappeared as part of the MEGAFAUNA EXTINCTION around 10 000 BC.

Wooton-style enclosure [MC]. Defended site of square or rectangular plan, up to 0.5 ha in extent and typical of the later Iron Age (1st–2nd century BC) of the south midlands of England. The defences generally comprise a single bank and ditch, an elaborate gateway, and timber stockades. These small farmsteads contained one or more round houses and four-posted storage structures.

word square [Ar]. *See* ACROSTIC.

workhouse [MC]. In Britain, a house maintained by the parish authorities after the Poor Law Act 1722 or by the Poor Law Union after 1834, in which the poor were housed and set to work where they were capable of it.

working floor [Co]. A scatter of debitage, spent raw material, cores, broken tools, and equipment associated with the production of flint or stone tools forming a definable surface or spread. When fully analysed it is sometimes possible to recognize the places where workers sat and something of the reduction sequences used.

working hollow [Co]. A scoop or artificially created depression in the ground in which one or more crafts were carried out. The scoop acted both to contain the activity itself and to provide a measure of protection from the elements; some working hollows show evidence of superstructures in the form of postholes or stone post-bases.

World Archaeological Congress (WAC) [Or]. An international forum for discussing the study of the past. Founded in 1986 following the repudiation by the existing international conference, the International Union of Prehistoric and Protohistoric Sciences, of a meeting organized in Southampton, UK, WAC is based on the need to recognize the historical and social role and political context of archaeology, and the need to make archaeological studies relevant to the wider community. WAC has particular interests in: education about the past; archaeology and indigenous people; the ethics of archaeological enquiry; the protection of sites and objects; the effect of archaeology on host communities; the ownership, conservation, and exploitation of the archaeological heritage; and the application of new techniques in archaeology. In addition to publishing newsletters, WAC has held a series of international conferences: Southampton, UK (1986); Venezuela (1990); New Delhi, India (1994); Johannesburg, South Africa (1998).

World Council of Indigenous Peoples [Or]. An organization founded in 1975 to represent peoples and communities of the Fourth World. The Council has observer status in the United Nations and a secretariat based in Canada.

World Heritage Convention [Le]. International convention concerning the protection of the world's cultural and natural heritage adopted by the general conference of UNESCO at its meeting in Paris on 16 November 1972. Since then it has been ratified by many states around the world. The aim is to recognize heritage sites of outstanding universal value, inscribe them on the World Heritage List, and thereafter ensure that each state that is party to the convention recognizes and fulfils its duties to protect, preserve, manage, conserve, and present its heritage sites.

world system (world system theory) [Th]. A concept developed by the American historian Immanuel Wallerstein to refer to an economic unit extending beyond the boundaries of an individual nation-state by virtue of trade networks and economic alliances. The example used by Wallerstein was the relationship that developed between Europe and the West Indies in the 16th century AD. As such it emphasizes that 'world systems' do not embrace the whole world, but do operate on a large scale. Implicit to the idea of a world system is the existence of 'core', 'periphery', and 'outer' zones; these distinctions form the basic principles for wider applications of the idea in capitalist and non-capitalist societies. The aim is to analyse the development of particular societies in terms of their position in relation to the full range of contemporary social systems and to ask what the scale of the economic systems within these societies was.

Worsaae, Jens Jacob Asmussen (1821–85) [Bi]. Danish prehistorian born in Jutland who early in life developed an interest in archaeology that later led him to be described as the first professional archaeologist. He studied law at Copenhagen University before assisting C. J. THOMSEN with the arrangement of collections in the National Museum. He was an enthusiastic exponent of the 'Three Age System', deducing support for it from his examinations of stratified and associated assemblages. In 1843, when he was only 22 years old, he published *Danmarks Oldtid oplyst ved Oldsager og Gravhoje* (Copenhagen), which was translated into English and published in 1849 as *The primeval antiquities of Denmark* (Oxford: Parkers). It was one of the first attempts to write a detailed account of the prehistory of a particular region. Worsaae travelled widely in Europe between 1843 and 1848, playing a major role in the adoption of the Three Age System in many countries. In 1846–7 he visited Britain, Ireland, and the Isle of Man studying the remains of Viking occupations. In 1848 he was appointed Inspector-General of Antiquities in Denmark, and in 1855 added to this an attachment to the University of Copenhagen that made him the first academic teacher of prehistory in Scandinavia. He resigned these posts in 1866 to succeed C. J. Thomsen as Director of the National Museum in Copenhagen.

[Bio.: J. Wilkins, 1961, Worsaae and British antiquities. *Antiquity*, 35, 214–220]

Wright, Thomas (1810–77) [Bi]. English antiquary, who spent his life editing medieval manuscripts. While an undergraduate at Cambridge he published *A history of Essex* (1831–6), incorporating archive and archaeo-

logical material. Some of his work has since proved to be hasty and careless, but the range is impressive, including papers and volumes on medieval literature, song, and language, as well as major contributions to Anglo-Saxon studies.

[Bio.: *Dictionary of National Biography*, 21, 1045–48]

wrist clasp [Ar]. Flattened piece of bronze, rectangular or triangular in shape, frequently gilded or inlaid with silver and decorated with animal ornaments. Mainly found in pairs in pagan Saxon graves in eastern England and adjacent areas of the continent. Dating to the 6th to 8th centuries AD, their purpose was to fasten the cuffs on tunics.

wristguard [Ar]. A thin stone plaque which strapped on to the inner forearm of an archer to prevent the arm from being grazed when the bowstring was released. Also known as a bracer. The stone used in making wristguards is generally of fine quality and they have one, two, or three holes at either end for attachment to what was presumed to be a leather strap. Well represented in the BEAKER CULTURE of early Bronze Age Europe.

writing [Ge]. The arrangement of letters or symbols in groups or sequences to express defined and recognized meanings, developed independently in three parts of the world at different times, usually in connection with the elaboration of administrative systems or the recording of ritual/ceremonial matters. Although some early ROCK ART might have employed combinations of symbols to represent meaning, the earliest writing as such is generally taken to be SUMERIAN CUNEIFORM which used an increasing range of phonetic syllable signs during the early 3rd millennium BC. This system developed over the succeeding centuries to form Akkadian, Eblaite, Elamite, Hititte, Hurrian, and Old Persian.

Egyptian hieroglyphic script developed about 3100 BC and changed little down to the Christian era. In India writing was developed in the Indus Valley from about 2500 BC. Finally, in Greece an indigenous hieroglyphic script was initiated in Crete in about 2200 BC, later to develop into Linear A around 1650 BC and Linear B around 1300 BC. The first true alphabet, with signs for individual letters/sounds, seems to have been developed in the Levant soon after 2000 BC, one of the earliest alphabetic inscriptions being from Serabit al-Khadim in Sinai which can be dated to about 1700 BC. The Ugaritic alphabet started with a script of 32 letters, but over succeeding centuries this was modified to a set of 22 letters. Proto-Canaanite script is generally held to be the direct antecedent of the three main alphabetic families: Arabic, Phoenician, and Greek.

A second cradle for the development of writing was in China where there is an uninterrupted literary tradition that can be traced back 3500 years to the pictography of the late SHANG DYNASTY around 1500 BC. The third independent development of writing was in the New World, where during the Late Formative Period of Mesoamerica logosyllabic scripts emerged around 300 BC to form four systems: epi-Olmec, Mayan, Oaxacan, and Izapan.

wrought iron [Ge]. A tough but malleable form of iron that has been beaten out or shaped by hammering rather than cast.

Würm [Ge]. Fourth and final glacial geostratigraphic stage of the PLEISTOCENE sequence represented in the Alps, spanning the period c.110 000–10 000 BC. Equivalent to the DEVENSIAN in the British Isles and the WISCONSIN in North America.

Xerxes [Na]. Ruler of the ACHAEMENID empire in the period 486–465 BC. He is remembered for his savage destruction of BABYLON and for his disastrous attempt to conquer Greece at Salamis in 480 BC.

X-Group [CP]. Post-MEROITIC culture in Lower Nubia dated to the period AD 350–600. Represented archaeologically by settlements such as Qasr Ibrim and cemeteries at Ballana and Qustul.

xoanon [Ar]. A primitive wooden image so unlike marble sculpture that it was supposed to have fallen from heaven and was deeply revered. Such an image of Athena was housed in the Erechtheum on the Athenian Acropolis and dressed in a new robe (peplos) at her great Panathenaic festival every fourth year.

Xochicalco, Mexico [Si]. Early fortified site and ceremonial centre of the late Classic Stage set on one of the string of hills in southern Morelos where it controlled access to the Balsas River basin. The centre of the site was constructed on an artificially levelled and terraced hill. The inhabitants of Xochicalco maintained close links with communities in the basin of Mexico, the Gulf Coast, and Maya Lowlands, and the centre may have been a satellite of Teotihuacán for a while. After the collapse of Teotihuacán, however, Xochicalco seems to have grown in importance.

[Rep.: C. A. Sáenz, 1962, *Xochicako, Temporada, 1960* (= Instituto Nacional al Anthropologia é Historia, Colección Informes 2). Mexico: Instituto Nacional al Anthropologia é Historia]

X-radiography [Te]. An imaging technique used to study the structure and composition of objects or materials. The specimen is placed on a radiosensitive surface, usually a photographic plate or real-time sensor, and then bombarded with short-wavelength high-energy electromagnetic radiation (X-rays). The image is recorded as darker and lighter tones according to the intensity of the X-rays that pass through the different parts of the sample material, the structure and composition of the material differentially absorbing X-rays. X-radiography is extensively used in archaeology to study metal objects, especially iron, where corrosion products mask the form of the original piece and any decoration that may once have been visible. It is also used to examine large objects prior to excavation under laboratory conditions (e.g. cremation urns; mummies), paintings and drawn images that have several layers to them, and human body parts and biological samples.

X-ray diffraction analysis [Te]. Destructive method for determining the mineralogy of crystalline materials such as ceramic, glass, stone, and corrosion products derived from certain kinds of metal. The sample is powdered and mounted either on a glass slide or on a platform to fit within an X-ray camera. Monochromatic X-rays are focused on the sample and the transmitted rays are then recorded using X-ray plates or photographic film. The spacing between crystal lattice planes in different mineral species and the incident angle of the X-ray beam determine the series of X-ray intensities that are transmitted through the sample and onto the recorder. The identification of minerals is based on the spacing between high-spots in the diffraction pattern while relative concentrations can be estimated using the intensity of signal recorded. Sample matching can be done manually or statistically to group similar materials and to relate such groups to potential source materials.

X-ray fluorescence spectrometry (XRF) [Te]. Non-destructive method for determining the elemental composition of natural and man-made materials such as ceramic, glaze, glass, obsidian, pigments, paint, and coins as an aid to determining their source, technology of production, and similarity to other examples of comparable style or form. A sample is exposed to an X-ray source causing it to fluoresce and emit secondary X-rays. The wavelengths of the released energy, known as fluorescent X-rays, are detected and measured as a spectrograph. Component elements can be identified on the basis of the unique wavelength of their fluorescent X-rays, while concentrations can be estimated from the intensity of the released X-rays. Since only the surface of an object is studied, care needs to be taken that corrosion and decay do not affect the analysis.

X-ray microscopy [Te]. *See* SCANNING ELECTRON MICROSCOPY.

X-ray milliprobe analysis [Te]. Specialized form of X-RAY FLUORESCENCE SPECTROMETRY involving the use of an instrument that allows a small and highly focused X-ray beam to be directed at a pre-selected point on the surface of a sample. Secondary X-rays emitted from the target point are directed to a detector and analysed as a spectrograph to reveal the presence and relative concentration of different elements. The great advantage of the technique is its ability to examine very small areas such as individual layers of paint or single minerals within a sample; there is, however, the associated danger that materials are characterized on the basis of unrepresentative samples.

X-ray style [De]. Manner of depicting humans and animals on rock art panels in which the skeleton and internal organs form part of the motif. Especially characteristic of rock art in northern Australia where most of it appears to have been produced over the last 3000 years, although some may be as old as 6000 BC.

XRF [Ab]. *See* X-RAY FLUORESCENCE SPECTROMETRY.

Yadin, Yigael (1917–84) [Bi]. Israeli soldier, archaeologist, and politician. At the age of sixteen he joined Haganah, the defence force raised in Palestine by the Jewish community. Later he commanded Israel's armed forces as acting commandant and, in 1948, was involved with the establishment of the state of Israel. In 1949 he was appointed Chief of the General Staff with the rank of major-general. Preferring archaeology to the military life, he was appointed to the Chair of Archaeology in the Hebrew University in 1963. His excavations included work at Hazor, Megiddo, and Masada. In 1966 he published the popular book *Masada: Herod's fortress and the Zealots' last stand* (London: Weidenfeld and Nicolson). In the early 1970s he entered politics and was eventually elected deputy prime minister, but he did not stand again after 1981.

[Obit.: *Antiquity*, 58 (1984), 169]

yam [Sp]. One of the earliest cultivated plants in southeast Asia, perhaps first domesticated in the northern mainland regions about 3000 BC before spreading to New Guinea and Melanesia. Two main species are represented: *Doscorea alata* and *Doscorea esculenta*. Yams were independently domesticated in tropical Africa and South America.

Yamnaya Culture [CP]. A late Neolithic pastoralist culture dating to 2000–1800 BC of the lower Volga and Don steppelands of Russia, also known as the Pit Grave Culture. Possibly a forebear of the Corded Ware Culture or Kurgan Culture in the area.

Yangshao Culture [CP]. Early Neolithic culture dating to 5000–3000 BC in north-central China, also known as the Painted Pottery Neolithic, named after the type-site of Yangshao in Mianchi Xian, western Henan Province. The agricultural economy was based on millet, complemented by domesticated dogs and pigs. Projectile points suggest that hunting was also practised. Their material culture includes coarse and painted pottery with many regional styles. Markings on some pottery have been interpreted as incipient writing. Some copper and bronze objects have been found associated with Yangshao pottery in the far western extent of the distribution of this culture.

Yanik Tepe, Tabriz, Iran [Si]. Multi-period site northwest of Lake Urmia, extensively excavated by Charles Burney in the 1960s. The earliest layers date to the late 7th millennium BC and were comparable to the Hajji Firuz Phase. These represent some of the earliest permanent settlements in the region. Nine phases were represented, characterized by rectangular houses with plastered floors. The early Bronze Age phases, dating to the later 5th millennium BC, included closely packed circular dwellings equipped with benches and storage bins all set within a stone walled enclosure. Exploration of the Iron Age levels included the initial discovery of painted triangle ware dating to the second quarter of the 1st millennium BC.

[Rep.: C. A. Burney, 1961, Excavations at Yanik Tepe, north-west Iran. *Iraq*, 23, 138–53]

yard [Co]. Open space within, adjacent to, or surrounding a domestic structure or dwelling. Typically wholly or partly paved or surfaced in some way and sometimes provided with drains, a well, and facilities for outdoor domestic activities.

Yarinachoca Phase [CP]. Provisionally defined almost entirely by ceramic styles found in the Rio Ucayali area of Amazonia and tentatively dated to *c*.AD 1–400.

Yasuni Phase [CP]. South American farming cultures found in the Rio Pastaza and Rio

Napo areas of Amazonia and tentatively dated to *c*.100 BC–AD 50. Characterized by their ceramic assemblages which belong to the Incised Rim Horizon Style of Amazonia.

Yayoi [CP]. A proto-historical period in Japanese history, broadly 300 BC to AD 300. The agricultural economy was based on wet-rice cultivation. Sites of the period include mound burials for Yayoi rulers, family burial grounds for others, and moated settlements. Genetically, Yayoi people are thought to be descended from the JOMON, and this link is visible in the succession of pottery styles, although links with other areas are also evident. Bronze and iron were used. Warfare and the degree of social differentiation present increased during the period.

Yeavering, Northumberland, England [Si]. Anglo-Saxon palace and royal centre extensively excavated by Brian Hope-Taylor in the 1950s. A series of foundations representing twenty or so large rectangular timber halls overshadowed by a large timber fort which may have been established by King Edwin in the early 7th century AD. There may also have been a church on the site, but the most extraordinary building was a semi-circular structure interpreted as a kind of grandstand for meetings and assemblies. It may have provided the platform from which Paulinus preached in AD 627.

[Rep.: B. Hope-Taylor, 1977, *Yeavering: an Anglo-British centre of early Northumbria*. London: HMSO]

yoke [Ar]. **1.** A wooden crosspiece fastened over the necks of a pair of oxen or horses. The yoke was connected to a plough, cart, or wagon so that the combined force of the two animals could be evenly distributed. **2.** A U-shaped stone, often elaborately carved, found widely in Mesoamerica, the Caribbean, and northern parts of South America. Believed to be stone imitations of protective belts worn by players in the ball-courts.

York, North Yorkshire, England [Si]. A major Roman fortress, settlement (Eboracum), early medieval ecclesiastical and trading centre of Anglian Northumberland (Eoforwic), a Viking trading centre (Jorvik), headquarters to one of the factions in the Wars of the Roses, and regional capital in medieval and later times.

The first Roman occupation was the construction of a legionary fortress on the north side of the River Ouse by the IXth Legion in AD 71. Built first in wood, during the 2nd century it was rebuilt in stone, the IXth Legion being replaced by the VIth Legion. In the early 3rd century AD a *colonia* was founded on the west bank of the Ouse under the emperor Septimus Severus. Commercial and industrial areas developed, as did cemeteries and suburbs. From the 5th through to the 9th centuries there is relatively little archaeological evidence, but settlement is believed to have continued within and around the former fortress, especially on the high ground between the rivers Ouse and Foss.

Between 850 and 1100 the settlement underwent a major replanning which gave the city a new shape and plan that has largely endured to this day. A thriving trading port was established focused on the river Ouse and its tributary the Foss. Tightly packed rectangular houses and waterfront facilities have been excavated, some of which are reconstructed in the Jorvik Centre in Coppergate. In 1067–8 an impressive Norman castle was built on the hilltop east of the River Ouse. The minster church was founded in AD 627, later to become one of the finest Gothic cathedrals in England. The town was walled, in some areas incorporating the remains of the defences of the former Roman fortress. Much of the medieval fabric of the city remains visible today and a great deal of excavation has taken place in the town, mainly since the formation of the York Archaeological Trust in 1972.

[Sum.: R. Hall, 1996, *York*. London: Batsford and English Heritage]

Yorkshire vase food vessel [Ar]. Distinctive early Bronze Age ceramic vessel found mainly in eastern England in association with inhumation burials. Characterized by coarse fabrics made into thick-walled vessels with flat bases, decoration on the shoulder and rim, and often with perforated lugs. Dates for this style of pottery centre on the period 1800–1400 BC.

York ware [Ar]. Style of wheel-thrown late Saxon pottery current in the period AD 850–1150, one of a series of regional industries of the period making cooking pots, jars, pitchers, flagons, bottles, jugs, bowls, and dishes. York ware is distinctive hard wheel-thrown quartz-gritted fabric, light red to brown or grey in colour.

Younger Dryas Phase [Ge]. A biostratigraphic subdivision of the late DEVENSIAN STAGE in which sub-Arctic conditions prevailed; the most recent of three subdivisions of the North Atlantic cold-climatic phase known as the DRYAS. Godwin's POLLEN ZONE III corresponds with the Younger Dryas in Britain, marked by the development of tundra and park tundra. The Younger Dryas spans the period from c.9000 BC down to c.8000 BC in northern Europe.

Yubetsu [CP]. A late Palaeolithic tradition of obsidian working in Japan dating from c.11 000 BC; also known as the Shirataki technique after the type-site at Shirataki-Hattoridai, Japan. The method of working was used widely from Mongolia to Alaska and involved a bifacial core which was then turned into a wedge-shaped core by flaking off one lateral edge.

yue [Ar]. A kind of stoneware ceramic with a yellowish-brown felspar-rich glaze produced in southeastern China during the HAN Dynasty and T'ANG period in the early centuries of the first millennium AD.

Yue [CP]. An ethnic group occupying the lower Yangtze region of China following its rise to power after the conquest of the Wu in 473 BC. Distinctive artefacts of the Yue are the fine swords of the kings, evidence of highly sophisticated metallurgical skills. The Yue were defeated by the Chu in about 433 BC, although the name lived on to describe the area around Shaoxing in Zhejiang Province.

Zakros, Crete, Greece [Si]. Minoan palace on the east coast of the Aegean island of Crete situated above a fine natural harbour. Extensively excavated by Nikolaos Platon in the late 1960s and early 1970s, the site has blocks of rooms used as living quarters, public areas, and storage facilities around a central court. Unlike many Minoan palaces, Zakros appears not to have been built until the late Minoan period, around 1700 BC. The occupants of the palace were probably involved in long-distance trade. The palace was destroyed by fire about 1450 BC, perhaps as a result of the eruption of Thera on Santorini. Associated with the palace is a terraced town with narrow streets.

[Sum.: N. Platon, 1971, *Zakros: the discovery of a lost palace of ancient Crete*. New York: Scribner]

Zambian Wilton [CP]. A microlithic stoneworking industry found in the drainage basins of the Kafue and Zambezi rivers in Zambia spanning the last 6000 years or so. Similar to the more widely distributed and fully studied Wilton Industry of South Africa.

Zamostje, Moscow Region, Russia [Si]. A series of closely related riverside and lakeside settlements in the upper Volga region discovered in 1987 by V. Sidorov and subsequently explored by Vladimir Lozovski (site 2) and Alexei Sorokin (site 5). The sequence of deposits, up to 5 m thick in places, has seven main units starting in the RESSETA CULTURE of the early HOLOCENE and extending through to the FATYANOVO CULTURE of about 2500 BC. Extensive waterlogging and later peat formation provides exceptionally fine preservation, especially for the Mesolithic (BUTOVO CULTURE) and Neolithic (LIALOVO CULTURE) levels. Until the early third millennium BC the area was occupied by hunter-fisher groups, in the Mesolithic focusing on elk and beaver hunting. Although elk remains prominent during

the Neolithic there is more interest in the exploitation of wild boar and Mustelidae than in earlier times. The rich material culture includes flint and bone projectile points, fishing equipment, and decorated bone and stone. A wooden platform and a possible fishtrap have also been uncovered, both probably of the later Mesolithic.

[Sum.: V. M. Lozovski, 1996, *Zamostje 2: the last prehistoric hunter-fishers of the Russian Plain*. Treignes, Belgium: Editions du Cedarc]

zangentor [De]. Literally 'scissors' or 'tongs-gate'. An entrance arrangement characteristic of later La Tène fortifications in Europe comprising a long entrance passage flanked by timber or stone revetments, across which double gates may be set to impede a direct line of access.

Zapotec [CP]. An early state-organized society flourishing in the highlands of Oaxaca, Mexico, during the Formative and Classic stages from about 200 BC through to AD 1000. Zapotec origins are obscure, but they emerge with Monte Alban as their capital, and distinctive material culture including grey ware pottery, in the period 200 BC to AD 200, and are fully developed by AD 300 when further expansion was hampered by the emergence of Teotihuacán. By AD 950 they have largely abandoned Monte Alban and relocated to other centres such as Mitla and Lambiteyeco. By the late Post-Classic stage the Mixtec had begun to infiltrate Zapotec society and they were later heavily absorbed into the Aztec empire. Only small groups remained in historic times. Zapotec culture includes a distinct language.

Zarzian [CP]. An epipalaeolithic industry dating to between 10 500 and 6000 BC and found at sites in and around the Zagros Mountains of Iran and Iraq. Initially defined in relation to finds from the cave site of Zarzi in northern Iraq, excavated by Dorothy Garrod in 1928, the industry is characterized by notched blades and backed blades.

Zawisza, Count Jan (1820–87) [Bi]. Polish antiquary specializing in research into the Palaeolithic. Between 1873 and 1886 he excavated at the Upper Palaeolithic levels in the Mamutowa Cave on the Kluczwoda River north of Krokow in southern Poland.

[Bio.: Partyka, J, 1992, Ojców i archeologia w latach 1871-1924. *Prądnik*, 6, 71–86]

Zebbuǵ Phase [CP]. A phase of the pre-temple Neolithic on Malta provisionally dated to 4100–3800 BC. The term is derived from a small cemetery at Zebbuǵ where five rock-cut tombs were discovered.

Zeliezovce style [De]. Late regional substyle of linear pottery characterized by angular incised lines relieved by lozenge-shaped incisions. Found mainly in Slovakia, Moravia, and southern Poland. Dates to about 4000 BC.

Zemi [Di]. ARAWAKAN deity recognized in northeastern South America and the Caribbean. Commonly represented on household implements as well as in places of worship such as temples built of organic materials and caves. Visualized in both animal and human form, Zemi is thought to be of Mesoamerican derivation.

Zeuner, Fredrick Everard (1905–63) [Bi]. In 1935 he was appointed Honorary Lecturer at the Institute of Archaeology in London, becoming Professor of Environmental Archaeology there in 1952. He was largely responsible for developing the study of environmental archaeology in the Institute and his personality and achievements as a scholar brought him an international reputation.

[Obit.: *The Times*, 8 November, 1963]

Zhizo [CP]. The local early Iron Age period between the 8th and 10th centuries AD in western Zimbabwe and the Limpopo Valley.

Zhob Culture [CP]. Chalcolithic culture in north Baluchistan, Pakistan, dating to the 4th and 3rd millennia BC. Well represented at Periano Ghundai and Moghul Ghundai. Among the distinctive artefacts is a class of red-on-black painted pottery. Rows of attenuated stylized humped cattle and buck were

popular motifs. Shapes include pedestalled dishes and deep goblets. Goggle-eyed hooded female figurines are especially distinctive of the culture. Bull figurines are also present and suggest connections with the HARAPPAN civilization. Buildings were of mud brick; burials were by cremation. In the succeeding **Incinerary Pot Phase**, cremations were placed in vessels under the floors of houses.

Zhou Dynasty [CP]. An ethnic group which established itself as a major Chinese dynasty after overthrowing the Shang Dynasty in about 1027 BC. Once established, the Zhou Dynasty was the longest lasting in Chinese history, surviving down to 256 BC. The dynasty is traditionally divided into two major phases, the Western or Royal Zhou (1027–771 BC) and the Eastern Zhou (770–221 BC). During the Zhou Dynasty many of the numerous small states which characterized China in the first millennium BC were united and organized into successively stronger groupings. Originally a pastoralist people, the Zhou kingdom was organized on a feudal basis. During the Eastern Zhou royal power declined and there was a concomitant growth in the feudal fiefs, some becoming quasi-independent kingdoms. Major developments during Zhou times included the discovery of iron-working, the introduction of coinage, the construction of defensive works that would later form part of the Great Wall of China, and the institution of tiered administration. The Zhou Dynasty was eventually conquered by its rivals, the state of Qin, in about 220 BC.

Zhoukoudian, China [Si]. Cave site on a steep hillside southwest of Beijing where numerous fossil hominid remains have been found. In ancient times the cave would have been overlooking the sea; more recently it is in an area of limestone mining. Initial excavations in the late 1920s by Davidson Black revealed thirteen main horizons within the cave, the investigation of which was continued by Franz Weidenrich, Black's successor, in the period 1935–7. In the lower levels more than 40 examples of HOMO ERECTUS, locally known as 'Peking Man', were discovered and reported. They date to about 300 000 BC. However, in 1941, when the Japanese were about to attack Beijing, the fossils disappeared after being packed for shipment to the USA. They have never been found, but more recent excavations by Woo Ju-Kang have found more early human remains together with stone tools and traces of the use of fire. In the upper levels there are skeletal remains of HOMO SAPIENS dated to about 25 000 BC.

[Rep.: L. Jia and W. Huang, 1984, *Excavations at Zhoukoudian 1984*. Tiagin: Tiagin Publications of Science and Technology]

ziggurat [MC]. Literally, the 'high point'. A temple-tower with a square or rectangular ground-plan and a stepped profile built as a series of superimposed platforms. There are sometimes steps for access up one or more sides. Mainly found in Mesopotamia (especially Sumerian, Babylonian, and Assyrian sites) and Mesoamerica. The platform on the top usually supports a building or temple dedicated to a particular deity.

zimbabwe [MC]. A court or house of a chief which comprises a series of walled enclosures built on top of a hill. The most famous is the GREAT ZIMBABWE which lends its name to the modern nation-state of Zimbabwe.

zinc [Ma]. White metallic element (Zn) occurring naturally as zinc blende used as a component of brass (together with copper) and for coating iron. Zinc was not extensively exploited until the 12th century AD in India and the 15th century AD in Europe. Although brass was used for making coinage from Roman times the zinc content is believed to derive from indirect sources.

Zinjanthropus [Sp]. The name given by Professor Louis Leakey to the fossil skull of an early hominid found in Bed I at OLDUVAI GORGE, Tanzania, in July 1959. Dated to the Lower Pleistocene, about 1.75 million years ago, the skull is that of a robust Australopithecine. At one time the Zinjanthropus skull was nicknamed 'Nutcracker Man' because of the large size of the teeth.

Złota Culture [CP]. Late Neolithic communities forming part of the GLOBULAR AMPHORAE CULTURE in the period 3200–2800 BC, occupying sites along the Vistula River in southeast Poland. Named after a cemetery site at Złota, Sandomierz, Poland, the Złota culture shares many traits with other nearby groups, especially the Baden Culture. Pottery includes corded ware, globular amphorae, and cups with upturned handles. Copper and amber or-

naments were used. The dead were buried laid in a contracted position on stone pavements in cist graves. The houses are square in plan, made of wattle and daub. The subsistence economy was farming, but Złota communities also exploited flint seams in the region by digging FLINT MINES.

zone [Ge]. A more or less precisely defined spatial region within a site, town, or landscape, the area of which shares certain characteristics.

zone of visual intrusion (ZVI) [Ge]. The area around a building, road, or some other construction or feature from which it can be seen by anyone standing at ground level. The ZVI can be changed by the introduction of screening through tree planting or mounding up banks of earth.

zong [Ar]. A tubular jade object with a square cross-section and a circular hollow in the centre. Found in Liangzhu, Shang, and Zhou culture contexts of Neolithic China. Sometimes decorated with t'ao t'ieh motifs perhaps representing a mythical animal figure. The purpose and symbolic significance of zongs are unknown.

zooarchaeology. *See* ARCHAEOZOOLOGY.

zoomorphic [De]. Based on the appearance or characteristics of an animal. In art this is usually some kind of depiction or three-dimensional representation, perhaps in stylized form, of the whole or part of one or more animals. The term can also apply to the attribution of animal form or nature to something else, for example a deity or supernatural being.

zoomorphic brooch [Ar]. A fastener for clothes which includes the representation of animal forms in its design or decoration.

zophorus [De]. The frieze of an entablature.

Zoser [Na]. King of Egypt during the Old Kingdom (3rd Dynasty). Well known for his stepped pyramid at Saqqara near Memphis in Lower Egypt, one of the earliest pyramids to be built as a royal tomb, and attributed to the architect Imhotep.

Zozimus [Na]. Greek historian living in the early 6th century AD who wrote a history of the last days of the western Roman empire, *Nea Historia*, which is especially important for understanding the collapse of Roman administration in Britain. However, living and working in Greece, Zozimus drew heavily on other works, particularly the twenty-volume *History* of Olympiodorus, an Egyptian Greek, who provided extensive commentary on late Roman times. Zozimus' own work is generally regarded as rather unreliable.

Zvejnieki, Latvia [Si]. Late Mesolithic and Neolithic cemetery on the northern shore of Lake Burtnieki discovered and excavated by Francis Zagorskis between 1964 and 1971. The site was found to comprise at least 304 graves. A broadly contemporary settlement is known nearby. The site had good preservation of organic materials and grave goods which allow the burials to be divided into two broad groups. The oldest were sprinkled with OCHRE and belong to the 5th and 4th millennia BC. The later group lacked ochre and date to the 3rd millennium BC. Grave goods included perforated elk-teeth pendants, amber pendants, and bone points.

[Rep.: F. Zagorskis, 1987, *Zvejnieku akens laikmeta kapulauks*. Riga: Zinatne]

ZVI [Ab]. *See* ZONE OF VISUAL INTRUSION.

Quick Reference Section

Principal international conventions and recommendations concerning the preservation of archaeological and historic sites and artefacts

Council of Europe, 1969, *European convention on the protection of the archaeological heritage.* London, 6 June 1969 (superseded by CoE, 1992)

Council of Europe, 1985, *Convention for the protection of the architectural heritage of Europe.* Granada, 3 October 1985

Council of Europe, 1989, *Recommendation of the Committee of Ministers to member states on the protection and enhancement of the rural architectural heritage.* Strasbourg, 13 April 1989. R(89)6

Council of Europe, 1990, *Recommendation of the Committee of Ministers to member states on the protection and conservation of the industrial, technical and civil engineering heritage in Europe.* Strasbourg, 13 September 1990. R(90)20

Council of Europe, 1991, *Recommendation of the Committee of Ministers to member states on measures likely to promote the funding of the conservation of the architectural heritage.* Strasbourg, 11 April 1991. R(91)6

Council of Europe, 1991, *Recommendation of the Committee of Ministers to member states on the protection of the twentieth century architectural heritage.* Strasbourg, 13 September 1991. R(91)13

Council of Europe, 1992, *European convention on the protection of the archaeological heritage.* Valletta, 16 January 1992

Council of Europe, 1993, *Draft recommendation to member states on the conservation and management of cultural landscape areas as part of landscape policies.* Strasbourg, September 1993

EC, 1985, *Directive on the assessment of the effects of certain public and private projects on the environment.* Brussels, 27 June 1985. 85/337/EEC

ICAHM, 1988, *Charter for the protection and management of the archaeological heritage.* Stockholm, September 1988

UNESCO, 1954, *Convention for the protection of cultural property in the event of armed conflict (the Hague Convention), with regulations for the execution of the convention as well as the protocols to the convention and the conference resolutions,* 14 May 1954. Paris

UNESCO, 1956, *Recommendation on international principles applicable to archaeological excavations,* 5 December 1956. Paris

UNESCO, 1960, *Recommendation concerning the most effective means of rendering museums accessible to everyone,* 14 December 1960. Paris

UNESCO, 1962, *Recommendation concerning the safeguarding of the beauty and character of landscapes and sites,* 11 December 1962. Paris

UNESCO, 1964, *Recommendation on the means of prohibiting and preventing the illicit export, import and transfer of ownership of cultural property,* 19 November 1964. Paris

UNESCO, 1968, *Recommendation concerning the preservation of cultural property endangered by public or private works,* 19 November 1968. Paris

UNESCO, 1970, *Convention on the means of prohibiting and preventing the illicit import, export, and transfer of ownership of cultural property,* 14 November 1970. Paris

UNESCO, 1972, *Convention concerning the protection of the world cultural and natural heritage,* 16 November 1972. Paris

UNESCO, 1972, *Recommendation concerning the protection, at national level, of the cultural and natural heritage,* 16 November 1972. Paris

UNESCO, 1976, *Recommendation concerning the international exchange of cultural property,* 26 November 1976. Paris

UNESCO, 1976, *Recommendation concerning the safeguarding and contemporary role of historic areas,* 26 November 1976. Paris

UNESCO, 1978, *Recommendation for the protection of movable cultural property,* 28 November 1978. Paris

World Archaeological Congress, 1989, *The Vermillion accord on human remains.* Vermillion, South Dakota, USA

QR2

Principal stratigraphic subdivisions of the Cenozoic era

Era	System (Period)	Series (Epoch)	Age
Cenozoic	Quaternary	Holocene	10 ky–present
		Pleistocene	2 my–10 ky
	Tertiary	Pliocene	7 my–2 my
		Miocene	26 my–7 my
		Oligocene	38 my–26 my
		Eocene	54 my–38 my
		Palaeocene	65 my–54 my

ky = thousand years ago
my = million years ago

Principal stratigraphic subdivisions of the Quaternary system in northwest Europe

System (Period)	Series (Epoch)	Geostrati-graphic stage	Age	Archaeologi-cal period	Cultural period
Quaternary	Holocene	Flandrian	10 ky–present	(see QR4)	(see QR4)
	Pleistocene	Devensian	120 ky–10 ky	Upper Palaeolithic	LUP / EUP / MOUSTERIAN
				Middle Palaeolithic	MOUSTERIAN
		Ipswichian	170 ky–120 ky		
		Wolstonian	200 ky–170 ky	Lower Palaeolithic	ACHEULIAN
		Hoxnian	300 ky–200 ky		
		Anglian	450 ky–300 ky		
		Cromerian	700 ky–450 ky		
			>700 ky		

LUP = Later upper Palaeolithic
EUP = Earlier upper Palaeolithic
Shaded geostratigraphic stages signify glacial phases

QR4

Principal geostratigraphic and biostratigraphic subdivisions of the late Devensian and Flandrian stages in the British Isles

	Series (Epoch)	Geostratigraphic stage	Biostratigraphic division or climatic phase	Pollen zone	Archaeological period
Post glacial	HOLOCENE	FLANDRIAN	Sub-Atlantic	IX	Roman and historic times
					Iron Age
			Sub-Boreal	VIII	Bronze Age
					Neolithic
			Atlantic	VII	
			Boreal	VI	Mesolithic
				V	
Late glacial	PLEISTOCENE	DEVENSIAN	Pre-Boreal	IV	Later Upper Palaeolithic
			Younger Dryas	III	
			Allerød Oscillation	II	
			Older Dryas	Ic	
			Bølling Oscillation	Ib	
			Oldest Dryas	Ia	

Shaded biostratigraphic divisions signify cold phases

Correlation of the principal geostratigraphic stages of the Pleistocene series on Europe and North America

Phase/age	North America	Northern Europe	Britain	Alps
Post-glacial 10 ky to present			Flandrian	
Last glaciation 120 ky–10 ky	Wisconsin	Weichselian	Devensian	Würm
Last interglacial 170 ky–120 ky	Sangamon	Eemain	Ipswichian	Riss-Würm
Penultimate glaciation 200 ky–170 ky	Illinoian	Warthe	Wolstonian	Riss
		Saalian		
Great interglacial 300 ky–200 ky	Yarmouth	Holstein	Hoxnian	Mindel-Riss
Glacial 450 ky–300 ky	Kansan	Elster	Anglian	Mindel
Interglacial 700 ky–450 ky	Aftonian		Cromerian	Günz-Mindel
Early glaciation 700 ky+	Nebraskan			Günz

ky = thousand years ago
Shaded subdivisions signify glacial or cold stages

QR6

Principal periods, industrial stages, and traditions of the British Bronze Age
(Based on C. Burgess, 1980, *The age of Stonehenge* (London: Dent) with additions from various other sources)

Meldon Bridge Period (3000–2750 BC)

> *Metalworking Stage I*—Castletown Roche industries (copper)
> *Metalworking Stage II*—Knocknague/Lough Ravel industries (copper)

Mount Pleasant Period (2750–2000 BC)

> *Metalworking Stage III*—Frankford industries (copper)
> *Metalworking Stage IV*—Migdale–Marnoch/Migdale–Killaha industries (copper, bronze, gold) (links to early Únětice/Reinecke A1 on the continent)
> *Metalworking Stage V*—Ballyvalley–Aylesford industries

Overton Period (2000–1650 BC)

> *Metalworking Stage VI*—Falkland industries. Wessex I: Armorico-British dagger series (Bush Barrow daggers) (influences from classic Únětice/Reinecke A2 metalwork on the continent)

Bedd Branwen Period (1650–1400 BC)

> *Metalworking Stage VII*—Arreton Down industries in southern Britain; Inch Island industries in Ireland; Ebnal industries in Wales and the Marches; Gavel Moss industries in Scotland. Wessex II: Snowshill–Camerton daggers (links to Reinecke A2/B1 or A3 on the continent)
> *Metalworking Stage VIII*—Acton Park industries in England; Killymaddy industry in Ireland; Caverton industries in the Scottish borders; Auchterhouse industries in Scotland (links to the European Tumulus Culture/Reinecke B1)

Knighton Heath Period (1400–1200 BC)

> *Metalworking Stage IX*—Taunton industries in southern England; Barton–Bendish industries in eastern England; Glentrool industries in Scotland; Bishopsland industries in Ireland. The ornament horizon (links to Frøjk-Ostenfeld Group of Montelius IIb-c in northern Europe, Tumulus Culture C stage in central Europe)

Penard Period (1200–1000 BC)

> *Metalworking Stage X*—Penard industries throughout the British Isles (links to the early Urnfield Cultures on the continent; Montelius III; Rosnoën in northern France; Hallstatt A1/A2)

Wilburton—Wallington Phase (1000–800 BC)

> *Metalworking Stage XI*—Wilburton and Wallington industries in England; the Poldar industries in Scotland; Roscommon industries in Ireland. This period sees the extensive use of lead-bronze (links to Hallstatt A2)

Ewart Park Phase (800–700 BC)

> *Metaworking Stage XII*—Carp's tongue/Bexley Heath industries in southeastern England; the Llantwit-Stogursey industries in the west of England and southeast Wales; the Broadward industries of the Welsh Marches; Heathery Burn industries in northern England; Duddington, Covesea, and Ballimore industries in Scotland; and the Dowris industries in Ireland (links to late Urnfield Culture and Hallstatt early C on the continent)

Llyn-Fawr Phase (700–600 BC)

> *Metalworking Stage XIII*—Widespread metalworking industries with little evidence of regional diversity; during this period iron begins to be worked (major links to Hallstatt C and Hallstatt D on the continent)

Principal cultural phases in the Americas

The following charts show the approximate duration of the main stages, traditions, and cultures recognized in the archaeology of the Americas from about 10 000 BC down to the present day. It should be noted that the earliest stages and cultures represented extend back well beyond 10 000 BC, although the full antiquity of human occupation in the Americas is not yet established.

For the purposes of presentation, the area is divided into two blocks, North and Mesoamerica, and South America.

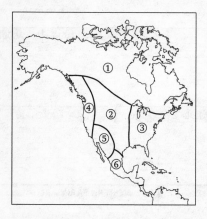

North America and Mesoamerica is subdivided into six regions as shown on the above map:

1. Arctic areas (including Alaska, Canada, and the islands off the north coast of Canada)

2. The Great Plains of central and western parts of the USA

3. The Eastern Woodland region of the USA east of the Mississippi

4. The west coast of the USA and western Canada

5. The southwest of the USA and northern Mexico

6. Mesoamerica: including southern Mexico, Belize, Guatemala, El Salvador, Honduras, and part of Nicaragua

South America is subdivided into five regions as shown on the above map:

1. Central America, including Costa Rica and Panama

2. The Caribbean

3. The Andes and the west coast, including Colombia, Ecuador, Peru, and Bolivia

4. Amazonia and the east coast, including Venezuela and Brazil

5. The far south, including Chile and Argentina

NORTH AMERICA and MESOAMERICA

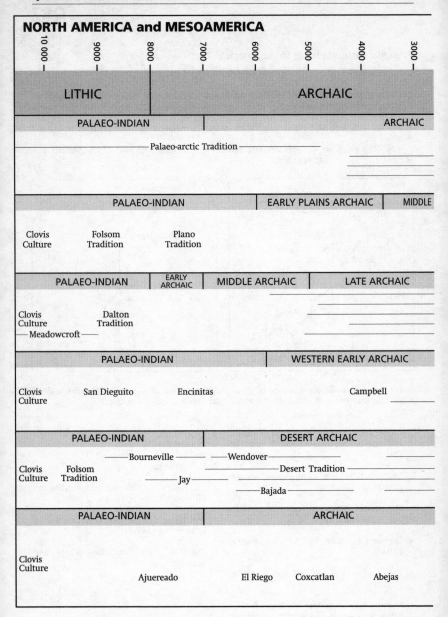

10 000	9000	8000	7000	6000	5000	4000	3000

| LITHIC | | ARCHAIC | | | | | |

| PALAEO-INDIAN | | | ARCHAIC | | | | |

————————— Palaeo-arctic Tradition —————————

| PALAEO-INDIAN | | EARLY PLAINS ARCHAIC | | MIDDLE |

Clovis Culture   Folsom Tradition   Plano Tradition

| PALAEO-INDIAN | EARLY ARCHAIC | MIDDLE ARCHAIC | LATE ARCHAIC |

Clovis Culture   Dalton Tradition
—— Meadowcroft ——

| PALAEO-INDIAN | WESTERN EARLY ARCHAIC |

Clovis Culture   San Dieguito   Encinitas   Campbell

| PALAEO-INDIAN | DESERT ARCHAIC |

————— Bourneville ————— ——— Wendover —————
————————————— Desert Tradition —————————————
Clovis Culture   Folsom Tradition   ——— Jay ———
————— Bajada —————

| PALAEO-INDIAN | ARCHAIC |

Clovis Culture

Ajuereado   El Riego   Coxcatlan   Abejas

APPROX. DATE	2000 BC	1000 BC	AD	500	1000	1500	Region
Willey & Phillips 1958		FORMATIVE			CLASSIC	POST-CLASSIC	

ARCTIC

MODERN

— Norton —
— Pre-Dorset — — Dorset —
— Arctic Small Tool Tradition — — Thule —
— Ocean Bay Tradition — — Birnirk —
— Kodiak Tradition — — Punuk —
— Old Bering Sea —

PLAINS

| PLAINS ARCHAIC | LATE PLAINS ARCHAIC | LATE PREHISTORIC | | PROTO-HISTORIC |

Woodland   Village

EASTERN WOODLANDS

| EARLY WOODLAND | MIDDLE WOODLAND | LATE WOODLAND |

— Shield Archaic —
— Maritime Archaic —
— Lake Forest Archaic —
— Mast Forest Archaic — — Weeden Island Culture —
— Central Riverine Archaic — Adena — — Mississippian —
— Poverty Point Culture — HopeWellian —

WEST COAST

| WESTERN MIDDLE ARCHAIC | WESTERN LATE ARCHAIC |

— Berkeley — — Hotchkiss —
— Windmiller — — Augustine —

SOUTH WEST

| BASKETMAKER | PUEBLO |

— Basketmaker I & II — — Basketmaker III — — Pueblo I —
— Pueblo II —
— Picosa Culture — — Anasazi —
— Cochise — — Hohokam — — Mogollon —
— Mimbres —

MESOAMERICA

| EARLY | PRE-CLASSIC MIDDLE | LATE | CLASSIC EARLY LATE TERMINAL | POST-CLASSIC EARLY LATE | MODERN |

— Pre-classic Maya — Classic Maya — Maya —
— Olmec —
— Zapotec —
Purron
— Toltec — — Aztec —
— Mixtec —

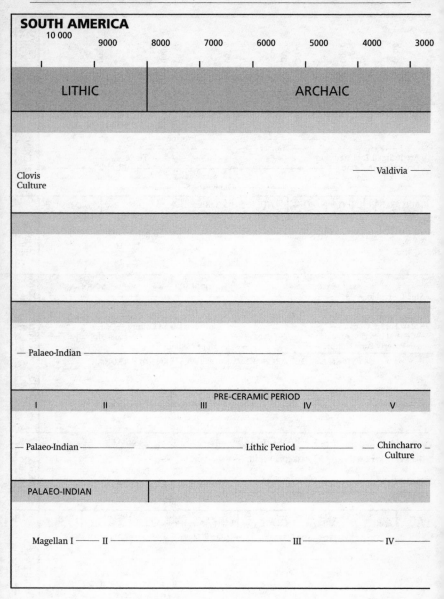

SOUTH AMERICA

| 10 000 | 9000 | 8000 | 7000 | 6000 | 5000 | 4000 | 3000 |

LITHIC | ARCHAIC

Clovis
Culture

— Valdivia —

— Palaeo-Indian ———————————————

PRE-CERAMIC PERIOD

| I | II | III | IV | V |

— Palaeo-Indian ——————— | ——————— Lithic Period ——————— | — Chincharro —
Culture

PALAEO-INDIAN

Magellan I ——— II ————————————— III ————————— IV———

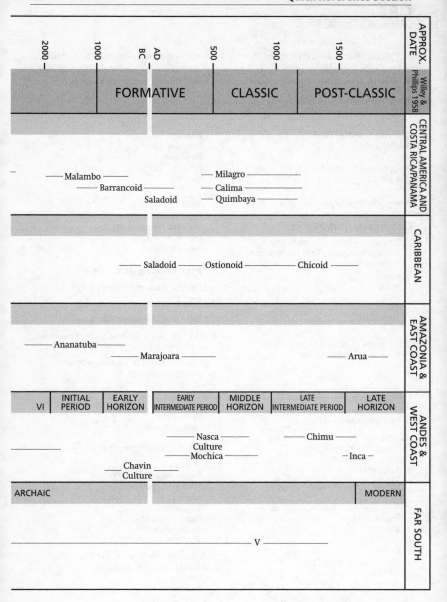

APPROX. DATE

2000 — 1000 — BC AD — 500 — 1000 — 1500 —

Willey & Phillips 1958

FORMATIVE   CLASSIC   POST-CLASSIC

CENTRAL AMERICA AND COSTA RICA/PANAMA

— Malambo —   — Milagro —
— Barrancoid —   — Calima —
Saladoid   — Quimbaya —

CARIBBEAN

— Saladoid — Ostionoid — Chicoid —

AMAZONIA & EAST COAST

— Ananatuba —
— Marajoara —   — Arua —

ANDES & WEST COAST

VI	INITIAL PERIOD	EARLY HORIZON	EARLY INTERMEDIATE PERIOD	MIDDLE HORIZON	LATE INTERMEDIATE PERIOD	LATE HORIZON

— Nasca —   — Chimu —
Culture
Mochica —   — Inca —
___ Chavin ___
Culture

FAR SOUTH

ARCHAIC   MODERN

— V —

QR8

Egyptian rulers and dynasties (Based on various sources, including: A. Siliotti, 1996, *Guide to the Valley of the Kings* (Luxor: Gaddis) and J. Baines and J. Malek, 2000, *Cultural atlas of ancient Egypt* (revised edition, New York: Checkmark Books).)

Badarian Culture—Neolithic culture (4500–3250 BC)

Predynastic—Nagada I and II/Amratian Culture (3250–2850 BC)

Proto-dynastic—Nagada III (2850–2789 BC)

Early dynastic (2789–2658 BC)

1st Dynasty—8+ monarchs including:
  Menes/Meni/Aha? (first king to achieve unification)
  Djer
  Wadj
  Den
  Adjib
  Semerkhet
  Qa'a

2nd Dynasty—10 monarchs including:
  Hetepsekhemwy
  Re'neb
  Ninetjer
  Peribsen
  Kha'sekhem

Old Kingdom (2658–2150 BC)

3rd Dynasty—5+ monarchs including:
  Zanakht (= Nebka)
  Djoser (Netjerykhet)
  Sekhemkhet
  Kha'ba
  Huni

4th Dynasty—?8 monarchs including:
  Snofru
  Khufu/Cheops
  Ra'djedef
  Dedefre
  Khephren (Ra'kha'ef)
  Menkaure (Mycerinus)
  Shepseskaf

5th Dynasty—?9 monarchs including:
  Userkaf
  Sahure
  Neferirkare' Kakai
  Shepseskare' Ini

Ra'neferef
Niuserre' Izi
Menkauhor
Djedkare' Izezi
Wenis

6th Dynasty
  Teti I
  Pepi I (Meryre)
  Merenre' Nemtyemzaf
  Pepi II (Neferkare)
  ?Queen Nitokris

First Intermediate (2150–2100 BC)

7th Dynasty—numerous minor kings

8th Dynasty—numerous minor kings

9th Dynasty—numerous minor kings

10th Dynasty (based in Nennisut)—19 monarchs, contemporary with the 9th Dynasty

11th Dynasty (based in Thebes)—6 monarchs
  Inyotef I (Sehertawy)
  Inyotef II (Wah1ankh)
  Inyotef III
  Nakhtnebtepnufer
  Nebhepetre
  Mentuhoteo II

Middle Kingdom (2100–1750 BC)

12th Dynasty
  Amenemhet I (Sehetepibre)
  Senuseret I (Kheperkare)
  Amenemhat II (Nubkaure')
  Senuseret II
  Amenemhat III
  Amenemhat IV
  Sebeknefru

13th Dynasty—70+ kings, some coeval with other dynasties, including:
  Wegaf
  Amenemhet V
  Harnedjheriotef
  Amenyqemau
  Sebekhotpe I
  Hor
  Amenemhet VII

Sebekhotpe II
Khendjer
Sebekhotpe III
Neferhotep I
Sebekhopte IV
Sebekhopte V
Aye
Mentuemzaf
Dedumose II
Neferhotep III

Second Intermediate (1750–1500 BC)

14th Dynasty—minor group of kings contemporary with 13th or 15th Dynasty

15th Dynasty—Hyksos rulers
Salitis
Sheshi
Khian
Apophis
Khamudi

16th Dynasty—minor Hyksos rulers coeval with other dynasties

17th Dynasty—numerous Theban kings, including:
Invotef V (1640–1550 BC)
Sebekemzaf I
Nebireyeraw
Sebekamzaf II
Taʿo I
Taʿo II
Kamose (1555–1550 BC)

New Kingdom (1550–1070 BC)

18th Dynasty
Ahmosis (1550–1525 BC)
Amenophis I (1525–1504 BC)
Thutmosis I (1504–1492 BC)
Thutmosis II (1492–1479 BC)
Hatshepsut (1479–1457 BC)
Thutmosis III (1479–1425 BC)
Amenophis II (1427–1397 BC)
Thutmosis IV (1397–1387 BC)
Amenophis III (1387–1349 BC)
Akhenaten—Amenophis IV (1349–1333 BC)
Smenkhare (1335–1333 BC)
Tutankhamen (1333–1323 BC)
Aya (1323–1319 BC)
Haremheb (1319–1307 BC)

19th Dynasty
Ramesses I (1307–1306 BC)
Sethos I (1306–1290 BC)
Ramesses II (1290–1224 BC)
Merneptah (1224–1214 BC)
Sethos II (1212–1204 BC)
Amenemesses (usurper during the reign of Sthos II)

Siptah (1204–1198 BC)
Twosret (1198–1196 BC)

20th Dynasty
Setenakhte (1196–1194 BC)
Ramesses III (1194–1163 BC)
Ramesses IV (1163–1156 BC)
Ramesses V (1156–1151 BC)
Ramesses VI (1151–1143 BC)
Ramesses VII (1143–1136 BC)
Ramesses VIII (1136–1131 BC)
Ramesses IX (1131–1112 BC)
Ramesses X (1112–1100 BC)
Ramesses XI (1100–1070 BC)

Third Intermediate (1070–712 BC)

21st Dynasty
Smendes (1070–1044 BC)
Amenemnisu (1044–1040 BC)
Psusennes (1040–992 BC)
Amenemope (993–984 BC)
Osorkon I (984–978 BC)
Siamun (978–959 BC)
Psusennes II (959–945 BC)

22nd Dynasty
Shoshenq I (945–712 BC)
Osorkon II (924–909 BC)
Takelot I (909 BC)
Shoshenq II (909–883 BC)
Osorkon III (883–855 BC)
Takelot II (860–835 BC)
Shoshenq III (835–783 BC)
Pami (783–773 BC)
Shoshenq V (773–735 BC)
Osorkon V (735–712 BC)

23rd Dynasty—various lines of kings recognized in Thebes, Hermopolis, Herakleopolis, Leontopolis, and Tanis, including:
Pedubaste I (828–803 BC)
Osorkon IV (777–749 BC)
Peftjauʿawybast (740–725 BC)

Late Dynastic (712–332 BC)

24th Dynasty—Sais
Tefnakhte (724–717 BC)
Bocchoris (717–712 BC)

25th Dynasty
Kashta (770–750 BC)
Piye (750–712 BC)
Shabaka (712–698 BC)
Shebitku (698–690 BC)
Taharqa (690–664 BC)
Tantamani (664–657 BC)

26th Dynasty
Necho I (672–664 BC)
Psammetichus I (664–610 BC)

Necho II (610–595 BC)
Psammetichus II (595–589 BC)
Apries (589–570 BC)
Amasis (570–526 BC)
Psammetichus (526–525 BC)

27th Dynasty—Persian period
Cambyses (525–522 BC)
Darius (521–486 BC)
Xerxes I (486–466 BC)
Artaxerxes I (465–424 BC)
Darius II (424–404 BC)

28th Dynasty
Amyrtaios (404–399 BC)

29th Dynasty
Nepherites I (399–393 BC)
Psmmuthis (393 BC)
Hakoris (393–380 BC)
Nepherites II (380 BC)

30th Dynasty
Nectanebo I (380–362 BC)
Teos (365–360 BC)
Nectanebo (360–343 BC)

31st Dynasty—second Persian period
Artaxerxes III Ochus (343–338 BC)
Arses (338–336 BC)
Darius III Codoman (335–332 BC)

Graeco-Roman period (332 BC–AD 395)

Macedonian Dynasty
Alexander III, the Great (332–304 BC)
Philip Arrhidaeus (323–316 BC)
Alexander IV (316–304 BC)

Ptolemaic Dynasty (304–30 BC)

Roman period (30 BC–AD 395)

Roman emperors (Based on Appendix II in P. Salway, 1981, *Roman Britain*. Oxford: OUP and other sources)

Julio-Claudians
Augustus (Octavian) 27 BC–AD 14 (sole ruler from 30 BC)
Tiberius 14–37
Gaius (Caligula) 37–41
Claudius 41–54
Nero 54–68
Galba 68–9
Otho 69
Vitellius 69–70

Flavians
Vespasian 69–79
Titus 79–81
Domitian 81–96
Nerva 96–8
Trajan 98–117
Hadrian 117–38

Antonines
Antoninus Pius 138–61
Marcus Aurelius 161–80
Lucius Verus 161–9 (with M. Aurelius)
Commodus 180–92
Pertinax 193
Didius Julianus 193

Severan House and its rivals
Septimius Severus 193–211
Clodius Albinus 193–7
Pescennius Niger 193–4
Caracalla 211–17
Geta 211–12
Macrinus 217–18
Elagabalus 218–22
Severus Alexander 222–35
Maximinus (Thrax) 235–8
Pupienus 238
Balbinus 238
Gordian I 238
Gordian II 238
Gordian III 238–44
Philip I (the Arab) 244–9
Philip II 244–9
Uranius 248–53
Pacatianus 248
Jotapianus 249
Decius 249–51
Herennius Etruscus 250–1
Hostilianus 250–1
Gallus 251–3
Volusianus 251–3

Aemilianus 253
Valerian 253–9/60
Gallienus 253–68
Macrianus 260
Regalianus 261
Aureolus 267–8
Laelianus 268
Marius 268

Gallic emperors
Postumus 260–9
Victorinus 269–71
Tetricus 271–3
Claudius II (Gothicus) 268–70
Quintillius 270
Aurelian 270–5
Domitian II uncertain
Vaballathus 270–1
Tacitus 275–6
Florianus 276
Probus 276–82
Saturninus 280
Carus 282–3
Julianus 283
Carinus 283–5
Numerian 283–4

The Tetrarchy
Diocletian 284–305
Maximian 286–305, 307–8
Constantius I (Chlorus) 305–6 (Caesar 293–305)
Galerius 305–11 (Caesar 293–305)
Carausius 287–93
Allectus 293–6 (Britain)
Achilles 296
Flavius Severus 306–7
Maximin Daia 310–13
Maxentius 307–12
Alexander 308–11
Licinius 308–24

House of Constantine
Constantine I (Constantine the Great) 306–37
Valens 314
Martinianus 323
Constantine II 337–40
Constans 337–50
Constantius II 337–61
Nepotianus 350
Vetranio 350

Magnentius 350–3
Claudius Silvanus 355
Juilian (the Apostate) 360–3 (Caesar 355–60)
Jovian 363–4

House of Valentinian
Valentinian I 364–75
Valens 364–78
Gratian 375–83
Procopius 365–6
Valentinian II 375–92
Magnus Maximus 383–8
Flavius Victor 384–8
Eugenius 392–4

House of Theodosius
Theodosius I (Theodosius the Great) 379–95

Western emperors
Honorius 395–424
Marcus 406 ? (in Britain)
Gratian 407 (in Britain)
Constantine III 407–11
Maximus 409–11
Jovinus 411–12

Constantius III (Flavius Constantius 421)
John (Johannes) 423–5
Valentinian III 425–55
Petronius Maximus 455
Avitus 455–6
Majorian 457–61
Libius Severus 461–5
Anthemius 467–74
Olybrius 472
Glycerius 472–80
Julius Nepos 473–80
Romulus (Augustulus) 475–6, etc.

Eastern emperors
Arcadius 395–408
Theodosius II 408–50
Marcian 450–7
Leo 457–74
Leo II 474
Zeno 474–91
Anastasius 491–518

House of Justin
Justin I 518–27
Justinian 527–65

Leaders, rulers, kings, and queens of England to AD **1066** (Based on Appendix III in
P. Salway, 1981, *Roman Britain*. Oxford: OUP and other sources)

Tribal rulers/petty kings of the 1st century BC/1st century AD

Note: the order of succession of these rulers, their dates of rule, and the geographical areas of influence are not known with certainty. For convenience, each is associated with one of the tribal areas identifiable in the later 1st century AD.

Brigantes
Queen Cartimandua
Venutius (?northern part)

Dobunni
Anted
Eisu
Catti
Comux
Corio (?southern part)
Bodvoc or Boduocus (?northeastern part)

Atrebates
Commius (originally from Gaul?)
Tincommius (son of Commius)
Eppillus (son of Commius)
Epaticcus (brother of Cunobelin)
Verica (son of Commius)
Cogidubnus

Catuvellauni
Cassivellaunus
Tasciovanus (son of Cassivellaunus)
Dubnovellaunos

Trinovantes
Mandubracius
Addedomaros
Cunobelin (?son of Tasciovanus)
Togodumnus (son of Cunobelin)
Caratacus (son of Cunobelin)

Cantii
Cingetorix
Carvilius
Taximagulus
Segorovax
Dumnovellaunus
Iovir
Adminius (son of Cunobelin)

Iceni
Anted
Ecen
Aesu
Saemv
Prasutagus, died AD 60
Queen Boudicca (widow of Prasutagus)

Govenors of Britannia from the time of the Roman conquest in AD 43
Aulus Plautius AD 43–7
Publius Ostorius Scapula 47–52
Aulus Didius Gallus 52–7
Quintus Veranius 57/8
Gaius Suetonius Paulinus ?58–61
Publius Petronius Turpilianus 61/2–3
Marcus Trebellius Maximus 63–9
Marcus Vettius Bolanus 69–71
Quintus Petilius Cerialis 71–3/4
Sexus Julius Frontinus 73/4–77/8
Gnaeus Julius Agricola 78–84 (or 77–83)
Sallustius Lucullus in period 83/4–96
Publius Metilius Nepos ?by 96
Titus Avidius Quietus ?97/8–?100–1
Lucius Neratius Marcellus ?100/1–3
Marcus Appius (or Atilius) Bradua perhaps 115–18
Quintus Pompeius Falco 118–22
Aulus Platorius Nepos 122–?5
Sextus Julius Severus *c*.131–2/3
Publius Mummius Sisenna ?132/3–5 or later
Quintus Lollius Urbicus 138/9–?44
Guaneus Papirius Aelianus by 146
Gnaeus Julius Verus by 158
Gnaeus Julianus Longus or Longinus 158/9–61
Marcus Statius Priscus 161/2
Sexus Calpurnius Agricola by 163/4–?6
Quintus Antistius Adventus in period 169–80
? Caerellius Priscus in period 169–80
Ulpius Marcellus by 180–?
Publius Helvius Pertinax 185?–7
Decimus Clodius Albinus 191/2–?
Virius Lupus 197–?200/2
Marcus Antius Crescens Calpuraianus acting governor ?202
Gaius Valerius Pudens 202/3–5 or later
Lucius Alfenus Senecio 205/7–?

Britannia Superior
Gaius Junius Faustinus Postumianus?
Titus Julius Pollienus Auspex?
Rufinus?
Marcus Martiannius Pulcher?
Titus Destcius Juba 253–5

Britannia Inferior
Gaius Julius Marcus by 213
Marcus Antonius Gordianus ?by 216
Modius Julius by 219
Tiberius Claudius Paulinus 220
Marius Valerianus 221–2/3
Claudius Xenephon 223
Maximus by 225
Claudius Apellinus in period 222–35
Calvisius Rufus in period 222–35
Valerius Crescens Fulvianus in period
   222–35

(T)uccianus by 237
Maecilius Fuscus in period 238–44
Egnatius Lucilianua in period 238–44
Nonius Philippus by 242
Octavius Sabinus in period 260–9

Diocese of the Britons (*vicarii*)
Pacatianus by 319
Falvius Martinus ?353
Alypius (soon after Martinus)
Civilis 368
Victorinus probably in period 395–406
Chrysanthus probably in period 395–406

Diocese of the Britons (governors)
Aurelius Arpagius (?Britannia Secunda) in
   period 296–305
Flavius Sanctus mid 4th century
Lucius Septimius (Britannia Prima)?

Kings and queens of the later first millennium AD

Northumbria
Ida 547–60
Aethelfrith 593–616
Edwin 616–32
Eanfrith 632–3
Osric 632–3
Oswald 633–41
Oswiv 641–70
Oswine 644–51
Alle 560–90
Aethelwald 651–4
Ecgfrith 670–85
Aldfrith 685–704
Oscred 705–16
Osirc 718–29

Mercia
Penda 632–54
Wulfhere 657–74
Aethdred 674–704
Ceolred 709–16
Aethelbald 716–57
Centred 704–9
Offa 757–96
Ecgfrith 796

Cenwulf 796–821
Ceolwulf 821–3

Wessex and England
Egbert 802–39
Aethelwulf 839–55
Aethelbald 855–60
Aethelberht 860–6
Aethelred 866–71
Alfred 871–99
Edward the Elder 899–924
Athelstan 924–39
Edmund 939–46
Cnut 939–46
Eadred 946–55
Eadwig 955–7
Edgar 957–75
Edward the Martyr 975–8
Aethelred 978–1016
Swein (king of Denmark and England)
   1014
Edmund Ironside 1016
Harald Harefoot 1035–40
Hardenut 1040–2
Edward the Confessor 1042–66
Harold 1066

Oxford Paperback Reference

A Dictionary of Chemistry

Over 4,200 entries covering all aspects of chemistry, including physical chemistry and biochemistry.

'It should be in every classroom and library ... the reader is drawn inevitably from one entry to the next merely to satisfy curiosity.'

School Science Review

A Dictionary of Physics

Ranging from crystal defects to the solar system, 3,500 clear and concise entries cover all commonly encountered terms and concepts of physics.

A Dictionary of Biology

The perfect guide for those studying biology – with over 4,700 entries on key terms from biology, biochemistry, medicine, and palaeontology.

'lives up to its expectations; the entries are concise, but explanatory'

Biologist

'ideally suited to students of biology, at either secondary or university level, or as a general reference source for anyone with an interest in the life sciences'

Journal of Anatomy

Oxford Paperback Reference

The Kings of Queens of Britain
John Cannon and Anne Hargreaves

A detailed, fully-illustrated history ranging from mythical and pre-conquest rulers to the present House of Windsor, featuring regional maps and genealogies.

A Dictionary of Dates
Cyril Leslie Beeching

Births and deaths of the famous, significant and unusual dates in history – this is an entertaining guide to each day of the year.

'a dipper's blissful paradise ... Every single day of the year, plus an index of birthdays and chronologies of scientific developments and world events.'

Observer

A Dictionary of British History
Edited by John Cannon

An invaluable source of information covering the history of Britain over the past two millennia. Over 3,600 entries written by more than 100 specialist contributors.

Review of the parent volume
'the range is impressive ... truly (almost) all of human life is here'

Kenneth Morgan, *Observer*

Oxford Paperback Reference

The Concise Oxford Dictionary of English Etymology
T. F. Hoad

A wealth of information about our language and its history, this reference source provides over 17,000 entries on word origins.

'A model of its kind'

Daily Telegraph

A Dictionary of Euphemisms
R. W. Holder

This hugely entertaining collection draws together euphemisms from all aspects of life: work, sexuality, age, money, and politics.

Review of the previous edition
'This ingenious collection is not only very funny but extremely instructive too'

Iris Murdoch

The Oxford Dictionary of Slang
John Ayto

Containing over 10,000 words and phrases, this is the ideal reference for those interested in the more quirky and unofficial words used in the English language.

'hours of happy browsing for language lovers'

Observer

Oxford Paperback Reference

The Concise Oxford Companion to English Literature
Margaret Drabble and Jenny Stringer

Based on the best-selling *Oxford Companion to English Literature*, this is an indispensable guide to all aspects of English literature.

Review of the parent volume
'a magisterial and monumental achievement'
Literary Review

The Concise Oxford Companion to Irish Literature
Robert Welch

From the ogam alphabet developed in the 4th century to Roddy Doyle, this is a comprehensive guide to writers, works, topics, folklore, and historical and cultural events.

Review of the parent volume
'Heroic volume ... It surpasses previous exercises of similar nature in the richness of its detail and the ecumenism of its approach.'
Times Literary Supplement

A Dictionary of Shakespeare
Stanley Wells

Compiled by one of the best-known international authorities on the playwright's works, this dictionary offers up-to-date information on all aspects of Shakespeare, both in his own time and in later ages.

OXFORD

Great value ebooks from Oxford!

An ever-increasing number of Oxford subject reference dictionaries, English and bilingual dictionaries, and English language reference titles are available as ebooks.

All Oxford ebooks are available in the award-winning Mobipocket Reader format, compatible with most current handheld systems, including Palm, Pocket PC/Windows CE, Psion, Nokia, SymbianOS, Franklin eBookMan, and Windows. Some are also available in MS Reader and Palm Reader formats.

Priced on a par with the print editions, Oxford ebooks offer dictionary-specific search options making information retrieval quick and easy.

For further information and a full list of Oxford ebooks please visit: www.askoxford.com/shoponline/ebooks/

Oxford Paperback Reference

The Concise Oxford Dictionary of Quotations
Edited by Elizabeth Knowles

Based on the highly acclaimed *Oxford Dictionary of Quotations*, this
paperback edition maintains its extensive coverage of literary and
historical quotations, and contains completely up-to-date material. A
fascinating read and an essential reference tool.

The Oxford Dictionary of Humorous Quotations
Edited by Ned Sherrin

From the sharply witty to the downright hilarious, this sparkling
collection will appeal to all senses of humour.

Quotations by Subject
Edited by Susan Ratcliffe

A collection of over 7,000 quotations, arranged thematically for easy
look-up. Covers an enormous range of nearly 600 themes from 'The
Internet' to 'Parliament'.

The Concise Oxford Dictionary of Phrase and Fable
Edited by Elizabeth Knowles

Provides a wealth of fascinating and informative detail for over 10,000
phrases and allusions used in English today. Find out about anything
from the 'Trojan house' to 'ground zero'.

Oxford Paperback Reference

The Concise Oxford Dictionary of Art & Artists
Ian Chilvers

Based on the highly praised *Oxford Dictionary of Art*, over 2,500 up-to-date entries on painting, sculpture, and the graphic arts.

'the best and most inclusive single volume available, immensely useful and very well written'

Marina Vaizey, *Sunday Times*

The Concise Oxford Dictionary of Art Terms
Michael Clarke

Written by the Director of the National Gallery of Scotland, over 1,800 entries cover periods, styles, materials, techniques, and foreign terms.

A Dictionary of Architecture
James Stevens Curl

Over 5,000 entries and 250 illustrations cover all periods of Western architectural history.

'splendid ... you can't have a more concise, entertaining, and informative guide to the words of architecture'

Architectural Review

'excellent, and amazing value for money ... by far the best thing of its kind'

Professor David Walker

More Art Reference from Oxford

The Grove Dictionary of Art

The 34 volumes of *The Grove Dictionary of Art* provide unrivalled coverage of the visual arts from Asia, Africa, the Americas, Europe, and the Pacific, from prehistory to the present day.

'succeeds in performing the most difficult of balancing acts, satisfying specialists while ... remaining accessible to the general reader'

The Times

The Grove Dictionary of Art – Online
www.groveart.com

This immense cultural resource is now available online. Updated regularly, it includes recent developments in the art world as well as the latest art scholarship.

'a mammoth one-stop site for art-related information'

Antiques Magazine

The Oxford History of Western Art
Edited by Martin Kemp

From Classical Greece to postmodernism, *The Oxford History of Western Art* is an authoritative and stimulating overview of the development of visual culture in the West over the last 2,700 years.

'here is a work that will permanently alter the face of art history ... a hugely ambitious project successfully achieved'

The Times

The Oxford Dictionary of Art
Edited by Ian Chilvers

The Oxford Dictionary of Art is an authoritative guide to the art of the western world, ranging across painting, sculpture, drawing, and the applied arts.

'the best and most inclusive single-volume available'

Marina Vaizey, *Sunday Times*

Oxford Paperback Reference

Concise Medical Dictionary

Over 10,000 clear entries covering all the major medical and surgical specialities make this one of our best-selling dictionaries.

'"No home should be without one" certainly applies to this splendid medical dictionary'

Journal of the Institute of Health Education

'An extraordinary bargain'

New Scientist

'Excellent layout and jargon-free style'

Nursing Times

A Dictionary of Nursing

Comprehensive coverage of the ever-expanding vocabulary of the nursing professions. Features over 10,000 entries written by medical and nursing specialists.

An A-Z of Medicinal Drugs

Over 4,000 entries cover the full range of over-the-counter and prescription medicines available today. An ideal reference source for both the patient and the medical professional.

 OXFORD

Oxford Paperback Reference

The Concise Oxford Dictionary of World Religions
Edited by John Bowker

Over 8,200 entries containing unrivalled coverage of all the major world religions, past and present.

'covers a vast range of topics ... is both comprehensive and reliable'

The Times

The Oxford Dictionary of Saints
David Farmer

From the famous to the obscure, over 1,400 saints are covered in this acclaimed dictionary.

'an essential reference work'

Daily Telegraph

The Concise Oxford Dictionary of the Christian Church
E. A. Livingstone

This indispensable guide contains over 5,000 entries and provides full coverage of theology, denominations, the church calendar, and the Bible.

'opens up the whole of Christian history, now with a wider vision than ever'

Robert Runcie, former Archbishop of Canterbury